D1361616

Reader's Digest

GREAT EVENTS OF THE 20TH CENTURY

How They Changed Our Lives

The Reader's Digest Association, Inc.
Pleasantville, New York Montreal London Sydney

The credits and acknowledgments that appear on pages 541-543
are hereby made a part of this copyright page.
Copyright © 1977 The Reader's Digest Association, Inc.
Copyright © 1977 The Reader's Digest Association (Canada) Ltd.
Copyright © 1977 Reader's Digest Association Far East Ltd.
Philippine Copyright 1977 Reader's Digest Association Far East Ltd.

Reproduction in any manner, in whole or in part, in English or in
other languages, is prohibited. All rights are reserved.

Library of Congress Catalog Card No. 76-23540

Printed in the United States of America

Great Events of the 20th Century

Editor: Richard Marshall
Art Director: Robert M. Grant
Associate Editors: James Cassidy, Fred DuBose, Ruth Goldeman, Anne C. Tupker
Assistant Editor: A. Denman Pierce-Grove
Copy Editors: Robert V. Huber, Susan Parker
Research Associates: Giza Braun, Laurel Gilbride, Patricia Selden
Art Staff: Dana Burns, Janet G. Iannacone, Dana Nordhausen, Marta Strait
Picture Researchers: Wesley Day, Laurie Drucker
Editorial Assistant: V. Frederick Veader

The editors of Reader's Digest wish to express their gratitude for the invaluable contributions of the following individuals:

Special Consultants

Nathaniel O. Abelson
Librarian, Map Collection Unit
United Nations

Thomas P. Barran
Department of Slavic Languages
Columbia University

Benjamin Bederson, Ph.D.
Chairman, Department of Physics
New York University

W. Tapley Bennett, Jr.
U.S. Deputy Permanent Representative
to the United Nations

Jan Bonalsky
Microbiology Laboratory
CIBA-Geigy Corporation

W. Stephen Childress, Ph.D.
Associate Professor of Mathematics
Courant Institute of Mathematics
New York University

Thomas G. De Claire
Reference Librarian
Geography and Map Division
Library of Congress

Colonel John R. Elting, USA-Ret.
Formerly Associate Professor
Department of Military Art and Engineering
U.S. Military Academy

David Lackenbruch
Editor, Television Digest

Jeff Magnes
Biophysics Department
Sloan-Kettering Institute for Cancer Research

William J. O'Donnell
Office of Manned Space Flight
National Aeronautics and Space Administration

Dom Pisano
Air and Space Library
Smithsonian Institution

John Riley, Jr.
Special Projects Historian
U.S. Navy Department

Richard E. Royal
Department of Political Science
Columbia University

Albert Rubin, M.D.
Professor of Surgery and Biochemistry
Cornell University Medical School

E. L. Schucking, Ph.D.
Professor of Physics
New York University

Timothy Wilson
Architect

CONTENTS

The Events That Changed Our Lives

THE PASSING OF THE OLD GUARD 1900-18

THE ROARING TWENTIES 1919-29

HARD TIMES 1929-39

THE WAR YEARS 1939-45

THE NUCLEAR AGE 1945-56

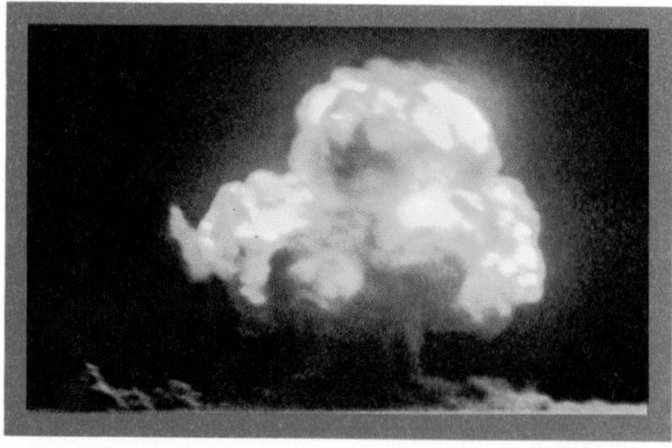

THE SPACE AGE 1957-76

1900-18 THE

PASSING OF THE OLD GUARD

There never was such a break-up. All the old buoys which have marked the channel of our lives seem to have been swept away.

—Lord Esher, friend and adviser of King Edward VII, commenting on the King's funeral, May 1910

1900-18

"Objects of dubious value," reads the caption of this 1906 German cartoon, in which Europe's monarchs nervously attempt to pawn their crowns. Time was indeed running out for the old order—and more rapidly than anyone realized.

On January 1, 1900, the world seemed a tolerably well-run place to the great men of Europe. The Continent had been at peace for three decades and looked forward to more of the same, thanks to a rising level of prosperity and a complex network of alliances among the major powers. Moreover, Europe was still the undisputed ruler of the world. The British Empire was at its height, with outposts on five continents and an enormous navy to safeguard the vital trade routes; France's colonial authority in Africa and Indochina was solidly entrenched; Russia was extending its domain eastward toward Manchuria and northern China; while Germany, a latecomer to empire building, had begun staking out its own claims in Africa and the Pacific.

Nevertheless, there were unmistakable signs of change on the political horizon. By the turn of the century two non-European nations were rapidly emerging as global powers: the United States, still basking in the afterglow of the Spanish-American War; and Japan, which stunned the world in 1905 with its victory at Tsushima against the Imperial Russian Navy. Russia was also shaken in 1905 by a bloody uprising that, though crushed by czarist troops, was only a prelude to the revolution that swept the old regime from power 12 years later.

At the same time, nearly every Western nation was feeling the side effects of rapid industrialization. The working classes of Europe, influenced by the socialist theories of Karl Marx and Friedrich Engels, had grown increasingly militant in their demands for social reform, and it was clear that the industrial world would soon have to accommodate them—or face dire consequences. Another potential threat to the turn-of-the-century status quo was a growing spirit of nationalism among the smaller nations of Europe, especially in the Balkan states ruled by the reactionary Austro-Hungarian Empire. Finally, the first 18 years of the century witnessed a leap forward in scientific achievement with so profound an impact that, in many ways, it marked the true birth of the modern world.

By June 1914, years of diplomatic maneuvering and military buildups had strained Europe's balance of power to the point of collapse. Then a gun was fired at Sarajevo, and the same web of alliances that had kept the peace pulled more than a dozen nations into a war unlike any before it—one that, with the aid of modern technology, produced a level of destruction never before imagined. In all, the fighting left a death toll in excess of 10 million, and a continent blighted by poverty, bitterness, and disillusionment. An era of history had ended: Europe's old order was gone, and with it a kind of innocence that could never be reclaimed.

1903

Wings for a New World

Taking off in the teeth of a wintry gale at Kitty Hawk, North Carolina, two brothers from Dayton make aviation history with the first successful flight of a self-powered heavier-than-air craft.

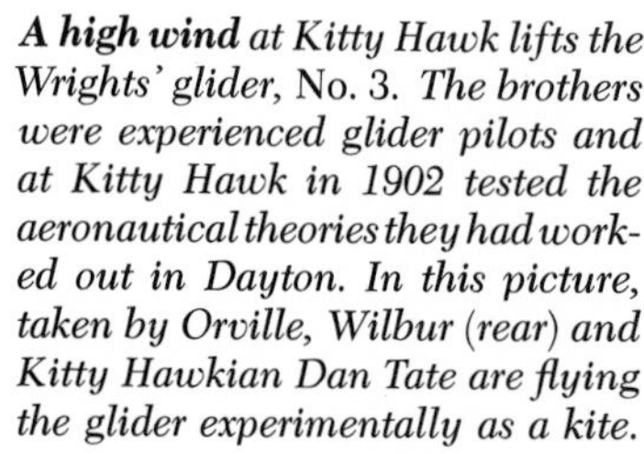

It was a curious-looking contraption, the machine that would become one of the most celebrated airplanes in history. Poised on a desolate stretch of sand at Kill Devil Hill, North Carolina, near the village of Kitty Hawk, it resembled a huge box kite, its muslin-covered wings spanning 40 feet, the bare bones of its body framework outthrust.

Thursday morning, December 17, 1903, was clear but freezing cold. A brisk 27-mile-per-hour wind blew in from the Atlantic, sweeping over the strip of dunes that separated the ocean from Albemarle Sound. Shortly after 9 a.m. the Wright brothers, Wilbur and Orville, inventors and builders of the aircraft, assisted by five men, hauled the 605-pound machine from its shed to a level stretch of sand at the base of Kill Devil Hill, a 100-foot-high dune.

The Wrights had devised a unique system for launching their craft, which they called the *Flyer*. The machine was placed on a trolley constructed to roll along the single rail of a greased 60-foot launching track. When the *Flyer*'s engine was started, the thrust from the whirling propellers would send both the plane and supporting trolley down the track. Theoretically, once flying speed was reached the craft would take to the air, leave the trolley behind, and land on the skilike runners attached under the lower wing.

By 10:30 a.m. the final adjustments were complete. The engine was started, and the two propellers began moving. Orville Wright, 32, four years younger than Wilbur, climbed aboard the *Flyer*. There was no pilot's seat; he lay face down in a cradlelike harness across the lower wing. From there he could manipulate wing and rudder controls by shifting his body. His hands were

***A high wind** at Kitty Hawk lifts the Wrights' glider,* No. 3. *The brothers were experienced glider pilots and at Kitty Hawk in 1902 tested the aeronautical theories they had worked out in Dayton. In this picture, taken by Orville, Wilbur (rear) and Kitty Hawkian Dan Tate are flying the glider experimentally as a kite.*

***The first of four** historic flights on December 17, 1903, was made by Orville Wright. Before strapping himself into the* Flyer, *he trained his camera on the end of the launching track and asked one of the men who had been helping out to snap the shutter if the plane became airborne. Wilbur (right), who had been running alongside holding the wingtip steady, has just released it.*

free to work the engine throttle and elevator lever, which controlled the up-and-down movement of the plane's nose and tail. Slowly Orville opened the throttle, bringing the 4-cylinder, 12-horsepower engine to full power.

Wilbur stood alongside, one hand steadying the right wingtip. At 10:35 Orville released the restraining wire, and the *Flyer* lurched forward, sluggishly at first, then picking up speed. Wilbur broke into a trot to keep up. A split second more and Orville pulled back on the elevator lever.

The *Flyer* responded immediately. It lifted and took to the air, while the trolley slowed to a stop. It was flying, flying on its own, pushed on by the churning propellers. The flight, far from steady, was later described by Wilbur as "somewhat undulating." Orville fought to keep the plane on an even keel. Suddenly, the *Flyer* swooped down, and its runners struck the sand. Undamaged, it skidded to a halt.

The flight had lasted 12 seconds, covered 120 feet, and reached an altitude of no more than 10 feet above the ground. But it marked a milestone in human progress. Orville made one more flight that day and Wilbur two. On the fourth and final flight Wilbur flew 852 feet in 59 seconds: The Wright brothers had proved controlled, heavier-than-air flight possible. One of man's most persistent dreams had come true.

From Balloons to Gliders

Men have always dreamed of being able to fly like the birds. During the Middle Ages many would-be aeronauts attached wings to their arms, flapped madly, and hurled themselves from church towers, cliffs, and hills. The results were always disastrous, frequently fatal.

When the Frenchmen Joseph and Jacques Étienne Montgolfier launched the first hot-air balloon in 1783, a whole new approach to flight opened up. Ballooning spread when hydrogen gas (discovered by Henry Cavendish in 1766) replaced hot air. But these gas bags were at the mercy of wind and weather.

The problems of balloon flight piqued the interest of many scientists, notably Sir George Cayley (1773–1857) of Yorkshire, England, who is considered the founder of the science of aerodynamics. Cayley became absorbed in heavier-than-air flight. Departing from the old wing-flapping theory, he evolved a glider with fixed wings and a tail unit, which in 1804 he flew successfully at his Yorkshire estate. Many historians regard this glider as the world's first true airplane.

The ascent of a toy helicopter, its straight-up flight powered by twisted rubberbands, was the spark that touched off the Wright brothers' fascination with flight. The helicopter, which the boys called a bat, was a present from their father, Milton, a bishop in the Church of the United Brethren of Christ. (There were five children altogether, two brothers considerably older than Wilbur and Orville and a younger sister. Wilbur was born in 1867, Orville in 1871. Both the younger boys were mechanically inclined.)

Enterprising and curious, the brothers began exploring airborne objects by building and flying kites. They ran a kitemaking business for the neighborhood children. In high school Orville published and sold a weekly newspaper printed on a press he and Wilbur built. The paper was so successful it became a daily (although only for four months).

In the early 1890's Wilbur and Orville took advantage of the bicycle craze sweeping the country and opened up a bicycle repair shop in Dayton, Ohio. They made a good business team: Wilbur, studious and

In the 1890's *Otto Lilienthal made more than 2,000 glides in craft built of willow and waxed cotton. These batlike wings folded for storage.*

In this odd "tail-first" biplane Alberto Santos-Dumont made Europe's first powered flight in 1906. Santos-Dumont, a Brazilian coffee heir, was an experienced balloonist.

This Type XI monoplane took Louis Blériot across the English Channel in July 1909. The 37-minute trip won him both fame and fortune: the London Daily Mail's *£1,000 prize.*

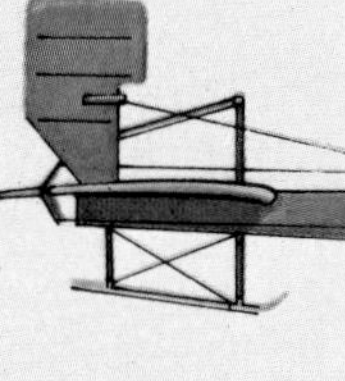

A Voisin-built biplane flown by Henri Farman in 1908 was the first in Europe to fly a circular course. The feat demanded a maneuverable plane and skillful flying.

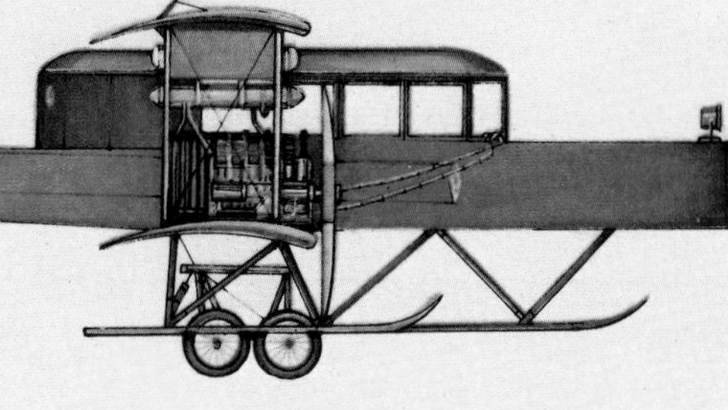

Le Grand, *the original four-engine biplane, was designed and manufactured by Igor Sikorsky, who first took it up in 1913.*

This Avro triplane was named for the English pilot A. V. Roe, the first Briton to build and fly his own powered airplane, in 1908.

EUROPE TAKES TO THE AIR

In Europe heavier-than-air flight was pioneered by the French and English. After the success of such men as the Montgolfiers in ballooning and the Yorkshireman Sir George Cayley in gliding, Europeans were shocked to learn that the first powered flight had taken place in the United States. For a time, in fact, they were convinced that Santos-Dumont (top right) had won that honor in France in 1906 with his short hops of 197 and 722 feet. But Europe did not lack men of the caliber of the Wright brothers, either in daring or expertise, and by 1913 European airmen had racked up an impressive number of their own aviation firsts.

practical; Orville, imaginative and quick to try out new ideas. Their enterprise acquired a title, the Wright Cycle Co., when the brothers began manufacturing a bicycle of their own design, the Van Cleve.

Not much was written about experiments in human flight in the late 19th century, but the Wrights read everything they could get hold of on the subject. Most interesting to them were reports of the extensive gliding tests being made by Otto Lilienthal in Germany and by Octave Chanute on the shores of Lake Michigan near Chicago. Everything they learned reinforced their decision to build and fly their own craft.

From Bicycle to Biplane

In 1899, using money from the bicycle business, the Wrights built a five-foot biplane, which they flew as a kite. After studying how the craft veered in gusty weather, Wilbur concluded that he could get lateral control by twisting or warping the wingtips at varying angles to the wind, moving them by sticks connected to strings. The experiment worked and had a profound effect on the Wrights' future success.

During 1900 Wilbur and Orville constructed their first glider. It was a biplane, with wires for wing warping and a front horizontal elevator to control up-and-down flight. They wrote to the U.S. Weather Bureau for information on a suitable testing area and were guided to the sand dune country near Kitty Hawk, North Carolina. There winds from the Atlantic blew at a fairly constant 20 miles per hour or better and would provide the lift needed for man-carrying gliders. The dunes, mostly clear of shrubs and trees, offered soft landing places, and, since the area was sparsely populated, no one (except possibly the pilots) would be endangered in test flights. In October 1900 the Wrights crated their glider and made preparations to travel to Kitty Hawk. There they made a number of successful manned flights.

Before the Wrights returned the next summer with a second glider, they built a small wind tunnel in their shop in Dayton, testing scores of miniature wing shapes for lift and drag. By 1902 they had built a third glider to which they added stationary vertical tailfins for better flight control. Later, this arrangement was replaced by a movable rudder that was connected with the wing-warping wires. Making mild banking turns was then possible. Between August and October 1902 the Wrights made about 1,000 controlled glider flights at Kitty Hawk, in winds of up to 36 miles per hour—an incredible achievement for the time. They were making world record flights. By then they had discovered that the calculations they had been using, based on Lilienthal's tables for air pressure, were wrong; so they were slowly working out their own.

During those years the brothers were writing to Octave Chanute, one of the foremost authorities on gliders. Chanute, nearly 70 when he first met the Wrights, gave them much valuable advice, visited them at Dayton and at Kitty Hawk, and was steadfast in his encouragement.

Finally, in the summer of 1903, Wilbur and Orville decided they were ready to try experiments with powered flight. They began building the biplane that was to become the famous *Flyer.* Since there was no lightweight gasoline engine available, they built their own—a 4-cylinder, water-cooled powerplant that produced 12 horsepower. It was installed in the *Flyer,* and two eight-foot wooden propellers were mounted well to the rear of the wings.

The *Flyer* was taken to the testing area in September 1903 and assembled at the site. December 14 was the date chosen for the first flight, and Wilbur was selected as the pilot by a toss of a coin. However, on the appointed day the *Flyer* stalled at takeoff and dropped to the ground. Wilbur escaped uninjured, but repairs to the *Flyer* took three days to complete. Then, on December 17, when all was ready again, it was Orville Wright's turn and his opportunity to become the first person in the world to fly a heavier-than-air craft.

In the late afternoon of December 17, 1903, after their four historic flights, the Wrights dispatched an exultant telegram to their father telling of their success and asking that the press be notified. Bishop Wright carried out his instructions, but the few papers that

***When fame caught up** with the Wrights, their simplicity charmed the public, as this early* Life *cartoon shows. The brothers were avid photographers: Wilbur took the portrait of Orville (right).*

No. 821,393

THE UNITED STATES OF AMERICA

TO ALL TO WHOM THESE PRESENTS SHALL COME:

Whereas Orville Wright and Wilbur Wright, of Dayton, Ohio,

Flying-Machines,

Now therefore these Letters Patent

Orville Wright and Wilbur Wright

SEVENTEEN

In testimony whereof

In 1908, two years after the Wrights were awarded the first patent for a flying machine (right), aviation claimed its first victim. Lt. Thomas Selfridge died at Fort Myer, Virginia, a passenger in the plane Orville Wright was demonstrating to the U.S. Army. In spite of the accident, the army purchased the plane a year later.

covered the story immediately after the event published inaccurate or distorted accounts.

The Wrights, although disappointed at the lack of recognition, went to work on a new machine when they returned to Dayton. By the spring of 1904 *Flyer No. 2* was completed, heavier and sturdier than the first and equipped with a more powerful 16-horsepower engine. The first trials were so successful that Wilbur and Orville invited members of the press to witness a demonstration at their Dayton flying field, a cow pasture they rented outside the city limits. Then their luck ran out. The wind dropped suddenly, which, combined with a balky engine, kept *Flyer No. 2* solidly earthbound on its launching track. The reporters left convinced that the Wrights' claim of having previously flown was a complete fake.

From then on the Wrights fought to vindicate their claim. To overcome the dependence on headwinds for takeoff, they added to their launching track a device that catapulted the *Flyer* down the track by the force of a falling weight. After that *Flyer No. 2* was in the air almost daily. On September 20 Wilbur succeeded in circling the flying field, the first such flight in history. Two months later he made two longer circular flights.

During the winter of 1904–05 the Wrights built a third *Flyer*, this time separating the wing-warping and rudder controls. They had discovered how to make tighter turns without stalling (by putting the nose down for greater speed) and could also make figure eights. In 1905 they flew 24 miles in 38 minutes—as far and as long as their gasoline supply lasted.

Most of these flights were made in full view of hundreds of people who rode past the flying field on interurban trolley cars. But no one seemed to feel they were witnessing anything extraordinary, and the local newspapers paid little attention to the experiments.

The Wrights, however, convinced they finally had the airplane they had dreamed of, decided to stop flying and begin safeguarding and marketing their invention. After a long delay Patent No. 821,393 for a flying machine was granted on May 22, 1906.

Recognition at Last

The brothers had repeatedly offered to sell their plane to the U.S. government, only to be turned down without even an inspection. Then in February 1908, prodded by an adventurous President, Theodore Roosevelt, the U.S. War Department proposed a payment of $25,000 for a Wright machine, on condition that it met certain requirements. It was to be capable of carrying two persons, have a top speed of 40 miles per hour, and a flying range of 125 miles.

A month later the Wrights accepted a French offer of $100,000 (with royalties to be paid later) to establish a Wright company in France. Again, the offer was contingent on passing specific tests. Since Wilbur and Orville had used the time of self-grounding to build three new *Flyers* they felt confident they would pass the two sets of tests.

Wilbur took on the overseas assignment and sailed for France. During the summer and fall he put on a series of aerial displays that stunned the French, many of whom had regarded him as a Yankee *bluffeur.* Orville staged similar demonstrations before packed crowds at Fort Myer, Virginia. The newspapers featured glowing accounts and pictures. For the first time the public became aware that there actually was a machine that flew, that it could be piloted by a man, and that it had been invented and flown by two brothers from Dayton, Ohio.

***Wilbur astonished Europe** with his banking and figure-eight flights at Le Mans in 1908. Here, he is congratulated by Alfonso XIII of Spain and Edward VII of England (at right).*

One tragedy marred Orville's Fort Myer displays: a crash in which a passenger was killed. Orville was injured, but he managed to complete the tests a year later. The War Department bought the plane, and the Wrights' airplane business expanded rapidly. Russia and Italy sent representatives to purchase Wright machines, and a Wright pilot training school opened in France. In 1909 Wilbur delighted New Yorkers by circling the Statue of Liberty and soaring up the Hudson from Governors Island to Grant's Tomb and back.

Yet at the time of their greatest success the Wrights' effort to control what they considered *their* invention was under attack. Airplanes were being designed and flown by other men in the United States and in France, Britain, and other European countries. Most of the aircraft used some sort of wing adjustment to maintain lateral control. Glenn Curtiss, a Hammondsport, New York, designer and builder of airplanes and a skilled pilot, used hinged flaps, called ailerons, between the wings. The Wrights claimed that these and all such devices infringed on the wing-warping detail covered by their U.S. patent. The *Curtiss* v. *Wright* lawsuit was the most bitter of 12 the Wrights fought in the U.S.A.

Wilbur Wright died of typhoid fever on May 20, 1912, in the midst of the Curtiss lawsuit; Orville stubbornly carried on the contest until, in 1915, he sold out his business interests in the Wright Co. and virtually retired from public life. The *Curtiss* v. *Wright* patent controversy was finally settled by a government-sponsored cross-licensing agreement in 1917 because the U.S.A. had entered World War I and manufacturers wanted the legal authority to build planes.

In 1914, still trying to prove that the Wrights' *Flyer* had *not* been the first heavier-than-air craft capable of flight, Glenn Curtiss persuaded the Smithsonian Institution to place on display Dr. Samuel P. Langley's *Aerodrome* monoplane, which had been built but not flown in 1903, with a notice stating that it was the first heavier-than-air machine capable of flight.

Orville, who felt that the Smithsonian had slighted his and Wilbur's achievements, refused the institution's later invitation to place the original Kitty Hawk *Flyer* in the museum for "perpetual preservation." Instead, in 1928 Orville sent the *Flyer* to the Science Museum at South Kensington, England. There it remained until 1943, when, at the request of President Franklin D. Roosevelt, Orville asked that the airplane be returned. Unfortunately, however, Orville did not live long enough to see the Wrights' *Flyer* installed in its place of honor in the Smithsonian. He died January 30, 1948. The following December 17, on the 45th anniversary of the first flight, the *Flyer* was placed on permanent exhibition, where it remains today. The exhibition label reads in part: "The original Wright Brothers' aeroplane/The World's first power-driven heavier-than-air machine in which man made free, controlled and sustained flight/Invented and built by Wilbur and Orville Wright/Flown by them at Kitty Hawk, North Carolina, December 17, 1903."

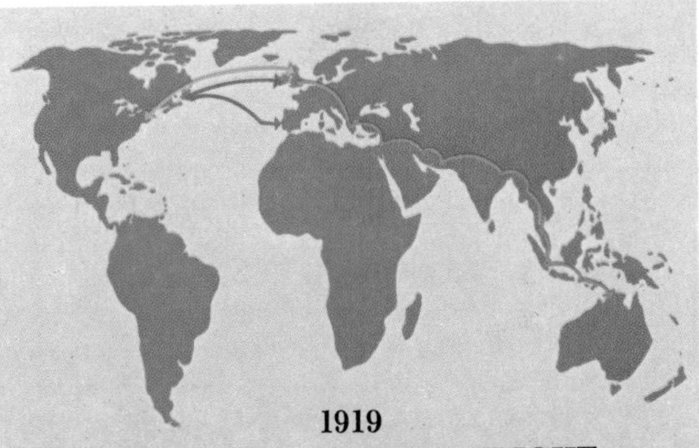

1919

THE GREAT YEAR OF FLIGHT

- The first west to east Atlantic crossing: Lt. Comdr. A. C. Read and crew, in the U.S. Navy's Curtiss flying boat *NC-4*, left Newfoundland May 16, stopped at the Azores, and landed in Portugal May 27.
- The first nonstop transatlantic flight: Two Englishmen, Capt. J. W. Alcock and Lt. A. W. Brown, left Newfoundland June 14 in a Vickers Vimy and flew to Clifden, Ireland, in less than 16½ hours.
- The first Atlantic crossing by dirigible: Maj. G. H. Scott commanded the British dirigible *R-34*, which left Scotland July 2 and reached Mineola, New York, July 6. The return trip to England took 75 hours.
- The longest flight to date: Australian brothers Ross and Keith Smith flew a Vickers Vimy 11,130 miles from England to Australia in a series of hops between November 12 and December 10.

1903

The Movies Come of Age

The Great Train Robbery, the first feature film to capture the public imagination, launches a powerful new form of popular entertainment.

The movies' first hit *was Edwin S. Porter's* The Great Train Robbery *(above and right). It involved audiences in a way no film had ever done, with action, realism, and a quick-as-lightning pace. Thrilled patrons crowded into small theaters to see the film again and again; it played for years in the United States and Europe, promoting an international interest in movies and helping to make them big business.*

The Edison Vitascope *(right) projected moving pictures onto a large screen and created a sensation when it was introduced in 1896. Color, albeit crude, was used in some early films, with each frame painstakingly tinted by hand.*

It was partially a show business gimmick that made Edwin S. Porter's 1903 film *The Great Train Robbery* the first great motion picture box office hit: Each reel shipped by the Edison Manufacturing Company included a melodramatic closeup of a mustachioed bandit firing his pistol "point-blank at the audience." The Edison catalog promised that "the resulting excitement is great" and suggested that "this scene can be used to begin or end the picture." Enthusiastic filmgoers sat through repeated showings just to experience the thrill of being safely shot at over and over again.

It was the basic structure of this first "western," however, that made it a milestone in the development of the cinema, the 20th century's first new art form. Before Porter, who worked for Thomas Edison, made his pioneering movies, the newfangled motion picture camera had been used primarily as a recording device, capturing everyday occurrences, news events, or scenes from stage shows filmed as if the stationary camera were a seated patron. Porter broke out of that mold. In one action-packed eight-minute reel divided into 13 distinct scenes, *The Great Train Robbery* tells of a band of daring bandits who take over a telegraph office and rob a train, only to be hunted down and captured by a hard-riding posse. Much of the movie was shot outdoors "on location" and seemed wonderfully real to 1903 audiences, even though it was filmed in New Jersey rather than the western desert, and featured untrained actors who were visibly frightened of their mounts. By cutting directly from one scene to the next—bridging the gap between scenes with the logic of the story rather than with titles or dissolves—Porter was able to build suspense and rivet audience attention, establishing the all-important editing technique that remains at the heart of moviemaking. His film became the standard attraction for the new movie theaters opening across Canada and the U.S.A.

Artists had long dreamed of portraying the motion as well as the look of the real world, but it was not until the early 19th century that men began seriously to puzzle out the problem. "Magic disks" became familiar parlor toys in Europe during the 1830's. By peering through a slit in a stationary disk while spinning another, the viewer saw the small drawings that lined its rim appear to move. Improved versions used mirrors and "magic lanterns" (elaborate light boxes) to project the drawn images onto a screen.

Coleman Sellers, a Philadelphia engineer, was the first to combine the new science of photography with the principle of the magic disks. In 1860 he pasted to the blades of a miniature paddle wheel six sequential photographs of his two sons hammering nails. The lifelike motion produced when the wheel was whirled delighted his neighbors. Ten years later fellow Philadelphian Henry Heyl projected views of a waltzing couple onto a screen by making still photographs of the models in each phase of action. During the 1870's Eadweard Muybridge used as many as 24 wire-tripped cameras to make still photographs of animals and people in motion. In 1882 French inventor Étienne Marey

used a single "photographic gun," combining a rifle stock and trigger with a rapid-firing shutter, to freeze the flight of birds on a revolving drum of photographic paper. In England William Friese-Green experimented with a camera that would record movement and a projector that would reconstitute it on a screen.

But it was in the New Jersey laboratories of Thomas Edison, inventor of the incandescent light bulb and the phonograph, that the first true motion picture camera and viewer were developed. Convinced that sales of phonographs would improve if customers could see as well as hear their favorite artists, he invested some $24,000 in the project. In 1889 his assistant, William Kennedy Dickson, finally devised a sprocket system for a 50-foot strip of inventor George Eastman's flexible celluloid film. The Edison "Kinetoscope," a peep-show device patented in 1891, was the precursor of all subsequent motion picture apparatus, and its film width (35 millimeters) has been an international standard ever since. Because it could not easily be synchronized with the phonograph, Edison saw little future in this invention and refused to pay an extra $150 fee for international patent rights, a decision that cost him a fortune as eager European imitators pirated his process and rushed into their own productions.

Kinetoscope parlors mushroomed across North America and Europe. For a nickel the passerby could look through a tiny peephole and catch a flickering, 15-second glimpse of real-life movement. A monumental sneeze by Edison lab worker Fred Ott was an early favorite. Later, cameramen covered (or re-created) news events and filmed diverse vaudeville turns in Edison's "Black Maria" studio in New Jersey.

The First Picture Shows

In 1895 two French photographers from Lyons, the brothers Louis and Auguste Lumière, devised an easily portable camera and a machine to project Kinetoscope reels onto a large screen. In December of that year they rented a basement at 14, boulevard des Capucines in Paris, equipped it with a hundred chairs, and gave the first showing of their invention to a paying audience. Film historians date the birth of the cinema from that wintry Saturday night—December 28, 1895.

The Lumières' pioneering, unaffected films of utterly prosaic subjects—a baby being fed, a train pull-

***Edison's "Black Maria" studio,** a tar-paper hut, pivoted on a circular track to take advantage of the light at any time of day. Sun shone in through an opening in the roof.*

ing into the station, factory girls leaving work for lunch—thrilled Paris audiences, spread to North America, and forced Edison to introduce his own projector, the Vitascope. The first public showing of the Vitascope in the U.S.A., at Koster and Bial's New York Music Hall on April 23, 1896, was a sensation. According to one enthusiastic reporter, it included "some precious young blonde persons dancing," a "burlesque boxing match," and "angry surf"—"all wonderfully real and singularly exhilarating." These first movies, which were rarely longer than two minutes, were used as bonus attractions for vaudeville shows; later they were shown alone at small movie houses.

But the novelty of simply seeing pictures move soon wore off, and the industry almost died in its infancy. The man who brought it back to life was Georges Méliès, a Parisian who first recognized the potential of film as a storytelling medium. By the early 1900's Méliès' films had become famous for their elaborate costumes, imaginative staging, and eerie special effects. In addition they employed an extraordinary range of film techniques that are still basic to moviemaking, including dissolves, slow motion and stop motion, fade-ins and fade-outs, and a crude form of animation. Such Méliès masterpieces as *A Trip to the Moon* (1902) and *The Impossible Voyage* (1904) drew large crowds and spawned scores of eager imitators. Yet for all their ingenuity his creations were little more than filmed stage shows. It was left to *The Great Train Robbery,* with its new editing techniques and active use of a moving camera, to free the new medium from the narrow confines of the stage.

Thanks to the storytelling skills of Porter and others, the profit-hungry scores of would-be producers and theater owners, and the universal desire for inexpensive entertainment, the movies were big business on both sides of the Atlantic by 1915. In the U.S.A. an attempt by Edison and other film pioneers to monopolize production and limit films to one reel through the Motion Picture Patents Company Trust had failed. Grimy nickelodeons were being replaced by plush movie palaces. Producer-director Thomas Ince and others had established the studio system in Hollywood, a sleepy Los Angeles suburb whose climate allowed year-round filming, and such early stars as William S. Hart, Mary Pickford, Douglas Fairbanks, Sr., and Charles Chaplin were familiar throughout the Western World. Still, most films were short, simplistic, and cranked out with little thought for detail.

David Wark Griffith, a courtly onetime stage actor who began his film career as an actor in a 1908 Porter potboiler, did more than any other man to change the movies from simple storytelling to an art. The director of 485 films, Griffith was a master of film editing and perfected or originated an entire arsenal of cinematic techniques, from extreme closeups to sweeping pano-

MÉLIÈS AND HIS MAGIC FILM

Films created a new kind of magic that was not possible on the stage. Audiences sat enthralled as figures on the screen disappeared, grew or shrank, or turned suddenly into birds or animals. The man who discovered the medium's extraordinary potential for these "special effects" was a French magician-turned-filmmaker, Georges Méliès. One day in 1896 Méliès was shooting a street scene when his camera jammed; a minute or so passed before it started again. Later, viewing the developed film, Méliès was astonished to see that a bus entering the scene just as the camera stopped turned inexplicably into a hearse when it started up again. Méliès saw in this unintended trickery a new way of performing illusions, and by 1900 he had made some 200 immensely popular "magical, mystical, and trick" films.

Méliès' film The India Rubber Head *(1901) features a scientist (Méliès himself) who appears to place his head on a table and then inflates it to great size.*

ramas, to make his audience "see," to heighten their emotional response. His most celebrated film, *The Birth of a Nation* (1915), a romanticized three-hour epic of the American South during Reconstruction, dazzled Virginia-born President Woodrow Wilson, who pronounced it "like history written in lightning, and all too true." Because it portrayed freed slaves as predatory and Ku Klux Klansmen as heroic, it outraged many historians and civil rights groups, but despite its gross inaccuracies, its unprecedented scope ultimately helped make the movies respectable to critics and upper-class theatergoers.

Soviet director Sergei Eisenstein (see pp. 310–313) further expanded the cinematic vocabulary in a series of historical films, such as *Potemkin,* in which he made use of several new devices, including montage, the rapid crosscutting of images.

The Movies Learn To Talk

It had taken the spirit of fantasy of Georges Méliès, the storytelling genius of Edwin Porter, the imaginative scope of D. W. Griffith, the technical virtuosity of Sergei Eisenstein, and the contributions of an international host of lesser known cinema pioneers to develop the rich variety of the silent screen. Only sound was lacking to make a reality of Edison's dream of true "talking pictures." Since the days of the early nickelodeons audiences had been accustomed to musical accompaniment, usually thumped out by a house pianist, but sometimes, as with the first run of *The Birth of a Nation,* played by a 70-piece orchestra. Technicians had succeeded in recording sound on movie film as early as 1923 and had used it for novelty "shorts"—usually filmed vaudeville acts—accompanying major silent attractions. But these caused little stir. Later, recorded musical scores accompanied some features, and soundtracks were added to newsreels; but it was not until 1927 that Warner Brothers produced the first talking feature, *The Jazz Singer,* starring vaudeville performer Al Jolson. Originally written to include only musical numbers, it became the first feature film to utilize speech when Jolson unexpectedly ad-libbed introductions to his songs. His first line, "You ain't heard nothin' yet," could have served as a slogan for the world movie industry as it entered its period of greatest prosperity. Films grew more lavish by the year, and people all over the world flocked to see them. By 1930 paid admissions to movie houses in the United States alone averaged 110 million per week.

Since that day in 1903 when *The Great Train Robbery* first caught the public's imagination, the movies, surviving war, the Depression, and even the television age, have been the world's foremost purveyors of romance, adventure, comedy, and glamour.

The Ideals: Fairbanks was dashing and Pickford was virginal.

William S. Hart was the first of the cowboy heroes.

THE NEW IDOLS

The names of actors in early films were kept secret by the movie studios, who feared that public recognition would lead to demands for higher salaries. But movie fans soon began to identify with the figures on the screen, and letters addressed to "The Tall Dark Man" or "The Poor Waif" flooded the studios. Moviemakers, realizing that a famous face would draw crowds, began to publicize their actors furiously, and the legendary "movie star" was born. Five stars set the style of Hollywood heroes and heroines for years.

Theda Bara, the antithesis of the all-American girl.

Chaplin—the tramp.

1903

A New Key to the Atom

Henri Becquerel observes the effects of a mysterious radiation, and the Curies trace its source to the heart of the atom.

One of the most exciting detective stories of the modern era unfolded in a leaky, tumbledown wooden shed on the outskirts of Paris at the turn of the century. There Pierre and Marie Curie labored for many years, tracking down, isolating, and examining the source of radioactivity in pitchblende. The long and twisting trail finally led to the discovery of two new elements, radium and polonium. In the process the Curies gathered invaluable knowledge about the nature of all elements and helped lay the groundwork for the new medical field of radiology. Their hard work and dedication set a model for scientists that has rarely been equaled, and in December 1903 they shared the Nobel Prize for Physics with Henri Becquerel, the French physicist who had discovered radioactivity in 1896 and whose work had originally inspired the Curies' investigations.

The work of the Curies and Becquerel spanned a decade of remarkable discoveries. Beginning with the discovery of X-rays in 1895 and ending with the publication of Einstein's special theory of relativity in 1905 (see pp. 38–43), scientific understanding of the world and of its basic materials was revolutionized. Most incredible of all, physicists unearthed evidence that within the tiny atom itself, long held to be the ultimate building block of matter, there was a restless and puzzling new world of subatomic particles.

The first surprise came in November 1895 when the German physicist Wilhelm Roentgen accidentally came upon a mysterious invisible radiation. Roentgen, a professor at the University of Würzburg, was experimenting with a new device called the cathode-ray tube, or Crookes tube, after its English inventor, William Crookes. When a high-voltage electric current flowed through the tube, its glass wall glowed, or fluoresced, but no one could fully explain why.

In the course of a routine experiment Roentgen had wrapped a piece of black paper around the tube, lowered the window shades in his laboratory, and then switched on the current. The room remained darkened except for a strange glow emitted by a fluorescent screen lying on a bench about three feet away from the tube. When Roentgen switched off the current, the glow vanished, but when he turned it on again, the glow reappeared. Apparently, something able to penetrate the glass and the black paper was causing the screen's eerie light.

***Marie and Pierre Curie,** the brilliant couple who isolated pure radium in 1902, appear in a contemporary caricature.*

Roentgen concluded that an invisible ray was the culprit and named it X, the scientific term for an unknown quantity. Then he began a careful, systematic study of X-rays, discovering that they could travel

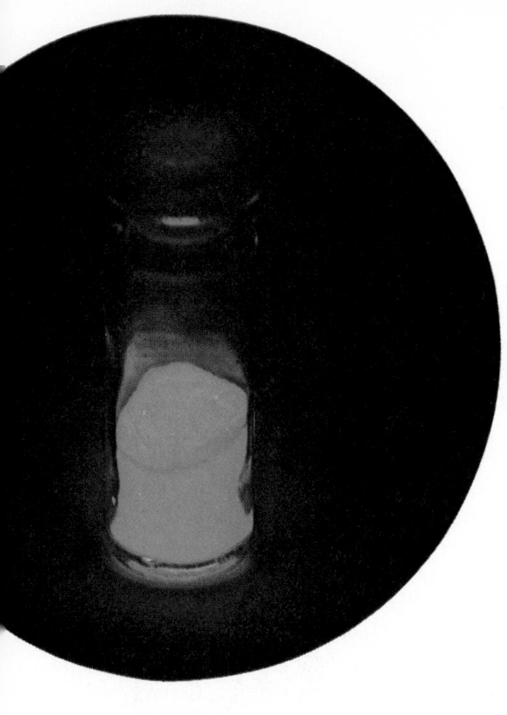

*The "**light of the future**" shines forth from a vial of radium salts (far left). Its mysterious glow comes from invisible charged particles, which flow spontaneously from within the radium atoms. Marie Curie, who termed this phenomenon radioactivity, took the name "radium" from the Latin word for ray,* radius.

***Henri Becquerel,** who shared the 1903 Nobel Prize for Physics with the Curies, accidentally discovered radioactivity in 1896. The revolutionary significance of his findings did not come to light, however, until Marie Curie observed that radioactivity was an atomic property and went on to discover and isolate two new radioactive elements, polonium in 1898 and radium in 1902.*

through almost anything—books, wood, rubber, even through thin metal. He also found that the rays passed through living tissue, producing on photographic plates ghostly images of bones beneath the flesh.

The publication of Roentgen's findings caused an international uproar. The idea of seeing the invisible immediately captured the popular imagination. Speculation abounded about the possible applications of the rays' see-through power, and one London company advertised X-ray-proof underwear. On the more practical side, doctors used X-ray photographs for diagnosis and surgery, and customs officials for scrutinizing luggage. Within a year more than 1,000 books, articles, and pamphlets had been written on the subject.

Excitement of a different kind spread through international scientific circles, as physicists pondered the implications of Roentgen's discovery. In Paris Henri Becquerel, a 44-year-old professor of physics at the Museum of Natural History, investigated the possibility that fluorescent minerals might generate X-rays. During his experiments he discovered a related but even more astonishing phenomenon—radioactivity.

Becquerel knew that certain minerals would fluoresce when they were exposed to sunlight. Beginning in January 1896, only weeks after Roentgen's discovery, he tested dozens of mineral samples, first exposing them to sunlight, then wrapping them in heavy black paper and placing them on photographic plates. Any rays that penetrated the paper and darkened the plate, he reasoned, would be X-rays. Only one of the samples, a uranium compound called potassium uranyl sulfate, seemed to be emitting such rays.

Then Becquerel made a surprising observation. One evening he accidentally placed a wrapped sample of potassium uranyl sulfate in a drawer on top of an unexposed photographic plate. A few days later he removed the sample and noticed that the plate had been darkened, even though the mineral had not been exposed to sunlight, or to any other energy source, beforehand. Whatever radiation it was emitting was therefore unrelated to fluorescence; indeed, it seemed to be flowing spontaneously from within the compound itself. In Becquerel's own understatement, the discovery appeared "very important and quite outside the range of the phenomena one might expect. . . ."

Abandoning his original hypothesis, Becquerel tested other uranium compounds and found that they too emitted these rays. He discovered that the radiation continued unabated for long periods and persisted even when the compounds had been melted or dissolved. By May he had established that pure uranium was more radioactive than any of its compounds.

Two New Elements

The consequences of this second surprise spread as rapidly as those of Roentgen's discovery. In Paris a young Polish-born graduate student named Marie Sklodowska Curie chose to study the Becquerel rays for her doctoral research project. For the time being her husband, Pierre, a professor of physics at the Sorbonne, continued his teaching and his research concerning the structure of crystals.

Marie Curie began where Becquerel had left off, refining and extending his observations. First she tested

Early radium workers unwittingly exposed themselves to dangerous—and often lethal—doses of radiation.

A DEADLY LEGACY

Radium's remarkable healing powers were more readily apparent than its destructive nature. For years radium technicians worked without protection. Thousands of innocents bought and used such radium panaceas as Radithor (at right), which promised to cure more than 160 ailments. Only after scores became sick and died from exposure to radium did men begin to understand its deadly powers.

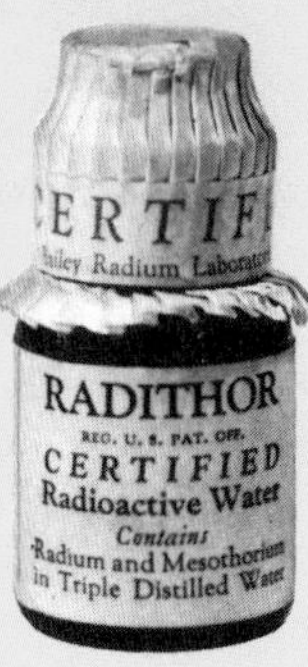

all the known elements and their compounds for evidence of radiation. Within weeks she discovered that another element, thorium, and its compounds also emitted Becquerel rays. None of the other elements, however, seemed to have this peculiar property, which she termed radioactivity. After exhaustive tests she realized that the phenomenon was not a chemical property but something new to science that came from within the atoms themselves.

Early in the spring of 1898 Marie found that pitchblende, an ore containing uranium oxide, was significantly more radioactive than pure uranium. Yet her own experiments and those of Becquerel had demonstrated indisputably that pure uranium was more radioactive than any of its compounds. There must be another element in the pitchblende, she concluded, whose radiation was even stronger than that of uranium but present in such minute quantities that no previous chemical analysis had detected it.

Marie Curie was determined to find and isolate the puzzling source of pitchblende's extra radiation. Her husband, Pierre, sharing her enthusiasm, decided to abandon his crystal research temporarily to help her in that difficult undertaking. When they began work in April 1898, neither of them realized how prodigious a task they had set for themselves. They assumed, conservatively, that the substance they were seeking composed about 1 percent of pitchblende's makeup. In fact, it was less than one ten-thousandth of 1 percent.

Working with barely a cupful of pitchblende, the Curies slowly separated and analyzed its components. It was an arduous undertaking, and the couple, who were also teaching and looking after their infant daughter Irène, worked long into the night in their tiny, cluttered laboratory. First they ground the pitchblende to a powder and dissolved it in acid. Then they repeatedly boiled, froze, and precipitated the acid solution to break it down into its separate parts. After removing all traces of uranium, they separated and discarded all the other known elements. At each step they checked to be sure that their remaining material was still radioactive.

In June Pierre and Marie had reduced their original sample to a handful of fine black powder, which registered 150 times more radioactivity than uranium. After additional refinement the powder became even more radioactive. By the end of the month Marie was convinced that they were finally closing in on their suspect. She decided to name the new element polonium, in honor of her native Poland.

A few months later they separated polonium from the powder. Then something wholly unexpected happened: They discovered that the residual powder was still radioactive. The pitchblende had contained not one but two unknown elements. The second was present in such minute quantities that it would take many months to separate it in pure form. Yet even in an impure state its radioactivity was 900 times that of uranium. The Curies had discovered radium.

A Labor of Love

It took another three years to isolate pure radium and to determine its atomic weight and number. First the Curies moved to a laboratory large enough to house the enormous quantities of pitchblende required for their work, a big, drafty shed that stood in a courtyard of the Sorbonne's School of Physics. In those miserable surroundings, described by one visitor as a "cross between a stable and a potato cellar," Marie and Pierre Curie were to spend the happiest and most rewarding years of their lives, completely absorbed in their work.

Next they had to find a plentiful source of pitchblende. Fortunately, the ore was considered almost valueless once its uranium had been removed, and the Curies were able to obtain the residues they needed at a low price from the Joachimsthal mine in Bohemia (now part of Czechoslovakia). Early in 1899 the huge sacks arrived, filled with tons of finely crushed brown rocks still mixed with pine needles and dirt. The work

AN ATLAS OF THE ELEMENTS: THE PERIODIC TABLE

In 1869 a Russian chemist named Dmitri Mendeleyev devised an ingenious catalog of the elements, the periodic table. He observed that the elements seem to fall into regularly recurring (periodic) families with similar chemical properties. Using this clue, he wrote the chemical symbol and atomic weight (see below) of all the known elements on cards and arranged them in order of increasing weight, placing elements with similar properties underneath one another. The resulting chart, the model for the modern version below, ordered the elements in a series of vertical families and horizontal rows or periods. Because of its unique chemical properties, hydrogen, the lightest element, is set slightly apart from the others.

In Mendeleyev's day scientists believed the atom was indivisible, but the discovery of X-rays and radioactivity suggested this was not true. Today we know that the atom is made up of three major particles—the proton, the neutron, and the electron. The protons and neutrons make up the nucleus of the atom; the electrons, which orbit the nucleus, determine its chemical properties and hence its position among the elements in the periodic table.

Simplified models of the atoms of elements in the family of alkali metals and those in the second period appear above the table. Notice that all alkali metals have a single electron in the outer orbit. It is this structural similarity that gives rise to their chemical similarities.

Within the second period the situation is quite different. Although every atom has two electron orbits, the number of electrons in the outer orbit varies. This structural difference makes for distinct chemical differences. As the number of outer electrons increases, the properties change from metal to nonmetal.

When the outer orbit is filled with eight electrons (neon), the second period is complete. Sodium, which begins the third period, has an additional electron orbit. The periods become longer and more complex as the number of electron orbits increases. The total number of electrons in each orbit grows as well. The heaviest atoms are also the least stable: All elements after bismuth (atomic number 83) are radioactive.

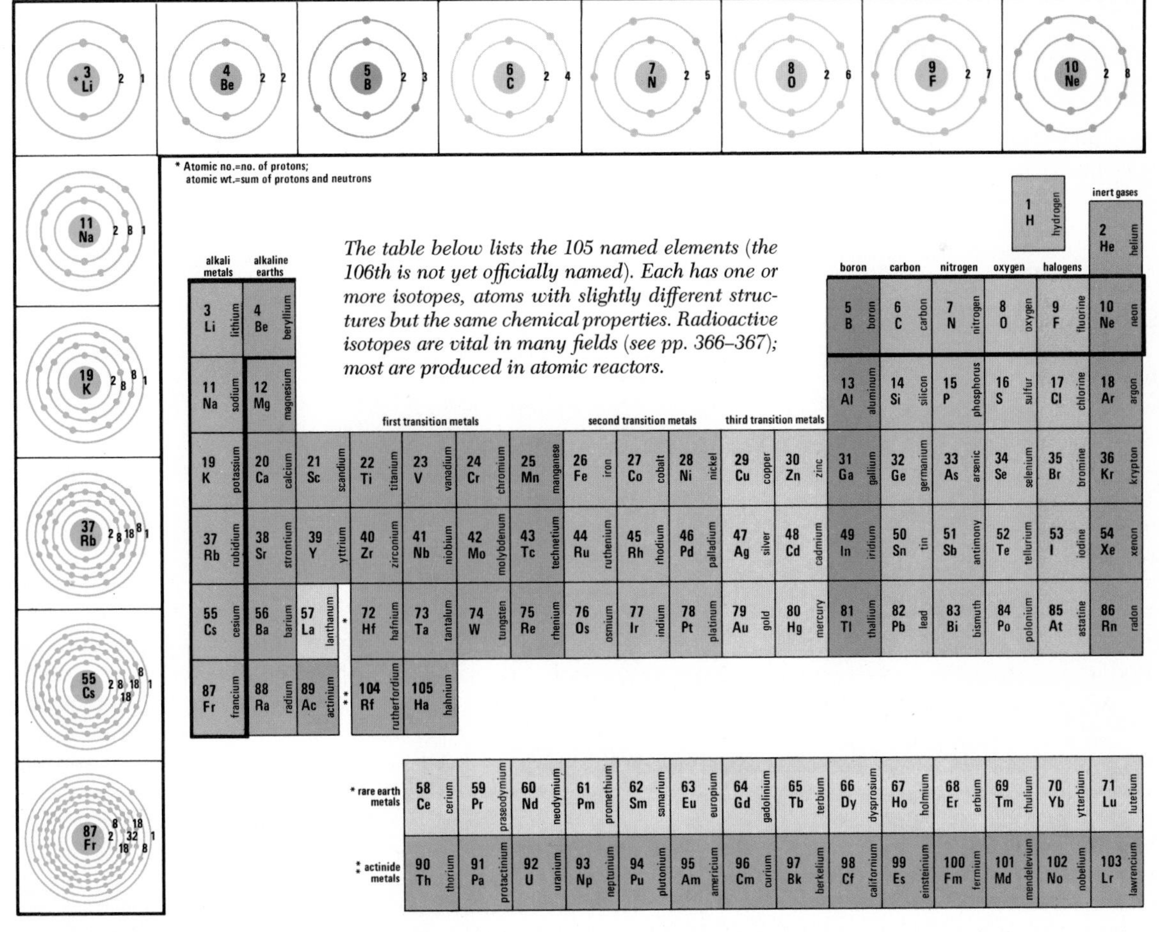

The table below lists the 105 named elements (the 106th is not yet officially named). Each has one or more isotopes, atoms with slightly different structures but the same chemical properties. Radioactive isotopes are vital in many fields (see pp. 366–367); most are produced in atomic reactors.

was almost on an industrial scale and involved exhausting physical labor. Marie later wrote of her work during those years: "I came to treat as many as 20 kilograms [44 pounds] of matter at a time, which had the effect of filling the shed with great jars full of precipitates and liquids. It was killing work to carry the receivers, to pour off the liquids, and to stir, for hours at a stretch, the boiling matter in a smelting basin."

Meanwhile, the daily exposure to radiation caused scarred fingertips and occasional bouts of weakness and nausea. The Curies never suspected the deadly source of their discomfort, and ignoring physical strain and illness, they continued to pursue their goal. By March 1902 they had isolated radium and supplied definite figures for its melting and boiling points, atomic weight, and other chemical properties.

Fame and Tragedy

The following year, when Pierre was 44 and Marie 36, they were invited to travel to Stockholm to receive the Nobel Prize for Physics along with their friend and colleague Henri Becquerel. Ill health prevented their making the journey. Their share of the prize money, 70,000 francs, brought them their first prosperity.

Less welcome were the instant fame and publicity that accompanied the prize. Radium and the modest couple who had tracked it down became overnight celebrities. The Curies' devotion to their work and to one another captivated the public, and articles in the press romanticized their life together.

Professional honors and speaking invitations were also heaped upon them. Marie, who had received her doctorate in June 1903, was given a university post in 1904. Later that year she gave birth to a second daughter, Eve. In 1905 Pierre was elected a member of the Academy of Science.

On April 19, 1906, Pierre was run over and killed by a freight wagon as he crossed a rain-slicked Paris street. Marie was deeply grieved by the loss of her husband and coworker. Slowly and painfully she resumed her experiments, and in the fall of 1906 took over the class Pierre had taught at the Sorbonne, becoming the first woman admitted there as a master.

In 1908 she published a corrected edition of her husband's scientific writings, and in 1910 a monumental, 1,000-page *Treatise on Radioactivity*, the first summary of existing knowledge on the subject. She was honored with a second Nobel Prize in 1911, this time in chemistry, for her descriptions of the chemical properties of the new elements. Poland established an institute of radiotherapy in Warsaw in 1913 in recognition of her achievements, and the Curie Radium Institute opened in Paris the following year.

During World War I radium and X-rays were used extensively for treating and diagnosing casualties. Radium produced dramatic cures in the case of tumors and was used widely in treating scar tissue, arthritis, neuritis, and various other afflictions. Its "miraculous" healing powers were also touted by unscrupulous medical quacks, who marketed a host of panaceas.

***X-rays and radiocarbon analysis** can help art experts determine the authenticity of paintings. The landscape at left, for example, by the 19th-century French artist Camille Corot, proved authentic after a radiograph revealed that an earlier Corot portrait (at right) lay beneath the landscape: A forger would probably not have painted over the original, but the real artist might have done so to save the cost of a new canvas.*

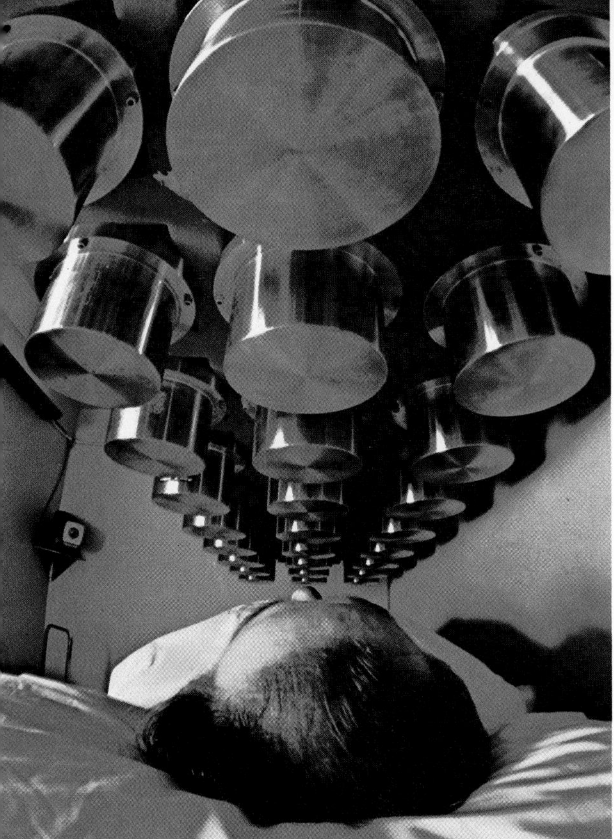

***Radiology** has been a boon to medical diagnosis and treatment, providing a means of peering inside the human body. With sophisticated scanning equipment (above), radiologists can trace the path of weakly radioactive substances in the body to gain otherwise unobtainable information about the size and location of tumors and the rate of metabolism.*

Meanwhile, scientists in France and other countries were extending the work begun by the Curies. Following the trace of Roentgen's X-rays, two physicists at Cambridge University, the British J. J. Thomson and his New Zealand-born colleague Ernest Rutherford, had begun to investigate the interior of the atom. Rutherford and others eventually identified three different kinds of radiation given off by uranium: alpha rays, beta rays, and gamma rays (see pp. 82–87). One of Rutherford's assistants, a German named Hans Geiger, helped fashion the first devices for counting the number of alpha particles emitted by uranium. These were forerunners of the Geiger counter.

More New Discoveries

Other radioactive elements had also been discovered. A friend and coworker of the Curies, André Debierne, discovered actinium in 1899, and in 1900 Rutherford isolated radon, a gaseous element produced by the radioactive decay of radium. Sixteen other radioactive elements have been added to the periodic table since then, one of them, curium, named after the Curies.

Today physicists understand a great deal more about radioactivity than was possible for the Curies and other pioneers. They know, for example, that radioactivity is a characteristic of heavy, unstable elements, which spontaneously emit particles—now known to be dangerous, even deadly—from within their own atoms, and that as the atoms decay, their structure changes and they become atoms of other elements. Thus radium decays into radon, which in turn becomes polonium, and so on, until its transformation into lead, a stable, nonradioactive element.

Ironically, Marie Curie, who devoted her lifetime to understanding that mysterious force, was one of its earliest victims. On July 4, 1934, she paid the price of a lifetime's work with radioactivity: A case of bronchitis led to anemic complications, and her bone marrow, weakened by years of exposure to radiation, could not overcome the illness. She was buried alongside Pierre at Sceaux, a Paris suburb. In 1935 her last scientific work was published. Its title was simple and to the point, neatly summing up the remarkable phenomenon which had inspired her tireless quest: *Radioactivity*.

NATURE'S ATOMIC CLOCK

Radiocarbon dating, developed by Willard F. Libby in 1947, has become a major tool in the exploration of human prehistory. Previously, the dating of prehistoric artifacts had been largely a matter of scholarly guesswork. Libby's system, for which he won the Nobel Prize in 1960, provided the first accurate means of dating objects as many as 50,000 years old. The yardstick is carbon 14, a radioactive form of carbon. All living plants and animals take in traces of carbon 14 during their lifetimes, but the process ceases at death. Thereafter, the unstable carbon 14 atoms, like all radioactive substances, begin to decay into stable atoms at a known rate. After 5,760 years half of the original carbon 14 atoms have decayed into stable nitrogen atoms. In another 5,760 years half of the remaining atoms have decayed, and so on. By carefully measuring the amount of carbon 14 remaining, Libby found he could calculate within a range of a few decades the age of bones, grain, seeds, ashes, wood, leather, or anything else that was once alive.

Since 1947 thousands of ancient objects have undergone radiocarbon analysis, often dramatically changing our ideas about early human life and evolution. As a result of recent findings, for example, archeologists have begun to revise the entire timetable of North American civilization. The time of the first human migrations to North America from Asia was once estimated to be 5,000 years ago, but radiocarbon tests indicate that civilized societies lived from coast to coast 10,000 years ago and suggest that the first people came to this continent at least 30,000 years ago and might even have arrived much earlier.

SCIENCE & TECHNOLOGY

1900-18

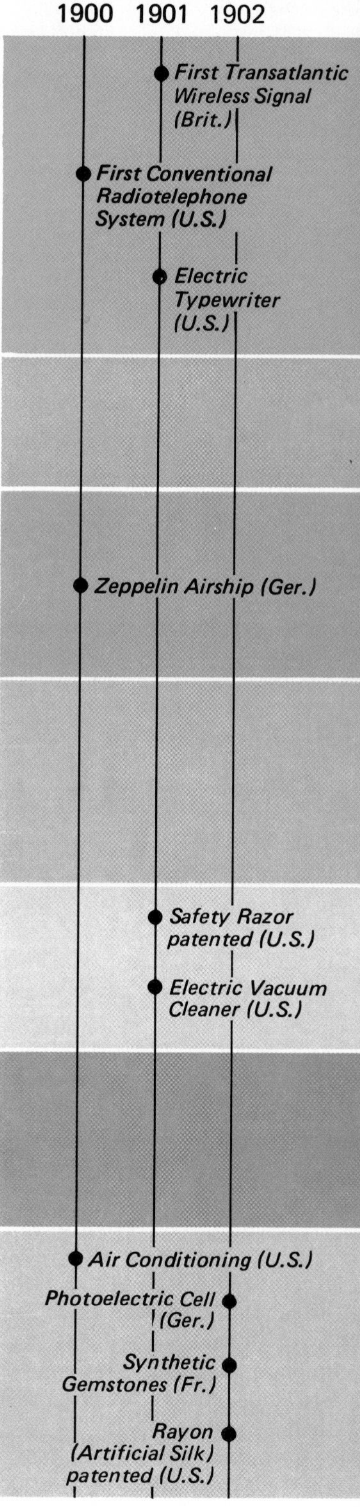

On Scale and Structure

In the opening years of the 20th century one of man's oldest ideas about the physical universe began to founder in the choppy seas of a scientific revolution. The idea, whose origin is lost in the mists of prehistory, was that the laws and structures of nature are consistent at every level of creation, from the cosmic to the minuscule, from the universe to the atom.

As late as 1911 this notion of universal symmetry was so widespread that when Britain's Lord Rutherford proposed his "solar system" model of the atom (see p. 86), the idea quickly became current that the solar system itself might be no more than an atom in some inconceivably immense molecule. In fact, though, Rutherford was one of the pioneers whose work finally helped to prove that the laws of nature are not so invariable after all. Tempests cannot really occur in teapots, for although molecules in the fragrant steam travel faster than hurricane-force winds, no air mass that small can sustain the complex processes associated with a storm; the sun, composed mostly of hydrogen, behaves very little like a hydrogen atom; and, in the domain of living things, we now know that the functions of life cannot exist below the level of the virus.

In short, it became clear during the first decades of the 20th century that the existing laws of science could not be applied without modification to every realm of nature; and, as science began to explore previously unimagined dimensions of space, time, velocity, and temperature, many established ideas had to be abandoned, or at least radically revised. Simultaneously, man's view of his own place in the history of the earth, in the hierarchy of living things, and in the entire cosmos of galaxies was severely jolted.

Pushing Back the Limits

By the middle of the 19th century geology and the theory of evolution had indicated that the earth was far older than formerly believed. Then, toward the end of the century, the new chronology was challenged by the British physicist Lord Kelvin, who concluded from his calculations of the planet's heat loss that life on earth could not be more than 20 to 40 million years old.

In 1907 new evidence emerged from yet another quarter: Ernest Rutherford suggested that heat from radioactive elements in the earth might invalidate Lord Kelvin's calculations, and an American specialist in radioactivity, Bertram Boltwood, soon showed that conditions suitable for life have existed on this planet for a few billion years. Eventually, the same radioactivity that warms the earth was found to provide a reliable basis for dating minerals and fossils (see p. 27), enabling scientists to form a clearer picture of our prehistoric origins.

At about the same time as the scale of geological time was thus being expanded, the earth's internal structure came under the scrutiny of the first pioneering seismologists. In 1906 Richard Oldham in England deduced the existence of a molten core from the way that earthquake waves travel, and by 1914 German seismologist Beno Gutenberg was

THE PACE OF INVENTION

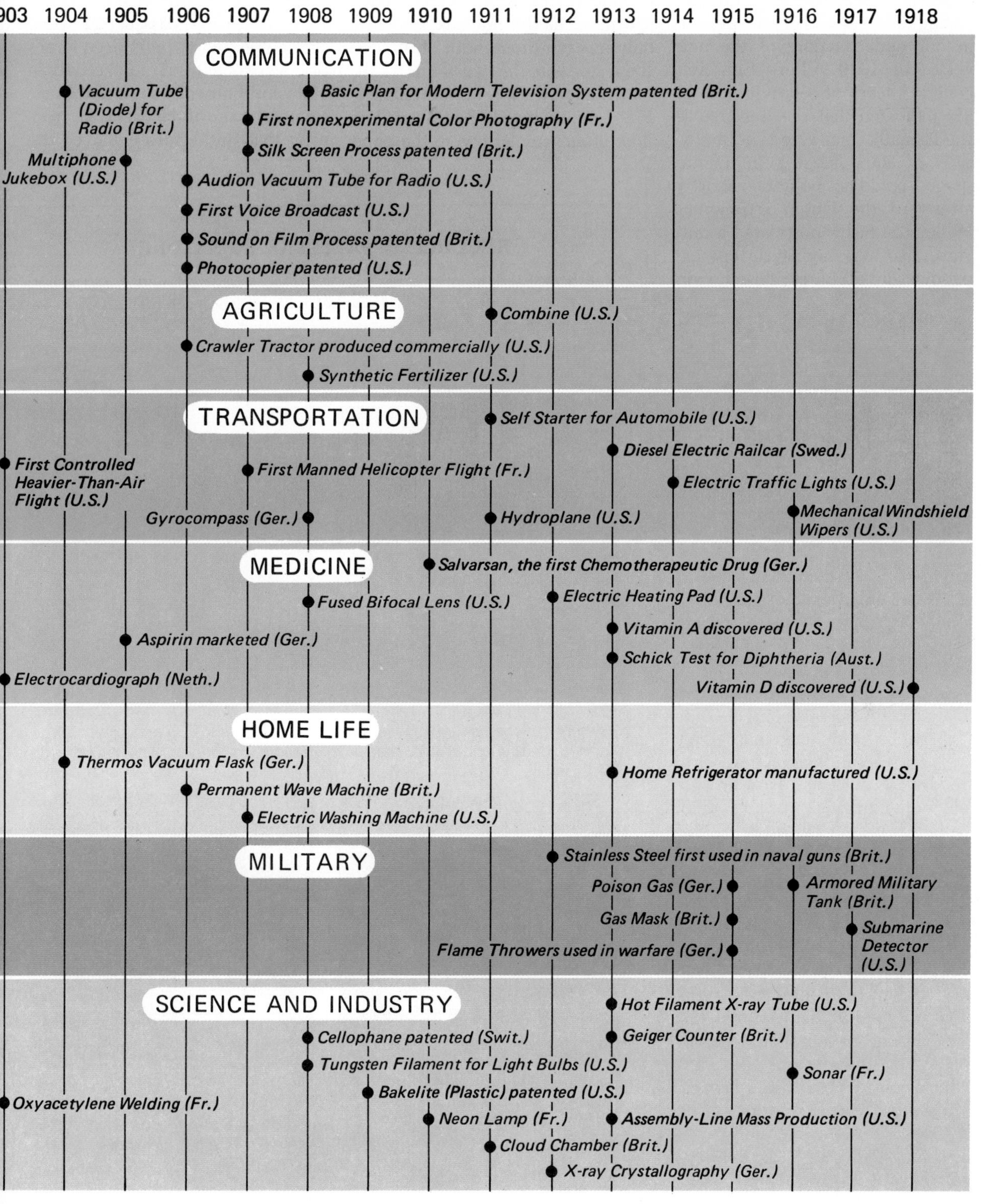

able to make a fairly accurate estimate of the core's depth beneath the planet's surface.

Meanwhile, other men were looking beyond the earth and preparing an extraordinary revolution in our understanding of the universe. In 1916 Albert Einstein's general theory of relativity (see p. 38) indicated that the universe as traditionally conceived—a multitude of stars hanging in infinite space—could not be stable. Shortly afterward the Dutch astronomer Willem de Sitter postulated a universe that was not static but expanding in all directions. Edwin Hubble, a U.S. astronomer, observed between 1922 and 1924 that many of the cloudy nebulae of gas and dust were not nearby, as had been believed, but faraway galaxies, as large as our own; by 1929 he realized that they were actually receding in all directions—as if the universe were indeed expanding.

The Atom's Inner Space

While some scientists were following lines of research that led to a vastly expanded sense of geological time and universal space, others were investigating the submicroscopic world of the atom.

At the turn of the century, though, many scientists still felt that such studies did little more than provide useful abstractions for chemists. But it was soon proven that atoms, although invisible (their diameters are on the order of one hundred-millionth of an inch), were quite real, and the work of discerning their size and structure began in earnest. J.J. Thomson, a British physicist, had identified electrons as charged particles in 1897, but it was 1914 before the American experimenter Robert Millikan isolated the electron and measured its charge. Rutherford used alpha particles (which consist of two protons and two neutrons) in his experiments for 20 years before the proton was isolated and named in 1920; the neutron was not discovered until 1932.

By the time of World War I it was known that the inner space of the atom is far emptier than the universe of the astronomers: Small as it is, most of the atom's mass is concentrated in the nucleus, which is only one ten-thousandth of its size. If our sun were the size of a golf ball, for instance, the most distant planet, Pluto, would be 617 feet away, but if an atom's nucleus were the same size, its outermost electrons would be about 3,500 feet away.

Vast as the geography of the atom proved to be, its exploration progressed with surprising speed. Eleven years passed between French physicist Henri Becquerel's discovery of natural radioactivity in 1895 and Boltwood's use of it to estimate the age of the earth; 11 years after that Rutherford achieved the

RECURRING PATTERNS IN NATURE

Nature repeats a number of basic structural forms throughout her vast realm. The spiral, the circle, bilateral symmetry, and the polygon recur at all levels of existence. Spirals generally indicate dynamic movement, while polygonal forms are more static. Circular and bilateral designs, most common in living things, also appear in river systems, water drops, and planetary orbits.

Natural spirals: the markings on an African waterbuck's horns (left), a chambered nautilus, and cloud formations (right, top and bottom).

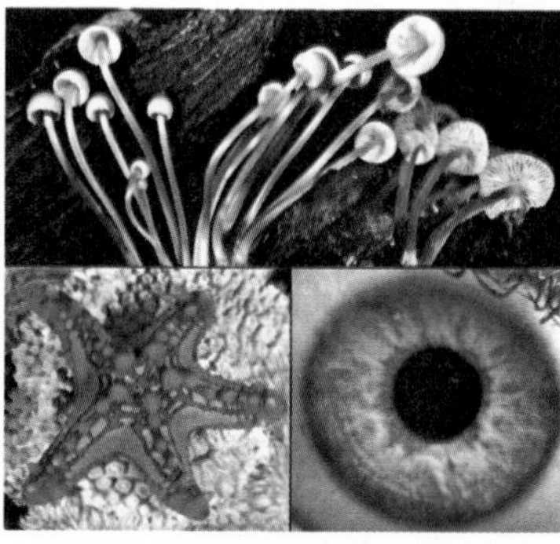

Radial symmetry: Mycena galerica *mushrooms (top), an African starfish, and the colored pigmentation of a human iris (bottom, left and right).*

Bilateral symmetry: a turkey vulture (top), the Wadi Hadhramaut in the Arabian Peninsula, and Calathea wiotiana *(bottom, left and right).*

Polygonal structures: a wild honeycomb (left), citrine quartz crystals, and the scaly skin of an agamid tree lizard (right, top and bottom).

ancient alchemists' goal of transforming one element into another. And although atomic fission was still years in the future (see p. 364), some physicists before 1920 began to look beyond it to the even more powerful process of atomic fusion, which sustains the sun and all stars.

Crystals and Cryogenics

The early years of the 20th century also saw great progress in man's understanding of structure above the atomic scale. Henry Moseley, a young British physicist, discovered that an atom's number of electrons determined its place in the periodic table (see p. 25), and in 1916 the American chemist Gilbert Lewis began relating this new information to all that was known about how atoms chemically bond into molecules. German physicist Max von Laue found in 1912 that Wilhelm Roentgen's X-rays were waves that could be diffracted by being passed through a crystal, just as a ray of light is diffracted by a prism. The following year in Britain a father-and-son research team, W. H. and W. L. Bragg, began to determine the internal structure of crystals by passing X-rays through them and interpreting the diffraction patterns produced on film. This technique eventually yielded synthetic fibers, plastics, and solid-state electronics.

In Holland the study of ordinary substances under extreme conditions was beginning in the laboratory of Heike Kamerlingh Onnes. Between 1911 and 1913 he was the first to study superconductivity, the low-temperature (near absolute zero, −460°F, the temperature at which all molecular motion ceases) phenomenon in which certain metals and alloys lose practically all resistance to the flow of an electric current. Like X-ray crystallography, cryogenics—low-temperature physics—grew as fast as researchers could supply new theories, typifying the accelerating growth that has remained the hallmark of all 20th-century scientific advances.

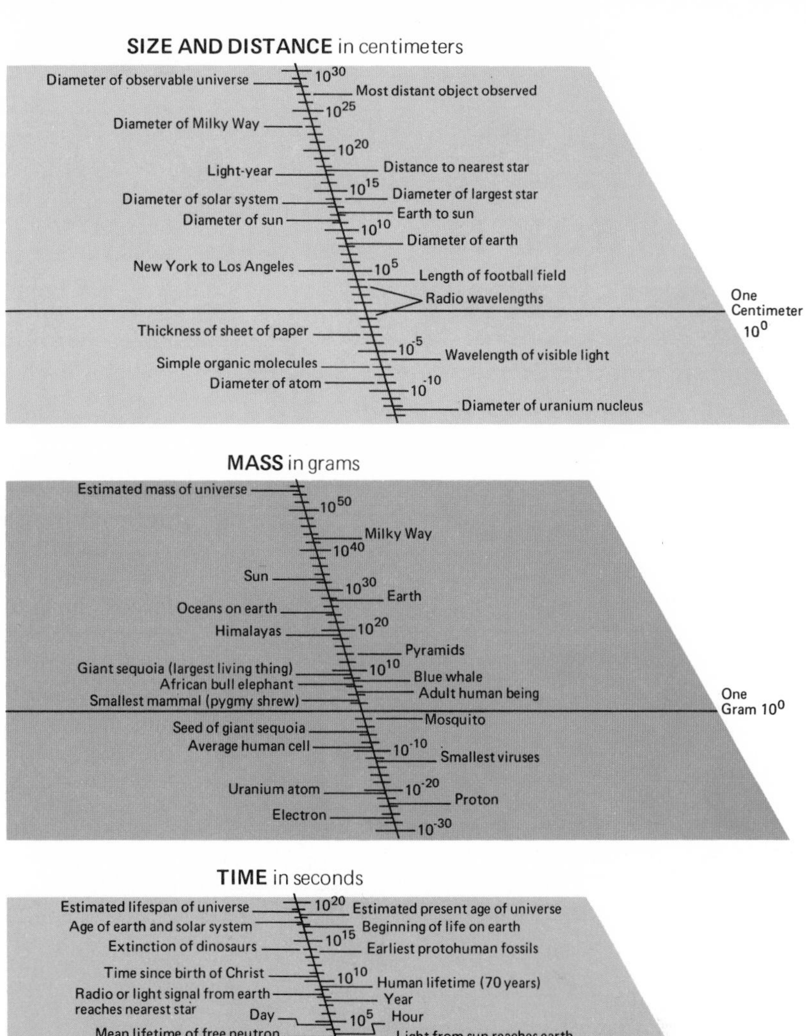

CHARTING NEW COSMIC AND SUBATOMIC DIMENSIONS

Since 1900 science has steadily expanded the known limits of distance, mass, and time, transforming traditional concepts of size and scale on both the cosmic and subatomic levels. These scales represent the present scope of our knowledge. Starting with 1, expressed as 10^0 (10 raised to the zeroth power), they increase or decrease by orders of magnitude (powers of 10): 10^1 equals 10, 10^2 equals 100; 10^{-1} equals 0.1, 10^{-2} equals 0.01, and so on. This system can express concisely the immense diameter of the cosmos as well as the brief lifetime of a subatomic particle. The mass of a human being falls roughly midway between the mass of an electron and that of the Milky Way—the ratio of the mass of an electron to a man is about the same as that of a man to the entire galaxy. In terms of mass, all living matter falls within a range of 10^{-13} to 10^9 grams. The universe itself may be bounded, but science has yet to find its limits.

1905
Showdown at Tsushima

Japan defeats Russia in one of the greatest sea battles of all time and joins the ranks of the world powers.

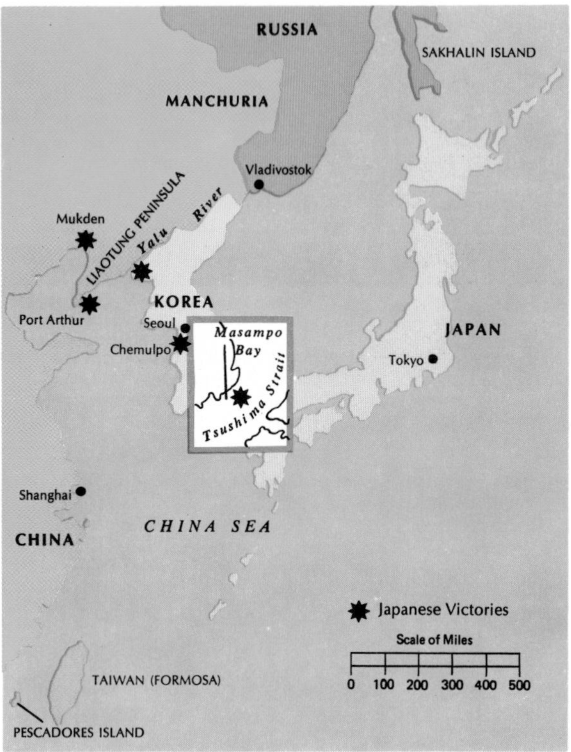

***Fierce fighting** in Tsushima Strait in May 1905 decided the Russo-Japanese War, the century's first major conflict. A Japanese woodcut of the battle (right) shows an imperial sailor slaying his foes. The war, fought between two expansionist powers for control of northeast Asia (above), erupted in February 1904 with a Japanese sneak attack on the Russian Fleet at Port Arthur. Despite repeated military defeats, the Czar refused to surrender until his navy was annihilated at Tsushima, spelling the end of his Asian empire and the rise of Japanese imperialism. By the Treaty of Portsmouth Russia renounced her claims to the Liaotung Peninsula, evacuated Manchuria, ceded southern Sakhalin Island to Japan, and recognized Japan's hegemony over Korea.*

"On this one battle rests the fate of our nation," Adm. Count Heihachiro Togo signaled the Japanese Fleet as he sighted the yellow and black smokestacks of the Russian battleships on May 27, 1905. His words were indeed prophetic. The encounter that day in the rough, misty waters of Tsushima Strait involved far more than victory or defeat; to a large extent, it would decide the future of Japan in the 20th century.

Newly industrialized and nationalistic, Japan was determined to join the ranks of world powers and establish her own colonial empire on the Asian mainland. But Russia, whose sprawling landmass stretched from Poland to Vladivostok, was equally determined to thwart her. Seeking a warmwater Pacific port, the czarist giant had already swallowed up southern Manchuria and seemed intent on absorbing Korea, Japan's presumptive gateway to the Asian continent.

Russia's designs on Korea had brought her to war with Japan 15 months earlier. Since 1895, when Japan forced China to withdraw from the peninsula and to recognize Korean "independence," the so-called Hermit Kingdom had become increasingly vital to Japan's economy. The fertile area supplied fibers, ores, timber, and other key raw materials for Japan's industries and provided markets for her exports. Japanese colonists had settled in Korean towns and cities, and Tokyo had

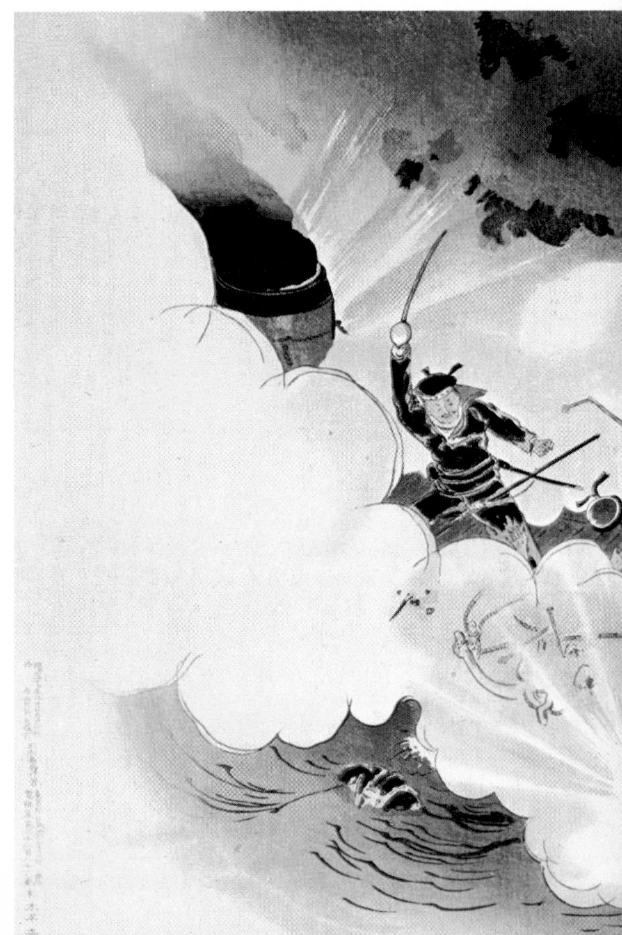

begun building a peninsular rail network. Government officials regarded Korea as rightfully Japanese, and they were prepared to go to great lengths—even to war if necessary—to protect their country's interests.

In 1902 Japan, alarmed by reports of secret Russian treaties with the weak Korean monarchy, offered to negotiate a pact recognizing Russia's dominant position in Manchuria in return for a similar concession regarding Korea. Negotiations dragged on for months. Meanwhile, Japanese intelligence reports in 1903 indicated the Russians had begun moving settlers and troops across the Yalu River into northern Korea.

On February 5, 1904, after long delays, St. Petersburg flatly refused to abandon her Korean interests. Never guessing that tiny Japan would be foolish enough to challenge her, Russia saw no point in further discussion. In response, Japan angrily broke off diplomatic relations and began preparing for war.

Tokyo's plans called for a quick, decisive victory that would overwhelm Russia's Far Eastern forces before help could arrive. Although Russia's total military manpower was vastly superior to Japan's, her scattered Far Eastern garrison numbered only 135,000 men and relied on the slow, uncompleted, 5,000-mile-long Trans-Siberian Railroad for supplies and reinforcements. Japan, on the other hand, could count on a total armed force of 850,000 trained soldiers, with 150,000 troops ready for immediate mobilization.

The Russian Navy was more than three times the size of Japan's; but the ships of the Czar's Pacific Fleet, divided between Port Arthur and Vladivostok, were less modern than those of the Japanese Imperial Fleet. Russia's larger Baltic Fleet lay halfway around the world, and her famed Black Sea Fleet was effectively blockaded by an international treaty preventing it from passing through the Dardanelles.

Hoping to catch the enemy unawares, Japan set plans in motion without formally declaring war. On the night of February 5, only hours after receiving Russia's final refusal to negotiate, Admiral Togo summoned his fleet commanders to the staff room of his flagship, *Mikasa.* "We sail tomorrow," he announced, "and our enemy flies the Russian flag."

The next day a small force sailed for the Korean port of Chemulpo (now Inchon), where it was met by a Russian cruiser. The cruiser was easily overcome, and the Japanese began landing troops on the Korean peninsula. Meanwhile, Togo, aboard the *Mikasa,* led his main force to Port Arthur.

Just before 10 p.m. on February 8, 10 Japanese torpedo boats stole into Port Arthur, where the Russian Pacific Fleet lay quietly at anchor. Unaware of the ap-

proaching enemy, the Russians mistook the attackers for their own patrol craft. The stationary, illuminated warships were perfect targets, and before the Russians could fire a shot, the Japanese had severely damaged two battleships and an armored cruiser. The next day, after a long-range duel with the shore batteries, Togo's battleships and cruisers blockaded the port.

On February 10 Japan formally declared war. The news was received with enthusiasm in St. Petersburg, where government officials expected an easy victory over the "little yellow monkeys." Spirits were equally high in Tokyo. Hundreds of Japanese young men volunteered for duty, a convicted murderer contributed his life savings to the war effort, and even the Empress found time to prepare bandages for the wounded.

Victory proved elusive, however, and the hostilities dragged on for months. Both sides missed opportunities, but the Russians were outstandingly inept. Unlike the Japanese, they had neither an overall plan of action nor any well-defined objectives; and their chain of command in the Far East—irreparably weakened by the death of their ablest naval commander, Adm. Stepan Ossipovich Makarov, during the Port Arthur blockade—was hopelessly inefficient and confused.

The siege of Port Arthur was long and costly to Japan. While Togo kept the Russian Fleet bottled up in the harbor, the Japanese infantry besieged the town by land. Vast numbers of lives were lost as waves of Japanese soldiers stormed the heavily fortified hills surrounding the port. The land siege began May 30 and ended seven months later, when the Japanese seized a vital hill above the harbor and bombarded the Russian Fleet. On January 1, 1905, Gen. Anatoli Mikhailovich Stoessel, military commander of Port Arthur, surrendered. His telegram to Czar Nicholas II reporting the defeat of his forces began, "Great Sovereign, forgive!"

The "Mad Dog Fleet"

Some months earlier the Russian Baltic Fleet had belatedly been ordered to the Pacific to relieve the battered Pacific Fleet. The Czar himself was on hand for the formal sendoff ceremony at Revel (now Tallinn) on October 9, 1904, and every leg of the journey received enthusiastic, if sometimes exaggerated or otherwise inaccurate, coverage in the world press.

The 18,000-mile voyage took nearly eight months and was fraught with misadventures, delays, and unforeseen difficulties. In command was 56-year-old Vice Adm. Zinovi Petrovich Rozhdestvenski, considered the best Russian naval leader since the death of Admiral Makarov. Most of his seamen, however, were untrained recruits from the Baltic peasantry, and the bulk of his officers were equally inexperienced. As for the 42 ships in his fleet, 4 battleships and 4 cruisers were brand-new; but many others, including one originally designed for sail, were badly outdated. Nonetheless, Rozhdestvenski, determined that his mission would succeed, did his utmost to overcome such shortcomings.

__The Russian giant__ makes a quick meal of his dwarflike Japanese adversary in a 1904 propaganda poster (left), but the real Japanese proved tougher. Zealous patriots signed petitions in blood (above) to show their eagerness to die for the Emperor. Many did die in the seven-month-long siege of Port Arthur (right), the Czar's Pacific naval stronghold which surrendered on January 1, 1905

The voyage went awry nearly from the start. About a week after leaving port, the fleet sighted a group of ships in heavy fog in the North Sea and concluded that they were Japanese torpedo boats ready to do battle. In panic, the Russians opened fire, sinking two of the "enemy" ships. Only later did they realize that the ships were British fishing trawlers. During the encounter a Russian battleship also scored four hits against one of the fleet's own cruisers. The incident caused a furor in England and earned the unit the derisive title of the "Mad Dog Fleet."

The long journey proved slow and demoralizing. When the fleet reached Madagascar in January, it learned of the fall of Port Arthur and received orders to proceed to Vladivostok instead. Meanwhile, the Czar, apparently reasoning that size would overcome the other deficiencies of his armada, dispatched a dozen ancient reinforcements from the Baltic. They joined Rozhdestvenski's fleet at Camranh Bay, Indochina, in early May. After a brief stopover for repairs and refueling, the armada set out on the final leg of its journey. To keep the motley fleet together, the admiral ordered his faster ships to reduce their forward speed.

Steaming northward through the East China Sea, Rozhdestvenski watched nervously for signs of the enemy. With fuel and morale running low, he had decided to take the direct route to Vladivostok through the narrow Tsushima Strait, counting on the usually heavy fog and mist to conceal his ships from the Japanese. Accordingly, he ordered a blackout of all but the running lights.

On May 26 the Russian admiral ordered all furniture and loose fittings thrown overboard. Crewmen made paddings out of hammocks, coal sacks, and tarpaulins and bound them to the ships' rails and fittings for protection from flying shell fragments. As a final precaution the decks were sprinkled with holy water.

Showdown

Meanwhile, Admiral Togo's ships lay in wait in Masampo Bay at the northern end of the strait. During the months since the fall of Port Arthur, Togo's fleet had been newly outfitted, and his crews, already seasoned in battle, had been drilling intensively for the upcoming encounter. Intelligence units dotted the coastline, ready to report the first sign of the Russians.

On the morning of May 27 Togo was awakened by news that the Russians were heading northward into the strait. By an unexplained oversight the Russian hospital ship *Orel* had failed to observe the fleet blackout and had been sighted in the heavy predawn mist. As he read the message, Togo reportedly smiled for the first time since the war began.

Togo immediately appeared on deck and ordered his fleet to prepare for battle. His men donned freshly laundered uniforms in honor of the occasion and as a precaution against infection if wounded. The gray Japanese warships were soon steaming southward to meet their adversaries. At their head stood the slightly built admiral, anxiously scanning the horizon.

Shortly after 1:30 p.m. Togo sighted the bright yellow and black smokestacks of the Russian Fleet. As the enormous enemy battleships bore down on the Japanese Fleet, Togo realized he must change course at once. If he continued on his original course, his ships would cross the enemy formation heading in the opposite direction. After an exchange of gunfire the "battle" would be over, and Rozhdestvenski's ships could proceed unopposed to Vladivostok.

To avoid such a catastrophe, Togo ordered his fleet to reverse direction immediately. The daring maneuver exposed Togo's battleline to enemy fire for nearly 15 minutes as each ship turned in sequence. The Russians quickly saw their advantage and opened fire; but although the Czar's inexperienced gunners scored 16 direct hits on the *Mikasa,* most shots went astray.

The Japanese, having completed their maneuver, steered a parallel course to the Russians and soon drew ahead of them, blocking their northward progress and forcing the enemy line to veer off course. Firing from close range, Japan's crack gunners concentrated their fire on Russia's four lead battleships, the *Suvorov, Oslyabya, Alexander III,* and *Borodino.*

From a nearby island a young boy watched as the two long lines of warships drew closer together and the waters erupted in the ferocity of full-scale battle. "Countless shells were flying around," he observed. "And as they fell into the sea they turned into hundreds of water columns. The guns flashed like lightning and roared like a thousand thunderstorms. . . ."

Japan's superior speed and marksmanship soon took its toll. The gray Japanese battleships, nearly invisible in the heavy mist, almost eluded the inexperienced Russian gunners aboard their all-too-visible warships. The Japanese had another decisive advantage in their deadly *Shimose* gunpowder, based on a secret French formula. The powder burst into flame on impact, producing unbearable heat and poisonous fumes.

Togo later boasted that the battle was virtually decided by 2:45 that afternoon, barely an hour after it had begun. By then the enemy formation was in complete confusion and all four lead ships had sustained direct hits. Minutes after 3 p.m. the captain of the *Oslyabya* gave orders to abandon ship. Half an hour later the huge vessel rolled on its side and sank.

About the same time the *Suvorov,* Rozhdestvenski's flagship, dropped out of line, badly crippled by an

TOGO'S WINNING STRATEGY

Admiral Togo (below) won the Battle of Tsushima in the first hours of fighting by a series of clever maneuvers (shaded on map; in detail below). As the Russians (red) approached the key area, Togo (yellow) was on a parallel course in the opposite direction and would have passed the enemy without engaging them. To prevent this, he executed four crucial maneuvers: (1) His fleet reversed direction, and both sides opened fire. (2) Togo, ahead of the enemy and on a parallel course in the same direction, forced them to veer to the south. Then, to maintain his advantage, he reversed course again. (3) The enemy looped back, hoping to escape to the north, but Togo countered with another turn. (4) Master of the contest, Togo could then keep ahead of and parallel to the enemy for the rest of the battle. He surrounded and captured the Russians the next day.

The Japanese first saw the Russian fleet at 4:45 a.m., May 27, 1905.

explosion on her conning tower. Rozhdestvenski, who had received a serious head injury from a flying shell fragment, was removed unconscious to a smaller ship. It would be hours before his second in command, Adm. Nicholas Nebogatov, learned that he had become acting commander of the Russian Fleet.

Meanwhile, the captain of the *Alexander III,* which had replaced the *Suvorov* as lead ship, tried to escape the enemy by turning westward; but Togo's ships blocked the way and continued their relentless bombardment. About 6 p.m. the *Alexander III,* her decks ringed with fire and smoke, fell out of line. She sank shortly after 7 p.m., carrying her entire crew of 900 men with her. The *Borodino* soon met a similar fate.

That evening Togo withdrew his battleships to the north to bar the enemy from escaping to Vladivostok, while his smaller destroyers and torpedo boats continued their assault through the night. By midmorning the next day Togo's fleet had surrounded what remained of the Russian Fleet, and Admiral Nebogatov raised the flag of surrender. He would later be court-martialed and sentenced to death for his action.

The Russian Fleet had been annihilated. Of the 38 ships that had entered the battle, all but 3 had been sunk, disabled, or captured. Some 4,800 crewmen and officers, nearly half the total manpower, had been killed. The Japanese, on the other hand, had lost only 3 torpedo boats and 117 men. In terms of tonnage lost, it was the greatest sea battle to date, surpassed only by the huge air-and-sea conflicts of World War II.

When news of the victory reached Tokyo, joyous crowds poured into the streets to celebrate. That night there was singing and dancing in Hibiya Park, with streamers flying and dazzling fireworks displays. The mood in St. Petersburg was quite different. For the discontented masses in Russia the humiliation was yet another example of the corruption, ineptitude, and inefficiency of the czarist regime. Mutinies by disgruntled returning veterans helped spark the abortive 1905 revolution. Twelve years later another disastrous war would precipitate a second revolution and overthrow the St. Petersburg dynasty (see pp. 132–139).

In the capitals of the world, leaders were stunned by Japan's remarkable achievement. Never in modern times had an Asian nation successfully challenged a Western power. Moreover, Japan had won using Western weapons and techniques. Thereafter, the Island Kingdom was recognized as one of the world's major naval powers.

Tsushima heralded Japan's emergence as the dominant power in eastern Asia. By the Treaty of Portsmouth, signed September 5, 1905, Japan gained control of the Liaotung Peninsula, including Port Arthur, and the southern half of Sakhalin Island. In addition, Russia agreed to evacuate her troops from Manchuria and to recognize Japan's exclusive rights in Korea; five years later Japan formally annexed the Hermit Kingdom. Only by skillful diplomatic maneuvering was Russia able to avoid paying a huge war indemnity and ceding more territory.

The repercussions of Tsushima were immense. Apart from the new status it bestowed upon Japan in the eyes of the world, it upset the balance of power in Europe as well as the Pacific. Russia, her dreams of Asian dominance frustrated, turned her expansionary efforts westward toward Turkey and the Balkans.

In Tokyo, despite bitter disappointment at the limits of the peace agreement, Japan's success provided a persuasive endorsement of the virtues of military might. To a very large degree the chauvinism and belligerence of Tokyo's future foreign policy were a direct consequence of Admiral Togo's fateful victory.

JAPAN'S ECONOMIC RENAISSANCE

Japan's new military might, resoundingly displayed in her defeat of Russia in 1905, grew out of a concerted national effort at modernization. In 1868 agrarian Japan launched an all-out drive to catch up with and surpass the West. Relying heavily on Western technical advice and financial aid, the government reformed the economy, sent students to study abroad, and imported foreign weapons, warships, machinery, and commercial vessels. Within a generation Japan had laid the foundations of a modern industrial state. Factories replaced home industries, roads and railroads were built, a merchant navy was developed, an efficient monetary system was introduced, new schools and universities were opened, the first iron and steel mills began operating, and the modern army and navy were established. By 1904 a strong independent Japan, inspired by the slogan "Rich Nation, Strong Army," had emerged, ready to challenge Russia for control of northeast Asia. Victory over Russia gave added stimulus to development, and by the end of World War I Japan's position as an international power was firmly established.

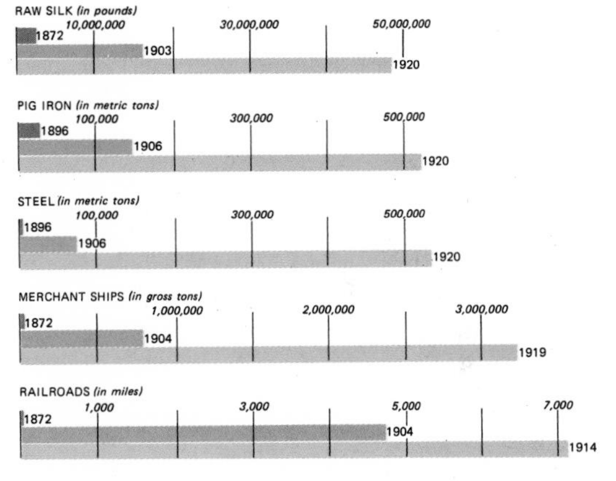

1905

Time, Space, and Einstein

A brilliant young physicist juggles the laws of time and space in his epoch-making special theory of relativity.

"I have no special gift—I am only passionately curious," Albert Einstein once said. That curiosity, expressed in two publications, on the special theory of relativity (1905), and on the general theory of relativity (1916), brought about a transformation in 20th-century man's view of the universe—and of space and time—more radical than any other in history.

The paper in which Einstein proposed the special theory of relativity was brief, one of the four revolutionary papers that he published in the German physics journal *Annalen der Physik* in 1905. In it the 26-year-old author (then a patent clerk in Berne, Switzerland) set forth "a simple and consistent theory of the electrodynamics of moving bodies based on Maxwell's theory of stationary bodies." Electrodynamics, the branch of physics that deals with electrical and magnetic fields, was pioneered by James Clerk Maxwell, the Scottish physicist, in the late 19th century. By applying his "passionate curiosity" to the electrodynamics of moving bodies, Einstein would soon lead his fellow physicists—and eventually the public at large—to the frontiers of a very strange world indeed.

Frames of Reference

In its broadest sense relativity is an everyday experience. If you are traveling in a train at 50 miles per hour and another train traveling at 70 miles per hour overtakes you, your impression of its speed will be quite different from the impression of someone standing by the side of the track; in everyday relativity, it all depends on your point of view.

The Italian physicist Galileo (1564–1642) described this kind of relativity some centuries ago. He also described a second, more puzzling kind, one that occurs within a closed frame of reference. Imagining a man on board a ship, in a closed cabin without portholes, he wrote: "So long as the [ship's] motion is uniform and not fluctuating this way and that, the man will discover

The great Andromeda galaxy *(left) is one of our nearest neighbors outside the Milky Way, yet it took the light in this picture 2 million years to reach us. What does it mean, then, to ask what is happening there "right now"? One of the "commonsense" ideas overthrown by Einstein was that the whole universe works within the same time frame. In fact, he said, the meaning of "now" depends entirely on where you are: When we look up at the heavens, for example, we are actually witnessing events that occurred in the remote past.*

A quiet, modest man *with a passion for truth, Albert Einstein produced a system of equations that overturned some of our most basic assumptions about the nature of the universe. His theories of relativity joined time, space, matter, and energy in ways never before imagined. Einstein subsequently sought to prove mathematically his belief in the underlying unity of all existence. Below, he explains an equation showing the density of matter in the Milky Way.*

no change" in the way an object falls, or in the amount of energy required to move it around the cabin. In other words, as long as the ship holds a perfectly steady course, without pitching, rolling, accelerating, or slowing down, no mechanical experiment can be made to determine whether or not the cabin is moving. Uniform motion (motion at a constant speed in a constant direction), Galileo realized, can only be demonstrated in relation to an external frame of reference.

The Speed of Light

In the period between Galileo and Einstein much had been learned about the nature of light. James Clerk Maxwell had shown it to be a form of electromagnetic radiation, and the general belief was that just as sound traveled through air, or waves through water, light traveled through an invisible, all-pervading medium called ether. Confident that not even Galileo's hypothetical cabin could be closed to the ether, Einstein's contemporaries held that it should be theoretically possible for the traveler with no windows on the world to set up an experiment using the speed of light (186,282 miles per second) to determine whether or not he was moving.

In this experiment the man would time the passage of a burst of light from one end of the cabin to the other, then reverse the direction of the light and time it again. If the cabin were moving, the light would in one case be traveling against the flow of the ether, and would therefore be slowed down; in the other case the light would be moving with the flow of the ether, and would therefore be speeded up. The slight difference between these two times would indicate that the cabin was in motion.

Not so, said Einstein.

His first step was to accept what almost none of his fellow scientists could bring themselves to accept (although it had been demonstrated in the famous Michelson-Morley experiment before 1905, and subsequently verified many times): that the speed of light is not variable, but always constant, regardless of the movement of the measuring apparatus; nor is it affected by the flow of the ether (whose existence had never actually been proven by an experiment, and which Einstein now denied).

Once he had taken this stance, Einstein was logically forced to conclude that the man in the cabin not only cannot perform any mechanical experiments to determine whether the ship is at rest or moving uniformly, but also cannot determine its rest or motion through any experiments involving the behavior of light, radio, or electrical currents.

Einstein admitted his conclusions were "apparently irreconcilable." For how could there be, on the one hand, a truly universal constant (the speed of light), and, on the other, no possibility of using it as a standard of reference? With the aid of an imaginary experiment such as he often used, we can see how Einstein approached the problem. Visualize a railroad car that can be set in motion at any uniform velocity. On it are a flashlight, a mirror, and a stopwatch.

First, while the car is at rest, send a light beam to the mirror and back. Traveling at the speed of light (usually designated *c*) it takes a certain amount of time, say *t*, to cover twice the distance between the light and the mirror. Call that distance *2d*.

Now start the car moving to the right at a very high speed, staying aboard it yourself. Again, you will observe the light traveling the distance *2d* in time *t*, as Einstein's theory holds it must, for otherwise you could use the time variation to determine whether or not you were in a state of uniform motion.

But wait! Try it again, this time getting off the car and watching it go by. From your new stationary point of view *this* is what you will see: It is obvious

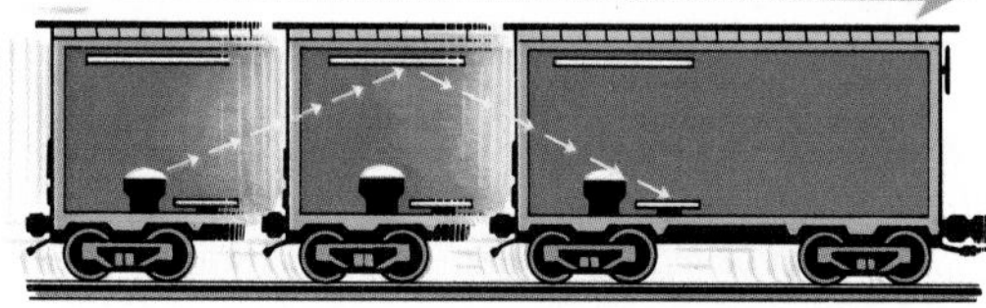

to you as a stationary observer that the light is traveling a distance considerably greater than *2d*.

Einstein's startling conclusion is the only way out of this paradox: In any system (such as our railroad car) moving at a very high speed, time itself *slows down* compared to a system at rest—in this case the earth.

A similar demonstration shows that space as well as time is affected by motion. If the beam of light is set up to travel in the direction of the car's motion, and synchronized clocks tell us how long it takes to travel from back to front, we have in effect a measurement of the car's length. For a stationary observer, though, the car's motion increases the distance the light must travel; again, to maintain the constancy of the speed of light and the length of time, the moving car must be *shorter* than it was at rest.

Neither of these effects would be noticed by an observer inside the car: If he timed the speed of light or measured the length of the car they would be unchanged—but only because his clock would be ticking more slowly (again, in relation to a stationary clock outside) and his tape measure would have contracted lengthwise in the same proportion as the car itself.

For example, a car measuring 100 feet long while stationary would, if rolling along at half the speed of light, still be measured at 100 feet by an observer traveling inside it; but a second observer standing beside the tracks as it passed would find that the car had shrunk to a length of about 85 feet. Moreover, if the two colleagues timed their experiment with identical, synchronized clocks, they would discover that the clock taken on the high-speed trip had fallen slightly behind its twin—not through any mechanical defects, but because time itself had been passing more slowly inside the car than outside.

In addition to time and distance, a third basic factor needed to describe any physical object or system is mass. In everyday terms there is little difference between mass and weight. Strictly speaking, though, mass is a measure of an object's resistance to a change in motion, that is, its inertia, while weight denotes the gravitational force with which objects are attracted to each other. In traditional physics it was taken for granted that when a force is applied to an object the object accelerates, and that more force produces more acceleration. Theoretically, no limits were seen to this process, for mass was assumed to be constant during acceleration and the universe had no speed limits. But in recognizing the constancy of the speed of light, Einstein realized that he had also found a universal speed limit—that nothing could ever travel faster than light in a vacuum. And therein lay a problem. For if mass is constant, what happens when you give a good push to something already traveling very close to the speed of light? Einstein's answer, as usual, was simple, logical, and astonishing: Mass is not constant. It increases with velocity, and the extra shove can never make the object travel at the speed of light; it can only make the object more massive.

At the time that Einstein predicted them, none of these "relativistic" effects had ever actually been observed—simply because the speeds encountered in our normal experience are far too slow to produce any measurable changes. (Even the astronauts of the Apollo program traveled at a paltry 1/27,000th of the speed of light.) But Einstein's predictions have been borne out beyond question by experiments with subatomic particles and by observations of the heavens. Electrons have been accelerated until they have hundreds of thousands of times their original mass, and cosmic-ray particles that should disintegrate before they reach the earth's surface do not do so because their "lifetimes" are extended by the dilation of time. Presumably, if any physical object—say a rocket ship—were to reach the speed of light, it would shrink down to nothing in the direction of flight, time aboard it would stop completely, and its mass would become infinitely large. However, Einstein's theory holds that no object can ever do so, for as one approaches the speed of light, more and more energy must be expended to achieve additional acceleration. To actually *reach* the speed of light, an infinite amount of energy would have to be expended! As far as we know, therefore, the speed of light is an absolute top speed limit for the universe, one that can never quite be reached by any material object. Photons (units of radiant energy) and neutrinos (particles created by radioactive decay), do travel at the speed of light, but they are not ordinary matter: They have no stationary mass and do not exist at any speed *less* than the speed of light.

Of the three relativistic effects discovered by Einstein, the increase in mass had by far the greatest implications. Before 1905 it had been accepted without question that the universe was composed of two basic elements: matter and energy. Each was meaningless without some sort of interaction with the other, but they remained fundamentally different things. Now, however, Einstein was forced to question this assumption. Since increased velocity produces an increase in the mass of an object, Einstein could only conclude that the extra mass was derived solely from the energy of the object's motion. In other words, energy *does* have mass. This was a truly revolutionary discovery. Matter and energy are not separate and distinct properties after all, but two sides of the same coin, two aspects of an even more fundamental reality.

$E = mc^2$: ENERGY + CONSERVATION

A tremendous practical benefit of Einstein's work is the possibility of producing boundless energy. If a controlled process of atomic fusion can be perfected, the mass of a single potato may one day yield as much energy as all the coal taken from this strip-mining site.

To be sure, the mass found in a given amount of energy would be almost imperceptibly small. As Einstein calculated it, the mass (m) is equal to the amount of energy (E) divided by the speed of light squared (c^2): in short, $m = E/c^2$. (Since physicists commonly use the metric system, m is normally calculated in grams, c in centimeters per second, and E in ergs.) More importantly, though, if energy has mass, Einstein realized that the reverse must also be true—that matter must have energy locked up inside it. To compute the amount of energy contained in matter one need only rewrite the equation in the form $E = mc^2$, and thus produce history's most famous equation.

The implications of this discovery were literally earthshaking. Einstein's formula helped explain the mysterious energy released by radioactivity (see pp. 22–27) and suggested that even a disintegrating atom (with tiny mass) might release a great deal of energy. Keeping in mind that c^2 means 186,282 miles per second × 186,282 miles per second, $E = mc^2$ reveals just how enormous the rate of exchange is from mass into energy. The total conversion of one ounce of any kind of matter would yield as much energy as the burning of 20 million gallons of gasoline. The technology needed to put this theory into practice was not yet available in 1905. It was only a question of time, though, and 40 years later a bomb detonated at Alamogordo, New Mexico, made it forever clear that Einstein's theory is far more than an abstract, theoretical way of talking about things.

The Cosmic Elevator

The subject of Einstein's 1905 publication is known as the special theory of relativity because it deals only with objects moving in a straight line at constant speed—a rather rare kind of motion. Indeed, most things in the universe, including our own planet and solar system, do not move uniformly. In his general theory of relativity, published in 1916, Einstein developed a system of laws that could be applied to nonuniform motion as well. In doing so, he again found himself questioning something long taken for granted —the universal phenomenon of gravity.

Newton's well-known law of inertia states that "every body continues in its state of rest, or of uniform motion in a straight line, unless it is compelled to change that state by forces impressed thereon." A car's acceleration presses us back against the seat, for example, or to the side against the direction of a sharp curve, because in each case our body is resisting a change in motion. In traditional Newtonian mechanics this force was considered a manifestation of the "inertial mass" of our bodies. We also feel a constant force, equal to our weight, pulling us toward the center of the earth; Newton called this the force of gravitation, and associated with it was "gravitational mass."

Newton also concluded that if equal force is applied to two objects with different masses, the object with less mass will accelerate faster than the more massive one. In other words, it is easier to push a shopping cart than a stalled automobile.

There was, however, one curious exception: As Galileo first demonstrated, two objects dropped from the same height will fall toward the ground with the same rate of acceleration, regardless of any difference in their masses. (A handkerchief and a rock might fall at different speeds, but only because of wind resistance; in a vacuum they would fall together. Millions of TV viewers saw an astronaut on the moon drop a hammer and a feather: They fell side by side to the moon's surface.) This presented Newton with a dilemma, since according to his laws of inertia a lighter object—one with smaller inertial mass—should offer less resistance to the earth's gravitational pull—and therefore fall faster—than a more massive object.

To resolve the problem Newton formulated a law of gravitation stating that the force with which the earth (or any other body) attracts another object varies in proportion to the mass of that object. Thus, the less massive object is pulled on less strongly by gravity than the more massive one, to a degree that exactly cancels its smaller inertial resistance.

For centuries the mass of an object, whether measured by its inertia or by its behavior in a gravitational field, always turned out to be the same. Einstein, however, found it very strange that these two figures should invariably coincide, since they were ascertained by different experimental methods and supposedly had distinctly different meanings; and he thought it too odd a coincidence that gravitational attraction is always just strong enough to overcome each object's inertia. He therefore asserted that inertial mass and gravitational mass are not merely equivalent, but, as he demonstrated with another of his imaginary experiments, indistinguishable. A man in an elevator drops a pencil, and it falls to the floor. He can account for this in at least three ways: (1) the elevator is at rest in a gravitational field (for instance, stalled between floors); (2) it is being pulled upward through space at a constant acceleration; or (3) the entire universe is accelerating past the stationary elevator car. Fanciful as it sounds, the point is important; there is *no way* for him to determine which of these explanations is "really" the case by any experiment within the closed elevator. The same is true if he drops his pencil and it floats in midair. Perhaps the elevator is falling without resistance in a gravitational field (i.e., the cable has broken); perhaps it is in orbit around the earth; or perhaps the elevator and the universe at large are stationary with respect to each other.

Since all the descriptions given above could be equally valid for the man in the elevator, Einstein concluded that inertial and gravitational mass are in reality *identical.* They therefore cannot provide, within a closed frame of reference, any clues to the detection of nonuniform movement, which is thus as relative as the uniform movement of special relativity.

Space Warp

Maintaining his skeptical view of accepted ideas, Einstein was deeply suspicious of the traditional notion of gravity as an invisible force that could reach across millions of miles and pull on an object like a fisherman reeling in his catch. But if the Newtonian description was wrong, just what was gravity? If gravitation is not such a force, what is it? Einstein's answer was that instead of invisibly tugging on other objects, a body creates a gravitational "field" around itself—the more massive the body, the stronger the field—and that within that field the basic geometry or shape of space is altered in a predictable way.

Thus, matter passing near a massive object is not "pulled" onto a "curved" path by a "force"; it continues on the shortest possible path—but the massive object so distorts the space around it that there *are* no straight lines in its vicinity.

Even as the scientific world was trying to absorb special and general relativity, Einstein was growing dissatisfied with them, and in 1916 started working on a new theory. In the special theory he had dealt with electromagnetic fields. In the general theory he had analyzed the outer cosmos of stars and galaxies, a realm governed by gravitational fields. Each theory contained its own system of laws and equations, and together they formed a more accurate picture of physical reality than any previous system. But Einstein was troubled by the fact that they were separate systems.

He believed that the four forces at work in the universe—electromagnetism, gravitation, and the strong and weak nuclear forces that hold the atomic nucleus together—could be expressed in a single unified field theory. In this theory no prior assumptions would have to be made about the nature of matter. It would be regarded neither as electrically charged particles (as in the special theory of relativity) nor in terms of gravitation (as in the general theory), but more probably as a sort of high intensity area—a wrinkle or convolution—in the field of space-time.

In 1950, at age 71, he published his new unified field theory, but he was not completely satisfied with it, and three years later produced a revised set of equations. The scientific world's reaction was mixed; some physicists believed the theory was adequately supported by

***Among the greatest** of Einstein's intellectual gifts was his capacity to unify, in mathematical formulas, apparently separate phenomena. One such achievement was to discern that the three physical dimensions of length, width, and height have no real meaning except in conjunction with a fourth dimension: time. Above, a carnation bud unfolds into full bloom: Its growth, like all phenomena involving movement, takes place not just in three-dimensional space but in a four-dimensional continuum of space and time.*

Einstein's new equations, but many others doubted whether such a theory was possible at all and felt that, in any case, even the rarified calculus used by Einstein was not advanced enough to settle the issue.

In the two decades since his death new developments in physics and mathematics have cast further doubts on Einstein's unified field theory—and indeed have led to some modifications of general relativity—but in the main his work has stood up well under the rigors of continual testing and reevaluation.

The Measure of Genius

"He who finds a thought that lets us penetrate even a little deeper into the eternal mystery of nature has been granted great grace." Einstein's words reveal his profound humility before the universe which he, more than any other man in this century, led us to interpret as a unified and harmonious structure. One of his colleagues has described the exhaustion that sometimes overtook Einstein in his later years, as, shaking his head, he would murmur, "I need more mathematics." Yet he never lost his faith that the universe is, after all, governed by laws that observation and reason can uncover: "God is calculating," he once said, "but He is not unkind."

Neither the difficulties of the unified field theory nor the apparent limits to our knowledge set by the quantum theory he helped to found (see pp. 82–87) was able to discourage him for long. His credo, in his own words, stands as a fitting epitaph:

> The most beautiful experience we can have is the mysterious. It is the fundamental emotion that stands at the cradle of true art and true science.

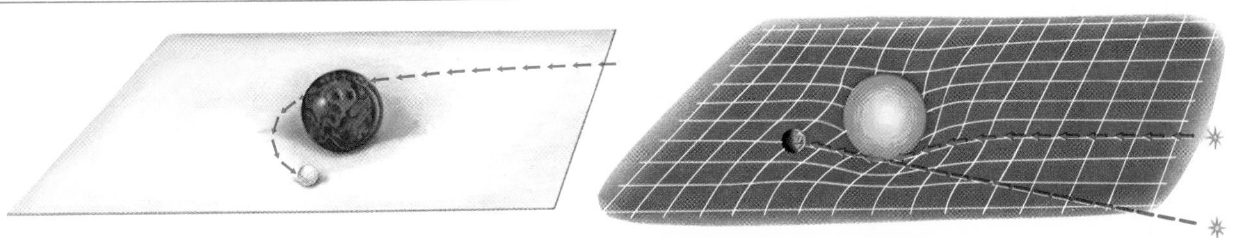

SPACE WARP: EINSTEIN'S UNIVERSE OF CURVES

Although gravity is an unavoidable fact of life, it is also one of the most misunderstood of all physical phenomena Yet as with so many of his insights, Einstein's analysis of gravity was fundamentally a simple one, as we can see with the help of a two-dimensional analogy (left): A bowling ball placed at the center of a trampoline will depress its elastic surface; if a golf ball is then rolled across that surface, it will naturally curve around the bowling ball. Now, someone seeing this from far enough above the trampoline that he could not perceive the warp of the surface might conclude, as Newton did about bodies in space, that the bowling ball is exerting some invisible "force" on the golf ball. But an observer standing beside the trampoline will readily see that the golf ball is only following the contours created by the bowling ball. This, in essence, was Einstein's view of gravity—that bodies distort the space and time around them—and in the first empirical test of his theory astronomers observed the behavior of starlight passing near the sun's edge during a 1919 eclipse. The results (right) dramatically confirmed his predictions. A star whose actual location was known appeared to have moved slightly, because its light rays were "bent" as they passed through the sun's gravitational field—and almost exactly to the degree that Einstein had calculated.

1906

The Birth of Broadcasting

An unpublicized Christmas Eve program broadcasts music and human voices for the first time, and heralds the beginning of a new era in communications.

Radio broadcasting, which was soon to become the most popular form of mass entertainment ever created, was inaugurated with a simple, unpublicized program on Christmas Eve 1906. This first broadcast was heard by a small and unsuspecting audience of shipboard wireless operators off the New England coast. Suddenly, at about 8 o'clock in the evening, they heard the startling sound of a man's voice through their earphones. He read the Christmas story from the Gospel of Luke, played the violin and a recording of Handel's "Largo," and wished them all a Merry Christmas. It was all over in a few minutes, and the familiar crackle of Morse Code signals began again.

The voice that made history that night belonged to Canadian-born Reginald A. Fessenden, an inventor who had long dreamed of broadcasting the human voice. He was speaking from his laboratory at Brant Rock, Massachusetts, not far from Plymouth. Fessenden, who had worked at the Edison Laboratory in New Jersey and had taught electrical engineering at several universities, had first conceived of voice radio in 1900, while conducting wireless experiments for the U.S. Weather Bureau. Two years later, with the help of two Pittsburgh financiers, he set up the Brant Rock laboratory and devoted himself to his dream of broadcasting not just the dots and dashes of Morse Code (which simply "chops up" a radio signal into long-short, on-off segments) but the sounds of the real world.

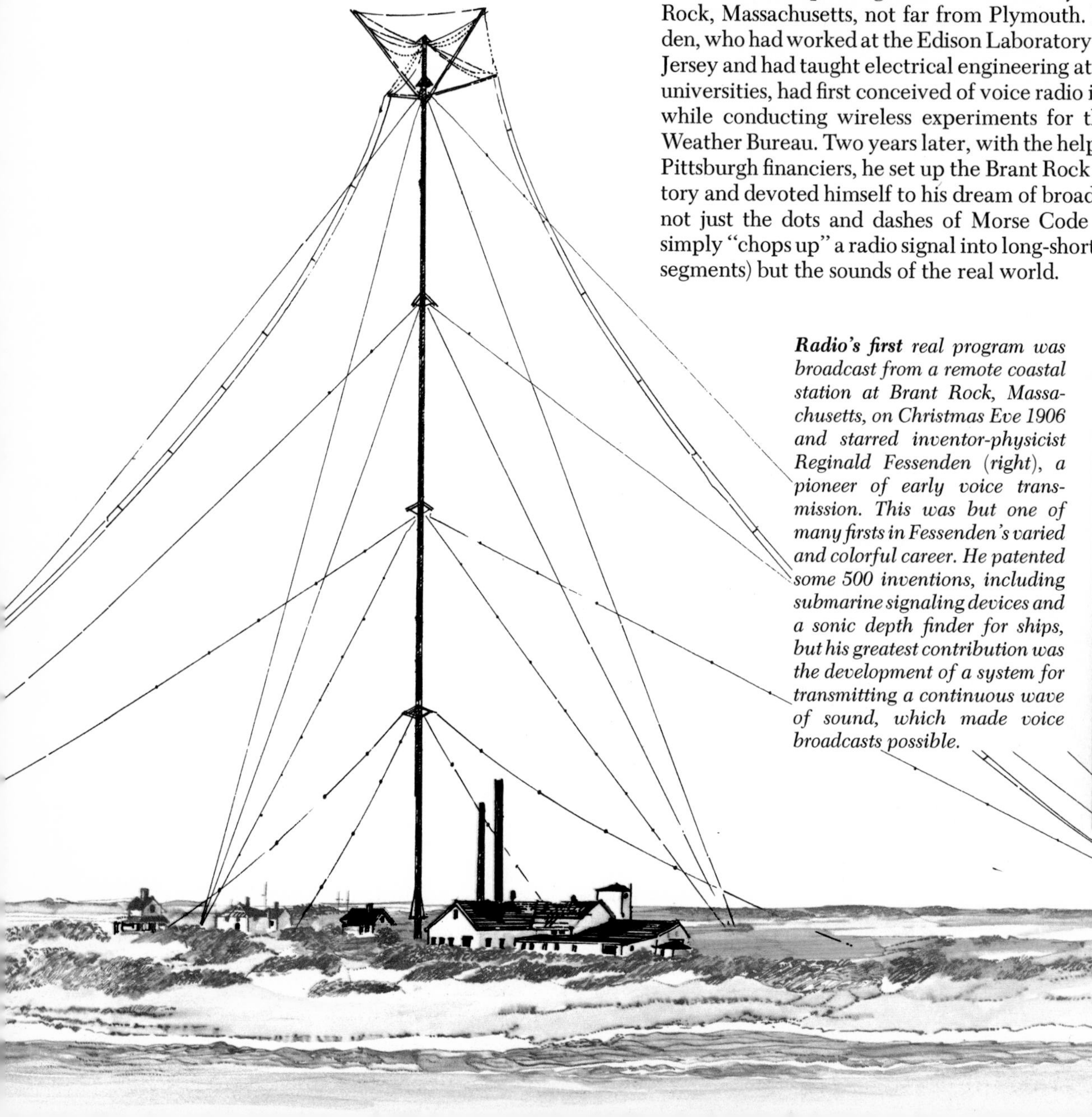

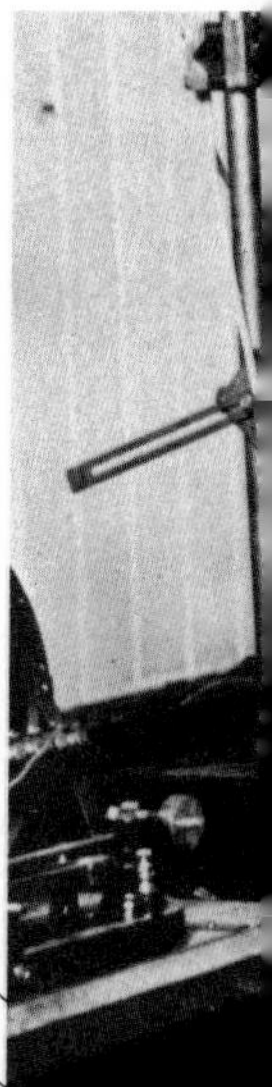

***Radio's first** real program was broadcast from a remote coastal station at Brant Rock, Massachusetts, on Christmas Eve 1906 and starred inventor-physicist Reginald Fessenden (right), a pioneer of early voice transmission. This was but one of many firsts in Fessenden's varied and colorful career. He patented some 500 inventions, including submarine signaling devices and a sonic depth finder for ships, but his greatest contribution was the development of a system for transmitting a continuous wave of sound, which made voice broadcasts possible.*

Fessenden's work at Brant Rock went slowly, with many false starts and minor setbacks. He spent long, lonely days and nights tinkering with wires, tubes, batteries, and antennas, searching for a way to transmit speech by modulating a continuous radio signal in accordance with the modulations of the human voice.

During the four years it took Fessenden to perfect such a system, another radio genius was working along similar lines. The man, Lee De Forest, an eccentric American physicist, patented his invention, a radio tube sophisticated enough to permit voice broadcasting, in 1907. The Audion, as he named it, soon became the standard tube in all radio sets. "I discovered," De Forest wrote, "an Invisible Empire of the Air."

The foundations of that empire had been laid only a decade earlier by a brilliant 24-year-old Italian named Guglielmo Marconi. His invention of the wireless in 1896, and his transmission of a radio signal across the Atlantic in 1901, had transformed international communication, providing for the first time a means of sending messages instantly between distant places. Before long a host of inventors, speculators, and enthusiasts began investigating the vast potential of the new medium, and by 1906 wireless had become the basis of a global network of communication.

For many years after Fessenden's 1906 broadcast voice radio remained an insignificant offshoot of wireless. Apart from a few prescheduled events, among them a program of live opera transmitted by Fessenden and De Forest from the stage of the Metropolitan Opera House in New York City, the airwaves generally carried more urgent information.

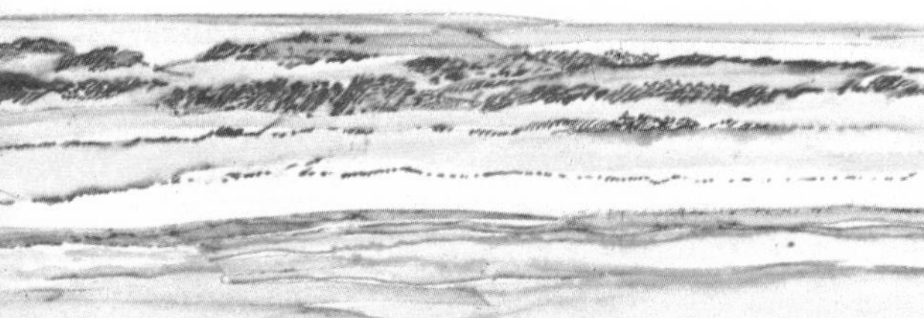

One reason for radio's prolonged infancy was that the equipment needed for mass voice communication had not yet been developed. Another was that the public was slow to accept the idea: Most people at first considered voice broadcasting an amusing but impractical oddity. Thus for 15 years or so voice radio was supported by a small but enthusiastic group of hobbyists called hams who programed and listened on headphones to impromptu talks and music played on phonographs. Their sets were cumbersome, unsophisticated, often homemade from copper wire and oatmeal cartons, and equipped with individual headphones.

A Radio Music Box?

Among the few who recognized the tremendous future of voice radio was David Sarnoff, a young wireless operator working for the Marconi Company of America. In 1916 the 25-year-old Sarnoff submitted a prophetic proposal to the management: "I have in mind a plan . . . that would make radio a household utility. The idea is to bring music into the home by wireless. The receiver can be designed in the form of a simple 'radio music box' and arranged for several different wavelengths which should be changeable with the throwing of a single switch or the pressing of a single button." Sarnoff was able to put his plan into effect a few years later at the Radio Corporation of America (RCA). The new design increased sales enormously.

Meanwhile, programing was also improving. In 1920 a Westinghouse executive, H. P. Davis, hoping to boost the sales of Westinghouse sets, asked Dr. Frank Conrad, a popular ham operator, to help him set up a commercial radio station in Pittsburgh.

On November 2, 1920, Conrad made radio's first commercial broadcast over station KDKA. (The term "broadcast" was coined by Conrad on one of his informal shows.) The scheduled event was the announcement of the returns of the Harding-Cox Presidential race, and an eager public heard the broadcast over public loudspeakers. The returns were phoned in to KDKA from a Pittsburgh newspaper office as soon as they arrived, and relayed by Conrad to the radio audience. In the lulls between returns Conrad played records, and two banjo players strummed tunes.

KDKA's tremendous success prompted other companies to venture into broadcasting, and within a year radio had become America's fastest-growing industry. In Detroit, Chicago, San Jose, and elsewhere local newspapers and merchants applied for call letters and set up transmitting towers. By the end of 1924 there were nearly 600 commercial radio stations from coast to coast. The rapidly increasing number of stations caused such chaos in the airwaves that the Federal Radio Commission (which became the Federal Communications Commission in 1934) was established in 1927 to assign frequencies.

These early ventures were designed purely to boost sales of radios, but as programing and equipment became more sophisticated, stations began selling time slots to advertisers to cover expenses. Station WEAF in New York City aired the first ad, sponsored by H. M. Blackwell, a real estate developer, on August 28, 1922.

Local stations soon began hooking up with one another to share programs. In 1926 RCA formed the first nationwide radio network, the National Broadcasting Company. NBC's initial coast-to-coast broadcast was the Rose Bowl Game from Pasadena, California, on New Year's Day 1927. In 1929 William S. Paley formed the Columbia Broadcasting System (CBS) by merging a group of smaller companies.

Networks, Stars, and Sponsors

Network broadcasting ushered in a golden era of radio, as stations competed for audiences and sponsors. Programs and stars proliferated in the late 1920's and the 1930's; the Hooper rating system kept track of the top ten shows. Listening to the radio became North America's favorite pastime, and in the midst of the Depression, while nightclubs stood empty and theater companies disappeared, radio sales boomed.

Radio started trends and shaped tastes on a massive scale. It captured the ears and imaginations of millions, reaching virtually every segment of the population. It popularized new expressions, suggested new ways of eating, dressing, and thinking, and brought news of faraway places directly into the living room. While some critics deplored the low standards of programing, millions of listeners liked what they heard.

What were they listening to? On a typical evening a family might hear a situation comedy, an opera program, a mystery, a variety show, a stage play, and a news report. Grouped around the Crosley or Philco console, they let their imaginations wander into the strange and unfamiliar world of *The Shadow*; settled back for a hearty laugh with comedian Ed Wynn, "The Perfect Fool"; dropped in at 79 Wistful Vista for a zany visit with *Fibber McGee and Molly*; or drifted back in time to "those thrilling days of yesteryear" and the adventures of *The Lone Ranger*.

Radio was equally popular in other countries, and between 1920 and 1924 stations appeared in every major nation. By 1930 broadcasts were heard throughout the world. Britain's first radio program was aired in 1919, and by 1921 there were stations in Canada, New Zealand, Australia, and Denmark. A year later France inaugurated regular broadcasts from the Eiffel Tower, and the first Soviet station opened in Moscow. By 1925 radio had spread to other European countries and to

A PAGEANT OF LIFE

In its heyday radio showered listeners with a rich variety of sounds and experiences. Like no other medium, it brought millions a generous sampling of life's diversity.

History Unfolding

"I have found it impossible to carry the heavy burden of responsibility and to discharge my duties as King . . . without the help and support of the woman I love. . . ."
—*King Edward VIII's abdication, December 11, 1936*

"Yesterday, December 7, 1941—a date which will live in infamy—the United States of America was suddenly and deliberately attacked by naval and air forces of the Empire of Japan." —*President Franklin D. Roosevelt, December 8, 1941*

German dirigible Hindenburg *burst into flames at its New Jersey mooring in 1937.*

RADIO'S BASIC TOOL

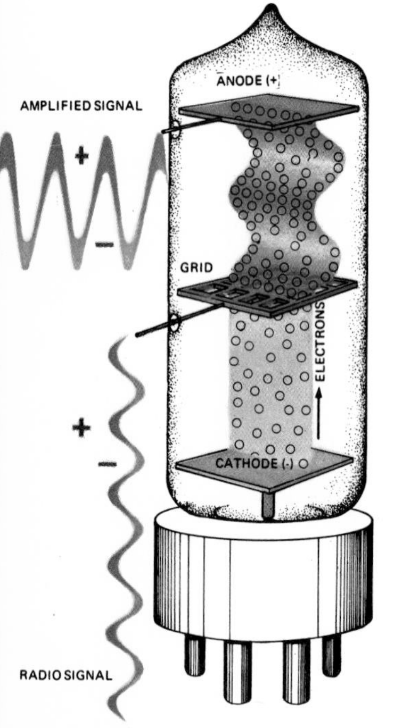

Lee De Forest's Audion tube, patented in 1907, made mass broadcasting possible by providing a simple, inexpensive way to amplify weak radio signals. The tube contains three basic elements: a cathode (negative); an anode (positive); and a grid, whose charge varies according to the fluctuating voltage of the incoming radio signal which is picked up by the antenna. A stream of electrons flows from cathode to anode, and the grid acts like a venetian blind in controlling this flow. When the incoming signal is positive (red), the grid lets all electrons through; when it is negative (yellow), the grid blocks most of the electrons. The result is an amplification of the signal.

Excitement, Adventure, and Entertainment
"... and Schmeling is down.... The fight is over.... Max Schmeling is beaten in one round."
—Joe Louis-Max Schmeling prizefight, June 22, 1938

"Incredible as it may seem ... those strange beings who landed in the Jersey farmlands tonight are the vanguard of an invading army from the planet Mars."
—Orson Welles' "The War of the Worlds," October 30, 1938

"A fiery horse with the speed of light, a cloud of dust, and a hearty 'Hi-yo, Silver!' ... The Lone Ranger rides again!"
—The Lone Ranger, *radio debut, January 30, 1933*

Real-Life Drama, Tragedy, and Suspense
"Charles A. Lindbergh ... landed at Le Bourget Airport, Paris, at 5:24 this afternoon, thus becoming the first person to fly from New York to Paris nonstop."
—Lowell Thomas, May 21, 1927

"It burst into flames ... oh my God ... this is terrible ... this is one of the worst disasters in the world...."
—The Hindenburg *air disaster, May 6, 1937*

Faith and Inspiration
"Hear, O ye Heavens ... and hearken ye people from afar...." *—Pius XI, first papal radio address, February 12, 1931*

"Let us therefore ... so bear ourselves that, if the British Empire and its Commonwealth last for a thousand years, men will say, 'This was their finest hour.'"
—Prime Minister Winston Churchill, June 18, 1940

Welles' "The War of the Worlds" shocked millions. The Lone Ranger fought for order in the West.

Joe Louis' first-round knockout clinched his 1938 bout with Max Schmeling.

Charles A. Lindbergh's 1927 solo flight made him a hero.

Mexico, Japan, and India. The first global regulatory body for radio was formed in 1927.

Radio in Britain followed a very different pattern from the one set in the United States. In 1927 a Royal Charter permitted the establishment of a public radio network, the British Broadcasting Corporation (BBC), to be financed by annual license fees on home sets, directed by a Crown-appointed board of directors, and responsible to the Postmaster General. This unique balance of interests was designed to insure the independence and impartiality of BBC broadcasts. Programs included news, concerts, opera, lectures, and dramas. All shows were broadcast "live" from BBC studios in London.

In the Commonwealth countries and Scandinavia radio followed a pattern similar to the BBC. Elsewhere, radio developed much as in Britain or the United States, or combined aspects of both.

The U.S.S.R. was the first country to use the airwaves exclusively for propaganda purposes. Under the first Five-Year Plan (1928) radio became a powerful instrument of the state, and by 1930 Soviet overseas programs were carried in 50 different languages and dialects. Italy, whose radio industry was commandeered by the Fascists in 1923, began foreign language broadcasts in 1936. After 1933 German radio was taken over by the Nazi Minister of Propaganda, Joseph Goebbels, who vowed "to make of broadcasting a sharp and reliable weapon for the government."

Democratic governments also used the airwaves politically, especially during World War II. The BBC sent wartime messages to resistance fighters in occupied Europe. The Voice of America, founded in 1943, carried American propaganda behind enemy lines.

Not long after the war radio's primacy was challenged by a new form of home entertainment, television (see pp. 278–281). During the 1950's millions deserted their radio sets to watch television programs. Television might have spelled the demise of radio if networks had not moved quickly to restructure their basic programing to emphasize things that television did not provide: up-to-the-minute news coverage, around-the-clock music and entertainment, and public service programs. People continued to buy radios to use at home, in the car, at the office, or at the beach. They kept listening to the little music box that David Sarnoff had predicted in 1916 would one day become a household utility.

THE ARTS 1900-18

Remaking All the Arts

A new age dawned in 1900—exuberant, fast paced, and above all hopeful. Radical change permeated almost every area of Western life. Thanks to his inventive genius and the wonders of industry, man was traveling in motorized vehicles and communicating instantaneously across continents and oceans. Urban workers, long the slaves of industrial bosses, began to clamor for power. Sigmund Freud was probing man's unknown inner being. Albert Einstein was calling into question the most basic assumptions of time and space. Nothing, it seemed, was sacred.

Inevitably, the arts mirrored this spirit of change. Music, drama, painting, sculpture, architecture, literature, and the dance were all transformed. Three of the era's greatest innovators were dancer Isadora Duncan, artist Pablo Picasso, and architect Frank Lloyd Wright.

Isadora Duncan. Serious dancing at the turn ot the century meant the classical ballet or its offspring, the romantic ballet. These dance forms could convey grace, beauty, and controlled emotion magnificently, but to a passionate performer their formality was somewhat limiting. At the beginning of the 20th century a young American dancer by the name of Isadora Duncan began to disregard the restrictions of ballet to dance in her own way. She was to become a global symbol of the artistic revolution of the early 20th century.

Isadora's dancing was something completely new. The dark-eyed, beautiful, and infinitely graceful girl rejected the stiff tutu and other confining ballet costumes. Instead, she wore only scanty Greek-style tunics and danced barefoot, seeking through improvised steps and gestures copied from Greek art to express the inner meaning of great music. Wherever she appeared she drew enormous audiences. Her new kind of dancing delighted the critics. "Not a single routine step is taken," wrote one, "and the whole dance seems like something that might have happened in ancient Greece." Another declared she had given the dance "a new form and life." Through a lifetime of public struggle and private anguish Isadora Duncan sought to do just that.

Isadora was born in San Francisco in 1878. A natural dancer, she taught dancing while still a small child and appeared on stage in her teens. She created a sensation at her solo dancing debut in New York City in 1898, displaying her bare arms and legs to the horror of society matrons, who stalked out of the theater in protest. The scandal established her reputation, and for the next two years she performed regularly in the elegant homes of New York's Four Hundred.

By 1899 she had scraped together enough money to sail to Europe, where she became the sensation of the London social season in 1900 and went on to subsequent successes in Paris, Budapest, Berlin, and Bayreuth. Some came to hiss, others to cheer, but all were fascinated by the sight of her graceful figure and the tremendous emotional intensity of her unforgettable performances.

***Wearing the Greek** robes that became her trademark (above), Isadora created a sensation in Paris with her dramatic interpretation of "La Marseillaise." She also founded a school to teach young dancers (right) her unique style.*

A born performer, *Isadora began giving dancing lessons while she was still a small child. In her midteens her mother took her to Chicago, where she made her stage debut as "The California Faun," dancing in a vaudeville show to the waltzes and mazurkas of Frédéric Chopin and the poetry of Omar Khayyam.*

In Moscow *Isadora's stormy, stirring performance of the "Internationale" (below) won enthusiastic applause from Lenin and other revolutionary leaders.*

Isadora was an outspoken rebel in virtually every area of life. She denounced marriage as deadening for any "true genius" and, declaring "the greatest thing in life is love," enjoyed a legion of lovers. Outraged by what she termed the "tyranny" of traditional ballet training, Isadora sought throughout her career to establish a permanent school where her theory of the dance might be taught to a new generation. But again and again her notoriety, extravagance, and total lack of business sense frightened away private backers. Finally, in 1921, the new revolutionary government of Russia invited her to come to Moscow and establish a school.

For a time she was happy there, winning enthusiastic applause from Lenin and other Bolshevik leaders. Then she became involved in a tempestuous affair with a flamboyant, peasant-born poet named Sergei Essenin, who was some 17 years her junior. Although neither Isadora nor Essenin spoke more than a few words of the other's tongue, they were formally married on the eve of a U.S. tour in the autumn of 1922.

The tour was a disaster. Isadora's reputation as a "loose woman" and Soviet sympathizer had preceded her. She and Essenin were harassed by immigration authorities and almost universally denounced in the press. Undaunted, Isadora infuriated conservative theatergoers by delivering revolutionary harangues between dances, while her husband drowned his sorrows in drink. When staid Bostonians objected to her politics and scanty dress, she defiantly bared her breast on stage, declaring that nudity is truth.

Evangelist Billy Sunday pronounced her a "Bolshevik hussy who does not wear enough clothes to pad a crutch." The mayor of Indianapolis forbade her to appear in his city. Frightened theater managers in other cities canceled engagements rather than risk riots. Finally, Isadora's citizenship was revoked. Weary and exhausted, Isadora returned to Moscow, where her marriage soon broke up. Essenin sank into chronic alcoholism, and in 1925 he hanged himself. Two years later, on September 14, 1927, Isadora too was dead, her neck broken by a trailing fringed shawl that had caught in the wheelspokes of the red Bugatti in which she was taking an evening spin. Isadora's death had been equally as bizarre as her life.

Isadora's Influence on Dance

Isadora Duncan's dancing was too intensely personal, too improvisational, to provide a systemized method of modern dance for posterity. Nevertheless, she had an effect on all forms of the dance. Michel Fokine, the Russian choreographer who, with the Russian impresario Sergei Diaghilev, went on to revolutionize ballet, was inspired by Isadora's dancing to inject more spontaneity and expressiveness into the older forms. "She reminded us of the beauty of simple movements," he wrote.

Without Isadora modern dance might never have come into being. Certainly it would not have been created so soon. The wide acceptance of her dancing in the early years of the century opened doors to others who were better able to establish schools and traditions. Among these were Ruth St. Denis and her husband, Ted Shawn, who helped codify modern dance and who established a school that taught some of the greatest figures in the field, including Martha Graham, Charles Weidman, and Doris Humphrey. Later in the century the revitalized classical ballet and the modern dance were fused into a new form, called modern ballet. All three forms are being performed today, giving the entire world of dance a new vibrancy, for which it is largely indebted to Isadora. She had dramatically demonstrated that the dance could reach beyond the restrictive boundaries of artificial convention and become "not the brain's mirror, but the soul's."

***The unorthodox cubist** style of Picasso and Braque abandoned traditional realism, breaking up objects into angular facets and planes. Color was minimal. The result was a muted "broken glass" effect, as in Braque's canvas "La Roche-Guyon" (left).*

***Italian futurism,** one of several artistic offshoots of cubism, used cubist techniques to create the effect of motion and energy, as in Umberto Boccioni's dynamic 1913 sculpture "Unique Forms of Continuity in Space" (right).*

*Spanish artist **Juan Gris**, who developed synthetic cubism, arranged simple geometric shapes and colors into semiabstract works, such as his "Still Life in a Chair" (above).*

***Picasso's "Les Demoiselles d'Avignon"** (left), completed in 1907, helped generate an artistic revolution. Its disregard of convention helped free painting from traditional bonds and paved the way for abstract art.*

Pablo Picasso. Isadora taught the world a new way to dance. Picasso taught it a new way to see. He was born in Málaga, Spain, in 1881. From 1900 to 1904 he traveled restlessly back and forth between Spain and Paris, a penniless artist. During this time he painted tramps and derelicts, predominantly in the melancholy colors that give this, his Blue Period, its name. In 1904 Picasso settled permanently in Paris and quickly became one of the city's most successful artists. His delicately colored, elegantly rendered paintings of harlequins, children, and women—the romantic products of his so-called Rose Period—fetched handsome prices.

Most artists would have been satisfied with this work, but not Picasso. In the spring of 1907 he began to work secretly on a large painting of five nude prostitutes. The subject was fairly conventional, if a little bawdy, but Picasso's new style overturned the conventions of nearly five centuries of painting.

Since the Renaissance, Western artists had been seeking to make the viewer feel as if he were glimpsing, through the window provided by the frame, either a real three-dimensional scene or the artist's interpretation of one. To give this impression on the flat canvas, artists developed conventions of perspective, lighting, and brushstrokes. In "Les Demoiselles d'Avignon" Picasso completely discarded such conventions in an attempt to present his subject not from one viewpoint but from all sides at once.

Before beginning to paint, he drew and redrew his subjects in scores of sketches, showing the figures from every conceivable angle, dividing them into simple geometric shapes and flat, intersecting planes. Then he reassembled them on canvas. The result was a deliberate distortion of anatomy, presenting displaced features and simultaneous profile and front views.

These extraordinary innovations did not spring full-blown from Picasso's brow. There are echoes of the crude but powerful Romanesque sculpture of Catalonia and of the mysterious, stylized wooden masks carved by West African tribesmen that were first exhibited in Paris at the time Picasso was completing his masterpiece. And, above all, there was the influence of Paul Cézanne, the reclusive turn-of-the-century French painter who declared that painting should be a "construction after nature" rather than a slavish imitation of it. Through arduous labor and dazzling brushstrokes Cézanne had shown how objects in the natural world could be refined down to the "cylinders, cones, and spheres" of which they were made.

But it was Picasso who synthesized these elements to create something altogether new, and he worked feverishly for months before he dared show the painting to even his closest friends. His reluctance proved well founded: Almost no one liked it. Although the canvas was sold in 1920, it was not exhibited in public until 1927, some 20 years after it had first been painted.

The Birth of Cubism

Too stubborn and confident of his own talent to be paralyzed for long by the critical opinions of others, Picasso doggedly pursued his new and independent path. Meanwhile, during the summer of 1908, his friend Georges Braque (who had initially been appalled by "Les Demoiselles") began painting a series of landscapes in which he did to the sun-baked countryside of southern France what Picasso had done to the human figure. Houses, mountains, figures, and foliage were all reduced to simple geometric forms and planes, then reordered.

Viewing these works, artist Henri Matisse is said to have remarked that they were filled with "little cubes," unwittingly christening the new movement, which has been known ever since as cubism. Simultaneously—and working miles apart—Picasso and Braque had

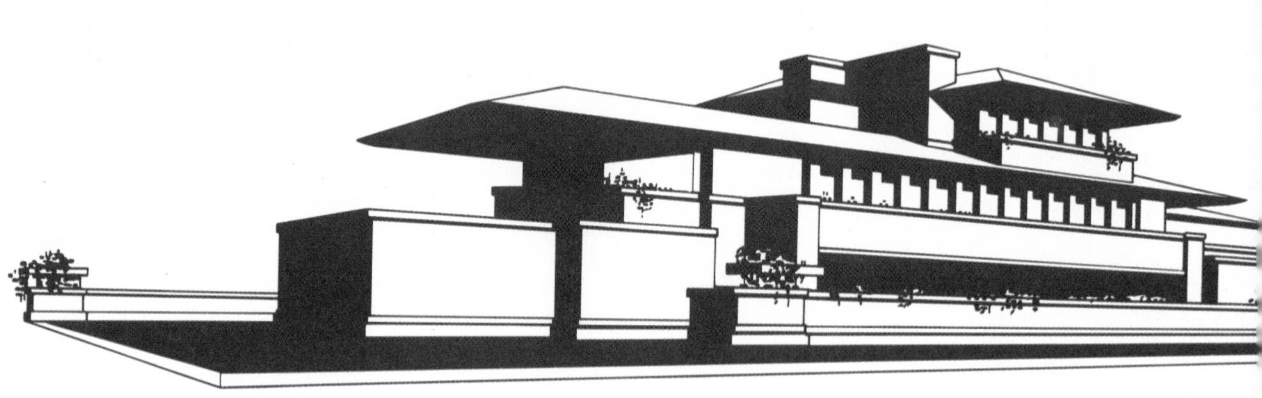

"invented" cubism, one of the most revolutionary and influential art styles of the 20th century.

Although critics remained generally hostile to cubism, young artists were soon drawn to the new style. By 1910 artists like Juan Gris, André Derain, Fernand Léger, and Marcel Duchamp were all busily reexamining their world on canvas, attempting, as Gris once said, "to create new objects which cannot be compared with any object in reality." Their innovations, in turn, spawned a host of minor art movements.

The most outstanding of these new styles were Orphism, which attempted to add a lyric quality to abstract painting by using facets of brilliant colors; futurism, which sought to show the subject in motion, reacting with its surroundings, through the use of broken colors and forms; and vorticism, which reduced art to its bare essentials—the arrangement of color and line in painting and of planes in sculpture.

Restless, mercurial, and awesomely prolific, Picasso himself soon moved beyond cubism. During a career that spanned almost three-quarters of a century, he produced a body of painting, sculpture, and graphics larger and more bewilderingly various than that of any other master, old or modern. Yet had he done nothing more than paint "Les Demoiselles d'Avignon," his position in the history of 20th-century art would have been established.

Frank Lloyd Wright. U.S. architect Frank Lloyd Wright was not a modest man. Fond of canes, flowing black capes, and broad-brimmed hats, unwilling to brook even the gentlest criticism, he once pronounced himself "the greatest architect who ever lived." Though few historians would echo such a sweeping claim, Wright was certainly among the most influential men in his field. Setting out to create a uniquely American building style, he succeeded in revolutionizing 20th-century architecture throughout the entire world.

Wright was born in Richland Center, Wisconsin, in 1869. As a young man he served a six-year apprenticeship in the Chicago studio of Louis Sullivan, whose monumental works and bold doctrines helped inspire his style. In opposition to the majority of U.S. architects of that time, who were building romanticized replicas of European landmarks, Sullivan taught that the form a building took should be dictated by its function, the use to which it was to be put. Thus, it was ludicrous to build modern banks that looked like ancient Greek temples or construct seaside vacation homes in the style of Moorish palaces. The world had changed, he argued, and its buildings and architectural styles would have to change with it.

Wright agreed. When he struck out on his own in 1893, he resolved to reject all historical models and evolve instead new, unorthodox forms, suited to modern life and employing modern building methods and materials. He began with the midwestern family home. "The usual Chicago prairie house lied about everything in it," he wrote. "It had no sense of unity at all, nor any sense of space as should belong to a free man among a free people in a free country." Conventional houses were ugly "boxes cut full of holes to let in light and air." Worse, he argued, these tall, narrow boxes were utterly unsuited to the broad, flat midwestern landscape.

The Prairie Houses

Wright believed a building must seem to be part of the site—"*of* the site, not on it." For almost a decade he wrestled with this problem, seeking to transform the old-fashioned vertical dwelling into a horizontal structure that would enhance and complement its surroundings. Between 1900 and 1909 he built a series of prairie houses, each more distinctive than the last.

The best known was the home he built for wealthy Chicago businessman Fred C. Robie in 1907. Its sprawling, horizontal plan is accentuated by flat, cantilevered roofs, horizontal bands of brick, and rows of long, narrow windows. Instead of being filled with traditional boxlike rooms, the interior is made up of free-flowing spaces centered on a single, central fireplace. There is no

The clean, horizontal lines and open spaces of Frank Lloyd Wright's buildings had an impact on modern architecture comparable to Picasso's on painting and sculpture. In the Robie House (left), built in Chicago in 1907 and most famous of his "prairie" homes, he blended design, function, and setting in an entirely new way.

attic or basement. The exterior resembles a cubist painting in its combination of intersecting planes and simple geometric shapes.

In his prairie houses Wright sought to integrate design, function, and materials to achieve an organic harmony. He selected natural materials, such as brick and unfinished wood, to harmonize with the surroundings. He also designed and chose fabrics and furniture styles that would blend in with and enhance the overall effect.

After 1914, when Taliesin, his home near Spring Green, Wisconsin, was destroyed by fire, Wright devoted much of his energy to designing monumental public buildings, including the famous Imperial Hotel in Tokyo (1915–22), the first earthquake-proof building. Its unique floating cantilevered construction survived the serious Japanese earthquake of 1923.

Before his death in 1959 Wright went on to build well over 600 buildings and to design a good many more that proved too daring or too costly to build. His most famous structures include the Guggenheim Museum in New York City and the Marin County Civic Center in California. Many of his creations are now recognized as masterpieces of modern architecture. But his early prairie houses are important as pioneers whose horizontal, smoothly flowing design set the pattern for 20th-century residential design.

A CHRONOLOGY OF THE ARTS: 1900-18

1900

- Polish-born writer Joseph Conrad published *Lord Jim,* one of a series of powerful novels noted for their moral and psychological insights.

1901

- Russian playwright Anton Chekhov's realistic masterpiece *The Three Sisters* was first produced by the innovative Moscow Art Theater.

1902

- U.S. photographers Alfred Stieglitz, Edward Steichen, and others organized the Photo-Secession to help establish photography as a fine art.

1903

- U.S. author Henry James published *The Ambassadors,* widely considered the best of his elegant novels about upper-class Americans and Europeans.

1904

- First U.S. feature film, *The Great Train Robbery* (directed by Edwin S. Porter), set the storytelling style for later movies.
- The Abbey Theater was founded in Dublin, Ireland. It helped popularize the works of W. B. Yeats, J. M. Synge, Sean O'Casey, and other writers.

1905

- Painters Henri Matisse, Raoul Dufy, Georges Rouault, and others—calling themselves *les fauves* ("the wild beasts")—opened an exhibit in Paris.
- French composer Claude Debussy completed his orchestral work *La Mer* ("The Sea"), the best-known example of musical impressionism.

1906

- U.S. dancer Ruth St. Denis performed her ballet *Radha* in New York. Based on Hindu dancing, it helped point the way toward modern dance.

1909

- Russian impresario Sergei Diaghilev brought his Ballets Russes to Paris and sparked a 20th-century ballet renaissance, highlighted by the dancing of Anna Pavlova and Vaslav Nijinsky and by avant-garde musical scores.
- Italian poet Filippo Marinetti initiated futurism, an artistic movement exalting energy, power, and the machine with his *Futurist Manifesto.*

1910

- Russian artist Wassily Kandinsky painted the first known purely abstract work—a watercolor made up of nothing but geometric forms and colors.

1913

- New York Armory Show introduced works of Vincent van Gogh, Paul Cézanne, Pablo Picasso, and other modern European masters to the U.S.
- French writer Marcel Proust published the first of seven volumes of *Remembrance of Things Past,* a monumental, semiautobiographical novel.
- Russian-born composer Igor Stravinsky's ballet *The Rite of Spring* was first performed in Paris by Sergei Diaghilev's Ballets Russes.

1914

- German architect Walter Gropius' model factory at the Cologne Werkbund Exhibition helped set the standard for modern industrial architecture.

1915

- U.S. filmmaker D. W. Griffith's epic *Birth of a Nation* made its debut.
- German writer Franz Kafka published *Metamorphosis,* one of the eerie, ambiguous works that made him one of the century's most powerful artists.

1916

- The Dada movement was launched in Zurich by Tristan Tzara.

1917

- U.S. poet Ezra Pound became foreign editor of the *Little Review.* In it he popularized Joyce, Eliot, William Carlos Williams, and others.

1918

- French artist Fernand Léger painted "Engine Room," one of the first of his monumental compositions glorifying machinery.

1908

Freud Unlocks the Subconscious

In the unexplored reaches of the human mind a Viennese analyst discovers important clues to the origin and treatment of neuroses and other mental disorders.

Sigmund Freud *(left, in a photograph taken about 1900) was born in the Austrian crownland of Moravia, in 1856. A youth of exceptional intellect, he entered the University of Vienna at the age of 17 to study medicine—primarily, he said, to gain knowledge of human nature. After research in the physiology laboratory of Ernst Brücke, he became interested in the work of Jean Charcot, the French neurologist who was formulating new theories about the human mind. Later, as a psychoanalyst, Freud opened a consulting room in Vienna.*

Freud's lifelong interest *in art was prompted by the belief that it often revealed the otherwise obscure workings of the psyche, and his consulting room overflowed with primitive and ancient works—busts, vases, statuettes, seals, coins, sphinxes, lamps. An engraving of Fuseli's 1781 painting, "The Nightmare" (left), hung in the foyer. Depicting a woman tormented by a demon in her sleep, it was an apt choice for the man who was to explore the darker side of dreams.*

The new science of psychoanalysis, *with Sigmund Freud (center left) as its leader, was well established when the International Congress of Psychoanalysis met in Germany in 1911. But C. G. Jung (near Freud) soon questioned Freud's theories, and in 1924 Otto Rank (left) also parted from him. Ernest Jones (far right) remained loyal.*

The First International Congress of Psychoanalysis meeting amidst the rococo splendors of Salzburg, Austria, in April 1908, caused barely a ripple outside the Salzburg Alps. Yet in retrospect it seems the very archetype of those small events that subsequently find a place in history: There was the tiny group of dedicated disciples; the usual angry wrangling over points of dogma; and most essential, the leader, who, although he sat at the head of a conference table, might have been speaking from On High. He was Sigmund Freud, father of psychoanalysis.

Freud, holding court in Salzburg, had come a long way in the eight years since he had written what he called "a respectable flop"—*The Interpretation of Dreams.* Although the book had been the product of three years of agonizing research and self-analysis, it sold only 123 copies in the first six weeks after publication; two years later the grand total stood at 351. But by the time of the 1908 conference its importance was unquestioned among psychologists. The book is still looked back on as a light blazing out of the darkness, for in it Freud presented the basic theories that secured his place in history as one of the first and greatest secular explorers of the subconscious mind.

The Uncharted Seas

Sigmund Freud discovered the subconscious after a long, tortured search through the uncharted seas of neurological medicine. Born in a small Austrian village in 1856, into a genteelly impoverished Jewish family, the young Sigmund suffered from the outspoken anti-Semitism of his time, and, perhaps because of it, determined to make his mark on the world. Freud studied medicine at the University of Vienna and became fascinated by the possibilities offered by a new drug, cocaine, in the treatment of "neurasthenia" (in the 1880's almost any illness that did not have a readily defined physical cause). In pursuit of more knowledge he went to Paris to work with the great French neurologist Jean Martin Charcot. Charcot had discovered that by using hypnosis he could relieve the symptoms of hysteria (for instance, paralysis or blindness) and that he could with equal facility produce those same symptoms in a healthy person. Clearly, Freud saw, it had been demonstrated that the mind had a great deal to do with the behavior of the body.

Returning to Vienna, Freud began to practice hypnosis on his patients. At the same time he collaborated with the eminent Viennese internist Josef Breuer, who had found that when the hypnotist helped to reveal those thoughts, memories, or desires that the conscious mind had "repressed" because they were too painful or forbidden, the patient experienced a kind of purging of the emotions, which, for a while at least, caused hysterical symptoms to disappear.

This new therapeutic technique had serious limitations, however: "Anna O.," the patient whose "cure" first aroused Freud's interest in Breuer, fell in love with her doctor, who quickly dropped both his patient and his method. Freud persevered, although he found that his patients often developed new symptoms to replace the old. The problem, Freud suspected, lay in the trance state, so he gradually developed a new way of bringing the hidden material to light. He asked his patients to loosen conscious control of their thoughts, to say everything that came into their minds. Through the rambling words Freud led the patient back to the forgotten events, the concealed ideas and feelings that caused his psychic problems. This technique of "free association" became a basic psychoanalytic tool.

Until 1896 Freud's published work had remained well within the limits of traditional medical practice. But then he aroused a tempest, the first of many he was to create. Addressing a medical meeting, he unveiled his "seduction" theory of hysteria: At the bottom of every case of hysteria lay a frightening sexual experience, suffered in early childhood. "I believe this to be a momentous revelation," he said. His colleagues did not agree and, rather shocked, stopped sending him their patients. The doctors did their best to ignore an even more scandalous theory propounded by Freud a few years later. Puzzled by the large number of parental seductions reported to him by his patients, Freud postulated that these horrendous events were actually just fantasies. All children, he said, were innocent possessors of sexual instincts and the creators of rich sexual fantasy lives involving themselves and their parents. The staid and respectable middle class of Vienna could not tolerate this muddying of the pure waters of childhood. "The void which formed itself about me," Freud wrote, "caused me gradually to realize that . . . from now onward I belonged to those who have troubled the sleep of the world."

The Interpretation of Dreams

Freud did indeed "trouble the sleep of the world," first by challenging and then by overturning long-cherished beliefs about human behavior. He began his revolution in 1897 with an investigation of dreams. He had noticed that during free association his patients often talked of their dreams. Encouraging them to articulate dream-related thoughts and memories as well, he found that those associations often revealed something that the dream itself did not disclose. He then outlined two levels of meaning in dreams: On the obvious level "manifest content" was the actual dream, but attached to it was the "latent content," the dream's true, though often disguised, meaning.

In Freud's view, dreams are the safety valves of sleep—the mind's attempt to relieve emotional tension without awakening the sleeper. The simplest form of such relief is a dream of "wish fulfillment." The hungry sleeper, for instance, dreams that he is eating a glorious meal; if he is on a diet, he may mask his appetite for food, and its gratification, as something else—a sexual encounter perhaps. When relating the dream, and his associations with it, the patient begins to realize that for him sex and food have a kind of emotional common denominator.

Most dreams are infinitely more complicated. It required a mind as subtle and sympathetic as Freud's to untangle the twisted threads of dreams and to make manifest the meanings knotted into them. After years of dream analysis he came to recognize a secret language of symbol and association peculiar to dreams and the workings of the subconscious mind. This strange language seems universal. Everyone uses it, and unlocking its code allowed Freud to begin to lay bare the tortuous, irrational, and yet strangely consistent processes of the human subconscious.

INSANITY: CONSTRAINTS TO CURES

Many cultures once accepted the harmlessly insane as special people, for whose well-being society was responsible. But in Europe about the 13th century an era of repression began: Along with Jews and witches, madmen came to be seen as instruments of the Devil. Many were burned at the stake. London's Bethlehem Hospital, once a haven for the sick, became "Bedlam," a house of horrors for the deranged.

Attitudes changed in the 18th century, when physicians began to seek "scientific" explanations for insanity and to attempt treatment on a rational basis. In 1793 the French doctor Philippe Pinel literally unchained mental patients in Paris. In 1796 in England the Quaker William Tuke built the York Retreat, an asylum dedicated to humane treatment.

About 1900 Sigmund Freud's work signaled a new era—that of exploration into the dreams, fears, and obsessions of the mentally ill for clues to their cure. It was a development that was to revolutionize the treatment of mental illness all over the world.

During the Renaissance water was thought beneficial, even curative, to madmen. The insane were crowded into boats to sail the seas and rivers of Europe. One such "Ship of Fools" was the subject of Hieronymus Bosch's 16th-century painting (left).

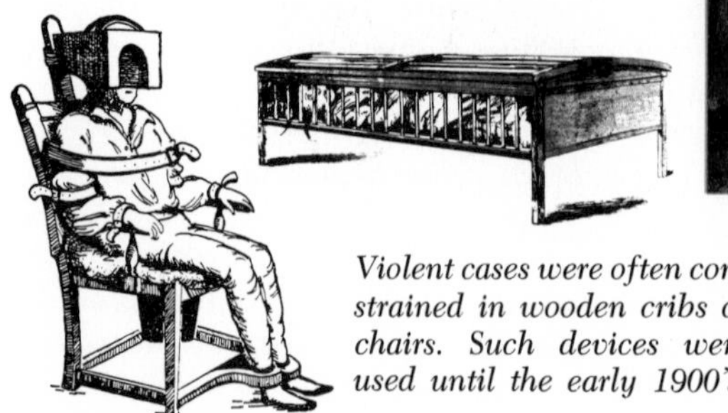

Violent cases were often constrained in wooden cribs or chairs. Such devices were used until the early 1900's.

Freud himself had always been a great dreamer; long before he realized the importance of dreams, he had felt that his own were in some way significant and prophetic. He then began an attempt to analyze himself, chiefly through the technique of dream association. The discoveries he made, combined with those he had gleaned from his patients, formed the basis for *The Interpretation of Dreams.* His fundamental insight was that sexuality is as much a part of childhood as it is of maturity: All men, he claimed, are subject to the Oedipus complex, a name he coined from the Greek legend that tells of the unfortunate Oedipus who unwittingly kills his father and marries his mother. "It is the fate of all of us . . . to direct our first sexual impulse towards our mother, and our first hatred and our first murderous wish against our father. Our dreams convince us that this is so." If the conflict is not resolved, if infantile sexual desires do not change their focus but remain in some way riveted on the mother, the personality disorder called neurosis is the inevitable result.

The "libido" was Freud's name for the sexual drive, and he attributed to the libido all the psychic energy that an individual possesses. Since society does not allow full and free expression of sexual desires, its members must learn to repress them or to express them in socially acceptable ways. Some creative men, for instance, have rechanneled—or sublimated—their libido energy into writing or painting. But the neurotic, mired in his Oedipal conflict, cannot free his libido from its forbidden object; his energies are devoted to defending himself against his desires, and he develops such "symptoms" of his psychic struggles as muscle tics or compulsive hand-washing.

Throughout his life Freud saw himself as a scientist whose theories were firmly rooted in observed fact. He asserted that his discoveries were not merely speculations, but basic psychological laws, and some disciples remained loyal Freudians throughout their lives. Others, opposed to his single-minded insistence that all neuroses are sexual in origin, broke away and established their own schools of analysis.

The first to fall away was Alfred Adler, a Viennese physician who had been Freud's close associate since 1902. For years the two had thrashed out theory between them, but by 1911 the break was complete and irreconcilable. The year 1913 saw the defection of Carl Gustav Jung, a Swiss psychiatrist. Jung's early work had been much admired by Freud, who saw in him "the Joshua destined to explore the promised land of psychiatry which Freud, like Moses, was only permitted to view from afar." (That Freud saw himself as Moses would probably come as no surprise to those who knew him.) Mixed with Freud's admiration, however, was an element of fear. At one analysis session,

ANNA O.'S "TALKING CURE"

Freud's interest in psychoanalysis was encouraged by a case involving Viennese physician Josef Breuer (below left). In 1880 Breuer treated a young woman, identified as "Anna O." (below), who had developed symptoms of hysteria—paralysis and impairment of sight and speech—after her father's death. One day Breuer asked Anna to describe her illness. As the girl talked, Breuer noted with astonishment that her symptoms began to disappear. Freud became interested in this mysterious "talking cure," as Anna called it, and collaborated with Breuer in further studies that helped spur him to his own discoveries.

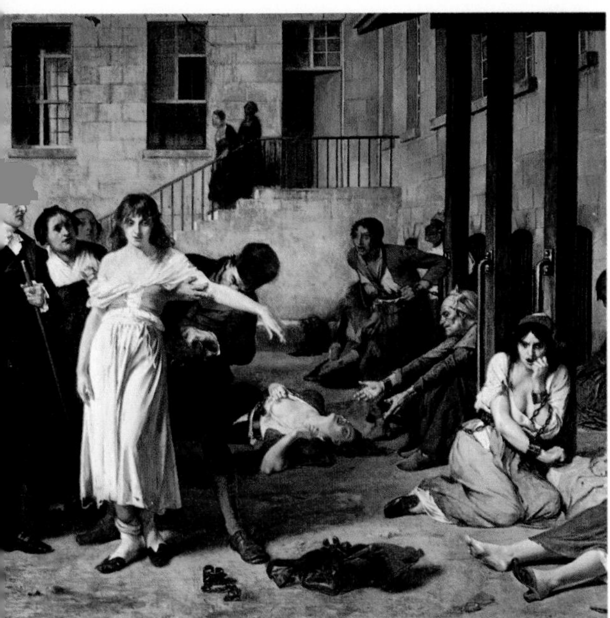

The 18th-century French reformer Dr. Philippe Pinel (left) was repelled by conditions at Salpêtrière, a Paris hospital for insane women, and ordered the wretched patients unchained. "I am convinced," he said, "that the people are not incurable if they can have air and liberty."

for instance, Freud interpreted a dream of Jung's as a wish to dethrone Freud and take his place. This ambivalence became more pronounced as the years passed. Jung, essentially a mystic and a religious man, found Freud's fanatic belief in sexuality as the root cause of all conflict to be a self-perpetuating vicious circle. "It is not the children of the flesh, but the children of God who know freedom," he wrote. Jung later evolved a mystically oriented theory of the subconscious mind.

A Society of Neurotics

Despite the disagreements, by the mid-1920's Freud's influence had grown well beyond the parochial limits of Vienna. His works had been published in other languages; hopeful students of psychoanalysis gathered around him; hundreds of patients in Europe and America underwent psychoanalysis. And, whether or not Freud was responsible, sex had come out of the closet. But greater sexual freedom did not augur, for Freud, an increase in human happiness.

In his *Civilization and Its Discontents,* published in 1930, he openly proclaimed a pessimism about the human condition that had been more or less latent in all his previous work. Societies, he theorized, may share with individuals the defects of neurosis. And when the demands a society imposes are impossible for most of its members to fulfill (the American "success ethic" is an example), the result must be individual guilt and widespread discontent.

While events in the 20th century provide ample justification for Freud's pessimism, interpretations of his theories have not remained so bleak, especially in America, the present stronghold of psychoanalysis. Since the 1930's American neo-Freudians have been altering Freud's views, adapting them to suit American optimism and contemporary mores. Therapist Karen Horney could not fully accept theories born in sexually repressed 19th-century Vienna. While she felt the Viennese were perhaps sexually obsessed, present-day Americans might not be. Other factors must be operative, too: culture, as a formative influence; the real-life situation of the adult patient, as well as his childhood memories. Horney's "neurotic personality of our time" is as much a result of the time itself as of Freud's immutable psychic laws. Harry Stack Sullivan, another American who founded his own school of therapy, traced emotional disturbance to a distortion of interpersonal relationships. The Sullivanian analyst does not assume the Freudian role of the patient's parent but becomes an active partner in an interchange that, ideally, will reflect the problems his patient has with other individuals.

For analyst and philosopher Erich Fromm *society* is the patient that must be cured. Beginning his work where Freud had only dared to speculate, Fromm maintains that nations possess an innate social character to

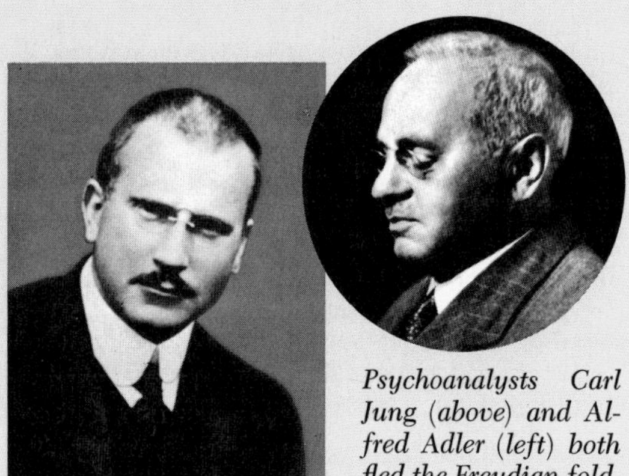

Psychoanalysts Carl Jung (above) and Alfred Adler (left) both fled the Freudian fold.

THE DISSIDENTS

Foremost among the dissidents who strayed from Freud's fold were Carl Gustav Jung and Alfred Adler. Jung taught a psychology that incorporated elements of mysticism and religion. The subconscious, he said, is not solely the repository for repressed material: It contains a deeper level, the "collective unconscious," common to all humanity—the "mighty deposit of ancestral experience accumulated over millions of years." These memories transmit through the generations a collection of "archetypes," timeless images and symbols whose latent emotional content is the same for everyone.

Mistrusting Freud's single-mindedness, Jung believed the energy at the core of human experience could not be described solely in sexual terms, but required a broader definition. In his ground-breaking theory of introverted and extroverted personality types, and in his goal of integrating the conscious "I" with all the levels of the subconscious mind, his views differed sharply with Freud's.

Adler, too, was unable to accept Freud's unswerving emphasis on sexuality. He formulated a theory of subconscious motivation, based on the infant's perception of his powerlessness in relation to his parents and the world: "Every neurosis can be understood as an attempt to free oneself from a feeling of inferiority in order to gain a feeling of superiority," he wrote. Today Adler's views are incorporated into a number of psychotherapeutic techniques.

One of Jung's "universal symbols" is a snake biting its tail (center) The German chemist Kekulé, researching the benzene molecule, claimed his dream of this ancient archetype led him to discover that the molecule was a closed carbon ring.

The inner turmoil of the insane is apparent in the work of Louis Wain, a turn-of-the-century English painter of cats. Wain developed symptoms of acute schizophrenia, and as his illness progressed, his paintings became more and more hallucinatory. It is the torment expressed in such visions that drug treatment attempts to control.

THE ALTERNATIVES TO PSYCHOANALYSIS

As Freud's theories gained acceptance, a new age of experiment began in the treatment of mental illness. Before long radically new methods and ideas appeared, ranging from physiological treatments (the use of drugs or electrical shocks) to the recent philosophy that some of those whom society regards as "insane" may in reality be saner than their critics suggest.

Electrical or insulin shock therapy has been found to relieve chronic depression and other symptoms of mental disorder; even surgery (lobotomy, in which the frontal lobes of the brain are severed) is used in especially severe cases. But the most important alternative to analysis has been chemotherapy—the use of drugs to control the graver symptoms of mental illness. As a result, mental hospitals have been able to abolish a good many of their more frighteningly repressive security measures.

Drugs have been found particularly effective in the treatment of schizophrenia, one of the least tractable conditions (see above). In recent years, however, some psychiatrists have campaigned against the ready use of drugs. Britain's R. D. Laing, for example, has taken the view that "insanity" may in some cases be a normal response to an intolerable situation. The patient may best be served, Laing suggests, by alleviating the circumstances lying at the root of his illness, and by providing an entirely tolerant environment in which his feelings can be vented rather than subdued by drugs or other traditional therapy. In a sense, Laing's view is the ultimate expression thus far of the attitude of tolerance that began with Sigmund Freud's research and theories.

which their citizens must conform. He does not agree that man is trapped in Freudian sexual dilemmas, for if the institutions that man creates can be changed for the better, there is hope that the state of man can be changed as well.

The behaviorist schools, on the other hand, believe that human behavior is determined by material factors—specifically, rewards and punishments. Not primarily concerned with questions of why, such men as B. F. Skinner attack the problem of *how* behavior is established or altered. The behaviorists derive much of their theory from clinical studies of animals, whose behavior, they say, can be radically changed by laboratory conditioning. But many psychologists believe that experiments with laboratory animals form an inadequate basis for the interpretation of human behavior, and discount many of behaviorism's sweeping claims; and many biologists are dissatisfied with the cavalier treatment of instinct in behaviorist theory. The critics charge that the behaviorists' work often suggests nothing so much as an instruction manual for building a sterile and superregimented society.

Despite these variations it is Freud's discovery that lies at the root of current psychotherapy—the discovery that the subconcious mind may provide clues to the cure for mental illness. In other fields, too, his work has had enormous influence. Modern theology, anthropology, and sociology bear the stamp, to some extent, of Freud's revelations. Moreover, contemporary writers and artists have found in Freudian psychology a fruitful and even liberating influence: The central character of 20th-century literature has become the Freudian man, in whom neurosis and insight go hand in hand. And such artists as the surrealists and abstract expressionists have been trying to penetrate beyond the conscious level of perception in their paintings and sculpture since the 1950's.

Freud died in London in 1939, having fled Vienna a year earlier when the Nazis came to power. He left behind a body of thought that has changed the consciousness of the Western World, ultimately forming the basis for a new way of perceiving mankind.

1908

Motoring for Millions

Henry Ford introduces the Tin Lizzie, and millions take to the road as motormania grips the U.S.A.

His name was Henry Ford. He was a farmer, woodcutter, machinist, businessman, tycoon, finally a symbol. Sometimes credited as a great inventor, he was in fact a borrower of ideas, with a genius for applying them to new uses. A leader in labor relations, he became one of the most criticized industrialists.

He was also a radical. The car he built, and the new way he found to build it, wrought revolutionary changes in the 20th-century lifestyle. In the way we work and get about, in the growth of industrial technology, in labor-management relations, even in the international economy, we are still feeling the effects of Henry Ford's work.

The car that started it all bore a humble enough name, the Model T, when it first rolled out of the Ford assembly plant in Detroit in mid-1908. It was not by any means the first car—or the first Ford—ever built. Practical automobiles had been around for more than three decades, and the T followed Models A, B, C, F, K, N, R, and S. Nor was the T much to look at. It was boxy, tinny-looking, and about as individualized as a pea in a very large pod. Yet the car was an overnight sensation, and for a reason that made it unique among the automobiles of the day: It was the first car especially designed to be driven, repaired, and above all *affordable* by the average workingman.

From Dearborn to Detroit

Perhaps Ford's humble origin inspired him to build for the average man. His grandfather John Ford had emigrated from Queenstown, Ireland, during the potato famine in 1847, settling with his family near Dearborn, Michigan, a day's oxcart ride west of Detroit. There William Ford, Henry's father, worked as a carpenter to help pay for the 80-acre farm they had bought for $350. At age 35 he married 21-year-old Mary Litogot, and their son Henry was born on July 30, 1863.

Right from the start Henry was a tinker. He disliked almost every aspect of farming except where machines were involved. When he was 13 he saw his first portable steam engine, hissing and clanking down the road under its own power. Awestruck, the boy questioned the operator about the mechanism, then quickly learned to fire and run it himself. The sight of this self-propelled vehicle, Ford later said, left an indelible impression on his mind.

When he was 16 he left Dearborn for Detroit and a series of jobs in machine shops, but returned at times to help on his father's farm. There he built his own shop, complete with forge, drill, hand lathe, and other tools. One day he had another instructive encounter with a steam engine. The engineer hired to run it had proved incompetent, so the owner appealed to Henry, and he began fiddling with it. "At the end of that first day," he later wrote, "I was as weary as I had been nervous at its beginning, but I had run the engine steadily, inducing it to stand up nicely to its work. . . . I was paid three dollars a day and had eighty-three days of steady work.

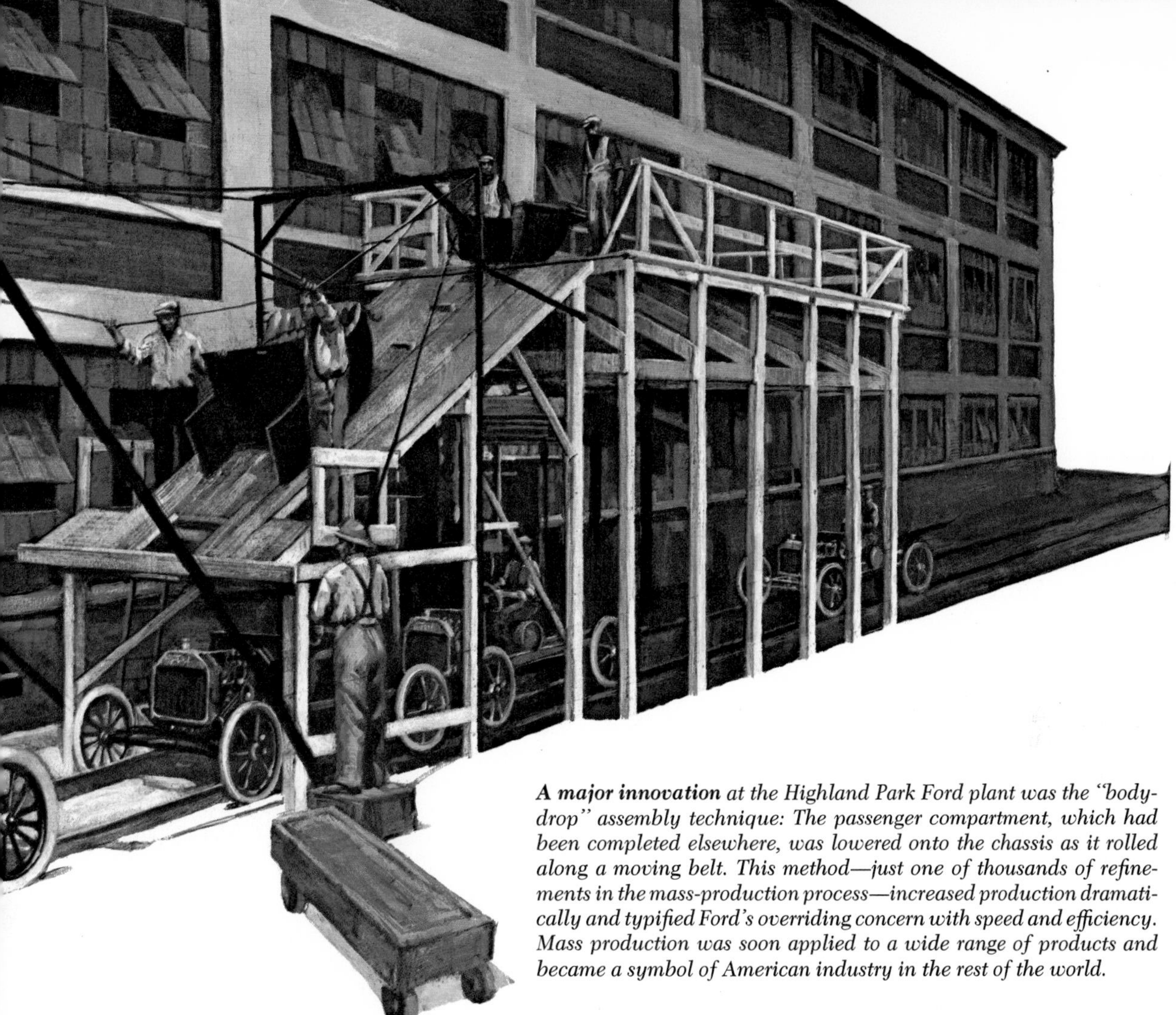

A major innovation *at the Highland Park Ford plant was the "body-drop" assembly technique: The passenger compartment, which had been completed elsewhere, was lowered onto the chassis as it rolled along a moving belt. This method—just one of thousands of refinements in the mass-production process—increased production dramatically and typified Ford's overriding concern with speed and efficiency. Mass production was soon applied to a wide range of products and became a symbol of American industry in the rest of the world.*

. . . I became immensely fond of that machine."

He returned to farming when he became engaged to Clara Bryant, daughter of a neighboring farmer. Then he went into the lumber business, felling trees and cutting boards with a rented steam engine. In his spare time, when not studying the mysteries of the new gasoline engine, he designed, cut the wood for, and built an attractive honeymoon cottage. But in 1891, just two years after they had moved in, Ford told Clara that for his career's sake they must move to Detroit. He had developed a passion to build a "horseless carriage."

He wasn't the only aspiring carbuilder. *Horseless Age*, a new magazine catering to cyclists, estimated that there were more than 300 American machinists and inventors working on plans for cars. Still, Ford's job as an engineer with the Detroit Edison Illuminating Co. was ideally suited to his hobby. He haunted the machine shops of the city, learning about engines, electricity, and tools, and he made valuable contacts among mechanics and businessmen.

With dogged persistence he also worked on his pet project: to assemble a car around the four-stroke Otto engine he had built in his kitchen sink. Finally, in the spring of 1896, Ford triumphantly drove his gas-powered buggy out of his garage workshop and onto the streets of Detroit. It was a real automobile, delivering just over 4 horsepower, and it could go 25 miles per hour. There were Fords in our future.

Mass Production

In the 17 years following that first automobile, Ford's genius for production techniques bore fruit. He developed the moving assembly line, leading America toward what some have called a second Industrial Revolution. Until the Model T, the automobile had rightly been considered a rich man's toy. Though refinements came rapidly (in 1900 Ford raced one of his early models at 70 miles per hour), most cars were both costly and scarce because they were still made by old handicraft methods. For although some improvements

—precision tooling and standardization of parts—were already being made in the manufacture of such popular products as bicycles, typewriters, and sewing machines, no one had yet found a workable combination of techniques for mass-producing a machine as complex as an automobile.

Henry Ford found it. In a Chicago meatpacking plant one day, he had been impressed with the efficiency gained by moving the carcasses from one worker to another by means of a moving overhead trolley. Time was saved by bringing the work to the man, instead of the other way around; and because each butcher specialized in one operation, he could do his cutting work much faster and more expertly.

In May 1913, at his new Highland Park automobile plant in Dearborn, Ford put a similar method into operation. His first experiment was with magnetos, which generate current for ignition. The results were astounding. Until then, one man worked on one magneto, the fastest worker in the plant completing the job in 18 minutes. Ford tried dividing the labor and sliding the magneto work down a line of men, each assigned a separate task. There was no wasted motion, and a completed magneto came off the line in 13 minutes. The time thus saved led to a 76-percent increase in the number of magnetos manufactured. Further refinements, such as using conveyor belts instead of gravity slides, reduced the operation to just five minutes.

Soon the entire car was being made this way, with spectacular effects. A chassis that used to take $12\frac{1}{2}$ hours to build now rolled off the line in an hour and a half. By early 1914 the cars were being *driven* off the line virtually complete. Production tripled between 1912 and 1915, and by 1924 there were 2 million new Fords on the road every year.

The Highland Park operation, as it mushroomed in size and complexity, was an enormous challenge to Ford's managerial skills. Within the plant, workers and foremen were encouraged to refine their assembly operations according to the virtues of accuracy (that is, standardization), continuity (keeping the parts moving), and, above all, speed. As they did, their new ideas created ever-changing patterns and adjustments, until the factory resembled a technological landscape, with mountains of parts flowing through rivers of feedlines into the causeways where assembly took place.

There was equal complexity outside the plant, as Ford handled, with exceedingly delicate timing, the precise amounts of coal, iron, nickel, brass, leather, rubber, lubricants, and other commodities needed. Careful management was crucial, for the prolonged failure of any supply would bring the whole operation

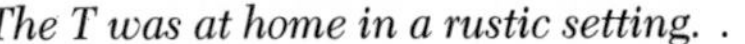
The T was at home in a rustic setting. . . . *. . . the Pierce-Arrow symbolized elegance.*

A CAR FOR THE MIDDLE-OF-THE-ROAD BUYER

Unlike the handsome, luxurious Pierce-Arrow, the Model T was truly a car for the common man. The secrets of its enormous popularity were its low price, dependability, and simplicity. Owners could replace parts cheaply and make most repairs themselves. Farmers even adapted the T for field work. As sales and production increased, Ford kept lowering his prices: A 1925 Runabout sold for only $265.

Ford's generous new wage policy brought huge crowds of eager jobseekers to his factory gates.

THE STAMPEDE FOR THE FIVE-DOLLAR DAY

One of Henry Ford's boldest experiments was the introduction in 1914 of a $5-a-day salary for his assembly-line workers, together with a profit-sharing plan. The radical move, which more than doubled the average daily wage, brought such a crush of applicants that the Detroit police force had to be called in to maintain order and prevent violence.

Ford himself was a fascinating eccentric, a mathematical wizard who read like a 10-year-old and dyed his hair with rusty water. But the characteristic qualities which he never lost, even after he became a millionaire, were his understanding of and feeling for the common man.

to a halt. Just how skillful a manager Ford was can be ascertained from a single amazing statistic: In 1924 every other car in the world was a Model T.

The Tin Lizzie

The car itself, though awkward looking, was distinguished by its lightness, simplicity of design, and superior power-to-weight ratio. It was dubbed the Tin Lizzie because it looked almost as flimsy as tin next to other heavier cars. Actually, Ford had begun exploiting the strong, lighter weight vanadium steel. Although its top speed was just 40 miles per hour, the Model T had good acceleration. Its high ground clearance was perfect for the rough roads of the time. Farmers hitched it up to their machinery as a power source, used it for outings and to haul produce.

Comfort was not the T's prime asset. In the earliest versions the front seat had to be lifted off to fill the gas tank, and the front and rear wheels were of different sizes, so two spares had to be carried. Until 1911, when the electric starter was invented, the motor had to be cranked up by hand—at the risk of breaking an arm when it kicked over. In compensation was the car's dazzling simplicity. It had no battery or complex wiring system. It required no brake fluid, special gasoline nor grease, nor sophisticated motor oil. Its popcorn-popper engine got excellent mileage, and its fenders and lights, if damaged, were easily replaced.

But what really attracted the buying public was the incomparable *fun* of driving. The T could go almost anywhere, clambering nimbly over rough (and even roadless) terrain. If a hill was too steep to climb, the car could be turned around and driven up backward. On flat ground the highly placed seats offered a pleasing view of the road and surrounding countryside. (The prudent driver often carried a raw egg or two along with the normal repair tools; if the radiator sprang a leak, the egg was dropped in and the hole would be sealed by egg fragments cooked hard in the hot water.)

Commercially the Model T was a huge success. The secret lay in Ford's crucial decision to build for the masses. He deliberately made it without frills and concentrated on keeping it cheap and practical.

Those two goals in a sense went together. To keep the price low, Ford excluded the custom features offered by other builders and made the cars as standardized as needles and pins. Standardization meant interchangeable parts, and this meant the average mechanically inclined man could do his own simple repairs. As production techniques were refined, the cost of the car dropped, once as low as $260. During the T's 19 years on the market its phenomenal popularity helped put the U.S.A., then the world, on wheels.

"Assembly-Line Blues"

But the cost of this universal car could not be measured in dollars alone. Mass production (known in Germany by the term *Fordismus*) soon spread to a host of other industries, becoming not just a fact of life but a *way* of life. It left behind centuries of craftsmanly tradition,

Fordland, U.S.A.: *Dozens of Model T's crowd the main street of Henderson, Texas, in 1927. The scene was typical of towns throughout the nation, for by that time—the final year of the T's production—some 15 million Tin Lizzies were on the road. Rival automobiles abounded, but none ever came so close to Henry Ford's grand dream of "the universal car."*

and workers began to feel as standardized and interchangeable as the parts they handled. Despite Ford's introduction of the "five-dollar day"—which nearly doubled the average man's wages—workers grew increasingly discontent with their tedious, repetitive jobs and impersonal surroundings.

In 1932 Aldous Huxley summed up the feeling in his devastating satire *Brave New World,* which prophesied a horrifying future ruled by industry. In the novel Ford's name was used as both a curse and an incantation. In 1936 Charlie Chaplin produced his classic film *Modern Times,* showing an assembly-line worker driven berserk by the routine and unrelenting pressure of his job. Many other critics have followed.

Meanwhile, the once-progressive Ford had become a captive of his own ideas. He was reluctant to change a winning formula, and by 1927, when he introduced the improved Model A, he had lost the lead in carmaking. He also resisted unionization, and this only added to his workers' discontent. Of the "Big Three" (Chrysler, Ford, and General Motors), Ford was the last to accept collective bargaining.

But the system Ford set in motion could hardly be done away with. A constellation of related industries, including steel, rubber, oil, and roadbuilding, swelled to meet America's insatiable taste for mobility. As these interests flooded Washington with campaign dollars and lobbyists, the automobile industry's role in fiscal planning grew ever more important. Charles Wilson, President Eisenhower's Secretary of Defense and an ex-president of General Motors, aptly summed it up: "For years I thought what was good for the country was good for General Motors and vice versa." It looked as though cars had begun to ride people.

Machines Making Machines

Mass production, the brainchild that started it all, seemed to take on a life of its own. As it grew more sophisticated, the role of the human worker shrank. A revolution was in the offing and at last arrived: the age of automation, in which machines were made by other machines. Across the land workers strove to hold onto their jobs, and unionism increased until Big Labor (the Teamsters, United Auto Workers, AFL, CIO, and others) stood eyeball-to-eyeball with Big Business. Following World War II, labor-management confrontations began an ominous cycle of crippling strikes, higher wages, and higher consumer prices.

THE ELECTRIC ALTERNATIVE

Soaring fuel costs and a huge pollution problem—nearly a ton of waste matter a year from the average gasoline-powered car—have revived interest in an old idea: the electric car. Compared with their ancestors, modern electrics have changed little. Their virtues remain the same: They require no transmission, cooling system, or motor oil and produce no exhaust or noise. But their drawbacks—a low top speed and a limited range—have not been eliminated. One problem is with batteries, which are still heavy and need frequent recharging. However, the concept has been found practical in England, where 40,000 electric trucks make short-run deliveries. The electric may yet prove an ideal second car.

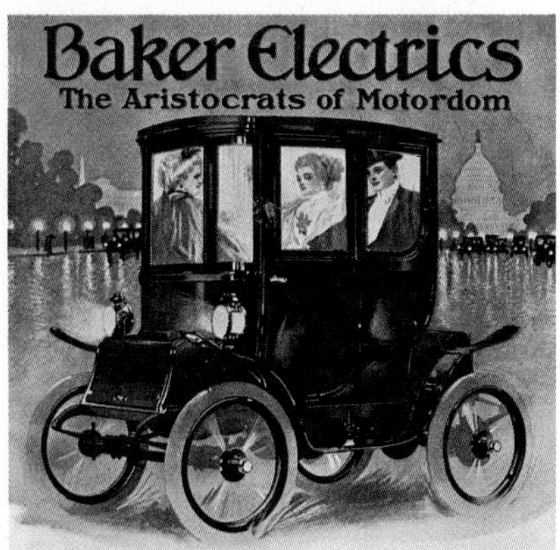

This 1909 Baker ran on 40 conventional batteries, arranged in trays. It could travel 70 to 100 miles at 15 miles per hour.

The 1966 Sebring (right) carries two passengers up to 50 miles at 28 miles per hour. It is small and streamlined to save energy.

In recent years some U.S. and foreign automobile manufacturers have responded to worker complaints about the depersonalizing effects of the assembly line. To foster individual effort at the Saab-Scania plant near Stockholm, workers have been grouped into teams, given flexible schedules, and permitted job rotation. The hated moving assembly line has been replaced by shoplike work "areas." Despite high initial costs and lower production, Saab found a lessening of absenteeism, turnovers, and strikes. U.S. car makers are watching the Saab and other Scandinavian experiments with interest. Differences in plant capacity and other economic and cultural factors make some aspects of the Scandinavian-style team approach impractical for U.S. manufacturers. In the mid-1970's, however, a small group of American workers visited the Saab plant to study its methods. The trip was sponsored, ironically enough, by the Ford Foundation.

Back to the Beginning?

In 1919 Henry Ford turned the presidency of the Ford Motor Company over to his son, Edsel, largely as a ploy to influence stockholders to sell their shares. He himself, however, retained control of the company. Edsel died in 1943 and Ford's grandson, Henry Ford II, became president in 1945. The elder Ford remained active in the company until his death in 1947. In his later years he devoted much of his time to Greenfield Village, the reproduction of an early American village at Dearborn, Michigan, which includes the building in which the first Ford cars were assembled.

By the mid-1950's the average American car differed radically from those simple, practical buggies. The emphasis had shifted from practicality to "performance" (usually meaning ever higher horsepower). Cars were bedecked with chrome trim and tail fins, and the term "superior styling" was used to describe the trendy new body styles.

In the early 1960's an increased demand for smaller cars became evident in the U.S.A. The energy crisis in the early 1970's brought shortages of fuel and higher prices for it. These factors combined with inflationary pressures to increase still further the demand for smaller, lighter cars. In addition, manufacturers explored the possibility of returning to steam or electricity to power automobiles. If the current trend continues, the old Tin Lizzie may well turn out to be another idea whose time has come—again.

1911

China: The End of a Dynasty

Asia's slumbering dragon begins to stir, ending the autocratic rule of the Manchus and thrusting China into the 20th century.

***Founder of China's** revolutionary movement, Western-educated Dr. Sun Yat-sen helped pave the way for the 1911 overthrow of the Manchus and the establishment of a republic. Later eclipsed by the warlords, Sun regained power in the south but died without seeing his ideals realized.*

The accidental explosion of a bomb at the headquarters of republican insurgents in Hankow, central China, on October 9, 1911, inadvertently touched off a nationwide revolution. When the police arrived, they arrested a handful of revolutionaries and confiscated arms, antimonarchist propaganda, and a list of members of the clandestine revolutionary movement. Then they began a systematic manhunt for all republican sympathizers in the area. Fearing arrest, leftist officers at the local military garrison revolted the next day, tearing down the yellow dragon flags of the Manchu Dynasty in Hankow and in the adjoining industrial cities of Hanyang and Wuchang. Within weeks garrisons in southern China joined the revolt. On February 12, 1912, the Emperor, a six-year-old child, was forced to abdicate.

Few Chinese mourned the passing of the Manchus, alien conquerors from Manchuria who had seized power in 1644. In the 19th century their rule had been weakened by corruption, inefficiency, peasant rebellions, and economic stagnation. Bloody court intrigues dominated the final years of the dynasty, as the reactionary Empress Dowager Tz'u Hsi maneuvered to preserve China's traditional order, a self-perpetuating oligarchy of the wealthy, highborn sons of mandarin officials and Confucian scholars. At the bottom of the scale were China's peasant masses, oppressed, exploited, and permanently excluded from power.

By the mid-19th century China had fallen into such a state of decay and impotence that Western nations were able to force the Manchus to bow to their demands (backed by military threats) for trading rights, special legal status, and missionary privileges. With each concession came a further erosion of national sovereignty, and by the turn of the century China had been reduced almost to the status of a colony. In Shanghai, Canton, Hong Kong, and Nanking, European merchants had established wealthy enclaves.

A ***prelude to revolution,*** *the Boxer Rebellion of 1898–1900 was he first outburst of Chinese nationalism. The Boxers, a ecret society, sought to rid China of the "foreign devil." In the ropaganda poster above, terrified European troops flee from heir invincible Chinese adversaries. The Boxers had the tacit upport of the reactionary Empress Dowager Tz'u Hsi (left), vhose ruthless suppression of all attempts at reform made revoution inevitable. It came three years after her death in 1908.*

Western entrepreneurs traveled inland to arrange lucrative deals with Chinese landlords and craftsmen. Christian missionaries roamed the countryside, spreading a religion alien to China's ancient culture.

Meanwhile, the Chinese watched the national resurgence of neighboring Japan with mingled fear and awe. Like China, Japan had been the target of colonial exploitation, but its leaders had reformed their government in 1868 and had launched an ambitious program of modernization. By 1894 Japan was strong enough to challenge China's control of certain Asian territories (notably Korea), and China suffered a humiliating defeat in the ensuing Sino-Japanese War. As a result, China agreed to give up Formosa and the Pescadores, and to recognize Korean "independence."

The Boxer Rebellion

China's deepening frustration at its helplessness and continued degradation by foreign imperialists exploded in the Boxer Rebellion of 1898–1900. The Boxers, a bizarre secret society that blamed all China's problems on the foreigner, led a campaign of terror against the "foreign devils." They slaughtered some 200 Christian missionaries and about 20,000 Chinese converts, murdered a Japanese envoy in Peking, and finally converged on the city's legation quarter. A combined force of British, American, German, French, Russian, and Japanese troops lifted the siege, subdued the Boxers, and dictated a harsh peace settlement. The Boxer Protocol charged the Chinese with crimes against civilization, demanded the execution of high officials who had supported the rebels, and levied a huge indemnity on the imperial treasury.

In time, the more progressive Chinese became convinced that China must follow Japan's example and modernize along Western lines in order to meet the foreign challenge. The most articulate advocates of such a national revival had been educated in England, France, the United States, and, in particular, Japan. On foreign soil China's youths were exposed to the ideas of democracy and independence that eventually found expression in the 1911 Revolution.

Among their prophets and spokesmen was Dr. Sun Yat-sen, a physician born in southern China in 1866. In 1894 the 28-year-old Sun organized the revolutionary China Renaissance Society in Honolulu, and a year later helped lead an abortive uprising against the Manchus in Canton. Forced to flee for his life, Sun traveled first to London and then to Tokyo, where he organized the influential Alliance Society. Its aims were to overthrow the Manchus, establish a republic, expel all foreign interests, and redistribute the land.

Sun's following in Tokyo became so great that the Manchus pressured Japanese authorities to expel him, and for the next few years he traveled through Indochina, Europe, and the United States to publicize his cause. Meanwhile, students returning to the mainland organized rebel bands, and between 1907 and 1911 Sun's supporters led a number of the proliferating but abortive uprisings in southern China. Then, on October 10, 1911, the revolt in Hankow and neighboring cities touched off the long-anticipated revolution.

The revolt caught the leaders of China's revolutionary movement off guard. Apart from their proclaimed objectives, they lacked a realistic, long-range program for China's national revival. They also lacked a strong leader. Sun Yat-sen, one likely candidate, was in the United States at the time of the revolution. As he hastened back to take command, the rapid onrush of events in China worked against his dream of bringing democracy to the Asian mainland. Before Sun could reach China and organize his followers, the single-minded Yüan Shih-kai, an ambitious general who commanded the Emperor's most modernized troops, was able to manipulate the situation to his advantage.

The vanguard of the revolution, *dissident army troops (above) rose against the Manchus in October 1911. From Hankow rebellion quickly spread through most of southern China. Its success was thwarted by the ambitious Gen. Yüan Shih-kai (right), who persuaded the Emperor to abdicate and convinced the rebels to make him President of the new republic. He dissolved parliament in 1913, tried to appoint himself Emperor two years later, failed, and died early in 1916, plunging China into the chaotic and turbulent decade known as the warlord era (1916–27).*

The Manchus' vast realm *stretched across Asia from Manchuria to Tibet (see map at right), but internal neglect and concessions to foreigners slowly alienated their Chinese subjects and gave rise to both the Boxer Rebellion and the 1911 Revolution.*

The Revolution Betrayed

Summoned by the Emperor to put an end to the spreading insurrection, Yüan gathered his forces and marched southward, easily overcoming republican resistance in Hankow and Hanyang. A less crafty general might have reestablished imperial rule throughout the south, but instead Yüan called a halt to the fighting and offered to negotiate with the revolutionaries. In return for promising to secure the Emperor's abdication, Yüan demanded he be named President of republican China. The rebels, acknowledging their weaker bargaining position, asked only that the capital be moved to Nanking (because of Peking's imperial ties) and that Sun Yat-sen be named President first and then be permitted to resign, as a face-saving gesture.

As he had promised, Yüan persuaded the Emperor to renounce the throne. The terms he offered were generous: The Emperor was allowed to retain his title for life, to remain in the imperial quarters in Peking, and to receive a large pension. On February 13, 1912, Sun resigned in favor of Yüan. A day earlier Emperor Hsüan T'ung (later called Henry Pu Yi) ended a 2,500-year-old tradition of dynastic rule in China.

At first Yüan seemed to support the revolutionary objectives. He agreed to adopt a republican constitution and arranged for parliamentary elections in 1912. His hastily organized Republican Party was heavily outnumbered by Sun's Kuomintang (Nationalist Party) in the new parliament, however, and Yüan soon became disenchanted with the republican experiment. In November 1913 he outlawed the Kuomintang and dissolved the legislature. With no means to oppose this illegal move (the President controlled the national army), Sun and the Kuomintang fled to Tokyo.

Meanwhile, Yüan assumed increasingly dictatorial powers, and in December 1915 announced plans to become China's new Emperor. Even his own military governors objected to this final outrage and forced Yüan to renounce his plan. He died a few months later, a broken man. Thereafter, China was plunged into a decade of internal chaos. Real political power rested chiefly with a dozen warlords, who controlled different segments of the country by sheer military might.

The warlords, or *tuchuns*, had originated as military governors during Yüan's regime. Too impoverished to send its own troops to maintain order over China's vast reaches, the national government was forced to rely upon local provincial chieftains to raise revenues and recruit militia. Some of the warlords were loyal officers who had served under Yüan in the Imperial Army; others were powerful local leaders. They were a mixed assortment of able administrators, land-hungry soldiers of fortune, and ambitious ex-bandits. In the decade between 1916 and 1926 they were almost constantly at war, serving intermittently as rivals and allies in often vicious campaigns of self-aggrandizement.

During these turbulent years China's nominal government at Peking was controlled by successive coalitions of northern warlords. In the south Sun Yat-sen, who had returned to China after Yüan's death and

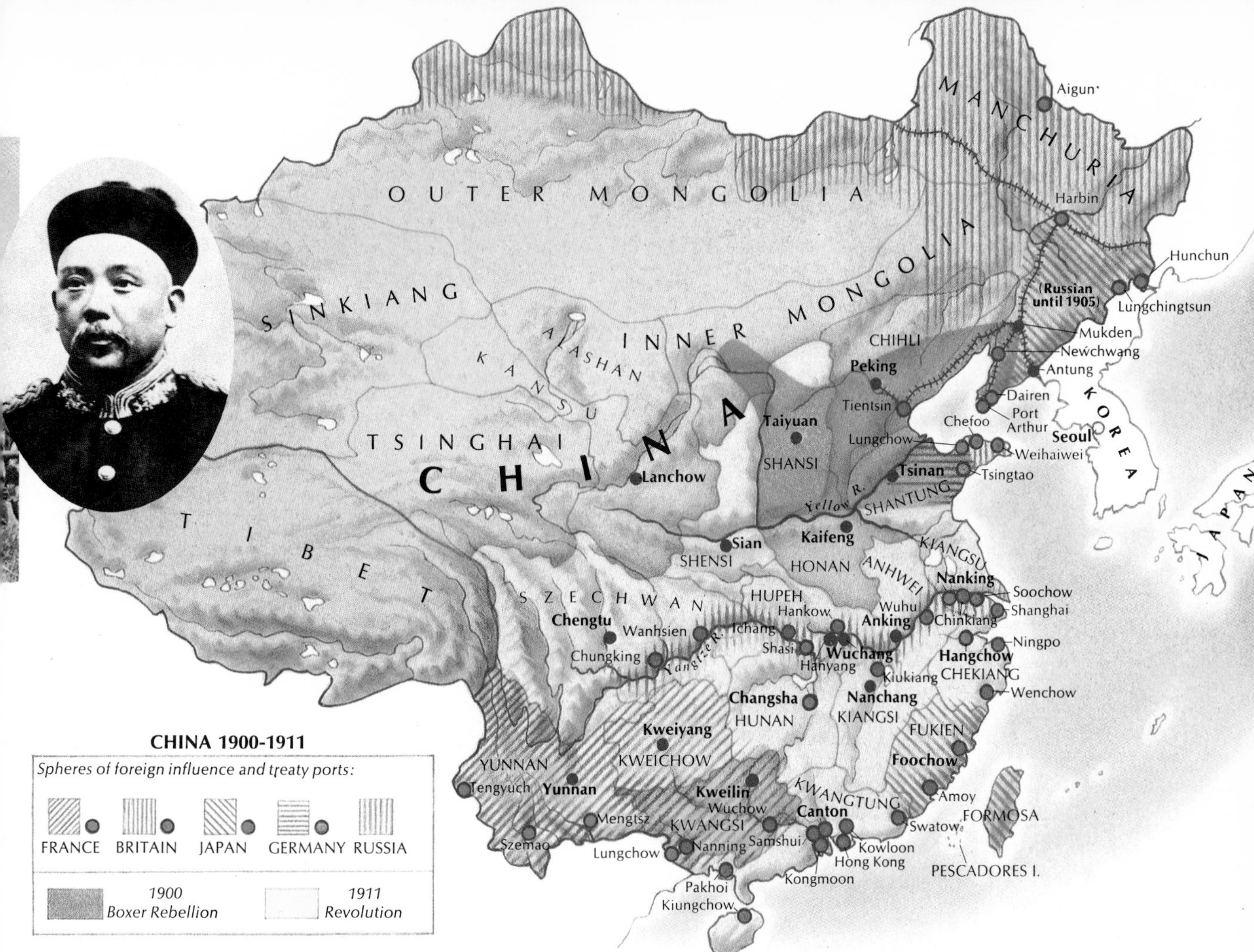

established a Kuomintang regime at Canton, maintained an uneasy alliance with the southern warlords. Although Sun claimed to represent China's only legitimate government, the foreign powers continued to deal exclusively with the leaders in Peking.

Meanwhile, the revolutionary initiative was taken up by a younger group of Chinese intellectuals and scholars who demanded a sweeping transformation of all aspects of Chinese culture and society. Dedicated, idealistic, and patriotic, they spearheaded the influential May Fourth Movement of 1919.

Foundations of a New Party

Like China's earlier reform efforts, the May Fourth Movement arose from a deepening alarm at the country's continued stagnation and its impotence in the face of foreign aggression. Its roots lay in China's 1915 submission to Japan's outrageous Twenty-one Demands, which gave Japan virtual financial and administrative control of the entire country. Publication of the agreement produced widespread indignation and concern among Chinese intellectuals, and they gradually formed a movement to rescue China from its disastrous course. The spokesman for the new group was Ch'ên Tu-hsiu, a Shanghai professor who founded the influential *New Youth* journal in 1915. Ch'ên exhorted China's youths to discard the "dregs of history" and "take up the task" of regenerating Chinese society. He foresaw the birth of a vital "Young China," in which the rigid traditions of ancient China would be replaced by a dynamic new order, based on principles of equality, humanitarianism, and rationalism.

The actual event from which the May Fourth Movement took its name was touched off by the 1919 Treaty of Versailles (see pp. 146–153). President Wilson's promises of self-determination and territorial integrity had given China's young idealists new hope for the restoration of national sovereignty over Shantung Province, a former German territory that Japan had occupied during World War I. They were therefore deeply shocked by the announcement of peace terms that confirmed Japan's sovereignty in Shantung.

Shouting "Down with the Traitors!" and "Return Shantung!" some 3,000 students marched through the streets of Peking on May 4, 1919, setting fire to the homes of pro-Japanese officials and demanding a boycott of Japanese imports. Their demonstration was followed by similar outbursts in other university cities,

Leaders of May Fourth Movement, *spurred by China's capitulation to Japan's Twenty-one Demands and the Versailles "betrayal," formed a Communist Party in 1921. (See map at top.) Above, Lenin and Asian leftists meet in Moscow.*

and their cry was soon taken up by Chinese businessmen, merchants, and laborers. Within a month Peking's leaders gave in to the students' demands: They released those youths they had imprisoned, dismissed pro-Japanese officials from the government, and refused to sign the peace settlement.

The May Fourth Movement gave China's intellectual reform leaders their first taste of political power and revealed widespread popular sympathy for their cause. Moreover, it marked the turning of Chinese revolutionary thinking away from the republican ideals of Sun Yat-sen and his followers toward a more radical solution. This leftist trend stemmed from the 1917 Russian Revolution (see pp. 132–139), an event that profoundly affected China's intellectuals.

At the time of the Soviet revolution many Chinese reformers had become disenchanted with the slow pace of democracy, but they were not aware of a viable alternative. The doctrines of Marx and Lenin, first introduced in China in 1917, seemed to promise a more expedient path to reform. After the May Fourth uprisings in 1919 Marxism became an active political force, and Ch'ên Tu-hsiu, Li Ta-chao, and other influential thinkers turned to communism.

In 1920 the Soviet Union sent Comintern agents to China to help organize a Chinese Communist Party. With their assistance Ch'ên established a small Communist cell in Shanghai and Li formed another in Peking. On July 1, 1921, the first official Congress of the Chinese Communist Party met in secret aboard a ship in Shanghai harbor. There, 12 delegates representing some 50 nationwide members elected Ch'ên Tu-hsiu party chairman. Among those present at that historic event was Mao Tse-tung, who had organized a small Communist cell in his native Hunan Province.

Communists and Nationalists

Comintern agents also established contact with Sun Yat-sen's Nationalist Government, which had been forced out of power by the southern warlords in 1922 and had fled to Shanghai. Sun, whose own thinking had taken a more leftist bent as a result of his repeated failure to find Western support or financial backing, welcomed the Comintern's offers of aid. In 1923 they negotiated an agreement of mutual friendship and cooperation, whereby Sun promised to open Kuomintang membership to the Communists in return for Soviet pledges to support his return to Canton and to help build an army to fight the warlords.

With Russian assistance, Sun reestablished a small political base in Canton and dispatched several aides to Moscow for six months of military training. Among them was a 37-year-old officer named Chiang Kai-shek, who in 1924 was chosen to head the new Nationalist military academy at Whampoa. Chiang's deputy political commissar was another officer destined to rise to national prominence, Chou En-lai.

That same year a warlord with revolutionary leanings came to power in the north and invited Sun to Peking to discuss a possible alliance. Sun accepted the invitation and arrived in the northern capital in December 1924, but negotiations were barely underway when he was hospitalized with terminal cancer. He died in Peking in March 1925.

Sun had not designated a successor, and a power struggle developed within the Kuomintang after his death. The fragile alliance between the Nationalists and the Communists became strained, as members divided into rightist and leftist camps. The leader of the rightists, Chiang Kai-shek, who had developed a profound distrust of Soviet motives in China during his sojourn in Moscow, finally gained the upper hand.

For the moment, however, Chiang managed to hold the shaky coalition together. On July 9, 1926, he launched a military expedition against the warlords. By January his army had conquered central and southern China and had captured the industrial tri-city of Wuhan (Hankow, Hanyang, and Wuchang). In March the Nationalists captured Nanking and Shanghai. Firmly in control of southern China, Chiang then moved against the Communists.

On the night of April 12, 1927, Chiang instigated a vicious purge of all leftists in Shanghai. At his orders more than 300 Communists and their sympathizers were executed. During the next year Chiang sanctioned a nationwide reign of terror against all Communists. In the face of this persecution Moscow's agents and advisers fled to the Soviet Union, but the Chinese Communists staged a series of desperate uprisings in southern Chinese cities. One such revolt was led by Mao Tse-tung in Changsha, capital of Hunan Province. Mao's uprising, like those attempted by his colleagues, met with dismal failure, and he went into hiding in the mountainous border region between Hunan and Kiangsi Provinces.

Chiang had gained absolute command of the Kuomintang, and in January 1928 he was proclaimed the head of the Nationalist government at Nanking. Resuming his northward advance, he led his armies into Peking in June, capturing the capital city with little effort. For the first time since 1916 China was united.

Outwardly, Chiang's victory appeared to be the long-delayed fulfillment of the 1911 Revolution. In actual fact, the Generalissimo had not brought real change to China but totalitarian, one-party rule backed by military strength. Ignoring China's urgent need for modernization and reform, he single-mindedly set about eradicating his enemies: warlords, Communists, and dissident Nationalists alike. Meanwhile, China remained underdeveloped, overpopulated, and internationally impotent. The revolution had failed, but its momentum had not been lost entirely. In China's remote countryside Mao Tse-tung was slowly rebuilding his battered party into a powerful revolutionary force.

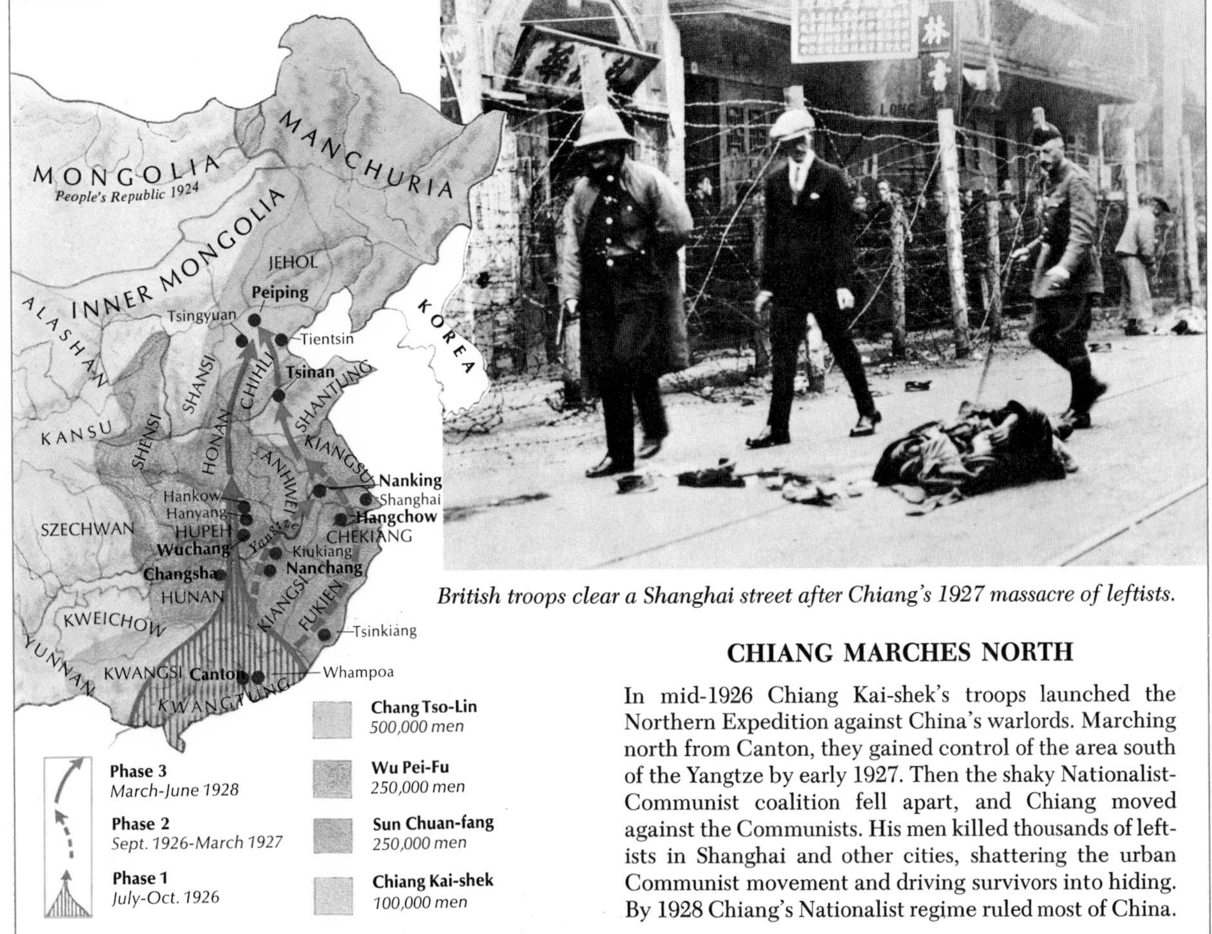

British troops clear a Shanghai street after Chiang's 1927 massacre of leftists.

CHIANG MARCHES NORTH

In mid-1926 Chiang Kai-shek's troops launched the Northern Expedition against China's warlords. Marching north from Canton, they gained control of the area south of the Yangtze by early 1927. Then the shaky Nationalist-Communist coalition fell apart, and Chiang moved against the Communists. His men killed thousands of leftists in Shanghai and other cities, shattering the urban Communist movement and driving survivors into hiding. By 1928 Chiang's Nationalist regime ruled most of China.

1913

Music in a Modern Key

Igor Stravinsky's passionate and unconventional ballet score The Rite of Spring *takes Paris by storm, giving music and dance a new dimension.*

On May 29, 1913, everyone who was anyone in Parisian society or the arts attended the premiere of *The Rite of Spring* (*Le Sacre du Printemps*) at the Théâtre des Champs Élysées. It was the third ballet that Igor Stravinsky, the most acclaimed new composer in Europe, had written for Sergei Diaghilev's Ballets Russes. Choreography was by Vaslav Nijinsky, the 23-year-old dancer whose soaring leaps and animal grace had already made him a legend.

The curtain rose on the scene of a verdant Russian landscape while eerie, dissonant sounds and pounding rhythm filled the theater. On stage 40 men and women, costumed in loose-fitting smocks as primitive tribesmen, seemed not so much to dance to the music as to react to it with awkward movement. Within two minutes the fashionable audience was in an uproar, divided into opponents and defenders of the production. Paris had never witnessed the like.

Shouts, whistles, and boos drowned the music. American writer Gertrude Stein recalled afterward how an outraged gentleman seated near her used his cane to smash the tophat of his overenthusiastic neighbor. Many in the theater saw an elegant woman slap a man next to her because he was hissing, whereupon her escort rose to exchange cards for a duel. From all sides abuse rained down on conductor Pierre Monteux and the orchestra, but they played on.

Nijinsky, his face chalk white, stood on a chair in the wings, shouting out the complicated rhythm so the dancers could remain in time to the music they could not hear. Stravinsky, furious at the ridicule heaped on his music, left in the middle of the performance.

Music—Or Madness?

Most music critics were outraged. They joked that *Le Sacre du Printemps* was in fact a *massacre du printemps.* One critic attacked Nijinsky as a man "devoid of ideas and even common sense" for his choreography of "epileptic fits" and "ugly movements." Only a few critics realized that "time would show the true worth" of the piece. The consensus was that *The Rite of Spring* was a negation of what music should stand for, and most Parisians agreed.

What the public wanted was music that could be understood. (Even musicians at the premiere found it hard to identify which of the instruments produced the piercing high notes and which the dark lower ones.) Good music was music already well known: the baroque works of Bach, the classical compositions of Haydn and Mozart, or unabashed romantic music, including that of Stravinsky's first two ballets, *The Firebird* and *Petrushka,* which had catapulted him to fame. Parisians also enjoyed the evocative music of Debussy and his fellow impressionists.

But *The Rite of Spring* was unlike any music heard before. In the place of melodies that one could remember was a discomfiting, dominating rhythm. Stravinsky had discarded the traditional steady rhythmic system and replaced it with his own, which consisted of constantly changing time signatures. (Understandably, the dancers—most of whom had not been tutored in music in the first place—found the score difficult to memorize. It took an unprecedented 114 rehearsals

Copyright 1926 by Edition Russe de Music. Copyright assigned 1947 to Boosey & Hawkes, Inc. Reprinted by permission.

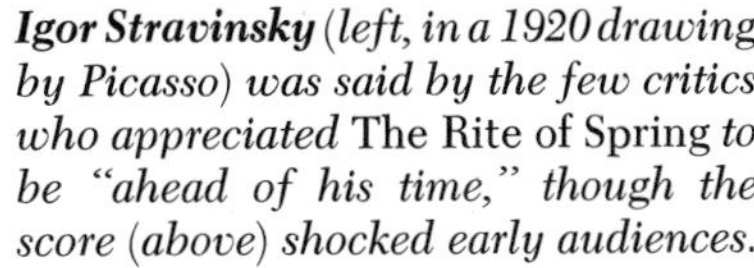

***Igor Stravinsky** (left, in a 1920 drawing by Picasso) was said by the few critics who appreciated* The Rite of Spring *to be "ahead of his time," though the score (above) shocked early audiences.*

Just as mystifying was Vaslav Nijinsky's choreography: The dancers (above and right) moved awkwardly, feet turned inward, shunning classical grace for a powerful, primitive style.

before they could synchronize their movements to it.)

Equally disturbing was the orchestration. Instrumental sounds failed to form a melody; instead, an unsettling series of loud notes—more reminiscent of squawks and shrieks—sporadically erupted above the bumpy rhythmic texture. Stravinsky did not seem to be trying to entertain his audience, but to shatter their composure instead.

Even Stravinsky's conception of spring was far removed from most composers' pastoral portrayal of the season. It came to him as a vision: "I saw in imagination a solemn pagan rite. Sage elders, seated in a circle, watched a young girl dance herself to death." Stravinsky was fascinated by the fear of primitive peoples that the earth would not renew itself after its long winter sleep unless a human being were sacrificed to the god of spring. His music tells the story of this ritual: A girl is offered as a sacrifice while, all around her, nature's process of rebirth begins.

Although the public reaction to *The Rite of Spring* angered him, Stravinsky's aim had not been to create yet another popular work. He wanted, instead, to develop the ingredients of music (harmony, tone, rhythm, orchestration) and assemble them in new ways. In his own words: "We have a duty towards music; namely, to invent it." Stravinsky continued to invent music throughout his 69-year career. His first compositions, scored for ballet, gave way to music unrelated to a story, and after the Russian Revolution of 1917 Stravinsky abandoned the use of Slavic folk tunes that had given so much of his earlier music a Russian sound. *Ragtime* (1918), a piece for 11 instruments, was based on American jazz, an idiom scarcely known in Europe at the time. Then, much to the public's surprise, he began to base his music on the techniques of past composers. But even Stravinsky's neoclassical pieces, such as *Pulcinella* (1920), were brilliantly fresh and unmistakably his own, even though they lacked the peculiar rhythm that was the driving force of *The Rite of Spring*.

Stravinsky Joins Diaghilev

The man who ushered in the era of modern music was born in 1882 into a noble Polish family that had emigrated to Russia in the 1800's. Stravinsky's father, a bass baritone opera singer, started his son on piano lessons at the age of nine. Later he sent Stravinsky to St. Petersburg to study law, but while at the university he devoted as much time to musical composition as to his legal studies. His music teacher was the great Nicolai Rimsky-Korsakov, dean of Russian nationalist composers. Before Stravinsky received his law degree in 1905, he abandoned all thoughts of a legal career.

THE IMPRESARIO

The founder and director of the Ballets Russes was by his own account "a great charlatan, a great *charmeur,* a man with a great quantity of logic, but with very few principles and no real gifts." Yet Sergei Diaghilev did possess one gift: the unerring ability to detect and stimulate genius in others. Stravinsky is perhaps his most famous discovery, but he employed other leaders of the early 20th-century avant-garde in art, music, and dance as well. Many attributed their success to Diaghilev's guidance and enthusiasm.

Diaghilev displayed the promotional instincts of a Hollywood producer, and could sometimes be a ruthless autocrat. He unhesitatingly fired members of the company he no longer wanted—including Nijinsky, his one-time lover and the leading male dancer. But he was also extremely generous with money for productions and friends, and cared little about personal gain. He lived his adult life out of suitcases and died penniless. By the time of his death in 1929, at the age of 57, the princely Russian impresario had revitalized the calm world of classical ballet with great daring and flamboyance.

A short, thin, energetic man with a large head, long nose, and round spectacles, Stravinsky looked the part of a scholarly lawyer or professor—or, according to a youthful contemporary, a "prancing grasshopper." He was a solicitous host, meticulously neat, deeply religious, and capable of harsh self-criticism. While he was still a young man, his cutting remarks about others earned him the reputation of being difficult. Once asked how he liked a famous composer's music, he replied: "I'll wait to answer until he writes some."

In the winter of 1910 however, this confident young man was only a promising newcomer to the music scene. Then Sergei Diaghilev, director of the Ballets Russes, heard a performance of Stravinsky's short piece "Fireworks," and asked the composer for a score to the *Firebird* ballet. Stravinsky enthusiastically agreed to write the music.

Diaghilev had already created a sensation in Paris with the first season of his Ballets Russes in 1909. His productions enthralled Parisian audiences with a new world of oriental mystery, eroticism, and myth. The fairies, princesses, and gentle peasants who were the stock characters of traditional ballets such as *Swan Lake* and *Giselle* were replaced by concubines, slaves, mythological creatures, clowns, and primitive tribesmen. They performed in ballets based on the *Arabian Nights* and Russian mythology and folklore, a dramatic contrast to the usual romantic stories of lovers winning eternal happiness or dying of broken hearts.

If the themes of Diaghilev's ballets were new, so were the steps and movements in them. Michel Fokine, the company's first choreographer, did not rely on the vocabulary of classical dance steps (which had originated at the French court in the 16th century), but revitalized ballet by using new forms to tell a story and express emotion. In his famous *Scheherazade* (1910), for example, an oriental king's favorite concubine and her forbidden lover lie on a pillow embracing, while all about the stage other members of the harem join their own lovers in a suggestive dance. Such daring and explicit sexuality was a far cry from traditional works. For example, in *Giselle,* the epitome of 19th-century ballet, Prince Albrecht tells Giselle he loves her by delicately folding his hands over his heart.

Blazing Jewels and Color

Most intoxicating of all in the early Ballets Russes productions were the rich sets and costumes. Dancers wore clothes that blazed with jewels and color; sets suggested the decadence of oriental palaces, the fairy-tale quality of St. Petersburg, or else the starkness of nomadic camps in Asia. Foremost among Diaghilev's designers were Alexander Benois, who used the technique of false perspective to create dazzling sets, and

The colorful, swirling costumes for the ballet Narcisse *(1911) were among Leon Bakst's most brilliant designs.*

Leon Bakst and Natalia Goncharova, whose flamboyant costumes were a complete departure from those of classical ballet. These designers, unknown until their discovery by Diaghilev, were to become among the most influential of the century.

With the onset of World War I Diaghilev could no longer rely solely upon Russian artists to work on his productions. Determined to keep his company going, he sought the help of the young, adventurous European artists he had met since coming to the West. As a result, the company lost its purely Russian character and became a showcase for the new artistic movements, such as cubism and surrealism, that were just beginning to make themselves felt in Europe.

The list of people who worked for the Ballets Russes constitutes an index of the most important artists in the first 30 years of this century—the modern masters. When Diaghilev hired them, many, like Stravinsky, were just beginning their careers. Others were known but not yet accepted by the public. Picasso, Braque, Derain, Matisse, Gris, Laurencin, Utrillo, Ernst, and Miró designed sets and costumes. In addition to Stravinsky, who composed nine ballets for Diaghilev, Richard Strauss, Poulenc, Fauré, Ravel, Satie, De Falla, Debussy, and Prokofiev composed for the company. All the choreographers who worked for Diaghilev achieved international reputations, and the last of them, George Balanchine, went on to found the New York City Ballet, one of America's finest companies. Many other former Ballets Russes dancers became well-known teachers and choreographers.

Diaghilev died, suddenly, in 1929, while on vacation in Venice, his favorite city outside Russia, and was buried there on the island of San Michele. The company did not long survive its founder. Little remains of the productions that so dazzled and outraged Parisians who had come of age in an era of long, bustled dresses and horse-drawn carriages. The famous sets and costumes have been destoyed or dispersed, and although the ballets themselves remain in the repertoires of many companies around the world, the choreography is often modified or changed altogether. Only the music has managed to remain intact.

The Rite of Spring is the most famous score Diaghilev commissioned. As the impresario sensed during its tumultuous premiere, it marked the beginning of modern music. By mid-century it had become part of the standard symphony repertoire. The composition that received such a stormy introduction in Paris no longer shocks, though it has not lost its power to move the listener and to cast a spell.

Many modern composers, including Roy Harris, Aaron Copland, and Bela Bartok, have carried Stravinsky's experiments even further. Compared to such contemporary forms of expression as electronic music or unpredictable music (for example, a piece by John Cage scored for radio frequencies and volumes), *The Rite of Spring* sounds almost old-fashioned. But in 1913 its debut helped to free music from some of the conventions that were no longer appropriate to a new age.

THE EXOTIC WORLD OF THE BALLET

The designer Alexander Benois wrote that the Ballets Russes was "conceived not by the professionals of the dance but by . . . artists, linked together by the idea of Art as an entity." Indeed, stage and costume design played as large a role as dance or music in Ballets Russes productions. Designers created opulent, often bizarre, sets sometimes using false perspectives; costumes, such as those the great Leon Bakst designed for Nijinsky, were devised as part of an artistic whole that included decor, music, and dance.

Benois created a "stage within a stage" for the 1911 ballet Petrushka.

Nijinsky, costumed by Constantine Korovin, performed Les Orientales *in 1910.*

1913

The Fight for Suffrage

A determined and articulate new breed of woman inaugurates an all-out struggle for freedom, equality, and the right to vote.

The scene was the racecourse at Epsom Downs, England, on Derby Day, June 4, 1913. As some of Britain's finest Thoroughbreds thundered around the track, a crowd of thousands cheered—then gave a sudden, collective gasp. A young woman named Emily Wilding Davison had run onto the track directly in the path of the King's prize horse, trying to seize the reins. The horse trampled her, and four days later she died.

To many of the onlookers the bloody spectacle was seen as an act of martyrdom on behalf of a cause that for years had gnawed at Britain's conscience. It was the culmination of a nationwide protest campaign that had by then brought the mighty city of London almost to a state of siege. As one commentator described it years later: "On stealthy midnight expeditions with brush and bucket [the raiders] painted out house numbers. . . . They poured jam down mailboxes, uprooted municipal flowerbeds, invaded picture galleries and mutilated paintings, cut telegraph wires, turned in false fire alarms, and damaged a home that Lloyd

A martyr for the cause of women's rights, *Emily Davison was trampled to death by the King's horse in the English Derby of 1913. The dramatic event, which shocked onlookers and stirred fellow suffragists, was vividly recorded in this early newsreel film. Despite some evidence that Miss Davison did not intend suicide, the Derby Day disaster strengthened support for the equal rights movement and became a rallying point for suffragists throughout Britain.*

George was building. Finally they began to set fires. Several railway stations, the refreshment pavilion at Kew Gardens, a football stadium in Cambridge, and even a few churches went up in flames."

Who were these guerrilla fighters, one of whom threatened Winston Churchill with a whip? What was their cause, that they would resort to such organized vandalism and violence? Why were they risking public ridicule, imprisonment, some of them even their own lives? Why were they provoking the government to take action against them?

The answer is disarmingly simple: They were the wives, sisters, mothers, and daughters of ordinary British subjects, and they merely wanted to vote.

The British suffragist movement, now often misremembered as the harmless highjinks of petticoated protest marchers, was really a decades-long struggle waged in deadly earnest. Its root causes went back to the Middle Ages and earlier, when the inequities of Roman and canon laws were carried over into English common law, so institutionalizing the inferior status of women that in feudal times a wife's legal status derived solely from her subservient role as the husband's wife and his children's mother.

Centuries of Subjection

Even in the "enlightened" 18th century the famous jurist Sir William Blackstone could safely negate the rights of married women. Since under common law husband and wife are held to be one person, he wrote: "The very being or legal existence of the woman is suspended during the marriage, or at least is incorporated and consolidated into that of the husband."

In 19th-century Britain the pattern still held true. A woman then reigned, but Queen Victoria's status was the spectacular exception. The lot of other women was decidedly different. If rich, they were pampered to the point of suffocation by a life of dinner parties and other social rituals. If poor, they were exploited as cheap labor in the factories. If middle class (as more were becoming), they hewed to the law of "respectability" and devoted their talents to culture and religion.

The worst oppression was borne by workingwomen during the first decade of the 20th century. By then virtually half the 4 million employed women were servants in other people's homes—menial drudges earning, on the average, about a third of what a workingman could make. A "respectable" woman could aspire to only two occupations—seamstress or, if she were educated, governess. Women of middle-class marriages, from whose ranks most suffragists came, fought the limitations of their lives as best they could.

The debate over votes for women had been simmering for decades. John Stuart Mill, the great libertarian, had effectively refuted Blackstone in his 1869 treatise *On the Subjection of Women,* noting that all women, not just wives, were a subject class. "[Women] are declared to be better than men," wrote Mill, "an empty compliment, which must provoke a bitter smile from every woman of spirit, since there is no other situation in life in which it is the established order . . . that the better obey the worse." Early suffragists used this work as their bible. The decisive struggle really began after 1903, when guerrilla bands of the Women's Social and Political Union (WSPU), led by the redoubtable Emmeline Pankhurst, began smashing up London.

Suffrage and Slavery in America

In North America it had once seemed less urgent that women get the vote. The pioneers settling the West needed all the "personpower" available; so distinctions based on sex were eased. The growing urban population needed factory workers and teachers, positions that were as ably filled by women as by men.

But gradually sex stereotyping set in, with the woman's "place" naturally in the home. This rankled

***The emancipation of the American woman** was championed in a colorful array of enameled pins like these, often featuring a rising sun to signify the dawning of a new day. Like their British sisters, American activists were harassed, derided, fined, and imprisoned by a society reluctant to accord women the same voting rights as men.*

Sir William Blackstone

John Stuart Mill

Mary Wollstonecraft

THE CAUSE OF EQUALITY: BEGINNING THE GREAT DEBATE

The British suffragist movement actually began in 1792 with the publication of *A Vindication of the Rights of Women,* an essay by Mary Wollstonecraft. She argued eloquently for women's rights in education and the professions, calling for an end to the "bitter bread of dependence" on the male. A society can be healthy, she wrote, only when true equality exists among the groups composing it—a view strongly at odds with that of Sir William Blackstone, the prominent 18th-century jurist. Blackstone's enormously influential *Commentary on the Laws of England,* published in 1765, set the tone of the times by stating that marriage suspended the "legal existence" of wives. Wollstonecraft answered that marriage "never will be held sacred till women, by being brought up with men, are prepared to be their companions rather than their mistresses."

Mary Wollstonecraft died from complications of childbirth in 1797 at the age of 38, but her essay continued to inspire suffragists, and in time a few men joined the struggle. John Stuart Mill, the 19th-century Utilitarian philosopher and economist, became a leading spokesman for the cause and in 1869 wrote *The Subjection of Women,* protesting against sex discrimination. The "legal subordination of one sex to the other," said Mill, "is wrong in itself, and now one of the chief hindrances to human improvement . . . it ought to be replaced by a principle of perfect equality, admitting no power or privilege on the one side, nor disability on the other." Mill was deeply influenced by Harriet Taylor, an invalid "woman of letters" who became his wife in 1851. Before they met, he declared, his belief in complete sexual equality in politics, in social relationships, and in the home had been "little more than abstract in principle." After his marriage Mill protested against the injustice suffered by all women as a class and the waste of talent this injustice involved.

such public-spirited women as Sarah and Angelina Grimké, who had begun speaking out against slavery in the 1830's. Male resistance to them, together with the fact that women were barred from the numerous antislavery societies of the 1830's, showed women that limitations on their freedom gave them a common cause with the slaves.

Toward midcentury, as the slavery debate became more heated, general awareness of the female's oppression increased. Women then numbered one-fourth of all those employed in manufacturing. Male abolitionists began demanding votes for women.

The Seneca Falls Conference

Lucretia Mott, daughter of a Nantucket whaling captain, was a teacher, Quaker minister, and a founder of the Philadelphia Female Anti-Slavery Society. At an 1840 World Anti-Slavery Convention in London she became friendly with Elizabeth Cady Stanton, also a staunch abolitionist. At the convention they shared a common grievance: Being women, they could not take part in the debates.

Eight years later they and their husbands met near the Stantons' home in Seneca Falls, New York, and resolved to call a convention on women's rights. They got valuable help from two men: Mrs. Mott's husband, James, who chaired the conference, and the famous black publisher and abolitionist Frederick Douglass. Some 300 people from as far as 50 miles away flocked to the two-day meeting. After hearing the speakers, 32 men and 68 women signed the Declaration of Prin-

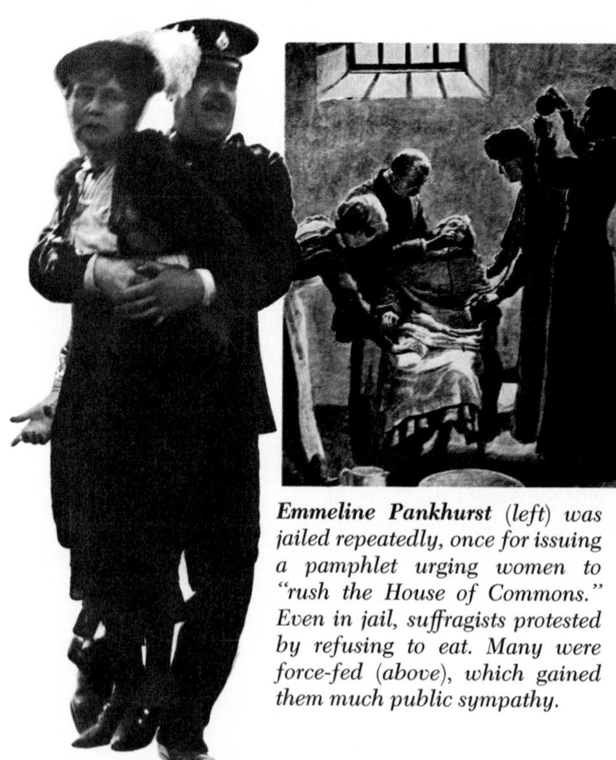

Emmeline Pankhurst *(left) was jailed repeatedly, once for issuing a pamphlet urging women to "rush the House of Commons." Even in jail, suffragists protested by refusing to eat. Many were force-fed (above), which gained them much public sympathy.*

ciples and Sentiments, a document which the feminists modeled on the Declaration of Independence.

The 1848 Seneca Falls Conference was the first public meeting in the United States held specifically to discuss women's rights. Its Declaration of Principles sounded a clarion call for the cause, and its spokeswomen became national figures. It launched a movement that spawned other suffragist organizations whose membership swelled into the thousands by 1900 and into hundreds of thousands by the time of the First World War.

On both sides of the Atlantic the success of the suffragists brought increasing male resistance—from the dais, in the headlines and the halls of government and especially from the pulpit. Men pointed to the so-called nature of women. They were illogical, fickle, and too fragile for the awesome responsibilities of the vote, it was said. Their proper role was to remain in the home and preserve familial, and hence social, stability. Besides, a more sinister argument went, by effectively doubling the electorate, the numbers of "poor, ignorant, and immoral" voters (meaning blacks, immigrants, and other presumed riffraff) would also double. To the women who had to answer these charges it was hard to tell which was worse: the condescending tone or the hypocritical substance.

In Britain the era of decorous debate ended in 1903 with Mrs. Pankhurst's formation of the Women's Social and Political Union. Tired of seeing their cause brushed off by Parliament, and dissatisfied with the sops thrown to earlier suffrage groups, she renounced "outworn missionary methods" and proclaimed instead the WSPU's goal: "immediate enfranchisement."

The organization's first target was the Liberal Party, which seemed headed for a landslide victory. In 1905 Christabel Pankhurst, Emmeline's daughter, invaded a party meeting carrying a placard bearing a simple challenge: "Will You Give Votes for Women?" The embarrassed members had her put out, but she then spat on a policeman, committing "technical assault" to ensure her arrest. Thus began not only a campaign of high visibility for the WSPU but a nationwide protest movement over the inferior status of women.

After that day no politician was safe from the demonstrators. Suffragists took to sneaking into meeting halls when they were locked out, shouting their challenge to the speaker, and being dragged away by the police. Then they moved on to street politics, scrawling "Votes for Women" on walls and sidewalks. Finally, they resorted to outright violence—firebombings, window smashings, and physical attacks.

Among their supporters in the government even the most progressive condemned these tactics as counterproductive. Violence, they said, would only alienate the unconverted and provoke a backlash. But so deep had the social inequities become, the reverse in fact happened. The suffragist movement galvanized a feeling of sisterhood among women of all ranks, and distinguished matrons were soon joining Manchester factory girls in what the Pankhursts called their army. With every act of protest this army grew larger and more prosperous. In one year alone it raised more than

In the vanguard of a social revolution, *these 1914 suffragists, marching in Washington, D.C., in support of equal voting rights for women, were accused by men of violating divine law and provoking atheism. Ratification of the 19th amendment was delayed until 1920, after American women had fully demonstrated their mettle in World War I.*

SUFFRAGE: NOT QUITE UNIVERSAL

Although suffrage movements began early in several countries, winning full equality was often a long hard struggle. Newly independent countries that mandated voting rights for women are not included in the following list.

1893 New Zealand
1902 Australia
1906 Finland
1913 Norway
1915 Denmark, Iceland
1917 U.S.S.R.
1918 Canada, Germany, Austria
1920 United States
1921 Sweden
1927 Ecuador
1928 Britain
1931 Spain
1932 Brazil, Thailand (then Siam)
1934 Sri Lanka (then Ceylon)
1934 Turkey, Cuba
1935 Burma
1937 Philippines
1944 France
1945 Italy
1946 Japan
1947 Argentina, China
1948 Belgium
1949 Chile
1951 Nepal, Greece
1953 Mexico
1955 Colombia, Peru
1956 Egypt
1963 Iran
1964 Afghanistan
1971 Switzerland
1974 Jordan

Today a few nations still deny women the vote. And while women have voted in most developed nations for years, few have been elected or named to high posts. By the mid-1970's only Sri Lanka, Argentina, India, the Central African Republic, and Israel had been headed by women.

The efforts of Japanese suffragists (shown at a 1912 convention) to get the vote succeeded only after World War II.

£37,000, far more than any of the "constitutional" suffrage societies had ever managed to collect before.

The government, meanwhile, could do nothing right. Leniency was seen as a sign of ineptitude, and repression chafed at the British conscience. Imprisoned hunger strikers posed the worst problem. Refusing to eat and courting martyrdom for their cause, the protestors finally had to be force-fed like so many French geese. Ugly stories of this treatment were luridly recounted by the press, further arousing pro- and anti-feminist passions.

The authorities' next move was an ingenious new measure aptly dubbed "The Cat and Mouse Act" by the suffragists. Prisoners, it said, were to be freed from jail when their health was in danger, but they could be returned when it improved. Under these provisions Mrs. Pankhurst and another of her daughters, Sylvia, were each imprisoned and released no fewer than 10 times in a span of a few months. Weak and emaciated, such women appeared at public meetings to serve as excellent advertisements of "official brutality."

Derby Day

The climax came in the Derby Day disaster of 1913. Emily Davison had been one of Mrs. Pankhurst's most ardent followers. Whether she had intended suicide is debatable, since a return train ticket to her home was found among her belongings; but to sympathetic spectators her martyrdom was unmistakable and sent shock waves throughout the land. Christabel Pankhurst would later write of Miss Davison: "Probably in no other way and at no other time and place could she so effectually have brought the concentrated attention of millions to bear upon the cause." At the young woman's funeral throngs of suffragists, veterans and the newly converted, marched behind a banner bearing this sentiment: "Thoughts have gone forth whose power can sleep no more. Victory. Victory."

The momentum for female suffrage was by then irreversible, but it took the cataclysm of a world war to effect the change. When hostilities broke out, Mrs. Pankhurst offered her well-organized brigades of women to the war effort; their valuable service helped win public support for the cause. In January 1918 British women over 30 were at last granted the franchise, and the following year the Sex Disqualification Removal Act opened many of the professions to women and entitled them to serve on juries. In 1928 the voting age for women was lowered to 21, the same as for men.

Like their British sisters, North American suffragists had to struggle long and hard for their rights. It was galling that the abolitionist cause they had championed in the U.S. succeeded—but left them behind; the 15th amendment to the U.S. Constitution granted the vote to black males but not to women.

Yet the leaders—Susan B. Anthony, Lucy Stone, and Carrie Chapman Catt—persevered. And the movement became more militant. In 1910 Harriot Stanton Blatch, daughter of Elizabeth Stanton, organized the first suffragist parade, and in 1917 Alice Paul led picket lines and hunger strikes in support of women's rights. Gradually, individual states began to relent—especially in the West. As in Britain, women's wartime service was decisive: On August 26, 1920, the U.S. Secretary of State certified the ratification of the 19th amendment to the Constitution, prohibiting disfranchisement because of sex, and the long, difficult struggle was over.

During the next four decades few direct changes in women's social status resulted from the 19th amendment. Some women, however, were noteworthy for their political accomplishments in this period: Jeannette Rankin, elected to Congress from Montana even before the passage of the 19th amendment; Nellie Tayloe Ross, first woman elected Governor in the United States; Frances Perkins, the first woman U.S. Cabinet member; and Hattie Wyatt Caraway, the first woman elected a U.S. Senator.

International Women's Year

In the 1960's, partially as a result of the libertarian spirit of the civil rights movement, the North American women's movement was revived. Betty Friedan's 1963 book, *The Feminine Mystique,* signaled the new beginnings. Steadily gaining in size and influence, scores of women's groups, ranging in type from the most radical to such long-established organizations as the League of Women Voters, have made significant gains against discriminatory laws and customs. They have opened the way to new freedoms for women in jobs, housing, and social behavior and have secured at least some legal guarantees of equality.

Other countries have changed at a less dramatic rate. It took Switzerland until 1971 to grant women the vote, and in some countries (including Kuwait, Saudi Arabia, Yemen, and Liechtenstein) women are *still* not enfranchised. Yet steady signs of progress in granting women more equality and greater opportunities can be seen in Sweden, France, Canada, Brazil, and other nations.

To promote equality between men and women, the United Nations designated 1975 as International Women's Year. Despite controversy about differing goals for developd and underdeveloped nations, many delegates to the Mexico City Conference considered it a success. To the British and North American suffragists who sacrificed so much for their cause, the emblem of the International Women's Year would have seemed fitting. It combines an equal sign with the biological symbol of woman to form the dove of peace.

Jackie finds that being a carpenter is much more rewarding than simply being "nice."

ELIMINATING SEXUAL STEREOTYPES

Many feminist organizations have charged that sexist attitudes are imposed upon children at an early age through the toys they play with, the games they play, and the books they read. Young girls are encouraged to play with dolls and assume a generally subservient role, while little boys are expected to play with guns and take on a more dominant role. Since 1970, however, many toy manufacturers have responded to feminist pressures by designing less stereotyped products, and children's book publishers have made a concerted effort to eliminate traditional male-female distinctions in their texts. They depict, for example, parents sharing household tasks, working mothers, and stay-at-home fathers.

Until recently, such sexual biases have been reinforced by school textbooks and courses, but in the past few years feminist efforts have sparked a growing reform movement. To date, 19 states have made some kind of effort to reduce sexual prejudices in the schools, and many localities have sponsored similar programs. Such formerly sex-segregated courses as home economics and industrial arts have been opened to all students. Teachers have been urged to select material that portrays women as logical and capable and to point out that men can be weak and scatterbrained at times. Offensive language has been purged from textbooks. By focusing on one of the root sources of sexual bias, feminists are making important strides toward a less sexist society.

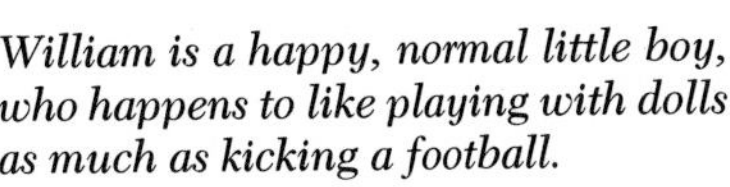

William is a happy, normal little boy, who happens to like playing with dolls as much as kicking a football.

1913

Inside the Atom: Order, Energy, and Enigma

With the help of Max Planck's radical new quantum theory Niels Bohr probes the atom and reveals its mysterious anatomy.

***No branch of the physical sciences** has had greater philosophical repercussions than quantum theory, for it described a radical discontinuity in the fabric of nature and seemed to suggest very definite limits to the scope of human inquiry. Working in the ambiguous landscape of the atom, where every phenomenon has, simultaneously, the aspects of both matter and energy, the pioneering quantum theorists, Max Planck and Niels Bohr, discovered that energy transactions do not occur smoothly but in sudden leaps and bounds—quantum jumps that give the substratum of reality a kind of irreducible graininess.*

A lily (above) and its pollen grains (right) photographed at increasing magnifications suggest the grainy reality of the quantum world. An electron-scanning microscope reveals the minute architecture of pollen dust; but at subatomic levels, represented in the smallest picture by the structure of an iridium crystal photographed through a field emission microscope (the closest thing to actually photographing an atom), architectural solidity becomes a system of energy transactions, occurring at unimaginable speeds in sudden, discontinuous leaps.

One night in October 1943 a small fishing boat crossed the narrow sea channel from Nazi-occupied Denmark to neutral Sweden. Aboard was Niels Bohr, the celebrated director of the University of Copenhagen's Institute for Theoretical Physics. The next morning the Gestapo arrived at the institute to arrest him—but by then Bohr, forewarned by the Danish underground, was on his way to England in an RAF bomber. Two months later he was working on the development of the atomic bomb in New Mexico.

Many of the scientists at Los Alamos had been Bohr's students and colleagues over the years, as had many of their fellows who remained in Hitler's Europe. No other single man was so familiar with nuclear research all over the world, or could estimate so closely German progress toward the atomic bomb. And certainly no other man could match Bohr's experience in applying atomic theory (abstract and mathematical as it had become) to the solution of physical problems. For much of what was known about the atom in 1943 had its origins in another journey by Niels Bohr more than three decades earlier, when he had undertaken the formidable task of developing our first reliably detailed model of atomic structure.

Arranging the Atom

The young Dane received his Ph.D. in 1911 and was granted a fellowship for further study in England. He went to Cambridge to work with J. J. Thomson, the discoverer of the electron (a tiny particle bearing little of the atom's mass but all its negative charge). The problem then under investigation by Thomson's research group concerned the location and behavior of electrons within the atom.

When atoms are stimulated by high temperatures, they emit electromagnetic radiation (e.g., the heat of red-hot metal or the brilliant yellow-white of the sun's gases). This radiation is characteristically different for each element, and for decades scientists had identified substances by the "fingerprints" of their spectral patterns—patterns of bright lines when the glow of heated matter was broken down by the prism of a spectroscope or of dark lines when white light (containing all colors) was filtered through a cooler sample of the substance. The means by which each kind of atom produced these characteristic "emission lines" and "absorption lines" was still not understood, and no matter how Thomson adjusted his conceptual model of the atom (in which electrons were scattered through a

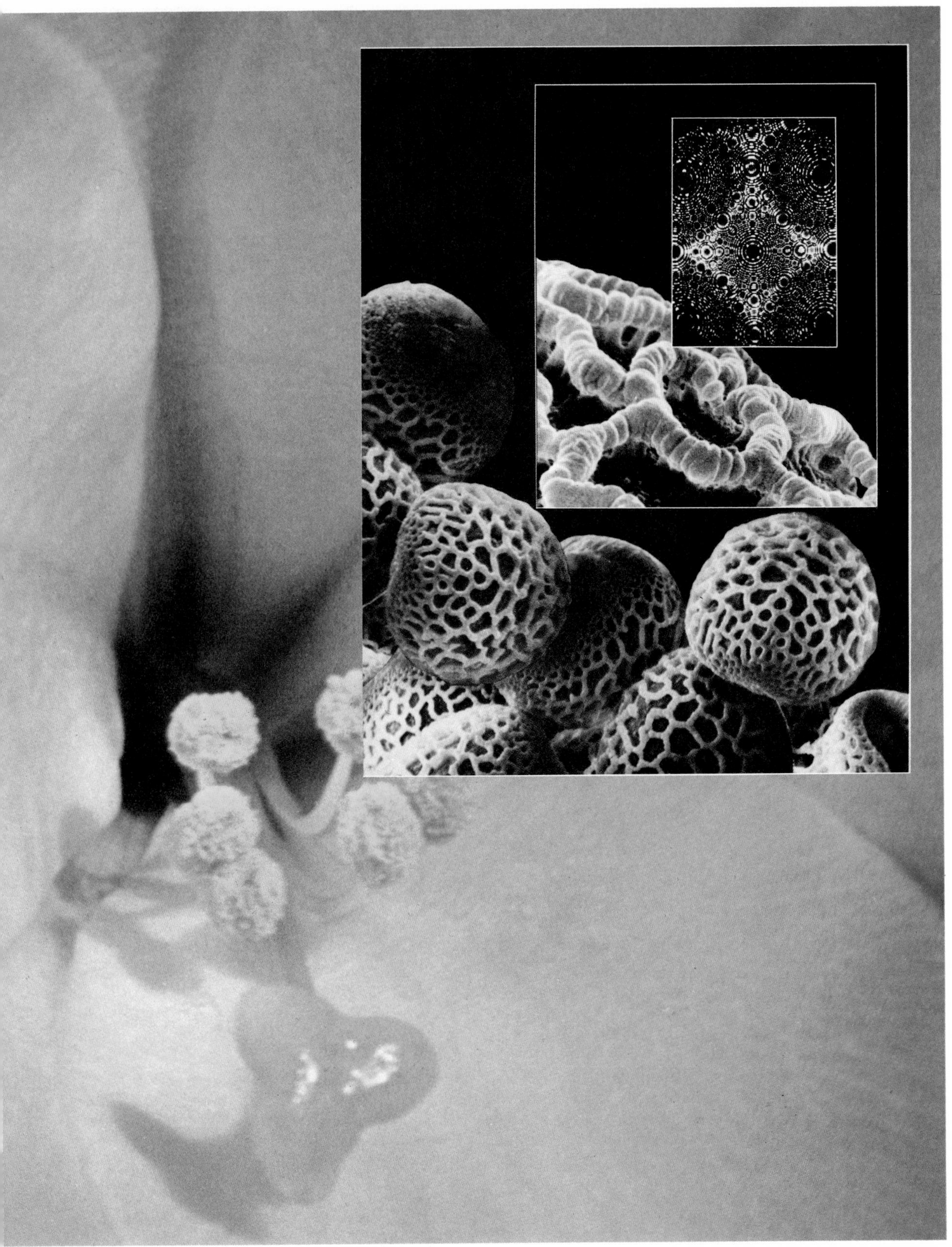

THE ELECTROMAGNETIC SPECTRUM

Complex as it is, the spectrum of visible light represents only one of many forms of energy radiating through the universe. By the early 19th century it was known that two types of "invisible light" exist just beyond the visible spectrum—infrared at one end and ultraviolet at the other. Then in the 1860's James Clerk Maxwell proposed his historic theory that light is a combination of electrical and magnetic impulses propagated through space in a wavelike manner and that there must be other invisible forms of "electromagnetic" radiation with different wavelengths. His predictions were later confirmed as scientists discovered the full extent of the electromagnetic spectrum.

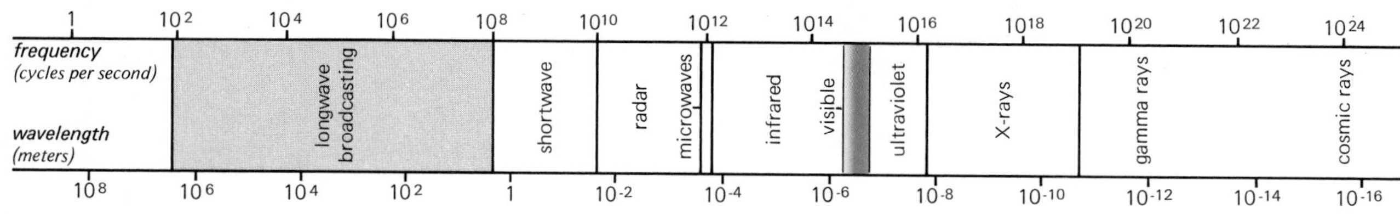

much larger positively charged mass), he could not get it to yield predictions in agreement with the observed spectra, even for the one-electron atom of hydrogen.

The problem was a knotty one, for there was (and still is) no way of directly observing atomic structure. It must be inferred from the behavior of large numbers of atoms, from their spectra or the way they affect particles which pass through them at high speed. To physicists of 1911 it was as if they had to determine the contents of a Christmas package but were allowed only two tests: shake it and listen to the rattling, or shoot bullets at it. Ernest Rutherford, a New Zealander who had been Thomson's assistant in the earlier electron work, was carrying out experiments of the latter sort at the University of Manchester. He directed a beam of positively charged alpha particles from a radioactive source at a thin sheet of gold foil. Most of the particles passed through with little or no deflection, but a few were widely scattered or even bounced back toward the source. Rutherford was convinced that this could only be explained by assuming that the atom had a relatively small, dense, positively charged nucleus and that electrons moved about this nucleus at great distances. But this model had its own drawbacks: Rutherford could not explain why the "orbiting" electrons did not steadily radiate energy and, energy all spent, fall into the nucleus.

However, Bohr believed that Rutherford's model was closer to reality than Thomson's, so he transferred to Manchester University. With him he brought the continental physicist's mathematical grounding and a gift for fruitful abstraction.

THE SPECTROSCOPE

In 1666 Isaac Newton discovered that white light passed through a prism is refracted into a spectrum consisting of all the colors of the rainbow. In 1859 Gustav Kirchhoff and Robert Bunsen developed the first spectroscope and found that each element, when vaporized and incandescent, emitted a unique pattern of light.

In 1913 Niels Bohr discovered why these patterns differed and in doing so arrived at the first accurate model of the atom. Applying the quantum theory to spectral lines, he deduced that when the element is incandescent, electrons move in quantum jumps from one orbit around their nucleus to another. During the jump they emit or absorb radiation at specific wavelengths, which show on the spectrum as lines of color. Since each element has a unique atomic structure, the jumps and the radiation differ for each element; thus each has its own spectral pattern.

Today the science of spectroscopy has numerous applications. It enables an astronomer to determine the chemical composition of a star; it is used in industry to detect impurities in metal; in police work it can identify the paint on a suspect's car. In addition, spectroscopy remains an essential tool in a broad range of scientific research.

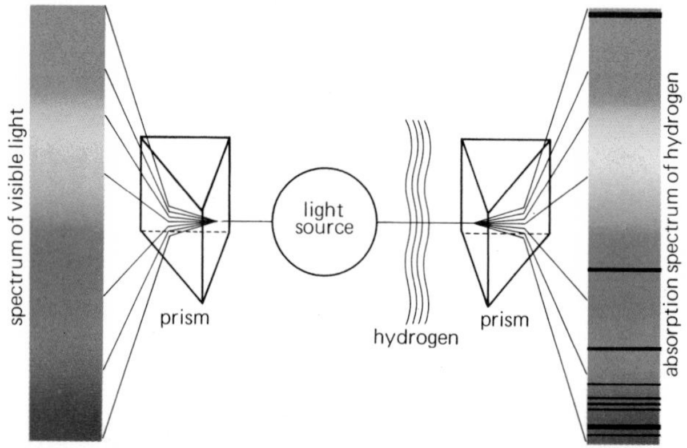

When light (which consists of many frequencies of electromagnetic radiation) passes through a prism, the high frequency waves (violet) are refracted more than low frequency waves (red), thus producing the familiar spectrum of colors. If the light passes through a gas before entering the prism, some frequencies are absorbed and appear as dark lines in the resulting "absorption" spectrum. The number and pattern of these lines (other techniques produce "bright-line" spectra) is a unique "fingerprint" for each element.

MAX PLANCK: UNWILLING PIONEER

For more than two centuries Newtonian physics appeared adequate to describe all events involving matter and energy. Then, in the 19th century, electromagnetic theory made it clear that energy could exist more or less independently of matter, as radiation of many wavelengths and frequencies. At the same time, the study of thermodynamics began to deal with problems of heat energy and its distribution in systems such as gases, where the individual particles were too small to be measured or observed. It was both impossible and pointless to predict the behavior of individual atoms or molecules, but the statistical laws of probability were applicable to the enormous numbers of such particles in even a small sample. In a gas at a given temperature some molecules would be moving very slowly, some very rapidly—but the *average* energy of all the moving molecules was exactly related to the temperature of the gas and the pressure it exerted on its container.

Max Planck was one of many scientists who attempted to apply the principles of thermodynamics to questions of radiation. In theory, a system containing radiation of varying frequencies should distribute its energy in the same way as a system containing gas molecules of many velocities—with one critical difference: Although there was an upper limit to a gas molecule's *velocity*, there was no comparable limit to the highest, most energetic *frequency* at which radiation could appear. Such a system would be like a piano with an unlimited number of shorter and shorter strings. Whatever note was struck, the piano would resonate with higher and higher frequencies as the energy of the original note was transmitted up the musical scale to infinity.

Planck attempted to explain why this theoretically predicted result did not, in fact, take place in radiation systems. At last he was forced to make a radical new assumption. In December 1900 he proposed at a scientific conference that radiant energy was produced and received in separate, indivisible packets, which he called *quantum* units from the Latin word for "portion." The energy of such a quantum depended on the frequency of the radiation and was related to it by a number that we now call Planck's constant. For any given frequency there is a *smallest possible amount of energy* that radiation of the frequency can bring into a system or take out of it.

Planck's theory implied that energy was not, as physics had always assumed, infinitely divisible. It said, in effect, that there was a smallest possible "push" that could be given and that below that level there could be no energy transfer. This "small change" of energy is very small indeed—the value of Planck's constant, written as h, is approximately .000000000000000000000000000000000662 joule-second in the meter-kilogram-second system—but on an atomic scale the size of quanta is very significant.

Packets of Energy

The breakthrough in atomic theory came after Rutherford returned to Manchester from a conference also attended by Max Planck and Albert Einstein. At the conference certain ideas were discussed that fired Rutherford's imagination, and on his return he shared them enthusiastically with Bohr.

The ideas derived from Max Planck's quantum theory, published in 1900 (see box). Briefly, Planck's discovery was that energy is not, as had always been thought, transmitted in a smooth, continuous stream, but in separate "packets" that he called quanta, after the Latin word *quantum*, meaning "portion."

Bohr seized on the idea of discontinuous energy transactions and its elaboration by Einstein and began to embody it in an atomic model that within two years solved the problems left unanswered by Rutherford, explained the spectral lines of stimulated atoms, and revealed the principle behind the periodicity of the elements (see p. 25).

In the Rutherford-Bohr atom electrons move around the nucleus at certain distances, in levels called "shells" or "orbitals." Their energy of motion at any one level remains constant; they give off and absorb radiation only when they make *quantum jumps*, sudden transitions to a lower or higher level. An electron cannot be made to move faster or slower within a given shell, nor can it occupy a position between shells. It cannot fall into the nucleus, for usually at the lowest level it possesses too little momentum to emit even a single quantum, and so cannot lose any more energy. Every spectral line corresponds to the transition of an electron from one shell to another. Also, Bohr suggested, the gradual filling up of levels, working outward from the nucleus, might account for the repetitive chemical behavior of the elements.

There were serious flaws in Bohr's 1913 model of the hydrogen atom, for in many respects it was still a makeshift combination of classical and quantum ideas, but the progress that followed more than justified the flaws. "That this insecure and contradictory foundation sufficed for a man of Bohr's unique instinct and sensitivity," Einstein wrote later, "appeared to me like a miracle."

Winged Lions

Most of atomic physics for a decade after 1913 was an elaboration and correction of the Rutherford-Bohr model. German physicist Arnold Sommerfeld modified it to include noncircular electron orbits and to take into account relativistic changes in electron mass; by doing so he was able to account for the "fine structure" variations in spectral lines. Wolfgang Pauli determined how and why electron shells are filled. Gradually the mathematics of quantum physics became more and more complicated, involving quantities which are impossible to visualize. Erwin Schrödinger put it this way: "As our mental eye penetrates into smaller and smaller distances and shorter and shorter times, we find nature behaving so entirely differently from what we observe in . . . our surroundings that *no* model shaped after our large scale experiences can ever be 'true.' A completely satisfactory model of this type is not only practically inaccessible, but not even thinkable. Or, to be more precise, we can, of course, think it, but however we think it, it is wrong; not perhaps quite as meaningless as a 'triangular circle,' but much more so than a 'winged lion.' "

The tantalizing ambiguity and ungraspable quality of the atom as revealed by quantum theory had parallels in other discoveries by Bohr's contemporaries. Louis de Broglie, for example, had revealed the curiously dual nature of matter in experiments that showed it could exist simultaneously as both waves and particles. In extending the quantum theory, Werner Heisenberg arrived algebraically at a theory with far-reaching philosophical implications, and Erwin Schrö-

ATOMIC MODELS

From the earliest speculations of the Greek philosophers until the early 19th century, the atom (from the Greek *atomos*, "uncuttable") was by definition the smallest possible unit of matter. It was imagined, in Sir Isaac Newton's words, as a "solid, massy, hard, impenetrable, moveable" particle, existing unchanged since creation, combining into different forms of matter but itself without inner structure. The 19th-century study of chemistry and electricity revealed regular patterns among the increasing number of elements and electrical properties that indicated the presence of negative charges that could be separated from the main mass of the atom. Then physicists like Niels Bohr (right) created a series of new models; the most important are shown below—though only mathematical equations can truly express the quantum atom.

1. ***Thomson Atom***
   Diffuse positive charge, electrons evenly distributed
2. ***Rutherford-Bohr Atom***
   Mass and positive charge concentrated at nucleus
3. ***Quantum Physics Atom***
   Electrons of uncertain position in "probability clouds"

dinger came to treat atoms as multidimensional wrinkles in a universe filled with vibrations.

Only the mathematical formulas of quantum physics have the flexibility and precision needed to describe such a subatomic world, where particles and antiparticles (see pp. 508–513) flash in and out of existence spontaneously, changing freely from matter to energy and back again.

Bohr went on to make a lifetime's work of the practice and the philosophy of quantum physics. In 1922 he won the Nobel Prize and the same year saw the creation of the Copenhagen Institute as his forum. It soon became a paradise for young physicists, a place where new ideas found sharp criticism but (if they held up) a warm welcome. George Gamow and others have left delightful accounts of the pleasure of working with Bohr, of all-night sessions that combined good Danish beer with intense speculative thought.

Bohr did honor to both Thomson and Rutherford by becoming in his turn one of the great teachers of the 20th century. In his writings he was able to develop the general principles of "complementarity" (every quantum term has a classical analogue) and "correspondence" (in large numbers discontinuous quantum events always approach the smooth continuity of classical mechanics).

The interplay of ideas between Bohr and Einstein provided some of the sternest tests for quantum physics, with the latter insisting to the end of his life that statistical uncertainty must betray some basic inadequacy in our understanding. Einstein kept saying, in one way or another, that "God does not play dice with the universe." Bohr, in exasperation, once burst out, "Stop telling God what to do!" Einstein was never able to imagine an experiment that would circumvent the uncertainty principle; however, his repeated attempts to do so greatly helped Bohr and others strengthen their thinking against some of the most pointed and subtle of challenges.

Among the strongest arguments in favor of quantum theory has been its success in predicting new particles. This success has now become something of an embarrassment, for there are now more known particles than there are chemical elements. Many theoreticians are trying to resolve this "subatomic zoo" into a few still more fundamental units, perhaps those called "quarks" or "partons." Their difficulties may be imagined when we consider that the energy required to break up some subnuclear particles is so great that the "fragments" are enormously energised in the process, and in consequence (by Einstein's mass-energy equivalence) have more mass than the original particle.

Quantum theory is of immediate practical application in almost every field of today's physics and technology: Lasers, plasma physics, solid-state electronics, and low-temperature physics would all be unthinkable without it. In extremely orderly systems such as crystals and supercooled fluids, even a single quantum jump may have a measurable effect. Devices known as light amplifiers can detect and multiply a millionfold a single photon from a faraway star; new computer memory elements are so sensitive that a few quanta can cause them to change states.

Niels Bohr's legacy as a creative and inspiring figure in science, like Einstein's, is one that stretches our mental horizons. We are beginning to realize that our understanding is very much a product of the scale we live on. Perhaps, as J. B. S. Haldane said, "The universe is not only a queerer place than we imagine—it may well be a queerer place than we *can* imagine." The challenge of Bohr's work is to continue the exploration that turns what was once unknowable into the merely unknown and then into the known and understood.

THE HEISENBERG UNCERTAINTY PRINCIPLE

Imagine, suggested Werner Heisenberg, that we want to ask conventional questions about an atomic particle, say an electron. We want to know where it is, how fast it is moving, and in what direction. To see where the electron is, we must use light or some other form of radiation: that is, photons must be produced by a source, they must encounter the electron, and they must "bounce back" to our eye or to an observing instrument.

Photons are so tiny as to have virtually no effect on large objects. We can shine the brightest light on the tiniest grain of sand without doing more than heating it up a bit. But when we study something as small as an electron, strange things begin to happen. For one thing, an electron is much smaller than the wavelength of visible light, so that it is impossible to get a sharp image—and hence impossible to know its position with accuracy. We could get a sharp image by using much shorter wavelengths, but those shorter wavelengths take the form of more energetic quanta, which are powerful enough to knock the electron completely off its original path. So if we observe the position of an electron exactly, we cannot know its velocity because the very act of observing changes that velocity.

Heisenberg showed that the combined uncertainty of a particle's position and its momentum could never be reduced below a certain minimum. It is impossible not only in practice, but also in principle, to know exactly what is happening (or to predict exactly what will happen) on a subatomic scale. While the basic properties of large numbers of particles are predictable (simply because they can be statistically "averaged out"), individual nuclear events are virtually random and entirely unpredictable.

1914

The Opening of the Panama Canal

An engineering team triumphs over unprecedented difficulties, separates two continents and opens up new opportunities for international commerce.

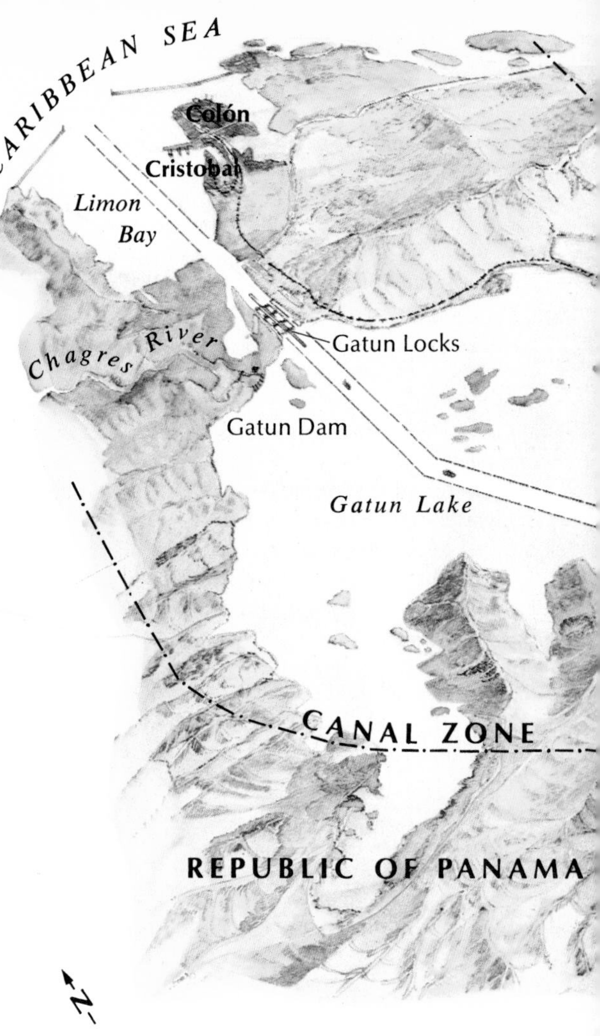

Canal Length: 50.72 miles between channel entrances

On August 15, 1914, cheered on by a festive crowd of engineers, workers, journalists, and dignitaries, an ungainly dredge named the *Ancon* made the first official transit through the newly opened Panama Canal. Nearly a decade of labor by a huge, U.S.-led task force had finally severed the mountainous land bridge linking the Americas; it was the fulfillment of a centuries-old dream.

Vasco Nuñez de Balboa, a Spanish adventurer who had explored the Caribbean side of the Isthmus of Darien (later called the Isthmus of Panama), was the first European to glimpse the Pacific Ocean, which he reached in 1513 and claimed for Spain. As early as 1524 King Charles V of Spain proposed a survey to study the possibility of a canal through the isthmus. But, although over the centuries other nations covetously eyed the slender neck that blocked passage between the Atlantic and Pacific, it was not until the 19th century that man's persistent dream of a canal showed any signs of finally coming true.

In 1876 a young French naval official, Lucien Napoléon-Bonaparte Wyse, grandnephew of Napoleon, arrived in Panama with enough money and resources to set a serious project in motion. After a thorough two-year survey of the isthmus Wyse obtained a concession from the Colombian government (which owned Panama) to build a sea-level canal along the path of the U.S.-built Panama Railroad. He submitted his proposal to the prestigious Geographical Society of Paris, whose president happened to be Wyse's mentor and close friend, Ferdinand de Lesseps, the man who had built the Suez Canal.

Early in 1879 De Lesseps called the society into special session to consider various proposals for a Central American canal. Two key decisions had to be made: the site, Panama or Nicaragua, and the type of canal to be built, sea level or lock. The assembly proved only a formality, for De Lesseps had already decided that the Wyse plan should be adopted and that he was the man to carry it out. Marshalling all his cunning and influence, he pushed through its formal endorsement with the bare minimum of debate.

Ironically, the only dissenting voice was that of a little-known engineer, Godin de Lépinay. He too had been to Panama and he was certain that because of the mountainous terrain the sea-level plan would never work. The alternative he proposed was deceptively simple: Dam up Panama's Chagres River to create an elevated lake and canal across the isthmus, then build locks at each end leading down to the seas. De Lépinay was shouted down by De Lesseps' supporters; 27 years later his ideas were successfully adopted.

The Failure of De Lesseps

De Lesseps launched a spectacular, year-long publicity campaign in Europe and the U.S. to raise funds for his newly formed Panama Canal Company. In Febru-

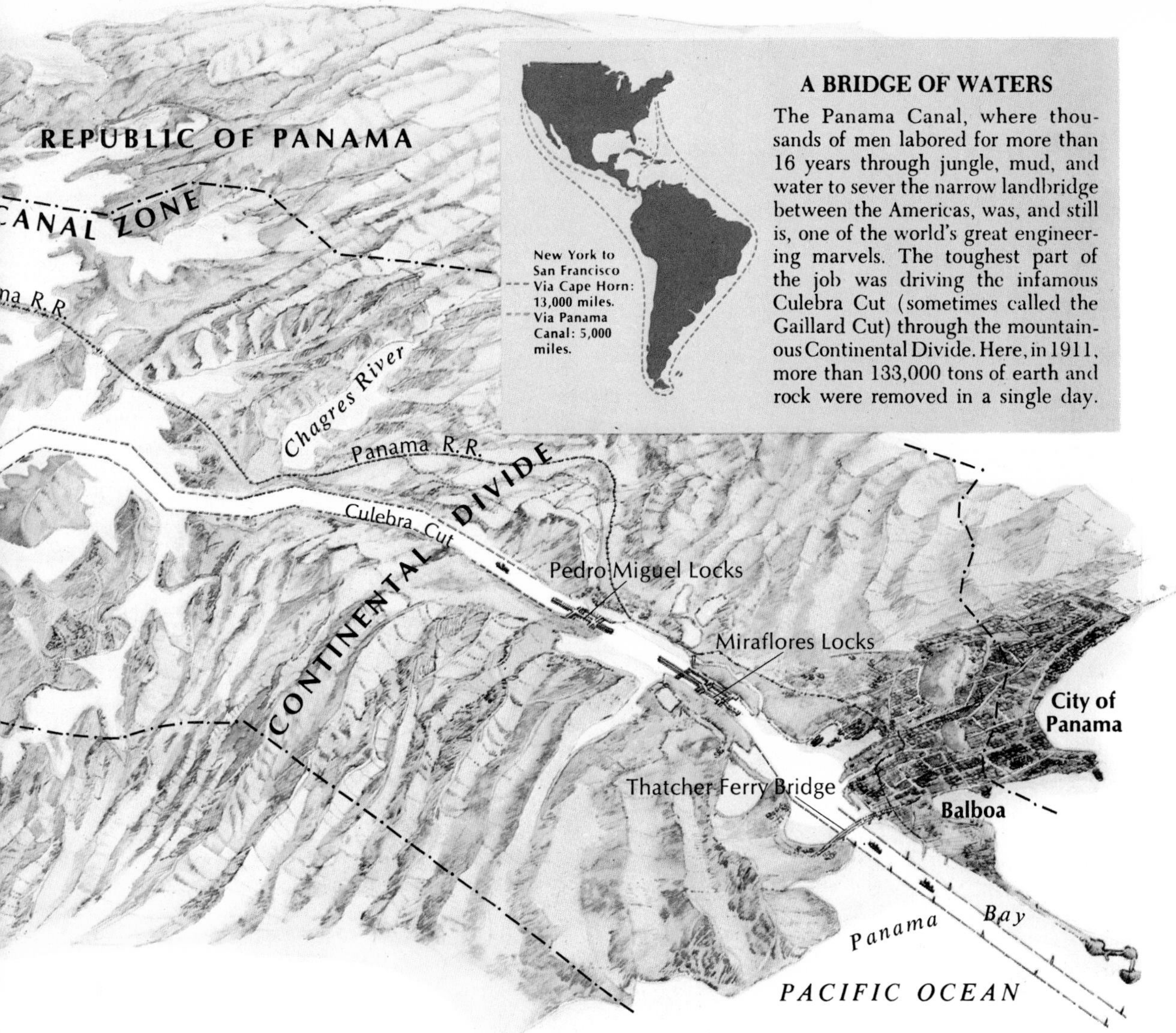

A BRIDGE OF WATERS

The Panama Canal, where thousands of men labored for more than 16 years through jungle, mud, and water to sever the narrow landbridge between the Americas, was, and still is, one of the world's great engineering marvels. The toughest part of the job was driving the infamous Culebra Cut (sometimes called the Gaillard Cut) through the mountainous Continental Divide. Here, in 1911, more than 133,000 tons of earth and rock were removed in a single day.

ary 1881 the first group of French engineers arrived on the isthmus. Eight years later, crippled by disastrous floods and landslides, financial scandals, and the ravages of tropical disease, the great venture collapsed into bankruptcy. De Lesseps, bitterly denounced by the press and public, was convicted of misappropriation of funds. He died, senile, in 1894.

In retrospect, the French tragedy in Panama can be traced to two fundamental errors. The first was De Lesseps' insistence on building the same type of canal he had built at Suez. The hard fact was that Panama and Suez were simply not comparable. The Suez Canal utilizes three existing lakes, and most of its route traverses low-lying land. The Isthmus of Panama, though only about 40 miles across at the point where the proposed canal was to be dug, proved a nightmare of geological faults and unstable rock formations, especially in the mountainous central region. Excavating down to sea level was virtually impossible with the equipment of the time.

The second error lay in De Lesseps' casual response to warnings about two diseases long known to thrive in Central America—yellow fever and malaria. Having visited Panama only during the mosquito-free dry season, he so underestimated their seriousness as to proclaim Panama one of the healthiest spots in the world.

It is unlikely that either of these errors by itself would have defeated the French. Together they proved insurmountable. By 1884 yellow fever had reached epidemic proportions, claiming thousands of lives and spreading panic among the workers. At the same time, technical problems encountered during excavation led to upward-spiraling costs, which went even higher because of widespread graft and profiteering. In 1898, hoping to recover some of their losses, the directors of the New Panama Canal Company offered to turn over all their assets to the United States for about $100 million. At first the offer aroused little interest. There was even opposition: The U.S. railroads feared the competition a canal would present to

"Is M. De Lesseps a canal digger or a grave digger?" asked American cartoonist Thomas Nast when he learned of the workers stricken on the Panama project.

TWO FLYING KILLERS ARE BEATEN

Ferdinand de Lesseps was roundly attacked when his Panama Canal venture failed, but the real villains of the story were two disease-carrying mosquitoes, *Aedes aegypti* and *Anopheles.* The man who finally conquered these pests was a U.S. Army doctor named William Gorgas, head of a camp for yellow-fever victims in Havana in 1898. Lacking any treatment for the fatal illness, he turned to the work of Carlos Finlay, a Cuban doctor who theorized that yellow fever was spread by the bite of *Aedes aegypti.* Gorgas methodically opened war on the insect. He had swamps drained, household water purified, buildings screened, and standing water—the mosquitoes' breeding ground—coated with oil in order to kill the *Aedes* larvae. The result: Yellow fever virtually vanished at the Havana camp. In 1904 Gorgas was transferred to Panama, where he rigorously applied the same techniques, and by 1906 yellow fever had disappeared in that area. A similar attack on the *Anopheles* mosquito reduced the incidence of malaria among canal workers from 82 percent in 1906 to 11 percent by 1912.

Anopheles *larvae suffocated in their breeding pools when an oil film interfered with their breathing apparatus. Hired swatters killed the adult mosquitoes.*

The Anopheles *larva*

The adult female Anopheles

their coast-to-coast freight business and lobbied in Congress to block acceptance of the French offer.

The entire matter might have remained in limbo but for an embarrassing incident in the Spanish-American War. Shortly after the war's outbreak in March 1898 the battleship U.S.S. *Oregon* was dispatched from San Francisco to the Caribbean. By the end of its 13,000-mile, 68-day voyage around Cape Horn, the war was almost over. Nothing could have more dramatically underscored the importance of a canal, and Congress was at last galvanized into action.

The Spooner Act, passed in June 1902, authorized President Theodore Roosevelt to purchase all French holdings (mainly the assets of the Panama Railroad) for a maximum of $40 million. A draft treaty with Colombia gave the U.S. sole rights to build a canal and administer a six-mile-wide Canal Zone for 100 years, in exchange for $10 million in gold plus an annual rental of $250,000 to be derived from canal tolls. The pact was ratified by the U.S. Senate in March 1903, but the Colombian senate first held out for more money, and then, in June 1903, angrily rejected the treaty.

Shaking the Big Stick

A wave of indignation swept over Panama, particularly among a militant faction that viewed independence from Colombia as the only way to guarantee the financial benefits of a canal. On November 3, 1903, with secret U.S. encouragement, a group of Panamanian rebels launched a revolution. The day before, a U.S. warship had cruised into Colón harbor. A contingent of marines, sent ashore on the pretext of protecting U.S. property, barred Colombian troops from reaching the scene of the uprising in Panama City. Three days later the United States officially recognized the Republic of Panama. The Hay-Bunau-Varilla Treaty, which was ratified in February 1904, granted the U.S. perpetual sovereignty over a 10-mile-wide Canal Zone across the isthmus in exchange for the $10 million payment and $250,000 annuity. By midsummer 1904, after the French canal company accepted the U.S. offer of $40 million, the first construction crews began arriving on the isthmus.

The assets they inherited from the French were considerable: 78 million cubic yards of earth already excavated, 47 miles of single-track railroad, ample (but antiquated) rolling stock, a huge amount of abandoned machinery, and, finally, an invaluable library of maps, surveys, plans, and records painstakingly compiled over the previous two decades.

In spite of all this the project got off to a terrible start. The Isthmian Canal Commission, a large, rather cumbersome military board chaired by Adm. John G. Walker and centered in Washington, was less attentive to conditions at the canal site than to political pressures at home. The public was impatient to "make the

The heartbreaking Cucaracha Slide was one of two major landslides in the Culebra Cut in 1913. The enormous mass of earth at right had to be removed before work could be continued, but the dedicated crew still met their deadline.

dirt fly," and Admiral Walker ordered work to begin before adequate preparations had been made. The result was almost immediate chaos. Excavations were begun piecemeal in the steaming, mountainous interior, with antiquated machinery and no way of disposing of the excavated material. Living quarters for the workers were overcrowded and unhealthy; food, drinking water, and medical facilities were all in dangerously short supply. Back in Washington requisitions for basic provisions went unread for weeks.

Amid this dismal spectacle Col. William C. Gorgas, chief sanitation officer of the canal project, stood out as a striking exception. His recent service in Havana had confirmed for the first time the link between certain species of mosquitoes and the two diseases, yellow fever and malaria, responsible for most of the 20,000 lives lost during the French attempts to build a canal. Precisely because this was a revolutionary breakthrough, Gorgas had trouble getting the support he needed. In December 1904 what Gorgas feared most happened: an outbreak of yellow fever. Panic spread among the workers and a mass exodus began. By the spring of 1905 the project was almost at a standstill.

The press played up the bad news. President Roosevelt, who shared the impatience and disappointment of the public, discharged the commission's officers and established a more flexible civilian board. Then he made what proved a crucial decision: He appointed John F. Stevens, a vice president of the Rock Island Railroad, to be the new chief engineer.

Stevens, well aware of the mistakes of his predecessors, immediately ordered a halt to all construction. He was determined to lay a solid groundwork on which work could proceed, regardless of the public's clamor for action. He began by giving Gorgas a free hand to combat the critical problem of disease. By 1906 Gorgas had eliminated yellow fever from the zone, and by 1912 only 11 percent of the workers were suffering from malaria (down from the 1906 high of 82 percent).

Stevens delegated to his assistants the job of providing for a work force that soon exceeded 42,000 men. Ample funds were made available to build comfortable houses and barracks, well screened against mosquitoes. A massive commissary system was organized to feed workers up and down the line.

The main reason Stevens succeeded in Panama was that he recognized the real problem was not excavating a channel but disposing efficiently of the enormous volume of excavated soil and rock. The key to the entire project was the old Panama Railroad, and using the original line as a nucleus, Stevens created a modern railroad system. He double-tracked the entire 47-mile roadbed, so trains could run simultaneously in both directions, conveyor-belt fashion, transporting men, machinery, supplies, and, most important, the mountains of excavated dirt, clay, and rock. He built a connecting network of spur lines and sidings, expanded the dockside facilities, and recruited experienced railroad men from the States to keep the cars rolling.

Finally, in the midst of all this, Stevens had to deal with a problem that proved political as well as technical: deciding between a sea-level canal and an elevated waterway using locks. At the end of 1905 an international board of engineers appointed by President Roosevelt split 8 to 5 in favor of a sea-level plan. In Congress the canal became the subject of a heated, six-month debate. The sea-level advocates cited esthetic considerations. And the fact that a lock canal would be cheaper to build than a sea-level canal made it suspect to those who felt cheaper couldn't be better.

Stevens, however, was able to convince Roosevelt that the lock canal was the best solution. The main reasons were that the violence of the Chagres River could be tamed only by dams and locks, and the amount of material to be excavated for a sea-level canal was probably still beyond the capacity of the most advanced systems and equipment. On June 21, 1906, Congress authorized construction of a lock canal.

By late 1906 real progress was being made on the isthmus, and on January 30, 1907, Stevens, who had always said that he would remain on the job only until success was assured, resigned. A workable plan had been approved, the necessary preparations had been made, and construction was underway. Stevens remained active as an engineer and railroad builder through much of his life. He died in 1943, aged 90.

Fortunately, Roosevelt found a highly competent man to carry on Stevens' work, Col. George Washington Goethals of the U.S. Army. The new chief engineer arrived in March 1907 and quickly convinced the workers of his ability. He said of his predecessor: "The real problem in digging the canal has been the disposal of soil, and no army engineer in America could have laid out the transportation system as Mr. Stevens did." Goethals vividly described the lock plan: "It is not so much a canal we are hoping to build as a bridge of water, consisting of lakes, locks and sea-approaches. . . ."

***The final barrier** to the "bridge of water" linking the Atlantic and Pacific went up in smoke on October 10, 1913, when President Woodrow Wilson pressed a button in Washington that signaled engineers to dynamite Gamboa Dam. Crowds of officials and journalists watched as an idea proposed four centuries earlier at last became a reality. The project had taken 10 years to complete and cost $387 million.*

***The canal** now serves more than 14,500 ships a year, carrying some 12 billion tons of cargo. The average transit, ocean to ocean, takes between 14 and 16 hours, and the average toll is about $7,000. Small ships go through unaided, but large ones, because of the pressure of their displacement, are towed by powerful locomotives called electric mules.*

Divide and Conquer
Goethals, in proper military fashion, organized the job into three sectors, the Atlantic, Central, and Pacific Divisions, each with its own director, work force, and timetable. The task of the Atlantic Division was to dredge an approach channel through Limon Bay and build a dam and locks at Gatun, which would form the north end of the new artificial Lake Gatun, fed by the Chagres River and its tributaries. The purpose of the dam was simply to back up the Chagres' powerful floodwaters and thus convert the 22-mile-long Chagres Valley into a stable, elevated waterway. Inevitably, construction on this scale posed enormous technical difficulties in addition to the periodic floods, mudslides, and other mishaps of nature, but the work force managed to stay on or ahead of schedule. By early 1913 the job had been completed.

At the southern end of the isthmus the Pacific Division was dredging a channel through Panama Bay and building two smaller sets of locks at Miraflores and Pedro Miguel. Though a dispute in Washington over where the locks should be located delayed them for more than a year, the section was completed before the end of 1913.

The greatest difficulties were met by the Central Division, whose territory encompassed the Chagres Valley and the mountainous, 10-mile-wide Continental Divide, through which a passage had to be excavated. The major battleground was a saddle-shaped notch at the peak of the divide called the Culebra Cut, later also known as the Gaillard Cut after the division's chief engineer, Maj. David Gaillard. Several rivers crossed the path of the excavation and had to be diverted or dammed. Because of the steep slopes and narrow confines of the working area, even a minor afternoon rainstorm could touch off a flash flood. Worst of all, the Continental Divide encompassed a bewildering array of rock types, geological faults, and volcanic cores. The combination of heavy rainfall and unstable earth made landslides frequent.

The Bridge of Water Rises
It was slow, tedious, backbreaking labor—6,000 men descending into the cut each morning to work for 10 hours in heat that often reached 120°F—but, amazingly, it went forward from 1908 to 1913 with hardly a delay. Even after two disastrous landslides in January 1913 the workers cleared away the tons of debris and finished on schedule. In the end, the Culebra Cut was 1,800 feet wide at the top and 400 feet deep. A stupendous total of nearly 150 million cubic yards of soil and rock had been dynamited and taken out.

By the middle of 1913 the work of all three divisions was substantially completed. On October 10 a dike at the south end of the Culebra Cut was dynamited and, 85 feet above sea level, the waters of the Atlantic and Pacific rushed together. The following year the *Ancon* made its inaugural transit through the canal, passing from Limon Bay to Panama Bay in slightly less than 10 hours. In the six decades since then that trip has been duplicated nearly half a million times.

Apart from its great economic importance, the canal represents a milestone in the history of applied science. Since the industrial revolution of the 18th century engineering projects in Europe and the Americas had become steadily more ambitious, but none approached the size and complexity of the Panama Canal. Indeed, seldom in history had so many men with so many skills ever been brought together to collaborate in a peaceful enterprise. The entire venture provided a prototype for the large-scale collective methods that have dominated 20th-century technology, and even today the Panama Canal remains one of the great engineering triumphs of all time.

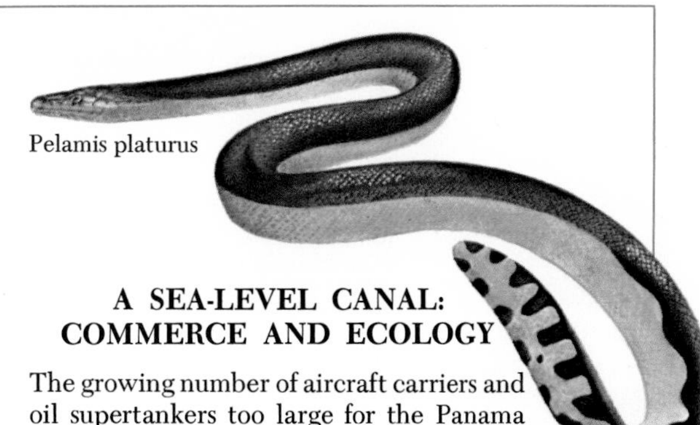
Pelamis platurus

A SEA-LEVEL CANAL: COMMERCE AND ECOLOGY

The growing number of aircraft carriers and oil supertankers too large for the Panama Canal has led to a U.S. proposal for a second waterway—a sea-level canal without locks. Though experts are in general agreement that an expansion of the Panama route is necessary, the proposal has stirred a controversy that typifies today's confrontation between the needs of nature and society.

A major question concerns the environmental impact of a design that would allow the waters of the Caribbean Sea and the Pacific Ocean to mix. (Mixing does not occur in the present canal; freshwater Gatun Lake forms an effective barrier.) The Pacific is colder than the Caribbean; and tides on the Pacific side run up to 18 feet, as compared to only 2 feet in the Caribbean. A mingling of the two waters, with a resultant change in temperature and tide level, could upset the balance of marine life in the area. For this reason the proposal for a sea-level canal needs careful study.

One of many possible hazards is the infestation of the Caribbean by poisonous sea snakes (*Pelamis platurus*) indigenous to the Pacific side. Marine biologists have theorized that if the snakes were to migrate eastward, slip through the new waterway, and multiply, they could become a deadly menace to swimmers as far away as Miami Beach. Such environmental threats may ultimately prove the most important considerations in planning a new sea-level canal.

THE LIFE OF THE TIMES 1900-18

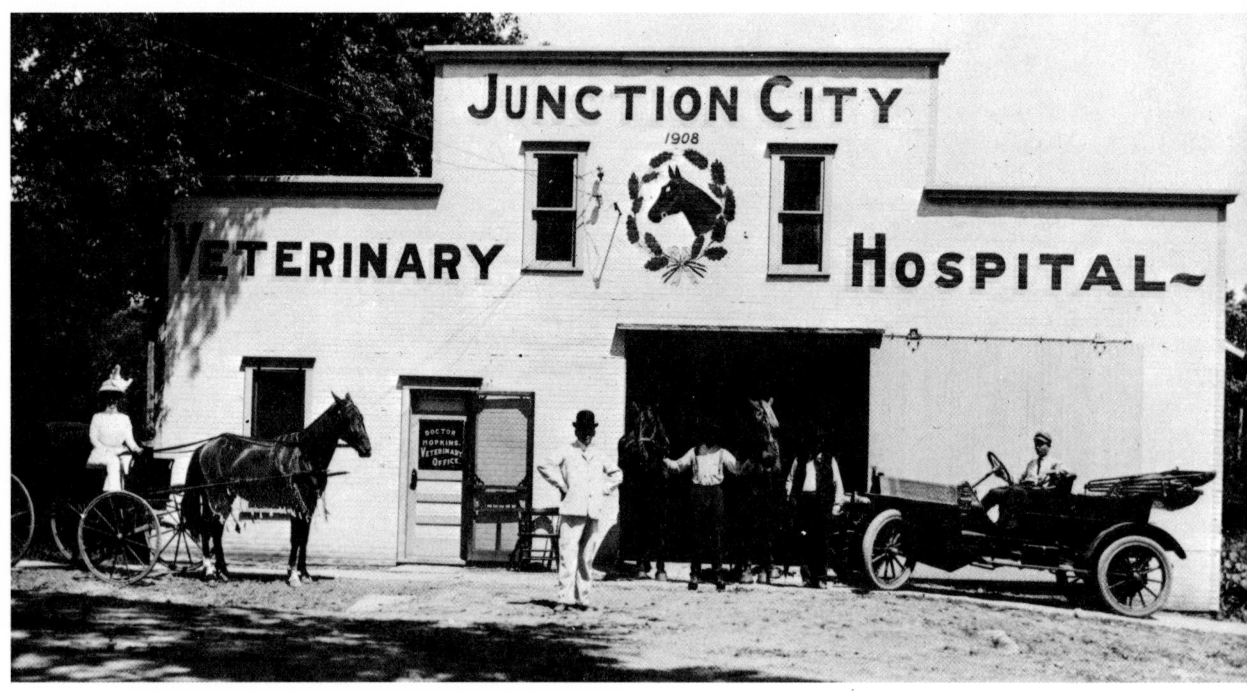

Aptly named *is this junction in Kansas, where the horse-drawn cart of the old age meets the motorcar of the new.*

A rubber tire her chariot, *a light bulb her inspiration, a technological angel bestows the bounty of the modern age.*

Looking back on it now, many Americans like to think of the first 18 years of our century as an "age of innocence." The era's gaslit, horse-and-buggy lifestyle certainly invites the name. But a closer look at the period—which saw the emergence of mass production, the Progressive movement, radical changes in the arts, and finally a world war—reveals quite a different picture: Far from being innocent, the opening decades of the 20th century were a time of rapid changes and profound new experiences.

To be sure, the country still had deep ties to the past as the calendar reached 1900. Three out of every five Americans lived in communities of fewer than 2,500 residents—places where the oldtimers could tell youngsters stories about the exciting days when long lines of Conestoga wagons passed through

***Only a tiny fraction** of rural American homes had electricity in 1905, but such laborsaving electric appliances as this Sears vacuum washer were a powerful incentive to get it.*

***Big-city diversions** included dazzling amusement parks like New York's Coney Island, or gay sing-alongs to the "sophisticated" new tunes that came out of Tin Pan Alley.*

***Smalltown outings** were held at the local picnic ground, which in many cases was just a small clearing with a few rough-hewn tables. Ankle-length dresses were* de rigueur.

on the way west, when the first telegraph wires went up, or when an all-important railhead was built.

The manner of life in these rural communities was not greatly changed from earlier generations. Most people continued to make their living from the land, got around chiefly with the help of a horse, and seldom traveled more than a day's journey from home.

Their entertainment was likewise simple and usually homemade. In a day when phonographs were still a novelty and radios were years in the future, people who felt like hearing a tune had to play it themselves. And they did: Local bands performed on the village green, young Romeos strummed banjos and guitars for their sweethearts, and no home was quite complete without an upright piano in the parlor for family sing-alongs.

During the summer, fishing, boating, and picnics were popular, as always, and on Saturday afternoons the young men of the town might choose up sides for a game of baseball. After the midday meal on Sunday, family and friends would gather on the front porch; on special occasions the girls would don their finest flowered bonnets, while their beaux sported striped jackets and boaters tilted to a rakish angle.

Thanks largely to the innovation of mail-order merchandising, pioneered by Montgomery Ward and raised to a high art by Sears, Roebuck and Co., the smalltown home was losing its austere look. For surprisingly low prices, people across the country could order all sorts of plain and fancy items from the huge Sears, Roebuck catalog—which, next to the Bible, was fast becoming America's favorite book.

One of the most popular songs of the same period was "In the Good Old Summertime," which was published in 1902 and sold a million copies in a single year. But it was not just those smalltown dwellers "strolling through the shady lanes" who bought the sheet music; more likely it was the city dweller, nostalgically remembering a time that for him had all but passed.

In the closing decades of the 1800's the last outposts of the West had been reached, charted, and settled, and Americans began to swell the nation's cities. They listened to "Hello! My Baby," "By the Light of the Silvery Moon," and other tunes, most of which were written on a section of New York City's West 28th Street called Tin Pan Alley. Irving Berlin got his start there as a singing "stooge"—a performer planted in a vaudeville or burlesque audience who, when a new song was introduced, would "spontaneously" echo the refrain and try to get the audience to join in.

Entertainment was big business in the cities. Huge crowds were drawn to the new amusement parks, built at the end of trolley lines and featuring Ferris wheels and roller coasters. Also popular was Thomas Edison's "little instrument which I call a Kinetoscope." Drop a coin in, peer down through a peephole at the top, and for a few minutes you could see the miracle of a picture that moved. (In some of these, on penny arcades, the moving picture was decidedly naughty.)

In 1905 the first nickelodeon was opened, where the moving picture was projected onto a screen, and it was an instant success (see p. 18). By 1908 about 10,000 nickelodeons were in operation, and in 1910 some 10 million people a week were flocking to local theaters.

The Gibson Girl: *America's ideal*

The automobile was another fast-growing source of amusement and could be had in an ingenious variety of steam, gas, and electric models. By far the biggest favorite was Ford's Model T, the Tin Lizzie, whose modest price soon made the open road the playground of the average American (see p. 60).

Chautauqua and the Churches

Movies quickened the slow pulse of life in the small towns, and the periodic descent of the circus revved it up to fever pitch. But to many, particularly in the Midwest, the high point of the summer was the arrival of the Chautauqua Circuit's traveling tent show.

The original Chautauqua Assembly was convened in 1874 on the banks of Lake Chautauqua in upstate New York. It was a summer cultural festival, complete with university-level courses, and turned out to be so successful that many commercial imitators staged festivals of their own. The Chautauqua Circuit shows, while preserving the wholesome tone of the founding institution, offered an incredible potpourri of events: band concerts, a little opera, lectures, arts-and-crafts exhibits, political oratory, Indian ceremonial dances, Hawaiians strumming their ukeleles—all this

The President's daughter, *Alice Roosevelt, typified the new, unfettered young woman, and the press followed her adventures with unprecedented fervor.*

Millions *of immigrants arrived at Ellis Island (left) between 1900 and 1910 with little more than a battered suitcase and an identification tag. For many of them, pursuit of the American dream began—and often ended—in the stifling ghettos of Manhattan's lower East Side (below).*

plus the climactic inspirational address on the true meaning of life and the key to happiness.

Church membership generally kept pace with population growth during these years, and church socials and services continued to fulfill their traditional functions. But change was in the air. Modernism was supplanting fundamentalism in many Protestant congregations, as the social gospel of service and brotherhood replaced the earlier emphasis on doctrine and afterlife.

While there were vast differences between rural and urban religionists, most were united on one issue: the evils of alcohol. In 1893 the Protestant churches of the United States had organized their first formal alliance in the Anti-Saloon League, and this grew steadily in power. The league joined forces with other prohibition groups to campaign for local and statewide prohibition. One minor but vivid figure in the crusade was Carrie Nation, who was arrested no fewer than 30 times for her "hatchetations" of what she called the joints. So great was the pressure of these groups that by 1917 two-thirds of the states were dry, and within three years Prohibition would be the law of the land.

The Gibson Girl Grows Up

In 1901 a short skirt was one that exposed the shoes. Hats were huge bun-shaped affairs, overhung with black-dotted veils that made the fashionable matrons wearing them look as if they were besieged by flies. And then there was the Gibson Girl. She was the perfect alternative to the matronly look and soon became every woman's ideal: dreamy-eyed, her mouth a Cupid's bow, hair piled in charming disarray, head held haughtily high on a swanlike neck.

The Gibson Girl sprang full-grown from the facile brush of artist Charles Dana Gibson. Her image graced the pages of *Life* (the early humor magazine) and appeared just about everywhere else—on dishes, pillows, calendars, and in countless real-life imitations. Glamour at last!

As the years went by, hemlines crept up. They had to, since women were taking a more active role socially, driving the new cars, playing Ping-pong, riding bicycles. A recent invention, the typewriter, was also drawing more women into the job market as secretaries. Teaching and nursing had traditionally been the proper fields of "women's work," and in 1870 fewer than 1,000 women worked in offices; by 1910 there were more than 386,000.

"That Damned Cowboy"

Female emancipation and suffrage were becoming prominent social issues, part of a wide-ranging popular movement called Progressivism. A spirit of energy and change was unquestionably in the air, and the

***By 1901 some hemlines** had crept up to the ankle, and the stuffy bustle had become passé among the fashionable.*

***Trade unionism gained ground** through thousands of strikes in the first two decades of the century. Clashes like this one at Lawrence, Massachusetts, in 1912 became common as workers demanded shorter hours and higher pay.*

Progress and peril: *New mass-production methods greatly improved industrial output in the U.S.A. (right), but worker protection still lagged. A fire in the Triangle Shirtwaist Factory in New York killed 148 workers.*

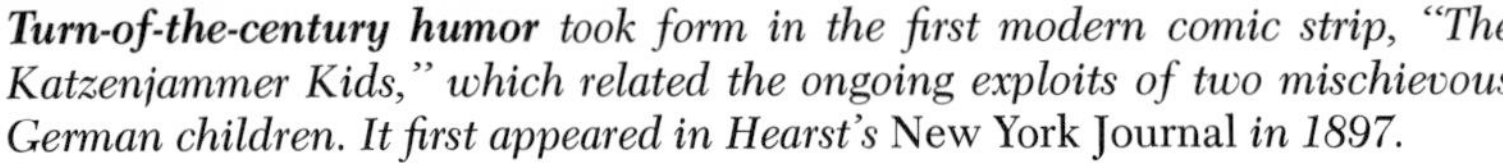

Turn-of-the-century humor *took form in the first modern comic strip, "The Katzenjammer Kids," which related the ongoing exploits of two mischievous German children. It first appeared in Hearst's* New York Journal *in 1897.*

nation could hardly have found a better embodiment of that spirit than its new vigorous President, Theodore Roosevelt.

At 42 the youngest man ever to occupy the White House, Teddy Roosevelt might at first have seemed more a throwback to the rough-hewn mold of Andrew Jackson than a harbinger of progress. Indeed, when he took office after the assassination of William McKinley in 1901, one of Roosevelt's fellow Republicans, Ohio Senator Mark Hanna, snorted to a colleague: "Now look! That damned cowboy is President of the United States."

But as it turned out, the "damned cowboy" was more than equal to the problems facing him. Instinctively sympathetic to the growing demands for social and political reform, Roosevelt found his high office "a bully pulpit" for arousing public opinion and needling his opponents in Congress and elsewhere.

The prime targets of the Progressive movement were the nation's huge industrial monopolies—such as John D. Rockefeller's Standard Oil Company—and the political graft they often engendered. Determined to "bust the trusts," break up the corrupt political machines in the cities, and improve conditions for the workingman, the Progressives grew steadily in influence through the first decade of the century. Though most of the activists came from the middle class, those who stood to gain most from their efforts were the hordes of impoverished immigrants—on the average, a million arrived each year from 1900 to 1915—who were being ruthlessly exploited in the labor market.

New mass-market magazines such as *McClure's* and *Cosmopolitan* became forums for the "muckrakers" (a term coined by Teddy Roosevelt), crusading journalists who wrote damning and fascinating exposés of the trusts. Perhaps the best muckraking novel of the period was Upton Sinclair's *The Jungle,* which, in exposing the deplorable state of the meatpacking industry, aroused the public and helped pressure Congress into passing the 1906 Pure Food and Drug Act.

In raising the consciousness of the middle class, the muckrakers helped Progressivism become a potent national movement. Three successive Presidents—Roosevelt, Taft, and Wilson—identified themselves with Progressive goals.

There was an appalling need for reform. In 1900 unskilled workers—many of them children—were earning less than 10 cents an hour for a 12-hour day. The nationwide weekly pay averaged less than $10; and with beef selling for a dime a pound and a man's shirt costing 50 cents, such wages could hardly feed and clothe a family.

Very slowly minimum wage laws were passed, industrial safety codes enacted, and the average workweek shrank from 59 hours in 1900 to fewer than 54 in 1918. Unionized workers had it better: Their hours declined from 53 to about 47.

"He's a bear!" was a favorite cry of high-steppers like these, who feverishly danced the grizzly bear, the cakewalk, and the turkey trot. They also bought sheet music in record numbers.

"Over There" became a spirited national theme song, glorifying America's role in the Great War. The cover for this song-sheet was by a young illustrator named Norman Rockwell.

The War in Europe Hits Home

In the American summer of 1914 Vernon and Irene Castle were dipping and gliding their way to fame in the Castle walk, foxtrot, and tango, and the rest of America did its best to follow. At the same time Europe, fatally locked into a network of opposing alliances, fell into the gorge of war.

President Wilson managed to keep America out of the fighting until the Germans sank three U.S. ships without warning, making further neutrality impossible. In April 1917 Wilson asked Congress for a declaration of war—which was promptly granted—and the nation began to mobilize with surprising speed. Taxes were increased. The Selective Service Act was passed on May 18, 1917, and on June 5, 9.5 million men registered for the draft. Liberty Loan drives began, netting nearly $17 billion. Women knitted socks for the boys at the front, and children amassed small mountains of peach pits for use in gas masks.

Anti-German sentiment grew rapidly, fed by such movies as *The Kaiser, Beast of Berlin.* With an almost missionary zeal the country rose up to challenge the Hun and make the world safe for democracy. The spirit was summed up in George M. Cohan's exuberant songs "I'm a Yankee Doodle Dandy" and "Over There."

By July 1918 more than a million American boys *were* over there, in France, and the exuberance was fast wearing off. Muddy, bloody assaults such as the Meuse-Argonne campaign, which left 120,000 doughboys dead or wounded, deflated the naive ideals of heroism. The suffocation of spirit in the war would be recorded by Ernest Hemingway, John Dos Passos, and others—a "lost generation" of U.S. writers.

Still, American determination never flagged, and it provided the extra strength needed to turn the tide against Germany. When the fighting was done, U.S. soldiers returned to a homeland now thrust into a new and unaccustomed prominence in international affairs.

In her rapid gearing up for war, the United States had entered into an expansive era of mass production and industrial might. Powerful at the dawn of the century, by 1918 she was the strongest, richest, and most highly industrialized nation on earth. And though Wilson's Fourteen Points and proposed League of Nations were doomed to futility, the United States was still secure in her new position.

If some innocence had been lost during these two eventful decades, much that was positive had been gained. In the world, the United States had begun to shed her provincialism and assume greater responsibilities in the international community. At home, Progressivism had come to grips with problems long ignored and brought into public consciousness issues that needed, and still need, constant reexamination. All things considered, the age of experience was well begun.

1914

World War I

Part One: Powder Keg, Spark, and Explosion

An assassination in a small Balkan state sparks a European conflict that soon spreads to the far corners of the world.

The first of the two great convulsions that tore Europe and much of the civilized world apart in this century began on August 1, 1914. In the opening days of that fateful month one of the most peaceful periods the Continent had ever known came to an end, and one by one each of Europe's great powers was drawn inexorably into a terrifying conflict. Recalling his country's decision to enter the war on the night of August 4, David Lloyd George, then Britain's Chancellor of the Exchequer and later Prime Minister (1916–22), said: "I felt like a man standing on a planet that had been suddenly wrenched from its orbit by a demonic hand and that was spinning wildly into the unknown." In the opposing camp German Chancellor Theobald von Bethmann-Hollweg predicted in Berlin: "This may be a violent storm, but short, very short. I count on a war of not more than three, or, perhaps at the very most, four months. . . ."

The storm was indeed violent, but beyond that the Chancellor was wrong: It would take not four months but four years to run its furious course. In the process approximately 8 million men in uniform would be killed and 12 million civilians would perish in the accompanying revolutions, famines, and epidemics. Three empires would fall, new nations would appear, and the societies of victors and vanquished alike would be radically transformed.

The war was set in motion by a wrong turn down a side street in Sarajevo, Bosnia-Herzegovina, on June 28, 1914. "Stop! You are going the wrong way!" shouted the general accompanying the visiting dignitaries. The driver stopped the car, but before he could turn it around a 19-year-old Serbian nationalist, Gavrilo Princip, stepped out of the crowd and began shooting. Archduke Franz Ferdinand, heir to the throne of the huge Austro-Hungarian Empire, and his wife, the Duchess of Hohenberg, were both killed.

A month later Austria-Hungary pressed on the tiny neighboring kingdom of Serbia an ultimatum demanding, among other humiliating terms, permission for Austro-Hungarian officials to enter Serbia to punish those persons involved in the assassination and "to put an end to those intrigues, which constitute a standing menace to the peace of the monarchy." The Serbians offered a conciliatory reply, agreeing to accept most of the conditions and to negotiate the others. Austria, refusing to back down on any of her demands, promptly broke diplomatic relations with Serbia, and on July 28, 1914, Emperor Franz Josef declared war.

Why Serbia? Ostensibly, the Vienna government had found evidence connecting high Serbian officials with the Sarajevo terrorists. However, imperial investigators uncovered no signs of Serbian government involvement. The Austrian government's true motives ran much deeper. In the eyes of Franz Josef and the overwhelming majority of his advisers, Serbia—and the Pan-Slavic separatist movement she had spearheaded in Bosnia and other southern Austro-Hungarian provinces—posed a serious threat to the continued existence of the Hapsburg Empire.

In 1914 Franz Josef's regime was desperately trying to hold together its unwieldy realm in the face of steadily rising nationalist pressures from its various ethnic groups. Fewer than half of its 50 million subject peoples belonged to the privileged nations that dominated the empire, the German-speaking Austrians and the Magyars of Hungary. There were also 8.4 million Czechs and Slovaks, 5 million Poles, 4 million Ruthenians, 5.5 million Serbs and Croats, and 770,000 Italians. Of these, the Slavs, who lived in the southern Balkan provinces of Croatia, Dalmatia, and Bosnia-Herzegovina, were the most vocal and best organized. Moreover, they had a champion and model for their cause in the neighboring kingdom of Serbia.

Six years earlier the two nations had nearly gone to war when Serbia opposed the Hapsburg's annexation of Bosnia-Herzegovina. Since then, the Imperial General Staff had come to regard war with Serbia as inevitable, and they waited only for an excuse to step in and squelch their feisty neighbor once and for all. Franz Ferdinand's assassination provided that excuse. "This is not the crime of a single fanatic. If we miss this occasion," warned the Austro-Hungarian Chief of

Silhouetted against a French battlefield, *a nameless infantryman watches a night bombardment. He was but one of millions of soldiers drawn into the four-year-long terror of World War I. Never before had a conflict been waged on such a vast scale. Never had opposing armies been so large or so well equipped to destroy one another. And never had so many men sacrificed their lives for such obscure reasons.*

Staff, Gen. Franz Conrad von Hötzendorff (generally called Conrad), "the monarchy will be exposed to new outbursts of South Slav, Czech, Russian, Romanian, and Italian aspirations. Austria-Hungary must wage war for political reasons." Thus despite the lack of evidence of any direct Serbian involvement in the assassination, the Dual Monarchy seized upon it to justify a punitive war against Serbia.

The Big Brother

Neither Austria-Hungary nor Serbia would have dared to let a diplomatic crisis turn into war without the support of their allies. For the Serbians that support came from Russia, the eastern colossus ruled by Czar Nicholas II. A longtime rival of Austria for control of the Polish and Ukrainian lands that were divided between them, Russia also had territorial designs in the Balkans. Like Austria, she wanted either direct control or influence over the strategic peninsula as well as the Dardanelles, the vital waterway connecting her Black Sea ports with the Aegean. Russia had vehemently opposed Austria-Hungary's 1908 annexation of Bosnia-Herzegovina, but military weakness after the disastrous Russo-Japanese War of 1904–05 (see pp. 32–37) had prevented her intervention. In standing by Serbia now, the Russians had a cause that satisfied at once their strategic interests, their Pan-Slavic sympathies, and their desire to discomfit an old enemy.

Austria-Hungary had already received similar assurances of support from her own "Big Brother," the Germany of Kaiser Wilhelm II. Germany, like Russia, was motivated by more than a simple desire to come to her ally's aid. In 1914 Germany was spoiling for a fight. No other European ruler was as outspoken on the subject of his nation's might as the Kaiser, who yearned for a Mitteleuropa (middle Europe) completely dominated by the Reich. Impatient to win for Germany the international recognition he felt she deserved, he was fond of announcing his readiness to "draw the sword," if necessary, to defend her "rights" abroad.

There was solid fact behind his dramatic pronouncements. In the quarter century before 1914 Germany had become Europe's most powerful nation. Her population had increased by 25 percent, her capital wealth by 50 percent, her national income by 100 percent. Steel production was three times that of England and four times that of France or Russia. A great wave of national confidence caused Germans to look beyond Europe for a place in the sun, a colonial empire and shipping network to match that of Great Britain.

The unprecedented swiftness of Germany's rise and, even more, the aggressiveness of her spokesmen alarmed leaders of other European states, who watched her warily and prepared for a possible test of strength. France, which had never forgiven the loss of Alsace and Lorraine in the Franco-Prussian War of 1870, had only two-thirds the population of Germany and was falling behind in industrial and military power. Her first step to counter this imbalance was the Franco-Russian Alliance of 1892, which obliged both countries to mobilize in the event of Germany's mobilization. The French and the Russians hoped that the prospect of a war on two fronts would serve to hold the Germans in check.

Britain felt less immediately threatened by Germany. After all, the Kaiser was Queen Victoria's grand-

August 1914: High-spirited soldiers *marched through the streets of London (left) and Berlin (above) with their wives, mothers, and children at their sides. In Paris cheering throngs bade their armies farewell. But others sensed impending tragedy. Commented British Foreign Secretary Sir Edward Grey: "The lamps are going out all over Europe; we shall not see them lit again in our lifetime."*

son and the cousin of George V, the reigning King since 1910. Many of the nobility of the two nations were similarly linked by kinship as well as by common traditions. With a vast and prosperous empire, Britain could afford to look condescendingly and critically at German expansion. Gradually, however, she came to realize that the Kaiser would not be satisfied with the best army on the Continent. He would also need to develop a strong navy.

It was this naval rivalry that finally aroused British fears. Her unchallenged command of the sealanes was more than a proud tradition; it was a vital necessity for an island nation dependent on her ships for food and raw materials. After 1906, when Britain launched the *Dreadnought*, the first of the superbattleships, the two nations became involved in a naval arms race. The British were determined to maintain their naval superiority under the "two-power standard," which held that her total naval capacity would never be less than the combined naval power of her two strongest rivals. These had traditionally been France and Russia; but when the Kaiser began building his own fleet of dreadnoughts and rapidly expanding his naval manpower, Germany became Britain's chief naval opponent.

Out of this reversal grew the Triple Entente, an understanding between Britain, France, and Russia providing for mutual defense in the event of a war with Germany. The Germans had already expanded their alliance with Austria-Hungary into the Triple Alliance with Italy. This intricate web of security, built of alliances, secret protocols, and military assurances, served to aggravate international tension and heighten mutual suspicions in the years before 1914. More important, it assured that when war actually did come, it would not remain a localized conflict between Austria-Hungary and Serbia but would explode into a general European conflagration.

Diplomacy on the Brink

On July 29, 1914, shells from Austro-Hungarian guns began to fall on the Serbian capital of Belgrade. The next day the governments in Vienna and St. Petersburg ordered full mobilization. Germany, hoping to limit the conflict to the Balkans, demanded that Russia halt her mobilization; when the Russians refused on August 1, the Kaiser ordered German mobilization on both eastern and western frontiers. His decision, prompted by his treaty obligations to Austria-Hungary, forced the French, who were pledged by treaty to mobilize against Germany if Russia did so, to follow suit. Germany declared war on Russia later that same day.

To avoid a war on two fronts, the German High Command moved at once against France, hoping to win a quick victory before Russia could fully mobilize her forces. German troops crossed into Luxembourg on August 1. Three days later they invaded Belgium, and Germany officially declared war on France, having failed to obtain a French pledge of neutrality.

Britain had been uncertain of how soon and how forcefully to put into practice her "understanding" with France, but the unprovoked German attack on Belgium tipped the balance. Not only was Britain (with all the other great powers) pledged to guarantee Belgian neutrality, she also recognized that she would be at a considerable strategic disadvantage if Belgium's Channel ports fell to Germany. When the Germans ignored her demand to withdraw from Belgium, Britain declared war on August 4. On the 6th Austria-Hungary declared war on Russia, and on the 12th France and Britain in turn went to war with Austria-Hungary. The die had been cast.

At the great stations of Europe's capitals enthusiastic crowds cheered and shouted "On to Paris!"—or Berlin, or St. Petersburg, or Belgrade—as trains loaded with troops departed for the fronts. At last the tension was broken, and diplomacy gave way to the test of arms. In this first flush of wartime enthusiasm few could have suspected how long and agonizing that test would be. "You will be home before the leaves have fallen from the trees," the Kaiser reportedly assured his troops as they departed for the front.

The Opening Campaigns of 1914

The German General Staff, headed by Gen. Helmuth von Moltke, had what it considered a foolproof plan. Based on the brilliant 1905 blueprint of Count Alfred von Schlieffen, it called for a major western offensive by seven German armies. (An eighth army would hold back the Russians along the heavily fortified East Prussian border.) The five armies of the attacking right wing would make a wide sweep to the west and south through Belgium and France, pivoting on the fortified area of Metz-Thionville, while two left-wing armies attacked the French to the south of Metz-Thionville, trapping them into an offensive in Alsace-Lorraine. The two northernmost armies would pass through neutral Belgium and invade France through the thinly defended Franco-Belgian frontier, making a wide swing to the west and south of Paris and attacking the French from the rear. If all went according to schedule, the French would be defeated within six weeks.

It almost worked. While German mobilization was underway, a special force attacked the Belgian border fortress at Liège on August 5. The city and its citadel surrendered two days later, but the valiant Belgian defenders refused to yield the outer forts. With the help of superheavy artillery, the Germans reduced the forts one by one, and the last fort fell on August 16. By that time the roads through Liège had been cleared, and the German armies had begun moving through Belgium. The remaining Belgian forces withdrew and took up positions around Antwerp, beyond the range of the outer German flank.

Meanwhile, the French Commander in Chief, Gen. Joseph Joffre, began putting his master plan into effect. A total of five armies was deployed. Four of these were to mount major offensives against the Germans to the north and south of the Metz-Thionville fortifications in Alsace-Lorraine. A fifth army was held in reserve, either to exploit a successful attack or to help extend the front northward in the unlikely event of a German attack through Belgium.

Joffre was so convinced that the main thrust of the German attack would come through Alsace-Lorraine that he was slow to react to reports of large troop concentrations in Belgium. But on August 15 he ordered the 5th Army northward to take up positions along the Belgian border between the Sambre and Meuse Rivers. Farther north the small but highly professional British Expeditionary Force (BEF) under Gen. Sir John French reached the area of Le Cateau on August 20. Joffre ordered a combined offensive against the advancing German armies, but he had underestimated the strength of the German right wing. This so-called Battle of the Frontiers (August 20–24) failed to halt the German advance.

Then suddenly, it was turned back at the Marne by a combination of luck and determination on the part of the British and the French and overconfidence and misjudgment on the part of the Germans. After the failure of the Allied offensive, Joffre ordered a retreat to the Marne and began massing a strong force to hold the line there. Moltke,meanwhile, buoyed by his successes, dispatched two corps from his right flank to reinforce the Russian front. This decision drained valuable troops from his western wing, already depleted by several corps that were left behind to contain the Belgian fortresses. Moltke's problems were compounded by his lax method of command and an inefficient system of communication. As a result, the Chief of Staff did not keep track of where his troops were at any one time, failed to control and coordinate their advance, and neglected to pass on vital information to his commanders. His men, moreover, were nearly exhausted by the long forced marches ordered to make up for the delays in Belgium and by growing supply shortages.

In the battle of the Marne, September 6–9, the Allies halted the German offensive and forced them to pull back to the Aisne River. In the first five weeks of fighting the combatants had lost more than half a million men, and the German advance had come so close to the French capital that taxis were commandeered to rush troops into battle. But the immediate threat of a quick German victory was dispelled.

In October and November the line of battle was extended to the Channel coast. Antwerp fell on October 9, although most of the Belgian forces escaped to join the BEF in Flanders, where they clashed again and again with superior numbers of Germans in the monthlong First Battle of Ypres. By the end of November a continuous front ran from Belfort on the Swiss border to the English Channel.

***Germany's violation of Belgian neutrality** became a heated issue in neutral countries. In a 1917* Life *cartoon, the United States rushes to save martyred Belgium from the Kaiser's brutal hands.*

GERMANY'S NEAR VICTORY: THE ADVANCE TO THE MARNE

On August 4, 1914, the first three armies of the German right wing began their sweep through Belgium. Liège fell on August 16, and on August 20 the German right wing—now five armies strong—was approaching the French frontier. French Commander in Chief Gen. Joseph Joffre called for a general offensive, but this Battle of the Frontiers failed to halt the German advance. Further attempts by the British Expeditionary Force (BEF) at Mons and by the French 5th Army at the Sambre River also failed to turn the Germans back. French offensives against the two German left-wing armies in Alsace-Lorraine were equally unsuccessful, and by August 24 the Allies were in retreat along the entire western front.

Alarmed by the progress of the Russian offensive in East Prussia, German Commander in Chief Helmuth von Moltke dispatched two corps to the eastern front. Joffre, meanwhile, formed a 6th Army to defend Paris and ordered the Allies to prepare for a counteroffensive. It began September 6 along the Marne, with the BEF and the French 5th and 6th Armies making the main thrust against the German 1st and 2d Armies. On September 9 a serious gap opened between these two German armies, exposing their flanks, and Moltke ordered a general withdrawal north of the Aisne River. At the same time, the French had halted the secondary German offensive in Alsace-Lorraine. In the next two months the front was extended northward to the Channel coast, as each side tried unsuccessfully to outflank the other.

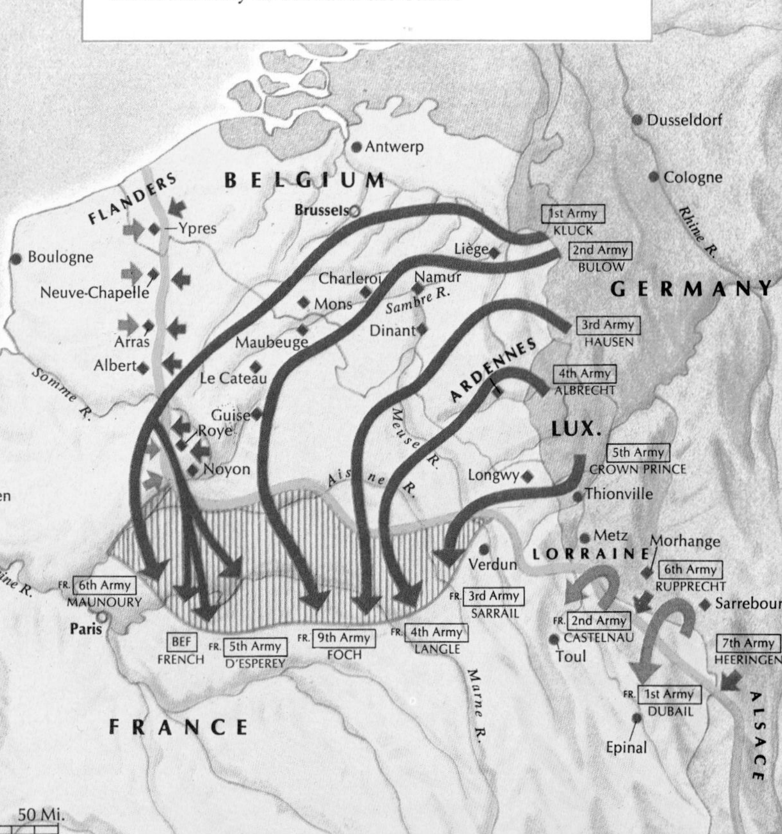

__At the height__ of the Battle of the Marne (September 6–9, 1914), an entire division of French infantry was rushed to the front in some 600 taxicabs gathered from the streets of Paris. The French capital itself had been transformed into an armed camp under the direction of Gen. Joseph Gallieni. (The government had fled to Bordeaux on September 3.) German troops came within 40 miles of the city, but they were turned back by the Allied counteroffensive at the Marne. Although the Allies had saved the day, their victory was not decisive. The war would go on.

The War in the East

In the east the Germans were granted a victory nearly as decisive as the one denied them in the west. By the terms of the Franco-Russian treaty the armies of Nicholas II were supposed to attack the Germans within 16 days of mobilization. In the event the first Russian soldiers crossed the border into East Prussia after only eight days, on August 7 (see map p. 121).

The Russians launched a two-pronged attack. One army, under Gen. Pavel Karlovich Rennenkampf, crossed the Prussian border east of the Angerapp River, while a second force, commanded by Gen. Alexander Vasilyevich Samsonov, entered farther south. The armies, like a giant pincer, planned to converge on the Germans to the south of Königsberg, the heavily fortified capital of East Prussia.

This bold plan might have succeeded had the timid German commander Max von Prittwitz had his way. He wanted to withdraw into Königsberg or even to abandon all territory east of the Vistula. Neither Moltke nor Prittwitz' gifted operations officer, Lt. Col. Max Hoffmann, agreed. On August 20 Moltke dismissed Prittwitz and rushed Gen. Erich Ludendorff, fresh from his successes against the Belgian forts, to become chief of staff of the eastern forces. His commanding officer, hastily recalled from the retired list, was the prestigious Gen. Paul von Hindenburg. The two took up their new posts on August 23.

Hindenburg and Ludendorff adopted Hoffmann's plan to concentrate all their forces against Samsonov in the south, hoping to annihilate his army before Rennenkampf came down from the northeast. Inexplicably, Rennenkampf's forces remained stationary for three crucial days while the Germans regrouped in the south. ("He need only have closed with us and we should have been beaten," Ludendorff wrote later.) Samsonov's army proved no match for the Germans in training, firepower, or tactics and was outflanked and cut to pieces near Tannenberg. Nearly 100,000 Russians were taken prisoner, and Samsonov shot himself. Centuries earlier the Teutonic knights had been slaughtered by the Slavs in the same spot.

A week later the Germans, strengthened by newly arrived reinforcements from the west, pushed Rennenkampf back across the border and gathered more scores of thousands of prisoners in the Battle of the Masurian Lakes. By mid-September the immediate threat to East Prussia had been averted.

To the south, meanwhile, the Russians faced an opponent almost as poorly equipped as themselves. The Austro-Hungarian forces, under Chief of Staff General Conrad, lacked the efficient railway network and highly skilled artillerists of their German ally. By late August Conrad's forces had crossed the Russian border and were advancing toward the vital Kiev-Warsaw railway, but Russia's sharp counterattacks drove them southward across the border and deep into Galicia.

In September and October German and Austro-Hungarian forces combined for a broad counteroffensive in southern Poland and Galicia. By then Russia had reached full mobilization, presenting a solid line of seven armies totaling 1.3 million men. In heavy fighting their general line finally held, but the losses of materiel, the expenditure of scarce ammunition, and the deaths of experienced officers weighed more heavily on the Russians than on the Germans.

Meanwhile, the all but forgotten war in the Balkans continued. The Austro-Hungarian campaign against

Serbia was led by Gen. Oskar von Potiorek, who predicted a victory over the small, poorly equipped Serbian Army within two weeks, but the Serbians under Gen. Radomir Putnik refused to give in so easily.

Twice Potiorek's forces penetrated into Serbia, and twice the Serbs caught them by surprise and hurled them back. In mid-December, more than four months after the war had begun as a result of Austria-Hungary's intent to "punish" Serbia, Putnik and his valiant soldiers had cleared Serbia of the enemy.

The War at Sea

As the armies of Europe's great powers took up battle positions across the Continent, the navies of Britain and Germany became engaged in a farflung contest for supremacy at sea. The initial test came in the Mediterranean in the first week of the war. Hoping to avoid a confrontation with the superior British Mediterranean Fleet, the German Admiralty ordered the battle cruiser *Goeben* and her consort, the light cruiser *Breslau,* to proceed at once to Constantinople, capital of the neutral Ottoman Empire. The German warships managed to evade the British Fleet completely and entered the Dardanelles unharmed. There they were sold to the Turkish government, which had been angered by Britain's unprovoked seizure of two Turkish warships being built in Britain. The *Goeben*'s flight thus paved the way for the Ottoman Empire's entry into the war in early November on the German side.

Elsewhere, German naval raiders wreaked havoc on British merchant shipping. By mid-October they had sunk or captured more than 40 British and Allied ships. The British and their allies, on the other hand, seized German bases in the Pacific, blockading the German East Asia Squadron from its home port at Tsingtao, China. The squadron's commander, Adm. Maximilian von Spee, decided to sail homeward. En route he sank two British warships at Coronel, off the coast of Chile, on November 1. Thereafter, Germany's luck at sea began to turn. The British were able to corner and capture most of the raiders, and on December 9, in a pitched battle off the Falkland Islands, the British Navy annihilated Spee's East Asia Squadron.

By the end of 1914 it was clear that the war had just begun to run its course. The British were masters of the sea, but on land no one held the upper hand. New fronts were opening up at Suez, Africa, and the Black Sea, as the forces of the Ottoman Empire began to mobilize against the British, French, and Russians. In Europe the fighting continued. In the east the Russians were battling the Germans and Austro-Hungarians in Galicia. And in the west the great armies of Germany, Britain, and France had begun digging in for a long and nightmarish war of attrition.

The Russian surrender at Tannenberg (above) made national heroes of Germany's winning generals Paul von Hindenburg and Erich Ludendorff (left).

TANNENBERG: THE MAKING OF A LEGEND

Germany's spectacular victory over Russia at Tannenberg in East Prussia in late August 1914 was engineered by the two generals who were to exercise a virtual dictatorship over Germany by the war's end, Paul von Hindenburg and Erich Ludendorff. Previously unknown outside military circles, they won overnight fame with their successes against the "Russian steamroller," spawning a popular legend of invincibility. Two years later the Ludendorff-Hindenburg team had risen to supreme command of the Kaiser's massive war effort.

1915-17

World War I

Part Two: The Western Front

Along a bloody 380-mile front the Allied and German armies are locked in a nightmare stalemate.

The First World War was destined to alter all previous concepts of war and to render the idea of armed conflict so horrible that rational men hoped it would never occur again. The almost universal enthusiasm and relief that had greeted its first calls to arms gradually gave way to a profound sense of disillusionment and disgust. As it ran its brutal course, the Great War refuted every traditional notion of victory, heroism, and glory. Along the western front—amid the trenches, barbed wire, and muddy wastelands littered with shell holes and rotting corpses—war became senseless, futile, and barbaric.

The Battle of the Marne in September 1914 marked the turning point of the war from the conventional spectacle of marching columns and pitched battles to the nightmare of trench warfare. The Germans, who had been denied a quick victory by the Allied Marne offensive, fell back and began building an almost impenetrable line of defense along the front stretching from Belfort on the Swiss border to the North Sea. Determined to hold fast to the Belgian and French territory they had gained in the first five weeks of fighting, they began digging in behind an elaborate network of trenches, underground tunnels and dugouts, and barbed wire.

The system was ingenious in concept. It was also devastating. From their entrenched positions the Germans could sight and mow down any attacking force as it advanced across the no man's land separating them from the opposing line of trenches the Allies were forced to construct. Whole regiments fell under the sweeping barrage of machinegun, mortar, and artillery fire without ever reaching their objective. By contrast, casualties among the troops holding trenches were initially comparatively light. As one British private observed: "Ten men holding a trench could easily stop fifty who were trying to take it." Even if some of the assailants managed to break through the barbed wire and reach the first line of trenches, there were two or more fortified lines beyond. Meanwhile, the defenders had had time to organize their main force for a counterattack, driving the battered assailants back over the ground they had just crossed, where scores of their comrades lay dead or wounded.

Since it was impossible to outflank this continuous defense system, the only possible operation was a penetration, designed to break through the front defenses and expose the enemy's rear. Surprise was possible—and often obtained—but the depth of the enemy defenses and the problem of moving the supporting artillery across the devastated no man's land and through the captured trench system limited the gains that could be achieved. Only where the German line bulged into the Allied defenses, creating a salient, was there some vulnerability and a chance for a two-pronged, nonfrontal attack. It was at such points that the leaders of both the French and British armies hoped to achieve the great breakthrough that would finally bring them a decisive victory.

Elaborate trench networks, *like the one below, which is based on actual maps of British and German positions in the Cuinchy sector of Artois, ran the length of the western front. First hastily dug as shelters, they evolved into complex defense systems, with several parallel trench lines and connecting communication trenches, concrete pillboxes, dugouts, firing bays, extensive underground tunnels, and mineshafts. Barbed wire entanglements protected the forward lines, and the rearmost lay beyond the enemy's fire. A desolate no man's land strewn with shells and craters lay between the camps. An intensive war was also waged underground, as each side tunneled toward the opposite camp. Engineers supervised clandestine digging operations to extend the forward line into no man's land or to plant explosives beneath enemy positions.*

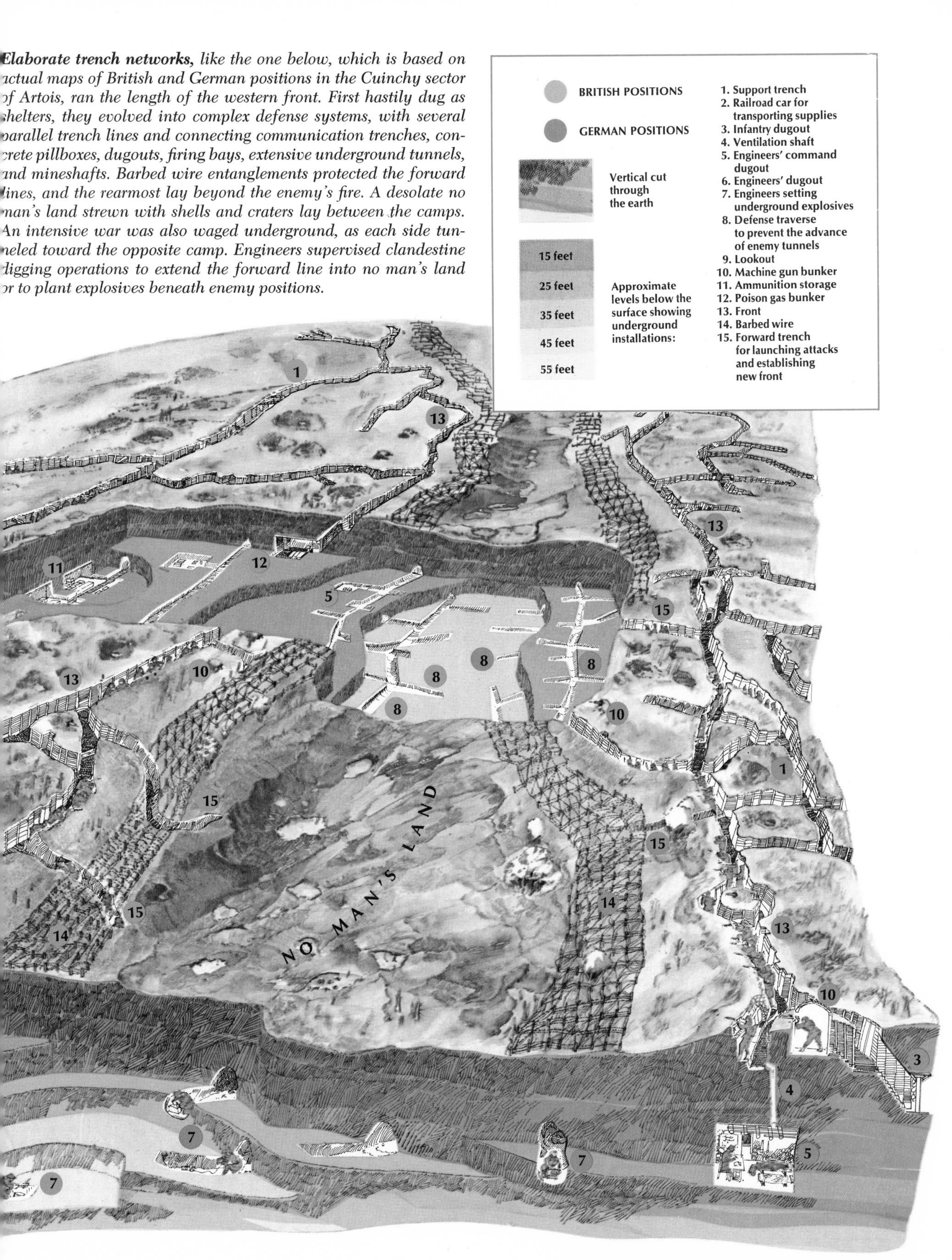

1915-17: STALEMATE

For three years the German and Allied armies held each other to a bloody stalemate along the western front, a nightmare of trenches, tunnels, barbed wire, and shell craters that stretched from Switzerland to the Belgian coast.

For three years each side believed it could make a decisive break through the enemy lines. The Germans dug masterly trench systems to defend their early gains in France and Belgium, and the Allies coordinated their attacks against the flanks of the great bulge in the German lines between the Flanders lowlands and Verdun.

But no matter how extravagantly the generals committed their men, no matter how heroically the troops fought, the assaults failed. New weapons were developed to break the deadlock along the 380-mile front: poison gas by the Germans, tanks by the British. The killing became more efficient and impersonal, but the impasse persisted.

The Triumph of the Defense

Leaders on both sides were slow to adapt to this totally new form of warfare. The result was a grueling war of attrition. The stalemate might have been broken sooner had the Allied leaders developed an offensive strategy capable of overcoming the vast superiority of the German trench artillery and defenses. It took time, however, to work out new tactics and develop and manufacture new weapons. In the meantime, commanders were forced to rely on traditional means of attack and on-the-spot improvisations. Their plight was further complicated by inevitable delays in producing sufficient guns and ammunition and recruiting and training the enormous number of soldiers needed merely to continue the fight.

Even when an assault gained its first objective, its advantage was often lost because of the failure of communication between the front line and the commanding general. Wireless equipment was too cumbersome to be carried by advancing units, and field telephone lines were vulnerable to shellfire. When they broke, commanders resorted to signal rockets, runners, or carrier pigeons to relay their orders, with resulting delays, confusion, and missed opportunities.

The only weapons that might have broken the deadlock, tanks and aircraft, were not utilized effectively until late in the war. Tanks were first employed by the British in the Battle of the Somme in 1916, but their performance was disappointing. They were finally successful against the German entrenchments in the summer of 1918. Even then they remained slow, mechanically unreliable, and difficult to maneuver. Although effective in mounting a major attack, they were incapable of sustained action. Airplanes, limited in the early part of the war to reconnaissance missions and artillery spotting, were used on a large scale against ground artillery and supply lines after 1916. Like the tanks, however, planes were relatively slow, vulnerable to infantry fire, and limited in firepower and accuracy.

The men themselves did their best to make up for tactical limitations. They attacked again and again, knowing that they would sustain enormous casualties. The French soldiers, with a fatal dependence upon elan, the "vital spirit of the attack," hoped to redress the humiliation of the Franco-Prussian War of 1870–71 when Germany defeated France and annexed the provinces of Alsace and Lorraine. But under the scything barrage of German artillery, their ambition to march on Berlin slowly gave way to a simple desire to clear French soil of the invaders; eventually even that ambition eroded to a numb, dogged determination to hold on to what they had at all costs.

They had doughty allies in the soldiers of the British Expeditionary Force (BEF), an army of sharpshooting professionals badly outnumbered by the German forces; in the first eight months of the war the BEF was nearly decimated. The new volunteer and conscript armies raised by Lord Kitchener, Britain's Secretary of

State for War, lacked the assurance, competence, and battlefield experience of their predecessors.

The Germans had an initial edge in trained manpower and equipment, particularly machineguns. They were also quicker to adapt to trench combat than the British and French. Moreover, the Germans exploited their defensive position to the fullest, abandoning that strategy only twice during the three-year impasse—at the Second Battle of Ypres in April 1915 and at the Battle of Verdun in February 1916. Under the leadership of Gen. Erich von Falkenhayn, who had replaced Gen. Helmuth von Moltke as commander in chief of the German forces after the Battle of the Marne in September 1914, the Germans adopted a fine defensive strategy in the west while conducting a successful offensive against the Russians in the east.

1915: Practice in Failure

The Allied strategy, in which Britain's Field Marshal Sir John French followed the lead of France's Chief of Staff Marshal Joseph Joffre, called for coordinated offensives against the flanks of the great bulge in the German lines between the lowlands of Flanders and Verdun. Throughout 1915 the French launched a series of unsuccessful offensives in Champagne at the southern flank of the bulge, while a combined Franco-British force led an equally futile campaign against the northern flank of the bulge in Artois.

In February and March the French lost more than 240,000 men for gains of less than a mile in Champagne, and the British made an even smaller dent at Neuve-Chapelle, near the Belgian border. Most of the British losses (nearly 10,000 men) came in the first three hours of a three-day battle that gained an advance of 1,000 yards. In mid-April the Germans attacked at Ypres, just across the Belgian border, using a new weapon: poison chlorine gas. The defending French force collapsed under the terrifying, choking, blinding fumes, but the Germans failed to exploit their advantage. Thereafter, both sides developed ever more effective gases, and from mid-1915 preliminary artillery bombardments by both camps included an assortment of gas shells.

In May and June the French launched costly, futile attacks against Souchez in Artois, and the British led an offensive at Festubert, to the south of Neuve-Chapelle. The Allies spent most of the summer assimilating new troops and planning a major offensive for September. On September 25 the French delivered the main thrust against the German lines in Champagne, and an Anglo-French force attacked in Artois. Nothing was gained, and by early November fighting had ceased. Each side suffered heavy casualties.

After the disastrous Battle of Loos in Artois in September, Field Marshal French was removed as commander in chief of the British forces, and his second-in-command, Gen. Douglas Haig, took his place. In France continued failure brought the downfall of René Raphael Viviani's government, and Aristide Briand became Premier. In an effort to intensify her war effort, Britain introduced a stepped-up recruiting system in October and enacted nationwide conscription the following January. At the same time, she stepped up the manufacture of arms and munitions.

1916: Verdun and the Somme

In December 1915 Allied leaders met in France to plan an all-out summer offensive for 1916. The blueprint called for a coordinated effort on all fronts, with French and British assaults in the west and Russian and Italian campaigns in the east. Italy had declared war on Austria-Hungary in May 1915, after signing the secret Treaty of London in which the Allies promised

WAR AND DISILLUSIONMENT

The idealism of an entire generation was shattered in the trenches of the western front. Like the handsome young British poet Rupert Brooke, who became their symbol, the young people of Europe had welcomed the chance to make noble and heroic sacrifices for their countries. The profitless butchery of the Somme, Verdun, and elsewhere, however, soon stripped away such illusions, and disenchanted poets such as England's Siegfried Sassoon wrote bitter, stark descriptions of the war's pervasive ugliness and futility.

THE SOLDIER

If I should die, think only this of me;
That there's some corner of a foreign field
That is forever England. There shall be
In that rich earth a richer dust concealed;
A dust whom England bore, shaped, made aware,
Gave, once, her flowers to love, her ways to roam,
A body of England's breathing English air,
Washed by the rivers, blest by suns of home.

And think, this heart, all evil shed away,
A pulse in the eternal mind, no less
Gives some where back the thoughts
by England given;
Her sights and sounds; dreams happy as her days;
And laughter, learnt of friends; and gentleness,
In hearts at peace, under an English heaven.

—Rupert Brooke

THE DUG-OUT

Why do you lie with your legs ungainly huddled,
And one arm bent across your sullen, cold,
Exhausted face? It hurts my heart to watch you,
Deep-shadowed from the candle's guttering gold;
And you wonder why I shake you by the shoulder;
Drowsy, you mumble and sigh and turn your head. . . .
You are too young to fall asleep forever;
And when you sleep you remind me of the dead.

—Siegfried Sassoon

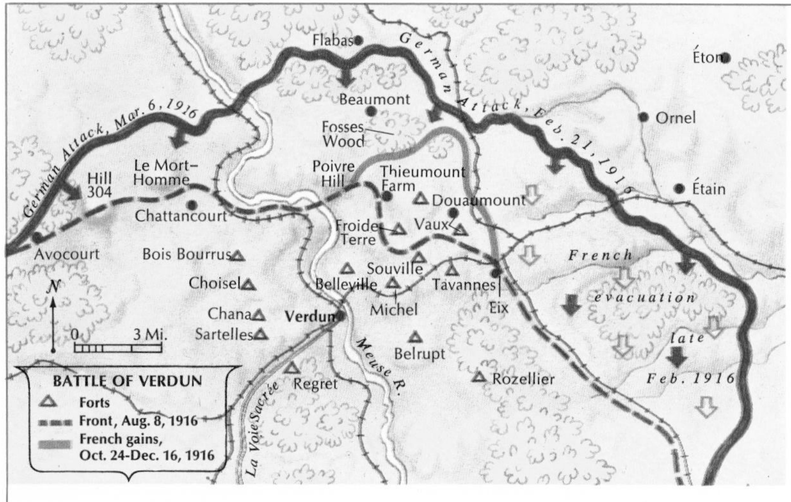

THE BATTLES OF VERDUN AND THE SOMME

The "Hell of Verdun," the five-month siege of France's legendary fortress complex, began on February 21, 1916. At dawn the Germans, bent on destroying the French Army by forcing it to defend Verdun to the death, loosed the most terrifying artillery barrage in history. By late afternoon, when the first infantry force crossed the east bank of the Meuse, the French front lines had been obliterated. On February 25 the Germans took Fort Douaumont, but the French halted their advance a few days later. A second German force attacked along the west bank of the Meuse on March 6, capturing Hill 304 and Le Mort-Homme. Fighting resumed east of the Meuse, and Fort Vaux fell June 9. Thereafter, the French line held, and in mid-July the Germans ended their offensive. That fall the French regained some ground.

On July 1 the British, with French support, attacked north and south of the Somme River after a week of artillery preparation. The British advance was halted in most places by nightfall with heavy casualties, but the French made considerable gains to the south. In the next months the Allies advanced a few miles but failed to break the German lines, and General Haig halted the fighting in mid-November. Together, Verdun and the Somme had cost the Allies and Germans more than 2 million casualties.

Verdun, 1916: Fort Douaumont (below, left), stripped of its guns to equip the French field armies, fell to advancing Germans on the fourth day of fighting. The Somme, 1916: The first British troops prepare to advance (right). Casualties the first day were staggering.

her Austrian territory at the war's end in return for her entry into the conflict on their side. She did not declare war on Germany, however, until August 1916.

The 1916 western offensive was scheduled for July along the Somme River in Artois, but before Allied plans had crystallized the Germans mounted a major assault at Verdun, the French fortress city astride the Meuse River on the Lorraine frontier. Falkenhayn hoped to "bleed France white" by forcing her to mass her armies in a life or death struggle to defend the fortress. One of a chain of bastions guarding the Franco-German frontier, Verdun was reputed to be the strongest fortress in the world. It was protected by a number of outlying forts, built on most of the commanding hills around the city, and a forward line of trenches. In fact, however, at the time of the German attack Verdun was very vulnerable. The front in that region had been quiet for many months, and Joffre (who became convinced after the fall of the Belgian fortress at Liège that conventional forts were useless) had transferred most of the garrison troops and many of the guns to more active fronts.

In the early weeks of 1916 Falkenhayn assembled the German 5th Army under Crown Prince Friedrich Wilhelm, a force of 140,000 equipped with more than 1,400 guns, including some 600 heavy artillery and a dozen 16.5-inch Big Bertha howitzers. On February 21 his gunners began an intensive bombardment of the French trenches. The shelling continued for the next nine hours without letup, completely demolishing the first line of entrenchment. Wrote one French soldier of the horror of the bombardment: "The pounding was continuous and terrifying. We had never experienced its like. . . . The earth around us quaked, and we were lifted and tossed about. Shells of all caliber kept raining on our sector. . . . Our blinded, wounded, crawling and shouting soldiers kept falling on top of us and died while splashing us with their blood. . . ."

That afternoon the guns fell silent, and the vanguard of the German troops advanced along the eastern bank of the Meuse and seized the crippled French forward positions. For the next three days they repeated the pattern, first shattering the French defenses with heavy bombardment and then advancing. By the 25th they had taken Fort Douaumont, mightiest of the outer forts, and were advancing on the inner strongholds.

Joffre, alarmed at the worsening situation, sent in the capable Gen. Henri Pétain to organize an effective defense. Determined to hold the fortress whatever the cost, Pétain ordered his men not to yield another foot, set up a supply route along the single access road to the fortress, and brought in massive reinforcements and artillery. At the height of the battle a 3,000-vehicle convoy made two daily trips over this vital lifeline, which became known as *La Voie Sacrée* ("The Sacred Way"), under constant artillery bombardment.

These measures revitalized the French position, slowed the German advance to a few yards a day, and forced Falkenhayn to mount a second offensive along the western bank of the Meuse. The Crown Prince's force met fierce resistance at every stronghold but gradually gained ground. Whole regiments perished in the monthlong bitter struggles for Le Mort-Homme (Dead Man's Hill) and Hill 304. By the end of May the Germans had broken through the last of the western defenses, and on June 9 they took the great fort of Vaux to the east after a desperate and bloody contest, which cost both sides heavy casualties.

As the Germans approached the gates of Verdun, the Russians began their planned offensive in the east, and Falkenhayn had to slacken the pressure at Verdun to provide reinforcements for the eastern front. At the end of the month the British, supported by a small French force, began their scheduled offensive on the Somme with five days of artillery bombardment. Falkenhayn drew off more troops from Verdun to reinforce his line on the Somme. On July 1 a large British force advanced along the northern bank of the river, and a smaller French force attacked to the south. The Germans were waiting for them, however. During the long preliminary shelling, they had hidden in deep underground bunkers, reportedly playing cards as the shells thundered overhead. Now they emerged unharmed to meet the advancing enemy.

The first wave of British troops was mowed down by German machineguns, and Haig ordered a second assault. British casualties ran high the first day, with 20,000 dead and 40,000 wounded or missing, but they continued their effort. The slaughter dragged on into August and September, with British losses mounting daily. Slowly they opened a wide, shallow dent in the German defenses, but they failed to win even one of their strategic objectives. On September 15 they employed tanks for the first time against the Germans, but the new weapons were too few and too mechanically unreliable to achieve a breakthrough. By mid-November the battle was over. The statistics reveal the gruesome cost: The Germans sustained some 650,000 casualties, and the Allies reported another 615,000 killed, wounded, missing in action, or taken prisoner.

Meanwhile, the fighting continued at Verdun. During the fall the French mounted a strong counteroffensive, regaining part of the lost ground and retaking Forts Vaux and Douaumont. By mid-December the threat to Verdun had been averted. The 10-month battle had been the longest and bloodiest of the war, claiming nearly a million casualties.

The costly impasse of 1916 brought new shifts in command. In August Kaiser Wilhelm II dismissed Falkenhayn and ordered Field Marshal Paul von Hindenburg, commander in chief of Germany's eastern forces, to come west with his chief of staff Gen. Erich Ludendorff to take his place. In December Joffre retired as French commander in chief; he was succeeded by Gen. Robert G. Nivelle, who had directed the successful French counter-offensive at Verdun and pledged to repeat that success on a larger scale. That same month a new Liberal government, headed by David Lloyd George, came to power in Britain, replacing that of Herbert Asquith.

More of the Same

To break the stalemate, Nivelle proposed another all-out Allied offensive along the Aisne River in Artois in 1917, but his plans were forestalled by Hindenburg. On his orders the German troops in the Somme sector pulled back an average distance of 25 miles to form a shorter, stronger defensive line along a 70-mile front stretching from Arras to the Aisne River. Before they withdrew they devastated the entire area and planted it thickly with mines and boobytraps. The new position was known as the *Siegfried Stellung* to the Germans and the Hindenburg Line to the Allies.

Nonetheless, Nivelle went forward with his plans. On April 9 the British sent 14 divisions against the German defenses at Arras, scoring initial successes but slowly losing ground after the second day of fighting. The only permanent gain was the capture of Vimy Ridge in a courageous assault by the Canadian Corps, the right wing of the British 1st Army. On April 16 Nivelle massed four French armies, more than a million men, to break through the German lines between Soissons and Reims. In a fortnight of fighting the French won no major objectives and lost some 100,000 men. At the beginning of May the French Cabinet called a halt to the fighting after mutiny broke out in many army units, and in mid-May Nivelle was replaced by Pétain. The spirit of the French soldier had reached the breaking point.

The British Army was left to shoulder the main burden of the war on the western front. Haig, who had been promoted to field marshal late in 1916, felt relieved of the need to follow the lead of the French commander and free to pursue his primary objective of clearing German forces from the coastal region of Flanders. In early June Gen. Herbert Plumer's 2d Army launched an attack against Messines Ridge, a German strongpoint six miles south of Ypres. After planting and exploding more than 500 tons of TNT beneath the ridge, Plumer's nine divisions captured the strategic ridge with little opposition.

The main assault was to take place at Ypres, but the lengthy preliminary bombardment broke up the precarious drainage system of the Flanders lowlands. When unusually heavy seasonal rains fell in August, the battle became bogged down in a sea of mud. Nevertheless, Haig continued the offensive, which deteriorated into a horrifying struggle around Passchendaele, seven miles northeast of Ypres. By early December the British had lost some 300,000 men, and the battle had been fought to a stalemate.

The last battles of 1917 were also indecisive. The French made a successful minor attack at Verdun, and the British sent a large, compact force of more than 200 tanks against the Germans at Cambrai, about 20 miles east of Arras. The latter, a surprise attack, was very successful at first, but the heavy losses of the Third Battle of Ypres had left Haig without enough reserves to exploit it. British momentum slowed, and a strong German counteroffensive eventually drove the British back almost to their original starting point.

In November, dismayed by their own repeated failures to turn the tide, the Allied heads of government met at Rapallo, Italy, and established a Supreme War Council to improve military coordination. Their position was critical. Although Pétain had put an end to the troop mutinies and punished the most serious offenders, French morale remained low and her armies faced serious manpower shortages. Britain was plagued by similar shortages, but her morale remained high. Moreover, Italy had suffered a disastrous defeat at Caporetto in October, and Russia had withdrawn from the war, signing a separate armistice with Germany at Brest-Litovsk after the successful Bolshevik Revolution in October.

Allied prospects for 1918 were mixed. The Russian collapse had freed German forces from the eastern front to strengthen her western forces for a major offensive. Only one hope remained to save the Allies from a crushing defeat: The United States, which had entered the war against Germany on April 6, 1917, could supply the manpower required to deliver a decisive blow on the western front. But it would be months before her armies could be recruited and trained and more months before they reached the battlefield. In the meantime the Allies would merely try to maintain the impasse. Three years of struggle without issue had proved that a decisive outcome on the western front was not within their power.

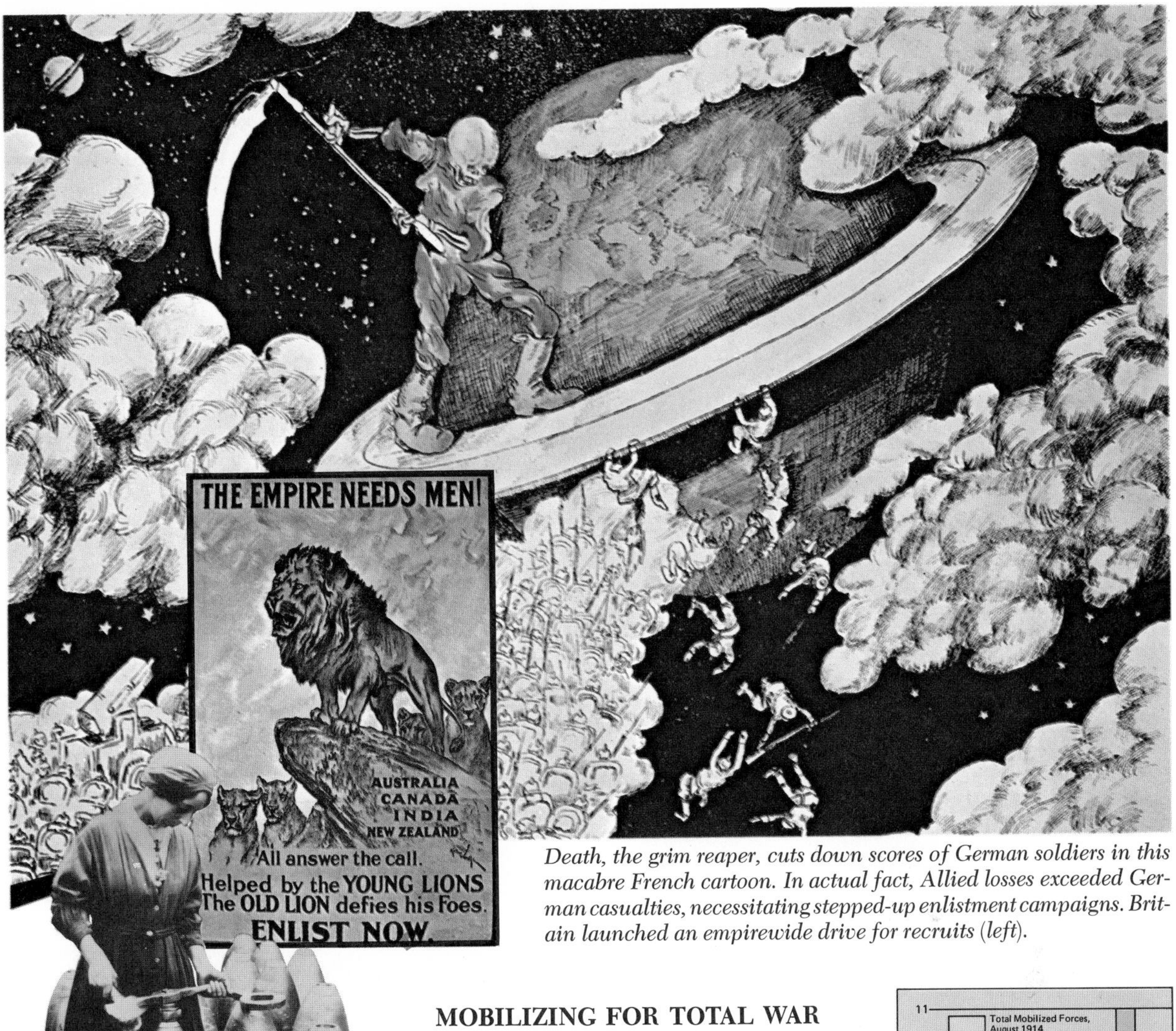

THE EMPIRE NEEDS MEN!

AUSTRALIA
CANADA
INDIA
NEW ZEALAND
All answer the call.
Helped by the YOUNG LIONS
The OLD LION defies his Foes.
ENLIST NOW.

Death, the grim reaper, cuts down scores of German soldiers in this macabre French cartoon. In actual fact, Allied losses exceeded German casualties, necessitating stepped-up enlistment campaigns. Britain launched an empirewide drive for recruits (left).

A female British munitions worker assembles a high explosive shell (above). Women in every major belligerent nation joined the labor force to replace men sent to the fronts. Many worked in factories, but others drove trucks and buses or tilled fields. Their contributions provided feminists with a strong argument for postwar sexual equality.

MOBILIZING FOR TOTAL WAR

The First World War was the first to draw whole societies into its midst. Germany, France, and Britain mobilized their entire resources to provide the massive armies and firepower needed to sustain the worldwide conflict. All able-bodied men aged 18 to 41 were called up, industries were placed on a wartime footing, economic controls were introduced, food and clothing were rationed, and women were recruited into industry.

These efforts brought impressive gains: The total number of Frenchmen under arms doubled from 1914 to 1918, Germany's armed strength grew by 150 percent, and Britain's increased ninefold. (See chart at right.) In all three countries the output of guns and munitions soared. Mobilization also accelerated social change by drawing women into the labor force and by introducing government regulation of most aspects of everyday life; yet for three years all these efforts failed to break the war's deadlock. In the end, however, the Allies were able to muster enough men and guns to achieve victory.

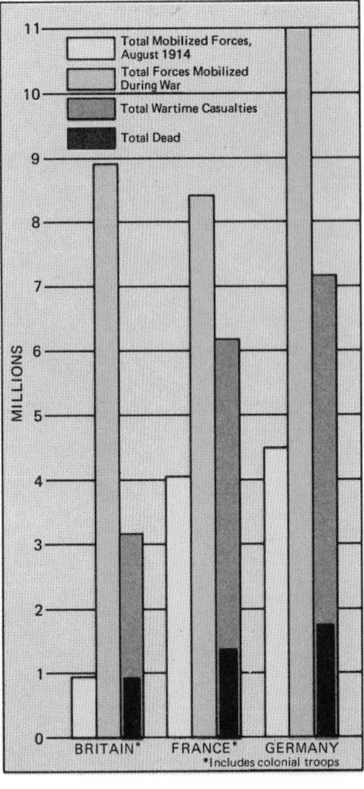

1915-18

World War I

Part Three: The World at War

For the first time in history a war explodes across the world, destroying the old order of things forever.

While the war along the western front ground to a terrible impasse, fighting flared again and again from the Baltic Sea to the Carpathian Mountains, in the Alps, the Balkans, Turkey, the Middle East, and Africa. There the armies of the belligerents fought pitched battles to gain large expanses of territory, and the concepts of victory and defeat still had full meaning. There, too, the war expanded, as both sides wooed neutral nations into the conflict. In November 1914 the Ottoman Empire joined the Central Powers, and in October 1915 Bulgaria followed suit. Italy declared war on Austria-Hungary in May 1915, and Romania joined the Allies in August of the following year. In April 1917 the most powerful of all neutrals, the United States, entered the war, committing its vast resources and manpower to the Allied cause.

The sprawling Ottoman Empire, the first of the neutrals to take up arms, stretched from the Black Sea to

the Persian Gulf and from the Caucasus Mountains to the Red Sea. Even before Turkey entered the war, the Germans had sent a military advisory mission, headed by Gen. Otto Liman von Sanders, to Constantinople to help reorganize the Sultan's armed forces. When war was declared late in 1914, Turkey's hotheaded Minister for War, Enver Pasha, immediately sent an army northeast to attack Russia's mountainous Caucasus frontier with Turkey. Enver envisioned a sweeping success followed by Turkish occupation of Russia's Caucasian and Georgian provinces. Instead, bitter winter weather, with blizzards, gale winds, and subzero temperatures, thwarted the offensive. In January 1915 the Russians drove the Turks back into Armenia. Enver's 150,000-strong army was destroyed: Barely one man in five survived the winter ordeal.

Throughout 1915 the Turks battled the Russians between Trebizond and Lake Van in Armenia. The Armenians, including those in Turkish Armenia, supported the Russians, and many joined the Russian Army. In reprisal for their disloyalty, the Turks savagely massacred hundreds of thousands of civilians in Turkish Armenia and deported thousands more to desert concentration camps. A 1916 Russian offensive led by Gen. Nikolai N. Yudenich succeeded in capturing all of Turkish Armenia by the year's end.

Meanwhile, Enver had dispatched a second force to seize the Suez Canal from the British. In January 1915 20,000 Turks, led by the German Col. Friedrich Kress von Kressenstein, marched across the Sinai Desert to the canal but were repulsed. In the spring of 1916 a British force under Lt. Gen. Sir Archibald Murray gradually cleared the Sinai Peninsula. They were followed by engineers and Egyptian laborers who laid a railway and water pipeline across the arid desert. By March 1917 the British were ready to attempt an advance

***Constantinople burns** after heavy British bombardment in April 1916 (left). Turkey's support of the Central Powers in World War I hastened the disintegration of the unwieldy Ottoman Empire.*

***Specially trained Alpine troops** (right) guard Austria-Hungary's mountainous Italian frontier. Italy declared war on the Dual Monarchy in 1915 and was badly defeated at Caporetto in 1917.*

***A Russian Orthodox priest** blesses his troops before a major battle (below). Russia's war with Germany and Austria-Hungary placed enormous strains on her resources and finally brought about the collapse of the weak czarist regime.*

***Advised by adventurous British officers,** such as Col. T. E. Lawrence (above), the Arabs supported Britain's Palestine campaign by disrupting Turkey's supply lines with raids on the Hejaz Railway. Britain's pledge of postwar Arab independence, however, was crippled by the Sykes-Picot pact, giving Britain control of Palestine and France of Syria.*

into Palestine, but they were twice repulsed in an attempt to break through the Turkish defenses in the Gaza-Beersheba sector. In June Murray was replaced by Gen. Sir Edmund Allenby, who was able to take Gaza and Beersheba in early November. Jerusalem surrendered in December.

Allenby's forces were aided by Arabs who had revolted against the Turks in 1916. Supplied and paid by the British, they were advised by a group of adventurous British officers including the famous Col. T. E. Lawrence. These Arabs annoyed the Turks by raids against the vital Hejaz Railway, which linked Turkey proper with Damascus, Amman, and Medina. The British in return promised to support Arab independence after the war, while secretly recognizing French postwar claims in Syria in the Sykes-Picot agreement. Their failure to make good their vow stirred deep resentment and distrust of the West in the Arab world.

Kut al Imara, Gallipoli, and Salonika

The British were less successful in other actions against the Turks. At the outbreak of Turkish hostilities, Britain sent a small force from India to Mesopotamia to protect British oilfields in southern Persia and the oil pipeline from Persia to Abadan Island. Landing at the head of the Persian Gulf, the combined Anglo-Indian force marched north along the Tigris River to establish a base at Basra. After taking that city and defeating Turkish counterattacks, they continued to advance northward, capturing Al Qurna, 'Amara, and Kut al Imara by September 1915. They next attempted to take Baghdad but were repulsed by the Turks at Ctesiphon, only 20 miles from their objective. The British retired to Kut al Imara. Too exhausted to continue their retreat, the 8,900 men dug in there. All attempts to relieve them failed, and Gen. Charles Townshend surrendered to the Turks on April 12, 1916.

The British defeat at Kut followed close on the heels of another major setback at the Dardanelles. Russia had appealed to the Allies to help divert Turkish troops from the Caucasus front in January 1915, and the British Admiralty began laying plans to seize control of the Dardanelles and the Bosporus, the strategic straits linking the Aegean and the Black Seas. (By that time the opening of the straits had become vital to speed delivery of Allied war supplies to Russia.)

During February and March 1915 British and French warships shelled the outer Turkish forts and entered the Dardanelles, but they found the waters heavily mined. After losing three ships the force withdrew. Britain's War Secretary, Lord Kitchener, then decided to launch a combined land-sea assault on the peninsula and sent Gen. Sir Ian Hamilton to direct the offensive. On April 25 some 75,000 troops landed at two points: A British force went ashore at Cape Helles at the southern tip of the Gallipoli Peninsula, and the Anzacs (Australian and New Zealand Army Corps) landed at Ari Burnu, thereafter known as Anzac Cove, about 15 miles to the north.

After some initial gains the offensive bogged down. The Turks, commanded by Otto Liman von Sanders, held tenaciously to the heights above the beaches, and the Allied forces were unable to break through. (Mustafa Kemal [Ataturk], who distinguished himself as the "Savior of Gallipoli," became ruler of Turkey after the war.) The stalemate dragged on into summer, aggravated by heat, insects, and malaria. Another Allied landing further north at Suvla Bay in August failed to achieve the hoped-for breakthrough, and the campaign lost its momentum. In the fall Hamilton was replaced by Gen. Sir Charles Monro, who wisely ordered a withdrawal in December and January.

The British failure at Gallipoli brought another neutral, Bulgaria, into the war on the side of the Central Powers. Both sides had tried to lure her into their

THE OTTOMAN EMPIRE'S WAR AGAINST THE ALLIES

Turkey's entry into the war opened up fronts in the Caucasus, the Dardanelles, Mesopotamia, and Palestine.

▲ **The Caucasus Front.** In November 1914 the Turks attacked Russia through the Caucasus Mountains but were repulsed. The Russians scored a major victory at Sarikamis in January 1915, and by the end of 1916 they had captured all of Turkish Armenia. The Turks regained the area after Russia's withdrawal from the war in late 1917.

• **The Dardanelles Campaign.** Russia appealed to Britain early in 1915 to help divert Turkish forces from the Caucasus, and the Allies made plans to seize the Dardanelles and reopen the strait (closed by the Turks in November 1914) to Russian shipping. After naval attacks in February and March 1915, two Allied forces landed at Cape Helles and Ari Burnu on the Gallipoli Peninsula in April. The Turks halted their advance. A third landing at Suvla Bay in August also met with failure. The attempt was abandoned in December.

▪ **The Mesopotamian Campaign.** At the war's outbreak Britain acted to protect her oil pipeline from Persia to Abadan Island at the head of the Persian Gulf. An Anglo-Indian force secured a base at Basra and advanced up the Tigris. Reaching Kut al Imara in September 1915, they marched on toward Baghdad but were repulsed at Ctesiphon and fell back to Kut, where they surrendered in April 1916 after a five-month siege. A second force took Baghdad in March 1917 and claimed the Mosul oilfields in November 1918.

◆ **The Palestinian Campaign.** In May 1916 a British army crossed the Sinai, reaching the Palestine border at El Arish in December. The force broke through the Gaza-Beersheba defenses in November 1917 after two attempts, took Jerusalem in December, routed the Turks at Megiddo in September 1918, and went on to Damascus and Aleppo. Turkish forces disintegrated. On October 28 Turkey sued for peace.

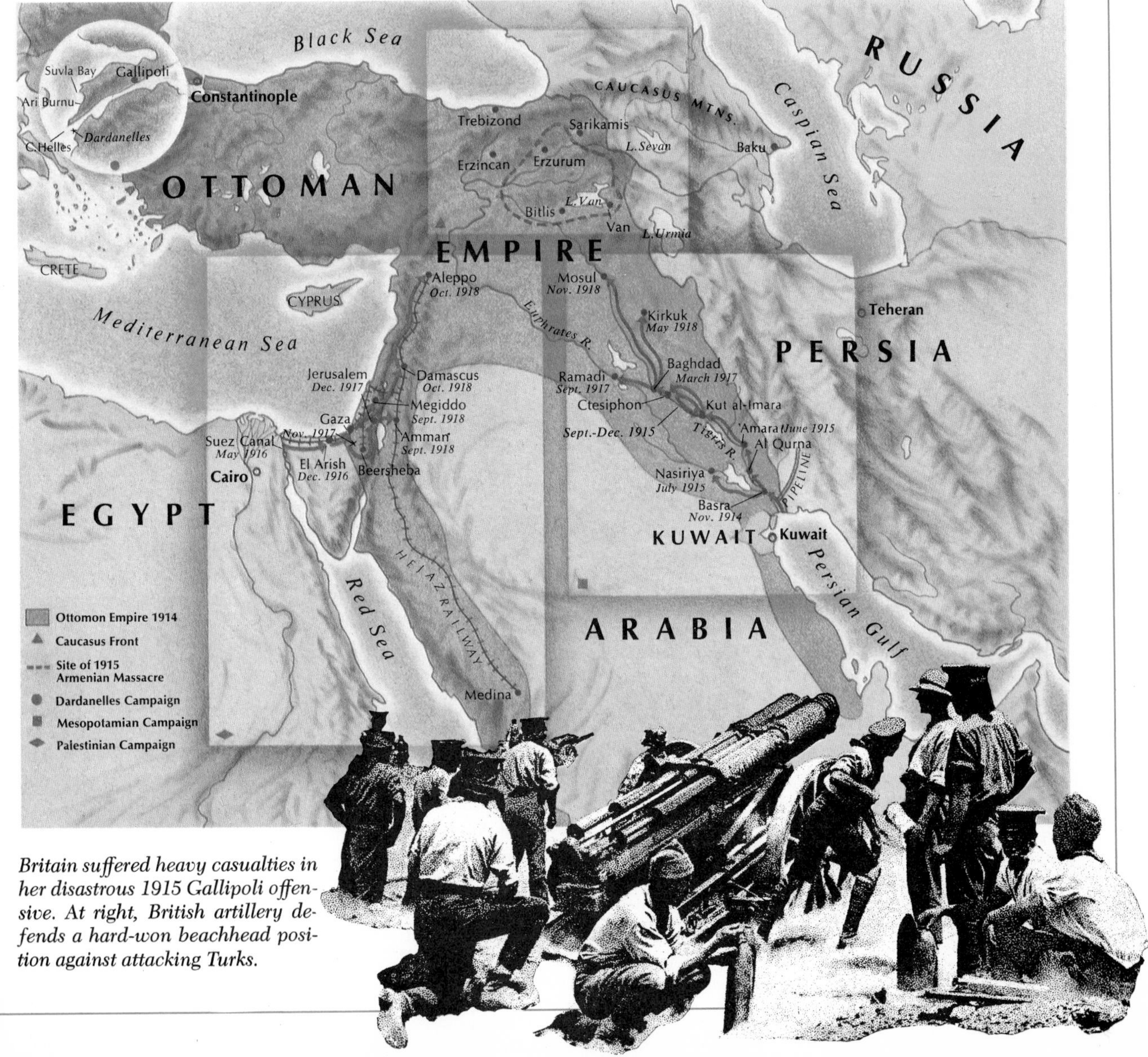

Britain suffered heavy casualties in her disastrous 1915 Gallipoli offensive. At right, British artillery defends a hard-won beachhead position against attacking Turks.

camp, but in the fall of 1915 she cast her lot with Germany, Austria-Hungary, and Turkey. By then Germany's Chief of Staff, Gen. Erich von Falkenhayn, had decided that Serbia must be crushed in order to open overland communications with Turkey. His plans called for a combined German, Austro-Hungarian, and Bulgarian offensive against the tiny Balkan kingdom. On October 6 German and Austro-Hungarian troops under Field Marshal August von Mackensen invaded Serbia from the north, capturing Belgrade two days later. Bulgarian forces attacked from the east October 14. By the end of November the Serbs, who were outnumbered two to one, had begun to retreat, crossing the rugged mountains into neighboring Albania and Montenegro and finally finding refuge on the island of Corfu. The Central Powers went on to invade Montenegro, which surrendered in January 1916.

When the Serbs had observed the massive buildup of enemy troops on their borders in the fall of 1915, they had appealed to the Allies for assistance. On October 5 a small Franco-British force of 13,000 men under French Gen. Maurice Sarrail landed at Salonika, just south of the Serbian border in Greece. Their attempt to advance northward to help the Serbs was blocked by the Bulgarians, however, and the Allies were forced to return to Salonika, where they gradually built up their forces for a future offensive in the Balkans.

SERBIA AND ROMANIA OVERRUN

In October 1915 the Germans, Austrians, and Bulgarians invaded Serbia to open the vital Berlin-Constantinople Railway. By late November the Serbs were retreating across Albania and Montenegro to the Adriatic island of Corfu. An Allied force, which had landed at Salonika, Greece, to aid the Serbs, was turned back by the Bulgarians at Veles. Romania joined the Allies and invaded Transylvania in August 1916 but was crushed by a German counteroffensive in mid-September. Bucharest fell on December 6.

The Brusilov Offensive

With the defeats at Kut al Imara, Gallipoli, and Salonika, Allied fortunes reached a low ebb by the beginning of 1916. On the western front German forces were advancing on Verdun, and their victory seemed at hand (see pp. 108–115). In June, however, a Russian offensive led by Gen. Alexei Brusilov helped revive Allied spirits and forced Falkenhayn to shift German forces from Verdun to the Russian front.

The Russians had been soundly beaten at the Battle of Tannenberg in August 1914, and German forces had driven them beyond the Masurian Lakes near the East Prussian border by the end of the year. The men responsible for this rout, Commander in Chief Gen. Paul von Hindenburg and his Chief of Staff Gen. Erich Ludendorff, acquired enormous prestige for their winning strategy. They ordered a second push in May 1915, taking Warsaw and Brest-Litovsk in August and advancing deep into Russian territory. By October the eastern front ran from Riga, Livonia, in the north, to Czernowitz, Romania, in the south. The Russians had lost all of Lithuania, Kurland, and Poland, as well as the territory previously gained in Galicia. In addition, some 2 million Russian soldiers had been killed, wounded, or taken prisoner; and the remaining forces were critically short of supplies and ammunition.

In the summer of 1916 there were disturbances in Petrograd, caused by Russia's continued battlefield defeats and increasing food shortages. In September Czar Nicholas II dismissed his Commander in Chief, the Grand Duke Nicholas, and assumed personal command of Russia's armed forces. This was a double mistake: It replaced a popular and able commander with a military incompetent, and it insured that if the war continued to go badly, the Czar would bear the blame.

The next six months saw a lull in the fighting, and Russia built up her forces and supplies. Early in 1916 the high command began laying plans for a major summer offensive to coincide with the anticipated British and French assault on the Somme (see p. 112). After the surprise German attack on Verdun in February, however, the French Commander in Chief, Gen. Joseph Joffre, appealed to the Czar for an immediate assault to divert German troops from Verdun to the east. Nicholas II obligingly ordered a frontal assault on German positions near Lake Naroch in northeast Poland. In the abortive 10-day assault the Russians suffered 70,000 casualties, five times the German losses. The attack utterly failed to affect the situation at Verdun and further damaged Russian morale.

THE EASTERN FRONT

On August 17, 1914, the Russian 1st Army invaded East Prussia, engaging German forces in an indecisive battle at Gumbinnen three days later. That same day the Russian 2nd Army invaded farther to the south, and the Germans shifted their forces to meet it, scoring a decisive victory at Tannenberg on August 31. Turning northeastward, the Germans attacked the Russian 1st Army near the Masurian Lakes region September 5–13, driving the Czar's soldiers beyond the Polish frontier. In November the Russians defeated the advancing Germans at Lodz.

Meanwhile, Russia's main forces battled the Austrians in Galicia from August 23 to September 11, penetrating deep within the Austrian border. A successful Austro-German counteroffensive from May 2 to September 30, 1915, drove the Russians 180 miles beyond Warsaw and moved the eastern front back to a line from Riga, Livonia, to Czernowitz, Romania.

On June 4, 1916, the Russian Gen. Alexei Brusilov (inset,above) launched a major offensive against Austria, advancing to the Carpathian Mountains before losing momentum September 20. Russia's last offensive in the summer of 1917 failed, and after the November Bolshevik Revolution the Central Powers moved into Estonia, the Ukraine, and the Crimea. Russia signed an armistice on December 15 and accepted German peace terms on March 3, 1918.

Meanwhile, plans went forward for the summer offensive. The huge assault was to strike along the entire eastern front on July 1. Gen. A. E. Evert's Western Army Group was to make the main effort in the center; the Northern and Southwestern Army Groups would make secondary attacks to fix the Austro-Hungarian forces on their fronts. In mid-May, before the Russian preparations were complete, the Austrians struck the Italians on the Trentino (South Tyrol) front, and the King of Italy begged the Czar for immediate help to divert the Austrians. Evert and the Northern Group were unwilling to risk a premature offensive, but Gen. Alexei Brusilov of the Southwest Army Group agreed to attack in June, if Evert would follow up his lead.

Brusilov began his attack on June 4, virtually shattering the opposing Austro-Hungarian defenses. The offensive continued its advance through September, striking deep into the Carpathian Mountains, despite Evert's failure to provide effective support. Brusilov had earned the distinction of leading the only offensive of the war to be named after its commander.

Brusilov's initial victories had far-reaching effects. They helped relieve the German pressure on Verdun as well as the Austrian pressure on the Italian front. Their success also encouraged Romania to declare war on Austria-Hungary on August 27. She immediately sent troops north to invade Transylvania in southern Hungary, an area of little strategic importance to the Allies but long coveted by the Romanians. By early September they had captured the provincial capital, but a strong counteroffensive drove them back across the border. By early December Bucharest had fallen to the Central Powers, and Romania's army had retreated into the northeastern corner of the country. As a result, the eastern front was extended southward through Romania to the Black Sea, communication between Turkey and her allies was improved, and Romania's rich oil and grain resources fell to the Central Powers.

The strain of Brusilov's offensive brought the Czar's armies to the brink of collapse. Exhaustion and chronic supply shortages weakened the morale of the soldiers. On the homefront, workers and peasants protested the deprivation they were forced to endure. Revolt broke out in the beginning of March 1917, supported by a majority of the Duma and military and civilian leaders, and the garrison troops in Petrograd defied orders to suppress demonstrations of factory workers and women demanding "bread, peace and land." When the Czar tried to return to his capital from army staff headquarters to gain control of the situation, rebellious troops and railwaymen halted his train en route. On March 15 Nicholas II abdicated, and power passed to a moderate provisional government made up of leaders of the recently dissolved Duma and of the soviets (unofficial but representative bodies elected by factories and regiments). In April the Germans, hoping to undermine the war effort, allowed exiled Bolshevik V. I. Lenin to travel through Germany to Russia.

The provisional government, headed by Alexander Kerensky, pledged to continue the war and ordered a new offensive that summer. This time, however, Brusilov's troops were more eager to return home and take advantage of the promised reforms than to continue fighting a frustrating war. Heavy German and Austro-Hungarian counterattacks halted the offensive by August, and the disheartened Russian forces began to disintegrate. Kerensky replaced Brusilov with Gen. Lavr Kornilov, but the military breakdown continued.

The Treaty of Brest-Litovsk

On November 7 Lenin's Bolsheviks came to power with a promise to end the war and secure a peace based on the prewar borders. The new government immediately sent representatives to meet the delegates of Germany and Austria-Hungary at Brest-Litovsk, and an armistice was signed December 15. The subsequent peace conference, however, became deadlocked when the Russians refused to accept the Central Powers' harsh terms. To force their hand, the Germans resumed their offensive February 18, 1918, advancing unresisted into Russian territory. On February 26 the Bolshevik government capitulated, and the Treaty of Brest-Litovsk was signed on March 3. Under its terms Russia renounced her sovereignty over Lithuania and Poland; recognized the independence of the Ukraine, Finland, Estonia, and Latvia; and agreed to cede territory on the Black Sea to Turkey.

The loss of Russian support was a major blow to the Allies. Moreover, in November 1917 another ally, Italy, had been nearly eliminated from the conflict by a devastating defeat at Caporetto. A former partner of Germany and Austria-Hungary in the Triple Alliance, Italy had agreed to enter the war on the side of Britain and France in return for promises of Austrian holdings in the Trentino and northern Dalmatia, the city of Trieste, and several islands in the Adriatic. She declared war on Austria-Hungary on May 23, 1915. (Italy did not declare war on Germany until August 1916.)

Italy's nearly 500-mile frontier with Austria-Hungary permitted only two avenues of attack. One was to the north through the Trentino, a rough, mountainous region, heavily fortified by Austria. The other lay to the east across the Isonzo River, toward the strategic Adriatic port of Trieste. Gen. Count Luigi Cadorna, the Commander in Chief of Italy's forces, chose the latter approach for his major offensive, and in June 1915 he launched the first of 11 assaults on the Isonzo. Although they achieved small advances here and there, the Italians failed to shatter the Austrian defenses and lost approximately a million men. Cadorna suspended the offensive in September 1917.

In mid-1916 an Austrian assault along the Trentino frontier gained as much as 15 miles before it was pushed back by the Italians, strengthened by reinforcements from the Isonzo front. Cadorna's men were less successful against a second Austrian offensive the fol-

Russian and German *soldiers embrace after the signing of an armistice in December 1917. Representatives of the new Bolshevik regime began peace negotiations with the Central Powers at Brest-Litovsk in January 1918 but balked at German demands. A month later the Germans resumed their advance into Russia, continuing until the Bolsheviks capitulated. They signed the Treaty of Brest-Litovsk March 3.*

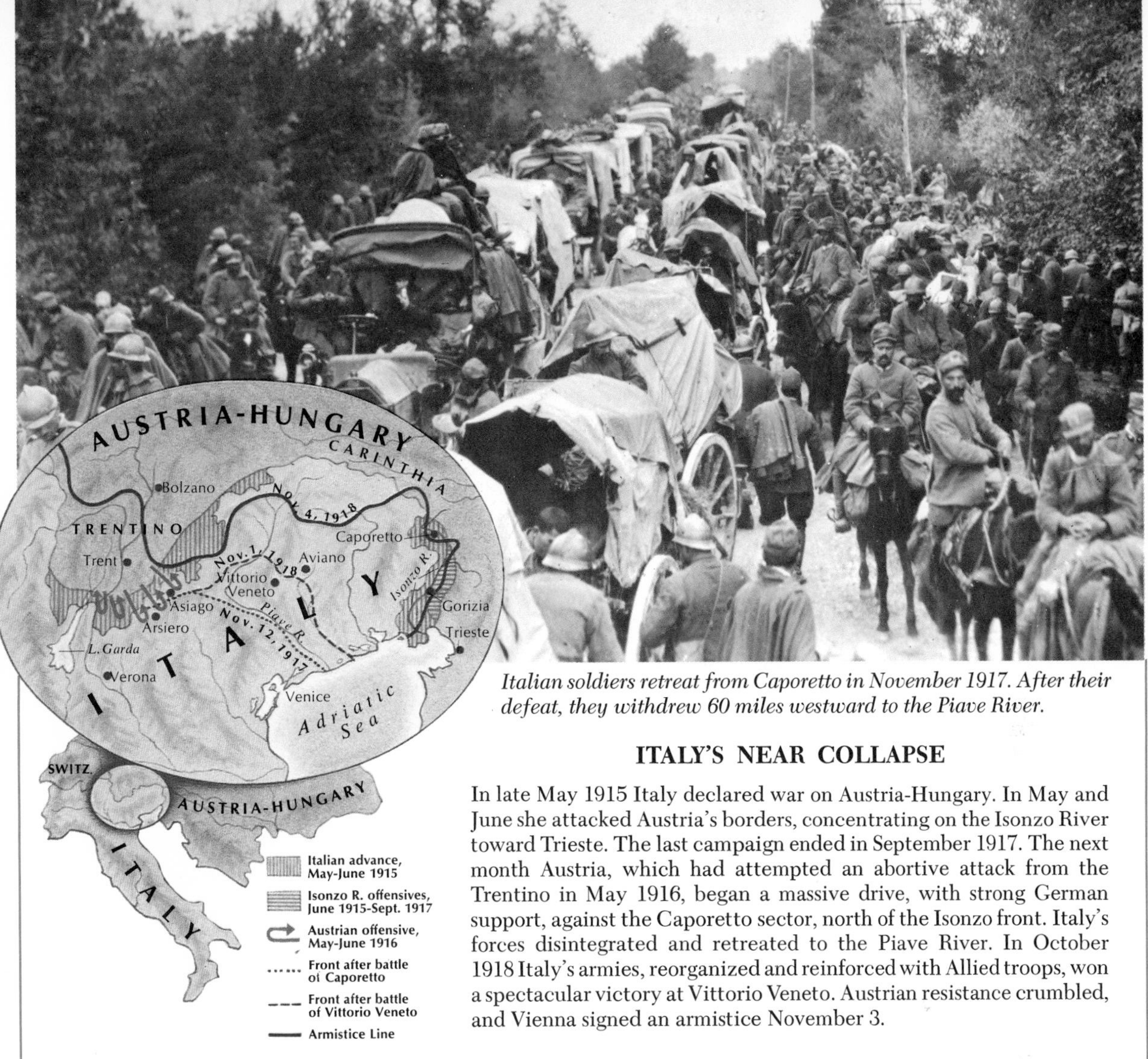

Italian soldiers retreat from Caporetto in November 1917. After their defeat, they withdrew 60 miles westward to the Piave River.

ITALY'S NEAR COLLAPSE

In late May 1915 Italy declared war on Austria-Hungary. In May and June she attacked Austria's borders, concentrating on the Isonzo River toward Trieste. The last campaign ended in September 1917. The next month Austria, which had attempted an abortive attack from the Trentino in May 1916, began a massive drive, with strong German support, against the Caporetto sector, north of the Isonzo front. Italy's forces disintegrated and retreated to the Piave River. In October 1918 Italy's armies, reorganized and reinforced with Allied troops, won a spectacular victory at Vittorio Veneto. Austrian resistance crumbled, and Vienna signed an armistice November 3.

lowing year. This time the Austrians, with German guidance and support, attacked at Caporetto on the Isonzo front. On October 24, barely six weeks after the failure of the 11th Italian offensive, the Austro-German attack opened with a short, intensive barrage, including a high proportion of gas and smoke shells. When the artillery had blinded the Italian defenses, the first wave of German shock troops attacked. The Italians, exhausted and demoralized by months of repeated failure, broke and retreated in disorder, eventually regrouping west of the Piave River by November 12. A total of about 40,000 were killed or wounded, and 275,000 were taken prisoner.

The humiliating defeat at Caporetto, coupled with continued setbacks on other fronts, convinced the Allies that they must act decisively to forestall defeat. England and France rushed reinforcements to Italy. Moreover, meeting at Rapallo, Italy, at the end of 1917, the Allied leaders agreed to create a unified command to coordinate an effective overall strategy. This Supreme War Council would eventually engineer an Allied victory under the aggressive leadership of French Gen. Ferdinand Foch.

At the end of 1917, however, the Allied future looked bleak. They had failed against the Turks at Gallipoli and Kut. They had suffered humiliating setbacks at Caporetto and Salonika. Four former Allies—Russia, Romania, Serbia, and Montenegro—had surrendered to the Central Powers, and a fifth—Italy—was hanging on by a slender thread. But there were indications that the tide was beginning to turn. In November a large British tank force broke through German lines at Cambrai, France. Although the attack was eventually repulsed, the Allies had discovered a way of ending the deadlock on the western front. In December General Allenby's army in Palestine captured Jerusalem and continued victoriously northward. Within a few months the first U.S. troops would reach Europe, bringing the Allies a source of fresh, enthusiastic manpower—and, above all, new hope.

1918

World War I

Part Four: Armistice

Peace finally comes to Europe and the world, as Germany, starving at home and exhausted in battle, is driven to accept the harsh terms of an Allied armistice.

The year 1918 was decisive. Although few could foresee it in January, the fighting that had ravaged Europe and much of the world for four years would end before December. Germany's sweeping spring offensive, by which Gen. Erich Ludendorff hoped to secure a decisive victory, failed to achieve its objective, but a massive Allied counteroffensive that fall finally brought the Kaiser's armies to their knees. Simultaneous Allied drives against the other Central Powers met with equal success, and beginning in late September Bulgaria, Turkey, and Austria-Hungary in turn sought to make peace with the Allies. Germany followed suit, and on November 11 in a railway car in the Forest of Compiègne, France, German delegates signed an armistice ending the war.

At the beginning of 1918, chances for an Allied victory on land seemed remote. At sea, however, their efforts had begun to achieve headway. By the end of 1917 the Allied blockade against Germany was succeeding, and the danger of the Kaiser's deadly submarines had been largely averted. Moreover, Germany's policy of unrestricted submarine warfare had convinced a powerful neutral, the United States, to join forces with the Allies. In the end, the combination of the blockade and U.S. support would tip the scales against the Central Powers.

Britain's wartime blockade of Germany began in August 1914, and the German High Fleet remained bottled up in the Baltic and North Seas for the length of the war. At first Britain's embargo applied only to ships carrying contraband war materials to Germany. At the end of 1914 the Kaiser ordered submarine attacks against British merchant ships, and in February 1915 the Germans declared all British waters a war zone and authorized the sinking on sight of any ship within British waters. In reply, the British Admiralty imposed a blockade on all ships bound for Germany.

German U-boats (from the German *Unterseeboot,* "submarine") destroyed a number of neutral ships bound for Britain, as well as the British luxury liner *Lusitania,* which sank May 7, drowning nearly 1,200 passengers and crew, including 128 U.S. citizens. This act provoked a furor in the United States, and President Woodrow Wilson threatened to enter the war if such attacks were not suspended at once. (It was later disclosed that the ship was actually carrying 173 tons of ammunition.) As a result, Germany called a temporary halt to unlimited U-boat warfare and resumed more conventional surface raids.

In late May 1916 the British and German Fleets clashed in the largest naval contest of the war, the battle known as Jutland to the Allies and Skagerrak to the Germans. The German High Seas Fleet under Adm. Reinhard Scheer had only 99 warships to the 149 vessels of the British Grand Fleet, and Scheer hoped to run the blockade without a showdown with the full British force. His plan was to lure a squadron away from the Grand Fleet, based at the northern Scapa Flow, and overwhelm it before the rest of the fleet could come to its rescue. Adm. Sir John Jellicoe, however, had picked up Scheer's coded wireless orders to his fleet and put to sea with the entire Grand Fleet in an effort to trap and crush Scheer.

The two fleets met off Denmark's Jutland Peninsula in the Skagerrak, the narrow waterway separating the North Sea and the Baltic, on the afternoon of May 31. The battle raged through most of the night and ended in a draw before dawn June 1. Neither side could claim a decisive victory. Although the British losses were double those of the Germans, the British retained strategic mastery of the North Sea. Scheer withdrew his fleet to its Baltic port at Kiel and did not venture out of the Baltic for the duration of the war.

After Jutland, the Germans again turned their attention to limited submarine warfare. Meanwhile, the British tightened their blockade measures and established a Ministry of Blockade to coordinate worldwide surveillance of cargoes bound for Germany. By the beginning of 1917 these measures had effectively stopped the flow of supplies and foodstuffs to the Reich, and Germany's masses were threatened by starvation. It has been estimated that as many as 750,000 German civilians—chiefly the very young, the aged, the poor, and the sickly—did die of disease and starvation as a result of the Allies' blockade.

Armistice Day, 1918: *Jubilant workers in London clambered aboard passing omnibuses, waving flags and banners (left). Men, women, and children danced and sang in the streets of Paris. Huge victory parades marched down New York's Fifth Avenue, and even in Berlin, the capital of defeated Germany, people welcomed the end of the war.*

The situation was so desperate that Gen. Paul von Hindenburg and Ludendorff (who had replaced Germany's top commander, Falkenhayn, in the summer of 1916) finally persuaded the Kaiser to resume unrestricted U-boat attacks against Allied shipping on February 1, 1917. The United States immediately broke diplomatic relations with Germany and armed American merchant vessels operating in the war zones. Soon after, British officials forwarded to President Wilson a telegram they had intercepted from the German Foreign Minister, Arthur Zimmermann, to his Ambassador in Mexico. It asked him to urge Mexico to go to war against the United States and to promise German aid in recapturing the former Mexican territories of Texas, Arizona, and New Mexico if the United States should declare war on Germany. In mid-March German U-boats sank three U.S. merchant ships.

These developments caused President Wilson to abandon his neutral stance, and the United States declared war on Germany April 6, 1917. In his war address to Congress, Wilson stated: "It is a fearful thing to lead this great, peaceful people into war—into the most terrible and disastrous of all wars, civilization itself seeming to be in the balance. But the right is more precious than peace."

The entry of the United States into the war greatly strengthened the Allied hand. The British had already demonstrated the effectiveness of the convoy system, and the U.S. Navy adopted it for transatlantic movements. American factories began turning out submarine-detection devices, depth charges, and mines to arm the ever-increasing number of ships that sped both to the Channel area and the Adriatic. U.S. troops, however, were slow in reaching the European front.

U-BOAT WARFARE: GERMANY'S DESPERATE GAMBLE

By early 1917 the Allied naval blockade (see blue lines on map at left for location of minefields and submarine patrol nets) had cut off the flow of food and supplies to Germany, and the German people faced severe shortages, disease, and starvation. In retaliation, German Chief of Staff Erich Ludendorff decided to resume unlimited U-boat warfare at the risk of provoking U.S. entry into the war, gambling that Germany could thus achieve victory before the United States completed its mobilization. On February 1 German U-boats began sinking Allied and neutral ships on sight. Allied shipping losses multiplied. By April Britain's food supplies were nearly exhausted. But Ludendorff had miscalculated. The United States declared war on April 6, making the blockade virtually total and adding U.S. naval strength to the antisubmarine campaign. By year's end the U-boat danger had abated. Germany's fate was sealed.

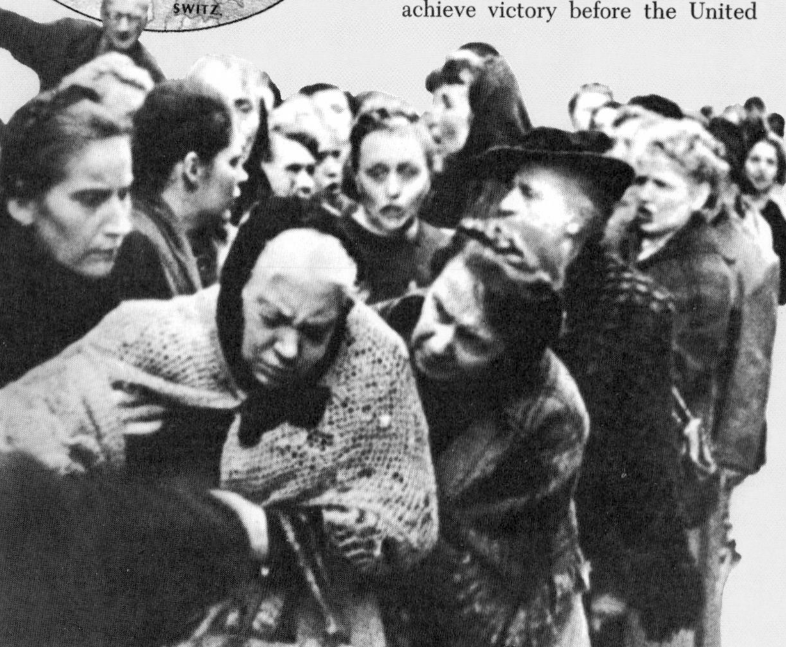

"U-boats go forth!" urges a German poster during the final effort to end the blockade and the long food lines (left) that it produced throughout Germany.

When war was declared, the U.S. Army numbered only 190,000 men, scattered in small units across the country. Selective Service was introduced in May 1917, but it took at least 6 months to process and train the recruits and another 30 days to transport them to their new posts. By March 1, 1918, almost a year after Congress declared war on Germany, there were only six U.S. divisions in France.

Germany's Final Offensive

Ludendorff, realizing that Germany must strike before U.S. troop strength had been built up, decided to attempt to destroy the British Expeditionary Force (BEF), which he considered the most dangerous force in Europe. By the early spring of 1918, German troops released from the eastern front after the collapse of Russia in November 1917 had reached the western lines, relatively fresh after weeks of rest and reoutfitting in Germany. Combined with his existing western front forces, they gave Ludendorff a total of 3,600,000 men for his final push. Against this, the Allies could muster a total of 3,400,000 soldiers, giving the Germans a slight manpower edge.

The Germans had the additional advantage of a unified command. The Allied front, on the other hand, was divided into two sectors, with the British armies defending the northern one in Artois and Flanders and the French holding the southern lines in Champagne. Moreover, in recent months the British had agreed to extend their front another 25 miles to the south. The French had built only sketchy defenses in this area, and the British had neither the manpower nor the time to complete them. To make matters worse, Prime Minister David Lloyd George, fearing a renewal of the futile slaughter of 1917, had refused to comply with British Commander in Chief Gen. Douglas Haig's repeated requests for reinforcements to replace the heavy losses his armies had sustained in 1917.

Ludendorff's strategy was to strike at the weakest part of the British defenses, separate the British forces from the French, and push the British back to the Channel coast, where they would be trapped. The key to success was a totally new method of assault, devised by Gen. Oskar von Hutier and first employed with tremendous success against the Russians at Riga in September 1917 and a month later against the Italians at Caporetto. Since the end of 1914, the war along the western front had been stalemated because neither side had devised a successful means of breaking through a well-organized defensive position and then maintaining the momentum of the attack. As a result, despite ever more elaborate and costly offensives, for three years the front had not moved more than a few miles in either direction. Hutier's brilliant tactical innovations were designed to break this impasse and restore the offensive to its rightful position.

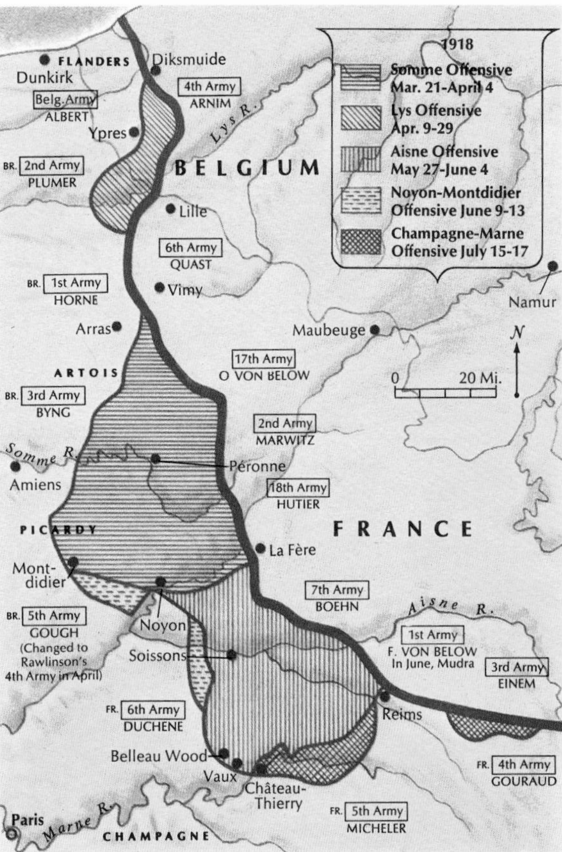

LUDENDORFF'S FINAL CAMPAIGN

On March 21, 1918, the Germans began their last offensive, shattering British-held lines between Arras and La Fère, but their advance was halted two weeks later by supply delays. On April 9 they struck again, in the Lys sector to the north near Ypres, denting—but not quite breaking—the British lines. The Allies stopped this advance on April 29. The third German assault began in the Aisne-Marne sector on May 27 and reached as far as Château-Thierry. A fourth drive on June 9 gained only nine miles, and the next push made even smaller gains. On July 18 the Allies launched a counterthrust, and two days later Ludendorff suspended his offensive.

Instead of the usual lengthy preliminary bombardment followed by a massive infantry charge against the enemy's front positions, Hutier suggested a brief but intensive artillery shelling, using large quantities of smoke and gas shells to render the defenders temporarily helpless. After about five hours of shelling, the German artillery began firing a rolling barrage, starting at the enemy front line and moving steadily forward at a rate of approximately one kilometer per hour. The leading infantry divisions, composed of handpicked, specially trained shock troops, followed the barrage as closely as possible, along routes that would take them between known enemy strongpoints. This portion of the attack was carefully controlled by the commanding general, but once the artillery had reached the limit of its range and ceased firing, regimental and battalion commanders took over, advancing as rapidly as possible in preassigned general directions. The shock troops bypassed strong centers of enemy resistance, leaving them to be mopped up by special units designated and equipped for that purpose. Small combat infantry teams, heavily armed with light machineguns and light field artillery, followed immediately behind the shock troops.

Hutier's system gave the Germans a new tactical flexibility that fully exploited the initiative and professional competence of the German officers. Its major weakness would prove to be Germany's lack of sufficient horses and motor vehicles to keep supplies, ammunition, and artillery moving steadily forward to support the advancing infantry.

The Allies were expecting a last-ditch German offensive in the spring. Haig and his French counterpart, Gen. Henri Pétain, had developed plans for sending troops to strengthen each other's lines when the attack came. Haig, who was fully confident that his soldiers would be able to repulse the anticipated German onslaught, boasted on March 2: "I am only afraid that the enemy [will] find our front so very strong that he will hesitate to commit his army to the attack. . . ."

Backs to the Wall

Ludendorff's great offensive opened before dawn on March 21, 1918, with a massive artillery bombardment along a 40-mile stretch of the British front between Arras and La Fère. Just before 10 a.m., the first wave of German shock troops swept forward. The effect was devastating. By the end of the day the British defenses had been shattered along the entire front. The German 18th Army under Hutier, which attacked the southern third of the front, achieved the most spectacular advances. On March 27 his troops took Montdidier, breaking through between the French and British armies. Hutier had outrun his supplies, however, and his men were exhausted. With some rather grudging help from the French, the British were able to seal the gap. The other two German armies, attacking on Hutier's right (northern) flank, were less ably led and faced stronger British defenses. There Haig's forces managed to hold the Germans to smaller gains.

An important consequence of the Germans' swift success was the appointment of a Supreme Allied Commander. The British had originally opposed such a development, but in the face of the German drive and Pétain's reluctance to divert French troops northward to assist the British, Haig backed down and offered to subordinate his command to French Gen. Ferdinand

The war in the air: *A 1919 painting by British artist G. H. Davis shows a German hunting pack* (Jagdstaffel) *of Fokker triplanes and D-VII's closing in on a squadron of British DH9A bombers flying in tight formation. Such aerial scenes were common only in the last year of the war, when the colorful dogfights of individual aces were replaced by combat formations of as many as 50 aircraft. Planes also strafed and bombed enemy positions during major ground offensives.*

U.S. infantrymen leave their troopship *at Brest, France, in April 1918 (left). Young, spirited, and eager to fight, they pumped fresh vitality into the war-weary Allied Armies.*

Foch "or some other determined general who will fight." On April 14 Foch was officially named Commander in Chief of the Allied Forces.

Meanwhile, Ludendorff pressed his advantage, striking in the north near Ypres April 9. The Germans broke through a sector that was held by a Portuguese division and advanced westward. (Portugal, a traditional friend of Britain, had joined the Allies in 1916.) A second thrust to the north the next day met with equal success, and the two German armies joined up and drove the British and their allies toward the Channel. With the help of reinforcements, the British managed to halt the offensive by April 29. The two drives had cost the Allies about 400,000 men. The Germans had lost about 350,000, most of whom were members of the elite shock troops and could not be replaced.

On May 27 the Germans began a third drive in the south against the French position along the Aisne River. Never losing sight of his primary objective, Ludendorff planned this thrust as a diversionary tactic to draw the French reinforcements—and possibly some British troops—from the northern end of the front, so that he might deliver a decisive blow against the depleted BEF in Flanders. The Germans easily broke through the French lines, advancing 13 miles in the first day. By May 30 they had reached the Marne near Château-Thierry, barely 37 miles from Paris, and Foch rushed reinforcements to the area. One division of Gen. John J. Pershing's American Expeditionary Forces (AEF) managed to prevent the Germans from crossing the river at Château-Thierry, while a second U.S. division counterattacked and broke through the bulge of the German position north of the Marne around Belleau Wood and Vaux.

To exploit his advantage, the German commander decided to mount two more diversionary offensives in the Aisne-Marne sector before launching a decisive assault against the BEF in the north. The first of these, which began June 9, gained nine miles but was stopped after three days by a fierce Franco-American counterattack. The second, which opened July 15 after a month-long lull in the fighting caused by a crippling influenza epidemic, was equally unsuccessful, and the Germans were halted two days later after managing to advance only four miles.

The failure of the July 15 offensive, which Ludendorff's men optimistically dubbed the *Friedensturm* (peace offensive), badly damaged German morale, already weakened by the month of inaction and the flu epidemic. Their spirit was finally broken by an Allied counteroffensive, which began July 18. On July 20 Ludendorff called off his planned attack on the BEF in Flanders. His final offensive had collapsed.

"The Black Day of the German Army"

The Allied counterstroke was remarkably well timed. By July the U.S. troop buildup in Europe was in full swing, and as many as 300,000 men were arriving per month. (Each U.S. division was at least twice the strength of the average French and British divisions.) Their presence, coupled with the disintegration of morale and discipline among the German armies, gave the Allies a decisive edge.

At the suggestion of French Gen. Charles Mangin, Foch ordered an initial thrust to regain the Aisne-Marne salient, which the Germans had overrun during their third and fourth offensives. On July 18 four French armies, including eight U.S., four British, and

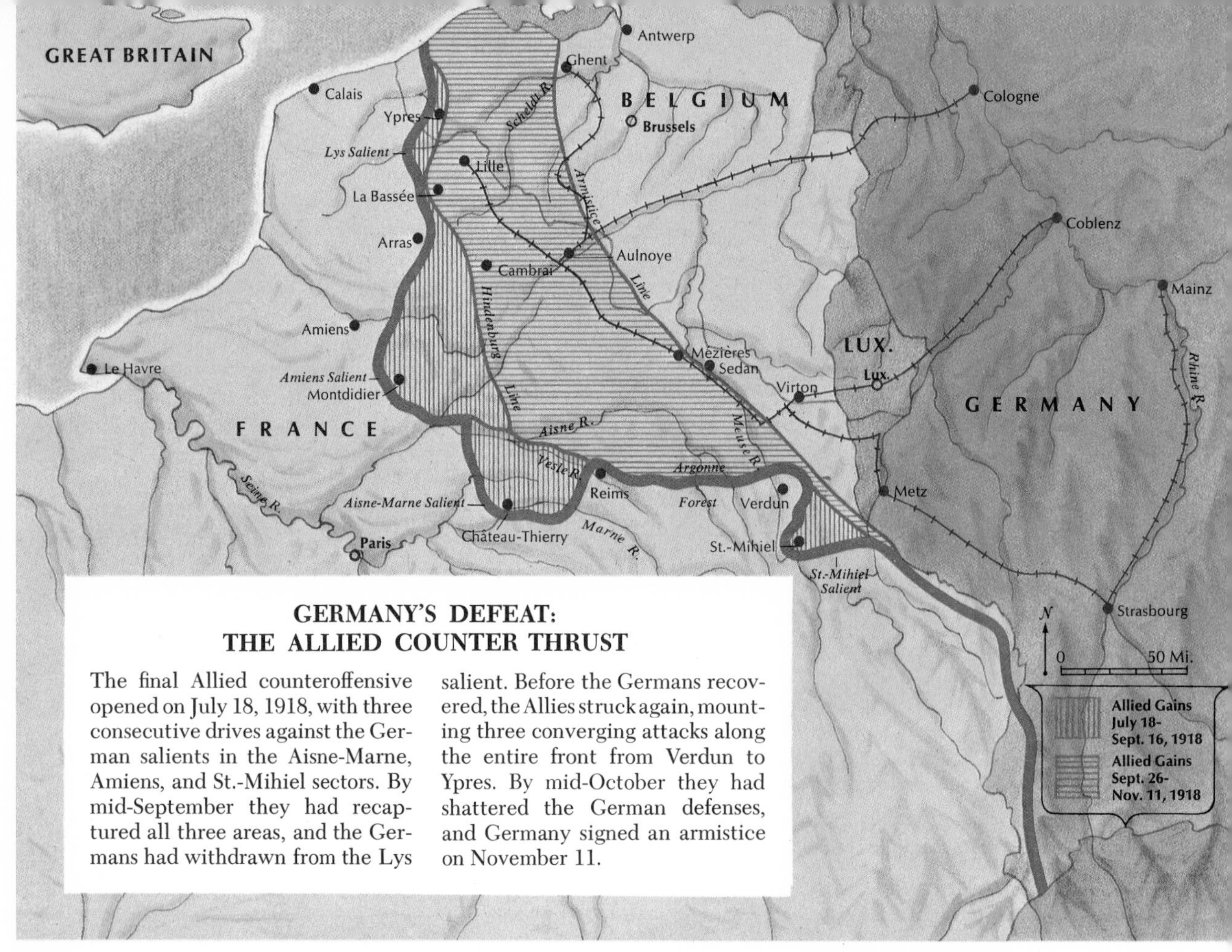

GERMANY'S DEFEAT: THE ALLIED COUNTER THRUST

The final Allied counteroffensive opened on July 18, 1918, with three consecutive drives against the German salients in the Aisne-Marne, Amiens, and St.-Mihiel sectors. By mid-September they had recaptured all three areas, and the Germans had withdrawn from the Lys salient. Before the Germans recovered, the Allies struck again, mounting three converging attacks along the entire front from Verdun to Ypres. By mid-October they had shattered the German defenses, and Germany signed an armistice on November 11.

two Italian divisions, attacked the salient from all sides. The French 10th Army under General Mangin was to launch the decisive attack against the northern German flank. His advance, which was preceded by a force of 350 tanks, met with considerable success. By August 6 the Germans had retreated behind the Vesle River in a methodical and orderly manner. The Allies had successfully eliminated the Aisne-Marne salient, and in recognition of his important achievements Foch was promoted to marshal.

The Allies moved quickly to exploit their advantage. On August 8, the date Ludendorff later called "the black day of the German Army," more than 20 divisions of British, Australian, Canadian, French, and U.S. troops, supported by more than 400 tanks, struck against German positions near Amiens. The Germans, who had not been expecting the assault, collapsed. By the beginning of September, the Allies had forced them back to the Hindenburg Line, their position before the spring offensive. Realizing that Germany could no longer hope to win the war, Ludendorff advised the Kaiser to seek peace negotiations. Meanwhile, Ludendorff would try to maintain his country's bargaining position by continuing to defend Germany's lines along the western front.

On September 12 the U.S. 1st Army, which included a few French units, began eliminating a third salient, which the Germans had held since 1914, in the area of St.-Mihiel in Champagne. The Germans had already begun to withdraw from the area, but the attack caught them by surprise. The Americans advanced quickly against weak resistance, managing to clear the entire salient in only 36 hours.

To Pershing's great dismay, Foch refused to let the Americans continue their advance, which had completely shattered the German defenses. Instead, at Haig's request, Foch ordered the AEF to strike northward, against the heavily fortified Argonne sector, to the west of Verdun, in order to support a renewed British offensive in the Amiens sector to the north.

Allied Victory and Armistice

Ten days later, on September 26, the Allies began the second phase of their offensive. Some 220 divisions attacked almost simultaneously at points along the entire front, beginning with a U.S.-French assault in the Meuse-Argonne. The next day 40 British divisions (with two U.S. divisions attached) struck to the north against the Hindenburg Line, and on the following day King Albert's 28 divisions (Belgian, British, U.S., and

French) mounted an attack in Flanders. German resistance withered under these successive blows, which strained their already exhausted strength to the limit. Slowly and steadily the Allies advanced, forcing the Germans back to the Scheldt River in the north and to Sedan in the south; but the Germans thwarted Allied attempts to cut off their lines of retreat. Realizing defeat was imminent, Ludendorff informed the Imperial Council of War on September 29 that Germany must seek an armistice on the basis of U.S. President Woodrow Wilson's Fourteen Points, a general platform for a peace settlement of mutual justice, which Wilson had proclaimed earlier in the year.

Meanwhile, Germany's allies were beginning to give way. Bulgaria was the first to seek an armistice, after an Allied force under French Gen. Louis Franchet d'Esperey marched north from its base at Salonika, Greece (Greece had joined the Allies in November 1916), and shattered Bulgarian defenses. Bulgaria signed a truce September 30. Turkey sued for peace a month later, after British forces under Gen. Sir Edmund Allenby had captured Damascus and Beirut, and a second British army had advanced deep into Asia Minor from Baghdad.

On October 24 the Italians, with considerable French and British support, began a concerted counteroffensive against the Austrians at Vittorio Veneto, and Austrian resistance crumbled. The enormous Dual Monarchy whose quarrel with Serbia had precipitated the war was on the brink of collapse. In mid-1918 the empire's Czech and Slovak, Polish, Yugoslav, Hungarian, and German minorities began pressing for independence, and on October 1 their representatives in the Vienna Reichstag had voted in favor of independence for each national group. A few weeks later they began setting up separate governments, and the Emperor belatedly renounced his sovereignty over the fragmented Hapsburg realm. On November 3 Austria signed an armistice with the Allies.

Germany herself was dangerously close to the breaking point. On October 3 the Kaiser appointed Prince Max von Baden Chancellor in the hope of creating a stable constitutional regime to replace Ludendorff's virtual dictatorship. But it was too late. Germany's war-strained population blamed the Kaiser for their country's misguided policy. During the lengthy negotiations following Prince Max's October 3 request to President Wilson for an armistice, mutiny broke out among sailors in the High Seas Fleet at Kiel, and revolt spread throughout the country. Workers' and soldiers' councils appeared in cities and along the front, and on November 7 Bavaria proclaimed the establishment of a Socialist Republic. Two days later Prince Max announced the Kaiser's abdication and then handed in his own resignation, asking Friedrich Ebert, a Social Democrat, to form a provisional government. Ludendorff had already resigned on October 27. On November 10 Kaiser Wilhelm II boarded a train to begin his exile in the Netherlands.

The next morning representatives of Germany and the Allied Powers concluded an armistice in a railway carriage in the Forest of Compiègne, France, north of Paris. Germany agreed to relinquish all conquered territory, to evacuate her troops to the west bank of the Rhine, to dismantle her fortifications in the Rhineland, and to surrender her fleet and the bulk of her war arsenal. At 11 a.m. on the 11th day of the 11th month of 1918 the Great War was over. Along the western front and in cities throughout Europe and much of the world, there was general rejoicing. At last the fighting had stopped, but the scars it left behind would linger, disfiguring the face of Europe for decades to come.

*"**To my son,** Since your eyes were closed mine have not ceased to weep." This simple and poignant message, etched on a plaque in the wall of Fort Vaux near Verdun, expresses the universal grief of parents, families, and sweethearts throughout Europe for the men who died in the fighting. Their countless graves dot the countryside of northern France and Belgium, haunting reminders of the war's terrible toll. More than 8 million soldiers were killed, and millions more were seriously wounded. For them and their loved ones, peace came too late.*

1917

Revolution in Russia: Lenin Seizes Power

After a riot-filled, rumor-torn summer the Bolsheviks seize power in Petrograd and establish the first Marxist state.

For weeks Petrograd had been gray and dreary, and its citizens had hurried about their tasks in bone-chilling rain and drizzle. But October 25,* 1917, dawned cold and clear. The sun shone on the Smolny Institute, until recently a finishing school for the daughters of Imperial Russia's aristocracy. Men in ragtag uniforms lounged against its imposing walls, whispering together or watching the constant flow of people. Inside, however, all was pandemonium.

There men with mud on their boots milled about. Most were members of the Petrograd Soviet of Workers and Soldiers' Deputies, a semiparliamentary body made up of representatives of factory workers and army units. Others, who arrived in increasing numbers as the day wore on, were members of similar soviets scattered throughout Russia. They were converging on the capital for a crucial meeting scheduled for that evening: the Second All-Russian Congress of Soviets.

These soviets had held a peculiar position since the overthrow of the Czar and the establishment of a provisional government seven months earlier. Officially they had no role in the new government, but in reality they had become the focus of power. As direct representatives of the armed workers and soldiers they had come to exert a far greater effect on the tide of events than the provisional government itself. As the year of revolution was drawing to a close, the Petrograd Soviet, the strongest and most influential of these bodies, and many of the other soviets in other cities and towns were on a collision course with the provisional government. Already troops and militia under the command of the Petrograd group had seized control of numerous public buildings and essential services in the capital. Before the dawning of October 26 the delegates assembling in the Smolny would witness and ratify the accession to power of a band of visionaries intent upon destroying the old oppressive order and creating the world's first socialist republic.

Some of the men in the Smolny that day wore the simple garments of factory workers, and some were shod in the felt boots of peasants. But the overall impression was one of drab army gray, for Russia was well into the fourth year of World War I, a war of disasters that had brought little but humiliating defeat, unimagined casualties, mass starvation, and revolution.

For Russia World War I was the death knell of an era. She was suffering the heaviest losses of all the Allies in the World War, and her troops were seriously demoralized, sometimes to the point of mutiny. Compared to the rest of Europe, Russia was a backward country; her industrial revolution had hardly begun. She was ill-equipped to supply and feed a vast army.

Although the serfs had been emancipated in 1861, the roots of serfdom were strong. Peasants still paid tribute to the landlords, who often took half of the crops. One-third of the peasants had no land.

The 1905 revolution had had few lasting effects. Czar Nicholas II retained all power as Czar of all the Russias; the Dumas he allowed to be formed were mere gestures toward parliamentary government. By 1917 the people were demoralized, the military restless and poorly led, and the food shortage extreme. The focus of the national tumult was Petrograd, where in 1917 two exiles, Vladimir Ilyich Lenin and Leon Trotsky, returned to direct the revolutionary movement.

A Battle for Bread Helps Topple the Czar

With a population of more than 160 million at his command, Czar Nicholas II had little difficulty in amassing an army of more than 12 million with which

*All dates refer to the Julian calendar used in Russia until 1918. It was 13 days behind the Gregorian calendar used in the West.

***Protesting workers** scattered and died when Alexander Kerensky sent the Petrograd police against them in July 1917. But repression only brought more defections to the Bolsheviks and hastened the day of all-out revolution.*

***In a painting** of the early 1920's, Lenin addresses an enthralled crowd of workers and peasants. The work is an altered version of an earlier painting by Russian artist Valentin Serov: Stalin and Trotsky have been painted in behind Lenin to show the solidarity of the Communist leadership. In fact, Stalin was already plotting to remove Trotsky from his place in the Politburo. Lenin's wife, Krupskaya, is shown in the foreground in a white shawl.*

Terror stalks the streets of Moscow in an anticzarist view of the massacres that followed the 1905 revolt.

BLOODY SUNDAY AND THE 1905 REVOLUTION

A grisly prelude to the October Revolution of 1917 was the abortive uprising that followed the Russo-Japanese War in 1905 (see pp. 32–37). It began on Sunday, January 9, when about 200,000 impoverished Russian workers rallied to demonstrate before the Czar's Winter Palace in St. Petersburg. Their leader was Father Georgi Gapon, a priest and well-known labor organizer. His followers carried a petition bearing these demands: the formation of a constituent assembly, the reduction of the working day to eight hours, and a minimum daily wage—for all workers—of one ruble.

The marchers gathering in the streets were unarmed and orderly—many sang hymns, carried icons, and joined in the anthem "God Save the Czar." But a spate of strikes had made the city's atmosphere tense. Phalanxes of soldiers and police appeared, ordering the crowds to disperse. When the workers refused to move, the troops opened fire, killing possibly as many as 500 and wounding hundreds more.

The news of what came to be known as Bloody Sunday electrified Russia. Millions of workers went on strike, and popular local councils (soviets) sprang up in many cities. The Czar's reaction was both shrewd and ruthless. First he wooed popular support away from the soviets with the liberal concessions in his October Manifesto; then he arrested the St. Petersburg Soviet en masse and smashed an armed uprising in Moscow. The 1905 revolution was ended, but from its unhealed wounds another, bloodier revolution would erupt 12 years later.

to battle the Germans and Austrians in World War I, which Russia entered in 1914. But how to transport such a mass of humanity, organize it into effective fighting units, arm and supply it from Russia's infant industries, and feed it were problems much too complex for Nicholas and his backward-looking advisers. From Russia's hard-pressed allies in the West, Britain and France, little help could be expected. Within months of the declaration of war Russian troops were on the defensive. Time and again Russian armies launched desperate attacks, only to be thrown back by the entrenched foe, whose superiority in firepower and tactical skill more than outweighed its inferiority in numbers. By early 1917 enemy forces had occupied most of the Czar's westernmost provinces and had struck deep into Russia. More than 9 million of Russia's sons had been killed, wounded, or taken prisoner.

Czar Nicholas, a weak-willed, slow-witted man, was dominated by his wife, Alexandra. Regal in appearance, deeply religious, the Czarina had one overriding ambition: to pass on total control of the empire to her hemophiliac son, the Czarevich. To this end she had long sought the advice of Grigori Rasputin, the "mad monk." He was a peasant and an eloquent, if poorly educated, drunken, filth-encrusted, lecherous, self-proclaimed holy man—but with an uncanny ability to ease the young Czarevich's suffering during his bleeding attacks. By the time the war began, Rasputin's influence over the Czarina, and through her the Czar, was virtually complete. On December 17, 1916, Rasputin was murdered by outraged aristocrats.

About two months before he was killed, Rasputin had prophesied Russia's revolution and civil war. The cataclysm began with a small incident. Throughout the winter the poor of Petrograd had suffered from an increasingly severe food shortage. On February 23, 1917, when the women of the city found that bakers were demanding still higher prices for bread, they began demonstrating against the regime. Hundreds of railway and factory workers carrying red flags marched through the streets with the women, demanding relief and an end to war.

The shock troops of the Czar, the Cossack cavalry, rode through the crowds, swinging clubs and whips to disperse the demonstrators. But to the experienced observer their old bloodlust seemed lacking. The next day, February 24, some 200,000 workers took to the streets, and the Cossacks, outraged by the slaughter of their comrades at the front and the suffering of the people at home, refused even a pretense of action.

When, on the 26th, a small unit of loyal troops was at last found to fire on the still rampaging crowds, other soldiers mutinied in army barracks throughout the city. They joined the throngs on the streets, and officers who tried to stem the tide were shot by their own men. The Czar ordered the Duma dissolved, but its usually compliant members refused to disperse and instead formed a provisional executive committee that claimed powers to restore order. That same day the Petrograd Soviet was reactivated to represent the local soldiers, sailors, and factory workers. This soviet would soon become a rival to the Duma committee for power and finally the agent of destruction of Russia's nascent parliamentary government.

To Czar Nicholas, who was with his troops at the front, the events in Petrograd seemed remote and unimportant. But very soon the Czar was forced to respond. On March 1, hearing that Moscow had allied itself with Petrograd in the revolution, he dispatched a handpicked force to pacify that city. But again the troops defected and joined the people they were ordered to subdue.

On March 2, 1917, abandoned by his troops, faced with demands for his abdication, and weary both in mind and body, Nicholas II, the last Czar of All the Russias, abdicated in favor of his brother, who refused succession to the throne the next day. The centuries-old Romanov dynasty slipped into history's shadows, emerging briefly in July 1918, when the captured royal family fell before a Bolshevik firing squad.

The abdication of the Czar cleared the way for the formation of Russia's provisional government, its ministers drawn from the leadership of the Duma. Nominally headed by Prince Lvov, a politically moderate nobleman, the regime was actually controlled by its most dynamic member, a moderate Socialist named Alexander Kerensky. His influence among the workers and his membership in the Petrograd Soviet gave him an unchallengeable authority—at least for a time. But Kerensky's attempt to establish a parliamentary-style democracy failed. It was a paper-thin facade of Western forms tacked on the decaying Russian state, and its members were involved in a complex charade in which the appearance of power substituted for the real power that was flowing into the hands of the soviets.

Enter Lenin

Vladimir Ilyich Ulyanov, known to his Bolshevik comrades and posterity as V. I. Lenin, was a steely-eyed intellectual of the revolutionary left. Born in 1870, the son of a school inspector, he was early attracted to leftwing movements. Lenin's brothers and sisters were also involved in radical groups and his older brother was executed for participating in a plot to assassinate Czar Alexander III. Lenin became thoroughly dedicated to the destruction of czarism and the creation of a socialist society. Twice arrested and twice exiled for his revolutionary activities, Lenin left Russia in 1900 but returned in 1905 to Petrograd (then St. Petersburg) for a stay of two years.

By the early 1900's Lenin's name was both respected and feared in radical circles. In 1903 his intransigence had split the Russian Social Democratic Party, then meeting in London, into two distinct factions. Ever militant, Lenin was an elitist who demanded that the party be organized along conspiratorial lines and its membership limited to dedicated revolutionaries prepared to follow orders with unquestioning obedience. Those who agreed with him came to be called Bolsheviks (from the Russian word for "majority"). His opponents, who wished to create a revolutionary mass movement closely linked to trade unions and following

THE MAD MONK

"Just a good, religious, simple-minded Russian," the Czar called him, but history would make the name Grigori Rasputin a synonym for evil. This self-styled holy man (actually an itinerant Siberian peasant) made use of his lowly status to pose as a spokesman for the masses. His hypnotic personality and reputed healing powers won him favor with the Czarina Alexandra and allowed him to influence the Czar's choice of men for important posts at court. In 1916 a few aristocrats, convinced that Rasputin was responsible for the decay of the Russian monarchy, conspired to murder him. The "mad monk" died slowly: Poison and two gunshots failed to kill him, and he was finally drowned in the Neva River.

Rasputin's power over Alexandra lay in his ability to alleviate the suffering of her son, a hemophiliac. Above: the royal family.

Monuments of imperial power: Clockwise from the far end of Nevsky Prospect were: the Admiralty (1), War Ministry (2), Winter Palace (3), Peter and Paul Fortress (4), the domed Tauride Palace (5), and the Smolny Institute (6).

an open program of reform, were called Mensheviks ("minority"). For them Lenin had only scorn.

World War I found Lenin in neutral Switzerland. There he wrote stirring articles for revolutionary journals, urging the workers to overthrow the Czar. When, to Lenin's surprise, the Czar was indeed toppled, the Bolshevik leader's thoughts turned toward the seemingly insoluble problem of traversing Germany and the German-occupied territory that separated him from Petrograd. Then the unlikely happened. The German imperial government, sensing that this revolutionary might lead a powerful movement to force Russia out of the war, permitted Lenin to return there via Germany. There is also a strong probability that German money found its way into Bolshevik hands.

Lenin arrived at Petrograd's Finland Station on April 3, 1917, and was almost overwhelmed by cheering well-wishers. Speaking to the crowd in a voice filled with ardor, he called for "worldwide socialist revolution." The next day he formally characterized Kerensky's provisional government as "imperialistic through and through," and demanded its overthrow in favor of a "republic of soviets. . . ."

To challenge the government was one thing; to overthrow it, another. Even in the Petrograd Soviet Lenin's Bolsheviks still constituted a small minority. But the program he espoused was one that found a ready response among the war-weary soldiers, the hungry workers, and the land-poor peasants.

In adopting the slogan "Peace, Bread, and Land," Lenin was promising the very things the provisional government could not, tied as it was to the Western Allies—who by then included the United States—by treaty obligations, massive loans, and bonds of honor. During 1917 conditions at the front deteriorated as increasing numbers of units mutinied or deserted. Kerensky's desperate gamble of an offensive along the southern front resulted in a disastrous retreat.

As in the army, so too in the cities and in the countryside. In Petrograd and Moscow runaway inflation, a worsening shortage of flour, and a breakdown in transportation was making bread as valuable as gold. On the vast estates where hired peasants tilled the soil, the word "revolution" meant land reform. Although the government was pledged to a legal redistribution of land, it refused to take decisive action.

The peasants, spurred on by revolutionary agitators, took matters into their own hands, burning down manor houses, driving off or murdering what nobles they could find, and seizing the land for their own.

PETROGRAD: HOST TO A REVOLUTION

On the night of October 25, 1917, Russia's rumor-haunted summer ended as Petrograd moved toward its strangely nonviolent revolution. People flowed onto Nevsky Prospect seeking information, banding together more out of curiosity than with any intent to demonstrate.

The ***Aurora,*** a Russian cruiser lying at anchor in the Neva River, played a key part in the Bolsheviks' carefully laid plans. Small military units had occupied Dvortsovy Bridge, the State Bank, power-houses, railroad stations, and the central telephone exchange since about 6 a.m. on October 25. That night the *Aurora* fired blank shots over the column in Palace Square to signal the attack on the Winter Palace. Cadres of Cossacks and officer cadets lined up to restrain the huge crowds assembling in the square, including armed members of the Bolshevik Red Guard.

The defenders were under orders from Kerensky's provisional government, which throughout the evening had waited desperately for reinforcements. None arrived. At the *Aurora's* signal the attackers broke through the outnumbered guards and charged into the opulent **Winter Palace,** whereupon the officials surrendered at once. They had no other option: Had they offered resistance, the palace would have come under attack from the cannons of the

Peter and Paul Fortress, taken earlier by the Bolsheviks.

In control of the coup was V. I. Lenin, mastermind of the revolution. Appropriately, he was attending the Second All-Russian Congress of Soviets, which ratified the revolution, meeting at the prestigious **Smolny Institute.**

Amid this chaotic atmosphere Lenin's tiny Bolshevik Party readily found support for a new upheaval. And it was soon to find its most powerful propagandist.

"All Power to the Soviets"

Lev Davidovich Bronstein, known as Leon Trotsky, was born in southern Russia in 1879, the son of a prosperous Jewish farmer. He was barely in his teens when he organized a strike of his father's employees. Like Lenin, he was twice arrested and imprisoned by the Czarist police. Between imprisonments he became well known in radical circles. When word of the February revolution reached him, Trotsky was editing a Russian émigré newspaper in New York. On May 4, 1917, he returned to Petrograd.

Trotsky, although he had in the past differed strongly with Lenin on party structure and theory, was now in full political agreement with him, and in a short time became one of Lenin's closest associates. After his election to the Petrograd Soviet Trotsky used his awesome powers of persuasion to overthrow the provisional government. He and Lenin united in the slogan, "All Power to the Soviets."

Initially this slogan seemed an odd one for the Bolsheviks to endorse. At the first All-Russian Congress of Soviets, held in Petrograd between June 3 and June 24, 1917, the Bolsheviks occupied only 137 seats out of 1,090. But in that mercurial atmosphere today's Menshevik might be tomorrow's Bolshevik. Pressure from street demonstrations, protests in factories, and army unrest made for rapidly shifting alliances. On July 2 thousands of soldiers and sailors joined street demonstrators. They surged through the Tauride Palace where the Petrograd Soviet was then sitting and threatened its leaders. The Kerensky government seized on the riots as an excuse to arrest Trotsky and other Bolshevik leaders. They suppressed *Pravda* ("Truth"), the Bolshevik newspaper, and declared Lenin, who fled to Finland, a German agent and a fugitive from justice.

When, on July 8, Kerensky was officially named Prime Minister, he acted quickly to weld a coalition of radical and moderate Socialist parties. To placate the right he ordered an end to the illegal land seizures. Hoping to weaken the Petrograd Soviet by isolating it, he transferred its headquarters to the Smolny Institute on the city's eastern edge.

Then came a blow from the right from which Kerensky never recovered. On August 28 Gen. Lavr Kornilov, commander of Russia's armies, launched an attempted coup on Petrograd. Against this threat

"Landlord property rights are abolished," *declared the Bolsheviks' "Decree on Land," and suddenly millions of peasants like these western Ukrainians began tilling their own soil. A half-billion acres were redistributed.*

Kerensky acted unwisely. He issued arms to the workers so they could fight Kornilov's troops. The coup failed; Kornilov's troops, subverted by agents of the Petrograd Soviet, deserted. Rumors circulated that Kerensky himself had participated in Kornilov's plot, and the Bolsheviks used the rumors to stir up the newly armed workers and the discontented soldiers.

A sudden change in mood swept the city. By September a Bolshevik majority was elected to the Petrograd Soviet. Kerensky, maneuvering with desperate speed, declared Russia a republic on September 14.

The Rebellion Succeeds

From his exile in Finland Lenin viewed these developments with increasing optimism and on October 7, still a fugitive, he returned to Petrograd. When, on October 9, Kerensky ordered many radical army units withdrawn from the city, the rumor was spread that the government planned to surrender the city to the Germans to forestall a Bolshevik takeover. In response the Petrograd Soviet authorized the creation of a Military Revolutionary Committee (MRC) to take command of the garrisons and arm the factory workers into Red Guard units. By then the Bolsheviks were so contemptuous of the Kerensky government that they were openly calling for rebellion. Trotsky rushed from factory to factory, from barracks to barracks, urging the workers and soldiers to prepare themselves for battle.

On October 23, without firing a shot, a Red Guard unit took control of Petrograd's ancient Fortress of Peter and Paul. With this act—though few recognized it then—the Bolshevik Revolution began.

At 11 p.m. on October 24 Lenin left his hiding place and made his way to the Smolny Institute. Dissatisfied with the pace of the rebellion and unsure of his majority in the Soviet, he had already issued a direct appeal for revolt to the people of the city. Small bands of armed Bolsheviks were moving about the city with caution, but they encountered no more than a hint of opposition. The agencies of the provisional government were simply collapsing. By 6 a.m., October 25, the central telephone exchange, the State Bank, the Treasury, the Central Post Office, the main railroad station, and the city's powerhouses were all in Bolshevik hands. And still hardly a shot had been fired.

The cruiser *Aurora*, flying the red flag of insurrection, lay at anchor on the Neva River. Its cannons were aimed directly at the Winter Palace, where a hesitant Kerensky was trying to rouse himself to action. Early on the morning of the 25th an aide brutally summed up his predicament: "There remains not one unit on which the government can rely." Hoping to raise a loyal army in the suburbs, Kerensky left the palace shortly before noon, and failing to rally support, fled into exile. Lenin, publicly addressing the Petrograd Soviet for the first time, declared triumphantly: "The state power has passed into the hands of the Petrograd Soviet. . . . Long live the revolution of the workers, soldiers, and peasants."

As darkness descended over the city, loyal troops took up stations in and around the Winter Palace. At 9:35 p.m. the cruiser *Aurora* fired a warning and the bombardment of the palace began. Most officials inside surrendered immediately to the Red Guards. Then the Bolsheviks rushed the palace, forcing the inevitable surrender of the government troops. Finally, at 2:10 a.m. on October 26, the last ministers of the provisional government made their formal capitulation.

Meanwhile, at the Smolny, the All-Russian Congress of Soviets had at last opened. Trotsky met charges of treason from anti-Bolshevik delegates with insult and scorn. "You are miserable bankrupts," he shouted, "Your role is played out; go where you ought to be: into the dustbin of history." The Bolshevik-controlled congress formally approved the insurrection and authorized a new government, with Lenin as Chairman, Trotsky as Commissar of Foreign Affairs, and Joseph Stalin, Lenin's disciple and the first editor of *Pravda*, as Commissar of Nationalities. The world's first government to call itself Communist had been born.

After the October Revolution came a devastating tidal wave of bloodshed, privation, misery, and death. From Petrograd rebellion quickly spread to other cities. In Moscow a unit of cadet officers loyal to Kerensky captured the Kremlin and slaughtered the Red Guard prisoners they had taken. On October 29 the Guards bombarded and broke through the Kremlin's thick walls. Four days later they stormed the ancient citadel, destroying the last center of opposition.

It was in the vast countryside that the future of the nation lay. Only by securing the loyalty of the peasants could the Bolsheviks stay in power. Their first task was to fulfill the promise of peace. In March 1918 Lenin, despite bitter opposition, forced the government to agree to Germany's harsh demands in the Treaty of Brest-Litovsk. Russia lost her Finnish province; the wheat-rich Ukraine; and her Polish possessions, Estonia, Latvia, and Lithuania. The losses comprised some 34 percent of the nation's population, 90 percent of her coal mines, and 32 percent of her agricultural land. (Russia eventually regained much of what she had lost.)

Meanwhile, the nation was plunged into a ruinous civil war. In May 1918 a White (non-Communist) army of Cossacks touched off the struggle. Other White armies soon joined the fray. Russia's wartime allies, fearful of revolutionary contagion, imposed a sea blockade, lent arms and supplies to the White forces, and finally supported them with troops. In the east Japan sent an army to occupy strategic points in Siberia. To the west the newly independent state of Poland, aided by France, launched an invasion against the Red Army. For more than three years Leon Trotsky, then Commissar of War, frantically shifted his limited forces to meet each new threat. One by one, at incalculable cost, he defeated his opponents.

Even nature seemed to conspire against Russia. In 1921 the drought was particularly severe. To feed the Red Army and the people in the cities, the Bolsheviks (by then called Communists) confiscated the limited grain supplies held by the peasants. Though hardly enamored of the Communists, most peasants loathed the Whites; and since the Reds at least assured them of their land titles, the peasants reluctantly supported them.

By the end of 1921 most threats to Communist power had ended. But the trials of the Russian people were far from over, for under Lenin terror was introduced as a means of dealing with political opposition. After his death, under Stalin's rule (see pp. 204–209), terror became an all-pervasive instrument in the building of a horrifying and monstrous police state.

***Leon Trotsky** was Lenin's closest ally and military leader of the October Revolution. He organized workers throughout Russia into small "labor armies" (right) that fought both the White Russians and foreign interventionists. After Lenin's death Stalin had Trotsky expelled from the Communist Party and exiled, and in 1940 he was assassinated in Mexico City, probably by one of Stalin's numerous secret agents.*

AN ALMANAC 1900-18

1900

Mar. 14 U.S. Congress approves adoption of the gold standard, marking victory of banking interests over farmers and other "cheap money" advocates.

June 12 Second German Naval Law initiates program to double number of German battleships and thus challenge Britain's naval supremacy.

1901

Jan. 1 Six Australian colonies unite to form Commonwealth of Australia, with Edmund Barton, federalist and protectionist, as Prime Minister.

Jan. 22 Queen Victoria dies after 63-year reign, the longest in British history; Edward VII becomes King.

June 12 Platt Amendment is added to Cuban constitution, empowering U.S.A. to intervene in island's affairs.

July 4 William H. Taft takes office as first U.S. civil governor of Philippines and proclaims amnesty for rebels who pledge allegiance to U.S.A.

Sept. 7 Boxer Rebellion, led by anti-foreign Chinese secret society, ends as 12 nations sign Boxer Protocol (see pp. 68–69).

Sept. 14 U.S. President William McKinley dies from bullet wounds inflicted by anarchist Leon Czolgosz. Theodore Roosevelt becomes 26th President.

1902

Jan. 30 Great Britain and Japan sign treaty recognizing independence of China and Korea.

May 31 Boer War in South Africa, between British and South Africans of Dutch descent, ended by Peace of Vereeniging, providing for self-government under British rule.

1903

Oct. 20 Boundary between Alaska and Canada adjusted in favor of U.S.A.

Nov. 3 Nationalist rebels declare Panama independent from Colombia; treaty on Nov. 18 puts Canal Zone under U.S. control (see pp. 88–93).

1904

Feb. 10 Russo-Japanese War declared, after Japanese attack on Russian Fleet at Port Arthur (see pp. 32–37).

Apr. 8 Under Entente Cordiale British and French settle colonial disputes and agree not to interfere with their respective interests in Egypt and Morocco.

Dec. 6 President Roosevelt, prohibiting European intervention, expands U.S. diplomatic activities in Latin America; policy later termed the Roosevelt Corollary to the Monroe Doctrine.

1905

Jan. 1 Russians surrender their Asian naval base, Port Arthur, to Japanese.

Jan. 22 (Jan. 9, O.S.*) "Bloody Sunday" massacre of unarmed protesting workers by Russian troops in St. Petersburg leads to general uprising against czarist regime (see pp. 132–139).

May 27-28 Japanese Navy destroys Russian Fleet in the Battle of Tsushima Strait (see pp. 32–37).

June 7 Norwegian-Swedish union dissolved. Prince Charles of Denmark crowned King Haakon VII of Norway on June 22, 1906.

Sept. 5 Treaty of Portsmouth, mediated by U.S. President Theodore Roosevelt, ends Russo-Japanese War.

Oct. 26 (Oct. 13 O.S.*) Russian workers in St. Petersburg set up first soviet (council). On Oct. 30 Czar Nicholas II signs manifesto, permitting formation of a national assembly.

1906

July 12 Controversial Dreyfus Affair, which had led to separation of church and state in France, ends when court declares Capt. Alfred Dreyfus' previous court-martial conviction "erroneous."

Sept. 29 Liberal revolt in Cuba results in U.S. military occupation and establishment of provisional government.

1907

Aug. 31 Anglo-Russian agreement is signed aligning Russia, Britain, and France against Triple Alliance of Germany, Austria-Hungary, and Italy.

Dec. 8 Gustavus V becomes King of Sweden on death of Oscar II.

1908

July 5 "Young Turk" military officers in Macedonia rebel against Ottoman authorities. On July 24 Sultan forced to restore 1876 constitution, permitting election of national assembly.

Aug. 20 Belgian King Leopold II transfers control of Congo Free State, previously his personal domain, to parliament; territory renamed the Belgian Congo (see pp. 442–449).

Sept. 16 Russia agrees not to contest Austrian annexation of Bosnia-Herzegovina, later part of Yugoslavia. Move creates tension between Russia's ethnic Slavs and Austrian government.

Oct. 5 Bulgaria declares itself independent of Ottoman Empire; Turkey offers no resistance.

1909

Oct. 24 Racconigi Agreement between Italy and Russia pledges to maintain status quo in Balkans.

Dec. 17 Albert I becomes King of Belgium upon death of Leopold II.

1910

May 6 George V of Britain accedes to throne on death of King Edward VII.

Aug. 22 Korea annexed by Japan after five years as a protectorate.

Aug. 28 Balkan principality of Montenegro proclaimed a kingdom by Prince Nicholas, who thereupon becomes King Nicholas I.

Oct. 5 Portugal declared a republic after successful revolt against King Manuel II, who fled to England Oct. 4.

1911

May 15 Under Sherman Anti-Trust Act U.S. Supreme Court orders Standard Oil and (Oct. 29) American Tobacco trusts dissolved.

May 25 Mexican President Porfirio Díaz resigns after Francisco Madero's revolutionary forces defeat government troops in Mexico's civil war. Madero becomes President Nov. 6.

Sept. 29 Italy declares war on Turkey; begins naval bombardment of Tripoli Oct. 3 and declares annexation of Tripoli and Cyrenaica Nov. 5.

Oct. 10 Chinese Revolution begins after revolt of military officers in Hankow. On Dec. 30 Sun Yat-sen elected provisional President of China by revolutionary assembly (see pp. 66–71).

1912

Feb. 12 A provisional Chinese republic is established after the last of the Manchu Emperors abdicates. On Feb. 15 Yüan Shih-kai replaces Sun Yat-sen as provisional President.

Aug. 2 With Lodge Corollary U.S. Senate extends Monroe Doctrine to include foreign corporations holding territory on both North and South American continents.

Oct. 18 First Balkan War begins as Bulgaria, Serbia, Greece, and Montenegro join forces against Turkey.

Oct. 18 Italian-Turkish Treaty of Lausanne gives Italy control of Tripoli and Cyrenaica. Turkey gets Dodecanese.

Nov. 5 Democrat Woodrow Wilson elected U.S. President over incumbent William H. Taft when Theodore Roosevelt splits Republican vote by running as third-party candidate.

Dec. 3 First Balkan War ended by armistice between Turkey, Bulgaria, Serbia, and Montenegro.

1913

Feb. 22 Mexican President Madero, overthrown by Gen. Victoriano Huerta, is assassinated while awaiting trial.

Feb. 25 Federal income tax becomes law in U.S.A. under 16th amendment.

June 30 Second Balkan War begun by Bulgarian attack on Greece and Serbia, who officially declare war on July 5–6.

July 10 Romania declares war on Bulgaria. Turkey attacks Bulgaria July 12, recaptures Adrianople by July 22, and forces Bulgaria's capitulation.

Aug. 10 Balkan States sign Treaty of Bucharest, ending Second Balkan War.

Oct. 6 Yüan Shih-kai confirmed as first President of Republic of China; proceeds to purge members of Sun Yat-sen's Kuomintang (see pp. 66–71).

1914

For further information on entries concerning World War I see pp. 100–131.

Apr. 21 U.S. Marines occupy port of Veracruz, Mexico, after anti-American incident. Dispute subsequently mediated by ABC Powers (Argentina, Brazil, and Chile), and U.S.A. withdraws its forces Nov. 23.

June 28 Assassination of Austrian Archduke Franz Ferdinand and his wife by Serbian revolutionary at Sarajevo precipitates outbreak of World War I.

July 28 Austria-Hungary declares war on Serbia after Serbia fails to comply unconditionally with ultimatum.

Aug. 1-3 Germany declares war on Russia and France, occupies Luxembourg, and invades Belgium.

Aug. 4 Great Britain declares war on Germany and, eight days later, on Austria-Hungary.

Aug. 6 Austria-Hungary announces declaration of war on Russia.

Aug. 10 France declares war on Austria-Hungary.

Aug. 15 U.S.A. officially opens Panama Canal to traffic (see pp. 88–93).

Aug. 20-30 German Army occupies Brussels and captures Lille and Amiens in France. On eastern front General von Hindenburg routs Russians at Battle of Tannenberg.

Sept. 6-9 First Battle of the Marne halts German advance toward Paris, leading into four-year general stalemate marked by trench warfare.

Oct. 15-20 Russians force Germans to retreat from Poland.

Nov. 1 Russia declares war on Turkey; on Nov. 5 France and England do same.

1915

Feb. 10 U.S.A. warns Germany against attacking neutral ships.

Feb. 18 Germany imposes submarine blockade against Great Britain; British counter with sea blockade Mar. 11.

May 7 Sinking of British ocean liner *Lusitania* by German submarine brings U.S.A. and Germany to brink of war.

May 23 Italy, previously neutral, declares war on Austria-Hungary after Allies secretly agree to Italian claims on Austrian territory. Italy enters war against Turkey Aug. 21.

1916

Feb. 21 Ten-month Battle of Verdun begins; casualties will exceed 1 million.

March 1 German Navy begins attacks on armed merchant ships in Atlantic.

March 15 U.S. troops enter Mexico to search for revolutionary bandit Pancho Villa after his raid on Columbus, New Mexico. Effort abandoned Feb. 5, 1917.

Apr. 24-May 1 Easter Rebellion in Dublin by Irish Republican Brotherhood suppressed by British after bitter fighting. Roger Casement and other rebel leaders executed Aug. 3.

May 31-June 1 Battle of Jutland in North Sea ends German hopes of naval supremacy over Britain.

July 1 Battle of the Somme begins.

Aug. 28 Italy officially enters war against Germany.

Nov. 21 Austro-Hungarian Emperor Franz Josef dies; succeeded by his grandnephew, Charles I.

Dec. 5 Asquith cabinet resigns in Britain; David Lloyd George becomes Prime Minister on Dec. 7.

1917

Jan. 31 Mexican Congress approves new constitution with provisions for broad social reforms.

Feb. 3 U.S.A. breaks diplomatic relations with Germany after Germans announce unrestricted submarine warfare against ships supplying Great Britain.

Feb. 23 German troops on western front begin withdrawal to Hindenburg Line; halt several Allied thrusts.

Mar. 1 Secret Zimmermann Note causes furor: German Foreign Secretary urged Mexico to attack U.S.A.

Mar. 8-15 (Feb. 23–Mar. 2, O.S.*) February Revolution in Russia overthrows imperial regime. Czar Nicholas II abdicates on Mar. 15 (see pp. 132–139).

Mar. 9 President Wilson orders arming of U.S. merchant ships.

Apr. 6 U.S. Congress declares war on Germany and, May 18, approves military conscription for men aged 21–30.

June 26 First detachments of U.S. troops arrive in France.

July 21 (July 8, O.S.*) Moderate Socialist leader Alexander Kerensky becomes Prime Minister of provisional Russian government.

Nov. 2 Balfour Declaration issued by British Foreign Minister, supporting the establishment of a national home for Jewish people.

Nov. 7 (Oct. 25, O.S.*) Bolshevik Party, led by V. I. Lenin, overthrows Kerensky (see pp. 132–139).

Dec. 15 (Dec. 2, O.S.*) Russia signs armistice with Germany and withdraws from war. Russian Civil War continues to 1921.

1918

Jan. 8 U.S. President Wilson proposes Fourteen Points for world peace, including "open covenants of peace openly arrived at" and League of Nations.

Mar. 3 By Treaty of Brest-Litovsk Russia loses borderlands to Germany.

July 16 Czar Nicholas II and his family executed by order of Bolsheviks.

Sept. 4 Germans retreat to Hindenburg Line in face of new Allied attacks.

Sept. 12-13 U.S. soldiers take 15,000 enemy troops at St.-Mihiel.

Oct. 24-Nov. 3 Italians break Austrian front line at Battle of Vittorio Veneto and capture Trieste.

Oct. 30 Turkey signs Armistice of Mudros with Allies.

Nov. 9 Kaiser Wilhelm II abdicates amid general uprising; provisional German republic established.

Nov. 11 Armistice signed, formally ending World War I. Estimates of servicemen killed exceed 8 million.

* *Dates followed by the initials O.S. refer to the Old Style (Julian) calendar used in Russia until 1918.*

1919-29 THE ROARING TWENTIES

Is everybody happy?

—Catchphrase of bandleader Ted Lewis

1919-29

While America reveled its way through the Roaring Twenties, Europe was preoccupied with the grimmer task of recovering from four years of war. An ominous sign of things to come was the rise of fascism in Italy, which glorified the warlike virtues of ancient Rome. Above, an anti-Fascist publication depicts Mussolini's ideal—a hooded killer roaming the countryside.

When the delegates to the Paris Peace Conference assembled in January 1919, they were confronted with no less a task than redrawing the map of Europe, and that of much of the rest of the world too. Yet even an occasion as momentous as this represented only one aspect of the new global order that emerged from the ruins of World War I. Conspicuously absent from the Paris conference was Russia, whose fledgling Bolshevik regime had arranged a separate peace with Germany in March 1918. For most of the next decade Russia remained a diplomatic outcast, but her presence was felt in every Western capital as fear of the "Red Menace" spread like an epidemic. In Italy it made possible Mussolini's dramatic rise to power, and 10 years later it likewise helped Hitler gain the support of more moderate factions in Germany.

If Russia represented a new, unpredictable force in the postwar world, this was equally true of the United States. Having just helped the Allies win the war, the American people abruptly ruled out further involvement in Europe's problems—including membership in the League of Nations. Without U.S. participation the league was doomed to ineffectiveness, and the deep social and economic ills afflicting Europe had little hope of being corrected. As a result, European industries in need of capital had to rely on private American investments and bank loans—a system that worked well enough so long as times were good. But when Wall Street's great bull market began to collapse in 1929, many investors who felt a desperate need for cash started to call in their overseas accounts, and in short order Europe's financial underpinnings had all but disappeared.

Of course, few people in the mid-1920's could have foreseen such a disaster. After the postwar recession of 1920–21 American business seemed to have entered a golden age that would go on forever. New industries were booming—automobiles, radios, motion pictures, household appliances, and the like—and the public was buying more than ever before.

In reality, things were not quite so rosy as they appeared. While the new industries were flourishing, some older and more basic ones—farming, mining, textiles, lumber—suffered a steady decline in prices that gradually undermined the country's entire economic structure. Nevertheless, the sensation of prosperity was real enough, and it had an intoxicating effect on American morals and manners, giving rise to the frenetic, frivolous era known as the Jazz Age. Even in Europe, still recovering from the war, the middle and late twenties saw a modest upswing in the tempo of life.

In many ways the economic and social trends of the decade were closely paralleled by the political climate. The Great War had been fought, in President Wilson's phrase, to "make the world safe for democracy," and for a while it seemed to have worked. With the exception of Lenin's Russia and Mussolini's Italy, virtually every country in Europe experimented with some form of representative government. In the end, though, the promising political trends proved as fragile as the economic boom with which they coincided. In Germany, especially, the old forces of reaction and militarism remained, and with the onset of the Great Depression they would find ample opportunity to reassert themselves.

1919

The Peace of Paris

Determined to set the postwar world firmly on its feet again, Allied leaders meet to hammer out the Treaty of Versailles.

"This is a peace conference in which arrangements cannot be made in the old style," Woodrow Wilson declared on his way to Paris in December 1918. A month later he and the other leaders of the victorious nations gathered in the French capital to draw up treaties they hoped would insure a just and lasting peace. The Great War, "the war to end war," had shattered the old order in a barbarous nightmare of blood, wreckage, and revolution. Finally the guns had fallen silent, and the world looked to the peacemakers to create a "new order of right and justice."

To that end, the peace conference delegates spent many months studying, discussing, and deciding a multitude of complex issues, claims, and proposals concerning the settlement with Germany and her allies. But amid the pressures of time, postwar bitterness, and conflicting national interests, the statesmen at Paris produced a hodgepodge of old and new that in many ways was neither right nor just.

In the end, the Treaty of Versailles with Germany and the four subsequent treaties with Austria, Hungary, Bulgaria, and Turkey satisfied neither the victors nor the vanquished. And 20 years later, in the shadow of World War II, a member of the British delegation would write: "We arrived at Paris determined that a Peace of justice and wisdom should be negotiated; we left it conscious that the Treaties imposed upon our enemies were neither just nor wise."

The harsh fact was that many of the ideals inspiring Wilson and his fellow peacemakers proved unworkable in the face of political reality. While delegates, citizens, and soldiers alike cheered the promise of a lasting peace, they could neither erase their bitterness nor ignore the loss and devastation caused by nearly five years of warfare. Although many openly championed the principle of national self-determination for all people, it had already been violated by secret wartime treaties and promises and the Allied occupation of German overseas territories. And despite the acknowledged wisdom of treating the enemy impartially, the harsh conditions of the 1918 armistice had already laid the groundwork for a punitive settlement.

***Germany signed the Allied peace treaty** on June 28, 1919, in the glittering Hall of Mirrors at Versailles, where nearly half a century earlier, in 1871, the triumphant German Kaiser had proclaimed the establishment of the German Empire and received Alsace and Lorraine from a defeated France.*

Meanwhile, anarchy and bolshevism threatened to upset the fragile peace of the armistice even before the negotiators at Paris had finished their work. Russia, a former ally, had been swept by a Bolshevik revolution in 1917, and the German and Austro-Hungarian monarchies had collapsed in the final days of the war. The Western powers, fearing that the mysterious "Bolshevik menace" would soon spread to the unstable new regimes in Central Europe, were anxious to establish strong states there as quickly as possible. Even as they met, Soviet agents were fostering revolution in Germany and the former Hapsburg lands. In the weeks before the conference convened, Marxist radicals had staged an abortive revolt in Berlin, and a few months later Hungary would install a Communist-led regime.

The overriding sense of urgency was quickened by the tense atmosphere of Paris, with its war-strained nerves and public thirst for security. The hotels and cafes of the French capital buzzed with rumors, speculations, and reports of each day's proceedings. The French Chamber of Deputies and the Parisian press

The Allies' "betrayal" of Germany *is vividly portrayed in this 1919 German cartoon, which shows the Allied leaders—Lloyd George, Clemenceau, and Wilson—preparing to behead their helpless victim.*

The Big Three *at the Paris Peace Conference (left to right): Britain's David Lloyd George, France's Georges Clemenceau, and America's Woodrow Wilson.*

clamored for revenge against the hated *Boche,* as the Germans were derogatively termed. One delegate observed that the strident headlines of the morning papers transformed the breakfast table into "a succession of intemperate yells." The voices of moderation were often drowned out by the general din.

Moreover, despite lofty public proclamations, each statesman came to Paris to accomplish a number of very specific aims, inspired less by a concern for the common good than by the narrow dictates of national self-interest. Great Britain wanted to hold on to the former German and Ottoman territories in Africa and Asia Minor that she had occupied during the war. Italy was determined to gain the former Austrian lands promised her by the secret 1915 Treaty of London as the price for entering the war on the Allied side. Romania wanted to make good the Allied pledge that she would receive the Hungarian province of Transylvania. Poland wanted part or all of Posen and German Silesia.

Other nations too saw the negotiations as an opportunity for self-aggrandizement. William Hughes, head of the Australian delegation, tersely expressed this general expansionist temper in reply to Wilson's query about Australia's plans for New Guinea and other former German territories. "Mr. Hughes," asked Wilson, "am I to understand that if the whole civilized world asks Australia to agree to a mandate in respect of these islands, Australia is prepared to defy the appeal of the whole civilized world?" Answered Hughes, "That's about the size of it, Mr. President."

The Politics of Peacemaking

To a great degree, the composition of the conference itself helped prejudice its final outcome. The more than 1,000 diplomats, advisers, and clerks who crowded the Crillon, Majestic, and other Parisian hotels and filled the stately conference rooms on the Quai d'Orsay represented only the Allied and Associated Powers. They included the major belligerents—France, Britain, the U.S., Italy, and Japan—as well as such distantly interested parties as Nicaragua, Liberia, and Siam, nations that had merely severed diplomatic relations with the enemy. There were also representatives of many colonial territories. One of them, Ho Chi Minh of French Indochina, had brought a petition for the independence of his homeland to present to President Wilson. The defeated Central Powers—Germany, Austria-Hungary, Bulgaria, and Turkey—were not invited to take part in the deliberations until the draft treaties had been prepared. (The Soviet Union, which had signed a separate peace with Germany after the 1917 Bolshevik Revolution, was also absent from the peace table.) No matter how many times its creators spoke of impartiality and equity, the Peace of Paris would be a dictated peace.

Even among the nations invited to participate, there was a sharp delineation of power. Although all 27 delegate nations were allowed to take part in the six plenary sessions, the real business of the conference was conducted by the Supreme Council, composed of the chief executives and foreign ministers of the five major negotiating powers: Georges Clemenceau and Stéphen Pichon for France, David Lloyd George and Arthur Balfour for Britain, Woodrow Wilson and Robert Lansing for the U.S., Vittorio Orlando and Sidney Sonnino for Italy, and Nobuaki Makino and Kimmochi Saionji for Japan. The other nations were invited to present their cases to the Supreme Council and were represented on various committees on specific issues and territorial claims, but all major decisions were made by the Great Powers. When Canada's representative protested this blatant curtailment of his nation's role, Clemenceau condescendingly replied, "We [the Great Powers] called together the entire assembly of interested nations . . . not to impose our will on them . . . but to ask their cooperation. That is why we invited them here. Yet we must ascertain how this cooperation is to be organized."

The embarrassing realities of global politics were equally visible in the choice of council members. Japan's contribution to the defeat of the Central Powers, for example, had been no greater than that of Belgium, but Japan was unquestionably a major power and Belgium was not. Even so, Japan's role on the council was limited to the realm of Asian affairs. Russia, who was the first major power to declare war in 1914 and who had made substantial contributions to the Allied war effort, was not represented at all, mainly because the Great Powers feared and distrusted her new Bolshevik regime. Italy was included by virtue of the sweeping promises the Allies had made to bring her into the war. When it became clear that Italy was not going to obtain all she had been pledged, Orlando and his delegation walked out of the conference.

The Big Three

Most decisions were actually made by three men: Georges Clemenceau, David Lloyd George, and Woodrow Wilson. Each combined great power with personal conviction, and each had a definite vision of the ideal postwar settlement. The three dominated the work of the conference, avidly defending their own causes, opposing what seemed at odds with them, and reluctantly giving ground on one issue to gain support for another. The Treaty of Versailles, which was composed in the six months these men were in Paris and upon which the remaining treaties were patterned, was largely their handiwork.

Georges Clemenceau, the 78-year-old "Tiger" of French parliamentary politics, was chairman of the conference. An imposing figure with massive forehead, bushy brows, and a bulky frame, the French Premier easily dominated council proceedings. His long career as a politician and statesman had made him master of the art of negotiation, a craft that served him well at the peace table. Profoundly nationalistic, his hatred for Germany went back to the Franco-Prussian War of 1870–71, in which Bismarck's victorious army had claimed the French provinces of Alsace and Lorraine.

Clemenceau's objectives, however, went far beyond the mere restoration of those areas to France. Like the

Bolshevik Bela Kun, seen here addressing his followers in Budapest, ruled Hungary from March through July 1919.

BOLSHEVISM: A NEW THREAT

As the Allies met in Paris, their hard-won peace was threatened by a new menance—bolshevism. Communist propaganda fanned the flames of revolution in Eastern Europe, and in the first half of 1919 leftist radicals staged uprisings in Berlin, Munich, Hungary, and Slovakia. In response, the Allies created a cordon sanitaire (safety zone) of small democracies in Central Europe and supported the counterrevolution against Lenin's Bolshevik government.

In truth, the Bolshevik specter was more imagined than real, and communism failed to take hold in Central Europe. A much graver danger grew out of the violent anti-Bolshevik reaction. Germany's shaky new regime used rightwing extremists to suppress Spartacist agitators, and Hungary's Communist-led coalition gave way to reactionary rule. The seeds of fascism had been sown and would flourish in years to come.

majority of his countrymen, he was determined to so weaken his enemy that no German soldier would ever again set foot on French soil. As for Wilson's Fourteen Points, Clemenceau reportedly remarked, "God gave us His Ten Commandments, and we broke them. Wilson gave us his Fourteen Points—we shall see."

Woodrow Wilson, whose Fourteen Points had been accepted by all belligerents as the basis of the forthcoming agreement, came to Europe as the Great Peacemaker. During his preconference tour of Europe the U.S. President had been welcomed by tumultuous crowds in Paris, London, and Rome, and he arrived at the conference in a strong bargaining position. His country's power had tipped the scales against Germany, and his terms had been accepted as the basis of the armistice. The Allies would need U.S. military backing, exports, and credits to rebuild Europe.

The idealist of the Big Three, Wilson reportedly instructed his advisers, "Tell me what's right and I'll fight for it." In fact, he had an extraordinarily strong conviction that he already knew what was right, at least in broad principle. The issues confronting him at Paris, however, were clouded by complexities that precluded simple judgments of right and wrong, and Wilson's lofty principles were often sacrificed in the interest of practicality or expediency.

David Lloyd George, Britain's fiery Prime Minister, was called upon more than once to mediate between Clemenceau and Wilson. The short, outspoken Welshman was considered adaptable by his admirers, opportunistic by his detractors. He could afford to be more flexible than his two colleagues because Britain's war aims had already been accomplished: Belgium had been liberated, the commercial and military competition of German seapower had been crushed, and Germany's overseas empire had been seized by the Allies.

Lloyd George was in general agreement with Wilson's aspirations insofar as they did not conflict with the prerogatives of the British Empire. He supported the principle of national self-determination, for example, so long as it was not applied to India and other colonies. On the issue of reparations, however, which he personally opposed, he was constrained by 1918 campaign promises to an electorate demanding that he "squeeze the German lemon till the pips squeak."

German Freikorps troops stationed at Berlin's Brandenburg Gate prepare to open fire on dissident Spartacist radicals.

A 1919 Bolshevik poster represents counterrevolutionary leaders as bestial agents of the U.S., France, and Britain.

Conflict and Compromise

One of the first items of business taken up by the peacemakers was the drafting of the Covenant of the League of Nations, which Wilson had insisted be written into the treaty with Germany. As chairman of the committee established for that purpose, he devoted his main energies to creating a workable blueprint for the league and enlisting support for his proposals. He was frequently forced to back down on other issues in order to win approval of various covenant provisions, but he felt justified in making such sacrifices because he believed the league would be able to correct any wrongs in the postwar settlement at a later date.

The covenant, which was adopted by the conference on April 28, 1919, represented a major victory for Wilson. It provided an open forum for settling international disputes; permitted joint action against aggressor nations; abolished secret treaties, the traditional bane of global relations; called for the limitation of armaments; and created an International Court of Justice. Ironically, Wilson encountered the strongest resistance to his plan among his own countrymen, who forced him to water down the proposed draft covenant and later refused to ratify the peace treaty. (The U.S. subsequently signed a separate peace with Germany.)

Program for the Peace of the World

By PRESIDENT WILSON January 8, 1918

I. Open covenants of peace, openly arrived at, after which there shall be no private international understandings of any kind, but diplomacy shall proceed always frankly and in the public view.

II. Absolute freedom of navigation upon the seas, outside territorial waters, alike in peace and in war, except as the seas may be closed in whole or in part by international action for the enforcement of international covenants.

III. The removal, so far as possible, of all economic barriers and the establishment of an equality of trade conditions among all the nations consenting to the peace and associating themselves for its maintenance.

IV. Adequate guarantees given and taken that national armaments will reduce to the lowest point consistent with domestic safety.

V. Free, open-minded, and absolutely impartial adjustment of all colonial claims, based upon a strict observance of the principle that in determining all such questions of sovereignty the interests of the population concerned must have equal weight with the equitable claims of the government whose title is to be determined.

VI. The evacuation of all Russian territory and such a settlement of all questions affecting Russia as will secure the best and freest cooperation of the other nations of the world in obtaining for her an unhampered and unembarrassed opportunity for the independent determination of her own political development and national policy, and assure her of a sincere welcome into the society of free nations under institutions of her own choosing; and, more than a welcome, assistance also of every kind that she may need and may herself desire. The treatment accorded Russia by her sister nations in the months to come will be the acid test of their good-will, of their comprehension of her needs as distinguished from their own interests, and of their intelligent and unselfish sympathy.

VII. Belgium, the whole world will agree, must be evacuated and restored, without any attempt to limit the sovereignty which she enjoys in common with all other free nations. No other single act will serve as this will serve to restore confidence among the nations in the law which they have themselves set and determined for the government of their relations with one another. Without this healing act the whole structure and validity of international law is forever impaired.

VIII. All French territory should be freed and the invaded portions restored, and the wrong done to France by Prussia in 1871 in the matter of Alsace-Lorraine, which has unsettled the peace of the world for nearly fifty years, should be righted, in order that peace may once more be made secure in the interest of all.

IX. A readjustment of the frontiers of Italy should be effected along clearly recognizable lines of nationality.

X. The people of Austria-Hungary, whose place among the nations we wish to see safeguarded and assured, should be accorded the freest opportunity of autonomous development.

XI. Rumania, Serbia and Montenegro should be evacuated; occupied territories restored; Serbia accorded free and secure access to the sea; and the relations of the several Balkan States to one another determined by friendly counsel along historically established lines of allegiance and nationality; and international guarantees of the political and economic independence and territorial integrity of the several Balkan States should be entered into.

XII. The Turkish portions of the present Ottoman Empire should be assured a secure sovereignty, but the other nationalities which are now under Turkish rule should be assured an undoubted security of life and an absolutely unmolested opportunity of autonomous development, and the Dardanelles should be permanently opened as a free passage to the ships and commerce of all nations under international guarantees.

XIII. An independent Polish State should be erected which should include the territories inhabited by indisputably Polish populations; which should be assured a free and secure access to the sea, and whose political and economic independence and territorial integrity should be guaranteed by international covenant.

XIV. A general association of nations must be formed under specific covenants for the purpose of affording mutual guarantees of political independence and territorial integrity to great and small States alike.

Woodrow Wilson's Fourteen Points, *intended to provide the framework for the negotiated peace, called for a just settlement based on democracy and self-determination for all.*

As a result, the scope and power of the new league were severely limited from the start.

The central issue at Paris, however, was the settlement with Germany, and it was here that the peacemakers deviated most strongly from their original intent. Even before the League of Nations committee had been appointed, the delegates took up the problem of dismantling Germany's large colonial empire. Although it was understood that the territories in question would be administered as mandates under the league, and despite vocal pledges to put an end to imperialism, the nations who were awarded mandates regarded them as colonies. As in previous wars, the victors gathered to divide the spoils.

Many powers came forward with claims, and committees met to study the problem of conflicting interests and to make recommendations to the Supreme Council. Their task was complicated by the fact that the various Allied armies that had occupied the German colonies during the war had not gone home. Japanese troops, for example, had dislodged the Germans from the Shantung Peninsula in China in 1915 and remained in occupation after the armistice. During the war the British and French had promised to uphold Japan's rights in Shantung in return for Japanese naval support, and they felt bound to honor that pledge. Wilson, on the other hand, did not feel bound by any such promises, arguing that Shantung was an integral part of China and should be returned to her. In the end, the moral weight of his argument proved less convincing than the very real strength of Japanese arms, and Shantung was awarded to Japan. (The Chinese protested this betrayal of their national sovereignty by refusing to sign the peace treaty.) With few exceptions, such practical considerations decided the disposition of all Germany's former colonies.

The problem of the postwar frontiers of Germany gave rise to some of the bitterest council debates. Under the terms of the armistice Germany had agreed to give up Alsace-Lorraine, but Clemenceau was determined to impose much harsher demands on the enemy. In passionate tirades he pressed for what amounted to a total dismemberment of the Reich, completely disregarding ethnic, geographic, and economic considerations in his single-minded pursuit of revenge.

Although Wilson and Lloyd George successfully resisted Clemenceau's most extreme proposals, the final agreement bore his unmistakable imprint. Germany was deprived of more than 13 percent of its territory and nearly 6 million people. In the west Alsace-Lorraine was ceded to France, and other territory went to Belgium. The coal-rich Saar region in the west and the northern province of Schleswig (which Germany had won from Denmark in 1864) were detached pending plebiscites to indicate the will of their people. In the east, Poland obtained most of West Prussia, Posen, and part of East Prussia to provide an access corrider to the Baltic Sea. This measure cut off East Prussia from the rest of Germany and placed several million German citizens under Polish jurisdiction. In the south the peacemakers recognized the new country of Czechoslovakia, which included within its borders part of German Silesia and some 3 million German-speaking people in Bohemia and Moravia. The treaty also stipulated that Austria, whose population was overwhelmingly German-speaking, could never unite with Germany, despite compelling ethnic and economic arguments in favor of such a union.

The military clauses similarly reflected Clemenceau's hardheaded determination to destroy Germany's power. They called for a 15-year Allied occupation of the left bank of the Rhine and the dismantling of all German fortresses on the right bank. Germany's air force was disbanded; her army was limited to 100,000 men; and her navy to 15,000 sailors and 6 light cruisers, 12 destroyers, and a few obsolete battleships. In addition, she was forced to surrender

THE POSTWAR WORLD AND THE NEW BALANCE OF POWER

The Allied peace treaties with the Central Powers drastically revised the map of Europe and the Middle East (below). The vast empires that had dominated those areas for centuries were carved up to form a bloc of independent nation-states stretching from the Baltic to the Mediterranean. Austria lost most of her former holdings to Italy, Poland, Romania, and the new states of Yugoslavia and Czechoslovakia. Hungary ceded land to Czechoslovakia, Romania, and Yugoslavia; and Bulgaria gave up territory to Greece and Yugoslavia. Germany was deprived of her overseas empire (see map at right) and relinquished territory to France, Poland, Czechoslovakia, and Belgium. In addition, the Rhineland was demilitarized, and certain regions were detached pending popular plebiscites. The Ottoman Empire was split into the independent states of Turkey, Armenia (whose independence lasted until 1921), and Kurdistan (whose autonomy was never ratified); and the mandates of Palestine (including Transjordan), Iraq, and Syria (including Lebanon). Territory also went to Greece and Italy. Russia, which did not participate in the peace negotiations, recognized the independence of Finland in 1919 and that of Estonia, Latvia, and Lithuania in 1920.

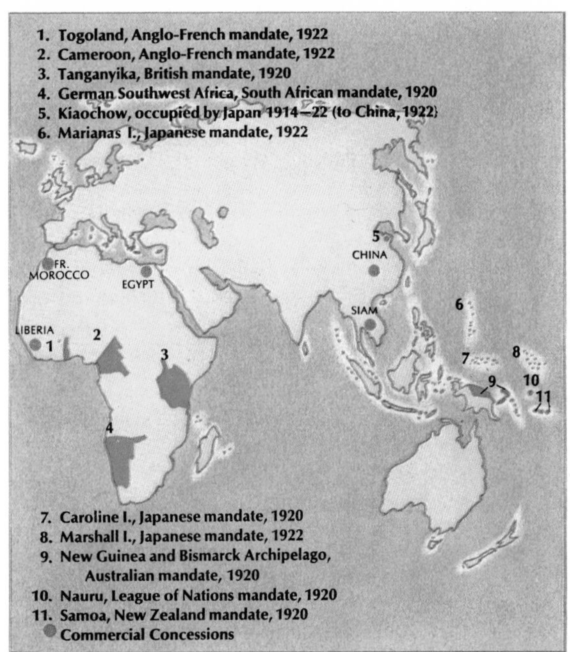

WILSON AND THE LEAGUE OF NATIONS

The founding of a world peacekeeping body was the key to U.S. President Woodrow Wilson's blueprint for the postwar world, and at Paris he devoted most of his energy to that end. When Wilson returned home in July 1919, however, the growing isolationism and strong Republican opposition, led by Senator Henry Cabot Lodge, threatened to defeat his proposed League of Nations. To rally popular support, Wilson began a strenuous cross-country crusade, but he collapsed from nervous exhaustion on September 25 and had to abandon the tour. Ironically, Wilson himself sealed the league's fate by urging Senate Democrats to vote against Lodge's diluted version of the covenant. The measure was rejected on March 19, 1920.

Wilson rides through Sioux City, Iowa, one of nearly 40 stops during his 8,000-mile nationwide tour in 1919.

French statesman Aristide Briand addresses a meeting of the league.

most of her wartime equipment, including all submarines, and forbidden to import arms or munitions.

The French Premier was equally intent on making Germany pay for the entire cost of the war. In the armistice, Germany had agreed to repay damages done to civilians and their property. These in themselves represented a large sum. In France, where much of the fighting had taken place, nearly 300,000 homes had been destroyed, some 6,000 factories dismantled, coal mines flooded, livestock slaughtered, and farmland ruined by shells and gas. Yet Clemenceau wanted Germany to pay for Allied military losses as well, increasing the amount in question from about $30 billion to as much as $200 billion. Wilson openly balked at this astronomical figure, but Lloyd George wavered, prompted by his conscience to follow Wilson and by his campaign promises to his countrymen to support Clemenceau. The result was a bad compromise, involving no definite total and extending the payment period for so long that a whole generation of Germans was doomed to live and work in a country whose living standards could not possibly improve.

Most damning of all, however, was the so-called "War Guilt" clause, in which Germany was charged with sole responsibility for the war and its devastation. The notorious Article 231 stated: "The Allied and Associated Governments affirm and Germany accepts the responsibility of Germany and her allies for causing all the loss and damage to which the Allied and Associated Governments and their nationals have been subjected as a consequence of the war imposed upon them by the aggression of Germany and her allies."

A Dictated Peace

Gradually, these and other lesser questions were debated, the conflicts were resolved, and the treaty took final shape. In the end it satisfied no one: It was too moderate for Clemenceau, too harsh for Lloyd George, and too flawed for Wilson. On May 7, 1919, the draft treaty was presented to the representatives of the Weimar Republic. They and their government were shocked by the severity of its terms, mistakenly believing that the Allies would base the treaty on the terms of the armistice agreement and Wilson's Fourteen Points. Instead, the victors had drawn up an extremely vindictive document. The Germans sought to mitigate the most severe terms, but the peacemakers refused to give ground on all but a few minor clauses. They also threatened to continue the blockade of Germany and resume hostilities if Germany did not sign.

On June 28 in the Palace of Versailles, where the French had been humiliated by Prussia in 1871, the Germans signed the peace treaty. No matter that the terms were milder than those contemplated in Germany's own victory plans, they were unmistakably those of a dictated peace. In future years the shame of the Versailles *Diktat* would feed the flames of Nazi fanaticism, and its alleged illegality and injustice would be used to justify Hitler's expansionist ambitions. In other countries, especially England, popular guilt over the treaty's shortcomings fostered the suicidal policy of appeasement toward Hitler.

After the official signing the Supreme Council disbanded and the Big Three went home. The lesser negotiators stayed on to draft the treaties of Saint-Germain, Trianon, and Neuilly, which outlined the peace settlement with Austria, Hungary, and Bulgaria respectively; and the Treaty of Sèvres, which disposed of the lands of the Ottoman Empire in the Middle East. These settlements were as crucial as the one with Germany and just as burdened with problems of wartime prejudices, secret treaties, and national rivalries.

Moreover, in the case of Austria and Hungary, the wartime regimes no longer existed. In the last days of the conflict the huge multilingual Dual Monarchy had collapsed into confused ethnic and political fragments. Its Slavic, Magyar, German, Italian, Polish, and other minorities were demanding that the Allies recognize their right of national self-determination. Two new countries had already come into existence: The Czechs and Slovaks had proclaimed an independent nation of Czechoslovakia, and the Croats, Serbians, and Slovenes had established the kingdom of Yugoslavia.

In attempting to redraw the map of Europe to satisfy the aspirations of its separate national groups, the negotiators were beset by a number of difficulties. Only rarely did ethnic boundaries coincide with geographic and economic divisions, and in most cases a strict adherence to ethnic lines would have created a patchwork of territories with little chance of economic or political survival. Thus self-determination was sometimes ignored in the interest of practicality.

Promises of self-determination aside, the Allies' overriding aim was to create a strong buffer zone of friendly Central European nations to check the westward expansion of bolshevism and to prevent the resurgence of Germany. Although plebiscites were held in some areas of mixed population to decide the will of the people, most disputed regions were awarded to Allied or friendly countries. When a serious conflict arose between Italy and Yugoslavia, both Allied nations, over Slavic lands promised to Italy by France and Britain in 1915, the peacemakers awarded all but the city of Trieste and adjacent territory to Yugoslavia, the weaker of the two nations. In no case were such conflicts decided in favor of former enemy nations.

Under the Treaty of Saint-Germain, Austria lost about 73 percent of her former territory and 75 percent of her population, including millions of Germans. The provinces of Bohemia and Moravia went to Czechoslovakia, the South Tyrol (Trentino) to Italy, and smaller areas to Yugoslavia, Romania, and Poland. Hungary was forced by the Treaty of Trianon to give up Transylvania to Romania, Slovakia and Ruthenia to Czechoslovakia, Croatia and Slovenia to Yugoslavia, and the city of Fiume to the Allies (pending a decision about its future): a total of 71 percent of her former empire and 60 percent of her population. Under the Treaty of Neuilly, Bulgaria was required only to give up her Aegean coastline to Greece and to cede four western districts to Yugoslavia.

After the signing of the Treaty of Sèvres with Turkey in Paris in August 1920, Allied statesmen turned to the problems of enforcing the peace. They had hoped to create a new order, but instead they had merely propped up the old one, masking its hypocrisies and contradictions with an idealism that was sometimes sincere and sometimes hollow. In the two decades that followed they trusted in the results of their work both too little and too much: too little to make the league an effective peace-keeping instrument against imperialism and fascism; too much to arm themselves when at last it became clear that only force would serve. And less than a generation later the enduring imbalances of 1914, the disruptive changes of the war years, and the uneasy compromises of 1919 would plunge the world into a second and greater conflict.

The fate of the peace settlement *was foreshadowed in this prophetic 1919 cartoon, which shows Clemenceau turning at the sound of a child weeping at the terrible future to which the handiwork of the Paris peacemakers has doomed him.*

1919

A New Look for the Machine Age

An innovative school in postwar Germany, the Bauhaus, profoundly changes the course of modern architecture and design.

***A voice of dissent,** Walter Gropius argued against "borrowing . . . our styles from antiquity." The insignia (above) of his Bauhaus art school reflected a new, austere approach to design; the school building itself (right), built in Dessau in 1925, prophesied the course that architecture would take for decades, although the Nazis closed the school in 1933.*

In the spring of 1919, 150 people converged on an old brick building in the German city of Weimar. To the staid burghers of that cultural capital the group must have looked strange. Most were young and penniless; many of the men were bearded, and a few of the women wore their hair in the scandalous new "bobbed" style. Their conversations were intense, enlivened by arguments over art, architecture, and the impact of the machine age on the way we perceive ourselves and our environment.

Presiding over the group was a radical 36-year-old architect named Walter Gropius. Within four years he and his followers—the first students and teachers of a new arts-and-crafts school called the Bauhaus—would be recognized throughout Europe as the pioneers of an entirely new approach to architecture.

Art and the Machine

For years Walter Gropius had argued against those schools of design that relied more on the inspirations of the past than on the techniques of the present. Dominating such schools for the last century had been the French École des Beaux-Arts. In a typical Beaux-Arts building, steel support beams were hidden behind heavy stone walls that only appeared to bear the building's weight, and concrete exteriors were disguised by rich ornamentation copied from historical pattern books. As a result, many private and public buildings at the beginning of the 20th century resembled Roman palaces, Greek temples, and Gothic cathedrals. Gropius and such fellow modernists as the Chicagoans Louis Sullivan and Frank Lloyd Wright believed that this kind of derivative architecture was a retreat from the realities of the modern age. By failing to exploit fully the properties of such new building materials as steel and concrete, the architects of the Beaux-Arts school were, in Gropius' opinion, ignoring the cardinal rules of good design: that form be integrated with function and that a designer keep his materials honest and undisguised. These were the guiding principles of the Bauhaus philosophy, and in time they became the most influential concepts in 20th-century design.

The atmosphere in postwar Germany was fully conducive to experiments in machine-age architecture. Rising from the ruins of Kaiser Wilhelm's war-shattered monarchy, the democratic Weimar Republic encouraged its artists and intellectuals to develop new ideas for rebuilding their country. In 1919 the city of Weimar invited Gropius to become director of its art school and its arts-and-crafts school. Gropius accepted, issued a manifesto proposing an innovative *bauhaus* ("house of building"), and united the schools under that name with full official backing. Within the year the new school had its first students.

A New Curriculum

The merging of the art school with the arts-and-crafts school illustrated the Bauhaus belief that every creative skill—whether painting, weaving, sculpting, or building—was in fact a craft that, under the right conditions, occasionally flowered into art. In this spirit, and ignoring traditional distinctions between the humble craftsman and the elevated artist, Gropius firmly set all of his students to work in craft workshops under the supervision of master craftsmen. To supple-

ment this technical training, Bauhaus students took courses in the social and physical sciences. They also studied under a number of modernist painters and sculptors whose job was to teach theory, inspire individual creativity, and act as "masters of form." Among the avant-garde artists on the staff, now recognized as founding members of the modern art movement, were Lyonel Feininger, a leading cubist and expressionist; Wassily Kandinsky, one of the first purely abstract painters; Paul Klee, who used symbols to develop a new language of form, space, and color in his paintings; and Laszlo Moholy-Nagy, now best known for his pioneering experiments with abstract and semi-abstract photography.

Training began with a six-month-long Beginner's Workshop designed to free students from their preconceptions about art and to encourage them to rethink solutions to design problems.

Josef Albers, later an internationally known painter and educator, was first a student at the Bauhaus, then a teacher in the Beginner's Workshop. On the first day of class one year he asked his students to construct from old newspapers "something more than you have now," without the aid of glue or scissors. Wishing them luck, he left the room. When he returned he found numerous boats, animal masks, and figurines, all of which he labeled "kindergarten products that would have been made better with other materials." He pointed out the only worthwhile solution he found: One student, a trained architect, had folded a single sheet of newspaper in half and set it on its edge like a screen. Albers explained that the limp, "lazy-looking" paper, visible on only one side when lying down, was now so stiff it could stand on its thinnest edge, and both sides could be seen. A problem had been solved simply and elegantly. Similar experiments using wood, cardboard, wire, matches, and metal fostered in students spontaneous, original attitudes toward ideas, design problems, materials, and creative methods.

The preliminary course was followed by three years of rigorous training in a craft of the student's choice—weaving, metalwork, pottery, furniture making, graphics, stage design, or printing. Each course was taught by both an artist and a craftsman, who, guided by the Bauhaus concept of cooperation and teamwork, strove to formulate an esthetic approach that recognized the machine as one of the most potent influences in contemporary design. Designs for mass production would have "clear, 'organic' form," Gropius said, ". . . unencumbered by lying facades and trickeries." The look of an object, whether a table lamp, a chair, or a building, would be determined primarily by its function and its suitability for machine production.

Prototypes suitable for machine production were made by students in the Bauhaus workshops. If a factory sought to buy one of these models, the student perfected his design by working in the factory. There he learned the capabilities of the machines that would be used to manufacture the product, a knowledge that enabled him to link his creative imagination to the realities of mass production.

In addition to workshop training, formal instruction was given in the nature of materials, geometry, construction, draftsmanship, modelmaking, color, and composition. After three years of training the student received a journeyman's diploma.

Architecture was essential to Gropius' idea of the Bauhaus: "The complete building is the final aim of the visual arts," read the Bauhaus Manifesto. Yet there was no formal study of architecture at the Bauhaus until 1927. Gropius saw no paradox in this. "The Bauhaus strives to coordinate all creative effort," he said, "to achieve . . . the unification of all training in art and design. The goal of the Bauhaus is the collective work of art—the building—in which no barriers exist between the structural and the decorative arts."

Uprooting the Radicals

Although the Bauhaus effort was intense, it was slow to produce tangible results, and Gropius worried that his students spent too much time theorizing and too little in actual production. To make matters worse, the citizens of Weimar quickly became suspicious of the school and its bohemian students, and resentful that taxpayers' money was being spent to maintain them. In 1923 the town council demanded that Gropius mount an exhibition of his students' work, believing that the school would surely be exposed in the process as the fraud of a charlatan and his eccentric followers.

Gropius would have preferred to wait until his students had accomplished more, but mounting the exhibition proved just the kind of cooperative venture the school needed to focus its energies. Before long, paintings, designs, and products of all kinds began to spill from workshops and classrooms into the corridors. Abstract paintings by already well-known masters like Klee, Feininger, and Kandinsky hung beside the works of younger artists exhibiting for the first time. Among those unknowns were Herbert Bayer, the man who was to modernize typography and graphic design, and Marcel Breuer, now an internationally known architect and designer.

One of the most talked-about exhibits was a model house fully furnished with Bauhaus designs. Its kitchen eliminated the traditional arrangement of a large worktable in the middle of the room and a separate pantry. Instead it featured a more efficient countertop workspace along the walls, with storage cabinets above and below. Today this "revolutionary" design is found in virtually all modern kitchens.

The show was an extraordinary success, hailed by art critics in Europe and America, but it failed to silence local criticism. With the 1924 election of a more conservative local government, complaints against the

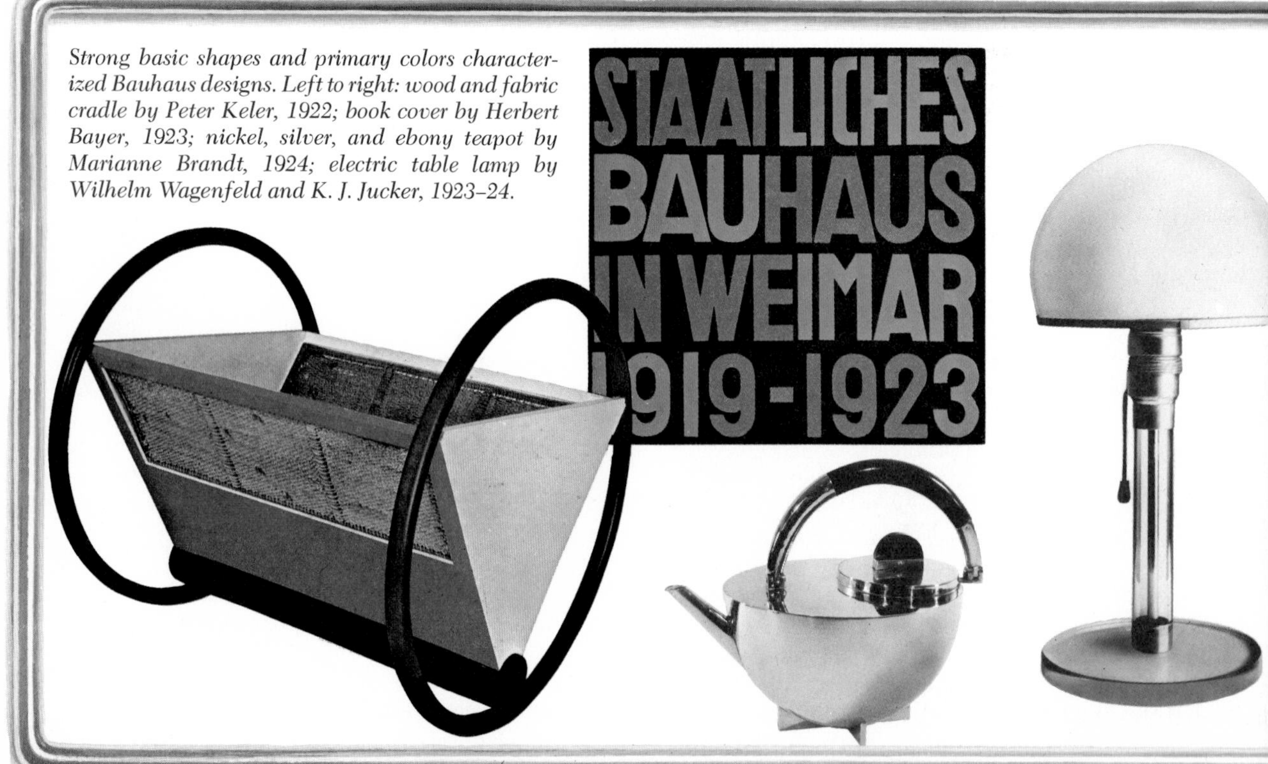

Strong basic shapes and primary colors characterized Bauhaus designs. Left to right: wood and fabric cradle by Peter Keler, 1922; book cover by Herbert Bayer, 1923; nickel, silver, and ebony teapot by Marianne Brandt, 1924; electric table lamp by Wilhelm Wagenfeld and K. J. Jucker, 1923–24.

Bauhaus received greater official attention, and Gropius was forced to close the school.

Undaunted, the Bauhaus staff and students resolved to continue their work together. When Dr. Fritz Hesse, the farsighted mayor of Dessau (a small industrial city in the coal mining region of Germany) offered backing for a new Bauhaus, Gropius gladly accepted. Hesse had seen that the school could be a cultural boon to his town, and an economic one as well, since local industry would benefit from the prototypes developed in the school's workshops. Although the drab atmosphere of a manufacturing center hardly seemed an inspiring background for artistic innovation, Dessau did provide support for the development of Bauhaus ideas and gave students the chance to cope with industrial conditions in a real commercial situation.

Funds were still in short supply, but the mayor and city council offered a commission for three major building projects: The Bauhaus' own facilities, a local housing complex, and a labor exchange. All the workshops became involved in the construction and furnishing of the new buildings. Local industries collaborated more willingly with the workshops than they had in Weimar. As a result the school not only became self-supporting, but perfected innovative designs for a number of products—for example, tubular steel furniture, built-in units, movable walls, aluminum light fixtures, light-reflecting and sound-absorbing fabrics—that are now a familiar part of our daily lives.

In Bauhaus philosophy every creative skill—from painting a canvas to building a skyscraper—was a craft. The Swiss-German painter Paul Klee and other abstractionists were as much a part of the Bauhaus school as the designers and craftsmen. Below: Klee's "Around the Fish," 1926.

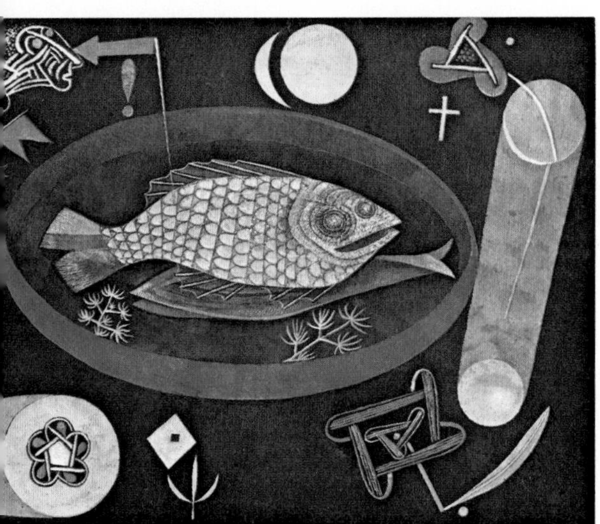

Thonet's bentwood chair, 1841

Thonet's Biedermeier chair, 1836

Breuer's chair, 1924

THE MACHINE VS. THE CRAFTSMAN

The transition from hand-made goods to machine-made goods was a difficult one, particularly in the making of furniture. The new mass-produced furniture was inferior in appearance and design, its makers trying to reproduce mechanically the ornamentation and workmanship of hand-made pieces. The machine, it seemed, was no match for the craftsman.

In 1830 a German furniture maker, Michael Thonet, perfected a machine process to make chairs from veneer strips saturated with glue and then heated in prepared molds. At first Thonet made chairs in the Biedermeier style, catering to the taste of the German middle class. And even though his chairs were lighter and cheaper, they did not meet the artistic standard of the hand-crafted ones.

In 1841 Thonet made a breakthrough. Abandoning the Biedermeier style, he began to produce furniture whose design reflected the material and process from which it was made. He used his molding technique to make simple bentwood chairs that were free of ornamentation, and whose beauty in fact derived from their machine processing.

Thonet's bentwood chair signaled a new esthetic in the design of mass-produced furniture, proving that machine-made pieces could indeed be beautiful. (And practical too: They could be shipped abroad in pieces and then easily reassembled.) The Bauhaus carried the idea a step farther in the 1920's by incorporating a true "machine expressionism" into their work. Their furniture proclaimed its machine origin through its simplicity, smoothness, and reproducibility. There could be no doubt, for example, that the tubular steel chairs of Marcel Breuer were produced by a machine, not by a craftsman. Breuer and his colleagues held that machine design was a totally new artistic form, without precedent. Their work marked once and for all a departure from the imitative commercial styles of the past.

The Bauhaus Legacy

A remarkable aspect of Bauhaus theory was that it never produced a fixed, instantly recognizable style. This was in keeping with Gropius' insistence that the form of products should grow "organically" from the materials used in them, as a flower grows from a bulb, and that they be "shaped by the presence of their own law," rather than by adherence to a fixed esthetic code.

In 1928 Gropius resigned from the Bauhaus, having accomplished his aims there, and resumed his private architectural practice. The administration of the school passed into the hands of the Swiss architect Hannes Meyer, an active leftist at a time when the National Socialist (Nazi) Party was coming to power. In 1930 Meyer resigned and another architect, Ludwig Mies van der Rohe, took over.

Although Mies immediately halted all political activity at the school, the Bauhaus, by Nazi standards, was not apolitical. In 1932 the Nazis seized power in Dessau and the town council closed the school down on charges of fostering bolshevism and decadence. Mies then opened a private Bauhaus in an abandoned telephone factory in Berlin, but six months later, in July 1933, the school was occupied by Hitler's Gestapo. After 14 years of intense artistic creativity the Bauhaus closed its doors for the last time.

But the closing of the school in Germany marked the beginning of its greatest international influence. Bauhaus students and teachers scattered to all parts of the world, continuing the search for new ways to make use of 20th-century technology in architecture and design. Moholy-Nagy opened a new Bauhaus in Chicago. Other schools patterned on Bauhaus principles opened in Japan, Hungary, the Netherlands, and Switzerland. Josef Albers went first to teach at Black Mountain College in North Carolina and later to the Yale University School of Design. Mies van der Rohe worked in Chicago at the Illinois Institute of Technology. Herbert Bayer joined a New York advertising agency as an art director. At least 20 Bauhaus graduates worked for a time in New York, leaving their stamp on the bold skyscrapers of the city.

Gropius himself was named head of the Harvard School of Architecture in 1937 and opened a private practice in Cambridge, Massachusetts, with Marcel Breuer. In 1946 Gropius formed The Architects Collaborative, an enterprise through which he remained one of the guiding forces of modern architecture.

The true legacy of Gropius and other Bauhaus members lies not only in the products they created, but in the new insights they offered into the processes of building and crafting. Fashioning a new union between art and machinery, they taught a vital, collaborative approach to design, the main purpose of which was, in Marcel Breuer's words "the civilizing of technology," a purpose still relevant today.

APPROACHES TO ARCHITECTURE: A FUSION OF TRENDS

Twentieth-century architecture has had a history of n directions and movements. Trends have merged or ov lapped, so that most modern buildings do not represent pure style but bear the stamp of many. Yet even thou there has been no single great tradition in modern arc tecture, certain key approaches to design have emerg

Functionalist architects—Louis Sullivan in Ameri Peter Behrens and Walter Gropius in Germany—had p haps the most profound effect on modern building. Th conviction that "form follows function" meant that design of a structure was determined by what would go inside it. The building "expressed" its function. Furth more, the building's materials remained undisguised order to express *their* functions: Thus steel frameworks w no longer hidden behind purely decorative blocks of st that appeared to support the building. The new functio

Habitat

Forecourt Founta

AEG Turbine Factory

Einstein Tower

buildings did not meet the prevailing standards of architectural beauty; they set new ones. Works like Behrens' massive AEG Turbine Factory were influential because they were conceived in a *structural*, rather than *architectural*, sense. The shape of the Behrens factory, for example, is determined by that of the huge steel girders that support it.

Functionalism was refined by Frank Lloyd Wright in his "organic" architecture. Wright held that the parts of a building should be integrated with the whole, growing organically to meet their intended functions. There should be perceived in form, line, and color, he said, "some fine fitness . . . to the purpose they serve." Falling Water, a home built in Bear Run, Pennsylvania, in 1936, illustrates Wright's philosophy most clearly; it is not only logical and functional but also integrated with its surroundings.

Falling Water

Some architects ignored functionalism, branding it a dehumanizing glorification of the machine age. These "expressionists" set about designing imaginative buildings to express the spirit rather than the function of architecture. Rejecting mere technology, they took delight in fantasy. Erich Mendelsohn's Einstein Tower, built in Germany in 1920–21, unfortunately now destroyed, was the best known of the expressionist works: A monument to individuality, it appeared to have been almost sculpted.

By the 1950's the expressionist philosophy was dead as an approach to architecture. But fluid, sculptural design remained—partly inspired by the expressionists and partly designed to counter the functional, geometric severity of the Bauhaus and what had become known as the International Style. The design of Jörn Utzon's Sydney Opera House (1954), for example, has no relation to the building's function as an opera house; it is designed primarily to be looked at. Built on a finger of land jutting into a harbor, it conveys the impression of white sails on the water. Nothing could be farther from the functionalists' philosophy.

Sydney Opera House

By the 1970's architects had begun to address themselves to the problem of the quality of life. Buildings such as Moshe Safdie's Habitat (1967) in Montreal met the need for high-density housing that retained a feeling of openness. Other projects enlivened city centers: Lawrence Halprin's Forecourt Fountain (1974) transformed a city block in Portland, Oregon, into a park of waterfalls and pools.

1921

Gandhi's Struggle for Freedom

A saintly but strong-willed patriot wields a formidable new weapon against British rule in India: passive noncooperation.

It was hardly an imposing start for a revolution—a small parcel sent from Mohandas Karamchand Gandhi to Lord Chelmsford, the British viceroy of India. Inside were three medals that the British government had awarded to Gandhi for his war service and his humanitarian work. With them Gandhi sent this message: "I can retain neither respect nor affection for a government which has been moving from wrong to wrong to defend its immorality."

That firm, courteous note was Gandhi's formal declaration of war on British rule, a weaponless war that would bring the world's mightiest imperial power to its knees. A fragile-looking little man was about to lead Britain's prize crown colony, India, to freedom.

When Gandhi sent the note, in August 1920, nationalism had not yet become a vital social movement. True, there were activists in the Indian National Congress, but the British for the most part ignored their decorous petitions. If protest grew violent it was brutally quelled. Besides, the great mass of Indian peasants was apathetic. Tied to the land for a bare subsistence, they could ill afford such grandiose ambitions as national independence.

Recent events, however, had changed the nation's mood. In 1919 London's announcement of a new constitution, called the Government of India Act, had raised Indian hopes of greater autonomy. But these hopes had been dashed by the passage on March 18 of the repressive Rowlatt Acts, which drastically curbed civil liberties. Then on April 13 came a climactic event: the Amritsar Massacre. The British fired on some 10,000 to 20,000 Indians peacefully gathered at Amritsar, killing or wounding more than 1,500.

Outrage was in the air when the Indian National Congress held their 1920 meeting. One member, Gandhi, came forward with a plan: massive—but passive—resistance. All aspects of the "satanic government" were to be rejected in a program of economic

***In India Gandhi Day** became the equivalent of Bastille Day in France or the Fourth of July in the U.S.A.—a celebration of the fight for independence and also of the Mahatma himself. The spinning wheel, on which homespun* khadi *is made, symbolized the Indians' rejection of British-produced textiles and goods and support of Indian self-sufficiency.*

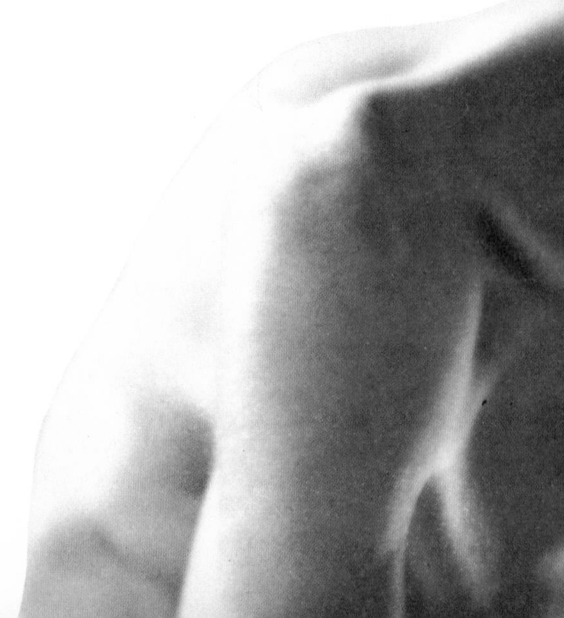

self-sufficiency called *swadeshi*. Indians were to renounce British titles and honors, desert British-run schools, boycott government offices, elections, and goods. The Congress eagerly endorsed the proposal. The goal was *swaraj*, or self-rule.

India was suddenly astir. Thousands of students wearing white "Gandhi caps" fanned out into mud-walled villages and teeming city slums to rally the poor. They preached the Gandhian gospel of nonviolence, literacy, hygiene, the establishment of cottage industries, and the ending of the untouchable aspect of the caste system. Strikes hurt the colonial economy, and for the first time in India's history Hindus and Muslims marched together in protest.

Gandhi himself tirelessly toured the countryside, winning converts to nonviolence. When the campaign ended in February 1922, its apparent achievements were small and civil liberties remained seriously curtailed. In fact, though, neither the nationalist movement nor India would ever be the same again. Gandhi had galvanized the people, transformed their Congress into a potent counterforce, and planned an irresistible strategy. The days of British rule were numbered.

From Commerce to Crown Colony: British India

British rule, though about three centuries old, began late in the history of India's exploitation. By the time Capt. William Hawkins first anchored off Surat in 1608, sent there by London's East India Company, Portuguese traders had been in India for more than 100 years, and Dutch agents controlled the coast.

They were all after a rich prize, for enormous profits could be made by trading cheap European goods and metals for exotic Indian spices, drugs, silk, and calico. Vanquishing their rivals, the British moved inland and took control of the subcontinent.

The company's original purpose was to trade, not govern, but as trade prospered more Britons settled in India, and the need for the protection of the British Army grew. In time, as Parliament slipped ever deeper into India's internal affairs, it gave a more noble coloration to its motives: Far from seeking to exploit India, Britain had come to "civilize" it.

Revolutionary changes were wrought. Hindu customs thought barbaric by the British—including female infanticide, ritual strangling, and the burning of widows on their husbands' funeral pyres—were forbidden. The British system of justice, based on equality before the law, replaced ancient Hindu codes that meted out punishments that varied by caste. The British crisscrossed the land with roads, railways, and canals. English became the official language in 1837.

But a turnabout came in the mid-19th century. It was the Industrial Revolution, which changed Britain from an importer to an exporter of fabrics and also wiped out the primary market for other Indian goods.

Indian handicrafts and urban industries collapsed, forcing jobless artisans to return to the already overcrowded soil. Famine became common, and by 1900 millions of Indians had starved to death.

Then in 1857 there was a widespread mutiny by Indian troops serving in the British Army. The revolt was swiftly crushed, but it profoundly frightened Britain and she ended the East India Company's rule. A year later India was made a crown colony, to serve as a captive market for British goods and a strategically vital military base. Crown rule brought more honesty and efficiency to the government and visible improvement in administration, health care, and communications. But the British so greatly feared another mutiny that they were reluctant to grant further freedoms, while poverty and racism worsened a potentially explosive situation.

Britain's greatest achievement in India was also perhaps her most ironic: Out of the welter of disparate regions, religions, castes, languages, and traditions there, Britain managed to fashion a fledgling nation—only to have it turn on her. With English as the common language, and with workable institutions such as the civil service, men and women for the first time began to see themselves as Indians, rather than Bengalis, Punjabis, or the like. But as this sense of national identity grew, so did Indian resentment of foreign rule.

Even more ironically, the new nationalist movements were often led by Indian lawyers trained in London. Since the 1830's Britain had sought to foster a new breed: Indian "in blood and color, but English in taste, opinion, morals, and intellect," to act as mediators between Crown and colony. Instead, exposed to British liberal writings and an even-handed code of justice, they became radicalized by the gap between British theory at home and colonial practice. The British-trained lawyers returned to India to spearhead the freedom movement.

Two main groups took up the nationalist cause. The first was the Indian National Congress, formed in 1885 and composed mainly of Hindus. The second was the All-India Muslim League, formed in 1906. Ancient Hindu-Muslim antagonisms and the Muslims' fear for their minority rights in an independent nation had prompted the separation. But both groups shared a growing impatience with Britain.

The British reaction was to temporize, to give up little power but with maximum public fanfare. By 1907 handpicked Indians served on all 11 provincial councils, but only as advisers. Real power still rested with the King's viceroy.

World War I brought matters to a head. In the hope that loyalty would bring more freedom later, most Indians rallied to the Crown. London's initial response was grateful, but after the war came the Rowlatt Acts—and Gandhi's resistance.

Sepoys, Indian volunteers trained by the British, fought on behalf of the Crown during World War I.

VALOR AND BETRAYAL

Demonstrating her loyalty in the hope of gaining greater independence, India offered all her resources to Britain for the war effort. Indian soldiers, a million strong by 1918, made significant contributions to the Allied cause, fighting valiantly throughout the conflict. These sepoys, 100,000 of whom were killed or wounded, were financed entirely by the Indian government at an average cost of £20 million a year—this in addition to war-time taxes totaling about £100 million. Yet the British, who had promised India a larger measure of autonomy in 1917, instead passed the repressive Rowlatt Acts in 1919, which authorized the jailing of political dissidents without trial. The next year Gandhi launched India's first nationwide noncooperation campaign: "In my opinion," he said, "noncooperation with evil is as much a duty as is cooperation with good." Many Indians agreed.

Gandhi was born in 1869 at Porbandar, son of a member of the merchant caste who was a *dewan,* or "prime minister". A shy, sensitive youth, he studied law in London and returned home as a barrister in 1891. Two years later he became counsel to a business firm and went to Durban, South Africa.

Less than a week after his arrival in Durban he experienced a racial incident that began his transformation from timid young lawyer to fearless revolutionary: He was manhandled out of a first-class railway compartment (for which he had a ticket). Rather than go to a third-class compartment, he spent the night shivering in an unheated waiting room. "My active non-violence," he later wrote, "began from that date."

Conquering his shyness, he rallied South Africa's large Indian community to protest discriminatory laws—at first through petitions, later through his doctrine of *satyagraha,* or "soul-force." He coupled the writings of Western reformers with centuries of Hindu tradition. Religion was joined with politics: Injustice was to be met with justice; violence with nonviolence.

From 1906 to 1914 Gandhi led a series of *satyagraha* campaigns and boycotts in South Africa, shaming the white rulers into repealing anti-Indian laws. When Gandhi left for India, the Boer Gen. Jan C. Smuts sighed, "The saint has left our shores—I hope forever."

Back in India Gandhi joined the Congress, traveled, and made speeches, awaiting a target for a national campaign of *satyagraha.* First the Rowlatt Acts, then the Amritsar Massacre, gave Gandhi the issues he sought. He made the most of them. The first noncooperation campaign galvanized the nationalist movement, and Gandhi, who had come to be known as the Mahatma ("Great Soul"), kept up unrelenting moral pressure. Bonfires of British goods lit the sky in thousands of towns and villages. *Khadi*-clad protesters halted trains by lying across the tracks. Club-swinging police met unflinching crowds of thousands. Visiting British officials were studiously ignored.

It was perhaps the central tragedy of Gandhi's life that only a few of his followers ever accepted nonviolence as anything more than a useful strategem and that he was never able to instill in others the purity of heart he regarded as a prerequisite to *satyagraha.* Even Jawaharlal Nehru, his political heir, abandoned nonviolence as a policy once he had become free India's first Prime Minister in 1947.

In fact, Gandhi's idealism often blinded him to political reality. Convinced that he and the Congress could fairly represent Muslims as well as Hindus, he never fully understood the Muslim's fear of Hindu rule. His refusal to agree to separate Muslim representation helped bring about the bloody dismemberment of the subcontinent in 1947, when Muslim Pakistan broke away from predominantly Hindu India (see pp. 390–395), and led to his own assassination in 1948.

Although Gandhi resigned from the Congress in 1934, he remained a highly influential figure. And by the mid-thirties he had led the Congress in bringing about dramatic changes in India. Gradually Britain gave ground, and the 1935 Government of India Act provided that popularly elected officials be guaranteed a share in the power. Thanks largely to Gandhi, the question was no longer whether India would be free, but when. On August 15, 1947, India was granted complete independence, and the British withdrew.

***With the 1930 Salt March** (left) Gandhi launched a massive protest against India's costly salt tax. He and about 60,000 followers were jailed, but by 1931 the government had given in to their demands.*

***Soon after his release** Gandhi played a major role at the 1931 Indian Round Table Conference in London. One of his primary goals was to make the British public more sympathetic to India's problems.*

SCIENCE & TECHNOLOGY
1919-29

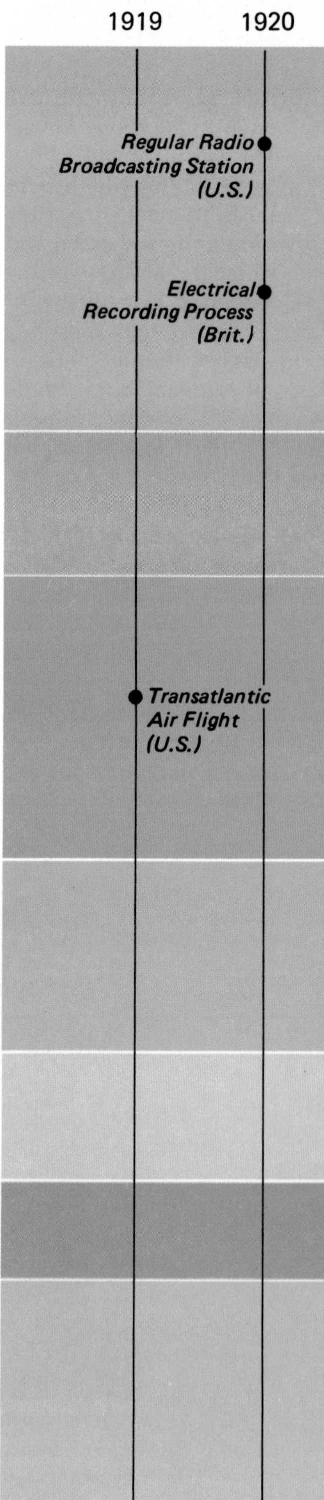

Science and Society

By the 1920's the distance between scientists and laymen seemed to be increasing and decreasing simultaneously. Men and women who had been born in a world without airplanes, radios, automobiles, or X-rays were beginning to feel the impact of the scientific revolution and to realize that technology was changing—and visibly improving—their lives at an unprecedented rate. The automobile, introduced in the early years of the century, had become a common sight, and manufacturers were producing ever improved and faster models. In 1920 Gaston Chevrolet won the Indianapolis 500 after driving for almost 6 hours at the incredible speed of 88 miles per hour. Airplanes, once reserved for hobbyists and war heroes, were offering commercial flights to more and more distant places. Radio provided a new form of family entertainment (see pp. 44–47), and new appliances, such as the automatic toaster and the spin drier, helped lighten the daily workload.

The future promised even swifter and more incredible technological advances. As early as 1920 the Smithsonian Institution in Washington, D.C., announced that Professor Robert Goddard had developed a rocket capable of traveling to the moon, and in 1926 Goddard made the first public test of his liquid fuel rocket (see pp. 192–197). In 1923 German physicist Hermann Oberth published a treatise on the possibility of interplanetary travel. Life itself seemed close to man's control when the July 1921 issue of *Scientific American* said that a doctor at the Rockefeller Institute in New York had succeeded in keeping the heart of an embryo chicken beating for more than eight years.

Science, it seemed, was capable of anything, and scientific methods were applied to virtually every area of endeavor: the arts, industry, agriculture, business, even government. Corporations and governments gathered teams of specialists and sponsored their work on specific projects. In 1923 British mathematician-philosopher Bertrand Russell summed up the attitude of his era: "It is science, ultimately, that makes our age different . . . from the ages that have gone before. And science is capable of bringing mankind into a far happier condition than any that he has known in the past."

At the same time, the nature of much scientific research was moving further and further away from the realm of common experience, and scientists were finding it increasingly difficult to express their theories in easily comprehensible terms. Einstein's theory of relativity postulated that time and space were not absolutes but variables and that mass and energy were equivalent and interchangeable (see pp. 38–43). German physicist Werner Heisenberg's uncertainty principle, published in 1927, stated that it was impossible to measure both the position and velocity of a subatomic particle at the same time (see p. 87). Three years earlier French physicist Louis Victor de Broglie suggested that electrons were not solid at all but had wavelike properties. His theory was incorporated into the

THE PACE OF INVENTION

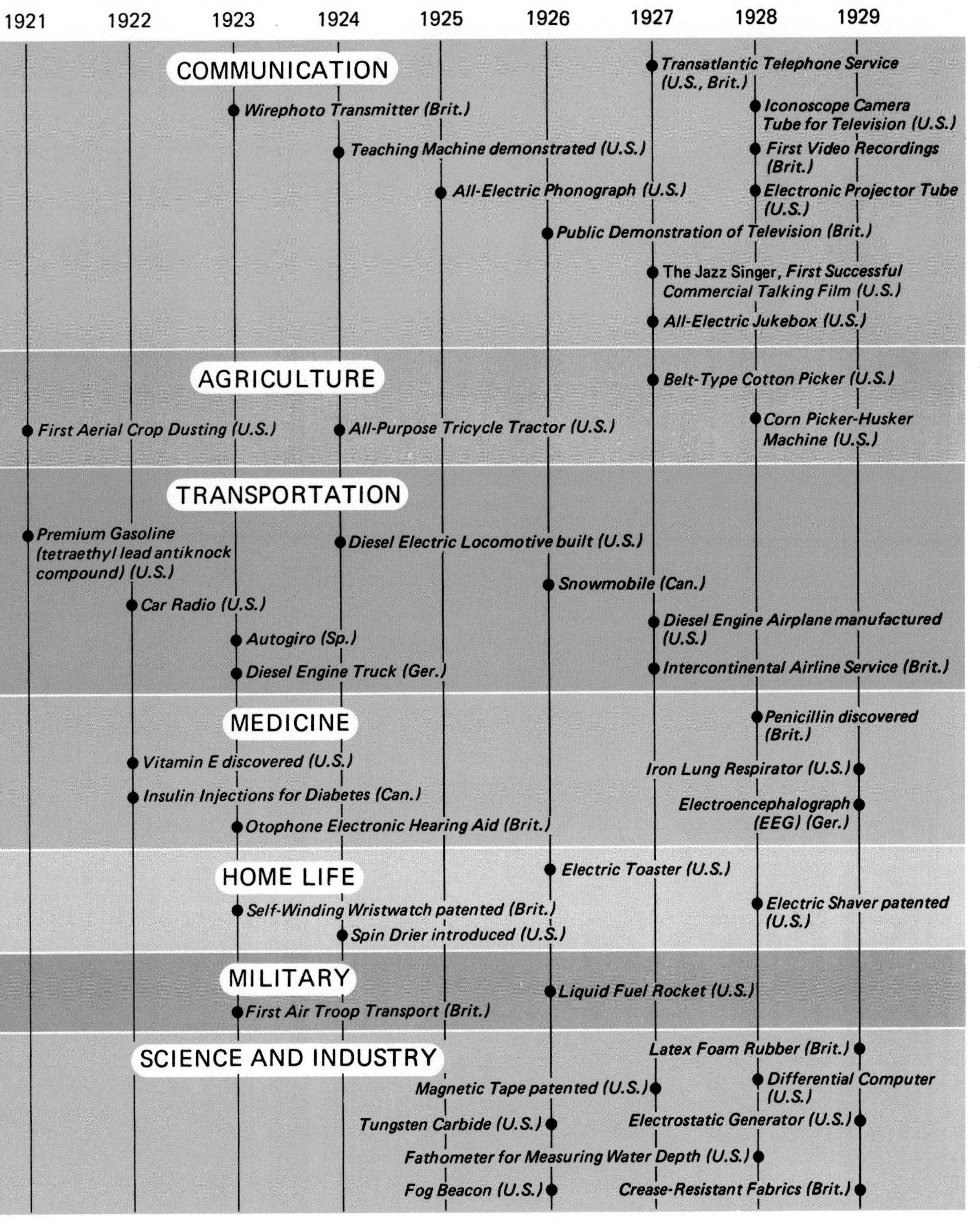

Evolution on trial: *Clarence Darrow, who defended John T. Scopes in the 1925 Tennessee trial, addresses the jury (above). His courtroom opponent, fundamentalist William Jennings Bryan, was caricatured by* Judge *magazine (right).*

systems of quantum wave mechanics developed by the Austrian and English physicists Erwin Schrödinger and Paul Dirac a few years later.

"Scientification"

The prevalent notion in the 1920's that "only two or three people really understand relativity," though untrue, comforted the average man or woman, who found such abstract, nonintuitive ideas virtually beyond their powers of comprehension. More palatable (and seemingly as likely) were the exciting futuristic adventures in the magazines of Hugo Gernsback, the first popularizer of science fiction. In 1926 Gernsback founded *Amazing Stories* magazine devoted exclusively to what he termed "scientification." Cartoons of the day featured the adventures of space-age heroes, such as Buck Rogers, and talked of "heat rays," "space ships," and "radio telescopes."

Since virtually anything seemed possible, then the stranger the better. People eagerly devoured newspaper and magazine accounts of all kinds of weird and otherwordly events. The *London Daily News* of September 5, 1922, carried a story about small toads falling from the sky for two days at Chalon-sur-Saône, France. The *London Evening Standard* of January 3, 1924, reported thousands of red worms falling in a snowstorm over Halmstad, Sweden. The *Scientific American* issue for July 1922 offered a lengthy description of an Argentinian water monster.

This general willingness to accept the extraordinary, especially if couched in scientific jargon, stimulated the development of a number of pseudoscientific theories. The Nazis in Germany, for example, resurrected long-discredited treatises on the origin of races to authenticate their belief in Aryan racial superiority. Other less sinister theories also gained acceptance. One, called the *Welteislehre* (World Ice Theory), held that the Milky Way was composed of blocks of ice. Another, the *Hoheweltlehre* (Hollow World Theory), claimed that the earth was really the inner surface of a globe, a bubble in a universe of solid rock. Neither seemed much less likely than Einstein's theories of the universe or De Broglie's formulas about atomic particles.

In Russia similar theories actually penetrated the scientific field of genetics, setting back progress in developing new strains of wheat for at least two decades. In the late 1920's and throughout the 1930's adherents of the unorthodox Soviet biologist I. V. Michurin gained control of the Russian agricultural complex. They held that parent plants could transmit acquired characteristics (rather than those inherent in their genes) to their offspring.

The New Religion

Elsewhere, science combined with religion to create a variety of pseudo-scientific religious cults. In Europe and North America self-proclaimed spiritual leaders spoke of "vibrational planes" and the "matter-spirit continuum," adorning their mystical speculations in terms borrowed directly from physics. A few scientists tried to establish philosophical frameworks for the recent scientific discoveries, but it was difficult to rival the colorful spiritualists.

Respect for science and scientific opinion was so strong that it remained unshaken by the verdict of the highly publicized Scopes trial in 1925 in Dayton, Tennessee. That contest between a biology teacher who taught Darwin's theory of evolution and Biblical fundamentalists focused on the age-old conflict between science and religion. Although John T. Scopes was convicted, most observers viewed the episode as the last skirmish on a battlefield conquered by science.

The public trusted and revered the new conquerors with a devotion generally reserved for religious figures. Clad in white laboratory coat and surrounded by test tubes or, in the manner of Einstein, unkempt in shabby cardigan, covering a blackboard with strange hieroglyphics, the scientist appeared as guardian of the deepest secrets of the universe. His vast knowledge, beyond the reach of most mortals, elevated him to a new status.

Only toward the end of the decade, when the stock market crash and a darkening world situation seemed to belie the scientific promise of creating an earthly Utopia, did people begin to question the ultimate value of scientific inquiry and to criticize the single-minded devotion to that quest. By then, however, science and the new technology it had spawned had established themselves far too firmly to be easily dislodged, and, despite warnings, they would become ever more dominant in the life of the century.

STRANGER THAN FACT, MORE AMAZING THAN FICTION

Science fiction of the 1920's wove fact and fantasy into exciting, mind-expanding tales. An account in Amazing Stories *for December 1929 (above) reads: "For an instant they were pressed crushingly against the floor, and then they floated strangely free. There was the earth rapidly dropping away..." The cover of a 1920's* Life *magazine features a city of the future (below left), and* Amazing Stories *for summer 1928 shows a scientist conducting a weird experiment (below right).*

1922

Mussolini's March on Rome

A journalist-turned-revolutionary leads a phalanx of blackshirted believers to an ominous victory for the reactionary political creed he calls fascism.

I tell you," the speaker intoned, "with the solemnity the moment calls for: Either the government will be given to us or we shall take it, descending upon Rome. It is now a question of days, perhaps of hours." With a single voice his audience, 6,000 blackshirted followers, shouted: "To Rome!"

Thus, on October 23, 1922, Benito Mussolini began to mobilize his Fascist legions for a march on the Italian capital. Four nights later some 25,000 of his private soldiers were clogging the roads to Rome, not knowing that their leader—Il Duce—was sitting in a theater in Milan; that, too late, he had sent a last-minute telegram canceling the march; or that the government they were marching to conquer was already on the brink of capitulation.

When they did enter the city gates the Fascists met no resistance. Parliament had torn itself into ineffectual factions, and King Victor Emmanuel, intimidated by exaggerated reports of Fascist strength, refused to marshal the army against them. On October 30 the new leader arrived at the Eternal City in a railway

sleeping car. It was a triumphant moment in a career that would end 22 years and 6 months later with his ignominious death at the hands of Italian partisans.

A Birthplace on a Battleground

Italy's north-central region of Romagna was indeed a fitting birthplace for Il Duce. For centuries the area had been the battleground for foreign invaders, and the poor who lived there were very poor. When the Russian anarchist Mikhail Bakunin traveled through the Romagna in 1864, his words reached responsive ears. Among those inspired by him was a blacksmith named Alessandro Mussolini, who became a passionate revolutionary. When his first son was born in 1883, Alessandro named him Benito, in honor of the Mexican revolutionary Benito Juárez.

Benito grew into a quarrelsome, restless child whose wild ways worried his devout schoolteacher mother. At the age of nine, despite his father's opposition, he was sent off to a strict Catholic boarding school—only to be expelled after two years for his violence and insubordination. Seven years later he managed to complete a teacher training course, and for a short time he was a village schoolmaster.

But his father's radical ideas had instilled in him an insatiable hunger for power, and at 19 he took up socialism and became an *agent provocateur* for the cause. Possessed of a certain skill with words, his extreme and violent rhetoric set him apart from the majority of more moderate Socialists. Mussolini left the Romagna for Switzerland, where he supported himself with odd jobs. He read the writings of Machiavelli, Nietzsche, Marx, and other radicals. He also mingled with revolutionary groups, even spending some time in jail for his revolutionary activities. While in jail he put his time to use by learning French and German and polishing his skills as a journalist.

The effort paid off. By 1912 the young activist was in Milan, the acknowledged leader of the burgeoning Italian Socialist Party, and editor of its influential daily journal, *Avanti!* ("Forward!"). Having found his cause he had also acquired a voice.

The eruption of World War I, in July 1914, gave Mussolini a major issue as well. Like most Socialists he demanded that Italy remain neutral; but in October his position suddenly and mysteriously changed. He resigned his editorship of *Avanti!* and within weeks began publishing a new daily, *Il Popolo d'Italia* ("The People of Italy"). Now he began exhorting Italy to join the Allies against Germany, the source of "everything which is treason, disgrace, deceit."

Mussolini's shift, which included a condemnation of Karl Marx himself, caused the Italian Socialist Party to expel him. How, his former comrades wondered, could the man who had been the voice of the party for so many years controvert its doctrines? And where, they wondered, was the virtually penniless Mussolini getting money for his new journal?

The identity of fascism's financial godfather remains a mystery. It could have been the French, who would have welcomed any ally against Germany, or it may have been those in Italy—King Victor Emmanuel III, the army, or members of the Italian nationalist movement—who, lured by the Allies' promise of new postwar territories, had clamored for their country to enter the war. Whoever his benefactor, Mussolini had joined those partisans.

In May 1915 Italy declared war on Austria. "O mother Italy," wrote Mussolini, "we offer thee . . . our life and our death." This pledge was dearly paid, as thousands died in the disastrous battles along the Austrian front (see pp. 108–115). Still writing impassioned dispatches for *Il Popolo d'Italia,* Mussolini served in the Bersaglieri (a light infantry corps) and fought in the trenches in the Carso. In 1917 he was wounded in the course of further training, was released from service, and returned to full-time work on his newspaper.

*"**Mussolini Reconsecrates** the Italy of Vittorio Veneto" boasts the headline in the October 30, 1922, edition of Mussolini's official newspaper.*

***The Quadrumvirate** and Mussolini: Fascism's strong man is flanked by four associates who led the march on Rome. From left, they are Italo Balbo, Emilio de Bono, Mussolini, Michele Bianchi, Cesare Maria de Vecchi.*

BELIEVE, OBEY, COMBAT!

Although fascism was spawned in the convulsions following World War I, it incorporated many ideas that had been circulating in Europe for decades. Chief among them were passionate anti-Marxism, the belief that democracy was a cancer on the sacred body of the state, and the idea (partly derived from half-understood readings in 19th-century biology) of an evolutionary struggle for survival. All three of these ideas were nourished by the most virulent form of nationalism, by a conviction of the state's supremacy over the individual, and by a pessimistic sense of social decay and mediocrity.

In Italy the symbol of fascism (and the origin of the name itself) was the fasces, the ancient Roman symbol of authority that Mussolini took as his party's emblem. A bundle of rods bound around an ax, it symbolized the role of the people (the rods) bound by unquestioning obedience to their warlike leader (the ax). At the same time it was a reminder of the ancient glory that the Fascists strove to regain for their country. The slogan "Believe, Obey, Combat!" became Mussolini's rejoinder to the Liberty, Fraternity, and Equality of the democracies he despised.

Pre-Fascist attacks on democracy had begun in the 19th century. Their most powerful spokesmen were both French, the political theorist Georges Sorel and Charles Maurras, a leader of the Action Française group. In essence, Maurras' argument was that the procedures of democracy allowed hosts of greedy, and for the most part worthless, individuals to prey upon the state at the expense of the general good. Only an absolute leader, completely identified with the state, would be above using it for his own ends; the democratic majority, when not venal, was stupid and destined only to achieve the state's destruction.

If the Fascists despised democracy, they feared Marxism, and for good, practical reasons. The Marxists had no sense of the glories of the past and saw history only as a catalog of oppression. They looked to the working classes for social revolution rather than to a great leader. Worst of all, they were internationalists, believing in a worldwide brotherhood of labor that was entirely opposed to the ideal of a nation made virile by devotion to a single man.

In Fascist Italy labor was organized according to a romantic conception of the medieval guild system. All workers belonged to corporations, according to their trade or profession, and at every level of each corporation were government representatives responsible for the national coordination of the corporation's work and aims. In theory, this corporate state would eliminate class conflict, since workers and managers were grouped together. But the electorate, voting by corporation rather than geographical area, was thoroughly fragmented, and before long all trace of representative government had disappeared.

The war ended in 1918, but Italy's problems did not. The demobilization of 2 1/2 million soldiers led to widespread unemployment and social unrest, and postwar inflation was strangling the economy. Even more dangerous was the bitterness felt by many nationalists, who thought that despite Italy's territorial gains, she had been cheated of her proper spoils—certain Austro-Hungarian lands that the Allies had held out as an incentive for Italy to enter the war. The United States had not been a party to this promise, and Woodrow Wilson, a champion of the principles of self-determination, balked at the idea of Italy's taking over these lands. The focal point of the issue was the Adriatic port of Fiume, claimed by Italians and Slavs.

D'Annunzio, Poet and Dictator

The fate of Fiume presaged, in miniature, the course of Italian history. In September 1919 the middle-aged poet and nationalist Gabriele D'Annunzio resolved to seize the city and for the purpose gathered around him a private army of shock troops. Many of these troops, called Arditi, were criminals released from jail on their promise to fight to the death. When the Arditi marched with D'Annunzio on Fiume, the generals of the regular army could have stopped them but, sharing their resentment, did not.

D'Annunzio set up an authoritarian regime in Fiume with himself as dictator. His bludgeon-wielding Arditi formed the occupying army, carrying out his will by, for example, forcing huge doses of castor oil down the throats of dissenters. The Arditi bore all the trappings that were later adopted as the symbols of fascism: a "Roman" salute, the anthem "Giovinezza" ("Youth"), a black flag with a white skull and crossbones, and a black uniform (reduced by Mussolini to the Fascist black shirt). For 15 months these thugs held sway in Fiume until the Italo-Yugoslavian Treaty of Rapallo made the city an independent state, whereupon D'Annunzio surrendered the city. Mussolini, who had raised money to support D'Annunzio, used the remaining funds to equip his first Fascist squads.

On March 23, 1919, a momentous meeting was held in a businessmen's club in Milan. Appealing for money and support, Mussolini told the businessmen that his former Socialist comrades had betrayed the proletariat and that he alone preserved the ideals and goals of the party. He made his Socialist claims more palatable to his conservative-minded listeners with a potent dash of nationalism and, most important, the promise of an unrestricted economy. The fact that his stated left- and right-wing goals were contradictory was, if anything, an advantage. As he himself boasted: "We allow ourselves the luxury of being aristocratic and democratic, reactionary and revolutionary. . . ."

Little immediate support was gained, and in the 1919 elections not a single Fascist was voted into

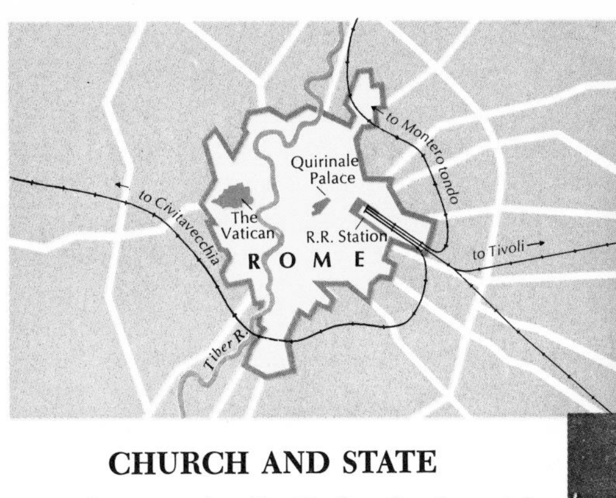

CHURCH AND STATE

Mussolini astutely allied Italian fascism with the Catholic Church in 1929. Right, Cardinal Gasparri and Mussolini sign the Lateran Treaty, making Vatican City a sovereign state within Rome (above). At the same time a concordat was also concluded. It made Catholicism Italy's official religion, passed church-approved laws affecting education and marriage, and exempted all church corporations from the obligation to pay taxes.

Mussolini signs the Lateran Treaty, assuring the Vatican's freedom.

office. But in 1920 the formation of the Italian Communist Party drove the business community into Mussolini's camp. A great wave of Communist-led strikes began among factory and farm workers, causing money from industry and the large landowning interests to pour into the Fascist offices in Milan. Soon Mussolini began to equip his Fascist *squadristi*—the blackshirted gangs that suddenly appeared everywhere, beating up Bolsheviks and terrorizing schools, clinics, and Socialist workers' clubs.

In 1921 the Fascists were elected to 35 of Parliament's 535 seats—though in the context of parliamentary disintegration their effective strength was far greater than their numbers implied. Since the King had little real power, and Parliament was reduced to a number of squabbling factions, no incisive action could be agreed on. As the economic and political crisis deepened, the *squadristi* flourished.

By the spring of 1922 Fascist squadrons occupied a number of Italian cities and, as in the Fiume episode, neither the army nor the police tried to stop them. By fall the country was in the throes of a general strike, and the government was ripe for a fall.

At a mass meeting in Naples on October 24 Mussolini issued his ultimatum: Either the government would give him its power or the Fascists would march on Rome. Four days later, when the 25,000 *squadristi* stood at the city's gates, Premier Luigi Facta persuaded his Cabinet to declare a state of siege. But the King refused to sign Parliament's declaration. Overestimating Fascist strength, Victor Emmanuel was convinced that opposition to Mussolini would mean the fall of the royal house and all-out civil war.

For his part, Mussolini had expected resistance. He had, in fact, returned to Milan to be near Switzerland, planning to flee there should the march fail. Instead, he received a series of calls and wires from the government begging him to come to Rome—first for a conference, then to help form a new government, finally to take over as Premier. He had won his war of nerves with a divided opposition.

The Kingdom of the Blackjack

At first Mussolini offered ministries in his new government to members of other political parties and promised to respect democratic traditions. But this period of cooperation soon ended. During the next few years he made a series of moves designed to lock the Fascist grip on all Italy.

The first move was made quietly and without opposition. In January 1923, by royal decree, the Fascist *squadristi* were given official status as the Voluntary Militia for National Safety. Mussolini's thugs were now paid and armed by the government. Il Duce later wrote: "When the militia was created, the death sentence of the old democratic system was sealed."

In the elections of April 1924 the Fascists, through a nationwide campaign of violence, intimidation, and murder, won 65 percent of the vote. In Parliament a young Socialist deputy named Giacomo Matteotti denounced Fascist violence and fraud. He moved that the elections be declared void and ended his speech with a prophetic sentence: "And now get ready for my funeral." Ten days later he was abducted and two months later his murdered body was found. The country was outraged. Parliament openly accused the

Fascists of the murder. Blackshirts were attacked on the streets. Mussolini, in panic, awaited his arrest.

But nothing happened. The opposition parties issued a manifesto of protest, then simply stayed away from Parliament. That was all. When the Fascists saw that there would be no reprisals, they finally and irrevocably took all power.

In 1925 Mussolini formally named himself dictator, forcing the resignation of all non-Fascist ministers. The opposition parties were dissolved, and the press became an organ of the government. All local decisions were delegated from Rome, and the Corporate State was created. The Corporate State was a huge government bureaucracy designed to control both employers and workers in all branches of the economy. Actually, this bureaucracy functioned inefficiently; many professionals and other workers went on much as they had before. Special Fascist tribunals judged and sentenced dissenters. Police spies proliferated. The kingdom of the blackjack had come at last.

Despite the regularizing of the train schedules (an accomplishment much admired by foreign visitors, who found that Fascist order and discipline made touring Italy much easier) and despite the building of huge public works and roads, plus a semblance of land reform, most Italians remained as poor as ever. The big landowners enlarged their holdings, while the number of landless peasants grew. Real wages continued to fall.

By 1935 the pressure of popular discontent was so strong that Il Duce decided to relieve it with attempts to gain territory and natural resources. In October he sent his army to conquer Ethiopia. The League of Nations protested, in vain, and Mussolini turned to the new German dictator, Adolf Hitler, for support. Along with Hitler, Mussolini intervened in the 1936 Spanish Civil War, sending arms and men to support the rebel general Francisco Franco. Early in 1939, emulating the German invasion of Czechoslovakia, Mussolini invaded Albania. In the same year he signed the Pact of Steel, pledging full military support to Hitler, even though Italy could ill afford an all-out war.

In June 1940 Mussolini committed the most disastrous folly of his career. Honoring the pact, he declared war on France and England. It was not a popu-

FROM GLORY TO INFAMY

Fortune's wheel turned swiftly for Mussolini, from his conquest of Ethiopia to his alliance with Hitler, his defeats in World War II, his narrow escape from capture by the Allies, and the final degradation of his image in Rome. "If I go forward," he once urged Italians, "follow me; if I yield, kill me; if I die, avenge me." He was killed to avenge those he had led to ruin.

1935: Il Duce taming "The Lion of Judah," Ethiopian Emperor Haile Selassie.

1937: Mussolini and Hitler in a review of the German Army. Mussolini had already benefited from Hitler's leadership and the greater resources at the Fuehrer's command.

lar move. He had little public support for the alliance with Germany, and indeed, the ordinary Italian was deeply confused to find himself at war with such countries as Belgium, Poland, and England, which he had always regarded as friendly.

Mussolini's other foreign campaigns, in Africa and in Greece, also brought humiliating defeat. With each new debacle antifascism and the resistance movement grew stronger. German troops came to Mussolini's rescue in both Africa and Europe—but they also descended on, and occupied, Italy itself.

When the Allies invaded Sicily in June 1943, Mussolini's opposition, weak and fragmented for more than 20 years, finally coalesced into action. The Grand Council, governing head of the Fascist hierarchy, voted to depose Mussolini, and he was put under what amounted to house arrest. A new government was formed, headed by Marshal Pietro Badoglio. On September 3 Badoglio signed an armistice with the Allies. In the streets of Rome a joyful people tore down the hated Fascist symbols and vandalized the images of the leader they had once called glorious.

On September 12 German paratroopers "rescued" Mussolini and took him to Lake Garda in northern Italy. Hitler's plan was to have Mussolini use what influence he still had to keep at least northern Italy loyal to the Axis Powers. But Il Duce was 60 years old, sick, and weary. His position was precarious in the extreme: He was hated by most of his own people and had become an obvious puppet of Hitler. There was little he could or wanted to do.

Near the end of the war a group of Italian partisans caught up with him. They fired off the questions that had been festering for so long: "Why did you betray socialism?" "Why did you make others carry out the march on Rome, while you were hiding in Milan?" "Why did you murder Matteotti?" On April 29, 1945, 22 years and 6 months after his first triumphant entry into Rome, Mussolini was gunned down, and his mistress, Clara Petacci, with him. In a final gesture of contempt and revulsion their bodies, and those of four Fascist followers, were taken to Milan and hung upside down for public display in a piazza. A tragic period of Italian history had come to its grim end.

1943: Arrested on orders of King Victor Emmanuel III, Mussolini was held in a hotel in the Abruzzi Mountains. Hitler arranged for him to be rescued in a daring paratroop raid, and he was flown to safety. Meanwhile, indignant Romans were smashing and mutilating Mussolini's statues by the hundreds. Seven months later he was assassinated.

1922

Satchmo: Jazz Grows Up

A rousing new style of American music, born and bred in the Deep South, sets an upbeat tempo for the twenties.

On a steaming July afternoon outside New Orleans a funeral procession, led by a small brass band, made its way to a local cemetery. The music was slow and subdued, perhaps a traditional spiritual like "Just a Closer Walk With Thee." Soon the ceremony was over, and the faces of the mourners brightened: Having lamented the loss of a friend, it was now time to celebrate his heavenly reward. A block or two from the graveyard the drummer tightened his snare and played a surging roll, as the members of the Tuxedo Brass Band broke into "Panama," "Didn't He Ramble," or some other hard-driving tune. Before long the returning procession became a parade, as scores of people danced along with the music; many found themselves caught up in the exuberant playing of a young cornetist.

The rollicking display was nothing extraordinary, for it was 1922 and funeral parades had become a familiar sight in New Orleans. Normally the band would proceed to a hall or tavern to continue the rejoicing, but today that had to be cut short. One of its members, the cornetist who had dazzled the crowd, was catching the train for Chicago. A warm goodby and he was off.

His name was Louis Armstrong. He was only 22 at the time, but it was already widely known in that jazz capital that he could blow any other horn player in town off the bandstand with his superb power and amazing inventiveness. During the past three years he had played in dancehalls and honky-tonks all over the city. He spent summers with Fate Marable's band on the riverboat *Sidney*, playing night excursions up the Mississippi. There he delighted the dancers and absorbed everything the other musicians had to offer.

He learned well, and by 1922 he held a secure place in the music world of New Orleans. Only one man could get him to leave: Joseph "King" Oliver, a legendary trumpeter who four years earlier had gone to play in Chicago and whose Creole Jazz Band had become a huge success. To Louis he was always "Papa Joe," who had helped and inspired him since he was a boy. As he boarded that train, Louis had little idea that within the next 10 years he would not only surpass Oliver but would go on to become the most famous, respected, and influential jazz musician in the world.

Jazz: An American Music

There was something supremely appropriate about the date of Louis Armstrong's birth: Independence Day, July 4, 1900. It was a new life in a new century, and a life that would become a monument to a new, uniquely American art form: jazz music.

Jazz was born *in the streets of the South, where black funeral bands celebrated the deceased's heavenly reward with an exuberant new music. In the 1920's jazz would sweep the country and a whole generation dance to its beat.*

Like America's society, jazz evolved out of a teeming diversity of peoples and cultures. Its earliest elements could be heard all over the South, whether in cities, the bayou country, or "turpentine" (lumber) camps. But the best jazz was played in New Orleans, the bustling, cosmopolitan trade center on the Mississippi delta. Here was a cultural crossroads that by 1900 was host to an amazing variety of musical styles, including remnants of African chants and work songs once sung by slaves, West Indian rhythms, stark Protestant hymns, sensuous Creole songs, marching brass bands, gospel music, folk music, country blues, and polkas, quadrilles, and other European dance music. In one way or another all these would contribute to the new alloy that came to be called jazz.

No one person invented jazz, but two men do stand out as great pioneers. One was a barber, scandal sheet publisher, and cornetist named Buddy Bolden, the other a sometime pool hustler and pianoplayer named Ferdinand "Jelly Roll" Morton.

At the seedy Tin Type dancehall in New Orleans Bolden won a reputation as the inventor of the "hot blues." He took the slow, mournful blues long heard in the country and played it with a lusty, lowdown flavor that suited the earthy atmosphere of the Tin Type. On fast numbers he would improvise breathtaking solos, playing with such power that he reputedly could be heard for miles. On slow tunes his cornet gave forth a passionate sound others soon strove to imitate. As New Orleans' first acknowledged "king" in the 1890's, Bolden was setting standards for the future.

Jelly Roll Morton, a friend of Bolden's, was the first great composer of jazz. In the nineties Scott Joplin's new "ragtime" piano style had come downriver from Missouri, and in the early 1900's Morton learned it, added the "stomping" left-hand beat that was his

trademark, and began writing tunes around it. In doing so he changed ragtime from piano music to band music, and right up to the thirties no jazz band's repertoire was complete without "King Porter Stomp," "Milenberg Joys," "Wild Man Blues," "The Pearls," or another of his lively compositions.

By 1900 jazz had acquired all the key ingredients that from that day to this have set it apart from other musical forms—a syncopated rhythm, improvisation, and the distinctive blue tonality achieved by adding two "blue" notes (a flatted third and a flatted seventh) to the standard eight-note European scale. Once these were adapted to rags, shags, shuffles, and other dance rhythms, music would never be quite the same again.

Storyville

The perfect setting for this early jazz was a very special area of New Orleans: Storyville, one of the few legalized red-light districts in the country. In its bars, cafes, and "sportin' houses" self-taught musicians could come down and play, developing their styles and learning from one another. At all hours of the day or night there were "cutting contests," when one advertising bandwagon would confront another. The rival bands would blow their loudest, finest tunes at each other until the crowd's applause would decide the winner. Joe Oliver's reputation was made one night when he singlehandedly cut down two of the city's top cornetists, Emanuel Perez and Freddie Keppard, without a band behind him. Like a gunslinger he strode to the porch of his saloon and began blowing toward the others' dancehalls. In minutes the crowds had poured into the streets: King Oliver was crowned.

Good times were to be had in the tenderloin, but Storyville could be rough, too. Bessie Smith, a graduate of the old 28 Club, recalled the spirit of that rowdy place in her song "Gimme a Pigfoot":

Check all your razors and your guns,
We're gonna be wrastlin' when the wagon comes.
Gimme a pigfoot and a bottle o' beer,
Send me, Gate, I don't care.
Gimme a reefer and a gang o' gin,
Slay me 'cause I'm in my sin.

Along Bourbon, Basin, Canal, and South Rampart Streets, long celebrated in song, there was a seemingly endless outpouring of jazz talent: Bunk Johnson, the fabled cornetist; clarinetists Alphonse Picou, Johnny Dodds, Albert Nicholas, and Jimmy Noone; Sidney Bechet, a genius on the soprano saxophone and the first international jazzman; influential white musicians Wingy Manone and Nick LaRocca and his Original Dixieland Jazz Band; and a number of performers who would be rediscovered at midcentury and lead a great New Orleans revival—Kid Ory, Kid Thomas Valentine, Big Jim Robinson, Billie and Dee Dee Pierce, George Lewis, and many, many more.

***Bessie Smith** translated her own sufferings into the raw, poetic jazz songs that earned her the label "Empress of the Blues."*

***Louis Armstrong** was a natural musician who coaxed notes from his trumpet in a way never heard before. No other figure in jazz history had such devoted followers.*

***King Oliver** and his Creole Jazz Band (left) invited Armstrong to play with them in Chicago in 1922 as jazz went North.*

When young Louis Armstrong went down to the district, he headed straight for the 25 Cabaret to stand outside and catch King Oliver's hot music. He was so ardent that Oliver took time to instruct him personally and even got him his first playing date. In 1917, dressed in an old police coat and cap, Armstrong played in a honky-tonk bar named Mastranga's for $1.25 a night and tips, using a cornet Papa Joe had given him. He was on his way.

But if 1917 marked the beginning of a career it also marked the end of an era, for with war approaching the Secretary of the Navy decided to close down Storyville because of the problems created by sailors on shore leave. Many sporting-house musicians were thrown out of work, and they joined the exodus to the more promising areas of the North and West. The way to New York was being paved by a white group, the Original Dixieland Jazz Band; an overnight sensation, it was also cutting the world's first records of authentic jazz. But most musicians flocked to the solid jazz communities that had been forming in Chicago, St. Louis, and Kansas City. In 1918 King Oliver joined the migration, opening at Chicago's Lincoln Gardens. By 1922, when Louis joined him, Chicago had become the new capital of the jazz world.

The Windy City and the Big Apple

You had to be good to make it in the Windy City. All over town they were blowing it hot and fast—the "Creole" (meaning black) bands on the South Side, and around the Loop such talented white groups as the New Orleans Rhythm Kings and the Wolverines, a band that featured the incredibly lyrical cornet of Bix Biederbecke. Prohibition was on, and, as in New Orleans, the musicians led a double life. Small groups played in the speakeasies while the big bands played their "sweet" music in the ballrooms.

But King Oliver still reigned. He had surrounded himself with the best musicians he could find, and his habit of scoring unwritten jazz numbers gave the band a large repertoire. Louis had learned to read "them little black dots," but with his uncanny jazz sense he didn't need to. Once Lil Hardin's four-beats-to-the-bar piano and Baby Dodds' biting cymbal had the band going, he and Oliver would step forward for one of their fierce, flawless breaks and, to the amazement of the listeners, charge through their duet without clashing on a single note.

"Whatever Mister Joe played," Louis later said, "I just put notes to it trying to make it sound as pretty as I could." They sounded so pretty together that in 1923 the Creole Jazz Band became the first black group to cut records. The nonelectric recording equipment of that day was crude—really just a large horn attached to a cutting needle—and when the band cut loose, their volume nearly ruined it. Louis had to stand 20 feet away to make his first recorded solo on "Chimes Blues." These early records helped whet the growing taste for jazz in the East, and the next year he got an offer to join Fletcher Henderson's popular 11-piece dance band in New York. The Oliver band had begun breaking up over money disputes, so in the fall of 1924 Louis took horn in hand once again and struck out for the performers' mecca known as the Big Apple.

Louis found success, but little musical satisfaction, in New York. He could handle Henderson's fancy arrangements all right, but the big-band setting made it hard for him to "stretch out," to play the way he felt. He stayed there just a year, but in that time he imbued the disciplined musicians of Henderson's orchestra with some of his own lighthearted spirit, and they developed a stronger jazz attack. In 1925 he returned to Chicago where he opened at the Dreamland, then joined the Vendome Theatre Orchestra. His popularity was growing rapidly, but behind the scenes he was putting another band together, one that was to virtually reinvent the sound of jazz. It was called the Hot Five, later augmented to the Hot Seven.

Satchmo the Great

Up to 1925 jazz had remained dance-band music, mainly restricted to ensemble playing with a few individual breaks and riffs. With his Hot Five, a group that played together only in recording sessions and didn't have to bow to the taste of the audience, Louis turned that tradition around. In one radical stroke he transformed jazz into a soloist's art, based on a series of freewheeling improvisational performances. The melody was still there, and some ensemble chorus work, but these merely formed the setting for the impromptu creations of the performers, who took turns giving spontaneous interpretations of the tune.

As if this weren't enough, Armstrong's cornet work was also revolutionizing the whole technique of jazz playing. Back in New Orleans Armstrong had learned a special way of playing—blowing his notes not precisely on the beat, as others did, but at times falling slightly behind or rushing forward. He was swinging wide of the beat, creating an effect that, once the big bands caught onto it, was to inaugurate a whole new jazz movement: the Swing Era.

In performance Louis' talents were nothing short of stupendous. Whether on cornet or trumpet (to which he switched in 1925), he had a breathtaking range and could produce perfect solos even in the highest register. His tone was so rounded and supple that he rarely needed the mutes and gadgets for special effects that others used. His musical imagination was inexhaustibly rich, always producing new ideas. So was his sense of rhythm, especially his surprising use of rests and pauses to intensify the beat. Finally there was his fabled endurance, which had developed over years of parade marches and late-night cabaret playing. For months at a time he was able to play afternoons and evenings at the Vendome, then rush over to the Sunset to play until dawn with only one intermission. The dancers drooped and his sidemen sagged, but Louis actually got stronger as the night wore on. When it came time to close with "The World Is Waiting for the Sunrise," he held those long high notes in perfect pitch.

At the Vendome Louis also began his career as a singer and entertainer *extraordinaire.* Clowning around onstage had been a stock-in-trade for many jazz musicians; the boisterous barrel-house crowds demanded it. Louis raised the practice to a high art. He donned a frock coat, walked onstage, and solemnly announced himself as the Reverend Satchelmouth—a name later shortened and immortalized as Satchmo. His feature number was "Heebie Jeebies," and he was always sure to include at least a few bars of the new kind of singing he had invented, the scat chorus, in which he replaced the words with nonsense syllables. Of course there were his other trademarks: the marvelous, gravelly voice ("I've got a cold," he used to explain), the ever-present white handkerchief, and the brilliant, infectious grin.

To understand his impact on other jazzmen of the time, one need only listen to some of his early records. Amid music that now sounds hopelessly dated, his swinging horn still comes through as crisply imaginative as anything played today. Throughout the twenties and beyond there was not a musician working who didn't have his stack of Hot Fives—or at least the *Fifty Hot Choruses of Armstrong* published by Melrose—and wasn't trying to learn Louis' tricks.

Their idol, meanwhile, was busy conquering the American public, appearing all over the country before wildly cheering throngs. Besides his incomparable playing, his warm personal style went far in freeing jazz from its stigma as a coarse music fit for bars and bawdy houses only. His tours and appearances in films made jazz familiar to many people who had

***From Europe to the Orient,** jazz made its mark. By mid-century it had developed an international character, as new performers such as British saxophonist John Dankworth (left) and French jazz violinist Stephane Grappelli (center) came of age. But no one was more instrumental in the worldwide popularization of jazz than Satchmo (right).*

barely heard about it before. Other musical styles would arise to challenge his brand of music, including swing in the thirties and forties, bop in the post-World War II years, and, later, cool "progressive" jazz. But no changes in musical fashion could dim Louis' personal popularity.

In the end he wound up conquering the world. Over the years jazz, by many considered the only unique American musical form, also inspired an enthusiastic audience in Europe, kept alive by a steady flow of records. Louis' records naturally made him something of a hero. A series of trips abroad after 1932, and the immensely popular album *Armstrong Plays Handy*, prepared the way for a triumphal European tour by "Ambassador Satch" in 1955. Then it was on to South America, Africa, and every other corner of the globe with his music. Even in the sixties, when the once mighty lip began to give out, his phenomenal popularity could make the vocals "Mack the Knife" and "Hello, Dolly" bestsellers from Kansas to Kenya.

Thanks largely to the Armstrong magic and what the French call *le jazz hot*, foreign performers have taken hold to give jazz an international spirit. London's John Dankworth, Stephane Grappelli of Paris, Belgian-born Django Reinhardt (the late Gypsy guitarist who was really a citizen of the world), and scores of others have made notable contributions. And the swinging, off beat Armstrong style is still a living presence in contemporary music, whether heard in the wailing blues guitar of B. B. King or the soulful singing style of Aretha Franklin.

When he died peacefully in his New York home on July 6, 1971, Louis Armstrong left a legacy that is unlikely ever to be matched. He had been the primary influence on at least two generations of musicians, and more than any other performer he had created a global audience for his music. To the millions whose affection he won, the notes he sounded will never cease to ring high and clear and true; as long as anyone, anywhere, is playing jazz, Satch lives.

The Artist as Celebrity

Unlike many of their more pampered ancestors, 20th-century artists have had to fend for themselves. The patronage system died out long before the turn of the century, as the industrial revolution transformed Western society. Forced to drum up enthusiasm for their work, artists found eager allies in the media, always in search of colorful copy and fresh sensations. Increasingly, artists have had to compete for attention with a host of rivals—politicians, athletes, entertainers, and the like.

The problems posed by celebrity —how to win it, and how to live with it once won—have troubled artists in many countries. But in America an artist who was both successful and glamorous was often so hounded by publicity that his life and art were affected. Examples are two of the most colorful American writers of the twenties, F. Scott Fitzgerald and Ernest Hemingway, and perhaps the most luminous actress in screen history, Greta Garbo.

F. Scott Fitzgerald's novel, *This Side of Paradise,* his first, tells the story of Amory Blaine, a handsome, wealthy Princetonian struggling to understand himself as part of a postwar generation "grown up to find all gods dead, all wars fought, all faith in man shaken." The book glorifies the revolution in morals that was sweeping American youth in the 1920's. Religion, culture, patriotism, and standards of decorum and morality were rejected with elaborate cynicism by many of Blaine's contemporaries, who found greater meaning in jazz, "petting parties," casual seduction, and bathtub gin. The book, published in March 1920, hit an instantly responsive chord. By the year's end some 50,000 copies had been sold.

Ironically, *This Side of Paradise* is not a great novel, and certainly not Fitzgerald's best. In spite of some memorable scenes and dazzling descriptions, it displays all the weaknesses of a fledgling author's work—naivete, pomposity, overripeness. Nonetheless, it unerringly caught the spirit of what Fitzgerald was the first to call the Jazz Age, and its enormous success made him, in one critic's phrase, a "kind of king of our American youth." Nothing could have pleased Fitzgerald more.

"1,000 Parties and No Work"

Like many of his fictional heroes, Fitzgerald was handsome, sensitive, ambitious, and a product of Princeton. But unlike them, he was never really rich, and he wanted very much to be—so much so that the "romance of money," as one critic termed it, ran through nearly all his writing.

Fitzgerald was born in St. Paul, Minnesota, in 1896, the son of a luckless commercial traveler who died young and an eccentric, book-loving mother, whose modest inheritance provided the family's only income. At Newman boarding school and then at Princeton, Fitzgerald was always among the most impoverished students. Dazzled by the glamour of Eastern society and hungry for fame and success, he relied on his great charm, his good looks,

Scott Fitzgerald *met Zelda Sayre (the portrait is by James Montgomery Flagg) in 1918 while he was stationed in Alabama. The success of* This Side of Paradise, *his largely autobiographical first novel, allowed him to marry her.*

***Fitzgerald,** flush with fame and money, moved his family (left) to the Riviera in 1924, where they were quickly taken up by the leaders of the expatriate society. But Scott could not hold on to the money he made, and after Zelda's breakdown he began drinking heavily. Jay Gatsby (below, the Newport mansion used in the 1973 film of* The Great Gatsby) *could have been Fitzgerald: a bedazzled midwesterner bent on living the life of the Eastern rich.*

and his developing talent for imaginative writing to gain acceptance.

In 1917 he left Princeton for the army, romantically hoping for combat duty overseas. Instead, he was assigned to stateside service. After the war he worked in a Manhattan advertising agency, using every spare hour to work and rework the manuscript that finally became *This Side of Paradise.* The novel won Fitzgerald instant fame—and a wife. For two years he had courted Zelda Sayre, the pretty, headstrong daughter of an Alabama judge, but he had been refused because he had so little money and so few apparent prospects. The novel's success persuaded Zelda to change her mind, and a month after its publication the two were married. Within weeks of their wedding the Fitzgeralds were New York society's most sought-after couple—handsome, engaging, ever eager to draw attention to themselves. They rode from party to party on the roofs of taxicabs and splashed in the fountain in front of the sedate Plaza Hotel. Scott brawled with doormen; Zelda danced on tabletops and became the quintessential flapper with her bobbed hair, short skirts, and flippant manner.

For 10 frenzied years the couple lived at fever pitch, a period the author later remembered as "1,000 parties and no work." They conquered the social world of the eastern seaboard and cavorted among American expatriates in Paris and along the Riviera.

Fitzgerald partially paid for the long bouts of drinking and almost desperate gaiety with short bursts of intensive work at the typewriter. Most of his 160-odd stories were of only momentary interest, written solely to meet current bills, but perhaps a third of them are among the finest ever produced by an American writer. Despite the great popularity of his magazine fiction and the substantial sales of his next two novels, *The Beautiful and the Damned* (1922) and *The Great Gatsby* (1925), Fitzgerald remained hopelessly mired in debt for most of his life.

The Crack-Up

By 1926 there were signs of the terrible anguish that was to haunt the rest of his career. Zelda came to resent her husband's fame and grew increasingly irrational when she failed in her artistic attempts. She finally broke down completely and had to be confined to institutions. In 1948 she died in a sanatorium fire.

Meanwhile, Fitzgerald's popularity plummeted almost as rapidly as it had risen. The Great Depression made his tales of the rich and well born seem frivolous and irrelevant, devoid of the social consciousness readers now demanded.

Fitzgerald slipped deeper into alcoholism—a process of disintegration he chronicled with chilling clarity in a memorable magazine series called *The Crack-Up.* After the commercial failure of his last completed novel, *Tender Is the Night* (1934), he devoted himself to screenwriting in Hollywood until his death in 1940.

Fitzgerald once wrote that "there are no second acts in America." In his own case, the wry perception was prophetic.

In 1939 Hemingway was writing For Whom the Bell Tolls, *a novel inspired by his experiences during the Spanish Civil War. It deals with the survival of comradeship and love amid the chaos of war. All his life Hemingway was fascinated by the way humans respond to extreme situations. Death intrigued him, and he was a devoted hunter. Right, on a pheasant shoot in Idaho in 1941.*

A passionate fisherman, Hemingway spun one of his most perfect fables, The Old Man and the Sea, *from the drama of a combat between man and fish.*

Ernest Hemingway was, like Fitzgerald, an international celebrity, one of the world's most famous writers for more than 30 years. And like Fitzgerald's, his turbulent career ended in tragedy.

Hemingway's first novel, *The Sun Also Rises* (1926), burst upon the literary scene like an artillery shell and made its author a star at age 27. It tells the story of a desperately carefree, mostly drunken band of American expatriates who journey from Paris to Pamplona to take part in the annual running of the bulls. They carouse, quarrel, risk their lives before angry bulls, fall in and out of love with one another—anything to escape the everyday world. In his distinctive prose style—terse, understated, dryly matter-of-fact—Hemingway brilliantly captured the mood of his contemporaries: weary, often cynical, groping for something to believe in. As with Fitzgerald, his art grew directly from his life.

Hemingway was born in Oak Park, Illinois, in 1899. His father, a physician, introduced him to hunting and fishing in the woods of northern Michigan, two passions that endured throughout his life.

A Life of Action

Resolving early to become a writer, Hemingway passed up college to work as a cub reporter for the Kansas City *Star*, then volunteered as an ambulance driver during World War I and was gravely wounded while serving on the Italian front.

Two years later Hemingway covered the Greco-Turkish War as a correspondent for the Toronto *Star*, and in 1922 settled in Paris, then a mecca for American artists and writers. Dubbed the Lost Generation by their unofficial leader, writer Gertrude Stein, the expatriates also included the poet Ezra Pound and (briefly) Fitzgerald. All three interested themselves in Hemingway's work: Pound and Stein helped him fashion his lean prose style and Fitzgerald induced his own publisher, Charles Scribner, to look at the young man's writing.

A volume of short stories, *In Our Time,* appeared in 1925 and caused a stir in literary circles. But *The Sun Also Rises* made him familiar to the general reading public.

Hemingway's abiding goal as a writer was to evoke remembered emotion, not by describing it but by putting down "what really happened in action . . . the sequence of

***The bullring,** Hemingway said in* Death in the Afternoon, *was "the only place where you could see life and . . . violent death now that the wars were over."*

motion and fact which made the emotion" and leaving the reader to experience it along with his characters. To this end every sentence was pared to the bone. Hemingway's powerful, tightly packed prose style was imitated by a whole generation of writers. "No novelist in the world," said British author C.P. Snow, "has produced such an effect on other people's writing."

The Legend
Even more than Fitzgerald, Hemingway became identified with his heroes. His protagonists were usually scarred veterans of war, distrustful of politicians and dogma, certain of little but the importance of complete honesty and the inevitability of death. They were also virile, restless, knowledgeable about food, wine, and women, and fond of the manly rituals of sport. All these qualities were visibly present in Hemingway's own complex personality and a part of his past.

The enormous success of his novel *A Farewell to Arms* (1929) enabled him to live the life he wrote about. He haunted the bullrings of Spain, becoming an expert on that gory drama. He traveled ceaselessly, boxing, skiing, spinning tales, and battling his critics—sometimes with his fists, sometimes in print.

He covered the Spanish Civil War, which was to serve as the background for his 1940 novel *For Whom the Bell Tolls*. While shells exploded outside his Madrid hotel, he worked on a play. In 1941 he covered the war in China. Three years later he was in Europe, fighting and drinking his way into Paris with the French Resistance and winning a Bronze Star for bravery.

Through all his turbulent adventures, however, he remained disciplined about his craft. "To work was the only thing," he wrote, "it was the only thing that always made you feel good."

But much of his later work seemed little more than an awkward self-parody. (One notable exception was *The Old Man and the Sea*, published in 1952, which won the 1954 Nobel Prize for Literature.) Hemingway entered a sad, downward spiral during the late 1950's. He became convinced he was being spied upon, bickered with old friends, underwent shock treatment for depression, and wept privately over his inability to summon up his youthful powers.

In the spring of 1961, while reworking *A Moveable Feast*, a bittersweet memoir of his Paris days, he found himself literally unable to write a line. The writer whose goal had been to transmit the joy of a life of action felt no joy. At dawn on July 2, at his home in Ketchum, Idaho, Hemingway killed himself with a shotgun. He could not bear to outlive his awesome talent.

Greta Garbo

If the personal fame and notoriety won by Fitzgerald and Hemingway was of far greater intensity than that generally bestowed upon writers, it was not new to entertainers. In the 1920's, however, the publicity heaped upon the stars of a new medium, motion pictures, was almost beyond belief. It was impossible for a movie star to remain at the top without surrendering to the spotlight of public attention. Only a few resisted. The best known of these was Greta Garbo, whose brilliant performances and magnetic personality made her the leading film actress of her time but whose loathing for hokum and love of privacy forced her to leave the screen at the height of her career.

Becoming the Greatest Actress
Garbo's early years offered few clues to her future. She was born Greta Gustaffson in Stockholm, Sweden, in 1905, the plump, pretty descendant of sturdy farmers. Her father died when she was 14, and she was forced to leave school and work at odd jobs to help support her family, but she was always interested in acting. She made her modest camera debut modeling hats for a store catalog, then appeared in two short advertising films. Later she won a scholarship to study at the Royal Dramatic Theater, where she caught the eye of Mauritz Stiller, one of Sweden's finest directors.

Stiller was convinced from the first that he could mold her into a great actress. He took over her life, accompanying her everywhere, changing her name, telling her how to dress, act, walk, and talk. "She is," he once said proudly, "like wax in my hands."

Garbo photographed well in her first feature, *Gösta Berling's Saga* (1924), but showed little acting skill. Then Stiller's direction won him an offer from movie mogul Louis B. Mayer to come to Hollywood. Stiller said he would accept if Garbo could come with him, and Mayer reluctantly agreed. Both went to Hollywood, but Stiller soon grew dissatisfied and returned to Sweden. Garbo stayed and underwent the standard studio buildup. She reluctantly gave interviews in broken English and posed for ludicrous publicity stills with a toothless MGM lion. Her first two U.S. movies were undistinguished, but in 1927 she made *Flesh and the Devil,* in which she played smoldering love scenes with John Gilbert, the screen's "perfect lover." This film, enhanced by rumors of an off-screen romance between the two, made Garbo a star. Her potent box-office appeal, however, involved more than her extraordinary beauty, and certainly more than any titillating gossip about her private life.

What mattered most was the fact that she could act, *really* act. Before Garbo, most stars represented types rather than fully rounded characters. Thus Mary Pickford was "America's sweetheart," cheerful and perpetually pure; Theda Bara was "the vamp," an exotic temptress always on the lookout for a naive young man to ruin; and Clara Bow was the "It" girl, sexy, bold, and brassy, the ultimate flapper.

Garbo could do it all. Though most of the parts Hollywood gave her were what she scornfully called "bad womens," she brought to them a sensitivity and cool intelligence never before seen in the movies. Actor Lionel Barrymore put it simply: "She was the greatest actress ever seen on the screen."

The Swedish Sphinx

Garbo's phenomenal success both pleased and bewildered her, for her fame brought with it the ceaseless glare of publicity. Without Stiller to shield her, uneasy in English, and dissatisfied with her roles, she became almost obsessively protective of her privacy. She shunned parties, barred onlookers (including studio executives) from her sets, refused interviews and autographs, traveled under assumed names, and hid the famous "face of the century" behind a spy's disguise of dark glasses, upturned collars, and cloche hats.

The result, of course, was the opposite of what Garbo wanted. As the mysteriously aloof "Swedish Sphinx," she presented the press with a constant challenge. News hounds haunted her every step; cameramen snapped her through windows; gossip columnists gushed about her romances with John Gilbert and conductor Leopold Stokowski and fabricated lurid details when she refused to provide them.

She put up with it all for 14 years while giving a long series of memorable screen performances, including those in *Grand Hotel* (1932), *Queen Christina* (1933), *Anna Karenina* (1935), *Camille* (1936), and *Ninotchka* (1939).

Then, in 1941, though just 36 years old, she simply quit. She had temporarily withdrawn from films before (until her salary demands were met), but this time she meant it. Though her return to the screen has repeatedly been rumored, she has turned down every script sent to her, continuing to seek the anonymity denied her by the 20th-century publicity machine. Garbo has become one of New York's millions.

Hollywood and her own genius *transformed Greta Garbo from a hopeful starlet (above, in 1925) into a celebrity and finally, via such roles as Camille (below, with Robert Taylor), into one of the alltime movie greats. But the statement by which the public knew her best was, "I want to be alone."*

***Icy and alluring** in* Mata Hari, *Greta Garbo came to typify the star who both attracts and shuns celebrity. She made her last film in 1941 and despite the demands of an ever-growing cult never stepped back into the limelight.*

A CHRONOLOGY OF THE ARTS: 1919-29

1919

- The Bauhaus school was established at Weimar, Germany, by architect Walter Gropius and others. It helped inspire the international style of architecture and strongly influenced modern art and design by insisting that they pay due regard to the role of the machine. (See pp. 154–159.)
- "The Six" was formed in Paris. A group of young composers, it included Darius Milhaud, Arthur Honegger, Francis Poulenc, Louis Durey, Georges Auric, and Germaine Taillefere—all major figures in modern music.

1920

- Eugene O'Neill's *Beyond the Horizon* opened in New York, launching the career of a great American playwright.
- French writer Colette published *Chéri,* perhaps the best known of her many novels and short stories on the theme of romantic love.
- U.S. writer F. Scott Fitzgerald published his first novel, *This Side of Paradise.* A tale of "flaming youth" on campus, it established its young author as the spokesman of the Jazz Age.
- English author D.H. Lawrence wrote his novel *Women in Love,* one of the finest of his powerful studies of English life and human passions.

1921

- Italian dramatist Luigi Pirandello penned *Six Characters in Search of an Author,* an innovative masterpiece in which characters "rejected" by the playwright appear on stage to interrupt and comment upon the action, underlining an intimate relationship between art and life.

1922

- U.S.-born critic, poet, and playwright T.S. Eliot wrote *The Waste Land.* Among the best-known poems of the century, it mirrored the despair felt by many postwar artists, and won its author international renown.
- Irish writer James Joyce published *Ulysses,* a milestone of modern literature. Highly praised for its dazzling language, it revealed epic meanings in the daily lives of ordinary Dubliners. Its frankness also made it a target of censors on both sides of the Atlantic. (See pp. 238–243.)
- U.S. novelist Sinclair Lewis published *Babbitt,* a savage lampoon of life in a small American town. The name of its central character became synonymous with the unrelenting pursuit of wealth and status.

1923

- Austrian composer Arnold Schoenberg perfected 12-tone music, freeing composition from the traditional major and minor keys. For each piece he created an original sequence of all 12 notes of the chromatic scale, then employed an elegant series of 48 interrelated variations, the basis of a system that revolutionized modern music.

1924

- French poet André Breton issued his *Surrealist Manifesto,* inspiring artists in many fields to explore the subconscious mind. (See pp. 186–191.)
- British novelist E.M. Forster published *A Passage to India,* an incisive look at the personal and cultural tensions underlying British colonial life.
- German writer Thomas Mann published *The Magic Mountain.* Considered by many critics the masterpiece of a long, distinguished career, it probed the intellectual pretensions of the era with sharp irony.

1925

- U.S. writer Theodore Dreiser published *An American Tragedy,* the most widely admired of his many realistic, impassioned assaults on U.S. society.

1926

- U.S. author Ernest Hemingway published his highly successful novel *The Sun Also Rises.* It painted a vivid picture of life among disillusioned expatriate Americans in France and Spain.

1927

- British novelist Virginia Woolf published *To the Lighthouse,* the best known and most accessible of her experimental, impressionistic novels.
- *The Jazz Singer,* the first talking feature film, opened.

1924

The Surrealist Manifesto

A radical new generation of artists explores the bizarre, uncharted landscape of the subconscious mind.

In 1924 a manifesto was published in Paris that struck a responsive chord in an entire generation of young writers, musicians, and painters. Inspired by its strange message and by its magnetically persuasive author, its adherents produced a body of powerful, disturbing work that substantially changed the way we view the world. They were the surrealists.

Their leading spokesman, the author of the 1924 manifesto, was André Breton, a French poet and a follower of Sigmund Freud. Breton had first noticed a kinship between art and madness while working with shell-shocked soldiers during World War I. In subsequent efforts to penetrate his own subconscious, he toyed with the occult, held seances, studied hypnotism, and tried writing while in a trance. In 1921 he and fellow poet Philippe Soupault published the first "automatic writing," a collection of literary fragments they created by allowing their subconscious reveries to provide words and images at random without regard for traditional sequence or meaning.

Three years later Breton issued the *Manifeste du surréalisme,* surrealist manifesto, which set forth his philosophy of art as an expression of the subconscious mind. Henceforth, he proclaimed, the artist in every field must abandon conventional logic and conscious thought to tap instead the boundless resources of his subconscious. "We must burst the bonds of reason," he declared. All pretense of talent must be forgotten, and every artist must seek instead to become the "modest recording device of his dreams." Those willing to create "free from any control by the reason" would encounter a new "absolute reality or super-reality."

Breton's perception of the mysterious power of the irrational and the "omnipotence of the dream" was far from new. The surrealist impulse had emerged before—in the 15th-century Gothic fantasies of the Flemish painter Hieronymus Bosch, in the grotesque hallucinations of the 18th-century Spanish artist Fran-

***The "automatic" drawings** of André Masson approached the surrealist ideal of "pure psychic automatism" (above, "Automatic Drawing," 1924). By rapidly tracing random scribblings on paper, he attempted to reveal the unconscious meanderings of his own psyche when freed from the restrictive bounds of reason and artistic convention.*

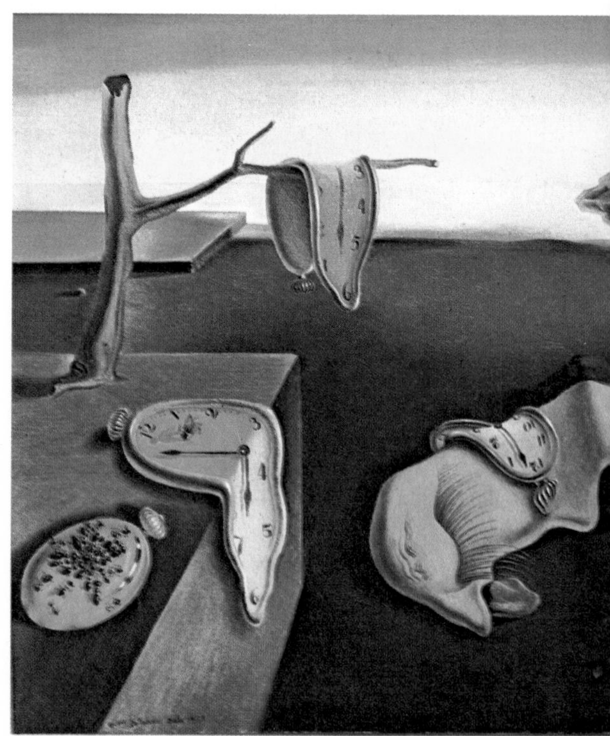

cisco Goya, and in the nightmarish imaginings of American writer Edgar Allan Poe. In France, Charles Baudelaire and Arthur Rimbaud were the poetic godfathers of surrealism, along with the Comte de Lautréamont and Guillaume Apollinaire.

But the oracle of the movement, the theorist whose revolutionary teachings helped Breton turn an impulse into an agenda, was Sigmund Freud, the man who first emphasized the extraordinary role of memory and the subconscious in shaping human behavior.

Freud believed that the waking mind, conditioned by the strictures of social convention, provides a limited and misleading impression of the true self; that on the deeper level of dreams men express their truest yearnings and anxieties by means of a secret language of symbol and association.

Freud himself had a strong interest in art and wrote lengthy essays on Leonardo's "Mona Lisa" and Michelangelo's "Moses," searching the works for hidden clues to the artists' psyches. Yet he never advocated the type of experimentation championed by Breton. In fact, when Breton explained his artistic exploration of the subconscious to Freud in 1921, the psychiatrist offered him very little encouragement.

"The Abolition of All Logic"

Surrealism's immediate predecessor was dadaism, an anarchistic art movement born amid the horrors of World War I. In 1915 young pacifists from all over

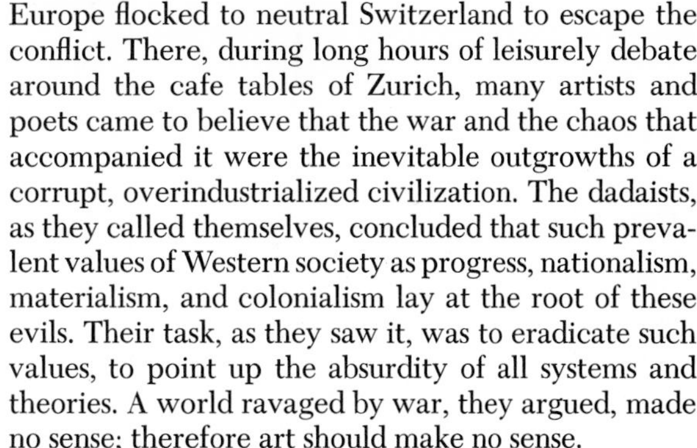

Europe flocked to neutral Switzerland to escape the conflict. There, during long hours of leisurely debate around the cafe tables of Zurich, many artists and poets came to believe that the war and the chaos that accompanied it were the inevitable outgrowths of a corrupt, overindustrialized civilization. The dadaists, as they called themselves, concluded that such prevalent values of Western society as progress, nationalism, materialism, and colonialism lay at the root of these evils. Their task, as they saw it, was to eradicate such values, to point up the absurdity of all systems and theories. A world ravaged by war, they argued, made no sense; therefore art should make no sense.

Their leader was Tristan Tzara, a Romanian-born poet with a gift for sloganeering, whose delight in shocking the public was infectious. His grandiose proclamations parodied the lofty declarations of contemporary statesmen. "We spit on humanity," he announced in 1916. "Dada," he declared, "is the abolition of all logic. . . . There is a great negative work of destruction to be done. We must sweep everything away and sweep clean."

To Tzara and his followers nothing was sacred because everything was meaningless. Even the group's name was nonsensical: Dada, which means hobbyhorse in French, was picked at random from the dictionary. Before long the government, the military, the church, the general public, art critics, and established artists all came under clamorous dadaist attack in magazines, paintings, and outrageous cabaret skits.

This self-styled "shock treatment for a crazed humanity" swiftly spread to other cultural centers. By the war's end there were groups of dadaists in Madrid, Berlin, Hanover, Cologne, and New York. Toward the end of 1919 Tzara carried dada to Paris, where its genial nihilism attracted the allegiance of a number of young writers, including Breton, Soupault, Louis Aragon, and Paul Éluard.

The unexpected juxtaposition *of unrelated objects, a surrealist innovation, inspired sculptress Meret Oppenheim to combine the fuzzy texture of fur with normally smooth-surfaced utensils in her 1936 composition, "Fur-Covered Cup, Saucer, and Spoon" (right).*

The strange hallucinations *of painter Salvador Dali, whom André Breton called "the incarnation of the surrealist spirit," introduced a new visual vocabulary of limp watches ("The Persistence of Memory," 1931, left), blazing giraffes, and other irrational images.*

***The irreverent surrealist impulse** also inspired dadaist Marcel Duchamp ("Nude Descending a Staircase, No. 2," 1912, left) and Giorgio de Chirico ("The Mystery and Melancholy of a Street," 1914, above).*

In Paris dada was primarily a literary and theatrical movement. Its most celebrated manifestation was a series of riotous stage performances in which weirdly garbed dadaists spouted gibberish verse while others drowned them out with drums and bells. The few words that reached the audiences' ears were often grossly insulting, and angry patrons sometimes retaliated by hurling rotten fruit at the stage.

"A Free, Revolutionary, Independent Art"

By 1920, however, dada was dying. The movement carried within it the seeds of its own destruction, as does any theory that holds all theories absurd. In their frantic search for ways to upset the status quo, the dadaists began to repeat themselves. Breton and his associates felt that some serious purpose was needed to focus dada's great energy and inventiveness. That purpose was embodied in surrealism.

Dada, Breton declared, had only been a "state of mind." Surrealism offered more, the creation of a "free, revolutionary, independent art." Breton and the surrealists, many of whom had been dadaists, shared dada's scorn for convention and its conviction that the world was mad. Unlike the dadaists, they envisioned a solution: a new reality achieved through a deliberate return to the innocence of childhood fantasies and the omnipotence of dreams.

An impressive roster of international artists eventually rallied to Breton's banner. Among them were Jean Arp, Max Ernst, Alberto Giacometti, René Magritte, André Masson, Joan Miró, Yves Tanguy, and Salvador Dali, in addition to Aragon, Soupault, and Éluard.

Because Breton was a poet, surrealism's first expression was written. Authors sought to banish all conscious thought in order to allow images, words, and phrases to flow unchecked from their subconscious depths onto the paper. They often achieved surprisingly powerful effects through the accumulation of apparently random thoughts and the juxtaposition of normally unrelated words and images. But surrealism's literary life was relatively short. The mere recounting of dreams and reveries eventually proved too limiting for Breton's most gifted disciples, and his authoritarian personality helped bring an early parting of the ways.

Handsome, grimly earnest, and given to oratory, Breton would have made a splendid political revolutionary. His true purpose was to effect a revolution in the realm of the mind, but he soon came to believe that

LA RÉVOLUTION SURRÉALISTE

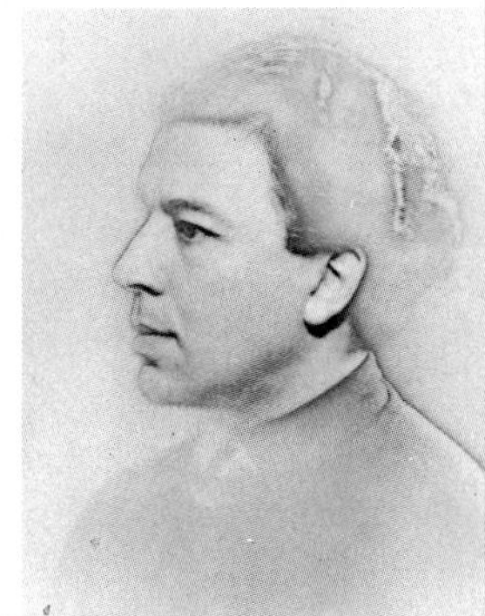

THE ORACLE OF SURREALISM

"I believe in the future resolution of the states of dream and reality . . ." proclaimed French poet André Breton (right, in a photograph by Man Ray) in 1924. His literary mouthpiece, *La Révolution Surréaliste* (above), publicized surrealist works.

his goal could not be achieved without first overturning the existing political and social systems. The early antics and publications of the surrealists, designed to shock the public into an awareness of its follies, merely antagonized. When Breton, Éluard, Aragon, and others disrupted a dignified literary banquet, even the press turned against them.

Thereafter the movement allied itself with the Communists, giving enthusiastic support to their goal of worldwide revolution. Breton entitled surrealism's official publication, which first appeared in 1925, *La Révolution Surréaliste.* In 1929 he published a second manifesto, placing his movement "at the service of the revolution." The creation of a new global order, he proclaimed, was art's "supreme task."

Yet the surrealists never agreed on a concerted political program. They were simply too individualistic to adhere to the strict dogma of official communism and perhaps, as intellectuals, too far removed from the proletariat to voice more than token sympathies for its plight. Political squabbling led to the expulsion of Aragon, Éluard, and others from surrealist ranks, and Breton himself was expelled from the French Communist Party for his unorthodox views in 1936.

A Landscape of Dreams and Nightmares

Surrealist paintings—the haunting canvases of Dali, Magritte, and others—had a much more profound and enduring impact than Breton's theories and writings.

Some artists developed new techniques for applying Breton's dictate of "automatism" directly to their work. French painter André Masson, for example, created semiabstract drawings from seemingly random doodles. German artist Max Ernst invented the technique of *frottage,* pencil rubbings of pressed flowers, wood, and other textured objects. Ernst also assembled eerie collages by combining painted canvas or magazine illustrations with bits of wood and other natural fragments. Spanish painter Joan Miró populated his canvases with colorful, amebalike forms suggesting whimsical human or animal silhouettes.

Other painters, including Belgian René Magritte, Frenchman Yves Tanguy, and Spaniard Salvador Dali, developed a style that might be called "fantastic realism," rendering weird, often nightmarish visions with an almost photographic clarity. Their unnerving juxtaposition of the familiar and the unknown lay at the heart of the surrealist impulse.

Some recurring images from Dali's works—melting watches, blazing giraffes, misshapen human figures—have become widely recognized examples of surrealism at its most flamboyantly bizarre. Dali was also given to surrealistic behavior: At a lecture he delivered on surrealism in London, he appeared in a diving helmet to emphasize his intention of submerging himself in his subconscious. On another occasion, during an interview with a *New York Times* reporter, he wore a lamb chop on his head. Dali's behavior proved so embarrassing to the movement that he was expelled in 1934, although he was permitted to continue exhibiting with his former colleagues.

The surrealists' activities were not limited to literary and graphic experimentation. Dali and others were quick to see that cinematic techniques such as dissolves, multiple images, and montages could create strong surrealistic effects.

In 1929 Dali collaborated with fellow Spaniard Luis Buñuel to produce the surrealist film *Le Chien Andalou* ("The Andalusian Dog"). Two years later the first showing of their film *L'Age d'Or* ("The Golden Age") provoked the audience to riot. Other surrealist film classics include *Entr'Acte* by René Clair (1924) and Jean Cocteau's *Blood of a Poet* (1931).

Surrealist Chic

After 1929 surrealism spread rapidly from Paris to other international centers, including London, New York, Prague, Brussels, Tokyo, and Copenhagen. Breton traveled to Czechoslovakia, Belgium, England, and the Canary Islands to expound his theories. In 1938 he visited Mexico, where he met the exiled Leon

Belgian surrealist *René Magritte wrote of his painting "The Human Condition" (1933): "In front of a window . . . I placed a picture representing exactly that part of the landscape which was masked by the picture. In this way the tree represented in the picture hid the tree standing behind it, outside the room. For the spectator the tree was at one and the same time in the room—in the picture—and, by inference, outside the room—in the real landscape. This is how we see the world; we see it outside ourselves and yet we have only a representation of it within us."*

The whimsical *"automatic" paintings of Joan Miró ("Person Throwing a Stone at a Bird," 1926, above) began as unconscious brushstrokes, which gradually emerged as men, birds, and other identifiable forms.*

Images of decay *and decomposition haunt the eerie landscape of Max Ernst's "Europe After the Rain" (1940–42). His highly individualistic style integrated two divergent surrealist impulses, combining the irrational visions of Dali and Magritte with the automatism of Miró and Masson.*

Trotsky and leftist painter Diego Rivera, who was also deeply committed to social reform. With Rivera, he published a manifesto entitled *Pour un Art Révolutionnaire Indépendant* ("For an Independent Revolutionary Art"), urging artists of the world to unite.

Earlier that year Breton had declared: "Never has civilization been menaced so seriously as today." To him and to many of his disciples the ominous rush of international events seemed almost as nightmarish as the surrealists' gloomiest artistic visions. While Prime Minister Neville Chamberlain led the forces of appeasement, Adolf Hitler was plotting the annexation of Austria. In Madrid the Spanish Republicans were preparing to evacuate, and in Paris the government had been toppled by an economic crisis. The madness of World War I seemed about to recur.

The growing global lunacy was mirrored in a massive international surrealist exhibition that opened at the Galerie des Beaux-Arts in Paris on January 17, 1938. Simultaneously the last gasp and the spectacular climax of the organized movement, it featured the works of some 70 artists from 14 nations. Other exhibitions had been held in London and New York to help spread surrealism abroad, but this was the first major show of the genre to be held in Paris, the city of the movement's birth. Breton and his followers spared no effort to make it the crowning statement of their aims.

Gone were all the conventional trappings of a gallery. Twelve thousand sacks of coal were suspended from the ceiling, and exhibition space was only dimly lit, producing a grottolike effect. Rumpled beds, some of them occupied by sleeping models, stood in the corners. The floor was littered with sticks and dead leaves. A machine roasting coffee beans sent their pungent odor wafting through the entire gallery.

But it was the art itself that drew the crowds. "Rainy Taxi," a Dali tableau that stood in the lobby, set the tone for the grotesque display within. In the back seat of an ancient, vine-covered taxi sat a seminude store-window mannequin surrounded by rotting vegetables.

Swiss sculptor *Alberto Giacometti translated the surrealist mandate into sculpture in "The Palace at 4 A.M." (1932–33).*

Live snails crawled across her face while a torrent of "rain" fell on her from ducts in the taxi roof.

Inside, exhibits included paintings, drawings, and collages by all the major surrealist artists. There were also 16 exotically garbed mannequins and a rich trove of curious objects and furniture, including a footstool with four silk-stockinged legs; a fur-lined spoon, cup, and saucer; and a vast umbrella made of sponges.

The show was a spectacular success. A milling throng of fashionably gowned women and their dapper escorts eagerly crowded the opening, stumbling through the semidarkness to view the exhibits by flashlight. When a lovely actress, clad only in chains, leaped up at a prearranged signal and splashed onlookers with muddy water, they were delighted. Surrealism, originally intended to outrage, had become chic.

Surrealists were prized dinner guests at smart Parisian homes. Their works were bought for handsome prices by rich art collectors who had read little Freud but enjoyed dabbling in dream analysis. Ever sensitive to the shifting cultural winds, advertising agencies on both sides of the Atlantic stole surrealist imagery to peddle a host of consumer products. So did the designers of department store windows. Soon eccentrically dressed mannequins and outsized liquor bottles looming over desert sands became visual cliches.

World War II brought the end of surrealism as an organized movement. With the fall of France in 1940, its adherents scattered across the globe. Breton, Ernst, and others fled to America, where they helped inspire the important postwar school of action painting.

Although the movement as such was dead, its influence continued. Most visibly, the surrealist technique of juxtaposing incongruous elements (a package of cigarettes swimming to the surface of a mountain pool, or a zipper on a human face) and of magnifying objects to enormous proportions have become part of the repertoire of modern advertising. In films (notably those of Luis Buñuel), surrealist techniques often indicate dreams, psychological associations, or fantasies. Pop artists such as Andy Warhol and Claes Oldenberg borrowed techniques indirectly from surrealism via outsized billboard advertisements.

The surrealists' most important contribution was to focus attention on the strange world of the psyche, illuminating its depths and complexities more vividly than any written theory of psychoanalysis could have done. By revealing their fantasies, by exposing the irrational and absurd sides of the human character, their antics provided, at the very least, a safety valve for a period still reeling in the aftermath of World War I. For those willing to take a longer, closer look, their work was more: a revelation of the subconscious drives that motivate individuals and societies alike.

A corporation's annual report *uses the same device as Magritte did in* The Human Condition*: the cover features a landscape superimposed on an identical scene, just far enough out of alignment to pique the reader's interest. In the highly competitive field of advertising a prime goal is to attract and hold the consumer's attention amid the thousands of voices and images urging him to spend. In today's media-saturated world the advertiser who makes an impression is likelier to get the dollar. Surrealistic art, with its powerful appeal to the unconscious, can catch the buyer on the run.*

1926

First Step to the Stars

Spurred by a vision of space travel, a Massachusetts physicist builds the world's first liquid-fuel rocket.

A dusting of snow covered the fields of the old Ward farm in Auburn, Massachusetts, as Dr. Robert Hutchings Goddard, physics professor at Clark University in nearby Worcester, finished his work in the deserted flatland below the farmhouse. There he and an assistant, Henry Sachs, had set up the metal framework of a rocket launching stand.

On the stand was an odd-looking rocket. Ten feet long, it had no cover or casing, and its motor and nozzle were mounted at the front rather than the rear. Two narrow metal tubes led from the motor to a pair of small tanks at the rocket's base. One tank contained gasoline, the other liquid oxygen, called lox.

The date was March 16, 1926, and the rocket was the culmination of many years of work by the tall, balding physicist. Since he was 17, Goddard had been intensely interested in rocket flight, at first experimenting with solid fuels (mostly varieties of gunpowder) as propellants, then turning to a highly explosive mixture of gasoline and liquid oxygen for extra power. Long, trying months of testing had seemed to justify his faith in the new fuel, but the final question, to be answered that afternoon, remained: Had he at last found the key to high-altitude rocket flight?

Arrows of Fire

Rockets were far from new at the time of Dr. Goddard's liquid-fuel experiment. The ancient Chinese, first known users of gunpowder, are also credited with the invention of the rocket. An account of the siege of Kaifeng in 1232 describes the terrifying effect that the Chinese "arrows of flying fire" had on the Mongol besiegers. A few years later, in 1241, the Tartars used rockets against the Poles at the Battle of Legnica, and in 1288 the Arabs launched a rocket attack against the Spanish town of Valencia.

In 1405 the first known theorist of rocketry, Konrad Kaiser von Eichstadt, published a treatise on fortifications, in which he described several different kinds of rocket. Throughout the 16th century a number of books dealing with the military and nonmilitary uses of rockets appeared, and in 1650 a Polish artillery expert, Kazimierz Siemienowicz, published several prophetic designs, including one for a multistage rocket.

The next developments in rocketry occurred in India, where toward the end of the 18th century Haidar Ali, Prince of Mysore, began to manufacture gunpowder rockets in tubular iron casings. After his death in 1782 his son, Tipu Sahib, continued to develop the weapons and equipped his expanded rocket corps with 6- to 12-pound missiles, thereby inflicting a number of heavy losses on the British Army between 1792 and 1799. The British were quick to learn from the experience and in 1807 they bombarded the city of Copenhagen with 25,000 rockets designed by William Congreve.

Congreve's rockets weighed up to 60 pounds, had a top range of two miles, and carried a variety of incendiary and antipersonnel heads. Despite their sophistication, however, they were unable (as the U.S. national anthem records) to dislodge the "star-spangled banner" from its appointed place above Fort McHenry during the War of 1812. But they were used to burn down the White House—not by being fired into it but by being wedged into the beams and ignited.

By the end of the 19th century improvements in artillery had made rockets obsolete for military purposes, and they were primarily used for signaling, firing lifelines to ships in distress, and spectacular fireworks displays. Only a few bold spirits dreamed that rockets might one day carry men beyond the earth.

That dream was ancient, dating at least to the second century A.D., when Lucan of Samosata imagined travelers carried up to the moon in a sailing boat propelled by a fierce gale. Thereafter, fictional space travelers were transported by an extraordinary variety of vehicles: Birds were popular, especially eagles, but demons, bottles of dew, giant springs, balloons, and antigravity substances were all proposed. The father of science fiction, Jules Verne, used a giant cannon in *From the Earth to the Moon* for his journey, and H. G. Wells turned the tables in his classic *War of the Worlds,* which related an invasion of Earth by creatures from Mars. Wells' novel caused a stir wherever it was read, but probably nowhere more than in the imagination of Robert Hutchings Goddard.

At Clark University *in 1924 Robert Goddard demonstrates how a rocket might travel to the moon. Above the diagram is one consequence of his work: a picture of the earth taken in 1972 by the Apollo 16 astronauts on their round trip to the moon. Apollo was powered by the Saturn 5 rocket, based on theories of liquid-fuel propulsion that were pioneered by Dr. Goddard more than 50 years earlier.*

MOON
limit of balloon, 20 miles
limit of atmosphere;
200 miles
6 miles/s
2 00,000
miles
1 lb
EARTH

A Practical Dreamer

When *War of the Worlds* was published in 1898, Robert Goddard was a 16-year-old schoolboy in Worcester, Massachusetts. Thin, threatened with tuberculosis, he had been forced to spend much of his time in bed, once for a period of two years. Young Goddard used the enforced rest for the study of mathematics and for scientific experimentation. He was constantly inventing new gadgets, from a tie press to an (unsuccessful) hydrogen-filled aluminum balloon.

On October 19, 1899—a date he afterward referred to as his Anniversary Day and every year recorded in his diary—he had a "vision." Goddard, who had just passed his 17th birthday, climbed a cherry tree at the back of the family house to cut off some dead branches. "It was one of those quiet, colorful afternoons of sheer beauty which we have in October in New England," he wrote in his diary. "And as I looked toward the fields of the east I imagined how wonderful it would be to make some device which had even the *possibility* of ascending to Mars." He envisioned a whirling machine that rose from the meadow below and upward into space. "I was a different boy when I descended from the tree," he noted. From that moment Goddard was driven by a dream of space travel, of building a craft that would liberate man from the tug of earth's gravity and lead him out from under the blanket of its atmosphere to soar freely among the stars.

In the years that followed Goddard immersed himself in the writings of the great physicist Sir Isaac Newton, and in 1904 enrolled in the physics class at Worcester Polytechnic Institute. He was a brilliant student, with ideas ranging far beyond the classroom. His notebooks for this period record speculations on the feasibility of ion propulsion: a method utilizing a beam of minute accelerated charged particles for thrust, which is now considered most suitable for long-distance space travel but is still far from practical realization. He also speculated on the possibility of harnessing the sun's rays in space by using a "solar boiler." In 1907, less than four years after the Wright brothers' first powered flight, Goddard wrote to the *Scientific American* proposing a scheme for stabilizing aircraft by means of gyroscopes. In 1909 he recorded his first tentative ideas for a liquid-fuel rocket, using hydrogen and liquid oxygen. These fuels are the staples of rocket propulsion today, but at that time were completely novel.

In 1911 Goddard completed his doctoral thesis and the following year was offered a research fellowship at Princeton University. Officially, he was there to investigate problems relating to the development of radio tubes. Although not yet ready to confide his preoccupation with rockets to the university authorities, at night and in his free time he continued working on his calculations, and by 1913 he had concluded

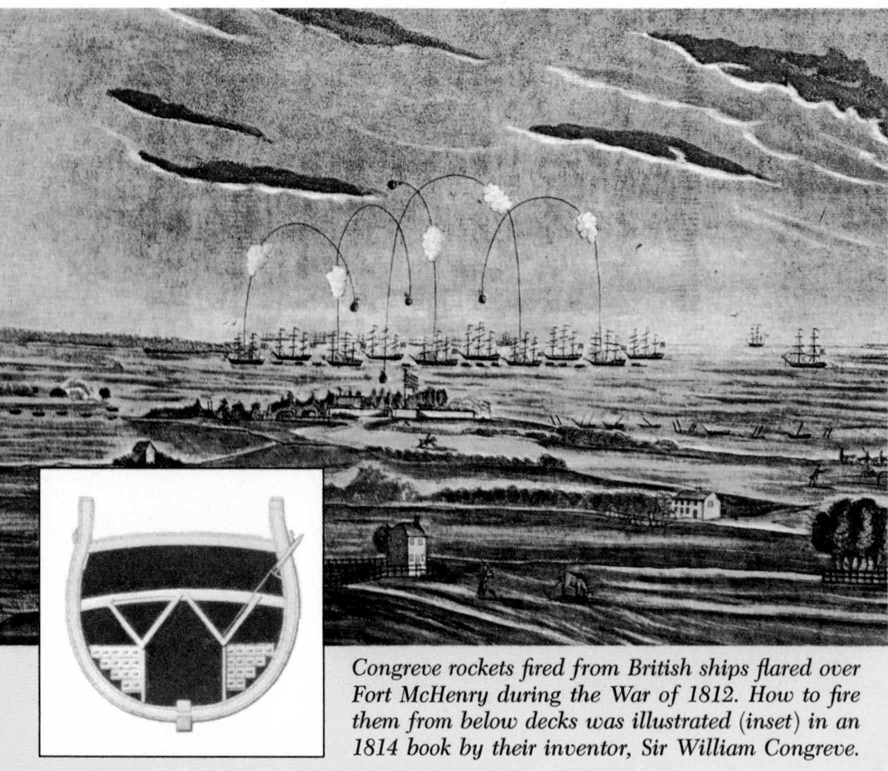

Congreve rockets fired from British ships flared over Fort McHenry during the War of 1812. How to fire them from below decks was illustrated (inset) in an 1814 book by their inventor, Sir William Congreve.

Konstantin Tsiolkovsky (below) theorized that plants could provide oxygen for space travelers.

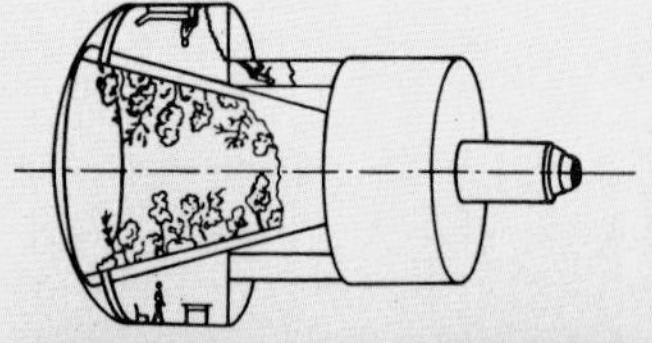

that a 200-pound rocket could be built that would be capable of propelling a 1-pound load beyond the earth's atmosphere and out into space.

A Patent and a Plea for Help

During the Easter vacation that year, Goddard discovered that he had tuberculosis. While confined to bed he worked steadily at the mathematical proofs of his theories, and in July 1914, having recovered his health, he took out his first patent. It was for a mechanism to feed explosive charges into a rocket combustion chamber and described in passing a modification that would allow liquid fuel and an oxydizer to be pumped instead. In the same month he patented another design embodying the idea of a multistage rocket, now the standard technique for space launches.

In retrospect it seems that the clarity of Goddard's vision should have assured him a quick success. But he was engaged in work that today requires whole teams of technicians—metallurgists, specialists in thermodynamics and aerodynamics, a wide range of structural, hydraulic, and mechanical engineers—and enormous financial resources. By 1916 Goddard was earning $1,000 a year as a researcher and teacher at Clark University in his native Worcester, Massachusetts. His limited private funds had gone for metals, especially the new light alloys, and for a variety of explosives. He had proved that a rocket would work in a vacuum and had calculated the effects of nozzle design on the thrust obtainable from various fuels, but without some financial support he could do no more. In September 1916 Goddard wrote the Smithsonian Institution in Washington, D.C., asking for help.

He explained that he had been experimenting for some years with ways of sending atmospheric recording instruments to greater altitudes than balloons could reach and gave a few details of his calculations. He also revealed that in static tests with a rocket motor he had achieved higher efficiency than had ever previously been realized by a heat engine. Before long Dr. Charles D. Walcott, Secretary of the Smithsonian, replied, asking for more details. Goddard was fully prepared and almost by return mail dispatched a neatly bound and boxed manuscript account of his work entitled "A Method of Reaching Extreme Altitudes." Goddard's manuscript was enthusiastically reviewed by the Smithsonian, which agreed to support his research program with a grant of $5,000.

In April 1917, when the United States entered the First World War, Goddard turned his attention to the military applications of rockets. With financial backing from the Army Ordnance Department he set up a new workshop at the Mount Wilson Observatory in California, and by November 1918 had developed a recoilless rocket launcher that could be fired by an ordinary soldier in the field. Four days after this fore-

LEAVING THE "CRADLE OF THE MIND"

U.S. astronaut Neil Armstrong's "giant leap" onto the moon on July 20, 1969, his Apollo spacecraft thrust there by a huge Saturn 5 rocket, marked the fulfillment of almost 2,000 years of dreams. But they had been dreams of little substance. Not until the end of the 19th century did a visionary realize that man could reach such a destination by means of an ancient military weapon, the rocket.

Rockets served sporadically in wartime from the 13th century until the early 1800's. Soon after the British used them against the Americans in the War of 1812, rifled artillery, far more accurate, appeared on the battlefield; rockets were relegated to sending distress signals and to hurling lifelines onto sinking ships and explosive harpoons into whales.

In the 1890's a Russian, Konstantin E. Tsiolkovsky, brilliantly depicted space travel via rockets. Calling earth "the cradle of the mind," he said that "man will not stay in that cradle forever."

Tsiolkovsky's farsighted work never went beyond the theoretical, however. In the United States Robert Goddard had come to the same conclusions concerning rocketry. He brought technology to theory and began experimenting with liquid-fuel rockets. In 1926, with the launching of his fragile 10-foot rocket, he set man on the most adventurous quest in history: the momentous quest for worlds beyond his own.

March 16, 1926: Dr. Goddard stands by his liquid-fuel rocket before its first successful launching. Soon science fiction heroes such as Buck Rogers were rocketing to the stars.

__Robert Goddard__ (left) and associates inspect a much more complex liquid-fuel rocket at his workshop in Roswell, New Mexico, in 1940. Despite the progress Goddard had made since his 1926 launching of the first such rocket, the U.S. military had scant interest in rocketry, and rockets played very little part in the American effort in World War II.

runner of the bazooka was successfully demonstrated, the war came to an end and with it Goddard's grant from the army. He returned to Worcester, to teach and to continue his research as best he could.

Moon Fever

In January 1920 the Smithsonian published Goddard's treatise "A Method of Reaching Extreme Altitudes." The Institution simultaneously released a press announcement mentioning the possibility, which Goddard had referred to only in passing, that the rockets being developed for atmospheric research might eventually lead to one that could land a magnesium flare, visible from the earth, on the moon. Newspaper editors across the nation pricked up their ears, and a barrage of provocative headlines descended upon Goddard, declaring to his embarrassment: "MODERN JULES VERNE INVENTS ROCKET TO GO TO MOON" (*Boston American*) and "AIM TO REACH MOON WITH NEW ROCKET" (*The New York Times*).

After World War I the German government realized rockets were not included in the ban on German rearmament in the Treaty of Versailles and gave large grants to a brilliant group of rocket researchers led by Hermann Oberth. Oberth wrote to Goddard requesting a frank exchange of information but received only guarded replies. As German successes grew, Goddard, whose secret notebooks were bulging with visionary and prophetic schemes, was chagrined to find himself criticized in Germany for his lack of foresight. Stung by the injustice, he sent the Smithsonian, in March 1920, a "Report on Further Developments of the Rocket Method of Investigating Space," amply demonstrating his vision as a theorist of space travel. Among the many topics he discussed were the control of unmanned space vehicles, ion propulsion, and a "solar sail"—a giant mirror 600 feet square—that would be unfurled in space to collect the sun's energy for propulsion. Goddard also suggested that contact might be made with other intelligent beings in the universe by way of a spacecraft carrying metal plates engraved with diagrams of the solar system, giving emphasis to the earth and moon. Similar plates were, in fact, eventually placed aboard the deep-space probe Pioneer 10 launched March 3, 1972.

Negative Information

Lack of vision never had been Goddard's problem. His problems were, and continued to be, a shortage of money and a plague of combustion chambers that burst, fuel-feeding mechanisms that refused to feed, and stabilizing mechanisms that did not stabilize. After many frustrating setbacks in his solid-fuel experiments, Goddard returned to his early notions of a rocket powered by liquid fuel, settling on liquid oxygen and gasoline as the most promising combination.

Between July 1920 and March 1923 Goddard spent his weekends and holidays at the Indian Head powder factory in south Maryland working under a $100-a-month grant from the Navy Bureau of Ordnance. In return for its modest investment the navy got plans for a depth-charge rocket and a rocket designed to carry an armor-penetrating warhead. In private Goddard pursued his experiments with liquid fuels, which continued to yield what he called "valuable negative information"—namely, failures.

When not at Indian Head he still taught at Clark University, which had given him a grant of $3,500 for rocket research. There Goddard, to all appearances a confirmed bachelor, met a pretty 17-year-old girl named Esther Kisk, who worked in the president's office. At first he asked her to type his papers, and later to be his wife. They were married in June 1924, and Esther became the official photographer and document keeper of Goddard's experiments.

By December 1925 she had something positive to record. During a test at Clark University, a lightweight rocket motor strained at its moorings and for 24 seconds lifted itself from the stand. The liquid-fuel mixture was doing its job. The next step was the flight test.

Lift-off

By March of the next year Goddard was ready. He chose the 16th, a Tuesday, his free day of the week. Loading the rocket motor, fuel tanks, and tubes and piping into wooden crates, and taking along two liters of liquid oxygen, he and his workshop assistant, Henry Sachs, set off for his testing area in Auburn. There the two men worked steadily all morning to assemble the rocket and its flimsy-looking launching tower.

At 1:00 p.m. Esther Goddard and Percy Roope, Goddard's assistant at Clark University, arrived. By 2:30 p.m. all was ready. Henry Sachs held a six-foot pole with a flaming blowtorch on the end. At a signal from Goddard, Sachs put the torch to the rocket's igniter, lit an alcohol stove beneath the motor, and dashed to join the others behind their sheet-iron shelter. After 90 tense seconds Goddard pulled the rocket's mooring release cord. The oxygen and gasoline burst into flame, and the first liquid-fuel rocket, forerunner of the V-2 and the ballistic missile, progenitor of the mighty Atlas space rocket, was on its way.

But only a short way, as things turned out. The flight lasted 2½ seconds, covered 184 feet, and reached an altitude of 41 feet—somewhat higher than an average man might throw a baseball.

The Goddards were jubilant!

In his diary for the next day Goddard noted that the nozzle had burnt out but that the rocket was "still going at a rapid rate" when it struck the ice and snow. "It looked almost magical as it rose, without any appreciable noise or flame," he added. The spectacle reminded Esther of "a fairy or an aesthetic dancer."

In the years that followed Goddard was to uproot his house and workshop and move to the desert of New Mexico to pursue his tests. Supported by famed transatlantic aviator Col. Charles Lindbergh and by the Guggenheim Foundation, he worked out new methods of gyroscopic stabilization. On May 31, 1935, he launched a liquid-fuel rocket that reached an altitude of 7,500 feet and flew beyond the speed of sound.

Robert Hutchings Goddard died August 10, 1945, after a throat operation. Up to the last he remained the dogged, secretive researcher he had always been, largely unrecognized by his fellow countrymen but driven by that vision of space travel that had visited him so many years before. He was a pioneer, drawn onward by the will-o'-the-wisp flame of the rocket engine he had created. That flame, that "magical, fairy dancer," has transformed our world beyond recognition. We owe it to a cold day in 1926, to a vision in a cherry tree, and to Robert Hutchings Goddard.

ROCKETRY IN GERMANY

The guiding spirit behind Germany's highly successful rocketry program was Romanian-born Hermann Oberth. Aware of Robert Goddard's experiments but working independently, Oberth published two works on liquid-fuel rockets and space travel, in 1923 and 1929. The military potential of his rocket soon attracted the attention of the German Army. At Peenemünde on the Baltic Sea the Germans, including Walter B. Dornberger and Wernher von Braun, developed the deadly V-2 rocket, which caused some 9,000 casualties in London. With the fall of Nazi Germany, V-2 components and rocket experts were taken to the United States and the Soviet Union. Both countries had long neglected rocketry and were eager to discover German advances. Oberth worked in the U.S.A. on an army rocket in the fifties.

A captured German V-2 rocket is wheeled to the launching site at the U.S. Army testing grounds at White Sands, New Mexico, in 1946.

Hermann Oberth on the set of Fritz Lang's 1929 futuristic film, The Girl in the Moon, *for which Oberth built a rocket.*

THE LIFE OF THE TIMES 1919-29

***In 1922 the hem** of a woman's bathing costume could go no higher than six inches above the knee. Here a bathing suit censor checks out a dubious case. Men had to cover their chests.*

***Clara Bow,** star of silent pictures, personified "It," or sex appeal. Press agents did their best to stimulate interest in her off-screen antics.*

***Cartoonist John Held** produced many magazine covers for* McClure's. *His flappers and playboys, moonfaced and stick bodied, still sum up the playful spirit of the Jazz Age.*

The decade of American life that became known as the Jazz Age, or the Roaring Twenties, ran its exuberant course from the election of President Warren G. Harding in 1920 to the catastrophic stock market crash of 1929. These two events were symbolically appropriate. The first confirmed what the Senate had indicated in 1919 when it refused to ratify the Versailles Treaty: a rejection of Woodrow Wilson's idealistic internationalism and a turning inward toward ease, prosperity, and the self-indulgent aspects of what was called Normalcy. The second showed the folly of such a course.

Between the two was a seemingly limitless joyride of jazz, vamps, flappers, and bootleg gin, or perhaps a "fling on the market" for some of that easy boom-time money. But the reckless gaiety of the period, so often documented in the movies, was really only half the story, for in the aftermath of the Great War there began a split in the national character between puritanical repression and conservatism on the one hand, and radical self-expression and profound cynicism on the other. It was a split that continues to trouble America to this day.

Bolsheviks and Bomb Scares

Americans had a special sense of their own importance after the war and saw their country as a fortress of democracy in an unstable world. It was to be expected, then, that they would be alarmed by a distant but portentous event: the 1917 Bolshevik Revolution in Russia.

As communism began to make inroads in Germany, Hungary, and other parts of Europe, and as American Communist groups sprang up in 1919, the lurid "yellow press" began to find sinister links between the situation abroad and the problems at home. The Bolsheviks were coming!—or, rather, were already here, infiltrating the unions, provoking widespread strikes, and corrupting our way of life.

The reading public, alarmed and credulous, was soon whipped into hysteria. Patriotic organizations crusaded against what they considered anti-American groups and ideas, and the Ku Klux Klan flourished anew. Attorney General A. Mitchell Palmer authorized nationwide raids against supposed subversives, thousands of whom were jailed on the basis of flimsy or nonexistent evidence.

Public fear crested with the discovery of a plot to assassinate cer-

The first Miss America, *Margaret Gorman, stands in solitary, flag-draped splendor on Atlantic City's famous boardwalk in 1921.*

The Ku Klux Klan *paraded in the streets of Tulsa, Oklahoma, in 1923 despite the efforts of local police to stop them. The white robes were part of the Klan's terrorist tactics.*

tain prominent men. Packages containing bombs had been sent to John D. Rockefeller, J.P. Morgan, Justice Oliver Wendell Holmes, and some three dozen others, presumably by Bolshevik revolutionaries, and in September 1920 a bomb exploded at the corner of Wall and Broad Streets in New York City, killing 35 bystanders and wounding 130 others. New York and California quickly outlawed groups that espoused violence; throughout the U.S.A. reprisal attacks by vigilantes claimed several lives.

In fact, the Bolshevik "uprising" in America was a classic nonevent. Though there were a few violently inclined Communists and Anarchists, support for their cause was practically nonexistent. Yet rumor bred rumor, and lawlessness in the name of patriotism spread. Most ominously, anti-Communist passions were transformed into a generalized distrust of all groups who were not considered "100-percent American," meaning Jews, Catholics, and blacks in particular.

Rise of the Flapper

The climate of fear and mistrust contributed to an almost desperate search for gaiety during the twenties. Among the most dramatic and highly publicized exponents of the new lifestyle were the modish young women known as flappers.

Short-haired, flat-chested, and daringly outspoken, the flapper was the antitype of the prewar society matron. In her looks and behavior she epitomized the emancipated "New Woman," who had at long last won the right to vote—and drink, and smoke—along with men.

The phenomenon of the flapper was just one part of a widespread reaction against the advent of Prohibition in 1920. Illegal alcohol was served in speakeasies to flappers and their boyfriends who danced the Charleston to the hot jazz bands of the era. The illicit tippling seems innocent enough now, but it supported a growing underworld of bigtime gangsters and racketeers.

These professional criminals took over the bootlegging business, then branched into gambling, loan-sharking, and related activities. In Chicago Al Capone's gang began an underworld reign of terror, gunning down rivals with a ferocity that made the city's name synonymous with violent crime.

In the end, Prohibition was bound to fail. Not enough men were budgeted to enforce it, and not enough people were willing to comply with it. Repeal came in 1933, but not before a whole new criminal class was rich and entrenched. Organized crime grew so powerful that the mob could, and did, control whole city governments.

Revolt Against the Masses

The official hypocrisy engendered by Prohibition, the rise of the Ku Klux Klan, and general disappointment in the failure of the Versailles peace agreement caused many intellectuals of the twenties to become disenchanted with American society. Prior to the war they had been in the vanguard of the Progressive movement, calling for reforms in favor of the working class; now they grew cynical.

A leading spokesman for these disillusioned writers, artists, and thinkers was the waspish H. L. Mencken. In his monthly magazine, *American Mercury,* Mencken applied his acid wit to democracy and idealism, organized religion, and the prim smugness of what he called the "booboisie." In a similar vein were Sinclair Lewis' condemnations of middle-class mediocrity in *Main Street, Babbitt,* and *Elmer Gantry.*

Other writers, members of the so-called Lost Generation, also chronicled their postwar disillusionment. F. Scott Fitzgerald's *The Great Gatsby* summarized the glitter and pathos of the Jazz Age and in *A Farewell to Arms* Ernest Hemingway attacked what he saw as the "phony idealism" of the war.

For playwright Eugene O'Neill the twenties were a productive decade; the six plays he wrote between 1921 and 1928 included "Anna Christie" and "The Emperor Jones." British novelist Aldous Huxley, widely read in America, captured the era's hectic atmosphere in *Chrome Yellow* and *Antic Hay.*

Harding and Teapot Dome

Without the support of the intellectual community social reform became a dead issue during the twenties. The boom, it was thought, would cure all ills. Presiding over the new prosperity was a man amply suited to not rocking the boat: Warren G. Harding. Harding was an easygoing, likable man who appears not to have had much sense of what was happening around him. Unremarkable in himself, his ineptitude was seized upon by a top aide who fashioned what was, until Watergate, the most infamous betrayal of the public trust in U.S.

***Prohibition,** which had become U.S. law in 1920, was doomed to fail chiefly because too many Americans wanted to drink. Another reason was lack of staff: There were never enough federal agents to find and destroy all the illegal alcohol in the country.*

***Baseball idol Babe Ruth** (his real name was George Herman Ruth) was also called the Sultan of Swat. In 1927, his best year, he hit a grand total of 60 home runs for the New York Yankees.*

***Gertrude Ederle,** the 19-year-old from New York City who swam the English Channel in 1926, was first woman to do so. It took her 14 hours 31 minutes; she broke the men's record by almost 2 hours. Grease protected her from cold water.*

Shipwreck Kelly, champion of one of the twenties' sillier sports, perches above a theater in Union City, New Jersey. At the height of his career, in 1929, Shipwreck spent a total of 145 precarious days atop flagpoles.

history: the Teapot Dome scandal.

The story broke in October 1923, three months after Harding had died. It was named for the rich Teapot Dome oilfield in Wyoming, one of several set aside for use by the Navy in case of emergency.

Harding had appointed a close friend, Senator Albert B. Fall of New Mexico, as Secretary of the Interior. One of Fall's first acts was to arrange the transfer of all the naval oil reserves to Interior. Then, without competitive bidding, Fall secretly leased the Teapot Dome and Elk Hills reserves to two friends who owned oil companies.

When the news leaked out, Fall invoked national security to justify his secrecy. But the smell of corruption was too strong. Investigations, suits, and trials involving the complex financial deals went on for almost a decade. They revealed that Fall's kindness to his friends had enriched him by about $400,000 and a herd of cattle for his ranch.

In 1927 the government won the right to cancel the leases awarded to Fall's cronies. Two years later Fall was sentenced to a one-year jail term and fined $100,000.

Coolidge and Hoover

Harding's successor, Vice President Calvin Coolidge, became President in 1923. This dour, colorless man was in most respects out of step with the times, but his honesty did much to repair the damage of Teapot Dome. In 1929 he was succeeded by Herbert Hoover, who shared with him an enthusiasm for an expanding, and almost completely unrestricted, economy.

Under these two men prosperity

***Al Capone** ruled the Chicago underworld with an army of 700 men. A product of Prohibition, he ran thousands of Chicago speakeasies and much of the bootlegging traffic east of the Mississippi.*

***The Teapot Dome scandal** embarrassed the Republican Party long after President Warren G. Harding died. Harding's cronies had benefited financially by leasing government oil reserves, one of which was Teapot Dome, near Casper, Wyoming.*

The execution of Nicola Sacco and Bartolomeo Vanzetti in 1927 caused a public outcry; many felt the two men had been convicted (of robbery and murder) through prejudice, not evidence.

In 1927 Charles Lindbergh made the world's first solo transatlantic flight. New Yorkers lined up 10 deep to welcome him back home, in one of the biggest ticker-tape parades ever seen. He was a perfect hero for those grown tired of cynicism.

grew like a gigantic bubble. It was a highly visible boom period, apparent in the giddily rising figures on the stock exchanges and the installment-plan mania for consumer goods. Despite a longstanding depression afflicting farmers, nearly everyone seemed to be getting rich.

As if to celebrate the national ebullience, a variety of faddish endurance contests came into vogue. There were marathon dance contests, coast-to-coast marathon runs, and, strangest of all, long-term flagpole-sitting exhibitions. An ex-fighter named Shipwreck Kelly won national fame for his ability to perch for days atop a pole, and his success testified to another feature of life in the twenties: the hunger for heroes.

By far the greatest hero of the decade was young Charles A. Lindbergh, the first man ever to make a nonstop solo flight across the Atlantic. His arrival in France, on May 21, 1927, seemed the ultimate triumph of American rugged individualism, and on his return he received what was probably the greatest outpouring of public adulation in our history.

Great Trials of the Twenties

If "Lucky Lindy's" feat was a sign of progress in what the advertisers were already calling the Air Age, the fate of another aviator, William "Billy" Mitchell, signaled the opposite. An army brigadier general, Mitchell publicly criticized the military hierarchy for its lack of interest in aeronautics and advocated a strong, independent air force. When he went so far as to charge the War and Navy Departments with "incompetency . . . and almost treasonable administration of the national defense," he was tried and convicted of insubordination. But his highly publicized court-martial made the issue of airpower a cause celebre and Mitchell himself something of a hero in the public eye.

The Mitchell court-martial was just one of several spectacular trials held in the twenties. In 1927 the public was outraged by the execution of two Italian anarchists, Nicola Sacco and Bartolomeo Vanzetti. Seized in 1920 as suspects in a holdup and murder, they had been held in jail despite considerable evidence in their favor. Once they came to trial, it became apparent that their politics, not their deeds, were at issue: Presiding Judge Webster Thayer had ruled against Vanzetti in an earlier case by instructing the jury that even though Vanzetti might not have committed the

***Low-flying barnstormers** thrilled crowds across the nation with their acrobatic stunts and did much to help make the 1920's airplane-crazy. Many of these men were ex-World War I pilots.*

STOCK PRICES SLUMP $14,000,000,000 IN NATION-WIDE STAMPEDE TO UNLOAD; BANKERS TO SUPPORT MARKET TODAY

PREMIER ISSUES HARD HIT

When stock prices plunged to an unprecedented low, leading financiers bought shares to reassure investors, but to no avail. The Great Depression was on its way. The headline is from The New York Times *of October 29, 1929.*

***Most fashionable women** had bobbed their hair by the late 1920's and were experimenting with dramatic makeup. In clothes, the mood was one of relaxed elegance. The lamé gown and velvet coat were designed by Créations Agnès of Paris.*

crime with which he was charged, he was "nevertheless morally culpable, because he is the enemy of our existing institutions."

After all the appeals courts and the Massachusetts Governor had upheld the guilty verdict, thousands gathered in the streets of Boston to protest what they felt was a miscarriage of justice. Sacco and Vanzetti were electrocuted nonetheless, and for many their deaths called into question the reality of America's claim of equality before the law.

Another controversial trial of the decade demonstrated the growing split between traditionalism and modernism: the "Monkey Trial" of teacher John T. Scopes in Tennessee. Scopes was convicted of violating a state law prohibiting the teaching of Darwin's theory of evolution in public schools. The law remained on the books, but the trial brought the issue of academic freedom sharply into focus for the public.

Black Thursday

Meanwhile, the economy, buoyed by recordbreaking investments each year, continued to soar. Like ordinary consumers, who were spending millions on the installment plan for radios, phonographs, and other new gadgets, speculators were literally banking on the future: "Margin buying" permitted investors to buy shares from brokers on credit for as little as 10 percent of their face value. The shares themselves were collateral for the loan; the investor benefited from any increase in the stock's value. As long as the market rose, the investor and his broker prospered; but a price decline could wipe out the investor's initial cash investment overnight and force the broker to demand payment of his loan. An investor who could not pay was forced to sell his shares. As a result, any drop in the market produced a chain reaction of selling.

The government did nothing. Regulatory agencies were tacitly discouraged from meddling in corporate affairs, so companies were free to practice the rankest kind of wheeling and dealing. Foreign governments, oblivious to the fact that countless stocks and bonds had virtually no real money to back them up, risked huge sums of their own on America's glittering, but hardly golden, prospects.

The day of reckoning came on October 24, 1929, forever after to be known as Black Thursday on Wall Street. For a few weeks the market had been wobbling, with the Dow Jones averages bouncing up and down and the financial headlines alternately optimistic and scary. On the floor of the Stock Exchange the tense brokers waited for dipping prices to start rising again.

Then the selling began. A small stock issue was unloaded here, a larger one there, and as if on cue there was a mad stampede to sell. Brokers were deluged with orders, and the ticker tape fell behind the action. Panic set in as investors lost track of their stocks' value. Sell! Cries went out for more margin, but no one was listening. Sell!

That day nearly 13 million shares were traded. The next day, Friday, there was a slight rise, then a dip again on Saturday. After that it was down, down, down, to a loss that by the end of the year would reach almost $40 billion. The joyride of the Roaring Twenties was over.

1928

Stalin's Rise to Power

A ruthless, resourceful tyrant secures undisputed control of the Communist state in Russia.

In the late afternoon of August 20, 1940, Leon Trotsky was visited in his home in exile near Mexico City by a young man known to him as Frank Jacson. Despite the heat of the Mexican summer, Jacson carried a long coat over his arm.

Shortly after 5:30 p.m. Trotsky—who with Lenin had plotted and led Russia's Communist revolution of October 1917—leaned over his desk to examine some papers; Jacson slipped a small ice ax from his coat pocket and smashed the pointed end through the older man's skull. Bodyguards, hearing Trotsky's cries, rushed in and subdued the assassin, sparing his life only in obedience to their leader, who cried: "No, no, he must not be killed—he must be made to talk."

Trotsky struggled to remain conscious as he was rushed to a hospital. With the last of his strength he called an associate to his side and painfully dictated a message to his followers: "I am close to death from the blow of a political assassin . . . Please say to our friends . . . I am sure of the victory . . . Go forward!" Leon Trotsky lapsed into a coma. On the next day he died.

Thousands of miles from Mexico City Iosif Vissarionovich Dzhugashvili, known to the world as Joseph Stalin (a name he derived from the Russian *stal*, meaning steel), greeted the news of Trotsky's death with satisfaction. The assassin, almost certainly acting under the authority of Stalin's secret police, had tracked the wily Trotsky, gained his confidence, then murdered him—the man whose very existence was both a reproach and a threat to Stalin. With his most formidable rival dead there was no one left to challenge his authority as dictator of Russia and as leader of the international Communist movement.

A New Triumvirate

When Vladimir Ilyich Lenin died in 1924, his closest comrades gathered in the Kremlin to pay their last respects. The man who had fathered the revolution of 1917 (see p. 132), who had been their guide and mentor throughout the subsequent period of rebellion, civil war, and famine, who had been their undisputed leader, was gone. Now, standing beside his coffin to pay him tribute and to jockey for position in the inevitable power struggle ahead, were the members of the Politburo, the ruling body of the Soviet Communist Party. Present were Grigori Zinoviev, who ruled the party organization in Petrograd (soon to be renamed Leningrad); Lev Kamenev, his counterpart in Moscow; Alexei Rykov, former chairman of the Supreme Council of National Economy; Nikolai Bukharin, theoretician and editor; and Joseph Stalin, Secretary General of the party.

On January 21, 1924, *Vladimir Ilyich Lenin died in Gorki, near Moscow. The 54-year-old leader of Soviet Russia had been ill for almost two years, suffering a series of debilitating cerebral hemorrhages. During his illness Russia had been led, unsuccessfully Lenin felt, by a triumvirate consisting of Grigori Zinoviev, Lev Kamenev, and Joseph Stalin (depicted at left in a German cartoon, with Commissar of War Leon Trotsky). The calm rows of mourners at Lenin's funeral in Red Square on January 27 (near left) belie the personal jealousy and bitter infighting existing among the Russian leaders at the time. Within four years Stalin had grasped virtually complete control of the Communist Party and of Russia. Within little more than a decade the other members of the quartet were dead: Kamenev and Zinoviev the victims of a firing squad in Stalin's great purge of the 1930's during which millions died; Trotsky the victim of a Stalin-directed assassination in 1940 while in exile in Mexico.*

Only one luminary of Soviet Russia was missing. Leon Trotsky was en route to the distant Black Sea resort city of Sukhumi, ordered there by his doctors to take a protracted rest. The brilliant and arrogant Trotsky had been a latecomer to Lenin's Bolshevik Party, but once they joined forces in June 1917, he rapidly became Lenin's closest collaborator, and his quick intelligence gave the Communist insurrection its cutting edge. Following the success of the Communist revolution Trotsky served as Commissar of Foreign Affairs and then became Commissar of War. He created a Red Army that swept the country clear of counterrevolutionary White forces and repulsed military and economic intervention from foreign powers, including Britain, Japan, France, Czechoslovakia, and the United States, in the Russian Civil War.

Of all Lenin's subordinates only Trotsky could claim a mass following of his own as a living symbol of revolutionary purity among Russia's idealistic youth. But Trotsky lacked warmth and compassion. He flaunted his brilliance and his dedication to communism, severely criticizing those less brilliant or less dedicated; he found only Lenin worthy of respect.

When Lenin died, Trotsky was his logical successor. Yet among those who mourned at Lenin's side, there was hardly one who did not agree that the heir apparent should never succeed to supreme power. Even as they mourned, the men who stood at the pinnacles of Soviet power were plotting. To ensure Trotsky's absence at the funeral, Stalin solicitously telegraphed the War Commissar that the "entire Politburo thinks that because of the state of your health, you should proceed to Sukhumi . . . the funeral will take place on Saturday, January 26th. You will not be able to return on time." In fact, as Stalin knew, the funeral was scheduled for the 27th. Trotsky's absence would be regarded as a lack of concern for the party and the state.

The Politburo members' common hatred of Trotsky was both political and personal. In the preceding two years Russia had achieved a degree of economic stability through a drastic "temporary" modification of communism that allowed some small-scale capitalism. Politburo leaders feared that the idealistic Trotsky would quickly move to collectivize agriculture and nationalize all industry, thus ending the more moderate policies adopted after the devastating civil war and threatening a period of renewed chaos. Knowing Trotsky's contempt for them and his ruthlessness, they also feared for their position and their power. Therefore, they united to strip Trotsky of his power before he could rally support. What his opponents—Kamenev, Zinoviev, Rykov, and Bukharin—did not know was that among them stood one who was a far greater menace than Trotsky. In the quiet, patient, and seemingly level-headed person of Joseph Stalin members of the Soviet revolutionary elite were soon to meet their master and their executioner.

The Making of a Tyrant

Joseph Stalin was the sole provincial among Russia's revolutionary leaders. Except for three brief trips abroad between 1905 and 1907 he had spent his entire life within the old Russian Empire. He adopted Marxism in the late 1890's but knew little of its subtleties or of the humanitarian impulse underlying Marx's work.

Born in the Georgian village of Gori in 1879, Stalin was the son of an impoverished cobbler and a washerwoman. His deeply religious mother had intended her son to become a Greek Orthodox priest and through the most extreme sacrifices managed to send him to a seminary in the provincial capital of Tiflis. Stalin chafed under the restrictions of seminary life, circulated revolutionary literature among his fellow pupils, and in 1899 was expelled. The next year he joined the political underground, working in the Caucasus with a band of revolutionaries who fomented labor strikes in the industrial cities of the region. Seven times between 1902 and 1913 Stalin was arrested and jailed, and seven times he easily escaped, lending weight to the view that he was an *agent provocateur* for the Okhrana, the Czar's secret police.

In 1913 Stalin was exiled to Siberia, where he remained until his release in 1917. He and Lev Kamenev, also just released from Siberia, went to Petrograd, where they edited the newspaper *Pravda* ("Truth").

Stalin's role in the October Revolution was considerably less crucial than Lenin's or Trotsky's, but after the victory he was awarded the post of Commissar of Nationalities. His bloody efforts to crush nationalist movements among non-Russian minorities (including the people of his native Georgia) were successful but earned him a reputation for butchery. In March 1922 he was made Secretary General of the Communist Party, a position scorned by his more intellectual peers as fit only for a master clerk. But Stalin eagerly sought the job and, realizing its unmatched potential as a power base, began filling the party ranks at all levels with ambitious careerists. Grateful for the appointments, their primary loyalty was to Stalin.

In May 1922 Lenin had his first cerebral hemorrhage. While he was incapacitated, a triumvirate composed of Zinoviev, Kamenev, and Stalin took control of the government. The following winter, when Lenin recovered sufficiently to govern, he found that the triumvirate had performed incompetently. He recognized the potential power of the Secretary General's office and began to doubt Stalin's qualifications to hold it. In December 1922 he wrote, in a document since known as Lenin's last testament: "Comrade Stalin, having become Secretary General, has concentrated enormous power in his hands; and I am not sure that he will always know how to use that power with sufficient caution." The next month he added this postscript: "Stalin is too rude . . . I propose to the comrades to find a way to remove Stalin from the position and appoint . . . another man . . . more patient,

***"We Have Routed the Enemy** Arms in Hand, We Shall Get Bread by Hard Work" proclaimed a Soviet postwar poster. The government's work programs faltered, however. The New Economic Policy (NEP) of 1921 failed to provide prosperity for the U.S.S.R. at a time when other nations were thriving. It was not until the Five-Year Plan of 1928–32 that the Soviets began to work their way into the front ranks of industry.*

The Soviet secret police have operated from the site of the Lubyanka prison (below, right) since 1918. During the great purge between 5 and 15 million people—estimates vary—were arrested. Below, Nikolai Yezhov, the "bloodthirsty dwarf," who was head of the NKVD from 1936 to 1938.

STALIN'S TERROR MACHINE

In 1917 the Bolsheviks formed a secret police organization named the Cheka, with the avowed purpose of crushing antirevolutionary elements in Soviet society. Modeled on the dreaded Okhrana, the Czar's secret police force, the Cheka arrested some 90,000 people and executed more than 11,000 during its first 18 months of existence.

For Stalin this bestial police force (known variously over the years as the GPU, OGPU, NKVD, NKGB, and now the KGB) was the essential tool of a regime shaped chiefly by paranoia and personal ambition. During the great purge of 1934–39 he used it without mercy and at least 3 million people died before firing squads, during torture, or as a result of the wretched living conditions in prisons and labor camps.

As Stalin's creatures the secret police were a privileged class, but not even they were immune to his bloodlust. Of the five directors in office between 1917 and 1956, only the first, Felix Dzerzhinsky, died a natural death.

more loyal, more polite. . . ." After Lenin's death his statement was partially suppressed by men like Kamenev and Zinoviev, who thought Stalin would be useful in the struggle against Trotsky.

Twists and Turns

Stalin, having assured Trotsky's absence, seized the spotlight at Lenin's funeral and made grandiose pronouncements of loyalty to the great man's memory that received wide notice in the Soviet press. "We vow to thee, Comrade Lenin," he said, "that we will not spare our lives to strengthen and expand the union of the toilers of the whole world." Then Stalin and his temporary allies turned to the work at hand: to isolate Trotsky by cutting him off from the levers of power.

Even before Lenin's death the Stalin-Kamenev-Zinoviev triumvirate had gained widespread control over the party and the nation. Rumors of Lenin's last testament circulated at the 13th Soviet Party Congress in May 1924, but the triumvirate prevailed upon the Politburo to keep the document secret from all but the members of the Central Committee. Speaking to that elite group, Zinoviev remarked: "But we are happy to say that on one point Lenin's fears have not proved well founded. I mean the point about our Secretary General. You have all been witnesses of our work together in the last few months; and like myself, you have been happy to confirm that Ilyich's [Lenin's] fears have not been realized." Leon Trotsky, confident that the triumvirate of second-raters would soon fall of its own weight, made no protest over the suppression of Lenin's will.

Stalin, Kamenev, and Zinoviev then opened a united propaganda campaign against Trotsky. They publicized his prerevolutionary statements opposing Lenin's Bolshevik programs as evidence of anti-Leninism. Trotsky's plan for a more rapid pace of economic development was characterized as "left-wing adventurism" that would lead to economic disaster. In January 1925 he was forced to resign as Commissar of War.

Once Trotsky was politically isolated, Stalin turned to eliminating his own allies and seizing their power for himself. Since the October Revolution a canon of communist doctrine had been that the success of the Leninist program ultimately depended on worldwide revolution, which would bring the advanced economies of the West to the aid of the Soviet regime. In pursuit of this goal the Third International, or Comintern, had been established in 1919 to unify the world's Communist parties and to foment revolution abroad.

Among the most fervent believers in worldwide revolution were Trotsky, Kamenev, and Zinoviev, the head of the Comintern. But in the postwar years the eagerly anticipated rebellions either failed to occur or, as in Germany, Hungary, and China, were crushed. In 1925 Stalin abandoned his hopes for world revolution, proposing instead, to the horror of Zinoviev and Kamenev, a course of "Socialism in One Country."

Stalin had calculated well, for his new slogan appealed to more conservative elements within the Politburo—particularly trade union chief Mikhail Tomsky, party theoretician Nikolai Bukharin, and Alexei Rykov, chairman of the Council of People's Commissars. It also appealed to Russian nationalism by implying that Russia, alone and unaided, could construct a new society that would be a beacon for the world. Kamenev and Zinoviev fought such isolationism furiously but in vain, and by the end of 1925 they were impotent against the new ruling collegium of Stalin, Rykov, Bukharin, and Tomsky.

Too late, Zinoviev and Kamenev realized they had been duped by Stalin. They frantically sought to regain the initiative by forming an alliance with Trotsky and attacking the leadership at every opportunity, but it was to no avail. Stalin and his new allies moved swiftly to break the back of the opposition, and in 1927 the three opposition leaders were expelled from the party. Zinoviev and Kamenev were later allowed to repent and temporarily return to the party, but Trotsky was exiled in January 1929.

With Trotsky abroad and the other opposition leaders cowed into silence, Stalin was free to attack Rykov, Bukharin, and Tomsky. Having long ridiculed Trotsky's program of industrialization and collectivization of agriculture, Stalin in 1928 adopted that course as his own. Rykov, Bukharin, and Tomsky fought back in the Politburo, warning that an emphasis on heavy industry at the expense of consumer goods would provoke the workers' hostility and that an attempt to collectivize the farms would lead to peasant rebellion and famine. But they too were outvoted by Stalin's men, divested of their high positions, and cast into the political wilderness. Now Stalin ruled supreme.

Having secured mastery of the Communist Party, Stalin moved to extend his tyranny over Russia's 160 million people. In 1928 he announced the first Five-Year Plan, intended to turn Russia into a major industrial power through nationalization of all private enterprise, both rural and urban. At the cost of millions of lives and the displacement of whole populations—mostly peasants who resisted collectivization of their farms—Stalin's goal was accomplished. By 1935 there had been an astonishing increase in Russia's industrial and agricultural production. It seemed to the world that almost overnight the U.S.S.R. had turned from an undeveloped nation into an industrial power.

The Communist Party meanwhile kept up a steady flow of propaganda that depicted Stalin as "the Lenin of today," a savior, a genius, a living saint. Those who objected or demurred were arrested and deported to slave labor camps. By the mid-1930's Joseph Stalin was carrying out a wave of political repression that made the czarist tyrannies pale by comparison.

The Great Purges

Stalin's great purges began in 1934 with the assassination of his close ally Sergei Kirov, Communist Party chief in Leningrad. Although Stalin himself is thought to have ordered the murder of Kirov, who was becoming a potential rival, blame was placed on the exiled Leon Trotsky and other old enemies of the dictator, all conveniently labeled Trotskyites regardless of their political orientation. Compounding fraud with absurdity, Stalin accused Trotsky, a dedicated Communist to the end of his life, of plotting with Nazi dictator Adolf Hitler and the Japanese against the U.S.S.R. Though long ago dismissed from power and officially disgraced, all of Stalin's rivals and erstwhile allies were imprisoned and interrogated by the NKVD. Eventually they were publicly tried, and to the world's astonishment, each, including Kamenev, Zinoviev, Bukharin, and Rykov, admitted to being a part of a Trotskyite-Nazi conspiracy to overthrow communism in Russia. As a final humiliation the accused were forced to beg the court for execution to expiate imaginary crimes, a request Stalin graciously granted. One by one Lenin's old comrades were dispatched with a bullet in the back of the head.

Even Stalin's second wife, Nadezhda (Nadya) Alliluyeva, could be called an early casualty of the purges. In 1932 Nadya pleaded with Stalin on behalf of a woman friend who had been exiled to a camp for political prisoners. When she defied Stalin by exchanging letters with her friend, Stalin had the friend and all who had played a role in the correspondence executed. Nadya committed suicide on November 7, 1932.

No element of Soviet society was spared. The army, as the only relatively independent force in Russia, had long been a thorn in Stalin's side. On May 31, 1937, the army purges began. Less than two weeks later eight top generals, including the chief of staff, had been condemned and shot. Before the year was out, most of the Soviet War Council, along with 30,000 other officers, were arrested, and many were liquidated.

By 1939 the worst of the purges and the trauma of industrialization had passed. Stalin stood alone, unchallenged and unchallengeable, secure in the absolute dictatorship that was to last until his death 14 years later. But, a man of infinite malice, he still had one score left to settle, and on August 20, 1940, in a villa near Mexico City, he settled it when he commissioned the assassination of Leon Trotsky.

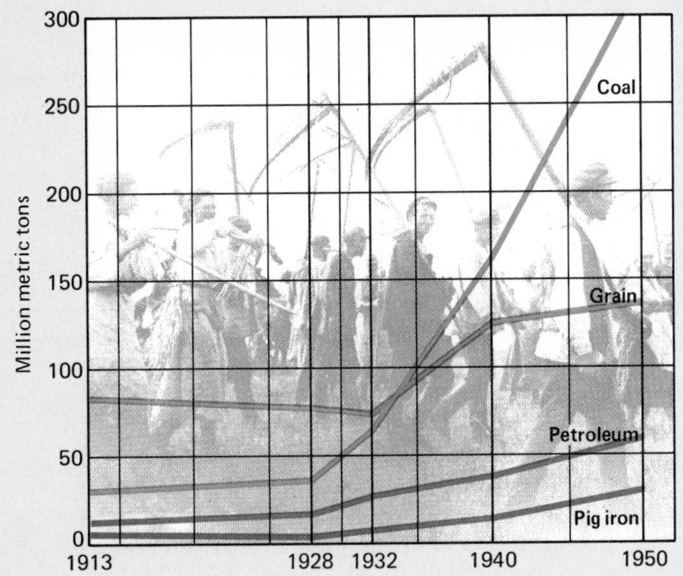

Agriculture and heavy industry in the U.S.S.R. made dramatic gains after the Five-Year Plans were instituted. The graph at left, with commodities measured in millions of metric tons, reflects the rise from undeveloped nation to world power in under 40 years.

Steel: While the U.S.A. and Europe suffered sharp declines in steel production during the Depression years, the U.S.S.R. surged forward as a result of the first Five-Year Plan, as shown in the comparative bar graph at right. Percentages are for the period from 1927 through 1934.

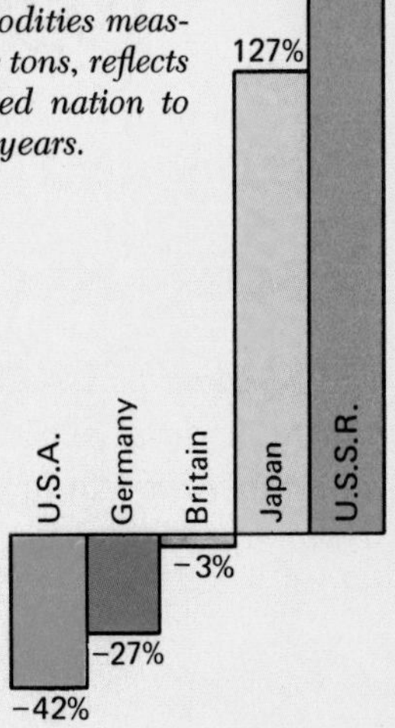

THE RUSH TO INDUSTRIALIZATION

Joseph Stalin's Five-Year Plan to nationalize all private enterprise and agriculture began in 1928. Millions of landholding, relatively prosperous peasants, especially the kulaks (peasants with enough land to use hired labor), fiercely resisted merging their land, tools, and livestock into giant collective farms. Determined to crush this opposition, Stalin ordered teams of workers and soldiers into the countryside to seize foodstuffs from the peasants, who responded by burning their crops and slaughtering for their own consumption more than half of Russia's livestock. Stalin retaliated savagely, branding all resisting peasants kulaks and deporting some 5 million to slave labor camps in Siberia between 1929 and 1934. (This is a conservative figure, for it does not take into account the millions more who died of starvation, disease, and overwork, or who were executed by the secret police.)

Stalin's massive program of rapid industrialization was enforced with all the brutality his extensive terror organizations could muster. Across Russia vast projects were begun to create electric power, build steel mills, drill oil wells, and exploit mineral and timber reserves. In 1931 collective bargaining was forbidden, and from then on workers were totally subject to the whims of the state. Absenteeism was severely punished and no worker was permitted to change jobs without official approval. By 1934 an industrial hierarchy had emerged, with some workers earning vastly more than their comrades. But Stalin had accomplished his goal of increasing industrial and agricultural production. The success of the first Five-Year Plan laid the groundwork for the future Five-Year Plans.

A propaganda poster from 1929 (right) pictures grossly caricatured enemies of the first Five-Year Plan: the rich, the bureaucrats, and the Imperial Army.

Kulak peasants (below) are forced to evacuate their villages and farms, leaving behind a centuries-old Russian way of life.

1928

Dr. Fleming's Wonder Drug

The accidental discovery of the first antibiotic drug, penicillin, sets the stage for a revolution in modern medical treatment throughout the world.

At St. Mary's Hospital in London the clutter of Alexander Fleming's laboratory matched the jumble of the Praed Street junk shops beneath his window. The Scottish bacteriologist liked having his cultures and equipment readily at hand and even teased his associates for being too tidy. His own practice, after initial studies of a bacterial culture, was to leave his little glass dishes standing for a week or so and then to check them for interesting changes. In just such a way he stumbled upon his greatest discovery.

Fleming later observed: "Had my lab been as up-to-date as those I have visited, it is possible that I would never have run across penicillin." Late in the summer of 1928 he was working on an article on the *staphylococcus,* a common bacterium that causes infectious skin boils and abscesses. Cultures of *staphylococci* were growing on plates in his cluttered lab.

One September afternoon Fleming was chatting with a colleague when he suddenly noticed something unusual. Stopping in midsentence, he took a closer look at one of his culture plates. "That's funny," he observed a moment later, indicating the green mold that was growing on the plate. The bacteria surround-

ing the mold had been dissolved. Instead of the usual yellow masses of bacteria, there were clear rings wherever the culture came in contact with the mold.

Realizing at once that he had unearthed something quite remarkable, Fleming set out to identify the mysterious mold. He scraped a bit of it from the plate and examined it under the microscope. The green flecks had the characteristics of a mold of the genus *Penicillium, Penicillium notatum,* which Fleming shortened to penicillin. Next he removed the remaining mold and stored it in a jar filled with nutrient broth. In a few days the penicillin had grown into a colony, and the clear broth had taken on a bright yellow hue.

Fleming began to devote his full energies to experimenting with the curious mold. He first determined that the mold was releasing its bacteria-killing substance into the broth in tiny golden droplets. The yellow liquid proved as effective against bacteria as the mold itself. Here was a simple fungus, not unlike the mold found on bread or cheese, that had a deadly effect on infectious germs. Yet his limited experiments indicated it was harmless to human cells and retained its power even when diluted thousands of times.

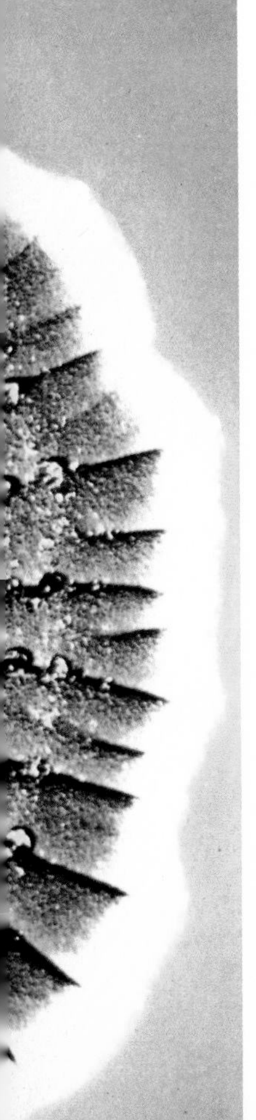

***Three pioneers in antibiotic** medicine (far left): Sir Alexander Fleming (featured), the Scottish bacteriologist who discovered penicillin in 1928; Dr. Howard Florey (center insert), who headed the Oxford University team that successfully tested the drug in 1941; and Dr. Ernst Chain (lower left), a member of the Oxford team that first isolated penicillin in its purified state in 1940. They shared the Nobel Prize for Medicine (lower right) in 1945 in recognition of their valuable joint contribution to man's fight against infection and disease.*

The wonderworking mold, Penicillium notatum *(at left), secretes the golden antibiotic liquid known as penicillin. Fleming observed its amazing ability to kill certain deadly bacteria without harming healthy human tissue in 1928, but he was unable to extract its active agent. It required an intensive effort by Florey and Chain to finally isolate a tiny amount of the purified drug more than a decade later. By then the wartime need for penicillin was so great that the United States government sponsored an intensive campaign to find more potent strains of the* Penicillium *mold and to improve production techniques.*

"Life Hinders Life"

For the 47-year-old Fleming the discovery represented the end of a lengthy quest for a cure for deadly infectious diseases. As a student at St. Mary's Hospital School of Medicine in London he had studied the discoveries of Louis Pasteur, the brilliant Frenchman who had revolutionized medicine with his germ theory of disease. Pasteur had demonstrated that certain diseases and infections are caused by minute living organisms, or germs, which invade the body and feed on its cells. In 1877 Pasteur had made an additional observation: Certain germs prey upon others, just as animals prey upon other animals. Even at the lowest level the struggle for survival continues. "Life hinders life," Pasteur had concluded, and in the 1880's the word *antibiosis* (from the Greek words meaning "against life") was coined to describe this natural opposition.

Pasteur's studies of microorganisms—bacteria, molds, and other tiny organisms—had laid the foundations for the interrelated sciences of immunology and bacteriology. In Fleming's student days scientists were making tremendous strides in both areas. Researchers had identified most disease-causing microorganisms and had developed vaccines to prevent typhoid fever, cholera, diphtheria, and other diseases. But no one had found a certain way to cure these and other deadly infections once a person had developed them. Fleming was determined to find such a cure.

"Magic Bullets"

His studies completed, Fleming joined the newly created Inoculation Department at St. Mary's, headed by Dr. Almroth Wright, a pioneer in immunology. One of Fleming's duties during his first years at St. Mary's was administering Salvarsan, a new drug that had shown dramatic effects in combating the microbe that caused syphilis, a major killer of the time. The new drug had been discovered in 1909 by the German doctor Paul Ehrlich. Earlier in his career Ehrlich had studied the interaction of chemical dyes and living cells. Under the microscope he observed that certain dyes stained only certain cells, leaving others uncolored, in what appeared to be a selective chemical process. To Ehrlich this process seemed akin to the way infectious microbes attacked specific cells in the human body. Thus tetanus germs attacked the nerve cells and tuberculosis microbes attacked certain cells in the lungs, kidneys, spine, and so on.

Ehrlich eventually reached the conclusion that scientists could develop chemical substances with a similar affinity for specific microbes, drugs that would attack and destroy germs but leave the other body cells unharmed. Ehrlich explained that "antitoxins and antibacterial agents are, so to speak, magic bullets which strike only those objects for whose destruction they have been produced."

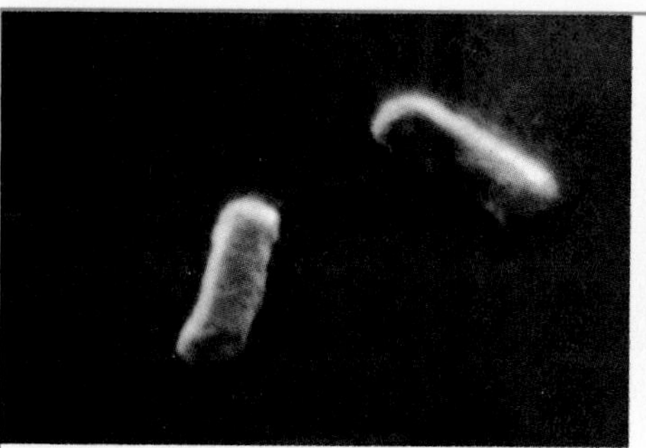

Untreated Escherichia coli, *bacteria that cause infections of the urinary tract.*

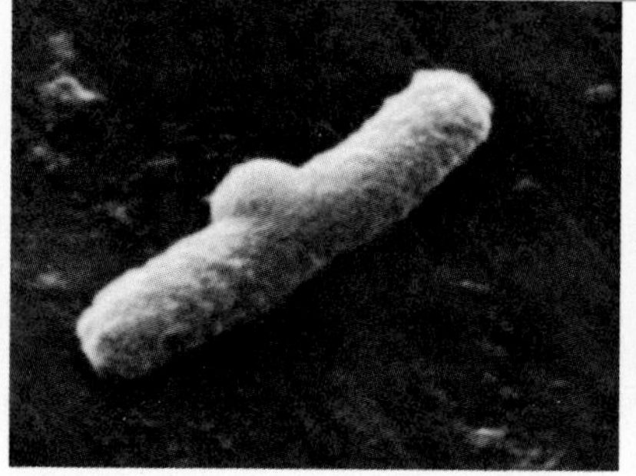

After a brief exposure to penicillin, a bulge begins to develop in the cell wall.

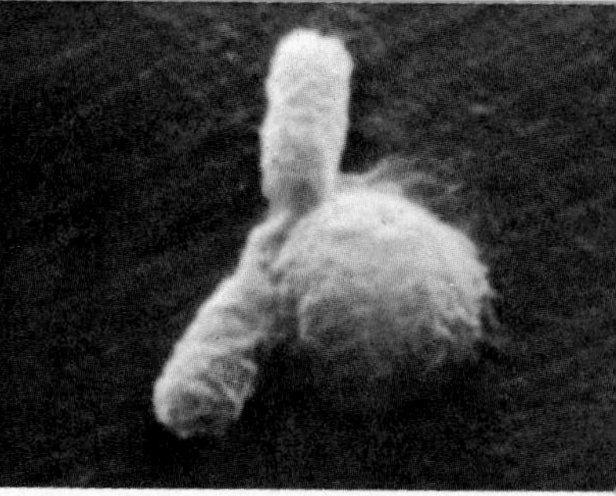

With longer exposure the bulge grows larger, stretching the cell membrane.

PENICILLIN AT WORK: HOW A MOLD DESTROYS BACTERIA

Penicillin's curative powers stem from its ability to interfere with a vital part of a bacterium's normal growth process, the expansion of the cell wall. By so doing, it causes the wall and membrane to weaken and eventually burst, which kills the bacterium. How does this happen?

All bacteria are made up of three basic parts: a tough protective exterior wall; an elastic inner membrane; and a dense liquid interior, the cytoplasm. Normally, the rigid wall expands as the cell grows. First a portion of the old wall dissolves, permitting the elastic membrane to expand. Then a new part of the wall is built from mucoprotein molecules, which are carried from the cytoplasm through the membrane to the cell wall by special transport enzymes. The latter are designed to link up with the mucoproteins, fitting together in a manner resembling a lock and key.

When penicillin enters this system, however, the process goes awry. Part of the penicillin molecule resembles the locking structure of the mucoprotein molecule, and the transport enzyme mistakenly binds to the penicillin molecule and carries it to the prepared mucoprotein site on the cell surface. The penicillin molecule does not fit properly into the site, creating a flaw in the new wall. As the cell continues to grow, exerting increased pressure on the wall, the flawed portion weakens and finally breaks. The elastic cellular membrane then bulges outward until it bursts, spilling out the cytoplasm and thus destroying the cell.

During World War I Wright and his staff at St. Mary's were asked to set up a field research laboratory at Boulogne, France, to study and cure the infections of wounded Allied soldiers. Casualties were brought there from the front as quickly as possible, but by the time they reached Boulogne their wounds were often already infected, and pathetically little could be done to combat such infections once they had entered the bloodstream. "Surrounded by all those infected wounds," Fleming said later, "by men who were suffering and dying without our being able to do anything to help them, I was consumed by a desire to discover . . . something which would kill those microbes, something like Salvarsan. . . ."

A Valuable Piece of Evidence

Fleming's first breakthrough came in 1922, several years after he had returned to St. Mary's from the front. As usual his laboratory was cluttered with plates of bacterial cultures. Fleming, who was suffering from a cold, decided to add some of his own mucus to one of the culture plates. Almost immediately the microbes surrounding the mucus began to dissolve. Apparently something in the mucus had a deadly effect on certain bacteria. Other experiments, using tears and even saliva, produced the same results.

Quietly elated by the discovery, Fleming concluded that the active substance in these secretions was part of the body's natural defenses against invasion by airborne microbes. He named it lysozyme because of its likeness to enzymes and its ability to dissolve, or lyse, the microbes. Unhappily, it was not as effective against more dangerous germs, and during Fleming's lifetime lysozyme was deemed of little use. After his death, though, a way was found to isolate the substance for use against diseases, and today it is an important tool of the microbiologist.

For Fleming, the great value of the discovery was a demonstration of how antibacterial substances work and as a spur to his search for more powerful ones. And when, six years later, he finally found such a substance, penicillin, it was his studies of lysozyme that helped him recognize its tremendous significance. Like lysozyme, penicillin dissolved the bacterial cell wall; beyond that, it was a natural enemy of staphylococcus, streptococcus, and other infectious microbes.

Unfortunately the Scotsman was unable to convince others of the significance of his discovery. On February 13, 1929, he presented a paper on penicillin to London's Medical Research Club. The audience listened politely and then turned to other matters. The published report of his findings also failed to arouse any

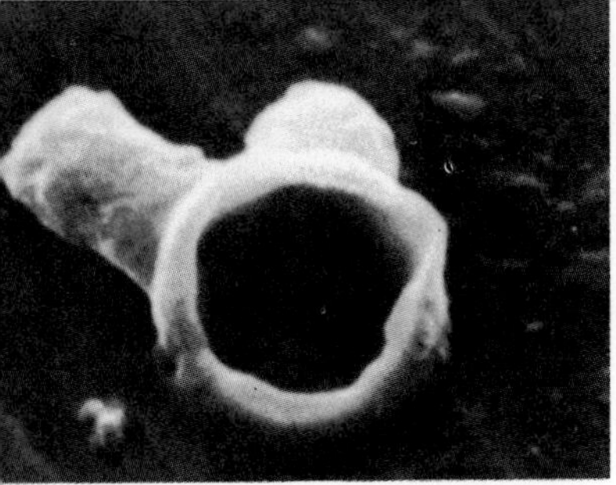

Stretched beyond its limits, the membrane finally bursts and the cell dies.

The cell wall of a healthy bacterium is composed of mucoprotein building blocks (blue). This wall has to expand continually to permit normal cellular growth, repair, and division.

To form new wall, part of the old wall is first dissolved. Transport enzymes (brown) pick up mucoproteins and carry them to the receptor sites. (Note that these sites are shaped to assure that the mucoproteins fit together solidly and in perfect alignment.)

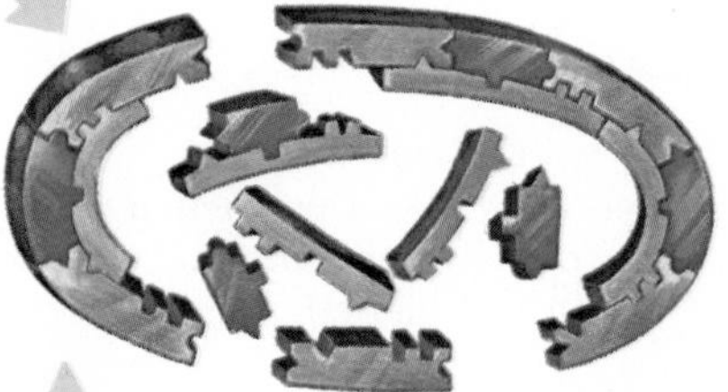

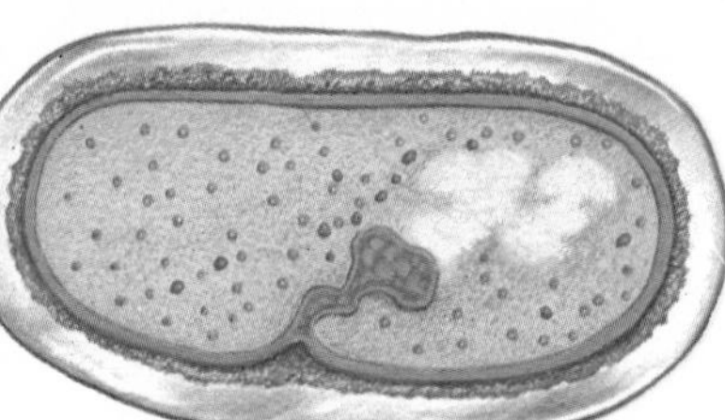

All bacteria have 3 basic parts: the wall (mauve), the membrane (gray), and the cytoplasm (pink). Antibiotics can kill them by hampering one of their vital life processes. Penicillin disrupts the expansion of the cell wall of certain kinds of bacteria.

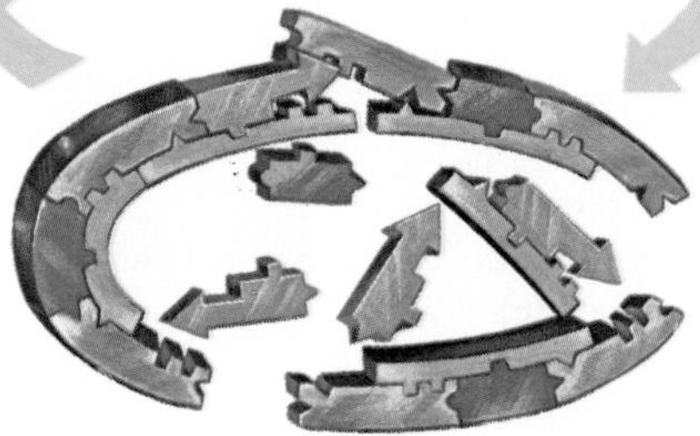

When penicillin (green) is injected, the transport enzymes pick up penicillin molecules instead of mucoproteins. The penicillin "fits" into the enzyme but not into the receptor site. The weakened cell wall soon breaks, the membrane bursts, the cytoplasm spills out, and the cell dies.

serious interest. Disappointed, Fleming resumed his other work, but carefully preserved his penicillin culture, waiting for the inevitable day when its powers could be put to their lifesaving work. It was to be almost 10 years before that day arrived.

Surprising News From Oxford

Elsewhere scientists continued to look for new germ killers. In the 1930's German researchers discovered the sulfa drugs, chemical compounds effective against such diseases as strep throat, spinal meningitis, gonorrhea, and even some viruses. The new drugs produced dramatic cures at first, but their effectiveness proved to be limited to a small range of diseases and many patients experienced serious side effects. Some even died from the administration of sulfa.

The shortcomings of the sulfa drugs stimulated a worldwide quest for effective but harmless germicides. One such search was organized at Oxford University by Dr. Howard Florey, an Australian-born professor of pathology, who gathered a team of researchers to study the properties of lysozyme. Late in 1935 Florey invited Dr. Ernst Chain, a 29-year-old biochemist, to join him at Oxford. Chain, a German-born Jew who had come to England in 1933, eagerly accepted, and in 1936 he began his own experiments with lysozyme. Intrigued by its antibacterial action, he decided to explore similar substances. In due course, he came across Fleming's long-forgotten paper on penicillin.

Chain was inspired by Fleming's description of penicillin's potential, and in 1939 he and Florey set out to isolate and test a sample. They found at Oxford a culture of *Penicillium notatum* that had originated in Fleming's lab. By the end of the year Chain had succeeded in isolating and purifying the drug in the form of a yellow powder with the consistency of cornstarch.

In their tests Florey and Chain discovered that the yellow powder retained its effectiveness even when diluted 30 million times. Its antibiotic action was 10 times as great as the strongest sulfa drug and 1,000 times more potent than Fleming's original droplets, with no apparent toxic effects.

Late in the spring of 1940 the Oxford team tested the drug's curative powers on a group of mice. The results were spectacular. Fifty mice were first given lethal injections of streptococcus germs; then half of them were given penicillin shots. The 25 untreated mice all died within 16 hours; all but 1 of the 25 mice that had been injected with penicillin survived.

When Fleming read the published report of the Oxford experiments, he went at once to meet the two men who had finally proved what he had long suspected.

Chain, astonished to learn that Fleming was still alive, later wrote: "He struck me as a man who had difficulty in expressing himself, though he gave the impression of being somebody with a very warm heart doing all he could to appear cold and distant."

From samples supplied by Fleming the Oxford team was able to produce an even more potent strain of penicillin. The process of purification was time consuming, though, and the yield small. Gradually they accumulated a tiny amount of the drug and stored it in a laboratory refrigerator for emergencies.

Promise in a Teaspoon

In February 1941 a policeman who had developed a staphylococcus infection and acute blood poisoning after cutting himself shaving was admitted to an Oxford hospital. The man's body was covered with abscesses, his temperature was 105°F, his lungs were weakened, and the infection had entered his bloodstream. Sulfa drugs failed to halt the progress of the infection; doctors gave him only a few days to live.

In so hopeless a situation the hospital agreed to let Florey and Chain try their new drug. The doctors arrived at the policeman's bedside with their entire supply of penicillin, a bare teaspoonful. They injected the drug every 3 hours, and within 24 hours his condition began to stabilize. After two days the patient's fever was down, and his sores had begun to subside. The policeman reported that he felt much better and even began eating again. As the tiny supply of penicillin dwindled, the doctors were able to recover more from the patient's urine, but in time even that supply was used up. Once the injections stopped, the infection took over again, and the policeman died.

Nonetheless, it was an encouraging beginning. As long as the penicillin had been available, it had dramatically halted the infection. Moreover, the patient had suffered none of the harmful side effects associated with sulfa drugs. A few weeks later Florey and Chain again demonstrated the miraculous powers of the drug: They saved the life of a youth who was suffering from a badly infected hip socket.

Help From Across the Sea

Other cures followed, but penicillin was in such short supply that it could only be given to a handful of patients. Ironically, it was World War II—then raging in Europe—that gave the needed stimulus for large-scale production. Florey and Chain first tried to enlist the help of British government and industry, but the country had marshaled all available resources for the war effort. Undaunted, Florey decided in June 1941 to travel to the United States, which had not yet entered the war. There he found the assistance he was seeking, and when the United States entered the war in December 1941, penicillin was declared a high priority war product. The Department of Agriculture, together with private industry, launched an all-out effort to find ways of mass-producing the new drug.

***High-yield strains of penicillin** are mass-produced today in enormous multistory fermentation tanks like the ones above, containing thousands of gallons of sterile nutrient broth.*

A factory in Peoria, Illinois, produced the first batches of penicillin, but its output was disappointingly small. The finicky mold would grow only in quart-sized containers, nourished by an expensive nutrient broth. As it needed air for survival, it grew only on the surface of the broth. The yield of hundreds of flasks of culture was barely enough to provide the daily dosage of penicillin for one patient. Clearly a more efficient process was needed.

By the end of 1942 three developments opened the way for large-scale production of penicillin. The first was the discovery of an abundant and inexpensive source of nutrient broth. The second was the development of a faster-growing strain of penicillin. A mold, identified as *Penicillium chrysogenum,* which had come from a rotting cantaloup in a Peoria grocery store, proved 200 times more productive than *Penicillium notatum.* In the laboratory scientists were able to develop an even more productive mutant form of the mold. The third breakthrough came with the perfection of a method of aerating huge tanks so that the mold could grow throughout the nutrient broth rather than only on the surface. Drug manufacturers began to build vats, nearly two stories high, that held 25,000 gallons of broth. Stirring rods the size of airplane propellers forced air through the tanks. As the mold grew, it produced enough warmth to heat a house.

Within a year a score of American companies were producing penicillin on a large scale, and by the end of the war they could supply enough of the drug to treat 7 million patients a year. The results were little short of miraculous. Never before had a drug demonstrated such potency against so wide a variety of diseases—and with so few harmful effects. Deaths from pneumonia, which had claimed 18 percent of those who contracted it in World War I, dwindled to less than 1 percent by the end of World War II. Penicillin showed an equally remarkable rate of cure against such once-certain killers as scarlet fever, strep throat, diphtheria, syphilis, and gonorrhea. It also proved effective in treating gas gangrene, blood poisoning, and certain forms of endocarditis and meningitis.

New Cures From the Soil

Penicillin's unprecedented success set off a worldwide search for other antibiotics. One of the pioneers of the new effort was Dr. Selman A. Waksman, a Russian-born biochemist. In 1943 Waksman discovered streptomycin, a substance produced by a soil-dwelling microbe. The new drug proved effective against a number of diseases, including tuberculosis, though its toxicity was higher than that of penicillin.

In the wake of Waksman's findings researchers began combing the world for new strains of molds and bacteria. Thousands of soil samples were collected and analyzed. In 1947 Chloromycetin, effective against a broad number of diseases, was isolated from a sample of Venezuelan soil. A drop of Missouri mud yielded Aureomycin, and Terramycin was found in Indiana soil. Gradually, however, the rate of discovery slowed, and efforts turned to the perfection of existing drugs.

Meanwhile, a number of problems began to develop. After a total of 100 million doses had been administered throughout the world, penicillin caused its first death. Experiments later revealed that as many as 10 percent of all people are allergic to the drug. Moreover, certain bacteria gradually developed resistance to penicillin, and though scientists have found ways to offset this by developing mutant strains of penicillin or by combining it with other antibiotics, the problem remains.

Alexander Fleming was knighted in 1944, and in 1945 he shared the Nobel Prize for Medicine with Florey and Chain. He was also publicly honored by governments and academic institutions from India to the Americas. When he died in 1955 at the age of 74, he was remembered throughout the world for his gentle charm and for his modesty in accepting the world's praise for his remarkable discovery.

DRUGS FOR ANIMALS AND PLANTS

More than half the antibiotics produced in the United States end up on farms, not in hospitals. Some are used in veterinary medicine, but many more are mixed into animal feed. For some as yet unexplained reason animals whose feed contains small amounts of antibiotics grow fatter faster. Farmers claim that drug-feeding has saved them millions of dollars and enabled them to keep pace with the rapidly growing demand. Today more than 80 percent of this country's supply of meat, poultry, and dairy products comes from drug-fed livestock.

There may, however, be drawbacks to this practice. With long-term drug-feeding, bacteria could develop resistant strains, and diseased livestock might not respond to antibiotic treatment. Worse, antibiotic residues in animal tissues might cause allergic reactions or promote a buildup of resistant bacteria among human consumers.

In 1969 a British task force concluded that antibiotics in animal feed are a health hazard, and the British government subsequently banned such use of most drugs. A similar study by the U.S. Food and Drug Administration in 1972 found no conclusive evidence and reported that such drugs "do not pose a known health hazard to humans."

Antibiotics also combat certain plant diseases, especially fire blight of pear and apple trees and lethal yellowing of coconut palms. In both cases whole groves of trees were destroyed before certain antibiotics were found to be effective.

Healthy steers receive periodic injections of antibiotics to prevent the spread of infection (below, upper left). A pear tree (lower right) receives a "shot" of Terramycin, a drug that combats pear decline.

AN ALMANAC 1919-29

1919

Jan. 16 18th amendment to U.S. Constitution, prohibiting sale and manufacture of alcoholic beverages, is ratified by last state, to take effect Jan. 16, 1920.

Jan. 18 Conference of 32 nations, including 5 British dominions, convenes in Paris to draft treaty ending World War I.

Jan. 21 Sinn Fein Party organizes Irish Parliament and declares Irish Republic and its independence from Great Britain. Fighting begins between British forces and Irish nationalists.

June 28 Treaty of Versailles signed. Key provisions concern Germany's territorial cessions, virtual demilitarization, and payment to victors for war damage (see pp. 146–153).

July 31 Germany adopts Weimar Constitution providing for democratic government under an elected President and a Chancellor appointed by President.

July 31 Bela Kun forced to declare soviet republic at an end as Romanian troops invade Hungary.

1920

Jan. 10 League of Nations becomes official. The Assembly, consisting of representatives from 42 nations, meets for first time at Geneva on Nov. 15.

Mar. 19 U.S. Senate formally notifies President Woodrow Wilson that Treaty of Versailles cannot be ratified. Senate opposition centered on treaty's provision for membership in League of Nations.

Apr.-Oct. Poles begin major offensive during Russian-Polish border dispute in western Ukraine.

July 23 British East Africa becomes crown colony of Kenya, its coastal region called Kenya Protectorate.

Aug. 10 Treaty of Sèvres between Allies and Turkey signed. Turkey gives up non-Turkish territory; Bosporus and Dardanelles are internationalized and demilitarized; Greek forces are permitted to occupy Smyrna. Sultan's acceptance of treaty causes final break between Ottoman government and Turkish nationalists led by Mustafa Kemal (Kemal Ataturk).

Aug. 26 19th amendment to U.S. Constitution certified, giving women right to vote (see pp. 76–81).

Nov. 2 Republican Warren G. Harding elected U.S. President over Democrat James M. Cox. Election returns carried by Pittsburgh station KDKA in world's first scheduled radio broadcast.

Nov. 8 Russian civil war ends as White troops evacuate Crimea.

Dec. 23 Government of Ireland Act by Britain provides separate Parliaments for Northern and Southern Ireland.

1921

Feb. 23 Anti-Bolshevik mutiny by Russian sailors at Kronstadt naval base crushed by Communists. Mutiny influenced adoption of Lenin's New Economic Policy.

Mar. 18 Treaty of Riga establishes peace between Poland and Russia and fixes their frontier; Russia abandons part of claim to Ukraine.

Mar. 24 Reparations committee declares Germany in default on war payments. On Dec. 15 German government notifies committee it is unable to pay debt. Moratorium granted May 31, 1922.

Aug. 24, 25, 29 U.S.A. signs peace treaties with Austria, Germany, and Hungary respectively.

Aug. 24–Sept. 16 Greek advance toward Angora (now Ankara) stopped by Turks in heavy fighting at Battle of the Sakarya.

Nov. 4 Takashi Hara, Premier of Japan, is assassinated.

Dec. 6 Liberal W. L. Mackenzie King elected Canadian Prime Minister.

Dec. 6 Treaty grants Ireland dominion Status as Irish Free State within British Commonwealth; officially proclaimed Dec. 6, 1922.

Dec. 13 Treaty between Great Britain, France, Japan, and U.S.A., signed during Washington Conference, guarantees that these nations will respect each other's island territories in Pacific. At same conference these four nations, as well as Italy, sign treaty with 10-year limit on naval armaments (Dec. 19).

1922

Jan. 30 Permanent Court of International Justice holds first meeting at The Hague in Holland.

Feb. 6 Achille Ratti is elected Pope (Pius XI), succeeding Benedict XV.

Feb. 28 Egypt declared independent; seven-year British protectorate at an end.

Mar. 18 Mohandas K. Gandhi, after his first civil disobedience campaign against British rule in India, is sentenced to six years' imprisonment (see pp. 160–163).

Apr. 16 Treaty of Rapallo establishes peace between Germany and Russia; both nations renounce payment of outstanding World War I debts.

July 18–24 League of Nations Council approves mandates for Palestine, Tanganyika, Togoland, and Cameroons.

Sept. 9 Turks enter Smyrna in successful drive to force Greeks out of Turkey. Nationalists abolish sultanate on Nov. 1.

Oct. 28 Fascist militants march on Rome and occupy city. Fascist government, with Benito Mussolini as Prime Minister, takes office on Oct. 31 (see pp. 168–173).

Dec. 30 Union of Soviet Socialist Republics is established by confederation of Russia, Ukraine, White Russia, and Transcaucasia.

1923

Jan. 11 French and Belgian troops occupy Ruhr district of Germany to enforce reparation payments.

July 24 Treaty of Lausanne replaces 1920 Treaty of Sèvres. Turkey recovers its European territory; Bosporus and Dardanelles remain demilitarized (but not internationalized). Turkish Republic is proclaimed by President Mustafa Kemal Oct. 29.

Aug. 2 U.S. President Warren G. Harding dies; succeeded by Calvin Coolidge the following day.

Nov. 8-11 Nazi leader Adolf Hitler attempts to overthrow Bavarian government in Munich, Germany, but fails. He is sentenced to five years' imprisonment but serves less than one year, during which he writes *Mein Kampf.*

1924

Jan. 21 Death of Vladimir Ilyich Lenin results in ferocious power struggle between opposing party factions led by Leon Trotsky and Joseph Stalin.

Jan. 22 First British Labour government formed under Ramsay MacDonald.

Feb.-Mar. Teapot Dome oil scandal, involving leasing of naval oil lands to private companies, revealed by U.S. Senate committee's hearings. Former Secretary of the Interior Albert B. Fall later found guilty of having accepted a bribe during Harding administration to lease lands.

May 1 Greece proclaimed a republic. King George II had been deposed (Dec. 18, 1923) by military coup.

May 26 U.S. Immigration bill signed by President Coolidge. It limits total number of immigrants from any one country each year to 2 percent of its nationals who were living in U.S.A. in 1890; Japanese immigrants are excluded entirely.

July 16–Aug. 16 London Conference approves Dawes Plan to stabilize German currency; loans and war reparations put under Allied control.

Oct. 2 League of Nations adopts Geneva Protocol providing for mutual assistance and alliances, reduction of armaments, and compulsory arbitration of all disputes between members.

Nov. 6 Stanley Baldwin announces Cabinet for Conservative government after British voters reject Labour Party in Oct. 29 elections. Winston Churchill, who had recently become a Conservative after serving for more than 20 years in the Liberal Party, is named Chancellor of the Exchequer.

1925

Jan. 5 Nellie T. Ross inaugurated to succeed her late husband as Governor of Wyoming, becoming first woman Governor of an American state.

Apr. 26 Paul von Hindenburg, retired field marshal, is elected President of Germany by million-vote margin. Communists poll 2 million votes.

May 4–June 17 Arms traffic convention of 45 nations, meeting at Geneva, bans poison gas as weapon of war.

Oct. 5–16 Locarno Conference drafts treaties guaranteeing security of Germany's frontiers with France, Belgium, Czechoslovakia, and Poland. Treaties also provide for demilitarization of Rhineland and Germany's entry into League of Nations (on Sept. 8, 1926).

Oct. 22–23 Greece invades Bulgaria after border clash. League of Nations settles dispute (Dec. 14) and fines Greece for the incursion.

1926

Jan. 8 Ibn Saud is proclaimed King of Hejaz and Sultan of Nejd at Mecca. He unifies two regions as Kingdom of Saudi Arabia in 1932.

Mar. 16 Dr. Robert H. Goddard begins Space Age with first flight of a liquid-fuel rocket (see pp. 192–197).

May 2 U.S.A. sends marines into Nicaragua after insurrection and civil war. Civil war ends May 4, 1927, after U.S. statesman Henry L. Stimson arranges elections under U.S. supervision.

May 3–12 General strike in England by 2.5 million union workers, who support striking coal miners, causes country's first full work stoppage. Miners continue their strike until Nov. 19 but do not achieve their demands.

May 12 Marshal Joseph Pilsudski leads a military coup d'etat in Poland. He controls country until his death in 1935.

May 26 Riff revolt against French rule in Morocco ends with surrender of Muslim rebel leader Abd-el-Krim.

June 28 W. L. Mackenzie King resigns as Prime Minister of Canada as result of corruption scandal in Customs Bureau. He is vindicated when he returns to office after elections of Sept. 14.

Sept. 24 New republican constitution goes into effect in Greece.

Oct. 23, 26 Stalin triumphs over Leftist opposition led by Leon Trotsky, Soviet Politburo expelling Trotsky and Grigori Zinoviev. Chief disagreement was whether Russia could build "socialism in one country" (Stalin) without having first promoted communist revolutions in other countries (Trotsky).

1927

Jan. 31 Allies end military control of Germany, with question of German rearmament put under jurisdiction of League of Nations.

Apr. 18 In the midst of civil war in China Chiang Kai-shek's conservative faction of Kuomintang splits from radicals at Hankow and sets up new government at Nanking.

May 20–21 Charles Lindbergh makes world's first solo nonstop transatlantic flight, from New York to Paris.

May 26 Britain breaks off diplomatic relations with Russia because of alleged hostile acts and propaganda.

Nov. 1 Mustafa Kemal unanimously reelected President of Turkey by National Assembly after being empowered to name all candidates of his People's Party, resulting in a monopoly.

Dec. 27 Soviet Communist Congress expels Trotsky and his followers from Communist Party, marking final victory of Stalin in Soviet power struggle.

1928

Apr. 9 Turkey ends legal status of Islam as the state religion.

July 19 King Fuad takes control of Egypt, dissolves Parliament, and suspends freedom of press and assembly.

July 28 China annuls "unequal treaties" with foreign states and begins to renegotiate treaties with 12 nations that had agreed to allow new Nanking government to set its own tariffs.

Aug. 1 In Yugoslavia Croats refuse to cooperate further with Belgrade government and set up their own Parliament (Oct.) at Zagreb.

Aug. 27 Kellogg-Briand Pact, outlawing war and providing for negotiation of international disputes, signed by 15 nations in Paris (and eventually by a total of 62 countries).

Aug. 30 Jawaharlal Nehru founds Independence of India League to work toward freedom from British rule.

Oct. 1 Stalin puts his first five-year plan into operation. Major goals are to develop heavy industry and collectivize farms (see pp. 204–209).

Oct. 6 Nationalist leader Chiang Kai-shek elected President of China by Kuomintang Congress.

Nov. 7 Republican Herbert Hoover succeeds President Coolidge, defeating Democrat Alfred E. Smith, first Roman Catholic to be nominated by a major U.S. political party.

1929

Jan. 19 Communist leftwing leader Leon Trotsky is exiled from Russia. On Nov. 17 Joseph Stalin expels rightwing opposition leader Nikolai Bukharin from Politburo of Soviet Communist Party.

Mar. 24 In Italy Benito Mussolini's Fascist Party is "victor" in one-party election.

June 5 Ramsay MacDonald forms Britain's second Labour Cabinet.

June 7 Lateran Treaty is ratified by Italian government and Papacy, establishing independent Vatican City with Pope as its sovereign ruler. From now on Popes are no longer the "voluntary prisoners" they became in 1870.

Aug. Arabs attack Jews in Palestine following disputes over Jewish use of Wailing Wall in Jerusalem.

Aug. 6–31 U.S. statesman Owen D. Young's plan for German payment of war reparations accepted by Germany at Hague conference. Allies in turn agree to evacuate Rhineland by June 1930. The Young Plan also provided for the founding of the Bank for International Settlements.

1929-39 HARD TIMES

Lord, I'm so low down, baby,
I declare I'm looking up at down.

—Big Bill Broonzy, blues singer

1929-39

The often bitter strife between business and the labor movement took on ominous dimensions in this 1938 cartoon from Ken *magazine.*

When the Great Depression began spreading across the world in 1930, little more than a decade had elapsed since the end of a war that left most of Europe in political and economic shambles. For a time there had been no way of knowing how many major nations might, like Russia and Italy, succumb to totalitarian pressure from the left or the right. Gradually, though, conditions had begun to improve, and by the late 1920's it appeared that democracy might prevail after all—even in Germany, where its prospects had seemed remote at best.

Then in October 1929 America's great stock market boom caved in on itself, setting off a shock wave that toppled the world's financial and economic systems one after another. In the wake of the collapse came far-reaching social and political repercussions. In some cases they led to basic and beneficial revisions in government policy, such as those enacted in the United States and Great Britain. Elsewhere, however, events took a different turn—most ominously in Germany, where a population still embittered by the harsh terms of the Treaty of Versailles lost faith in the slow-moving processes of representative government. Increasingly, they hungered for simple solutions and decisive leadership, and the one man who seemed to offer both was Adolf Hitler.

In retrospect, the movement of history through the 1930's was marked by all the ironies, accidents, misjudgments, and cross-purposes of a classical Greek tragedy. The Nazis' rise in Germany was paralleled in Japan where, with the onset of the Depression, a liberal republican government gave way to an authoritarian, militaristic regime with its own dreams of conquest. And it happened that the Fascists began to flex their muscles precisely at a time when the world's other leading powers were least prepared to resist them. England, France, and the U.S.S.R.—all with good reason to fear Germany's sudden resurgence—were nevertheless too preoccupied with their own internal problems to take any decisive action. On the other side of the globe, China was in the throes of civil war and virtually helpless against Japan's growing power and aggressiveness.

Meanwhile, the United States remained cloaked in stubborn isolationism, trying to recover its own economic health and to avoid what were scornfully referred to as "foreign entanglements." The League of Nations, while occassionally useful in settling disputes among smaller countries, proved utterly powerless to restrain the aggressions of larger ones.

Thus the world stood by, appalled by what it saw but unwilling or unable to act. By 1938 it had become clear enough that a global confrontation between fascism and its opponents was approaching. But those opponents still hesitated, divided among themselves, clinging to their hope that the inevitable might yet be averted—that China might somehow unite itself to beat back the Japanese; that Mussolini might abandon his dream of a new Roman Empire around the Mediterranean; above all, that Hitler's latest territorial demands might really be his last.

By the time the world realized its mistake, it was too late. All that remained for Hitler were the final preparations, which he completed in August 1939 with an astonishing diplomatic coup: a nonaggression pact between Germany and the Soviet Union. With this, the last obstacle was removed. Nine days later, on September 1, German troops crossed the border into Poland, and the nightmare of the Second World War began.

1929

The Great Depression

The New York stock market crashes, precipitating a decade of economic and social strife around the world.

The resounding collapse of the American economy in October 1929 caught most of the country's financial community off guard. On October 24, the day history has memorialized as Black Thursday, the New York Stock Exchange opened for business in a deceptively normal mood. For nine heady years its soaring market had symbolized America's unprecedented prosperity. In his 1929 inaugural address President Herbert Hoover had confidently predicted that the final triumph over poverty was near at hand. Many Americans agreed. Financiers and industrialists became popular heroes, and some 1.5 million Americans were already eager investors.

Until 1925 most of the country's growth had rested solidly on massive industrial expansion; afterward the growth was spurred on by hundreds of thousands of large and small investments. The interest (up to 10 percent) paid on money borrowed by investors to trade on margin had in turn lured further investment, building a pyramid of paper profits based only on the hope for a perpetually rising market. But behind this facade of prosperity had been some ominous signs. Construction and industrial production were declining, automobile sales were off, and wholesale prices were falling. In September stock prices began dropping as well.

Trading proceeded normally at first on the 24th, but by 11 o'clock there were far more orders to sell than to buy. A frenzy of selling suddenly swept the floor. Prices shot down. Panicky brokers shouldered one another out of the way, bellowing offers to sell cheap. Telegraph and telephone lines were jammed with orders to sell. A vast, anxious crowd gathered outside the exchange. The stock ticker fell behind, so that frightened investors were powerless to know their fate. Beleaguered brokers issued frantic calls for margin payments that spelled bankruptcy for thousands of small investors. Elsewhere local exchanges closed their doors in a futile effort to stop the price slide. Finally a

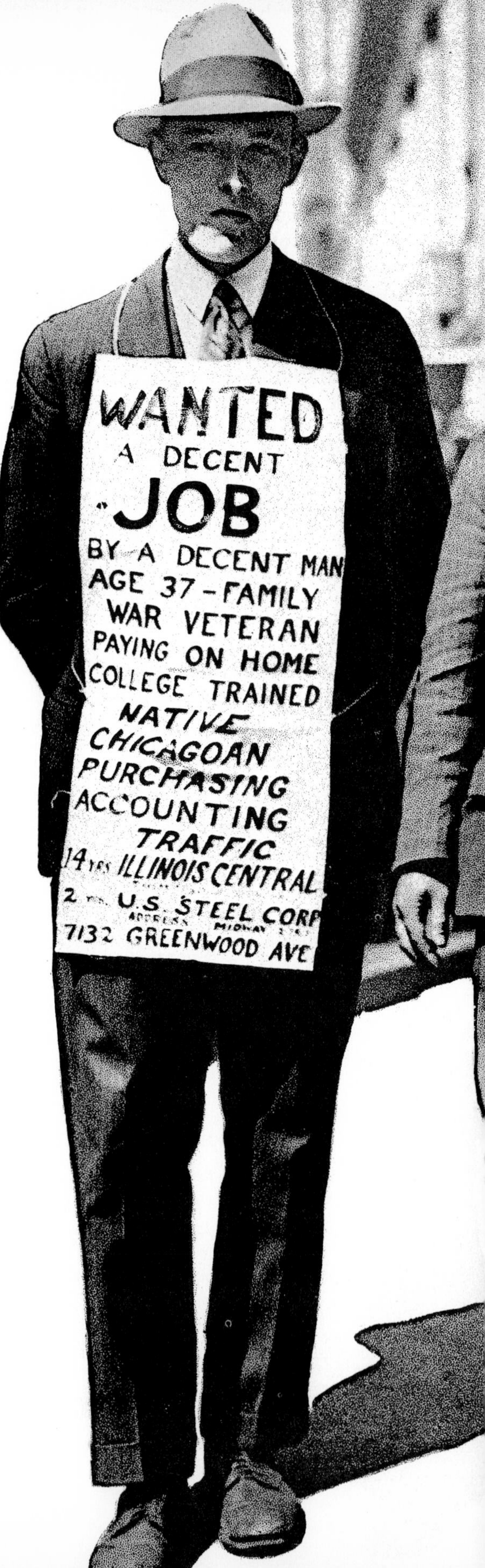

Instead of hawking apples, *some men became their own billboards. This scene was photographed in Chicago in 1934, but similar ones occurred during much of the Depression in cities across the land. People unable to find a decent job were often grateful to earn a few cents an hour for piecework.*

group of powerful bankers pooled their resources and bought shrewdly to restore confidence. By the close of business, although a record 13 million shares had changed hands, the market had leveled off.

No further damage was done on Friday, October 25, and Hoover urged calm, stating that the "fundamental business of the country . . . is on a sound and prosperous basis." But the following week the market tumbled sharply again. On Tuesday the 29th alone the Dow Jones average fell 40 points. Many of those who had bought cheap the week before were forced to dump their shares at ludicrously low prices. Sixteen million shares were sold. As the slide continued into November, large investors as well as small went under.

Black Thursday, or the even blacker Tuesday, the 29th, did not cause the Great Depression. The economy was already in deep trouble when the opening gong sounded on those fateful days. But the panic of selling that took place called a sudden, jarring halt to a decade of sunny business optimism. Pessimism and retrenchment set the tone for business. Almost overnight the soaring spiral of rising prices reversed itself and became an equally dizzying spiral of decline. The result was economic disaster, starting in the United States and spreading worldwide—the worst and longest depression in modern history.

The Great Prosperity of the Roaring Twenties

The decade of prosperity that the crash ended had been dazzling. In 1919 the war was over, and the nation had turned its attention to making money. It succeeded beyond its wildest dreams. With a friendly Republican government in Washington fully committed to business growth, U.S. industry mushroomed. Mechanization, electrification, and the spread of assembly-line techniques led to a manufacturing output increase of 64 percent between 1919 and 1929. Wages and real earnings rose, but profits rose far higher.

The business boom was based largely on two great industries, automobiles and construction. By 1929 a finished car rolled off Henry Ford's Detroit assembly line every 17 seconds, and there were 26 million autos and trucks on U.S. roads, or one for every five Americans. The auto business led to the rise of a host of related industries; boosted consumption of oil, steel, and rubber; and helped spur a nationwide clamor for better roads. Increased mobility led to the growth of suburbia, which boosted still higher the already prosperous construction industry. U.S. cities grew not only up but out as gleaming skyscrapers rose in the city centers and commuter suburbs spread around them.

America's inventive genius, her new need to fill leisure time, and the spread of electrification all fitted perfectly with the advertising industry's newly developed talent for making luxuries seem like necessities. Factories could hardly keep up with the demand for

***Armies of homeless men** roamed the country fruitlessly seeking work. In the cities these men congregated in what were often called hobo jungles. Reginald Marsh's painting "East 10th Street" illustrates such an area in New York.*

consumer goods and household appliances. Tourism and entertainment became multibillion-dollar industries. Sports became big business. Radio, movies, and phonograph records brought even the tiniest towns up to date. Americans were caught up in a new craze for possessions and the social status they conferred. The national attitude toward money changed. For the first time in U.S. history, thrift was disparaged in favor of spending and conspicuous consumption.

The Flaws Behind the Facade

Yet beneath the decade's glittering surface lurked hidden fissures, early and unheeded signs of the collapse to come. Under Presidents Warren Harding and Calvin Coolidge (and to a lesser extent under Hoover), the government sought to identify the nation's welfare with that of the businessman. The conventional economic policy of laissez-faire was based on the idea that if the government kept from "interfering" with the economy, business profits would be shared with workers in the form of wages; the workers, in turn, could invest in stocks and thereby partake of the general wealth. Most Americans shared this view. Coolidge went so far as to state that "this is a business country and wants a business government," and his Secretary of the Treasury, millionaire Andrew Mellon, acted accordingly. Federal spending was slashed. So were taxes for the well-to-do (so their earnings could be reinvested in expansion). Antimonopoly laws were eased to encourage consolidation and boost efficiency. The stock market was allowed to soar without regulation. Tariff walls shielded U.S. industries.

These government policies delighted businessmen. Corporate profits soared 62 percent between 1923 and 1929. But the average worker's real income rose only 11 percent. Since wages did not go up proportionately to industrial production and profits, workers could not buy the ever-increasing quantity of goods. More plant space had been created than could profitably be used, and production chronically outstripped demand. Thus the refusal of business to share profits with workers actually helped bring about a business downfall.

By 1929 the richest 5 percent of the population had one-third of all personal income. The possibility of making vast sums inevitably lured the unscrupulous, and the ugly aftermath of the crash laid bare massive frauds by once respected financiers. Some 6,000 banks buckled during the four-year period 1929–32.

Another flaw in the system was the fact that some elements of the economy had no share in the national prosperity: Several key industries (notably coal and textiles) never regained their prewar levels; unemployment was high, and wages were alarmingly low. Greater efficiency, improved farming methods, and new fertilizers and machinery enabled farmers to greatly increase their yields, but a chronic glut resulted, and farm prices fell steadily. Between 1919 and 1929 agricultural income fell 22 percent.

Thus, despite bland assurances by government, the prosperity of the twenties contained within it not just the seeds but the well-rooted weeds of disaster.

A Good Man in Bad Times

When Herbert Hoover entered the White House in 1929, he was among America's most universally admired men; he left it four years later in largely undeserved disgrace. An able engineer and self-made millionaire, he had given up private gain for public service during World War I. Known to his admirers as the Great Engineer, he seemed ideally suited to guide the nation through any crisis. But the crash that shook the country only seven months after his inauguration shattered America's confidence both in business and in Hoover. Suddenly thousands of holding companies and investment trusts were bankrupt. So were many of the people who relied on them.

On December 11, 1930, in New York City, the powerful Bank of the United States collapsed, destroying the savings of half a million depositers. Some 2,300 banks collapsed in 1931 alone. Manufacturers with overstocked inventories cut losses by shutting down plants; between 1930 and 1933 an average of 64,000 workers joined the ranks of the unemployed each week. By 1933 some 13 million Americans were out of work. Most of those with jobs had their wages slashed. Manufacturing output slid back to 1916 levels.

These grim statistics can only hint at the human suffering caused by the Depression. The old virtues—thrift, tenacity, and willingness to work—seemed no longer to make any difference. Many workers were unsure whether or not they would be able to feed their families. Thousands were threatened with actual starvation. Hundreds of thousands of jobless men and boys roamed the countryside, stowing away on freight trains and haunting hobo jungles.

An activist, Hoover refused to heed the advice of laissez-faire conservatives who urged him to do nothing. People were suffering, and Hoover believed the government should help them, at least up to a point. He sought first of all to bolster public confidence, promising again and again that prosperity was "just around the corner." Hoover also acted with bold vigor. He created the Reconstruction Finance Corporation to bail out failing banks, state governments, and railroads; used the Federal Reserve Board to encourage business borrowing and industrial growth; stepped up public works to provide jobs; cut taxes to encourage consumer purchasing; and tried to maintain farm prices by buying up crop surpluses for sale abroad.

Much of Roosevelt's New Deal legislation had its origin in the measures Hoover took to relieve the suffering of the unemployed. But although Hoover also encouraged the shift from private charity to aid by state and local governments, he could not go so far as to sanction direct federal aid. And aid in massive amounts by the federal government was what was called for: In 1931 the unemployment rate had reached 16 percent and was still climbing.

The Crisis Spreads to Europe

The effects of the U.S. stock market crash were felt very quickly around the world. Australia and Canada,

***The anguish and dignity** of the dispossessed were documented in this widely published Farm Security Administration photograph by Dorothea Lange.*

***Derisively dubbed "Hoovervilles"** by the inhabitants, shantytowns like the one above in Brooklyn were built of any scrap available.*

THE GLOBAL DEPRESSION

The repercussions of the American Depression were worldwide. Japan lost its lucrative U.S. market for silk exports (which had provided an essential income for Japanese farmers and textile workers), and in Latin America the withdrawal of U.S. loans left many governments in the middle of ambitious projects for which they no longer had funds. In Europe the collapse of the largest Austrian bank, the Creditanstalt, in May 1931 produced shock waves of panic and a bank run that forced many smaller banks, unable to meet their obligations, to close. International efforts to aid the Creditanstalt had succeeded only in draining needed money from other banks.

In Germany half the men between 16 and 30 were out of work, and in Australia the unemployment rate went from less than 10 percent in 1929 to more than 30 percent in 1932; around the world more than 30 million people were unemployed. While hungry men and women in the cities searched for food in refuse cans, thousands of acres of grain were allowed to rot in the fields because harvesting and shipping were unprofitable. In Brazil millions of pounds of coffee were burned for the same reason.

In September 1931 Great Britain abolished the convertibility of the pound into gold, thus spelling the end of the gold standard. As nations retreated behind barriers of high tariffs, import quotas, competitive devaluations, and other attempts to protect their own industries, international trade began to collapse, and national self-interest took the place of the international cooperation that might have speeded recovery. As it was, the real stimulus to economic recovery came from German rearmament, whose own roots lay deep in the Depression. In terms of lives and suffering, it was a stimulus that would prove costly beyond experience or imagination.

Demonstrations such as this London march of jobless men in 1930 (center) reflected unemployment figures that rose to 2.5 million by December.

Police and unemployed skirmish during a 1931 march in London. Unemployment insurance had been introduced in 1911, and coverage was extended in 1920. With 23 percent of insured workers jobless, national finances were greatly strained.

At hard-money markets (left, in Berlin) Germans, remembering the inflation of 1923, exchanged paper money for metal coins. The Salvation Army annually gave bread and soup to Berlin's destitute on Christmas Eve (below).

France was slow to recover from World War I, and its prosperity, regained late in the 1920's, was short-lived. By 1931 unemployment was as severe as elsewhere (above).

primarily agricultural countries, suffered from the sharp drop in farm prices. Early in the spring of 1931, just as the U.S. economy was beginning to show signs of a slight upturn, events abroad conspired to send it tumbling down again.

Since World War I European economies had depended heavily on U.S. dollars in the form of loans, goods exported to America, and (after the war) tourism. When the 1929 crash withdrew those dollars, Western Europe was staggered. Hardest hit were Germany and Austria, each saddled with heavy reparations payments to the Allies and wracked by unstable currencies and political strife. The two nations sought to merge their economies in a desperate effort to survive. But in March 1931 France, partly for political reasons, demanded immediate repayment of German short-term notes. A Viennese bank, the Creditanstalt, a traditional mainstay of central European economies, collapsed in May, and finally the desperate German government, with nowhere else to turn, appealed to Washington for help, but in vain.

A decade of lofty U.S. tariffs on foreign imports had severely restricted foreign trade. Thus the United States had made it hard for European nations to earn the dollars with which her former allies could pay their war debts and her former foes their reparations. Hoover saw that a radically different policy was needed, for if Europe's financial institutions failed, European gold would be withheld from the already battered U.S. banks. He called for a yearlong moratorium on reparations payments. But it was too late. Within weeks after the Creditanstalt and other Viennese banks collapsed, most European nations were in deep trouble. By 1932 some 6 million Germans were unemployed. In Britain, where 3 million were without jobs, public anger toppled the ruling Labour Party. Britain had abandoned the gold standard in 1931—a radical move swiftly imitated by 40 other nations. As Hoover had feared, more U.S. banks failed, and the national economy resumed its slide.

The President's policies had failed. His unwillingness to take bolder action was solidly rooted in principle, but points of doctrine meant little to the hungry. Hoover's frequent predictions of imminent upturn were mocked; his offers of aid to business, coupled with his refusal of direct aid to jobless workers, seemed less principled than uncaring. He became the dour symbol of all that had gone wrong. Stung by criticism (much of it cruel and unfair) and baffled by the continuing crisis, Hoover retreated into resentful silence. Although few could have anticipated it in 1931 and 1932, the Depression was to last many bitter years. The U.S.A. did not recover until well into World War II. In the autumn of 1932 the American people abandoned Hoover and elected Franklin D. Roosevelt to lead them in the struggle for recovery.

SCIENCE & TECHNOLOGY

1929-39

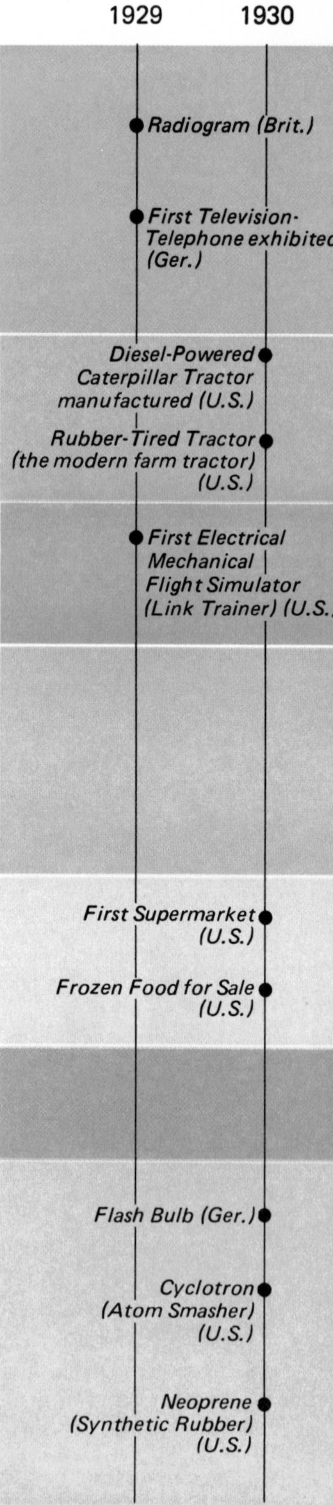

Tools and Techniques

A writer in the mid-19th century, discussing the limits of human knowledge, chose the chemical composition of the stars as an example of something mankind could never know. Twenty years later helium was detected in spectrograms of the sun and subsequently added to the periodic table of the elements. Today the chemistry of stars is routinely analyzed by spectroscopy (see p. 84), and the greatest challenge is no longer to discover what they are made of, but to put our knowledge to work—in this case to develop a process of controlled hydrogen fusion that would enable us to tap the same source of energy that fuels the sun.

So it is that the tools and techniques of science help transform the unknowable into the commonplace. The tools of early scientists were generally homemade, requiring at most the skills of a lens grinder or metalsmith. But as research grew more complex, the design of scientific apparatus became increasingly important, especially after the great surge of discovery at the turn of the century, when decades were needed for the technology of instrument making to catch up.

It was during the 1930's that much of this progress was achieved, making it possible for scientists to evaluate a growing list of new ideas. One such innovation of major importance was the electron microscope, first built in 1931 by the German physicists Ernst Ruska and Max Knoll. The early instruments tested by Ruska and Knoll magnified only a few hundred times, but within a few years improved models were producing magnifications of 100,000 times and more, greatly accelerating the pace of research into viral diseases and a widening range of other topics.

The thirties also saw a great advance in the instrument that had helped give rise to modern science three centuries earlier—the telescope. During the decade a major effort was launched to construct a reflector telescope 200 inches in diameter—twice the size of the largest one then in existence. Beset by numerous delays and technical problems, the massive project was finally completed in 1948, when the Hale telescope was installed at the Mount Palomar Observatory in California.

The thirties also marked the appearance of an unexpected new astronomical tool, the radio telescope, first developed in 1931 by a young American engineer, Karl Jansky. Used to detect and track down radio emissions from outer space, the new device was able to provide a great deal of information unavailable through optical telescopes (see pp. 494–497).

At the smaller extreme of magnitude, Marie and Pierre Curie's discovery of radium (see pp. 22–27) had given scientists a revolutionary new method of investigating the structure of the atom—that is, by using a radioactive substance as a "gun" with which to fire subatomic particles at another element and then observe the effects. As of 1930 only two components of the atom had actually been proven to exist—the positively charged proton in the nucleus and the negatively charged electron orbiting around it. As early

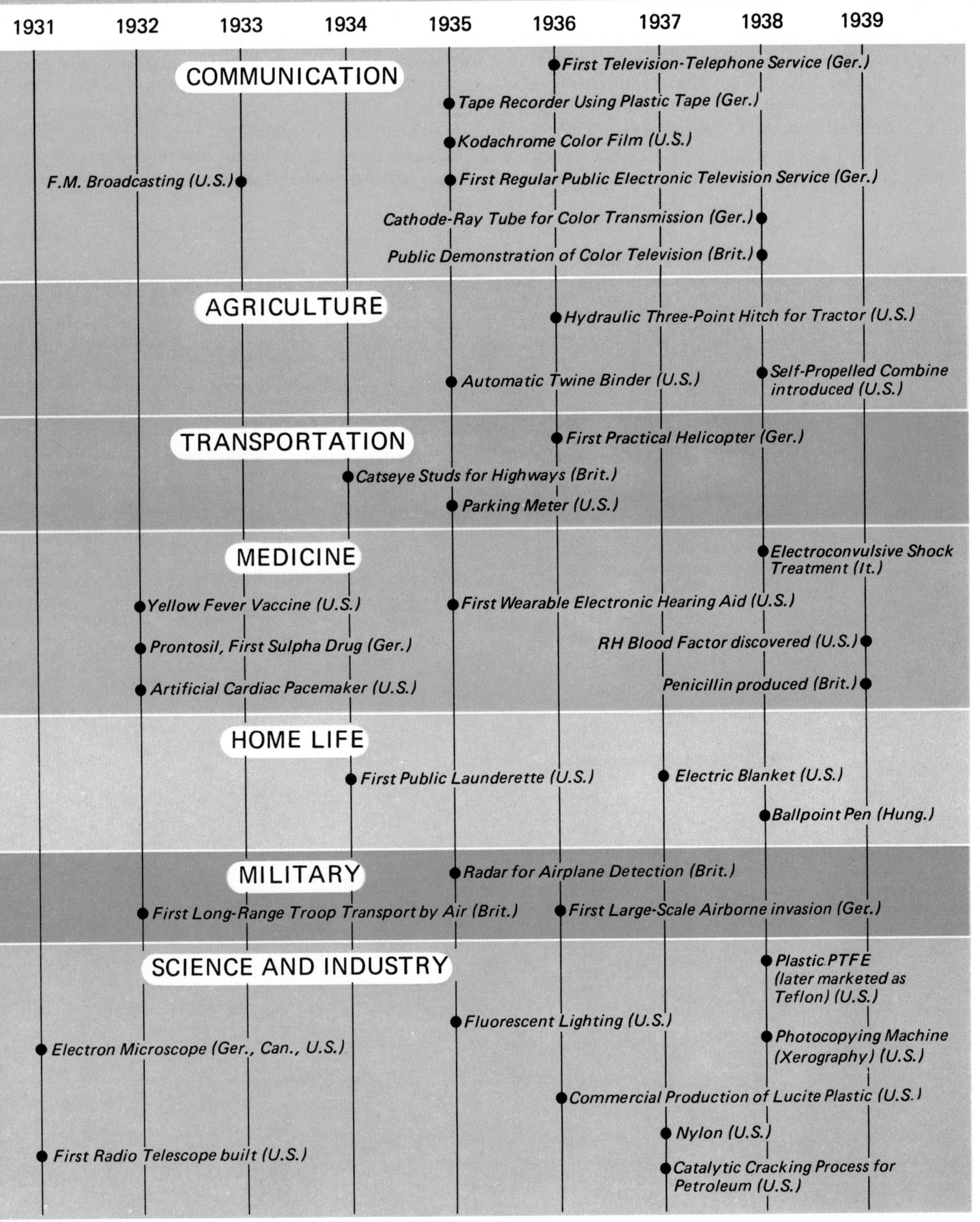
THE PACE OF INVENTION
1931
1932
1933
1934
1935
1936
1937
1938
1939
COMMUNICATION
First Television-Telephone Service (Ger.)
Tape Recorder Using Plastic Tape (Ger.)
Kodachrome Color Film (U.S.)
F.M. Broadcasting (U.S.)
First Regular Public Electronic Television Service (Ger.)
Cathode-Ray Tube for Color Transmission (Ger.)
Public Demonstration of Color Television (Brit.)
AGRICULTURE
Hydraulic Three-Point Hitch for Tractor (U.S.)
Automatic Twine Binder (U.S.)
Self-Propelled Combine introduced (U.S.)
TRANSPORTATION
First Practical Helicopter (Ger.)
Catseye Studs for Highways (Brit.)
Parking Meter (U.S.)
MEDICINE
Electroconvulsive Shock Treatment (It.)
Yellow Fever Vaccine (U.S.)
First Wearable Electronic Hearing Aid (U.S.)
RH Blood Factor discovered (U.S.)
Prontosil, First Sulpha Drug (Ger.)
Artificial Cardiac Pacemaker (U.S.)
Penicillin produced (Brit.)
HOME LIFE
First Public Launderette (U.S.)
Electric Blanket (U.S.)
Ballpoint Pen (Hung.)
MILITARY
Radar for Airplane Detection (Brit.)
First Long-Range Troop Transport by Air (Brit.)
First Large-Scale Airborne invasion (Ger.)
SCIENCE AND INDUSTRY
Plastic PTFE (later marketed as Teflon) (U.S.)
Fluorescent Lighting (U.S.)
Electron Microscope (Ger., Can., U.S.)
Photocopying Machine (Xerography) (U.S.)
Commercial Production of Lucite Plastic (U.S.)
Nylon (U.S.)
First Radio Telescope built (U.S.)
Catalytic Cracking Process for Petroleum (U.S.)

as 1920, though, several physicists had theorized the existence of another subatomic particle, and in 1932 the British physicist James Chadwick used the new research techniques to confirm their predictions, finding particles dislodged from the nuclei of beryllium that had about the same mass as protons but no electrical charge. These he named neutrons, and their discovery provided the last major piece of the jigsaw puzzle of atomic structure.

The same period also saw the development of a research instrument of enormous importance: the particle accelerator. Since the Curies' time physicists had depended on the particles spontaneously given off by radioactive substances to study the atom. It became clear, though, that the atomic nucleus was held together by forces far stronger than anything science had dealt with before, and that to break it apart would require more powerful ammunition. With this in mind, British physicist Sir John Cockcroft and his Irish colleague, Ernest Walton, developed a machine in which a series of electrical impulses accelerated protons to many times their normal velocity. In 1932 they succeeded in breaking the nucleus of lithium in two. For the first time an atomic nucleus had actually been split—and,

Right, a protozoan drawn by Anton van Leeuwenhoek, who pioneered microscopy in the late 1600's. Below, a modern microscope reveals the animal's means of locomotion—minute, hairlike cilia, unseen through early instruments.

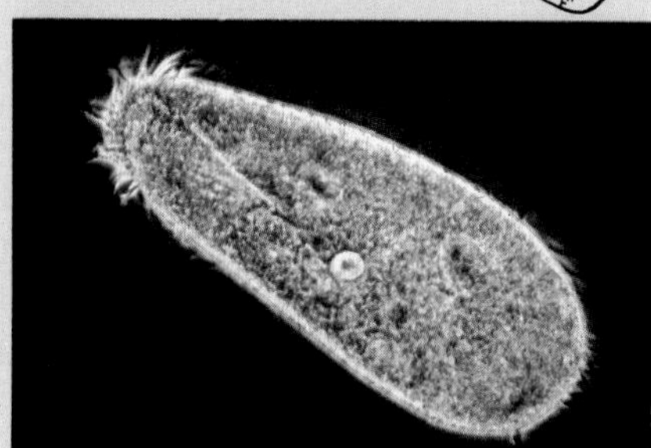

WINDOWS ONTO UNSEEN WORLDS

The scientist's tools, in essence, are no more than extensions of his hands and senses. They extend his powers of observation, allow him to measure what he observes, and provide the raw material of his inquiry. In the 1930's two radically different new tools, functioning beyond the limits of visible light, were developed. These tools, the electron microscope and the radio telescope, opened windows onto unseen and hitherto unimagined worlds.

By 1930 conventional microscopes seemed to have reached their limits, producing a top magnification of around 2,000 times. Anything too small to be seen at that magnification is small enough to "slip through" the wavelengths of light, as a small fish slips through the holes in a coarse net. In the electron microscope the finer "net" is a stream of electrons, focused by magnets rather than glass lenses and viewed on a specially coated screen. With such an instrument magnifications of more than 100,000 times are possible.

At the other extreme of magnitude, another ultimate seemed to have been reached with the development of the giant Hale telescope at Mount Palomar. Then an entirely different kind of instrument was built, recording not light but natural radio emissions from outer space. Before long such radio telescopes had dramatically increased man's understanding of the universe.

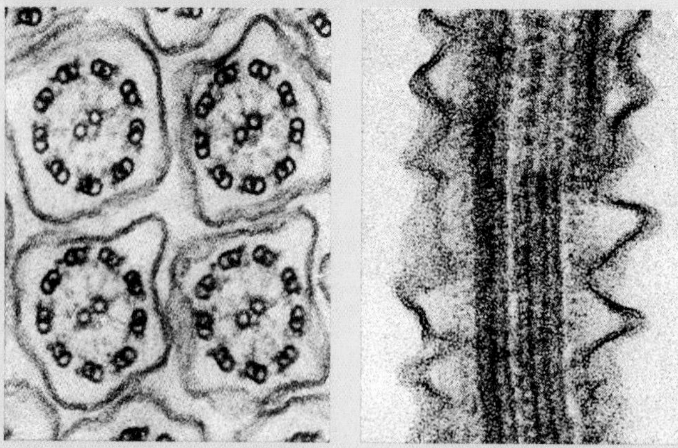

Above, an advanced electron microscope provides dramatically closer views, in cross section and lengthwise, of the cilia of a tetrahymena *protozoan magnified more than 100,000 times. The schematic drawing at right was based on such pictures, which have enabled biologists to understand ciliate structure and function.*

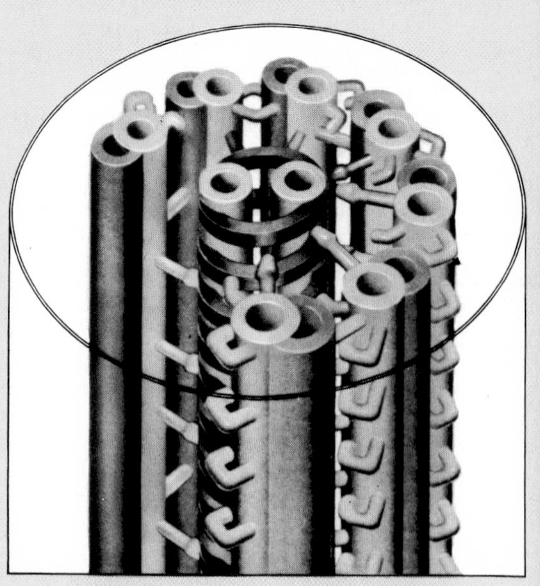

more importantly, it turned out that the two halves of a nucleus had a slightly smaller combined mass than the original, intact nucleus, the difference having been released in the form of energy. Cockcroft and Walton thus provided the first experimental proof of Albert Einstein's 1905 theory on the transformation of matter into energy (see pp. 38–43) and showed that the process conformed exactly to the century's most famous equation, $E = mc^2$.

Seven years later high-speed neutrons were used to bombard the unstable element uranium: The effect was the same as when lithium was used, except that the splitting of the uranium nucleus released a much larger amount of energy (200 million electron volts, to be precise; an exploding molecule of TNT releases 10 electron volts). Moreover, it was soon discovered that the splitting, or fission, of a uranium nucleus released other neutrons that might then collide with adjacent nuclei, thus starting a rapidly multiplying chain reaction.

The implications of this were, in 1939, little known outside the realm of theoretical physics. But the onset of war led to a massive mobilization of America's scientific resources, and the world would soon learn of the power inside the atom.

This panorama of our galaxy, the Milky Way, is a composite of several photographs taken through the wide-angle Schmidt telescope, used in conjunction with the 200-inch Hale telescope at the observatory on Mount Palomar, California (right). The 60-foot-long, million-pound Hale telescope has given astronomers a visual range of 2 billion light-years.

A radically different view of the galaxy is provided by a radio telescope, which measures radio signals from stars and interstellar clouds of hydrogen. The brighter areas on the map, near the galactic nucleus, indicate signals of greater intensity. Right, the 250-foot radio telescope at Jodrell Bank, England, can be precisely focused on any point in the sky.

1933

The Fuehrer Takes Command

An act of arson at the German Reichstag provides Adolf Hitler with a golden opportunity to gain absolute power.

On the night of February 27, 1933, less than a week before the German people were to elect a new national government, the Reichstag building, home of the German legislative assembly in Berlin, was set on fire and badly damaged. Adolf Hitler, who had become Chancellor only a month earlier, hurried to watch firemen bring the blaze under control. Even before police had finished questioning a suspected arsonist, Hitler was at work on a proclamation charging that the fire had been the signal for a Communist revolution, and promising to move swiftly against the threat. Before dawn on February 28 police began to arrest more than 4,000 of Hitler's known opponents; later that day Hitler was granted special emergency powers "for the protection of the people and the state"—powers he would not give up until his death.

In the months before the fire the German electorate had given Hitler's National Socialist (Nazi) Party enough support to bring him to the head of a coalition government. In a move to obtain a majority, Hitler had then called for new elections on March 5. During the campaign, the Nazis had used official powers to harass their opposition; the Reichstag fire provided them with an excuse to suppress it. Although the Nazis have often been accused of starting the fire, the case against them has only recently been proved; their arson was to augur a holocaust.

The Weimar Republic

The government that Hitler brought down in 1933 had come into existence on the eve of the Armistice ending World War I. Led by the three prorepublican parties and ratified by the German people in the election of January 19, 1919, it met first in the town of Weimar—a site symbolically associated with the Germany of peace and philosophy, and removed from the unrest current in Berlin. The liberal Weimar constitution was an attempt to replace the autocracy of Kaiser

***In 1930 Hitler** (left, leaving his headquarters) was well on the way to consolidating the power he needed to rule Germany. In 1933 he became Chancellor, and when the Reichstag was set on fire shortly after the elections (above), he took advantage of the event, using it as a pretext to justify the stringent repression of all his political opponents.*

Wilhelm II, and his rubberstamp wartime parliament, with democratic representation. No similar attempt in this century has failed so disastrously.

In the first Weimar elections the three moderate parties received more than three-quarters of the popular vote. The Nazis had not yet organized themselves and the Communists, committed to a workers' revolution, had boycotted the campaign. In June 1919 Chancellor Philipp Scheidemann resigned rather than accept the stringent terms of the Treaty of Versailles. But under the allied threat of blockade and invasion the new government submitted and signed the treaty on June 28, 1919.

That year millions of German soldiers came home to an economy nearly paralyzed by shortages, to cities and states in turmoil after Communist uprisings, and to a civilian population humiliated and disillusioned by defeat. Many former soldiers, unable to find work or adjust to civilian status, joined the Freikorps ("Free Corps"), quasi-military gangs that engaged in street fighting against the Communists, in banditry, murder, and assassination. Even so, the government reluctantly found itself in need of the Freikorps thugs to maintain even a semblance of civil order. When the prestigious Gen. Erich von Ludendorff announced that the war had not been lost by the armed forces, but that the army and General Staff had been "stabbed in the back" by politicians at home, the government's position became even weaker. In the elections of June 1920 the center coalition's share of the vote fell below 50 percent. It would never again attain a majority.

The moderate leaders of the fledgling Republic were unaccustomed to the exercise of power. Too often between 1918 and 1933 they argued among themselves rather than uniting to defend their common principles; too often they allowed civil rule to give way to the brute force of Freikorps, army, or Nazi paramilitary groups; too often they made deals with extremists, hoping to "tame" them by involving them in government.

But a new constitution could not instill democratic habits overnight in a people whose experience for centuries had been the least democratic of any industrialized nation. Weimar's moderates would have been considered conservatives elsewhere. Its judges consistently favored right-wing terrorists and plotters over their left-wing opponents, and many teachers and professors continued to spread the doctrines of power politics and Teutonic superiority that had helped bring about World War I. Many of its citizens began to look back on the war years with nostalgia, preferring memories of martial glory to a present marked by political wrangling and economic disorder. The longing for a return to unity and discipline may have been inevitable, but its consequences were fatal.

The Austrian Corporal

Adolf Hitler was born in 1889 in Braunau, Austria, near the German border. From 1907 until 1913 he lived in Vienna, where, after failing the entrance exam for the Academy of Fine Arts, he turned his energy to reading and talking politics. Later he would foster the impression that he was desperately poor in these years; in fact, his government pension as an orphan (his father had been a customs official), small inheritances from his father and mother, and occasional jobs as a postcard and advertisement painter sustained him adequately. Vienna at that time was rife with anti-Semitism, the bigotry that had supplied Europe with scapegoats throughout the centuries. Hitler adopted it eagerly and went further: "Disgusting to me was the conglomerate of races which characterized Vienna, disgusting the whole mixture of peoples, of Czechs, Poles, Hungarians, Ruthenians, Serbs and Croats, etc...." He

THE FUEHRER SPEAKS

Though Hitler often seemed to be carried away by the power of his own oratory, he actually made a careful study of dramatic gestures and facial expressions. This 1929 photograph by Heinrich Hoffman shows Hitler rehearsing gestures while listening to a recording of his speech. Anyone who watched him speak at a mass rally was struck by the hypnotic power of his presence and voice. He relied particularly on his large, expressive eyes, which he would widen theatrically at climactic moments. The clenched fist, the hands raised and spread apart in horror or held, palms up, in suppliance, were all practiced beforehand for maximum effect. Always Hitler played on the same themes: the Jews, whom he blamed for Germany's woes; the jobs he promised the unemployed; and Germany's glorious destiny, so long postponed, which he alone could bring about. As Hitler's control grew, he began indoctrinating young children. Boys joined the Deutsches Jungvolk at 10, the Hitler Youth at 14, taking part in sports and military exercises while absorbing Nazi doctrine. The Reich school system was geared to teach Nazi doctrine.

Your child belongs to us already.

—Adolf Hitler, November 6, 1933

In the presence of this blood banner, which represents our Fuehrer, I swear to devote all my energies to the savior of our country, Adolf Hitler. I am willing and ready to give up my life for him, so help me God.

—The oath sworn by 10-year-old German boys upon joining the Jungvolk organization

burned to fulfill the Kaiser's dream of German domination on the Continent. When he left Vienna for Munich in 1913, he believed that a worldwide conspiracy of Jews and other inferior peoples was working to destroy Germany. His political and economic ideas were vague and contradictory, but he hated and feared both bolshevism and democracy.

During World War I the young Austrian volunteered for service with an infantry regiment from the Bavarian region around Munich. As a dispatch runner he was five times decorated for bravery in some of the western front's worst fighting and was promoted to corporal. He remained in the army until April 1920, first as a POW guard, then as an instruction officer for troops being demobilized, lastly as a political agent for the Munich district command. Munich was a tumult of Freikorps and Communist activity, and Hitler had a chance to observe firsthand the strengths and weaknesses of these groups.

Rise of the Nazis

While Hitler was still in the army, he had joined the tiny German Workers' Party, becoming its fifty-fifth member and the seventh man on the steering committee. He was an effective orator, and his impassioned denunciations of the Berlin government brought many veterans into the party. By mid-1920 he was the party's chief spokesman and ideologue. The name was changed to the National Socialist German Workers' Party (Nationalsozialistiche Deutsches Arbeiterpartei), shortened to Nazi. Its program was an ill-assorted combination of pan-German nationalism, radical economic ideas, and Hitler's own brand of hatred. In large part it was an extension of his personality. Authority was exercised only from the top down, and responsibility only from the bottom up. The Fuehrer ("Leader") could not be wrong.

By 1922 the Nazis numbered ten thousand. The following winter French and Belgian troops marched into the heavily industrialized Ruhr to force Germany to pay her war reparations. The Weimar government counseled passive resistance; the workers responded with strikes and sabotage. Paralysis of coal and steel production in the Ruhr spurred an already galloping inflation. The mark's dollar value dropped from 400 to 1 in mid-1922 to 7,000 to 1 in late 1923. The Republic seemed ready to fall apart. In late 1923 the Nazis in Bavaria joined forces with a strong local separatist movement that opposed the federal government in Berlin. Beginning with the Beer Hall Putsch—an armed attempt to overthrow the local government assembled for a political rally in a Munich beer hall—Hitler planned to make himself dictator of all Germany. But he failed to win enough support from the army and police, and his own Sturmabteilung (SA—"storm troopers") were too few. The putsch collapsed in a burst of state police gunfire and Hitler was arrested and tried for treason.

The Weimar government was suicidally lenient with extremists who cloaked themselves in patriotism; sympathetic judges allowed Hitler and the Nazis' party newspapers to turn the trial into a forum for attacks on the government. Although Hitler was sentenced to five years in the comfortable Landsberg prison, he served only nine months before his parole; he used the time to dictate the first part of *Mein Kampf* ("My Struggle"). Paroled from prison, he returned to Munich to find the Nazis in disarray. Forbidden by law to speak in public, Hitler devoted his time to party organization and consolidation.

Meanwhile, conditions in Germany had improved. Financial reforms had curbed inflation, and political violence had declined. The federal and state governments reconciled some of their differences, while Foreign Minister Gustav Stresemann improved Germany's international position and brought his country into the League of Nations in 1926. Friedrich Ebert, the Republic's President since its foundation, died and was replaced by Field Marshal Paul von Hindenburg, the 77-year-old war hero. His prestige reassured the nationalists that the Republic would not become too democratic.

After reestablishing his leadership of the Nazi Party, Hitler, mindful of his abortive putsch, prepared for a new struggle to win power by constitutional means. He began to purge the party of those who took its "socialist program" seriously and set out to win the trust of the army and financial support from the conservative classes. To counterbalance the SA he created the SS, or Schutzstaffel ("defense squadron")—an elite corps of personal guards, loyal only to himself. And he gained the unswerving allegiance of Joseph Goebbels, the Nazi newspaper editor who later became the most brilliant mass psychologist of the century. Nazi Party membership reached 60,000 in 1928, when Nazis got 2.6 percent of the vote in Reichstag elections.

Depression and Disaster

In October 1929 Stresemann died. He was perhaps the only Weimar statesman who could have eased the crushing impact on Germany of the American stock-market collapse that month and the worldwide depression that followed. German prosperity depended on American credits and active international trade; when both dried up, unemployment quickly soared to levels of 20 percent or more. Voters lost faith in the moderates who had created the Weimar Republic, and both Nazi and Communist strength multiplied.

The government of Chancellor Heinrich Brüning (March 1930–May 1932) was the last relatively stable one before Hitler. Brüning was a conservative Catholic of the Center Party who exploited President von

THE MEN AROUND HITLER

Three men crucial to Hitler's success were caricatured in a wartime series of Soviet cartoons. Paul Joseph Goebbels, an intellectual with a Ph.D. from Heidelberg, wrote in his diary in 1926: "Hitler spoke for three hours. Brilliantly. He can make you doubt your own views." As the Reich's Minister of Propaganda, Goebbels put the press, radio, and the arts under rigid control. He took poison in the chancellery bunker with Hitler. Heinrich Himmler, a Bavarian farmer, became head of the SS (Schutzstaffel, popularly known as the Blackshirts) in 1929. He also headed the Gestapo (Geheime Staatspolizei, or "Secret State Police") and administered the wartime concentration camps. Himmler took poison when he was captured after the German surrender. Hermann Goering, World War I fighter ace, lent a necessary note of prestige to the Nazis. He and Ernst Roehm built up the SA (Sturmabteilung). Air Minister and second in command to Hitler during the war, Goering also took poison during the trials at Nuremberg to escape death by hanging.

Hindenburg's constitutional powers to override the Reichstag and rule by decree. In 1932 the Reichstag passed only 5 laws but issued 60 decrees. Germany, which had lost the moderate political base needed for a stable democracy, was now giving up the forms of democracy as well; for although the decrees Brüning persuaded Hindenburg to issue were wage and price orders to combat the depression, measures against extremist violence, and the like, their effect was to make government by executive order seem normal.

Like all Hitler's opponents, Brüning underestimated the Nazi threat until it was too late. During his administration the Nazis maneuvered for military support and gained the backing of industrialists; the SA and SS became fully equipped private armies, and the police forces were infiltrated by Nazi sympathizers.

In early 1932 Hindenburg's seven-year term expired and he ran for reelection against Hitler and other minority candidates. A runoff gave him 53 percent of the vote, with 37 percent going to Hitler and 10 percent to Ernst Thalmann, the Communist candidate. Brüning belatedly awoke to the danger of SA and SS violence during this campaign and persuaded Hindenburg to decree their suppression. The army refused to comply. Brüning's Defense Minister, then Brüning himself, resigned under heavy pressure. Hindenburg named as Chancellor an aristocrat and political novice named Franz von Papen. Papen's own Center Party expelled him for conniving at the fall of Brüning, but he was an adequate pawn. He called for new elections on July 31, 1932, and helped spread authoritarian rule to the state level by naming himself Reich Commissioner for Prussia and deposing the elected state government. Street fights broke out daily and martial law was proclaimed in Berlin.

Papen remained Chancellor until November 17. Hindenburg offered Hitler the Chancellorship if he could gain a Reichstag majority for a Nazi program —or the Vice Chancellorship under Papen in yet another administration by decree. Scenting blood now, Hitler refused to serve under Papen, and Hindenburg appointed Gen. Kurt von Schleicher, his chief adviser for several years and a man whose intrigues had helped bring down Brüning and Papen. Schleicher held office for only 57 days before intrigue toppled him also. He had tried to split the Nazis by offering a Cabinet post to Gregor Strasser, but Strasser resigned from the party. The Nazis united in their refusal to cooperate.

Victory and Opportunity

Hitler's great moment came at last on January 30, 1933, when Hindenburg appointed him Chancellor, heading a Cabinet of conservative and Nazi ministers. With government-owned radio and press in their hands, the Nazis broke up their Reichstag coalition and called for elections on March 5. Hermann

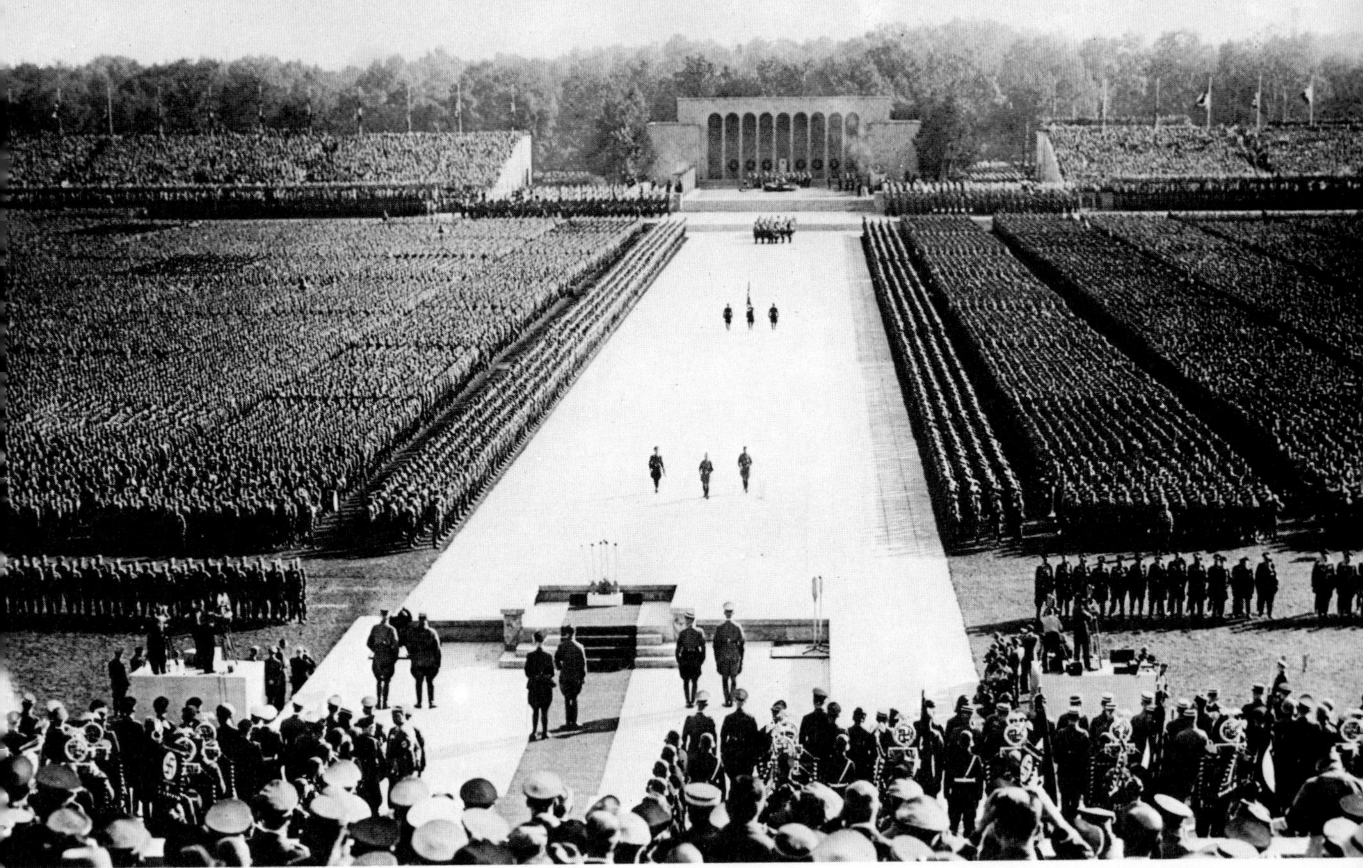

***The most impressive** of the Third Reich's frequent festivals were the annual Nazi Party rallies at Nuremberg. Hitler's architect Albert Speer (see p. 306) used thousands of flags for color; at night powerful searchlights sent columns of light deep into the sky, turning the stadium into an immense temple to Hitler and the Nazi regime he had built up.*

Goering, Prussia's Nazi Minister of the Interior, forbade Communist demonstrations and banned Socialist publications. He urged police to use force against anti-Nazis, hinting that any policeman who shot to kill would be protected. SA gangs broke up the meetings of moderate and leftist candidates. It seemed that nothing could make Hitler's preparations more effective.

Marinus Van der Lubbe, a 24-year-old Dutch Communist, entered Germany in early February 1933. Toward the end of the month, bent on harassing the Nazis, he set several small fires in Berlin. It has been said that he was half-witted, or a Nazi dupe, or could not have started the Reichstag fire singlehandedly —but the evidence suggests that when he was captured in the burning building and freely admitted to arson, he was telling the whole truth. Three Bulgarian Communists and the Communist leader in the Reichstag were tried with him, but were acquitted. If the Nazis had laid a plan for the fire, they would surely not have failed to convict all the accused. Van der Lubbe paid with his head (literally) in January 1934. His execution was illegal, as the law setting the death penalty for arson was passed only after the Reichstag fire, but by then such illegalities were overlooked.

Between the Reichstag fire and the March 5 elections, Adolf Hitler became virtual dictator of Germany. By a Presidential decree accepted by the Cabinet and Reichstag, freedom of speech and press and assembly, immunity from search without warrant and confiscation of property without due process, privacy of mail and telephone conversations were all suspended "until further notice." Death penalties were introduced for a wide range of crimes.

Hitler and Goebbels spoke at great rallies all over Germany, hammering home the message that only national socialism could save the country from Red anarchy. On March 5 they were rewarded with a Nazi-Nationalist majority. Soon Communists were excluded from the legislature and some Socialist deputies were arrested on trumped-up charges. Trade unions were dissolved. The SA and the SS began building concentration camps for political prisoners. The following year would bring the bloody purge of Ernst Roehm and his followers in the SA, cementing Hitler's relations with the armed forces; Hindenburg would die, and Hitler would become President as well as Chancellor. Barely a week after the Reichstag fire, Hitler began to build the Third Reich in earnest.

1933

Literature Goes on Trial

The problem of censorship is reexamined as James Joyce's brilliant novel Ulysses *wins a landmark decision on obscenity.*

***One of the 20th century's** most brilliant and controversial writers, James Joyce had a profound impact on the style and content of modern literature. Above, a view of College Green in Dublin as it appeared at the turn of the century. The setting for all of Joyce's novels, Dublin itself is at least as vital a part of* Ulysses *as any of its characters.*

In the spring of 1933 a copy of James Joyce's novel *Ulysses* was seized by customs officers in New York City. The book, which had been sent from Paris to Bennett Cerf, president of Random House publishers, was held for trial on charges of obscenity. The Customs Office's act surprised no one: Despite the growing stature of Joyce's work in the literary world, to most people *Ulysses* was simply a dirty word.

During the frenetic Roaring Twenties *Ulysses,* like alcohol, had become one of life's illicit pleasures. Copies were being smuggled in from Europe through Canada, and in the United States counterfeit "first editions" were selling for up to $50. But with his book under the censorship ban, Joyce received not a penny for these sales.

Censorship had in fact plagued *Ulysses* from Joyce's earliest attempts to publish it. The novel, begun in 1914, first appeared in serial form in a London review called *The Egoist* but was suppressed after five issues. Then in March 1918 the *Little Review* in New York began a serialization and by 1920 had published about half the book. The next year a suit was brought by the New York Society for the Suppression of Vice, and when the society won its case the Post Office made a bonfire of the *Review*'s copies.

The first complete version of *Ulysses* was published in 1922 by Shakespeare and Company, a Paris bookshop which became a publishing house for just that purpose. The first edition amounted to only 1,000 copies, but that was enough to ignite a widespread controversy over the novel's startling sexual frankness. Poet and critic T. S. Eliot lent his considerable prestige to Joyce's defense, hailing *Ulysses* as "the most important expression the modern age has found." Most readers of the time, however, seemed to agree more with the playwright George Bernard Shaw who, having read only fragments of the novel, attacked it as a "revolting record of a disgusting phase of civilization." The second Paris edition, sent to England and the U.S.A., got no farther than "the King's chimney" in Dover, where it was burned, and the Hudson River in New York, where it apparently was drowned.

Thus when Bennett Cerf's copy was seized in 1933 and threatened with "forfeiture and confiscation and destruction," the action was hardly a surprise. But the trial that followed would prove a landmark in the old and often bitter struggle between the adherents of censorship and the advocates of free expression.

Ulysses

Just what is this most profound, innovative and outrageous of modern novels all about? On the simplest level *Ulysses* tells the story of two men involved in the routine of an ordinary day in Dublin—June 16, 1904. Their paths cross, interweave, and eventually join. The entire action unfolds over a span of just 19 hours, but Joyce's painstaking chronicle of the characters' inner and outer lives ultimately fills more than 700 pages. The leading character ("hero" would not be quite the right word) is an advertising salesman named Leopold Bloom—a clownish, inept, goodhearted, complex, and preeminently human specimen. His chief supporting character is Stephen Dedalus, a scholarly, rather arrogant young poet presently earning his living as a schoolteacher. (The same Stephen Dedalus, a year younger, had been the protagonist of Joyce's autobiographical first novel, *A Portrait of the Artist as a Young Man.*) Though totally unlike each other on the surface, Bloom and Stephen develop an oddly intimate relationship, much like that of a father and son, as they make their way through a night of dreamlike revelry in Dublin's red-light district.

A third key figure is Bloom's wife Molly, little heard from until the final section of the book, but appearing recurrently in Bloom's thoughts throughout the day. A locally prominent singer, younger than her husband, voluptuous and uninhibited, Molly takes few pains to conceal her adulterous affairs—the latest of which, as it turns out, is consummated during the afternoon of this altogether ordinary day. It is to Molly that Joyce devotes the final section of *Ulysses,* presenting an uninterrupted transcript of Molly's thoughts as she lies beside her sleeping husband. Of this extraordinary passage even Arnold Bennett, the British author who roundly condemned what he called the book's "staggering indecency," went so far as to say, "I have never read anything to surpass it, and I doubt if I have ever read anything to equal it."

This literary technique, often referred to as an "interior monologue" or "stream of consciousness," was only one of several innovations Joyce used in an attempt not merely to record the thoughts and deeds of his characters, but to explore their innermost sensations—to give the reader an impression of what it *feels* like to be Bloom, or Stephen, or Molly. *Ulysses* in fact does not have one style but many, moving freely between fantasy and reality, blending conventional narrative, Shakespearean parodies, dialogue with stage directions, and other techniques into a complex, carefully wrought pattern. Overlying all is the framework of the Homeric epic *The Odyssey,* in which Bloom becomes a vulgar, distinctly unheroic Ulysses, Stephen a feckless version of Ulysses' son Telemachus, and Molly a travesty of his faithful wife, Penelope.

It was not, of course, the Homeric elements or stylistic innovations that made *Ulysses* the focus of an international controversy, but the frequently earthy language and subject matter. Joyce was not content, as most Victorian writers had been, to screen out certain areas of experience in deference to current standards of propriety or to gloss them over with polite euphemisms. Instead he sought to depict his characters honestly and completely, with all their imperfections, their misbehavior, even their bad language.

This new emphasis on psychological realism, however, especially Joyce's concern with the mysteries of sex, infuriated members of the so-called vice societies, who maintained that the sole purpose of literature must be to elevate and ennoble its readers. In his reckless pursuit of what really goes on in the human mind, they felt, Joyce had violated human decency.

The Rise of the Vice Societies

When the legal battle lines were drawn up for the *Ulysses* trial, the legions of censorship had a wealth of tradition on their side. A series of 19th-century British and U.S. court decisions had been won by morality-minded groups whose crusade for "pure" literature had taken on an evangelical fervor over the decades.

One of the earliest and most important of these was handed down in England in the 1868 case of *Regina* v. *Hicklin.* Justice Alexander Cockburn, ruling against an allegedly indecent pamphlet, set forth standards for obscenity that dominated legal thinking well into the 20th century:

> Whether the tendency of the matter charged as obscenity is to deprave and corrupt those whose minds are open to such immoral influences, and into whose hands a publication of this sort may fall.

The reasoning in this so-called Hicklin Test was challenged on two main grounds: First, it reduced all acceptable literary material to the level of what is morally proper for the young; and second, it allowed a book to be condemned for isolated passages taken out of context, without regard for the work's artistic integrity. The criticism was futile, though, and the standards of the Hicklin Test endured on both sides of the Atlantic for the next 50 years.

Vice Societies in America

Buoyed by the success of the British censorship groups, similar organizations spread across the United States. The first and most energetic was the New York Society for the Suppression of Vice. Founded in 1873, its guiding spirit was the redoubtable Anthony Comstock, who argued simply that "books are feeders for brothels." In Boston the Cabots, Lowells, and other prominent families closed ranks in defense of public morality, declaring that "all reading and conversation must be of the most pure and elevating character."

Such sentiments, however, were destined to collide with an artistic trend that began early in the 20th century and grew steadily more forceful: an interest in human sexuality. Sigmund Freud's analysis of sex as a basic force in character development proved too compelling an idea to be ignored, and as Freudian theory gained wider acceptance, the theme was taken up by increasing numbers of writers.

On the opposite side, the austere moral code of the World War I period and the subsequent triumph of the Prohibition movement encouraged censorship groups to make a concerted attack on these liberal tendencies. What was intended as a frontal assault, however, proved to be an increasingly lonely rearguard action.

Lowering the Barriers

At the instigation of John Sumner, head of the New York Society for the Suppression of Vice, a bookseller named Halsey was arrested in 1917 for selling Théophile Gautier's 1835 French classic, *Mademoiselle de Maupin.* Acquitted of the obscenity charge, Halsey sued the society for damages and won. The

TWO GLIMPSES OF *ULYSSES*

The various prose styles in *Ulysses* include more-or-less conventional descriptions, altered just slightly by a character's passing thoughts. Below, a dog on a beach momentarily reminds Stephen Dedalus of a coat of arms, described with the heraldic terms "tenney" (meaning tawny), "trippant" (one forepaw raised), "proper" (naturally colored), and "unattired" (without horns).

"Their dog ambled about a bank of dwindling sand, trotting, sniffing on all sides. Looking for something lost in a past life. Suddenly he made off like a bounding hare, ears flung back, chasing the shadow of a lowskimming gull. The man's shrieked whistle struck his limp ears. He turned, bounded back, came nearer, trotted on twinkling shanks. On a field tenney a buck, trippant, proper, unattired. At the lacefringe of the tide he halted with stiff forehoofs, seawardpointed ears. His snout lifted barked at the wavenoise, herds of seamorse. They serpented towards his feet, curling, unfurling many crests, every ninth, breaking, plashing, from far, from farther out, waves and waves."

Much of the controversy over *Ulysses* focused on the 45-page, unpunctuated record of Molly Bloom's thoughts as she lies in bed in the early hours of the morning musing on her past and present life, including a number of her sexual adventures. Below, the conclusion of her famous "interior monologue."

". . . yes and those handsome Moors all in white and turbans like kings asking you to sit down in their little bit of a shop and Ronda with the old windows of the posadas glancing eyes a lattice hid for her lover to kiss the iron and the wineshops half open at night and the castanets and the night we missed the boat at Algeciras the watchman going about serene with his lamp and O that awful deepdown torrent O and the sea the sea crimson sometimes like fire and the glorious sunsets and the figtrees in the Alameda gardens yes and all the queer little streets and pink and blue and yellow houses and the rosegardens and the jessamine and geraniums and cactuses and Gibraltar as a girl where I was a Flower of the mountain yes when I put the rose in my hair like the Andalusian girls used or shall I wear a red yes and how he kissed me under the Moorish wall and I thought well as well him as another and then I asked him with my eyes to ask again yes and then he asked me would I yes to say yes my mountain flower and first I put my arms around him yes and drew him down to me so he could feel my breasts all perfume yes and his heart was going like mad and yes I said yes I will Yes."

New York Appeals Court decision was one of the first to modify the 50-year-old Hicklin Test, establishing the principle that "books must be considered broadly and as a whole," rather than on the basis of isolated passages, and that expert testimony was admissible in judging literary merit.

Undaunted, Sumner in 1921 proceeded against the *Little Review* for its serialization of *Ulysses,* winning the case and burning the offending copies. The next year he helped launch a campaign in New York State in support of an obscenity bill that would reaffirm, point by point, the standards of the Hicklin Test.

By the time the bill came to the floor of the state legislature in 1923, it had already sparked considerable controversy. The deep antagonism between pro- and anti-censorship forces polarized the lawmakers, who became immersed in a long and bitter debate. Then dapper Democrat Jimmy Walker, leader of the bill's opponents, strode to the floor and won himself a small place in literary history: "No woman," he declared, "was ever ruined by a book." The bill was defeated.

Liberalization of censorship laws on the federal level followed a somewhat more complicated path. Congress first acted to prevent off-color imports in 1842 when it denied entry to "all indecent prints, paintings," and other graphic material (chiefly in an attempt to keep "dirty" French postcards out of the country). Import restrictions were expanded in 1922 to include printed matter, on the strength of which a Customs Court decision in 1928 reaffirmed the *Ulysses* ban, holding the work to contain language "of the rottenest and vilest character." A year later the House of Representatives voted to tighten the import standards still further, but in the Senate that proposal was eloquently opposed by Senator Bronson M. Cutting of New Mexico, who warned against allowing customs officials "to dictate what the American people may or may not read." At length, his limitations on federal censorship were incorporated in the 1930 Smoot-Hawley Tariff Act, which transferred final authority in obscenity questions from the Customs Office to the courts. The bill also provided that books in federal cases must be judged in their entirety, as was already true in New York and other states.

With this the stage was set for the 1933 showdown over *Ulysses,* the first work of fiction to be prosecuted under the new federal guidelines. The chances for a successful defense seemed as good at that point as they were likely to be, primarily because *Ulysses'* reputation in the literary world had grown enormously during the previous decade. In addition, public support for censorship had plummeted drastically in reaction

Nazi Germany's *spectacular book burnings in 1933 made it clear that censorship ultimately involves far more than a few "dirty" books. Coinciding with the* Ulysses *trial, Hitler's fiery purge of all "anti-German" literature caused protests across the U.S.A. and hastened the decline of such self-ordained censors as John Sumner (left, in hat), head of the New York Society for the Suppression of Vice.*

Two poles of judicial opinion: *(inset) Federal Judge John M. Woolsey who presided over the 1933* Ulysses *trial, and (right) Chief Justice Warren Burger of the U.S. Supreme Court, who wrote a 1973 decision reversing the liberal trend of previous rulings. Woolsey's decision, the strongest affirmation up to that time of an individual's right to read what he chose, dominated four decades of legal thinking. The ruling by Justice Burger, which strengthened the power of local authorities to ban books, movies, and other works, has led to a wave of new uncertainties—and a promise from the Court to clarify its ruling in future decisions.*

to the chilling spectacle of mass book burnings conducted throughout Nazi Germany in May of 1933.

The presiding judge in *United States* v. *One Book Entitled "Ulysses"* was John Munro Woolsey, a 50-year-old native of South Carolina, who had devoted a full month to a careful reading and rereading of the work. The case itself was argued the first week in December, and on December 6 Judge Woolsey released his lengthy, eloquent decision finding *Ulysses* innocent of the obscenity charge. At the heart of his reasoning was the legal definition of the word "obscene": "Tending to stir the sex impulses or to lead to sexually impure and lustful thoughts." Nowhere in *Ulysses,* he said, despite its "unusual frankness," did he detect "the leer of the sensualist." On the contrary, he observed, "whilst in many places the effect of *Ulysses* on the reader undoubtedly is somewhat emetic, nowhere does it tend to be an aphrodisiac."

Trying To Draw the Line

The effects of Judge Woolsey's decision proved historic indeed. In addition to legalizing the sale of a literary masterpiece, it dealt a symbolic *coup de grace* to the old-line vice societies, acknowledging at a high judicial level the gradual change that had occurred in the public's attitude toward censorship.

In the decades following the *Ulysses* trial the U.S. Supreme Court found itself increasingly drawn into the censorship question, most of the cases centering on First Amendment guarantees of the right to free speech and a free press. Some cases concerned themselves only with individual books or narrow points of law, but others had far broader implications, as in the 1948 decision that officially acknowledged movies as a "legitimate" form of expression:

> We have no doubt that moving pictures, like newspapers and radio, are included in the press, whose freedom is guaranteed by the First Amendment.

Time and again state obscenity convictions were reversed by federal courts, and in 1957, hoping to reduce the volume of such cases, the Supreme Court for the first time in this century set forth an official definition of obscenity. Stating that First Amendment protection should extend to "all ideas having even the slightest redeeming social importance," the Court adopted as its yardstick:

> Whether to the average person, applying contemporary standards, the dominant theme of the material taken as a whole appeals to prurient interest.

Over the next several years the Court further liberalized its policies, requiring that any item to be banned must be utterly lacking in "literary or scientific or artistic value or any other form of social importance," and that the "contemporary community standards" used to judge it must be those prevailing in the nation as a whole. One result of these decisions was the legalization of several long-suppressed works by serious 20th-century writers, including D. H. Lawrence's novel *Lady Chatterley's Lover* in 1959 and Henry Miller's *Tropic of Cancer* in 1964. But as the law's tolerance increased, so did the flood of hard-core and soft-core magazines, tabloids, movies, plays, and books, and in the mid-1960's, the Supreme Court began edging away from its earlier position. In separate 1966 rulings the Court upheld a Massachusetts ban on John Cleland's 18th-century classic *Fanny Hill* and let stand a five-year prison term for a magazine publisher charged with sending "pandering" advertisements through the mail. Then in 1969 it ruled that, while an individual has the right to enjoy any material, obscene or otherwise, in the privacy of his own home, he does not necessarily have the right to *buy* it.

Finally, in 1973, the legal backlash was climaxed by a decision in the case of *Miller* v. *California,* in which the Court held by a five-to-four vote that states and local communities could henceforth ban books, magazines, movies, plays, revues and other works that:

> taken as a whole, appeal to the prurient interest in sex, which portray sexual conduct in a patently offensive way, and which, taken as a whole, do not have a serious literary, artistic or scientific value.

The wording of this passage had the effect of shifting the burden of proof in an obscenity case from the prosecution to the defense. Previously a work had to be "utterly without redeeming social value" to be obscene, and it was up to the prosecutor to prove that. Now the defendant would have to prove its value. Further, obscenity would hereafter be determined by local tastes, not by a uniform national standard, though the ruling did not specify what was meant by "local." (As one lawyer asked, "is it a state, a town, a county, or a mosquito-abatement district?")

Indeed, the ruling seemed to reactivate the very problem it was intended to settle: how to define obscenity. Several members of the Court, having grappled with that question for years, had reached the conclusion that it simply can't be done with the kind of precision the law requires. Instead, they seemed to favor dropping most sanctions against pornography, preserving only those that would keep it away from minors and from adults who find it offensive. As Justice William O. Douglas noted, "There is no 'captive audience' problem in these obscenity cases. No one is being compelled to look or listen."

Chief Justice Warren Burger, writing for the majority, denied that the ruling would in any way hamper "the free and robust exchange of ideas." But amid a wave of subsequent obscenity prosecutions, blatantly hard-core pornography has not been the only target of censorship. Such widely respected novels as *The Grapes of Wrath* by John Steinbeck, J. D. Salinger's *The Catcher in the Rye,* and William Golding's *Lord of the Flies* have been banned in some areas. Elsewhere the movies *Carnal Knowledge* and *Last Tango in Paris* were barred, though both had been praised by critics.

Thus, an unintended result of the Court's 1973 decision has been to reopen the perennial controversy over freedom of expression. Supporters of censorship argue chiefly that pornography threatens to undermine traditional moral values and therefore must be suppressed. Their opponents reply that the government has no right to tell a citizen what he can and cannot read or look at—particularly since (as Chief Justice Burger himself admitted) there is no evidence that pornography encourages criminal or antisocial behavior.

The only point on which there seems to be unanimous agreement is that the issue has yet to be resolved, and that perhaps it never will be resolved once and for all. The day after the Court's 1973 decision the head of Random House recalled the *Ulysses* case and remarked, "it seems strange that now, 40 years later, we have to start all over again."

STRUGGLE IN THE SCHOOLS

In recent years perhaps the most bitterly contested aspect of the censorship question has concerned books used in public schools. Since the 1973 Supreme Court decision "clean books" advocates across the country have redoubled their efforts to purge classrooms and school libraries of books they find objectionable—aided in some cases by such highly organized groups as the John Birch Society and the Ku Klux Klan. Nowhere has this struggle been more heated, and in fact violent, than in Kanawha County, West Virginia, where a months-long protest was waged in 1974 over books some parents considered irreligious and disrespectful of authority. Elsewhere less publicized but equally emotional battles have taken place, often aimed at widely respected works. In one North Dakota town 32 copies of Kurt Vonnegut's *Slaughterhouse-Five* were burned because of some four-letter words; fundamentalists in a southern community had *Jonathan Livingston Seagull* banned on religious grounds; conservative whites in many areas have fought the use of Eldridge Cleaver's *Soul on Ice* because of its antiwhite attitudes, while black activists have sought to ban *Huckleberry Finn* for tolerating white racism; New Hampshire legislators debated a bill to ban all schoolbooks containing "obscene" words—including works by Shakespeare and Chaucer. Thus the battle to control the use of language—and the exchange of ideas—continues in the 1970's much as it has been since the invention of the written word.

Religious and political beliefs dominated the 1974 textbook battle in Kanawha County, West Virginia. As in many other such conflicts, the real issue was not obscene language but unpopular ideas.

THE ARTS 1929-39

Out of the Ivory Tower

Throughout history, artists have enlisted in social and political causes at times of crisis. The global Depression of the 1930's was such a time. Unemployment, economic chaos, and the growing menace of fascism all served to convince many creative people that the old order no longer worked. Most turned to Marxism as an alternative, directing their talent and energy toward a worldwide proletarian revolution. In their hands art sometimes became a weapon, and sometimes merely a polemic.

Some socially conscious creators, like German dramatist Bertolt Brecht, became faithful followers of the Communist Party. Others, like Mexican painter Diego Rivera, threw themselves with equal vigor into the class struggle, but strictly on their own terms. Still others, like the German photographer August Sander, strove only to document the social scene with a clear, unprejudiced eye and expressed no other ideology than a human concern for their fellow beings.

Bertolt Brecht was born at Augsburg, Bavaria, in 1898, the son of a prosperous paper manufacturer. He seemed destined for a career as a physician when he was sent to serve as an orderly in a World War I field hospital. The hideous results of that struggle's mechanized carnage permanently seared Brecht. During the immediate postwar years he became a dissolute haunter of Munich cafes, strumming the guitar and singing his own cynical songs to earn a living at night and writing angry, iconoclastic poems and plays during the day.

In 1924 Brecht moved to Berlin, where he learned stagecraft firsthand as an assistant to director-producers Max Reinhardt and Erwin Piscator. He also became known for his savage social satire. His play *In the Jungle of the Cities* (1924) and his garish musical dramas *The Threepenny Opera* (1928) and *The Rise and Fall of the City of Mahagonny* (1929), both with scores by Kurt Weill, mercilessly parodied the moral and political disintegration that characterized the pre-Nazi era. The Nazi Party denounced Brecht as "decadent," and Brownshirts routinely broke up performances.

In Berlin Brecht adopted Marxism. World War I and the economic and political disorder that followed it had persuaded him that man's worst enemy was man himself. Marxism offered a new villain, capitalism, and a political program with which to defeat it.

Whether Brecht was ever officially a member of the Communist Party is uncertain. He once denied it under oath, but he rarely deviated from the party line, and even supported Stalin's purges.

Art and Instruction

Few of Brecht's plots originated with him. He ransacked newspapers and history books for subject matter and adapted the works of other writers. But his style made even the most familiar plots seem fresh and alive. The current trend in dramatic writing was realism, and playwrights were seeking to evoke the viewer's empathy, forcing him to share the characters' joy and pain.

Brecht sought to sweep all that away. The theater was a means of aiding the struggle against capitalism. "I do not believe in the separability of art and instruction," Brecht wrote. Theater would appeal "less to the feelings than to the spectator's reason. . . . Instead of sharing an experience, the spectator [should come] to grips with things."

No effort was spared to create "critical distancing" between audience and actors, to destroy every vestige of the old-fashioned "theater of illusion." Scenery was minimal and shifted in full view of the audience, both stage and spectators were bathed in the same bright light, slogans flashed on and off, performers impersonated "types" rather than real people, and dramatic scenes were underplayed and interrupted with songs and ironic monologues. Every theatrical device was used to move the audience to political or social action—not through the "witchcraft of realistic producers who make a dream world of reality," but through persuasion.

At his best, Brecht created a powerful fusion of art and instruction. His major works are among the most memorable in modern theater history. They include *Mother Courage*

In Brecht's theater *ideas were more important than characters, and his actors played types rather than individuals. Below, the highly stylized cast of* A Man's a Man, *premiered in 1926.*

and Her Children, The Life of Galileo, The Good Woman of Setzuan, and *The Caucasian Chalk Circle.*

Exile and Return

In 1933, the year that Hitler gained absolute power, Brecht fled Germany to begin a 16-year exile. His citizenship was revoked, his plays were banned, and his books publicly burned. He lived and worked in many countries, striving to stay one jump ahead of the German legions: Czechoslovakia, Austria, Switzerland, France, Denmark, Sweden, and Finland. Everywhere he went he eloquently denounced the Nazi regime that had enslaved his homeland and threatened all of Europe.

Finally, he fled to the United States, settling near Hollywood, California, in 1941 amid an exile colony that also included novelist Thomas Mann and composer Arnold Schoenberg. Always a good Marxist, Brecht was appalled by American luxury. He was unhappy in Hollywood—calling it the place "where lies are bought"—and when the House Un-American Activities Committee summoned him to explain his political views in 1947, he lost little time in taking flight again.

West Germany refused him entry, but in 1949 he accepted an offer from the Communist government of East Germany to come to East Berlin and head his own handsomely subsidized theater. There, with his actress-wife Helene Weigel, he spent his last years.

Although his Berliner Ensemble won international fame for its brilliant productions, Brecht himself produced no further work of importance. He also remained conspicuously silent on the subject of Communist curtailment of civil liberties, even after Soviet tanks brutally crushed the 1953 workers' revolt in East Germany. His lifelong loyalty to communism was rewarded with the Stalin Peace Prize in 1955, a year before his death. A fierce foe of one dictator, Brecht was seemingly incapable of recognizing the monstrous cruelty of another.

***Having fled** Nazi Germany in 1933, Brecht returned in 1949 and settled in East Berlin, where he successfully established his own theater, the Berliner Ensemble.*

Diego Rivera, the world's most celebrated revolutionary artist, began work on what was to be the most controversial project of his turbulent career in the same month that the Nazis seized Germany. He had been commissioned to create an enormous mural for the newly completed Rockefeller Center complex, New York City's glossiest monument to the success of corporate capitalism.

The mural was to be entitled "Man at the Crossroads Looking With Hope and High Vision to the Choosing of a New and Better Future." It was to show a central figure, representing Man, surrounded by heralds of a hopeful, distinctively socialist future—the wonders of science and technology and the triumph of the workers over their masters. It was also to include reminders of the capitalist past and present—war, decadence, disease, and brutality. Despite their obviously revolutionary message, the preliminary sketches were enthusiastically approved by Nelson Rockefeller, executive overseer of the building. Rivera and seven associates began painting in early March 1933.

All went well until about May 1, when the figure of a labor leader in the center panel began to look remarkably like Lenin. On May 3 Rivera received a letter from his employer. Rockefeller professed to find the mural "thrilling," but he was afraid that a portrait of Lenin "might easily offend a great many people." Rivera replied that he was willing to add portraits of Lincoln and other U.S. heroes for balance, but he would not remove Lenin. The portrait had appeared in the approved sketches, he insisted, and removing it would render his mural meaningless. When the controversy reached the press, messages supporting Rivera flooded in from artists of every political persuasion, and long lines of chanting leftists circled Rockefeller Center. But Rockefeller stood firm and finally paid Rivera what was owed him and had the unfinished mural boarded up. Later it was secretly destroyed.

Angry but undaunted, Rivera used his "Rockefeller money" to paint two Manhattan murals without charge, then returned to Mexico City. There, he re-created the Rockefeller Center mural in the Palace of Fine Arts. The new version included an acid caricature of Nelson Rockefeller's father, John D. Rockefeller, Jr.

A Revolution on the Walls

Like his mammoth murals, everything about Rivera seemed larger than life. He was born at Guanajuato, Mexico, in 1886, the son of a luckless mineowner. He began drawing at the age of three and showed the first signs of "radicalism" at five: During Mass one Sunday he loudly announced to his embarrassed family that the Virgin Mary was simply a

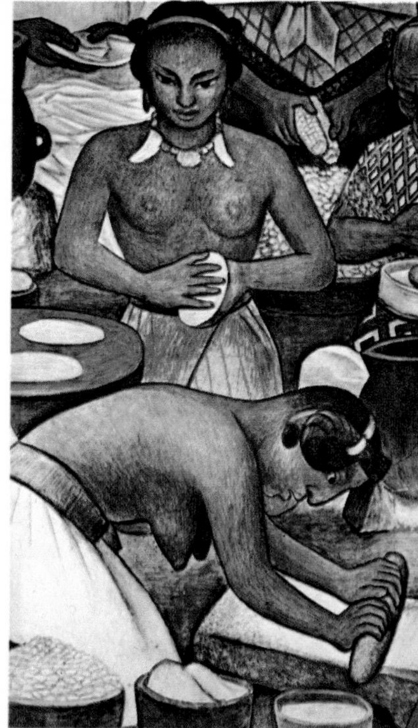

RIVERA'S VERSION OF MEXICAN HISTORY

Rivera's murals teem with figures. They excoriate the rich and the clergy, glorify peasants and workers, recount the horrors of the Mexican past, and trumpet the glories of the socialist future. These illustrations are samples from the walls of the National Palace in Mexico City. At the top is a detail from "Cultivation of Corn" in what Rivera saw as Mexico's golden age—the days before the Spanish arrived to degrade the Indians and turn them into slaves and beasts of burden (above). Then (opposite top) come prominent figures from the Revolution of 1910: the bemedaled dictator Porfirio Díaz, surrounded by his arch-capitalist friends, and (center right) the idealistic revolutionary Francisco Madero. Finally, Rivera's dream of Mexico's future (right)—through Marxism and the unity of the workers.

wooden statue, deaf to prayers. Enrolled in art school at 10, he became the prize pupil of two of Mexico's leading landscapists, received his academic art training in Spain, and became a fashionable success among wealthy collectors in his homeland. Later he spent a decade in Paris, where he became an enthusiastic cubist—until he discovered Marxism. He had always been sympathetic to the plight of his nation's peasant poor. Communism provided him with a focus for his feelings and the ideological underpinnings for an entirely new approach to painting.

Art was a weapon, Rivera came to believe, and "to be an artist one must first be a man, vitally concerned with all problems of social struggle, unflinching in portraying them." He pronounced easel painting "unnatural" because it was

meant to be seen only by a privileged few, and abandoned cubism and all other forms of "modernism" as empty exercises for the esthetic pleasure of other painters. Only the mural—vast, vivid, profoundly public, and filled with uplifting political content—could offer authentic "art for the masses."

In 1921 Rivera returned to Mexico in search of walls on which to unleash an artistic revolution. The reformist regime of President Álvaro Obregón proved eager to cooperate. Anxious to rally peasant support, it offered up the exteriors of a host of public buildings around the country. During the next busy decade Rivera covered hundreds of thousands of square feet with his angry, crowded compositions.

Many of his works are dominated by monumental figures symbolizing abstractions like "Progress" and "Fecundity." But they escape the blandness of most official art because of Rivera's brilliant color and powerful stylized drawing—both derived in part from the wall paintings of his Aztec forebears in whom he took fierce pride.

Although Rivera's credentials as a Communist were impeccable, he had far too rebellious a spirit to accept party dictates for long. Visiting the U.S.S.R. at Moscow's invitation in 1927, he dared denounce the bureaucratic sameness of Soviet art, urging instead a bolder, more colorful style based upon Russia's rich heritage of folk art.

Two years later he resigned from the party, and subsequently offered Soviet exile Leon Trotsky sanctuary in his home. After years of party praise he became a pariah overnight: Leftist critics began to denounce his painting as crude, slovenly, and even antirevolutionary. Meanwhile, conservative critics railed at Rivera's "Uglyism," and termed his attacks on the clergy blasphemous.

Rivera continued to paint for another quarter century, paying little heed to the growing opposition on all sides—though he sometimes felt obliged to wear a pistol in his belt while he worked to guard against political assassination. Then, in 1954, the Mexican Communist Party reinstated Rivera in a last-ditch effort to add prestige to its dwindling ranks. He died three years later and was buried in Mexico's Rotunda of Illustrious Sons after a clamorous funeral. Rivera's pious family overruled his desire to be cremated; the Communist Party insisted on draping the Red Flag over his coffin; fistfights ensued. A battler to the end, Rivera would probably have loved it.

***A**ugust Sander* chose to reveal the personal, nonpolitical face of the world in a decade when most artists were striving to express their political beliefs. A photographer, he chose for his lifework the immense task of portraying, neither cynically nor idealistically, representatives of the entire German race.

Beginning with the peasants of his native Westerwald, Sander eventually photographed people belonging to all levels of rural and urban society, producing a gallery of portraits whose subjects are both individuals in their own right and archetypes of German life.

For this achievement, Sander fell foul of the Nazis. In their grotesque dream of an Aryan master race there was no place for the clarity of his vision, and in 1934 his book *Face of Our Time* was destroyed. Many of his negatives survived, however, and preserve a piece of history that might have vanished forever.

***At right** is a student teacher at the village school in Sander's Westerwald.*

***Below left,** a pastry cook, photographed in his cavernous kitchen in Cologne in 1928.*

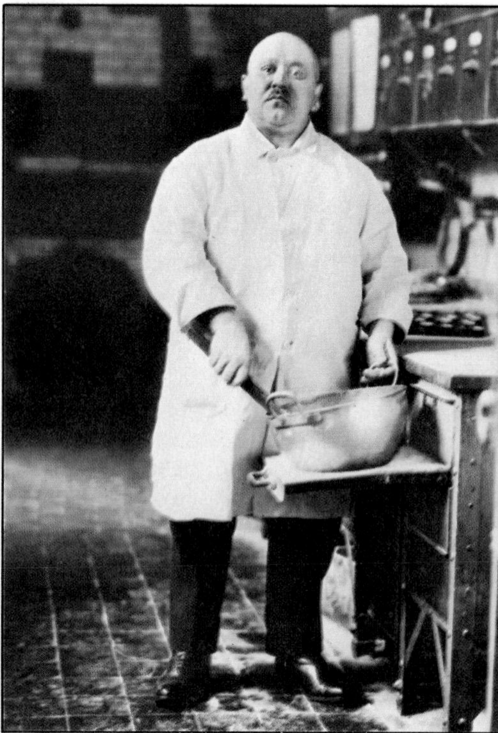

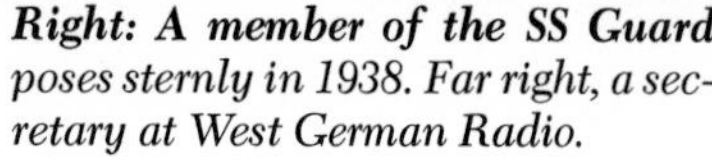

***Right: A member of the SS Guard** poses sternly in 1938. Far right, a secretary at West German Radio.*

***Above, a student** shows his dueling scars; below, a high school teacher. They symbolized two of the opposing elements in the doomed Weimar Republic.*

A CHRONOLOGY OF THE ARTS: 1929-39

1929

- Swiss artist Paul Klee held his first one-man show in Berlin. A dazzling painter and eloquent theorist, Klee was an inexhaustible source of pictorial ideas and artistic wit.
- U.S. novelist William Faulkner published *Sartoris,* the first of 16 books detailing the history of the fictitious Mississippi county of Yoknapatawpha.
- German architect Mies van der Rohe designed the German pavilion at the Barcelona International Exposition. Its flowing inner space, broken only by slender marble slabs and columns of chrome steel, influenced scores of industrial architects all over the world.

1930

- French poet Jean Cocteau produced his first and best known film, *Blood of a Poet.* An experimental, semisurrealist work, it marked a high point in the career of this lifelong popularizer of the avant-garde.
- U.S. poet Hart Crane published *The Bridge,* his most celebrated poem. Although he committed suicide at 33, just 2 years later, Crane has since been recognized as one of the century's finest American poets.

1931

- Lithuanian-born U.S. painter Ben Shahn first won fame with a series of 23 gouaches inspired by the Sacco-Vanzetti trial. A master of many media, Shahn went on to become one of the most influential creators of his era, a major figure in both commercial and fine art.

1932

- Russian author Maxim Gorki became the first president of the Soviet Writers' Union. Already internationally known for plays like *The Lower Depths* and novels like *Mother,* Gorki—previously chief of the Soviet propaganda bureau—helped make socialist realism the official Soviet style.
- British novelist Aldous Huxley published *Brave New World,* a chilling look at a future devoted to pleasure and controlled by totalitarian tyranny.

1933

- U.S. painter Edward Hopper held his first one-man show at the Museum of Modern Art. His eerie, desolate, almost photographic American scenes influenced the pop and superrealist schools of the late 1960's.

1934

- The Nazi regime forbade public performance of Paul Hindemith's opera *Mathis der Mahler,* and denounced him as a spiritual non-Aryan.

1935

- U.S. composer George Gershwin produced his opera, *Porgy and Bess* (based on the novel *Porgy* by lyricist DuBose Heyward). It marked the peak of a musical career that sought to fuse jazz with older musical forms.

1936

- U.S. novelist John Dos Passos published *The Big Money,* the third volume of his *U.S.A.* trilogy. His work combined current events, newspaper headlines, brief biographies, and interweaving fictional narratives.
- André Gide, French novelist, playwright, and diarist, published *Return from the U.S.S.R.,* a disillusioned leftist's notebook in which he urged fellow artists to remain aloof from political movements.
- Spanish poet-dramatist Federico García Lorca was killed by Falangists during the Spanish Civil War. Among his finest works are the play *Blood Wedding* and the poem "Lament for the Death of a Bullfighter."

1938

- Russian writer Isaac Babel was banished to Siberia (where he subsequently died in a concentration camp) for having "defamed" heroes of the Russian Revolution in his short stories about the 1917 struggle.
- Nikos Kazantzakis, perhaps the greatest Greek writer of the century, published his verse epic, *The Odyssey: A Modern Sequel.*

1939

Irish novelist James Joyce published his last book, *Finnegan's Wake.*

1934

The Long March of Mao Tse-tung

An astonishing feat of endurance saves the insurgent Chinese Communists from destruction and produces a brilliant young leader.

It was the most remarkable march in history. In October 1934, surrounded by the Nationalist forces of Generalissimo Chiang Kai-shek, nearly 100,000 Communists abandoned their Kiangsi-Fukien base area in southern China and set off in search of refuge. Toting military supplies and all the paraphernalia of their rebel government—printing presses, machinery, gold bullion, propaganda, and documents—they retreated westward and then northward until they finally found sanctuary a year later in the remote northwestern province of Shensi. They had marched 6,000 miles through 11 provinces, skirmishing with pursuing Nationalist forces, with regional warlord armies, and with hostile tribesmen, as they crossed a formidable landscape of rivers, mountains, and swamplands. Of their original number only 1 man in 13 had survived the ordeal of the harsh year-long trek.

To Chiang and other observers, it appeared that the enemy had finally been eradicated. But under the clever and determined leadership of Mao Tse-tung, the Communists turned their seeming defeat into a victory. Slowly and carefully establishing a strong following in Shensi, they rebuilt their movement. Fourteen years later the Communists, led by the invincible hard core who had survived the Long March, again performed the seemingly impossible. On October 1, 1949, Mao Tse-tung proclaimed the triumph of his Marxist revolution from the Chinese capital of Peking.

The Communist retreat in 1934 was part of a larger struggle for political control of China that had been raging for decades. The Revolution of 1911 (see pp. 66–71), inspired by Sun Yat-sen, had established a republic, but Sun's followers were forced to relinquish power to Gen. Yüan Shih-kai, who as President of the republic gradually assumed dictatorial powers. His death in 1916 ushered in a decade of domestic chaos during which provincial warlords fought for power.

Meanwhile, Sun Yat-sen attempted to establish his republic in southern China, but in 1922 the southern warlords forced him into exile in Shanghai. There Soviet Comintern agents offered financial support if he would agree to an alliance with China's infant Communist Party, founded a year earlier at Shanghai. With Soviet backing Sun's Kuomintang, or Nationalist Party, returned to Canton and began building up an army. After Sun's death in 1925 Chiang Kai-shek, head of the Kuomintang army and dedicated anti-Communist, launched a military expedition against the warlords, gained control of most of China by 1928, and set up a national government at Nanking.

In 1927 Chiang had turned against the Communists, outlawed the Communist Party, and ruthlessly annihilated the urban Communist movement. All Soviet advisers fled to Moscow, and most surviving urban Communist leaders escaped to remote hideouts in the countryside. Mao Tse-tung retreated with a few followers to the mountainous Chingkangshan border region between Kiangsi and Hunan Provinces. There they began to organize a revolutionary movement.

***The Red army's** heroic crossing of the Tatu River, one of the most perilous feats of the Long March, is commemorated in a recent Chinese painting. To halt the Reds' progress, the Nationalists had removed half the planks from an ancient chain bridge across the river's gorge. According to an eyewitness account by Yang Cheng-wu, a regiment leader, "The attack began at four in the afternoon. The buglers of the regiment gathered together to sound the charge, and we opened up with every weapon we had. The noise ... reverberated through the valley. The twenty-two heroes ... climbed the swaying bridge in the teeth of intense enemy fire. Each man carried a tommy-gun, a broad sword and twelve hand grenades." Midway, the soldiers climbed onto the planks and charged the enemy redoubt. Then they replaced the missing planks, so that the others could cross.*

The epic trek involved many other rigorous challenges. "Victory was life," observed P'eng Teh-huai, deputy commander of the 8th Route Army, "defeat was certain death." When it was over, Mao Tse-tung composed this poem:

The Red Army, never fearing the challenging Long March,
Looked lightly on the many peaks and rivers.
Wu Liang's Range rose, lowered, rippled,
And green-tiered were the rounded steps of Wu Meng.
Warm-beating the Gold Sand River's waves against the rocks,
And cold the iron-chain spans of Tatu's bridge.
A thousand joyous li of freshening snow on Min Shan,
And then, the last pass vanquished, Three Armies smiled!

Old Hundred Names

China's peasantry was ripe for change. For centuries the Old Hundred Names, as her rural multitudes were called, had endured poverty, famine, floods, wars, and epidemics. In the 20th century, however, these traditional ills had been aggravated by population pressures and critical land shortages. During the warlord era (1916–27) conditions deteriorated further as greedy provincial strongmen conscripted peasants into their armies and levied heavy taxes—sometimes collected decades in advance—to finance their military ventures. Their soldiers raided fields and villages and ravaged local women. Landlords fled to the safety of towns and cities, leaving bailiffs to collect their rents. The latter often exacted several times the amount due, lining their own pockets with the difference.

Under these desperate circumstances Mao's exhortations to "Arise! Overthrow those who have oppressed you and who have benefited at your expense!" found an immediate welcome. Long-simmering resentments exploded as groups of peasants rose violently against their landlords and local officials. After these initial passions had been vented, the Communists helped villagers redistribute the land, organize village soviets, and elect local party representatives.

The Red army formed an integral part of the peasant movement. The force was founded in 1927 by Chu Teh, who led a mutiny of Nationalist forces at Nanchang and later joined Mao at Chingkangshan. By 1929 Chu had recruited some 10,000 men for his guerrilla army. According to Mao it was a ragged, motley corps, armed with "spears and old fowling pieces" and a few captured weapons. Yet what it lacked in equipment, it made up for in spirit and determination.

The Red army's first test came in December 1930, when Chiang Kai-shek, alarmed by reports of Communist-led peasant uprisings in Hunan and Kiangsi, sent 100,000 men, armed with rifles and machine guns, on the first of several "Bandit Extermination Campaigns." This first encounter ended in a disastrous defeat for the Nationalists, but Chiang launched three more anti-Communist drives in 1931 and 1933. Each time his forces suffered a humiliating defeat.

Using Mao's guerrilla warfare tactics, based on his theory: "The enemy advances, we retreat. The enemy halts, we harass. The enemy tires, we attack. The enemy retreats, we pursue," the Red army overcame its decided disadvantage in numbers and weapons. Its stunning victories boosted troop morale and rallied other peasants as well as disgruntled Nationalist soldiers; by the end of 1931 the Red army had grown to 30,000. That same year Mao proclaimed a provisional soviet republic at Juikin in the border region between Kiangsi and Fukien Provinces.

Chiang sent nearly 700,000 Nationalist soldiers to besiege the whole south-central Kiangsi area in October 1933. Working methodically, they encircled the region, sealing off the entire area with an elaborate network of barbed wire and cement blockhouses. Then they waited. As the months wore on, Mao and his followers suffered increasing shortages of such essentials as salt, cloth, and medical supplies. At the end of a year they realized their situation was hopeless, but they refused to surrender. Instead, they decided on a daring plan: to break out of the blockade and retreat to Shensi Province in China's extreme northwest.

The Making of a Legend

Dividing into small groups, the Communists fought their way out of the blockade and headed directly westward, through the rugged border areas of Kiangsi, Kwangtung, Hunan, and Kwangsi Provinces. Along the way they suffered heavy losses in battles with the Nationalists, who anticipated the path of the Red Army and took advantage of the slow pace of Mao's heavily encumbered legions. By the time the Reds reached Kweichow, they had lost a third of their force.

In Kweichow they discarded all nonessential baggage and developed diversionary tactics. While the main force continued its westward march, smaller divisions tried to distract the Nationalists. Meanwhile, Chiang deployed thousands of soldiers to prevent the Communists from crossing the Yangtze River into Szechwan. The Nationalists destroyed bridges, ordered ferries removed to the far bank, and set up roadblocks and barriers on all approaches. As a result, the

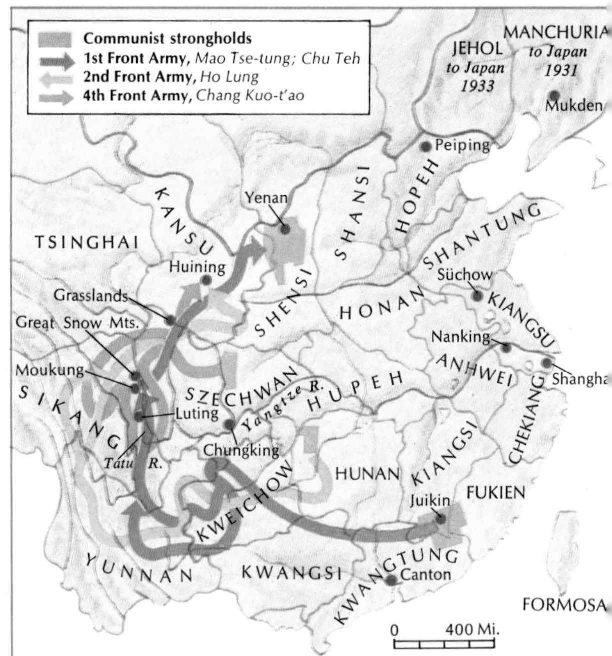

THE ROUTE OF THE LONG MARCH

Setting out from Kiangsi in October 1934, the First Front Army under Mao Tse-tung traveled 6,000 miles before reaching Shensi a year later. Two other Red armies also took part in the Long March. The Fourth Front Army joined Mao at Mouking in July 1935 but chose a separate route, entering Shensi a few months after Mao. The Second Front Army marched farther south and west and did not join Mao's group in Shensi until the fall of 1936.

Communists spent four months avoiding, encircling, and attacking enemy forces in Kweichow before turning southward into the wilds of Yunnan Province and crossing the high Yangtze at Chou P'ing Fort.

The Communists encountered another major obstacle at the Luting Bridge of the Tatu River, a Yangtze tributary. At Luting the Tatu flows through a deep gorge nearly 100 yards wide. The only possible crossing was a primitive bridge built by the Emperor in 1701 out of 13 huge iron chains, secured at either side by massive pegs and spanned by wooden planks. To block the way, the Nationalists had removed the planks to a point midway across the gorge. The Reds used a bold tactic to secure the bridge. Under covering fire 22 volunteers, armed with knives and hand grenades, swung hand over hand across the gorge until they reached the middle. The remaining planks provided a kind of protective shield from enemy bullets. Nonetheless, three men were hit and plunged into the abyss. Midway, the Reds climbed onto the planks and charged the enemy redoubt, hurling hand grenades. The Nationalists fled. Then the Reds replaced the missing planks, and the others crossed unharmed.

Other grueling challenges lay ahead. After a six-week rest at Moukung on the Sikang-Szechwan border, they crossed the Great Snow Mountains in western Szechwan. There they endured snow, hail, fierce winds, and bitter cold. Farther north lay the Grasslands, a vast rainswept swampland, overgrown with tall grasses. The Reds found neither food nor shelter for the duration of the 10-day crossing.

A Dedicated Hard Core

After another six weeks of marching the Communists reached Yenan, on the western fringes of Shensi Province. Only about 7,000 of the original 100,000 had survived the ordeal. With them were another 15,000 who had been recruited along the way. In the next year Mao's group was joined by two other armies of Communists who had also fled from Chiang's soldiers.

The Long March laid the foundations of a legend of Communist invincibility. The men who survived the

ao Tse-tung addresses a oup of his followers at their enan headquarters in Chi-i's northwestern Shensi ovince (below, left).

hensi peasants celebrate the ommunists' land reforms ight). Long March veteran hou En-lai (below, right) as the Reds' top diplomat.

A REVOLUTION TAKES HOLD IN CHINA'S NORTHWEST

From its new base in Shensi Province, the Red army launched a rural revolution. When U.S. journalist Edgar Snow visited the area in 1935–36, he was impressed by its progress. The Reds had "liberated" peasants from landlords, redistributed land, lowered taxes, outlawed usury and child slavery, reformed local politics, and set up schools. Observed one Shensi peasant: "Here everybody is the same. It is not like the White [Nationalist] districts, where poor people are slaves of the landlords and the Kuomintang. Here everybody fights the landlords and the White bandits."

THE SINO-JAPANESE WAR: 1937–45

Japan began a full-scale invasion of China in July 1937. By the end of 1938 two-thirds of the country was in Japanese hands, and Chiang Kai-shek's government had retreated to remote Chungking. Despite much U.S. aid, Chiang was reluctant to fight back, preferring to save his resources for the postwar fight against the Communists. The Reds, however, led an active resistance movement behind enemy lines, winning popular support and gaining strength for the upcoming civil war.

The beleaguered Chungking regime of Gen. Chiang Kai-shek (left) relied on the Burma Road (above) for supplies. It was also vital in World War II.

Crammed into crowded railway cars (right) Chinese families fled inland before the advancing Japanese troops.

Long March had endured attack, disease, hunger, pain, extreme heat and cold, and the most spartan of existences. They formed a dedicated hard core of tough, experienced leaders. Moreover, during the march the Red army had made contact with large numbers of China's rural population—not as marauding bandits in the traditional manner of Chinese armies, but as sympathetic, fair-minded peasants like themselves. In later years the favorable impression so carefully cultivated by Mao's army was not forgotten.

Mao himself emerged from the Long March as the undisputed leader of the Chinese Communists. The experience of the Kiangsi soviet period and of the trek itself had vindicated his brand of peasant communism and helped discredit the Russian-based theory of the proletarian uprising. From then on Chinese communism would be a rural-based movement, and its philosophy and program would be dictated by the uniquely Chinese writings and theories of Mao Tse-tung.

Meanwhile, China was drifting inevitably toward a war with Japan. A confrontation had been looming since 1931, when Japanese soldiers occupied Manchuria, China's rich northeastern industrial province, and set up the puppet state of Manchukuo. Apart from an angry protest to the League of Nations, Chiang did nothing to oppose the occupation. The Communists, however, immediately declared war on Japan.

In 1933 the Japanese seized Jehol Province and began to penetrate into Inner Mongolia and northern China. Such blatant aggression caused a groundswell of nationalism among China's people and aroused widespread resentment of Chiang's avowed policy of "first pacification, then resistance." Ignoring Japan's incursions, the Generalissimo pressed doggedly forward with his antibandit campaigns, alienating many supporters, who thought his priorities were wrong.

Unable to persuade the stubborn Chiang to abandon his disastrous course, one group resorted to force. In

December 1936, when Chiang was visiting Shensi Province to arrange yet another extermination campaign, the local warlord arrested him and demanded that he join in an alliance with the Communists against the common enemy, Japan. Chiang reluctantly made peace with the Communists.

Japan, whose greatest fear was a strong, united China, decided to strike before the country had time to rally its forces. On July 7, 1937, fighting broke out at the Marco Polo Bridge near Peking (then Peiping), and China and Japan went to war. Chiang's badly organized and poorly equipped forces fell back in the face of Japan's efficient war machine. Nanking fell in mid-December, and the Nationalists moved their government first to Hankow and then to Chungking. By October 1938 Japan had conquered two-thirds of the country, most major industries, and all ports of entry. Yet from his provisional capital at Chungking, Chiang refused to capitulate. He was convinced that Japan would eventually provoke the United States into war in the Pacific and that his beleaguered government would be saved by American help.

In occupied northern China the Communists began organizing guerrilla resistance. Their program of opposition to the invader and immediate land reform appealed to China's peasants. In village after village the Communists organized farmer-worker-soldier teams, which took turns harassing the enemy and making the land more productive. As the years of occupation dragged on, their following increased.

In 1941 the United States went to war with Japan and began supplying the Nationalists with artillery, trucks, tanks, airplanes, guns, and ammunition to fight the Japanese. U.S. Gen. Joseph Stilwell was appointed to serve as Chiang's chief of staff. Despite U.S. aid, however, Chiang failed to undertake a serious campaign against the Japanese and refused to comply with Stilwell's urgent requests to reform his inefficient chain of command. Instead, he husbanded his new weapons and best troops for the inevitable postwar conflict with Communists. In 1944 Chiang demanded —and obtained—Stilwell's recall to Washington.

The end of the war in August 1945 saw the resumption of the Nationalist-Communist conflict, as both sides scrambled to reclaim the territory vacated by the Japanese. U.S. attempts to mediate the impending crisis failed, and full-scale civil war erupted throughout China in June 1946. At the outbreak of hostilities Chiang's troops outnumbered the Communists four to one. The Nationalists also had superior weapons and an air force. For the first two years of the conflict fighting centered in Manchuria. Despite early gains and massive American aid the Nationalists finally were defeated. By the end of 1948 the People's Liberation Army, as the Red army had been rechristened, under Gen. Lin Piao, had taken Manchuria.

Surging southward, the Communists claimed victory after victory. As Chiang's defeats multiplied, his economy collapsed, and his policies became increasingly repressive; his supporters joined the Communists in ever-growing numbers. The high morale, dedication, and competence of the Red army appealed greatly to China's war-weary multitudes. It seemed that nothing short of a miracle could stem the tide.

The decisive battle of the civil war began in November 1948 at Hwai-Hai, a crucial railway junction in central China. It was one of the epic battles of all time: For 65 days some 500,000 Communist soldiers fought 500,000 Nationalist regulars to decide the future leadership of China. In the end the Nationalists were nearly annihilated, and soon afterward Chiang fled with his remaining supporters to set up a government-in-exile on the offshore island of Formosa.

On October 1, 1949, a triumphant Mao Tse-tung mounted the rostrum of Peking's ancient Gate of Heavenly Peace and proclaimed the establishment of the People's Republic of China. The dreamed-for revolution had finally come to pass, and for the first time in decades the country was at peace. The road to victory had been long and tortuous and by no means certain. Yet Mao's movement had survived the 1927 massacres, Chiang's vicious extermination campaigns, the rigors of the Long March, the privations of Japanese occupation, and a bitter civil war. Ahead lay new and even more rigorous challenges.

***Communist Victory:** Mao Tse-tung proclaims the People's Republic of China in Peking on October 1, 1949.*

1936

America Ratifies the New Deal

President Roosevelt and his sweeping economic policies win a resounding vote of confidence in the 1936 election.

Up from the ashes of the Depression rose office buildings, schools, factories, and dams in thousands of government-sponsored work projects. New Deal agencies gave work to everyone, from roadbuilders to artists and writers. At right, detail from William Gropper's WPA mural, "Construction of a Dam."

"That man in the White House," Republicans called him; yet FDR was to do more to change the social structure of America than any President since Lincoln. As a result of the New Deal, labor unions became more powerful, farmers got government subsidies for the first time, and big business took a back seat.

His pince-nez gleaming red in the reflected light of torches and flares, President Franklin Delano Roosevelt flashed his famous grin and waved greetings to old friends from the porch of his Hyde Park, New York, home. It was election night 1936. Returns had poured in all evening and, as the awesome scale of Roosevelt's triumph became clear, a cheering crowd of local Democrats led by an American Legion band arrived to salute their illustrious neighbor.

Surrounded by beaming family, friends, and campaign aides, FDR had every reason to be jubilant. He had won an unprecedented victory, swamping his hapless Republican opponent, Gov. Alfred M. Landon of Kansas, by the widest popular margin in history. Every state but Maine and Vermont ended up in the Roosevelt column. When the 531 electoral votes were tallied, FDR had won 523. And his lengthy political coattails had added to the already heavy Democratic majorities in the House and Senate.

This expression of overwhelming public support was a ringing endorsement of his New Deal, the furthest reaching program of government action and social and economic change in United States history.

Facing the Crisis

When FDR entered the White House in March 1933, the nation was facing its gravest crisis since the Civil War—the Great Depression. While thousands of Americans faced starvation, Washington withheld direct aid to the needy, as President Herbert Hoover argued that "the primary duty of this government . . . is to hold expenditures within our income."

Fear and despair gripped the nation, and the system of democratic government embodied in the Constitution seemed finally to have failed. Roosevelt was short on concrete proposals, but he did promise a "new deal for the American people," a fundamental "reappraisal of values." He saw clearly that America yearned for bold, persistent action. It was common sense, he said, when faced with so awesome a challenge, "to take a method and try it: If it fails, admit it frankly and try another. But above all, try something." In that pragmatic spirit he began his first term as President in 1933.

His New Deal was not long in coming. Everyone was eager for action, and FDR responded with vigor. Proclaiming in his March 4 inaugural address that "the only thing we have to fear is fear itself," he called for "broad Executive power to wage a war against the emergency." Congress cooperated and in the "First Hundred Days" of the Roosevelt administration more innovative federal legislation was enacted than in any similar period in the nation's history.

When Roosevelt was inaugurated, four-fifths of the nation's banks had been closed to forestall further

financial panic. The following day the President declared a four-day bank holiday, then called Congress into special session to ratify his bold action. Banks in sound condition were licensed to reopen; some 200 weak ones were liquidated. Depositors' savings were guaranteed by the newly established Federal Deposit Insurance Corporation. Public confidence in the banking system was restored, and more than $1 billion that had been hoarded flowed back into the economy.

"The Forgotten Man"

But it was in providing direct relief for the neediest that the New Deal had its most immediate impact. Congress created the Federal Emergency Relief Administration (FERA), which disbursed some $500 million to state agencies for direct aid to jobless citizens. It was the first tangible sign in four bitter years that the government in Washington cared about the citizen whom FDR called "the forgotten man at the bottom of the economic pyramid."

Desperate farmers, plagued by low prices and overproduction, were aided by the creation of the Agricultural Adjustment Administration (AAA), which paid federal subsidies to farmers for crop reduction, marketing quotas, and loans. To hasten the AAA's effectiveness, farmers were paid to slaughter some 6 million pigs (100 million pounds of the pork were distributed to families on relief) and to plow under 10 million acres of cotton in 1933.

The New Deal's early hopes for economic recovery were pinned on the ambitious National Industrial Recovery Act (NIRA) which established the National Recovery Administration (NRA). Based on the principle of self-regulation, it stressed that improved distribution and intelligent production planning, rather than industrial expansion, were better solutions for the economic problems facing the nation. The NIRA authorized businesses to draft industrywide codes of fair practices, exempt from antitrust laws, which were to control production and prices. The workers' right to "organize and bargain collectively through representatives of their own choosing" was guaranteed, a national system of maximum hours and minimum wages was established, and the sweatshop was virtually abolished. The NIRA also set up the Public Works Administration (PWA) to boost consumer buying power and stimulate industrial activity by providing federal jobs on some 34,000 public projects, including road building and home construction.

Although much of the early New Deal was slapdash and wasteful, it seemed to work. By the spring of 1934 the economy had begun to climb out of the Depression's worst depths, and the large groups of grateful Americans to whom New Deal programs had meant survival and renewed hope stood firmly together behind their jaunty President.

A Second New Deal

FDR's enormous popularity helped elect even more Democrats to Congress in the off-year elections of 1934, but recovery soon slowed again. Critics at both ends of the political spectrum began to make their voices heard. Leftists accused Roosevelt of being too cautious, while equally vocal conservatives were frightened and appalled by him and all his works. Businessmen now were expected to share their power with labor and farmers, and the New Deal was steadily expanding Washington's power to regulate business. Many agreed with former President Herbert Hoover's statement that Roosevelt's radical programs represented a "stupendous invasion of the whole spirit of liberty," and they called the wealthy and well-born President a demagogic "traitor to his class."

FDR wavered for a time, wary of further alienating either camp, but in January 1935 he asked Congress to enact a new program of reform aimed at providing greater security for every citizen. The need for such legislation was intensified when, in May, the Supreme Court declared the code-making provision of the NIRA an unconstitutional delegation of Congress' legislative power.

Massive dams (left) were built by the WPA to stem floods and control the disastrous soil erosion of Midwest farmlands.

The Triboro Bridge (below) in New York City was a WPA project completed in 1941.

BUILDING A NATION

One of the most significant legacies of the relief agencies established as a part of the New Deal is that of the Works Progress Administration, created by Congress in April 1935. Under its $11 billion umbrella some 8.5 million skilled workers of every kind, from artists and writers to bricklayers and steamfitters, were put to work for the public good. Though branded a handout program by conservatives, some 651,000 miles of streets and roads, 78,000 bridges, 125,000 public buildings, as well as parks, airports, public utilities, and recreational facilities had been built, refurbished, or improved by the time the WPA was phased out in 1943.

Thousands of miles of streets and roads were built by the agency's workers.

Projects for small towns included schools like the one above, city halls, and post offices.

To provide the still-unemployed with jobs rather than handouts Congress established the Works Progress Administration (WPA) in 1935. Unlike the older Public Works Administration (PWA), which worked through grants-in-aid to cities and states, the WPA set up and directly controlled projects to aid the jobless. In addition, the Social Security Act offered protection against penniless old age and provided aid for the disabled. That this law was compulsory and required employers to pay part of the cost outraged conservatives, who routinely denounced Social Security as revolutionary or worse. Actually it only brought the U.S.A. into concert with other Western nations, like Germany and England, that had long provided such security for their citizens.

With a forceful record to run on, Roosevelt reentered the Presidential lists in 1936, crisscrossing the continent to denounce the "economic royalists" who opposed him. His GOP challenger, Alf Landon, was an able, progressive governor. Yet, thanks to FDR's oratorical skills and the unrestrained anti–New Deal denunciations made by Landon's backers, Landon was seen as a reactionary whose election would threaten continued recovery. FDR's smashing electoral triumph marked the peak of his career.

The 1936 election demonstrated overwhelming popular backing for the New Deal, and Roosevelt continued to dominate the heavily Democratic Congress. But the Supreme Court struck down a dozen laws that FDR considered central to his program. Finally, in 1936, a New York State minimum wage act was ruled invalid in terms that seemed to indicate that both the Social Security Act and the Wagner Act, which had established a powerful National Labor Relations Board, might soon be overturned as well.

The New Deal was still incomplete, and the Depression was far from over; indeed, the economy had begun to slide dangerously again. Roosevelt pledged to aid the one-third of the nation that remained "ill-housed, ill-clad, ill-nourished." The narrow view of the Constitution held by some of the "nine old men" of the Court (with an average age of 72 in 1936) seemed to threaten everything FDR had achieved. He resolved to fight back and settled upon a "court-packing" plan that would have permitted him to appoint a new justice for every sitting judge who failed to retire at the age of 70. This would increase efficiency, Roosevelt said, by adding younger men to the bench. But most Congressmen, including many ardent New Dealers, refused to tamper with the balance of power between the executive and judicial branches of government.

Suddenly and without explanation the Court itself began to change its tune. On April 12, 1937, it upheld the Wagner Act. Thereafter it became more difficult for Roosevelt's spokesmen to charge that the "horse and buggy" Court was behind the times or unreasonably hostile to change. Roosevelt's plan was defeated, marking what his own supporters conceded to be the worst political mistake of his administration.

Roosevelt prepares to deal the American people a brandnew hand in this 1930's cartoon.

THE ROAD TO THE PRESIDENCY

In many ways Franklin D. Roosevelt was an unlikely savior. Born in Dutchess County, New York, in 1882, the pampered son of a wealthy family, he was educated at Groton, Harvard, and Columbia Law School. As a young Democratic state senator (1910–13) Roosevelt was at first considered merely a handsome political lightweight by his peers. Although his famous name and strong personality won him his party's 1920 Vice-Presidential nomination, he and his runningmate James Cox were easily crushed by Republicans Harding and Coolidge.

In 1928 Roosevelt was elected Governor of New York, and after establishing an excellent gubernatorial record, he mapped a classic campaign to win the 1932 Democratic Presidential nomination. No longer a lightweight, FDR was a shrewd politician genuinely committed to using government to bring about reform. He ran an almost perfect campaign against Hoover. His self-confident air and vibrant voice caught the imagination of a battered country, and he was borne to power by a landslide majority.

The Roosevelt Legacy

The New Deal did not halt the Depression. Some 10 million Americans remained jobless in 1938, and only the massive defense spending that began the following year would get them back to work. Nor had it been consistent or uniformly effective. But its achievements were enormous and long-lasting. In the light of history, the New Deal seems to have saved capitalism from its own excesses, kept the U.S. free when some other depression-wracked nations turned in desperation to totalitarianism, and established a more equitable balance among the competing forces that have helped to shape modern society.

1936

The Spanish Civil War

In a tragic prelude to World War II General Franco and his Fascist allies overthrow Spain's legal government.

For nearly 40 years the fate of Spain was tied to the ambitions and destiny of one man—an autocrat as puzzling to outsiders, and as contradictory, as Spain itself: Generalissimo Francisco Franco. In 1936 he led a revolt against the elected government and, after a bloody three-year civil war, assumed full power in his country. The scars of that conflict and of his subsequent iron rule are still not completely healed.

Franco was born in El Ferrol, Galicia, in 1892. He was commissioned a second lieutenant in 1910 and engaged in the tough fighting between Spanish troops and the Moroccan nationalists who resisted Spanish rule. By the time he was 23, his qualities of bravery and leadership had won him promotion to the rank of captain, the youngest in Spain's Moroccan army. By 1920 he was second in command of the Spanish Foreign Legion. During the twenties Franco became convinced that men like himself, tested in combat and steeled by the discipline of army life, should lead Spain—rather than the politicians who were whittling away at the power of King Alfonso XIII.

In fact, Franco had good reason to distrust the politicians, for in the early years of this century Spain was boiling over with political strife. Although she was primarily an agricultural nation, her land resources were underexploited, and between the peasantry and the landholding aristocracy there was only a small middle class. Geographically cut off from the heart of Western Europe by the rugged Pyrenees Mountains, she had become isolated culturally and economically too. The Catholic Church had retained a quasi-medieval grip on society, but many, especially the poor, resented its power, and militant anticlericism had long been on the rise. In the few big cities leftist trade unions attracted thousands of members, and strikes were frequent. Against this background of geographical and cultural isolation, sharp class division, and general unrest, Spain was ripe for civil war.

When it came, Spaniard fought Spaniard not so much for money or land as for ideals, which ranged from an anarchist or socialist utopia to a Catholic monarchy recalling the glorious days of imperial Spain. Yet the 600,000 men and women who died in the war failed to establish their ideals. Instead, foreign nations, by injecting men, money, and arms, helped establish Franco, and nearly 40 years of repression.

A Society of Extremes

Four centuries ago Spain led the emergent nations of Europe in extent and wealth of empire. Then, under an absolute monarchy whose bulging coffers maintained society at a near-feudal level, Spain began to stagnate. Meanwhile, her less wealthy competitors were spurred to new political and economic developments, and by the end of the 18th century Spain had been eclipsed as a world power.

During the Napoleonic period the Iberian Peninsula became a battleground for the French and British, and Spain's colonies in the New World and in the Pacific began to slip from her grasp. Within her borders, the army, the church, the wealthy landowners, and the monarchy fought for dominance, while the workers (centered around the textile mills of Barcelona and the ironworks of Bilbao) and peasants began to develop their own political awareness. Anarchism gained a large following among the trade unionists, and regional separatism was strong in Catalonia and elsewhere, while the traditions of the monarchy and the church were cherished by the relatively well-to-do peasants of Navarre and Old Castile.

At its highest levels, the Spanish church, the most conservative in Europe, was intimately allied with the King and landowners, and was itself the largest single landowner in Spain. Even when the liberals finally obliged it to sell its lands in 1837, the proceeds left the church Spain's richest corporate entity. Many poor Spaniards reacted bitterly, and for more than a century local uprisings brought with them the burning of churches and the killing of priests.

The Slow Revolution

In this politically corrosive environment the government of Alfonso XIII gradually crumbled until, by 1923, the King had become merely a figurehead. Dictatorial power was held for about 6½ years after-

Political prisoners *labored on the Valley of the Fallen, Franco's huge memorial to the 600,000 who died in the Civil War. Many of those who were killed in the war are buried there, as was the Generalissimo himself in 1975.*

As the Nationalists rampaged *through Catalonia in January 1939, France opened her border to the Republican refugees. Some 500,000 people fled Spain during the Civil War, in fear of Falangist reprisals and mass executions.*

ward by Gen. Miguel Primo de Rivera, who with French help ended the drawn-out Moroccan campaign in 1927. Although Primo de Rivera censored the press and dissolved the Cortes (the legislative assembly), most historians regard him as a relatively benevolent despot who did much to modernize Spain.

The Great Depression toppled Primo de Rivera's rule, and after an ineffectual attempt to resume power, Alfonso XIII went into exile in 1931. The leaders of the Cortes became founders of the Second Spanish Republic, and Manuel Azaña, the second man to serve as Premier, emerged as a dominant figure.

Azaña, who feared the army as a rival, tried to reduce its size. Injudiciously he demanded that officers sign an oath of loyalty to the Republic, but allowed those who refused to retire on full pay; many who did so used their new leisure to conspire against the Republic. An attempted coup d'etat (or, in Spanish, *pronunciamiento*) led by Gen. José Sanjurjo was put down in 1932. In late 1933 Azaña was unseated by a moderate-conservative coalition backed by the church and the landowners. The new Premier, Alejandro Lerroux, tried to turn back the clock, ending the redistribution of land and sabotaging other reforms. There followed the *bienio negro* ("dark two years") for Spain's poor, which brought strikes and increasingly violent government reprisals. Troops were called out to crush separatist revolts in Catalonia and the Basque provinces.

The most violent upheaval occurred in the Asturias region, in late October 1934. Some 30,000 militant, mostly leftist miners succeeded in taking over much of the province. The government sent Gen. Francisco Franco and his crack Foreign Legion and Moorish troops to put down the rising. But the troops were not withdrawn even after the miners surrendered, and hundreds of civilians, including many miners, were killed after the insurrection was over.

Lerroux was less willing to use force against the right. In fact, he pardoned Sanjurjo, and had allowed known rightwing conspirators to travel to Italy to confer with Mussolini, who promised them his support. Armed bands of monarchists and members of the quasi-Fascist Falange (Phalanx), who aped Mussolini's Blackshirts, drilled openly to prepare for the overthrow of the Republic.

In the next elections, February 1936, a broad coalition of Radicals, Socialists, Anarchists, and even the small but influential Communist Party, returned Azaña to power. This Popular Front coalition won approximately 4.2 million votes, as against 3.8 million for the Right and 600,000 for the Center. In a reaction against the conservatism of the *bienio negro*, many Spaniards began to force the pace of revolutionary change. There were more than 100 general strikes, and churches were burned all over Spain. Peasants occupied farmland even before Azaña could resume the land reform program, and many towns formed their own "socialist militia" to oppose the hated Civil Guard.

The Generals Plot a Coup

At the same time three generals were making plans for a coup d'etat. Sanjurjo would lead the insurrection, Gen. Emilio Mola would lead his troops against the Republic in the north of Spain, and Franco would rally the veterans of the colonial army in Morocco.

The spark that set off the rebellion came in July, when Falangist assassins killed a lieutenant in the Asaltos, or Republican Guard. In revenge, Guardsmen shot José Calvo Sotelo, a conservative leader in the Cortes. The rising began in Morocco as scheduled on July 17, although Franco did not arrive there until the 19th. On July 18, Franco had broadcast the rebel Manifesto from the Canary Islands, and on that day, all over Spain, garrison commanders led their troops into the streets. But large numbers of Spaniards responded with vigorous support for their elected government. In Barcelona, Madrid, Toledo, and scores of other cities and towns the workers' militias and the Republican Guard led mass risings against the scattered army garrisons. In a few days the government had regained control of two-thirds of the country. Navy crews rebelled against officers who supported the conspirators. General Sanjurjo, flying to rebel headquarters at Burgos, died in a plane crash.

By late July Azaña was confident that the rebellion, from then on led by Franco, could be put down. A majority of the population was in Republican-held territory. The industrial centers in Vizcaya and around Barcelona were secure. The rich gold reserve of the Bank of Spain was in government hands, and the Republicans enjoyed diplomatic legitimacy.

But already Franco's forces—the Nationalists—were receiving aid from abroad, as German and Italian transport planes appeared in Africa to lift Moroccan and Spanish Foreign Legion troops over the sea blockade set up by the Republicans.

Then Azaña discovered that the Republic could not buy the arms needed for its defense. Traditionally, international law permitted the sale of arms to a legitimate government and forbade their sale to rebels. But France, though sympathetic to the Spanish Republican cause, did not dare risk a domestic political split by selling weapons to Spain, nor was she willing to antagonize Hitler and Mussolini. Britain forcefully advocated an arms embargo to both Republicans and Nationalists. And the United States, under the terms of the Neutrality Act of May 1937, was prohibited from selling arms to any belligerent nation. The label France, England, and the United States applied to their policy was "nonintervention." Germany and Italy signed a nonintervention pact in August, but continued to increase their military aid to Franco.

THE FALL OF REPUBLICAN SPAIN

On July 17, 1936, antigovernment uprisings occurred in the Spanish Army garrisons at Melilla, Ceuta, and Tetuán in Morocco, at Palma de Mallorca, and in Spain at Granada, Córdoba, Seville, and Pamplona. The next day there were further insurrections at Salamanca, Burgos and Valladolid, and on the 20th at Saragossa, Vigo, La Coruña, and Oviedo. On the 28th German transport planes began to airlift Franco's troops from Morocco to the mainland, and by the end of the month the Nationalists controlled most of northern Spain. By the end of August they had formed a continuous front.

From October 1936 to March 1937 the Nationalists, united under Franco, consolidated their gains against the fragmented Republican coalition of left-wing and liberal groups. By October 1937, backed by massive German and Italian aid, they had overcome a stubborn pocket of resistance in the northern provinces (Map 2).

During the next nine months Franco's troops pushed westward to the coast, and by July 1938 had driven a 100-mile-wide wedge between Catalonia and the rest of the Republic (Map 3). By February 9, 1939, the Catalonian provinces had fallen, and in the last days of March the Republican garrisons around Madrid surrendered. On April 1 the Nationalists took control of the Spanish capital.

In quick succession Francisco Franco became the youngest captain, major, colonel, and general in the Spanish Army.

The moment of death for a Republican soldier. With him died hundreds of thousands of others who tried to defeat Franco's Fascist rebellion.

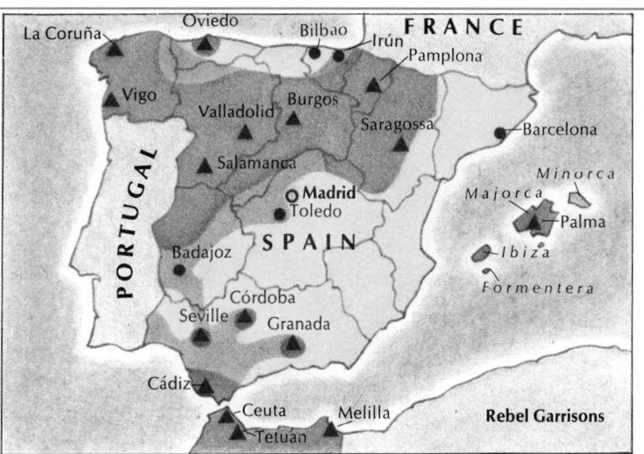

NATIONALIST INSURRECTIONS AND EARLY GAINS
Nationalists gains: ☐July 1936 ☐Aug.–Sept. 1936 ▲Garrisons

VICTORY IN THE SOUTHWEST AND NORTH
Nationalist gains: ☐Oct. 1936–March 1937 ☐April–Oct. 1937

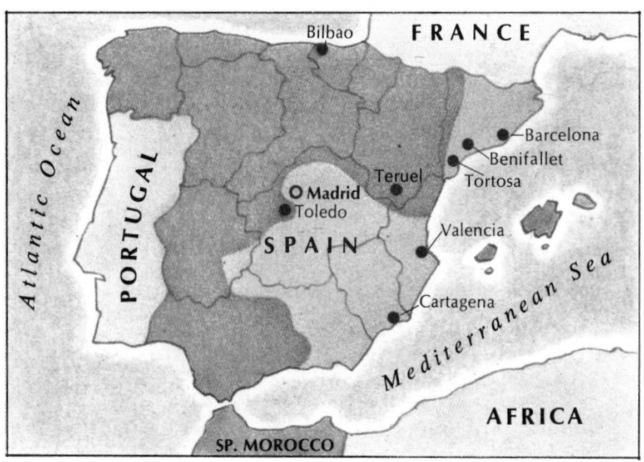

THE DRIVE TO THE SEA AND FINAL VICTORY
Nationalist gains: ☐Nov. 1937–July 1938 ☐Aug. 1938–April 1939

Inevitably the military balance began to tip against the Republic, as Franco's forces, advancing from the south, joined with General Mola's troops near Badajoz. The *pronunciamiento* was now a full-scale civil war, and violence behind the lines became out-and-out terrorism. Peasants and workers in Republican Spain killed priests, factory owners, and soldiers whom they had besieged in their barracks. In Nationalist territory, labor leaders and Republican officials were shot without trial, and Franco's Moorish troops were encouraged to commit massacre.

When it was clear that Britain and France would not aid the Republic, Azaña appealed to the Soviet Union. Soviet aid (food and medical supplies, followed by arms and high-level military advisers) began to flow to Spain. As a result, the Spanish Communist Party attracted more followers, and in the elections of September 1936 Azaña was replaced by the more radical Francisco Largo Caballero. Only weeks later, on October 1, 1936, Franco was proclaimed head of the Nationalist state by General Mola.

Volunteers from other countries began arriving to form the International Brigades—men fleeing Hitler and Mussolini, and liberals, anti-Fascists, Communists, and anarchists from England, Canada, France, Mexico, the United States, and other countries. They first saw action at a desperate stage—in the defense of Madrid in November 1936. Thereafter, they and the Spanish shock troops, organized and led by Communist advisers, were the most dependable troops the Republic could field while it was turning its militiamen into soldiers.

On the Nationalist side, foreign troops in far larger numbers were available. At the battle of Guadalajara in early 1937 some 30,000 Italian soldiers took part —Mussolini's best Blackshirt divisions. Fewer Germans were in Spain, but those that were made up 80 percent of the rebel air force and helped Franco plan his key air attacks. With this support, the Nationalists were able to capture the isolated Basque provinces on Spain's northern coast in the spring of 1937. Heinkel and Junker bombers of the German Condor Legion smashed the town of Guernica, leaving 2,500 dead or wounded and foreshadowing the aerial terror of World War II.

In May 1937 Catalonia exploded with an anarchist uprising. Largo Caballero, now under heavy pressure from the Communists he had helped bring into the government, used Republican troops and Communist assault squads to break down the anarchists' street bar-

THE POLITICS OF INTERVENTION: MEN, MONEY AND IDEALS

In many ways Spain was a testing ground for World War II. There Germany rehearsed the mass-bombing of civilian populations, and Britain, France, and the U.S.A. practiced the appeasement policies that led to Munich; the U.S.S.R. sought to plant communism there, and there thousands of volunteers gained an insight into the coming horrors of global war.

Germany needs to import ore. That is why we want a Nationalist government in Spain, so that we may be able to buy Spanish ore. *—Adolf Hitler, June 27, 1937*

It was in Spain that men learned that one can be right and yet be beaten, that force can vanquish spirit, that there are times when courage is not its own recompense. It is this, doubtless, which explains why so many men, the world over, regard the Spanish drama as a personal tragedy.

—Albert Camus, French author

You have thus helped to strengthen confidence in the new German Army and in the excellence of our new weapons.

—Hitler addressing members of the returning Condor Legion, June 6, 1939

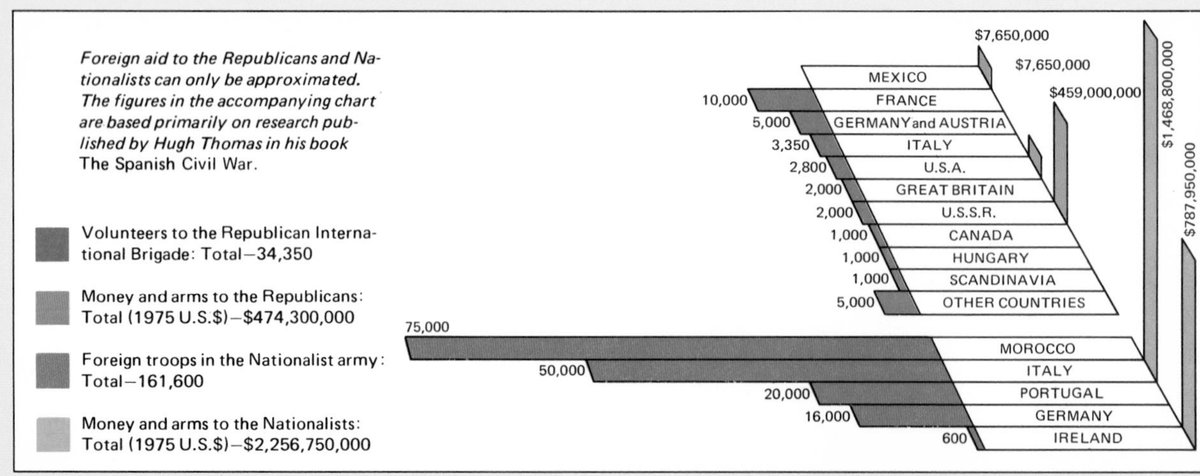

ricades. Thereafter the Communists exercised increasing control over the government. The Socialist Juan Negrín, deeply sympathetic to Russian communism, became Premier in mid-May 1937.

In the winter of 1937–38 the Republicans captured Teruel but were driven out again after two months. Franco followed up with a spring offensive that carried Nationalist troops to the Mediterranean in late April 1938, severing Catalonia from the rest of the Republic. Nightly bombardment, which Madrid had been suffering for more than a year, began at Barcelona. A Republican attack across the Ebro River regained a little of the lost ground, but the pressure of superior arms and training was inexorable, and through the winter of 1938–39 Nationalist troops drove their opponents north toward the French border. Barcelona fell on January 26, and hundreds of thousands of Republican refugees fled into France. Many thousands never returned to their native land.

Madrid was the last center of Republican resistance. After Hitler's bloodless triumph at Munich (see p. 272), Negrín and his colleagues could no longer hope for a change in the attitude of the French, British, or Americans. In the last days of March 1939 four Nationalist armies surrounded the city. There were persistent (and, as it turned out, well-founded) reports of a "fifth column" of Franco sympathizers ready to welcome him to Madrid.

The Generalissimo

As the Popular Front had collapsed under the pressures of defeat and isolation, so Franco's personal prestige had grown. His only possible rival, General Mola, had, like Sanjurjo, died in an airplane accident. The various rightist groups had been amalgamated by Franco in 1937 into a new organization, which upon his victory became the ruling (and only) party in Spain.

During World War II Franco shrewdly disassociated himself from Hitler and Mussolini. He did send the Blue Division of Falangist volunteers to fight with Hitler's army on the Russian front, but mineral exports promised to German arms manufacturers somehow became unavailable, then appeared at British ports; interned Allied nationals were allowed to go home.

For the Republican losers in Spain, the process of arrest and summary execution continued. Tens of thousands were imprisoned. Franco had promised to restore the "traditional values" of Spain; his interpretation of those values proved to be a dictatorship as absolute as any in Spanish history.

"Help Spain" cries the cover of this pro-Republican pamphlet, produced in France and painted by the exiled Spanish artist Joan Miró.

Hot soup warms volunteers of the International Brigade during their first winter of fighting.

In August 1936 the great poet Federico García Lorca was murdered by Nationalist troops and buried in an unmarked grave. These lines for a dead friend, a famous bullfighter, are from one of his last works, "Lament for Ignacio Sánchez Mejías." They also stand as an appropriately bitter elegy for all those who died during the Civil War.

The bull does not know you, nor the fig tree,
nor the horses, nor the ants in your own house.
The child and the afternoon do not know you
because you have died for ever.

The back of the stone does not know you,
nor the black satin in which you crumble.
Your silent memory does not know you
because you have died for ever.

The autumn will come with small white snails,
misty grapes and with clustered hills,
but no one will look into your eyes
because you have died for ever.

Because you have died for ever,
like all the dead of the Earth,
like all the dead who are forgotten
in a heap of lifeless dogs.

Translated by Stephen Spender and J. L. Gili

THE LIFE OF THE TIMES 1929-39

***Belongings packed** into an old car, thousands of families followed the example of the 19th-century pioneers and rattled across the plains in search of a better life on the west coast.*

***January 1932:** While Congress debated the establishment of the Reconstruction Finance Corporation, the streets of the capital were jammed with people who were demanding direct action.*

For many Americans the good times of the twenties seemed so good, and the future so bright, that it was hard to imagine living any other way. Employment was up, wages were up. Production, profits, the Dow Jones Index—all were advancing steadily every year, pointing in the general direction of Utopia.

Then something unexpected happened. In October 1929, after years of frenzied speculation and sky-rocketing paper profits, Wall Street's bubble finally burst. Prices mysteriously began to slip, nervous investors started to sell, the decline steepened, and before anything could be done a full-fledged panic had set in.

Across the country there was a rush to withdraw deposits from banks, many of which collapsed under the pressure and wiped out the life savings of millions of ordinary citizens. Then, with fewer and fewer people able to buy as freely as before, industry was forced to curtail production; workers consequently lost their jobs or had their wages cut; and so ran the relentless cycle. Hard times were here.

One of the most perplexing aspects of the Depression's early years was the reluctance of President Herbert Hoover to recognize how bad things actually were. In March 1930, with almost 3 million already out of work, the President predicted that prosperity would return within two months. True to his word, if not to reality, he met a delegation of concerned businessmen that July with the good news: "Gentlemen, you are six weeks too late. The crisis is over."

Two Julys later unemployment had passed the 10 million mark, a "Bonus Army" of jobless war veterans had just been routed from Washington by federal troops, and Hoover's Presidency was in ruins. The public's mood by that time could be summed up in a popular anecdote about a hitchhiker who crossed the country in record time with the help of a sign that warned: "Give me a lift or I'll vote for Hoover."

The Plight of the Farmer

The nation's farmers had had trouble enough trying to survive the recent "prosperity." Throughout the twenties overproduction of crops and the iron law of supply and demand had combined to keep farm revenues perilously low; then in the first three years of the Depression, farm prices dropped a staggering 60 percent—nearly twice the decline in other industries. Unable to meet mortgage payments, thousands of small farmers were dispossessed by the banks, their crops went unharvested, and people in growing numbers began to question the virtue of a free enterprise system that allowed them to go hungry while tons of grain rotted in midwestern store-

This family *of refugees from the Oklahoma drought (right) probably made the trip to California with hope, but etched in their faces is the discouragement that awaited most of those who went west.*

Photographed for *the Farm Security Administration by Arthur Rothstein, this Arkansas sharecropping family typified rural poverty in the U.S.A.*

Veterans participating *in the Bonus Army march try to protect their shelters from the police.*

houses. (Indeed, normally law-abiding citizens were sometimes driven to take matters into their own hands. In one memorable instance an Iowa judge who seemed too quick to approve bank foreclosures was dragged from his courtroom by a mob of local farmers and encouraged to mend his ways with the threat of a lynching.)

To make things even worse, the Great Plains were beset by a two-year plague of duststorms, beginning with the nightmarish "black blizzard" over South Dakota in November 1933. From Canada to Texas millions of acres of crops were ruined in the next few years, leaving behind the vast Dust Bowl of barren earth. Out of this wasteland came bands of so-called Okies, migrating westward like some devastated species toward the still-green valleys of California. There at least they could eke out a lean existence as field hands and day laborers, if they were lucky.

The TVA

In contrast to the drought-stricken Plains states, the Tennessee Valley suffered from an excess of rain. Each year, when the Tennessee River flooded it drastically affected life in the seven river valley states.

One of the few bright spots for farmers during the Depression was the establishment of the TVA, the Tennessee Valley Authority. It was one of the most popular of Roosevelt's progressive measures, and no wonder. Broad, almost visionary in scope, it was the highly successful precursor of much of modern regional planning.

The goal of flood control was achieved, but the first direct benefit was to put thousands of people in the valley to work, clearing forests and building roads and the dams themselves. Thousands more were employed to run the TVA after the system was set up.

Besides flood control, which made farming both possible and profitable in areas previously given up as hopeless, the dams produced hydroelectric power. And electricity opened up a new way of life to many thousands of farm families.

The Cities

Their counterparts in the cities, with nowhere else to go, did whatever they could to weather the economic storm. As unemployment rose, the soon-to-be-familiar symbols of poverty, soup kitchens and breadlines, proliferated across the country. In front of the fashionable stores on New York's Fifth Avenue, well-dressed men who had once been stockbrokers or business executives sold apples for five cents apiece. Artists made chalk drawings on the sidewalk in the hope of eliciting a few coins from appreciative passers-by. When stores went out of business, their display windows were often commandeered by hucksters to hawk worthless medicines, cheap clothes, toys, trinkets, novelties—anything.

Along what is now a scenic park on the West Side of Manhattan there appeared a "hobo jungle" of lean-tos and tar-paper shacks for those with nowhere else to live. These dismal shantytowns—better known as Hoovervilles—sprang up near railroad yards in virtually every U.S. city, their ranks swollen by a steady influx of families thrown out of their apartments for nonpayment of rent. By 1933, with evictions numbering some 17,000 a month in New York City alone, landlords were probably exceeded only by bankers as objects of popular resentment.

FDR Offers a New Deal

Apart from the immediate problems of finding food and shelter, the most disheartening aspect of the Depression was the way it kept getting worse. At length, after a dozen years of "normalcy" under Harding, Coolidge, and Hoover, the American electorate in 1932 was more than ready for a change. In November they got it, voting a Democratic majority into both Houses of Congress and a new President, Franklin D. Roosevelt, into the White House. In his acceptance speech at the Democratic Convention the previous July, Roosevelt had set the tone for his forthcoming campaign for the Presidency: "I pledge you, I pledge myself, to a New Deal for the American people."

It was what the people needed to hear, and when FDR took office in March 1933 he made it clear that the New Deal was more than a slogan. Deploying every area of government to do battle with the Depression, he called Congress into a special session and declared a nationwide bank holiday. Only those banks deemed reliable by federal inspectors were allowed to reopen. During the "First Hundred Days" of the Roosevelt administration the Congress passed an unprecedented array of bills aimed at putting the country back on its feet.

Before long the public was introduced to a bewildering series of so-called alphabet soup agencies: the AAA, CCC, NRA, SEC, TVA, WPA, and so on. The Blue Eagle, symbol of the National Recovery Administration (NRA), became a ubiquitous sight in factories, offices, and store windows across the country.

Perhaps as important as the legislation he pushed through Congress was the psychological lift, the renewed sense of confidence that

John L. Lewis *began working in the coal mines at 15. A gifted orator, he rose to head the United Mine Workers and helped establish the* CIO.

Louisiana Senator *Huey Long, nicknamed the Kingfish, won a national following in the Depression with his "Share the Wealth" program.*

Roosevelt instilled in millions of people. Not the least of his innovations were the "fireside chats" carried by radio from his White House office into living rooms across the country. The first broadcast—on Sunday night, March 12, just eight days after the inauguration—opened with the words that would become as familiar as his upturned cigarette holder: "My friends. . . ."

He spoke that night about the bank crisis, what caused it and what was being done about it, and he did so in such a clear and reassuring way that most of his listeners came away feeling they really *were* his friends. Roosevelt had often expressed concern for the plight of "the forgotten man." As the noted humorist Will Rogers quipped: "I will say one thing for this administration. It's the only time when the fellow with money is worrying more than the one without it."

Of course the ones without money, or without enough of it, still had plenty to worry about, but at least there was some cause for optimism. The National Industrial Recovery Act (NIRA), a keystone of the New Deal, contained an historic clause establishing the right of collective bargaining for workers. The NIRA was ruled unconstitutional in 1935, but most of its prolabor provisions were retained the same year in the Wagner Act, which opened the way for an enormous upswing in union organizing.

The emerging champion of the workingman in the mid-1930's was John L. Lewis, the brilliant and colorful president of the Congress of Industrial Organizations (CIO). In 1937, a landmark year for the labor movement, Lewis personally induced two industrial Goliaths, General Motors and U.S. Steel, to sign union contracts, and so effectively did he mobilize public opinion that never again could government or business leaders safely ignore the voice of organized labor. The trade unions still had many difficult—and sometimes bloody—battles ahead of them, but by the time Lewis stepped down from CIO leadership in 1940, their ultimate victory was assured.

Chasing the Blues Away

Needless to say, even during the Depression there was more to life than political and economic issues. Throughout the thirties at least one industry flourished as never before: the movies. Every week an estimated 85 million fans paid their 25 cents admission (give or take a nickel) to get away from reality for a couple of hours and perhaps to win the raffle or door prize that many theaters were offering as an extra attraction.

Epitomizing the escapist trend, the two biggest hits of the era were Walt Disney's animated version of *Snow White and the Seven Dwarfs* and the film of Margaret Mitchell's bestselling novel of the decade, *Gone With the Wind*. In general, the

***A relieved, departing President Hoover** shakes the hand of a jaunty Roosevelt on Inauguration Day, March 4, 1933.*

***New York City's Central Park,** near the reservoir, was a natural place for the homeless to set up housekeeping.*

***Two little** English girls who caught the public fancy were the daughters of King George VI, Elizabeth and Margaret Rose, posing here with their grandmother.*

***The pageantry and pathos** of the South in the Civil War came alive in* Gone With the Wind. *Clark Gable shone as Rhett Butler, the gambler-profiteer and soldier; Vivien Leigh was Scarlett O'Hara.*

***Fred Astaire and Ginger Rogers** danced the Depression blues away in lighthearted, highstepping musicals. Reading up, scenes from* Top Hat, Carefree, Swingtime, *and* Shall We Dance.

most reliable box office formulas were musicals—Busby Berkeley's extravaganzas (one featured 100 girl pianists), Fred Astaire and Ginger Rogers tripping the light fantastic, Nelson Eddy and Jeanette MacDonald singing their hearts out—and comedies of the sort concocted by the Marx Brothers, W. C. Fields, and Laurel and Hardy.

The thirties also produced a pair of saccharine child superstars, little Shirley Temple and the only slightly larger Mickey Rooney. For more hardnosed audiences there was a durable lineup of tough guys headed by James Cagney, Edward G. Robinson, and George Raft.

In addition to all this, there appeared an impressive array of serious actors—Charles Laughton, Walter Huston, Fredric March—and intelligent, enduring films. These ranged from sophisticated comedies like *It Happened One Night* to searching political dramas like Paul Muni's *The Life of Émile Zola* to such excellent government-sponsored documentaries as Pare Lorentz' *The River* (which was hailed as "the epic of this century" by no less an authority on the subject of epics than James Joyce).

Voices in the Air

Outside the theaters, too, there was usually something to divert people's attention from their problems for at least a little while. Radio, like the movies, enjoyed a phenomenal growth in the thirties, bringing big-city entertainment (and even a little highbrow culture) into households in the remotest parts of the country.

Boys and girls raced home from school to follow the latest adventures of their favorites: Dick Tracy, Jack Armstrong (the All-American Boy), and Little Orphan Annie, who made the transition from the comics. Kids by the thousands joined the clubs dreamed up to sell the sponsors' products. They proudly flashed badges, membership cards, and secret code rings, helpful in decoding broadcast messages.

Evening shows like *The Shadow* and *The Whistler* were popular with children and adults. Sound effects—creaking doors, manic laughs, and footsteps approaching ever closer—added shivers to suspense shows. Comedy stars Jack Benny, Fibber McGee and Molly, and Fred Allen had huge followings.

The weekly schedules offered everything from *Amos 'n' Andy* to *Aïda*, and major news events were covered with a kind of immediacy never before possible, as when H. V.

ootlight Parade, *a typically lavish Busby Berkeley-Lloyd Bacon film, rew on art deco for its sets. Ranks of imaginatively costumed showgirls ere filmed from many angles, particularly above, for maximum effect.*

Radio came into *its own in the thirties; gravel-voiced George Burns and his flighty wife, Gracie Allen, were one of many comedy teams.*

In Disney's 1937 film *the seven dwarfs and the evil Queen upstaged a rather saccharine Snow White.*

Kaltenborn, the nation's star newscaster, made 85 broadcasts in 18 days to report the developing crisis at Munich in September 1938.

In the arts and literature of the period the predominant theme, not too surprisingly, was one of sympathy for the plight of the common man. It was reflected by artists such as Ben Shahn, who depicted the joylessness of city streets; by dramatist Clifford Odets in *Waiting for Lefty* and *Awake and Sing;* by novelist John Dos Passos in his scathing trilogy *U.S.A.,* and by John Steinbeck in *The Grapes of Wrath,* which pictured the desperate life of impoverished farmworkers forced out of the Dust Bowl toward the illusory promised land of California. Two novelists who drew on their southern background for inspiration launched their literary careers in 1929: Thomas Wolfe, with his autobiographical *Look Homeward, Angel,* and William Faulkner, with *The Sound and the Fury.*

At the same time, such literary lions of the twenties as F. Scott Fitzgerald and H. L. Mencken fell from popular esteem almost as abruptly as the stock market crashed. The reading public simply seemed to lose its taste for the frivolous decadence of Fitzgerald's rich heroes and heroines and for Mencken's bilious commentaries on the American cultural scene.

The Gathering Storm

In the end, it was not domestic reforms but events abroad that broke the grip of the Depression. While the U.S.A. remained preoccupied with its own problems, Europe and Asia were moving inexorably closer to the second great holocaust in 20 years. Japan invaded China. Hitler seized total power in Germany. Mussolini conquered Ethiopia. Spain erupted into civil war.

Through all this the U.S.A. tried to preserve its old policy of isolationism, hoping that the storm clouds on the horizon would keep their distance. At the 1939 World's Fair in New York City, which took as its theme "The World of Tomorrow," the future was glowingly depicted as an age of efficiency, prosperity, and international harmony. But one visitor to the fair, a member of the British Parliament, injected a note of realism into the festivities. "We shall not be able to enjoy ourselves again," he reflected, "until Franco's widow tells Stalin on his deathbed that Hitler has been assassinated at Mussolini's funeral."

1938

Appeasement at Munich

Great Britain's Neville Chamberlain makes an eleventh-hour attempt to avert total war with Hitler's Germany.

The fate of Czechoslovakia was precarious in the fall of 1938. Central Europe's most successful postwar democracy was the focal point of a major international crisis brought on by Adolf Hitler's demand that the strategic Czech frontier region known as the Sudetenland, with more than 3 million German inhabitants, be annexed to the Reich. By mid-September war seemed inevitable. Nazi troops were reported massing on Germany's southeastern border, and Czechoslovakian President Eduard Benes ordered full mobilization. At the same time Hitler informed Britain and France that he was prepared to go to war if not granted his demands at once.

Western leaders weighed their course of action. Hitler, they feared, would not hesitate to make good his threat of war if he were denied, but if his troops were permitted to occupy the Sudetenland peacefully, there was a slender hope that war might be averted.

On September 21 Winston Churchill warned of the futility of appeasing Hitler. "The belief that security can be obtained by throwing a small state to the wolves," he cautioned, "is a fatal delusion." But Britain's government was of a different mind. On September 27, Prime Minister Neville Chamberlain stated his position: "However much we may sympathize with a small nation confronted by a big and powerful neighbor, we cannot . . . involve the whole British Empire in a war simply on her account."

Two days later Chamberlain and French Premier Édouard Daladier (France was pledged by treaty to defend Czechoslovakia against foreign aggression) flew to Munich to meet with Hitler and Italian leader Benito Mussolini. Il Duce, Hitler's ally, had persuaded the Fuehrer to hold the conference in the hope of averting a war. On September 30 the four issued a joint agreement granting Hitler's demands almost to the letter, and German troops entered the Sudetenland. Czechoslovakia was not even consulted.

As the Nazi shadow lengthened over Central Europe, Chamberlain returned to London in triumph. Waving a copy of the Munich Agreement on his return, the Prime Minister proclaimed: "This is the second time there has come back from Germany to Downing Street peace with honour. I believe it is peace for our time." Events soon proved him wrong. Within a year Germany marched into Czechoslovakia, conceding parts of the dismembered country to Hungary and Poland; next, she invaded Poland itself.

Appearement and Aggression

The Munich Agreement represented the tragic culmination of the policy of appeasement pursued by Britain and France from 1933 to 1939. Underlying this policy was the assumption that Germany, which had been treated unfairly in the 1919 Treaty of Versailles (see pp. 146–153), should be restored to her rightful place among nations. Once Hitler's seemingly reasonable demands had been granted, the advocates of appeasement believed—as Hitler assured them—that Germany would be satisfied.

The roots of appeasement were many. The leaders of Britain and France misguidedly placed their trust in the power of the League of Nations and the Geneva Disarmament Conference to limit armaments and prevent armed conflict—indeed, so deep-seated were the British and French public's horror of war that their governments steadily reduced armaments appropriations from 1926 to 1933. By 1938 Britain's rearmament program was not yet in full swing. The French, on the other hand, had developed an almost mystical faith in the Maginot Line, and many Frenchmen felt they could make concessions in Central Europe without endangering their own security.

Unwittingly, the advocates of appeasement contributed directly to the success of Hitler's plans for Germany's resurgence. To avenge the hated Versailles Treaty, Hitler withdrew from the League of Nations and the Geneva Disarmament Conference in 1933, and a year later secretly authorized a full-scale buildup of Germany's armed forces, which had been severely restricted by the treaty. In March 1935 Hitler publicly disclosed plans to create an air force and conscript an army; a year later German troops reoccupied the Rhineland, which had been demilitarized in the peace treaty. The Western powers responded with little more than halfhearted protests.

In November 1937 the Fuehrer met secretly with his top political and military aides to present his plans for expansion into Central Europe to obtain more *Lebensraum* ("living space") and natural resources. The first step would be the consolidation of Austria and Czechoslovakia into the Reich. Then Germany could push eastward into Poland and the Ukraine.

In February 1938 Hitler proclaimed to the Reichstag that one of the primary concerns of his regime was "the protection of these fellow Germans who live beyond our frontiers and are unable to ensure for themselves the right to a general freedom, personal, political, and ideological." The first target of the Fuehrer's concern was Austria, whose population was 96 percent

***Hitler's prestige** ran high as he entered Carlsbad in Czechoslovakian Sudetenland in October 1938. Already in control of Austria, he had gained Sudetenland without a shot. Next, at his urging, Poland and Hungary absorbed Czech areas with Polish and Magyar minorities. In 1939 Hungary occupied Ruthenia; Germany took Bohemia, Moravia, and later Slovakia, and also took the seaport of Memel from Lithuania. Italy, emulating Germany, invaded Albania. With Czechoslovakia dismembered, Hitler prepared to invade Poland.*

German-speaking, but which had been expressly forbidden in the Versailles Treaty to unite with Germany. Despite an agreement of mutual respect concluded with Germany in 1936, the weak Austrian government, headed by Chancellor Kurt von Schuschnigg, found it impossible to resist the Nazis' growing power. In February 1938 Hitler presented Schuschnigg with an ultimatum demanding that Arthur Seyss-Inquart, an Austrian Nazi, be given command of Austrian security forces, that a general amnesty for Nazis be issued, and that the Austrian Army be integrated into the Wehrmacht. When Schuschnigg tried to resist, Hitler threatened to invade Austria. Schuschnigg resigned, and Seyss-Inquart requested German intervention to help put down alleged disturbances. On March 12 and 13 German troops marched into Vienna.

None of the signatories of the Versailles Treaty tried to prevent the Nazi takeover of Austria. Britain and France ignored their pledges to guarantee Austrian independence, preferring to view the situation as a "family affair," rather than run the risk of another war.

Operation Green

Meanwhile Hitler, emboldened by his success, pressed forward with Operation Green, the code name for the German occupation of Czechoslovakia. This time, however, the situation was more complex. Czechoslovakia, created in 1918 out of the heart of the old Austro-Hungarian Empire, was the strongest and most democratic of the small nations in Central Europe. It was also the best defended, with a miniature Maginot Line along the Bohemian border and a well-equipped army of 205,000 men. Under its first two Presidents, Thomas Masaryk and Eduard Benes, the country had achieved economic prosperity and relative political stability. Moreover, the maintenance of Czechoslovakia's independence was the key link in an intricate network of treaties and pledges designed to protect Central Europe from domination by either of its powerful neighbors, Germany or the U.S.S.R.

Czechoslovakia, however, had not overcome the problem of her ethnic minorities. In addition to 10 million Czechs and Slovaks, the country included nearly 1 million Hungarians, half a million Ruthenians, 80,000 Poles, and more than 3 million Germans. The most vocal and numerically powerful of the minorities were the Germans, who lived in the Sudetenland, and Hitler masterfully used them as a pretext for intervening in Czech affairs.

From the very start the Sudeten Germans had resented their inclusion in a Slavic state, but until Hitler came to power in Germany, they had no radical reform movement. With Hitler's encouragement, however, embittered Sudeten citizens joined the extremist Sudetendeutsche Partei ("Sudeten German Party," S.D.P.), which supported full autonomy for the Sudetenland. By 1938 the S.D.P. had become the main spokesman for the Sudeten Germans.

HITLER'S COVERT REARMAMENT

Because the Treaty of Versailles limited German arms manufacture, Hitler skillfully disguised his first preparations for war. The network of highways that would soon facilitate troop movements was begun in 1933 to provide work for the unemployed; clubs and youth organizations that seemed to encourage sports and exercise actually gave military training and Nazi indoctrination. In 1935 Hitler announced publicly that Germany was rearming.

1933: Hitler opens a roadbuilding project, while Goering's aides (right) train pilots at a glider club.

In March 1938 Hitler summoned the S.D.P. leader, Konrad Henlein, to Berlin and instructed him to take an increasingly uncompromising stance, fomenting internal dissension whenever possible. At an S.D.P. rally at Carlsbad (now Karlovy Vary) on April 24 Henlein called for recognition of an autonomous German region, politically aligned with Nazi Germany. The Benes government rejected the demand outright.

In Berlin, a few days before the Carlsbad speech, Hitler had secretly ordered his chief of staff, Gen. Wilhelm Keitel, to draw up plans for the invasion of Czechoslovakia. Meanwhile, Britain and France, in total ignorance of the German role in Sudeten affairs, urged the Czechs to compromise with the S.D.P.

Serious clashes between Czechs and Sudeten Germans erupted during local election campaigns in May, and on May 20 German troops were reported near the Bohemian border. President Benes ordered partial mobilization, and Britain, France, and the U.S.S.R. informed Hitler that they were prepared to defend Czechoslovakia. Hitler reluctantly backed down. A few days later, however, he ordered Keitel to prepare to invade Czechoslovakia on October 1.

Under further pressure from France and Britain to find a peaceful solution to the Sudeten problem, President Benes agreed to hold negotiations with Henlein, and talks opened on June 23. The S.D.P., however, refused to compromise. To break the deadlock Britain sent a fact-finding mission headed by Lord Runciman to Czechoslovakia as "mediator and adviser." His delegation was not acquainted with Central European problems nor with the complexities of Czechoslovakia's minority situation. Moreover, this British intervention in an internal Czech problem thrust the Sudeten German issue into the international arena. Inadvertently the British had given Hitler his excuse to intervene at an opportune time.

Under pressure from the Runciman mission, Benes conceded point after point to the S.D.P., but Henlein insisted that the Carlsbad program be granted in full, and that the treaties of alliance between Czechoslovakia, France, and the U.S.S.R. be abandoned. On September 5 Benes, anxious for continued French and

At the age of six, boys donned the uniform of the Hitler Youth Organization and attended open-air camps (left). Below: other youthful Nazis wait to see a film and touring exhibition in a massive propaganda truck.

Chamberlain, *Daladie Hitler, and Mussolin appear somber at th September 29 Munic meeting. Outside, tw Czech representative wait nervously to hea the fate of their country*

British support, agreed to grant all demands. Unprepared for this turn of events, Henlein broke off negotiations. Hitler, who wanted a pretext to occupy not just the Sudetenland but all of Czechoslovakia, was equally alarmed by Benes' sudden generosity.

With the deadline for Operation Green drawing near, the Fuehrer instructed Henlein to toughen his stance. The S.D.P. leader rejected Benes' concessions and insisted that the Sudetenland be granted full self-determination. Amid mounting tension Hitler delivered an emotional tirade at a Nazi Party rally at Nuremberg on September 12, blaming Benes for the present crisis and demanding self-determination for the "oppressed" Sudeten Germans.

The speech provoked mass demonstrations in the Sudetenland, and armed clashes between Czechs and Germans broke out in Carlsbad and other Sudeten cities. The government in Prague declared martial law, and calm was temporarily restored. Henlein and several thousand supporters fled to Germany.

The French government, hopelessly divided over its response, turned to Britain for leadership, and Chamberlain decided to fly to Germany to confer personally with Hitler. At the meeting at Berchtesgaden on September 15 the Fuehrer insisted that the Sudetenland be given full self-determination and emphasized his willingness to go to war. Returning to London, Chamberlain met nervously with his Cabinet and Daladier, and on September 19 the British and French presented

Sudeten Germans *eagerly saluted this sign in Klein-Philippsreut on October 1, 1938. "Sudeten German comrades!" the announcement read. "The hour of liberation has come. German troops are about to take your country under the supremacy of the Reich."*

After the Munich *Agreement was signed, Hitler exclaimed angrily: "That fellow Chamberlain has spoiled my entry into Prague!" But he was not delayed long. On March 15, 1939, his troops entered Prague, and Hitler proclaimed, "Czechoslovakia has ceased to exist."*

a new proposal to the Czech government, calling for an immediate plebiscite to arrange for the transfer of all Sudeten areas where Germans were in the majority. When the Czechs rejected the plan, Britain and France warned that they would not feel bound to defend Czechoslovakia in the event of a German invasion. The Czechs reluctantly accepted the plan, explaining in an official communique that: "We had no choice, because we were left alone."

With Czechoslovakia's approval in hand, Chamberlain flew to meet Hitler at Bad Godesberg on the Rhine on September 22, but the Fuehrer angrily rejected the plan, which guaranteed the integrity of the rest of Czechoslovakia. He demanded that the territories in question (including all of Bohemia and Moravia) be occupied by the German Army prior to the October 1 plebiscite, or he could not be responsible for the consequences. Chamberlain asked Hitler to delay military action until he could again confer with members of his Cabinet and with the Czech leaders.

On September 23 rumors of German troop concentrations on the Sudeten border were confirmed in Prague, and President Benes ordered a full mobilization. Three days later Hitler delivered a vicious attack against Benes and threatened an immediate invasion if the Czechs did not concede. "It is the last territorial claim which I have to make in Europe," he insisted, "but it is the claim from which I will not recede. . . ."

The Munich Agreement

The next evening Chamberlain announced to the British nation that his government was not prepared to go to war to defend Czechoslovakia. On the 28th he told a cheering House of Commons that he would again fly to Germany, this time to attend a summit meeting with Hitler, Mussolini, and Daladier.

Neither Czechoslovakia nor the U.S.S.R., which was standing by its treaty to guarantee the Czech borders, was invited to the conference. The talks opened at 12:45 p.m. on September 29, and an agreement was concluded in the early hours of September 30. It provided for immediate German military occupation of the Sudetenland and called for a plebiscite to determine areas for additional annexation. France and Britain agreed to guarantee the post-plebiscite boundaries.

Apart from a few minor concessions, the final agreement granted all of Hitler's demands. At one stroke he received some 11,000 square miles of territory and 3.6 million people, including nearly 800,000 Czechs. Without firing a shot, Germany had captured Czechoslovakia's border defenses and at least 75 percent of her industrial resources.

"We are in the presence of a disaster of the first magnitude which has befallen Great Britain and France," cried Winston Churchill above his fellow countrymen's general applause of the Munich Agreement. In the next months Hitler pressed forward with his plans to absorb the rest of Czechoslovakia. On October 5 President Benes resigned and went into exile. His successor, Emil Hacha, fought in vain to preserve his country's integrity, but his position grew ever weaker. On March 14, 1939, Slovakia and Ruthenia, prompted by Hitler, declared their independence from Prague. That same day Hitler bullied Hacha into accepting a German Protectorate over Bohemia and Moravia. Within 24 hours the Wehrmacht had occupied Prague, and Hitler triumphantly proclaimed to the German people that "Czechoslovakia has ceased to exist."

This final betrayal at last laid bare the folly of appeasement. Against the tyranny of Nazi Germany, the democracies of Britain and France could not hope to preserve the peace indefinitely. At most, by throwing Czechoslovakia to the Nazi wolves, the West gained a little time to prepare for the by then unavoidable nightmare of another world war.

1939

Live From New York City: Television!

Combining the magic of radio and the movies, a new communications medium makes its American debut.

On the afternoon of April 30, 1939, hundreds of thousands of visitors jammed Flushing Meadow in New York City to watch the ceremonies officially opening the World's Fair. The theme of the fair was "The World of Tomorrow," and in at least one aspect it was indeed a harbinger of the future. Amid the familiar battery of radio microphones on the speakers' platform was a conspicuous intruder: a television camera. The National Broadcasting Company (NBC), under the auspices of its parent company, the Radio Corporation of America (RCA), was telecasting the ceremonies as part of its exhibit, and thereby initiating the first regular television service in the United States.

The show began at 12:30 p.m. with a view of the fair's already famous symbols, the Trylon and the Perisphere. The camera moved across the Court of Peace for a panorama of the crowds, fountains, and flags, then focused on the approaching parade of U.S. servicemen, foreign delegations in native dress, and thousands of fairground workmen decked out in gleaming white overalls and caps. The huge procession was led by New York's high-spirited mayor, Fiorello H. LaGuardia, who startled NBC's personnel by walking right up to the camera and smiling into the lens. A short time later President Franklin D. Roosevelt's car arrived at the reviewing platform. After the parade was over, the camera remained fixed on the podium for a series of speeches, ending with the fair's official opening a few minutes after 3 p.m.

Several hundred viewers had the novel experience of watching the telecast on 9- by 12-inch viewing screens at the RCA exhibit. In addition the program was relayed by cable from the fairground to NBC's transmitter on top of the Empire State Building, and seen by audiences at Radio City Music Hall. Within days people were lined up by the thousands in Manhattan department stores to see demonstrations of the new device, and thousands more flocked to the fair at night to watch NBC's hour-long variety shows.

The Beginnings of Television

Television's slow, complex evolution had begun at least as far back as 1884, when a Russo-German inventor named Paul Nipkow patented a device for relaying pictures. The heart of Nipkow's system was a "scanning disk," a rapidly spinning wheel, perforated with holes. Behind the disk was an illuminated scene. As the disk spun, its perforations broke up the scene into dots of light and shadow. The dots were then converted into electrical signals and telegraphed to a receiver with an identical, synchronized disk, where a reverse process reconstructed a crude image.

The device, however, could not scan quickly enough or with sufficient precision to achieve high quality pictures. In the early 1920's a Russian immigrant to the U.S.A., Vladimir Zworykin, developed an electronic scanning system. In 1923 he filed a patent application for his Iconoscope, a television camera tube that became the basis of modern picture transmission. Inside the tube was a plate covered with a light-sensitive metal. When the camera was focused on a scene, dots formed by an electron beam became electrically charged in proportion to the intensity of the light striking them. An electron gun continuously scanned the plate, passing over each dot just long enough to pick up its charge. After this information, transmitted as an electrical code to a receiving set, was decoded, another electron gun "painted" the picture on a phosphorescent viewing screen.

While Zworykin was trying to perfect his Iconoscope a number of scientists were working along similar lines. Among them were Philo T. Farnsworth, a prodigy who demonstrated his first closed-circuit system when he was barely 21, and Allen B. Dumont, who developed the first high-quality picture tubes. By the late 1920's, however, the clear lead in television research in the United States was held by RCA, which had hired Zworykin in 1929. RCA made the first experimental broadcast of an all-electronic video

***When TV became** part of American life, so did some of its stars. Among the most enduring, and endearing, have been (clockwise from the top): Doc, Kitty, and Matt Dillon of* Gunsmoke; *Big Bird,* Sesame Street*'s unlikely learning aid; Jack Paar, who led the field of talk shows for five years; Lucy, whom everybody loved as queen of the comedies; Edward R. Murrow, who told it as it was on his news show,* See It Now; *Ed Sullivan, the variety king who launched the Beatles; and Dr. Kildare, the handsome healer with winning ways. In the center, the moment when it all began: David Sarnoff at the New York World's Fair in 1939, giving the first-ever publicly televised speech. He called it "Birth of an Industry."*

system in 1933, and in April 1939 RCA made its public debut at the New York World's Fair. Network television had begun.

But World War II nearly halted the growth of American television. Electronics factories converted to wartime production; only six television stations continued broadcasting. For the few who had purchased home sets, RCA's programs were supplemented by those of two rival companies, the Columbia Broadcasting System (CBS) and the Dumont Television Network.

On the other side of the Atlantic the British Broadcasting Company (BBC) had launched its first television service on November 2, 1936, with daily two-hour broadcasts. In 1937 the BBC's coverage of King George VI's coronation was seen by some 50,000 viewers, and by 1939, when the government suspended television broadcasting for the duration of the war, about 20,000 homes in Britain had TV sets.

The Postwar Boom

Television did not come into its own until after the end of the war. In 1946 the BBC resumed regular programing and the U.S. government lifted its ban on the manufacture of new sets. In the United States, between 1949 and 1951, the year of the first coast-to-coast broadcast, the number of television sets jumped from 1 million to more than 10 million. By 1958 there were 523 stations and nearly 47 million home sets.

In an amazingly short time the public abandoned other forms of entertainment and began staying home by the millions to eat TV dinners in front of the living room screen. Movies, newspapers, and magazines all suffered precipitous declines, and even radio had to fight for its survival, abandoning comedy and drama for around-the-clock music and news.

A typical evening's fare on U.S. television might have included a stage play on the "General Electric Theater," baseball or boxing on the "Gillette Cavalcade of Sports," headlines on the "Camel News Caravan," and light entertainment on Milton Berle's "Texaco Star Theater." As the names suggest, early programs were sponsored by individual companies, which bought regular time slots from the networks and provided their own shows. Even though production costs were huge in comparison with those of radio, a sponsor could produce his own 39-week series for about $1 million. By the mid-1950's, however, production expenses had risen so high that sponsors were forced to share their time slots with other advertisers.

In contrast, British television began as a noncommercial enterprise. As a nonprofit public corporation financed by annual license fees on radio and television sets, the BBC from the start leaned more toward cultural and educational programing than the lighter, more commercial American style.

In 1955, however, the British government ended the BBC's exclusive use of the airwaves by permitting the creation of commercial networks under the control of the Independent Broadcasting Authority.

In the U.S.A. in the 1950's the first local noncommercial, or educational, stations began to operate. In 1967 Congress established the Corporation for Public Broadcasting to oversee their activities. Community Antenna Television (CATV), financed by monthly fees from subscribers, brought additional alternatives to network broadcasts. Originally designed as a means of improving home reception in certain areas, CATV, or cable television, gradually began offering nonnetwork shows and exploring such areas as two-way video relay systems.

Television in Other Countries

Worldwide, the growth of regular television broadcasting was slower than in the U.S. and Britain, not beginning in most countries until the 1950's. In Latin America the new industry developed on the U.S. pattern, with commercially sponsored programing subject to varying degrees of government control or censorship. In Argentina, Brazil, and Mexico, for example, all programs must be approved by the government before they are aired. At first most Latin American broadcasts were of imported U.S. shows, but recently there has been an increase in the number of domestically produced programs.

European television, on the other hand, followed the British model, with broadcasting controlled by a public or semipublic corporation financed by license fees on home receivers. Television in Japan, New Zealand, Australia, and Canada developed along similar lines. Rising production costs, however, forced a number of countries—notably France, Italy, and Germany—to begin selling commercial time to advertisers. A similar combination of public and commercial interests dominates Swiss and Swedish television.

Television broadcasting in the Soviet Union, Poland, Czechoslovakia, Romania, Bulgaria, Yugoslavia, and Hungary is controlled and financed by the state. The same is true in many African and Asian nations.

A "Global Village"?

In the United States radio had taken two generations to become a household necessity; television became seemingly indispensable in less than one generation. Partly because of television's meteoric growth, and despite its phenomenal popularity, remarkably little is known about its social impact. But critics have begun their widely different assessments.

To Marshall McLuhan, the oracle of the modern communications media, the television screen has become an extension of the viewer, putting him, since satellite transmissions began in 1962, in immediate and

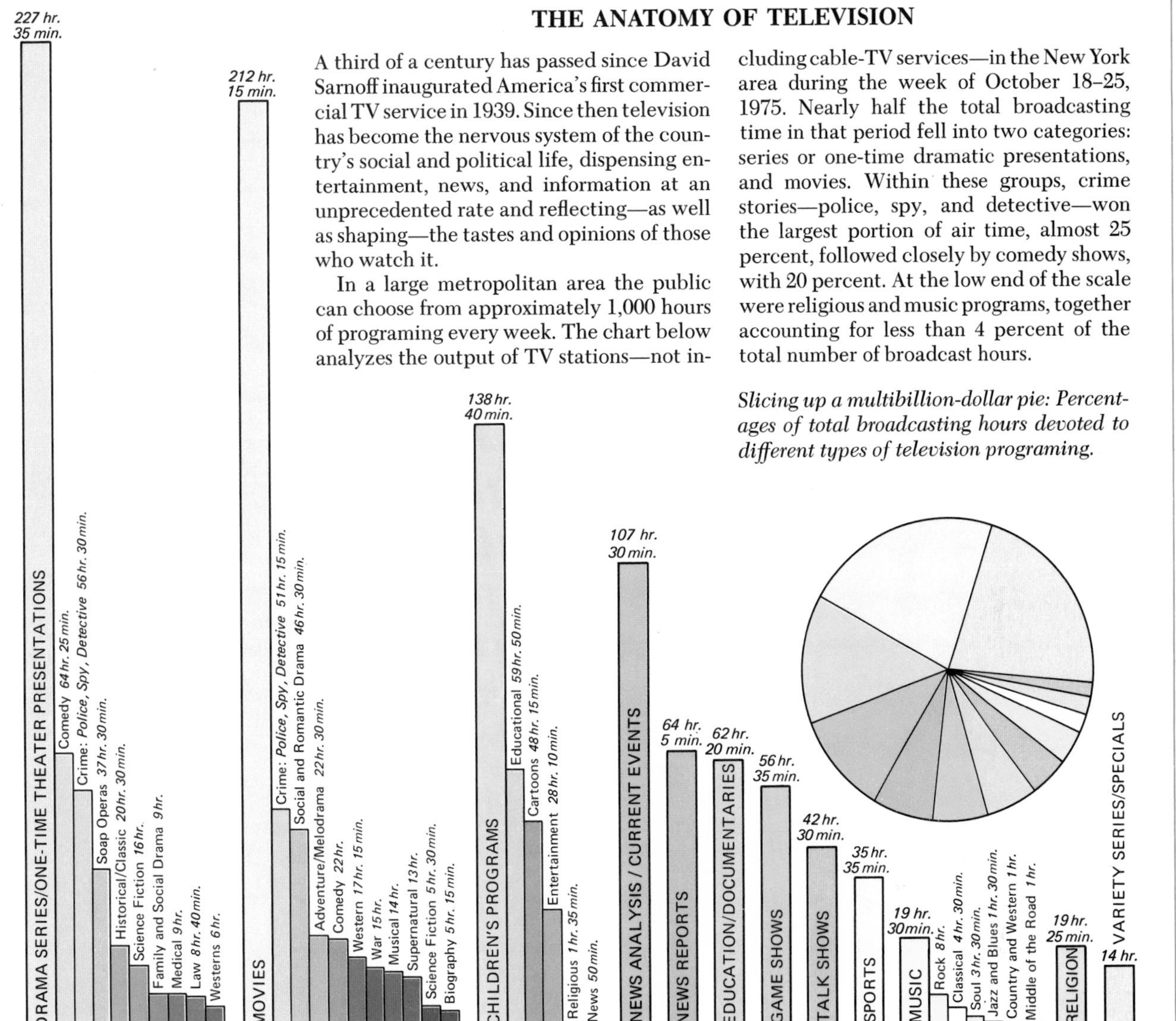

THE ANATOMY OF TELEVISION

A third of a century has passed since David Sarnoff inaugurated America's first commercial TV service in 1939. Since then television has become the nervous system of the country's social and political life, dispensing entertainment, news, and information at an unprecedented rate and reflecting—as well as shaping—the tastes and opinions of those who watch it.

In a large metropolitan area the public can choose from approximately 1,000 hours of programing every week. The chart below analyzes the output of TV stations—not including cable-TV services—in the New York area during the week of October 18–25, 1975. Nearly half the total broadcasting time in that period fell into two categories: series or one-time dramatic presentations, and movies. Within these groups, crime stories—police, spy, and detective—won the largest portion of air time, almost 25 percent, followed closely by comedy shows, with 20 percent. At the low end of the scale were religious and music programs, together accounting for less than 4 percent of the total number of broadcast hours.

Slicing up a multibillion-dollar pie: Percentages of total broadcasting hours devoted to different types of television programing.

intimate touch with events all over the earth. "Ours is a brand-new allatonceness," writes McLuhan. " 'Time' has ceased, 'space' has vanished. We now live in a *global* village . . . a simultaneous happening." Other critics claim that, on the contrary, the TV screen has become a kind of barrier to community experience; that it promotes vicarious living at the expense of actual contact with other people and places.

No one, however, denies that television has changed social patterns. On-the-spot coverage of political conventions, congressional hearings, and United Nations sessions has opened to public scrutiny a realm of activity formerly reserved for a privileged few. Political careers have been made, destroyed, and sometimes resurrected through television. Horrors of all kinds —battle footage from Vietnam, race riots in Newark, and starvation in Africa—have literally been brought home, to shock or numb the conscience of millions of viewers while a relentless parade of advertisements drums out the doctrine of consumption. As technology expands its powers, the debate over television's potential impact will continue.

For television has invaded many more areas of our world, from spy-in-the-sky TV satellites to computer monitors and street-corner cameras that serve as electronic policemen; from cameras lodged in the noses of bombs to direct them to their targets to the wall-sized viewing screens, video casettes, and three-dimensional pictures that the industry foresees. Whether we like it or not, the tiny screen that first began to glow for the American public at the World's Fair in 1939 is already providing much of the light by which we lead our lives.

AN ALMANAC 1929-39

1929

Oct. 29 The New York Stock Exchange suffers record losses, ushers in a worldwide depression (see pp. 222–227).

1930

Jan. 28 Spanish Premier Miguel Primo de Rivera resigns following student agitation and military revolt, but widespread unrest continues.

Mar. 12 Indian leader Mohandas K. Gandhi begins his second civil disobedience campaign to protest British government's salt tax.

Apr. 22 London Naval Conference ends with agreement on partial naval limitation and disarmament signed by Japan, Great Britain, and U.S.A.

June 17 President Hoover signs into law protectionist Smoot-Hawley Tariff, despite strong opposition of more than 1,000 economists. Other nations soon retaliate by raising their own tariffs, contributing to worldwide depression.

July 16 German President Paul von Hindenburg authorizes budget by decree after Reichstag rejects it—a step toward totalitarian government.

Sept. 8–22 Canadian Parliament emergency legislation to combat depression includes tariff increases and government-sponsored public works.

Sept. 14 Adolf Hitler's National Socialists (Nazis) emerge as a major party in German Reichstag elections; they oppose payment of war reparations and stress national pride.

Oct. 14 In Finland rightwing coup directed against Communist influence fails, but the government takes strong measures to curb communism. Similar coup attempt in 1932 also fails.

Dec. 12 Allied soldiers evacuate Saar region of Germany, which they have occupied since World War I.

1931

Mar. 4 With signing of Delhi Pact, Gandhi ends second civil disobedience campaign and British release nonviolent political prisoners.

May 11 Financial collapse of Central Europe begins with failure of Austria's largest bank, the Creditanstalt.

June 20 President Hoover proposes one-year moratorium on all debt and reparation payments for World War I. Most governments accept quickly.

June 28 The Republican-Socialist coalition wins majority in Spanish elections. On Nov. 12 assembly forbids return of exiled King Alfonso XIII.

July 13 All banks in Germany close following Danatbank failure.

Sept. 18 Japanese troops attack Mukden, Manchuria; conquer three eastern provinces by Feb. 1932. China appeals to League of Nations.

Sept. 21 Great Britain abandons gold standard because of worsening world financial situation; value of pound falls.

Dec. 9 Spain adopts constitution as Second Republic. Government empowered to nationalize church property.

1932

Jan. 4 Colonial government of India arrests Gandhi, who later begins "fast unto death" to win suffrage for "untouchables."

Jan. 7 Secretary of State Henry Stimson, protesting Japanese occupation of Manchuria, says U.S.A. will not recognize territory gained by force of arms.

Feb. 2 Geneva Disarmament Conference opens and deliberates until July; fails to agree on disarmament terms or international police force.

Feb. 18 Japan establishes puppet state of Manchukuo (Manchuria).

Mar. 9 Eamon De Valera becomes head of Irish Free State government after his republican party scores a victory in parliamentary elections.

Apr. 10 Paul von Hindenburg reelected President of Germany, defeating Adolf Hitler by 6 million votes; Nazis excluded from Cabinet.

July 5 Antonio de Oliveira Salazar elected Premier of Portugal; establishes new, essentially Fascist state.

July 28 "Bonus army" of ex-servicemen demanding money driven from Washington, D.C., by federal troops.

July 31 Nazi Party gains significant number of seats in Reichstag elections.

Nov. 8 Democrat Franklin D. Roosevelt defeats President Hoover by wide margin in U.S. election.

1933

Jan. 30 Adolf Hitler was appointed Chancellor of Germany by President Hindenburg; coalition cabinet formed.

Feb. 23 Japanese troops attack Chinese land north of Great Wall. By truce signed May 31, province of Jehol is added to Manchukuo.

Feb. 24 League of Nations censures Japan for actions in Manchuria and adopts policy of nonrecognition of Manchukuo. Japan gives notice Mar. 27 it will withdraw from league.

Feb. 27 Reichstag fire gives Hitler excuse to round up Communists and to acquire dictatorial powers (see pp. 232–237).

Mar. 6 President Roosevelt, 2 days after his inauguration, closes banks and prohibits export of gold. Within one week nation's sound banks reopen.

Mar. 23 Reichstag's Enabling Act sets aside constitution and allows Hitler to bypass Reichstag, thus establishing Nazi dictatorship in Germany and enabling Hitler to suppress labor unions and political parties.

Apr. 1 Nazi persecution of Jews becomes official with nationwide boycott of Jewish businesses.

Apr. 19 U.S.A. abandons gold standard.

May 12 U.S. Congress passes Federal Emergency Relief Act authorizing $500 million to aid unemployed.

July 14 Nazi Party is declared the only legal political party in Germany.

Oct. 14 Germany quits League of Nations and Geneva conference.

Nov. 16 U.S.A. establishes diplomatic relations with U.S.S.R. after 16 years.

Dec. 5 Prohibition in U.S.A. repealed by 21st amendment to Constitution.

1934

Feb. 8 National Union coalition cabinet formed in France to avert civil war after rightwing riots in Paris.

Feb. 12 Four days of civil war in Austria follow ban by Chancellor Engelbert Dollfuss on all political parties except his own. Social Democratic Party destroyed.

June 30 Ernst Roehm and many other Nazi leaders executed for allegedly plotting against Hitler. This bloody purge strengthens Hitler's hand; he becomes President of Germany after Hindenburg's death on Aug. 2.

July 25 Austrian Chancellor Dollfuss murdered during attempted Nazi coup.

Sept. 18 U.S.S.R. admitted to membership in League of Nations.

Oct. 9 King Alexander of Yugoslavia assassinated at Marseilles by Macedonian revolutionary. League of Nations is successful in averting war between Yugoslavia and Hungary.

Oct. 16 Mao Tse-tung's Chinese Communist guerrillas begin their famous Long March (see pp. 250–255).

Dec. 1 Sergei Kirov, close associate of Stalin, assassinated following Stalin's purge of about 1 million Russian Communists from the party. Stalin makes assassination excuse for new purge.

Dec. 19 Japan renounces Washington treaty of 1922 on Japanese naval arms.

1935

Mar. 1 Saar basin returned to Germany following plebiscite.

Mar. 16 Hitler denounces Versailles treaty clauses limiting German armaments and reintroduces conscription.

May 27 U.S. Supreme Court declares unconstitutional National Industrial Recovery Act passed two years earlier.

June 12 Three-year Chaco War between Bolivia and Paraguay ends.

July 25–Aug. 20 Comintern, worldwide association of Communist parties, urges Communists in democratic countries to unite with moderates in "popular fronts" against fascism.

Aug. 2 Great Britain's Government of India Act divides India into 11 self-governing provinces, but British Parliament retains ultimate control.

Aug. 14 Social Security Act takes effect in U.S.A.; provides pensions for workers from age 65, financed by new taxes on employees and employers.

Sept. 15 Nuremberg Laws deprive Jews of German citizenship and ban intermarriage with Germans. As a result many Jews leave Germany.

Oct. 3 Mussolini's army invades Ethiopia. League of Nations brands Italy the aggressor; imposes economic sanctions.

1936

Jan. 20 Edward VIII becomes King of England upon death of George V.

Feb. 16 Popular Front coalition of leftist parties wins Spanish elections.

Mar. 7 Germany reoccupies Rhineland in violation of Versailles treaty and Locarno Pact.

Apr. 28 Sixteen-year-old Farouk becomes King of Egypt upon death of his father, King Fuad; signs mutual defense treaty with Britain in August.

May 5 Italy occupies Addis Ababa; formally annexes Ethiopia (May 9). On July 4 League of Nations lifts economic sanctions against Italy, marking failure of international body to keep peace.

June 4 Popular Front government established in France under Socialist Premier Léon Blum.

July 17 The Spanish Civil War begins with army revolt in Morocco; spreads to mainland (see pp. 260–265).

Aug. 19–23 In Moscow Communist leaders publicly confess to a conspiracy against Stalin. (It will later be disclosed that brain washing and torture were used to extract confessions.)

Oct. 1 Gen. Francisco Franco named head of Spanish state by Nationalists. Germany and Italy send weapons and "volunteers" to help Franco; U.S.S.R. aids Spanish Loyalists.

Oct. 25 German-Italian Pact marks beginning of Berlin-Rome Axis.

Nov. 3 U.S. President Roosevelt re-elected in sweeping victory over Republican Alfred M. Landon.

Dec. 10 King Edward VIII abdicates British throne to marry divorced woman, U.S.-born Mrs. Wallis Warfield Simpson, after Baldwin government reaffirms opposition to the marriage. Edward's brother becomes King George VI.

Dec. 12 Sian Incident. Gen. Chiang Kai-shek kidnaped by Chinese warlord; forced to declare war on Japan. Making some concessions to Communists, Chiang wins wide support throughout China and is released Dec. 25.

1937

Feb. 5 President Roosevelt asks U.S. Congress for power to appoint more Justices to Supreme Court but is refused.

Apr. 26 Guernica, the "holy city" in Spain's Basque region, bombed by German airplanes; first major bombing of civilian population in history.

May 1 U.S. Neutrality Act, forbidding arms exports to warring nations, signed by President Roosevelt.

May 28 Stanley Baldwin retires and Neville Chamberlain becomes Prime Minister of Great Britain.

June 12 Eight Soviet generals executed after secret court-martial convicts them of conspiring with Germans and Japanese.

July 7 Following incident at Marco Polo Bridge Japan launches full-scale but undeclared war on China. Bombing and atrocities outrage world opinion.

Dec. 12 Sinking of U.S. gunboat *Panay* in Yangtze River by Japanese aircraft causes diplomatic crisis. Japan apologizes; promises that she will pay reparations to U.S.A.

1938

Feb. 20 Anthony Eden resigns as British Foreign Secretary to protest Chamberlain's policy of appeasing Fascist dictators.

Mar. 2–15 Moscow trials of Nikolai Bukharin, Alexei Rykov, and others end with conviction and execution.

Mar. 12 German Army invades Austria without resistance; Austria officially annexed Mar. 13.

Mar. 18 Mexico seizes U.S. and British oil properties valued at $450 million.

Mar. 28 Japan sets up puppet Chinese government at Nanking.

May 20 Czechs mobilize in anticipation of possible German aggression to attain Sudetenland Germans' demands for autonomy. France and Great Britain strongly support Czechoslovakia.

Sept. 7 Sudeten Germans break off relations with Czech government amid public disorders. Chamberlain meets Hitler Sept. 15, agrees to his annexing German areas of Czechoslovakia.

Sept. 30 Munich Agreement between Chamberlain, Hitler, Mussolini, and Premier Daladier of France accepts Germany's claim to some 11,000 square miles of Czechoslovakian territory.

Oct. 1 Germany marches into Sudetenland. Czech President Eduard Benes resigns Oct. 5. Poland and Hungary seize Czech frontier areas Nov. 2.

Nov. 9–10 Nazi anti-Semitic pogroms in Germany lead to sending thousands of Jews to concentration camps.

Dec. 23 General Franco's armies begin their campaign in Catalonia.

1939

Jan. 26 General Franco's rebel forces capture Barcelona. Within two weeks they conquer Catalonia. Franco's government is officially recognized by Britain and France in late Feb.

Mar. 15 German troops invade Moravia and Bohemia in Czechoslovakia, then set up a German protectorate. It is now clear that Adolf Hitler has territorial ambitions beyond that of the German-inhabited areas of other countries. Appeasement policies dropped.

Mar. 28 Spanish Civil War ends when Madrid surrenders to General Franco.

Mar. 28 Poland rejects Hitler's demand that the Free City of Danzig be ceded to Germany; Britain and France pledge to support Poland.

Apr. 7 Italian troops invade Albania; King Zog flees into exile. Albania's union with Italy proclaimed Apr. 12.

1939-45 THE WAR YEARS

We shall fight on the beaches, we shall fight on the landing-grounds, we shall fight in the fields and in the streets, we shall fight in the hills; we shall never surrender.

—Winston Churchill, Speech on Dunkirk, House of Commons, June 4, 1940

1939-45

Although the art of propaganda reached new levels of sophistication during World War II, certain themes were used again and again. The most popular, on both sides, was that of a woman and child bestially menaced. Another, favored by the Allies, portrayed the Nazis' contempt for religion with daggers or jackboots smashing through stained glass windows.

Even today, more than 30 years after the end of World War II, it is difficult to assess its total cost precisely. Some 55 million men, women, and children died, the greatest number in East Asia and Eastern Europe. In most belligerent countries the civilian death toll was greater than that of the military; Britain, Canada, and the United States were among the exceptions. Aerial bombardment flattened whole cities, destroying great medieval cathedrals and priceless museums as well as factories and homes. Centuries of man's noblest, most deeply humane accomplishments in the arts and in learning were consumed in the flames.

Lives were disrupted; families were wrenched apart. Millions of people were first psychologically humiliated, then deprived of their basic human rights, and finally killed because they were of the wrong race or the wrong religion or were "politically unreliable."

There were echoes of another war. As in World War I, Great Britain, France, and the 47 countries that fought alongside them were called the Allies. Germany, Italy, Japan, and the nations aligned with them were the Axis. One view of history is that the two wars were part of the same conflict, the years between only an armed truce.

But the weapons that were new and primitive in World War I were perfected by World War II, and the techniques of warfare gained a deadly sophistication. The German blitzkrieg ("lightning war")—a closely coordinated offensive combining attacks by air, tanks, and infantry—was a new development. It proved particularly effective against Poland, France, and the Low Countries. After the astonishingly swift defeat of France, Britain was left to face the German onslaught alone. In the Far East Japan soon overran Burma, Thailand, Hong Kong, Malaya, the Netherlands East Indies, and the Philippines.

Although the U.S.A. entered the war late, most historians agree that her contribution was decisive. Without her fighting men and without her overwhelming production of bombs, ships, and planes, the Allies might well have been defeated. There were other factors—such as Hitler's strategic mistakes—but U.S. participation, and before it the provision of arms and other supplies to Britain, was crucial.

In 1942 the tide began to turn for the Allies, first with the Battle of Midway in the Pacific and later in the other war theaters. The invasion of Normandy in 1944—an amphibious operation of unprecedented magnitude—set in motion a series of events that led to the liberation of Western Europe from the Nazis. One of the last and most critical major European engagements was the Battle of the Bulge in Belgium and Luxembourg, in which most of Hitler's reserves were destroyed.

The war brought many changes. Scientific research in the prevention of jungle diseases led to the development of DDT, which would greatly benefit a peacetime world. Jet engines and radar revolutionized travel. The atomic bomb, which so devastatingly ended the war, introduced new fears.

Political changes were perhaps the most far reaching. With the end of the war, new differences became apparent among erstwhile allies. In Europe countries were divided, borders shifted, and the Continent split into a Red east and a democratic west. In Africa and Asia nationalism gained a new potency, and revolution spread in former colonies. Six years of bloody war had ended, but peace was to bring new problems.

In all World War II maps the following color code is used: ■ Allies, ■ Axis and Cobelligerents, □ Countries Controlled by Axis or Cobelligerents, ■ Neutral Countries.

1939

Blitzkrieg!

In the early months of World War II the Third Reich conquers Poland and Western Europe with a radically different kind of warfare.

On September 1, 1939, the armies of the Third Reich invaded Poland, and two days later Britain and France declared war on Germany. For the second time in a quarter of a century the nations of Europe took up arms. This time, however, there were no cheering throngs to send the troops off to battle as there had been in August 1914. In Berlin a gloomy silence greeted Adolf Hitler's announcement of war against Poland. In London Prime Minister Neville Chamberlain, whose foreign policy had aimed at preserving peace by appeasing Hitler, told a downcast House of Commons: "This is a sad day for all of us. . . . Everything that I have worked for, everything that I have believed in . . . has crashed into ruins."

To the end, the German Fuehrer had been convinced that Britain and France would not go to war over Poland. For five years he had managed to gain his objectives without war, playing on the military weakness and divergent interests of Britain and France and skillfully exploiting their insecurity, mutual suspicions, and fear of war. One by one Hitler had unilaterally removed the restraints placed upon Germany by the post-World War I peace settlement—the hated *Diktat* of the Treaty of Versailles—and had steadily undermined the system of collective security designed by the victorious Western Allies to uphold it.

This time, however, Britain and France were not taken in by assurances that he was only interested in restoring to Germany what was rightfully hers. The Fuehrer's aggression in Czechoslovakia following the Munich agreement of September 1938 (see pp. 272–277) had made any such deception impossible, and after Germany's seizure of the Czech provinces of Bohemia and Moravia, Britain and France, resolving to toughen their stand against further aggression, began to rearm. When Hitler, turning his attention to Poland, demanded the return of the Free City of Danzig, transit rights through the Polish Corridor to East Prussia, and better treatment of Poland's German minority, Britain and France announced that they would back Poland if Germany tried to force the issue.

Discounting these pledges as idle threats, Hitler continued to aim for a quick, localized war against Poland. On April 3, 1939, he directed the Army High Command (OKH) to complete preparations for Plan White, the invasion of Poland, by September 1. Meanwhile, he set about strengthening his alliances to isolate Poland politically. During the spring and summer he signed nonaggression pacts with Slovakia, Lithuania, Latvia, and Estonia; concluded an economic pact with Romania; and received pledges of friendship from Romania, Hungary, Bulgaria, and Yugoslavia. In May he negotiated the Pact of Steel with Mussolini, pledging mutual support in the event of war. Finally, in a masterful diplomatic reversal, Germany concluded a nonaggression treaty with her archenemy, the Soviet Union, on August 23, 1939, barely a week before German tanks rolled into Poland. This Nazi-Soviet pact contained secret protocols, not made public until the war's end, carving up Poland and Eastern Europe into German and Russian spheres of influence.

The German Invasion of Poland

At dawn on September 1 the German armed forces launched the most terrifying air and ground attack the world had ever seen. Hitler's blitzkrieg (lightning war) took the Poles completely by surprise. German fighter planes and Stuka dive bombers wiped out the Polish Air Force within 48 hours, before most planes had time to leave the ground, and bombed Polish marching columns and rail lines. Meanwhile, the German Navy seized Danzig and cut off Polish access to the sea, and German panzer (armored) divisions and motorized infantry units invaded from three sides.

The speed and intensity of the German attack threw the Polish ground forces into complete confusion. Their chain of command was irreparably disrupted, and many units never reached their assembly areas. Moreover, although the Poles fought valiantly, their outdated tactics and weapons were no match for the enemy. (At one point a division of Polish cavalry armed with lances and sabers reportedly charged oncoming German tanks.) By September 5 the Germans had sealed off the Polish Corridor, and three days later the first German tanks reached the outskirts of Warsaw. In less than three weeks virtually all of western Poland had been overrun.

The Russians, who were startled at the swiftness of the German advance, invaded Poland from the east on September 17 under the pretext of protecting the White Russian and Ukrainian minorities in eastern Poland, but in reality to claim their share of the bounty as promised in the secret protocols of the Nazi-Soviet pact. The Russians encountered little resistance, and Russian and German troops met at Brest-Litovsk on

From north, west, and south *German troops poured into Poland on September 1, 1939. From the east Soviet forces invaded to seize their share of the booty. In five weeks a nation of more than 150,000 square miles was overrun, conquered, and divided between its two most powerful neighbors. Hitler's conquest of Poland, the first battle test of his blueprint for world domination, was a success. His soldiers were better equipped and more skillfully led than the Poles, and his generals used surprise, coordinating air and ground forces to greater advantage.*

September 18. Ten days later the Germans and Russians partitioned Poland between them.

Although Britain and France had declared war on Germany on September 3, the speed of Germany's campaign had not given them time to mobilize in Poland's defense. Now, his conquest completed, the Fuehrer publicly offered to make peace if Britain and France would recognize his latest acquisitions and return some of Germany's pre-World War I colonies. In private, however, Hitler had already begun laying plans for an invasion of Western Europe should his peace offer be refused. Once France was defeated, he reasoned, Britain could be persuaded to make peace. Then, his western flank secure, he could return to his main objective, the eastward expansion of the Reich. On October 10 Hitler told his generals to prepare for the earliest possible attack on the West and at the end of October set the invasion date for November 12.

"The Phoney War"

Thus far there had been no serious fighting in the West, and as the lull continued, people began referring to the "phoney war" or *Sitzkrieg* ("sitdown war"). While the Germans finalized their invasion plans, the Allies stayed put behind their border defenses. In November bad weather forced Hitler to postpone his Western offensive until mid-January, and in early January he was forced to delay still further after some of the plans for the opening campaign accidentally fell into Belgian hands. The offensive had to be delayed until a new strategy could be worked out.

In the interim Hitler's admirals persuaded him to undertake the conquest of Norway before Britain could occupy it or blockade Norwegian territorial waters. If the Allies gained control of Norway, they argued, Germany would be subject to a crippling blockade, as in World War I. Worse, she would be cut off from her major source of iron ore, which traveled by rail from northern Sweden to the Norwegian port of Narvik and was then shipped along the Norwegian coast to Germany. In mid-December naval commander in chief Admiral Erich Raeder introduced Hitler to a Norwegian Nazi named Vidkun Quisling (a man whose name would soon become a synonym for traitor), who offered to arrange a coup d'etat in conjunction with the German invasion.

On April 9, 1940, German forces moved against Norway, relying on speed and surprise rather than on overwhelming numbers. Naval detachments seized the main Norwegian ports, and paratroopers captured Norway's principal airfield. Nazi troops overran Denmark and were ferried across to Norway. The startled Danes capitulated immediately, but the Norwegians resisted. They could not hold out indefinitely, however, without Allied assistance. The Allies managed to land a few brigades on Norway's coast, but they were beaten back by German air and ground attacks and forced to evacuate at the beginning of June. Norway surrendered on June 12. In Britain disagreement over the conduct of the war in Norway forced Chamberlain's resignation on May 10. He was succeeded by Winston Churchill, First Lord of the Admiralty.

The Fall of France

At dawn that same day, more than eight months after they had invaded Poland, the Germans opened their offensive in the West. Plan Yellow, the code name for the offensive, called for a coordinated drive against the Low Countries and France by three German Army groups deployed along a 150-mile front. Army Group A, headed by Gen. Gerd von Rundstedt, would make the main thrust at the center of the front through the Forest of Ardennes. To the north, Army Group B, under Gen. Fedor von Bock, would launch a simultaneous attack on Holland and Belgium; to the south,

***Germany's assault** on Denmark and Norway in April 1940 brought swift success: Denmark surrendered within one day, and Hitler wrested control of the Scandinavian waters from the British Navy and quickly built up an 80,000-man force in Norway to defeat the Norwegians and the 40,000 Allied troops that had landed to assist them. Thereafter, he established air and submarine bases along the Norwegian coast. At left, the Norwegian town of Elverum, virtually leveled by German bombers in April 1940. King Haakon VII, who had sought refuge there, escaped to England to lead the government in exile.*

***Civilians who survived** the blitzkrieg, like this Belgian family, often had only burned-out ruins to go home to.*

***Blitzkrieg in the west:** From May 10 to June 5, 1940, the German armies swept across the Low Countries and northern France to the Channel coast. Turning southward, they overran much of France before fighting ceased on June 25. Italy attacked France on June 21 but gained little ground.*

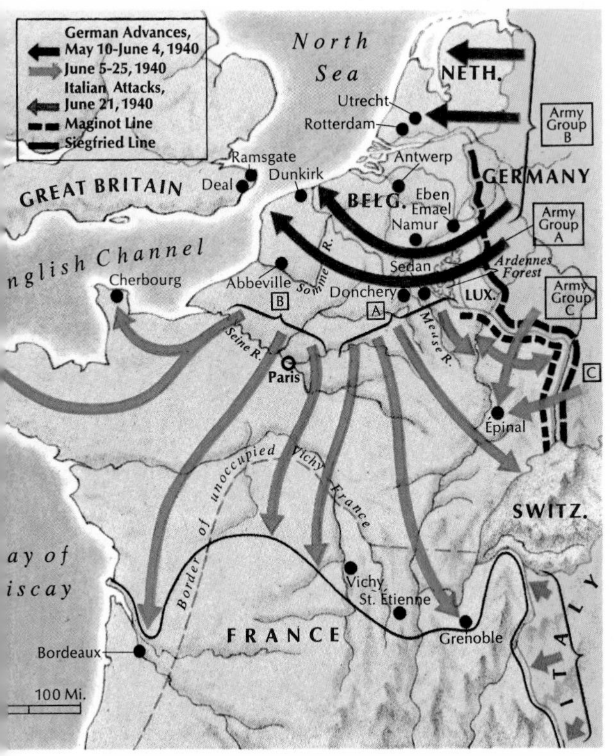

Army Group C, under Gen. Wilhelm von Leeb, would remain on the defensive facing the Maginot Line.

Allied tacticians, however, expected a German strategy similar to that of World War I. As a result, French Gen. Maurice Gamelin, the Allied commander in chief, concentrated most of his mobile forces in the north along the Franco-Belgian border, where the German breakthrough had occurred in 1914. The Ardennes region (where the French thought the terrain too difficult for major troop movements) and the Maginot Line were more weakly defended.

In numbers and equipment the opposing armies were nearly equal. French, British, Dutch, and Belgian forces totaled some 135 divisions as against 136 German divisions. The Allies' tank strength was slightly greater than the Germans' and of comparable quality. The Germans had a small edge in airpower, particularly in dive bombers and transport planes.

Allied organization, tactics, and morale, however, were decidedly inferior. Until the last minute the Dutch and Belgians maintained strict neutrality, thus preventing the development of a coordinated Allied defense. French and British armored units were of equal or better design than the German, but were intended to provide infantry support rather than independent operations, and thus were scattered in small groups along the entire front. The Allies were completely unable to cope with the huge tank formations, the combined air and ground tactics, and the enormous mobility and coordination of the German assault. Moreover, German morale, bolstered by the spectacular victories in Poland and Norway, was vastly superior to that of the Allies, especially the French.

Holland suffered the most crushing defeat. While German armored forces smashed westward across the border, Nazi paratroopers were dropped behind the lines to seize key bridges and airfields. The Dutch resisted, demolishing canal locks to flood the lowlands in a desperate attempt to slow the German advance, but they could not halt the invaders.

Within four days the Dutch Army had sustained 25 percent casualties but still held northern Holland, Rotterdam, and Utrecht. The Germans threatened to destroy these cities if the Dutch refused to surrender and bombed Rotterdam on May 14. Holland surrendered that same day, after Queen Wilhelmina and her government had escaped to London.

The attack on Belgium was simultaneous with the one on the Netherlands. German paratroopers captured Belgium's main border stronghold, Fort Eben Emael, in a daring night attack on May 10–11, while other airborne units secured major bridges and airfields. At the same time German tank and infantry divisions began pouring across the border. Gamelin, who had been expecting such an advance, immediately dispatched French and British troops eastward to aid the Dutch and Belgians, but by the time they linked up, the Germans had already crossed the Meuse River into central Belgium and were deep within Holland.

The reputedly impregnable Maginot Line, *part of which appears above, had given the French a false sense of security and left them unprepared for the German advance.*

Meanwhile, the Germans were delivering their heaviest blow not in central Belgium, as the Allies believed, but farther south through the Forest of Ardennes, between Namur and Sedan. There seven panzer and three motorized divisions, comprising some 1,800 tanks in all, broke through the Ardennes, unhindered by its narrow roads and hilly terrain. Behind them came 45 divisions of German infantry. The Belgian light infantry and French cavalry defending the Ardennes passes were overwhelmed. By nightfall on May 12 the Germans had reached the east bank of the Meuse and had begun constructing bridges across the river, while German dive bombers flew ahead to soften the French defenses. Two days later the Germans captured Sedan and Donchery.

Although Gamelin immediately ordered French reserve divisions to the Ardennes sector, they arrived there too late. Delayed along roads clogged with soldiers and civilians fleeing in terror, they found their assigned positions already occupied by the enemy. By May 16 the Germans had advanced as much as 20 to 30 miles west of the Meuse at some points, and four days later reached Abbeville near the French coast and turned northward. The Belgian Army, the British Expeditionary Force (BEF), and three French armies were trapped in Belgium between two converging German forces, one marching west through Belgium and the other north along the French coast.

On May 19 General Gamelin was replaced as Allied commander in chief by 73-year-old veteran Gen. Maxime Weygand, who began organizing a last-ditch Allied counteroffensive. His efforts came too late, however. The Belgian Army was collapsing, and on May 28 King Leopold III surrendered unconditionally. Two days before, the British had realized that the only alternative to surrender or destruction was an evacuation by sea from Dunkirk on the French coast to Britain. On the 26th the British Navy had begun evacuating troops, hoping to rescue 45,000 soldiers before the Germans overran the beaches. As it turned out, nearly 340,000 men, including 198,000 British and some 140,000 French and Belgian soldiers, were evacuated because of a German blunder.

On May 24, when German tanks were nearing Gravelines, only 13 miles south of Dunkirk, Hitler and Army Group A Commander Rundstedt ordered them to halt for two days, giving the Allies enough time to strengthen their defenses and complete the evacuation from Dunkirk. While Royal Air Force (RAF) fighter planes battled the Luftwaffe overhead, a motley armada of more than 700 vessels—including destroyers, Channel steamers, barges, and sailboats—made trip after trip ferrying soldiers across the choppy Channel waters to Deal and Ramsgate. The evacuation

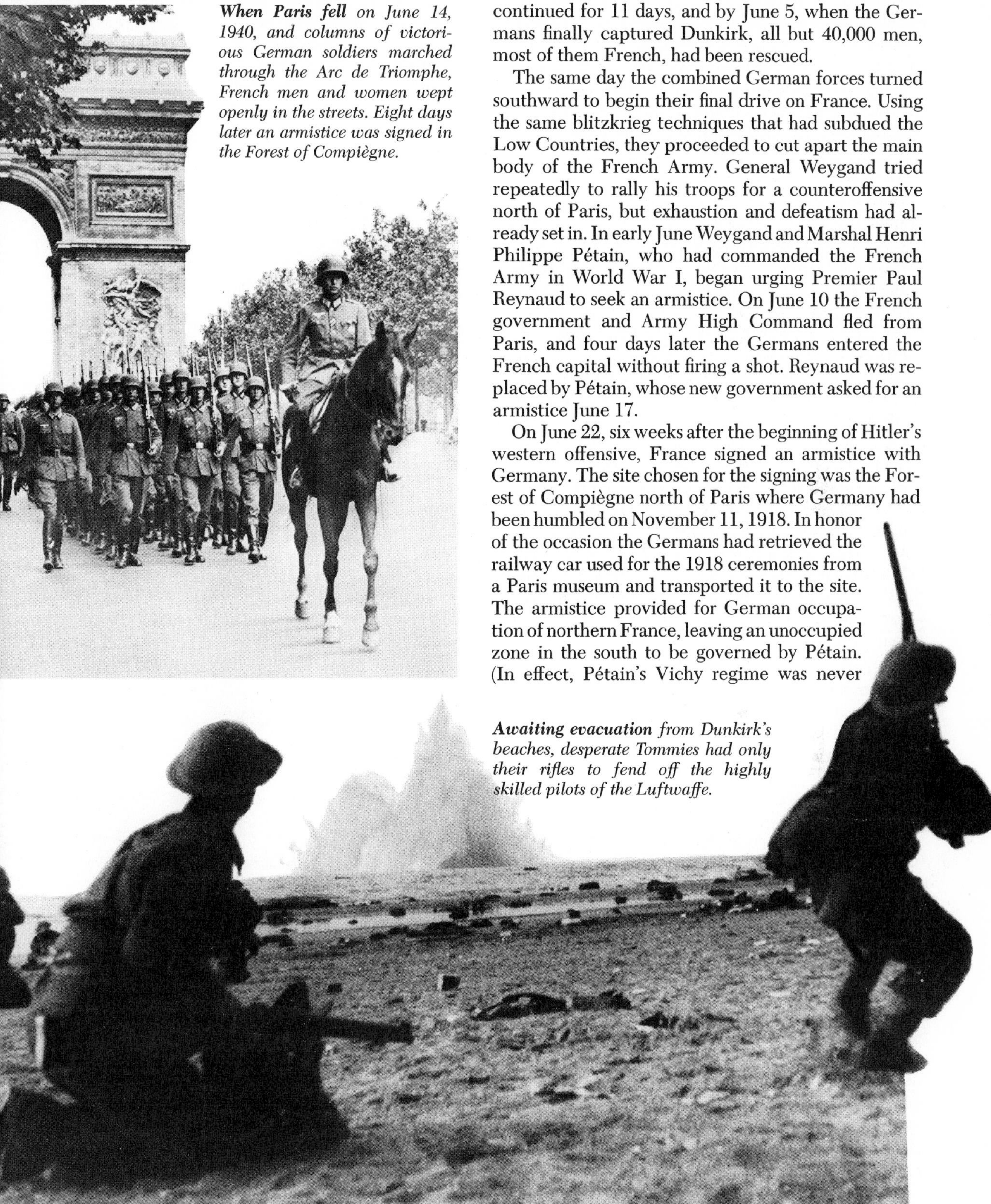

***When Paris fell** on June 14, 1940, and columns of victorious German soldiers marched through the Arc de Triomphe, French men and women wept openly in the streets. Eight days later an armistice was signed in the Forest of Compiègne.*

continued for 11 days, and by June 5, when the Germans finally captured Dunkirk, all but 40,000 men, most of them French, had been rescued.

The same day the combined German forces turned southward to begin their final drive on France. Using the same blitzkrieg techniques that had subdued the Low Countries, they proceeded to cut apart the main body of the French Army. General Weygand tried repeatedly to rally his troops for a counteroffensive north of Paris, but exhaustion and defeatism had already set in. In early June Weygand and Marshal Henri Philippe Pétain, who had commanded the French Army in World War I, began urging Premier Paul Reynaud to seek an armistice. On June 10 the French government and Army High Command fled from Paris, and four days later the Germans entered the French capital without firing a shot. Reynaud was replaced by Pétain, whose new government asked for an armistice June 17.

On June 22, six weeks after the beginning of Hitler's western offensive, France signed an armistice with Germany. The site chosen for the signing was the Forest of Compiègne north of Paris where Germany had been humbled on November 11, 1918. In honor of the occasion the Germans had retrieved the railway car used for the 1918 ceremonies from a Paris museum and transported it to the site. The armistice provided for German occupation of northern France, leaving an unoccupied zone in the south to be governed by Pétain. (In effect, Pétain's Vichy regime was never

***Awaiting evacuation** from Dunkirk's beaches, desperate Tommies had only their rifles to fend off the highly skilled pilots of the Luftwaffe.*

***The Germans bombed London** 57 nights in a row during the fall of 1940. But British factories continued to turn out planes; and the RAF, radar, and antiaircraft measures were eventually successful in defeating the German Luftwaffe.*

***RAF pilots scramble** to meet a German attack. Outnumbered nearly three to one, they were Britain's last, impenetrable line of defense.*

more than a puppet government.) The French Navy was to be demobilized, and its ships were to be interned in French ports.

On June 25 Pétain's government signed an armistice with Italy, which had declared war on France June 10 to claim her share of the spoils. The Italian Army, however, had not been able to attack until the 21st, and had only advanced a few hundred yards. The armistice permitted the Italians to occupy that territory and established a demilitarized zone.

After the fall of France Hitler again sought to persuade Britain to make peace, but the British flatly refused to negotiate unless he first withdrew from all occupied territory. In a speech to the Reichstag on July 19 Hitler made a final appeal: "I feel it to be my duty . . . to appeal once more to reason and common sense in Great Britain . . . I am not the vanquished begging favors, but the victor speaking in the name of reason. *I can see no reason why this war must go on.*"

Hitler had not counted on a war against Britain, and his generals had not drawn up plans for such a possibility. Only three days before his final appeal for peace the Fuehrer had reluctantly ordered the High Command to begin preparations for Operation Sea Lion "to eliminate the British homeland as a base for the carrying on of the war against Germany and, if it should become necessary, to occupy it completely." He delayed his final decision on the exact date for launching such an invasion, however, for another two months, until September 15.

Meanwhile, realizing that a successful conquest of Britain could only be achieved once Germany had gained complete mastery in the air, Hitler ordered Field Marshal Hermann Goering, commander in chief

During the Battle of Britain anti-aircraft crews provided a last-ditch defense against German bombers. The Dornier bomber above was hit over the London docks. The big fight, however, was in the air, where British Spitfires outperformed German Messerschmitts. Hitler's plan to destroy the RAF and soften English morale in preparation for a full-scale invasion proved a failure.

of the Luftwaffe, to organize a major air offensive to destroy the RAF and cripple British shipping.

The British had realized that they would be the next target of Hitler's aggression and had begun strengthening their coastal and air defenses. Churchill appointed Lord Beaverbrook head of the new Ministry of Air Production, organized to step up manufacture of fighter planes and air defense equipment. At the same time Air Chief Marshal Sir Hugh Dowding, head of the RAF Fighter Command, tightened and coordinated existing defenses. More coastal radar stations were built, and fighter command and tracking operations were placed underground. This excellent system gave the RAF detailed advance warning of the size, altitude, flying position, and direction of all German squadrons as they approached the coast.

The Battle of Britain

The Battle of Britain officially opened on July 10, although the RAF and Luftwaffe had engaged in sporadic air attacks since the evacuation from Dunkirk. Until August 19 German bombers concentrated on British Channel and North Sea ports and shipping. Thereafter Hitler ordered an all-out air offensive against the RAF. Britain's aircraft factories and fighter bases, especially the central RAF airfields ringing London, became targets of an intensive assault. Day after day Goering's huge fleets of Dornier and Heinkel bombers swept in on British airfields, while Messerschmitt fighter planes fought off the RAF Hurricanes and Spitfires that rose to engage them. Damage was extensive and RAF losses mounted. Goering boasted to Hitler that the RAF had been decimated. Even the British were beginning to lose heart.

Then a fortuitous turn of events caused the Germans to change their strategy. On the night of August 23 German bombs accidentally hit London, and Churchill immediately ordered the RAF, which had been bombing other German cities since May 15, to shift its night raids to Berlin in retaliation.

In late August Hitler suddenly ordered Goering to suspend the attacks on British airfields and begin massive bombing of London and other industrial centers. On September 7 a huge air armada attacked London, setting fire to a large section of the city's East End docks. Daily raids continued thereafter. Meanwhile, the British, fearing invasion, began bombing the Channel and North Sea ports where the German Navy had begun assembling its fleet.

The change in German tactics gave the RAF time to repair its damaged airfields and fighters, and on September 15 RAF planes inflicted severe losses on Goering's air fleet. Four days later Hitler postponed Operation Sea Lion indefinitely and ordered the invasion fleet withdrawn to safer waters. In October he rescheduled the operation for the spring or early summer of 1941, but in effect the plan had been abandoned. Although German bombers continued night raids on British cities, the Battle of Britain was over. The Nazis had suffered their first major defeat.

By then Hitler had turned his attention eastward toward the Soviet Union. Thus far he had skillfully avoided provoking a war on two fronts, but now he decided to take the risk, counting on Britain's weakness to prevent her intervention. It proved to be a fatal gamble. Germany's decision to push eastward gave Britain valuable time to build up her manpower and armaments for a future counteroffensive. Hitler's attack on the U.S.S.R. signaled the beginning of the end.

Scientists at War: The Secret Battlefront

Without question, the great shaping force of the 20th century has been the phenomenal growth of scientific knowledge—and never has that knowledge been more vigorously pursued than in times of war.

In 1940 President Franklin D. Roosevelt established the National Defense Research Committee to initiate a crash program to develop new weapons, the first such high-level undertaking in the country's history. A year later the larger Office of Scientific Research and Development (OSRD) was created to direct the entire range of war-related research. Organized in conjunction with scientists in Great Britain and Canada, OSRD programs encompassed fields as diverse as medicine, engineering, agriculture, metallurgy, and linguistics.

Two notable results were the first large-scale production of penicillin (see pp. 210–215) and the development of a new pesticide, DDT, which brought wartime outbreaks of typhus and malaria under control and dramatically increased world food production after the war.

The most fateful example of the OSRD's work, of course, was the Manhattan Project (see pp. 360–367), which produced an atomic bomb just $6\frac{1}{2}$ years after the uranium atom was split for the first time. In addition, technical innovations were applied to a wide variety of conventional weapons, resulting in more powerful explosives; new types of mines, torpedoes, and depth charges; better airplane engines; and more accurate bombsights and artillery.

With the exception of the atomic bomb, though, by far the most important new scientific tool of the war was radar, first developed in England in the 1930's. In December 1940, as German bombers were making nighttime raids over Britain almost at will, the head of the RAF made the terse prediction that "night bombing will be greatly reduced by spring." He was right: German aircraft were soon being shot down with enough regularity to bring the Battle of Britain to an end—thanks to new radar devices carried aboard RAF fighters. As the war progressed, radar was adapted to a variety of other purposes—locating submarines, for instance, or focusing antiaircraft fire automatically on fast-moving targets. Radar was also the basis for one of the most ingenious inventions of the war—the proximity fuse, developed jointly by Canadian and U.S. researchers. Equipped with a miniature radar system, the fuse electronically detonated an antiaircraft or artillery shell that came close enough to cause damage.

Behind Closed Doors

Another technological campaign, further removed from the battlefront, centered on the esoteric science of cryptanalysis, or codebreaking. By 1941 U.S. intelligence agents had succeeded in deciphering the top-level Japanese military and diplomatic codes and then in constructing a replica of the complex decoding machines used in Japanese embassies. Unfortunately, the Japanese were careful not to mention their planned attack on Pearl Harbor even in coded messages, thereby preserving its secrecy until the morning of December 7, 1941. But this sophisticated eavesdropping proved invaluable later in the war, providing enough information to surprise the Japanese Fleet at the crucial Battle of Midway in 1942. Perhaps the war's greatest intelligence coup was scored by the British in 1939 when they obtained a copy of the Nazis' highest level code machine, known as Enigma, enabling the Allies to intercept most of the communications between Hitler and his generals throughout the war. So vital was this machine that Winston Churchill decided in November 1940 not to evacuate Coventry when it was learned that the city would be the target of a major bombing, for fear of alerting Germany that the code was broken.

This battle of wits and technology, of course, was not one sided. Many of Germany's early successes relied on their ability to penetrate British and U.S. codes. Eventually Allied cryptanalysis proved more efficient, furnishing countless pieces of information that helped accelerate the collapse of the Axis.

In Germany two other critical matters, atomic fission and the development of improved radar equipment, were given relatively low priorities—fortunate decisions for the Allies, in view of the high caliber of German scientists. Perhaps only in the field of jet and rocket propulsion did German science live up to its full potential—in part because rockets had not been among the weapons ban-

THE PACE OF INVENTION

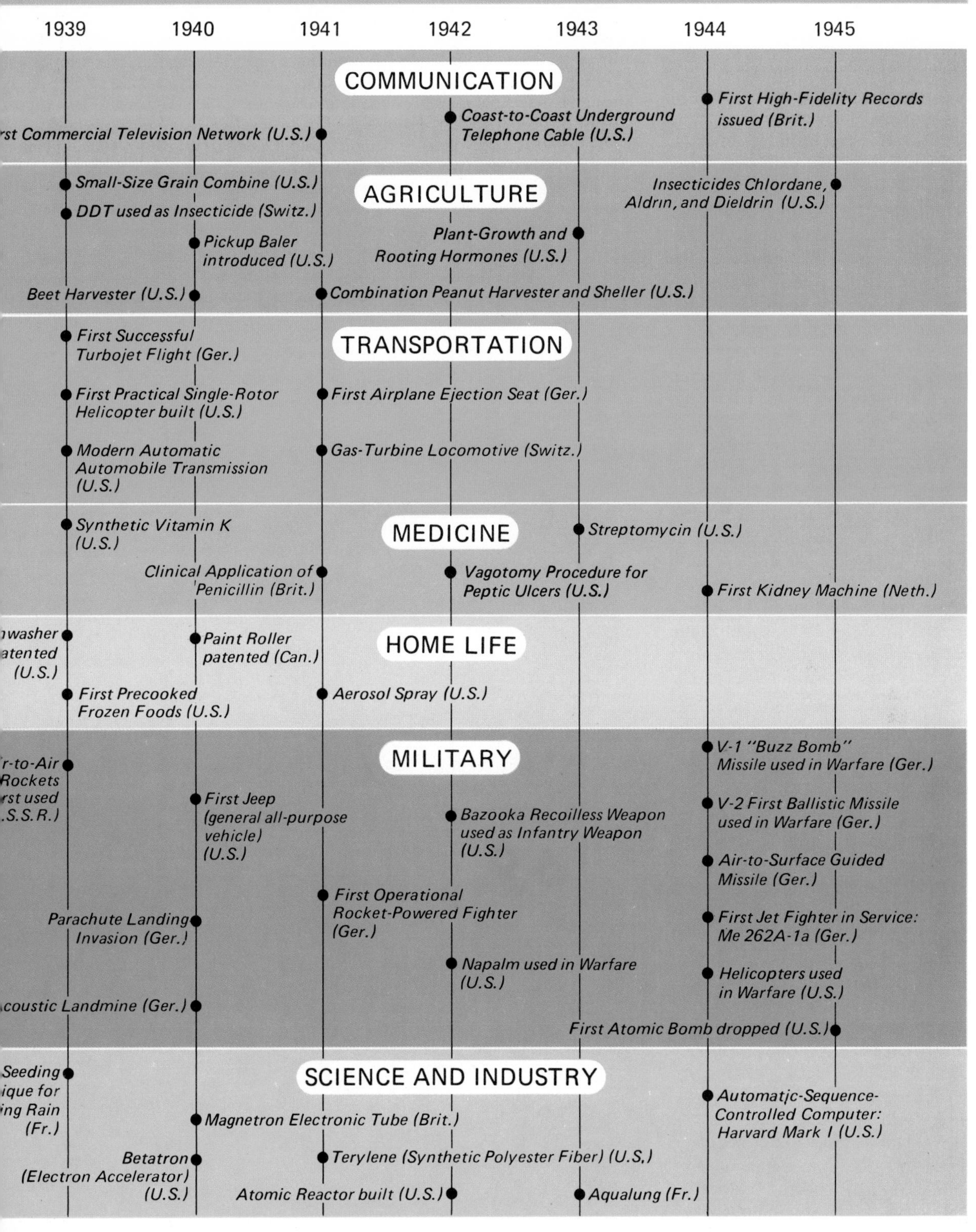

ned by the Treaty of Versailles and therefore had been actively researched in Germany from the 1920's onward (see pp. 192–197). This early work made possible the development of the jet-powered V-1 "flying bomb" and the supersonic V-2 rocket, both impressive feats of technology. They were not ready for use, however, until late in 1944, too late to alter the war's outcome.

In the end, the mobilization of science not only helped the Allies win the war, it also set a pattern that would profoundly influence the postwar world. The partnership between government and the scientific community proved too successful—and too attractive to both sides—to be dissolved when the fighting ended. Indeed, it would grow steadily thereafter, giving rise to major political and social issues as the United States became locked into an arms race with the Soviet Union that consumed an increasing portion of the nation's wealth. It would also pose a difficult and urgent question within the scientific community—that of a scientist's moral responsibility for the ultimate results of his work. Clearly, in a world suddenly vulnerable to nuclear self-destruction, it was a matter of more than academic interest whether an atomic physicist, for example, could afford the same detached, "ivory tower" attitude that so often characterized his predecessors. For without a governing sense of social and political realities, the possibility grew stronger that technology might simply outrun man's ability to control it. Such a fear was voiced by J. Robert Oppenheimer, director of the Los Alamos center where the atomic bomb was developed, who observed: "One thing that is new is the prevalence of newness, the changing scale . . . of change itself, so that the world alters as we walk in it, so that the years of man's life measure not some small growth or rearrangement or moderation of what he learned in childhood, but a great upheaval."

THE BOYS IN THE BACK ROOM

One of the unforeseen byproducts of World War II was a new, increasingly com plex relationship among science, industry, and the military—a relationship tha has become one of the predominant forces in modern political and economic life From 1939 onward a kind of war-within-a-war was waged in laboratories an testing centers on both sides of the Atlantic, each party seeking to outpace it enemies in technological innovation and ingenuity. When German U-boats bega to use torpedoes guided by sound, the British developed a noisemaking device tha was towed at a safe distance behind a ship; likewise, Germany's magnetic mine were counteracted by a process called degaussing, in which electric current wa run through special cables in a ship to neutralize the magnetic effect of its hull. I the air war the British confounded German radar by dropping metallic strips fron their planes; then when the Germans modified their radar to overcome this strata gem, the RAF introduced more sophisticated electronic jamming devices. One o the most ingenious feats was an Allied air raid in 1943 that destroyed two massiv hydroelectric dams in Germany with bombs designed to skip along the surface o the water, then settle against the dam's base. To be sure, the war was ultimatel won by ground troops at the front and by the factory workers who kept then supplied; but never before had so large and diversified a role been played in an military campaign by "the boys in the back room."

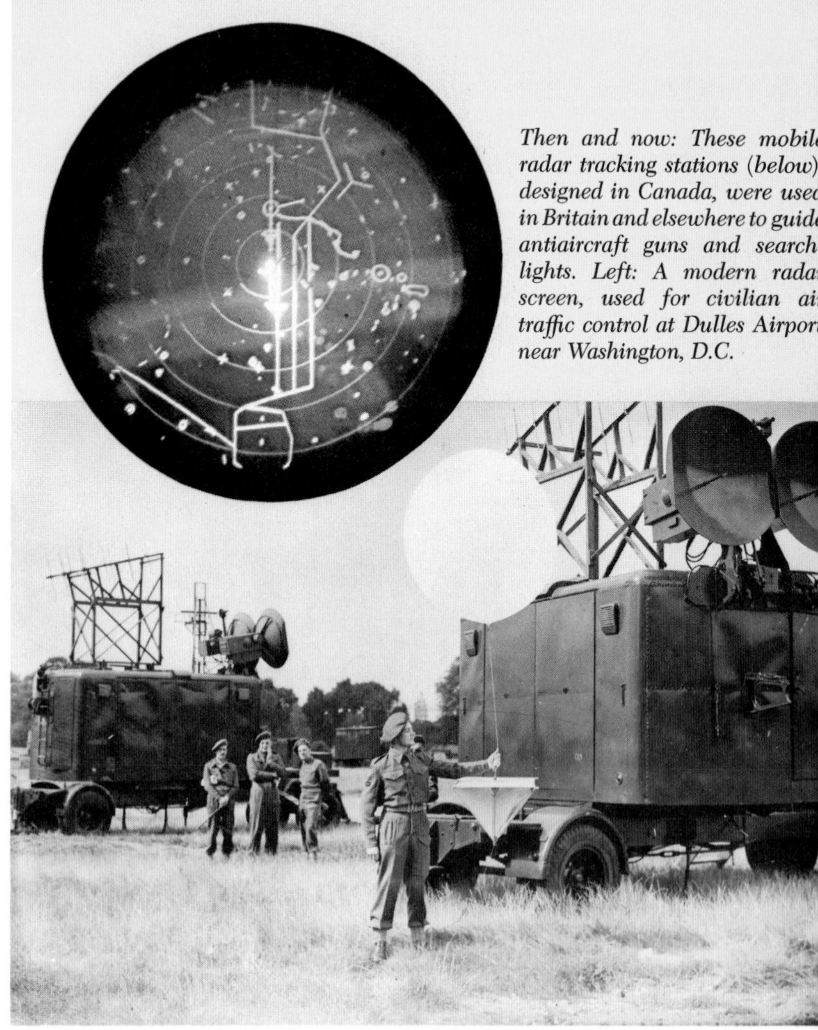

Then and now: These mobil radar tracking stations (below) designed in Canada, were use in Britain and elsewhere to guid antiaircraft guns and search lights. Left: A modern rada screen, used for civilian ai traffic control at Dulles Airpor near Washington, D.C.

A German V-2 rocket being prepared for launch; a scientific triumph, it appeared too late to ward off military defeat.

This telegram (right) sent to Tokyo on December 6, 1941, reported that the U.S. Fleet was still at Pearl Harbor. Though decoded, its significance was not known until the next day.

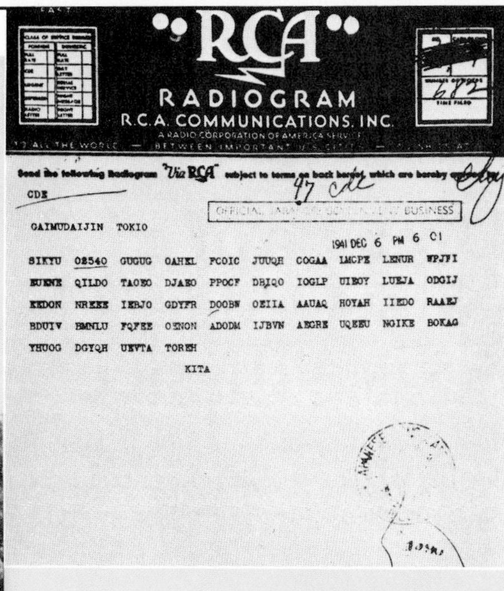

RCA
RADIOGRAM
R.C.A. COMMUNICATIONS, INC.
A RADIO CORPORATION OF AMERICA SERVICE

Send the following Radiogram "Via RCA" subject to terms on back hereof, which are hereby agreed to

CDE

OFFICIAL JAPANESE GOVERNMENT BUSINESS

GAIMUDAIJIN TOKIO

1941 DEC 6 PM 6 01

SIKYU 02540 GUGUG OAHKL FCOIC JUUQH COGAA LMCPE LENUR WPJFI
BUKNE QILDO TAOEO DJAEO PPOCF DBIQO IOGLP UIEOY LUEJA ODGIJ
KEDON NREKE IEBJO GDYFR DOOBW OEIIA AAUAQ HOYAH IIEDO RAAEJ
BDUIV BMNLU FQFEE OENON ADODM IJBVN AEGRE UQEEU NOIKE BOKAG
YHUOG DGYQH UEVTA TOREH

KITA

The Ultrasecret: Unknown to the Nazis, a copy of their highest-level cipher machine, the Enigma (right), was obtained by the British in 1940, enabling the Allies to monitor nearly all important German communications. Far right: William Friedman, whose U.S. team broke Japan's top codes.

1940

Dreams of a New Order: The Axis Alliance

A new pact between Germany, Italy, and Japan links the three aggressor nations in a quest for worldwide domination.

By September 1940 Adolf Hitler had reached the pinnacle of his career. Only a year after he had provoked the Second World War by invading Poland, he was master not only of Poland, but of Denmark, Norway, the Netherlands, Belgium, Luxembourg, and France. Across the Channel an isolated but determined Britain had survived the Luftwaffe's summer bombardment, but it was doubtful that she could hold her own indefinitely against the seemingly invincible German war machine.

On September 27 the Fuehrer presented the world with still another coup. At a glittering gala ceremony in Berlin, Germany, Italy, and Japan signed the Tripartite Pact, pledging mutual support "with all political, economic, and military means" in the event of an attack "by a power at present not involved in the European war or in the Sino-Japanese conflict." Specifically, this meant the United States (the U.S.S.R., the only other nonbelligerent, had pledged neutrality with Germany in 1939); the Axis powers hoped that their threat of a war on two fronts would dissuade the U.S.A. from entering the conflict. The pact also divided Europe and Asia into spheres of influence, recognizing German and Italian leadership of a "New Order" in Europe and Japanese ascendancy in East Asia.

Ostensibly, the pact formally linked three kindred nations. Western fascism and eastern militarism seemed to have forged an unshakable global alliance. On closer inspection, however, the three aggressor nations were vastly different and their alliance was subject to constant strains. Moreover, the New Order that Hitler and his Italian and Japanese partners intended to impose upon their conquered subjects was based on concepts of national interest that precluded peaceful coexistence with other nations and races. Had they ever been able to carry out their grandiose schemes, the Aryan Nazi conquerors, the heirs of the Roman Empire, and the people of the Chrysanthemum Throne would certainly have come to blows.

*The **Tripartite Pact** linked Germany, Italy, and Japan in a 10-year military and economic partnership. Ambassador Saburo Kurusu reads Japan's declaration; Italy's Foreign Minister Galeazzo Ciano and Hitler are to his left. In secret negotiations that followed, Hitler attempted to bring the U.S.S.R. into the alliance by including her in the proposed spheres of influence shown on the map. ■ German ■ Soviet ■ Italian ■ Japanese ■ German, Italian, and Soviet ■ Territory in dispute between U.S.S.R. and Germany. At right, Hermann Goering, head of Germany's Luftwaffe and second only to Hitler in the Nazi hierarchy, Italy's Benito Mussolini, and Japan's Hideki Tojo are led, in chains, by the grim reaper Death in a 1942 caricature from* Esquire *magazine.*

The Rome-Berlin Axis

The October Protocols, signed by Germany and Italy in 1936, were the beginning of the Rome-Berlin alliance. Italy's dictator, Benito Mussolini, coined the term Axis on November 1, when he mentioned an "Axis round which all those European states which are animated by a desire for collaboration and peace may work together." Thereafter the fates of Germany and Italy were inextricably joined, and in May 1939 this informal partnership was extended into a formal 10-year military alliance, the Pact of Steel.

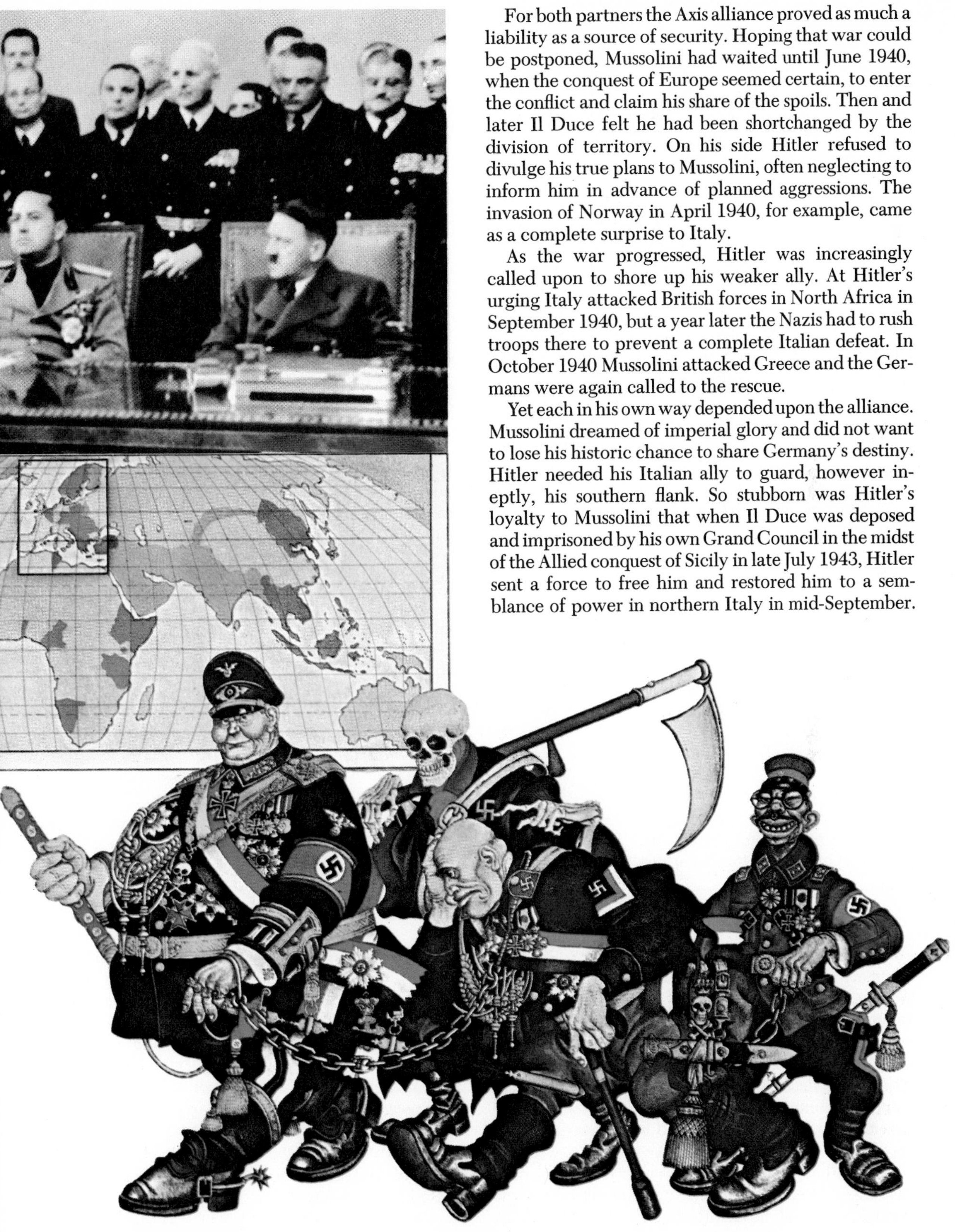

For both partners the Axis alliance proved as much a liability as a source of security. Hoping that war could be postponed, Mussolini had waited until June 1940, when the conquest of Europe seemed certain, to enter the conflict and claim his share of the spoils. Then and later Il Duce felt he had been shortchanged by the division of territory. On his side Hitler refused to divulge his true plans to Mussolini, often neglecting to inform him in advance of planned aggressions. The invasion of Norway in April 1940, for example, came as a complete surprise to Italy.

As the war progressed, Hitler was increasingly called upon to shore up his weaker ally. At Hitler's urging Italy attacked British forces in North Africa in September 1940, but a year later the Nazis had to rush troops there to prevent a complete Italian defeat. In October 1940 Mussolini attacked Greece and the Germans were again called to the rescue.

Yet each in his own way depended upon the alliance. Mussolini dreamed of imperial glory and did not want to lose his historic chance to share Germany's destiny. Hitler needed his Italian ally to guard, however ineptly, his southern flank. So stubborn was Hitler's loyalty to Mussolini that when Il Duce was deposed and imprisoned by his own Grand Council in the midst of the Allied conquest of Sicily in late July 1943, Hitler sent a force to free him and restored him to a semblance of power in northern Italy in mid-September.

SOLDIERS OF THE SWASTIKA AND RISING SUN: THE WAR THROUGH AXIS EYES

When you consider the progress of the last ten war months—the destruction of Poland, the heroic battle of Narvik, the capitulation of Holland and Belgium, the smashing of France—it is quite unbelievable. Here brilliant military strategy has been wedded to statesmanship of exceptional power; our marvellous Wehrmacht, so integrated, was forcefully supported by home production; but above everything else, how obvious it is that the Almighty has blessed us in this struggle!

We are aware of our strength! We know that at the conclusion of this struggle will be the most glorious victory of history; we fear nothing, no one. For after all, the Führer has said how incomparably we are armed for this last phase of the struggle, how immense are our arms and munition, our supplies, petrol and fuel, our inexhaustible fund of raw materials . . .

But despite all this: once more the Führer has appealed to reason. As a soldier, as a human being, as victor! Once more he has given England and the world the possibility of ending this senseless battle. What a man!

—Lt. Wilhelm Prüller, July 19, 1940

About four o'clock I stood on a hill overlooking the entire gulf, where a vast armada of ships formed a weird silhouette against the setting sun. Suddenly thick, black clouds began to cover the convoy; a sound like distant thunder reached our ears. The clouds were the smoke of antiaircraft guns. Several speck-like things dashed into the clouds of smoke from every point of the sky—our suicide planes!

"It's our kamikaze attack!" I shouted to some passing soldiers. They came running. A black speck flew into the smoke, then another, and another. The attack lasted about ten minutes. Gradually the smoke cleared, and I could see in the gathering haze some ships ablaze in the distance.

Was this mission necessary? I wondered. Was it worth the lives of young people to sink a few ships out of such an armada? Volunteers or not, both they and their parents were victims of this reckless type of warfare.

"That's the damnedest, silliest thing the top brass could think of!" said a soldier indignantly.

—Tetsuro Ogawa, a Japanese officer in Luzon, Philippines

The Rising Sun

Germany's alliance with Japan was quite different. Whereas the Fuehrer was fully aware of Italy's economic and military weaknesses, he had no doubts about Japan's ability to conquer East Asia, believing her capable, if necessary, of defeating the British and U.S. Pacific fleets. In certain ways Japan seemed the Oriental counterpart of Germany. Both nations had industrialized late, and both had been shaped by the experience into proud and warlike nations.

Their alliance, however, was not inspired by an awareness of their common destinies, but by their mutual hatred of Soviet Russia, the Eurasian giant lying between them. In 1936, a month after the formation of the Rome-Berlin Axis, Japan and Germany signed the Anti-Comintern Pact, publicly vowing to resist Communist subversion, but privately agreeing to aid each other against Soviet aggression. Italy joined the pact the following year.

Like most of Hitler's alliances, the one with Japan was merely an expedient, a scrap of paper to be torn up whenever it ceased to serve his purposes. Thus in August 1939, when the Fuehrer needed Soviet assurances of neutrality before he invaded Poland, he negotiated the Nazi-Soviet Pact, a bilateral nonaggression treaty with the U.S.S.R.

A year later Hitler reversed himself again, bringing the Japanese into the Axis with the signing of the Tripartite Pact. The alliance was mutually advantageous. Japan, having watched the progress of Hitler's conquest of Europe, wanted to take advantage of his successes by seizing the isolated Dutch and French colonies in the Far East, particularly in French Indochina and the Netherlands East Indies. Hitler, for his part, wanted the Japanese to put pressure on the British by attacking Singapore and other British possessions. (Ironically, although the Nazis had begun laying plans for an attack on the U.S.S.R. by then, they specifically avoided urging the Japanese to attack the Soviets from the east. At the time, Hitler believed Germany could defeat Russia without outside help.)

Soon after the Tripartite Pact was signed, Germany tried to secure Soviet membership by offering her, in return for a free hand in eastern Europe, dominion over a sphere reaching to India and the Persian Gulf. The Russians, however, were more ambitious, and the negotiations broke down.

In April 1941 Japan signed a five-year nonaggression pact with the U.S.S.R. and held to it despite subsequent German pleas for an invasion of the Soviet's eastern front. For her part, Russia declared war on Japan only on the eve of the Allied victory, after being assured of postwar territorial gains.

Hitler did not inform Japan of his plans to invade Russia, and Japan in turn gave Germany no warning of her attack on Pearl Harbor. Nonetheless, Hitler unhesitatingly honored the Tripartite Pact and declared war on the U.S.A. on December 11, 1941. The decision was fateful, for he thereby engaged the world's largest industrial power at a time when his armies were beginning to bog down in Russia and Britain still posed a threat in the Mediterranean and North Africa.

The New Order

Perhaps the strongest link between the three Axis powers was their desire to create a new political and economic order at home and in their conquered territories. In Italy Mussolini, who came to power in 1922 (see pp. 168–173), established a one-party Fascist dictatorship. The cornerstone of this system was the corporate state, through which the government exercised control over the country's economic life. Mussolini ruthlessly suppressed all forms of opposition, censored the nation's press and media, and regimented many aspects of everyday life. Though his policies were never as extreme as Hitler's, he did, at Hitler's urging, proclaim the "Prussianization" of Italy, enact anti-Jewish legislation, and pass laws regulating behavior and dress to help "purify" the Italian race.

Mussolini's fondest dream was to make Italy into a modern-day Roman Empire, but his poor and overpopulated country had neither the resources nor the army for such an undertaking. In fact, most of Italy's military ventures were disastrous. Against her will she found herself increasingly dependent on German economic and military support and eventually became little more than a satellite of the Third Reich.

Japan came much closer than Italy to achieving her goal of foreign domination. The military clique that came to power in 1940 pledged to build a New Order in East Asia by establishing the Greater East Asia Co-Prosperity Sphere. Having gained control of Manchuria and much of China in the 1930's, the Japanese wrested Indochina from Vichy France after Hitler's victory in 1940. The bombing of Pearl Harbor in December 1941 signaled the opening of a large-scale expansionist campaign (see pp. 314–321). Within a year the Land of the Rising Sun had captured the Philippines, British Malaya, the Netherlands East Indies, and other Pacific islands, to whom the New Order meant military rule and economic exploitation.

Although the Japanese were harsh overlords, they never instituted an overall system of terror like the one imposed in lands under Nazi rule. The Kempeitai, Japan's military secret police, were every bit as ruthless as the Gestapo and SS, and there were many instances of Japanese atrocities and inhuman treatment of prisoners of war and civilians; but in general they were less dedicated to terror than the Germans.

The Nazis, on the other hand, developed an intricate and efficient system of brutality. Throughout the lands they came to rule, but especially in the Slavic nations to the east of the Reich, the New Order meant total subjugation to the German *Herrenvolk* ("master race"). Administered by Heinrich Himmler's SS (Schutzstaffel), the New Order imposed a reign of torture, execution, kidnap, deportation, slave labor, and genocide throughout Europe.

Hitler never drew up a detailed plan for his 1,000 Year Reich, but his conversations, speeches, and orders clearly indicate the sort of empire he had in mind. His primary concern was Eastern Europe: Poland, Czechoslovakia, the Ukraine, and the U.S.S.R. The Fuehrer had long coveted those rich eastern expanses, and dreamed of securing them for *Lebensraum* ("living space") and for their rich natural resources. These lands and their Slavic populations, which Hitler termed *Untermenschen* ("subhumans"), were to be ruthlessly exploited for the benefit of the Reich.

After the conquest of Poland in 1939, Hitler began to execute his plans. On October 7, 1939, he appointed SS Chief Heinrich Himmler to take charge of establishing the New Order in Eastern Europe. Special SS and Gestapo units were set up to supervise the operations: rounding up and deporting men and women to Germany, eliminating Poland's ruling gentry and intelligentsia, and herding the Jews of Warsaw and other cities into walled ghettos.

THE WAR WITHIN A WAR: SUFFERING AND SABOTAGE

Although the full horrors of the Nazi death camps were not revealed until the war ended, most people in occupied Europe saw Gestapo brutality at first hand. In many countries, however, resistance began very slowly. People listened to their exiled leaders broadcast from London on the BBC. Clandestine newspapers, passed from hand to hand, helped combat Nazi propaganda and gave people hope.

As anti-Jewish violence and other repressive measures increased, resistance became more active. Countless individuals and small groups, necessarily ignorant of one another, played their part in the silent, dangerous game to thwart the enemy. Factory and transport workers delayed vital shipments or sent goods to the wrong destination.

The British Special Operations Executive (SOE) trained and supplied agents who committed key acts of sabotage and relayed vital information by radio. By 1943 the resistance network was helping thousands to escape. It proved invaluable in preparing the ground for Allied victory.

This well-fed SS guard (above left), arrested after the war at the Bergen-Belsen camp, had authority over starving prisoners.

A Czech victim of an SS death squad about to be shot (above); fellow prisoners had just dug the mass grave in front of him.

Half-dead of typhoid, a naked victim of the death camps faces her liberators. Disease was rampant at most of the Nazi camps.

The clandestine press (here powered by bicycle) fueled the resistance movement, boosting morale and spreading news.

This symbol of loyalty to exiled King Haakon VII (inside the V for victory) appeared all over Norway. Below, Dutch saboteurs pose by their handiwork.

In the summer of 1941 Himmler's deputy, Reinhard Heydrich, was instructed to draw up plans for the "final solution" of the Jewish problem. (In Hitler's mind the Jew was the archenemy of civilization and the source of all evil in the world.) Heydrich formulated two solutions. One was to send mobile extermination squads behind the Wehrmacht as it marched into eastern Poland and the U.S.S.R. (Germany had invaded the Soviet Union in June 1941, see pp. 328–335) to kill all Jews and local Communist leaders on the spot. The other plan involved building enormous extermination camps, equipped with efficient gas chambers and modern crematoria, in Poland. In the next four years nearly 6 million Jews were transported to Auschwitz, Treblinka, Belsen, and other sites, where they were systematically slaughtered.

Those who attempted to undermine the New Order by sabotage, subversion, or armed resistance were brutally punished. In some cases whole villages were destroyed in reprisal to discourage other would-be resisters. After Heydrich's car was blown up by the underground outside Prague in late May 1942 (mortally wounded, Heydrich died June 4), the Nazis surrounded the nearby village of Lidice, rounded up its citizens, and shot every male over 16 years of age. The women and children were separated and carried off to concentration camps. Then the village was burned. Another target of Nazi reprisal was the small town of Oradour-sur-Glane near Limoges, France. On June 10, 1944, SS units stormed into the town, locked up the men in barns and the women and children in a church, riddled the buildings with machinegun bullets, and then set fire to them.

The Jews of Warsaw staged a desperate, month-long uprising in the spring of 1943, after all but 60,000 of the original 450,000 had died or been taken to the death camps. When the SS tried to remove the remaining Jews from the Warsaw ghetto in mid-April, they resisted, and the angry SS commander ordered his men to besiege the ghetto with tanks, guns, flamethrowers, and dynamite. Resistance collapsed in mid-May, after the SS blew up the Warsaw synagogue, where the few hundred survivors had sought refuge.

Although such acts of brutality discouraged many from opposing the Nazis, they did not completely destroy the spirit of resistance. Throughout occupied Europe small groups of men and women organized underground newspapers, established spy networks, and planned and carried out sabotage operations. They gathered valuable intelligence about German activities and aided Allied agents, downed aviators, and escaped prisoners of war. Perhaps just as important as the work they did was that such groups provided at least some people of occupied Europe with a shred of hope that they might one day be able to throw off the intolerable yoke of Hitler's 1,000 Year Reich.

The Artist as Propagandist

Among the advanced technologies that made World War II global were those of communications. Without them, strategies could not have been coordinated nor supply lines kept open. Just as important, the hearts and minds of whole populations could not have been so readily mobilized for the conflict.

It was in this last area that artists on both sides did their bit. Three who far exceeded the call of duty were Hitler's architect Albert Speer, American poet Ezra Pound, who lived in and sided with Fascist Italy during the war, and Soviet filmmaker Sergei Eisenstein.

Albert Speer A few days after the fall of France in June 1940 Adolf Hitler made an unannounced early-morning tour of Paris. That evening, back at field headquarters in northeast France, he summoned the 34-year-old Albert Speer, who had been his companion during the three-hour excursion. "Wasn't Paris beautiful!" the Fuehrer exclaimed to his favorite architect. "But Berlin must be made far more beautiful. I have often considered whether we would not have to destroy Paris," he continued. "But when we are finished in Berlin, Paris will only be a shadow. So why destroy it?"

Hours later Hitler dictated instructions for Speer: "By a top-speed reconstruction program Berlin is to be given an architectural style commensurate with the grandeur of our victory and suitable to the capital of a powerful new Reich. I expect you to complete this project by the year 1950." The city would be renamed "Germania."

Architecture is a classic medium for national propaganda, and the idea of building a showcase capital for the Thousand-Year Reich had obsessed Hitler since the early 1920's. Like the ancient Athenian leader Pericles, who first envisioned the Parthenon as a display of his city's imperial greatness, Hitler had a highly detailed idea of what he wanted. Pericles had entrusted the actual design and execution to his friend, the sculptor Phidias. Nevertheless, the project was a close collaboration, and the result has ever since proclaimed the glory that was Greece. Hitler needed a new Phidias to transform Berlin.

Young Speer first attracted Hitler's attention in summer 1933 when, as a volunteer, he designed the magnificent setting for the first Nuremberg party rally—gratis. Inviting him to dinner afterward, Hitler asked Speer to do it again the following year and submit a bill.

For the 1934 rally, documented by filmmaker Leni Riefenstahl in her famous *Triumph of the Will*, Speer created a vast torchlight pageant. Tens of thousands of flags and marching men advanced in darkness toward the Fuehrer's eagle-crowned platform, to surround it on three sides within a space ringed by 130 antiaircraft searchlights, which blazed straight up into the night sky to a height of 25,000 feet, where they merged into a general glow. British Ambassador Nevile Henderson wrote: "The effect, which was both solemn and beautiful, was like being in a cathedral of ice."

Speer's fortunes skyrocketed as he rapidly became the leading confidant and achiever of his master's grandiose dreams. Inexhaustibly inventive, he gave those dreams tangible form, and each year brought new triumphs, new honors.

January 1939 witnessed completion of the New Chancellery (in the ruins of which the Fuehrer was to die six years later). Upon moving into his new residence, Hitler had a large 1 : 1,000-scale model of Germania set up in former exhibition rooms of the Berlin Academy of Arts

Albert Speer *designed a new chancellery to be built when Germany won the war. He chose artist Werner Peiner (a Goering protégé) to decorate its great hall with tapestries. Left, a detail from Peiner's design.*

For Nuremberg *party rallies Speer designed a giant stone installation and the famous "cathedral of light" effect (right), which was immortalized by Leni Riefenstahl's film* Triumph of the Will. *From 1934 onward Speer put in hundreds of hours at the drawing board with Hitler (below right), planning the grandiose Berlin of 1950. Hitler planned to rename the city "Germania."*

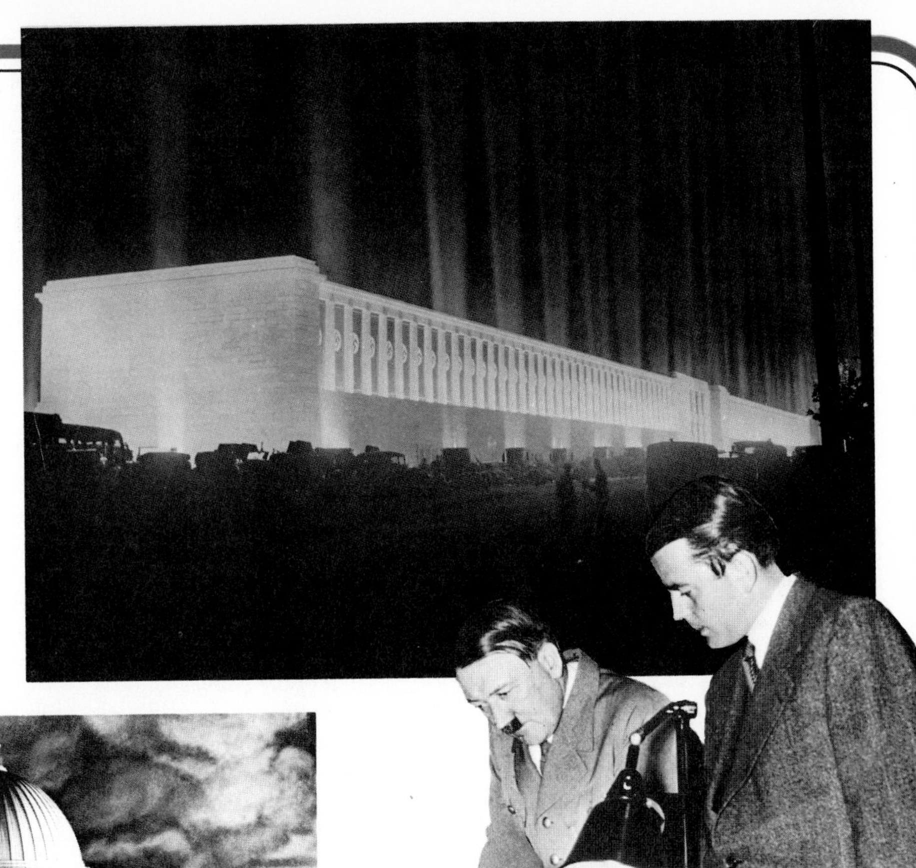

Jointly designed *by Hitler and Speer, the Great Hall of the German People was to symbolize the capital of the victorious Third Reich.*

next door. Hand-shaped and painted in lifelike detail in accordance with Speer's specifications by a team of master woodworkers, the 100-foot-long model simulated an overview of midtown Berlin along an axis formed by a grand boulevard which, like much else in the project, was Hitler's own brainchild. At its southern extremity a triumphal arch three times the size of Napoleon's Arc de Triomphe in Paris crowned the station plaza of an ultramodern rail terminal. From it future state visitors would emerge to a vista that could only leave them stunned.

Each night the avenue would become a Great White Way flooded with pleasure-seekers. This three-mile-long splash of sound and light was to culminate at the gaudy Adolf Hitler Platz, in front of a 726-foot-high dome, the tallest on earth. The dome, standing at the nerve center of Europe's capital, would symbolize nazism for all time to come, as St. Peter's in Rome had for centuries symbolized Christendom.

The interior of the great domed hall would hold 200,000 people standing. Outside, its copper-sheathed dome would be surmounted by a 132-foot turret, which in turn would be crowned by an eagle perched on a globe, emblem of Germany's world leadership. Adolf Hitler Platz would be closed to motor traffic, so that visitors might admire undisturbed the hall's colonnaded front with its delicate marble friezes and columns of red Swedish granite, flanked at either end by colossal sculptures of Atlas and Tellus bearing blue-enameled spheres representing Earth and the vault of the heavens, their respective continents and constellations stamped in gold.

The second-biggest building on Adolf Hitler Platz would be Hitler's own palace, with its facade of red mosaics, white marble pillars, bronze lions, and gilded silhouettes—the only openings the steel entrance gate and a door to a balcony five stories up, from which the Fuehrer could appear to the crowd.

All neighboring buildings would be likewise equipped with steel shutters and doors. Iron gates for closing off the square would enable the guards' regiment garrisoned there to transform Adolf Hitler Platz quickly into a citadel.

These were the dream Germania's highlights, and Hitler never tired of playing tour guide, taking intimates and honored guests to view the models. Under the spotlights he could unbend, growing lively and voluble in the make-believe 1950 sun. Beside him Speer grew ever stiffer and more taciturn.

The fantasy tours wore on into their third year. By autumn 1941 Speer was using a labor force of 65,000—tearing up large sections of midtown Berlin, sinking foundations, and building a fleet of ships to bring in granite and marble from abroad. Costs reached nearly 4 percent of the total annual volume of the German construction industry. Speer clearly foresaw the end; he begged the Fuehrer to release the laborers for repair work on communications lines in Russia. Shocked at the mere suggestion, Hitler ordered the work to continue.

Called to Hitler's rooms at 1 a.m. on February 8, 1942, for another session of city planning, Speer made a supreme effort to play along. It worked. "That night our dreams were transformed into realities; we had once again worked ourselves up to a hallucinatory optimism."

Next morning, startled out of sleep by a bedside phone, Speer learned that production minister Dr. Fritz Todt had died in a plane crash minutes earlier. That same day Hitler designated Speer as Todt's successor.

Four weeks later, acting in his new capacity as Minister of Armaments and War Production, Speer had to kill the Germania project.

Ezra Pound Just after 6 p.m. on December 7, 1941, shortwave radio listeners in Great Britain and North America who were tuned in to Rome Radio heard a thin, strained voice. In a flat Pennsylvania accent it touched on a variety of topics, including Confucius, monetary reform, international finance, fascism, and the British and U.S. governments. Addressing a nation that had just been shocked by the Japanese attack on Pearl Harbor, the speaker declared: "Lord knows I don't see how America can have fascism without years of previous training." The voice (which had been heard twice weekly—same time, same station—since January 1940) was that of the American poet and critic Ezra Pound.

Long recognized as a literary giant, Pound was best known for his epic *Cantos,* a poetic reconstruction of the story of civilization. His famous cry, "Make it new!" had become the motto of a whole generation, including Robert Frost, Ernest Hemingway, E. E. Cummings, T. S. Eliot, and James Joyce, whose careers he had furthered and in some cases singlehandedly launched. Whenever Pound embraced a new cause, be it imagism, futurism, or the New Criticism, he always managed to create a flurry of interest. By 1939, when he persuaded Italian officials to let him use Rome Radio as a soapbox, fascism had been his favorite cause for a decade or more.

Pound had lived in Italy since 1925, in the Ligurian seaside town of Rapallo. A believer in the Fascist ideal of the "corporate state," in which all would be represented in government by men of their own trade or profession, rather than by geographical area as in a democracy, he had published a book likening Mussolini to Thomas Jefferson. Both, after all, were shapers of their respective national revolutions. The Duce's aims (Pound argued) were as noble as Jefferson's had been, in that Mussolini was animated by "a vast will for the welfare of Italy, not Italy as a bureaucracy, or Italy as a state machinery stuck on top of the people, but for Italy organic, composed of the last ploughman and the last girl in the olive-yards."

Like many before and since, the poet believed that the modern world was choking on its own economics. He had perceived the increasing concentration of big money—and power—in the hands of a relatively small number of competing financiers. The only remedy was to establish credit without interest—thereby abolishing the practice of money earning money, which Pound viewed as the world's main evil. Modern banking, he argued, was really just plain usury.

Fascism would soon find a way to put an end to usury, Pound hoped, and would topple the financial czars—the Rothschilds, Morgans, Mellons, Rockefellers, and the rest—who Pound believed had actually provoked and cruelly protracted the Great War of 1914. It had been a mere struggle for markets and for the aggrandizement of territories, spheres of influence, power, and money. As a humane man who had lost some of his dearest friends in the war, Pound was deeply shocked at the idea that millions had been done to death, crippled, or crazed in such a struggle—all for the sake of a few bankers. Succumbing to a fallacy then widespread, he became a believer in the so-called Jewish conspiracy and an anti-Semite. Such was his state of mind on Pearl Harbor Day 1941, and since he viewed the present war as a repetition of the last, it was as good a day as any to denounce Roosevelt as the puppet of Wall Street.

*"**Does anyone** have the slightest idea what I said?" Ezra Pound asked while debating whether his Rome Radio talks constituted treason or lawful exercise of the right of free speech. This photo shows him returning to face U.S. treason charges in November 1945.*

Following this final sally, Pound left Rome and retired to Rapallo "to seek wisdom from the ancients. I wanted to figure things out."

The poet contemplated returning to the U.S., but when offered passage he declined, unwilling to risk his family's lives. His parents, who had come years earlier to spend their retirement in Rapallo, were now very old, and Homer (the elder Pound) was bedridden. He was equally loath to endanger the younger family, which included a daughter, Mary. These private problems were further complicated when the U.S. Chargé d'Affaires in Rome allegedly told Pound he could not return in any case, and a diplomatic train left Rome for Lisbon carrying all remaining Americans except the poet's family.

Unable to decide what to do, Pound sat at his father's bedside reading out loud to him from the works of Aristotle and Henry James.

Pound finally made up his mind "to use Rome Radio for personal propaganda in support of U.S. Constitution" and returned to Rome from Rapallo. The announcer, reintroducing him to listeners on January 29, 1942, added: "He will not be asked to say anything whatsoever that goes against his conscience, or anything incompatible with his duties as a U.S. citizen." Taking the microphone, Pound had strong words to say: "The U.S. has

"EUROPE CALLIN', POUND SPEAKIN'"

In the Middle Ages *usura* ("usury") meant the charging of any interest on a loan. Both the civil and canonical laws of Western Christendom forbade the practice. Ezra Pound was obsessed with the idea and engaged in a one-man crusade against modern banking, which he denounced as "usura." One medieval alternative had been a free-credit system. That, the poet asserted, had worked splendidly and should be restored. His celebrated "Canto XLV" deals with the evil consequences of "usura." Pound read the poem over Rome Radio in 1942. The headline above was his call signal.

Canto XLV

With Usura
With usura hath no man a house
of good stone
each block cut smooth and well fitting
that design might cover their face,
with usura
hath no man a painted paradise on
his church wall
harpes et luthes
or where virgin receiveth message
and halo projects from incision,
with usura
seeth no man Gonzaga his heirs and
his concubines
no picture is made to endure nor
to live with
but it is made to sell and sell quickly
with usura, sin against nature,
is thy bread ever more of stale rags
is thy bread dry as paper,
with no mountain wheat, no strong flour
with usura the line grows thick
with usura is no clear demarcation
and no man can find site for
his dwelling.
Stone cutter is kept from his stone
weaver is kept from his loom
WITH USURA
wool comes not to market
sheep bringeth no gain with usura
Usura is a murrain, usura
blunteth the needle in the maid's hand
and stoppeth the spinner's cunning.
Pietro Lombardo
came not by usura
Duccio came not by usura
nor Pier della Francesca; Zuan
Bellin' not by usura
nor was 'La Calunnia' painted.
Came not by usura Angelico; came
not Ambrogio Praedis,
Came no church of cut stone signed:
Adamo me fecit.
Not by usura St Trophime
Not by usura Saint Hilaire,
Usura rusteth the chisel
It rusteth the craft and the craftsman
It gnaweth the thread in the loom
None learneth to weave gold in
her pattern;
Azure hath a canker by usura;
cramoisi is unbroidered
Emerald findeth no Memling
Usura slayeth the child in the womb
It stayeth the young man's courting
It hath brought palsey to bed, lyeth
between the young bride and
her bridegroom
CONTRA NATURAM
They have brought whores for Eleusis
Corpses are set to banquet
at behest of usura.

been misinformed. The U.S. has been led down the garden-path and maybe down under the daisies. All through shutting out the news."

The reaction among U.S. intellectuals was an angry one. Years later, a well-known poet was wont to say, "He sounded just like Hitler!" This theme was repeated often.

Actually, Pound did not sound at all like Hitler. Much of the time, he sounded like an oldtime vaudeville comedian. He had a gift for mimicry and could easily serve up a dozen or more ethnic and dialect gags in the course of any quarter-hour show. (Joyce had once aptly dubbed him "the ventriloqual agitator.") He talked a lot about Confucius ("the original philosopher of Fascism") and sometimes of fellow artists—Eliot, Cummings, and Céline, for example. At other times he would come on the air to rant against the betrayal of America in 1863 by northern financiers, denounce Churchill, or reply to a BBC statement that "Japs" were "barbarous jackals," citing Noh drama as proof that "would convince any man with more sense than a peahen of the degree of Japanese civilization."

Once Pound admitted his occasional inability to think clearly: "I lose my thread at times. . . . This war is proof of such vast incomprehensions, such tangled ignorance, so many strains of unknowing, I am held up, enraged. . . ."

Then, one evening in the summer of 1943, Pound chanced to hear over the BBC that he had been indicted for treason by a federal grand jury in Washington, D.C. Stunned, he wrote to Atty. Gen. Francis Biddle: "I do not believe that the simple fact of speaking over the radio, wherever placed, can in itself constitute treason. I think that must depend on what is said, and on the motives for speaking." Undaunted and convinced of his mission as a man of truth, Pound kept on broadcasting.

Shortly thereafter, in September 1943, when American tanks were rolling into the southern end of Italy, Pound hiked out toward the northern end, provided only with the clothes on his back, a knapsack, three eggs, a map, and a walking stick. He traveled 450 miles northward, mostly on foot, sleeping under the stars. American troops entered Rapallo a year and a half later, in April 1945. Pound was translating a Chinese philosophical work when they came to arrest him.

Orders came from Washington to place him in the maximum-security isolation section of the "Disciplinary Training Center," which U.S. Military Police had set up next to a highway outside Pisa for the confinement of soldiers under sentence of death and other dangerous offenders. Mystified and frightened, the 60-year-old man found himself in a roofless steel cage with a cement floor. The only furniture was one blanket and one bucket, to be emptied once a day. The cage was narrow, barely high enough for Pound to stand up.

After a week's isolation in the summer heat, glare, ear-splitting noise, and all-night floodlights focused on the roadside cages, the old man's features twisted into a strange grimace. Uncontrollably, his eyebrows lifted as high as they could go and stayed that way for two weeks. One day, delirious with fever, Pound went out of his mind.

Recovering, he found himself still in the Pisan camp, but in a tent. Later, allowed pencils, paper, and school exercise books, he wrote the *Pisan Cantos,* a 100-page manuscript often called his finest work.

Returned to Washington, D.C., in November 1945, Pound was declared mentally unfit to stand trial and was confined in St. Elizabeth's Hospital, an insane asylum. He remained there until early 1959, when the Justice Department agreed to drop the treason charges on condition that he return to Italy. This he gladly did. Death came on November 1, 1972, in Venice, where nearly 70 years earlier he had written verses to the "Venice of dreams."

At the climax *of* Ivan the Terrible, Part I, *the Stalin-like Czar Ivan, in self-imposed exile at Alexandrov monastery, is approached by a procession of Muscovites, who petition him to return to Moscow and resume his fight against the aristocracy and the church. "Each take represented an Eisenstein sketch," Nikolai Cherkasov, the star of* Ivan, *was to write years later. "He composed each shot just so, and tried to make each take a finished tableau." Above, some of Eisenstein's sketches and, right, the processional scene from the film itself.*

Sergei Eisenstein Soviet Kazakhstan had a freak heat wave during April–May 1942. For 16 days it was like breathing in an oven, each breath parching the nostrils, sinuses, and lungs. The temperature is said to have gone as high as 140° F on occasion. But there was no provision for heat waves in the production schedule of *Ivan the Terrible;* so director Sergei Eisenstein started filming on the scheduled date, April 22.

In the heat at the barren outdoor filming location, people and things seemed to be swimming in midair—the sound truck parked in the buffalo grass, the parasol under which there floated a 35-mm movie camera, and behind it Eisenstein, a thickset man with an enormous face, blue eyes, quivering lips, and pointed ears under a pith helmet.

All efforts focused on the actors—make-believe soldiers and princes of 16th-century Muscovy besieging the Mongol citadel of Kazan.

Ivan the Terrible—story of Ivan IV (1530–84), the first Czar, who destroyed the independence of the aristocracy and welded Russia into one nation under his command—had been commissioned by the Soviet film trust MOSFILM on Stalin's special orders. The project was entrusted to Sergei Eisenstein because of the filmmaker's tremendous popular success with *Alexander Nevsky* (1938)—story of the invasion of Russia by Teutonic Knights in the year 1242. At the climax of the earlier film (much heightened by composer Sergei Prokofiev's exciting musical score), the great hero Alexander Nevsky leads Russians in battle on the ice of Lake Peipus and sends the invaders to their doom in the frozen waters of the lake. All over the U.S.S.R. children dressed in Nevsky-style chain mail made of paper clips drove the Teuton invaders from their courtyards with broomstick lances. The delighted Stalin exclaimed half-jokingly to Eisenstein, "Sergei Mikhailovich, you're a good Bolshevik after all!"

These were indeed barbed words. The Great Purge was still at its height; the film industry had been hard hit; Eisenstein's position as the maker of the greatest Communist propaganda film ever, *Battleship Potemkin* (1925), story of a successful sailors' mutiny during the 1905 revolution, was no guarantee of immunity from arrest and imprisonment or even execution. *Potemkin* had influenced intellectuals the world over. But Eisenstein's position in Stalin's Russia was shaky until he made *Alexander Nevsky*.

Not only was *Nevsky* the best propaganda piece yet in the government's campaign to reawaken nationalist feeling and prepare the Russian people for war with Germany, but it pointed to the role of national hero which Stalin intended to play during the coming war.

Mindful of Lenin's dictum that "Cinema is the most important of all the arts," and wanting to build up his personal image even more in the minds of the masses by associating it with the legend of Ivan the Terrible, founder of the Russian state, Stalin instructed Eisenstein to make an *Ivan* that would outdo *Nevsky*.

Eisenstein had been at work on the script for Part I of the projected two-part *Ivan the Terrible* for six months when the Nazi invasion came. Then, in mid-October 1941, with the Germans at the gates of Moscow, his entire studio was packed aboard a train ("a modern Noah's ark," he quipped) and transported to Alma-Ata, capital of Kazakhstan, in Central Asia.

By summer 1942 shooting was in full swing. Prokofiev arrived to collaborate with Eisenstein on the score. Typical suggestions from the director were: "At this point the music must sound like a mother tearing her own child to pieces," or "Do it so that it sounds like a cork rubbed down a pane of glass."

Nikolai Cherkasov (star of both *Nevsky* and *Ivan*) was later to write

***Dressed up** in the imperial robes by Ivan, Boyarina Euphrosyne's son Vladimir dies as his mother's plot to kill the Czar backfires—the assassin has mistaken Vladimir for Ivan. "Vladimir has crashed down to the stone floor on his face . . . Euphrosyne has come running: 'Behold, O people! Ivan is finished: the beast is dead! Russia shall bloom under a boyar Czar . . . Vladimir!' She has stopped, suddenly. The rows of Lifeguards have made room. And, from the depths, toward her, slowly . . . Ivan advances."*

***A snapshot** (below) of the director in a joking mood was made by his cameraman, who labeled it: "S. M. Eisenstein, showing disgust and anger to cameraman because the composition of the scene was no good, prepares to scourge him with an old whip used to flog rebel Indian workers."*

that each take corresponded to a finished Eisenstein drawing—not the mere sketch that would satisfy other directors. "He tried to make every take a finished tableau. He modeled his scenes like sculpture."

Meantime Eisenstein wrote in his notebook: "Cherkasov's incomparably lithe and flexible body will practice long and tiringly to produce the tragic bend of Czar Ivan's figure as I spontaneously fixed it on paper. These drawings are no more (but also no less) than those Japanese paper toys that, when cast into warm water, unfold and develop stems, leaves, and flowers of fantastic and surprising shape."

Eisenstein's working method—the drawings, the formalism akin to that of the classic Kabuki theater of Japan—was in fact taking a heavy physical and emotional toll on his actors. In the end, the realism-oriented Cherkasov was on the edge of a nervous breakdown.

Following its Moscow premiere at the beginning of January 1945, *Ivan the Terrible, Part I,* was an instant triumph. Eisenstein, however, went straight back to Alma-Ata. In less than a year he completed the even more formalistic and subjective *Part II,* with its savage finale in which the Czar destroys his power-hungry aunt and her effeminate son, by means of whom she had aimed to seize state power. This part is shot on captured German color film. Its bloodcurdling beauty combines with a tightly involuted formalism: *Ivan the Terrible, Part II,* is no propaganda film, whatever hopes Eisenstein may have had for it.

Eisenstein's friends threw a party for him in February 1946, the day he finished editing *Part II.* With difficulty, they extricated him from the cutting room. His Stalin Prize, First Class, for *Ivan the Terrible, Part I,* was announced to the guests. Toasts were drunk, and Eisenstein appeared elated. He flirted with the women, was jovially expansive with the men. He told friends of plans for a *Part III,* which would complete the *Ivan* cycle.

One of his actresses, the young and beautiful Vera Maretskaya, appeared. Eisenstein asked her to dance. They took a few turns on the floor, then stopped dancing. Eisenstein staggered backward and collapsed, a terrible pain in his chest.

Ignoring the advice of a doctor who was saying, "If you move, you are a dead man," he struggled up and left on the arm of a friend who drove him to the hospital.

After a painfully slow recovery, he learned that *Part II* was banned, following a Central Committee resolution condemning the sequences in which Ivan's police became "like a band of degenerates" and Ivan himself "something like Hamlet."

He replied with a public self-criticism: "Like a bad foundryman, we light-mindedly allowed the precious stream of creation to be poured over sand and become disposed in private, unessential sidelines." At the same time, he wrote privately to Stalin, begging to be allowed to continue with *Part III.* Stalin invited him and Cherkasov to tea and treated them with hospitable warmth. Nothing was changed, he assured them. *Part III* would start as soon as Eisenstein's health permitted.

But his heart disease got steadily worse. Late at night on February 2, 1948, he suffered a final heart attack while alone in his apartment. The unfinished manuscript of a treatise on color film that he had been writing lay on the table in front of him.

A CHRONOLOGY OF THE ARTS: 1939-45

1939

- Release of film classic, *Gone With the Wind,* about the U.S. Civil War.

1940

- Charlie Chaplin starred in *The Great Dictator,* a film satirizing Hitler.
- The concluding section of Mikhail Sholokhov's epic novel of World War I, *Quiet Flows the Don,* was published in the U.S.S.R.
- Prehistoric wall paintings discovered in the Lascaux Cave, France.
- German novelist Ernst Jünger published his masterpiece *On the Marble Cliffs.* Elements of antitotalitarian allegory caused German authorities to order the book withdrawn.
- Nordahl Grieg, a Norwegian patriot who had earlier fled from the Nazis to England, published the anthology *Norwegian War Lyrics.*
- U.S. author Ernest Hemingway published *For Whom the Bell Tolls,* a novel of the Spanish Civil War as experienced by the Republicans.

1941

- In the U.S.A. Orson Welles produced, wrote, directed, and starred in *Citizen Kane,* a film depicting the rise and fall of a newspaper tycoon.
- Romans acclaimed the play *Hero Without a Tragedy,* by G. Cenzato.
- Leftist German playwright Bertolt Brecht arrived in Hollywood, where he worked throughout the war years as a screenwriter.

1942

- Some 10,000 U.S. artists organized the Artists' Council for Victory.
- U.S. author John Steinbeck published a new bestseller, *The Moon Is Down.* The book argued the effectiveness of passive resistance.
- U.S. poet Edna St. Vincent Millay published a book-length poem, *The Murder of Lidice.* Lidice was a Czech village demolished by German troops after they had massacred its male inhabitants in reprisal for the assassination of deputy Gestapo Chief Reinhard "Hangman" Heydrich.
- In July leaders of the U.S. movie industry publicly resolved to depict Negroes as an integral part of American life and of the "world at war"; black performers would no longer be restricted to comic and menial roles.
- U.S. artist Jackson Pollock has his first one-man show, in New York City.

1943

- French philosopher Jean-Paul Sartre published his monumental *Being and Nothingness,* the first full statement of existentialist philosophy.
- Anglo-American poet and critic T. S. Eliot published *Four Quartets,* a meditation on the meaning of history.
- The 30-year-old Welsh poet Dylan Thomas, who had joined the British Army in 1940, published *New Poems.* The raging violence of Thomas' imagery proclaimed a world of pain and terror.
- *Oklahoma!*—by Rodgers and Hammerstein—opened in New York.

1944

- New York witnessed an unprecedented number of one-man abstract shows, as U.S. artists (and collectors) came increasingly to favor withdrawal from the social realism of the thirties and early war years.
- With the liberation of Paris, the literary men of the hour included novelist André Malraux, who had fought in the underground; Algerian-born novelist, playwright, and philosopher Albert Camus, also an activist; and the poets of the French Resistance, Paul Éluard and Louis Aragon.
- In Germany director Veit Harlan finished his historical film *Kolberg,* in which a German town stands fast against an enemy of overwhelmingly superior strength. A color spectacular that featured 187,000 soldiers and 6,000 horses, it was to open in Berlin on January 30, 1945, the day Germans would commemorate the 12th anniversary of the Third Reich.

1945

- In May the U.S. 101st Airborne Division displayed art treasures pillaged by Hermann Goering. Valued at $200 million, they were discovered hidden away in a Bavarian cave by a counterintelligence unit of the 7th Army.

1941

The War in the Pacific

Japan inaugurates her war of conquest with a sneak attack on the United States Pacific Fleet at Pearl Harbor.

Just before 8 a.m. on Sunday December 7, 1941, the skies above the island of Oahu in Hawaii were suddenly filled with Japanese warplanes. Minutes later a huge air fleet of nearly 200 fighters, dive bombers, and torpedo planes attacked the island's airfields and the United States Pacific Fleet at Pearl Harbor. At 8:25 they withdrew and another group of warplanes appeared, carrying on the devastating air strike until 9:45. In less than two hours the Japanese had crippled the main force of the U.S. Fleet, sinking or badly damaging seven battleships, three cruisers, two destroyers, and four auxiliary vessels. They had also

wiped out the island's air defenses, destroying most of the planes before they got off the ground. Altogether, 2,403 U.S. sailors, soldiers, marines, and civilians were dead, and another 1,178 had been wounded.

The next day an angry U.S. President Franklin D. Roosevelt described December 7 as "a date which will live in infamy," and Congress declared war on Japan. On December 11 Germany and Italy, Japan's allies, declared war on the United States, and Congress immediately reciprocated. With shocking swiftness a nation that had remained neutral for more than two years of war in Europe was brought into World War II.

A menacing Japanese bat *carrying a bomb hovers above its target, Pearl Harbor, in a 1942 cartoon from the U.S. magazine* Collier's *(left). The bold sneak attack succeeded in temporarily immobilizing the entire U.S. Pacific Fleet while Japan conquered a sizable Asian empire.*

The Japanese attack on Pearl Harbor *(below), December 7, 1941, was photographed by a Japanese pilot. Exploding bombs sent up huge waterspouts (center), destroyed U.S. naval and air power, but failed to damage the island's vital oil storage tanks (background, right).*

At the time of the attack Japan controlled Korea, Manchuria (renamed Manchukuo), and much of eastern China, including China's coastal ports and the offshore islands of Formosa and Hainan. In addition, she exercised mandate rights over three groups of islands in the Pacific: the Carolines, Marshalls, and Marianas (except for Guam, a U.S. possession). She also held the southern half of Sakhalin, the Kurile Islands, and the Ryukyu, Bonin, and Volcano Islands.

In late June 1940 the success of the German blitzkrieg in Europe (see pp. 288–295) gave the Japanese an unprecedented opportunity for expansion into the French, Dutch, and British colonies in Southeast Asia, an area rich in tin, oil, rubber, and other resources vital to Japan's continued growth. A new Cabinet, dominated by the military, came to power in Tokyo in July 1940 and resolved to bring the Southern Resources Area (which included French Indochina, Burma, Thailand, Malaya, and the Netherlands East Indies), the Philippines, and northern New Guinea into Japan's Greater East Asia Co-Prosperity Sphere.

Accordingly, in September 1940 Japan forced the puppet Vichy regime in France to permit Japanese troops to occupy northern Indochina, where they built airbases for bombing the Burma Road, China's only remaining lifeline to the outside world. Subsequent air raids forced the British to close the road temporarily. The United States, which was sending supplies to Chiang Kai-shek over the Burma Road, retaliated by increasing aid to China and placing a total embargo on the sale of aviation fuel, scrap iron, and steel to Japan on September 26. The next day Japan joined the Axis by signing the Tripartite Pact (see pp. 300–305).

Diplomatic efforts to wring concessions from colonial authorities in the Netherlands East Indies, however, failed. An Imperial Conference in January 1941 discussed the use of force to secure the needed resources in the Netherlands East Indies, and Admiral Isoroku Yamamoto, Commander of the Japanese 1st Fleet, suggested the possibility of a sneak attack on Pearl Harbor to neutralize U.S. naval forces while Japan completed her conquests.

Meanwhile, Japan moved to cover her flanks by signing a five-year nonaggression pact with the U.S.S.R. in April 1941 and by concluding a neutrality pact with Thailand. In July Japan occupied southern Indochina. The United States reacted by freezing all Japanese assets in the U.S.A., and Great Britain and the Netherlands East Indies immediately joined the U.S. trade embargo against Japan. Tokyo, dependent on imports for survival, began laying plans for war.

The Japanese strategy called for a three-stage operation. During the first phase the U.S. Fleet at Pearl Harbor would be destroyed, and Japanese forces would seize Hong Kong, Thailand, Malaya, the Philippines, and the Netherlands East Indies, establishing a

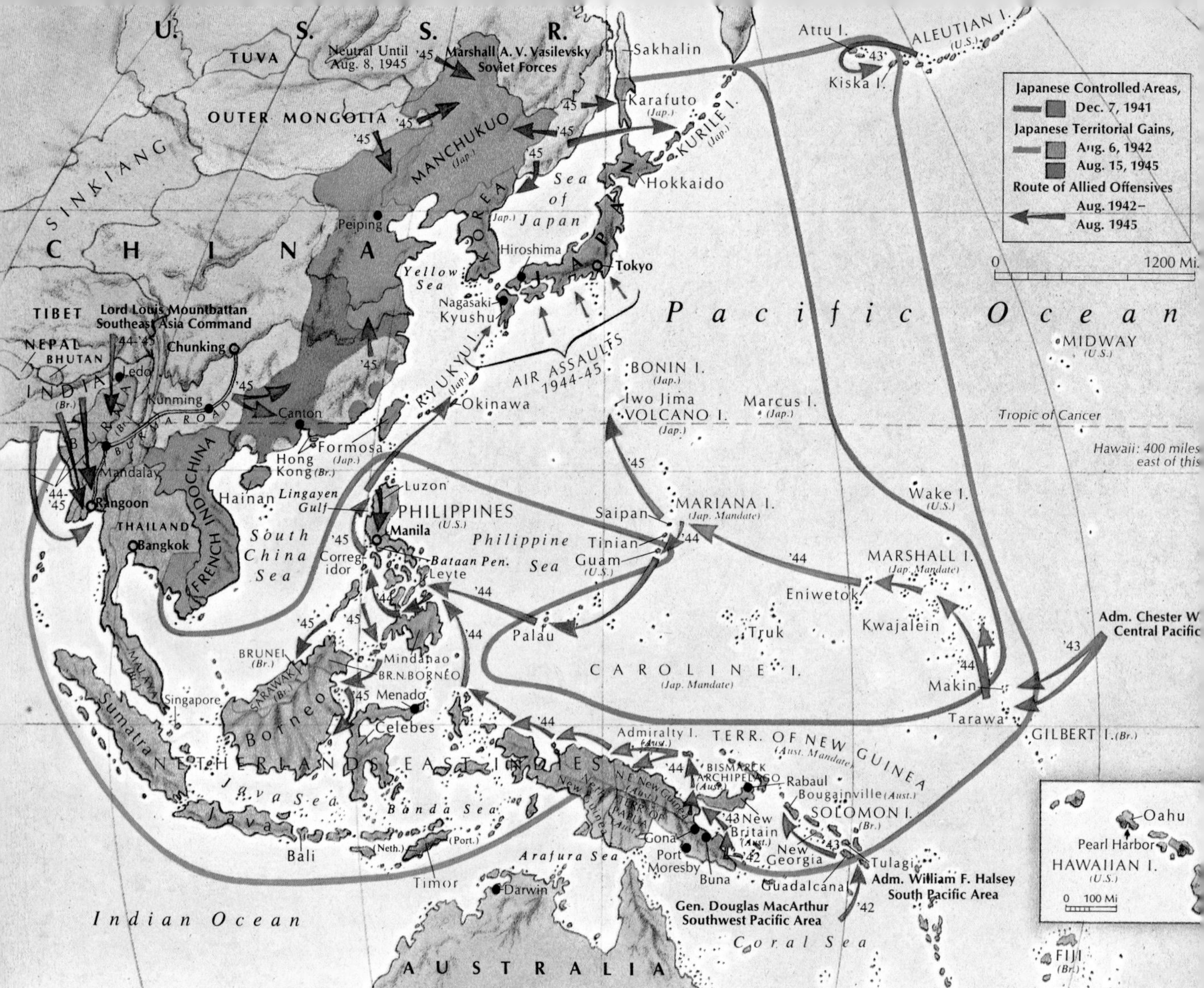

defensive perimeter from the Kurile Islands through the central Pacific to Burma. Phase two would be devoted to firmly establishing the defensive perimeter in preparation for phase three, when Japan would be forced to defend her new acquisitions. In this scenario the enemy would eventually despair of success and accept Japan's conquests.

In the meantime the Japanese continued their efforts to reach a negotiated settlement with the United States. On November 5 they dispatched a special envoy to Washington, but the talks made little progress. On December 1, five days after the United States rejected Japan's final proposals, an Imperial Conference formally decided to go to war.

A special Japanese task force of six aircraft carriers, two battleships, and several destroyers and cruisers had already assembled in secret and had begun steaming toward Hawaii on November 26. Maintaining radio silence, they reached their destination some 200 miles north of Oahu at 6 a.m. on December 7.

Japan's Spectacular Victories

In the short run the attack on Pearl Harbor was a brilliant success. The United States did not recover from its losses for months to come, giving Japan ample time to complete her Asian conquests. In the long run it proved to be a serious blunder. The U.S. Pacific Fleet's three aircraft carriers, which were away from their base at the time of the raid, were not harmed. Their survival was to prove significant.

Within hours Japan followed up her triumph at Pearl Harbor with attacks throughout the Pacific. Fighting in most cases against inexperienced and poorly equipped colonial troops, Japan's forces achieved spectacular victories. On December 8 her bombers struck at three more U.S. Pacific bases: Midway, Wake, and Guam. The attackers destroyed the airbase at Midway and then withdrew, but small forces captured Guam on December 10 and Wake on December 23. The British Crown Colony of Hong Kong fell on Christmas Day.

THE WAR IN THE PACIFIC

The success of Japan's overall strategy in World War II hinged on the attack on the U.S. Fleet at Pearl Harbor. By thus weakening the American naval forces, she hoped for complete freedom to carry out her planned expansion into Southeast Asia, including the capture of sizable oil, tin, and rubber resources.

In fact, three aircraft carriers escaped destruction at Pearl Harbor and gave the U.S.A.—which promptly launched the most massive program of shipbuilding and arms manufacture in history—a nucleus with which to fight back. Even so, the first months of the war saw a series of Japanese victories. Then the tide turned and in three years of bitter and costly fighting the Allies wrested one island after another from the Japanese forces, who resisted them with suicidal determination.

U.S. marines dash from their landing craft onto the beach at Guadalcanal during the Allied campaign in the Solomon Islands.

At the same time, Japanese forces advanced from Indochina into Thailand and down the Malay Peninsula. By the end of January 1942 the British colonial forces had withdrawn to the island of Singapore at the tip of the Malay Peninsula. Singapore, the symbol of British strength in the Far East, fell on February 15, opening up the Indian Ocean and the Netherlands East Indies to the Japanese.

Meanwhile, only hours after the attack on Pearl Harbor, Japanese warplanes had blasted the heavy bombers on the runways at Clark Field on Luzon, largest of the Philippine Islands, a U.S. possession. Two days later Japanese troops went ashore on northern Luzon; a second force debarked on southern Luzon on December 12. By January 7, 1942, U.S. and Filipino troops under Gen. Douglas MacArthur had been pushed back to the narrow Bataan Peninsula and the adjacent island fortress of Corregidor. Cut off from all outside relief, the garrison resisted bravely; but as rations dwindled, disease and malnutrition took their toll. On March 12 MacArthur was evacuated to take command of Allied forces in the southwest Pacific, and in April the Bataan garrison surrendered. Corregidor, last U.S. stronghold in the Philippines, fell on May 6.

In January and February Japanese forces overran Borneo, Sumatra, Bali, Java, and other islands in the Netherlands East Indies. The weak Dutch colonial forces were overwhelmed by Japan's swift, coordinated drives, and an Allied naval force sent to defend Java, capital of the Netherlands East Indies, was nearly annihilated in the Battle of the Java Sea in late February. On March 9 the Dutch colonial authorities surrendered the islands to Japan.

Other Japanese forces landed simultaneously in northeastern New Guinea, the Bismarck Archipelago, and the Solomon Islands to establish bases on the southeastern perimeter of the conquered territory. By July Japan had occupied the port of Rabaul in the Bismarcks, the entire northern coast of New Guinea, and islands in the northern Solomons.

In barely five months, with a speed that startled even themselves, the Japanese had completed phase one of their original plan. Phase two called for entrenching themselves within the outer defense perimeter. But Japan's leaders, inflated by their success, had decided to expand that perimeter to include the southern Solomons; Port Moresby in southeastern New Guinea (Papua); the islands of New Caledonia, Fiji, Samoa, and Midway in the north-central Pacific; and the Aleutian Islands off the coast of Alaska.

The islands in the southern Solomons were secured by mid-July, but the Allies intercepted the Japanese naval force sent to seize Port Moresby. The ensuing Battle of the Coral Sea, May 4–8, 1942, ended in a tactical draw: The Americans lost the carrier *Lexington,* and the Japanese lost the light carrier *Shoho;* each side shot down or damaged nearly 100 enemy aircraft. This, the first naval battle ever to be fought entirely by airpower, was nonetheless a strategic victory for the Allies. For the moment at least, they had prevented the Japanese from establishing a stronghold at Port Moresby, within striking distance of Australia.

A month later the Allies thwarted Japan's attempt to seize Midway. Located more than 1,000 miles west-northwest of Hawaii, Midway was to be the key to Japanese control of the northern Pacific. Admiral Yamamoto hoped to destroy the remainder of the U.S. Pacific Fleet in the Battle of Midway, but the contest, which raged from June 3–6, 1942, was an overwhelming U.S. victory. Planes from the U.S. carriers *Hornet, Yorktown,* and *Enterprise* sank the Japanese carriers *Akagi, Kaga, Hiryu,* and *Soryu* (all members of the Pearl Harbor task force), along with many of their aircraft and veteran pilots. Japan's long-range striking capacity, based on powerful aircraft carriers and well-trained pilots, had been effectively destroyed.

Farther north simultaneous Japanese landings against the outlying Aleutian Islands of Attu and Kiska had succeeded; but without the base at Midway the Japanese would be hard pressed to defend them.

1943: Guadalcanal and New Guinea

For the Allies, Midway was a significant turning point. Their victory shattered the myth of Japanese invincibility and encouraged them to adopt a more aggressive policy. Moreover, by mid-1942 the Allied military buildup had begun to accelerate. The 3 U.S. carriers remaining in the Pacific—the *Yorktown* was damaged at Midway and later sank—would eventually be joined by 23 more. (Japan had 6 carriers in service and 18 under construction, of which 12 were finally built.) As time went on, there would be more American pilots, more and better planes for them to fly, and more ships to transport them across the far-flung Pacific battlefront than Japan could hope to match. On land as well, Allied tactics, weapons, and manpower were improving rapidly, and the overall coordination of Allied operations and logistical support was gradually becoming more efficient.

The Allied commanders in chief planned a two-pronged offensive in the southwest Pacific beginning in mid-1942. One force would attack Guadalcanal in the southern Solomons and advance up the Solomon chain. The other would move from Australia through New Guinea. Eventually both prongs would converge on Rabaul, Japan's main base in the southwest Pacific.

U.S. marines began landing on Guadalcanal on August 7 and moved inland, encountering light Japanese resistance. Opposition increased in the next weeks, however, and both sides sent in reinforcements. The battle for the island dragged out into a long, seesaw contest, but the U.S. troops slowly gained ground against the fanatic Japanese defenders, who chose to fight to the death rather than relinquish their positions. In December U.S. troops mounted a final offensive, capturing the last pocket of resistance on February 9, 1943. They found only a few Japanese. The bulk of their forces had been evacuated during the last week of fighting. Other U.S. forces continued the advance through the Solomons in 1943.

The New Guinea campaign, a combined U.S.-Australian effort under the direction of General MacArthur, was scheduled to open at the same time as the Guadalcanal landing but was delayed by a renewed Japanese effort to take Port Moresby. On July 22 Japanese troops landed on the northeastern coast, then headed overland toward Port Moresby. Their advance was slowed by Australian troops, and MacArthur's counterattack at the end of September forced the Japanese into retreat. By mid-November they had been beaten back to the coast, where they held out until January 22, 1943. Some 12,000 Japanese had died rather than surrender. The Allies, on the other hand, had lost only about 3,000 men.

Throughout 1943 the Allies continued their advance up the Solomons and along the northern New Guinea coast. By the end of the year Rabaul had been isolated, and the Allies decided an assault would be unnecessary. Elsewhere in the Pacific there was little fighting during 1942 and most of 1943. After Midway U.S. forces in the central Pacific limited their activities to submarine attacks on enemy shipping and air and naval raids on Japanese island bases. In May and July 1943 the United States recovered Attu and Kiska Islands. On the Asian mainland the Japanese had occupied Burma by May 1942 and closed the Burma Road into China. Allied counteroffensives from September 1942 to May 1943 failed to regain any ground. Meanwhile, the Chinese government in isolated Chungking received supplies from India via an emergency airlift over the 500-mile Himalayan "hump," and the Allies had begun building a new overland supply route to Chungking from Ledo, India.

The Road to Victory

By mid-1943 the Allies had sufficient land, air, and naval power to launch a large-scale offensive. Their plans called for a two-pronged assault on the Philippines. The U.S. Pacific Fleet under Adm. Chester W. Nimitz would approach westward from Hawaii through the Gilbert, Marshall, Caroline, and Mariana Islands. General MacArthur would direct a simultaneous amphibious drive along the northern New Guinea coast toward the Philippines.

Japan's military strategists altered their plans in September 1943. To gain time to rebuild their striking power, they decided to shorten their defensive perimeter to a new line extending from the Kuriles through the Bonins, Marianas, Carolines, western New Guinea, and the Netherlands East Indies to Burma. Japanese forces stationed outside of the new line were ordered to fight to the death to delay the Allies as long as possible while the Japanese fortified their inner bases.

In late November Nimitz opened his campaign with landings on Tarawa and Makin in the Gilbert Islands, which Japan had seized in December 1941. Japanese resistance was fierce but hopeless, as it was on Kwajalein in the Marshall Islands in February 1944. From the Marshalls Nimitz' forces continued westward, reaching the Marianas in June. On June 15 U.S. forces landed on Saipan, administrative center of the Marianas and a vital link in Japan's inner defensive perimeter. Saipan's 30,000-man garrison resisted with incredible bravery. Finally cornered at the northern tip of the island, 4,300 Japanese survivors staged a suicidal night attack; nearly 3,000 of them died. Some 3,000 Americans were killed and 10,000 wounded during the month-long effort.

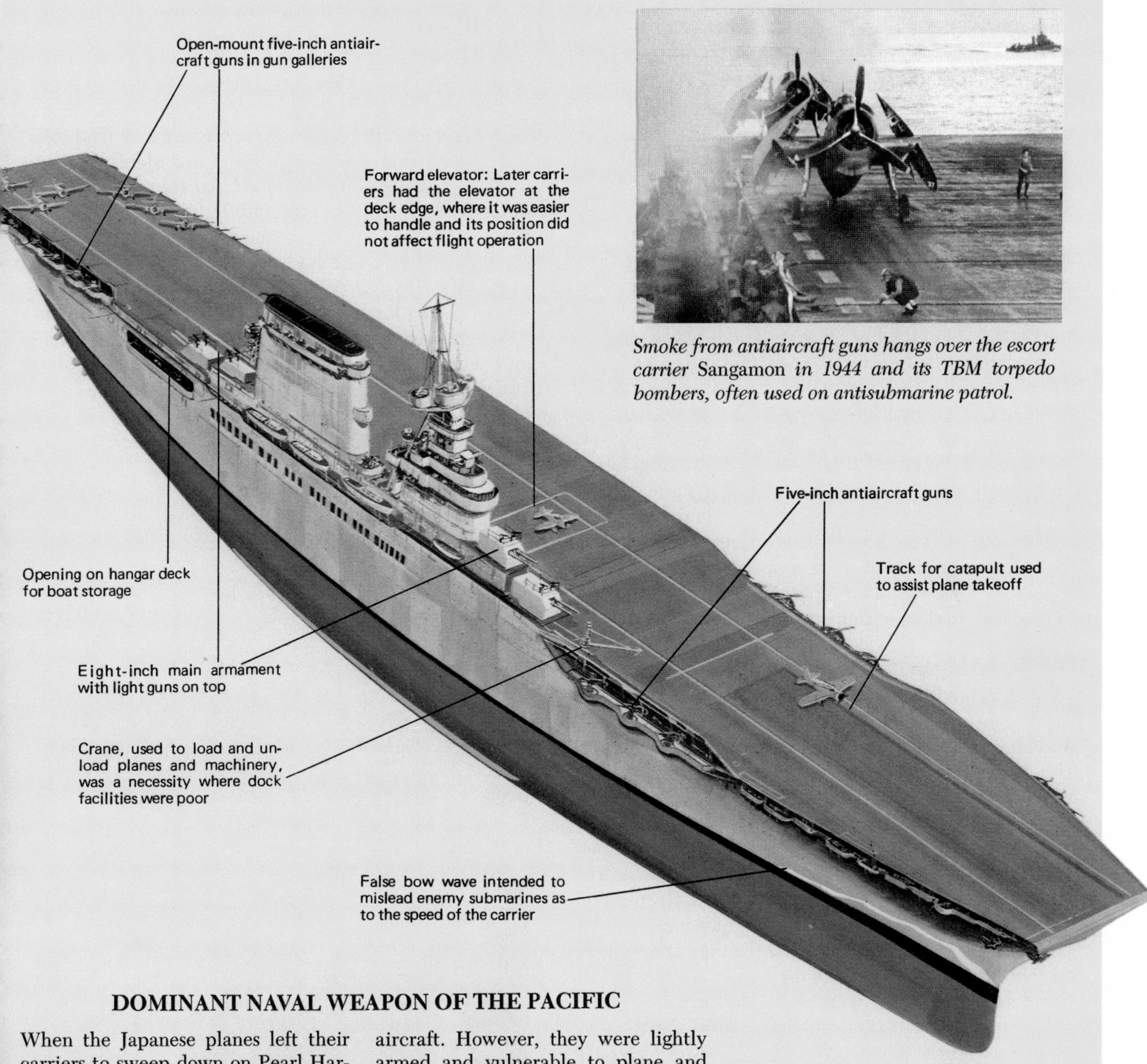

Smoke from antiaircraft guns hangs over the escort carrier Sangamon *in 1944 and its TBM torpedo bombers, often used on antisubmarine patrol.*

DOMINANT NAVAL WEAPON OF THE PACIFIC

When the Japanese planes left their carriers to sweep down on Pearl Harbor, the three U.S. aircraft carriers in the Pacific—the *Lexington,* the *Saratoga,* and the *Enterprise*—almost half of the entire U.S. carrier force of seven, were away from the base. Their survival was critical during the early stages of the war in the Pacific, since it took between one and two years to provide a fully operational carrier, even under wartime crash programs.

Although the first plane takeoff from a ship had been accomplished in 1910, it was not until World War II that carriers played a major role in naval warfare by increasing the striking range of aircraft. However, they were lightly armed and vulnerable to plane and submarine attack, so each carrier task force included a protective screen of battleships, cruisers, and destroyers.

In spite of this protection, carriers were often damaged or sunk; for example, submarine attacks twice sent the *Saratoga* to a repair yard for months. *"Sara"* was also severely damaged by kamikaze pilots but was not finally sunk until 1946 in U.S. atomic tests.

The *Lexington* was sunk after the Battle of the Coral Sea in May 1942. The *Enterprise,* although damaged in nearly every major Pacific battle, was one of the few to survive the whole war.

The Lexington *as she appeared in the spring of 1942, when the U.S. shipbuilding program was moving into high gear. When she was lost after the Battle of the Coral Sea, her name was given to one of the new* Essex-*class carriers that became mainstays of the Fast Carrier Force between 1943 and 1945.*

While fighting raged on Saipan, Nimitz' armada eliminated Japan's carrier-based airpower in the Battle of the Philippine Sea on June 19–20, 1944. The Japanese lost 395 planes, the remainder of their veteran pilots, and 4 aircraft carriers and sustained severe damage to several other vessels. Although Nimitz lost 130 planes, not a single American ship was sunk or disabled. In July and August U.S. forces seized the Marianas, piercing Japan's inner perimeter.

The way was now open for General MacArthur's return to the Philippines. Since February Allied forces had been moving up the New Guinea coast and into the Bismarck and Admiralty Islands in preparation for the assault. On October 20 some 200,000 U.S. troops began landing on Leyte in the central Philippines. The Japanese, expecting the Allies to land on outlying Mindanao first, had left Leyte thinly defended. Reinforcements were sent, and the weakened Japanese Navy was ordered to attack the U.S. landing force. From October 23 to 26 a series of sharp air and sea contests was fought in the narrow straits to the north and south of Leyte. This Battle of Leyte Gulf saw the first kamikaze air strikes, desperate suicide missions against U.S. vessels. The Japanese lost, however, and their battered fleet withdrew on October 26.

Victory in the Pacific

Leyte was finally cleared by early 1945 after months of bitter fighting that cost the Japanese 70,000 casualties and the Americans 15,584. On January 9, 1945, the U.S. 6th Army went ashore on central Luzon, and other U.S. forces landed on the 29th and 31st. By early February Manila was surrounded, but the city was not cleared of enemy forces for another month. As elsewhere, many Japanese fought fiercely to the death, against overwhelming odds. Bataan and Corregidor were cleared by late February, but thousands of Japanese troops escaped to the central mountains, where they held out until the end of the war. In all the Luzon campaign claimed the lives of 170,000 Japanese. U.S. casualties totaled 38,000, including 8,000 killed.

Farther north Admiral Nimitz' forces were preparing to land on Iwo Jima and Okinawa, within striking distance of Japan. On February 19, 1945, the U.S. Marines opened their operation against Iwo Jima, capturing Mt. Suribachi in the south on the 23d after heavy fighting, and marching northward against stiff opposition. Organized resistance ended in mid-March. Of an original force of 21,000 Japanese only 216 surrendered. The capture of Iwo Jima gave the U.S.A. a base for fighter escorts for B-29 raids on Japan and for emergency landings by returning bombers.

On April 1 some 50,000 U.S. troops went ashore on Okinawa, advancing slowly in heavy fighting. They took two months to break through the heavily fortified Shuri Line and another three weeks to mop up the last pockets of resistance. Both sides suffered severe losses. The campaign, the last major contest of the Pacific war, cost Japan 117,472 casualties, including 110,071 dead. Some 12,520 U.S. troops died, and 36,631 were wounded. Now the Allies had secured a base for bomber and other offensive operations within 350 miles of Kyushu, Japan's southernmost island.

By the spring of 1945 it was clear that Japan could not win the war. Her naval and air forces had been irreparably weakened, and her armies had sustained shattering losses. She had already been forced to relinquish a sizeable part of her scattered Pacific conquests and no longer possessed the resources to mount a successful counterattack. The war in Europe had ended in early May, freeing thousands of Allied troops and war materiel for the war against Japan. Moreover, Japanese shipping losses were mounting daily. In four years of war her merchant shipping had declined by

U.S. marines land on Iwo Jima, scene of one of their costliest campaigns. Prior bombing had little effect, for the Japanese had tunneled into the island's volcanic rock. Soft volcanic ash prevented tractors from moving supplies up the beach; marines and tanks were hit by fire from concealed pillboxes.

nearly 60 percent. Yet Japan refused to surrender. Instead she began fortifying the home islands for a final struggle against the upcoming Allied invasion.

The Allies were rapidly gaining ground throughout the Pacific. Allied forces in Burma were pushing the Japanese back toward Rangoon and Mandalay. The Australians were beginning a campaign against Borneo in the Netherlands East Indies. The Americans were accelerating their air bombardment of strategic targets in Japan in preparation for a future U.S. invasion. Regular B-29 raids began in earnest after the capture of Iwo Jima in March and continued throughout the spring and summer. The effect was devastating: According to Japanese estimates, bombing by U.S. B-29 Superfortresses killed 260,000 people, injured another 412,000, and left 9.2 million homeless.

On August 6 the United States dropped an atomic bomb on Hiroshima, destroying 60 percent of the city. Three days later a second atomic bomb fell on Nagasaki (see pp. 360–367). That same day, August 9, the Soviet Union joined the war against Japan and began to invade Manchuria and Outer Mongolia. On August 14 the Japanese finally agreed to an unconditional surrender. It was signed aboard the U.S.S. *Missouri* in Tokyo Bay on September 2. (A formal peace treaty did not go into effect until April 28, 1952.)

After nearly four years of some of the bitterest and most difficult fighting in the history of warfare, the war in the Pacific had ended. Through a combination of military setbacks, economic strangulation, and strategic bombing, the people of the Chrysanthemum Throne had lost their bid for Asian domination; they had sacrificed the best of their manpower, resources, and national pride for a brief moment of glory, and now they were forced, in Emperor Hirohito's words, to endure the unendurable and suffer the insufferable.

Okinawa, crucial to Allied strategy, *lay only 350 miles from the major Japanese island of Kyushu. Above, an Okinawan civilian surrenders to U.S. forces. Only 7,000 defenders were captured; some 110,000 others died in battle or committed suicide in fear of American reprisals.*

Gen. Douglas MacArthur *kept his promise to return to the Philippines when he landed on Leyte island in October 1944. While the 6th Army fought the entrenched Japanese, kamikaze planes attacked U.S. ships in Leyte Gulf. After a bitter two-month battle Leyte was in U.S. hands.*

THE LIFE OF THE TIMES 1939-45

At the 1939 New York World's Fair, *in which 63 nations took part, the Trylon and Perisphere symbolized the World of Tomorrow for 45 million optimistic visitors.*

Very simply and very bluntly," President Franklin D. Roosevelt said in a speech only weeks before the Japanese attacked Pearl Harbor, "we are pledged to pull our own oar in the destruction of Hitlerism . . . in the face of this newest and greatest challenge . . . we Americans have cleared our decks and taken our battle stations."

Before and after Pearl Harbor war news dominated the newspapers. Many Americans did take their battle stations, in factories and shipyards, in lonely aircraft spotters' posts. American boys and men enlisted or were drafted into military service, and the country backed them in a spirit of determined patriotism. And, on the homefront, from 1939 to 1945 the lives of millions were changed, heightened, and speeded up by war.

The Rumble of War

In 1939 the United States was still extricating herself from the effects of the Great Depression. Although the worst was over, close to 10 million people remained unemployed. The mood of the country for a decade had been turned inward, as government and private citizen alike struggled with overwhelming economic problems. In the mid-1930's Congress had passed three neutrality acts, and the prevailing trend was isolationist.

Uncle Sam, almost awash, *still sits on neutral ground in this 1940 cartoon.*

***Outraged by Japanese aggression** at Pearl Harbor, Americans mustered a grim determination as they prepared to join in battle with the desperate Allied forces in World War II.*

I AM AN AMERICAN

***After Pearl Harbor** Japanese-Americans declared their loyalty in vain: 110,000 spent the war in detention camps.*

***Roosevelt and Churchill,** meeting on a warship off Newfoundland in August 1941, affirmed Anglo-American unity.*

***By 1943 U.S. troops were fighting** in all theaters of war, and posters appealing to history fanned the patriotic spirit.*

But by 1939 radio commentators such as H. V. Kaltenborn and Gabriel Heatter were hammering home the same ominous themes—Japan was on the march, Hitler would never be satisfied until he controlled all of Europe—and, however reluctantly, Americans were beginning to believe them.

President Roosevelt, backed by a coalition of southern and eastern Democrats, intellectuals, some businessmen, and many newspapers, was able to prevail against prominent isolationists like Republican Senator William E. Borah of Idaho and Col. Charles A. Lindbergh. In September 1939, when Great Britain and France declared war against Germany after the invasion of Poland, the arms embargo section of the latest neutrality act was lifted, enabling Britain to purchase weapons. Roosevelt promised that the United States would become the "arsenal of democracy."

Ordinary Americans reacted to Hitler's conquest of Europe with an apprehension that at times approached panic. Some thought the Germans, once Britain fell, would invade the Americas. A poll taken in March 1940 showed that 43 percent believed a German victory would menace their security. By July the figure reached 69 percent.

The Lend-Lease Act, which went into effect in March 1941, was a step toward total U.S. commitment to the Allied cause. Through it Congress gave the President the power to lend or lease any war material to any government whose defense was considered vital to U.S. security.

In the months before the United States entered the war, Nazi submarines were sinking ships twice as fast as British and American shipyards could replace them. Bodies and debris from sunken ships washed up on Cape Hatteras, North Carolina, and Montauk Point, New York. The Coast Guard patrolled and fenced off headlands and beaches to keep news of the U-boat menace from the public. When a U.S. destroyer was torpedoed in the

North Atlantic on October 27, with 11 men missing, the U-boat secret could no longer be kept.

Pearl Harbor

But it was the Japanese militarists, not Hitler, who plunged the country into war. The attack on Pearl Harbor, in which more than 2,400 Americans died and half the Pacific Fleet was wiped out, canceled all isolationist doubts and unified the United States more completely than in any other war it had ever fought.

Within a few weeks after the formal U.S. declaration of war against the Axis Powers, draft boards all over the country went into action. All told they registered some 31 million men, of whom almost 10 million were eventually inducted. (The number rejected for poor health, malnutrition, or mental instability came as a shock to many.) The Army Air Corps received priority. It grew from less than 300,000 men to 2.3 million by 1945. The women who volunteered to serve at home or overseas, in the WACS, WAVES, SPARS, and Marine Corps, released more than 200,000 men for combat.

One of the darkest episodes on the homefront was the internment of loyal Japanese-Americans. By early 1942 prejudice against Japanese-Americans living on the west coast, particularly in California, had led to many acts of violence. On February 19 the President authorized the army to take control of civilian affairs in the Pacific Coast states. The commanding general, John L. De Witt, ordered the rounding up of all Japanese-Americans. Before long, 110,000 men, women, and children had been herded into relocation camps—hastily built barracks on government lands in the interior. The camps were sur-

***Alluring pinups** of Rita Hayworth (above) cheered lonesome GI's while women on the job—riveters, welders, secretaries—boosted war production to record heights.*

***Liberty ships, used for cargo,** were built at a feverish pace in Henry Kaiser's shipyards. In October 1942 President Roosevelt was on hand to witness the launching of the* Joseph N. Teal, *completed only 10 days after its keel was laid.*

rounded by barbed wire and patrolled by guards, and the Japanese were not allowed to leave them and return home to try to rebuild their lives until December 1944.

A Booming War Economy

By 1943, thanks to U.S. industrial might, American military men were the best equipped in the world. Government and industry, working together, set priorities, allocated vital materials, and imposed rationing and controls. They accomplished a miracle of production that, thanks to the heroism of the Merchant Marine, supplied not only the American armed forces but also a large number of the British, French, and Russian troops. There were conflicts, confusion, waste, and inefficiency, but the job got done. In September 1943 the Allies began sinking German submarines. At last the supply line to Europe was clear.

The war solved most Depression-related problems, giving employment to 7 million people who were still out of work. Nearly 8 million more—women, teenagers, and older people—found work, many for the first time in their lives. Women took on tough, dirty, boring jobs: riveting airplanes, tanks, and ships; shoveling coal; making bullets.

Whole industries converted to war production. Automobile makers and their suppliers turned out planes and tanks; electronics and appliance manufacturers made radar devices and fuses for shells. The total value of war production, only $8.4 billion in 1941, topped $30 billion a year later. Farmers, the group hit hardest during the Depression, saw their income triple.

Nightclubs and restaurants drew capacity crowds of big spenders night after night: soldiers on leave and civilians making more money than ever before. Luxury goods, such as fur coats and diamond rings, were bought on the spot for cash.

Trains were jammed to the aisles with soldiers and preoccupied civilians on urgent missions: relatives rushing to meet a serviceman on leave at some midway point; businessmen hurrying down to Washington, D.C., or out to Chicago, to help the nation gear up for war.

Service wives set up housekeeping in strange new parts of the country. New Yorkers went to Georgia; Californians landed in St. Louis. The housing shortage was extreme. Home was often a makeshift attic or basement apartment.

Bobby-soxers and Big Bands

In the forties a group of people, called variously by the press teenagers, teeners, or bobby-soxers, discovered itself. It was the first time adolescents had a separate sense of

***An American hostess** and a British sailor dance the Lambeth Walk in Brooklyn, New York. Left, city backyards and rooftops took on a rural air as Americans grew their own vegetables in wartime victory gardens.*

Early editions of the New York Sunday Mirror *for April 29, 1945, ran this premature report. President Harry Truman proclaimed victory in Europe on May 8.*

FINAL

Sunday Mirror

NEW YORK, SUNDAY, APRIL 29, 1945

EXTRA

REPORT GERMANY GIVES UP

SAN FRANCISCO, April 29 (AP).—Germany has surrendered to the allied governments unconditionally, and announcement is expected momentarily. It was stated by a high American official today.

The official, a member of the American delegation at the United Nations Conference here, dictated a statement for use by the press with the expected announcement.

One other equally high official said he had the same information, but others in the American and in other delegations here declined comment or said they knew nothing of the reports.

The official said that announcement of the surrender presumably would be made through Gen. Dwight D. Eisenhower, Supreme Allied Commander.

The announcement had been expected at 4 P. M., Eastern War Time, in Washington, he said—but was delayed.

The American official said:

"There were no strings attached to the surrender."

He said that while he was not informed of all the details, the surrender was made to all three of the major allied powers.

Secretary of State Stettinius suddenly left the

(Continued on Back Page)

***The Japanese** accepted Allied surrender terms on August 14, 1945. That night the biggest crowd that has ever gathered in Times Square went wild.*

identity, complete with their own version of English and special clothes. Girls in particular wore what amounted to a uniform: pleated skirts and baggy sweaters for school, blue jeans and a man's shirt on weekends. Bobby socks and loafers went with both outfits.

For these young people the outstanding entertainer was Frank Sinatra, a skinny, soulful-eyed crooner whose meticulous phrasing and pleasantly husky voice were usually drowned by the screams of hysterical fans. Girls tore pieces of his clothes off for souvenirs and saved the dirt he walked on.

The forties were the age of the big band as well as the crooner. Sinatra got his start singing with Harry James and his orchestra, then with Jimmy Dorsey. Glenn Miller played smooth, Woody Herman bouncy jazz, Stan Kenton loud and hot. Sentimental songs about the war, such as "The White Cliffs of Dover" or "My Shining Hour," alternated with fast, slangy numbers like "G.I. Jive" and "Boogie Woogie Bugle Boy." The Andrews Sisters, dressed in the squared-off, padded-shoulder suits or dresses of the era, delivered a bouncy, cheerful sound in close harmony. Teenagers also favored the cornball lyrics and realistic sound effects of Spike Jones and His City Slickers. One of his biggest hits was the "Hawaiian War Chant."

Movies and Musicals

Ingrid Bergman and Gary Cooper starred in *For Whom the Bell Tolls,* one of the most popular movies of the war years. Gary Cooper's portrayal of the title role in *Sergeant York* was the highlight of an unusually perceptive war movie.

Casablanca, starring Bergman and Humphrey Bogart, was a successful blend of wartime intrigue and romance. It opened, fortuitously enough, a week after the Allied landing in North Africa.

The musical *Oklahoma!* began its long run on Broadway in 1943, taking Americans' minds off the war and back to the more peaceful days of the settling of the West, when the only feuds were those fought between farmers and cattlemen.

A Time of Change

Under the stress of war, factories were built, such industries as synthetic rubber and plastics developed, and industrial capacity rose.

The very face of the country changed. More than 27 million people moved during World War II. Industry—shipyards, aircraft fac-

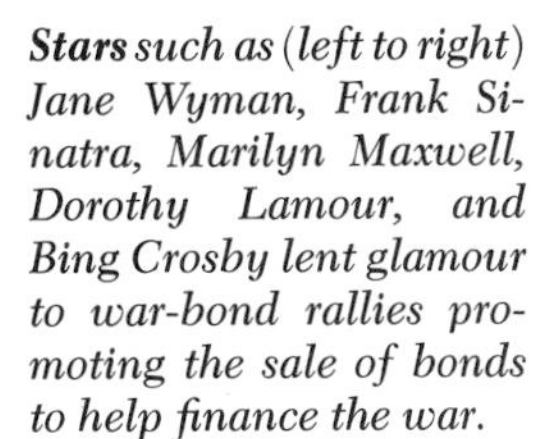

***Stars** such as (left to right) Jane Wyman, Frank Sinatra, Marilyn Maxwell, Dorothy Lamour, and Bing Crosby lent glamour to war-bond rallies promoting the sale of bonds to help finance the war.*

***"The Homecoming"** by Norman Rockwell was* The Saturday Evening Post*'s cover for May 26, 1945. In one family's joy at a soldier's safe return it summed up the emotions felt all over America.*

tories, even a steel mill—spread to the Pacific coast, starting a westward population trend that still continues. Farm laborers left the rural South for jobs in the North or in newly booming southern cities.

The marriage rate, as always in wartime, jumped. Three million children were born each year in 1942 and 1943, as opposed to 2 million a year before the war. Fathers were deferred as long as they could be spared, but eventually over a million were inducted.

Inevitably, the frenzied pace of wartime America took its toll. Marriages broke up, although many divorces had to be postponed until soldiers returned home. A new term, "juvenile delinquency," became current as younger and younger children roamed the streets while their mothers worked.

Southern Negroes employed in northern defense plants clashed with whites, some of whom had also recently moved north. A 1943 race riot in Detroit claimed 34 lives. One bright spot was the establishment of the Fair Employment Practices Committee, which worked to prevent racial discrimination at home all through the war. By 1944 approximately 2 million Negroes were employed in the defense industry.

The Bomb Brings an End

By the early spring of 1945 the last great drives were underway in Europe. But Franklin Roosevelt, President for over a decade, did not live to see the war's end and the birth of the United Nations. He died suddenly of a massive cerebral hemorrhage at Warm Springs, Georgia, on April 12. A shocked Harry Truman asked for the nation's prayers. He would need them. After a joyous V-E Day it was Truman who made the decision to hasten V-J Day by sanctioning the use of the atomic bomb against the Japanese. The destruction of Hiroshima and Nagasaki jolted the whole world.

In the United States the cost of the war in lives was low compared with the losses of the rest of the world. It has been estimated that about 17 million fighting men were killed, of whom about 300,000 were Americans. The United States was hardly touched by shells and never occupied. But the war had overturned and changed virtually the whole world. The very fact that the United States was spared what most of the world suffered would force her into the role of helper and leader in the years that followed the end of World War II.

1942

Hitler Marches East: The Battle of Stalingrad

The armies of the Third Reich experience their first major defeat in the city named in honor of Soviet dictator Joseph Stalin.

At 3 a.m. on the morning of June 22, 1941, Germany launched the greatest military offensive in history. Along a 1,100-mile front 3 million soldiers of the Third Reich pushed eastward toward Leningrad, Moscow, Kiev, and the oil-rich Caucasus beyond. Easily overcoming the U.S.S.R.'s hastily organized defenses, they advanced with incredible speed. By October 20 German tanks were within 40 miles of Moscow, and the Nazis seemed about to add yet another triumph to their dazzling string of successes in Poland and western Europe.

Victory eluded them, however. The Russians, drawing on their vast supply of manpower and resources, slowly toughened their defenses, strengthened their armies, and stepped up their production of armaments. In the winter of 1942–43 they struck back, annihilating the German 6th Army at Stalingrad and gradually forcing the remaining German forces into retreat. Stalingrad, the first major defeat for Hitler's army since the outbreak of the war, was a significant turning point. Thereafter, although the war continued for more than two years with many fierce battles, the Germans never fully regained the initiative.

Hitler had long believed that Germany would one day go to war against the Soviet Union. The struggle would be much more than an ideological contest between nazism and communism. The Fuehrer looked upon the conquest of the U.S.S.R. as a historic mission to subdue the Slavic *Untermenschen* ("subhumans") in the East and gain living space and food supplies for his superior Aryan master race. Nonetheless, he had entered into an alliance with the Russians in August 1939. His reasons for doing so were purely expedient. At that time he was planning to invade Poland, thereby risking a war with France and Britain, and could not simultaneously chance war with the U.S.S.R. The Nazi-Soviet nonaggression pact of 1939 pledged both parties to neutrality in the event of war and contained a secret protocol providing for the division of eastern Europe into German and Soviet spheres of influence. The U.S.S.R.'s domain was to include eastern Poland, Finland, Latvia, Estonia, and the Romanian province of Bessarabia (all of which she had lost at the end of World War I). Germany's share comprised western Poland and Lithuania.

While the Wehrmacht (the German Armed Forces) was overrunning western Poland, Denmark, Norway, the Low Countries, and France, Soviet dictator Joseph Stalin wasted no time in claiming his share of the spoils. Between September 1939 and June 1940 the Red Army seized eastern Poland, occupied the Baltic States (including Lithuania, which had been allotted to Germany), and waged a brief winter war with Finland, forcing the Finns to cede territory to the north of Lake Ladoga and on the Karelian Isthmus north of Leningrad. In June Stalin annexed Bessarabia and the northern Bukovina in Romania. The U.S.S.R. had no historic claims to the latter, and it had not been mentioned in the Nazi-Soviet pact.

Disturbed by the U.S.S.R.'s aggressive movements, Hitler established a German protectorate over the rest of Romania and concluded arms agreements with Finland in the summer and fall of 1940. On September 27 he signed the Tripartite Pact with Italy and Japan (see pp. 300–305). The pact obliged each member to provide economic, political, and military support if one of its allies was attacked by one of the major powers not already involved in the war.

Although the Tripartite Pact was ostensibly aimed against the United States and specifically ruled out a conflict with the U.S.S.R., Stalin was alarmed. When his Foreign Minister, Vyacheslav M. Molotov, demanded an explanation, Hitler offered to admit the U.S.S.R. to the Axis if she would redirect her expansion from eastern Europe to south-central Asia. When Molotov demanded additional concessions, Hitler refused, and the talks broke down. A few months later the Soviet Union signed a neutrality pact with Japan. (In the event of a confrontation with Germany, the U.S.S.R. would not be threatened by a two-front war.)

Operation Barbarossa

Time was quickly running out on the Nazi-Soviet alliance. In the summer of 1940, when all of western Europe was under Nazi rule and Britain was isolated and alone, Hitler's thoughts had turned to an invasion of the Soviet Union, the only remaining obstacle to German dominance of the entire Continent. Intelligence reports indicated, moreover, that Soviet forces were greatly inferior to Germany's, and the Fuehrer was convinced that he could win another lightning victory. Then, when he had all Europe under his sway,

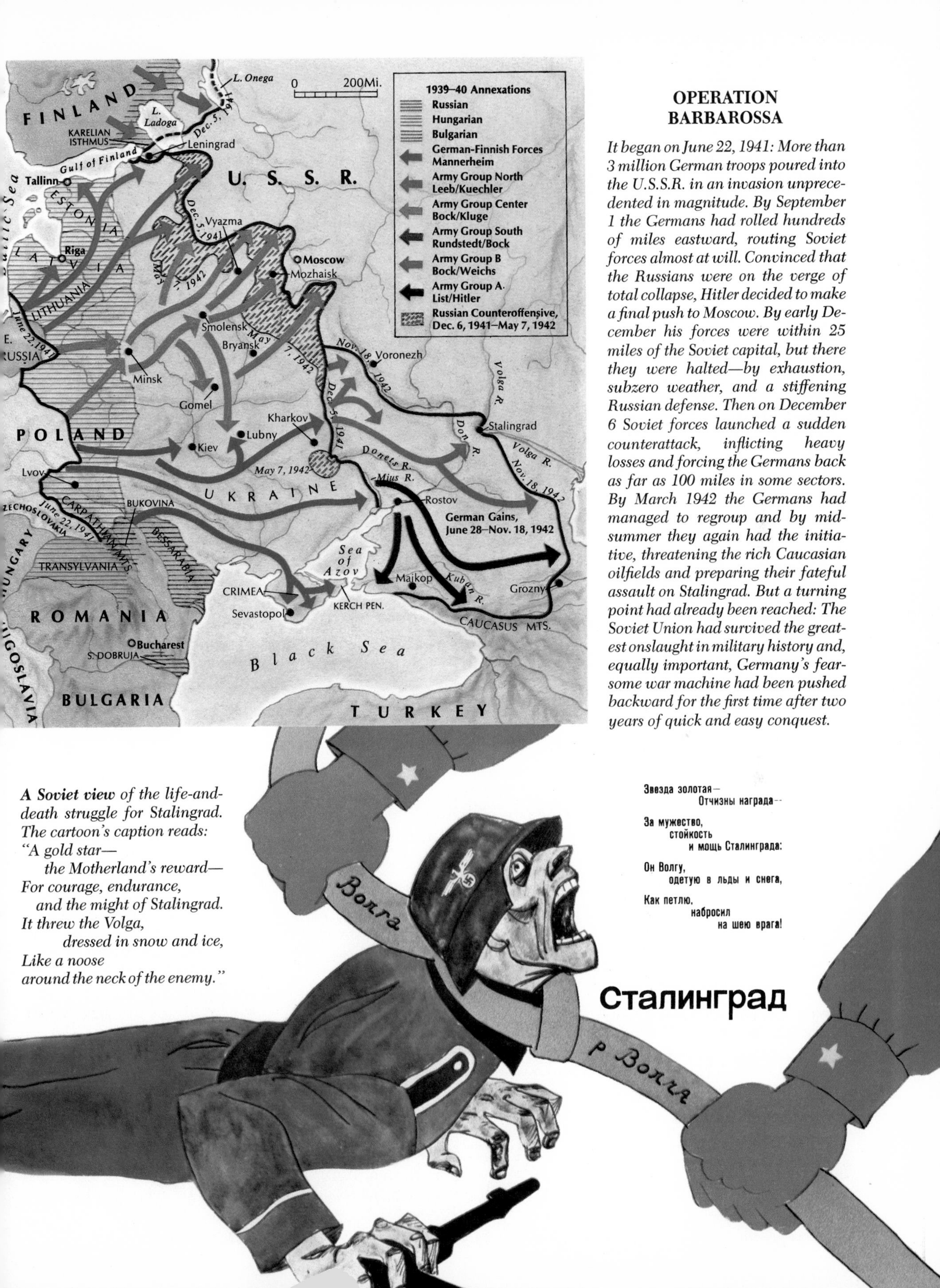

OPERATION BARBAROSSA

It began on June 22, 1941: More than 3 million German troops poured into the U.S.S.R. in an invasion unprecedented in magnitude. By September 1 the Germans had rolled hundreds of miles eastward, routing Soviet forces almost at will. Convinced that the Russians were on the verge of total collapse, Hitler decided to make a final push to Moscow. By early December his forces were within 25 miles of the Soviet capital, but there they were halted—by exhaustion, subzero weather, and a stiffening Russian defense. Then on December 6 Soviet forces launched a sudden counterattack, inflicting heavy losses and forcing the Germans back as far as 100 miles in some sectors. By March 1942 the Germans had managed to regroup and by midsummer they again had the initiative, threatening the rich Caucasian oilfields and preparing their fateful assault on Stalingrad. But a turning point had already been reached: The Soviet Union had survived the greatest onslaught in military history and, equally important, Germany's fearsome war machine had been pushed backward for the first time after two years of quick and easy conquest.

A Soviet view *of the life-and-death struggle for Stalingrad. The cartoon's caption reads:*
"A gold star—
the Motherland's reward—
For courage, endurance,
and the might of Stalingrad.
It threw the Volga,
dressed in snow and ice,
Like a noose
around the neck of the enemy."

Britain would finally be forced to realize the hopelessness of her position and come to terms.

On December 18, 1940, Hitler issued a directive for Operation Barbarossa, the invasion of Russia. The German offensive, named for the conquering 12th-century Teutonic Emperor, Frederick Barbarossa, was scheduled to open in mid-May 1941. The Soviet defeat, Hitler estimated, would be accomplished before the onset of the harsh Russian winter.

In the spring of 1941, however, the Germans became embroiled in a brief war in the Balkans and were forced to postpone the start of Operation Barbarossa. Italy had attacked Greece in late October 1940 without informing Hitler of her plans. The Italian campaign was a disaster, and Greek troops drove out Mussolini's forces in early November. Unable to go forward with his eastern campaign as long as Greece remained hostile, Hitler decided to crush Greece.

To secure safe passage for his troops, Hitler pressured Hungary, Romania, Bulgaria, and Yugoslavia into joining the Axis, but Yugoslavia reversed her decision after an anti-Axis coup in March. On April 6, therefore, Germany invaded Yugoslavia as well as Greece. Yugoslavia fell on April 17, and on April 22 mainland Greece surrendered. (A small British force sent to aid the Greeks was evacuated in mid-April.)

With his southern flank secured, the Fuehrer ordered Operation Barbarossa to begin on June 22. The Russians were caught completely off guard by an onslaught unmatched before or since in its magnitude and initial success. Across the width of the Continent an enormous phalanx of more than 120 infantry and 19 panzer (armored) divisions moved eastward. To the north and south they were supported by an additional 34 divisions of Finns and Romanians. This incredible striking force—more than 3 million men strong—was organized into three main army groups. Army Group North under Field Marshal Wilhelm von Leeb drove through the Baltic States toward Leningrad. At the same time, a small German-Finnish force advanced toward Leningrad across the Karelian Isthmus. Army Group Center under Field Marshal Fedor von Bock struck toward Minsk, Smolensk, and Moscow. Army Group South under Field Marshal Gerd von Rundstedt pushed into the Ukraine toward Kiev, Kharkov, and the Caucasus oilfields.

Against this formidable array the U.S.S.R. could immediately deploy some 158 infantry divisions and 40 tank brigades. There were additional troops in Siberia, but it would take time to transfer them to the distant fighting front. Soviet aircraft greatly outnumbered the Germans', but most planes were obsolete. The Russians had 10,000 tanks, but they were employed in small units for infantry support.

In the first weeks of fighting, Germany's superior tactics and organization were decisive, shattering the Soviet lines and carrying the invading army well within the enemy borders. Army Group Center's advance was particularly spectacular. On July 19 it closed its pincers around Smolensk, capturing some 100,000 prisoners and a large store of tanks and guns. Hitler's generals urged the Fuehrer to continue the drive to Moscow, despite the slower advance of his northern and southern flanks. Instead, Hitler decided to halt the drive on Moscow until the cities of Leningrad and Kiev had been taken.

Army Group South took Kiev on September 19, and the German 11th Army pushed southward toward the Crimean peninsula. By August 31 Army Group North had advanced to within 10 miles of Leningrad, and by early September the Finnish force had reached the pre-1940 Russo-Finnish border.

On September 6 Hitler suddenly ordered the attack on Moscow resumed, but plans were not completed for several weeks, with the drive not actually underway until the end of September. Meanwhile, the Russians, who viewed the delay as a miracle, had gained six weeks' time to dig in and organize their defenses for the upcoming offensive and to reinforce their lines with seasoned troops from Siberia.

The German drive on Moscow began on September 30 and achieved complete surprise. The Soviet forward positions were broken within a week, and Bock's forces captured some 650,000 prisoners around Bryansk and Vyazma. Their progress was slowed, however, by the autumn rains, which began on October 7, turning the roads to mud and miring Bock's tanks and trucks. Yet the Germans pushed stubbornly forward, taking Mozhaisk, only 40 miles from Moscow, on October 20. In early November the rains stopped, and on November 15 the Germans began a final push. Despite stiff Soviet resistance, the Germans' vanguard came within 25 miles of the Soviet capital, but the arrival of winter, with heavy snow and subzero temperatures, finally halted the German advance on December 5.

On December 6 the Russians, under Gen. Georgi K. Zhukov, opened a counterattack, pushing the Germans back from the capital. Bock requested permission to retreat, but Hitler refused. On December 18 the Fuehrer replaced Bock with Field Marshal Hans Günther von Kluge. The next day Hitler, who blamed the failure of the campaign on his General Staff, announced he was taking personal command of the German Army and ordered his troops on the Moscow front to fight for every inch of ground. The Red Army continued to push them back nonetheless, and on February 15 Hitler agreed to a withdrawal. By the end of February the Germans were 75 to 200 miles west of Moscow. The Soviet offensive ended in May.

1942: On to Stalingrad

The first months of fighting had taken a heavy toll in lives and equipment on both sides. The Red Army had lost more than 4 million soldiers, 15,000 armored vehicles, and 9,000 aircraft. The Germans had sustained more than 1 million casualties (a third of their original force), and their tank divisions were about half their 1941 strength. Realizing he did not have sufficient forces for another general offensive in 1942, Hitler decided to concentrate on the southern front for a major drive toward the Caucasus, which provided more than 90 percent of the U.S.S.R.'s oil supply. By cutting off this vital area, Hitler hoped to cripple the Soviets and bring his erstwhile ally to her knees.

In preparation, Hitler divided Army Group South into two new groups: Army Group A under Field Marshal Wilhelm List and Army Group B under Bock. (Rundstedt, who formerly commanded Army Group South, had been dismissed.) The Fuehrer also sent in 21 Romanian, Italian, and Hungarian divisions, but these troops were of dubious value: Their training and

A tank-supported *German infantry action south of Stalingrad (left). One of the fatal flaws in Hitler's eastern campaign was his failure to concentrate his forces on a few key targets. Instead, he spread them out along a 1,000-mile front, diluting their impact and making it difficult to provide vital supplies.*

A German antiaircraft battery *(far left) guards a bridge across the Desna River at Bryansk, an important rail junction captured during the early months of Operation Barbarossa.*

equipment were inferior to that of the Germans, and the Romanians and Hungarians hated each other more than they hated the Russians.

The campaign plan called for a series of quick converging attacks. One force from Army Group B (the 4th Panzer and 2d Armies) would encircle Voronezh and march southward, linking up with a second force (the 6th Army) advancing from Kharkov. The combined forces would then drive southwest across the industrial Donets Basin to the bend of the Don River. Meanwhile, Army Group A would march eastward from the Mius River and secure the lower Don, linking up with Army Group B at the Don bend west of Stalingrad. Both army groups would hold the Don line, while the 6th Army encircled Stalingrad and cut the Volga River supply line. The main force would then march into the Caucasus, capturing the wheatfields and the oilfields of this rich area.

In early May the German 11th Army began a preliminary campaign to complete the conquest of the Crimea, with its Black Sea port at Sevastopol, and to secure the strategic Kerch Peninsula. Army Group B launched its offensive on June 28. On July 6, after heavy fighting, Voronezh fell, and the next day the 2d, 4th Panzer, and 6th Armies linked up to the south of Voronezh. Then, on July 9, Army Group A struck east from the Mius River, advancing along the Don River against scattered Soviet resistance. But before the two army groups had completed the next phase of the plan, linking up at the Don bend, Hitler altered his plans. On July 13 he ordered Army Group A to turn south and cross the Don River east of Rostov, gateway to the Caucasus. Army Group B would go to Stalingrad.

Initially, the new strategy met with considerable success. Rostov fell on July 23, and Army Group A surged southward. On July 29 List's forces severed the last Soviet rail connection with the Caucasus. By late August they had driven to the foothills of the Caucasus Mountains, but then they encountered strong Soviet resistance in the mountain passes and increasing supply delays. On September 9 Hitler dismissed List and took personal command of Army Group A.

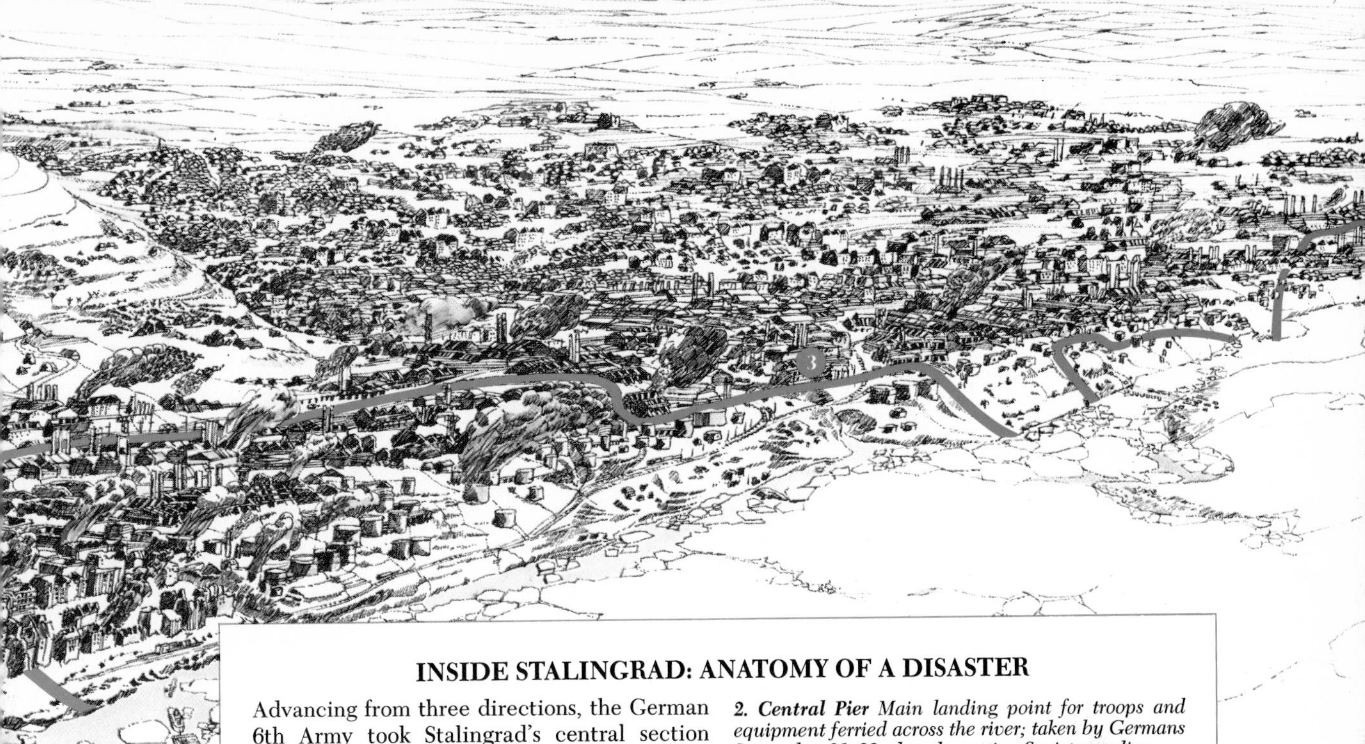

INSIDE STALINGRAD: ANATOMY OF A DISASTER

Advancing from three directions, the German 6th Army took Stalingrad's central section (left), then captured Mamai Hill after two months of fierce fighting. By mid-November they held most of the industrial area and had isolated the defenders in several pockets along the river. They went no farther: Surprised by a Soviet counterattack on November 19, the encircled Germans surrendered in January 1943.

1. ***Mamai Hill*** *Site of Soviet command post until September 13; located between central city and industrial section, within shooting range of Soviet ferry landings, it changed hands repeatedly.*

2. ***Central Pier*** *Main landing point for troops and equipment ferried across the river; taken by Germans September 21–22, sharply cutting Soviet supplies.*

3. ***Red October Metallurgical Plant*** *Object of some of the fiercest fighting in Stalingrad; Germans captured most of the grounds by November 11, placing them within 400 yards of the river.*

4. ***Pavlov's House*** *Located on the perimeter of the main Soviet bridgehead, it was named for Sgt. Jacob Pavlov, who defended it with a handful of civilians for 50 days against repeated German assaults.*

5. ***Univermag Department Store*** *Situated in the heart of the city, it was the focal point of intense fighting in September and, on January 31, the scene of field Marshal Paulus' formal surrender.*

Gradually, he became obsessed with the capture of Stalingrad, originally planned as a minor action in conjunction with the Caucasus offensive. The city, named for the U.S.S.R.'s ruthless dictator, stretched along the western bank of the Volga River. It had been the site of a minor victory by Red Army troops under Stalin during the Russian Civil War in 1920. Now it was a great industrial center with a population of 500,000. Tens of thousands of workers lived in the northern districts around the tractor and gun factories, the Lazur Chemical Works, and the Red October Metallurgical Plant. Residential suburbs, grain elevators, and warehouses lay to the south. In the center were shops, businesses, the main railway station linking Moscow and the Caucasus, and the central ferry dock connecting the city with the Volga's east bank.

For the past month Stalingrad had been frantically preparing for the German attack. Stalin had ordered the city to stand firm and had sent in a military commander to organize its defenses. Women, children, and old men had been evacuated to safer ground, and the approaches to the city had been fortified. Supply dumps, artillery positions, and airfields had been hastily set up across the river.

The onslaught began on August 23 with a terrifying air raid, which reduced much of the central city to rubble. The next day German artillery shelled Soviet positions on the northern rim of the city; a day later more German troops attacked from the south. Simultaneously, the German 6th Army under Gen. (later Field Marshal) Friedrich Paulus began closing in.

After a series of delaying actions, the Soviet 62d Army pulled back into Stalingrad on August 29 and began digging in under the able command of Gen. Vasily Chuikov. Chuikov divided his men into small "storm groups" and deployed them at strategic locations throughout the central area. He organized a lifeline of ferries and makeshift foot bridges across the Volga. Under constant enemy fire, it provided food, ammunition, and reinforcements throughout the siege. Chuikov's greatest resource, however, was the fierce determination of his troops.

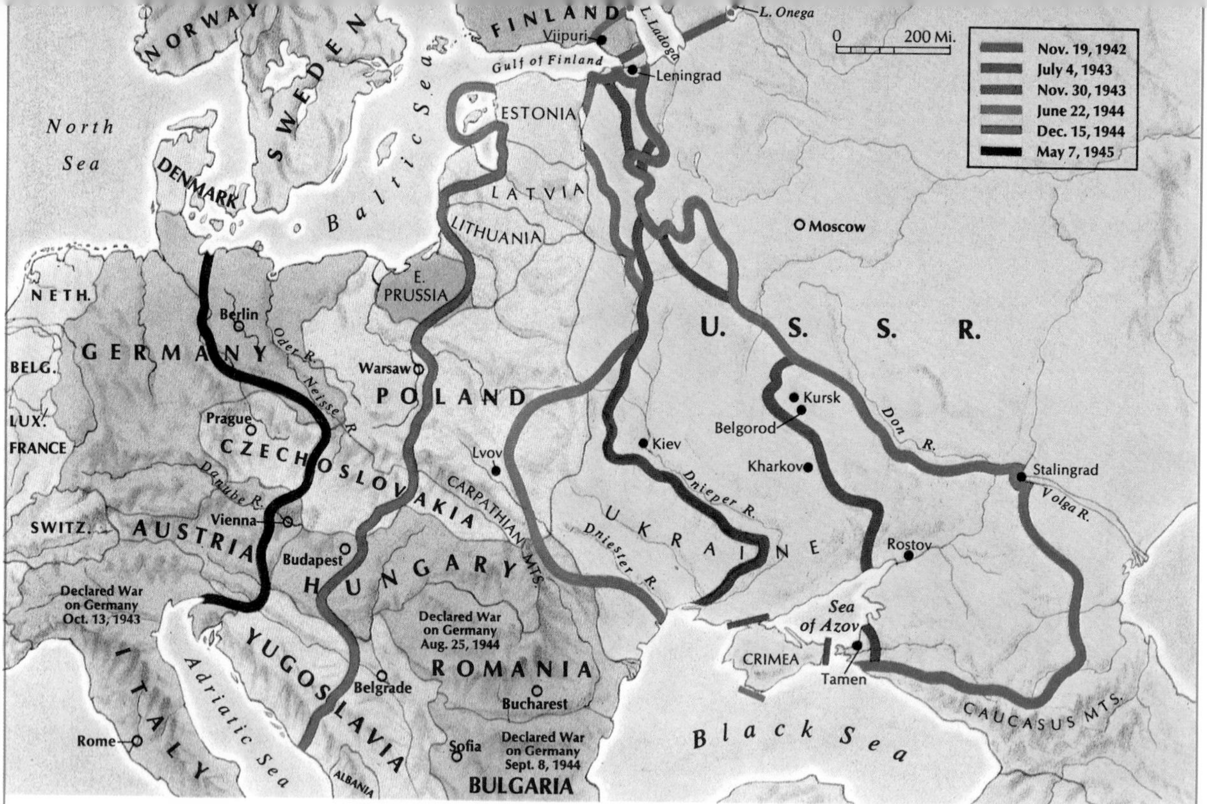

FROM STALINGRAD TO BERLIN

While Stalingrad looms in retrospect as a crucial turning point in the war, there remained hope in Germany that the Russian offensive might again be stopped as it had been the previous winter—a hope fueled by the dramatic German triumph at Kharkov in March 1943. But the next major battle, at Kursk in July, ended in a Soviet victory that, coinciding with the Anglo-American landing on Sicily, dealt the Germans a severe psychological blow. The war was still far from over, but Germany would spend the rest of it on the defensive as the Red Army pushed its way from the east, mile by mile, toward the heart of the Third Reich.

Gen. Vasily Chuikov directing Stalingrad's defense from his command bunker in October 1942. His German counterpart, Field Marshal Friedrich Paulus, was forced to surrender after his troops were encircled in the Soviet counterattack.

German Field Marshal Paulus

Soviet Gen. Vasily Chuikov

When Paulus' men pushed into the central city in mid-September, they encountered heavy resistance. Unseen Soviet snipers fired on them from windows, railroad overpasses, and foxholes amid the rubble. Each night the snipers slipped away silently through the city's sewers and underground tunnels to take up new positions. For the first time in the war the Germans found themselves engaged in a vicious street-to-street, house-to-house, room-to-room struggle. Their tanks were blocked by debris, and air raids endangered their own men as well as the Russians. Casualties on both sides ran as high as 60 percent.

Progress was painfully slow. By the middle of October Paulus' forces had broken the Soviet defenses into three separate bridgeheads, but the enemy refused to give up its remaining positions. Meanwhile, outside the city Red Army troops under General Zhukov, who had orchestrated the Soviet victory at Moscow, were preparing a major counterstroke. Zhukov's plan was to break through the flanks of the German Army to the north and south of Stalingrad and trap the German 6th Army within the city. Additional forces would strike against the German lines along the upper Don and then drive toward Rostov, while another force counterattacked in the Caucasus.

On November 19 Zhukov struck with a force of 1 million soldiers. They easily shattered the weak German flanks, held by inferior Romanian recruits, and by November 23 had encircled the 6th Army within Stalingrad. A day earlier Paulus had requested permission to fight his way out with his 285,000 men, but Hitler refused. His decision was based on the assurances of Luftwaffe commander Field Marshal Hermann Goering that his planes could airlift the required minimum of 600 tons of supplies per day to Stalingrad. In fact, the Luftwaffe only managed to supply Paulus' men with an average of 70 tons per day.

On November 20 Hitler appointed Field Marshal Fritz von Manstein to head the new Army Group Don—formed from the remnants of Army Group B—and ordered him to restore the German positions along the Don and relieve Stalingrad. By December 19 Manstein's advance forces were within 35 miles of the city, and he ordered Paulus to break out and join up with his forces. While Paulus stalled, waiting for Hitler to approve the order, Manstein was forced into retreat. (Meanwhile, the simultaneous Soviet counteroffensive in the Caucasus had forced Army Group A to begin withdrawing northward. By early February its forces had reached the Taman Peninsula, whence they were evacuated by air to reinforce Manstein.)

On January 10, after Paulus failed to reply to a final surrender ultimatum, the Red Army broke into the city. Although weakened by the long ordeal and lacking shells for their artillery, Paulus' men resisted. They were no match for the Russians, however, and within six days their stronghold had been cut in half. By January 24 both airports had fallen, severing the Germans' last ties with the outside world. On January 31 Paulus capitulated, and two days later all German resistance collapsed. The Russians netted 91,000 prisoners, all that remained of the German 6th Army.

Paulus' stand had given Army Groups Don and A time to complete an orderly withdrawal. Shortly after Paulus' defeat, Manstein retreated to the general line held before the 1942 German offensive. In March 1943 his troops retook the town of Kharkov, but their advance was halted soon afterward by the spring thaw. These were to be the last major German victories in the war against the Soviet Union.

1943: The Way West

By the spring of 1943 Soviet production was coming into high gear: Behind Soviet lines factories worked around the clock, turning out T-34 tanks, artillery, and Yak-9 fighter planes in abundance. Red Army conscription was in full swing, drawing on reserves three times greater than Germany's. American and British lend-lease aid was supplying 10 percent of the Soviets' direct war needs and considerably more of machine tools, aluminum, foodstuffs, clothing, and other essentials. Soviet generals, meanwhile, had had two years to study German strategy and tactics and to adapt them to their own advantage.

By contrast, Germany's airpower, weaponry, and personnel were being steadily depleted in combat or transferred to other fronts. German wartime production had not yet reached its maximum level. In addition, growing Allied pressure in the west was straining the Reich's resources to the limit. On November 8, 1942, the Allied invasion of North Africa, Operation Torch, opened (see pp. 336–343), and in January 1943 U.S. Flying Fortresses began their first daylight raids on strategic German targets. In May Axis forces in North Africa surrendered to the Allies.

The Germans were still not defeated, however, and in the summer of 1943 Hitler ordered an offensive around Kursk in an attempt to achieve a victory that, in Hitler's words, "would shine like a beacon around the world." The attack, optimistically code-named Operation Citadel, began in early July and made slight gains, but on July 13 the Fuehrer was forced to suspend it. The Allied invasion of Sicily had begun on July 10, and Hitler needed to transfer troops and armor westward for the defense of Italy.

Thereafter the U.S.S.R. gained the initiative, forcing German withdrawals on the southern and central fronts. By the end of July the Russians had advanced beyond Kursk and Belgorod, and Kharkov was recaptured on August 23. In late September some of Manstein's forces were pushed back behind the Dnieper River, and on November 6 the Soviet forces retook Kiev. On Hitler's orders the German armies adopted a scorched-earth policy, demolishing mines, factories, power plants, railroads, fields, and all other resources as they withdrew.

By the end of 1943 the Red Army outnumbered its opponents by nearly 3 million men, 6,100 tanks, and 12,000 heavy guns. The U.S.S.R. kept up its pressure all along the front into the spring of 1944, and by May, despite some minor victories, the Germans had fallen back to a line running south from the Gulf of Finland through the Pripet Marshes to the border of Romania. Then in June, in conjunction with the Allied D-day landings in Normandy, the Red Army surged across the prewar Polish and Romanian frontiers. Within a year they would sweep up to the gates of Berlin.

1943

The Allies Fight Back

Anglo-American campaigns fought in North Africa, Sicily, and Italy help weaken the Axis empire.

On December 11, 1941, following Japan's attack on Pearl Harbor, Adolf Hitler supported his ally by declaring war on the United States. With that almost casual gesture the Fuehrer added the world's greatest industrial power to his long list of foes. It was to prove a fatal miscalculation, for Hitler grossly underestimated the potential strength of the United States. Several months earlier he had reportedly observed to the Japanese Foreign Minister Yosuke Matsuoka that in the event of war America was confronted by three possibilities: She could arm herself, she could assist England, or she could wage war on another front (the Pacific, see pp. 314–321).

In the end the United States accomplished all three feats with an enormous multibillion-dollar effort involving more than 16 million men under arms, 300,000 aircraft, 85,000 tanks, and more than 20 million tons of shipping. She was able to arm herself and provide substantial aid not only to Britain but to the Soviet Union, China, and other Allied nations as well. And at the same time she managed to fight a two-front war in Europe and the Pacific.

She was able to do so, however, only after overcoming some enormous obstacles. The most serious early difficulty was transportation. The vast distances that protected the American homeland and its vital factories from enemy attack also created the problem of delivering men and war materiel safely to farflung battlefronts. Once this was solved, there were the additional problems of putting troops ashore on territory already held by the enemy and of maintaining supply lines that sometimes stretched halfway around the globe. To a large degree the success of the United States depended as much on merchant vessels, shipbuilding schedules, landing craft, and weather charts as it did on the effectiveness of her armed forces.

The United States had begun playing an active role in the Allied war effort well before the formal declara-

***The men who led the campaigns** in North Africa and Italy were, clockwise from left: Lt. Gen. Bernard Law Montgomery, commander of the British 8th Army; Field Marshal Erwin Rommel, head of the German Afrika Korps; Field Marshal Albert Kesselring, who led the German Army in central Italy; Gen. Dwight D. Eisenhower, head of Operation Torch; Lt. Gen. George Patton of the U.S. 7th Army; and Gen. Sir Harold Alexander, British commander.*

tions of war between herself and the Axis Powers. On the eve of the German invasion of Poland in September 1939 President Franklin D. Roosevelt had urged Congress to revise the 1937 Neutrality Act, which banned the sale of American arms to all belligerent nations. Two months later the statute was amended to permit the British and French to buy U.S. arms on a cash basis if they provided the means of transport. The Nazi blitzkrieg against France and the Low Countries in 1940 brought a few more concessions: The United States agreed to provide more weapons and ammunition to Britain, to train Royal Air Force pilots, and to repair British ships. In September 1940 Congress authorized nationwide conscription and agreed to exchange 50 American destroyers for the right to establish U.S. bases in Newfoundland and in British colonies in the Caribbean.

In December 1940 British Prime Minister Winston Churchill appealed to Roosevelt for increased aid. Britain had exhausted her monetary reserves and could

A convoy *steams off the English coast in the first winter of the war. Canadian and U.S. convoys, consisting of troop and supply ships escorted by destroyers and other warships, suffered relatively few losses until the fall of France made French ports available to the Germans as submarine bases.*

From the deck *of the U.S.S.* Spencer, *U.S. coastguardsmen watch as a depth charge hits a German submarine. Depth charges, which were propelled from the ship's stern, were preset to detonate at depths determined by underwater detecting devices. The struggle for supremacy in the Atlantic was one of the most bitterly contested and crucial battles of the entire war effort.*

no longer afford to import arms. Moreover, her own arms production would not be in full swing for more than a year, and her shipping losses to German U-boats in the Atlantic were reaching a critical level. In response Congress passed the Lend-Lease Act in March 1941; the act pledged wartime aid not only to Britain but also to all nations under Axis attack.

The Atlantic Alliance

For almost a year before the attack on Pearl Harbor, the U.S. Navy had become increasingly involved in the naval warfare between German U-boats and British and Canadian merchant shipping in the Atlantic. By early 1941 special U.S. naval task forces patrolled the Caribbean, the Gulf of Mexico, and the eastern coasts of the United States and Canada, keeping track of the location of German submarines and warning Anglo-Canadian convoys of their whereabouts. With the military occupation of the Danish territories of Greenland and Iceland (Denmark had been occupied by Germany in 1940) in the spring and summer of 1941, U.S. surveillance was extended to the North Atlantic. On May 27 Roosevelt announced that the Battle of the Atlantic was "coming very close to home" and declared an unlimited national emergency. After the German U-boat attack on the U.S.S. *Greer* on September 4, the U.S. Navy began waging an undeclared, semisecret war against Germany.

Meanwhile, U.S. and British military planners had already begun mapping their joint strategy in the event of full U.S. entry into the war. In January 1941 they agreed that if the United States went to war with both Germany and Japan, her first priority would be the defeat of Germany. In August Roosevelt and Churchill set forth general guidelines for achieving peace in Europe in the Atlantic Charter, which became the ideological basis for their wartime alliance.

Immediately after the U.S. declaration of war, Anglo-American strategists reaffirmed their earlier "Germany first" policy. They decided to weaken the Axis position initially by striking at Germany's Atlantic U-boat fleet, by bombing strategic targets in Europe, and by mounting an offensive against Axis forces in North Africa. That done, the Allies would launch an invasion of the Continent, either across the Mediterranean through Sicily and Italy or across the English Channel through France. They also established the Combined Chiefs of Staff (CCS), consisting of the heads of the U.S. and British Armed Forces, to help plan and coordinate the war effort.

The first U.S. ground troops arrived in Northern Ireland in January 1942, and shortly thereafter the first U.S. airmen reached England. In August U.S. bombers flew their first mission over Europe. Meanwhile, in late June Lt. Gen. Dwight D. Eisenhower assumed command of U.S. operations in Europe and began supervising the buildup of American forces in Britain for Operation Torch, the Anglo-American invasion of North Africa. Preparations were undertaken at once for an offensive to begin in late 1942.

The 1,400-mile North African coastal strip between Tripoli, Libya, and Alexandria, Egypt—the so-called Western Desert—was the scene of more advances and retreats than any other combat zone of the war. Fighting there was simply an extension of the war in Europe to the belligerents' colonial possessions. At the war's outbreak France held Algeria, French Morocco, and Tunisia, with naval bases at Bizerte, Algiers, and Oran. Italy held Libya. Egypt had granted Britain the right to station troops at the Suez Canal and other points and to maintain a naval base at Alexandria.

Upon the fall of France in June 1940 the French North African territories recognized the rule of the puppet Vichy regime in unoccupied France and agreed to cooperate with the Axis. In September Italy, Germany's ally, attacked Egypt from Libya. Her objective was Alexandria and the Suez. British forces commanded by Gen. Sir Archibald Wavell halted the Italian advance to the east of Sidi Barrani, some 60 miles inside the Egyptian border. In December the British Western Desert Force led by Lt. Gen. Richard O'Connor opened a counteroffensive, recaptured Sidi Barrani, and pushed the Italians back to Benghazi by early February. The spectacular 500-mile advance brought all of Cyrenaica (eastern Libya) under British control and cost the Italians 130,000 prisoners. British casualties totaled 1,928.

Meanwhile, British warships gained temporary control of the Mediterranean. In July 1940 they sank or damaged Vichy French ships at Oran and Mers-el-Kebir, Algeria, and impounded all French ships at Alexandria. (The main French Fleet had been interned at Toulon, on the Mediterranean coast of France, and Germany had pledged to leave it alone.) After losing a few gun duels to the British Fleet, the large, modern Italian Navy withdrew to the harbor of Taranto. In November British aircraft from the H.M.S. *Illustrious* sank or badly damaged three battleships and two cruisers. On the night of March 28, 1941, British attacks crippled a small Italian squadron off Cape Matapan, Greece, damaging one battleship and sinking at least five cruisers and destroyers.

British supremacy in North Africa and the Mediterranean, however, was soon challenged by Germany's invasion of Yugoslavia and Greece in April 1941. (Italy had invaded Greece the previous fall and had suffered a disastrous defeat; Hitler was then forced to come to Mussolini's aid.) Britain, who considered the defense of Greece vital to her position in the Mediterranean, decided to transfer most of her North African forces to the Greek mainland. The expedition proved futile, for by the end of April the German Wehrmacht had occupied Greece and forced the British to evacuate their troops. A few weeks later German paratroopers and airborne infantry seized the Greek island of Crete, despite a valiant defense by New Zealand forces under Maj. Gen. Bernard Freyberg (which cost the Germans so heavily that Hitler never again attempted a large-scale airborne offensive).

Tobruk and El Alamein

The Greek expedition also weakened Britain's position in North Africa. In February 1941 Hitler sent the newly formed Afrika Korps, commanded by Lt. Gen. Erwin Rommel, to aid the flagging Italian effort in North Africa. In late March the Korps struck against the depleted British forces in Cyrenaica. Rommel's tactical daring and his brilliant grasp of armored warfare, gained in France the previous year, caught Wavell's men off guard, and by mid-April the Germans had reached the Egyptian border, captured General O'Connor, and isolated the port of Tobruk, where an Australian garrison still struggled to hold out.

Wavell urgently requested reinforcements, and in May his troops were sufficiently strengthened to stage a counteroffensive. Despite some initial success, the offensive failed. A second offensive in June also failed. In July Wavell was relieved, and Gen. Sir Claude Auchinleck took command. Over the next six months Auchinleck supervised the buildup of British and

Commonwealth strength in North Africa and began planning a campaign to relieve Tobruk and recapture Cyrenaica. After an abortive attempt to relieve Tobruk in November, Auchinleck's troops finally lifted the siege on December 10. His men pressed forward to Benghazi, which they occupied December 24.

The British success proved temporary. On January 21, 1942, Rommel struck back, and by the 28th Auchinleck's forces had retreated to a line just west of Tobruk. After a lull of nearly four months Rommel resumed the offensive on May 27. By the end of June the Afrika Korps had almost reached El Alamein, only 55 miles from Alexandria and the Nile Delta. Thereafter Rommel's momentum faltered, and his men began to suffer increasingly from supply shortages. (On June 16 an Anglo-American convoy had reached Malta and succeeded in lifting the German air offensive against the island. Later in the month Allied planes from Malta began attacking Axis supply convoys to North Africa; and by mid-July only one Axis ship in four was able to reach its destination.) Auchinleck's men were able to hold the line, and on July 10 they began a series of limited counterattacks. By the end of the month both sides were too exhausted to continue the offensive, and Auchinleck called off the attacks.

In August Auchinleck was replaced as commander in chief by Gen. Sir Harold Alexander, and Lt. Gen. Bernard Law Montgomery took over as field commander of the Western Desert Force, rechristened the British 8th Army. Alexander reorganized the British defense line and ordered his men to hold their ground. On August 31 Rommel renewed the offensive against El Alamein, but could not drive the British back. On September 2 the Desert Fox, as Rommel was called by both sides, began withdrawing his forces and ordered them to take up the defensive. He himself left for sick leave in Germany at the end of the month.

In the next weeks Montgomery directed the largest buildup of tanks, guns, and men that had been seen in the desert war. At the same time he trained his troops rigorously and boosted their self-confidence. On October 23 he launched his meticulously planned offensive with a huge artillery barrage against the German position. Within three days Rommel (now a field marshal) had cut short his sick leave and returned to the front, organizing a stubborn defense that gave

THE MEDITERRANEAN THEATER AND THE DESERT WAR

After a grueling series of inconclusive battles in the North African desert, England finally defeated Rommel's crack German and Italian troops at El Alamein in the fall of 1942. Rommel, pursued by the British, retreated toward Tunisia, where Hitler was hastily sending in German and Italian reinforcements. Meanwhile, new British and American forces, supplemented by British veterans from El Alamein, converged to defeat the Axis in Tunisia.

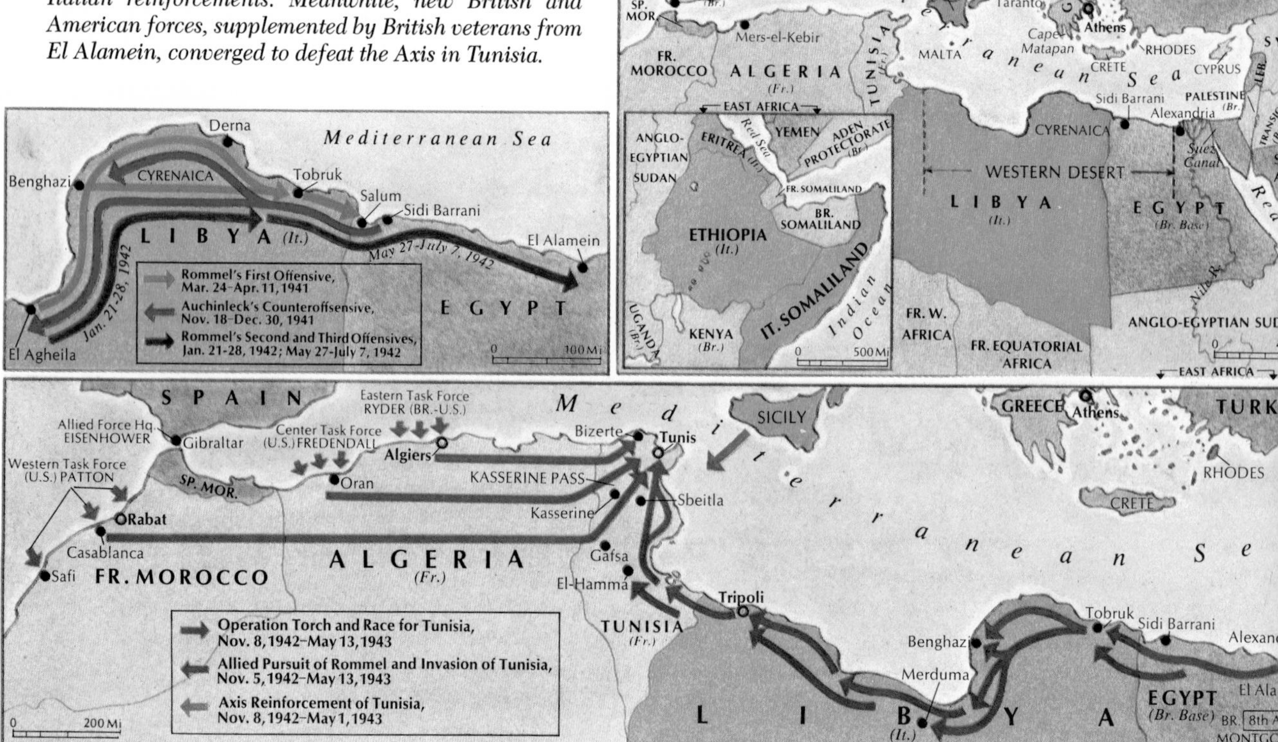

way only after 12 days of heavy fighting. Axis losses were more than 26,000 compared to the Allies' 13,500.

On November 5 Montgomery renewed his offensive, and by nightfall the Afrika Korps had begun withdrawing toward Sidi Barrani. Three days later, hundreds of miles to the west, more than 100,000 Anglo-American troops landed in French North Africa in the first phase of Operation Torch. By November 11 Algiers, Oran, and Casablanca had been occupied by the Allies, and all French resistance in Algeria and Morocco had ended. Despite orders from the Vichy regime to fight on, Adm. Jean Darlan, the French High Commissioner in North Africa, ordered a cease-fire and urged the French Fleet at Toulon to escape to North Africa. However, Hitler had anticipated such a move; he occupied Vichy France on November 11 and ordered his troops to seize the French warships at Toulon. Faced with the difficult choice of surrender to Germany or treason against the Vichy government, the French naval officers decided to scuttle their ships instead, denying them to both sides.

Meanwhile, the Allies advanced quickly eastward along the North African coast, as Hitler rushed troops to northern Tunisia to seize and expand a beachhead vacated by retreating French troops. The Allied march bogged down to the west of Bizerte in the winter rains, and in December the Axis forces began a series of sharp counterattacks. For the first time the unseasoned U.S. troops faced the veteran German forces, and they were badly beaten in the Gafsa-Kasserine-Sbeitla area in February 1943. Meanwhile, as American soldiers gained valuable battle experience in Tunisia, Montgomery continued his successful advance into Libya. Tobruk had been recaptured on November 13, 1942, and Tripoli fell on January 23, 1943. In March Rommel, by that time seriously ill, was replaced by Gen. Dietloff Juergen von Arnim.

In early May the Allies began a final assault in Tunisia. Arnim fought a strong, mobile defense, but his position was untenable. On May 13 he surrendered some 275,000 Axis troops, including 125,000 Germans. The Allies had gained control of North Africa at a cost of 275,000 casualties. Axis losses were even greater.

The Invasion of Sicily and Italy

At the Allied Conference at Casablanca in January 1943 the United States and Britain had disagreed over Allied strategy after the completion of Operation Torch. U.S. General George Marshall favored an invasion of France in 1943, but Churchill supported a campaign against Italy, the "soft underbelly" of Europe. There were powerful arguments in favor of the latter course of action. In August 1942 an Anglo-Canadian force had attempted a small-scale raid to test the effectiveness of Allied amphibious tactics at

***Australian soldiers** in the Western Desert are nearly hit by an exploding German shell as they send a gun carrier to the rear for repair.*

The Allies *gained experien in amphibious warfare in t Sicilian campaign. The It ians suffered heavy loss surviving Axis troops, most German, retreated to Italy.*

German propaganda *leafl dropped to Allied troops mo their long struggle to captu the town and monastery Cassino, on the way to Rom*

A year after *the Sicily lan ings, on June 4, 1944, the lies finally took Rome. T Germans, aided by the ru ged terrain and bad weath held on in central and nor ern Italy until May 1945.*

Dieppe on the French coast. The disastrous outcome of the raid indicated that the Allies needed more time to perfect their amphibious operations before attempting a full-scale invasion of France. Moreover, sufficient transport for such an invasion was unlikely before early 1944. In the end Britain and the United States reached a compromise: They would strike Sicily and Italy in mid-1943 and begin preparing at once for a cross-Channel invasion in 1944.

General Eisenhower, who had directed Operation Torch, was again called upon to head Operation Husky, the invasion of Sicily. Britain's General Alexander was placed in charge of Allied ground forces. On July 10 two Allied forces, numbering nearly half a million men, landed on the southeast shore of Sicily. The U.S. 7th Army under Lt. Gen. George S. Patton, Jr., pushed northwest to Palermo and turned eastward along Sicily's northern coast. Simultaneously, the British 8th Army under General Montgomery pressed northward on either side of Mount Etna toward Messina. Within five weeks the last Axis resistance had been crushed and Sicily was in Allied hands. Axis losses, most of them Italian, were eight times as great as Allied losses, which totaled about 20,000. Another 100,000 Axis soldiers escaped across the narrow Strait of Messina to Italy.

On July 25, three days after Patton's troops took Palermo, the Fascist Grand Council deposed Premier Benito Mussolini (see pp. 168–173). King Victor Emmanuel III assumed control of Italy's armed forces and appointed Marshal Pietro Badoglio to replace

Il Duce as Premier. The new government pledged it would continue the war, but immediately opened secret armistice negotiations with the Allies. On September 3 Badoglio secretly signed a truce. (The agreement was not announced publicly until September 8.) Hitler, alarmed by the sudden coup, ordered his troops in Italy to seize and disarm Italian soldiers and sent

reserve forces to hold the northern Italian passes. German troops under Rommel in northern Italy and under Field Marshal Albert Kesselring in central and southern Italy swiftly occupied the country. A few months later Hitler restored Mussolini to power in northern Italy, but the regime never amounted to much more than a puppet government.

Meanwhile, Eisenhower went ahead with plans for an invasion of the Italian mainland. On September 3 troops of the British 8th Army under General Montgomery crossed the Strait of Messina to Calabria, at the toe of the Italian boot. Six days later the U.S. 5th Army, under Lt. Gen. Mark W. Clark, went ashore at Salerno, on Italy's southwest coast. On the same day British troops seized the Italian naval base at Taranto.

Although the U.S. 5th Army met determined resistance from Kesselring's forces, it managed to break through and make contact with British 8th Army troops by September 13. The Germans withdrew northward, destroying the harbor at Naples on the way. On October 1 the 5th Army occupied Naples and began restoring its harbor. By the 12th the Allied front ran across the Italian peninsula from Termoli on the Adriatic to a point just north of Naples. The next day Italy declared war on Germany.

The developments in Italy had created increasing demands on Germany's military manpower. Hitler was forced not only to occupy central and northern Italy, but also to replace Italian forces in Axis-occupied Yugoslavia and Greece with additional German troops. And yet, Germany's position was far from hopeless. The rugged Italian terrain provided a series of natural defensive positions that in effect multiplied German strength. Kesselring erected a strong defensive line in central Italy, using the jagged passes and swift-running streams of the Apennine mountains to their best advantage. His winter position was actually a series of defensive lines, organized in depth. Its strongest sector was the so-called Gustav Line (see map).

In late October and early November the Allied armies fought through Kesselring's southernmost positions, but after a series of bloody encounters their advance was halted at the Gustav Line by January 15, 1944. At the same time, Eisenhower left for Britain to direct plans for the upcoming invasion of France. Montgomery had already left on December 30, and the transfer of Allied troops and supplies westward in preparation for D-day had begun in November. However, Allied commanders still considered the capture of Rome an essential objective, and on January 22 an Allied force of 50,000 men landed at Anzio, to the north of the Gustav Line and south of Rome. At first the new troops encountered no enemy opposition, but German reserves rushed south from Rome and soon encircled their beachhead. During the next four months the Allies failed repeatedly to break out. They suffered heavy casualties: Some 30,000 dead and wounded were evacuated from the Anzio beachhead.

Farther south the Allied armies suffered one costly defeat after another in an attempt to capture the town of Cassino, a key position near the Gustav Line. In February and March the Allies bombed Cassino and its ancient Benedictine monastery, and in mid-May they finally broke through the Gustav Line west of Cassino. On the 23d the Anzio forces broke out of their encirclement, and two days later they joined the other Allied troops advancing on Rome. On June 4 they entered the Eternal City without firing a shot. The Germans had already withdrawn farther northward.

Two days later, on June 6, the Allies opened their campaign against France with the D-day landings on the beaches of Normandy. From then on, although the Italian campaign would continue on a reduced scale, Italy would serve primarily as an airbase for Allied attacks on German industry and communications networks. The fighting there and in North Africa had provided a costly training ground for the final crusade in the west. It had given the green Allied armies the battle-hardened edge they would need to push forward from the coast of Normandy, across France and the Low Countries, and into the heart of Germany.

1944

D-Day: The Road to Victory

The Allied invasion of France opens with landings on the coast of Normandy, and Allied armies begin closing in on the Third Reich.

"Under the command of General Eisenhower, Allied naval forces, supported by strong air forces, began landing Allied armies this morning on the coast of France." The announcement from Supreme Headquarters, Allied Expeditionary Force (SHAEF) came on D-day, June 6, 1944, exactly four years and two days after the last British forces had been evacuated from Dunkirk to escape the Nazi blitzkrieg of June 1940. The night before, the largest amphibious assault force the world had ever seen had assembled off the coast of Normandy, and at dawn more than 150,000 Allied soldiers had begun landing on Utah, Omaha, Gold, Juno, and Sword beaches.

Operation Overlord, more than a year in the planning, was finally underway. By nightfall on the 6th American and British forces had established a foothold

in German-occupied Europe, and in the next days and weeks they pushed forward. Although the Germans fought back stubbornly, they could not stop the Allied advance. By September 11 the first American patrol had crossed the German border.

The idea of a cross-Channel invasion of western Europe had long been discussed, but such an ambitious undertaking became feasible only after the United States entered the war in December 1941. Even then Allied strategists disagreed on the time and place of the invasion. The Americans favored a cross-Channel assault as early as 1943, but the British sought to delay it until enough troops and arms could be amassed to assure success, preferring first to weaken Hitler's empire with air bombardment and ground assaults in North Africa and the Mediterranean.

At the Casablanca Conference in January 1943 the Combined Chiefs of Staff tentatively agreed to schedule a landing on the French coast for the spring of 1944, and Allied planners began drawing up the first blueprints for Operation Overlord. That December President Franklin D. Roosevelt appointed Maj. Gen. Dwight D. Eisenhower, who had directed the successful 1943 Allied campaigns in North Africa and Sicily (see pp. 336–343), to be supreme commander of all Allied ground, air, and naval forces involved in the D-day landings and subsequent operations. In mid-January 1944 Eisenhower went to England to take charge of the newly created SHAEF command. British Gen. Sir Bernard Law Montgomery, commander of British troops in North Africa and Italy, would lead the British and direct Overlord ground operations.

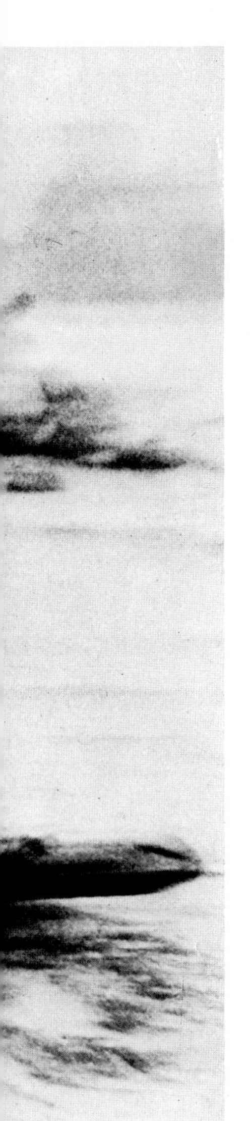

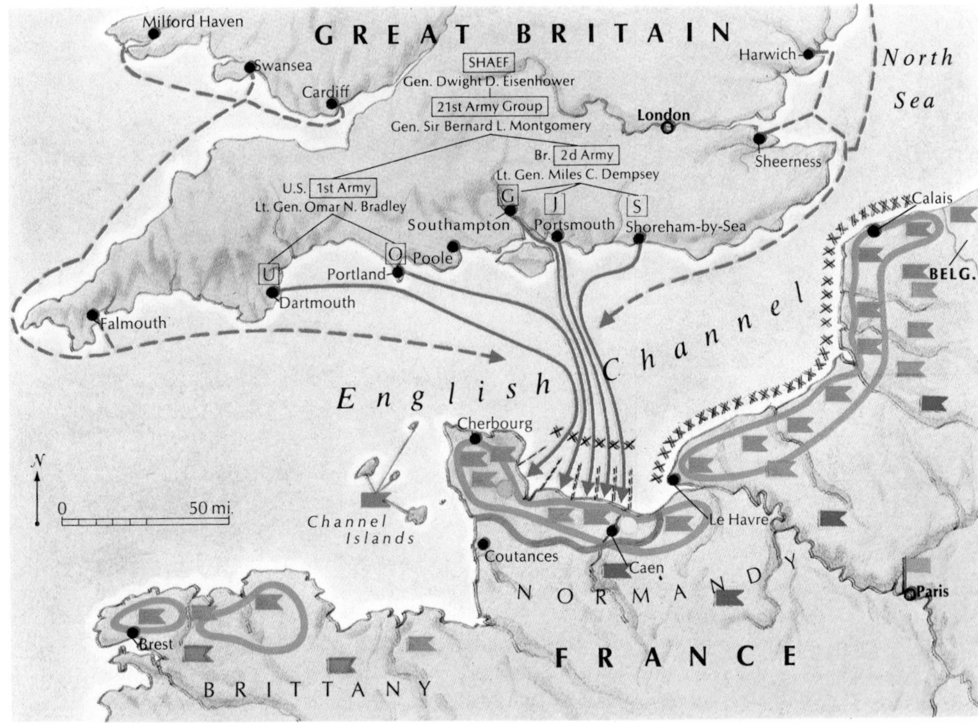

In the gray dawn of D-day a U.S. soldier swims through bodies and debris toward the shore. The photograph was taken by Robert Capa, who accompanied one of the first assault waves at Omaha Beach. The devices in the water, set by the Germans to disable landing craft, also provided cover for U.S. troops from the unexpectedly heavy German fire.

Invasion of Normandy, Operation Overlord, June 6, 1944

- U — Utah Beach Assault Force, U.S. 4th Infantry Division
- O — Omaha Beach Assault Force, U.S. 1st Infantry Division
- G — Gold Beach Assault Force, Br. 50th Infantry Division
- J — Juno Beach Assault Force, Can. 3d Infantry Division
- S — Sword Beach Assault Force, Br. 3d Infantry Division
- Followup Forces
- Paratroop Landings, Br. 6th Airborne Division
- Paratroop Landings, U.S. 101st and 82nd Airborne Divisions
- Allied Line of Advance, July 24, 1944

German Dispositions

- ××× German Minefields
- Atlantic Wall (front line of German defenses)
- Static Divisions (understrength and underequipped garrison units manning the Atlantic Wall)
- Infantry Divisions
- Panzer Divisions
- Paratroop Divisions
- HQ, Western Armies

Final invasion plans were completed in the spring of 1944. The initial landings were scheduled to take place in early June along the French Channel coast between Caen and Cherbourg in Normandy. The site was chosen for its good beaches, favorable tides, and comparatively weak coastal defenses. Southern England became a giant military base as an enormous Allied force began assembling. By early June some 3 million soldiers, sailors, and airmen, as well as thousands of tanks, guns, and other supplies, had been readied for the assault. Preparations were also completed for the laying of a cross-Channel fuel pipeline and for two huge prefabricated harbors, designed to serve as port facilities until the Allies had captured Cherbourg and other French ports. Special landing and amphibious vehicles were tested and built, and new kinds of minesweepers were developed. Allied bombers struck railheads, bridges, and roads in Normandy in an effort to seal off the invasion area.

Since it was impossible to conceal this tremendous buildup, the Allies developed an elaborate scheme to

Soldiers help a wounded comrade *ashore at Utah Beach (above). During Operation Overlord 9,000 ships ferried over a million men and more than 170,000 vehicles to the beaches of Normandy, supported by 702 warships and over 200 minesweepers. Three more divisions were airlifted by nearly 1,400 transport planes and 867 gliders. At top, a view of the elaborate post-D-day operations on Omaha Beach.*

convince the Germans that the major thrust would come in the Pas-de-Calais region some 150 miles northeast of the actual landing site. German opinion already favored the Calais area because of its close proximity to England, and the Allies reinforced this misconception with false radio messages, offshore naval maneuvers, and other indications of an impending assault. So successful was the deception that even after the D-day landings had begun, the German High Command was convinced they were only diversionary efforts and ordered the 15th Army to remain in the Calais area for the main assault.

In June 1944 there were only 58 German combat divisions in all of France and the Low Countries, and more than half of them were understrength and deficient in equipment and training. Most of Hitler's best troops had been transferred to the eastern front to fight the Soviets (see pp. 328–335). For the same reason, German airpower in France had been seriously depleted, and almost half the remaining warplanes were grounded awaiting repairs or spare parts. Field Marshal Gerd von Rundstedt, commander in chief of German forces in western Europe, exercised only nominal power. German air and naval forces were under separate commands, and Rundstedt's orders to his own field commanders were subject to Hitler's approval. (Since early 1943 the Fuehrer had exercised supreme command of all Germany's armed forces.)

Field Marshal Erwin Rommel, who had been in charge of German Army Group B in northern France since December 1943, was only partially subordinate to Rundstedt. Moreover, he disagreed with Rundstedt's strategy for opposing the upcoming invasion. Whereas Rundstedt favored light coastal defenses backed up by mobile striking forces, Rommel wanted heavy coastal fortifications held by strong local units. For the past six months he and his troops had been strengthening the Atlantic Wall along the French coast, building pillboxes, setting up obstacles, and laying mines to prepare for the Allied assault.

The landings had been scheduled for June 5, 6, and 7, a time when the tides would be most suitable for amphibious operations. On the 4th some 5,000 warships and other craft were poised for the assault, when Eisenhower postponed the landings because of unfavorable weather. The next day, however, despite continued bad weather, he decided to go ahead with the assault rather than risk another delay. Shortly after midnight on June 6 Allied minesweepers began clearing the area and marking off lanes of approach, and RAF bombers attacked strategic targets along the Channel coast. Between 1 and 2 a.m. three divisions of Allied paratroopers were dropped behind German lines to secure the western and eastern flanks of the beachhead, and just before 6 a.m. Allied warships opened fire on the German coastal fortifications. Some 11,000 planes massed above the landing site to provide a protective umbrella against German bombers.

At 6:30 a.m. U.S. troops under Gen. Omar N. Bradley began splashing ashore at Utah and Omaha beaches. At 7:20 a.m. British and Canadian forces commanded by Lt. Gen. Sir Miles Dempsey landed at Gold, Juno, and Sword beaches. With the exception of Omaha Beach, where heavy seas and strong currents scattered the landing craft and forces ran into unexpectedly strong coastal defenses, casualties were lighter than anticipated. By dusk some 155,000 men were ashore.

The Germans were caught completely off guard. They had thought that the uncertain weather and high seas would rule out an assault at that time. Rundstedt had no armored divisions at his direct disposal, and Rommel, whose command included three armored divisions, was in Germany when the landings took place and did not reach Normandy until the evening of June 6. Hitler had four panzer divisions under his personal control, and they could not be moved without his permission.

Once ashore the Allies encountered varying degrees of resistance—sometimes desperate, sometimes light, but always determined. By June 11 the landing beaches were linked in a continuous front. By the 17th nearly 600,000 men and 100,000 vehicles were ashore; and by July 2 a million men, half a million tons of supplies, and 177,000 vehicles had landed. Slowly at first, the Allies began expanding their beachhead toward Cherbourg and Caen. While Bradley's 5th and 19th Corps fixed the Germans along the lines reached by June 13, his 7th Corps fought its way toward Cherbourg. On June 27 the German garrison at Cherbourg surrendered, but only after destroying the port facilities. (The Allies did not have them in working order until August 7.) Bradley's forces then surged southward. On July 28 they broke through the German lines near Coutances. The German's had massed most of their armored units to halt the drive on Caen by Dempsey's 1st and 8th Corps. Dempsey's forces did not break through to the south of Caen until July 24.

In early July Rundstedt, despairing of success, was replaced by Field Marshal Hans Günther von Kluge. Rommel stayed on, but on July 17 he suffered serious skull and facial wounds when his car was wrecked by the strafing of an Allied fighter plane, and Kluge assumed command of Army Group B. On July 20 Hitler was injured by a bomb planted by a group of German officers seeking to assassinate him and end the war. The conspirators were executed, but thereafter Hitler completely refused to trust his subordinates.

From late July onward the Allied advance gained momentum, leaving the German forces too little time between assaults to organize an effective counterattack. Allied forces were reorganized with the creation of the U.S. 3d Army under Lt. Gen. George S. Patton and the Canadian 1st Army under Lt. Gen. Henry Crerar. By July 30, U.S. troops had captured Avranches. The 8th Corps turned southwestward to secure Brittany and its vital ports, while the main force marched eastward toward Paris. On August 20 some 50,000 German soldiers were trapped 20 miles south of Falaise. Kluge was replaced by Field Marshal Walter Model. (Kluge later committed suicide.) Five days later, on August 25, U.S. and Free French forces made a triumphal entry into Paris. The first phase of Operation Overlord was over. In less than two months the Allies secured Normandy and most of Brittany, inflicting some 530,000 German casualties.

On August 15 a second Allied invasion force, consisting of U.S. and French troops under Lt. Gen. Jacob L. Devers, had landed on the Mediterranean coast of France between Cannes and Toulon and began advancing northward. The Germans withdrew rapidly, covering their retreat with skillful rearguard actions that blocked Allied efforts to cut off any large forces. On the 17th Hitler ordered them to withdraw to the Vosges Mountains. By September 11 the two Allied invasion forces had made contact.

Meanwhile, the Allied armies in northern France pushed into Belgium, Luxembourg, and Alsace. Antwerp fell on September 4, although its port facilities, blocked by the German grip on the Scheldt estuary, were useless to the Allies until November 28.

By mid-September the Allied front ran from the Vosges Mountains along the Siegfried Line of Germany and across the southern border of Holland. Thereafter the advance was slowed by logistical problems and stiffening German resistance. Hitler rightly concluded that the tremendous speed of the Allied conquests and his troops' dogged refusal to surrender the French and Belgian ports had prevented the establishment of an efficient Allied supply network. He ordered his men to hold the line while he prepared a counteroffensive and on September 5 reinstated Rundstedt as German commander in western Europe.

In mid-September a daring Allied armored and paratroop attack, code named Market-Garden and designed to seize the bridges across the Meuse, Waal, and lower Rhine Rivers in Holland and gain a foothold on the east bank of the Rhine, ran into tough German opposition. Although the Meuse and the Waal were secured, the attempt to seize the lower Rhine failed. Elsewhere the Allies also encountered difficulties, and by early October their progress had been effectively checked.

Throughout the fall of 1944 Hitler had secretly mustered all Germany's remaining resources for a decisive counterstroke. The Third Reich still had nearly 10 million men under arms, and by expanding the draft ages and converting service, naval, and air

***French civilians** joined with soldiers in a last-ditch battle against the Germans in the Bois de Boulogne on August 25, 1944, the day Paris was liberated by the Allies.*

***Excited Parisians** (below) push forward to greet Gen. Charles de Gaulle, who led a triumphal procession down the Champs Élysées to mark the end of Nazi occupation.*

personnel into infantry troops, Hitler was able to create another 25 divisions. Moreover, despite the intensive Allied bombing of German industries, war production continued. While soldiers and engineering crews worked feverishly to refurbish the Siegfried Line fortifications, Germany's armored divisions were strengthened and regrouped for the final onslaught.

The Battle of the Bulge

At dawn on December 16, 22 German armored and infantry divisions struck the thinly held Allied lines in the Ardennes sector of the front, attempting to break through to Antwerp and cut the Allied forces in half. Startled by the sudden offensive, the six U.S. divisions holding the area fell back everywhere. While Eisenhower rushed in reinforcements to contain the flanks of the growing bulge, the 101st Airborne Division managed to hold the important road junction at Bastogne. By the end of December the Allies had stopped the Germans east of the Meuse. On January 8 Hitler, realizing that his bold plan had failed, ordered his panzers to withdraw. By the 16th the Allies had reestablished an unbroken front. The Battle of the Bulge cost the Germans about 100,000 casualties, 600 tanks and assault guns, and 1,600 planes. The Allies suffered nearly 76,000 casualties.

A second German offensive began on January 1, 1945, to the south, in Alsace-Lorraine. U.S. forces there had been depleted to reinforce the Ardennes front, and the offensive was successful at first. The Allies quickly reorganized their defenses, however, and by January 26 they had halted the Germans about 12 miles short of their objective, the Saverne Gap, which was the main route through the Vosges Mountains.

The Allied armies *pushed slowly outward from their narrow beachhead in June and July 1944 (see map below right). While British and Canadian forces pinned down the bulk of German armor around Caen, U.S. troops captured Cherbourg and the Cotentin Peninsula and broke through German lines near St. Lô, surging southward toward Brittany and turning westward toward Paris. A second Allied invasion force landed on the southern French coast on August 15 and began marching northward. By mid-September the Allied advance into the Low Countries and Alsace-Lorraine had slowed, and by December 15 the front had temporarily stabilized along the line indicated on the map.*

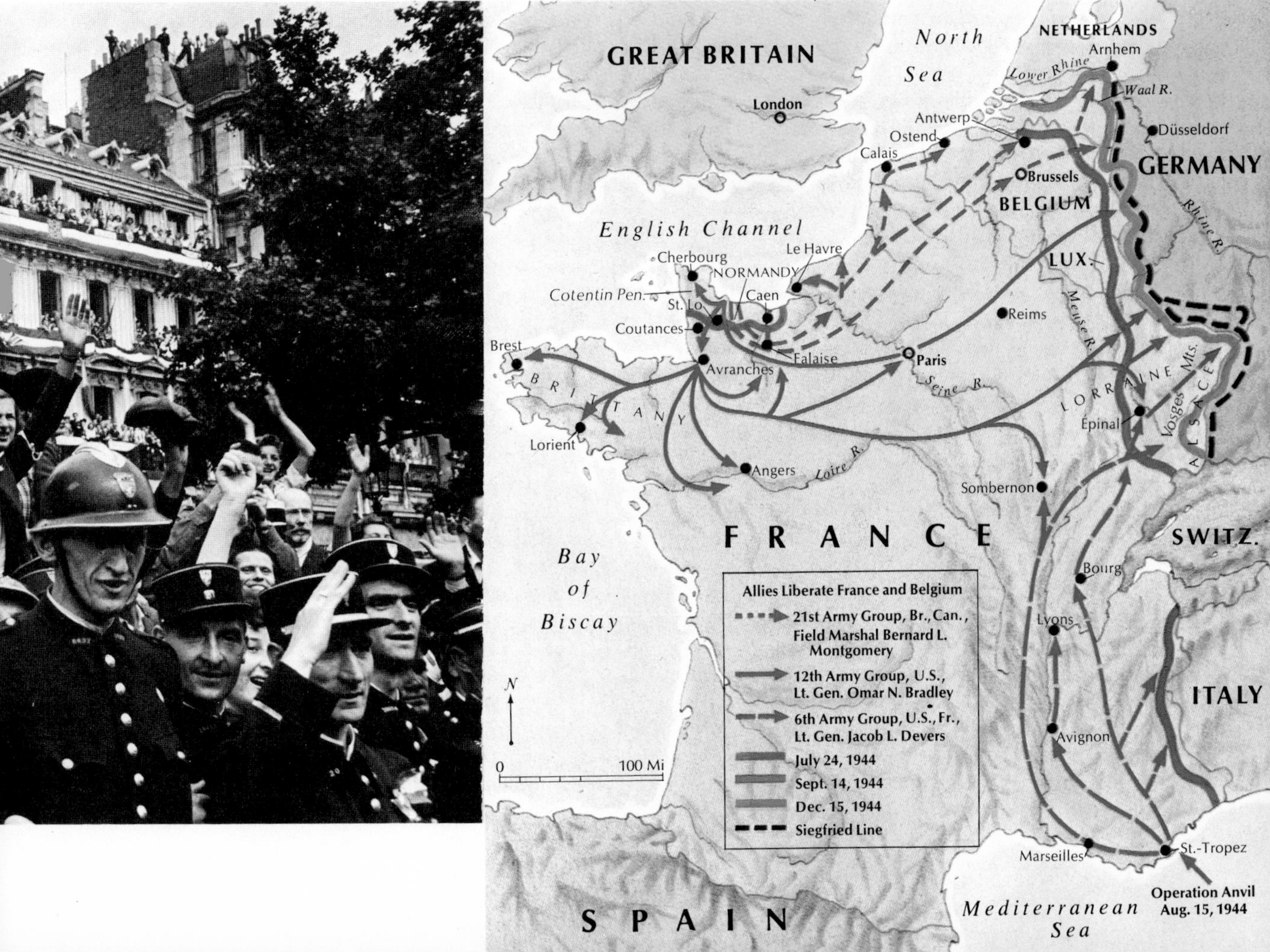

With the failure of this latest gamble, a kind of madness seemed to overtake the leaders of the Third Reich. Despite the unmistakable signs of defeat on all sides, Hitler and his closest associates continued to hope for a miracle. Refusing to draw the obvious conclusion from the developments of the last few months, they convinced themselves that the Allied fortunes would change; that the Soviets would turn against their British and American allies (or vice versa); that the new secret weapons, the V-1 and V-2 rockets and the Messerschmitt jet, would wreak such destruction that the Allies would plead for mercy; that somehow Germany could hold out long enough for a stroke of good fortune. In the meantime Hitler called upon all able-bodied men between the ages of 16 and 60 to form a Home Guard (Volkssturm) and ordered his field armies to fight to the last man.

With victory approaching, the Allied heads of state met to discuss the coordination of the final offensives against the Third Reich, the fate of Germany and Poland after the war's end, the Soviet Union's role in the defeat of Japan, and the proposed United Nations (see pp. 372–377). Talks between Roosevelt, Churchill, and Stalin were held from February 4–11 at Yalta on the Crimean peninsula. Thus far the pressures of the war had overshadowed the very different war aims of the Big Three powers, but at Yalta the unmistakable conflicts began to surface.

The postwar reconstruction of Poland aroused the most heated controversy. The Red Army had already liberated much of Poland, and Stalin clearly desired the installation of leaders sympathetic to Soviet influence, not only in Warsaw but throughout Eastern Europe. Churchill was firmly opposed to such a development. The British Prime Minister, convinced that a strong and independent Poland would check Soviet influence in Central Europe, supported the Polish government-in-exile of Stanislaus Mikolajczyk. Stalin stubbornly insisted that Mikolajczyk's government was less representative of the Polish people than his chosen leaders. Although Roosevelt tried to mediate, there was little room for negotiation: The Soviet Army had already occupied most of Poland, and Stalin had already recognized the provisional Polish government at Lublin as the legal government of Poland a few days before the Yalta Conference. In the end Stalin agreed to form a "Polish provisional government of national unity" by asking "democratic" Polish leaders to join the Lublin regime; but given the reality of Soviet military and economic domination, the concession was meaningless. The Allies did give in to Stalin's insistence that the new Soviet-Polish frontier be drawn to the west of the prewar frontier (thus giving Stalin all the Polish territory he had received in the 1939 Nazi-Soviet Pact). In compensation for this loss of territory, Poland was promised that it would gain part of eastern Germany at the war's end.

As for Germany, the Big Three agreed to divide the country into four separate zones of occupation by the United States, Britain, France, and the U.S.S.R. Berlin,

fter the failure of German counteroffensives *in the rdennes (December 16, 1944–January 16, 1945) and e Saverne Gap area (January 1–26, 1945), the Allies liminated the Colmar pocket in early February. On ebruary 8 they launched their final offensive against e Third Reich, overrunning the Ruhr on April 18 nd sweeping forward across Germany. At the same me the Red Army closed in from the east and other llied forces pushed into northern Italy. Faced with nternal collapse and defeat on all fronts, Germany, fter a few last-ditch efforts, surrendered on May 7.*

he Allied air offensive *in Europe was a key factor in he success of Operation Overlord and subsequent llied campaigns. Primary targets included fuel lants and other war-related industries, airfields, ocket bases, railways, roads, bridges, and urban cen- ers. Allied fighters and bombers also played a critical ole in ground operations, cutting off areas from out- ide support, saturating enemy positions before as- aults, and providing air cover during offensives. The omposite picture at right shows U.S. B-17 Flying ortresses dropping bombs above Wesel, Germany, here heavy Allied bombing in March 1945 left the ity in ruins. In all, some 537,000 German civil- ns were killed and 834,000 injured by Allied bombs.*

lying within the Soviet zone of occupation, was to be administered by all four powers. Plans for the administration and eventual reunification of Germany, another probable source of conflict, were left to be decided at a later date. The issue of reparations was also left open. Roosevelt and Churchill favored reparations against Germany, but they objected to setting a definite figure until after the war was over and they could determine how much she could afford to pay, arguing that the enormous sums levied after World War I had brought political and economic disaster to the Weimar Republic. Stalin, on the other hand, wanted Germany to pay heavily for the 17½ million Soviet civilian and military war dead and the terrible destruction Hitler's retreating armies had inflicted. To preserve Allied unity, the issue was referred to a reparations committee, and the Soviet figure of $20 billion was accepted as a basis for discussion.

Roosevelt was anxious for the Soviets to join the war against Japan as soon as possible. Although he knew at the time that the atomic bomb would soon be ready, he was not sure that it would work. If not, Japan might hold out for another year, forcing the United States to mount a costly invasion. Soviet support might help convince the Japanese that their case was hopeless and speed their surrender. At Yalta Stalin pledged to Roosevelt that the U.S.S.R. would declare war on Japan two or three months after Germany's surrender.

With all its conflicts, the mood at Yalta was relatively cordial and optimistic. Roosevelt left the conference convinced that a frank and friendly attitude would overcome the Russian leader's suspicions and that he and Stalin could work out any disagreements in the future. Churchill, however, did not share his belief. The British Prime Minister strongly suspected that Stalin would readily forego Roosevelt's good will should Soviet interests so demand. Stalin had reason to be pleased. Making few concessions, he had won guarded acceptance of his principal goals.

The Last Days of the Third Reich

In early February the Allied armies had launched a coordinated drive to the Rhine. British and Canadian forces made short gains against strong German opposition in the north. Elsewhere the Allies advanced more rapidly, despite vicious German counterattacks. On March 5 U.S. soldiers captured Cologne. Two days later a U.S. armored division discovered that the Germans had failed to demolish a bridge across the Rhine and captured it intact, while the Germans were trying to blow it up. (Hitler was infuriated and dismissed Rundstedt, installing Field Marshal Albert Kesselring, who had led the German armies in Italy, as commander in chief.) By the end of March Allied troops held the west bank of the Rhine from Arnhem, Holland, to the Swiss border. They had broken through Hitler's fabled Siegfried Line fortifications in all but the southernmost sector, which lay east of the Rhine. Allied bombers had stepped up their air offensive in March. In day and night raids they dropped 245,000

The Big Powers at Potsdam: British Prime Minister Winston *Churchill (upper left), his successor Clement Attlee (top center), Soviet Premier Joseph Stalin (upper right), and U.S. President Harry Truman (bottom, left of center).*

The Allies divided postwar Germany and Austria *into U.S., British, French, and Soviet occupation zones and placed Berlin and Vienna under joint four-power control. In 1945 Poland, with Soviet backing, unilaterally seized all German territory east of the Oder and Neisse Rivers.*

tons of bombs on German cities, factories, fuel plants, railways, and other strategic targets.

As the Allied armies in western Europe smashed into the Third Reich, the Red Army was closing in from the east. By late February Russian forces had reached the Oder-Neisse Line, within 40 miles of Berlin. Meanwhile, the Allied forces in northern Italy had pierced the Gothic Line in places and were preparing a final offensive against Hitler's battered forces.

On April 1 the U.S. 1st and 9th Armies enveloped the Ruhr, seat of Germany's vital coal and industrial resources. After several abortive attempts to break out, the encircled German forces disintegrated, and by April 18 the Allies had overrun the area, capturing some 320,000 enemy soldiers. (Model himself reportedly committed suicide.) Thereafter German resistance collapsed, except in a few areas where fanatical troops fought to the death, and the Allied armies swept across the country.

The Soviets mounted their final assault on Berlin on April 16 as the British marched northeastward toward Hamburg and Lübeck, and the Americans headed southeast toward Munich and the Czech and Austrian borders. Refusing to believe what was happening, Hitler called for the formation of a German guerrilla force (the Werewolves) to resist the invaders; ordered Nazi officials to destroy all German resources; and pushed nonexistent German divisions about his map board. His only good news during this period was of the death of Roosevelt on April 12.

By April 22, however, even the Fuehrer realized the end was near. He decided to remain in Berlin, but most other highranking Nazi officials fled. Finally, on April 30, Hitler committed suicide, convinced to the end that he had been betrayed by his subordinates and that history would vindicate him. His will named Grand Admiral Karl Doenitz, architect of Germany's U-boat campaign, as his successor.

A day earlier, on April 29, German forces in Italy had surrendered, and in the next days Nazi armies in the Netherlands, Denmark, and northwestern and

NUREMBERG: NAZI WAR CRIMINALS STAND TRIAL

Long before the war's end the Allies had begun collecting evidence against leading Nazi officials, and special intelligence units accompanied the advancing armies to round up as many suspects as possible to be tried before an international military tribunal for wartime atrocities. The first and most highly publicized of 13 such war crimes trials held at Nuremberg, site of the great Nazi Party rallies, opened on November 20, 1945. Among the 22 defendants were Hermann Goering, head of the Luftwaffe and the number two man in Germany until just before the end of the war; Adm. Karl Doenitz, Hitler's chosen successor and former German naval commander; Gen. Wilhelm Keitel, armed forces Chief of Staff; Gen. Alfred Jodl, chief of operations; Joachim von Ribbentrop, German Foreign Minister; Albert Speer, Hitler's chief architect and armaments production expert; Alfred Rosenberg, Nazi Party "philosopher"; Arthur Seyss-Inquart, the Austrian Nazi leader who helped Hitler seize Austria in 1938; and Rudolf Hess, Hitler's former deputy. Martin Bormann, deputy chief of the Nazi Party, had vanished without a trace and was tried *in absentia*.

Evidence presented at the trial—films of the liberation of German concentration camps, the diary of Nazi legal authority Hans Frank, the secret protocols of the 1939 Nazi-Soviet pact, official documents, and eyewitness testimony—revealed the monstrous extent of Nazi brutality. Sentencing took place on October 1, 1946. Three men were acquitted, three were committed to life imprisonment, and four received lesser sentences. The remaining 12, including Goering, Keitel, Jodl, Ribbentrop, Rosenberg, Seyss-Inquart, and Bormann, were sentenced to death by hanging. Ten men were executed two weeks later. Goering committed suicide, and Bormann, who probably fled to South America, was never found.

southern Germany followed suit. The Germans signed an unconditional surrender at Reims on May 7. The next day all fighting officially ceased. At Stalin's insistence the surrender was formally ratified by a ceremony in Berlin on May 9.

Potsdam: An End and a Beginning

Peace had finally been achieved, but the exact nature of the postwar settlement remained to be delineated. For this purpose Churchill, Stalin, and Roosevelt's successor, Harry S. Truman, met at Potsdam outside Berlin from July 17 to August 2, 1945. (In the midst of the talks Churchill was replaced by the new Prime Minister, Clement Attlee.) At this, the last summit meeting of World War II, the Allied leaders again failed to agree on a joint policy for postwar Germany and put off the touchy questions of reparations and settlement of the new Polish-German border. The division of Germany into separate Soviet and Western occupation zones had already begun, and Poland had unilaterally seized territory in eastern Germany and expelled all German nationals.

On other issues, however, the Allies did reach agreement. They established a Council of Foreign Ministers to hammer out peace treaties with Italy, Romania, Finland, Hungary, and Bulgaria. They determined to destroy all traces of National Socialism and militarism in Germany and to set up an international tribunal to try leading Nazi officials for the "terrible crimes" they had committed while in power. They resolved that all Germans living in Hungary, Czechoslovakia, and Poland would be transferred to Germany as soon as possible. Yet these problems were relatively minor. Bigger issues went unresolved or were ignored.

The atmosphere at Potsdam was noticeably chilly. Truman was determined not to be "pushed around." As Vice President he had never been fully briefed on wartime diplomatic and military matters, and he set himself to carry out Roosevelt's policies as he saw them. Truman could well afford to take a hard line. The day before the conference opened, the United States had successfully tested the world's first atomic bomb, and he knew he no longer had to depend on Soviet support to win the war against Japan.

Near the end of the conference Allied leaders issued a joint demand for Japan's unconditional surrender. When she did not respond, Truman authorized the use of the new weapon. Atomic bombs were dropped on Hiroshima and Nagasaki on August 6 and 9 (see pp. 360–367), and Japan surrendered on August 14. Nearly six years after the Nazi invasion of Poland, World War II had ended. It had been the most destructive and most widespread conflict in history. It was also the deadliest, taking the lives of nearly 17 million fighting men. Some 6 million Jews had been murdered in Nazi concentration camps, and as many as 30 million other civilians around the world had died as a result of strategic bombing, starvation, disease, and other war-related causes.

Yet at its end, the prospect of a "fresh start" in international affairs seemed even dimmer than it had after World War I. Despite the creation of the United Nations the postwar world would be dominated by just two countries: the United States and the U.S.S.R., both immensely strong and growing more antagonistic as time went by. In a very short time less powerful nations would be drawn into one camp or another, building the precarious equilibrium of the cold war.

AN ALMANAC 1939-45

1939

May 22 Hitler and Mussolini sign the so-called Pact of Steel, pledging a 10-year political and military alliance.

May 23 British plan for an independent Palestine approved by Parliament. Plan denounced by Jews and Arabs.

Aug. 23 Nazi-Soviet pact of nonaggression startles Western liberals, gives Hitler a free hand to attack Poland. British Prime Minister Neville Chamberlain warns that Britain will stand by Poland.

Sept. 1 German Army invades Poland in first Nazi blitzkrieg ("lightning war").

Sept. 3 World War II begins when Great Britain and France declare war on Germany.

Sept. 17 U.S.S.R. invades Poland. Besieged from both east and west, Polish government withdraws to Romania.

Sept. 27 German troops capture Warsaw; Poland surrenders and is divided between Germany and U.S.S.R.

Nov. 4 U.S. Neutrality Act amended to permit Britain and France to buy arms on a "cash and carry" basis.

Nov. 26 Finland rejects Soviet demand for military bases on her territory.

Nov. 30 Soviets bomb Helsinki and cross into Finland but meet stubborn resistance. The League of Nations expels U.S.S.R. for aggression Dec. 14.

Dec. 13 In battle of the River Plate, Uruguay, British ships chase German battleship *Graf Spee* into Montevideo harbor. Germans scuttle ship Dec. 17.

1940

Mar. 12 Russian troops breach Finland's Mannerheim Line. Finland accepts terms in Treaty of Moscow, giving up Baltic seaports and other territories but retaining independence.

Apr. 9 German forces invade Norway and Denmark. British and French troops land in southern Norway Apr. 14 but are forced to withdraw May 3.

May 10 Germans invade Netherlands, Belgium, and Luxembourg. Chamberlain resigns and Winston Churchill becomes new British Prime Minister.

May 14 Dutch Army capitulates and German Army crosses Meuse River to begin blitzkrieg against France.

May 26–June 4 After Belgian Army surrenders on May 28, British intensify rescue operations, evacuating almost 340,000 Allied troops from Dunkirk.

June 10 Italy declares war on France and Britain; invades southern France.

June 12 Norway surrenders.

June 14 German troops enter Paris and cross Maginot Line. Paul Reynaud resigns as French Premier; Marshal Henri Pétain replaces him (June 16).

June 22 France signs armistice with Germany, and three days later with Italy, surrendering some three-fifths of France to Germany. Gen. Charles de Gaulle, leader of the Free French, vows from London to fight until France is liberated. In July the Germans install a puppet French government at Vichy, France, under Marshal Pétain.

July 10–Oct. 31 Battle of Britain begins with German attempt to destroy British airpower; peaks in large-scale air raids on London and other cities. But Royal Air Force foils Nazi attempt to bomb England into submission as prelude to German invasion.

Sept. 27 Japan signs 10-year military and economic alliance with Germany and Italy, the Tripartite Pact.

Oct. 28 Italy invades Greece. Greek Army counterattacks and by Dec. 3 occupies one-fourth of Albania. Germans must reinforce Italian armies.

Nov. 5 U.S. President Franklin Roosevelt reelected to third term.

Nov. 14 English industrial city of Coventry heavily damaged in night air raid.

Dec. 9 British open offensive in North Africa.

1941

Mar. 11 U.S. Lend-Lease Act promises all-out aid to Britain and other countries at war with Axis Powers.

Apr. 6 British forces capture Addis Ababa, Ethiopia, from Italians.

Apr. 6 German troops invade Greece and Yugoslavia; Yugoslav government surrenders Apr. 17; Greeks sign armistice Apr. 23.

Apr. 13 Japan and U.S.S.R. conclude a treaty of neutrality.

May 20 Germans invade British-held island of Crete in Mediterranean. British forces evacuated by May 31.

May 27 German battleship *Bismarck* sunk by British Navy in North Atlantic.

June 22 Operation Barbarossa begins as Germans invade U.S.S.R. on 1,100-mile front. They besiege Leningrad (Aug. 31) and move on Moscow.

Aug. 14 Atlantic Charter, signed by Churchill and Roosevelt, states peace goals that include "freedom from fear and want" for all peoples.

Nov. 29 Soviet Army begins successful counterattack in Moscow sector.

Dec. 6 Britain declares war against Finland, Hungary, and Romania. Soviet Army begins counterattack against Axis forces.

Dec. 7–8 Japan attacks U.S. naval base at Pearl Harbor, Hawaii, by air, destroying most of U.S. Pacific Fleet. Japanese troops attack Philippines and Hong Kong, invade Thailand and British Malaya (see pp. 314–321). U.S.A. and Britain declare war on Japan.

Dec. 11 Germany and Italy declare war on U.S.A.; Congress recognizes state of war with both nations.

Dec. 23 Marines on Wake Island surrender to Japanese after 15-day siege.

Dec. 25 British Crown Colony of Hong Kong surrenders to Japanese.

1942

Jan. 11 Japanese invade Netherlands East Indies.

Feb. 1 Vidkun Quisling installed to head Nazi puppet regime in Norway.

Feb. 15 Japanese, attacking from Malaya, seize Singapore.

Mar. 7 British evacuate Rangoon and Japanese conquer Burma.

Mar. 9 Dutch surrender Netherlands East Indies to Japanese.

Apr. 9 Gen. Jonathan Wainwright's U.S. forces on Bataan Peninsula in Philippines surrender to Japanese; fort of Corregidor in Manila Bay falls May 6.

May 4–8 Battle of Coral Sea halts Japanese expansion in southwest Pacific.

June 3–6 Japanese naval force attacks Midway Island in central Pacific but is stopped by U.S. ships and planes in turning point of war in Pacific.

June 21 German Army under Gen. Erwin Rommel captures city of Tobruk in Libya; then Rommel invades Egypt.

Aug. 7 U.S. Marines land on Guadalcanal in Solomon Islands.

Aug. 19 Canadian and British troops (as well as 50 U.S. Rangers) suffer heavy casualties in raid on Dieppe, France.

Sept. 14 German offensive in U.S.S.R. meets fierce resistance at Stalingrad. Soviet counteroffensive begins Nov. 19.

Oct. 23–Nov. 4 Heavy air support helps British, under Gen. Bernard Montgomery, defeat Rommel's Afrika Korps at Battle of El Alamein. Germans forced out of Egypt by Nov. 12.

Oct. 26 Battle of Santa Cruz: Japanese inflict heavy losses on U.S. naval forces but fail to reinforce Solomon Islands.

Nov. 8 U.S. and British troops, commanded by Gen. Dwight D. Eisenhower, land in North Africa.

Nov. 11 Germans take over remainder of unoccupied France, confirm Pierre Laval as head of Vichy regime.

Nov. 23 Soviets encircle German Sixth Army within Stalingrad.

1943

Jan. 17–27 Churchill and Roosevelt meet at Casablanca, Morocco, to plan Allied invasion of Hitler's Europe.

Jan. 31 German Field Marshal Friedrich Paulus surrenders at Stalingrad.

Feb. 7 Last remaining Japanese forces evacuate Guadalcanal, ending six months' stubborn resistance.

Apr. 19 Jewish uprising in Warsaw ghetto begins. In several weeks Nazis massacre more than 50,000 Jews.

May 7 U.S.-British troops capture Tunis and Bizerte in North Africa.

May 13 Axis forces surrender in North Africa.

June 30 Gen. Douglas MacArthur's "leap-frogging" campaign in Pacific begins with landing in New Guinea.

July 10 Allies invade Sicily, complete conquest of island Aug. 17.

July 25 Mussolini is overthrown by Grand Council; held prisoner until rescued Sept. 12 by Germans, who use him as a puppet ruler until his assassination.

Sept. 3 Allies invade southern Italy; Italian government signs truce with Allies. German resistance and winter weather slow Allied advance.

Oct. 13 Italy declares war against Germany.

Nov. 21 U.S. forces invade Tarawa and Makin in Gilbert Islands. In three days they crush Japanese resistance.

Nov. 22–26 Churchill and Roosevelt meet with Chinese President Chiang Kai-shek at Cairo and agree on military strategy against Japan.

Nov. 28–Dec. 1 Churchill, Roosevelt, and Stalin, at Teheran Conference, make final plans against Germany.

Dec. 31 Soviets regain Zhitomir, following capture of Smolensk (Sept. 25) and Kiev (Nov. 6). At end of year U.S.S.R. has recaptured two-thirds of territory taken by Germany.

1944

Jan. 22 Allied troops establish beachhead at Anzio, Italy.

Jan. 27 Soviets relieve besieged defenders of Leningrad, begin to drive Germans back into Estonia and Poland.

Feb. 6 U.S.A. invades Kwajalein and (Feb. 21) Eniwetok in Marshall Islands.

Feb. 20–26 U.S. aircraft bomb German industrial cities, inflict heavy damage.

Apr. 22 U.S.A. outflanks Japan in Netherlands New Guinea.

May 18 Allied army drives Germans off stronghold at Cassino, Italy.

June 4 U.S. 5th Army marches into Rome, earlier declared an open city, not subject to bombardment.

June 6 D-day. Allied troops land in Normandy for final assault on Hitler's Fortress Europe.

June 13 First German flying bombs, V-1 rockets, fall on London.

June 15–19 U.S. troops invade Saipan in Marianas, defeat Japanese in 24 days.

July 20 German officers' plot to assassinate Hitler fails.

Aug. 10 U.S.A. regains Guam.

Aug. 15 Allies land on southern coast of France.

Aug. 21 Representatives of Britain, U.S.A., and U.S.S.R. meet at Dumbarton Oaks Conference to plan for an international peacekeeping organization.

Aug. 25 General de Gaulle leads Allied armies into Paris.

Sept. 3 Allied troops liberate Brussels, then cross into Germany Sept. 11.

Oct. 20 General MacArthur fulfills pledge to return to the Philippines, leads U.S. invasion of Leyte.

Oct. 20 Soviet troops and Yugoslav guerrillas enter Belgrade.

Oct. 23–26 In Battle of Leyte Gulf Japanese suffer heavy losses; U.S.A. wins air and sea superiority in Philippines.

Nov. 7 Roosevelt reelected to fourth term, defeating Thomas E. Dewey.

Dec. 16 Battle of the Bulge begins; Germans drive U.S. front back to the Meuse River; Allies relieve U.S. troops at Bastogne, Dec. 26.

1945

Jan. 17–19 Soviet armies push back Germans in Poland, capturing cities of Warsaw, Tarnow, Cracow, and Lodz.

Jan. 20 New Hungarian government signs armistice with Allies.

Feb. 4–11 Yalta Conference: Churchill, Roosevelt, and Stalin plan Allied occupation and control of Germany and eastern Europe after defeat of Nazis.

Feb. 19–Mar. 16 U.S. Marines land on Iwo Jima. Despite heavy casualties they raise American flag on Mount Suribachi; resistance ends in mid-March.

Mar. 7 U.S. 1st Army crosses the Rhine on the bridge at Remagen, establishes invasion bridgehead in Germany.

Mar. 9 Heaviest bombing of Tokyo by U.S. B-29's destroys 16 square miles of city, killing some 85,000 Japanese.

Apr. 1 U.S. forces invade Okinawa, only 350 miles south of Japan. Japanese resistance includes 1,900 kamikaze attacks, but by June 21 battle ends.

Apr. 12 U.S. President Roosevelt dies of a massive cerebral hemorrhage at Warm Springs, Georgia. Vice President Harry S. Truman succeeds him.

Apr. 20–25 Soviet troops enter Berlin. Soviet and U.S. units join up in Germany, at Torgau on Elbe River, Apr. 25.

Apr. 28 Mussolini tries to reach Switzerland, is killed by Italian partisans.

Apr. 30 Hitler commits suicide; two days later Berlin surrenders to Soviets.

May 1 German Army in Italy surrenders to Allied forces.

May 3 Rangoon captured by British.

May 7 Germans surrender unconditionally at Reims, France.

May 8 V-E Day in Britain and U.S.A. celebrates the surrender of the German armies to the Allied forces.

May 9 Soviet forces capture Prague and begin purge of Nazi collaborators.

June 5 Allies assume full control of Germany; divide country into four occupation zones: U.S.A., Britain, the Soviet Union, and France.

June 26 At San Francisco Conference 50 nations sign United Nations Charter.

July 5 General MacArthur announces liberation of the Philippines.

July 17–Aug. 2 Potsdam Conference held by leaders of Allied powers.

July 26 British voters oust Churchill's Conservative government in favor of Clement R. Attlee's Labour Party.

Aug. 2 Potsdam Declaration, issued by Truman, Attlee, and Stalin, imposes harsh peace terms on Germany.

Aug. 6 U.S.A. drops atomic bomb on Hiroshima; three days later second bomb dropped on Nagasaki.

Aug. 14 Japan surrenders; formalities signed Sept. 2, celebrated as V-J Day.

1945-56 THE NUCLEAR AGE

My God, what have we done?

—Robert A. Lewis, copilot of the *Enola Gay*, after dropping the atom bomb on Hiroshima

1945-56

As cold war tensions grew between the Soviet Union and the United States, so did stockpiles of nuclear weapons. To many people it seemed that the world had become a gigantic multifused bomb. To others, who embraced the idea of the nuclear deterrent, an arms race seemed the only sane policy in the face of Communist aggression; and to a few others nuclear weapons seemed mainly a prelude to the peaceful uses of atomic power that held such immense promise.

On August 6, 1945, an atomic bomb was dropped on Hiroshima, and the world was profoundly changed. Even the devastation of the previous six years seemed to pale in comparison with the nightmarish power of this weapon. It ended the Second World War, but it also cast a shadow over the peace that followed.

In many ways the postwar era was scarcely a period of peace at all. Before the armistice in Europe, the United States and the Soviet Union had carefully maintained good relations as allies. However, once Germany was defeated, the Soviets peremptorily took over Eastern Europe and part of Germany, and the euphoria of victory gave way to mistrust and mounting tension.

In March 1947 U.S. President Harry Truman announced: "It must be the policy of the United States to support free peoples who are resisting subjugation by armed minorities or by outside pressure." This statement, which came to be known as the Truman Doctrine, marked the beginning of the cold war and the struggle that would dominate the next quarter-century.

The guiding principle of American foreign policy after the war became the containment of communism. In Europe that goal seemed to have been achieved by 1950. Elsewhere, however, the late 1940's and early 1950's were years of almost unrelieved turmoil, and the increasing tensions—and potential dangers—of the cold war could be felt virtually everywhere.

Following its independence in 1947, India under Nehru embarked on a course of neutrality, seeking as much assistance and attention as it could attract from both sides of the Iron Curtain. This policy of nonalignment set a pattern for other emerging nations. By playing off the two great powers against each other, the underdeveloped nations of the Third World would before long come to exert an influence out of proportion to their military or economic strength.

Ten years after the end of World War II, the world in many ways seemed as tense as it had in 1914 or 1939. The United States and the Soviet Union, both by then armed with weapons of global destruction, appeared to be permanently poised on the brink of war. Moreover, the demise of European colonialism and the birth of new nations had released a wave of savage violence in Southeast Asia, India and Pakistan, Algeria, and elsewhere that so far showed no signs of abating.

In spite of all this, there were still some grounds for hope. To the surprise of many, the United Nations, unlike its predecessor, proved itself capable of effective action—most notably during the Korean War and again in the 1956 Suez crisis. Perhaps a greater surprise was the rapid economic recovery of West Germany and Japan, both of which had organized stable democratic governments and were enjoying steadily increasing prosperity. In the field of technology, the transistor and electronic computer greatly increased man's capacity for instant communication and the processing of vast amounts of information at lightning speed.

Above all was the fact that, despite a buildup in nuclear armaments and a steady exchange of threats and counterthreats, the United States and the Soviet Union had thus far managed to avoid World War III. Indeed, it was argued, the very existence of nuclear weapons had become a deterrent to full-scale war, the prospect of mutual destruction forcing both sides to act with greater caution than they might otherwise have done. In introducing man to weapons of such nightmarish power, therefore, the nuclear age had also provided him with the very best of reasons not to use them.

1945

Hiroshima: "A New and Most Cruel Bomb"

In these six words Emperor Hirohito describes the weapon that devastated Hiroshima and Nagasaki, ending the war and unleashing the possibility of worldwide devastation.

Early on August 6, 1945, the industrial port city of Hiroshima on the main Japanese island of Honshu was stirring. The city had so far been spared the blistering firebombings by American B-29's that had devastated Tokyo and other urban centers, but its inhabitants expected trouble because Hiroshima was a major military post and supply depot. In anticipation of an incendiary attack, the population had been reduced through evacuation from about 400,000 to 245,000 people.

Shortly after 7 a.m. an air-raid warning sounded as a single U.S. weather plane flew over the city. The appearance of such planes was a common occurrence, and most people did not bother to take shelter. At 7:32 the all-clear sounded. At just after 8 a.m. Japanese radar operators detected three more aircraft approaching Hiroshima at high altitude, but these were presumed to be reconnaissance planes, and there was no second alert.

A few seconds after 8:15 two of the high-flying planes made tight, diving turns in opposite directions. As they turned, one plane dropped three parachutes carrying blast-recording equipment; the other dropped an atomic bomb that was set to detonate 1,850 feet above the city.

The bomb exploded in a brilliant flash of light, followed by an expanding fireball so intense that it incinerated thousands of people near Hiroshima's center and burned others as far away as 2½ miles. Then came the blast, carrying the impact of a 500-mile-per-hour wind and leveling almost everything within a radius of more than two miles. Loose bits of wood, brick, tile, and glass became deadly missiles; the stone columns of a hospital directly below the explosion were driven straight into the ground. Water mains were ripped to pieces, and fires, started by thousands of overturned charcoal stoves still hot from the preparation of the morning meal, finished the work that the heat and blast had begun. Every building within five square miles of the hypocenter was destroyed. The city of Hiroshima was flattened.

Huge drops of condensed moisture from the mushroom-shaped cloud rising 50,000 feet above the city fell as black, greasy rain. Finally, those who had headed for the rivers and parks to escape the flames were engulfed by a great "fire wind" that blew toward the city's center, uprooting trees and churning up high waves in the rivers, drowning many who had sought refuge in the water.

At least 78,000 people, and possibly many thousands more, were killed or fatally injured in Hiroshima. As great a number were injured, and all their dwellings were damaged or destroyed. The city's military garrison was wiped out. Only a handful of doctors remained alive, and most hospitals and medical supplies were destroyed. Citizens of neighboring towns described the burned, living and dead, as no longer recognizably human, with their flesh raw and blackened, their hair gone, and the features melted on their faces.

The day after the bombing Gen. Seizo Arisue was sent to Hiroshima by the Japanese Supreme Command. Arisue described the aftermath of the bomb: "When the plane flew over Hiroshima there was but one black dead tree, as if a crow was perched on [the city]. There was nothing there but that tree. As we landed at the airport all the grass was red as if it had been toasted. There was no fire anymore. Everything had burned up simultaneously . . . the city itself was completely wiped out."

Arisue had not heard of the atomic bomb, but a Japanese nuclear physicist who came to the city on August 8 knew the source of the destruction. The Japanese Supreme War Council met on August 9 to discuss surrender, but they were too late to avert another disaster. At 11:02 a.m. that day a second atomic bomb was exploded over the city of Nagasaki.

Later, when the bomb's nature was understood, the Japanese would call it by the oddly poetic name *genshi bakudan* ("original child bomb"). The new words *hibakusha* ("explosion-affected person") and *higaisha* ("victim" or "injured person") are used even now in preference to *seizonsha* ("survivor"), because the latter's emphasis on living is considered to be unfair to those who were killed.

The face of survival: *Thousands of* hibakusha, *survivors of the Hiroshima and Nagasaki bombs, would bear psychic as well as physical scars for the rest of their lives. Many were beset by feelings of severe guilt over their own survival, by fears of bomb-related disease in themselves and their children, and by a pervasive "psychic numbing" that tragically isolated them from the rest of their countrymen.*

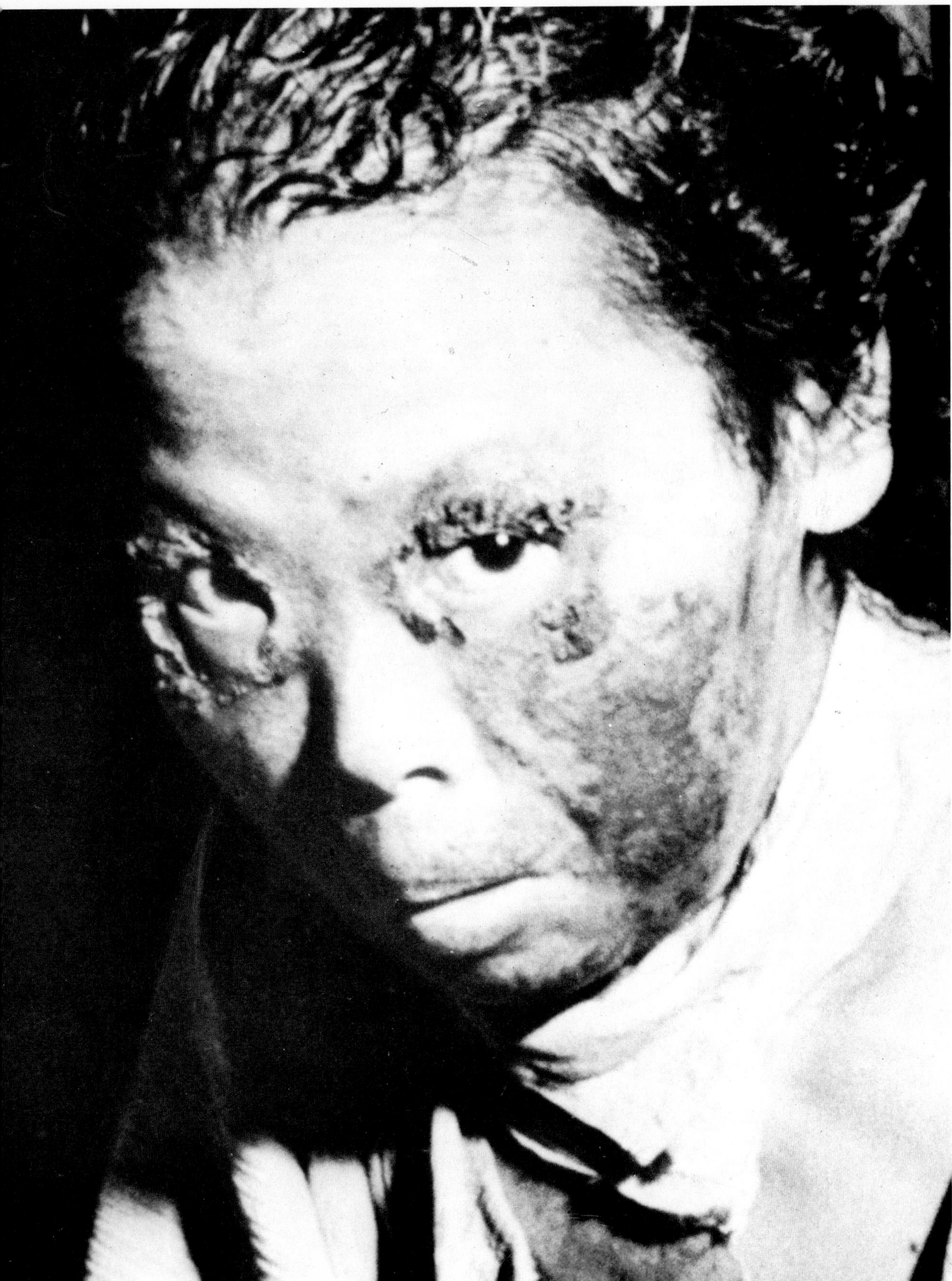

The Decision Is Debated

Responsibility for the decision to use the atomic bomb—described by Winston Churchill as "the Second Coming in wrath"—has been endlessly debated by historians. The final decision came from President Harry S. Truman, who had taken office at the death of Franklin D. Roosevelt on April 12, 1945. As Vice President, Truman had not been told of the top-secret Manhattan Project that created the bomb; as President, he alone could authorize its use.

By the summer of 1945, with Germany defeated and Japan the sole threat to the Allies, Truman's advisers on the Interim Committee—a civilian council on atomic policy headed by Secretary of War Henry L. Stimson—issued a report urging that the bomb be used. They recommended that the target be both a military installation and a large population center susceptible to maximum blast effect. The committee believed, and Truman agreed, that the bomb would preclude a mass invasion of the Japanese home islands, which, according to predictions, could have cost more than a million American casualties. Another factor influencing the President and his advisers was their growing fear of the Soviet Union. The Soviets had already seized control of eastern Europe and had expressed their eagerness for a major role in any invasion and occupation of Japan.

Many scientists and even some top military men urged alternatives—warning the Japanese, demonstrating the bomb on an unpopulated area before using it on a major city, or concluding the war by conventional means—but their suggestions were rejected as impractical. Japan's determination was well known, and conventional warfare would take too long, especially in view of the Soviet threat. Any warning might prove unpopular at home and might give the Japanese time to intercept an atomic mission. Whether the decision was morally justified is still a matter of bitter contention. But the question remains whether it was possible, by the summer of 1945, not to use the bomb. J. Robert Oppenheimer, the physicist who was in charge of the actual construction of the bomb, expressed the dimensions of the dilemma when he recalled: "The decision was implicit in the project. I don't know whether it could have been stopped."

A Race Against Time

The nuclear age might well have been born in Nazi Germany had Adolf Hitler paid more heed to the work of his own scientists. In December 1938, at the Kaiser Wilhelm Institute of Chemistry in Berlin, Otto Hahn and Fritz Strassmann succeeded, after six years of experimentation, in splitting the uranium atom—a process previously thought contrary to natural law. Their work implied the possibility of a controlled chain reaction and the release of enormous quantities of energy. Word of their accomplishment spread

***The 10-foot-long uranium bomb** dropped on Hiroshima—dubbed "Little Boy" to distinguish it from the larger plutonium bomb used at Nagasaki—was relatively simple in principle. At 1,850 feet above ground a radar signal detonated an explosive charge that fired a "bullet" of U-235 into a larger target of the same material. Together they formed the critical mass needed to produce a nuclear explosion.*

Uranium Target
Uranium Wedge
Gun Barrel
High Explosive
Radar Antenna

quickly through the scientific world: The great Danish physicist Niels Bohr (see pp. 82–87) learned of it from two colleagues who had fled the Nazis. In early 1939 Bohr sailed to the U.S.A. and passed his knowledge along to American scientists. Most notable were two refugee physicists, the Italian Enrico Fermi and Leo Szilard of Hungary. But subsequent efforts to convince the U.S. government of the atom's military possibilities bore little fruit until Szilard persuaded Albert Einstein, America's most famous scientist and himself a German-Jewish refugee, to sign a letter written to President Franklin D. Roosevelt in October 1939.

Although Roosevelt was convinced in theory, for the next two years progress in government-sponsored atomic research was slow and halting. Still, the process had begun, and in 1939 the question facing scientists was not whether to develop atomic weapons but how to do it before the Nazis did. It was on December 6, 1941—one day before the Japanese attack on Pearl Harbor—that Vannevar Bush, head of the U.S. Office of Scientific Research and Development, finally got Presidential approval for an all-out effort in atomic research. The scientific-military-industrial program that followed was characteristic of the U.S.A., with its relative invulnerability to attack, its enormous industrial capacity, and its faith in science and technology.

Nuclear physicists knew, at least in theory, that sufficient quantities of two uranium derivatives—U-235 and the manmade element plutonium—could be made to undergo rapid fission, or chain reaction. Dr. Ernest O. Lawrence had already solved one basic problem by using a cyclotron, or "atom smasher," to produce the fissionable materials. But the scientists now faced three critical problems: how to control a chain reaction, how to produce sufficient quantities of the fissionable material, and how to translate their theories into a workable bomb. The first problem was resolved by Fermi on December 2, 1942, when, in an improvised laboratory under the University of Chicago athletic stadium, he presided over the first controlled chain reaction. The experiment was crude, but it demonstrated that nuclear fission could be started, sustained, and stopped.

The remaining questions—how to produce enough fissionable material and the bombs to carry it—became the responsibility of Brig. Gen. Leslie R. Groves of the Army Engineers. On September 17, 1942, General Groves was appointed chief of the top-priority, top-secret Manhattan Project. Groves drafted captains of industry and Nobel Prize-winning scientists, coaxed $2 billion in secret funds from the Treasury (the project had previously been financed by Executive order), imposed total secrecy on the thousands of workers employed in the project, and selected the isolated sites where the actual work was done. A city sprouted at Hanford, Washington, where plutonium was produced; and rural Oak Ridge, Tennessee, where U-235 was separated, became the fifth-largest urban center in the state. Major theoretical work had already begun at several American universities. In the spring of 1943 at Los Alamos, New Mexico, where the work was most dangerous and the security tightest, a team led by Oppenheimer undertook the designing of a workable bomb that would fit inside the new B-29 long-range bomber.

Scientific luminaries were commonplace in the Manhattan Project: Oppenheimer, Lawrence, Arthur and Karl Compton among the native-born Americans; Szilard, Fermi, Bohr, James Franck, and Edward Teller among the European refugees. They worked in an atmosphere of urgency, excitement, and secrecy. The various phases of the project, especially at Los Alamos, were rigidly compartmentalized. Few scientists knew what their colleagues were doing. Everyone and everything had a code name: Fermi was "Henry Farmer," the bomb was "the beast," or simply "it,"

The first nuclear reactor *(left), shown here nearing completion late in 1942, was a 19-foot-high, 24½-foot-square assembly of uranium and graphite bricks, an arrangement that gave rise to the informal term "atomic pile."*

A genius haunted *by his own success, J. Robert Oppenheimer oversaw the design and assembly of the first atomic bombs at Los Alamos. He later advocated international controls of atomic energy and opposed U.S. development of the hydrogen bomb —factors leading to the controversial revocation of his security clearance in 1954 due to alleged Communist ties.*

Morning

They dream:
A workman dreams, lowering his pickax,
his sweat turned into scars by the flash.
A wife dreams, bending over her sewing
machine, midst the diseased odor of her
parted skin.
A box-office girl dreams, her hidden scars
like crab's claws, on both arms.
A match-seller dreams, with pieces of
shattered glass sticking in his neck.

They dream:
That through an element made from
pitchblende and carnotite
By means of an endless chain of energy,
Famished deserts are changed into fertile
fields;
Bright canals run round the base of
crumbling mountains,
Under artificial suns, in the wastelands of
the Arctic.
Cities and towns are built of pure gold.

They dream:
That festival flags wave in the shade of
trees where working people take their
rest, and legends of Hiroshima are told
by tender lips.

They dream:
That those swine in man's shape
Who do not know how to use the power
from the earth's center except for
slaughter
Survive only in illustrated books for the
little ones.
That the energy of ten million horsepower
per gram, one thousand times as strong
as high explosive,
Be delivered, out of the atom into the
hands of the people.
That the rich harvest of science
Be conveyed, in peace, to the people
Like bunches of succulent grapes
Wet with dew
Gathered in
At dawn.

—Sankichi Toge

and the British atomic program—begun in 1941 and rather reluctantly coordinated with its American counterpart—was the "Directorate of Tube Alloys."

Trinity and Potsdam: Point of No Return

At least six months before the Nazi surrender in May 1945, U.S. intelligence discovered that Germany was hopelessly behind the Allies in atomic research. But the Manhattan Project went forward. In December 1944 Groves had warned a group of high-ranking aides that "if this project fizzles, each of you can look forward to a lifetime of testifying before congressional investigating committees." That year Stimson, the only official in the government kept informed on all aspects of the project, finally revealed its nature to a few top congressional leaders who could guide money bills through the Legislature without discussion.

On July 16, 1945, at an isolated corner of the Alamogordo airbase in New Mexico—a site dubbed "Trinity" by Oppenheimer—the first plutonium bomb was tested. Code-named "Fat Man" because its bulging shape resembled Churchill's, the bomb exceeded all expectations. (The U-235 bomb was never tested because the scientists were confident it would work.)

Truman had inherited, along with the atomic project, a secret aide-mémoire made by Roosevelt and Churchill on September 19, 1944, which stated that "when a 'bomb' is finally available, it might, perhaps, after mature consideration, be used against the Japanese, who should be warned that this bombardment will be repeated until they surrender." The document did not mention the possible use of atomic weapons against the Nazis, even though Germany's defeat lay eight months away, and there is little evidence that top policymakers ever considered such a move.

Whether the choice of target was dictated primarily by the virulence of anti-Japanese feeling in the U.S.A. or by Allied confidence that Germany was near the end, no one can say. By September 1944 the United States and Britain were concerned about the Soviet Union's lack of cooperation, and the Roosevelt-Churchill agreement specifically urged that no atomic information be leaked to the Soviets. Indeed, it has been argued that the atomic bombing of Japan was not the final act of World War II but the first move—as a warning to the U.S.S.R.—in the cold war.

On July 4, 1945, another Anglo-American agreement to use the bomb against Japan was signed. Time was running out. The U.S.A. knew that the Japanese were on the brink of defeat and had been seeking a negotiated peace through the Soviet Union. (Japan was unaware of the Soviet agreement with the other Allies to enter the war against Japan in August.) But the Americans did not encourage Soviet-mediated negotiations. American leaders were equally unwilling to negotiate on their own for anything less than unconditional surrender: The memory of Pearl Harbor followed by years of anti-Japanese propaganda made prolonged negotiations a risk no U.S. politicians were likely to take. In June a final plea from a scientific committee under James Franck stated that the atomic bombing of Japan would place the United States in an untenable moral position, but the plea was rejected.

At the Potsdam Conference Truman received a detailed report on the success of the Trinity test. On July 26 the U.S.A., Britain, and the Republic of China jointly issued the Potsdam Proclamation. The document warned the Japanese to surrender unconditionally or face "prompt and utter destruction." Although the proclamation promised that the Japanese would not be "enslaved as a race or destroyed as a nation," it did not mention the atomic bomb or another vital issue—the retention of the revered imperial dynasty. An earlier version of the proclamation had mentioned the possible retention of the Emperor, but this paragraph was struck out because U.S. Secretary of State James F. Byrnes agreed with his predecessor, Cordell Hull, that it sounded "too much like appeasement."

On receiving the Potsdam ultimatum, the Japanese government, torn between pride and desperation, arrived at a fatal "compromise": On July 28 Prime Minister Kantaro Suzuki publicly belittled the Allied terms without rejecting them. The Japanese were stalling for time, but the United States misinterpreted the response as a flat refusal, and the machinery for delivering the bomb ground on.

By July 23 Stimson, who was with Truman at Potsdam, had been informed that "Little Boy" (the gun-type U-235 bomb used on Hiroshima) would be ready on or about August 1 and that "Fat Man" (the Nagasaki bomb) would probably be available by August 6. The special air force unit assigned to drop the bomb —the 509th Composite Group and its flying nucleus, the 393d Squadron, commanded by Col. Paul W. Tibbets, Jr.—was awaiting orders at Tinian island in the Marianas. For a year the 509th had been undergoing rigorous secret training in visual bombing on a clear day, because Groves felt radar bombing was unreliable. The planes it was using were modified B-29 Superfortresses, stripped of most armaments for speed and to accommodate a single atomic bomb weighing 10,000 to 13,000 pounds.

On July 25 a directive prepared by Groves and Army Chief of Staff George C. Marshall was issued to

***Just three days after Hiroshima** a second bomb was dropped on Japan, this time destroying the city of Nagasaki and claiming as many as 70,000 lives. The mother and child at left, holding rations of rice balls, were among the thousands injured and left homeless in Nagasaki. The poem "Morning" was written by Sankichi Toge, a survivor of the Hiroshima blast who died in 1953, aged 36.*

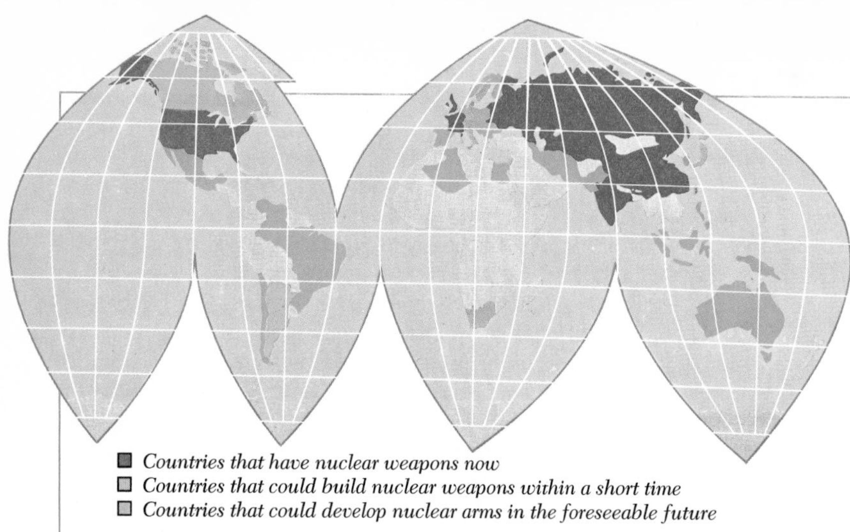

■ *Countries that have nuclear weapons now*
□ *Countries that could build nuclear weapons within a short time*
□ *Countries that could develop nuclear arms in the foreseeable future*

THE NUCLEAR CLUB

Since Hiroshima the spread of peacetime atomic technology has created an urgent need to curb the proliferation of atomic weapons. Success has been limited, though. The 1970 Nuclear Nonproliferation Treaty, the most ambitious effort yet made in that area, has proven difficult to enforce—as evidenced by India's test of an atomic device in 1974—and unless better controls can be devised, the "nuclear club" seems certain to keep growing.

Gen. Carl A. Spaatz, commanding general of the U.S. Army Strategic Air Forces: "The 509th Composite Group, Twentieth Air Force, will deliver its first special bomb as soon as weather will permit visual bombing after about 3 August, on one of the [approved] targets: Hiroshima, Kokura, Niigata and Nagasaki. . . . Additional bombs will be delivered on the above targets as soon as made ready by the project staff. . . ." On August 7 Truman sent a second order to Spaatz to "continue operations as planned unless otherwise instructed." Thus the decision to use additional bombs was left to the military where the view prevailed that at least two would be needed—one to convince Japan of the weapon's power, a second to demonstrate that the U.S.A. had more on hand.

"Little Boy" Erases a City

At 2:45 a.m. on August 6 the B-29 *Enola Gay* took off from Tinian. The plane, piloted by Colonel Tibbets and named after his mother, barely cleared the runway with its heavy load. The bomb was armed in the air to avoid the possibility of a nuclear accident on takeoff. With an instrument plane and a photographic plane, the *Enola Gay* headed for Japan, and Tibbets informed the crew: "This is for history, so watch your language. We're carrying the first atomic bomb."

Three weather planes had gone ahead to scout the target cities: Hiroshima, Kokura, and Nagasaki. Just after 7:25 a.m. Tibbets received a coded message from Maj. Claude Eatherly's weather plane, the *Straight Flush*, that the sky was clear over Hiroshima.

Enola Gay approached the city at 31,600 feet with no interference: Japan had no fighters to waste on a few high-flying aircraft. At 8:15 a.m. plus 17 seconds the bomb was released. At 8:16 the mission's crew members, wearing special goggles to protect their eyes, saw the purple flash. "My God," said the copilot, Capt. Robert A. Lewis, "what have we done?"

Three days later Japan received two more crippling blows. At 1 a.m., Tokyo time, on August 9, the Soviet Union attacked the Japanese Army in Manchuria. Ten hours later, while stunned members of Japan's Supreme War Council met in Tokyo to consider Emperor Hirohito's expressed wish that hostilities be ended, a "Fat Man" plutonium bomb was exploded over Nagasaki's suburb of Urakami. The bombardier had missed his target by three miles, but estimates of the death toll ranged from 38,000 to nearly twice that number.

Even after Nagasaki, the Emperor was forced to override his two top military advisers and suffer a brief revolt in his name by members of the Imperial Guard before he was able to accept the Allied surrender terms. On August 15 the Emperor made an unprecedented radio speech, addressing the nation in the language of the court: "We are keenly aware of the inmost feelings of all ye, Our subjects. However, it is

THE ATOM IN PEACETIME

The most widely used products of the nuclear age are the manmade sources of radioactivity known as radioisotopes. Many medical disorders, for example, are diagnosed with the aid of a radioactive liquid swallowed by a patient and traced as it passes through the body. Disposable syringes, surgical instruments, and some foods are sterilized by irradiation. The thickness of such products as metal foil, paper, and rubber can be constantly monitored during production by the amount of radiation they absorb; heavier radiation is also used, much like X-rays, to examine machinery and castings for hidden defects. In addition, plastic can be forced into wood and bonded there by irradiation, producing a flooring material that retains a high gloss with very little maintenance.

according to the dictate of time and fate that We have resolved to pave the way for a grand peace for all the generations to come by enduring the unendurable and suffering what is insufferable." Three years and eight months after Pearl Harbor the nation that had vowed to fight to the death finally capitulated. On V-J Day, September 2, the surrender was formally signed aboard the U.S. battleship *Missouri* in Tokyo Bay.

In the autumn of 1945 the world's hope for peace seemed to lie in the newly formed United Nations, but the delegates who had signed its charter on June 26, 1945, were unprepared for the nuclear age. In June 1946 an American proposal for a U.N.-sponsored international atomic development authority was undermined by Soviet insistence that the U.S.A. destroy its stockpiles before any inspection system was arranged.

The United States set up its own civilian program for the secret development of nuclear energy, the Atomic Energy Commission, and tested a fourth atomic bomb over Bikini Atoll in the Pacific. By 1947 the terms "Iron Curtain" and "cold war" were familiar. In 1948 the U.S.A. and the U.S.S.R. seemed on the brink of war over Berlin. In 1949 the Soviet Union exploded its first atomic device. Until the Nuclear Test-Ban Treaty of 1963, which France and China refused to sign, the fear of contamination from nuclear fallout was felt worldwide.

In the U.S.A. the fear of Communist subversion led to the anti-Red drive of the 1950's, personified by Senator Joseph R. McCarthy, who built a brief but spectacular career on political witch hunting. In 1951 Julius and Ethel Rosenberg were convicted of atomic spying, after a trial that remains highly controversial, and were executed for treason in 1953. In the same year J. Robert Oppenheimer, who had opposed the development of the hydrogen bomb and favored international civilian control of atomic energy, was denied further access to secret government data on the grounds that he was a security risk, although his left-wing associations had long been known.

The acceleration in secrecy and international suspicion has been matched by the growth of nuclear technology. The explosive force of thermonuclear "superbombs" came to be measured not in tons but in megatons (millions of tons of TNT), and delivery systems have become increasingly sophisticated. After the war few people believed that any nation would dare use nuclear weapons again. But like the process that brought Hiroshima, the nuclear race continues. In the words of Albert Einstein, "Every step appears as the unavoidable consequence of the preceding one."

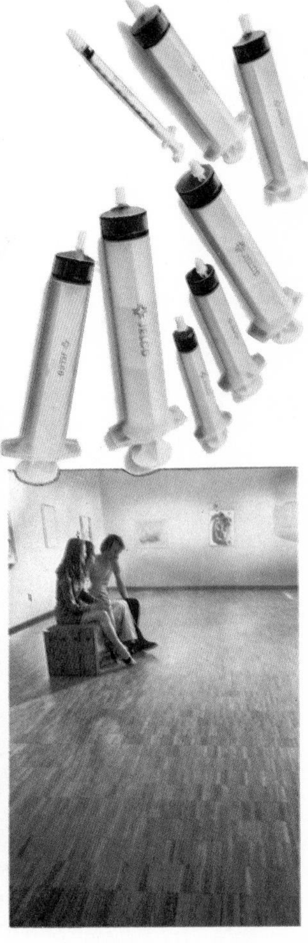

SCIENCE & TECHNOLOGY

1945-56

Science and Communication

In the summer of 1947 American newspapers found a new subject to intrigue their readers: flying saucers. In the years to come UFO's (unidentified flying objects) were seen over every continent, and it seemed to many that man might be on the brink of communicating with beings from another world.

If such space travelers had indeed been keeping a watch on our planet during the 20th century, monitoring mankind as one vast organism, they might well have concluded that our "nervous system"—our own capacity for communication—was coming along nicely.

They would have seen that the main channels of communication—roads, railways, rivers, and oceans—were already well established when, shortly before the turn of the century, networks of telegraph lines and electric power cables began to reach out over the land, followed closely by telephone lines. If their vision were subtle enough, they might next have seen the networks of electronic communication that followed: Guglielmo Marconi's first transatlantic transmission in 1901, worldwide radiotelephone stations in the late 1920's, radar in the 1940's. They would deduce, rightly, that we had learned first to deal with electrical currents in metallic conductors, then with free electrons in low-pressure, or vacuum, tubes (see p. 46).

A third stage in communications began during World War II, when scientists, mathematicians, and engineers were developing the electronic computer (see pp. 378–383) and with it a new discipline, cybernetics, to analyze the problems of control and communication. In 1947 three physicists at the Bell Telephone Laboratories in New Jersey—William Shockley, John Bardeen, and Walter Brattain—made a discovery that was to ensure the growth of the computer and revolutionize electronics.

Recognizing the need for an improved method of amplifying electrical signals, Bardeen, Shockley, and Brattain had been studying the class of materials known as semiconductors, substances whose electrical conductivity is midway between that of good conductors, such as metals, and nonconductors, such as glass and rubber. Specifically, the Bell team was studying germanium and silicon crystals.

It was already well known that crystals had useful electrical properties. They had been used in early radios, and phonographs made use of the piezoelectric effect, by which a crystal under pressure produces minute electrical currents, but how these properties arose was scarcely understood at all. The great breakthrough came with the discovery that by applying a small current between closely spaced contacts on a tiny piece of germanium or silicon, a much larger current to a third contact on the semiconductor could be regulated—and amplified. The first successful test of the device, on December 23, 1947, produced a power amplification of 18 times. Before long, power gains of 40 and 100 times were achieved. In 1950 Shockley introduced the improved junction transistor, using semiconductors made with other materials.

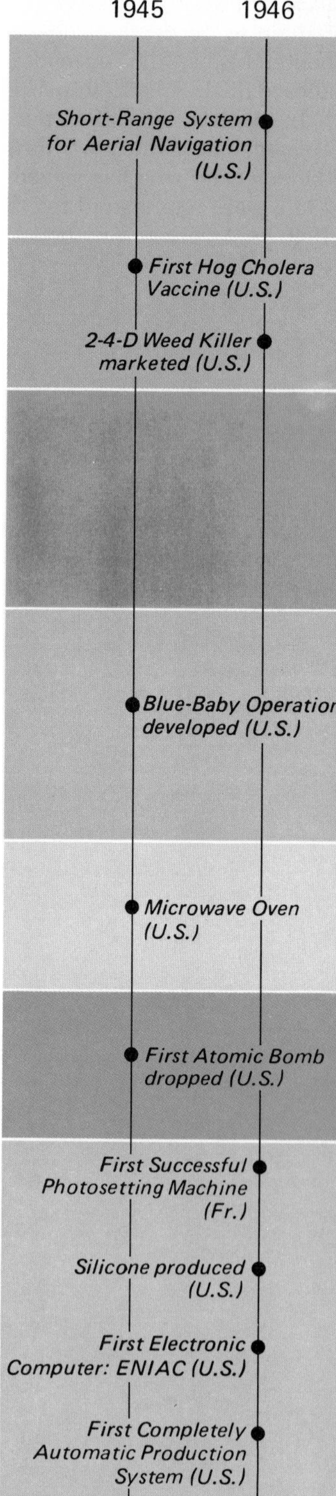

THE PACE OF INVENTION

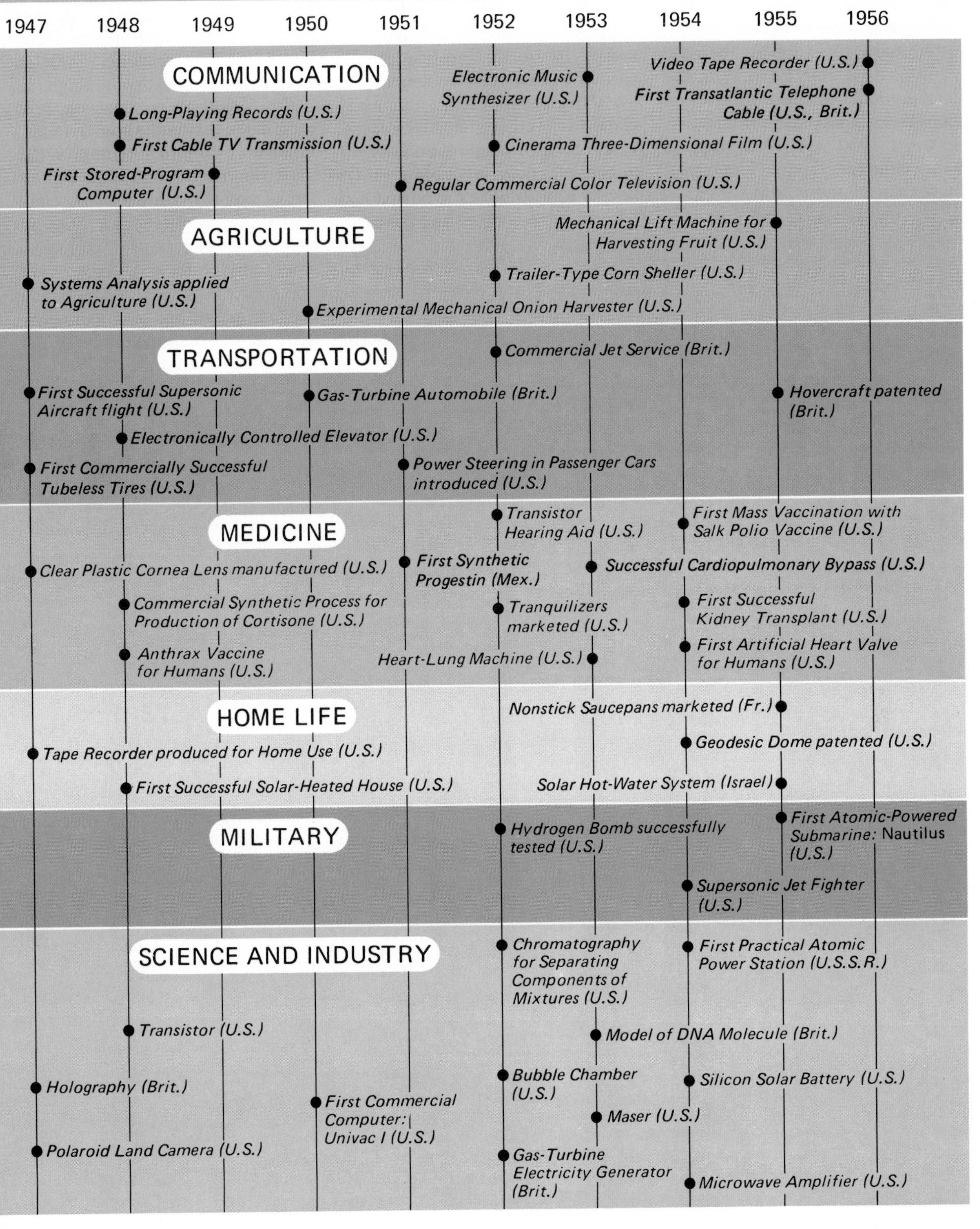

In addition to its small size, the transistor (its name is a contraction of "transfer resistor") offered other advantages: It consumed very little energy, produced virtually no heat, and, containing no fragile filaments, lasted many times longer than the traditional vacuum tube. With the development of mass-production techniques it was also far cheaper. Between 1950 and 1960 sales of semiconductor devices increased more than a hundredfold.

Almost overnight radios shrank, television sets became smaller and less expensive, and reliable high-speed computers were built. The exploration of space became possible, for without solid-state electronics, modern rocketry and miniature instruments for satellites would be unthinkable. Via satellite links a worldwide network of instant communication by radio, telephone, and television was established.

The Sixth Sense

Even as the transistor was hastening the development of electronics, another form of communication had begun to intrigue some scientists: extrasensory perception, or ESP.

In 1932 U.S. psychologist Joseph B. Rhine had established a parapsychological laboratory in the psychology department of Duke University in North Carolina. In his earliest experiments subjects were asked to guess which of a number of cards, each bearing one of five signs, would be turned up by an assistant in another room. According to the laws of probability each person had a 1 in 5 chance of guessing the cards correctly—of making 20 correct guesses in 100 cards, 200 in 1,000, and so on. In fact, some people achieved a much higher degree of accuracy, though the odds against doing so by chance were millions to one. Ruling out chance, therefore, Rhine concluded that telepathy must be at work. For the first time ESP research had been standardized and had yielded positive results.

For most scientists, however, the idea of ESP remained unacceptable. Then in 1943 and 1944 Rhine published even more controversial data, indicating that certain people could influence events, such as the fall of dice, at a distance—the phenomenon now known as psychokinesis, PK for short. By 1950 his experiments had been successfully repeated at the University of Pittsburgh in Pennsylvania and at Cambridge University in England.

But despite these successes, ESP remained a spasmodic phenomenon, impossible to predict despite the most rigorously controlled experiments, and this caused many scientists to regard the whole field of psychic research with suspicion. In 1949 the Cambridge philosopher C. D. Broad offered the following explanation of the seemingly random nature of psychic events: "It looks as if telepathically received impressions have some difficulty in crossing the threshold and manifesting themselves in consciousness. There seems to be some barrier or repressive mechanism which tends to shut them out from consciousness, a barrier which is rather difficult to pass, and they make use of all sorts of devices for overcoming it. Sometimes they make use of the muscu-

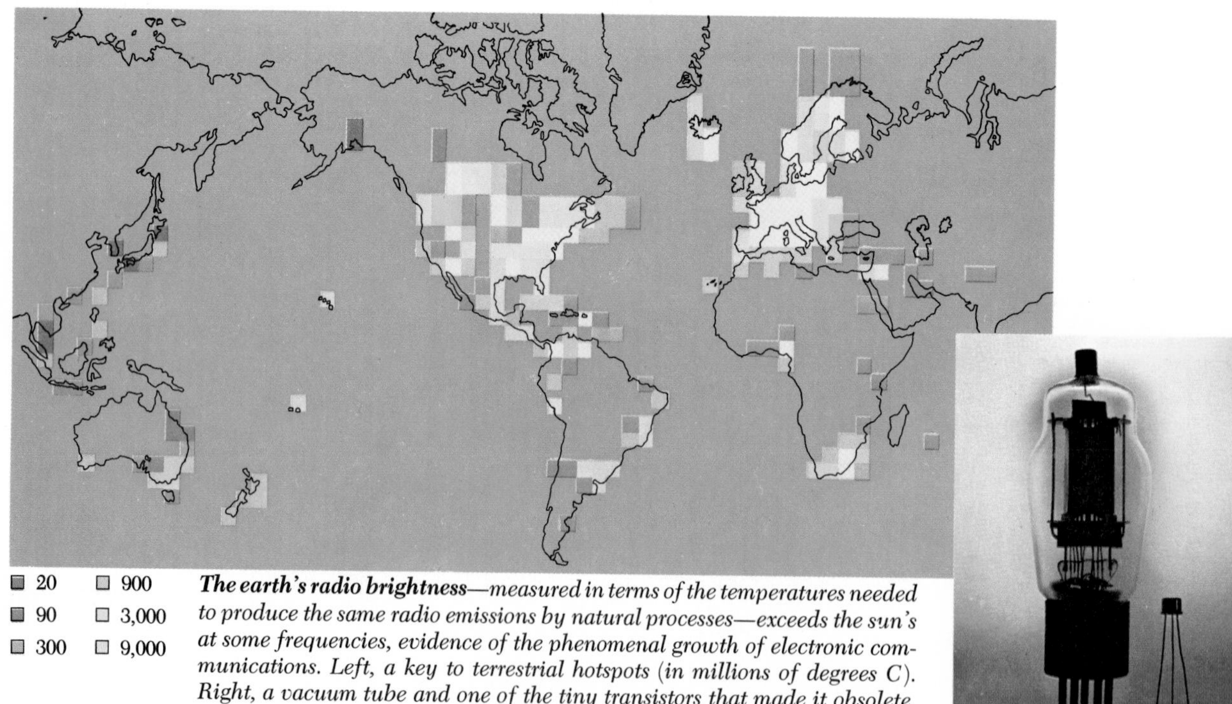

The earth's radio brightness*—measured in terms of the temperatures needed to produce the same radio emissions by natural processes—exceeds the sun's at some frequencies, evidence of the phenomenal growth of electronic communications. Left, a key to terrestrial hotspots (in millions of degrees C). Right, a vacuum tube and one of the tiny transistors that made it obsolete.*

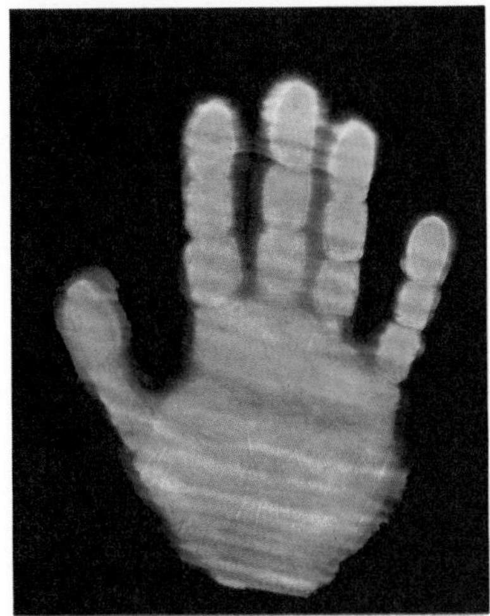

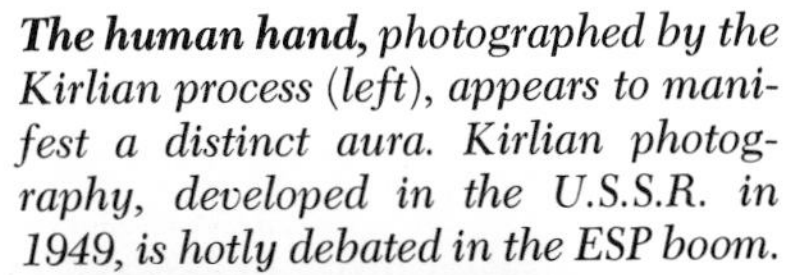

__J. B. Rhine__ (right) of Duke University, North Carolina, put parapsychology on the scientific map in the 1930's and 1940's, documenting thousands of ESP tests with Zener cards (above).

__The human hand,__ photographed by the Kirlian process (left), appears to manifest a distinct aura. Kirlian photography, developed in the U.S.S.R. in 1949, is hotly debated in the ESP boom.

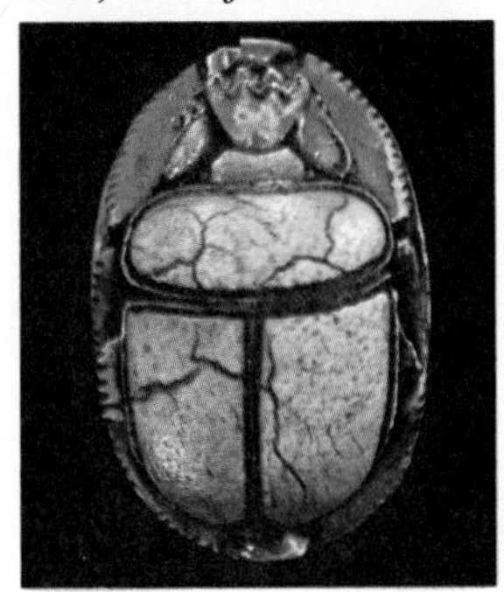

The psychologist C. G. Jung *theorized that some psychic events might be governed not by the usual rules of cause and effect but by undiscovered laws of coincidence. In one of numerous such coincidences a patient dreamed that a scarab beetle (right) flew into her room. At that moment in the dream she felt a great sense of relief. Suddenly a real scarab beetle flew into Jung's consulting room—and she felt the relief she had just been describing to him.*

lar mechanisms of the body, and emerge in the form of automatic speech or writing. Sometimes they emerge in the form of dreams, sometimes as visual or auditory hallucinations. And often they can only emerge in a distorted and symbolic form (as other unconscious mental contents do). It is a plausible guess that many of our everyday thoughts and emotions are telepathic or partly telepathic in origin, but are not recognized to be so because they are so much distorted and mixed with other mental contents in crossing the threshold of consciousness."

Although most psychologists remained skeptical of ESP research, theories were being developed in other fields of science that made Rhine's work seem less absurd. In 1949 Richard Feynman, a physicist at the California Institute of Technology, proposed that a mysterious atomic particle named the positron was in fact an electron that had gained a positive electrical charge by moving backward in time.

For those involved in parapsychological research the idea that time might, in certain cases, move backward had obvious appeal. The frontiers of brain research offered further encouragement, for in 1953 Sir John Eccles, an Australian physiologist, published *The Neurophysiological Basis of Mind.* In it he theorized that a single neuron (nerve cell) in the brain might be sensitive enough to respond to a "field of influence" produced by the "will" and to transmit that influence to hundreds of thousands of connected neurons. In 1965 Adrian Dobbs, a young mathematician and physicist working at Cambridge University, combined Eccles' idea with advanced quantum theory (see pp. 82–87) and postulated the existence of what he called psitrons. These insubstantial particles, conceived of as the agents of Eccles' "will influence," had their existence, he theorized, in a universe possessing five dimensions, three of space and *two* of time. In one of these temporal modes a multiplicity of potential events, each the product of numerous subatomic possibilities, explored a variety of routes toward actualization, creating a "psitronic" wavefront, perceptible by certain highly sensitive neurons and conveying information about the probable disposition of future events (though not information processed in any conventional way).

Today the existence of parapsychological phenomena has been established beyond reasonable doubt. In 1963 NASA confirmed that it was examining telepathy with a view to developing "new communications media"; as part of the effort to reach the first frontiers of space, telepathy—the last frontier in communication—was finally becoming respectable.

1945

Swords Into Plowshares

A world racked by the war just ended and aware of new dimensions in mass destruction takes the first halting steps toward peace through unity.

During the waning days of the Second World War, representatives of 50 Allied nations gathered in San Francisco to lay what they hoped would become the foundation for a lasting peace. On the day they convened, April 25, 1945, the Soviet Union announced that Berlin had just been surrounded: The war that had devastated Europe and the Far East for more than five years was almost at an end. Buoyed by the approaching victory, the men who met at San Francisco confidently resolved that such a holocaust must never be allowed to happen again. In the preamble to the United Nations Charter, signed on June 26, they proclaimed their unanimous determination "to save succeeding generations from the scourge of war . . . to reaffirm faith in fundamental human rights . . . to establish conditions under which justice and respect for . . . international law can be maintained, and to promote social progress."

It was not the first time in the century that such an ambitious task had been undertaken. A similar body, the League of Nations, had been created after World War I, and for 20 years its members had striven for peace—with some success, but ultimately in vain.

The United Nations was likewise the offspring of war, taking its name from the military alliance formalized in the Declaration by United Nations issued on January 1, 1942. Signed by the United States, Great Britain, the Soviet Union, and 23 other countries, the declaration was naturally concerned first with the war effort against Germany and Japan. But even at that low point in their military fortunes the Big Three gave high priority to the foundation of a world peacekeeping body. In preparation for the San Francisco conference, emissaries of the Big Three and China met in 1944 at Dumbarton Oaks, an estate in Washington, D.C., to draw up a plan for the United Nations. With only a few exceptions their proposals provided the blueprint for the organization's charter.

The architects of the U.N. were keenly aware of the flaws which had undone the League of Nations. Its membership, first of all, had never been a true reflection of the world's political realities. Although Woodrow Wilson had staked his Presidency on acceptance of the league, the United States never joined, having chosen to avoid further involvement in foreign problems. In addition, the countries of Western Europe, fearing the threat of bolshevism, excluded the Soviet Union from membership until 1934—by which time both Japan and Germany, in response to criticism of their growing militarism, had simply walked out.

The league, moreover, had never been able to back its decisions with military force. Although it could exert a certain amount of pressure through verbal censure and economic sanctions, it was powerless to act in cases of blatant armed aggression. When Japan took Manchuria in 1931, when Italy invaded Ethiopia in 1935, and again when Germany annexed Austria in 1938, the Geneva peacekeepers could merely protest.

Mindful of these shortcomings, the founders of the U.N. sought to be more pragmatic than their predecessors, who had naively hoped that the mere existence of such an organization would guarantee peace. An instructive note of restraint was sounded by the U.S. Senate Foreign Relations Committee, which, while recommending approval of the charter, cautioned that "Neither this Charter, nor any other document or formula that might be devised, can prevent war. . . . the United Nations will at best be a beginning toward

the creation of those conditions of stability throughout the world which will foster peace and security."

While the structure of the new body was similar to the earlier one, there were differences that reflected the lessons of the previous quarter century. The charter provided for a General Assembly of all member states and a smaller Security Council composed of five permanent members—the U.S.A., Britain, the Soviet Union, France, and China—and 6 nonpermanent members (later increased to 10) chosen by the General Assembly on a rotating basis. In contrast to the League of Nations, decisionmaking power in the U.N. would be centered in the Security Council, and particularly in the five permanent members, who alone had the right to cast a veto. Moreover, all members of the General Assembly were pledged to comply with any action by the Security Council—including, if necessary, a call to arms. Thus if the U.N. was somewhat less "democratic" than the league—in which any member could veto any decision—it was at least a closer approximation of the real balance of power in the postwar world.

It was hoped that this new system would enable the U.N. to move quickly and decisively in times of crisis and that the major wartime powers would continue to cooperate in the interests of world peace. That ex-

***The United Nations** General Assembly has seen many moments of high drama in the decades since its founding. Here Fidel Castro denounced an earlier U.S.-Cuban agreement, and Nikita Khrushchev obliged the press with histrionics and pithy Russian proverbs. When the U.S.A. finally lifted its ban on the seating of Red China, the Nationalist Chinese delegation walked out—as did Israel's representatives when Yasir Arafat, head of the Palestine Liberation Organization, addressed the Assembly. Also pictured during visits to the U.N.: President Idi Amin of Uganda, Israeli Prime Minister Golda Meir, U.S. President John F. Kennedy, and Pope Paul VI.*

pectation, as it turned out, proved wrong. The wartime alliance, which had begun to show signs of strain at the Yalta and Potsdam conferences, disintegrated completely in the months after the fighting ceased. As early as March 1946, in a speech at Fulton, Missouri, Winston Churchill warned that the Soviet Union had lowered an "Iron Curtain" across the center of Europe, tightening its grip on the countries it occupied at the end of the war. A year later President Harry S. Truman announced a major program of aid to the governments of Greece and Turkey, both seriously weakened by Communist insurgencies, and he declared that the United States was prepared to support any other nation threatened by a Communist takeover.

The Cold War

So began the long, bitter contest between the world's two most powerful nations, a cold war that would dominate international affairs for the next generation. This cold war was fought primarily with words rather than bullets, on economic and political fronts; but there was no guarantee that it would not suddenly erupt into armed—even nuclear—conflict.

Inevitably, one of its earliest battlegrounds was the United Nations, which seemed fated to go the way of its impotent predecessor. Repeated use of the veto in the Security Council, especially by the Soviet Union, effectively ruled out U.N. intervention in most cold war crises—which came to include almost every international dispute, no matter how far removed from the direct interests of the two superpowers.

A sign of things to come was the stalemate that developed over the fighting in Greece from 1946 to 1949. In essence, the U.S.A. charged the Soviet Union and her satellites with aiding the rebellion against Greece's legitimate government, whereupon the U.S.S.R. accused the Western powers of propping up a decadent and unpopular regime. A central issue in the case, and one that would recur elsewhere, was whether the uprising was truly indigenous—and therefore outside U.N. jurisdiction—or dependent on foreign support, in which case the U.N. would be obliged by its charter to intervene.

Unhappily, this question remained an academic one, since the Soviet veto barred any serious thought of U.N. military action. As would so often happen, the issue was ultimately settled outside the U.N.—in this case the Greek government, backed by American aid, successfully put down the insurrection.

One of the few instances of cooperation between the cold war powers involved the infant state of Israel, created by the United Nations in 1948 (see pp. 396–403). During the ensuing Arab-Israeli War the U.N. was instrumental in arranging an armistice and in maintaining the cease-fire lines by establishing in 1949 a truce supervisory organization that still exists.

Another area of U.S.-Soviet agreement—different though their motives were—concerned the independence of longtime European colonies. From its opening session in 1946 the United Nations tried to moderate an increasingly bitter struggle in Indonesia against Dutch colonial rule. After several cease-fires had been arranged and then broken, the Security Council set a deadline of July 1950 for Indonesian independence and brought enough pressure to bear on the two sides to see its decision carried out.

THE BERLIN AIRLIFT

One of the cold war's most dangerous confrontations was the 11-month Soviet blockade of Berlin, which provided a sobering example of the U.N.'s inability to deal with crises involving the two postwar superpowers. When the only road linking Berlin to West Germany was suddenly sealed off in 1948, the U.N. was barred by a Soviet veto from taking action, leaving the United States and its allies no recourse but to respond on their own. Rather than use force, they decided to mount a round-the-clock airlift of vital supplies—and hope the flights would not be intercepted by Russian fighters. Ultimately the plan succeeded: An armed conflict was avoided, and Berlin did not starve. But that success, welcome as it was, offered little encouragement to those who had looked to the U.N. for leadership in the search for peace.

THE UNITED NATIONS AT WAR: KOREA AND THE CONGO

When North Korean troops suddenly crossed the 38th parallel in June 1950, the United States viewed the invasion largely as a test of its willingness to resist Communist expansion and decided that South Korea must therefore be saved. But it also hoped to avoid unilateral action, and because of the Soviet boycott the means to do so was found in the Security Council resolution. For practical purposes the resulting war effort was American: While 22 nations took part, more than 90 percent of the non-Korean troops under the U.N. flag were Americans. Ultimately a July 1953 armistice restored the 38th parallel as a cease-fire line—at a cost of almost 2 million dead, mostly civilians—but no peace treaty was ever signed, and a large U.S. military force remains in South Korea more than 20 years later. While the U.N. has attempted no other actions on so large a scale, it intervened forcibly in the 1960 Congo crisis and has used peacekeeping troops to stabilize numerous flareups that might otherwise have spread into full-scale war.

Below, Turkish soldiers fighting with the U.N. forces in the Korean War in 1951 attack North Korean and Communist Chinese antitank troops. Right, three soldiers—American, Swedish, and Moroccan—serving with a special U.N. force guard the streets of Leopoldville during the violent upheavals that followed the Belgian withdrawal from the Congo.

The Indonesian case proved only the first of many in which the U.N. would play an active part in speeding up the process of decolonization—and it demonstrated what the world body could accomplish when its two most powerful members were in accord. But such rare occasions became even rarer in the period from 1948 to 1952, which saw the most dangerous escalations of cold war tensions.

In 1948 the Soviet Union sealed the borders of East Germany to all traffic, with the aim of cutting off supplies to West Berlin and so forcing the Allies to abandon their part of the city. The Western Powers in this case avoided a direct confrontation—and won an important psychological victory—by organizing a massive airlift which fed the city until the blockade was lifted almost a year later.

Then in October 1949 Communist forces led by Mao Tse-tung gained full control of the Chinese mainland and established the People's Republic of China (see pp. 250–255), while the deposed Nationalist leader, Chiang Kai-shek, set up a government-in-exile on the island of Taiwan. Chiang's pro-Western regime had been given one of the five permanent seats on the Security Council at its inception. Now, however, that position was challenged in a resolution sponsored by India to replace the Nationalist delegation with representatives from the new Communist government. The United States, which at the time commanded a heavy majority in the General Assembly, successfully blocked the measure when it came to a vote in January 1950. Enraged, the Soviet delegation denounced the action and began a boycott of all U.N. functions.

That boycott was still in effect the following June when Communist troops from North Korea launched a sudden invasion of South Korea. The United States immediately brought the issue before the Security Council, and in the absence of the Soviet delegation the Council unanimously condemned North Korea as an aggressor, recommending that "members of the

United Nations aid the Republic of Korea in repelling the armed attack . . ."

It was a momentous step in the life of the U.N. For the first time a major army was mobilized under the flag of an international organization. Further, while the war effort was preponderantly an American one, the fact that it went forward under the United Nations' aegis set an important precedent for future crises.

Yet another major step was taken as a result of the Korean crisis, less dramatic at the time but ultimately of sweeping importance to the power structure within the U.N. It was clear that, had the Soviet Union been present in the Security Council, the decision to send troops to Korea would have been summarily vetoed. In the hope of circumventing that obstacle in the future, the United States secured General Assembly approval in November 1950 for the so-called Uniting for Peace resolution. The equivalent of a charter amendment, it authorized the General Assembly to act in international crises whenever the Security Council failed to

THE WAR AGAINST POVERTY

While the U.N. was envisioned first and foremost as a peacekeeping body, its founders also intended it to assume responsibilities in a wide range of economic, social, cultural, and humanitarian affairs. Since its first hectic years, when the U.N. helped rebuild postwar Europe and resettled millions of refugees, a proliferation of new programs have made substantial contributions to the reduction of illiteracy, disease, hunger, and poverty across the world. Most of this work is administered through more than a dozen affiliated agencies, among them the World Health Organization (WHO), the U.N. Educational, Scientific, and Cultural Organization (UNESCO), and the Food and Agriculture Organization (FAO). By 1975 the total funds available for all U.N. activities, including loans and investments, approached $7 billion—a sum reflecting the enormous growth and diversification of the world body in its first three decades.

Election day in La Campana: Residents of an isolated village in Colombia choose a governor as part of a U.N. program to improve conditions among South America's highland Indians.

Third World industrial development is one of the chief goals of the U.N.'s economic programs. Above, molten metal is cast in a foundry at Ahwaz, Iran, where an industrial complex was planned and built with U.N. aid.

A young patient is examined at the N'Djili Health Center in the Congo (right), one of the numerous clinics established by the World Health Organization to provide basic medical training and services in areas where none had been available before.

"exercise its primary responsibility for the maintenance of international peace and security."

Ironically, though aimed at undercutting Soviet veto power, the resolution had the long-term effect of diminishing the United States' own influence in the U.N., shifting the balance of power from the Security Council to a General Assembly that in years ahead would no longer furnish automatic voting majorities for U.S. positions.

This process was a gradual one, coinciding with the slow "thaw" in East-West relations that began after the Korean War. For almost 10 years cold war antagonisms had created a near-deadlock in admitting new members to the U.N., each side barring nations friendly to the other. By 1950, in fact, only 9 of 31 applicants had been granted admission. The stalemate was finally broken in 1955 by a U.S.-Soviet compromise which allowed the admission of 16 new states, 8 favoring the West and 8 leaning toward the Soviet Union. Thereafter, membership began to rise rapidly as former colonies in Africa and Asia gained their independence—often with U.N. help—and were promptly admitted to the world body.

While the two sides seemed willing at least to talk with one another, the cold war continued. In 1956 the Soviet Army crushed a popular uprising in Hungary, again spotlighting the U.N.'s impotence in matters involving one of the superpowers. Although the Uniting for Peace resolution had given the General Assembly authority to *recommend* action in such cases, no member states were obligated to comply; and since none of the major Western nations was willing to become involved in an armed conflict, the Assembly could do no more than issue a series of condemnations. Similarly, when U.S. marines were sent into the Dominican Republic in 1965 to suppress what was thought to be a Communist rebellion, the U.N. was not consulted. Again, mounting U.N. criticism of America's escalating war in Vietnam was consistently ignored, as was the U.N.'s denunciation of the Soviet invasion of Czechoslovakia in 1968.

Despite these rebuffs, though, the United Nations did succeed in defusing a number of volatile situations, arranging cease-fires, and maintaining peacekeeping missions in the Middle East in 1956, 1967, and 1973, the Congo in 1960–62 (see pp. 442–449), Cyprus in 1964–74, Kashmir in 1947–72, and elsewhere.

The U.N. and the Third World

By the mid-1960's subtle but fundamental changes were making themselves felt in the world organization, reflections of changes in the world at large.

With the formal dissolution of Europe's colonial empires in the 1950's and 1960's, the last vestiges of an old historical era were being replaced by the first stirrings of a new one. Gradually, the two opposing factions that had dominated world politics since the end of the war became aware of another group, the newly independent countries of Asia, Africa, and Latin America. These Third World nations, as they came to be called, suffered enormous liabilities: Most were militarily weak, politically unstable, and extremely poor, with few industrial or educational resources to draw upon. Yet they made up a large percentage of the world's population; some had natural resources of great value; and—perhaps most important—they were committed to neither side in the cold war.

Their first attempt to establish some form of political solidarity took place in April 1955 at the Afro-Asian world conference in Bandung, Indonesia. Though the results of that conference were generally inconclusive, it did reaffirm their intention to remain "nonaligned" and, in effect, to make use of cold war rivalries to improve their own conditions.

Since then the Third World nations have emerged as an unpredictable but important factor in global politics, tending in many cases to balance and moderate the actions of the superpowers. In the U.N. particularly their strength as a voting bloc has given them a pivotal voice in virtually all policy decisions. It was at least in part a result of their increased prominence that the United States, after 21 years, finally acquiesced in 1971 to the admission of the largest and most powerful of the Third World nations: Mao Tse-tung's China.

Thus, almost by accident, the original goals of the United Nations Charter seemed in many ways closer to fulfillment than ever before. World peace, or at least world survival, had been secured during a period that could have marked the end of recorded history. A modicum of power had been transferred from the superpowers to some of the lesser ones, and an increasing percentage of the world's population was represented in the world body; in three decades its membership had risen from 50 nations to 144.

The future, of course, would not be without problems. As their power eroded, the major nations would become less eager to finance the world body—particularly in the wake of actions they opposed, as when the Soviet Union, France, and others refused to pay their assessed shares for the costly intervention in the Congo. Such a threat was again raised following the controversial vote of November 1975 in which the General Assembly, led by the Arab nations, passed a resolution labeling Zionism a form of racism.

Nonetheless, there remained the simple, heartening fact that even at moments of the greatest tension, no nation had yet repudiated its membership in the world body—a far cry from the stormy walkouts in the old League of Nations. Various countries at various times would doubtless continue to find fault, but never again, it seemed, would the principle or the importance of the United Nations seriously be questioned.

1946

The Computer Revolution

The success of ENIAC, the first electronic computer, leads to machines that will produce the most rapid social and economic revolution in history.

One of the major revolutions in human culture began quietly in the months after World War II. Its improbable agent was a gigantic metal machine called the Electronic Numerical Integrator and Calculator, or ENIAC for short. Designed by John Presper Eckert and John W. Mauchly at the University of Pennsylvania and completed late in 1946, ENIAC was the world's first all-electronic digital computer. The upheaval it engendered has been called the computer revolution. ENIAC had been developed by the U.S. Army for a specific wartime purpose: to calculate trajectory tables for field artillery. To compute a single trajectory, which told gunners the range of their fire at different barrel elevations, air temperatures, wind velocities, and so on, required some 200 steps and took a trained mathematician using the most sophisticated desk calculator anywhere from 7 to 20 hours. ENIAC could do the same work in 30 seconds. In just two hours it could complete elaborate calculations in nuclear physics that would take an engineer an entire century.

Such dizzying speeds would have astounded the inventors of ENIAC's predecessors: the abacus, said to have originated in Babylonia some 5,000 years ago; the knotted strings of pre-Columbian tribes in South America; and the pebbles the ancient Romans called *calculi.* Nonetheless, their essential purpose was the same. All were tools invented by man to help him complete the tedious work of adding up columns of numbers more quickly and accurately.

The first significant step beyond such simple tallying devices was an ingenious system for multiplying known as Napier's bones, which became popular in early 17th-century Europe. It was devised by the Scottish mathematician John Napier (who also invented logarithms) and consisted of a pocket-sized set of bone or ivory rods engraved with the digits 0 through 9 and their multiples. The numbers were arranged in such a way that the answer to a complex multiplication problem could be found after rotating the rods by hand and adding the relevant figures.

Wheels, Gears, and Punched Cards

In 1642 French philosopher-mathematician Blaise Pascal invented the first mechanical adding machine, a metal box containing rotating cylinders, wheels, and gears. The digits 0 to 9 were engraved on 10 exterior wheels, which were attached to gears with 10 corresponding teeth. Numbers were entered by turning the wheels to the appropriate digits and the calculation carried out by turning a crank. A further refinement, the Stepped Reckoner, was designed by German philosopher-mathematician Baron Gottfried Wilhelm von Leibniz in 1694. Besides adding and subtracting, it could multiply, divide, and find square roots.

The real father of modern computing, however, was an eccentric mid-19th-century English genius named Charles Babbage. His revolutionary design for an Analytical Engine (devised over a century before the completion of ENIAC) anticipated nearly all the central features of present-day computers. Babbage envisioned a machine that could solve complicated mathematical problems, involving a series of separate calculations, all by itself. He realized that such a machine would require at least five separate elements: (1) an input mechanism for feeding the machine the necessary information for setting up and solving the problem; (2) a storage unit, where the input material could be kept until the machine needed it; (3) a mathematical unit to perform the actual calculations; (4) a control unit to tell the machine when and how to use its stored information; and (5) an output device to deliver the answer in printed form. A very similar formula was followed by the men who designed the first electronic computers.

"The whole of arithmetic now seemed to be within the grasp of mechanism," Babbage later wrote of his inspiration. "A vague glimpse ... of an Analytical Engine at length opened out, and I pursued with enthusiasm the shadowy vision." Unfortunately, despite heavy government subsidies, Babbage's vision never materialized. The factories of Victorian England simply could not produce the highly refined parts he needed to build his Analytical Engine. When Babbage

***The world's first** electronic computer, ENIAC (inset), contained 18,000 vacuum tubes and occupied an entire room. Within 30 years the general purpose microcomputer had been developed. Two inches square, less than a quarter of an inch thick, and weighing less than two ounces, it incorporates more than 100,000 transistors and has 120 input-output leads, 30 along each edge. The sophistication of such instruments is one measure of the scale and speed of the revolution that began with ENIAC, a revolution that has reached into virtually every corner of modern life.*

THE ON-OFF CODE THAT HELPS COMPUTERS COUNT

Since 1950 computers have used a form of arithmetic that allows any number to be written with combinations of only two digits instead of the usual ten. Although numbers expressed in this binary form are much longer than their decimal equivalents, their great advantage, for a computer, is that the two signs can correspond to the "on" and "off" states of an electrical circuit. Today special programs exist to convert ordinary decimal numbers into binary form for the computer and to convert the computer's binary output into a decimal form for readout.

Building Numbers in the Decimal System

Any number can be built with the ten digits (0–9) used in the decimal system. The position of each digit in a number

702 Third Position Second Position First Position

indicates a certain size of unit; each unit, working from right to left, is 10 times as large as the one preceding:

Third position	Second position	First position
Unit(s) of 100	Unit(s) of 10	Unit(s) of 1

The digit indicates how many of the units must be used:

7	0	2
Units of 100	Units of 10	Units of 1
=700	=0	=2

The value of the number is the sum of the units so indicated.

700+0+2=702

***The forerunners** of today's punched computer cards (center) were used to guide the Jacquard looms (above), invented in France in 1801. Each card allowed only certain of the loom's needles to penetrate the cloth through its punched holes, thus weaving the desired pattern. The holes in a computer card allow mechanical or electrical contacts to be made, thereby registering a series of numbers. Below, a modern card-sorting machine.*

died in 1871, he left behind a library of detailed plans, drawings, and instructions for his ingenious machine, providing posterity with a wealth of insight into the functional principles of computing.

Among Babbage's inspirations was the idea of using coded cards punched with holes to automate the computing process, a concept he borrowed from the Jacquard power loom. Invented in 1801 by French textile manufacturer Joseph Jacquard to automate the weaving of silk brocades, the loom had shuttles guided to weave a certain pattern by the arrangement of holes in punched cardboard cards. The system worked something like the perforated music roll on a player piano. As Lady Lovelace, one of Babbage's most ardent disciples, explained: "We may say most aptly that the Analytical Engine weaves algebraical patterns just as the Jacquard Loom weaves flowers and leaves."

Jacquard's ingenious system inspired other inventors, including Herman Hollerith, the U.S. statistician who in 1896 founded the Computing Tabulating Recording Company, which later merged with two other companies to form the International Business Machines Corporation (IBM), the first company to produce electronic computers in volume. Hollerith's original punched card system—used to sort, count, and tabulate the results of the 1890 census—could process information three times as fast as conventional adding machines. Early in this century such mechanisms, based on the ideas of Hollerith and others, came into wide use in business and accounting.

Building Numbers in the Binary System

In the binary system any number can be written using only two digits instead of the ten used in the decimal system. The digits used are 1 and 0. In binary notation 702 is written 1010111110. As in the decimal system, the position of the digits indicates a certain size of unit. The difference is that in the binary system each unit is twice *as large as the one before it (instead of ten times, as in the decimal system):*

Fifth Position	Fourth Position	Third Position	Second Position	First Position
Unit(s) of 16	Unit(s) of 8	Unit(s) of 4	Unit(s) of 2	Unit(s) of 1

The Sequence of Binary Units

The digit 1 indicates that the unit in the corresponding position will be used; the digit 0 indicates that the unit in the corresponding position will not be used. Thus 27 is written as follows in the binary system:

Each subsequent unit is twice as large as the one preceding it.	16	8	4	2	1
	1	1	0	1	1
	16 +	8 +	0 +	2 +	1 = 27

Long Numbers, Fast Calculations

A larger number, such as 702, is written according to exactly the same procedure, except that it requires a longer sequence of binary units. Since computers work at such high speeds, this presents no real problem.

512	256	128	64	32	16	8	4	2	1
1	0	1	0	1	1	1	1	1	0
512 +	0 +	128 +	0 +	32 +	16 +	8 +	4 +	2 +	0 = 702

Babbage's dream of a completely automatic computer was not realized until 1944, with the completion of the IBM-Harvard Mark I. Part mechanical and part electrical, it was both the last of the mechanical computers and the forerunner of the all-electronic brains to come. The Mark I's cogged gears, wheels, clutches, and relays were driven by an electric motor. Information was fed into the machine on punched paper tapes and processed in its memory, arithmetic, and control units. The results of its computations appeared on punched cards. Compared to conventional mechanical calculators, the Mark I was incredibly fast: It could add or subtract two 23-digit numbers in one-third of a second and multiply them in six seconds.

ENIAC: The First of a New Breed

Then, barely two years after the completion of the Mark I, Eckert and Mauchly unveiled ENIAC, which immediately rendered the Mark I and all mechanical calculators obsolete. The secret of its spectacular success was electronics. Eckert and Mauchly had replaced the Mark I's 760,000 moving parts with some 18,000 vacuum tubes, several miles of copper wire, and half a million soldered connections. Messages were carried by swift electrical impulses at speeds 1,000 times faster than the Mark I's mechanical relay system.

By virtue of speed alone, ENIAC was clearly the first of a new breed. Yet compared to its descendants, it was bulky, temperamental, inefficient, and expensive to operate. ENIAC weighed more than 30 tons, occupied more than 1,500 square feet of floorspace, and consumed 150 kilowatts of electrical power. Moreover, the granddaddy of electronic computers required almost constant attention. Its thousands of vacuum tubes generated so much heat that the room had to be cooled by air-conditioning, and the tubes themselves needed frequent replacement.

ENIAC's moment of glory was brief. Even before it was finished, engineers had begun working to improve its design and to produce more efficient and reliable machines. One of the leading innovators in early computer technology was mathematician John von Neumann of the Institute for Advanced Study at Princeton, New Jersey. Von Neumann helped build ENIAC's successor, EDVAC (Electronic Discrete Variable Automatic Computer), which began operating in 1950. EDVAC embodied two design concepts that have since become standards of computer engineering: the stored program and the binary numeral system.

ENIAC's programers had to wire in every single step of instructions each time they wanted to solve a new problem. Realizing that this process was both time-consuming and wasteful, Von Neumann developed the idea of stored programs. He saw that the complicated operation sequence constituting each program was built up out of a series of simple steps and that most of these steps were repeated in every program. If these steps could be stored in a memory unit in the machine, Von Neumann reasoned, the process could be speeded up considerably. Rather than spelling out each new program in its entirety, the programer could simply direct the machine to consult specific pigeonholes in its memory unit and follow the instructions stored there.

In this sense all a computer really needs to know is how to add and subtract. All more complicated operations are part of its stored programs. Even the most complicated input procedure consists mainly of references to steps or whole programs already stored in the machine's memory. Many of today's machines are even hooked up to auxiliary reference units, where they can look up necessary information and supply it where and when it is required.

EDVAC also inaugurated the binary number system of arithmetic notation. This type of notation is much better suited to the computer's electronic makeup than the traditional decimal system based on the total number of digits on the human hands. Just as an electric switch has only two positions, off and on, the binary number system uses only two digits, 0 and 1. If the 0 corresponds to off and the 1 to on, we have established a simple, efficient basis for all computer operations. Since EDVAC most electronic computers have used binary arithmetic to carry out calculations.

Since 1950 technology has brought us increasingly more compact and speedier computers, largely as the result of improved electronic components. ENIAC's power-hungry tubes gave way to smaller transistors, which in turn were supplanted by miniature integrated circuits, a fraction of the size of a postage stamp. Today's computers are a million times faster than ENIAC. The time required to extract or store a bit (one binary digit) of information in the machine's memory unit is measured in nanoseconds (billionths of a second), and other operations are nearly as fast. A computer designed today to handle the same scope of operations as ENIAC would cost about $1,000 and would be about the size of a standard typewriter.

BIG BROTHER'S DATA BANK?

To a growing number of people the sheer capacity of computers to receive, store, and disgorge almost limitless amounts of information with incredible speed and efficiency represents a potential menace. Their primary concern is the possible misuse of the huge amount of computerized personal data on file with various state and federal agencies. Most of this material is collected for such routine and ostensibly harmless purposes as vehicle and driver's license applications, income tax returns, Social Security records, census reports, and armed services registration; but some is gathered clandestinely by the police, FBI, and other organizations for security purposes.

Until recently the average person had no way of knowing how such information was used, no means of finding out whether inaccurate or outdated material was included in his files, no guarantee that such information would not be used for unauthorized or illegal purposes. In the case of certain police and security records, many people were not even aware that such files existed. Most ominous of all, there was no way to prevent the consolidation of all existing records under one mammoth, centralized agency—a situation foreshadowed by the nightmare world of George Orwell's *1984,* where the state authority—Big Brother—sees all, knows all, controls all.

To forestall such a development, state legislatures have passed laws safeguarding the individual's right to examine, correct, and limit the use of existing government records about himself. The Federal Privacy Act, which went into effect on November 27, 1975, extends these guarantees to the national level. While such laws represent a major step forward, they deal only with the public sphere, overlooking the equally vast—and potentially damaging—amount of computerized data in the hands of banks, insurance agencies, and other large private concerns.

Marvel or Monster?

No one in 1946 could have foreseen the enormous impact computers would have in the years ahead. Today they are as much a part of our daily lives as television—and far more essential. They perform myriad tasks from recordkeeping to writing music. In business and industry computers are used in supervising payrolls and billing, keeping tabs on inventory levels, evaluating marketing statistics, designing new products, and guiding management policy. They help scientists in virtually every field, solving problems, conducting and monitoring experiments, simulating complex situations, and probing unexplored areas like the ocean floor and outer space. Computers book seats on airlines, calculate odds on games of chance, oversee the flow of traffic on highways and in cities, and even run whole factories.

For most people, however, the computer remains a remote, bewildering, and often frustrating intruder. Many have never even seen the seemingly omniscient machines that process their paychecks, figure their bank balances and credit ratings, total up their bills, and silently accumulate all kinds of information about their preferences, habits, and aspirations. Such terms as flowchart, hardware, software, data processing, critical path, feedback, and information retrieval have entered our vocabulary, but few people could actually define them and fewer still could explain how the computer itself operates. A real understanding of the world of the computer is confined to a relatively small number of experts and technicians, who have been specially trained to run, program, design, sell, or otherwise direct the machines.

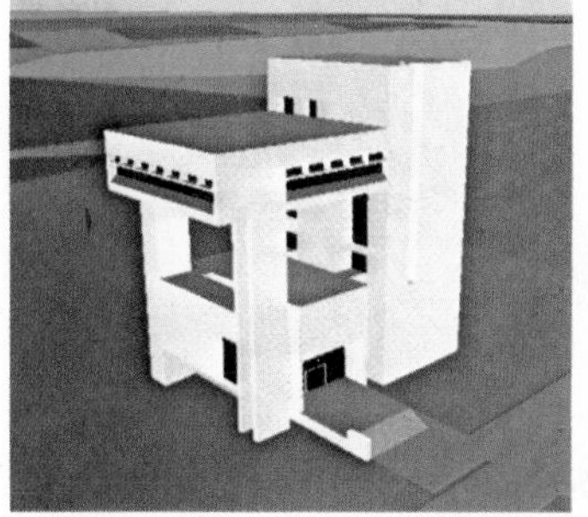

Innovative programing enables computers to generate varied perspective views of a planned university building.

This trim computer terminal of The New York Times *data bank replaces traditional newspaper "morgue" files.*

Data to build pictures of Mars are processed by this high-speed digital recorder at the rate of 16,200 bits per second.

VERSATILE TOOLS FOR A FAST-PACED WORLD

Today computers perform an incredible variety of sophisticated tasks, ranging from corporate decision making to producing graphic art. Patrolmen use computer data banks to provide instant descriptions of crime suspects. Cartographers use computers to draw accurate maps from aerial photographs. Architects and engineers build models and test their designs by computer. Researchers have taught computers to play games, compose music, even write brief plays. The possibilities seem endless, and the only limits may be those imposed by our own imagination.

From our present vantage point in the midst of the computer revolution it is difficult to evaluate the machine's long-range impact. To be sure, it has enabled man to keep up with the hectic pace of change that has deluged modern society. It has also provided a means of coping with the demands of our rapidly expanding population. Computers too have increased and multiplied: from about 4,000 worldwide in 1961 to an estimated 100,000 by the mid-1970's. But its very speed and efficiency in dealing with the complexities of present-day life may be adding momentum to the accelerating rate of change. Critics of the computer fear that this machine, designed as a tool, may be hurling us prematurely into a future that our slow-paced brains are not yet capable of dealing with.

Until recently the computer was restricted to the linear input and output of punched cards and magnetic tape, but recent input and output devices have begun to catch up with the computer's internal sophistication. Today artificial intelligence researchers are equipping computers with cameras, microphones, and other sensory input units and adding such innovative output units as television screens and plotting tables. Who can say what other uses may yet be found for these machines that are only beginning to be able to "see" and "hear" for themselves?

The fact of the matter is that we probably do not yet understand ourselves well enough to ask whether a machine might learn to do what we can do. What do we mean by terms like "think," "reason," and "create"? It may well be that the current research into artificial intelligence will tell us as much about our own mysterious inner workings as about the potential applications of the machines we have created.

Anxiety and Existentialism

The horrors of World War II had made a mockery of the political sloganeering of the 1930's. And the new threat of nuclear annihilation that dominated the postwar decade made what should have been a tranquil period an anxious and agonizing time. Artists reacted in various ways. Three who triumphed in those troubled years were Swiss-born Alberto Giacometti, whose attenuated figures evoked the spiritual isolation of modern man; American painter Jackson Pollock, who made the act of painting itself his "subject"; and the Irish-born playwright Samuel Beckett, who re-created the absurdity of modern life for the stage.

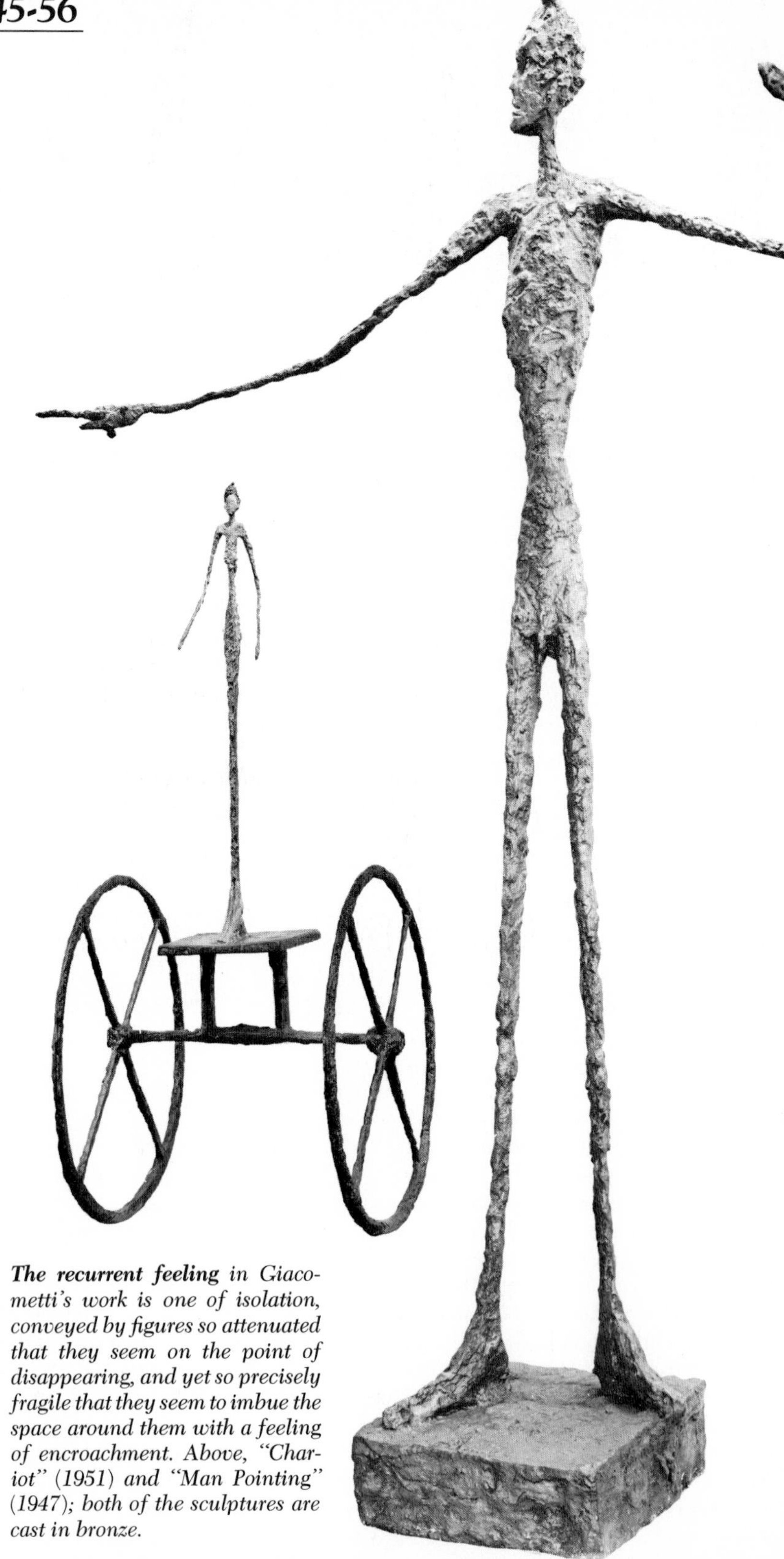

The recurrent feeling *in Giacometti's work is one of isolation, conveyed by figures so attenuated that they seem on the point of disappearing, and yet so precisely fragile that they seem to imbue the space around them with a feeling of encroachment. Above, "Chariot" (1951) and "Man Pointing" (1947); both of the sculptures are cast in bronze.*

Alberto Giacometti As of 1945, when Alberto Giacometti began working on the agonized, pencil-thin sculptures that were to make him world-famous, *Being and Nothingness* by existentialist philosopher Jean-Paul Sartre had been in print for two years. It is not surprising that the reclusive Giacometti counted its author among his few close friends, for his art reflects Sartre's bleak vision of the world.

Like Sartre, Giacometti considered life a brutal business. Like Sartre, he believed that each man is alone, cut off from God and from other men with whom he lives in constant conflict; since life is essentially meaningless, each man is forced to find his own way. Sartre held that men are all "cursed" with free will. Yet this same existential freedom also renders man noble,

***Giacometti,** hunched against the Paris rain, echoes his own sculpture in this photograph by Henri Cartier Bresson, in which he too seems besieged by invisible forces.*

makes him "like God" as he endlessly struggles and endlessly fails.

Giacometti was a genuine existential hero. He once wrote, "All that I will be able to make will only be a pale image of what I see . . . I do not know whether I work in order to make something, or in order to know why I cannot make what I would like to make."

Alberto Giacometti was born in Stampa, Switzerland, in 1901, the son of Giovanni Giacometti, a post-impressionist landscape painter. Encouraged by his father, Alberto became an accomplished draftsman by the age of 9 and a talented sculptor at 13. After a single year of formal art training, he went to Italy and began a lifelong fascination with the old masters. He also studied ancient sculpture, particularly the slender, stylized figures of the Etruscans and Egyptians. In 1922 he settled in Paris; there, for the most part, he lived, studied, and worked hard until his death came in 1966.

An Existential Quest

Giacometti's earliest works were rooted in realism, but, dissatisfied with this style, he experimented with cubism and surrealism. In 1935, still unhappy with his work, Giacometti returned to working from nature. For five long, laborious years he worked from dawn to dusk each day, using his infinitely patient brother, Diego, and his bride-to-be, Annette Arm, as models. Still he could not satisfy himself, and after 1940 he again began to work from memory. But he fared no better, for in peeling away everything to the essence, he shrank his sculpture to a minuscule size—often less than an inch in height. "To my terror," he said, "the sculptures became smaller and smaller, they had a likeness only when they were small, yet their dimensions revolted me, and tirelessly I began again. . . ."

Trying To Do the Impossible

It was not until after World War II that Giacometti returned to full-size figures and found them truest to his vision when made tall and slender.

When he worked he was indefatigable. He labored over his figures for months, building them up, paring them down, and then, as often as not, smashing them to pieces and starting over. He was constantly in search of his private and unattainable ideal.

Man's isolation was his constant theme. He was the first artist to make his figures look as if seen from a distance. The facial features are indistinct; edges are blurred.

Giacometti's figures appear in groups, as in "City Square" (1949). They seem invariably alone and set apart. They constitute a timeless testimony to man's ability to endure.

Jackson Pollock The art of Jackson Pollock is everything Giacometti's is not—enormous, explosive and impassioned. Yet it, too, mirrored its time. A victim of the anxiety that characterized the world around him, Pollock retreated into his works and concerned himself with the processes of art, attempting to let the works create themselves.

Pollock gained prominence with a showing that opened on January 5, 1948, at the Betty Parsons Gallery in New York City. The artist was a familiar, if controversial, figure in New York, celebrated both for his powerful abstractions and his frequent bouts with alcoholism. But the 17 vast canvases in his new exhibit were unlike anything anyone had ever seen.

Over the preceding year Pollock had devised a new way of painting. Abandoning the easel, brush, and palette, he spread gigantic strips of canvas on the floor of his studio, then dripped and spattered paint onto the surface in enormous, apparently random patterns. What emerged were dense, tangled, multicolored skeins of paint without apparent beginning or end.

The show created a sensation. Some critics were bewildered; others were angered at what seemed a tasteless artistic joke aimed at a gullible public. But Pollock was serious, and his example helped stir a revolution in the world of art.

Jackson Pollock, with good cause called an action painter, nailed his canvases to the floor and charged over them with paint and brush. Out of the intricate net of drops, swirls, and spatters he cast came works pulsating with life and vigor.

***Pollock's** "Blue Poles" (16 ft by 6 ft. 11 in.) was bought in 1973 by the Australian National Gallery, Canberra, for $2 million. It is typical of his large-scale action paintings. His unorthodox methods and spectacular results helped make New York the home of abstract expressionism during the 1950's.*

A Painter's Progress

Pollock was born on a ranch near Cody, Wyoming, in 1912. His father's chronic ill luck forced his family to move often. Young Pollock's formal education ended when he was expelled from Los Angeles Manual Arts High School.

Determined to become "an artist of some kind," Pollock went to New York City in 1930 and studied at the Art Students League with muralist Thomas Hart Benton. Benton's realistic regional works reflected pride in his midwestern heritage and scorn for what he dismissed as "modernist dirt." From him Pollock learned the joy of working on a mammoth scale, the importance of craftsmanship, and the power of Renaissance masters. But Pollock did not swallow Benton's teaching whole. "My work with Benton," he later recalled "was important as something against which to react very strongly."

Several artists besides Benton influenced Pollock's works, including Picasso, German expressionist Max Beckmann, and Mexican muralist David Siqueiros, who first taught him to use spattered house paint. But Pollock was most affected by the European surrealists, especially André Masson. Pollock came to share the surrealists' belief that all art should grow directly from the subconscious, but he took it one step further. While the earlier surrealists probed the subconscious in search of eerie images to re-create on canvas, Pollock was able to make the emotional impulse to paint in itself the focus of his art.

From 1935 to 1943 Pollock worked for the New Deal's Federal Art Project, swapping a painting every eight weeks for a monthly stipend of $100. During this time he suffered from periods of intense anxiety and drank heavily. He spent hours in psychoanalysis, tried chemotherapy, and endured six months in a mental hospital. Nothing helped.

At last, Pollock's lot began to improve. In 1942 Peggy Guggenheim opened her Art of This Century Gallery in New York City. She placed Pollock under contract and offered him an opportunity to display his bold, calligraphic abstractions. During this same period he met Lee Krasner, a talented painter who later married him and dedicated herself to furthering his career and easing his anxiety.

By 1945 poet-critic Clement Greenberg had hailed Pollock as "the strongest painter of his generation," and Pollock had become the unofficial leader of a band of young abstractionists that included Arshile Gorky, Willem de Kooning, Robert Motherwell, and Mark Rothko. But he remained unsatisfied with his own work and with the traditional tools and techniques of his art.

Then, in 1947, he developed his drip-and-splatter technique. Painting on the floor appealed to him, he later wrote, because it made him feel "more at ease. I feel nearer, more a part of the painting, since in

this way I can walk around it, work from the four sides and literally be *in* the painting."

Reluctant Hero

Other artists—such as De Kooning and Gorky—were experimenting along similar lines. Their work came to be called abstract expressionism or action painting because of its emphasis on the *act* of painting rather than on subject matter.

Pollock's novel method and explosive canvases made him an instant symbol of the new movement. Popular magazines dubbed him Jack the Dripper. Picture spreads showed him furiously at work. Even his admirers often misunderstood him. Because he was a rancher's son, some European enthusiasts hailed him as a sort of artistic cowboy. Others thought they saw elaborate symbols in passages of pure painting or applauded him for having made talent and training obsolete.

Troubled, turbulent, intensely private, and with an abiding distrust of all intellectualizing about art, Pollock rarely sought to defend himself. He hoped his work would speak for itself. Abstract painting, he once said, "should be enjoyed just as music is enjoyed"—for its own sake and on its own terms, without murky theorizing. He also sought to minimize his own role. "The painting has a life of its own," he once wrote. "I try to let it come through."

Controversy continued to swirl about the man and his work, and finally the notoriety took its toll.

By 1952 Pollock had become the nation's most celebrated artist; the pressure to produce, to surpass himself, finally proved too much. Although some of his finest works, including "Blue Poles" (1952), date from these last difficult years, Pollock was unable to paint at all for long, bitter periods. He drank himself into a stupor almost daily and quarreled with friends and strangers alike. On August 10, 1956, Pollock and a woman companion were instantly killed when a car he was driving plunged off the road near his Long Island home and overturned. He was only 44.

Pollock helped free artists from the confines of tradition and demonstrated the power of fresh materials and methods. His explosive action painting also helped to make the U.S.A. the center of avant-garde art for the first time in history.

Samuel Beckett In Paris, on January 5, 1953, *Waiting for Godot* was first performed. The extraordinary play established its 49-year-old author, Samuel Beckett, as one of the great dramatists of the 20th century and a leader of the international Theater of the Absurd.

Waiting for Godot tells no story in the traditional sense. In Act One, two grizzled tramps, Vladimir and Estragon, are passing time on a country road by a scraggly tree. They are waiting for Godot, with whom they have an appointment. They discuss a wide variety of topics—including the state of Estragon's feet (bad) and his memory (worse)—in order to make the time go faster. They also talk with two passersby, a rich man named Pozzo and his slave Lucky. Pozzo brutalizes Lucky; the two tramps take the slave's side until Lucky kicks Estragon. At the end of the act a young boy announces that Godot has been delayed until the next day.

In Act Two the tramps are again waiting for Godot. Everything seems to be the same, yet small details suggest that a long period of time has elapsed. Pozzo and Lucky pass through again, but this time

Pozzo is blind and Lucky is dumb. Upon leaving, Pozzo gives a speech that sums up the mood of the play: "They give birth astride of a grave, the light gleams an instant, then it's night once more."

But in spite of all their frustrations and suffering, the characters go on. At one point, Vladimir exclaims, "I can't go on," but immediately realizes the implications of his statement and cries out, "What have I said?" At the end of the play a boy again announces that Godot will come the next day. Godot is never identified. Is he God or the Second Coming of Christ? (Biblical allusions abound in the play.) Does he exist at all outside the tramps' dim imagining, or is he a symbol that keeps men from understanding their plight? Beckett refuses to provide guidance. "If I knew," he once said, "I would have said so in the play."

Whoever or whatever Godot is, the wait proved worthwhile to audiences, for the play was an instant hit, running 400 performances during its first engagement while foreign producers clamored for it. What so intrigued the public?

First, there was the spare beauty of Beckett's language. There are no wasted words; although the dialogue can be maddeningly repetitive, it is filled with poetry, puns, and gags. At one point, for example, the waiting becomes unendurable, and the tramps resolve to end it by hanging themselves with the rope Estragon uses to hold up his pants. In a scene resembling a Laurel and Hardy routine the rope breaks, and Estragon's pants fall down.

Beckett uses the comedy routines and the seemingly meaningless chatter of the characters to probe the desolation of the human condition. As critic Martin Esslin has pointed out, Beckett's protagonists prattle endlessly because to do otherwise would force them to heed the inner voices that warn of their isolation, the meaninglessness of their lives.

Theater of the Absurd

Critics have classified Beckett's works as "Theater of the Absurd," a group of plays that reflect the irrationality of the modern world. The movement was launched in 1950 with Eugene Ionesco's play *The Bald Soprano. Waiting for Godot* followed in 1953, as did other plays by Beckett and Ionesco and their fellow dramatists, particularly Arthur Adamov, Jean Genet, and Edward Albee. All share the same essentially pessimistic view of man's predicament and the same scorn for traditional storytelling theater. As Ionesco described it, the absurd is "that which is devoid of purpose." Because modern man is "cut off from his religious, metaphysical and transcendental roots," he is "lost; all his actions become senseless . . . ."

The known facts of Beckett's life are almost as spare as his works. He was born near Dublin in 1906, studied and lectured in modern languages, and has lived in France

***Samuel Beckett** (left) casts a sardonic eye over his play* Happy Days. *In it a woman (played by Dame Peggy Ashcroft in this scene from Britain's National Theater production) holds forth in a strangely vaudeville mixture of poetry and desperate philosophy, as garbage gradually engulfs her.*

for all but a few years since 1928. He was a youthful intimate of Irish expatriate novelist James Joyce. During World War II Beckett served in the French Resistance until Nazi pursuers forced him to go into hiding in 1942. Beckett generally writes his works in French and translates them into English himself. He began writing essays, stories, and poems as early as 1929 and went on to publish the now-celebrated novels *Murphy* (1938), *Watt* (1945), and *Malone Dies* (1948). He remained little known, however, until *Waiting for Godot*. *Godot* was followed in 1957 by *Endgame*, a play in which the end of mankind seems imminent. In subsequent plays, monologues have increasingly replaced dialogues, and Beckett's style has grown ever more terse. The dialogue in the one-act play *Krapp's Last Tape* (1958) is between an old man and tape recordings he had made in previous years. The two-act *Happy Days* is virtually a monologue by a woman who is slowly sinking into a mound of earth and rubbish. *Not I* (1973) features only a spotlit woman's mouth.

In recent years Beckett has lived in a remote farmhouse in the south of France, shunning interviews, ignoring critics, and refusing to attend literary "events." In 1969 he was awarded the Nobel Prize for Literature—but did not acknowledge it.

A CHRONOLOGY OF THE ARTS: 1945-56

1945

- Swiss-born sculptor Alberto Giacometti began fashioning the nervous, attenuated figures that made him one of the world's best-known artists.
- Tennessee Williams' semiautobiographical play, *The Glass Menagerie*, was given its first Broadway production.
- British novelist George Orwell published *Animal Farm*, a brilliant barnyard fable excoriating totalitarianism and Stalin's Russia.
- English composer Benjamin Britten's *Peter Grimes* was first produced. It paints a brilliant picture of life in a small English fishing village.

1947

- The third symphony of U.S. composer Charles Ives, written in 1911, was first performed. A reclusive genius, Ives employed such innovations as atonality and polytonality long before European composers.
- British novelist Malcolm Lowry published *Under the Volcano*, a grimly symbolic tale of an alcoholic artist in Mexico. Undervalued during his lifetime, Lowry's reputation has soared in recent years.
- Algerian-born French author Albert Camus published *La Peste* ("The Plague"), an allegory of occupied France and the hopelessness of the human situation. In his books, plays, and essays Camus sought to define man's responsibilities to himself and to others.

1948

- U.S. painter Jackson Pollock exhibited his first abstract canvases.
- U.S. novelist Norman Mailer established his reputation with *The Naked and the Dead*, a tough, profane account of World War II in the Pacific.

1949

- *Death of a Salesman* by Arthur Miller was first produced. The play examines the relationship and responsibility of the individual to himself, his family, and the world in general.

1950

- Romanian-born playwright Eugene Ionesco's *The Bald Soprano* was first produced in Paris, launching the so-called Theater of the Absurd.

1951

- French artist Henri Matisse designed the dazzling vestments, murals, furniture, and stained glass of the Chapel of the Rosary at Vence, France.
- U.S. composer John Cage's *Music for Changes*, employing notes chosen at random, was first performed.

1952

- Welsh poet Dylan Thomas wrote, directed, and starred in his radio play, *Under Milk Wood*, for Britain's BBC. The work is filled with the same rich, ripe writing that has made his poetry internationally popular.
- U.S. novelist Ralph Ellison published *The Invisible Man*, a much acclaimed novel about what it means to be a black in America.

1953

- Irish dramatist Samuel Beckett's *Waiting for Godot* was first presented.

1954

- Swiss architect Le Corbusier began designing a complex of government buildings for Chandigarh, the new capital of India's Punjab state.
- English writer William Golding published *Lord of the Flies*, a story about schoolboys on a desert island and an allegory of human cruelty.

1955

- Russian-born novelist Vladimir Nabokov published *Lolita*. A witty look at U.S. society through the eyes of a jaded European visitor with a weakness for young girls, the novel's sexual overtones made it a bestseller but obscured its dazzling language and devastating satire.

1956

- British playwright John Osborne's *Look Back in Anger* was first staged in London. A bitter glimpse of British middle-class life, it was the best-known work of the group known as the Angry Young Men.

1947
The Partition of India

As Britain withdraws from India, Hindu fights Muslim in a struggle that rocks the subcontinent. Hundreds of thousands on both sides die in the chaos that follows Partition.

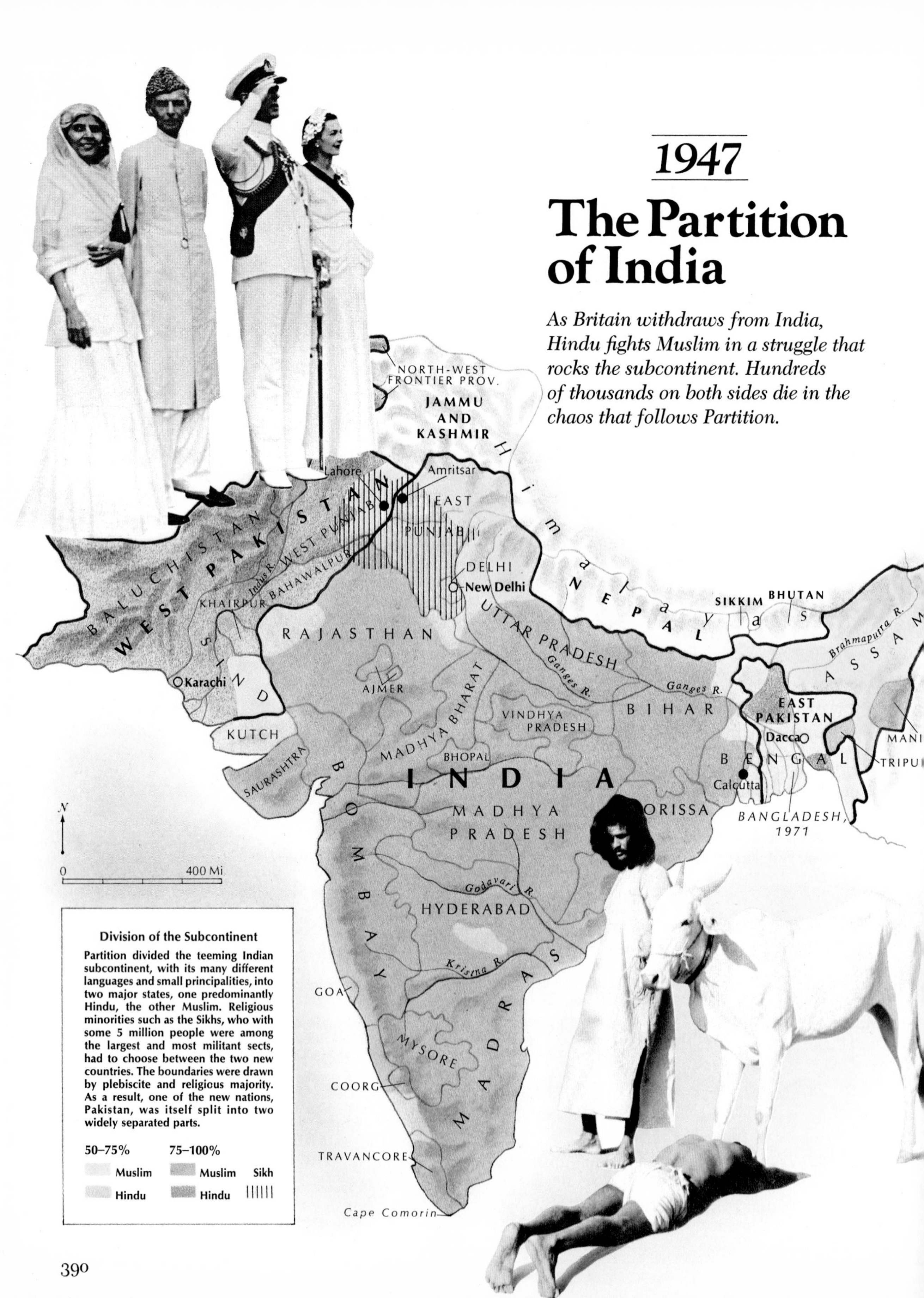

Division of the Subcontinent

Partition divided the teeming Indian subcontinent, with its many different languages and small principalities, into two major states, one predominantly Hindu, the other Muslim. Religious minorities such as the Sikhs, who with some 5 million people were among the largest and most militant sects, had to choose between the two new countries. The boundaries were drawn by plebiscite and religious majority. As a result, one of the new nations, Pakistan, was itself split into two widely separated parts.

50–75%	75–100%	
Muslim	Muslim	Sikh
Hindu	Hindu	||||||

August 15, 1947, should have been a day of jubilant celebration throughout the Indian subcontinent. At midnight three-quarters of a century of struggle culminated in India's independence from Britain. The saffron, green, and white flag of free India flew proudly from the Himalayas to Cape Comorin, fireworks lit the night sky, parades and mass assemblies filled a thousand towns and city squares, and patriotic oratory was heard everywhere. In the capital city of New Delhi India's first Prime Minister, Jawaharlal Nehru, and Britain's last Viceroy, Lord Louis Mountbatten, rode together through cheering throngs.

But Mohandas K. Gandhi, the 77-year-old "father of the nation," was away from New Delhi on another, more somber mission: He was in Calcutta trying to stop Hindus and Muslims from butchering one another. His lifelong dream of a free and united India had become a hideous nightmare; amid appalling carnage his beloved Hindustan had been divided into two antagonistic nations—Muslim Pakistan and a secular (but mostly Hindu) India.

To some Westerners the main difference between the two groups can be summed up in a crude generalization: The Hindus worship the cow; the Muslims eat it. To Indians, however, the differences are many and complex and frequently irreconcilable.

Islam, the Muslim faith, was carried into India by conquerors. Beginning in the eighth century a succession of zealous Muslim invaders from Persia, Turkey, and Afghanistan poured through the Himalayan passes, laying waste Hindu kingdoms and temples. On the ruins they established the mighty Mogul Empire, which remained predominant until the 17th century and sowed the seeds of religious rivalry.

Both Islam and Hinduism are still practiced with intensity, and mutual incompatibilities abound. Muslims worship one god, Allah; Hindus acknowledge many. Muslims are beefeaters, forbidden to eat pork; Hindus venerate the cow. Muslims require quiet five times a day for prayer; occasionally at those same hours Hindu processions playing music, which is forbidden in Muslim religious devotions, pass by a mosque. Despite their common language, history, and race (most Indian Muslims are descended from Hindus who were forcibly converted in the Mogul era), Hindus and Muslims rarely mingle.

When, in the 17th century, the British began to replace the Mogul rulers as the dominant force in the subcontinent, antagonisms grew even more complex. Both groups were resentful of the Westerners, but the Muslims, who saw themselves as displaced heirs to a glittering dynasty, found adjustment especially hard. And as the industrial age dawned, their traditions held them back still more. Their holy book, the Koran, stressed religious rather than secular education, and its doctrines conflicted with the new commercial practices. As a result, many Western-trained Hindus rose to positions of power and wealth, further embittering those Muslims who remained poor.

The emergence of the Indian nationalist movement in the late 19th century created yet another problem for the Muslims, who numbered only about a quarter of the population. They hated British rule but feared that in a free India, ruled by the mainly Hindu Indian National Congress, their fate might be even worse.

A short-term answer was found in the All-India Muslim League, established in 1906. This rival political organization agitated for separate electorates to safeguard Muslim rights, and the Indian National Congress and the British government acceded to some of its relatively modest demands. As independence became more feasible, certain visionaries within the League began to dream of an autonomous Muslim state. Its name, Pakistan, took on a magic sound.

Symbols *of the political and religious orders that shaped Partition: Far left above, the outgoing Governor General of India, Lord Louis Mountbatten, attends the ceremony marking Pakistan's independence. He is flanked by his wife and the new Governor General of Pakistan, Mohammed Ali Jinnah, with his sister, Fatima. Below, a Hindu prostrates himself before a white cow, symbol of divine providence.*

Jinnah, Founder of Pakistan

Pakistan might well have remained merely a golden dream without the single-minded zeal of one implacable man—Mohammed Ali Jinnah. This London-trained lawyer grew from a dandified pragmatist into a political moderate, then into an activist, and finally into a revolutionary leader. Almost singlehandedly he made Pakistan a reality.

Jinnah began his political career as a Congress Party nationalist, urging Hindu-Muslim unity and spurning the Muslim League until 1913, when it joined the Congress in making Indian home rule its prime objective. However, after Gandhi became the leader of the Congress in 1920, Jinnah resigned from the Congress, although he continued to advocate Hindu-Muslim unity.

Jinnah disliked Gandhi and distrusted his pious Hinduism. He also feared that the wholesale democratization proposed by Gandhi would result in Hindu domination at the expense of Muslim rights. In 1930, disgusted with Gandhi's tactics of passive resistance and with dissension in the Muslim League, he went into self-imposed exile in London.

Five years later Jinnah returned to resume leadership of the League, and his burning intensity of purpose galvanized India's Muslims. "Islam is in danger!" was the rallying cry. The League sprang into action, setting up thousands of village cells, circulating lurid accounts of real and imagined Hindu atrocities, and

***The Sikhs** shown demonstrating at right belong to a 500-year-old sect that, though combining elements of both Hinduism and Islam, has an ancient animosity toward Muslims. With a majority in the old Punjab state, the Sikhs, perhaps the most martial of India's many peoples, reacted violently to the partition of their state between India and Pakistan, and several months before Partition, riots began. In the city of Amritsar in East Punjab, which was to be awarded to India, the Sikhs and Hindus were in the majority and they fell ferociously upon the Muslims. Thirty-four miles away in Lahore, which was to become part of Pakistan, the Muslims attacked the Sikhs. The violence spread to the countryside, and tales of atrocities carried to both sides by refugees further fanned the flames. In the fighting that broke out all over the subcontinent, the Punjab area was the worst hit. By September 1947, when the holocaust was nearly spent, much of the cities of Amritsar (above) and Lahore had been reduced to piles of smoking rubble, and thousands lay dead.*

spreading rumors of the alleged horrors that would follow the establishment of a Congress government.

In 1937 the Congress confirmed Jinnah's accusations by refusing the British proposition that it form a coalition with the League. Perhaps unwittingly, the decision intensified the Hindu-Muslim schism. Then Nehru, who was president of the Congress, compounded the effect with a declaration that seemed to deny the political significance of India's approximately 90 million Muslims. "There are only two forces in India today," said Nehru, "British imperialism and Indian nationalism as represented by the Congress."

Construed as willful indifference to Muslim claims, the statement had a devastating effect on the prospects for unity. Here, Jinnah was quick to argue, was hard evidence of Hindu perfidy and of the religious disenfranchisement that would come with rule by the Congress. The issue became central to Jinnah's accelerating campaign for a separate state.

An incident during World War II further strengthened Jinnah's position. In 1942 the Congress passed a resolution calling upon Britain to quit India immediately and began a nationwide campaign of civil disobedience when London refused. Charging wartime sedition, Britain suppressed the revolt and jailed all leaders of the Congress. For the next three years Jinnah was without rivals, and he made the most of it by capturing power in Muslim provinces and hardening his demands for the creation of a Muslim state.

By the mid-1940's a climax was approaching. Britain, wearied by decades of Indian recalcitrance and weakened by World War II, proposed a coalition government with equal representation by Hindus and Muslims, but when the Congress refused to let Jinnah appoint all the League's Muslim leaders, he rejected the proposed coalition. Elections for a new constituent assembly early in 1946 showed the world what Jinnah already knew—that while the Congress truly represented most of India's 296 million Hindus, most of her 93 million Muslims followed the League.

***Above, one of the several Muslim** members of India's Constituent Assembly signs a copy of the Indian Constitution, completed in November 1949. At the leadership level of India and Pakistan, the transfer of power from the British was carried out with solemn dignity and with high hopes for the future; but for many of the common people Partition was an occasion for fear and rage, and often for exile.*

***Jawaharlal Nehru,** below right foreground, meets with Hindu and Sikh delegates in the city of Lahore during the Punjab riots. Nehru became Prime Minister of India at independence, and until his death in 1964 his strong leadership, emphasizing socialism and industrialization, kept India on a parliamentary path and helped unify her many and diverse peoples.*

***The intricate Hindu caste system,** now officially abolished, is still deeply embedded in Indian society and still provides a code of behavior for its members. Vaishnava Brahmins (left, below) exchange formal greetings.*

The Violent Climax

On August 16, 1946, flashpoint was reached. In May the British Cabinet Mission had issued a new plan calling, in principle, for a free but united India with no provision for a separate state of Pakistan. The Muslim League agreed until the Congress rejected part of the plan. Charging betrayal by both Britain and the Congress, Jinnah withdrew his consent and designated August 16 as Direct Action Day, a day on which Muslim outrage was to be demonstrated. He pointedly refused to renounce violence.

In most places the day was marked only by black flags and protest marches; but in Calcutta, the teeming, volatile heart of Bengal, there began a four-day orgy of hatred that left more than 5,000 dead. The Great Killing of Calcutta sparked reprisals throughout Bengal and Bihar. The aged Gandhi hurried to the troubled region, making his way on foot from one smoking village to another. But his calming presence could not hold back the firestorm for long. The chant "blood for blood" was taken up on both sides, and for Jinnah and his followers it was to be Pakistan or havoc.

Eager now to be out of India's affairs, the British government announced on February 20, 1947, that withdrawal would be completed by June of the following year and that Lord Louis Mountbatten would begin at once to oversee the transfer of power. Lord Mountbatten, a skilled diplomat, tried hard to work out a plan on which both sides could unite, but Jinnah

India's problems in aiding the destitute refugees (below, a mother and child) were intensified when cholera struck the camps (below right) and hastened the decision to enter the war against Pakistan. When Indian aid had assured victory, some Bengalis (top right) took summary revenge against captured West Pakistanis.

remained adamant, insisting that Pakistan was the only answer. Meanwhile, the killing continued.

Faced with civil war or partition, Lord Mountbatten, filled with misgiving, gave in early in June 1947. He announced that the subcontinent would be partitioned into two dominions—and several hundred small Indian states—just six weeks hence. Nehru and the Congress reluctantly agreed. Jinnah, whose health was failing, had secretly doubted he would live to see Pakistan a reality. Now he was jubilant. Gandhi mourned India's "vivisection."

Elections and plebiscites were held in haste to determine the Muslim majority regions. There were two such regions, one in the northeastern and one in the northwestern corners of India, with more than 900 unfriendly miles between. Jinnah's request for a connecting corridor was rejected by the Congress. As bureaucrats raced to divide up files, allocate funds, and distribute resources, an ill-equipped British commission drew up the new boundaries. Using antiquated maps and obsolete data, the commission tried to arrange the separation of Hindus and Muslims who had lived together for centuries.

Caught in the middle were some 5½ million Sikhs living in the Punjab region of northwest India. These members of a casteless offshoot of Hinduism had once endured Mogul persecution and they had long hated Islam. When partition cut them off from many of their holy places, they exploded into violence.

Partition forced some 14 million refugees to flee for their lives. Hindus and Sikhs trekked southward and Muslims hurried north (though about 45 million elected to stay in India). At least 600,000 died along the way, murdered by roving bands of fanatics. Jinnah, now Pakistan's first Governor General, had won Muslim independence at a high price.

Although the worst violence had subsided by late September, the subcontinent's tragedy did not end

BANGLADESH: A NATION BORN OF A BLOODBATH

East and West Pakistan were separated by more than distance. Language, culture, and racial composition posed barriers that could not be overcome by a common religion and fear of India.

East Pakistan, formerly part of the Indian province of Bengal, was smaller than West Pakistan, but had a larger, more homogeneous population. Yet the capital city was located in West Pakistan, and Urdu rather than Bengali was chosen as the official language. East Pakistan's exports of jute helped pay for projects in West Pakistan. Most of the army and the civil service was composed of West Pakistanis. The East Pakistanis felt they were treated as second-class citizens and gave increasing support to the Awami ("People's") League, which advocated autonomy.

In the elections for a national assembly held in December 1970 the Awami League won a sweeping victory in East Pakistan, giving it an overall majority and slating its leader, Sheikh Mujibur Rahman, for the office of Prime Minister of Pakistan. However, President Yahya Khan postponed the national assembly, and the Bengalis rioted in protest. A new flag symbolizing Bangla Desh ("the Bengal nation") appeared on rooftops in Dacca, the capital of East Pakistan. Fearing secession, the government flew troops into Dacca. On March 25, 1971, they were unleashed.

Mujib and others summarily were rounded up. Tanks and machineguns riddled anyone moving in the streets. At the university hundreds of students were shot. The troops moved into the countryside where they razed villages and killed thousands of peasants.

Some 10 million Bengalis fled to India. Barely able to feed her own people, India finally sent troops to help the Bengali resistance on December 3. After a two-week war with India in the east and west, the Pakistanis surrendered. Four days after that, Yahya Khan resigned. He was succeeded by Zulfikar Ali Bhutto, Pakistan's first civilian President in 13 years.

East Pakistan became the separate nation of Bangladesh. Mujib was freed and became head of the new state. Bangladesh, with 75 million citizens, became one of the most populous nations in the world.

The nine months of terror had left some 3 million Bengalis dead and a legacy of lawlessness that impeded reconstruction and climaxed in the murder of Mujib during a 1975 coup. Moreover, a series of floods and cyclones destroyed yet more lives, ruined the rice crop, and battered down recent repairs. Even in 1976, despite more than a billion dollars of aid, the new nation was still beset by famine, disease, and chronic economic problems.

with Partition. Within a month the two new nations were at war over the Muslim state of Kashmir in the first of several exhausting and inconclusive territorial clashes. Within a year both Gandhi and Jinnah were dead—Gandhi murdered by a Hindu who thought him too tolerant of Muslims, Jinnah the victim of a heart attack. Finally, for more than a quarter of a century, both nations had to turn their efforts to fighting a host of internal problems, including poverty, disease, illiteracy, and overcrowding.

The final, tragic irony emerged in 1971 when Pakistan was itself torn in two. The Bengali-speaking people of East Pakistan, rejecting the rule of the Punjabi government of West Pakistan, declared their independence as the new nation of Bangladesh. In the ensuing struggle (in which the Indian Army finally took part) perhaps as many as 3 million lives were lost. Once again, a new nation had been born amid bloodshed. Violence had bred violence.

Indira Gandhi, *the daughter of India's first Prime Minister, Jawaharlal Nehru, attained the same office in 1966. Facing court action for abuse of her office during the 1975 elections, she took sweeping measures to preserve and extend her powers, replacing the comfortable jacket that her father had made fashionable with a political straitjacket.*

1948

Return to Zion

The armies of five Arab nations attended the birth of the State of Israel. Zionism had won its ancient land, but the war at Israel's founding foretold a stormy future.

In the late afternoon of May 14, 1948, throughout Jewish Palestine there was a universal hush, a quiet filled with both tension and expectation. From the ancient city of Safad in the north to the wastes of the Negev desert in the south, from the winding alleys of Old Jerusalem to the sun-washed squares of the new city of Tel Aviv, the 650,000 Jews of Palestine gathered around radios and waited. Then, at precisely 4:00 p.m., through a crackle of static came the familiar voice of their longtime leader, David Ben-Gurion. His voice filled with emotion, the old warrior-pioneer began to read: ". . . by virtue of the national and historic right of the Jewish people and the resolution . . . of the United Nations: [We] hereby proclaim the establishment of the Jewish State in Palestine—to be called Israel."

Their expectations fulfilled, their tensions momentarily dissipated, the Palestinian Jews—now the new citizens of the State of Israel—rose to acclaim the mo-

ment with the anthem of their Zionist cause, the haunting "Hatikva," the song of hope. Indeed, at that moment of national birth hope seemed Israel's primary weapon. For arrayed against the newborn state stood the armies of five Arab nations, their troops already massed at the borders; their arsenals boasting tanks, aircraft, and light and heavy artillery; and their leaders vowing to throw the Jews into the sea. As if to underscore the peril, minutes after Ben-Gurion's voice had faded from the airwaves, the grating howl of the air-raid alarm pierced the Tel Aviv atmosphere, sending thousands scurrying for shelter. That this alarm was false, that no bombers appeared, made little difference. All Israelis knew and had known for months that their 40 million Arab neighbors were determined to crush them. Arab leaders had made clear their intention to turn Israel's U.N.-established borders into a "line of blood," and to consign Israel's banner, emblazoned with the Star of David, to history's junk pile.

Endings and Beginnings

Shortly before David Ben-Gurion proclaimed Israel's independence, another ceremony took place 50 miles north of Tel Aviv, in the port city of Haifa. There a smartly uniformed Englishman, Sir Alan Cunningham, the last British High Commissioner for Palestine, took the salute from a contingent of his troops. He then boarded a motor launch and headed out into the Mediterranean, where a cruiser lay offshore awaiting him. With this simple ceremony 31 years of British rule in the Holy Land ended. It had begun during World War I, when, in December 1917, British troops marched into Jerusalem to wrest Palestine from Turkish control and to begin carrying out a pledge made by British Foreign Secretary Arthur Balfour to the Anglo-Jewish scientist Chaim Weizmann. The pledge, embodied in what came to be called the Balfour Declaration, had been formally issued earlier that year, and it stated that "His Majesty's Government view with favour the establishment . . . of a national home for the Jewish people . . . [and] nothing shall be done which may prejudice the civil and religious rights of existing non-Jewish communities in Palestine."

Britain's decision to sponsor a revival of Jewish nationalism in Palestine came about through a variety of circumstances. From the late 1890's numerous influential Jews in a number of countries had begun to organize a worldwide Zionist movement to foster Jewish immigration to the Holy Land. Among the leaders of this movement was Weizmann, a world-renowned chemist who made persistent efforts on behalf of Zionism among Britain's political elite. During World War I Weizmann had contributed several important scientific discoveries to Britain's war effort, and it was certainly in some measure due to his influence that the Balfour Declaration was made. But there were other reasons as well, not the least of which was London's hope of rallying worldwide Jewish support for the Allied cause. Thus the world war and Britain's interest in controlling the strategic Middle East lands of the crumbling Ottoman Empire gave the Zionists an unequaled opportunity to realize their fervent dream. Balfour, sympathetic to the cause of Zionism, seized that opportunity and in so doing committed the British Empire to an experiment in nation building whose repercussions would be felt through the decades. In 1922 the League of Nations confirmed Britain's tem-

Divided by culture, language, *and conflicting national aspirations, Palestine's Arabs and Jews clashed from the start of post-World War I Zionist colonization. The establishment of a Jewish state in 1948 precipitated a bitter war between the Arabs (far left), who were fiercely determined to oust the Jews from Palestine, and Jewish settlers (left), who just as stubbornly defended their new homeland.*

porary title to the Holy Land, conferring a mandate to carry out the principles of the Balfour Declaration.

For Britain, Palestine was only one of many responsibilities in the Middle East. During the war London had secured Arab support against the Turks by holding out the hope that Britain would sponsor the creation of a vast Arab nation, which would include most of the Arabian Peninsula. Even though Palestine lay directly in the center of this projected Arab nation, the Arabs at first seemed willing to delay discussion about the Holy Land until after the war. Soon, however, the reality of power politics intruded.

Britain, it seemed, had yet a third commitment in the Middle East—to herself and her wartime ally France. Ignoring Arab protests, London and Paris carved up the Middle East between them: Britain would continue her longstanding suzerainty over Egypt, to which she added control of Iraq, the region of Palestine east of the Jordan River (soon to be called Transjordan), Palestine itself, and certain areas along the southern and eastern coasts of the Arabian Peninsula. France occupied Syria and Lebanon. Furious, the Arab emirs, princes, and chieftains cursed this betrayal of their trust. But since they lacked the power to defy the two Western nations, they turned their fury on the growing Jewish settlements in Palestine.

By 1922 some 85,000 Jews were living in Palestine (among about 650,000 Arabs). Many of the Jews were either refugees from turn-of-the-century anti-Semitic outbursts in eastern Europe or descendants of Jews who had remained in the Holy Land since Biblical times. The rest were idealistic immigrants who had arrived in the preceding two years under the auspices of the modern Zionist movement. Alarmed by the rapid growth of the Jewish population and embittered by British Middle Eastern policy, Arab leaders in Palestine instigated anti-Jewish riots in 1920—the first of many such disturbances to inflame the Holy Land.

The Pace Quickens

Not until the 1930's, however, did the flood of Jewish immigration begin. Prodded by the anti-Semitic policies of the new Nazi government of Germany, hundreds of thousands of German Jews fled their homeland between 1933 and 1939, many of them settling in Palestine. But early in 1939, on the eve of World War II, Britain changed its Palestine policy. London, anxious for Arab support in the forthcoming conflict, produced a white paper on Palestine, limiting the number of immigrants to 75,000 during the next five years. In that time millions of Jews would be trapped in Nazi-occupied Europe, and 6 million would die in the gas chambers of Hitler's concentration camps.

Recognizing that Hitler's legions represented the ultimate threat to Jewry, thousands of Palestinian Jews enlisted in the British armed services.

Yet as the fight against Hitler went on, so too did the Zionist effort to save as many Jews as possible from Germany's wrath. During the early years of the war, when a few southern European ports still remained open, several shiploads of Jewish refugees were taken aboard leaky, barely seaworthy boats to be smuggled into Palestine. Few of these refugees ever made it. The British, determined to halt illegal Jewish immigration, established a strong sea patrol off the Palestine coast to intercept the refugee ships, at first forcing them to return to their ports of embarcation, then rerouting them to British-occupied territory in central Africa.

Such examples of British callousness caused waves of anger to sweep Jewish Palestine. Haganah, the defensive arm of the Jewish Agency, gradually became more aggressive. But this was nothing to the fury that was felt when, in 1945, after World War II had ended, the British announced that their policy would remain unchanged. Where six years before, British fears of an Arab fifth column had dictated London's policy, now fear of Soviet penetration into the oil-rich Middle East was the rationale for keeping the homeless remnants of Europe's Jews out of the Holy Land. Jews in Palestine took to arms, not just in their own defense against bands of Arab raiders, as before, but to lash out at those they considered oppressors.

Their targets were British soldiers and installations. In 1946 and 1947 members of underground terrorist organizations roamed the country, relieving their pent-up frustrations with a bloody campaign of ambushes and swift bombing attacks on the 100,000-man British garrison. Two terrorist organizations, Irgun Zvai Leumi and the Stern group, stepped up their campaigns of violence against the Arabs. Meanwhile, other Zionist militants, like Ben-Gurion and Golda Meir (both would one day be Israeli Prime Ministers), concentrated their energies on smuggling arms into the country, smuggling refugees past British patrol ships, and arousing the world against British policy. Harassed on all sides—by Arabs who demanded no softening of policy, by Jews who insisted that Zion's gates be thrown open, by U.S. President Harry S. Truman, who supported the Zionists—Britain in 1947 turned the problem over to the United Nations.

The Arabs Rally

On November 29, 1947, after weeks of intensive debate, the United Nations General Assembly voted 33 to 13 (with 10 abstentions) to partition Palestine into two independent states, one for its 1.1 million Arabs, the other for its 650,000 Jews. For the Jews this was a moment of victory. If the lands they had been assigned were considerably smaller than the region proposed by the Jewish Agency, at least the U.N. decision promised the beginnings of a viable state, which would be a refuge for the survivors of Hitler's death camps.

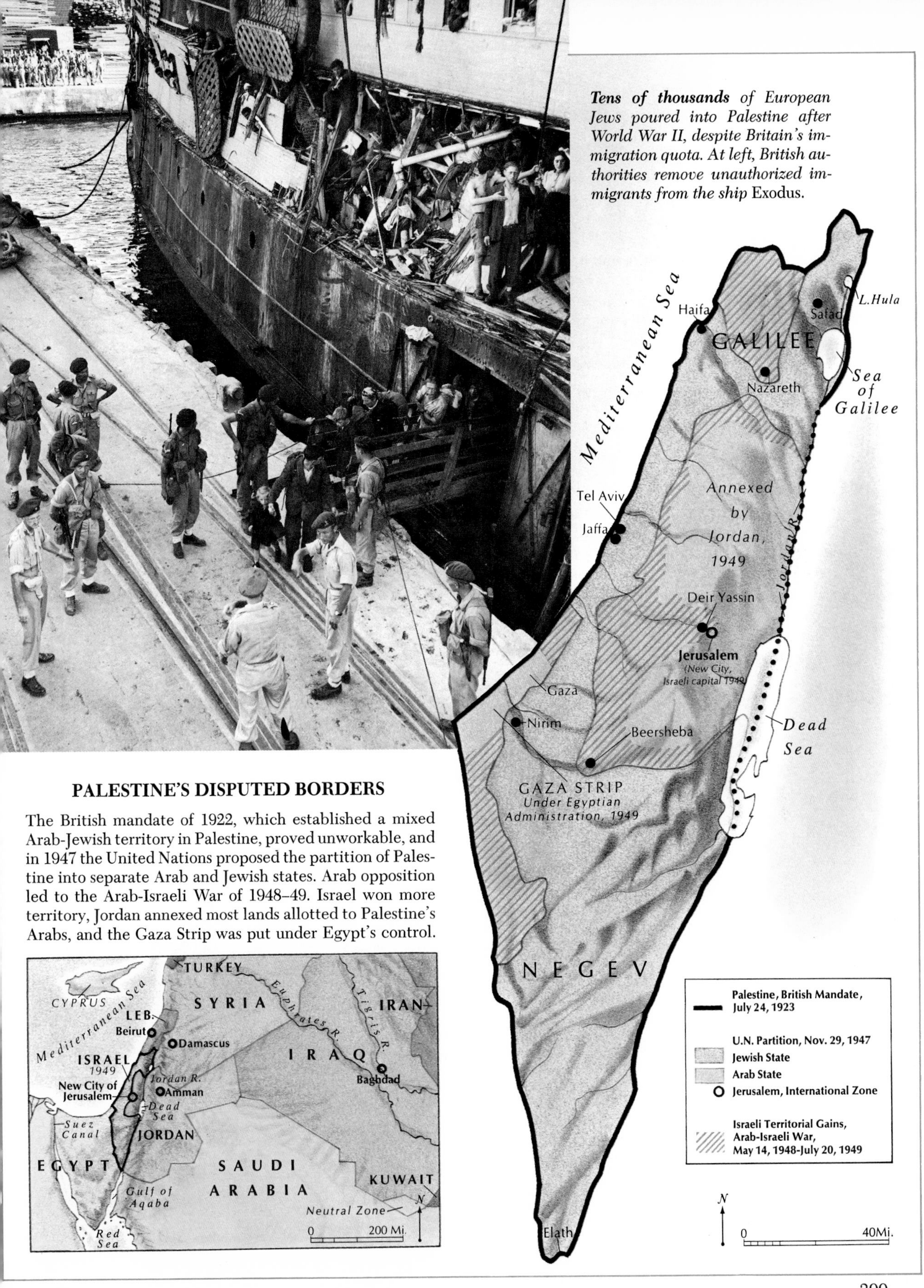

Tens of thousands of European Jews poured into Palestine after World War II, despite Britain's immigration quota. At left, British authorities remove unauthorized immigrants from the ship Exodus.

PALESTINE'S DISPUTED BORDERS

The British mandate of 1922, which established a mixed Arab-Jewish territory in Palestine, proved unworkable, and in 1947 the United Nations proposed the partition of Palestine into separate Arab and Jewish states. Arab opposition led to the Arab-Israeli War of 1948–49. Israel won more territory, Jordan annexed most lands allotted to Palestine's Arabs, and the Gaza Strip was put under Egypt's control.

To the Arabs, however, the decision was an outrage, a dismemberment of a region they had long claimed as their own, an insult to be avenged in blood. Almost immediately they struck back. Arab mobs in Jerusalem attacked and murdered their Jewish neighbors, Arab bomb squads detonated explosives in marketplaces, Arab guerrilla bands, drawn both from Palestine and neighboring states, besieged Jewish settlements and cut communications lines. By December 1947 Palestine was in a state of virtual civil war, and the slowly evacuating British forces declined to intervene.

To hold on, to yield nothing, was the Jewish order of the day. Armed mostly with rifles, settlement after settlement held off intensive Arab attacks. In the six months between the passage of the partition resolution and the declaration of statehood not a foot of Jewish-held territory was lost, for the Jews had two keys to victory the Arabs lacked: unity and organization.

For decades Jewish affairs in Palestine had been run by a semiofficial elected body, the Jewish Agency, which became in time a shadow government, ready to take control of the country upon Britain's departure. Although there were Jewish dissidents, such as those organized into the terrorist groups, the vast majority of Palestine's Jews recognized the authority of the agency, and its leaders were anxious to follow its directives. While the various Arab nations on Palestine's borders were united in their distaste for Zionism, they lacked one strong leader and, as it turned out, had seriously overestimated their ability to defeat such a small and youthful nation.

Against this backdrop of Arab disunity the Jews of Palestine were soon able to take the offensive. In the spring of 1948 the Haganah seized control of all major cities within the U.N.-proposed Jewish state. These included the crucial port of Haifa; the all-Arab city of Jaffa; Safad, near the Syrian border; and the New City of Jerusalem. The latter, together with the neighboring and much smaller Old City, had been designated an international zone by the U.N. As the Jews advanced from one city to the next, hundreds of thousands of Arab residents fled. Distrustful of Jewish Agency assurances that their lives and property would be safe, believing instead they would return to their homes in the wake of victorious Arab armies, the Arabs of Palestine hurriedly began packing their belongings and by boat, bus, cart, and car streamed across the borders into the safety of neighboring states. There most of them were forced into refugee camps. This pitiful flight was turned into a stampede by an outrageous

As independence approaches, *Syrian soldiers maintain a tense vigil along their frontier with Palestine (left).*

Across the border *Syrian mountain troops, supported by mule trains, begin moving into battle positions (below).*

act of brutality by the Irgun and Stern groups, who defied the Jewish Agency and brutally murdered 254 Arab civilians at a village called Deir Yassin on April 10, 1948. By 1949 about half a million Arabs—three-quarters of the original population—had fled Palestine to seek refuge in neighboring countries.

To hold off Arab mobs was one thing; to defeat Arab armies, another. What the Jews needed most of all was arms and the money to buy them. To secure funds the Jewish Agency, in early 1948, sent Golda Meir to the United States where, in a whirlwind tour lasting but a month, she raised $50 million from American Jews. In the surplus supply depots of half a dozen European nations the arms were purchased—machineguns, rifles, bazookas, Flying Fortresses, and, ironically, several German Messerschmitt fighter planes whose swastikas were replaced by the Star of David. But except for small quantities that could be smuggled into Palestine, this desperately needed materiel had to remain outside the projected state until midnight, May 14, the moment of official British withdrawal, when His Majesty's fleet would cease patrolling the waters off Palestine to prevent the importation of arms. It was also the moment when the armies of the Arab nations were scheduled to invade.

***Violence mounted** in the weeks preceding Israel's independence as Arab and Jewish terrorists grew increasingly ambitious. Above, rescuers remove some of the victims of an Arab bombing from the Jewish business section of Jerusalem.*

The Invasion Begins

The Arab plan of operations was simplicity itself. From the south a strong Egyptian army of two 5,000-man brigades would sweep up the Negev, one brigade making for Tel Aviv, the other for Jerusalem. From the east Transjordan's Arab Legion—about 10,000 men trained and staffed by British officers—would cross the Jordan River, quickly occupy those regions of central Palestine the U.N. had determined should be part of the Arab state, capture the Old City of Jerusalem, and lay siege to the New City. From the north elements of the Lebanese, Syrian, and Iraqi armies would smash through Galilee, sweep into Haifa, and then head down the coastal plain toward Tel Aviv. In a week, perhaps two at most, the Jewish state would be extinguished, its citizens the victims of what one Arab leader predicted would be a "Mongol massacre."

With seemingly limitless supplies and with some 21,500 presumably frontline troops at their command (drawn from a far bigger population than Israel's), such Arab leaders as Egypt's King Farouk and Transjordan's King Abdullah appeared to have few worries. Opposing them was a striking force of some 60,000 Israeli troops, including men and women drawn from the underground army, backed by field troops and local defense forces. Although the Israelis outnumbered the Arabs, the Israelis began the war poorly equipped: In all, on May 14, 1948, they could muster barely 10,000 rifles, each with 50 rounds of ammunition; four ancient artillery pieces; and 3,600 submachineguns.

As in the months before, the Israeli strategy was to hold fast, to contest every inch of territory, to turn each settlement into a fortress, to abandon nothing so long as a single bullet remained in a single rifle. By such tactics the Israelis hoped to slow the Arab advance and gain time while arms were delivered and recruits trained to use them. With luck, a broad offensive might eventually be mounted to sweep the invaders back behind their own borders. It was a risky tactic, but it was the only one that offered even a slim hope of survival, much less victory.

Under cover of darkness, on the night of May 14–15, the Egyptian invading army moved across the border into the Negev desert. A large force drew up to the outskirts of a small Jewish settlement called Nirim, whose armaments consisted of 17 rifles, 1 light machinegun, and 4 submachineguns. Against this barbed wire-enclosed commune the Egyptians launched a furious artillery barrage. This was followed by a frontal assault of several hundred infantrymen, backed by four tanks, several armored cars, and self-propelled light artillery. The settlers held their fire until the infantrymen were within rifle range. Then, as the Egyptians approached the barbed wire, they found themselves under intense fire. Having anticipated little resistance, the conscripted peasant soldiers fell back in panic.

This 1967 aerial photograph of Jerusalem shows the walled Old City (above, center) and the sprawling New City, where most of the fighting in the 1948 war occurred. The 24-day siege of Jerusalem by Arab Legion troops was broken on June 11, 1948, when the first Israeli convoy made its way into the city. Trucks traveled on a road Israeli workers had built, mostly at night, around Arab gun emplacements. The truce that followed the siege gave the Israelis time to recoup.

Several times the Egyptian officers regrouped their men, formed them into a skirmish line, and sent them into the teeth of the Israeli positions. Each time the result was the same. At length the Egyptians decided to bypass Nirim and make for the coastal road they were sure would lead them to Tel Aviv and Jerusalem.

The fighting at Nirim established a pattern on both the southern and northern fronts. Arab officers proved timid tacticians, wary of pressing their advantage. Their men, prepared for easy victories, were consistently thrown into confusion by stiff Israeli resistance. To make matters worse, numerous Arab politicians, particularly those in Egypt, had seen the war as a chance for quick profit. Funds earmarked for food, boots, and weapons made their way into politicians' pockets instead of being used to support the soldiers in the field, and what had been billed as a triumphant Arab sweep to Tel Aviv soon turned into a stalemate.

The Battle for Jerusalem

Only on the eastern front did the Arabs make impressive progress. There the superbly trained, well-armed, highly disciplined Arab Legion of Transjordan thrust quickly toward Jerusalem, laying siege to the New City on May 19 and capturing the Old City on May 28. About 100,000 Jews lived in the New City, which the Israelis then intended to make the capital of their nation. But with Arab shells pouring into the New City and its supply lines cut, it appeared virtually certain that Israeli-held Jerusalem would yield either to Arab Legion assaults or to starvation. Time and again shock troops of the Israeli Army attempted to storm legion positions commanding the highway to the coast, and time and again they were driven off with heavy casualties. Finally, in desperation, the Israelis determined to build a detour, a three-mile-long road skirting the legion's artillery nests. Working under constant bombardment, along terrain that a goat might have had difficulty traversing, Israeli work crews raced against time to complete the road before starvation forced Jerusalem's surrender. So certain were Arab Legion officers that the road would never be completed that aside from the harassing artillery fire they made scant efforts to prevent the work. But on the morning of June 11, 1948, the first Israeli convoy rumbled down the new road into the city. The 24-day siege was broken and Jerusalem was saved. The lead truck bore the words of the ancient Hebrew prayer: "If I forget thee,

THE PALESTINE LIBERATION ORGANIZATION

After the war of 1948 about half a million Palestinian Arabs left Israel to seek new lives in neighboring Arab States. Some were fortunate, but many were detained in dismal refugee camps in Jordan, Syria, the Gaza Strip, the occupied West Bank, and Lebanon, where an estimated 644,000 still live. In 1964 it became clear that the Palestinians could not rely on a united Arab front to press their claims, and the Palestine Liberation Organization—the PLO—was founded. After Israel's takeover of Arab territories in the 1967 war (see pp. 484–487), the Al Fatah wing of the PLO, led by Yasir Arafat, became prominent, aiming to regain Arab lands by eliminating Israel. In 1974 the PLO, whose terrorist factions include the Popular Front for the Liberation of Palestine and the Black September movement, was recognized by Arab leaders as the legitimate representative of the Palestinian people. Israel, however, consistently refused to negotiate with the organization.

Haganah soldiers drive Arabs out of the vital port of Haifa.

O Jerusalem, may my right hand forget its cunning."

On the same day Jerusalem was relieved, the clamor of battle in the Holy Land suddenly ceased. After a fierce debate in the U.N. the Arab states agreed to a month-long truce mediated by Count Folke Bernadotte of Sweden. (Bernadotte was assassinated by the Stern group on September 17, 1948.) Having failed in their efforts to crush Israel, the Arabs now fell to wrangling among themselves, each nation blaming the others for the failure. With each passing day the morale of the Arab troops sank lower and lower, the high expectations of May yielding to the undeniable fact of defeat in June. The Israelis, however, put the truce to good advantage. Weaponry recently imported was distributed, and new army units were formed, many made up of refugees only days off the boats from Europe.

From Truce to Rout

When fighting resumed after the truce period, on July 8, 1948, demoralized Arab armies found themselves confronted with a vastly improved foe, and in a 10-day offensive the Israeli armed forces swept the fields of battle, clearing Galilee of the Syrian, Lebanese, and Iraqi salients and opening the old highway to Jerusalem. In little more than a week they had achieved their objectives and were ready to turn their attention to the Egyptian salient in the south, when a new U.N. truce temporarily ended the combat. In the fall of 1948 and the winter of 1948–49 a series of truce violations gave Israel the opportunity to move against the Egyptians. First, Egyptian troops were cleared from a salient on the Negev's northern edge, then they were routed from the depths of the Negev itself, leaving Israel with a reasonably secure southern flank.

By the first anniversary of independence it was clear that a new power had arisen in the Middle East. Israel had not only survived but had extended its territory by about a third. Yet survival had cost the nation dearly. Some 6,000 Israelis had been killed, almost 1 percent of the population. Arab deaths were even greater. The defeat was made more bitter for the Arabs by their feeling that they had been treated unfairly. During the next quarter century Israel would fight three major wars to ward off Arab threats to its existence. Yet despite the cost and suffering, Zionism in 1948 had, against overwhelming odds, realized a dream of centuries: The wandering Jew of history had secured a home in the land of his ancestors.

THE LIFE OF THE TIMES

1945-56

*The "**GI Bill of Rights,**" the Servicemen's Readjustment Act of 1944, eased the transition to civilian life for World War II veterans. Its benefits enabled nearly 8 million ex-servicemen to continue their education, often while raising a growing family.*

The postwar decade promised to be a safer, better time for Americans. The most devastating war in history had ended, and millions of veterans thankfully packed away their uniforms, bought new "civvies" with their mustering-out pay, pinned "ruptured duck" discharge buttons on their lapels, and set out to enjoy the fruits of peace. Although much of the world was in ruins, the United States was more powerful than ever.

After 15 years of economic hardship and wartime disruption young men and women wanted more than anything to build a happy, secure future. They were determined that their own children would enjoy all the comforts and advantages they had missed. The generous loan and assistance provisions of the GI Bill of Rights, passed in 1944, offered millions of veterans the opportunity to obtain a free college education, a good job, and a comfortable home. In 1946 nearly half of the 2 million U.S. college students were war veterans. Millions more were buying their own homes with little or no money down and 30 years to pay.

To meet this sudden demand for new housing, builders bought up vast tracts of vacant land outside urban centers and rushed to put up thousands of look-alike houses. Before long a new kind of community, the suburb, had become the hub of the American middle class.

Most suburban homes were built on such popular designs as the ranch, the split level, the colonial, and the Cape Cod, the last two imitating more traditional Georgian and New England styling. Many came with the latest conveniences, including huge freezers for storing the new timesaving frozen foods, and clothes washers and dryers. Picture windows, carports, and backyard patios were standard features, as were unfinished attics or basements, which could be converted into family rooms.

Almost everyone seemed to be planning a large family. Public opinion polls in 1945 reported that the average American woman hoped to have four or more children, and the country was soon experiencing a prodigious "baby boom." By the early 1950's some 5 million more children were crowding the nation's classrooms.

Under the guidance of Dr. Benjamin Spock's 1946 manual, *Common Sense Book of Baby and Child Care,* parents were taking a new approach to child rearing. Spock's bestselling guide was read, reread—and frequently misread—by millions of postwar mothers and fathers. He urged them to replace the sterner methods of older generations with more sympathy and understanding. Asserting that "there's no such thing as a bad boy," he encouraged fathers to become pals with their sons.

Suburban lifestyles reflected these new attitudes toward children, and most homes were designed to promote family togetherness. Mom, Dad, and the kids gathered in the family room each night and on

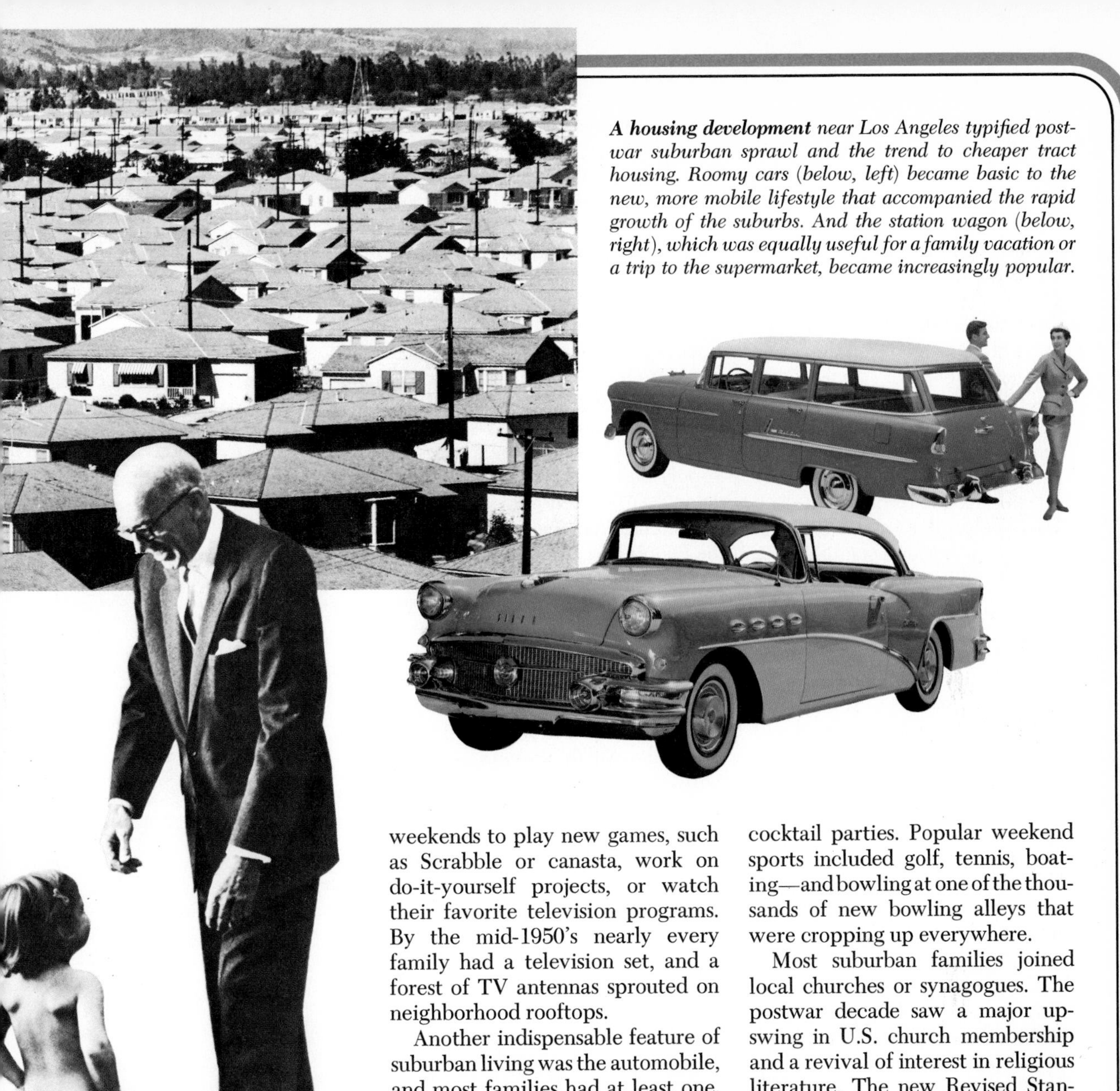

***A housing development** near Los Angeles typified postwar suburban sprawl and the trend to cheaper tract housing. Roomy cars (below, left) became basic to the new, more mobile lifestyle that accompanied the rapid growth of the suburbs. And the station wagon (below, right), which was equally useful for a family vacation or a trip to the supermarket, became increasingly popular.*

***Dr. Benjamin Spock** (above) advocated a new permissiveness in his* Common Sense Book of Baby and Child Care, *published in 1946. Millions of American mothers relied on his down-to-earth approach for guidance and reassurance, as they and their children weathered the Terrible Two's and other challenging phases of childhood.*

weekends to play new games, such as Scrabble or canasta, work on do-it-yourself projects, or watch their favorite television programs. By the mid-1950's nearly every family had a television set, and a forest of TV antennas sprouted on neighborhood rooftops.

Another indispensable feature of suburban living was the automobile, and most families had at least one. Mother doubled as the family chauffeur, dropping Dad at the station to commute to his urban office, taking the kids to their piano or dancing lessons, scout meetings, and Little League practice. In between she could do the grocery shopping and other errands at one of the new suburban shopping centers. Detroit's answer to these demands was the station, or ranch, wagon, designed to carry groceries, dogs, and children comfortably and to load and unload easily.

Suburban social gatherings were informal. Entertaining consisted of family-style backyard barbecues or cocktail parties. Popular weekend sports included golf, tennis, boating—and bowling at one of the thousands of new bowling alleys that were cropping up everywhere.

Most suburban families joined local churches or synagogues. The postwar decade saw a major upswing in U.S. church membership and a revival of interest in religious literature. The new Revised Standard Version of the Bible topped nonfiction bestseller lists from 1952 to 1954, and books like Lloyd C. Douglas' *The Big Fisherman* (1948), Fulton Oursler's *The Greatest Story Ever Told* (1949), and Norman Vincent Peale's *The Power of Positive Thinking* (1952) were widely read. Hit tunes included "The Man Upstairs" and "I Believe," and such revivalists as Billy Graham preached to recordbreaking crowds.

An Age of Anxiety

While the postwar years brought an unprecedented degree of prosperity and material comfort to the American people, they did not bring the peace that had been promised. The war in Europe and the Pacific was followed by another kind of conflict, in some ways more sinister and alarming than its predecessor. As the late forties passed into the early fifties, the American way of life, indeed the future existence of the human race, seemed threatened by the hostile force of Soviet communism and the possibility of nuclear warfare between the United States and the U.S.S.R.

In the final days of World War II the Soviet Union, whose armies had liberated Eastern Europe from Nazi occupation, began establishing a series of satellite states there. As one country after another fell into the Soviet sphere, British statesman Winston Churchill warned in March 1946 that "an Iron Curtain has descended across the Continent [of Europe]." With most nations of Western Europe weak and in ruins, it was feared that they would be the next target of Communist expansion. In 1947 U.S. President Harry S. Truman announced a new foreign policy aimed at containing communism by supporting anti-Communist forces in Europe and throughout the world. A year later the Marshall Plan began providing billions of dollars to rebuild the economies of Western Europe. When the Soviet Union responded by temporarily blockading Berlin, the United States, Canada, and 10 other nations formed a military alliance, the North Atlantic Treaty Organization, or NATO.

In September 1949 the American public was stunned by news that the U.S.S.R. had broken the U.S. monopoly on nuclear weapons by developing its own atomic bomb. The next month Mao Tse-tung declared the People's Republic of China, and the world's most populous nation became Communist. In June 1950 troops from Communist North Korea invaded U.S.-supported South Korea. When the United States sent troops to aid the South Koreans and Red China sent troops to aid the North Koreans, a third world war seemed imminent.

The Red Scare of the early fifties reached a climax in the case of Julius and Ethel Rosenberg, convicted in 1951 of passing atomic secrets to Soviet agents. Their death sentences touched off worldwide protests—as well as such counter-demonstrations as the one below. Though much of the evidence was questionable, higher courts upheld the sentence, and in 1953 the Rosenbergs were electrocuted. Below: Senator Joe McCarthy, whose frequently reckless charges against public officials spurred the anti-Communist frenzy.

***Not many fallout shelters** were as elaborate as this fortress-home in Washington State (above), but by the late 1950's thousands of more modest versions had been built in basements and backyards across the country.*

The Beat Generation *first gained the public's attention in the mid-1950's through the work of two young writers, Jack Kerouac (above) and Allen Ginsberg (right). Ginsberg's best-known poem, "Howl," published in 1956, startled readers with the bitter, provocative tone of its opening (upper right).*

I saw the best minds of my generation destroyed by madness,
starving hysterical naked,
dragging themselves through the negro streets at dawn
looking for an angry fix. . . .
—From "Howl" by Allen Ginsberg

To prepare for it, Congress passed the Civil Defense Act of 1950, authorizing the creation of public fallout shelters across the country and providing instructions for what to do in the event of a nuclear attack. Many families began building backyard shelters and stocking them with water and stores of nonperishable canned goods. In school air-raid drills children learned to duck under their desks and cover the back of their necks with their hands. Civil defense volunteers took to the rooftops to scan the skies for Soviet bombers, and a rash of reports of unidentified flying objects (UFO's) raised fears of invasion from outer space. President Truman announced on January 31, 1950, that U.S. scientists had begun work on developing a hydrogen bomb, with a force equal to several hundred atomic bombs, in an effort to restore America's deterrent power and world military leadership.

The Red Scare

Meanwhile, there appeared to be evidence of Communist infiltration at high levels of the U.S. government. In 1948 the House Un-American Activities Committee (HUAC) began investigating charges by a former Soviet agent that Alger Hiss, a former State Department official, had passed secret documents on to him. Hiss denied the charges but was later convicted of perjury. Then, in October 1949, 11 high-ranking officials of the U.S. Communist Party were found guilty of violating the Smith Act, which forbade the teaching of doctrines advocating the violent overthrow of the U.S. government. A few months later the British government announced that it had arrested Dr. Klaus Fuchs, who had worked at the Los Alamos atomic bomb project, and that he had admitted leaking atomic secrets to the Soviets. A subsequent roundup of his alleged accomplices in the U.S.A. resulted in the still-controversial trial, conviction, and execution of Julius and Ethel Rosenberg.

These disclosures caused a wave of public hysteria. After the Hiss trial the House Un-American Activities Committee began a frantic search for hidden Communists and their associates (known variously as pinkos or fellow travelers). During public hearings informers, protected by congressional immunity, brought charges against scores of men and women for subversive Communist activities. Among them were a number of Hollywood scriptwriters, university professors, intellectuals, and others—including, most surprisingly, J. Robert Oppenheimer, head of the U.S. A-bomb development program.

In the midst of this panic-ridden atmosphere Wisconsin Senator Joseph McCarthy launched a vicious four-year smear campaign in an attempt to further his own political career. In February 1950 McCarthy declared he had proof (which he never revealed) that the State Department was riddled with Communists. Cloaked in congressional immunity, McCarthy used slander and innuendo to attack whomever he chose. His targets included Professor Owen Lattimore of Johns Hopkins University; Philip C. Jessup, a U.S. representative to the United Nations; Gen. George C. Marshall; Gen. Dwight D. Eisenhower; Secretary of State Dean Acheson; and President Truman. Although many criticized the tactics of the Senator's Communist witch hunt, a large number of people supported him, including members of the Republican Party, who hoped to make political hay out of his charges that the Democratic administration was soft on communism. When McCarthy began attacking the U.S. Army for covering up subversive activities in its ranks, however, his fortunes changed. The series of televised hearings on the army charges exposed the shabbiness of McCarthy's tactics, and public revulsion set in. In December 1954 the Senate passed a vote of condemnation against him, and thereafter he faded rapidly from the public scene, leaving behind a string of ruined reputations and careers and an overriding public fear of nonconformity and all forms of extremism.

The Eisenhower Years

The end of the McCarthy era at home coincided with a temporary easing of international tension. Soviet dictator Joseph Stalin died on March 5, 1953, and a truce was signed in Korea later that year. In January 1953 a new President, embodying the American ideals of decency, self-reliance, and hard work, took office. Under his leadership the United States embarked on a safe middle-of-the-road course at home and abroad. One of the most popular Presidents in U.S. history, former Gen. Dwight D. Eisenhower was reelected in 1956 by a landslide.

In contrast to the turbulent, uncertain time of the Truman administration, the mood of the Eisenhower years was secure and tranquil. In the mid-1950's, however, some Americans began to rebel against their society's restrictions. One such group, known as beatniks, protested the conformity and commercialization of American life. The Beats, as they called themselves, were a group of poets, performers, and artists who collected on the east and west coasts in the mid-1950's. Bohemian in their habits and appearance, they were united by a common sense of detachment from the contemporary world. Some of their works, notably Allen Ginsberg's poem "Howl" (1956) and Jack Kerouac's novel *On the Road* (1957), have since become literary landmarks.

More ominous were the motorcycle and street gangs that plagued some parts of the country in the mid-1950's. These youthful hoodlums (or hoods for short) roamed city streets and interstate highways in vandal wolfpacks, drinking, stealing, and committing violence. Their

On Broadway, *musicals integrated the lyrics and story more closely with dance.* South Pacific, Guys and Dolls, *and* The King and I *were among the stream of popular productions, but the poster at right is from the musical that broke all attendance records,* My Fair Lady.

Jackie Robinson *(below) became the first black baseball player in the modern major leagues when he joined the Brooklyn Dodgers in 1947. His acceptance opened the way for other blacks, some of whom became the sport's greatest stars. In 1962 he also became the first black to be elected to the Baseball Hall of Fame.*

James Dean, *Hollywood's symbol of rebellion, was less articulate than Ginsberg and the Beats, but his roles and his personal life fulfilled teenage dreams so well that a cult centered around him lasted long after his death in a car crash in 1955. He had been in Hollywood a year and acted in only three films. His fans saw them again and again.*

rootless lifestyle was depicted in popular movies like *The Wild One* with Marlon Brando (1954) and *Rebel Without a Cause* starring James Dean (1955). Many teenagers aped their insolent manners, slicked their hair back in ducktails, wore black leather motorcycle jackets and tight jeans, and borrowed expressions like "cool," "way out," and "square."

Perhaps the most dramatic outgrowth of the new teenage culture was its music. In 1955 a song by Bill Haley and The Comets, "Rock Around the Clock," became an overnight hit, introducing the new style of rock and roll. A year later a greasy-haired crooner named Elvis Presley burst on the scene wearing tight jeans, gyrating to the new beat, and driving a whole generation crazy with "Hound Dog," "Heartbreak Hotel," and a dozen other hits. Parents were horrified, but their teenage sons and daughters mobbed Elvis' personal appearances and bought millions of his records. It was the first sign of a widening gap between the two generations.

In the South another type of rebellion was brewing, and it would become a major theme in the next decade: The U.S. Negro, long treated as a second-class citizen, had begun to demand equal rights. Although some states passed civil rights legislation, such illegal Jim Crow practices as segregated seating on public transportation were common in the South. And "gentlemen's agreements" among real estate brokers and clients prevented the sale or rental of property to certain minority groups, particularly blacks, throughout the country.

In 1954, however, the Supreme Court ruled that segregation in public schools was unconstitutional, and three years later President Eisenhower called upon federal troops to enforce integration in Little Rock, Arkansas. In 1955 a young Baptist minister, Martin Luther King, Jr., organized a peaceful boycott of buses in Montgomery, Alabama, to protest the arrest of a black woman for refusing to give her seat to a white. Much more would be heard of him in the years to come.

***Between 1945 and 1955** Norma Jean Baker (right) metamorphosed from a photographer's model for cheesecake magazine covers to blonde Marilyn Monroe (below, in the film* Bus Stop*), the object of every American man's dreams. Yet, underneath her smiling facade were complex problems that ultimately led to her death from an overdose of barbiturates in 1962. The decade for which she was a symbol would also turn from a surface normality to violence.*

***Teenage girls** screamed and fainted when Elvis Presley came near. "Elvis the Pelvis," as he was known for the pelvic gyrations that accompanied his performances, actually had a good voice. Some of his imitators who became popular did not.*

1955

Jim Crow Is Dead!

Martin Luther King, Jr., a charismatic black minister, leads his people in boycotts, sit-ins, and marches that help end legal segregation in the U.S.A.

On Thursday evening, December 1, 1955, Mrs. Rosa Parks, a middle-aged black seamstress, boarded a nearly empty bus in downtown Montgomery, Alabama. "Bone weary," as she later remembered, and laden with groceries, she paid the 10-cent fare and sat in the first seat she came upon, a seat that by law and local custom was in the section set aside for whites only. The bus filled up as it rolled along, until other black passengers were standing at the rear. Then, in front of the Empire Theater, six more whites got on. The driver called out matter-of-factly, "Niggers move back," and three blacks meekly rose to give up their seats to the newcomers.

But Mrs. Parks refused to move. "I don't know why I wouldn't move," she later recalled. "There was no plot or plan at all. I was just tired from shopping. My feet hurt." The angry, disbelieving driver called a policeman. Mrs. Parks was arrested, booked, fingerprinted, and briefly jailed for violating a city ordinance that required busdrivers to tell passengers where to sit. A hearing was set for the following Monday.

Rosa Parks' personal rebellion was not the first protest against the indignity of segregated seating aboard city buses. Three earlier attempts had been made but had caused little stir. Mrs. Parks, however, was well known in the Negro community. She had acted as secretary of the local branch of the National Association for the Advancement of Colored People (NAACP), and news of her arrest angered virtually all of Montgomery's 50,000 black citizens. A group of 25 Negro ministers met at the Dexter Avenue Baptist Church to consider a community-wide expression of support for her spontaneous gesture of defiance. Encouraged by the 1954 U.S. Supreme Court decision in *Brown* v. *Board of Education of Topeka* that had declared segregated public education unlawful, many blacks believed the time was ripe to move against segregated public facilities as well. After some discussion the ministers settled upon a one-day black boycott of the city buses to coincide with Mrs. Parks' trial.

Because the Negro population was traditionally divided along strict class lines, few believed that such a boycott could succeed. Yet thanks to fervent pulpit appeals for unity on Sunday morning, and despite the real hardships it imposed on the city's Negro poor (some of whom had to trudge six miles to and from work), the boycott proved over 90 percent effective. Meanwhile, Mrs. Parks was found guilty; her attorneys immediately appealed the verdict.

The "Weapon of Love"

The ministers then called for the boycott to continue until three relatively modest demands were met: Black passengers were to be treated with courtesy, black drivers were to be assigned to primarily black routes, and seating was to be on a first-come, first-served basis with whites starting from the front of the bus, blacks from the rear. As their leader the pastors elected the newly appointed 26-year-old minister of the host church, Dr. Martin Luther King, Jr. The son and grandson of activist ministers, King had been trained at Atlanta's Morehouse College, Crozer Theological Seminary, and Boston University. His fellow pastors hoped his erudition and oratorical skills would help sustain the boycott and make him an effective negotiator with the white community. Few suspected that in choosing him they were launching the meteoric career of the most important civil rights champion of his time.

King had already discovered the "spirit of passive resistance" in the teachings of Jesus and had learned how to apply them to social and political issues from studying the life and work of the father of free India, Mohandas Gandhi (see pp. 160–163). The boycott gave him a chance to use what he termed "the weapon of love" to alter century-old patterns of legally enforced segregation.

Under King's inspiring leadership the boycott continued and quickly demonstrated the peaceful power the once-powerless Negro community could wield. Bus revenues fell 65 percent. Downtown business declined. Citywide carpools were formed, and black taxi drivers transported black passengers for a dime. Biweekly rallies, enlivened by King's charismatic preaching, helped keep morale high.

In March, three months after the bus boycott had been launched, King and 89 other black leaders were

The 1955 arrest *of seamstress Rosa Parks (lower right) for refusing to vacate the "whites only" section of a Montgomery, Alabama, bus sparked the public career of black leader Rev. Martin Luther King, Jr. At the high-water mark of the civil rights movement in August 1963, King (center, with his coworker Rev. Ralph Abernathy) exhorted over 150,000 Freedom Marchers with his famous "I have a dream" speech.*

"I have a dream today. I have a dream that one day every valley shall be exalted, every hill and mountain shall be made low, the rough places will be made plains, and the crooked places will be made straight, and the glory of the Lord shall be revealed and all flesh shall see it together . . . and if America is to be a great nation this must become true. So let freedom ring. From every mountainside, let freedom ring... When we let freedom ring, when we let it ring from every village and every hamlet, from every state and every city, we will be able to speed up that day when all of God's children will be able to join hands and sing in the words of the old Negro spiritual, 'Free at last! free at last! thank God Almighty, we are free at last!'"

—Martin Luther King, Jr.

found guilty of violating an obscure 1921 antilabor law forbidding boycotts; they immediately appealed. The following November the city went to court again, demanding an injunction to halt the carpools and seeking massive damages for the loss of tax revenues caused by the boycott. "This may well be the darkest hour before dawn," King warned his followers. "We have moved all these months with daring faith . . . we must go on with that same faith." November 13 was set for a hearing; if the boycott leaders lost, many believed, 11 months of effort would have been in vain, and southern segregation would survive intact.

The Emergence of Jim Crow

Segregation had a long and sordid history in the United States. The Civil War freed some 4 million slaves, and for a time it seemed that the postwar federal government would insure that the freedmen would enter the mainstream of American life. Yet hopes for an integrated South were short lived. When Reconstruction ended and federal troops were withdrawn in 1877, white southerners lost little time in reasserting their supremacy. With the blessings of a conservative Supreme Court, southern states began producing a blizzard of segregationist Jim Crow laws (so called after an old minstrel song, "Jump Jim Crow"), and by the early 20th century black people throughout the South were legally barred from white-only schools, theaters, restaurants, hotels, streetcars, cemeteries, parks, and virtually every other type of public facility. In addition, an ingenious system of laws—poll taxes, preposterous literacy tests, and "grandfather clauses" excluding anyone whose grandfather had not been a voter—prevented the vast majority of blacks from voting.

In the face of such barriers two organizations were formed—the National Association for the Advancement of Colored People (NAACP) and the National Urban League—that lobbied together for decades to promote greater legal and economic equality. The 1954 school desegregation decision (won by NAACP lawyers) accelerated the momentum for social change, and when Rosa Parks refused to give up her seat on a Montgomery bus a year later, she sparked the imagination—and the conscience—of millions of Americans.

But as Martin Luther King, Jr., entered the Montgomery courtroom on November 13, 1956, he was near despair. The presiding judge was the same one who had found Mrs. Parks guilty almost a year earlier. An injunction halting the carpools that had formed the boycott's backbone seemed inevitable, and King feared that further calls for sacrifice from the weary black community might go unheeded. Brooding at the defense table, he barely heard the lawyer's arguments. Then, near noon, a reporter handed him a tele-

Education was a hot issue *in early civil rights confrontations. In September 1957 President Dwight D. Eisenhower ordered 1,000 federal paratroopers to Little Rock, Arkansas, to assure the admission of nine black children to Central High School (below left). The black students had been barred from the school by Governor Orval A. Faubus. In 1962, when Air Force veteran James Meredith became the first black student at the University of Mississippi, federal marshals were assigned to escort him to and from classes (below). Within a decade the focus of the battle for educational equality was to switch to the teeming urban centers of the North.*

type message from one of the wire services: The U.S. Supreme Court had upheld a district court ruling that made segregated seating on buses unconstitutional.

"God Almighty has spoken from Washington, D.C.!" shouted one exuberant onlooker. The boycott had worked. Characteristically, King urged his followers to be magnanimous. Their victory, he said, was a victory for all Americans, not just Negroes. It took more than a month for the ruling officially to reach Montgomery, but on December 21, 1956, King and a white minister boarded a city bus and rode together without incident. Though a few outraged whites continued to resist, peppering integrated buses with buckshot and bombing several churches, the Montgomery movement had demonstrated the effectiveness of peaceful protest, and it had made Martin Luther King a nationally known figure.

For the next dozen years King was the inspirational symbol and sometime leader of the peaceful struggle for civil rights in the United States. Through his Atlanta-based Southern Christian Leadership Conference (SCLC), established in 1957, he sought to foster "creative tension" in southern cities and towns through firm but peaceful defiance of laws and customs that he considered evil. Warning white authorities that "we will wear you down by our capacity to suffer," he trained his thousands of adherents to endure indignity, imprisonment, violence, even the threat of death, to shame the nation into righting century-old wrongs. He was not always successful. Some city administrations proved utterly intransigent, willing to shut down parks, public pools, and libraries rather than share them with all their citizens. King's old-fashioned pulpit style annoyed and embarrassed some young blacks. So did his constant assurances to whites that however he and his followers were treated, "we will love you." To fiery black nationalists like Malcolm X, who worked in the tough big-city ghettos of the North, such talk seemed unnatural, weak, and even cowardly. Conservative blacks, on the other hand, worried that King's activism was too radical.

Even while King and his SCLC lieutenants mapped a systematic city-by-city assault on Southern segregation, events elsewhere added fuel to the fires of the "Negro revolution." Southern defiance of school desegregation court orders brought a somewhat reluctant federal government into the struggle.

In 1957 the Governor of Arkansas pleased his white constituents but embarrassed the nation by sending National Guardsmen with bayonets to keep black pupils from attending Little Rock's all-white Central High School. Though President Dwight Eisenhower privately believed the 1954 school decision had "set racial progress back 15 years," he sent in paratroopers who successfully upheld the law and safeguarded the students' right to a desegregated education.

The same year Congress enacted a civil rights law that empowered the federal government to move

*"**If Martin Luther King** hadn't come to this county, people wouldn't have been able to register to vote. King gave us the courage that nothing would happen to us . . . King got us to the place where we wasn't afraid. And he told us to be together. We needed someone to stand for us who wasn't afraid."* —*Joseph Lee Anderson of Camden, Alabama.*

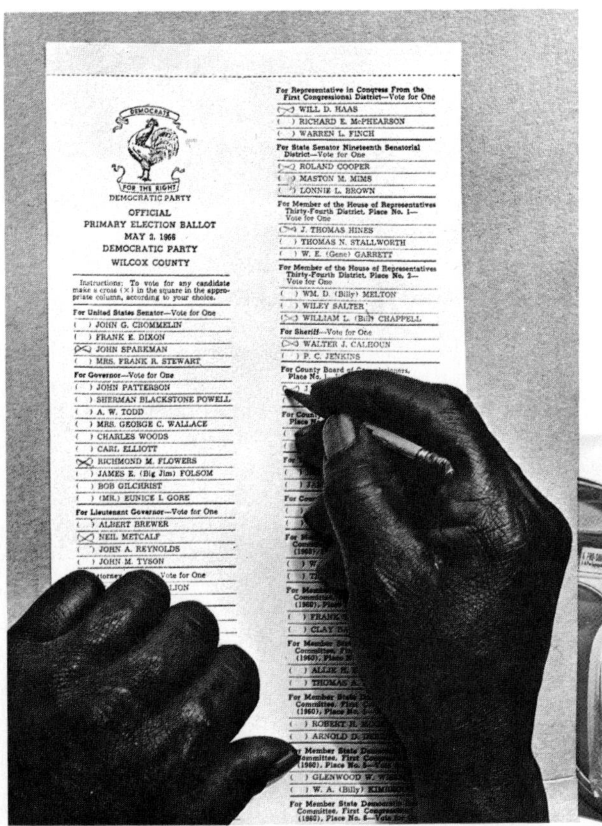

Defiant segregationists *in the mid-1950's sought to stem the South's movement toward integration and civil liberties.*

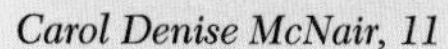

Carol Denise McNair, 11

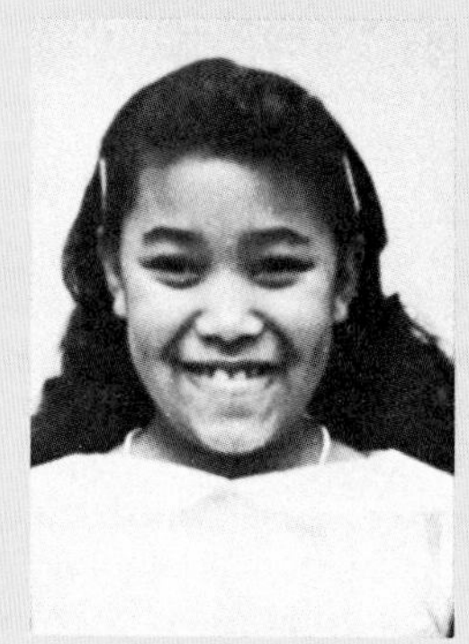

Carole Robertson, 14

Addie Mae Collins, 14

Cynthia Dianne Wesley, 14

"If they can find those fellows they ought to put medals on them. It wasn't no shame they was killed. Why? Because when I go out to kill rattlesnakes, I don't make no difference between little rattlesnakes and big rattlesnakes . . . I say good for whoever planted the bomb."—Klan speaker, commenting on the deaths of four black Sunday school students in the bombing of a Birmingham, Alabama, church in September 1963.

KKK: THE INVISIBLE EMPIRE

"Murders of Negroes are so common as to render it impossible to keep accurate accounts of them," a congressional committee was advised in 1871. The speaker was describing the actions of the Ku Klux Klan, an organization of bedsheet-wearing terrorists whose "fundamental objective" was "the maintenance of the supremacy of the white race in this republic." Despite declining membership, the Klan persists today, wallowing in the legacy of its invisible empire: burnings, shootings, floggings, maimings, bombings of churches and homes. Aiming a steady stream of racist filth at black people and Jews, the United Klans of America coordinates its grotesque efforts to divide the nation with those of the neo-Nazi National States Rights Party and simultaneously soft-pedals its advocacy of violence in an effort to win new recruits to its malignant cause.

against some forms of discriminatory voter registration. It was a relatively weak bill, but as the first civil rights statute since 1875, it had great symbolic impact. So did the successful struggle of blacks on the African continent to overthrow colonial rule. For the first time in living memory large numbers of Africans in the homeland were running their own affairs. American Negroes took a new pride in their ancestry.

The Rush Toward Freedom

Almost from the first King found himself racing to catch up with his eager followers. In February 1960 four Negro college freshmen at Greensboro, North Carolina, entered an F. W. Woolworth store and sat at the lunch counter. (Throughout the South blacks were encouraged to shop in department stores but forbidden to eat at lunch counters open to white patrons.) The shocked waitress avoided the students until closing time, but when they returned the next morning with 25 friends, all were arrested. News of their bold nonviolent protest swept southern campuses. With King's encouragement, and under the supervision of the newly formed Student Nonviolent Coordinating Committee (SNCC), similar demonstrations spread throughout the region. Students conducted "sit-ins" at restaurants and lunch counters, "wade-ins" at public pools and beaches, "sleep-ins" in hotel lobbies. They were jeered, spat upon, beaten, and jailed, but by the end of the year four department store chains had agreed to desegregate, others were about to follow suit, and nightly television news coverage had alerted the nation—and much of the world—both to the ugly reality of racial segregation and to the new determination of Negroes to end it.

In the spring of 1961 the Congress of Racial Equality (CORE), an interracial activist group founded in 1942, dispatched bands of black and white Freedom Riders aboard buses into the Deep South to test local compliance with court rulings that forbade segregated seating in bus terminal waiting rooms. While local officials stood by, some riders were beaten senseless by irate mobs. Buses were set ablaze. Finally, U.S. Attorney General Robert Kennedy sent in 400 federal marshals to protect the Freedom Riders' right to travel. In September the Interstate Commerce Commission forbade segregation on interstate carriers or in the terminals from which they operated.

The rush of events forced the federal government to become at least a part-time partner in the Negro struggle. In 1956 Autherine Lucy, a black woman, won admittance to the University of Alabama by court order; but Washington remained silent when the institution first suspended her for having "caused" whites to riot by her presence, then expelled her for daring to object. Six years later, when the Governor of Mississippi, in open defiance of a court order, sought to bar

James Meredith, a Negro air force veteran, from the University of Mississippi at Oxford, Kennedy dispatched federal marshals and 12,000 federalized National Guardsmen to the campus. In a night of rioting two men were killed and dozens were wounded, but Meredith was enrolled. In 1957 Governor George C. Wallace of Alabama, who had vowed to maintain "segregation today, segregation tomorrow, segregation forever," and who had promised to "stand in the schoolhouse door" rather than allow blacks and whites to attend the same schools, acquiesced in the enrollment of two Negroes at the University of Alabama.

Meanwhile, King and others fought their peaceful battles in the dusty streets of scores of southern cities and towns, courageously facing threats of violence and even of death. In 1963, the centennial of the Emancipation Proclamation, there were some 10,000 racial demonstrations in the United States. In April of that year Birmingham, Alabama—perhaps the South's most segregated city—became King's prime target. Several weeks of peaceful marches had resulted in little progress and a record 2,500 arrests at the hands of public safety director Eugene "Bull" Conner, a tough segregationist who sported a large button that read "Never." Daily marches—in which large numbers of children took part for the first time—were met with ever-increasing white anger. In early May photographs and news film of burly policemen clubbing prostrate women, snarling dogs ripping the clothing of unarmed black men, and children knocked to the ground by powerful firehoses circled the globe and produced an international outcry of shock and anger. President John F. Kennedy had already called for a new civil rights bill to integrate virtually all public accommodations. "We are confronted primarily with a moral issue," he declared, ". . . as old as the Scriptures and . . . as clear as the American Constitution." The brutal tactics of Bull Connor did much to win its eventual passage.

Sensing defeat, diehard segregationists struck back with cruel violence. Medgar Evers, NAACP field secretary for Mississippi, was shot to death on his Jackson doorstep; four black girls were killed while attending Sunday school when their church was bombed in Birmingham; churches suspected of harboring civil rights meetings were razed; local leaders were beaten.

On August 28, 1963, King and a host of other civil rights leaders led some 250,000 blacks and whites in a "march on Washington for jobs and freedom." Gathered on the vast mall before the Lincoln Memorial, a

***A second generation** of black leaders like Eldridge Cleaver (lower right among the posters) radicalized the feelings of frustration and aimlessness that gripped the civil rights movement in the late 1960's. Espousing black power, separatism, and violent confrontation, they appealed to young, urban blacks left leaderless as a result of the death of Martin Luther King, Jr., and the declining prestige of his Southern Christian Leadership Conference. Their model and inspiration was pioneer black militant Malcolm X (below). One of the earliest proponents of separatism, Malcolm X renounced violence and black racism shortly before his death; he was assassinated in 1965, probably by a militant faction of the black Muslims.*

deliriously cheering throng heard King speak dramatically of his "dream that one day this nation will rise and live out the true meaning of its creed: 'We hold these truths to be self-evident; that all men are created equal.'" The jubilant, peaceful march—and the extraordinary speech—marked the high tide of King's influence in the civil rights struggle. The following year King was awarded the Nobel Prize for Peace.

Thanks in part to the legislative adroitness of the new President, Lyndon B. Johnson, the Kennedy civil rights bill was passed in June 1964. Any person who operated an establishment that catered to the passerby had to serve anyone asking for service. Among the notables who crowded around the President's desk to watch the signing of the historic bill was Rosa Parks, the courageous Montgomery seamstress.

New Progress and Old Problems

But the new bill's voting rights provisions were still inadequate to ensure full black access to the polls; local registrars evaded the law by unfairly administering registration tests. Accordingly, in the summer of 1964 a coalition of civil rights groups dispatched some 1,000 black and white student organizers into rural Mississippi, where discrimination at the polls was most blatant. Local whites fought back hard: Three civil rights workers were murdered, 1,000 arrests were made, and 35 black churches were set afire.

In February 1965 King led long lines of would-be voters to city hall in Selma, Alabama, a city in which the population was almost equally divided between blacks and whites, while the voter rolls were 99 percent white. Again demonstrators were beaten and jailed. When a local black woodcutter was killed, King called upon his followers to march on the state capitol at Montgomery. Governor Wallace forbade the march, and at his orders mounted deputies and club-swinging policemen waded into the would-be marchers, bludgeoning defenseless men and women to the ground.

News film of this horrifying scene produced a new outcry for federal action. President Johnson responded by proposing a new voting rights bill, then sent armed troops to guard the line of march. Some 25,000 black and white supporters followed King into Montgomery, the scene of his first nonviolent victory. The new law was passed with stunning swiftness: It suspended all literacy tests where less than 50 percent of the adult population had voted in 1964 and empowered federal registrars to move into areas where overt discrimination was being practiced. By the end of 1965 alone, a quarter of a million new black voters had been registered, and Negroes were already running for (and winning) local and state offices in places where they had not dared even to vote before.

All this activity helped spawn ferment among Negroes throughout the nation. The successful civil rights revolution led by King and directed primarily at the visible, statutory segregation of the South had not touched the lives of northern ghetto dwellers. Despite all of King's efforts, the yawning economic gap between blacks and whites continued to widen. Northern Negroes also began demanding change, a way out of the choked, crime-ridden, urban nightmare to which they were doomed by job discrimination and de facto housing segregation. As early as 1960 ghetto anger and frustration had erupted into violence in several cities. It grew steadily worse each year thereafter. Between 1964 and 1967 riots occurred in 58 cities. Whole neighborhoods were ravaged by arson and vandalism.

***For many American blacks** the assassination of Robert F. Kennedy on June 5, 1968, completed a triptych of civil rights martyrdom which included his brother, John F. Kennedy, and Rev. Martin Luther King, Jr. Emerging from a funeral at the Dixie Grove Baptist Church in Wilcox County, Alabama, two years later, a local woman displays a cardboard fan immortalizing the three Freedom Fighters with photographs and excerpts from their speeches. But it was the murder of King in April 1968 that generated the greatest feelings of despair and anger among blacks. The quiet protest of Boston youths on the day after the killing (above right) contrasted with a wave of rioting and arson that swept 125 cities in a spontaneous outburst of rage and grief.*

INTEGRATION AND THE BUSING CONTROVERSY

In the 1970's the familiar yellow school bus became the symbol of bitterness and breakdown in the drive for racial integration in America's classrooms.

Since the Brown decision in 1954, the federal courts have held that public schools must be desegregated under the Constitution. But because of segregated patterns in housing, particularly in northern cities, it has become increasingly obvious that the only way to integrate urban schools is by busing black and white students to schools far away from their homes. Such court-imposed plans have increasingly been greeted with parental opposition, violence, and questions challenging the basic philosophy of school integration.

Even assuming the beneficial effects of school integration, some blacks are beginning to doubt the value of busing, which seems to spur racial hostility and provide an excuse for rejecting desegregation, without improving the lot of the urban black student. To many, improvement of the schools seems a better solution than a temporary improvement in the racial balance of their students, who too often are viewed merely as ciphers in a political struggle.

King and his lieutenants tried but failed to make northern conditions yield to the nonviolent weapon they had honed in the southern struggle. A two-year SCLC campaign for open housing and more jobs for blacks in Chicago yielded little, and King himself was stoned by an angry white mob in the suburb of Cicero. Calling for a "reordering of national priorities" and a massive "Marshall Plan" to end poverty and discrimination in America, King came to view U.S. involvement in the Vietnam War as the major obstacle to domestic progress. His outspoken antiwar stand alienated both the once-friendly Johnson administration and moderates within the Negro movement itself. At the same time, his refusal to endorse violence or any form of black separatism drew the bitter scorn of the increasingly militant young. First SNCC and then CORE abandoned the goal of integration in favor of black power, an intentionally vague but deeply felt concept first popularized by SNCC firebrand Stokely Carmichael. To some it meant that blacks should control their own affairs within the American system, just as other ethnic minorities had tried to do; to others it meant black separatism. To nervous whites and some angry big-city blacks it simply meant "get whitey" and was a rallying cry for roaming, mindless rioters.

In the spring of 1968 King called for thousands of poor people of all races to come to the nation's capital that summer to dramatize their plight. He hoped such a massive, peaceful demonstration would rekindle the nonviolent movement and serve as an alternative to further violence. But in early April he went to Memphis, Tennessee, to show support for striking Negro garbage workers. There, on April 4, 1968, he was assassinated by James Earl Ray, a white ex-convict. Tragically, King's death sparked a new wave of urban rioting. In one week violence tore at 125 cities, killing 46 people, wounding 3,500, and destroying $45 million worth of property. For the first time in its history, the nation's capital was patrolled by tanks and armored cars to guard against the fury of its citizens.

The violence eventually subsided, but the struggle against racism clearly had not ended. In 1968 a Presidential commission that had studied the riots warned that "the nation is moving towards two societies, one black, one white, separate and unequal." Nonetheless, thanks largely to King and thousands of unsung followers, a century of statutory segregation had been swept away—though, in practice, the struggle for full equality for all Americans was still far from over. But King himself provided a hopeful view of the future. How long would it take to achieve full equality? he asked at the climax of the 1965 Montgomery march and then answered his own question in his characteristic cadences. "It will not take long," he said, "because truth pressed to earth will rise again. How long? Not long, because no lie can live forever. How long? Not long, because you still reap what you sow. How long? Not long, because the arm of the moral universe is long, but it bends toward justice."

AN ALMANAC 1945-56

1945

Aug. 6 Atomic bomb is dropped on Hiroshima, Japan, leading to end of World War II (see pp. 360–367).

Aug. 9 Soviet Union declares war on Japan, invades Manchuria.

Aug. 9 Atomic bomb explodes over Nagasaki, Japan.

Aug. 14 Japan agrees to terms for surrender presented by Allies with previous proviso of retaining Emperor.

Sept. 2 World War II ends; Japanese officials sign surrender documents on U.S. battleship *Missouri*.

Oct. 24 Birth of United Nations (see pp. 372–377).

Nov. 20 Nuremberg tribunal begins trial of 22 Nazi leaders.

1946

Feb. 14 Bank of England nationalized by new Labour government.

Mar. 5 Winston Churchill, in a landmark speech, warns the West of Soviet Iron Curtain across Europe and of Communist expansionist policies.

June 2–3 Italian voters approve referendum in favor of a republic. King Umberto II deposed.

June 3 U.S. Supreme Court rules racial segregation on interstate buses unconstitutional.

July 4 The Philippines gain independence after 47 years of U.S. rule.

Sept. 1 In national plebiscite Greeks approve a monarchical system and return King George II to throne.

Sept. 30–Oct. 1 The Nuremberg war crimes tribunal sentences 12 Nazis to death. (One, Hermann Goering, commits suicide Oct. 15.) Seven receive prison terms. Three acquitted.

Nov. 3 In Japan, the new constitution transfers political power from Emperor to elected bicameral legislature (Diet).

1947

Jan. 1 British Labour government nationalizes the coal mining industry.

Jan. 29 U.S.A. abandons its efforts to mediate in China between forces of Chiang Kai-shek and Mao Tse-tung.

Mar. 12 U.S. President Harry S. Truman announces Truman Doctrine: aid to countries threatened by communism.

June 5 U.S. Secretary of State George C. Marshall proposes the Marshall Plan, a program of massive economic aid to Europe by the United States.

June 23 The Taft-Hartley Labor Act, curbing powers of big labor unions, is passed by Congress over Truman's veto.

Aug. 8 South Africa refuses U.N. trusteeship of Southwest Africa.

Aug. 15 India, Pakistan, and Indian states become independent and separate (see pp. 390–395).

Sept. 2 Nineteen American republics sign the mutual assistance Treaty of Rio de Janeiro.

Oct. 5 Nine European Communist Parties establish the Cominform (Communist Information Bureau) to coordinate their activities.

Dec. 30 King Michael of Romania abdicates under pressure; Communist-controlled republic set up.

1948

Jan. 4 Union of Burma becomes an independent republic.

Jan. 30 Indian leader Mohandas Gandhi killed by an anti-Muslim fanatic.

Feb. 25 The coalition government in Czechoslovakia overthrown by Communist coup d'etat. Foreign Minister Jan Masaryk dies under mysterious circumstances Mar. 10; President Eduard Benes resigns June 7.

May 14 Independent State of Israel is proclaimed in Palestine; immediately attacked by five Arab states (see pp. 396–403).

June 24 Soviet forces block rail traffic between Berlin and West Germany (road traffic had already been halted). Western powers begin airlift of supplies to West Berlin a few days later.

June 28 Cominform expels Yugoslavia. Marshal Tito maintains charges against U.S.S.R. while denying hostility; wins mass support and party vote of confidence from Yugoslavs.

July 5 British National Health Services Acts provide free medical care for everyone "from cradle to grave."

Aug. 15 Republic of Korea established below 38th parallel; North Korea proclaimed Communist Sept. 9.

Nov. 2 Harry S. Truman wins reelection as U.S. President.

Nov. 12 War crimes tribunal sentences former Premier Hideki Tojo and six other Japanese leaders to death. Sixteen more receive life imprisonment.

Dec. 27 Hungarian Cardinal Mindszenty arrested for protesting nationalization of Catholic schools.

1949

Jan. 1 India and Pakistan agree to a cease-fire in disputed state of Jammu and Kashmir. Divide area between them in July.

Apr. 1 Newfoundland becomes 10th Canadian province.

Apr. 4 North Atlantic Treaty, providing for mutual defense against aggression, signed by U.S.A., Canada, and 10 Western European nations.

Apr. 18 Republic of Ireland proclaimed. On May 17 Great Britain reaffirms Northern Ireland's status within United Kingdom.

May 12 Soviets lift blockade of Berlin.

May 23 West Germany becomes separate state (German Federal Republic) under Allied control; East Germany established as German Democratic Republic under Soviet commission Oct. 7.

July 16 Generalissimo Chiang Kai-shek starts evacuating Nationalist troops from mainland China to Formosa.

Aug. 3 War in Indonesia ends. Dutch give Indonesia independence Nov. 2.

Sept. 18 Great Britain devalues pound from rate of $4.03 to $2.80. Other European nations subsequently devalue their currency in relation to U.S. dollar.

Sept. 23 U.S. monopoly of atomic power ends with announcement of Soviet atomic explosion.

Oct. 1 Communists proclaim People's Republic of China.

Oct. 16 Three-year Greek Civil War comes to an end.

1950

Jan. 25 Alger Hiss, former U.S. State Department official, convicted of perjury: revealed as former Communist agent.

Jan. 31 President Truman approves development of hydrogen bomb.

May 9 Schuman Plan, to pool German and French coal and steel, proposed.

June 25–28 Korean War begins when Communist North Korean forces invade South Korea.

July 20 Senate subcommittee rejects charges by Senator Joseph R. McCarthy that State Department is "infested" with Communists. But on Sept. 23 Congress passes law requiring Communists to register with government.

Sept. 15 U.N. forces under Gen. Douglas MacArthur land at Inchon, South Korea. Seoul retaken Sept. 26. South Koreans cross 38th parallel Oct. 1.

Oct. 7 U.N. General Assembly votes to reunify Korea; U.N. troops invade North Korea.

Oct. 25 Chinese Communists invade Tibet; control it by May 1951.

Nov. 5 U.N. forces retreat from Yalu River border. Chinese Communist troops cross 38th parallel into South Korea Dec. 29.

1951

Jan. 4 North Korean and Chinese Communist troops capture Seoul.

Feb. 26 Twenty-second Amendment to U.S. Constitution, limiting President to two four-year terms, ratified.

Mar. 14 U.N. forces recapture Seoul and stabilize positions along 38th parallel by Mar. 31.

Apr. 5 Convicted U.S. atomic bomb spies Julius Rosenberg and his wife, Ethel, sentenced to death for transmitting atomic secrets to Soviet agents; executed June 19, 1953.

Apr. 11 Truman fires General MacArthur for publicly opposing administration policy in Korea.

July 1 Communists agree to discuss a Korean cease-fire; talks begin July 10.

Sept. 8 Japan signs World War II peace treaty with 48 nations.

Oct. 25 Conservatives overturn Labour Party in British elections; Winston Churchill again Prime Minister.

1952

Jan. 24 Vincent Massey becomes first Canadian-born official to serve as Governor General of Canada.

Feb. 6 King George VI of Great Britain dies and is succeeded by his daughter Queen Elizabeth II.

Mar. 1 Jawaharlal Nehru's Congress Party wins large majority in India's first national elections.

July 26 King Farouk I abdicates throne of Egypt three days after military officers stage a coup d'etat.

Oct. 20 Great Britain declares a state of emergency in Kenya because of Mau Mau violence against whites.

Nov. 4 Republican Dwight D. Eisenhower elected U.S. President.

Nov. 6 U.S. successful in first major explosion of hydrogen weapon.

Dec. 3 Czechoslovakia announces execution of former Communist Secretary General Rudolf Slansky and 10 other party officials in high positions.

1953

Jan. 12 Yugoslavia adopts new constitution; Tito becomes President Jan. 14.

Mar. 5 Joseph Stalin, ruler of U.S.S.R. for 29 years, dies at 73. Georgi M. Malenkov succeeds him as Premier; Nikita S. Khrushchev later named Communist Party First Secretary.

Mar. 31 Dag Hammarskjold of Sweden elected Secretary General of U.N.

May 29 British expedition reaches summit of Mount Everest. New Zealander Edmund Hillary and Sherpa guide Tenzing Norkay are first to scale the world's highest mountain.

July 27 Armistice ending Korean War signed by U.N. and Chinese Communist delegates at Panmunjom.

Aug. 20 Iran announces arrest of Premier Mohammed Mossadegh.

Dec. 23 New post-Stalin regime executes Lavrenti Beria, chief of the Soviet secret police, and six aides.

1954

Apr. 18 Lt. Col. Gamal Abdel Nasser becomes Premier of Egypt for second time in two months, replacing Maj. Gen. Mohammed Naguib.

Apr. 26 Nationwide testing of the Salk polio vaccine begins in U.S.A.

May 7 French stronghold of Dienbienphu in Vietnam falls to Vietminh Communists after 55-day siege.

May 17 In landmark decision, *Brown* v. *Board of Education of Topeka, Kansas,* Supreme Court outlaws racial segregation in U.S. public schools.

June 27 Communist-controlled government of Guatemala resigns in wake of national revolt and is replaced by military junta.

July 21 Geneva Accords divide Vietnam at 17th parallel. Vietminh to control North Vietnam; State of Vietnam (pro-Western nationalist) and French troops to control South Vietnam until projected elections in July 1956.

Sept. 8 Southeast Asia Collective Defense Treaty, pledging mutual aid to resist armed attack and subversive activities, signed by U.S.A. and seven other nations.

Oct. 19 Egypt and Great Britain sign pact for British evacuation of Suez Canal Zone.

Dec. 2 Senate "condemns" Senator Joseph McCarthy after hearings on Communist infiltration of the military.

1955

Apr. 5 Sir Winston Churchill resigns as Prime Minister of Great Britain. He is succeeded by Sir Anthony Eden.

Apr. 28 Vietminh insurgents rebel against Premier Ngo Dinh Diem's regime in South Vietnam.

May 5 Allied occupation of West Germany ends and its sovereignty is restored with ratification of the Paris agreements in Bonn.

June 2 Yugoslav President Tito and Soviet Premier Nikolai Bulganin sign cooperation agreement.

July 27 Austria becomes independent when Great Powers end occupation.

Sept. 19 Argentine President Juan Perón resigns and goes into exile after army revolt deposes him.

Oct. 25 South Vietnam declared a republic after referendum favors Premier Ngo Dinh Diem over Emperor Bao Dai.

Dec. 5 Dr. Martin Luther King, Jr., civil rights leader, leads blacks in Montgomery, Alabama, bus boycott.

1956

Feb. 14 Soviet leader Khrushchev denounces the late dictator Stalin at a secret Communist Party meeting.

Mar. 10 Britain deports Greek leader Archbishop Makarios from Cyprus.

Apr. 21 Egypt, Saudi Arabia, and Yemen sign military alliance.

June 22 Nasser elected President of Egypt under new constitution.

June 28–30 Polish workers riot in Poznan to protest restrictions and living conditions. Government crushes demonstrations with heavy loss of life.

July 26 President Nasser nationalizes Suez Canal after U.S.A. and Great Britain decline aid for Aswan High Dam.

Oct. 23–Nov. 14 Hungarian Revolution: Students and workers demonstrate for human rights and withdrawal of Soviet troops. Soviets put down rebellion; death toll estimated at 25,000 Hungarians and 7,000 Russians. Premier Imre Nagy ousted, replaced by Janos Kadar.

Oct. 29–31 Israeli troops launch attack against Egypt in Sinai Peninsula in cooperation with British and French; British bomb Egyptian airfields.

Nov. 4 British and French paratroopers land at Port Said, Egypt.

Nov. 6 U.S. President Eisenhower reelected by a 9-million-vote plurality.

Dec. 5–22 British and French withdraw from Egypt; Israeli troops remain in the Sinai until March.

1957-76 THE SPACE AGE

The exploration and use of outer space, including the moon and other celestial bodies, shall be carried out for the benefit and in the interests of all countries . . . and shall be the province of all mankind.

From Article One of the International Treaty on the Exploration and Uses of Space, January 27, 1967

1957-76

As man reached for the stars, a booming population threatened to destroy the quality of life on his home planet —and even its chances for survival.

When the Soviet Union launched Sputnik 1 in October 1957, the bond of gravity that tied man to the planet earth was broken, and limitless space was suddenly open to his exploration. Within a few years visits to the moon by U.S. astronauts became almost commonplace, and unmanned space vehicles sent back volumes of scientific information from other planets.

Ironically, this space-age technology appeared at a time when the inhabitants of the earth seemed driven by some strange madness to destroy one another and possibly themselves. The two nuclear superpowers, the United States and the Soviet Union, were locked in a cold war, and unimaginable destruction became a very real possibility during the crises over Berlin and Cuba. The antagonists managed to pull themselves back from the brink, but the potential sources of mass extermination continued to multiply. France, China, and India developed their own nuclear weapons, and other nations—including Egypt and Israel—were known to have the capability of producing them.

Meanwhile, international relations grew increasingly strained. China and the U.S.S.R. experienced a major ideological break that brought about open border fighting in 1969. The attempt of the United States to halt the spread of communism ended in a disastrous defeat in Vietnam. And a new element was added to global politics by the emerging Third World, composed mainly of economically depressed former colonies that relied on richer nations for aid but at the same time resisted alignment with either side in the cold war.

The mood of the space age was largely one of protest and increasing violence, as greater gulfs opened between black and white, young and old, rich and poor. In many countries the steady economic growth of the early 1960's declined sharply as the decade drew to a close, further aggravating already severe problems of social and political tension.

In addition to all the immediate threats of violence, mankind faced the long-range dangers of overpopulation, pollution of the air and water, and the exhaustion of numerous natural resources.

But the picture was not entirely bleak. Science moved forward on many fronts. Access to unlimited solar energy was becoming practical; medical research all but eliminated such scourges of past generations as polio and smallpox; lives were prolonged by organ transplants and other new techniques. Lasers, computers, satellites, and comparably important developments in biology opened up horizons of tremendous promise.

Even so, the ancient question remains: Can man, the most creative and destructive creature on earth, learn to control himself?

1957

Sputnik

The Soviet Union puts the first manmade satellite into orbit, shocking the world and winning the first stage of the "space race."

***Only the beginning:** A model of Sputnik 1 (above), first in the pioneering series of satellites that gave the Soviet Union an early lead in space exploration. Since then the U.S.A. and the U.S.S.R. have launched nearly 2,000 spacecraft into earth orbit and beyond, though the fierce competitiveness of the 1960's has largely given way to a spirit of cooperation.*

***A giant Soviet booster,** comprising five separate engines (right), in transit to its launch site. Developed in the mid-1950's, these liquid-fuel engines—the RD-107 and RD-108—were far more powerful than any available in the United States, evidence of the Soviets' intensive rocketry program after World War II. Not until the 1960's did the U.S.A. develop a launch vehicle of comparable power.*

The world's space age—and everything the phrase implies for mankind's new hopes, fears, and fantasies—opened officially on October 4, 1957. On that day a mysterious electronic beep emanated from radio and television sets around the world, creating some bewilderment, much fear, and many angry calls to local repairmen. The mystery was soon dispelled: The Soviet Union proclaimed that it had launched the first manmade orbiting satellite. Sputnik was its name and the beeps were a coded message of the observations it was making as it sailed through the skies.

The Russians had accomplished what then seemed a miracle of technology. American rocket scientists had been trying, and failing, to put up their own satellite; and it seemed ominous that a nation considered strong mainly in its belligerent intentions could have marshaled the money and expertise to accomplish what the United States, with its much vaunted technological know-how, could not. Thus, the rich and powerful United States began to question some of the assumptions it had been taking for granted: that American science was the best in the world, that American education produced the most competent citizens, and that the United States could do whatever it set out to do. For the first time in the 20th century Americans began to suffer from an inferiority complex.

The Soviet triumph was unquestionable. Using a rocket whose power was greater than anything available to the Americans, they had hurled into orbit around the earth a metal sphere, 22.8 inches in diameter, weighing 184 pounds, and equipped with instruments for recording and transmitting atmospheric data. According to Soviet news releases the multistage launching rocket reached an altitude of 587 miles before moving parallel to the earth at about 18,000 miles per hour; the satellite then detached itself from its burnt-out rocket and established its own orbit some 550 miles above the earth. Sputnik circled the globe every 96.2 minutes and, because of the earth's rotation, ranged over every continent and nearly all inhabited areas. No Westerner, in that time of pervasive cold war, could help but feel that he had lost the skies to the enemy. Russian scientist Leonid I. Sedov, basking happily in his country's triumph, said: "The American loves his car, his refrigerator, his house. He does not, as the Russians do, love his country." While this statement hardly explained how the Soviet Union had achieved the triumph, it seemed to many in the West an adequate analysis of the U.S. failure.

A month later Sputnik 2 was launched. It weighed half a ton and carried the first living creature into orbit, a dog named Laika, indicating that the Russians might soon send a man into space. Shortly after Sputnik 2 the Americans attempted to put a Vanguard satellite into orbit. At a heavily publicized launching at Cape Canaveral the rocket "toppled slowly, breaking apart . . . with a tremendous roar." To most of the world that roar was the decisive signal that American technology had come out second best to the Soviets.

The Postwar Rocket Race

The immediate forerunner of the Russian and American space rockets was the German V-2, developed at Peenemünde on the Baltic coast by Wernher von Braun for the Nazis during World War II. In 1945 the V-2 installations at Peenemünde were captured by the Russians, but they found little of value there. The machinery had been destroyed by the Germans, the staff had been evacuated, and Von Braun and some 150 V-2 scientists and engineers had surrendered to the U.S. Army. This rare haul—almost the entire top V-2 establishment—became the nucleus of the later American rocket program.

Even before the end of the war the U.S. military had begun preliminary studies into the possibilities of rocket weapons and rocket-propelled satellites. In those early stages the army's efforts were separate from the navy's, and the programs were carefully shrouded in top-secret classifications. Postwar America was, at first, unwilling to fund vast programs for its military, especially if they threatened to develop weapons even more deadly than those the war had so horribly demonstrated. The military space programs were killed, leaving only one small rocket research project in existence: Wernher von Braun and his Peenemünde team, augmented by American scientists, were experimenting in New Mexico, using V-2's. During the Korean War interest in long-range rockets, armed with nuclear warheads, revived. Von Braun's team built the army's Redstone missile, launched in 1953. By 1956 the team had perfected the Jupiter C rocket, which, without its fourth satellite stage, had an astonishing 3,300-mile range.

On January 31, 1958, four months after the flight of Sputnik 1, a Jupiter C rocket launched Explorer 1, an 18-pound satellite whose 115-minute orbit took it from a low of 219 miles to an apogee of 1,587 miles above the earth. Chattering away in code—which had been published for all ham and professional radio stations to pick up and read—it announced, among other things, the presence of a cloak of radiation, held around the earth by its magnetic field, extending 40,000 miles out into space (as confirmed by later satellites). This, the Van Allen belt (after James Van Allen, who identified it), was the first major scientific discovery to result from the space race. In the years that followed hundreds of others were to be made, and space science became an arena for some of the world's best minds.

Since 1957 satellites launched by the Soviet Union and the United States (and in 1965 by France and in 1970 by Japan and China) have: refined our knowledge of the earth's shape; transmitted photographs of the

Monitoring our planet's environment *has been the task of the U.S. Earth Resources Technology Satellite (ERTS), launched in 1972. Using cameras sensitive not only to visible light but to infrared and other forms of radiation, ERTS has amassed valuable data on agricultural and mineral resources, pollution control, oceanography, and other subjects. Against a composite satellite view of the U.S.A., the inset above shows part of Holt County, Nebraska, color-coded by computer to distinguish separate crops of field corn (red), popcorn (salmon), alfalfa (dark blue), and sorghum (blue).*

earth and skies via television; mapped the earth's magnetic field; circumnavigated the moon and photographed its far, never-before-seen side; provided global TV and telephone transmission; served as weather monitors; and detected nuclear explosions.

Skylab, a manned space station launched by the United States in May 1973, spent a total of 172 days orbiting the earth at an altitude of 270 miles. In their weightless environment the crews measured the effect on their bodies of prolonged sojourns in space. They also photographed the sun with sophisticated instruments, generating an enormous amount of data that may revolutionize the field of solar physics.

But the launching of Sputnik had effects far beyond the realm of science. As the skies and planets have become open to human inquiry, culture and consciousness have changed too. In the United States one immediate effect is still obvious: a great rebuilding and expansion of the educational establishment.

The Challenge of Sputnik

In the wake of Sputnik Americans began to suspect that their system of education was not, perhaps, the best in the world. After all, the Soviet Union, despite its poverty and supposed backwardness, had been able to educate enough engineers and scientists to launch a satellite. For the first time since the end of the war articles praising the U.S.S.R. began to appear, especially articles describing and analyzing Soviet education. At the same time there was much anguished recitation of unfortunate figures relating to the U.S. system: In early 1958 less than half of all high school graduates went on to college; most high school students had no science or math education of any significance; the number of college-trained math and science teachers was shrinking. The President's Committee on Scientists and Engineers urged an intensification of scientific training to bring the nation's scientists up to the Soviet level. The Joint Atomic Energy Committee warned that the atomic energy program was "in serious danger of lagging unless something drastic is done immediately" to expand scientific education.

The solution seemed obvious to U.S. legislators: a vast expenditure of money. In 1958 Congress passed the National Defense Education Act (NDEA), which authorized approximately $1 billion for federal and state education programs providing new equipment for elementary and secondary schools, loans for college students, graduate fellowships, and special programs in the sciences, mathematics, and foreign languages.

As a result of the NDEA and legislation passed in the ensuing years, the number and size of educational

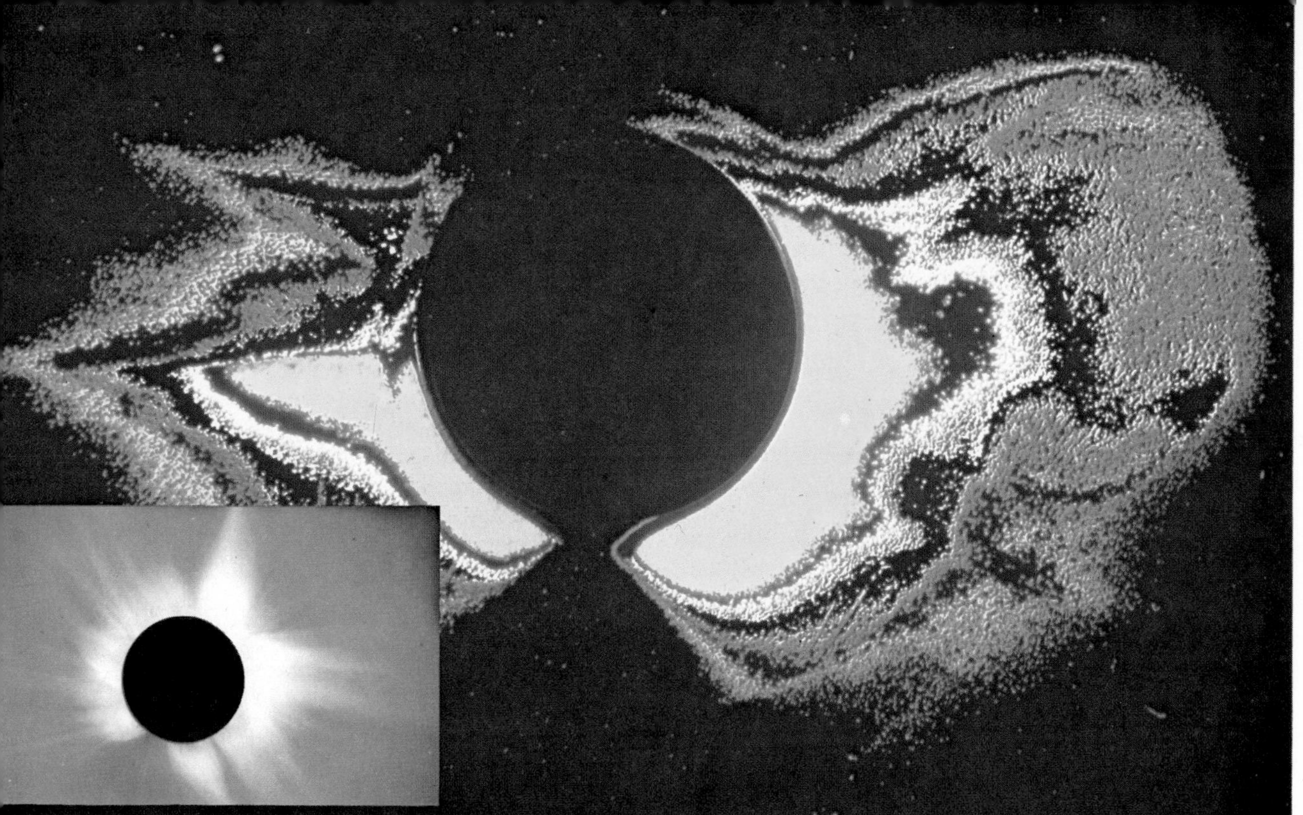

***The most elaborate spacecraft** yet launched, Skylab was home to three teams of U.S. astronauts in 1973–74, whose duties included photographic observations of the sun to study forms of solar radiation normally filtered out by the earth's atmosphere. Above, a simulated eclipse made possible this dramatic view of the sun's corona, color-coded to show levels of brightness. It revealed an awesome and hitherto unseen phenomenon: the ejection of a huge ball of gas through the corona (right), an event repeated every 48 hours. Inset, a view of the corona during an eclipse by the moon.*

institutions, the number of trained teachers, and the number of college students have all increased beyond the most optimistic expectations. In 1957, the year before the NDEA, 3,037,000 students were enrolled in institutions of higher learning. In 1968 the number had risen to 6,928,000—an increase of 128 percent. In the same period the total expenditure on scientific research and development in the areas of defense and space rose by 124.7 percent. By 1972 total expenditures on education in the nation had risen to $83.3 billion—7.8 percent of the gross national product. (In 1945, by comparison, expenditures had been some 2 percent of the gross national product.) Of all the branches of society only the military receives more federal money than the educational establishment.

Another immediate effect of the Soviet satellite was the suddenly increased influence of scientists in government and in top national policymaking. The two weeks following Sputnik saw an unprecedented stream of scientists meeting with President Eisenhower. The Office of Special Assistant to the President for Science and Technology—a vital post that fell into disuse only under President Nixon—was established in November 1958; and the President's Science Advisory Committee was given new quarters in the White House. The scientists were charged with setting the goals of a national space program, and, even more important, they were asked to appraise the U.S. weapons programs. The lofting of Sputnik had proved that the Soviet Union was capable of producing rockets—and thus long-range armed missiles—far more powerful than anything the U.S. military could have imagined. The American ballistic missile program was accelerated. And in both the U.S.S.R. and the United States the two competitions—the space race and the arms race—became essentially one rivalry: The rocket technology needed to send satellites and men into space was the same as that necessary to send bombs across the world. Many of the rockets used for space shots are modifications of intercontinental ballistic missiles (ICBM's). And all of the military services, especially the air force, have been intimately involved in the research and development programs of the National Aeronautics and Space Administration (NASA).

The Systems Approach

The brilliant success of the U.S. space program—with its giant mobilization of scientists, technologists, workers, and military men, all funded by huge appropriations of money—has inspired a new discipline using the same techniques of systems analysis that worked so well at NASA. The systems approach—a methodology for the solution of complex problems—works today on any subject that can be expressed in numerical terms: Mathematical models can be made of situations as complex as the criminal climate in a large city (with the goal of predicting where and when crimes will occur) or as seemingly simple as the scheduling of nurses in a hospital. Wherever a problem has a multiplicity of factors—urban transportation, for instance, or pollution control—systems analysts can chart possibilities and suggest solutions.

Space technology has been directly responsible for advances in a variety of other fields as well. Revolutionary progress in computer technology has been made possible by new developments in micro and solid-state electronics developed for satellites (see pp. 378–383). There have been improvements in medical technology, due especially to the new instruments devised to test the physical responses of astronauts; in food processing and preservation; in environmental and pollution control systems; in new tools and materials for industry. In fact, there is almost no area of life today untouched by space age skills—down to the latest high-speed dental drills, which use the same tiny ball bearings first developed for scientific satellites, or the new heat-retaining aluminized plastic used both in satellites and in swaddling newborn babies.

Important far beyond the new techniques and tools that have evolved as a result of the space projects, the opening of the heavens to man's first probes has also given rise to new scientific problems. The argument for the possibility of life existing on other planets is an old one. But it was necessary to find some scientific, rather than divine, explanation for the origins of life before that question could be approached in detail.

Life Among the Stars

In 1952 experiments reproducing the conditions of the primordial earth succeeded in creating some of the complex molecules of amino acids that form the basis of protein chains—and of life. Since, as the experiment proved, life had probably emerged from such conditions on earth, it may very well have begun the same way elsewhere. The evidence for the chemical origins of life has accumulated; the latest, supplied in part by satellite, is the discovery of amino acids among the particles of dust retrieved from interstellar space.

The creation of a theory describing the possible origins of life has led, on the one hand, to an increasingly serious search for extraterrestrial civilizations and, on the other, to a widespread belief that the earth itself is the subject of exploration by extraterrestrial beings. The phenomenon of the UFO (unidentified flying object) is not unique to our time, but much that was, until quite recently, considered impossible has now become reality. Tiny manmade moons circle the earth, men explore the moon itself, and space probes nudge the edges of our solar system: The possibility of alien visitors to our own planet no longer seems utterly fantastic. Although most UFO reports prove to have been sightings of weather balloons, high-flying kites, earth satellites, or unusual meteorological phenomena, there remain enough inexplicable sightings to keep UFO seekers hopefully on the watch.

Whatever the current status of UFO enthusiasts, most scientists agree that the probability of there being other inhabited planets in the universe is enormous. Carl Sagan, professor of astronomy and space science at Cornell University, estimates that there may be advanced civilizations on perhaps 1 million of the planets in our galaxy, concluding that, "There appears to be a fair chance that advanced extrater-

A SPACE-AGE WIRELESS

Since 1962, when the experimental Telstar 1 was launched, a new generation of communications satellites have made instantaneous around-the-world television and telephone contacts a routine occurrence. More recently a number of satellites have been introduced to provide the same service for domestic American communications, particularly in remote areas of the country. The first three of these "domsats" were launched in 1974 into synchronous orbits (that is, stationary in relation to the earth's surface) about 22,300 miles above the Equator. By the end of 1976 a total of eight such satellites will be available for television, telephone, radio, and photographic transmission; they will ultimately cost less to use than conventional systems. Similar satellites launched in 1976 have made possible reliable ship-to-shore communications, regardless of atmospheric conditions.

restrial civilizations are sending radio signals our way." He also points out the difficulties inherent in receiving such signals, given the great number of stars that would have to be monitored on a wide range of frequencies. But, although such a project would require large amounts of time, money, and dedicated monitors, a number of scientists feel it would be well worth pursuing. Sputnik 1 long ago vanished from the sky, burnt up by the earth's atmosphere as it lost orbital speed and fell groundward. But the sciences that created Sputnik have grown and flourished. They have not only changed the material quality of our lives but have also given us a new awareness of our earth as a small island in the cosmos and a new urge to discover who may share the universe with us.

Its giant antenna unfolded in a preflight testing chamber (left), the ATS-6 domestic communications satellite, the most powerful and complex to date, was launched by the U.S. government in 1974. Through a network of ground relay stations like the one below, the ATS-6 provides such services as two-way TV connections for medical consultations between patients in isolated areas and doctors hundreds of miles away.

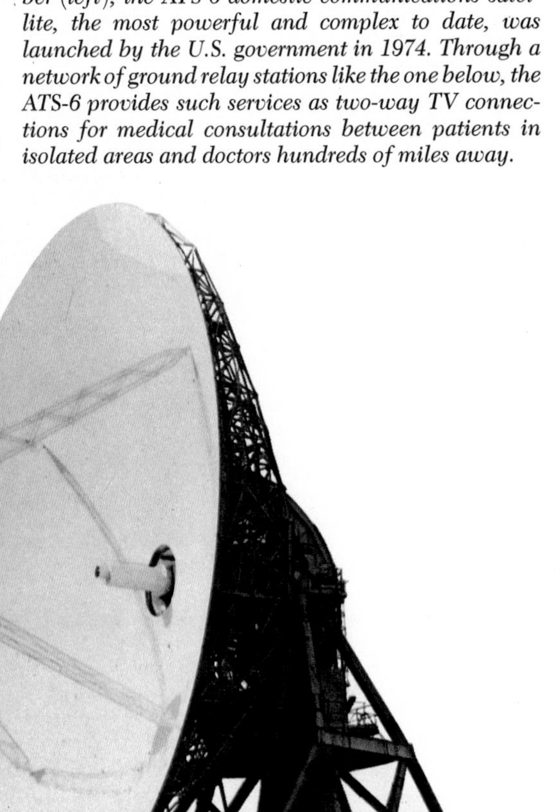

SATELLITES, LASERS, EARTHQUAKES, AND GRAVITY

Launched in 1976, the Laser Geodynamic Satellite (LAGEOS) is designed to provide information about movements of the earth's crust and may lead to the development of techniques for predicting earthquakes. The process involves bouncing laser beams off the satellite, timing their return to the earth, and thereby measuring the satellite's distance from various terrestrial tracking stations.

Laser-satellite measuring techniques have also been proposed as a possible means of detecting gravity waves, the hypothetical equivalent, for gravity, of electromagnetic radiation (see p. 84). In theory, bursts of gravitational energy would reveal themselves by jarring the satellites in their orbits. However, such effects might well be too small to be registered by current laser techniques, and to date the most convincing effort to verify the existence of gravity waves has been made by Dr. Joseph Weber of the University of Maryland. Employing two $3\frac{1}{2}$-ton cylinders of solid aluminum, 600 miles apart and thoroughly insulated from local vibrations, Weber was able to detect (with equipment sensitive enough to record movements as small as one-hundredth of the diameter of the atomic nucleus) simultaneous vibrations in the cylinders for which no known phenomena could be responsible. One cause of the vibrations could be bursts of gravitational energy.

If further experiments prove this to be the case, we may stand at the brink of a revolution in physics as great as the one heralded by the discovery of electromagnetic radiation in the 19th century. For in our understanding of gravity we are only a little more advanced than the ancient Greeks were in regard to electricity. They were familiar with electricity's static and magnetic forms but knew nothing of its third manifestation, the invisible waveforms that make possible radio, television, and numerous other phenomena now taken for granted. If society is to undergo another major revolution, its technological roots may ultimately prove to lie in the efforts now being made to detect gravity waves.

1959

The Cuban Revolution

Rebel leader Fidel Castro ousts the corrupt Batista regime—and brings the cold war to North America's doorstep.

***Fulgencio Batista** seized effective power in Cuba after a military coup in 1933 and was elected President in 1940. His name became synonymous with corruption and repression.*

Few political events of the mid-20th century generated as much controversy as the Cuban Revolution of 1959 and its aftermath. Was it a Communist revolution? A classic Marxist revolt of the workers? Of the peasants? Was it inspired by the Soviet Union, or did the U.S.A. in effect drive Cuba into the Soviet camp by imposing a trade embargo? To what extent did Castro become a brutal tyrant? Although the answers to these questions are still disputed, some things are relatively clear. First, that a social, political, and economic revolution unique in modern Latin America has been consolidated only 90 miles off the coast of the United States, providing the Soviet Union with its first firm base in the Western Hemisphere; second, that the significance of the revolution was seriously misunderstood and underestimated by authorities in the U.S.A.; and third, that the effects of Cuba's example and direct influence on Third World countries have only just begun to be felt.

A Caribbean Protectorate

Cuba's history is a tale of revolutions made and betrayed. In 1868 the island rose up against its Spanish conquerors, triggering years of bitter unrest. The hero and martyr José Martí united the people in 1895 in a climactic struggle to throw off the Spanish yoke, and left to their own devices the rebels might well have won their fight for independence. But the mysterious sinking in Havana harbor of the U.S. battleship *Maine*—which the American press blamed on Spain—created a fervent sentiment in the United States for intervention. America entered the war in 1898. Spain was beaten, and Cuba found herself free—but in name only; in fact, she had become a virtual protectorate of the United States.

American businessmen, attracted by Cuba's proximity to the United States and the open-door policies of various Cuban administrations, had for years been buying up vast sugar, tobacco, and mining properties in Cuba, and by 1896 their holdings totaled $50 million. With this enormous investment to protect, the United States did not end its military occupation of Cuba after the war against Spain, nor did the U.S.A. recognize the victorious rebel government. Instead, the U.S. government instructed Cuba to call a constitutional convention in 1901 and to include in the new constitution a special amendment favorable to U.S. interests. This agreement—the Platt Amendment—declared that the United States could intervene to preserve Cuban independence and government and

Fidel Castro greets exuberant supporters after ousting President Batista in January 1959. His revolution was accomplished in three years, with relatively little bloodshed.

that Cuba must "sell or lease to the United States land necessary for . . . naval stations." As a result, the United States built the still-operating naval base at Guantánamo Bay. By 1902, when the four-year U.S. military occupation of Cuba came to an end, American investment in the island had doubled, yellow fever had been eliminated (see p. 90), and a railway linking Havana and Santiago de Cuba had cut travel time between the two cities from 10 days to 24 hours.

From their independence from Spain in 1898 to Castro's revolution in 1959, the Cuban people lived under a variety of governments, most of them marred

Ernesto "Che" Guevara, an Argentine, was one of four non-Cubans in Castro's original army. A revolutionary and a medical doctor, Guevara fled to Mexico from Guatemala in 1954, after the radical Arbenz regime had been overthrown. In Mexico he met Castro and helped him plan the invasion. Guevara led the assault on Santa Clara (see map), cutting Batista's military communications and insuring the rebel victory. After Castro's takeover he became Cuba's unofficial foreign minister.

PARTNERS IN REVOLUTION

Castro's camp in the rugged Sierra Maestra (above) was photographed in October 1957, after newcomers had reinforced the 12 survivors of the original 82-man invasion group. Eventually the guerrillas numbered about 300, opposing some 12,000 demoralized government troops; in May 1958 Batista launched a series of actions against them, but his efforts failed on Christmas Day 1958 and Castro entered Santiago. Fulgencio Batista fled to safety in the Dominican Republic on January 1, 1959.

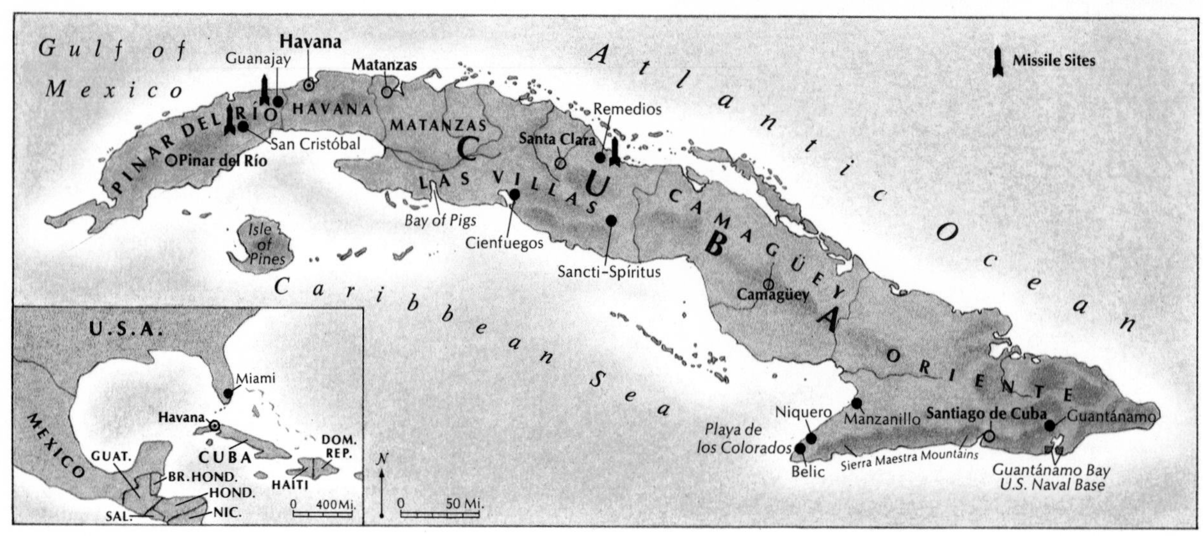

by corruption and gross inefficiency. U.S. troops, under the provisions of the Platt Amendment, intervened in Cuba in 1906, 1912, and 1917 to quell uprisings. In 1922 the United States withdrew its troops but continued to send advisers to the Cuban government.

Gerardo Machado, a wealthy businessman and onetime cattle thief, was elected President in 1924. After an auspicious start he became increasingly unpopular as sugar prices fell and economic chaos threatened. Machado, feeling his grip on the government slipping away, turned tyrant and insured his reelection through terrorism and brutality. He was overthrown by a military coup in 1933. The new President, Carlos Manuel de Céspedes, lasted four months before being overthrown. His successor, Ramón Grau San Martín also held office for four months before another coup, this one engineered by an ex-army sergeant named Fulgencio Batista, displaced him and installed Carlos Mendieta as President. With the installation of this new government in 1934, which the United States considered "stable," President Franklin D. Roosevelt annulled the Platt Amendment.

Although he did not head the new government, Fulgencio Batista, now a colonel, was a powerful figure, functioning as the army's political chief. He served quietly behind the scenes while three relatively liberal but ineffectual Presidents ruled over administrations that were at least as corrupt and inept as those of the past. In 1940 Batista helped to draft a new, democratic constitution that provided for free elections and in that year was himself elected President. Having amassed considerable wealth after four years in office, he left government service when his party lost the elections of 1944, returning eight years later as head of an army group that overturned the government and made him Cuba's dictator. Two years later he was elected President.

Under Batista's rule Cuba was fertile ground for U.S. investment. In 1956 the U.S. Department of Commerce reported: "American participation [in Cuba] exceeds 90 percent in the telephone and electric services, about 50 percent in public service railways, and roughly 40 percent in raw sugar production."

The Young Revolutionary

A few weeks after Batista's 1952 coup d'etat, a young lawyer filed suit with Havana's Court of Constitutional Guarantees, accusing the dictator of having violated the Cuban civil code, of illegally holding the offices of "President, Prime Minister, Senator, Major General, Civil and Military Chief," and demanding that he be punished for crimes against the constitution. The judges refused, and the lawyer, 25-year-old Fidel Castro, began to make his plans for revolution.

Fidel Castro was born on August 13, 1926, in Oriente province, Cuba. His father, who had entered the country as a Spanish immigrant laborer, owned a prosperous sugar plantation by the time of Fidel's birth, and the boy led the comfortable life of the Cuban middle class. He was later to characterize his father as a wealthy *latifundista* (owner of a large estate), who exploited the peasants, paid no taxes, and "played politics for money"—a typical capitalist-farmer. Young Castro was sent to a Jesuit high school in Havana where, according to his yearbook, "his record was one of excellence, he was a true athlete, always defending with bravery and pride the flag of the school." In 1945 he entered the University of Havana to study law. Castro was a brilliant student, although he insists that he "never went to class, never opened a book." He was also involved in the violent factional strife between radical student groups at the university.

In 1952 Castro, having gained his law degree, was a candidate for the Cuban Congress and might have been elected if Batista had not seized power. But after March 10, 1952—the day of Batista's coup—all the usual processes of democracy became empty gestures.

It was therefore as a gesture, and without hope of any real response, that Castro had petitioned the Cuban courts to punish the illegitimate Batista regime. With the energy and single-mindedness that have marked his entire career, Castro then began to create a revolutionary army. He gathered together a group of young men and women who pooled what money they had to buy arms, gave up jobs and careers, and trained in secret for more than a year. On July 26, 1953—a day that is now a national holiday in Cuba—the revolution began. Castro's tiny army, perhaps 160 in all, attacked the Moncada Barracks, a 1,000-soldier garrison near Santiago. The attack failed, however, and the army scattered and hid as Batista's troops scoured the streets and fields to find them. Many were killed, nonparticipants as well as revolutionaries. Batista's men arrested and executed indiscriminately. Although Castro's life was saved by a sympathetic army officer, he and his surviving comrades were captured and imprisoned. Some of his followers were tortured. On September 21 the prisoners, handcuffed and escorted by heavily armed guards, were put on trial in a courthouse in Santiago. Castro, as a lawyer, demanded and was given the right to conduct his own defense.

Castro had been held in solitary confinement for 76 days when he made the impassioned speech that was the culmination of his defense. Addressing the judges, prosecutors, and 100 armed guards, he traced in outline the entire scope of Cuban history, its economic and social conditions and governmental repression. He cited statistics, quoted the philosophers of social justice, and defined his own program for revolutionary change. He spoke without notes. The only record of the speech was reconstructed later by Castro himself, in prison, in sentences written in lime juice between the lines of letters smuggled out to his friends. Painstakingly pieced together, the speech was published as a pamphlet, its title borrowed from Castro's final lines: "I do not fear the fury of the wretched tyrant who snuffed out the lives of 70 brothers of mine. Condemn me. It does not matter. *History will absolve me.*"

The publication of "History Will Absolve Me" went virtually unnoticed by the majority of Cubans and unpunished by Batista. Whether he was scornful of the threat Castro represented, or simply oblivious to it, Batista released Castro and his followers from jail in May 1955, as part of a general amnesty following his own reelection. Returning to Havana, Castro restricted himself to nonviolent agitation. The results were negligible, and with a few of his followers he sailed to Mexico, where he hoped to organize a small but well-trained and well-equipped army that would return to Cuba as a force of liberators. The name chosen for his movement was the "26th of July."

Fighting the War

It was in Mexico that Castro formed the nucleus of what at first would be a successful revolutionary army and later a functioning revolutionary government. Ernesto ("Che") Guevara joined Castro there. A young doctor from an upper-class Argentine family, Guevara had already been active in leftist movements in Latin America. He fled to Mexico in 1954 in the wake of the overturn of the radical Arbenz regime in Guatemala. Joining the Cuban movement was the inevitable next step for this revolutionary-without-a-country, and having joined, Guevara served Castro with a passionate dedication until his death on a revolutionary mission in the Bolivian wilderness in 1967.

There were 82 men in all when the time came to return to Cuba. Money had been collected, much of it from Cuban exiles in the United States; arms had been bought and months spent training in the techniques of guerrilla warfare. Castro had already announced to the world that he would return to Cuba: "In 1956 we will be free or we will be martyrs." Despite the absence of any organized support in his own country and the pleas of his sympathizers to postpone the invasion, he kept his promise. (He had little choice, in fact: The Mexican government had raided his camp, seized some arms, and informed Batista.)

On November 25, 1956, Castro's invasion army crammed into the battered yacht *Granma* and embarked for Niquero, west of Santiago. Their arrival on November 30 was to be coordinated with a series of guerrilla attacks in Santiago, led by a 24-year-old revolutionary named Frank País. After rendezvousing with País they would move on Manzanillo and engage Batista's army. País and his 300-man army executed their part of the plan well and briefly had control of Santiago. Another attack on Guantánamo and a 24-hour general strike added to the anti-Batista ferment.

However, the passage from Mexico to Cuba was a stormy one; the yacht was driven off course, the men were seasick, and the plan fell behind schedule. On

***Propaganda posters** stress Cuban solidarity with worldwide victims of capitalist oppression. Far left: a poster commemorating the Geneva Accords and demanding self-determination for Vietnam and the withdrawal of all foreign troops. Near left: Another poster announces a day of solidarity with the people of Laos. Right, below: the text of a poster expressing solidarity with North American blacks. It appeared soon after the assassination of Martin Luther King, Jr. In 1960 Castro visited the U.S.S.R. and met with Premier Khrushchev (right). That year Cuba began receiving economic, technical, and military aid from the Soviet Union. Since then the Cubans have given more than propaganda to their selected causes: The Congo, Algeria, Guinea, Bolivia, and several other countries, including Angola, have all seen Cuban troops in action.*

December 2 the *Granma* hit swampy ground at Playa de los Colorados near a small fishing village in the vicinity of Belic. The yacht was abandoned, along with some of the weapons and ammunition, and for three hours the men sloshed through mud to reach shore. Then they turned toward the Sierra Maestra mountains. In the days that followed, they were betrayed by one of their peasant guides and split into groups to avoid Batista's pursuing army. Most were killed in ambushes, and of the 22 who survived, 10 were taken prisoner and only 12 reached safety in the mountains: Castro, his brother Raúl, Che Guevara, and 9 others.

The small group was in a wilderness, without food or support, surrounded by hostile soldiers. Yet Castro's fanatic conviction of success and the help of a local bandit leader, Crescencio Pérez, kept him and his men alive. In the months and years ahead the number of his followers grew slowly, the peasants of the mountains came gradually to support him, and word of his movement filtered into the slums of the cities. Acts of insurrection, by *Fidelistas* and other revolutionary groups, grew more numerous, and Batista's counterrevolutionary measures grew increasingly brutal.

At first Batista had tried to deny, at least in public, that a revolutionary movement existed. But by the beginning of 1958 Castro, who set up a radio transmitter and began nightly broadcasts "from the Territory of Free Cuba in the Sierra Maestra," had become too successful. In May an infuriated Batista announced that he would exterminate the ragtag army and its leader. Twelve thousand men, armed with the newest equipment, marched into the Sierra Maestra.

SOLIDARITY WITH THE AFRICAN AMERICAN PEOPLE AUGUST 18, 1968

SOLIDARITE AVEC LE PEUPLE AFRO-AMERICAIN LE 18 AOUT 1968

SOLIDARIDAD CON EL PUEBLO AFRO-NORTEAMERICANO 18 DE AGOSTO, 1968

تضامن عالمي مع الشعب الافروامريكي ١٨ آب ١٩٦٨

The odds were 40 to 1: 12,000 soldiers against Castro's army, which had grown to 300 men. To counter this superiority of arms and numbers, the revolutionaries had only the wild terrain in their favor—and the fact that most of the government troops had little desire to die for Batista. The few soldiers captured by Castro were treated benignly, propagandized, and sent home to spread the word of his kindness. Within weeks Batista's men were defecting in droves. (In March Batista received a bitter blow: The United States suspended almost all arms shipments to him. Some U.S.-made weapons had been reaching Castro through supporters in the U.S.A.) Still, Batista had enough napalm-armed planes and professional soldiers to keep the hide-and-seek guerrilla fighting going for months. It seemed to the *Fidelistas* that the only way to win decisively was to come down from the mountains. In August Che Guevara began to lead some 200 veteran fighters on a gruelling march westward across two-thirds of the island, aiming to cut communications between east and west. They moved at night, constantly fending off government troops. In 31 days, one man wrote, they ate just 11 times, once "a mare, raw, without salt." Five months later they reached the city of Santa Clara; it fell on December 29.

Meanwhile, on Christmas Day Castro's Sierra Maestra troops had marched into Santiago, the key city of Oriente province. Throughout the island bands of guerrilla fighters blew up army installations and harassed Batista's troops. On New Year's Day 1959 Gen. Fulgencio Batista fled to refuge in the Dominican Republic, with a fortune of some $300 million.

The New Regime

In the United States Castro's revolution caused great confusion. Many newspapers either ignored or misreported the events of the war, and as Castro and his army rode in triumph from one end of the island to the other, there were reports of a bloodbath in Cuba. Yet few revolutions in history had been initially so untainted with bloody revenge as the Cuban revolt. Certainly there were injustices—property was seized and enemies were maltreated—but it was the execution, at first after rough trials and later by revolutionary tribunals, of some 200 "war criminals"—prisoners accused of torturing and assassinating pro-Castro rebels—during the first three weeks of the revolution that aroused the foreign press and public.

The majority of Cuban people approved the executions to avenge the thousands of victims Batista had murdered (possibly as many as 20,000)—it was the "justice" Fidel had promised them—but the outrage felt by many Americans would blacken U.S.-Cuban relations for many years after.

On July 6, 1960, in retaliation for the seizure of U.S.-owned Cuban sugar mills and oil refineries, the U.S. Congress authorized President Eisenhower to reduce by 95 percent the Cuban sugar quota, depriving Cuba of the single largest market for its single largest product. By the end of 1960 Cuba had expropriated all U.S. investments, and in 1972 the U.S. Foreign Claims Settlement Commission certified claims for compensation amounting to $1,851,057,358. Early in 1961 the United States broke off diplomatic relations with Cuba, and Cuba found a new friend, the Soviet Union. Given Castro's mistrust of the United States and U.S. fear of communism, the events of 1960–61 may have been inevitable. Yet the U.S. Ambassador to Cuba during that crucial period, Philip W. Bonsal, would later write: "We did not force them [Cuba] into the arms of the Soviets, but we were . . . unwisely cooperative in removing the obstacles to their chosen path."

When Fidel Castro came to power, he had no ideological or political ties with the Soviet Union, or so he claimed on January 16, 1959, at the grave of Eddy Chibas, an anti-Communist revolutionary; and in 1964 Che Guevara also declared that Castro had not been a Communist when he seized power. Certainly the Cuban Communist Party opposed him almost to the very day of his victory. But the mutual repulsion that then existed between the United States and Cuba produced the only alignment possible for Castro. In 1960 Cuba signed the first trade-and-aid agreements with the Soviets. The U.S.S.R. agreed to buy 5 million tons of sugar from Cuba in a five-year period at the then current world rate of up to three cents per pound. In

***The Cuban missile crisis** of October 1962 flared when U–2 spy planes photographed the construction of Soviet nuclear missile bases in Cuba. For days the world stood near the brink of nuclear war. On October 22 President Kennedy imposed a naval blockade on "all offensive military equipment" headed for Cuba. Above: On October 25 U.S. Ambassador to the United Nations Adlai Stevenson (right) confronted the Soviet delegation (left) with the photographs. On October 28 Premier Khrushchev backed down, ordering the missile sites to be destroyed and all missile-bearing ships to return to the U.S.S.R. Right: The* Metallurg Anosov *heads for home.*

addition, Cuba would receive a $100 million credit repayable at 2.5 percent interest in 12 years. Much of the credit was to be in the form of heavy machinery. The agreements produced such U.S. apprehension that, in 1961, U.S.-backed forces invaded Cuba.

The invasion, which came to be known as the Bay of Pigs debacle, has been described as the strangest tragedy of errors in which the U.S. was ever involved. It entangled two U.S. Presidents (Dwight D. Eisenhower and John F. Kennedy), the U.S. Central Intelligence Agency (CIA), and the most fervent of the thousands of anti-Castro Cubans who poured into Florida in the years following the revolution. Fourteen hundred exiles returned to Cuba on April 17, 1961, to a place called the Bay of Pigs. They had been trained by the CIA, had come in U.S. boats, and were supported, to a small extent, by U.S. planes. They expected that their invasion would trigger a counterrevolution in Cuba, but effective counterrevolutionary forces did not exist. There was no uprising but instead rout, capture, and utter defeat for the invaders. In 1962 Castro traded 1,179 prisoners for $50 million in food and medicine from the U.S.A. In December of that year he contradicted his earlier statement by announcing that he had always been a Communist. For Castro the Bay of Pigs was a glorious victory; for the United States, many believed, it was a symptom of irrational fear engendered by the cold war.

***Guantánamo Bay** naval base, leased by the U.S.A. from Cuba since 1903, is always guarded against Cuban seizure.*

At the Brink of War

Yet within a year U.S. apprehensions of a Communist state almost on its borders proved rational after all. With gifts of Soviet weapons and technicians, Cuba was well on its way to becoming the most heavily armed country of Latin America. In July 1962 Castro agreed to allow the placement of Soviet missiles in Cuba, missiles poised to strike at U.S. targets. The work was completed, the missiles were in place, and from October 22–28 the world teetered on the brink of nuclear war, until the Soviet Union agreed to U.S. demands to remove the weapons.

In the years that followed, many Cubans turned against Castro and left the country. By 1975 an estimated 600,000 Cubans had fled, many to the United States. They traced their bitterness to Castro's betrayal of promises made before the revolution and to the repressiveness of his regime. In 1965 Castro himself estimated that there were 20,000 political prisoners in Cuba, half of them in "rehabilitation" programs; other estimates are higher. The number of those executed may have been 5,000 by 1970. Among the promises not kept were those pledging the restoration of free elections, free speech, free press, and an independent judiciary. Castro further alienated the middle and upper classes by expropriating private property. Other promises were fulfilled, however: land reform, the ending of unemployment, reduction of rents, the creation of a functioning educational system, of public housing, of an effective public health program, and the ending of corruption in government.

By the mid-1970's Castro remained a dictator in the truest sense of the word, with all power still held by him and his nine-man advisory committee. Although he tried to foment revolutions in other Latin American countries, for a few years Castro seemed to lose interest in such provocative ventures. Nor was the United States so strongly apprehensive of his ability to subvert her hemispheric sisters. Two U.S. Senators visited Cuba in the autumn of 1974, and U.S. television crews were allowed to film interviews with Castro himself. A rapprochement, unthinkable in the 1960's, was a possibility in the 1970's. But U.S.-Cuban relations have continued to fluctuate, and in 1976, when 12,000 Soviet-armed Cubans intervened in Angola, they took a decided turn for the worse.

SCIENCE & TECHNOLOGY

1957-76

Science and Life

In the first decades of the 20th century a revolution took place in the science of physics; it was to change the course of history in ways that no one then could even imagine. During the last few decades another revolution has been in progress, this time in the life sciences; in its impact it will almost certainly be as profound, and in its consequences as unpredictable, as the one with which the century began.

For hundreds of years the inanimate world was far better understood than the world of living things. Physicists began their studies by examining such fundamental qualities of matter as mass, force, and motion, which have been applied in every field from the astronomic to the microscopic. Biologists, on the other hand, had no comparable universals on which to base their science; for among living things no single set of characteristics seemed more fundamental than another, nor was any applicable to the whole range of organisms: The skin temperature of a mouse is no more "fundamental" than its skill at mastering a maze, and equally "basic" information can be obtained from a study of its eating habits or of the nerves in its tail; moreover, such data will have no relevance to the biology of earthworms or ants.

Throughout most of its history, therefore, biology tended to be either very general or very specific: general in that it made use of such concepts as "reflex" and "digestion" long before they could be adequately explained, and specific in that what was learned from tomato plants might well not apply to corn, and even less to pine trees or Persian cats. Consequently it seemed beyond hope, until fairly recently, that biology could yield the kind of broad, comprehensive understanding that physics had achieved.

In the last 20 years, though, the life sciences have found revolutionary ways to connect the general and the specific. The first breakthrough came in 1953 when two scientists at Cambridge University announced their discovery of the structure of DNA (see pp. 454–461). The realization that virtually all life on earth uses the same complex molecules to store and transmit genetic information resulted in a new understanding of living things. Their kinship became measurable with the same kind of precision that physicists had been able to employ in describing mass, regardless of whether they were dealing with a feather or an ingot of gold. Today biochemists can determine, for example, that the sequence of amino acids in a certain protein molecule differs in a pig at 4 points from that of the same protein molecule in a rabbit, at 11 points from that in a frog, at 27 points from that in a moth, and at 47 points from that in a cauliflower.

Genetic Engineering

Once molecular biology had begun to reveal the continuity of life at the subcellular level, biologists gained a new freedom to manipulate their material and a new ability to predict the consequences of their work. In 1970 H. G. Khorana of the University of Wisconsin successfully synthesized a gene, the fundamental unit of heredity, and for the first

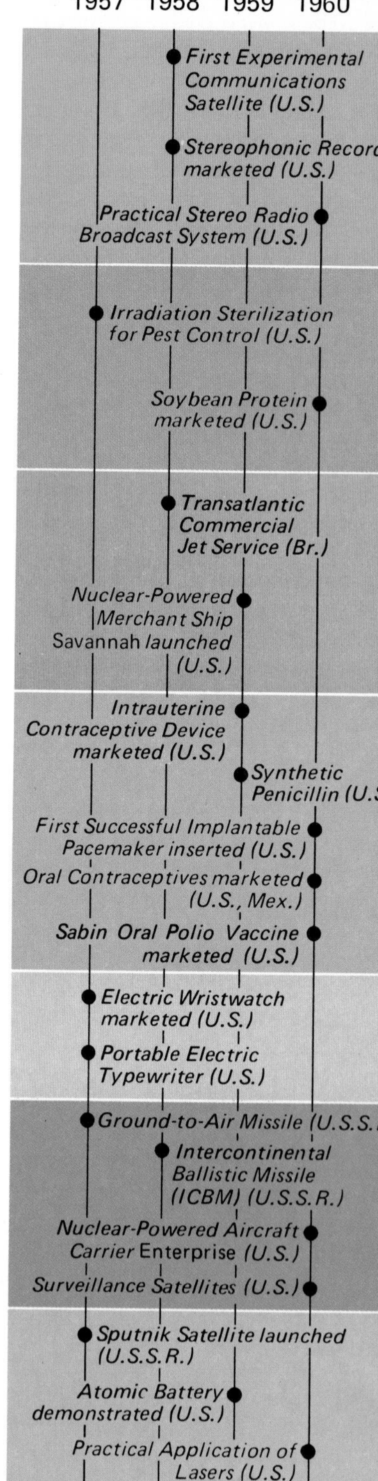

THE PACE OF INVENTION

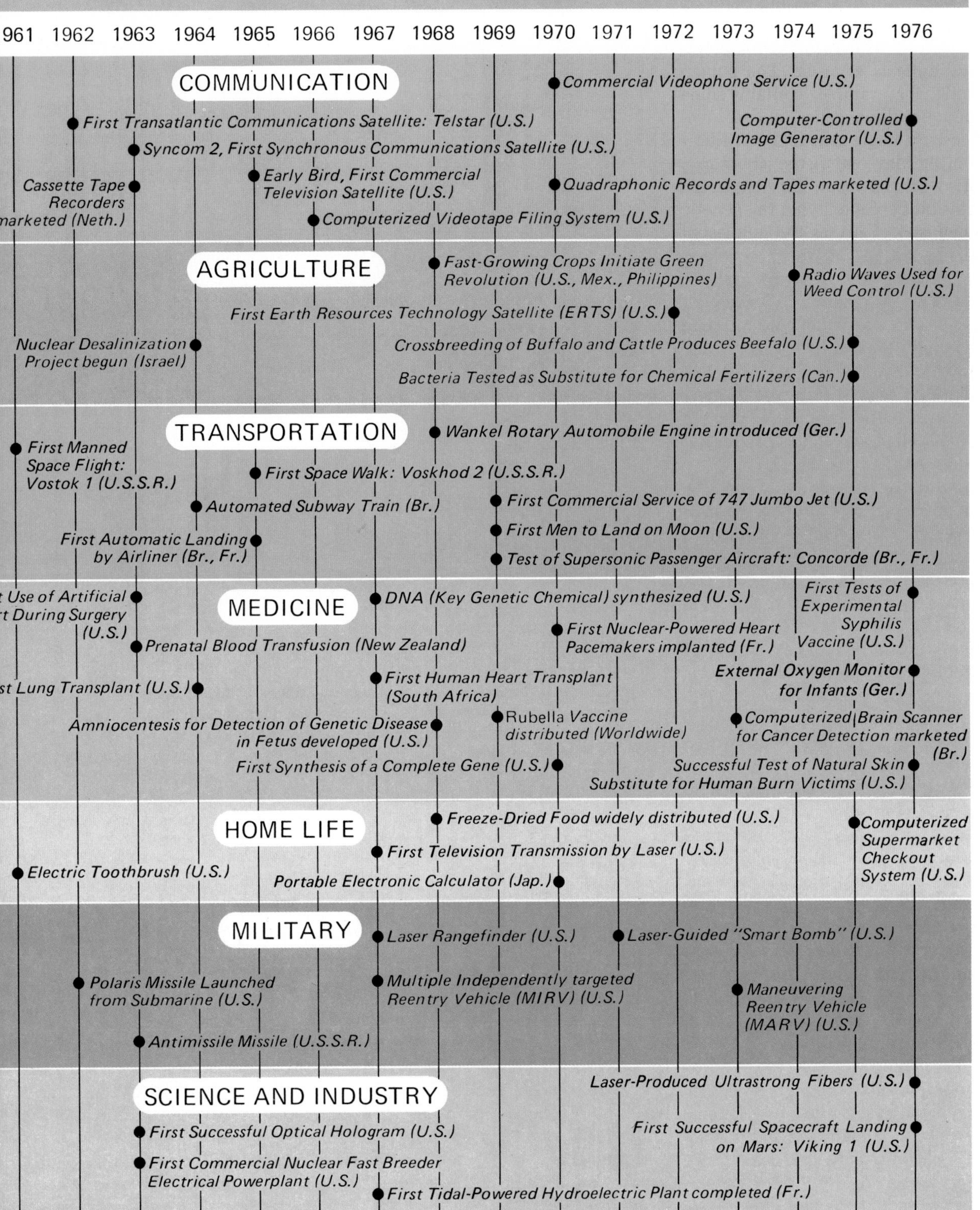

time genetic engineering began to seem a practical possibility.

Although Khorana's achievement was a historic breakthrough, it by no means signified that science was ready to start manufacturing plants and animals to order. The human body, for example, contains some 2.3 quintillion genes, and to synthesize a single gene had cost Khorana five long years in the laboratory. His work, however, did suggest the possibility of modifying the genetic chemistry of viruses, the simplest of all living organisms, by adding manmade genetic material to them. From such "engineered" viruses it may soon be possible to prepare vaccines that will stimulate the body to produce new genes. Through such therapy genetically diseased patients—the victims of sickle-cell anemia, for example—may eventually be cured.

More direct forms of genetic engineering may also be feasible, given the increasingly sophisticated instruments now available. Electron microscopes (see pp. 228–231) can currently magnify up to 1 million times, and improved instruments, operating within a few degrees of absolute zero (−460° F) and employing the phenomenon of electrical superconductivity, may soon make possible the direct observation of single molecules.

At the same time, methods of preparing specimens for the microscope have greatly improved, and the ultramicrotome developed by H. Fernandez-Moran of the University of Chicago employs a diamond blade sharp enough to section the large molecules of starch. In combination with the most powerful microscopes, such instruments may one day make molecular surgery an everyday event.

Although the electron microscope is normally used to magnify, it can also be used, like a telescope in reverse, to miniaturize. In this way electronic circuits less than one-thousandth of a millimeter in size have already been made, and it may be possible to shrink them still further, to the size of a large molecule. Such circuits could be implanted in the living nervous system (perhaps to correct such deficiencies as those leading to paralysis) and might also serve as links between the human nervous system and an external computer, with staggering diagnostic and other possibilities.

As the molecular processes underlying growth and heredity became known, improved methods of cultivating living organs in the laboratory were providing new insights into embryonic development and into the effects of hormones.

But despite their discoveries at the molecular and embryonic levels, biologists still lacked the theories

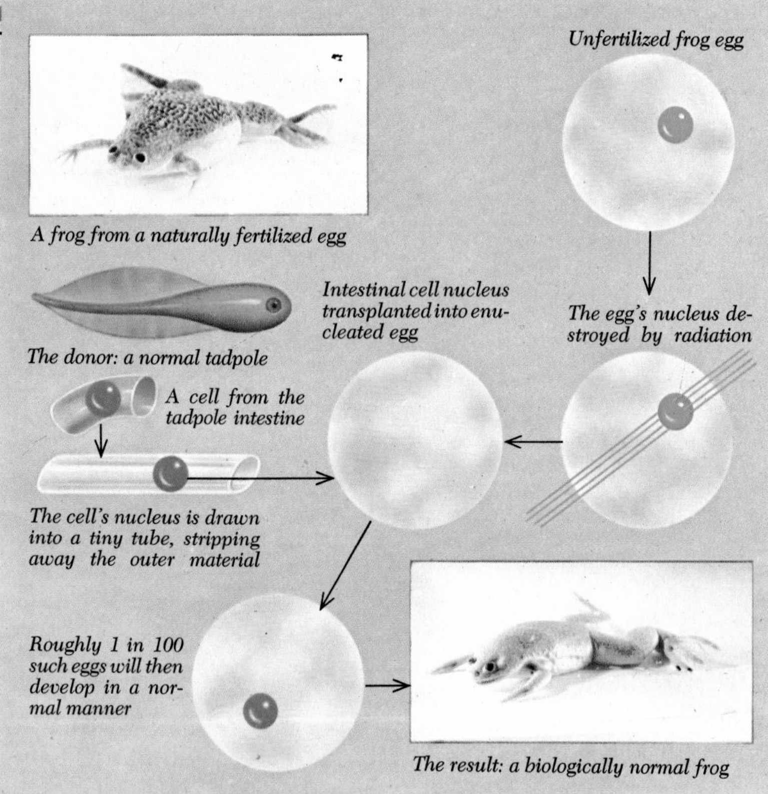

CLONING: THE MODEL T FROG?

Among the most sinister visions of the future are those in which an elite governing class superintends an antlike society of clones—genetically identical humans, test-tube bred for specific tasks. To date, carrots, tobacco plants, and frogs have been cloned, and in theory mammals could be cloned too, and one day there may be, for example, cloned herds of identical high-yield beef or dairy cattle.

In frog cloning the nucleus of a cell taken from a donor animal is transplanted into an egg (minus its own nucleus) taken from another frog. The egg is then maintained in the same conditions it would normally encounter after fertilization. All being well, an embryo matures into an adult genetically identical to the donor of the nucleus.

Although the success of current frog-cloning experiments is only about 1 percent, they do shed light on the genetic process (see pp. 454–461). For the layman there is something both ominous and marvelous in the fact that each cell in his body contains a latent blueprint for every other cell and for their organization into his own replica.

that might unify their work in the same way that the equations of Maxwell and Hertz had helped to unify studies in electromagnetism.

Then, in 1968, René Thom, a French mathematician, published his catastrophe theory, a series of equations and visual models designed to explain discontinuities ("catastrophes" in Thom's language) as diverse as a stock market crash or the sudden changes in a living cell.

For biologists Thom's theory offered an entirely novel way to explain why living organisms attain the shape they do and why various events in the growth process occur when they do.

Although the theory has already been applied to such fields as the differentiation of amphibian cells and the treatment of *anorexia nervosa,* a nervous complaint, it will be many years before catastrophe theory becomes an everyday biological tool. It may, however, already represent a final stage in the revolution that began with the discovery of DNA, providing biologists with the kind of predictive ability that allows astronomers to calculate the gravitational field of a distant planet. Allied with the possibilities of genetic engineering, the result could be an upheaval as great as any so far unleashed by nuclear physics.

CATASTROPHE THEORY

Biologists gained a powerful conceptual tool when French mathematician René Thom proposed his catastrophe theory in 1968. An extension of topology, the branch of geometry that deals with the study of surfaces, the theory offers an entirely new way of visualizing processes in which sudden discontinuities occur. Such events range from the specialization of cells in a growing embryo to the development of geological faults, from fluid dynamics to prison riots and (above and right) the simple cusp catastrophe of boy meets girl. Thom's analysis of such events yielded seven topological forms, which, alone, in sequence, or in combination, help reveal both the totality and the otherwise hidden properties of a fleeting or complex process.

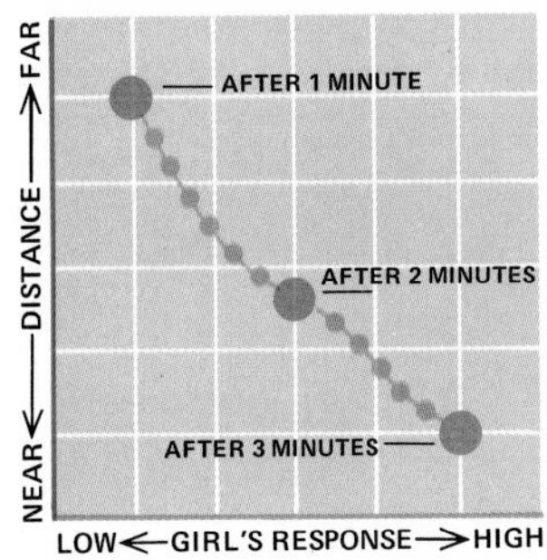

Any process that can be described by the relationship between two variables can be graphed, using one axis for each variable. Above: Boy meets girl, plotted here in terms of the distance between them and the girl's response.

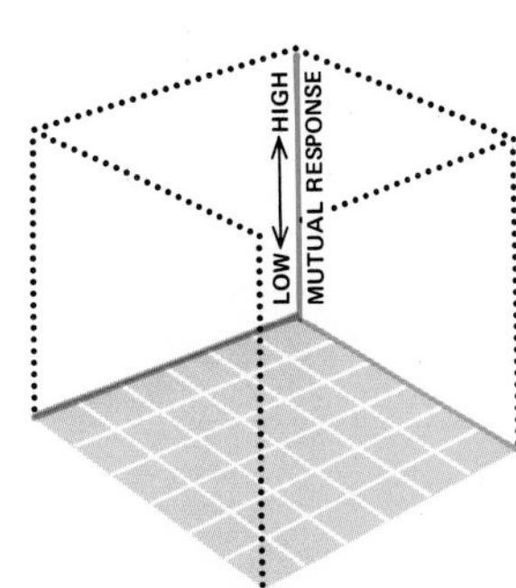

For the sake of a more complete description of the process, the effects of a third variable can be shown on the graph. Above: A measure of the mutual interest between the boy and girl is plotted on a third, vertical, axis.

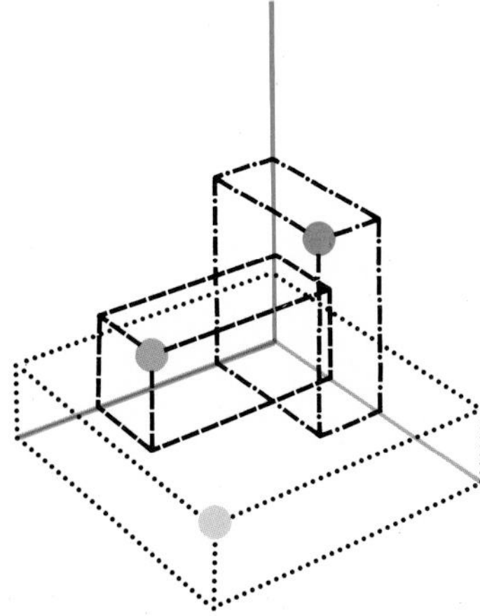

When three axes are used, the position of each point is determined by three coordinates. The resulting points cannot now lie along a single plane (as in Figure 1); rather, they can only be plotted in three-dimensional space.

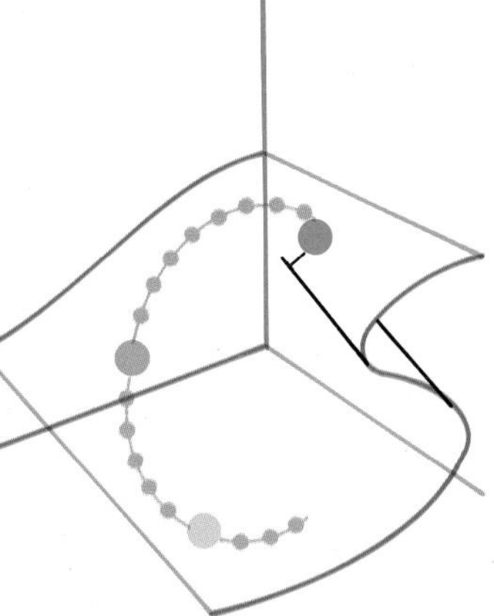

If enough examples of the process are plotted, the sum of the resulting points will define an undulating plane known as the behavioral surface. A specific example of the process will appear on this plane as a single line (above).

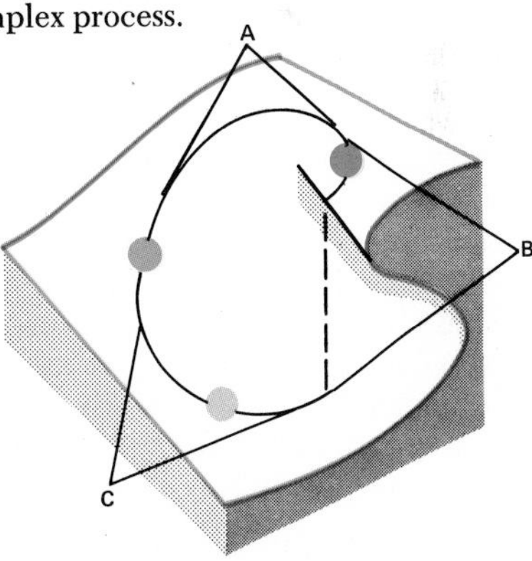

A. Boy approaching girl: distance decreasing; girl's response increasing; mutual interest increasing
B. Familiarity breeds contempt: interest decreasing; distance increasing. Catastrophe! Girl slaps boy; relationship falls to a new, low, level
C. Interest low, response low, distance increasing.

If the process lends itself to such analysis, the plane describing it will be one of seven catastrophic forms, in this case the cusp. Discontinuities are predicted as the line plotting a specific example approaches the cusp.

1960

Civil War in the Congo

Emerging from years of colonial rule, the Congo shakes Africa in a convulsive national awakening.

The year 1960 was a jubilee for black Africa, a time of liberation and confidence for what had been known only a century before as the Dark Continent. Seventeen former colonies achieved their independence that year, and in most of them the political transition was orderly. But in one nation, the Democratic Republic of the Congo (now Zaire), the coming of freedom was marred by riot, bloodshed, and civil war. For five years after independence the chaos continued. There was mutiny in the Congolese Army; fighting between tribes; military occupation by the country's former colonial master, Belgium; the secession of Katanga, its richest and most vital province; and a bitterly debated intervention by the United Nations. At one point there were four self-proclaimed governments ruling different areas. Only with the establishment of a military dictatorship in 1965 did relative calm settle over the Congo.

Some Western powers pointed to the collapse of order in the Congo as proof that Africans were incapable of self-government; yet many of the nation's troubles could be traced directly to the colonialism of the late 19th century, when European powers carved Africa into portions as large as their strength and appetite allowed. The great 19th-century explorers who mapped Africa's interior—John Hanning Speke, Sir Richard Burton, and David Livingstone among others—were soon followed by European agents who established "protectorates" or garnered trade concessions from tribal chiefs. Working for their monarchs or nations, these Europeans established new empires whose borders often fragmented tribes and ethnic groups—and just as often lumped traditional enemies together. That these colonial territories had no geographical or cultural logic mattered little to their new masters, who were scarcely aware of the existence of African cultures and were determined, in any case, to "civilize" their subjects in the Western mold.

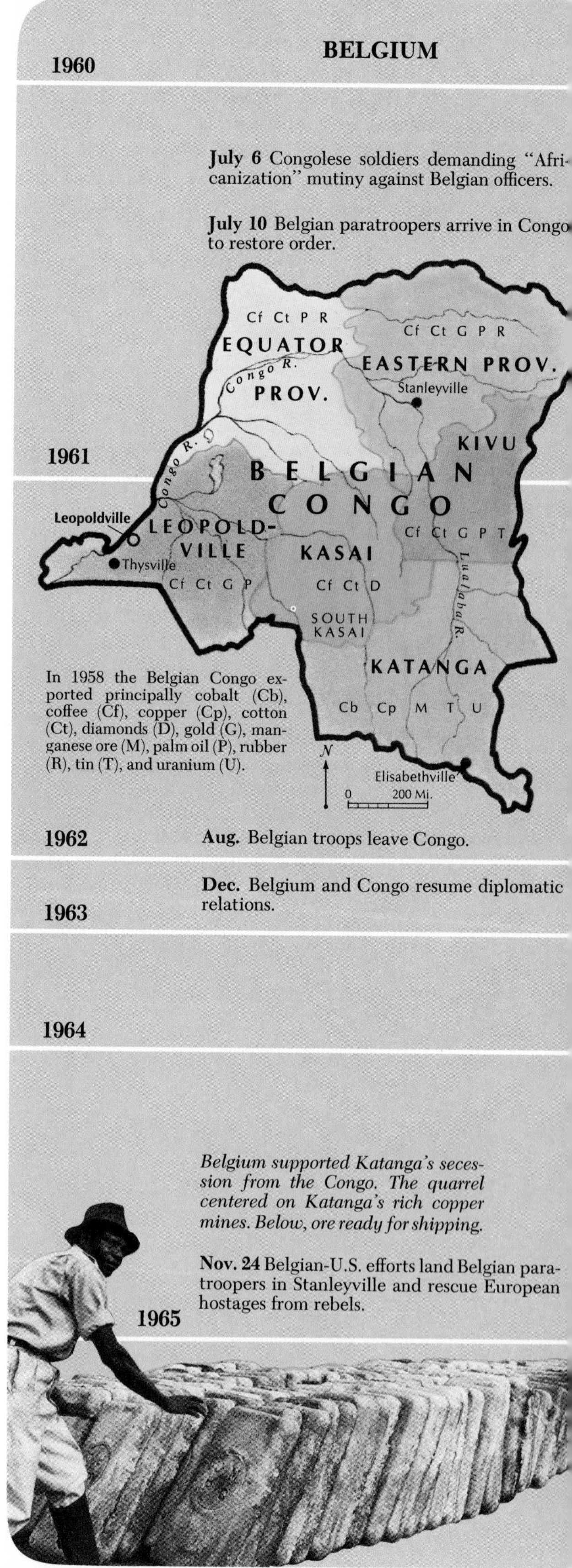

Belgium supported Katanga's secession from the Congo. The quarrel centered on Katanga's rich copper mines. Below, ore ready for shipping.

CONGO	SECESSIONS	UNITED NATIONS
June 30 Independence. President, Joseph Kasavubu; Premier, Patrice Lumumba. **July 6** Congolese soldiers mutiny, demanding that Africans replace the Belgian officers who still run the army. **July 10** Belgian paratroopers arrive to restore order. Congo government requests U.N. aid against foreign aggression. **July** Lumumba, dissatisfied with U.N. refusal to interfere in Katanga, says he will request Soviet aid. **Aug.** Congolese Army runs amok in action against South Kasai. **Sept. 5** Kasavubu, fearing Soviet influence, dismisses Lumumba, who in turn tries to dismiss Kasavubu. During deadlock army head Joseph Mobutu takes over.	**July 11** Moise Tshombe declares secession of mineral-rich province of Katanga. Supported by South Africa, Belgium, and colonial nations of Europe. **Aug. 9** Mining province of South Kasai secedes. **Aug. 25** Kasai and Katanga form confederacy. 	**During the year** 17 newly independent African nations gain admittance to the U.N. **July 10** Kasavubu and Lumumba request U.N. military aid against "foreign aggression" from Belgium. Also request U.S. aid. **July 15** First U.N. troops arrive in Leopoldville. No mandate to interfere in internal Congolese conflict. *In Elisabethville, Katangan boys throw stones at Swedish U.N. troops in 1961.*
July U.N.-protected meeting in Leopoldville approves coalition government with Cyrille Adoula as Prime Minister.  *Above, Lumumba after arrest.* *Left, General Mobutu as President.*	**Feb. 12** Lumumba murdered in Katanga. **Feb. 13** Anger at Lumumba's death helps his associate Antoine Gizenga to form a government in Stanleyville. This, the fourth government in the Congo, is recognized by Soviet bloc and radical African states. **July** Gizenga joins central government as Vice Prime Minister, but stays in Stanleyville; gradually loses popular support. **Sept.** U.N. and central government begin campaign to expel 500-odd white mercenaries in Katanga service. **Dec.** U.N. forces recommence action in Katanga. Tshombe reopens negotiations.	**Feb.** U.S.S.R. charges Belgium and U.N. Secretary General Dag Hammarskjold with complicity in Lumumba's murder. **Feb. 21** U.N. Security Council resolution gives U.N. forces greater authority. Kasavubu's government protests parts of resolution as violation of sovereignty. **July** Delegations from all parts of Congo meet in Leopoldville under U.N. protection. **Sept. 18** Dag Hammarskjold, U.N. Secretary General, killed in mysterious plane crash en route to negotiate with Tshombe. U.N. action temporarily halted. **Dec.** Leopoldville representative to U.N. charges arms supplied to Katanga mercenaries through Northern Rhodesia.
All year Fighting and discussions with Katanga continue.	**Jan.** Arrest of Gizenga ends Stanleyville regime and its threat to central government.	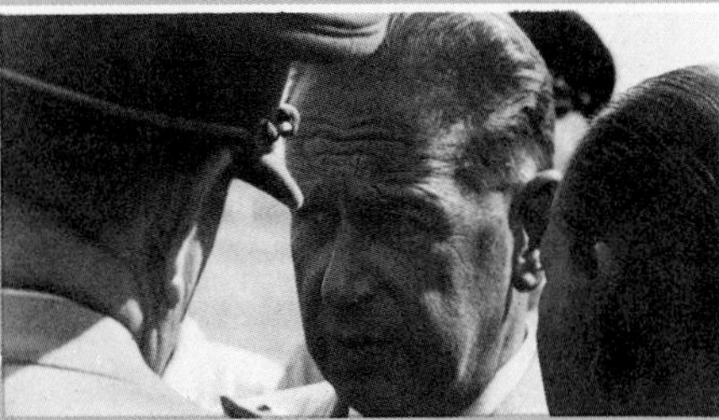 *U.N. Secretary General Dag Hammarskjold died while trying to unite the Congo.*
Sept. 29 Kasavubu dissolves Parliament, deadlocked over new constitution. Growing acts of unrest, particularly in the capital, cause Kasavubu to declare state of emergency.	**Jan. 14** End of Katanga secession. Kasai secession ends a few months later.	
May Congolese Army unable to contain rebellion sweeping across Congo. **June 26** Kasavubu dismisses Adoula as inadequate, calls in Moise Tshombe from exile. **July 9** Tshombe installed in government; recalls Katanga *gendarmerie* and mercenaries. **Aug. 5** Rebels capture Stanleyville and make it their capital.	**Jan.** Rebellion in Kwilu led by former Minister in Lumumba regime. **May** Rebellion in Kivu sweeps across northeast Congo. **Aug. 5** Rebels capture Stanleyville. Take European hostages. Atrocities mount on both sides.	**June 30** U.N. troops leave Congo, ending four-year mission. **Nov. 24** U.N. debates U.S.-Belgian rescue action in Stanleyville.
May Election results give Tshombe a parliamentary majority. **Oct. 13** Opposition to government of Tshombe grows in Leopoldville. Kasavubu dismisses him. Parliament deadlocks over formation of new government. **Nov. 25** In military coup General Mobutu becomes President.	*Moise Tshombe, shown here at the height of his power in 1964, was disliked by African leaders for his use of white mercenaries in Katanga and then in the Congo.*	

The Belgian Heritage

By 1900 much of Africa had been colonized by Britain, the Netherlands, France, Portugal, Germany, and Italy. But more than 905,000 square miles of the Congo River basin, an area rich in copper, cobalt, and diamonds, had been annexed not by a government but as the personal fief of Belgian King Leopold II, who had sent American explorer-journalist Henry M. Stanley to negotiate trade concessions with the area's tribal rulers in 1878. By 1885 Leopold and his financial backers had organized the Congo Free State, and the King, who never visited his African empire, became the world's most powerful absentee landlord.

Leopold's exploitation of his holdings was ruthless. Profit was the only measure of his colonial rule, and forced labor in the mines and on the plantations was rigorously enforced by white overseers, who frequently disciplined the unruly, the rebellious, and the merely inefficient by cutting off their right hands. Under Leopold's rule some 5 to 8 million Congolese died, and even in the Western World, where Africans were often considered no more than beasts of burden, the stench arising from the Congo was too overpowering to be tolerated. In 1904 international pressure forced Leopold to appoint a commission of inquiry into abuses there, and in 1908 he ceded his Congo Free State to the Belgian government.

The Belgians were anxious to improve conditions, but they were also anxious to exploit their new domain. They thus arrived at a policy combining paternalism and profit. The Congolese, who seemed like children to the Belgian administrators, would be given steady employment, churches and missions, housing, recreational and health facilities, and schools; in return, the Congolese would provide a labor force for European investors.

The Belgians did indeed improve the lot of the Congolese. By the 1950's the colony could boast that its literacy rate and its standard of living were among the highest in black Africa. But there was a flaw: Schooling stopped at the elementary level; few Congolese had access to a high school and virtually none to a university. Unlike the British and French, the Belgians saw no need to train a native elite, as Brussels considered even limited self-government in the Congo to be decades, perhaps centuries, away.

Certainly a cursory examination of conditions in the Congo in the early 1950's tended to support the Belgian view. Almost nowhere in colonial Africa was there less ferment. The Congo's large, semiurbanized working class was bereft of leadership but appeared satisfied to the point of lethargy. Had it not been for the momentous events sweeping over other parts of Africa—the "winds of change" in the words of British Prime Minister Harold Macmillan—Belgium might well have kept its empire for decades.

In the wake of World War II the structure of African colonialism began first to crack and then to crumble. The Western European powers, weakened by the war, found themselves unable and unwilling to maintain the military forces necessary to control their African possessions, though they made some effort to retain their sovereignty in the face of rising native opposition. In Kenya Britain fought a long and bloody war against the Mau Mau guerrillas, but eventually their leader, Jomo Kenyatta, became Kenya's Prime Minister in 1963. By then much of Africa had already been freed. Even in those cases where a colonial power exerted every effort to maintain control of its possessions, the attempt proved both costly and futile. Portugal, whose territories included Angola, Mozambique, and Portuguese Guinea, threw her limited resources into a battle against native guerrilla movements. For its pains the Portuguese government reaped only revolution at home and, in the mid-1970's, the loss of its territories abroad. Only in those few areas of Africa where Europeans formed a substantial part of the population was the tide stemmed: In South Africa and Rhodesia white regimes mobilized well-equipped armies to maintain their supremacy, even in the face of worldwide hostility.

But as the movement toward independence mounted, Belgium looked the other way. When Prof. A. A. J. van Bilsen, a prominent Belgian political theorist, suggested in 1955 that the Congo be prepared to assume independence in 30 years, his proposal was met with derision and fury. Few, if any, of his countrymen could conceive of a Congolese nation emerging in a mere three decades. In fact, in just five years the Belgians would be scrambling out of the Congo even faster than they had once scrambled in.

By 1957 the Belgians found themselves less and less able to isolate their huge colony from events in the rest of Africa. That year Brussels allowed a token measure of self-rule: Three Congo cities were permitted to elect African burgomasters, city officials armed with the symbols of power but with little of its substance. Gradually the movement for national independence gained tempo as more and more people joined political groups. Most of the new parties were formed around local interests and tribal groups—and one of the burgomasters elected in Leopoldville was Joseph Kasavubu, leader of the powerful Bakongo tribe and soon to become the Congo's first President.

The Road to Independence

In December 1958 Ghana's fiery Pan-Africanist leader Kwame Nkrumah held an All-African People's Conference in Accra. The Congo was represented by Patrice Lumumba, the radical young leader of its first nationally based political party, the Mouvement National Congolais (MNC). After returning to the Congo,

"THE WINDS OF CHANGE": AFRICA TRANSFORMED

By 1912, when France and Spain established colonial rule in Morocco, all Africa except for Liberia (which became independent in 1847) and Ethiopia was governed by European powers. After World War I Germany's African possessions were mandated to the League of Nations, and Africa remained a colonial continent until the late 1950's. Even Ethiopia was temporarily seized by Mussolini. In 1954 the major Algerian struggle for independence from France began (it succeeded in 1962), and in 1957 the British Gold Coast became the nation of Ghana. Other states soon followed, and within a decade Africa was transformed (below).

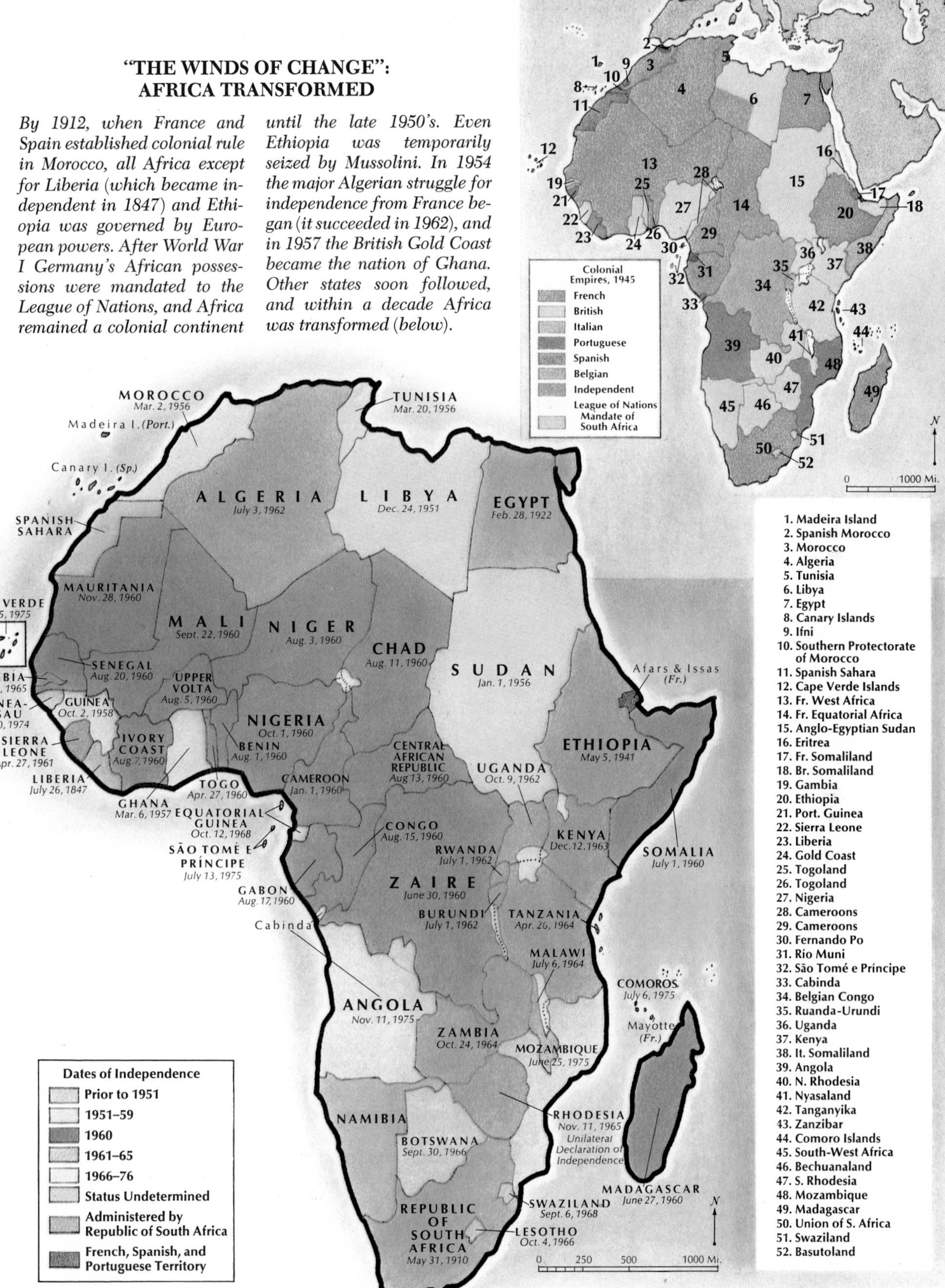

THE MAU MAU TERROR

On October 21, 1952, Kenya's governor declared a state of emergency and began a campaign to stamp out the Mau Mau, a terrorist organization drawing its membership mainly from the Kikuyu tribe and aiming to expel Kenya's white settlers and establish Kikuyu rule over an independent nation. Binding its members to secrecy with ritual oaths, Mau Mau became a byword among both Europeans and Africans for ruthlessness and sudden death. In fact, its tribalism and the viciousness of its attempts to coerce Kikuyu into membership provoked virtual civil war and proved the Mau Mau's undoing.

For four years British and Kikuyu troops waged war on the terrorists. By 1956, 11,000 Mau Mau had been killed, along with 2,000 of their Kikuyu opponents and 100 Europeans. Some 20,000 Kikuyu were confined to detention camps and exposed to what the British termed "political reeducation." Among them was Jomo Kenyatta, a Mau Mau leader who had first come to minor political prominence in 1946. When the state of emergency ended in 1960, two political parties emerged: the Kenya African National Union (KANU), supported by the Kikuyu and Luo tribes, and the Kenya African Democratic Union (KADU), drawing support mainly from smaller tribes. In the elections of May 1963 KANU, headed by Jomo Kenyatta, defeated KADU, and when Kenya became independent on December 12, 1963, Kenyatta became his country's first Prime Minister.

After his capture General China (below right), leader of the Mau Mau on Mt. Kenya, helped persuade his troops to surrender.

Lumumba addressed a huge rally in Leopoldville and in an explosive speech demanded Congolese independence. Immediately after the rally, rioting broke out in the city. Lumumba fled but was later imprisoned by the Belgian authorities, who held him responsible for the disorders. By then the youthful independence movement was being fueled by economic recession and widespread unemployment. Intertribal competition for the few jobs available increased tensions. Suddenly panic-stricken, the Belgian government promised reforms. The colonial regime that had so recently denied all possibility of change found itself virtually besieged as hungry mobs of Africans began to riot throughout the Congo. Unwilling and unable to mount an expensive colonial war to maintain their hold, the Belgians hastily began to dismantle the elaborate edifice of their empire.

In early 1960 the Belgians convened in Brussels to decide the future of the Congo. Among the native leaders attending was Patrice Lumumba, recently released from prison. The Africans came prepared for prolonged negotiations and considerable opposition to their demand for independence within five years. But Belgium was weary of the Congo; and the Africans were startled to discover that rather than oppose their demands, the mother country was all too eager to sever the ties—despite the fact that the native leaders had had precious little time to develop their own programs. So independence day was set not five years in the future but a scant half year away.

Days of Hope and Fear

The Congo's national elections, held in May 1960, brought a coalition government to power. Lumumba, who was supported by urbanites and subsistence farmers, as well as by several small southern tribes, became the Premier, while his archrival Joseph Kasavubu became President. Thus the lines were already being drawn between the nationalist supporters of Lumumba and the regionalist members of Kasavubu's ABAKO (Association of the Lower Congo). Kasavubu and the Belgian-backed Moise Tshombe in Katanga Province were determined to make the new state a loose federation in which tribal and regional interests prevailed. But Lumumba was intent on forging a strong central government. This conflict between regional groups (many of them outgrowths of ancient tribes and kingdoms) and nationalist aspirations is familiar in Africa, but in the Congo it soon erupted into a protracted and deadly struggle—as it would six years later in Nigeria. To complicate matters, Belgium's hasty exit had left no time for the Africanization of the administration or the Congolese Army; both remained largely in Belgian control at the time of independence.

On independence day, June 30, 1960, Belgium's young King Baudouin addressed a rally in Leopoldville in terms that Premier-designate Patrice Lumumba considered markedly paternalistic. Replying to the King, Lumumba spat out these words: "We are no longer your monkeys." Five days later the Congolese Army began the revolt that would bring the new nation to the edge of collapse.

The mutiny started in Thysville and Leopoldville, where Congolese enlisted men, infuriated by the refusal of their Belgian officers to promote them, locked up the white officers and their families. Within days the rebellion had spread to the entire army, and Belgian nationals, fearing for their lives, began to flee the country in panic. Stories of murder, rape, and arson —some of them true, some exaggerated—were headlined in European and American newspapers, setting off demands that the white population of the Congo be protected. By July 10, 1960, Belgian soldiers were being flown to Elisabethville and other places in the Congo to protect Europeans and their property.

The Belgian troops added fuel to an already explosive situation. Most Congolese had expected that independence would bring all sorts of benefits to each individual. When these did not immediately materialize, the people were easily recruited by dissident groups. Though bitterly divided among themselves, tribalists and nationalists all looked to profit from the confusion. On July 11 Moise Tshombe, leader of the mineral-rich Katanga Province, declared that region independent, thus threatening to deprive the Congo of its primary source of revenue. Katanga's secession was backed by Union Minière, the vast international company that controlled the province's enormous reserves of copper and cobalt. With his nation invaded by Belgian troops, with his own forces disaffected, and with rivals carving out independent empires from Congolese territory, Patrice Lumumba made a frantic appeal for U.N. intervention to restore the territorial integrity and sovereignty of his nation.

THE PAINS OF NATIONHOOD: STRIFE AND UNITY

The difficulties of welding disparate tribes into single nations have plagued Africa since the 1960's. Intertribal hostility erupted in the Congolese secessions, and a key Mau Mau aim was to establish the dominance of the Kikuyu tribe over an independent Kenya. Nigeria's northern province, fearing domination by another tribe, threatened secession in 1967, and in the east the Ibos actually did secede: Declaring themselves the new state of Biafra, they fought desperately (right) for 30 months until starvation and federal troops overcame them.

In contrast, opposition to white rule, which still prevails in South Africa and Rhodesia, has been a unifying force on the continent. A heritage of repression, and such events as the Sharpeville Massacre of March 1960, in which white police fired on African demonstrators, have made reactions to minority white rule increasingly bitter.

During the Nigerian Civil War some 2 million Ibos died either fighting (right) or from malnutrition.

The Sharpeville Massacre in South Africa left 69 dead (above) and approximately 180 wounded.

Chaos Compounded

Although a U.N. peacekeeping force was dispatched to the Congo, its mandate was far from clear. Some Western interests, with millions of dollars invested in Union Minière, were less than anxious to see Tshombe's Katanga regime overthrown. When U.N. Secretary General Dag Hammarskjold hesitated to launch a direct attack upon Katanga, Lumumba retaliated by refusing to permit the U.N. troops to disarm the mutinous Congolese soldiers, whom he now hoped to rally for his own attack upon Katanga.

The Congo's independent neighbors in Africa, who had supplied most of the troops for the U.N. contingent, had their own misgivings about the role they were playing. On the one hand, they were highly sensitive to the possibility of tribal and regional breakaway movements within their own boundaries and saw in Katanga's bid for independence a portent of disaster for themselves. On the other hand, most African nations were hesitant to establish the precedent of interference in the internal affairs of a neighboring state. But all of them detested the specter of neocolonialism represented by Tshombe's Western backers and on the whole supported Lumumba's defiant stand—though they were powerless to prevent his downfall.

When Lumumba threatened to appeal to the Soviet Union for help, official sympathies in the West began to shift from tacit backing of the Tshombe regime in Katanga to open support. On September 5 Congolese President Kasavubu dismissed Lumumba—to the relief of both Washington and Brussels—but the Premier refused to step down and in turn dismissed Kasavubu. The situation was resolved nine days later when a young Congolese Army colonel, Joseph Mobutu, took control of the government, placed Lumumba under house arrest, and expelled the Soviet technicians who had already arrived. Mobutu became, for a time, the real power in the Congolese government, but less than two months later he turned the government over to Kasavubu and installed himself as commander in chief of the armed forces.

In January 1961 Lumumba was transferred to Katanga into the hands of his archenemy, Tshombe. Within a month Lumumba was dead, Tshombe claiming that he had been shot while attempting to escape. Lumumba immediately became a potent symbol of African nationalism. Worldwide riots followed the news of his murder, even reaching into U.N. headquarters when angry blacks demonstrated in the General Assembly Visitors Gallery on February 15, 1961.

By the fall of 1961 fighting had become intense between U.N. units and the Katanga Army (led by white mercenaries), with U.N. forces occupying Katanga's capital, Elisabethville. In a last-ditch attempt to pacify the nation and reunify the Congo, Secretary General Hammarskjold arranged a meeting with Tshombe

***Angola's November 1975 independence** from Portugal heightened the long struggle for control among three established guerrilla factions: the National Front for the Liberation of Angola (FNLA), led by Holden Roberto and supported by Zaire and China; the pro-Western National Union for the Total Independence of Angola (UNITA), led by Jonas Savimbi; and the pro-Soviet Popular Movement for the Liberation of Angola (MPLA), led by Agostinho Neto.*

Below, FNLA troops head toward one of their camps in Zaire, where Roberto has personal ties with President Mobutu. Both Zambia, which supports UNITA, and Zaire depend on Angola's ports and railroad to export their copper and so have a vital interest in Angolan events. Below right is UNITA's Savimbi with a Cuban soldier captured from the MPLA. Savimbi and Roberto joined forces in 1975, but by the beginning of 1976 the MPLA controlled most of Angola and in February was recognized as its legitimate government by the Organization of African Unity.

to be held in the city of Ndola in Northern Rhodesia (now Zambia). As Hammarskjold's plane approached the Ndola airport, it went out of control and crashed, the Secretary General dying in the wreckage. The cause of the crash still remains a mystery.

Peace Restored

In the wake of Hammarskjold's death, worldwide resentment focused on Katanga, its President, and its mercenary-led army. It was not until December 1962, however, that U.N. forces launched their final drive against the secessionists to bring the province under the central government once more. By then much of the rest of the Congo was in rebellion, with the political heirs of Lumumba attempting to install a leftist regime, while the tribalists, some of them with their own private armies, sought regional autonomy and sometimes even independence. The situation was made to order for a military strongman, and in November 1965 Gen. Joseph Mobutu launched a bloodless coup against Kasavubu and took over the Presidency.

Mobutu's accession marked the end of large-scale civil strife in the Congo, for with the army behind him he quickly strangled the secessionist movements. Also dead, however, was the effort to build a parliamentary democracy in the former Belgian possession. In the 1960's this scenario was to become familiar in Africa, as numerous nations—Dahomey, (now Benin), Sierra Leone, Ghana, Uganda, and Nigeria, among others—jettisoned democratic forms in favor of military rule. Other nations, like Tanzania, Zambia, and Kenya, fell into the hands of nondemocratic civilian authorities in regimes ranging from the enlightened rule of such leaders as Zambia's Kenneth Kaunda and Tanzania's Julius Nyerere to the bombastic and bloodthirsty tyranny of Uganda's Gen. Idi Amin.

In military rule the Congo found a peace that had eluded it under earlier regimes. In an effort to eliminate the reminders of colonial rule the name of the country was changed in 1971 to Zaire (the local name for the Congo River); Leopoldville became Kinshasa. Far more important, however, has been Mobutu's exploitation of Zaire's resources for the primary benefit of its citizens. In 1966 he nationalized Union Minière and began a drive to increase cobalt and copper production, welcoming foreign investment but carefully maintaining national control over the country's resources. The general also proved politically adroit, attracting huge amounts of aid, particularly from the United States, while maintaining friendly ties with the Third World countries and the Communist bloc.

It remains to be seen whether the calm imposed by Mobutu has been institutionalized or will end with the disappearance of his leadership. In Zaire, as in much of black Africa, intertribal jealousies and competing ideologies remain a constant threat to nationhood.

THE ORGANIZATION OF AFRICAN UNITY

When civil war rent the Congo, the new African nations, which until then had glowed with the ideals of pan-African unity, found themselves split into two major blocs, one supporting the federal Congolese government and the other the breakaway provinces. Not until May 1963 were the two blocs able to settle enough of their differences to join each other in the Organization of African Unity (OAU), founded to promote peace and cooperation on the continent and to eliminate the remaining vestiges of European colonialism.

In pursuit of these aims the OAU tried unsuccessfully for several years to persuade the three guerrilla factions in Angola to unite against their Portuguese masters, and the members argued bitterly over the question of recognizing any faction separately.

Such a failure was perhaps inevitable, for the varied backgrounds and interests of the OAU members have frequently led to friction—former French colonies versus former English colonies, or black nations versus Arab states—and the organization's pledge of noninterference in the internal disputes of its members renders it virtually helpless during civil wars. It has, however, achieved some successes, notably in resolving border disputes, and is now a firmly established mediator of African affairs.

1960

Population and the Pill

A revolutionary method of birth control offers new hope in the crisis of the world's population explosion.

In the mid-1940's public awareness of science was dominated, understandably enough, by the field of physics, which only recently had produced such technological marvels as television, radar, supersonic rockets, and, of course, the atomic bomb.

But far from the public eye, and in a different scientific discipline, equally significant events were building. A small group of chemists and biochemists in Mexico City were studying a group of chemicals called steroid hormones, vital substances produced in minute quantities in certain human glands. Within 15 years —by 1960—their work would result in a simple pharmaceutical tablet that would have a profound effect on our moral, social, and cultural values, on the state of the human condition and the quality of individual life.

The steroids themselves had been known for years. They were classified into two main groups, the sex hormones, controlling the reproductive systems of both sexes, and the adrenocortical steroids, regulating the body's metabolism. Of the sex hormones there are three types: androgens, or male hormones; estrogens, or female hormones; and progestins. Progesterone, the pregnancy hormone, is the dominant progestin.

As the researchers explored the properties of hormones, provocative questions arose. If progesterone was necessary for pregnancy, would injections of extra progesterone help prevent habitual miscarriages? If estrogens were necessary to a healthy menstrual cycle, would supplementary doses help stop menstrual disorder? And if the fatal Addison's disease was caused by a lack of adrenocortical hormone, could patients with this condition be saved by administering a laboratory-made duplicate of the natural hormone?

In time the answer to all these questions emerged; it was "Yes." But the supplies of the replacement hormones were limited. They were derived from pregnant mares' urine, bulls' testicles, and sows' ovaries. Synthesis was difficult, and prices high—a single gram sold for $100. The race to discover a plentiful and inexpensive source of steroids began in earnest.

One of those engaged in the search was Russell E. Marker, an eccentric genius working at Pennsylvania State College. Having developed an efficient method for converting certain plant materials called sapogenins into progesterone, he began hunting for a plant source rich in sapogenin, examining some 400 plant species gathered in the American Southwest and Mexico. After two years he left the university and established his laboratory in an old pottery shed in Mexico City. In the jungles of southern Mexico he found a wild yam, *cabeza de negro*, that met his requirements. In just two months Marker produced 2,000 grams of progesterone, more than anyone had ever seen before, and established a commercial venture called Syntex, S.A. Within two years Marker had a falling out with his partners and left the firm, taking the secrets of his process with him. He formed another company in Mexico but became steadily more reclusive until, in 1949, he vanished totally from the field of organic chemistry. In the meantime, Syntex hired George Rosenkranz, a Swiss-trained chemist who soon discovered Marker's methods, and by 1948 the company was selling all the natural hormones that were then known to be medically valuable.

***An ally** against overpopulation: Mexican women (above, in a detail from a mural by David Siqueiros) harvest the wild yams from which the first commercial oral contraceptive was synthesized.*

***"Happiness** Is a Two-Child Family," according to a poster (top left) used in the Indian government's family-planning campaign. The campaign has had so little impact that compulsory sterilization after two children is a strong possibility.*

***Parents** in many poor countries have no security except their children and resist official attempts to reduce the birth rate. Left, a traditionally large family in Africa.*

The Miracle Drugs

In the spring of 1949 two scientists at the Mayo Clinic in Minnesota, Edward C. Kendall and Philip S. Hench, made an electrifying announcement: a steroid called Kendall's E had shown a remarkable power to alleviate the crippling symptoms of rheumatoid arthritis. Kendall's E was soon known worldwide as the miracle drug cortisone.

The supply of cortisone was only a trickle compared with the millions of arthritis sufferers in the world, and another dramatic race began. Four research groups solved the problem, using progesterone (at 48 cents per gram) as a starting material to supply much of the needed cortisone. An entirely new horizon of steroid research now opened up, and scientists began synthesizing variations of the steroids at a breathtaking pace. Early in 1951 a Syntex team synthesized a new progestin called norethindrone. Over a year later a research team at G. D. Searle & Co. produced a slightly different variation, norethynodrel. On testing, both drugs demonstrated a biological potency never seen before. The technology required for an oral contraceptive had arrived.

One last giant step remained to be taken before chemical contraception became a reality—the thorough testing of the new compounds—and at this point Margaret Sanger, the great feminist, enters the story. Sanger believed strongly in every woman's right to plan the size of her family and had devoted herself to removing the legal barriers to publicizing the facts about contraception.

In 1951 Margaret Sanger met with Gregory Pincus, a reproductive biologist, and urged him to seek the most effective possible means of birth control. Pincus was already interested in clinical applications of progesterone, and with C. M. Chang and other colleagues, he undertook the necessary laboratory studies. In the fall of 1956 clinical trials began in a housing project in a suburb of San Juan, Puerto Rico. They were conducted with the help of Dr. John Rock, a gynecologist, and Celso-Ramon Garcia and financed by Margaret Sanger's wealthy friends.

By the end of 1959, studies with more than 1,200 women had shown that Searle's norethynodrel was an effective oral contraceptive. To market such a pill, however, was a very sensitive matter. How would the public react? At this point, Dr. Rock, who happened to

THE GREEN REVOLUTION

As the world's population increases, more and more people find themselves on the brink of starvation. According to conservative estimates some 460 million people in 44 nations are already so undernourished that any crop failure or increase in agricultural costs could precipitate mass famine. Less conservative sources estimate that 2 billion people are undernourished or actually starving. Since 1943, when Dr. Norman Borlaug, a U.S. agronomist working in Mexico, began developing a new strain of high-yield wheat, hopes of averting global hunger have been pegged to the so-called Green Revolution.

However, although plant geneticists have produced high-yield varieties of corn, rice, sorghum, and other cereals, supergrains alone will not solve the food crisis. Many of them are more vulnerable to diseases and insect pests than conventional crops, and all need far more water and fertilizers. Unfortunately, most poor countries lack the technology to build modern irrigation systems, and the continuing energy crisis has curtailed the production and increased the cost of fertilizer. Thus it becomes increasingly clear that the problem of world hunger will not be solved until political and technological remedies are applied with equal force; for those who are already starving, the danger is that such remedies may come to be regarded as political tools, rather than as instruments of compassionate fellow-feeling.

be a prominent figure in Boston's Roman Catholic community, provided the needed reassurance. Searle took the plunge, and in 1960 norethynodrel was introduced under the trade name Enovid.

For the first time in history a method of contraception was available that was safe (as far as anyone knew then), simple, virtually guaranteed to work, and completely separated in time from sexual intercourse.

Although important questions soon arose about the long-term effects of the new contraceptive, most women—and a majority of their doctors—accepted it enthusiastically. By the 1970's the pill was being used worldwide by between 20 and 30 million women. In the developed countries it has become the most common form of contraception. In poor countries it has had less impact, being comparatively expensive, and is used by only about 4 percent of couples.

The Population Explosion

An irony of the world's current population problem is that medical science not only provides effective methods of birth control but also reduces the rate of infant mortality and increases the average life span—especially in those underdeveloped countries most subject

A clinician explains *the use of an intrauterine contraceptive to an Indian mother. Unless its birth rate declines, India will have to feed another 150 to 200 million people by 1985. Family-planning clinics are already reaching out into the villages, where three-quarters of the population lives, but so far their only real impact has been in the cities.*

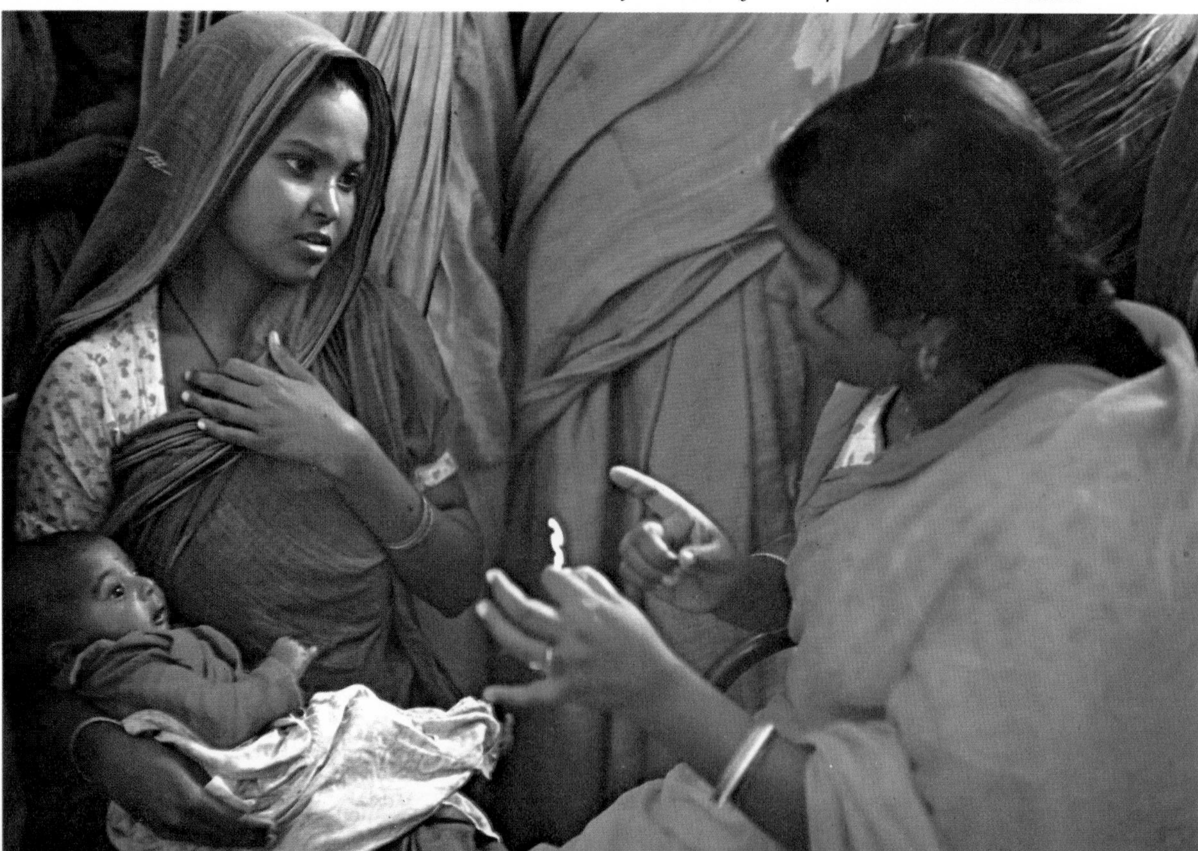

to disease. Thus the population snowballs, at a current rate of some 71 million people per year. By A.D. 2000 the population will have climbed from more than 4 billion in the mid-1970's to 6.2 billion, a rate representing a doubling every 39 years (compared with a doubling rate of 1,200 years in the period between the birth of Christ and the beginning of the Industrial Revolution in 1750). At this rate, according to an Einsteinian calculation by Ansley Coale, of the Office of Population Research at Princeton University, within 700 years there will be one person for every square foot of the earth's surface, within 1,200 years the human population will outweigh the earth, and within 6,000 years the mass of humanity will form a sphere expanding away from the earth at the speed of light.

There are two main schools of thought on the population problem. The first is that it portends an immense catastrophe that can only be averted by the most vigorous efforts to reduce the world's birth rate. An extension of this view is that population pressures not only create famine and disease but may dispose those who suffer them to violence: during the World Population Conference held at Bucharest in 1974 it was estimated that such pressures played a part in over 80 percent of a sample of 45 violent conflicts in Africa, Asia, and Latin America between 1945 and 1960.

The second view is that the real problem lies not so much in the birth rate of the underdeveloped nations as in the inequitable distribution of food and energy between the developed nations and the Third World. In this argument the industrialized countries (and especially the United States, whose per capita energy consumption is 6 times greater than the world average and over 200 times that of the poorest region, West Africa) are seen as urging population control on poorer nations in preference to undertaking a thoroughgoing redistribution of their own wealth.

According to calculations made by Roger Revelle, professor of population policy at Harvard University and director of Harvard's Center for Population Studies, such a reorganization could enable the world to provide food for between 38 and 48 billion people. His estimate assumes that, with proper management, the world's available farmland could be made as productive as farmland in the state of Iowa.

Until that happens—if it ever does—the poor of the world will probably continue to regard their children as the only reliable source of aid in the struggle for food and the only possible investment they can make for the future. Against such feelings, which reflect ancient social traditions, birth-control programs are at a disadvantage. Many governments, therefore, choose to sugar the pill with economic incentives and pay volunteers to be sterilized. Others favor disincentives —withholding maternity benefits after the birth of a second child, for example—and in India coercive sterilization programs are already being developed.

Meanwhile, the search for improved contraceptives continues, for the pill, in its current form, still presents many uneducated women with the problem of remembering when and when not to take it. Research projects have included developing a pill for men, a pregnancy vaccine, and a subcutaneous implant that would provide up to a year's contraceptive protection. Intense studies are also being made of the pill's long-term safety, since some evidence already links prolonged use with thrombosis and some forms of cancer.

If the problem of overpopulation and its attendant misery is to be solved, every means possible, short of forced sterilization, should probably be employed—including, in the opinion of many experts, a more equitable distribution of wealth. The failure to curb population growth will result in a dehumanizing poverty for the world at large and, for those few who may briefly remain privileged, a retreat into apathy.

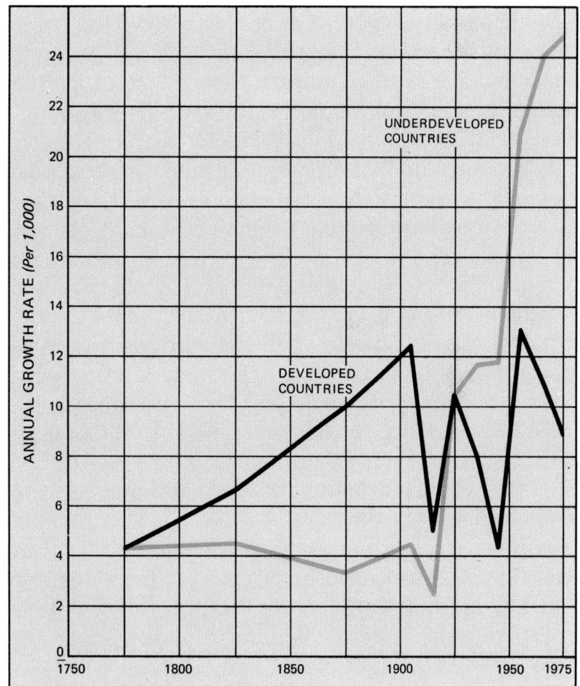

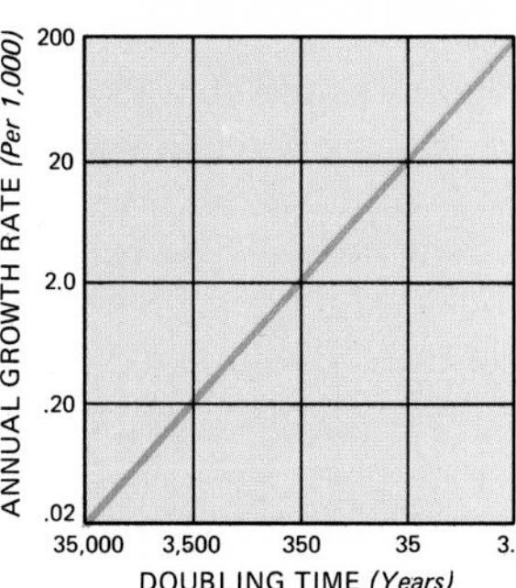

***Fifty years ago** the developed nations had a higher birth rate (numbers of children born per thousand of the population) than the rest of the world. Today the birth rate is falling in the developed nations, skyrocketing elsewhere. Left, the doubling time of the world's population: at present, less than 40 years.*

1962

The Spiral Key: DNA and the Spark of Life

Three scientists receive the Nobel Prize for discovering the highly complex genetic codes contained in the DNA molecule.

The key to one of life's great mysteries, the secret of heredity, was discovered in 1953 by two scientists at Cambridge University. Working with clues from widely scattered sources, they pieced together the unique molecular structure of DNA (deoxyribonucleic acid), the fundamental genetic material. Their now-famous double helix (spiral) model opened the way for investigations of the genetic code, the elaborate chemical language by which DNA controls and directs the process of protein synthesis. In 1962 these two men, James Watson, an American biochemist, and Francis Crick, a British biologist, shared the Nobel Prize for Physiology and Medicine with Maurice Wilkins, the British biophysicist whose detailed studies of DNA crystals had been basic to their investigations.

The work of Watson and Crick was the culmination of long years of scientific inquiry into the nature of heredity. The path that ended in the discovery of the double helix began in a remote Austrian monastery nearly a century earlier. It was there that the Austrian scientist-monk Gregor Mendel, the "father of genetics," first applied mathematics and controlled testing to explain why certain characteristics are passed on from a parent to its offspring.

In the garden of the monastery Mendel experimented with more than 20 varieties of garden peas, crossing two varieties differing in a single characteristic and recording the results. Mating tall with short plants and purple-flowered with white-flowered plants, he inferred that each offspring inherits a full set of traits from each parent, that certain traits are more likely than others to appear in the offspring, and that even traits not visible in the offspring can be passed on to the next generation. Most important, Mendel demonstrated that heredity was actually governed by a well-defined set of mathematical probabilities.

From Garden Peas to Sea Urchins

Mendel published his revolutionary findings in 1866, but no one realized their significance until much later. In the meantime the theories of Charles Darwin established the importance of natural selection in evolution, and biologists, with the help of the microscope, discovered exciting new facts about cell division and reproduction. In 1875 the German embryologist Oskar Hertwig watched the sperm cell of a sea urchin enter an egg cell and join with its nucleus. As he looked on, the fertilized cell began to divide into two new cells. Hertwig had witnessed, for the very first time, the creation of new life. Four years later another German, Walther Flemming, observed that just before a fertilized cell divided, the long threadlike fibers within its nucleus duplicated themselves. Copies went to each of the new cells. Biologists named these threads chromosomes (from the Greek word *chroma*, "color") because the threads had been stained with dye for the purpose of identification.

Had Mendel's work been known at the time, Flemming and his successors would doubtless have linked the chromosomes with heredity. However, it was not until 1902, two years after the rediscovery of Mendel's theories, that Walter Sutton, an American biologist, proposed such a connection. Then about 1915 researchers observed that the chromosomes were made up of smaller units called genes (from the Greek word *genea*, "kind"), and the study of heredity became the science of genetics.

Early chemical studies of the cell nucleus, where the chromosomes are located, indicated that they were composed of protein and nucleic acids, RNA (ribonucleic acid) and DNA (deoxyribonucleic acid). Little was known of the function or composition of RNA and DNA, and scientists concluded that they played a minor role in the cell's activities. The importance of proteins to all living things had been firmly established, and for many years biologists assumed that chromosomes must be made of complex protein molecules.

Into the Protein Factory

In the early 1940's, however, evidence began accumulating that DNA was in fact the crucial ingredient in the genetic process. Experiments conducted at that time by researchers at the Rockefeller Institute in New York City demonstrated that DNA from a virulent strain of pneumonia bacteria could transform a harmless pneumonia bacterium into a virulent one. Most scientists dismissed these findings as inconclusive and continued to insist that protein was the genetic material, but in 1952 researchers at the Carnegie Institution at Cold Spring Harbor, New York, proved beyond a doubt that DNA was the key to heredity.

The Carnegie team used a bacteriophage, or phage, a virus that attacks bacterial cells. The simplest of all

THE PROTEIN CONNECTION

The basic materials from which living things are made are all ultimately derived from proteins, which include such vital chemicals as the enzymes and hormones that mediate the life process. Proteins themselves consist of enormously long chains of much simpler chemicals known as amino acids, which are either taken into the body as food or synthesized from other materials. The task of arranging and linking these amino acids into the correct sequence is accomplished inside the cells of the body by certain substances manufactured within the cell nucleus.

Sometimes a chemical accident occurs and an incorrect sequence of amino acids is produced, radically changing the properties of the protein. Such mutations can alter the appearance or behavior of the animal concerned, perhaps improving its chances of survival and thereby allowing it to produce more offspring than its fellows. If the offspring also possess and transmit the mutation, it may eventually become normal for the species.

Most mutations, however, are disadvantageous; fortunately, even these occur only infrequently, and most parents continue to produce offspring resembling themselves. This is because the genetic code is stable, and instructions for protein manufacture are rarely garbled; this efficiency is primarily due to the structure of DNA.

***Natural selection in action:** As pollution darkened the bark of trees around cities in Britain, black variations of the peppered moth became less conspicuous to predators than the normal pale gray variety (top). They therefore survived to produce more offspring than the gray moths and eventually became the dominant form around cities. As antipollution laws took effect, tree bark again became lighter and the pale moths regained their previous advantage (bottom); the black forms, once again more obvious to predators than their pale relatives, again became exceptions to the norm. Such variations commonly arise throughout the animal kingdom as a result of variations introduced for one reason or another into the genetic coding for protein manufacture.*

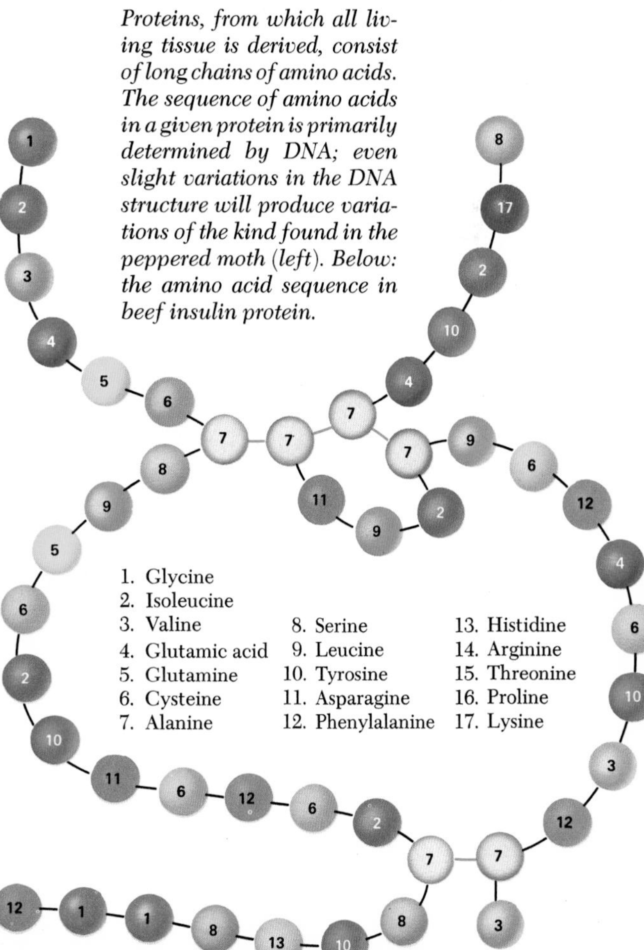

Proteins, from which all living tissue is derived, consist of long chains of amino acids. The sequence of amino acids in a given protein is primarily determined by DNA; even slight variations in the DNA structure will produce variations of the kind found in the peppered moth (left). Below: the amino acid sequence in beef insulin protein.

Chromosomes, found in the nucleus of all plant and animal cells, are the repositories of genetic information. Each of the 60 trillion cells in the human body has 46 of them, and each is roughly five one-thousandths of a millimeter long. Laid end to end, all the chromosomes in a human body would reach to the moon and back 16 times. Below, a greatly magnified illustration of fruit fly chromosomes. 1

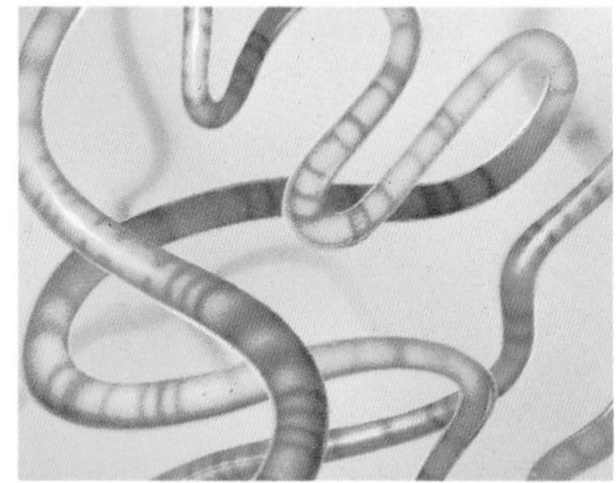

2

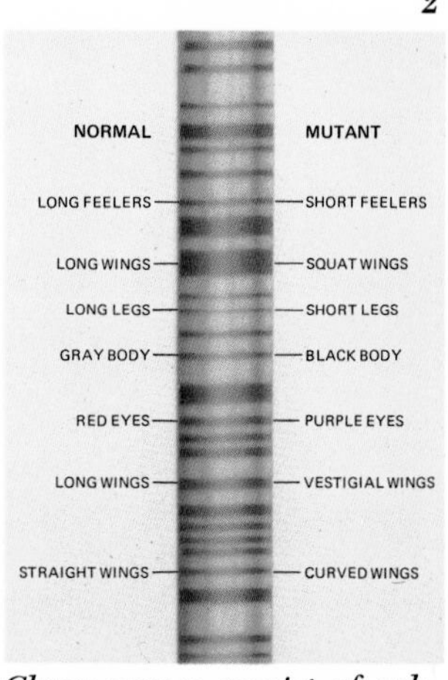

Chromosomes consist of subunits called genes, each of which controls a specific feature. Changes in genes cause mutations: above, part of the genetic map of a fruit fly.

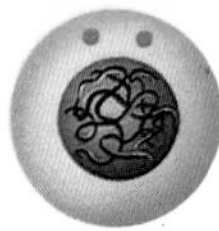

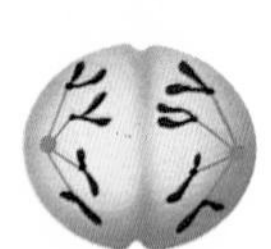

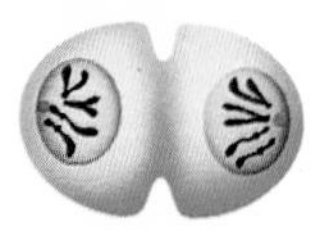

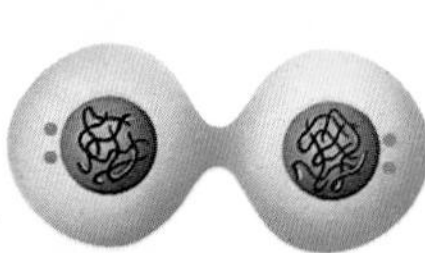

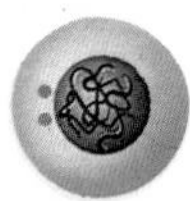

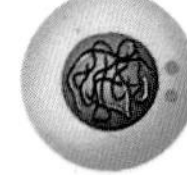

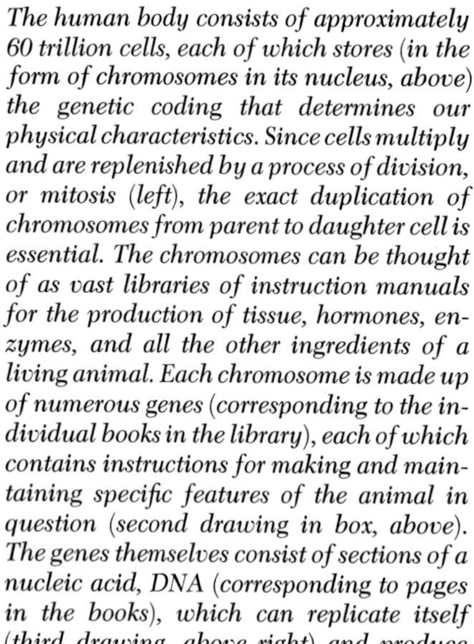

LIFE AT A CELLULAR LEVEL

The human body consists of approximately 60 trillion cells, each of which stores (in the form of chromosomes in its nucleus, above) the genetic coding that determines our physical characteristics. Since cells multiply and are replenished by a process of division, or mitosis (left), the exact duplication of chromosomes from parent to daughter cell is essential. The chromosomes can be thought of as vast libraries of instruction manuals for the production of tissue, hormones, enzymes, and all the other ingredients of a living animal. Each chromosome is made up of numerous genes (corresponding to the individual books in the library), each of which contains instructions for making and maintaining specific features of the animal in question (second drawing in box, above). The genes themselves consist of sections of a nucleic acid, DNA (corresponding to pages in the books), which can replicate itself (third drawing, above right) and produce three kinds of another nucleic acid, RNA. The nucleic acids themselves are composed of nucleotide bases, phosphates, and sugars (fourth drawing, far right); these correspond to the letters of the language in which the many genetic volumes are written.

living organisms, the phage consists of a core of DNA surrounded by a protein sheath. Because it cannot reproduce on its own, the phage invades a bacterial cell and takes over its genetic machinery, causing it to produce phages instead of more cells.

To pinpoint which substance in the phage was responsible for this process, the Carnegie researchers tagged the protein and the DNA with different radioactive tracers, then analyzed the cell contents before and after the phage attacked it. The results showed that before entering the cell wall, the phage shed its protein covering; only DNA entered the cell's nucleus, and therefore DNA, not protein, was the phage's genetic instrument. Thus researchers were forced to conclude that DNA was the long-sought agent of heredity.

Once the role of DNA had been identified, the investigation of its chemical makeup began in earnest. It was already known that DNA molecules are long chains of organic compounds called nucleotides and that each nucleotide link contains a sugar, a phosphate, and one of four nitrogen bases: adenine, thymine, guanine, or cytosine—commonly shortened to A, T, G, and C. It still remained, though, for someone to determine how these substances combine to create a DNA molecule, and this task was taken up in several European and North American laboratories.

At the University of London Maurice Wilkins, a student of DNA, was attempting to determine its molecular structure by the painstaking technique of X-ray crystallography. X-rays were passed through purified DNA crystals and scattered, forming a cloudy pattern of points and rings on a photographic plate. The shadowy

3

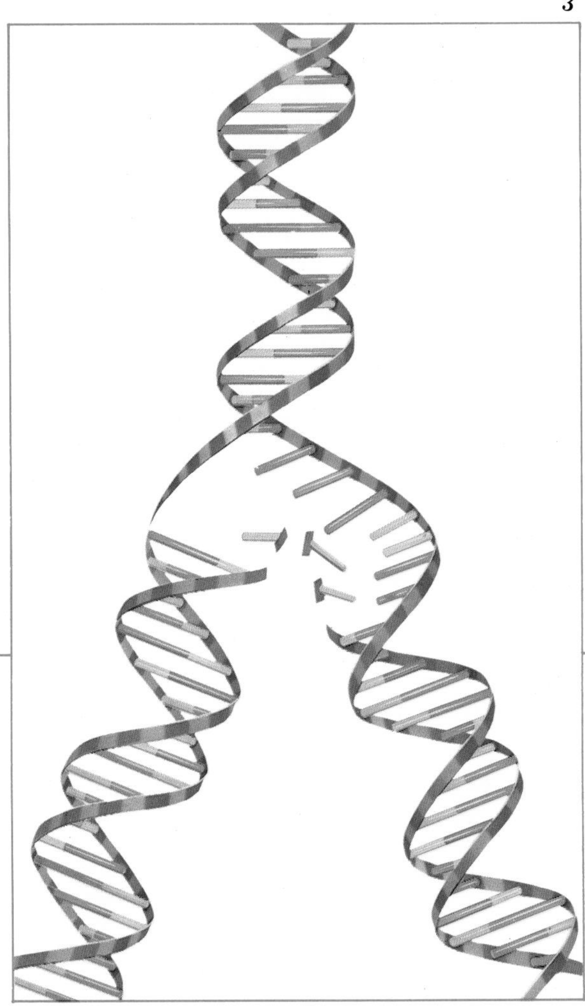

Genes consist of DNA, a nucleic acid whose molecules are arranged in a double spiral. When a cell is ready to replicate itself, an enzyme, DNA polymerase, causes the two strands of the DNA spiral to "unzip." On each of the unzipped strands nucleotides, previously floating free in the nucleus, link up in a sequence dictated by, and complementary to, the order of bases on the two free strands (below). When the process is finished, two complete DNA molecules have been formed, each one of which is identical to the original.

4

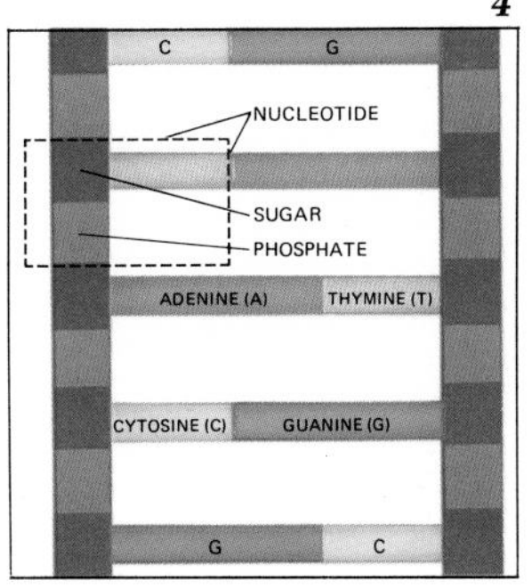

DNA molecules are formed from subunits called nucleotides (inset), each composed of a sugar and phosphate molecule attached to one of four bases—adenine, thymine, guanine, or cytosine. The sugars and phosphates form the backbone of each DNA strand, while the bases on one strand bond to those on the other, as shown here.

outlines of the X-ray photographs lent themselves to a number of different interpretations, but Wilkins concluded that they most likely indicated some type of helical (spiral) structure.

In May 1951 Wilkins met another DNA enthusiast, James Watson, at a scientific conference in Naples. Watson was then studying the chemistry of DNA and RNA in Copenhagen. He was excited by a photo Wilkins had brought with him, which showed the DNA crystal with remarkable clarity. That fall the 22-year-old Watson transferred to the Cavendish Laboratory at Cambridge University, where he met Francis Crick. Before long Watson and Crick discovered their common fascination with DNA and began collaborating. Studying photographs obtained from Wilkins and gathering other chemical evidence, they began building models of the mysterious DNA molecule.

At the California Institute of Technology Linus Pauling (who was to win a Nobel Prize for Chemistry in 1954 and another for Peace in 1962) was also building models. In the summer of 1951 he unveiled a model of the alpha helix, an important protein structure, and at the beginning of 1952 he completed his own model of the DNA molecule. Pauling's version, composed of three helical strands, soon proved erroneous—much to the relief of Watson and Crick.

The Coding Machine

During the next 18 months Watson and Crick set up and demolished numerous models in their attempt to understand the structure of DNA and its mode of replication. Working first with twisted metal wires, they later had parts machined in the Cavendish workshop, obtaining the precise measurements they needed from the studies of Wilkins and his colleague Rosalind Franklin. One piece of information was to prove especially valuable in the final, hectic days of their work. Erwin Chargaff, a biochemist at Columbia University in New York City, had found that in every DNA sample he analyzed there was an equal amount of adenine and thymine and an equal amount of guanine and cytosine. He also discovered that the ratio of A and T to G and C differed from one kind of organism to another but remained constant within a particular species.

By fits and starts the Cavendish team made progress. In his book *The Double Helix* Watson has described the combination of restless curiosity, personal frictions, discouraging setbacks, and sudden intuition that characterized his collaboration with Crick. From the start they assumed that the molecule had a helical structure with "backbones" of sugar and phosphate. Like Pauling they began by tinkering with three-stranded helices, some with inner and some with outer backbones.

Early in 1953 they decided to try a double helix with two outer backbones. In this model each base would be connected at one end to one of the backbones and at the other to another base, the bases meeting at points between the two spiraling strands of sugar and phosphate. This double helix fitted all the known data precisely, but the sequence of the bases presented a major problem. At first they paired like bases, A's with A's, T's with T's, and so on, but this made for an awkward configuration, since the base molecules were of different sizes, and the matching pairs created a ripple along the outer backbones.

In a moment of insight Watson found the solution: If an A were paired with a T in a certain way, the resulting molecule was the same size as a G paired with a C. Such a pairing eliminated the ripples in the backbones and accounted for the equal amounts of A and T bases and of G and C bases observed by Chargaff. Here at last was a three-dimensional configuration of the DNA molecule. Maurice Wilkins' photographs confirmed that they had indeed solved the mystery of DNA.

"It is a strange model," Watson and Crick conceded in a note to the British scientific journal *Nature*, requesting publication of their findings. "However," they continued, "since DNA is an unusual substance, we are not hesitant in being bold. . . . It has not escaped our notice that the specific pairing [of bases] we have postulated suggests a possible copying mechanism for the genetic material."

As conceived by Watson and Crick, the DNA molecule resembles a spiral ladder. The two winding strands of sugar and phosphate that form the sides are held together by "rungs" composed of joined pairs of bases. Only A's can join with T's, and only C's with G's, but any sequence of paired bases is possible. In a human cell the entire DNA ladder is about a yard long and contains as many as 6 billion rungs. A single human gene, giving the information necessary to manufacture one of thousands of proteins, might be a length of the ladder with 2,000 rungs.

When a cell reproduces, the DNA ladder comes apart at the center in something like an unzipping action. Each linked pair of bases separates, and the separated halves obtain new partners from free-floating molecules in the cell's nucleus. All A's link up with new T's and all G's link up with new C's, and so on, until they form two exact replicas of the original. In this way the parent cell can divide into two new cells, each one carrying identical DNA molecules.

Transmitting the Message

Once Watson and Crick had discovered how DNA reproduces itself, and thereby insures that subsequent generations of cells continue to transmit the same genetic message, scientists began looking for clues to an

Many biochemical processes, including those involving DNA, are mediated by enzymes, which bring chemicals with little natural affinity into close enough proximity for bonding to occur. They do this by virtue of their own affinity for the chemicals. After bonding, the enzyme (left) drops out of the process.

In addition to replicating itself, DNA also serves, in the presence of the appropriate enzymes, as the template for other nucleic acids, including messenger RNA (below) and transfer RNA (bottom). These are formed in the same way as DNA, except that they are all single, not double, stranded, and the thymine base is replaced by uracil (U).

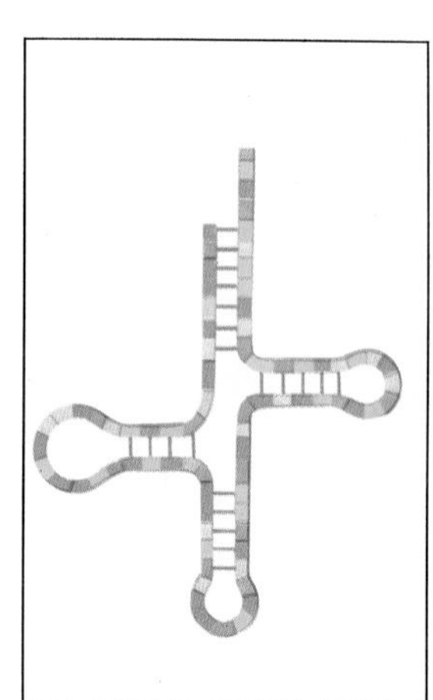

At one end of the transfer RNA molecule (right) the same group of three bases (adenine and two cytosines) always occurs; with the help of an enzyme it serves as the bonding point between the tRNA molecule and its specific amino acid. At the other end a group of three variable bases (the anticodon), in conjunction with a ribosome, mates with a complementary group of three bases (the codon) on the messenger RNA chain.

PARTNERS IN THE DANCE OF LIFE

Protein manufacture demands that amino acids be linked into long chains, in specific sequences that determine the protein's chemical characteristics. This is accomplished within the cell's cytoplasm by messenger RNA (mRNA), transfer RNA (tRNA), and ribosomes—aggregations of ribosomal RNA and protein. The process begins when a ribosome starts to move along an mRNA chain. As a binding site on the ribosome engages an mRNA codon—a group of three bases—the ribosome halts, allowing a tRNA molecule, with an amino acid attached, to bind to the codon. Once the mRNA-tRNA-amino acid bond has formed, the ribosome moves along the mRNA chain, breaking the mRNA-tRNA bond. As it pauses at the next codon, another tRNA molecule, again with an amino acid attached, bonds with the new codon. At this point the amino acids attached to the first and second tRNA molecules bond together; as this happens, the first tRNA molecule becomes detached from its amino acid, leaving the second tRNA with a two-link amino acid chain. In some of the larger and more complex protein molecules a chain of this type may be more than five hundred amino acids in length.

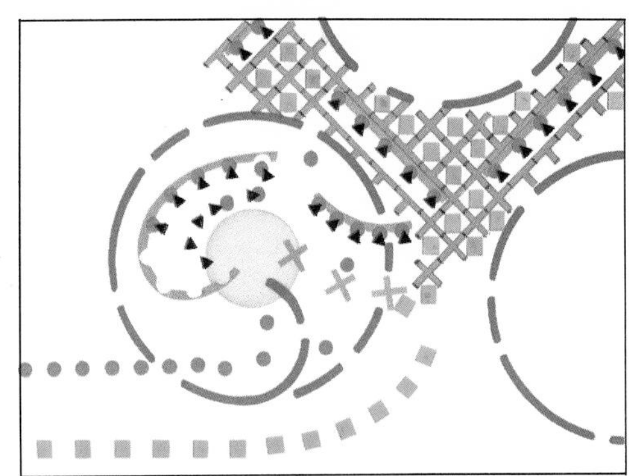

Proteins have numerous biochemical uses. In bone cells (above) nutrients ● acted on by certain enzymes ▲ yield the protein collagen . The nutrients also provide the raw material for other bone-producing proteins: enzymes that organize collagen into fibers, and other enzymes — that make the cell wall permeable to these fibers. Bone is formed when further enzymes + cause minerals ■ to precipitate around the collagen.

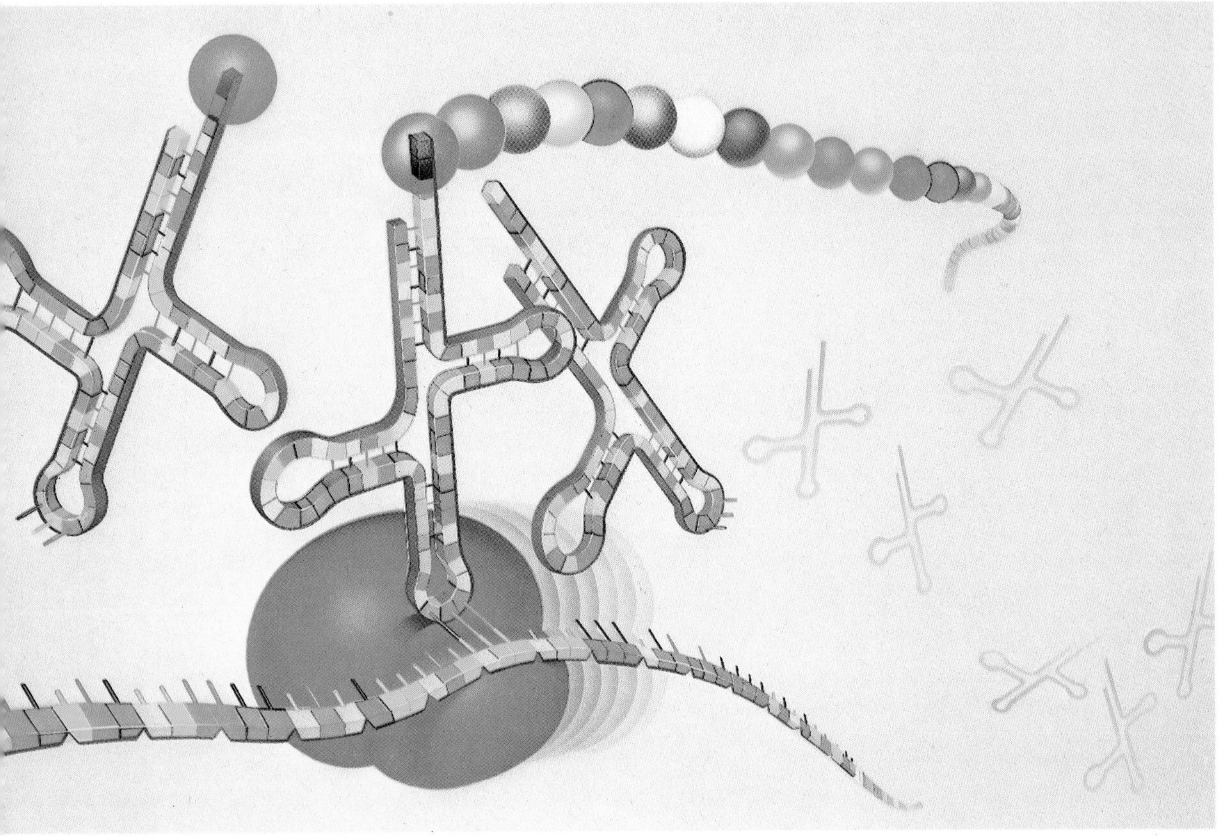

Each codon on the mRNA chain is highly selective and will bind only to a tRNA molecule whose anticodon is complementary. Since tRNA molecules are themselves highly selective of the amino acids they will bind to, mRNA codons in effect select specific amino acids. Thus the sequence of mRNA codons, itself determined by the original sequence of bases on the DNA template, determines the sequence of amino acids in an amino acid chain—that is, in a protein.

CELLS GONE WILD: CANCER AND THE DANCE OF DEATH

All living things are potentially subject to cancer. Among humans the rate of death due to the disease has tripled during the century, and all signs indicate that an even more rapid increase is imminent. So far, though, there is no clear understanding of what causes cancer or of how it may finally be cured. In fact, there are over 100 distinct varieties of cancer, each caused by different factors—perhaps including some not purely biological: Researchers have found evidence that emotional stress, for example, may sometimes trigger renewed activity in a long-dormant tumor.

Tumors—aggregations of mutant cells in a state of uncontrolled proliferation—can originate in virtually any tissue. Benign tumors may become quite large, but are contained within the tissue of their origin; malignant tumors may involve adjacent tissues and frequently spread to distant parts of the body via the blood and lymphatic systems. This migration (metastasis) is what makes cancer lethal.

Today scientists are more and more convinced that the major causative agents of cancer (carcinogens) are environmental rather than genetic. Every day we are exposed to an alarming number of carcinogens—in the food we eat, in the drugs we take, in the smoke we inhale, in the chemicals we absorb, and in the radiation we receive. And since the incubation period for cancer is relatively long (20 to 35 years of exposure to a carcinogen, by most estimates), it is difficult to predict in advance the possible effects of any new substance entering into general or industrial use. One tragic example of this delayed-action effect involves the daughters of women who, in the 1940's and 1950's, took the synthetic estrogen diethylstilbestrol (DES) to prevent miscarriage; these young women are now proving particularly susceptible to an often fatal form of vaginal cancer. If the contraceptive pill should prove to be similarly carcinogenic (definitive results will not be obtained until it has been in general use for at least 20 years), the result could be a cancer epidemic of unimaginable proportions.

Currently, there are four levels of cancer treatment: surgical removal of the tumor; radiation therapy to kill any remaining traces of it; chemotherapy to impede regrowth; and, to a lesser extent, immunotherapy—attempts to stimulate the body's own immune system into destroying cancerous cells. So far none of these methods, singly or in combination, has proved to be a certain cure for cancer, and less than 50 percent of all patients are permanently cured. Since a cancer cure-all is not immediately foreseeable, hopes of controlling the disease are pegged to improvements in prediagnostic methods of prevention and in early diagnostic techniques, as well as in the treatments used after diagnosis.

even more mysterious process: the way in which the message is received and translated into living tissue. Basically, this involves the continual production of new proteins in the cytoplasm (the part of the cell surrounding the nucleus). Proteins, incredibly versatile and complex substances, are the building blocks of life. They form most bodily fibers and tissues as well as hemoglobin, hormones, antibodies, and enzymes. In chemical terms a protein is a long chain of amino acids. (Some proteins, such as hemoglobin, consist of several such chains.) Since there are 20 kinds of amino acids and since a protein chain can be thousands of links long, the variety of proteins, and thus of the biochemical tasks they can perform is almost unlimited. A mammalian cell, for example, may be able to synthesize well over 1 million different proteins.

Watson and Crick had postulated that protein is not manufactured directly by DNA but through an intermediary, RNA (ribonucleic acid), a close relative of DNA. It was this substance that proved to be the essential link in the genetic process. RNA is similar to DNA in its chemical makeup, with a sugar-phosphate backbone and four nitrogen bases. It differs in two important ways: RNA molecules are single stranded, and they contain the base uracil (U) instead of thymine (T). Like thymine, however, uracil can bond with adenine but not with guanine or cytosine. RNA is synthesized by DNA in a process similar to the one by which DNA reproduces itself. An enzyme (RNA polymerase) causes the DNA molecule to become partially "unzipped," and on one strand (which serves as a template) RNA is formed as a single, nonhelical strand with a complementary sequence of A, U, G, and C bases.

In the early 1960's researchers identified three different kinds of RNA, each synthesized by DNA and each with a specific function; messenger RNA (mRNA), transfer RNA (tRNA), and ribosomal RNA (rRNA). Messenger RNA acts as template for linking amino acids into the proper sequence to form a specific protein. Transfer RNA, with the help of certain activating enzymes, "selects" the appropriate free amino acids and serves as an adaptor to fit them to the mRNA template. The actual linking of amino acids (via mRNA and tRNA) to form proteins always occurs on the surface of spherical particles called ribosomes, which may account for as much as one-quarter of a cell's mass. Ribosomes are the gathering points for the three kinds of RNA and consist of approximately two-thirds RNA and one-third protein. Ribosomal RNA (rRNA) does not have the same kind of template function as the other two forms but constitutes the ribosome and orientates them correctly for the business of protein synthesis.

As the ribosome moves along the mRNA chain, a group of three bases (a codon) on the mRNA chain contacts a binding site on the ribosome and renders it specific to a particular tRNA molecule. The appropri-

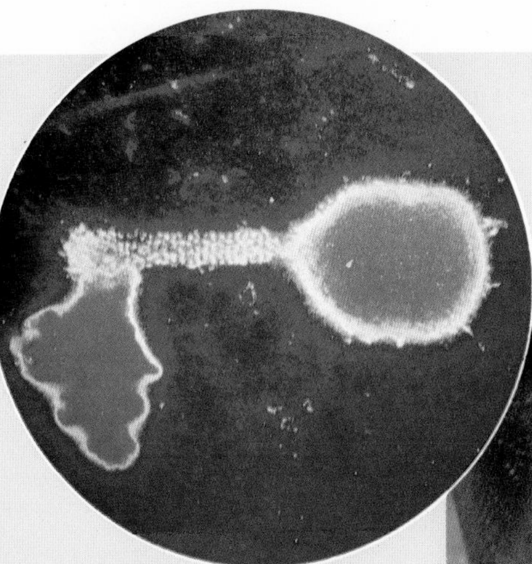

According to the repressor gene theory, the wild proliferation of cells—that is, cancer—is prevented by specific repressor genes, unless carcinogens render them inactive. The genetic structure of viruses like the one at left has been mapped with great precision, and mutated viruses have served as tools in genetic engineering. If the theory is correct, and if more complex human chromosomes can be mapped accurately enough, it may one day be possible to repair damaged repressors.

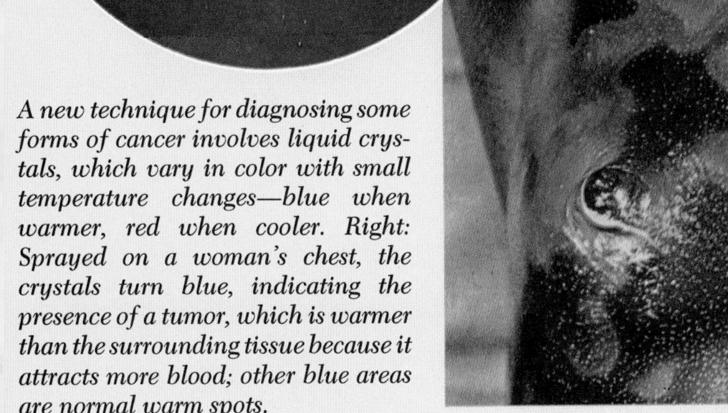

A new technique for diagnosing some forms of cancer involves liquid crystals, which vary in color with small temperature changes—blue when warmer, red when cooler. Right: Sprayed on a woman's chest, the crystals turn blue, indicating the presence of a tumor, which is warmer than the surrounding tissue because it attracts more blood; other blue areas are normal warm spots.

ate tRNA molecule, which is already carrying a specific amino acid at its other end, then bonds to the mRNA and ribosome at that point. The ribosome then moves along the mRNA chain, displacing the first tRNA molecule and bringing another codon into contact with the binding site. The binding site is thereby modified again to receive another tRNA molecule bearing another amino acid. As the first tRNA molecule detaches from the binding site to make way for its successor, the amino acid it was carrying bonds to the amino acid borne by the second tRNA molecule and becomes detached from its own tRNA molecule. As the ribosome passes over successive codons of mRNA this process is repeated, and a chain of amino acids—a protein—is formed. Once the protein chain is complete, the ribosome is free to work with another mRNA molecule.

The Language of Life

We now know that 61 of the 64 codons embodied in messenger RNA in the genetic vocabulary relate to the 20 amino acids (GAA codes for glutamic acid, CAU for histidine, and so on), while the remaining three codons serve as punctuation marks in the instructions needed to create a particular protein. At the same time, though, genetic chemistry has become even more complex than it seemed at first. New varieties of DNA and RNA have been discovered, and some viruses are now known to be capable of synthesizing DNA from RNA. There are also indications that some RNA may be stored in the cell's outer membrane, where it can communicate with and help regulate the growth of adjacent cells. If this is so, malfunctioning RNA might be partly responsible for the uncontrolled cell reproduction associated with cancer.

The biggest questions now being asked of the genetic code concern its self-regulation. How does DNA "know" when to start and when to stop producing each of the three main varieties of RNA? And how do they in turn "know" exactly what quantities of proteins are required from one moment to the next?

Science has now read a few pages written in the language through which molecules, cells, and tissues communicate. One result (especially of those readings in the sophisticated dialogue maintained between giant molecules and cells) is that the traditional distinction between living and nonliving material has been blurred, if not eliminated; the same is true of traditional distinctions between biology on the one hand and chemistry and physics on the other. Another result is the awareness that chapters, volumes, and whole libraries written in this language are still waiting to be read and that within them may lie the answers not only to the most vexing scientific questions—those concerning the origins of cancer, for example—but also to others more philosophical, concerning the relationship of mind to matter.

THE ARTS 1957-76

Technology and Art

The launching of the Soviet satellite Sputnik in 1957 marked the beginning of an all-out race among nations for technological supremacy. The achievements of that race—including moonwalks, interplanetary probes, and telecommunications satellites—have changed the way man looks at himself. This change is evident in the world of art: Since the launching of Sputnik there has been an unprecedented wedding of art and technology.

Although artists have always used whatever technological developments pertained to their crafts, since the late 1950's they have been emphasizing the importance of technology itself. Two of the most prominent figures have been American artist Robert Rauschenberg and German composer Karlheinz Stockhausen. Rauschenberg has worked alone and with groups to create a new kind of art that will appeal not only to the sense of sight, but to the other four senses as well. Stockhausen is generally considered the leading composer of electronic music.

Robert Rauschenberg On an indoor tennis court illuminated by 48 lights, two players volleyed. Every time a player hit the ball his racket, which was rigged with a contact microphone and Actan switches, made a loud bong and turned out one of the lights. When the building was reduced to darkness, 700 people entered the court area, talking softly, and then went out again. The audience was able to see these people only through two infrared television cameras. When the throng had gone, the artist entered, carrying a woman wrapped in a canvas bag. While he marched solemnly across the tennis court the woman sang softly. The artist then exited with his mysterious package, and the piece ended in the reverent way some liturgical celebrations end—in silence, in darkness.

The piece, called "Open Score," was created by Robert Rauschenberg and engineer Jim McGee for Nine Evenings: Theatre and Engineering, an exhibition organized by Rauschenberg and Swedish-born engineer Wilhelm (Billy) Klüver. Nine Evenings involved 9 artists—including Rauschenberg, Robert Whitman, and composers John Cage and David Tudor—and 19 engineers, most of whom were colleagues of Klüver, who was working on electron beam and laser research at Bell Laboratories. The show was given in October 1966 at New York City's 69th Regiment Armory, the site of the historic Armory Show of 1913, which had introduced to Americans the avant-garde works of leading European artists. Like its predecessor, Nine Evenings presented a controversial challenge to the art world. It was the first attempt by U.S. artists and technicians to work together on a project on a grand scale. Such a collaboration was the natural outcome of the works and views of Rauschenberg, who, consciously or unconsciously, had been working toward it through most of his adult life.

Rauschenberg was born in Port Arthur, Texas, in 1925. He served in

The Pepsi Pavilion *(above) at Japan's Expo '70 was the most ambitious (and expensive) project undertaken by EAT, the avant-garde association cofounded in 1966 by Robert Rauschenberg and Billy Klüver.*

Capped by five *rotating disks (right), Canada's futuristic Palace of Mirrors likewise combined disparate art forms with the newest in electronic technology to create its own multimedia environment.*

the U.S. Navy during World War II and then studied art at the Kansas City Art Institute, the Académie Julien in Paris, Black Mountain College in North Carolina, and the Art Students League in New York City. At Black Mountain Rauschenberg came under the influence of the innovative composer of electronic music John Cage, who taught him to incorporate into his work materials found in the environment.

Living in New York City in the late 1950's, Rauschenberg combed the thrift shops and junk stores of Manhattan's Lower East Side for materials for his paintings—old clothes and photographs, street signs, scrap paper. These he worked into combine paintings—works created with traditional artists' tools to which outside materials are added. The most significant of Rauschenberg's combine paintings was "Broadcast" (1959), a work of assorted materials, including three radios tuned to different stations. When the viewer turned the knobs protruding from the canvas, the radios exploded with independent bursts of sound.

In discussing his combine paintings of the 1950's Rauschenberg later commented: "I felt as though I were collaborating with the neighborhood." This collaboration made him one of the most important figures in the pop art movement of the 1960's, a movement that focused on the banal, vulgar, and commercial objects that make up the contemporary industrial environment.

Nine Evenings

In the early 1960's Rauschenberg was continuously expanding the scope of his work, introducing an increasing amount of technology into his artistic collaborations with the neighborhood. Collaborating with the neighborhood, he argued, means collaborating with nature, and technology is "contemporary nature."

In 1965 Rauschenberg worked with Billy Klüver in constructing "Oracle," a highly sensitive radio-controlled sculpture in five parts. While working together both Rauschenberg and Klüver, who had previously worked on art projects with the Swiss junk sculptor Jean Tinguely and pop artist Andy Warhol, became convinced of the need for a large scale collaboration of artists and technicians. At the time there were a number of groups of artists in Europe who were successfully collaborating on works of art. The first of these, Group Zero of Germany, had recently given shows in the United States, exhibiting a number of works that incorporated technology. Encouraged by such shows, Rauschenberg and Klüver produced Nine Evenings in October 1966. Working on a shoestring budget, the engineers, who donated more than 3,000 hours to the project, were unable to work out all the technological kinks before the opening of the show. Nevertheless, Nine Evenings managed to achieve a great deal of technical success and marked the dawning of a new and totally different artistic age.

EAT and Its Work

Elated over the success of Nine Evenings, Rauschenberg, Klüver, and a few other artists and engineers founded Experiments in Art and Technology, Inc. (EAT), an organization designed to bring together

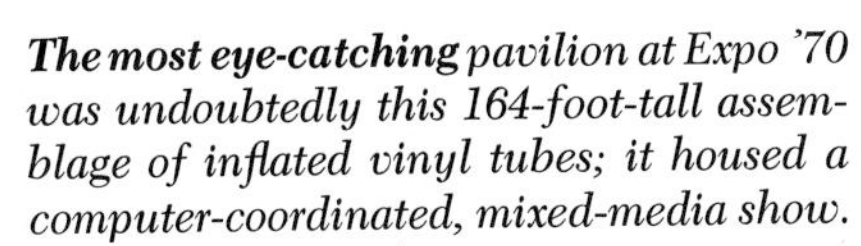

***The most eye-catching** pavilion at Expo '70 was undoubtedly this 164-foot-tall assemblage of inflated vinyl tubes; it housed a computer-coordinated, mixed-media show.*

***Portrait of the artist:** Robert Rauschenberg (right) in his New York City studio with one of his distinctive combine paintings.*

artists and engineers from all parts of the United States. The purpose of EAT, announced Rauschenberg and Klüver, "is to catalyze the inevitable active involvement of industry, technology, and the arts" and, in addition, to develop "an effective collaborative relationship between artists and engineers."

EAT soon attracted the attention of some major corporation executives and received a number of grants from big business firms. By the early 1970's its national membership included 3,000 artists and 3,000 engineers.

In its first few years EAT sponsored close to 500 collaborative works and 2 major projects—Some More Beginnings, an exhibition at the Brooklyn Museum in 1968, and the Pepsi-Cola pavilion at Expo '70, the 1970 world's fair at Osaka, Japan. EAT also promoted numerous artists-in-residence and museum-based engineers-in-residence programs that were sponsored by industrial firms. It established Japanese chapters of artists and engineers and organized Projects Outside Art, programs that brought together educators, scientists, engineers, and artists to experiment with new kinds of learning environments and related problems.

In spite of the controversy it spurred, the Pepsi-Cola pavilion at Expo '70 was one of EAT's most successful projects. The project was directed by Billy Klüver, who was once referred to by a museum official as "the Edison-Tesla-Steinmetz-Marconi-Leonardo da Vinci of the American avant-garde." More than 30 engineers and artists worked for two years in developing a space age setting that would allow spectators to participate actively in a 21st-century environment. The spherical pavilion was rigged with a light and sound system that responded to the movements and sounds of the spectators. A technologically produced cloud of fog hovered over the dome. Other features of the pavilion included the world's largest spherical mirror, which produced three-dimensional reflections of the audience on the domed ceiling, and a Japanese garden area with a landscape of slowly moving sculptures.

Artistically and technically the pavilion was a huge success, but a few weeks after its opening its creators were abruptly dismissed by the

Compared with *the technological avant-garde, Francis Bacon, perhaps the most important English painter of the century, is a traditionalist, whose paintings directly express his emotions. Right: his "Study After Velásquez's Portrait of Pope Innocent X"; above: Diego Velásquez's original (c. 1647). In Bacon's version, the former symbol of spiritual and worldly power becomes a helpless figure, trapped and twisted in a glass box extrapolated from the papal chair.*

Chuck Close, *a New York photorealist, chose a black-and-white photograph as the starting point for his 9-foot-high portrait "Keith." He then followed the technology of the camera meticulously, even re-creating, in places, the shallow depth of focus of the camera lens.*

TECHNIQUES AND INTERPRETATIONS

As more and more artists first came to terms with, and then embraced, the technology of the 1960's and 1970's, a major trend emerged. It was characterized by a cool, detached manner, and its exponents—such as the conceptual artists and the photorealists—tended to forego emotion in favor of more intellectual and ironic moods.

Other artists, resisting this trend, followed a more humanistic tradition; by the mid-1970's they were in the minority, but among them were some of the period's most eminent painters.

The differences between these two trends, the technological and humanistic, reflect two quite different views of the artistic process and of the artist's role in society; they can perhaps be most easily understood when representatives of the two schools, such as Chuck Close (above) and Francis Bacon (left), re-create an existing work in their own terms and thereby reveal their intentions through the divergence between the new work and the old.

Pepsi-Cola Company as the result of a long-standing controversy over money and esthetics. Officials at Pepsi-Cola said the dismissal was prompted largely by EAT's failure to keep within the agreed-upon operating budget. EAT claimed the dismissal came because of esthetic differences—their project, which would have featured 24 different programs by 24 different artist-programers, was a far cry from the more orthodox Disneyland-type productions sponsored by other companies at Expo '70. EAT worked out a settlement with Pepsi-Cola and continued working on a variety of projects for five more years. In 1975 Experiments in Art and Technology, Inc., came to a quiet end, and Rauschenberg, Klüver, and the other artists and engineers who had been associated with it went on to other things.

In its nine-year history EAT had created a climate for the increased acceptance of the collaborative efforts of artists and technicians and had set the stage for a greater collaboration between artists and leaders in industry. If the efforts of EAT were uneven, it was at least partly because the artists needed more time to master and learn to integrate a staggering number of new materials, including video tape, laser light, and computers. Rauschenberg had summed up the problem when he commented: "I think that in the beginning collaborative work is going to be necessarily self-conscious about the technology, no matter who the artist is; parallel to the first drawings he did with a pencil. A mature esthetic is the result of familiarity with, and accomplishment in, your medium."

Although the artists of the art and technology movement have yet to produce major works with their new materials, they have opened up a new direction for art. The first experiments of the artists and technicians in the 1960's and 1970's may prove to be the preliminary sketches for the great works of the future.

Karlheinz Stockhausen As some graphic artists were redefining the boundaries of art through their experiments with new technological materials, many composers were exploring similar paths in music. Like Rauschenberg, they worked with the latest technological innovations, particularly in the field of electronics.

In the late 1940's the French composers Pierre Schaeffer and Pierre Henry carried out the first significant experiments in music and electronics. Exploring related musical regions with the magnetic tape recorder, they created *musique concrète,* tape collages of natural sounds produced by man and his environment. In the early 1950's Otto Luening and Vladimir Ussachevsky of Columbia University composed works for tape recorder and orchestra. In 1959 Luening, Ussachevsky, and composer Milton Babbitt founded the Columbia-Princeton Electronic Music Center, where they worked with an electronic music synthesizer. A technological device developed in 1955 by the Radio Corporation of America, the synthesizer greatly facilitates the mixing of taped sounds.

A number of other composers experimented further with tape recorders, synthesizers, digital computors, and other electronic devices. Sounds of all kinds—both natural and manmade—were arranged, mixed, distorted, slowed down, speeded up, or otherwise manipulated to create artistic works. These electronically processed sounds—usually on magnetic recording tape—were used as individual works in themselves or were mixed with music performed by live instrumentalists or singers.

The use of electronic processing greatly extended the range and variety of sounds available to composers, and soon electronic music, as it naturally came to be called, was attracting worldwide attention. The opportunity to write music using an entirely new technology proved irresistible. Of the many composers who began creating electronic works, the most outstanding was Karlheinz Stockhausen.

Electronic and Spatial Music
Stockhausen was born near Cologne, Germany, in 1928. After following a rigorous four-year music program at Cologne's Hochschule für Musik, he became interested in the unlimited possibilities of electronic music. From 1952 to 1954 he studied physics and acoustics at the University of Bonn. In 1953 he joined the Studio for Electronic Music, a newly formed workshop at a Cologne radio station.

The studio proved ideal for composing and broadcasting electronic music. During his first years Stockhausen composed *Electronic Studies 1 and 2* (1953), *Contacts* (1960), and one of his best works, *The Song of the Youths* (1956) for a boy's voice and electronic sound. The work reflected Stockhausen's commitment to exploring music beyond the limits of performed instrumental and vocal sounds.

In addition to composing, Stockhausen did all he could to promote electronic music. He developed a system of notation for electronic sounds, and in 1955 he helped found *Die Reihe* ("The Row"), a music journal for which he wrote many articles on electronic music.

Stockhausen combined his concern for an open-ended experimentation in sounds with a preoccupation with what he called "new musical time space," that is, spatial, or directional, music. Unlike traditional performances, in which the music reaches the listeners from only one direction—usually from a raised stage—spatial music comes from several directions. The effect is similar to that achieved by quadraphonic sound.

One of the best and most exciting examples of Stockhausen's spatial music is *Groups* (1959), which is performed simultaneously by three orchestras in three separate parts of the concert hall. Stockhausen has remarked about this work: "They play . . . partially independently in different tempi; from time to time they meet in common rhythm; they call to each other and answer each other; for a whole period of time one hears only music from the left, or from the front, or from the right. The sound wanders from one orchestra to another."

The Cosmic Composer
Stockhausen's music sometimes seems to be almost without boundaries. It is constantly reaching out beyond the known. "If the stars are not made for me," Stockhausen once remarked, "then I wouldn't be interested in the universe. My music must receive those universal vibrations like some fantastic radio. Ultimately we are all looking for unity with the Divine. I believe the moment has come in the Western Hemisphere to move from intelligence to intuition, to the irrational, where spirit replaces flesh."

This cosmic spirit is best reflected in *Anthems for Electronic and Concrete Sounds* (1967), an evening-long composition. *Anthems* is divided into four "regions," each of which features the national anthem of a different country. An orchestra plays the anthems to the accompaniment of miscellaneous sounds, ranging from the heavy breathing of the orchestra members to the recorded sounds of jungle animals. It is a mystifying work, a 21st-century hymn to the universe.

Few of technology's new inventions are more readily adapted to the uses of art than the laser, which can produce a virtually infinite variety of three-dimensional designs with intense, uncommonly clear colors. Left: images from Laserium, a laser-and-music "concert."

***Man and machine:** Karlheinz Stockhausen superintends (below left, standing) as his associates set up a synthesizer and other advanced equipment for an open-air performance of the electronic music he helped elevate from a novelty to a serious art form.*

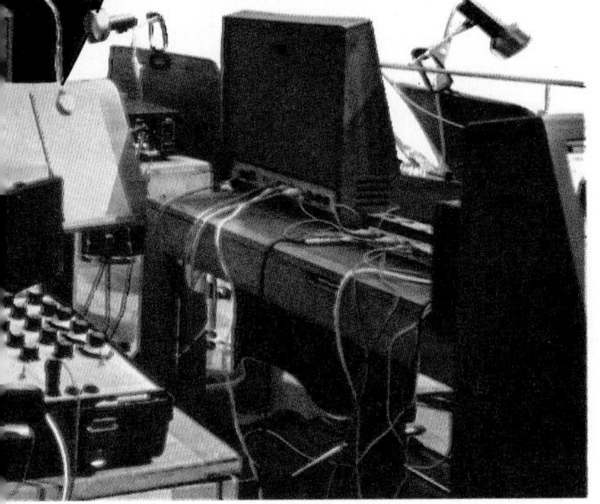

Stockhausen still helps to shape the music of the 1970's, influencing even the most traditional composers. He has been called a genius and a prophet, yet many critics find his work enigmatic. In his own view, creating any work of art "is like building a city—like New York—and putting all kinds of people into it. You must have courage to let forces bang against each other and establish harmony. Music is a state of being. Sometimes the more strange it is, the more layers of yourself you can wake up. It's not just for the evening when you're tired, it's not to be used as a meeting ground. It's a means to a new awareness—music will transform people, we will become like music, more open, cosmically oriented."

A CHRONOLOGY OF THE ARTS: 1957-76

1957

• French writer Albert Camus, author of *The Stranger, The Plague,* and other works, won the Nobel Prize for Literature.

1958

• The young, little-known U.S. pianist Van Cliburn became the first American to win the prestigious Tchaikovsky Competition in Moscow.

1959

• French filmmaker François Truffaut's *The 400 Blows* inaugurated the New Wave trend in motion pictures, typified by fast, low-budget production and a loose, improvisational style.

1961

• U.S. novelist Henry Miller's *Tropic of Cancer* was legally published in the U.S.A. for the first time after a 27-year ban for obscenity.

1962

• Edward Albee was established as a major U.S. playwright with *Who's Afraid of Virginia Woolf?,* a searing portrait of two married couples.

1963

• German dramatist Rolf Hochhuth sparked an international controversy with *The Deputy,* which centered on the failure of Pope Pius XII to speak out against Hitler's extermination of the Jews.

• Works by Andy Warhol, Robert Rauschenberg, Jasper Johns, and others were featured in an exhibit of Pop Art at New York's Guggenheim Museum.

1964

• The Beatles, Britain's sensational rock group, made their U.S. debut.

• *A Moveable Feast,* Ernest Hemingway's memoir of the Paris literary scene in the 1920's, was published posthumously.

1965

• Russian-born virtuoso Vladimir Horowitz, considered by many the world's greatest pianist, returned to the concert stage after a 12-year period of seclusion.

• U.S.-born poet and critic T. S. Eliot, a towering literary figure whose works included *The Waste Land* and *Four Quartets,* died at age 76.

1966

• Floods in Italy destroyed or damaged thousands of art treasures in Florence and Venice; a massive rescue effort prevented further losses.

1968

• The innovative rock musical *Hair* opened on Broadway, celebrating the youthful counterculture and launching a trend toward nudity onstage.

1969

• More than 400,000 young people gathered near Bethel, New York, for the three-day Woodstock Music and Art Fair.

1971

• The John F. Kennedy Center for the Performing Arts in Washington, D.C., opened with the premiere of Leonard Bernstein's *Mass.*

• Russian-born composer Igor Stravinsky, whose ballet score *The Rite of Spring* heralded the birth of modern music, died at the age of 88.

1973

• Spanish-born painter and sculptor Pablo Picasso, generally acknowledged to be the most important artist of the 20th century, died at 91.

1974

• Nobel Prize–winning Soviet author and political dissident Alexander Solzhenitsyn was expelled from the U.S.S.R.

• Two prominent Soviet defectors, Mikhail Baryshnikov and Natalia Makarova, appeared together with the American Ballet Theatre.

1975

• The 50th anniversary of the Martha Graham Dance Company was celebrated with a benefit performance of her new work, "Lucifer," by Rudolf Nureyev and Dame Margot Fonteyn.

1962

The Second Vatican Council

Pope John XXIII convenes an ecumenical council and initiates a far-reaching program to modernize the Roman Catholic Church.

Some 2,500 cardinals, archbishops, bishops, and heads of major men's religious orders, clad in vestments of white, red, and purple, gathered in St. Peter's Basilica on October 11, 1962, for the opening of the Second Vatican Ecumenical Council, the 21st such council of the church. They had been summoned there by Pope John XXIII to participate in an unprecedented effort to "unsettle the dust that has been gathering on the throne of Peter since Constantine." In the years ahead these powerful prelates from the four corners of the world—these sons of peasants and princes, lawyers and stevedores, merchants and tribal chieftains—would work together to bring their ancient and complex institution into the 20th century.

Council Origins

Pope John had decided to call the historic council shortly after his elevation to the papacy in 1958. An idealistic, compassionate leader, he had been deeply disturbed by the church's inadequate response to the world's problems of war, injustice, and poverty. He was also aware of the acute need for an *aggiornamento,* a "bringing up to date," of the church. He felt that an ecumenical council would be the most dramatic way for the church to assess its role in the world and become a greater source of hope for mankind.

When he first broached the subject of a council to his close aide, Domenico Cardinal Tardini, the Pope was overwhelmed by the enthusiastic response: "Si, Si! Un concilio!" Encouraged, Pope John next revealed his plan to members of the Roman Curia, the Vatican's central governing body. To his great disappointment, they responded with an icy silence and in the following days tried to persuade him to abandon or at least delay the calling of the council.

Their opposition reflected the fear that a council might undermine the delicately balanced ecclesiastical chain of command, which they controlled. As officers of the Roman Curia, they headed the sacred congregations in charge of all aspects of church life. Conservatives who equated change with weakness, they were opposed to any movement that might threaten the hallowed traditions of the church. Their most outspoken representative was Alfredo Cardinal Ottaviani, head of the Sacred Congregation of the Holy Office, which governed all matters of faith and morals, from banning books to silencing heretics.

The Pope, however, was determined to hold the council at the earliest possible date. The aging prelate wanted to see his dream realized within his lifetime. On the very day of his election he observed that the reigns of all his namesakes had been brief. Almost at once he began making preparations for the council. In May 1959 he appointed Cardinal Tardini to supervise the task of gathering suggestions for the agenda from bishops and Catholic universities throughout the world. In June 1960 he established 10 preparatory commissions, headed by the cardinals of the Curia, to draft proposals for the council's consideration.

Some 800 theologians and scholars were summoned to Rome to help sift through and organize all available data on the existing state of ecclesiastical affairs. The findings of these commissions were ultimately summarized in a body of 73 schemata, which were presented to the council when it convened in 1962. Meanwhile, in December 1961, Pope John issued an Apostolic Constitution formally convoking the Second Vatican Council, the first such gathering since the Vatican Council held in 1869–70, and only the second since the Council of Trent in 1545–63.

In June 1962 the pontiff invited all separated Christian churches and all non-Christian religious sects to send delegates to observe the sessions of the council. The invitation was warmly received, and, in a new spirit of friendship and ecumenism, most of the world's major religious denominations sent delegates to the council. The council's first session was held from October 11 to December 8, 1962. Pope John's dream had become a reality.

The beloved pontiff was not to see the end of his dream, however, for he died on June 3, 1963, six months after the first session. His successor, Pope Paul VI, presided over the final three sessions, which convened in the autumns of 1963, 1964, and 1965. Although Pope Paul supported the council and endorsed it as "a bridge toward the contemporary world," his tendency was to steer it toward a more conservative course than the one set by Pope John.

The Council at Work

The preparatory commissions had been dominated by the most conservative church minds, and many, including most Curia members, expected that the council itself would provide a rubber stamp for their pro-

***Vatican II opened** in the golden splendor of St. Peter's Basilica. Council fathers—bishops, cardinals, and patriarchs from the world over—fill the foreground, dressed in white vestments and miters. The solemnity of the occasion gave no hint of the controversy that would split conservative and liberal factions during the working sessions. It would take all of Pope John's tact to initiate the changes he judged essential.*

***When Angelo Roncalli** was elected Pope in 1958 (left), he closed his address to the College of Cardinals with the words, "My children, love one another. . . ." This warm and deceptively plain-spoken man enjoyed the company of others and sought their advice. His goals for the Second Vatican Council were to modernize the church and to reconcile all Christians.*

***The Roman Catholic and Eastern Orthodox** Churches have been divided by a schism that began in 1054, when the reigning Pope and Patriarch excommunicated each other. After Vatican II Pope Paul (left) met Patriarch Athenagoras; in 1965 the excommunications were lifted. In 1975 the Pope kissed the feet of the envoy of the present Patriarch, Demetrios I (right), hinting at a complete reconciliation.*

posals. Instead, the gathering provoked a dramatic confrontation between liberals and conservatives.

Opposition surfaced as early as the first working session of the council, when Eugène Cardinal Tisserant, dean of the Sacred College of Cardinals and president of the council, tried to rush through the vote on members to the permanent commissions. Liberals, led by Achille Cardinal Liénart, Bishop of Lille, France, and Joseph Cardinal Frings, Archbishop of Cologne, Germany, balked at Cardinal Tisserant's proposal to elevate the members of the preparatory commissions to permanent status. The members passed by a wide margin Cardinal Liénart's motion to delay the vote until they had time to draw up a more representative slate of candidates. As a result, the committees, although still headed by Curia members, provided a more accurate reflection of the council's general temper. None of the 73 draft proposals was adopted in its entirety, and many underwent radical changes before they were endorsed.

Council sessions often erupted into stormy exchanges between liberals and conservatives. On one such occasion Cardinal Frings attacked the clandestine operations of Cardinal Ottaviani's Holy Office as "a source of harm to the faithful, and of scandal to those outside the church." During the proceedings, which lasted a total of 12 months over a period of 4 years, the intransigent Ottaviani emerged as the leading conservative spokesman. His supporters included Ernesto Cardinal Ruffini, Archbishop of Palermo, Italy, who spoke oftener than any other of the council fathers, and Frane Franic, Bishop of Split, Yugoslavia. They were backed by the Roman Curia. Voting on major issues, however, indicated that the sympathies of the council were more on the side of such progressives as Cardinals Frings and Liénart; the gentle Augustin Cardinal Bea of the Secretariat for Promoting Christian Unity; the intellectual Leo Joseph Cardinal Suenens, Archbishop of Malines-Brussels, Belgium; the leftist Raúl Cardinal Silva Henríquez, Archbishop of Santiago, Chile; and the persuasive Paul Émile Cardinal Léger, Archbishop of Montreal, Canada.

The Work of the Council

By the time the council ended on December 8, 1965, after four long years of on-the-scene and behind-the-scenes deliberations, it had enacted a total of 16 texts—4 constitutions, 9 decrees, and 3 declarations. The council's most significant achievements and resolutions included the following:

The 30,000-word *Dogmatic Constitution on the Church* redefined the nature of the church and its hierarchical structure. It stressed that the Pope, although still absolute ruler of the church, should not isolate himself from the other bishops of the world but should work closely with them in ruling the universal church. This concept of collegiality was one of the most controversial topics of the council. In response to its adoption Pope Paul instituted an international synod of bishops to meet with him regularly and, in addition, he urged the formation of national and continental conferences of bishops to share in the exercise of the church's authority.

As a result of the *Constitution on the Sacred Liturgy*, sweeping changes were made in the church's centuries-old methods of worship. The Mass was put into the vernacular, replacing the traditional Latin (and Greek), and the service was changed in order to effect the more active and meaningful participation of the congregation. Variations in rites were sanctioned to accommodate customs and traditions of people in different parts of the world.

The *Pastoral Constitution on the Church in the Modern World* examined the problems of man in the world today, discussing family life and social, economic, cultural, and political life in relation to man's duties to God and the church. It stressed the beauty of conjugal love in marriage but did not include the views of a minority of bishops who argued against the church's condemnation of birth control. In its concluding sections the constitution condemned genocide and all forms of discrimination and recommended mutual nuclear disarmament of all nations as a step toward world peace.

Four of the council's texts—the *Decree on Ecumenism*, the *Decree on Eastern Catholic Churches*, the *Declaration of the Relationship of the Church to Non-Christian Religions*, and the *Declaration on Reli-*

gious Freedom—urged friendship and understanding among all religions of the world. Christian churches were encouraged to work together toward ultimate unity, and religious discrimination—particularly anti-Semitism—was condemned. No government or other agency, the council said, should force a person to accept or reject a form of religion.

The *Decree on the Apostolate of the Laity* urged laymen to take a more active part in the work of the church. Other texts dealt with religious orders, priestly life, the pastoral duties of bishops, missions, education, the relationship between revelation and tradition, and the moral duties of those making use of the modern communications media. Indirectly, the opinions expressed at the council led to a restructuring of the Roman Curia, begun by Pope Paul in 1967.

The Church After the Council

The teachings of the Second Vatican Council have deeply stirred the Catholic clergy and laity in all parts of the world. While most Catholics have—willingly or reluctantly—accepted the changes wrought by the council, many have fought bitterly to retain the old ways—especially the Latin Mass—while others have carried the council's progressive ideas much further than had ever been intended.

Throughout the world news stories of clerical marriages, rock and folk Masses, radical worker-priests, and Catholic political activists have made front-page headlines. Some striking changes have occurred in Latin America, a bastion of Catholic traditionalism.

At the meeting of Latin bishops held at Medellín, Colombia, in 1968, clerics endorsed a program of socialism and anticapitalism. As a symbol of their willingness to become a church of the poor, some bishops have begun disposing of church lands and property and exchanging their rich robes for humbler trappings. Many priests, following the example set by the bishops, have given up the privileges accorded them in the past and are living like their poor parishioners.

In addition, a climate of dissent and defiance has emerged among the clergy in all parts of the world. Large numbers of priests have left the clergy in protest against rigid church policies, and the number of young men entering the priesthood has declined. Many of those who have remained within the church have lost their traditional timidity and have strongly opposed recent Vatican rulings. Among the most outspoken critics is Bernard Cardinal Alfrink, Archbishop of Utrecht, the Netherlands, who has led a vigorous renewal campaign within the Dutch church. His controversial policy of allowing Protestant participation in the communion ceremony and his support of loosened restrictions on birth control and clerical celibacy have provoked strong Vatican opposition.

For the most part Pope Paul VI has tried to counter dissent by reasserting his papal authority. His success has been limited, and few Catholics believe that the rift within their ranks can be easily closed. If it can be closed, though, the church may yet demonstrate its capacity for major, far-reaching changes, and so fulfill the dream of Pope John XXIII.

THE CHURCH IN LATIN AMERICA

After Vatican II many Latin American bishops and priests, long identified with the ruling elite, came into sharp conflict with their governments. In Chile the church is becoming a focus of resistance to the junta; priests in Paraguay have preached revolution; Colombian churchmen have taken part in antigovernment guerrilla activity. In Brazil Archbishop Camara of Recife organized a protest movement against the country's repressive military regime. In 1975 a large group of bishops meeting in São Paulo accused the Brazilian government of murdering and torturing political prisoners, including priests.

Brazilian Archbishop Camara, a leader in the movement against government-sanctioned repression.

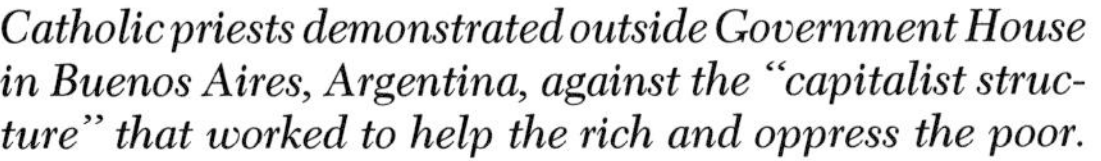

Catholic priests demonstrated outside Government House in Buenos Aires, Argentina, against the "capitalist structure" that worked to help the rich and oppress the poor.

1964

Vietnam: The Bitter Ordeal

The Gulf of Tonkin resolution opens the way for massive U.S. involvement in a seemingly endless war in Southeast Asia.

The first reports began to reach the Pentagon around 8 a.m. Washington time. In Vietnam it was 8 p.m. of the same day: Tuesday, August 4, 1964. The information, though spotty and confused, indicated that a naval encounter was in progress in the Gulf of Tonkin, off the coast of North Vietnam. By 10 a.m. Washington had received messages that two U.S. destroyers, the *Maddox* and the *C. Turner Joy*, were being attacked, evidently by North Vietnamese patrol boats. Sporadic signals continued to come in, and by midday President Lyndon Johnson was meeting with his top advisers to determine a course of action.

Shortly after 6 p.m. Johnson called congressional leaders to the White House to inform them of the incident—and of his decision to retaliate with bombing strikes against North Vietnamese coastal installations. The President also asked for an official resolution making it clear that such retaliatory measures were endorsed by Congress as a whole. The leaders of both the Democratic and Republican Parties gave their assurances, and before midnight U.S. fighter-bombers from the aircraft carriers *Constellation* and *Ticonderoga* were attacking their designated targets.

The next day, in an atmosphere heavy with impending crisis, a joint meeting of the Senate Foreign Relations and Armed Services Committees was held to vote on a resolution supplied by the administration. The document would empower the President not only to repel armed attacks against U.S. personnel but also "to take all necessary steps including the use of armed force to assist any member . . . of the Southeast Asia Collective Defense Treaty requesting assistance in defense of its freedom." After brief deliberations the joint committee recommended passage of the measure. Two days later, on August 7, the Senate passed the resolution by an 88-to-2 margin, the only dissents coming from Wayne Morse of Oregon and Ernest Gruening of Alaska. In a statement after the vote Senator Morse said, "I believe that history will record that we have made a great mistake. . . . We are in effect giving the President . . . warmaking powers in the absence of a declaration of war."

Few others shared his misgivings, at least in public. Despite the seemingly open-ended wording of the resolution, Johnson assured the Congress and the country that the role of the United States in Vietnam would remain limited, that he had no intention of sending "American boys to do the fighting for Asian boys."

Hours after the Senate action the House of Representatives followed suit with a unanimous vote of the 416 Congressmen present, and the Tonkin Gulf resolution assumed the full force of law. Indeed, it was to become the sole legal basis for the massive war effort that followed. Without realizing it, Congress had just authorized the longest and most bitterly divisive foreign war in the nation's history.

Involvement by Proxy

In a broader sense the passage of the Tonkin Gulf resolution was not so much the beginning of a war as it was the culmination of a policy originated more than 10 years earlier. The United States had become involved in Southeast Asian affairs in the early 1950's, when France was struggling in vain to retain the colonial control it had held over Vietnam since the 19th century. The fight to expel the French was being carried on by the Vietminh, a nationalist guerrilla movement that had spearheaded Vietnamese resistance against Japanese invaders during World War II. Its leader was Ho Chi Minh, acknowledged even by opponents as the country's most popular figure. What concerned the United States was that Ho was a Communist, determined not only to defeat the French but also to establish Vietnam as a unified and independent Marxist state.

Domestic political pressures prevented direct U.S. involvement in the Indochina War, but increasing economic aid was given until, by 1954, the French war effort was being financed almost entirely by U.S. money. But the financial aid bought poor results. After seven years' effort France was still unable to defeat the elusive, resilient Vietminh. And when the French failed to lift a long bloody siege of their key fortress at Dienbienphu in early 1954, they finally gave up.

In April of that year a 14-nation peace conference was convened in Geneva to work out a political settlement for Vietnam. The negotiations produced an agreement that temporarily divided Vietnam into two sections, separated by a demilitarized zone (DMZ) along the 17th parallel. The Vietminh agreed to withdraw to the north, where Ho's regime would be in control, while the southern half was to be administered by the French-backed Emperor Bao Dai. Finally, internationally supervised elections were to be held in

A war without fronts, *Vietnam proved a tactical nightmare to U.S. military leaders, most of whom were veterans of World War II and unaccustomed to the elusive, hit-and-run methods of the Vietcong. Only in early 1975, as North Vietnamese tank columns rolled southward toward Saigon, did the fighting begin to resemble conventional warfare—and by then the outcome was inevitable.*

The greatest tragedy of the fighting in Vietnam was the toll it took among civilians, millions of whom were killed, maimed, or left homeless by a war few of them even understood. To a South Vietnamese mother grieving for her dead infant (above) and to countless others like her in North Vietnam, Cambodia, and Laos, it scarcely mattered from which side the fatal bomb or artillery shell had come.

July 1956 to reunify the country—elections that, in the absence of organized opposition in the south, the Communists expected to win easily.

Events did not follow as planned. In mid-1954 Bao Dai called on Ngo Dinh Diem, a member of an influential Catholic family, to form a new government in Saigon. Bolstered by a pledge of U.S. support from President Dwight D. Eisenhower, Diem set about consolidating his authority in the south. In October 1955, having eliminated potential rivals in the army and elsewhere, Diem deposed Bao Dai and named himself President of the Republic of Vietnam. The next year he canceled the scheduled elections, counting on increased U.S. assistance to strengthen his regime. By the end of 1955 some 600 U.S. military advisers had been sent to train South Vietnamese troops, and in the next five years more than 75 percent of all U.S. aid to Saigon went to Diem's army and secret police.

First Steps into the Quagmire

Following the 1954 partition some 90,000 Vietminh troops (many of them southerners by birth) had been withdrawn north of the 17th parallel as required by the Geneva agreement. Others, however, had returned to their villages in the south—some to conduct propaganda activities but most simply to wait for reunification. Nonetheless, Diem continued to view them all as a mortal threat, and through 1956 and 1957 he conducted a campaign of censorship, imprisonment, and terror that succeeded in destroying what remained of the Vietminh organization in the south. At the same time, however, a hard core of well-trained Communist partisans evaded Diem's troops and secret police by fleeing into the same jungle and swamp areas they had used as sanctuaries during the war with the French. In the next three years the rebels regrouped and laid the groundwork for resistance. They raided government outposts for weapons, recruited new members, and organized revolutionary committees in villages around the countryside. Finally, in December 1960, they formed the National Liberation Front (NLF) to serve as the political arm of the rebellion. The military arm of the movement came to be known as the Vietcong.

Although the NLF was often accused by the Saigon and U.S. governments of being controlled by North Vietnam, it remained a more or less indigenous South Vietnamese force. In late 1961 U.S. intelligence reports estimated that 80 to 90 percent of the NLF's 15,000 recruits were southerners and that most of their weapons were stolen from ARVN (Army of the Re-

THE PENTAGON PAPERS

Commissioned by Defense Secretary Robert McNamara in 1967, the Pentagon Papers were intended to be a candid, top-secret study of U.S. involvement in Vietnam from 1945 onward. Compiled by 36 Defense Department analysts, the completed study encompassed some 7,000 pages of narrative and government documents. In mid-1971 *The New York Times* (and later *The Washington Post*) began to publish excerpts of the study based on copies furnished by Daniel Ellsberg, a former Pentagon employee. Largely because of their sensitive (and often embarrassing) contents, the publication of the classified documents became the focus of a major legal and political storm. Below are some of the papers' most important revelations.

Why Are We in Vietnam?

For 20 years the primary official goal of U.S. policy in Vietnam was to enable the South Vietnamese to determine their own political future. The Pentagon Papers revealed, however, that U.S. leaders were in fact determined throughout to control events there. Immediately after the end of the 1954 Geneva conference, the United States made it a matter of policy to prevent the reunification elections scheduled for 1956 and sent agents into North Vietnam to initiate a sabotage campaign. A decade later, when support seemed to be growing in Saigon for a neutralist or coalition government that would include Communists, President Lyndon Johnson made it clear to Henry Cabot Lodge, U.S. Ambassador to South Vietnam, that "nothing is more important than to stop neutralist talk wherever we can by whatever means we can." Other documents made it equally clear that the primary concern of the Johnson administration and its predecessors had not been to aid the South Vietnamese people but to prevent a blow to America's prestige—a view summed up in a secret memorandum to Secretary McNamara estimating U.S. goals in Vietnam by percentages:

"70 pct.—To avoid a humiliating U.S. defeat (to our reputation as a guarantor).

"20 pct.—To keep SVN (and then adjacent) territory from Chinese hands.

"10 pct.—To permit the people of SVN to enjoy a better, freer way of life.

"Also—To emerge from crisis without unacceptable taint from methods used.

"NOT—To 'help a friend' . . ."

Saigon 1963: A Buddhist monk immolates himself in an anti-Diem protest.

public of Vietnam) outposts, not supplied by Hanoi.

As the guerrilla war intensified, Diem's forces proved less and less able to cope with the rebels, and urgent requests were made to Washington for more help. President John F. Kennedy, fearful of the political effects of a Communist victory, responded with a major increase in the U.S. commitment. By the end of 1961, 900 military advisers had been sent to South Vietnam; a year later the number was over 11,000, accompanied by an avalanche of military hardware.

The Vietcong nevertheless continued to outfight government troops and gained control over large areas of the countryside. In addition, Diem's increasingly repressive security measures—most of them orchestrated by his brother Ngo Dinh Nhu—were alienating large segments of the population. In the cities hundreds of non-Communist politicians and intellectuals were jailed for dissent of almost any kind. In the countryside local elections had been abolished, and government officials were being appointed solely on the basis of personal loyalty to Diem and his family.

At length, mounting public resentment burst into the open, sparked by an uprising of Buddhists in May 1963. Within a month demonstrations—gruesomely dramatized by the self-immolation of several Buddhist monks—had spread across the country, focusing world attention on Diem's dictatorial policies.

The uprising—and Diem's ruthless attempts to suppress it—proved the final blow to his already dwindling support in Washington. In the early autumn it was quietly made known to key South Vietnamese generals that the U.S.A. would not oppose a coup, and on November 1, 1963, the regime was overthrown with almost no resistance. The following morning, as crowds celebrated in the streets of Saigon, Diem and his brother Nhu were found hiding in a church. They were taken outside and shot.

The Upward Spiral

The popular leader of the coup, Gen. Duong Van Minh, was deposed only three months later, and for the next year and a half a succession of inept regimes paraded in and out of power. It was in the midst of this turmoil that the Tonkin Gulf resolution was passed by Congress. Not until after his January 1965 inauguration, however, did President Johnson begin to wield the full authority he had been granted. Early in February U.S. airstrikes were made against enemy strongholds above and below the DMZ, and on March 2 Johnson launched what was to become a heavy and

The Tonkin Gulf Incident

Regarding the fateful naval incident of August 1964, the Pentagon Papers disclosed crucial information that had been withheld from Congress when it was considering the Tonkin Gulf resolution. During Congressional hearings on August 6 Defense Secretary McNamara was asked about reports that boats with South Vietnamese crews had attacked two North Vietnamese islands the previous week. He answered that "our Navy played absolutely no part in, was not associated with, was not aware of, any South Vietnamese actions, if there were any . . . . I did not have knowledge at the time of the attack on the island."

The Pentagon Papers, however, revealed that the United States had in fact been conducting a secret military campaign against North Vietnam, code-named Operation Plan 34A, since the previous February. Carried out chiefly by South Vietnamese personnel but directed by the U.S.A., the 34A actions included commando raids, infiltration of sabotage teams, and the shelling of North Vietnamese coastal installations. The Pentagon documents also established not only that Secretary McNamara had received regular reports on the 34A missions, but that he himself had recommended the program to President Johnson in December 1963. Finally, though the U.S. destroyers *Maddox* and *C. Turner Joy* were not part of the 34A operations, it is known that the North Vietnamese believed they were; and since the latest 34A attacks had taken place just the night before, the incident was hardly the unprovoked act of aggression the administration claimed it to be. Thus, while it is possible that Congress might have passed a similar resolution at some later date, the fact remains that the sole legal authorization for the Vietnam War was granted on the basis of incomplete and misleading information.

Saigon 1968: Police Chief Nguyen Ngoc Loan summarily executes a Vietcong suspect during the Tet offensive.

***One more patrol:** A group of U.S. infantrymen jump from their helicopter to conduct reconnaissance near a South Vietnamese hamlet. By 1973 more than 2 million of their countrymen had participated in the war and 55,000 had died.*

continuous bombing campaign against North Vietnam. Within the week another portentous step was taken: On March 8, 3,500 U.S. marines came ashore at Da Nang, the first U.S. combat troops to arrive in Vietnam. Sent at the request of Gen. William Westmoreland (named commander of U.S. forces in Vietnam in June 1964), the marines were intended only to guard the U.S. airbase at Da Nang. But in May the Vietcong launched an offensive that decimated South Vietnamese forces, and Westmoreland responded with a call for an immediate major deployment of U.S. troops. His request was granted, and the upward spiral began in earnest: In August 1965 there were 90,000 U.S. troops in South Vietnam; by the end of the year the number had jumped to 184,000. The United States was now committed to a large-scale (if still undeclared) war, and for the next three years the escalation continued, peaking at more than 540,000 U.S. troops in 1968.

But even this massive infusion of manpower—along with the heaviest bombing campaign in history—proved inadequate. Like the Vietminh, the Vietcong proved themselves a skillful, stubborn, and resilient enemy. Supplied now with arms from the Soviet

*"**We had to destroy it** in order to save it." So said a U.S. officer in 1968, referring only to one village but to a great degree summing up the American role in South Vietnam. Aiming to deny shelter to the Vietcong, the U.S. systematically leveled hundreds of villages—and in the process alienated the very people it claimed to be defending.*

Union and China, they were willing to accept heavy casualties and seemingly were prepared to fight on until the Americans decided the war was no longer worth the price.

The Tet Offensive

Finally, the U.S. public began to question this distant conflict. In 1965 leaders of the Johnson administration had pledged to "bring our boys home by Christmas"; in 1966 they spoke of "turning the corner" in Vietnam and of seeing "the light at the end of the tunnel." But draft calls kept mounting, casualties continued to rise, and the fighting dragged on. At the same time press reports about the ARVN's lackadaisical performance, as well as the rampant corruption and dictatorial methods of the Nguyen Cao Ky regime, which had been installed in South Vietnam in mid-1965, forced a growing number of Americans to wonder what sort of government their soldiers were fighting to preserve.

By 1967 the U.S. antiwar movement had reached major proportions across the country. Then at the beginning of 1968 President Johnson's last hope of vindicating his policy was crushed by the most sudden and dramatic development of the war: the Tet offensive. On January 30, 1968—the first day of Tet, the Lunar New Year—the Vietcong and North Vietnamese launched a massive and totally unexpected assault against almost every city and town in South Vietnam. In the early hours of the campaign the enemy penetrated to the heart of Saigon and briefly occupied the grounds of the U.S. Embassy. Elsewhere, more of the same: 5 major cities, 36 provincial capitals, and 64 district capitals were seized for varying periods.

In mid-March, after six weeks of desperate fighting, the campaign ended. Though the Tet offensive failed to bring down the Saigon government, its impact on the U.S. public was devastating. Within weeks several leading news publications and a number of previously hawkish Congressmen openly criticized the war for the first time, and public support for Johnson's policy dropped to 35 percent in the opinion polls. In the New Hampshire Presidential primary in March Senator Eugene McCarthy's antiwar campaign won a surprising 42 percent of the vote, and a few days later Senator Robert F. Kennedy announced that he too would challenge Johnson for the Democratic nomination.

Faced with this gathering political storm, the President finally relented. On March 31, 1968, he appeared on national television to announce a major new peace initiative: All bombing of North Vietnam above the 20th parallel was being halted immediately in the hope of encouraging Hanoi to begin peace talks. Then, at the end of his address, Johnson stunned the nation by announcing that he would not run for reelection.

Hanoi soon agreed to meet for preliminary negotiations, and on May 13 the talks opened in Paris. No progress was made for several months, however, and in a final effort to break the deadlock before election day Johnson ordered an end to all bombing of North Vietnam on October 31, 1968.

Five days later Richard M. Nixon barely defeated Hubert H. Humphrey in the U.S. Presidential election. During the campaign Nixon had made frequent references to a "secret plan" to end the war, and as he took office in January 1969 many Americans anticipated an early breakthrough in the peace effort.

"Peace With Honor"

Throughout the spring and summer, however, there was little evidence of any policy change. Ground fighting rose to its highest level since the Tet offensive, with proportionately heavy casualties, and the air war was dramatically intensified. At length, faced by growing congressional impatience and renewed antiwar protests, President Nixon delivered a major television address in November 1969 to explain his war policy. Describing his ultimate goal as "peace with honor," he announced a plan for the gradual withdrawal of U.S. combat troops and a simultaneous "Vietnamization" of the war. He concluded by citing the importance to U.S. prestige of preventing an overthrow of Nguyen Van Thieu's regime (which had replaced the Ky regime in September 1967) and appealed for support to "the great silent majority of my fellow Americans."

Reactions to the policy were sharply divided in Washington, but a majority of the nation seemed to approve, and the President's Vietnamization program went into effect. By the end of 1969 U.S. troop levels had been reduced from more than 540,000 to 479,000, and a year later the number was down to 339,000.

At the same time, though, the overall level of violence was scarcely decreasing. To compensate for the troop cutbacks, U.S. bombing raids were intensified to an unprecedented degree. Between January 1969 and March 1971 U.S. aircraft dropped 2.5 million tons of bombs over Indochina—more than U.S. planes had dropped in all of World War II. Meanwhile, the remaining U.S. troops continued to engage in search-and-destroy missions and to suffer heavy casualties: During President Nixon's first three years in office some 15,000 GI's were killed and more than 100,000 others were wounded.

Though the continued fighting prompted a resurgence of antiwar activities—particularly during the allied "incursions" into Cambodia and Laos—President Nixon's troop cutbacks generally succeeded in neutralizing the peace movement. By mid-1972 U.S. troop strength was down to about 50,000, and the President was able to announce that he had withdrawn half a million troops since taking office. In a sense, though, the figures were illusory, since by 1972 an equal number of servicemen had become directly or indirectly involved in the vastly increased air war over North and South Vietnam, Cambodia, and Laos.

The final bloody chapter of U.S. participation in the war began on March 30, 1972, the first day of a major new North Vietnamese offensive. Like the Tet offensive of 1968, the countrywide campaign caught government forces badly unprepared. On May 8, with the fighting at its peak, President Nixon announced his decision to mine North Vietnam's harbors and begin an intensive bombing campaign against Hanoi, Haiphong, and all rail lines bringing supplies from China.

The move touched off another storm of protest, but the bombing went on without pause for the next 5½ months. During that period Nixon's national security adviser, Henry Kissinger, began a series of secret negotiations with North Vietnam's Le Duc Tho—circumventing the off-again, on-again official conference. By mid-October rumors abounded that a settlement was imminent, and the speculation heightened when Nixon suddenly suspended bombing north of the 20th parallel on October 24. Two days later Dr. Kissinger dramatically announced that "peace is at hand," predicting that the remaining details of a cease-fire could be ironed out in a matter of days. The impact was not lost on the U.S. electorate, which on November 7 reelected the President by a landslide over his Democratic challenger, George McGovern.

Just after the election, however, the promised settlement seemed to evaporate as quickly as it had appeared, and on December 17 Nixon resumed the massive bombing of North Vietnam. For the next 13 days—broken only by a short Christmas pause—U.S. B-52's carried out the heaviest air raids of the entire war, pounding cities and the countryside with 500-pound bombs on an around-the-clock basis.

At length, on December 30th, after Hanoi had agreed to resume the cease-fire negotiations, Nixon announced that the airstrikes against northern population centers would again be halted. A week later the talks reopened in Paris, and on January 27, 1973, a cease-fire agreement was signed by representatives of the United States, North Vietnam, the Saigon govern-

***The Vietnamese people** were not the war's only victims: The countryside itself was devastated by U.S. bombing (above) and chemical defoliation that left huge areas scarred and useless.*

***A human flood** of refugees like those at left moved southward in the spring of 1975 as North Vietnamese tank columns advanced toward Saigon. Most returned to their homes when the long-feared Communist "bloodbath" failed to occur.*

ment, and the NLF. The accord provided for the withdrawal of all U.S. servicemen within 60 days, concurrent with the release by the enemy of all U.S. prisoners of war. The agreement also gave equal recognition to the Thieu regime and the NLF in the areas controlled by each side as of January 28. Finally, an international commission would supervise the truce while a national council of Saigon and NLF delegates worked out a political settlement for the country.

In effect, the cease-fire agreement was a face-saving device for the United States. Saigon had not been toppled by the Communists, the prisoners were coming home, no more Americans were dying in combat. President Nixon could thus claim to have achieved his goal of "peace with honor." But in Vietnam, as in Cambodia and Laos, talk of peace was sadly premature. From the outset the cease-fire was marred by frequent violations, and within months the fighting in many areas had resumed the intensity of full-scale war. Through 1973 and 1974 the United States continued to pour aid into Saigon; in the meantime President Thieu canceled the elections stipulated in the Paris accords.

In short, it seemed to have started all over again—but with one crucial difference: U.S. combat troops and B-52's were no longer there, and without them the South Vietnamese army proved no match for its opponents. Month by month Communist forces widened their control of the countryside, nourished by a steady influx of fresh troops and equipment from the north.

At length, in early 1975, the final chapter unfolded with breathtaking swiftness. A large-scale North Vietnamese offensive at the beginning of March forced Thieu to pull his troops out of the Central Highlands, and the ARVN withdrawal soon turned to panic as the Communist forces quickened their southward pace. Within six weeks almost every important city and town north of Saigon had been captured, often with no resistance, and the capital was virtually encircled.

At this point the North Vietnamese paused, choosing to wait for the Saigon government to collapse rather than mount a climactic bloody assault on the city. They did not have long to wait.

On April 21 President Thieu, after eight years in power, announced his resignation and shortly fled the country. On April 28 Gen. Duong Van Minh was named as his successor; the next day the last U.S. officials and troops were evacuated from Saigon, and on the morning of April 30 President Minh announced his government's unconditional surrender.

So ended the long agony, 10 years, 8 months, and 23 days after the passage of the Tonkin Gulf resolution. The United States had come and gone—at a cost of more than 55,000 American lives and well over a million Asian lives—but the war had continued, propelled by its own logic and momentum. The long-term effects of the war on the United States—on its role in the world, the use of its power, the relationship between Congress and the President—would be revealed only by history. But if Americans had learned anything after a decade of fighting in that small, ravaged country, it was that the future of Vietnam finally had to be determined by the Vietnamese.

TRAGEDY ACROSS THE BORDER: THE WAR IN CAMBODIA

Like an innocent bystander in the wrong place at the wrong time, the small, historically unwarlike nation of Cambodia found itself caught up almost by accident in the ever-widening conflict in South Vietnam. As early as 1963 Cambodia's head of state, Prince Norodom Sihanouk, had reluctantly permitted Hanoi's troops to use the eastern part of his country as a staging area for raids into South Vietnam rather than risk an invasion of Cambodia by North Vietnam. By the late 1960's the North Vietnamese had armed and revitalized Cambodia's Communist insurgents, the Khmer Rouge, and were in virtual control of the region adjacent to the Vietnamese border. In response to growing public resentment, Sihanouk sought to reduce the North Vietnamese presence, but without success. Partly as a result of that failure, he was overthrown in March 1970 by the U.S.-supported Premier Lon Nol, who promptly broke off relations with Hanoi and mounted a full-scale military campaign against the Khmer Rouge.

Shortly afterward, on April 30, U.S. and South Vietnamese troops launched an invasion into Cambodia against North Vietnamese sanctuaries, an action that turned out to have little effect on Communist operations in South Vietnam. (The Cambodian invasion did, however, cause a storm of renewed antiwar protests at hundreds of U.S. colleges—including Kent State University in Ohio, where National Guardsmen fired without warning into a crowd of students, killing four and wounding nine others.)

So began a five-year civil war in Cambodia that would end in a victory for the Khmer Rouge, who took the capital of Phnom Penh after a long siege on April 17, 1975. Immediately after their takeover Cambodia's new leaders sealed the country off from the outside world and began reorganizing its society by brute force. Some 2 to 3 million residents of Phnom Penh and other population centers were marched off into the countryside at gunpoint, with little provision for food, water, or medical care. Details of the forced marches may never be known, but tens of thousands are believed to have died along the way from hunger, disease, and exhaustion. At the end of 1975 yet another mass migration was decreed by the government, pushing the overall death toll to an estimated 600,000—about 10 percent of the population—and adding to the revulsion felt in the non-Communist world over the unrestrained brutality of the new regime.

1966

The Red Guard Revolution

Following Chairman Mao's philosophy of continuous revolution, youthful bands of Red Guards throw China into turmoil.

Nearly a million young students from all parts of China began to assemble in Peking's enormous Tien An Men Square before dawn on August 18, 1966. As part of Mao Tse-tung's Red Guards, they would serve as the shock troops of one of the most puzzling and momentous movements in modern Chinese history, the Great Proletarian Cultural Revolution.

Precisely at sunrise the crowd broke into a deafening roar as Mao Tse-tung, father of China's Communist revolution and the nation's most venerated leader, climbed the ramparts of the colossal Gate of Heavenly Peace to the triumphant strains of "The East Is Red." Amid the thunderous applause the aged hero, clad in his familiar military tunic, raised his hands in greeting.

During the day-long rally that followed, speakers from across the country urged the people to "smash the old world, create a new world, and decisively carry out the great proletarian cultural revolution." Then the Red Guards marched in review before the assembled dignitaries, singing, chanting revolutionary slogans, and holding aloft their red-bound copies of *Quotations From Chairman Mao Tse-tung.* At nightfall a brilliant fireworks display brought the rally to a close.

In the next months the Red Guards brought Mao's cultural revolution to every city, town, and village in China. Their assigned task was to attack the "four olds"—old culture, old ideas, old customs, and old habits. And with schools closed that autumn, China's youth went on a countrywide rampage, uprooting everything smacking of "bourgeois" or "Western" influence. They destroyed ancient Confucian scrolls and Buddhist statues, abused anyone dressed in either traditional Chinese or Western-style clothes, and tore down street signs bearing colonial names. They plastered walls and buildings with huge posters denouncing officials suspected of "taking the capitalist road," paraded the offenders before the local citizenry, and forced them to make humiliating "self-criticisms."

To most Western observers it seemed that China had fallen into utter chaos. Yet those more familiar with China and its leaders saw meaning behind the Red Guards' frenetic campaign. Part social revolution, part educational reform movement, and part political power struggle, the Great Proletarian Cultural Revolution was above all an attempt to bring China closer to Mao Tse-tung's vision of a Communist utopia.

Such convulsive mass movements had erupted from time to time throughout China's history, and from its earliest days the Chinese Communist Party had relied on similar campaigns to initiate its radical reform programs. After the Communist takeover in 1949 the new leaders inaugurated a program of sweeping changes designed to transform China into a strong, prosperous, and unified nation. During and after the Civil War of 1945–49 they had carried out a radical land reform program, seizing the acreage held by wealthy landlords and redistributing it among the peasantry. Then in 1953 China embarked on an ambitious program of industrialization. Peking borrowed about $430 million from Moscow, imported many skilled Soviet technicians, and harnessed the manpower of China's enormous population. The results were impressive: At the end of the First Five-Year Plan (1953–57) industrial production had more than doubled; elementary education and health care were available in the most isolated rural areas; factories, roads, dams, and irrigation ditches had been built. At the same time, China's rural areas were organized into village agricultural cooperatives or collectives. Although this radical step met with stiff opposition from the peasants, who were understandably reluctant to give up ownership of their newly won lands, by mid-1957 some 97 percent of the land had been collectivized.

The Great Leap Forward

As the First Five-Year Plan drew to a close, another Maoist program, the Hundred Flowers campaign, was introduced. In the spring of 1956 Mao called upon China's intellectuals to come forward with criticism of

Chairman Mao, *to most Chinese, is a hero who in two decades led China out of poverty to her present position as a world power. The number of those killed by the Maoists to achieve this is unknown, but estimates range as high as 20 million. Nonetheless, Mao is revered as few men in the 20th century have been, with a zeal reinforced by such rites as this 1967 display of loyalty (right).*

*"**All our literature** and art are for the masses," says Mao; "An army without culture is a dull-witted army, and a dull-witted army cannot defeat the enemy." For decades China's leaders have waged an intensive literacy campaign (above). As the goal of nationwide literacy draws nearer, the educated classes, who long since ceased to be landlords, are also losing their monopoly on the best jobs, and so China moves toward its classless ideal.*

*"**The army** must become one with the people so that they see it as their own army. Such an army will be invincible."*(Quotations From Chairman Mao Tse-tung) *In addition to its regular army, China maintains the People's Militia comprising some 5 million members drawn from all segments of society. A key element in Mao's program for the Great Leap Forward of 1958–59, the militia served not only as a model for his ideal society of citizen-soldiers, but also as a coercive instrument available if needed to help maintain or restore order—thus illustrating another of Chairman Mao's maxims: "Political power grows out of the barrel of a gun."*

his regime, "Letting a hundred flowers blossom and a hundred schools of thought contend." Reluctantly at first, and then with ever-increasing vehemence, scholars, writers, and artists unleashed a scathing storm of critical commentary, attacking some of the most fundamental aspects of Communist rule. Indeed, the reaction far surpassed Mao's expectations, and in mid-1957 the government abruptly halted the campaign and silenced its harshest critics.

Despite its success, the First Five-Year Plan had also opened a deep rift within the party concerning the country's future development. One group favored the continuation of Soviet-style central planning. The other, led by Mao, advocated a program to mobilize the population into teams that would serve alternately as soldiers, farmers, and workers. Such a program would be a major step toward achieving Mao's vision of "pure" communism, and with this goal, he launched the Great Leap Forward at the beginning of 1958.

The new economic program, based on the decentralization of industry and agriculture, was designed to maximize local productivity by amalgamating the farmlands of adjacent villages into larger units called communes. Citizens were to be conscripted into paramilitary work brigades, moving from one locale to another as conditions demanded.

Initially the campaign proved a reasonable success, at least in terms of agriculture and industrial production. But problems soon became evident. Decentralization led to severe transport and supply difficulties. The quality of industrial goods was lamentable. The zealous young party members in charge of the labor brigades, anxious to meet or exceed production goals, placed harsh demands on workers. Moreover, the severe disruption of family life—traditionally the core of Chinese society—produced widespread resentment.

Conditions were exacerbated by poor harvests in 1959 and 1960 and by the abrupt termination of Soviet technical aid in 1960. Gradually the party began to relax its most extreme requirements, and in January 1961 the abortive Great Leap Forward was officially brought to an end.

One result of its failure was Mao's temporary withdrawal from active participation in party policymaking. Liu Shao-chi, another veteran of the Long March, replaced him as State Chairman in 1959, though Mao retained his post as Party Chairman. In his absence a group of liberal economists, favoring such policies as agricultural mechanization, material incentives, and capital investment, gained ascendancy.

Mao was violently opposed to this drift toward capitalism and individualism, which he felt would encourage a fragmentation of society into "elitist" groups of professionals, bureaucrats, intellectuals, and others. With his influence in the party at a low ebb, Mao enlisted another powerful instrument to help reverse this trend: the People's Liberation Army (PLA), headed by one of Mao's oldest allies, Defense Minister Lin Piao. In the early 1960's the PLA command was divided over fundamental issues. One camp wanted to build the PLA into a professional standing army, while the other, led by Lin Piao, wanted to preserve the PLA's traditionally informal, militia-type structure. By 1965 Lin had gained the upper hand, and with his victory the Maoists were assured of PLA support.

Cultural Politics

What actually triggered the Cultural Revolution was a play, *The Dismissal of Hai Jui*, which dealt with the firing of an upstanding party official. A thinly veiled critique of Mao's dismissal of Defense Minister P'eng Teh-huai during the Great Leap Forward, the play was interpreted as heresy by loyal Maoists.

***In 1950 the Chinese invaded Tibet,** later embarking on what the International Commission of Jurists would describe as a policy of genocide. A hundred thousand Tibetans fled their homeland to escape torture, execution, forced labor, sterilization, and the mindless fury of Red Guards bent on destroying an incomparable tradition of Buddhist philosophy and practice. Most of the refugees (above) still live in India, Nepal, Sikkim, and Bhutan, hoping against the odds to preserve their ancient and unique cultural heritage.*

DETENTE WITH THE DRAGON

As cordiality between Red China and the U.S.S.R. cooled into hostility, the Western World was slowly reaching the conclusion that its refusal to recognize the established government of a major nation was foolish. In 1971 mainland China was admitted to the United Nations, and in February 1972 President Richard Nixon visited Peking. His trip, the first ever made to China by a U.S. President, signaled the end of 22 years of overt hostility between the two countries and opened the door to improved Chinese relations with other Western nations. It also demonstrated to the world—and to the Soviet Union in particular—that China was no longer isolated.

Nixon and Chairman Mao exchange reading matter and smiles; Chou En-lai clutches his own copy of the Little Red Book.

In September 1965, confident of PLA backing, Mao and his supporters began an attack on Peking's intellectuals, focusing initially on *The Dismissal of Hai Jui*, but gradually broadening the campaign into a nationwide drive against "revisionist" tendencies in China's arts, educational system, and news media. The country's high schools and universities soon became the center of ferment, and during the spring of 1966 hundreds of thousands of zealous students were organized into bands of Red Guards.

Then in August of that year the Central Committee of the Communist Party announced the beginning of a nationwide Cultural Revolution—launched at the mass rally in Peking—designed to root out revisionist attitudes and policies not only in China's educational and intellectual establishments, but also among the party bureaucracy. Under the supervision of the PLA the Red Guards became the driving force behind the Cultural Revolution. Their campaigns throughout the country aroused villagers and townsmen to help ferret out local leaders and party members who had departed from strict Maoist ideology.

Like the Great Leap Forward, however, the movement soon began to suffer from excesses. Schools were shut down entirely, and production and transportation were disrupted. Street fighting frequently erupted between Red Guards and workers, or among the Red Guards themselves. Thousands of Chinese died.

Meanwhile, the movement brought about a major shake-up in the Communist Party hierarchy that came to focus on two of its top figures, President Liu Shao-chi and Secretary Teng Hsiao-p'ing. The capital was ablaze with red wall posters denouncing them, and they were finally bullied into public confessions of their "capitalist" policies.

By 1969 it was evident that continued turmoil would cripple China's political and economic life. Thus, as he had a decade earlier, Mao bowed to suggestions that the restoration of order take precedence over revolutionary objectives. The PLA was gradually able to restrain the new "revolutionary committees" from excesses. The Red Guards returned to school, and under the guidance of Premier Chou En-lai, cooler party leaders began to take charge of day-to-day decisionmaking and to reconstruct and build up the morale of the battered party hierarchy.

Like the Great Leap Forward and earlier revolutionary programs, the Cultural Revolution brought China a step closer to Mao's concept of the ideal Communist state. Indeed, when the convulsions finally ended, the Maoist scheme was more firmly embedded than ever in the fabric of China's society: in its schools, its farming and industry, in its daily life and political hierarchy, in the mingling of military and civil affairs.

Even in old age, then, the man who had brought his country into the 20th century and restored it to world prominence continued to shape its rapid evolution. Mao's leadership, although controversial—and, by Western standards, profoundly repressive—has imposed a degree of stability and national unity rare in Chinese history. In little more than 25 years, his radical programs have brought literacy, medical care, an adequate diet, and a measure of prosperity to China's 800 million people.

With no clearly designated heir, China's future after Mao remains in doubt. In his absence the Chinese, like the Russians after the death of Lenin, may abandon his ideals. On the other hand, Mao has gone to enormous lengths to implant his ideology, and only time will tell how strongly its roots have taken hold.

1967

The Six-Day War

Israel's spectacular offensive against her hostile Arab neighbors gains valuable time and territory for the Jewish state but fails to secure a lasting peace in the Middle East.

For the people of the tiny dagger-shaped State of Israel, the early months of 1967 were as tense as any in their country's 19-year history. From Egypt to the west, Syria to the north, and Jordan to the east, a powerful coalition was building that had one avowed purpose: to destroy the Hebrew nation.

Israel had always been a Jewish island in a hostile Arab sea, and total war had been its lot twice before. In 1948, immediately after the creation of the new State of Israel (see pp. 396–403), Palestine's Jewish settlers had defeated combined Arab armies, and eight years later Israeli troops swept into the Sinai desert, smashed Cairo's army, and occupied the Suez Canal. Under a United Nations cease-fire agreement, Israel soon withdrew its troops; the Sinai was demilitarized and a United Nations Emergency Force (UNEF) established a buffer zone between the Israelis and the Egyptians.

To the Israelis' great advantage, the Egyptian fortress of Sharm al-Sheikh, overlooking the narrow Strait of Tiran at the southern tip of the Sinai, was included in the demilitarization plan. For years Egypt had used this fort to prevent Israeli shipping from entering the Gulf of Aqaba, the Jewish state's only outlet to the Red Sea. With the Egyptian blockade lifted, and with the U.N. troops patrolling the Sinai, Israel's southern border at last seemed secure.

In the north, however, there was no such security. Syria, perhaps the most hostile of all Arab states, held commanding positions on the frontier's Golan Heights. From strong fortifications atop this plateau Syrian artillery could attack Israeli settlements below, and by the spring of 1967 shellings had become daily occurrences. In the east, too, there was a constant threat. Jordanian troops occupied a huge slice of pre-1948 Palestine, including the Old City of Jerusalem abutting the Israeli capital, the New City. Although Jordan's King Hussein was the most moderate of the Arab leaders, the presence within his country of thousands of displaced Palestinian refugees forced him into a militant posture, as did the prodding of the influential Egyptian leader Gamal Abdel Nasser and the fiercely anti-Israel governments of Syria and Iraq.

To the Brink of War

In mid-May the slide toward war in the Middle East gained momentum. Syria, claiming that the Israelis were mobilizing, stepped up the shelling of Jewish settlements and called on Nasser to prepare for war. On May 16 Nasser ordered the UNEF to evacuate the Sinai, including the fortress at Sharm al-Sheikh. To the world's astonishment, U.N. Secretary General U Thant, citing Egyptian sovereignty over the desert peninsula, immediately agreed to the withdrawal of U.N. troops. Within days 80,000 Egyptians, equipped with Soviet jets, tanks, and other materiel, had garrisoned the Sinai and clamped a new blockade on the Strait of Tiran.

At first Israel appeared to hesitate, for the odds against her success in a war seemed overwhelming: In addition to the Egyptian force in the Sinai, backed by a reserve army of 60,000 men on the west bank of the Suez, she faced the 50,000-man Syrian Army—also armed with the latest Soviet equipment—and a Jordanian force of equal strength. Israel could muster an army of 70,000 backed by 230,000 reservists and equipped with U.S., British, and French weapons. To strike first, hard, and swiftly seemed to offer the Israelis their only hope of survival.

Over the Brink

In the early morning of June 5, 1967, wave upon wave of Israeli fighter-bombers swept in from the Mediterranean at altitudes so low they were undetected by Egyptian radar. In a textbook display of precision bombing and strafing, they devastated Nasser's air force on the ground, leaving some 300 Egyptian planes in ashes by nightfall. Other Israeli air units simultaneously attacked airfields in Jordan, Syria and Iraq, destroying about 100 aircraft. Before the dawn of June 6 Israel had secured complete control of the skies, at a cost to its 300-plane air force of 19 fighters.

Meanwhile, Israeli ground troops, including reserves summoned to a predetermined rendezvous by code words announced over the radio, were mobilizing, and by nightfall on June 7 Israel had 235,000 troops armed and ready for battle.

Ironically, news of the Israeli offensive was met with frenzied enthusiasm in Cairo, Damascus, and Amman, for the disaster that had already overtaken their air forces had been kept secret from the people. "Now we will teach Israel the lesson of death," shrieked Radio Cairo, and Radio Damascus echoed, "We will destroy Israel in four days." Eager to participate in the victory to come, thousands of Arabs surged to recruiting stations throughout the Middle East.

***Israel's third life-and-death struggle** with her Arab neighbors began on June 5, 1967, after Egypt cut her vital oil supplies by blockading the Strait of Tiran. Regarding this as an act of war, Israel launched an all-out attack on Arab airfields. Within hours the Israelis had virtually destroyed the Egyptian and Jordanian Air Forces and had badly damaged those of Syria and Iraq; by June 7 Israel held most of the Sinai. Above: An Israeli plants his country's flag by the Suez Canal. Upper right: An Israeli plane maneuvers over Jerusalem. Lower right: Egyptians demonstrate against Israel before the war.*

Blitzkrieg in the Sinai

The first and most crucial theater of operations was the Sinai desert, occupied by the largest and best-equipped Arab force, the 80,000-man, 1,000-tank Egyptian Army. On the heels of the initial air strikes 30,000 Israeli troops, led by 800 tanks, surged across the border from the Negev desert to destroy Nasser's forces. So effective was the Israeli assault that the massed Egyptian border force, after several hours of tank warfare and hand-to-hand combat, panicked. Those who did not surrender began to flee west toward the Suez Canal. Israeli jets crisscrossed the skies, bombing and strafing at will, knocking out scores of Egyptian tanks, trucks, and weapons carriers, and frustrating every Egyptian attempt to regroup. Within three days hundreds of Egyptian tanks had been destroyed, all border positions had been overrun, and the vital fortress at Sharm al-Sheikh had been captured. Through the wastes of the Sinai, Israeli armored columns moved forward without pause, driving westward to outflank the fleeing Egyptians.

For all practical purposes the Battle of the Sinai was over. In the following days there would be only one major encounter. In the mountains just east of the Suez Canal Egyptian tanks were trapped within the narrow confines of the Mitla Pass. On June 8 Israeli tanks caught up with them, and in an armored battle reminiscent of the desert warfare of World War II, 1,000 tanks traded fire, often at pointblank range. When the smoke cleared, the remainder of Nasser's Soviet-built armored force lay smoldering. The path to the Suez Canal was clear, and on June 9 Israeli troops planted the Star of David banner on its eastern shore.

Jerusalem Reunited

Meanwhile, warfare was flaring on another front. On June 5 the Israeli government had offered Jordan's King Hussein an informal nonaggression agreement. But in keeping with his obligations, Hussein refused the offer and instead opened an artillery barrage on the New City of Jerusalem. For two days, while the main Israeli thrust was concentrated in the Sinai, the bombardment continued, killing or wounding some 500 people. At the same time Jordanian tanks assumed offensive positions in readiness to attack the New City and push west to the sea, cutting Israel in half.

To counter this threat, several Israeli units were hurriedly reassigned from the southern front, and air attacks were launched against Jordanian positions and convoys. Reservists, backed by tanks, moved inland from the coast, capturing along the way scores of towns and villages that had been in King Hussein's domain since 1948. By dawn on June 7 two Israeli tank columns had surrounded the Old City, and the Jordanian forces, under constant attack by Israeli aircraft, had no choice but to retreat.

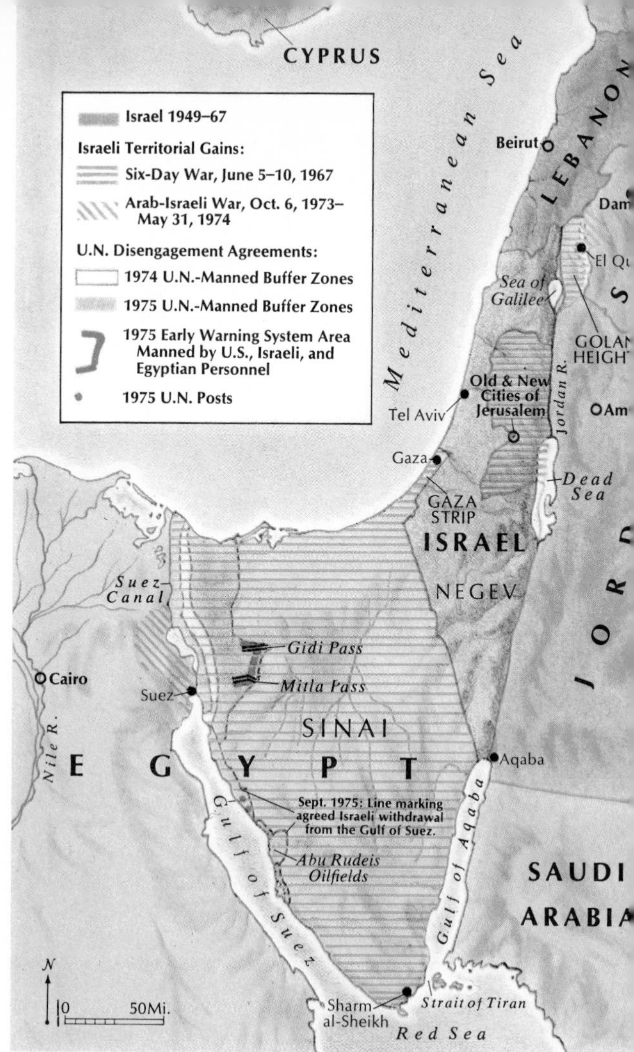

In 1974 and 1975 Israel, responding to the increasing military and political strength of the Arabs, began negotiated withdrawals from strategic areas gained (along with much other territory) during the wars of 1967 and 1973–74.

While Arab delegations at the United Nations headquarters in New York, stung by the unexpected rout, were in the process of agreeing to a cease-fire, handpicked commando units were beginning to lead the Israeli assault on the Old City. To their astonishment, they found that most of the Arab defenders had fled. By 10:00 on the morning of June 7, Jews stood in prayer before Old Jerusalem's Wailing Wall.

Assault on Syria

With its objectives in the south and east accomplished, Israel turned northward to the Golan Heights. First came the sweptwing fighter-bombers, raining bombs and rockets on the deeply entrenched Syrian artillery positions. Then, in a desperate effort to push their enemy off the heights before a U.N. cease-fire became effective, the Israelis launched a tank and infantry assault up the steep, rock-strewn slopes. The battle for the Golan Heights was fierce and bloody, but the Israelis continued to advance. Once atop the plateau, their forces fanned out, one column capturing the provincial capital, El Quneitra, another moving up the then-open road toward Damascus. When the cease-fire finally came into effect on June 10, Israeli forces were in sight of the towers of the Syrian capital.

After six days of combat a nation that had comprised just 8,000 square miles now had 26,500 square miles under its control. Israel had captured or destroyed 430 enemy aircraft and 800 tanks while inflicting 15,000 casualties on Egypt, Jordan, and Syria. The cost to Israel was some 40 planes destroyed and 803 deaths.

The Uncertain Future

Despite its overwhelming victory, Israel did not find peace. In the years that followed, the Arab nations, with Soviet aid, rebuilt their shattered forces. On Yom Kippur, October 6, 1973, the most solemn of the Jewish High Holy Days, Egypt and Syria launched attacks that began the fourth Arab-Israeli war. Initially unprepared, Israel rallied, crossed the Suez Canal into Egypt, and invaded Syria. On October 17 the Arab oil-producing nations announced an embargo on oil supplies to the United States and other allies of Israel. On the 29th a U.N.-sponsored cease-fire between Egypt and Israel took effect with the arrival of a U.N. Emergency Force in the Sinai peninsula. Fighting between Israel and Syria continued sporadically until a disengagement agreement was signed on May 31 of the following year.

Since then an uneasy peace has prevailed, disturbed by a continuing campaign of Palestinian terrorism and Israeli retaliation and by growing unrest in the Israeli-occupied West Bank. The U.N. has become a stage for the mouthing of much anti-Zionist venom, and Israel has been condemned as a racist and imperialist power, not only by those committed to her total destruction but by other nations seeking the benefit of assured oil supplies. Israel has refused to negotiate directly with the terrorists and has pointed out the irony that their supporters include such notable racists as Uganda's governing tyrant, Idi Amin. As the conflict continues, the people of Israel, remembering the ovens of Auschwitz and Dachau, steel their will to survive.

***During the Yom Kippur War** surface-to-air missiles (above, a SAM 3) supplied to Arab forces by the U.S.S.R. greatly reduced Israel's crippling air superiority.*

***Israeli artillery crews** man their camouflaged tanks in the barren sea of the Sinai desert. Though still a major weapon, the new missiles rendered tanks less potent in 1973 than they had been during the Six-Day War.*

THE LIFE OF THE TIMES 1957-76

Evangelist Billy Graham (above, left) drew nearly 2 million people to Madison Square Garden in 1957 during a 16-week New York campaign. His spellbinding style of preaching won him worldwide fame.

Pat Boone's relaxed style and wholesome image have sold more than 20 million records since the late fifties. Boone (above, sitting) was also a familiar figure on TV.

John Foster Dulles (above, right), Eisenhower's Secretary of State, shaped U.S. foreign policy during the cold war. He advocated containment of Communist expansion.

Mick Jagger (left), neither relaxed nor, apparently, wholesome, drove The Rolling Stones to stardom in the post-Boone years with a blend of showmanship and hard rock.

As the fifties came to a close, many Americans felt that they and their country were well on the way to a prosperous and peaceful future. President Eisenhower, as popular a man as ever sat in the White House, played golf and administered the most powerful nation in the world. True, the cold war continued. Secretary of State John Foster Dulles preached a hard line against the Reds abroad—some journalists called his threats of nuclear retaliation "brinkmanship"—and in Guatemala and Lebanon the forces of communism had been repulsed by modest invasions of U.S. marines. Even so, East-West tensions were far less severe than they had been in the first half of the decade. Senator Joseph R. McCarthy, the chief architect of the "Red scare," had died of cirrhosis of the liver in May 1957. The term "McCarthyism" would live as a description of witch-hunting and irre-

More inclined to détente than brinkmanship, Henry Kissinger meets North Vietnam's Le Duc Tho during the Paris peace talks.

***Women of all ages,** and some men, took part in the nationwide Women's Strike for Equality Day on August 26, 1970, the 50th anniversary of the women's suffrage amendment. In New York City thousands of women, including some of the first suffragists, marched down Fifth Avenue.*

***Many young people** spurned convention in the late 1960's, preferring communal living to conformity. Left, the dome home of a group in Drop City, Colorado.*

sponsible accusation, but domestically the Communist Party seemed to have become a dead issue.

The great crop of "war babies" was growing up in the vast new suburbs across the United States. Girls swayed enthusiastically in their "hula hoops." Boys played baseball on the popular Little League teams; in 1957 the country was startled by the victory of a Mexican team in the 11th Little League World Series. *The Saturday Evening Post* continued to display those reassuring Norman Rockwell covers of jolly grandparents, understanding parents, freckled children, and lovably awkward teenagers. The leather-jacketed youths who sped past the family car on motorcycles were a noisy minority. "Good" kids drank soda pop and listened to Pat Boone sing songs like "April Love"—although growing numbers of them, to the alarm of their elders, were bringing home loud rock records by an ex-truck driver named Elvis Presley. Adults read the novel *Doctor Zhivago* and watched *The $64,000 Question* on TV. "Senior citizens" (the new name for older people) were being attracted to retirement communities like Sun City, Arizona; in an increasingly youth-conscious society it was rare to find grandparents living with their families as they formerly had.

Beneath the country's relatively calm exterior, though, there were tensions. The unemployment rate was up to 6.8 percent by the end of 1958, and a sharp recession was in progress. Black people were increasingly determined to gain the same rights enjoyed by whites. Many whites agreed with them and were active in civil rights movements, and the federal government—under court orders—was behind them. In September 1957 President Eisenhower sent 1,000 paratroopers into Little Rock, Arkansas, to protect nine black students entering a previously all-white school. That same year Martin Luther King, Jr., a young black minister, founded the Southern Christian Leadership Conference to aid blacks in their fight for civil rights. Dr. King's leadership was predicated on nonviolence; peaceful boycotts, demonstrations, and "sit-ins" characterized the movement's progress through the South.

This period also saw the publication of two books that were harbingers of things to come: *Profiles in Courage* by the young Senator John F. Kennedy in 1956 and *On the Road* by Jack Kerouac in 1957. The next decade would be deeply influenced by the politics and lifestyle of the Kennedy family and by the surge of nonconformity that began with the poets and novelists of the Beat generation.

By the end of the 1950's the United States had been surprised and shaken by two events: the Soviet Union's successful orbiting of Sputnik, the first manmade space satellite, and Fidel Castro's rebellion and establishment of a Communist government in Cuba.

During the next decade and a half the pace of life would accelerate, and many cherished beliefs would be severely tested. Dozens of new words and phrases would find their way into the language, each recording a new idea or trend in American society: "consumerism," "women's liberation," "environmentalism," "consciousness-raising," "credibility gap," "transplants," and "tripping" would all become familiar concepts to young and old alike.

In the midst of such changes some Americans felt elation and a new sense of personal responsibility for the world around them. Others felt confused, threatened, and unable to adapt to new ways. Typical of the latter, perhaps, might be a young man, living in the suburbs, working for a corporation, married, with two young children, and, as the 1950's drew to a close, with an expectation that his ensuing years would be quietly successful.

Yet in the next 15 years this young man, raised to respect his parents and to believe that the federal government (especially the Presidency) was always victorious and honorable, would witness the debacle of Vietnam and the crisis of Watergate and, perhaps, see his children drifting into drug use and defiance.

He might also find that the once-friendly Negroes at the carwash were now scowling at him—a bewildered "honky" whose car (a Detroit gas guzzler, already condemned as a death trap by Ralph Nader) began costing a fortune when the country realized that it was running out of cheap fuel.

At home (and worst of all) his once submissive wife might now be demanding her own rights, finally tired of housework and wanting, at last, to find herself. Even his job, probably insecure for the first time

***His family** mourns slain President John F. Kennedy on November 25, 1963. Rumors of government coverups spread rapidly after Lee Harvey Oswald, the presumed assassin, was murdered.*

***July 20, 1969:** Neil Armstrong and Edwin Aldrin make the first moon landing. Right, Aldrin sets up an experiment near the lunar module.*

***The victim** of an oil spill: Ruined beaches, ravaged wildlife, and unbreathable air rallied many Americans to environmental issues in the 1960's and 70's.*

in his working life as a result of the worst recession since the end of World War II, might no longer offer much satisfaction.

So where might our now middle-aged citizen look for an answer? The newsstands were full of pornography, and psychoanalysis, encounter groups, and meditation all seemed faintly absurd. What was happening to America?

Feeling that their traditional values were under attack, many citizens came to blame the communications media for the state of society. Undoubtedly the media, especially TV, had been an active influence in America's evolution since 1960. It was on the television screen that most social changes were witnessed and publicized. Indirectly, television caused the demise of several of America's most influential mass-circulation magazines: *Look, Life,* and the venerable *Saturday Evening Post.* In a time of rapid social and political developments they were unable to compete with the impact of instant news and entertainment on TV and could not hold their advertisers. By 1974 more than 96 percent of all U.S. homes with electricity had at least one TV set.

It was on the TV screen that so many shocked Americans witnessed the funeral of their President and the murder of his assassin during the bleak November of 1963. President John Kennedy himself had been the first candidate to fully utilize television as a source of popular influence: His personal charm and appeal, rather than his arguments, had caused most of the viewing public to regard him as the "winner" of the 1960 campaign debates against Richard Nixon. After a brief three-year "Camelot" in which President Kennedy and his wife, Jacqueline, "glamorized" the White House with guests from the art and entertainment world, the nation entered a decade of turmoil. The Kennedy years had been full—the Peace Corps and the Bay of Pigs invasion in 1961; the Cuban Missile Crisis, Freedom Marchers, and the orbiting by NASA of both an astronaut (John Glenn) and a communications satellite (Telstar) in 1962; a mass civil rights rally in Washington and a nuclear test-ban treaty with Russia in 1963—but in comparison with what followed, they would seem positively tranquil. During the next several years three great developments left their indelible marks on America: Vietnam, the black rights movement, and the youth culture.

From 900 military "advisers" in 1961, the American presence in South Vietnam had escalated to more than 500,000 soldiers, sailors, airmen, and marines by 1969. And there were already more than 30,000 American dead. Public protest against the war was insignificant at first, but it rose as U.S. involvement increased and as people became sickened by suffering made evident everyday on television and in the press. Ultimately, President Lyndon Johnson chose not to run for office in 1968 rather than face a likely defeat. The next President, Richard Nixon, eventually ended the most unpopular war in U.S. history, but only after another 15,000 Americans had died and U.S. planes had dropped more bombs on Southeast Asia than they had dropped everywhere during World War II.

Throughout the middle sixties American blacks had increasingly pressed their demands for equal rights. The initially peaceful movement, under the influence of Martin Luther King, Jr., gave way to the bloody urban riots that erupted in Chicago, Los Angeles, Detroit, and dozens of other cities between 1964 and 1968. Radical black groups coming out of the northern ghettos showed no desire to protest peacefully or to work with the whites. The Black Panthers, the Student Non-

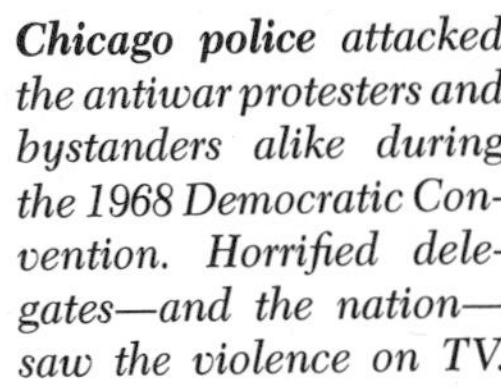

***Chicago police** attacked the antiwar protesters and bystanders alike during the 1968 Democratic Convention. Horrified delegates—and the nation—saw the violence on TV.*

***Angela Davis,** a leading black radical of the early seventies, was on the FBI's "ten most wanted" list. She was acquitted of kidnap, murder, and conspiracy charges in 1972.*

For three days at Woodstock *500,000 fans enjoyed a nonstop rock concert.*

The slow demise *of Richard Nixon's credibility was watched by millions during the Senate's televised investigation of the Watergate scandal.*

violent Coordinating Committee (SNCC), and the Black Muslims were interested in black progress, but not in integration. In the meantime, court-ordered busing of public school children to achieve integration became a national political issue that continued into the seventies. The assassination of Martin Luther King, Jr., in April 1968, and the assassination of Robert Kennedy a few months later, left the civil rights movement fragmented. By the mid-1970's, with black unemployment at about 14.7 percent (the overall national figure was about 8.5 percent), racial activism had temporarily subsided. The black community in America had a new awareness of itself, however, and would do its best never to allow things to be quite the same again.

The Woodstock Generation

In 1964 *The Ed Sullivan Show* welcomed a new group of Englishmen to America: the Beatles. Their songs, along with those of the American Bob Dylan and dozens of popular rock groups, expressed the new attitude of a generation unwilling to fully accept the values of its parents. In the next five years the country was confronted with a phenomenal change in its youth. The "silent generation" of the fifties gave way to the loudly protesting generation of the sixties. Campus protests that began over free speech, student rights, and other local issues were rapidly replaced by nationwide demonstrations against the Vietnam War.

In the late sixties young people began to *look* different. Men began to wear their hair long and to grow beards; women began to wear less makeup and adopted a "natural" look. Both wore the universal uniform of youth: blue jeans. Drugs, especially marijuana and LSD, became very popular, even among high school students. Across the land hippies, then "flower children," and finally "Jesus freaks," commune-livers, and "dropouts" shocked their elders. Many of the young flocked to such centers of the counterculture as the Haight-Ashbury section of San Francisco and the East Village of New York City.

With the 1968 Democratic Convention in Chicago, all of the tensions between the generations (and the classes—most college students and hippies were from middle-class families) erupted when the Chicago police attacked antiwar demonstrators in what an investigation later termed a "police riot." Millions witnessed the melee on TV, and the Democratic candidate, Hubert Humphrey, went on to lose the election to Richard Nixon.

The next year about 500,000 young people made their way to a farm near Woodstock, New York, to attend an outdoor rock festival. It was a peaceful occasion and, in a way, marked the climax of the youth movement. But the new generation of Americans continued to feel strongly inclined to challenge big business and big government, and a growing number of older citizens had begun to share their concern with the quality of life in the United States and to try to change it.

Nixon and Watergate

The first three years of the Nixon administration marked a period of domestic reaction to the liberalism of the sixties and of international détente with America's longtime antagonists, the Soviet Union and Communist China. At home, however, opposition to the Vietnam War spread, especially after 1970,

Homosexuals came out *into the open in the 1970's, protesting against harassment and discrimination. Parents and children paraded for Gay Pride.*

Alvin Ailey's Revelations, *featuring Judith Jamison, celebrates the religious and joyous moments that enriched the Negro experience on the plantations of the Old South.*

During a religious revival *that began in the early 1960's North Americans turned in increasing numbers to the yogic traditions of the East. Hinduism gained new adherents, and so did Buddhism. One stimulus was the arrival in the West (following the Chinese invasion of their homeland) of Tibetan lamas, guardians of perhaps the most sophisticated battery of meditational techniques still surviving. Above, a Buddhist rosary, or* mala, *from Tibet, made of bone, coral, pearl, and silver. Practicing a less austere form of Buddhism than Zen (although identical in its aims), the Tibetan schools stress the use of mantras (brief chants with calculated vibrational characteristics) and complex visualizations designed to calm the mind, to produce feelings of compassion for all creatures, and to foster latent psychic potentials.*

when four young people, taking part in a demonstration at Kent State University in Ohio against the U.S. incursion into Cambodia, were shot dead by troops of the National Guard. The next year over 12,000 antiwar demonstrators were arrested in Washington, and the publication of the "Pentagon Papers" revealed the government's efforts to conceal the full truth about America's involvement in the war. In 1973 U.S. forces finally withdrew from South Vietnam, but America's longest and most futile war had scarred the nation and severely damaged its self-esteem.

That same year, amid increasing inflation and unemployment, the greatest political crisis in U.S. history began to unfold. It had actually started the previous summer of 1972, when a group of men were arrested after breaking into the Democratic National Campaign Headquarters in the Watergate office building in Washington, D.C. It was later learned that the money for their operation had come from President Nixon's reelection campaign fund.

The Watergate scandal, great as it was, turned out to be just the tip of the iceberg. Testimony before Senator Sam Ervin's investigating committee revealed that it was only one part of a network of political spies, burglars, informants, extortionists, and agitators acting on orders from high White House officials.

The shock waves generated by the disclosures quickly spread to all areas of the executive branch, followed by scores of lawsuits, investigations, and ultimately the resignation of Nixon himself in August 1974. The Vice President, Spiro Agnew, had resigned a year earlier in response to an unrelated charge of income tax evasion resulting from charges that he had accepted bribes when Governor of Maryland.

Nixon was pardoned later in 1974 by his successor, President Gerald Ford, whom Nixon himself had nominated to replace Vice President Agnew. The Watergate scandal had lasting repercussions as the federal government moved to prevent similar abuses and tried to restore the public's trust in the Presidency.

Although the nation entered its bicentennial celebrations in 1976 facing severe problems—economic recession, continuing racial friction, and a deteriorating environment—it could take pride in having recently survived one of the most critical periods in its history. And although the future might hold even greater problems, the American people approached it with a degree of confidence and, in some quarters, with a renewed concern for those principles upon which their country had been founded.

1967

Strange Beacons in the Depths of Space

A faint but very regular pulsebeat from outer space betrays the presence of a baffling, and previously unknown, heavenly body.

For thousands of years men have been beguiled by the twinkling stars, seeing them in their minds' eye as the arbiters of destiny, as the abodes of departed heroes, and even finding a place for them in lullabies and romantic ballads. In the 17th century the invention of the telescope allowed scientists to observe more of the light from outer space, and in the 19th century the spectroscope (see p. 84) enabled them to analyze that light for clues to the composition and inner workings of the sun and other stars.

Yet there were limits to the traditional modes of observation. The twinkling of the stars marks the passage of their light through the earth's atmosphere, a deep ocean of air that, like a dirty window, filters out much incoming radiation. Moreover, man's "window" onto the stars was inevitably narrow, being confined to radiations in the spectrum of visible light. In recent years, though, the rapid development of electronics

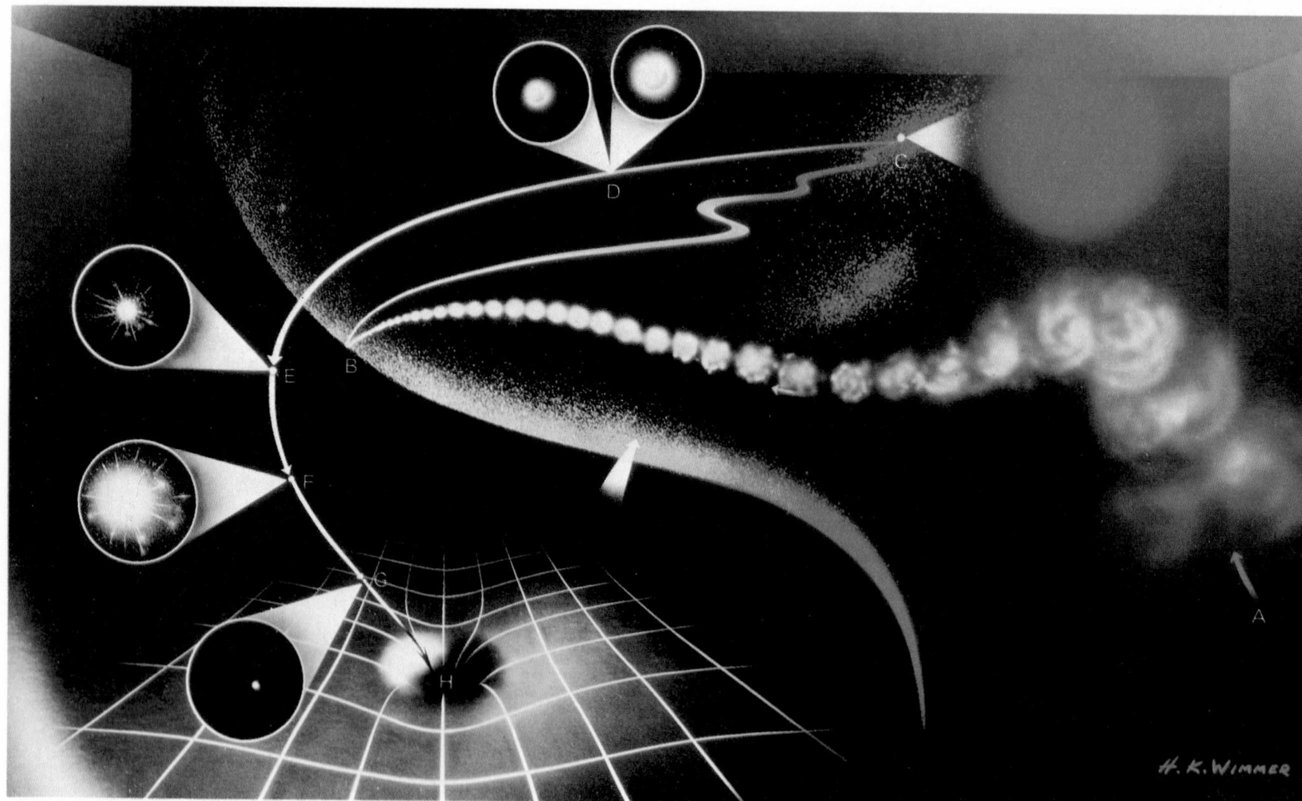

***The astronomical discoveries** of the last 15 years have radically altered and enlarged our understanding of the universe, especially regarding the complex process of stellar evolution. The multibillion-year life cycle of a star, represented in the painting above, begins as a huge cloud of cosmic dust and gas (A) coalesces and grows hotter until nuclear fusion begins in the core and it joins the mainstream of stars (B)—commonly diagramed by astronomers along a diagonal curve—where it spends most of its life. When its hydrogen has finally been consumed, the star becomes a red giant (C), then when all other nuclear fuels have been used up it becomes a pulsating star, varying in size and brightness (D). Under special conditions it may explode into a nova (E). A very massive star can explode into a far more spectacular supernova (F), thereafter collapsing into a small, extremely dense neutron star (G) or, beyond that, into a mysterious, superdense black hole (H), where gravitational forces are so great that our laws of physics have no meaning.*

and the ability to send instruments beyond the atmosphere have vastly extended our observational window, and the science of radio astronomy, working with unseen wavelengths of energy, is producing an explosion of startling data about the universe.

The first investigations of radio waves from sources outside our own solar system were made in the early 1930's by Karl Jansky (see pp. 228–231), a researcher at The Bell Laboratories in New Jersey. Jansky found that behind manmade radio signals and the continuous radio "noise" of the earth's atmosphere are far fainter radio waves coming from the central regions of our galaxy, the Milky Way.

The development of radio astronomy as a major science had to await the advances in electronics that came with the use of radar in World War II. After the war large radio "dishes" and other types of antennas began to appear all over the world, and these new devices at last made astronomers independent of atmospheric conditions. Radio signals pass through the atmosphere without much distortion, often bringing information from regions of the sky where cosmic dust and gas block visible light. Among the most important of the recent discoveries have been pulsars, mysteriously regular radio sources that were first half-jokingly called "LGM sources," for "little green men." Since they were first observed in 1967, the effort to explain the pulsars' cosmic beeping has opened astonishing avenues of research at the opposite extremes of scientific study, subatomic physics and cosmology.

The Invisible Universe

The first indication that radio astronomy might reveal entirely new orders of heavenly phenomena came in the early 1960's. In 1962 Australian radio astronomers studying a radio source known as 3C-273 were able to fix its position with great accuracy by noting the instants at which it vanished behind the moon and reappeared. They knew that similar sources had been identified with faint, unremarkable blue stars visible through optical telescopes, and they expected such an identification when they sent data on 3C-273 to Maarten Schmidt, a Dutch astronomer working at Mount Palomar. Schmidt, however, found that the spectrum of 3C-273 was very different from that of ordinary blue stars, and in early 1963 he came to the tentative conclusion that it was located about 1½ billion light years away, far outside our own galaxy. Too small to be a galaxy itself, yet far too bright to be a star or even a huge exploding star (a supernova), 3C-273 turned out to be the first of a new category of quasi-stellar objects—quasars—whose prodigious outpouring of energy remains to be explained.

Then in late 1967 radio astronomers at Cambridge University in England encountered an even more provocative phenomenon, the pulsars. A graduate student, Jocelyn Bell, noticed a "regular irregularity"—a series of pulses—in the record of cosmic radio waves. At first the project director, Anthony Hewish, and others believed that the pulses must be some form of local noise; during one series of followup observations university students in the countryside around the antenna appealed to motorists to stop their engines for a few minutes so that the electrical impulses of their ignition systems would not interfere with the work.

But the strange pulses continued, and the Cambridge group was soon monitoring such signals from four separate points in the sky. Each had its own rate, varying from four pulses per second to one every 1.3 seconds, but all were extremely regular—so much so that for a time it was thought they might be messages from far-off civilizations. By early 1968, though, astronomers realized that the signals were not originating from a planet but must be coming from a previously unknown radio source of stellar origin—the pulsar. Since then scores of other pulsars have been located. The first visual identification of one was made in 1969 when astronomers at the University of Arizona observed a flashing light at the site of a known pulsar in the center of the Crab Nebula, the remnant of a supernova whose spectacular explosion had been observed and documented by the Chinese in A.D. 1054.

The Death of a Star

The discovery of a connection between a supernova and a pulsar proved to have a bearing on a number of major astronomical puzzles. Astronomers already knew that when an average-size star (roughly the size of our sun) has burned up all its hydrogen fuel, it begins to compress under its own gravitational pressure. At this point the star's core is composed mainly of helium—the "ash" left over from hydrogen fusion—which itself begins to burn, temporarily halting the contraction. But when the helium is used up, the contraction resumes, until finally the entire mass of the star is reduced to a white-hot ball about the size of the earth. Such a star is known as a white dwarf, and it is so greatly compressed that, as one astronomer put it, 10 tons of its material could be kept in a matchbox.

When the notion of a superdense white dwarf was first proposed in the 1920's, it was greeted with a skepticism that gave way only after considerable supporting evidence had been gathered. Then in the 1930's a new theory prompted even greater incredulity. It suggested that when a larger-than-average star had consumed all its hydrogen, it would initially follow the same sequence of events as a smaller star. However, because of its great mass, the large star's gravitational compression would drive temperatures in its core up to incredible levels—as high as 100 *billion* degrees—climaxing in a supernova, a stupendous explosion 10 billion times brighter than the sun that would hurl part

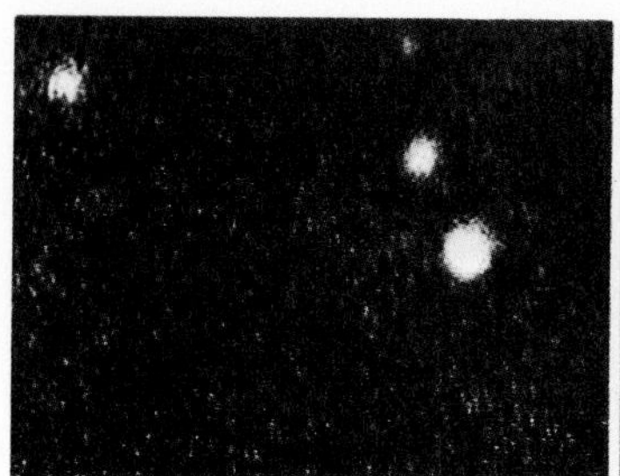
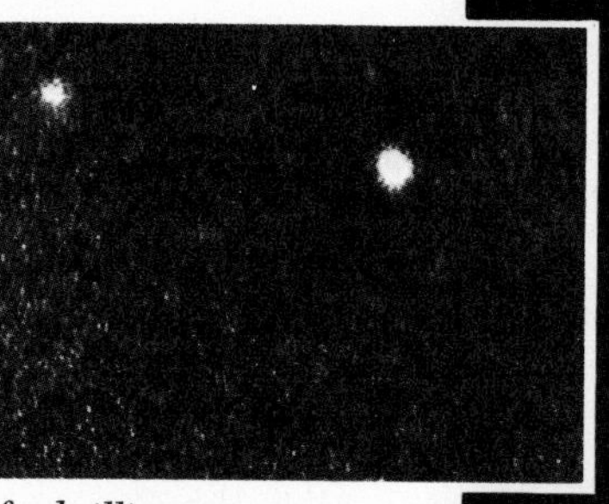

The Crab Nebula (right), remnant of a brilliant supernova seen on earth in A.D. *1054, is the site of the first pulsar to be located visually (arrow). Astronomers in 1969 used a specially designed high-speed camera system to take the above photographs of the pulsar, which flashes on and off with extraordinary precision 30 times per second.*

of the star's mass out into space. The remainder would continue to compress, though, and with such force that it would not stop at the white dwarf stage. When atoms are subjected to intense heat and pressure, the electrons are driven out of their usual "orbits" around the atomic nuclei and merge into a strange "electron sea" on the stellar surface. Because the electrons move at high speeds, their motions generate enough pressure to halt the compression of a white dwarf. In the case of a larger star, though, calculations indicated that its weight during contraction would overpower the electrons' resistance, forcing them into so intense a compression with the positively charged protons that they would cancel out each other's electrical charges and combine into neutrons (particles with no electrical charge). Finally, then, only neutrons would remain, locked into a fantastically dense body that the theorists called a neutron star.

Such a body would represent a radically new state of matter, in comparison with which the densest known material would seem a mere cloud. To make a neutron star, a mass greater than the sun's would have to be packed into a sphere about 10 miles across—one cubic inch of which would weigh 10 billion tons!

The Stellar Connection

While there were no obvious flaws in the calculations, most astronomers and physicists simply found the conclusion impossible to accept, and for 30 years the neutron star was regarded as little more than imaginative speculation. But with the discovery of pulsars and the effort to understand them, all that changed.

So far as was known, there were only three possible sources for the pulsars' radio signals. The first was a "pulsating" star—that is, one that expands and contracts regularly, giving off radio emissions in the process. While many such stars have been observed, none of them pulsates rapidly enough to produce four separate signals in one second. The second possibility was a pair of stars orbiting around each other, one of them a radio source whose emissions are interrupted as its partner passes between it and the earth. Such two-star systems are common, but none has an orbit fast enough to account for the pulsar signals. The only other possible source was a star rotating on its axis and emitting a narrow radio beam that would sweep the sky much like a lighthouse beam. While no ordinary star can spin so fast, a white dwarf is theoretically capable of four rotations per second. This seemed the most promising explanation until November 1968, when radio astronomers discovered the pulsar at the center of the Crab Nebula, which emits an astounding 30 signals per second. Even a body as dense as a white dwarf would fly into pieces before it reached that rate of spin. Just as an ice skater spins faster when he pulls his arms in close to his chest, so an astronomical body rotates faster as it contracts, and any massive object rotating 30 times a second would have to be much more compressed than a white dwarf. Such an object could only be the elusive neutron star.

Since this discovery it has become generally accepted that neutron stars not only exist but are quite numerous. This conclusion has added weight to long-ignored theories postulating the existence of objects in the universe even more dense than neutron stars, remnants of extremely massive stars (more than twice the mass of the sun) that do not stop collapsing at the level of a neutron star. Such a body continues contracting until its mass is concentrated into an area no more than three or four miles across. This so-called black hole would create gravitational forces so enormous that nothing—no particles, no radio waves, not even light—could escape from it.

Since a black hole by definition would be invisible, its presence could only be ascertained by its effect on other objects in its vicinity. One such piece of indirect evidence might be found in a double-star system in which only one of the stars is detectable. In addition, astronomers calculate that when a black hole's gravity pulls interstellar gas or other matter into it, extreme heat will be produced, which in turn will generate powerful X-rays.

Although X-rays cannot penetrate the earth's atmosphere, they can be readily detected by a satellite, and in 1970 the United States launched one for just that purpose. In several years of operation the satellite located nearly 100 X-ray sources. One of these sources was identified as a two-star system, one of which is a visible supergiant while the other is invisible but far too massive to be a white dwarf or a neutron star.

While this observation and others have furnished strong evidence that black holes do exist, important questions remain to be answered before they can be accepted as proven fact. If the black hole theory is confirmed, though, it could provide the key to one of the ultimate mysteries in science: How is the universe held together? It is known that virtually all the galaxies in the cosmos are moving away from each other at immensely high speeds, but their velocities seem to be diminishing gradually because they cannot escape the combined force of each other's gravity. All the visible matter in the universe, however, adds up to only a tiny fraction of the amount that would be needed to substantially slow the galaxies' outward flight. It may be, then, that much of the remaining gravitational power emanates from black holes.

Some astronomers have also theorized that enormous black holes at the center of distant galaxies might produce enough energy (by pulling whole solar systems into them, for instance) to account for the still-unexplained quasars. It has even been proposed that a quasar is the "other end" of a black hole, a brilliant "white hole" through which matter is flowing from origins unknown—from elsewhere in our universe, or perhaps from some entirely *different* universe.

Such thoughts are not merely the speculations of science-fiction writers, but serious topics of consideration among theorists in astronomy and physics around the world. While no definitive answers are likely to be found in the near future, the astronomical discoveries of the past two decades have raised the possibility that even our most firmly held notions about physical reality may prove as imperfect as our ancestors' quite reasonable belief that the sun revolved around the earth.

FIRE FROM THE SKY: THE UNSOLVED SIBERIAN MYSTERY

Shortly after 7 a.m. on June 30, 1908, the remote, sparsely populated Tunguska region of Siberia was the scene of an explosion unlike any the world had ever experienced. Virtually every tree within a 20-mile radius was charred and leveled; 250 miles away a "pillar of fire" could be seen in the sky; 150 miles beyond that horses were reportedly knocked down by the shock wave. Seismic readings recorded as far away as Washington, D.C., indicate that the blast was considerably more powerful than the atomic explosion at Hiroshima 37 years later. What could have caused such a cataclysm? Explanations that would normally seem most likely—that it was caused by a giant meteorite, or possibly by a comet—did not fit the evidence. There was no sign of a crater, as would have been caused by a meteorite's impact, and a comet could hardly have approached the earth unobserved. This left only more exotic possibilities—among them that a miniature black hole plunged into the Siberian forest, or even that an alien spacecraft burned up like a meteorite in the earth's atmosphere, causing its atomic-powered engine to explode. Each view has some scientific supporters, but perhaps the most plausible theory is that the explosion was caused by a small chunk of antimatter entering the atmosphere. The existence of "antiparticles" was confirmed in 1932 with the discovery of the positron, identical to the electron in every way save that its electrical charge is positive, not negative. It is now known that nearly every subatomic particle has an oppositely charged twin, and most physicists believe that antimatter, made up of antiparticles, would be indistinguishable from ordinary matter. But if the two came into contact, they would annihilate each other in a violent burst of radiation. If this was the cause of the Siberian explosion, two questions remain: Where did the "antirock" come from? And what is the chance of a recurrence?

More than 20 years later, the effects of the 1908 Siberian explosion were still dramatically visible.

1969

A Small Walk on Another World

In one of the truly momentous steps in human history, the voyage of Apollo 11 lands the first men safely on the moon.

They were the first visitors to a lifeless world, but they were not alone. "Be advised," came the radio message from the Manned Spacecraft Center at Houston, Texas, "there are lots of smiling faces in this room, and all over the world." The reply flashed back from the moon: "There are two of them up here." Just a moment before, at 4:17 p.m. (EDT) on July 20, 1969, the lunar module (LM) carrying Apollo 11 astronauts Neil Armstrong and Edwin Aldrin, Jr., had touched down on the plain called the Sea of Tranquility. Six hours later Armstrong eased his bulky space suit through the hatch of the *Eagle* and climbed down its short ladder. As he did so, hundreds of millions of people—more than had ever witnessed any single event—were able to watch the historic moment on their television screens. "I'm going to step off the LM now," Armstrong reported. "That's one small step for a man, one giant leap for mankind."

His words climaxed an intensive U.S. effort to put a man on the moon, inaugurated by President John F. Kennedy in 1961. Two events that year had jolted U.S. pride and self-assurance: On April 12 Soviet cosmonaut Yuri Gagarin became the first man in space, making a 108-minute one-orbit space flight; a week later the U.S.-sponsored Bay of Pigs invasion of Cuba met with disastrous failure. Kennedy resolved to restore national prestige by launching a new phase in the U.S. space program. On May 25 he spoke to Congress: "I believe that this nation should commit itself to achieving the goal, before this decade is out, of landing a man on the moon and returning him safely to earth." To finance this undertaking, Kennedy requested additional funds for the National Aeronautics and Space Administration (NASA), the civilian space agency created in 1958 in response to the Soviet launching of Sputnik 1 (see pp. 424–429). Congress responded swiftly, approving the first of the more than $22 billion that would eventually go into Project Apollo. Spending on the project averaged 3 percent of the annual federal budget. By far the greatest part went to the 16 aerospace firms that designed and produced the Saturn 5 rocket and the main components of the Apollo spacecraft. In addition, the mammoth effort involved 12,000 subcontractors and the resources of more than 100 of the nation's universities. In all, a total of 400,000 people worked on some phase of the project.

First on the Moon

From the beginning the national effort to place the first men on the moon was seen as a race, an opportunity to demonstrate once and for all the superiority of U.S. technology over that of the Soviet Union. Unlike the explorations of previous eras, the goal of Project Apollo was not land or other natural wealth. Nor was it primarily scientific knowledge: Much, though not all, of the data gathered in Project Apollo could have been obtained by unmanned probes at far less expense. And while Apollo did give the United States valuable experience in the tools and techniques of space exploration, it was not part of a systematic plan to that end.

Although Kennedy's scientific advisers had assured him the United States was capable of achieving a manned lunar landing in six to nine years, there were enormous problems to be solved. One of the first was the development of a rocket powerful enough to thrust the 45-ton Apollo payload away from the pull of the earth's gravity. Another was finding out enough about the moon itself to select a favorable landing site and develop equipment suited to the moon's environment. There were other difficulties too: of shielding the astronauts from the incredible heat of reentry into the earth's atmosphere, of developing the sophisticated guidance and tracking systems needed to send a spacecraft to the moon and back, of testing and perfecting the technical maneuvers involved, and of minimizing the possibility of human or mechanical error.

Two manned space programs, Mercury and Gemini, and three unmanned series of lunar probes, the Ranger, Surveyor, and Lunar Orbiter, preceded the first Apollo mission. On May 5, 1961, Alan Shepard became the first American in space. His 15-minute suborbital flight in a Mercury space capsule made him a national hero. Nine months later John Glenn made the first U.S. orbital flight in a 3,700-pound Mercury capsule, the *Friendship 7*. The Mercury series, which ended with Gordon Cooper's 22-orbit flight in May 1963, tested the astronauts' ability to withstand the stress of acceleration and to function in the weightlessness of space. The astronauts had accumulated more than 50 hours of in-flight experience. The ground teams were beginning to gain the expertise in planning, control, and communication they would need for more ambitious flights.

Meanwhile, the Soviets continued to achieve impressive space firsts: two- and three-man missions in

Man's first steps *on the moon (right, Edwin Aldrin, his visor reflecting Neil Armstrong) augured a new age of space technology. Some scientists believe that one of its most valuable results may be the establishment of enormous self-sustaining colonies (above and p. 502) between the earth and moon. Most of the technology needed to build these settlements already exists.*

***The successful** Apollo 11 moon landing spurred probes into deeper space, among them the orbital survey of Mars begun in 1971 by Mariner 9 (above). It revealed that conditions suitable for life may once have existed there or may even now be in the process of forming. The investigation of that possibility was a major goal of Viking 1, an unmanned U.S. spacecraft that landed safely on Mars in July 1976. The stunningly clear photographs Viking 1 transmitted to earth confirmed that the Martian surface (right) is reddish, and they revealed that the sky varies from off-white to pink. In addition, a preliminary analysis of the soil disclosed a surprisingly high level of oxygen, lending new weight to speculations that some microscopic form of life may yet be found.*

the Voskhod capsules, beginning with the three-man crew of Voskhod 1 in October 1964 and a space walk by Alexei Leonov in Voskhod 2 on March 18, 1965. In contrast to the highly publicized U.S. moon project, the Soviet missions were shrouded in secrecy. No one could say with assurance that they were even participating in the race to put a man on the moon. Their continued lead in space technology, however, meant that they might well be planning to do so and intensified U.S. determination to get to the moon first.

On March 23, 1965, Virgil "Gus" Grissom and John Young flew in the first of 10 two-man Gemini missions, during which U.S. astronauts learned to modify their orbit at will, to maneuver their craft into position for orbital rendezvous and for docking with other capsules, to walk in space, and to deal with emergencies, such as a fuel-cell failure on Gemini 5 and a misfiring thruster on Gemini 8. When the series ended in November 1966, it was apparent that the Gemini was a more sophisticated craft than the Voskhod. The United States had gained an edge over the Soviets.

There were other indications that the U.S.S.R. space effort was beginning to lag. The leaders who replaced Premier Nikita S. Khrushchev in 1964 seemed less interested in space firsts than he was. No doubt the death of Sergei Korolyov, the chief Soviet rocket designer, in 1966 contributed to the overall slowdown in the space program. Throughout 1966 and 1967 Soviet spokesmen placed increasing importance on the merits of unmanned space probes and hinted that they considered the construction of a permanent space station to be more worthwhile than a "hasty visit to the moon."

At the same time unmanned spacecraft from both nations were busily gathering data about the moon. After six unsuccessful tries three U.S. Ranger probes sent back thousands of closeup photographs before crashing into the lunar surface. In early 1966 the Soviet Union's Luna 9 achieved a soft landing on the moon, and Luna 10 gave the world its first view of the moon's far side. Seven U.S. Surveyors soft-landed on the moon between 1966 and 1968 to test the texture and composition of the soil and to take ground-level photographs of the lunar landscape. From August 1966 to August 1967 five Lunar Orbiters mapped the entire surface of the moon, enabling Apollo's planners to select the best site for landing.

The Final Stages

Apollo flights had begun in October 1961 with the first unmanned launch of a Saturn 1 rocket. But it was not until 1967 that the first flight test of the Saturn 5 moon rocket was to take place. The Saturn 5 was the heaviest, most complex, and costliest device ever to leave the ground. Its three stages stood more than 290 feet tall. There were five F-1 engines burning kerosene and liquid oxygen in the first stage, five J-2's burning hydrogen and oxygen in the second, and one J-2 in the third. In the first 2½ minutes of flight the first stage would generate 7.6 million pounds of thrust, burning more than half a million gallons of propellant and accelerating the rocket to 10 times the speed of sound (6,100 miles per hour). On the ground and in flight a 5,000-pound instrument and computer unit automatically controlled its speed and course.

The Apollo craft itself consisted of three parts, or modules: the service module (SM), the command module (CM), and the lunar module (LM). The largest was the service module, housing the engine that would curve Apollo's outward path into a lunar orbit and later start it on its homeward journey. The SM also carried the main long-distance antenna, oxygen reserve, fuel cells, and attitude-control jets. Everything in it was designed as simply and reliably as possible. The two components of its fuel were mixed by gas pressure rather than pumps, and they ignited on contact. The thrust chamber and nozzle had coatings that burned away steadily and needed no cooling system. Any one of the three fuel cells could supply enough electricity for a safe return.

Atop the SM, and drawing on its facilities for all but a few hours of the trip, was the astronauts' command module. It was a triumph of design. Only its blunt conical shape was reminiscent of Alan Shepard's Mercury capsule. Inside, there was four times more space. The CM carried a compact computer with a storage capacity exceeding that of Project Mercury's ground control computer. Outside, it was protected against the heat of its reentry into the earth's atmosphere by a heavy honeycombed metal-resin-fiber heat shield.

The lunar module resembled nothing ever seen before, although it was often called the "bug." Its outer covering was of metal foil, and it had four insect-like legs to support it after landing on the moon. To facilitate its takeoff from the lunar surface, every part of the LM was painstakingly designed to minimize weight. It did not even have couches or chairs. The astronauts used light body harnesses for support during takeoff and landing. The LM would weigh a total of 24,000 pounds when it started its descent to the moon. Most of that was fuel that would be consumed, and the lower part of the LM, which served as a landing platform, would remain behind on the moon. On takeoff the LM would be no heavier than a large automobile.

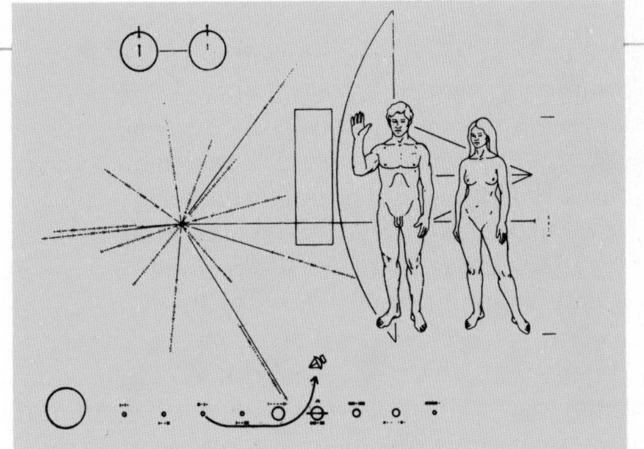

The 6- by 9-inch plaque carried aboard Pioneer 10.

IS ANYBODY OUT THERE?

For years astronomers have searched for evidence of intelligent life beyond our solar system. Since the short-lived U.S. Project Ozma in 1960, radio telescopes have monitored hundreds of stars, though without picking up any noteworthy signals as yet. The U.S. space probe Pioneer 10, launched in 1972, used another approach: a plaque designed to communicate in the language of science. The hydrogen atom (the most common element in the galaxy) is shown schematically at the top. The radiating lines of binary numbers (see p. 380) below represent specific pulsars, arranged to show the position of our sun. The humans in front of the craft illustrate the kind of creatures that built it. At the bottom is our solar system, indicating which planet is ours.

The first manned orbital flight of the Apollo CM was scheduled for February 1967. During a preflight simulation exercise on the afternoon of January 27, fire broke out in the sealed capsule, which had been pressurized with pure oxygen. There were muffled cries from the three astronauts inside, but in less than a minute Gus Grissom, Edward White, and Roger Chaffee were dead of asphyxiation and burns. An investigation of the tragedy revealed that a faulty wire had set fire to some synthetic webbing, and the flames had spread with lightning speed in the 100-percent-oxygen atmosphere. The capsule's hatch did not have a quick-release lever, although one was planned for later models. Investigators also found that the capsule interior contained far too many flammable materials.

Project Apollo came to a near standstill while the CM was redesigned and rebuilt. A few months later a second space tragedy occurred, this time in the U.S.S.R. Cosmonaut Vladimir Komarov, veteran of the first Voskhod flight, was killed during reentry on April 24, 1967, when the parachute, designed to brake his Soyuz spacecraft's descent, failed to open and the capsule plunged to the ground.

By late 1968, however, the United States was ready to resume its manned Apollo flights. After two more unmanned missions to check the LM and Saturn 5 rocket, three astronauts orbited the earth for 11 days in Apollo 7 in October 1968. In December Apollo 8 and its three-man crew orbited the moon 10 times, and in March 1969 the crew of Apollo 9 practiced rendezvous and docking maneuvers with the LM and tested the bulky space suit that would be worn on the moon. In May *Snoopy*, the LM of Apollo 10, descended to an altitude nine miles above the Sea of Tranquility. Everything was ready for the actual moon landing.

Nearly a million spectators jammed the roads around Cape Kennedy, Florida, for the liftoff on the morning of July 16. With a prolonged roar the enormous Saturn 5 rose skyward and angled out over the ocean. Three days later the crew—Neil A. Armstrong, the civilian commander of the mission, Edwin E. "Buzz" Aldrin, Jr., an Air Force colonel with a doctorate in astronautics, and Michael Collins, the Air Force lieutenant colonel who would remain in the command module while Armstrong and Aldrin took the *Eagle* down to the Sea of Tranquility—began orbiting the moon. In the early afternoon of the 20th *Eagle* and its two-man crew separated from the CM and dropped first into a low orbit that took it down to 50,000 feet above the moon's surface. At a programed moment Armstrong began the final 10-minute descent. As the *Eagle* neared the lunar surface, Armstrong realized that they were heading directly for a boulder-strewn crater and quickly took over the controls to steer the craft to a safer landing site, where he brought the *Eagle* gently to rest. Then he radioed: "Houston, Tranquility Base here. The *Eagle* has landed."

The New World—and Beyond

Armstrong and Aldrin spent more than 21 hours on the moon, about two of them outside the capsule. For protection from the harsh, airless lunar environment, where temperatures range from −250°F to 250°F and micrometeoroids shower down at speeds of 64,000 miles per hour, they wore special insulated and pressurized suits, boots, gloves, helmets, and visors, and carried portable life-support systems on their backs. On earth the equipment would have weighed nearly 190 pounds, but on the moon, where the pull of gravity is about one-sixth that of the earth, they weighed only 32 pounds. As he walked on the moon, Armstrong described it as having "a stark beauty all its own. It's like much of the high desert areas of the United States." Aldrin called it "magnificent desolation." The two men studied the terrain in the immediate vicinity of the LM, set out equipment for three scientific experiments, and gathered samples of lunar dirt and rocks before reboarding the *Eagle*. Their takeoff and reunion with *Columbia* went according to plan, and on July 24, some 195 hours after liftoff, the CM splashed down in the Pacific Ocean. After more than two weeks to guard against the remote possibility that they had brought back lunar micro-organisms, they received unprecedented heroes' welcomes in the United States and throughout the world.

There were five more Apollo flights. The Apollo 12 LM landed in the moon's Ocean of Storms in November 1969, and its crew inspected the remains of Surveyor 3 and found them to be almost unaffected by the 2½ years of exposure to the moon's vacuum and temperature extremes. The flight of Apollo 13 in April 1970 was cut short when an oxygen tank in the SM exploded

NO LONGER SCIENCE FICTION

Within a few years of the moon landing, scientists were seriously discussing the benefits of colonizing space, and by 1975 advanced technology had made such a project feasible. The colonies, built mainly with minerals mined on the moon and ferried to the construction sites by space shuttle, would be placed in stable orbit at libration points between the earth and moon—points at which the gravities of the earth, sun, and moon are in perfect balance. The colonies would grow their own food, and, by beaming solar energy in the form of microwaves to the earth for conversion into electricity, would quickly repay the cost of their construction.

The first small space colony for about 10,000 inhabitants might look like the design below. A profile (lower right) shows the numerous amenities of the living area; it would be separated by a partition from the humid farming area.

Some proposed space colonies would be cylindrical, with mirrors along the sides to reflect the sun. On average they would be about 19 miles long and 4 miles in diameter.

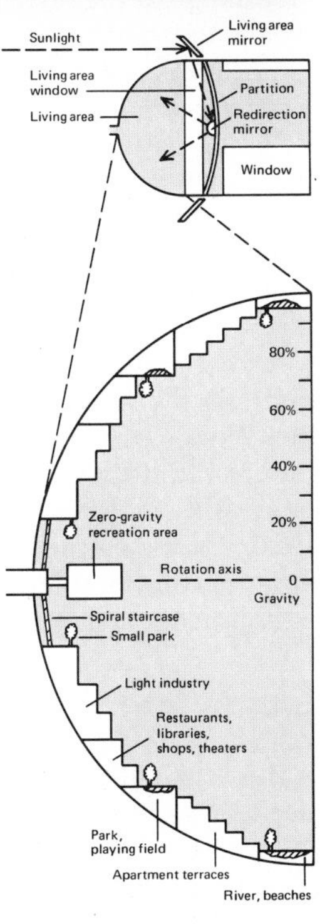

on the way to the moon, and only an ingenious temporary repair allowed the astronauts to draw on the LM's electrical and life-support systems for a tense, chilly return flight. In February 1971 Apollo 14's LM took Alan Shepard and Edgar Mitchell to Fra Mauro site, and on three longer stays the landing teams from Apollos 15, 16, and 17 used a "lunar rover" vehicle to cover more of the lunar surface and gather hundreds of pounds of rock and soil samples.

Apollo 17, in December 1972, marked the last of man's first series of visits to the moon. Since then emphasis has shifted to discovering what men can do during extended orbital missions and to sending unmanned spacecraft to explore the planets. The Soviet Union sent up the first orbiting space station, the 18-ton Salyut 1, equipped with a biological laboratory and special scientific instruments, in April 1971. The first tests aboard Salyut 1 were carried out by two members of the three-man crew of Soyuz 2 in June 1971. Tragically, all three were killed during their return to earth at the end of their 24-day mission. The U.S. Skylab space station was orbited in 1973. In all, it gave nine astronauts in three visits more than 3,000 hours in orbit and demonstrated that valuable knowledge about solar physics, the earth's resources, and man's reactions in space could be gained by tests and observations conducted in a permanent orbiting space station. From May to July 1975 two Soviet cosmonauts lived and worked aboard the Salyut 4 space station for 63 days, and in mid-July Apollo and Soyuz capsules linked up in orbit and remained docked for two days.

Meanwhile, in the mid-1970's unmanned U.S. and Soviet probes began reaching out to the planets. The Soviet Union's Venera spacecraft penetrated Venus' hot, corrosive clouds and soft-landed on its surface to radio back data about that mysterious planet's atmosphere and geological composition. American Pioneer probes scanned Jupiter and Saturn, and two U.S. Viking robot landing craft were sent to look for evidence of life on Mars, the first landing safely in July 1976.

Future manned space voyages will probably have to await the development of reusable rockets and spacecraft. Otherwise, the tremendous cost and waste involved in one-shot missions will render them impractical. NASA planners favor the development of a space shuttle to ferry men and equipment between the earth and the moon via a permanent orbiting space station. Such a system may eventually open the way to establishing colonies in space and on the moon and the planets and to making exploratory voyages beyond the solar system. It will take many more years and billions more dollars to carry out these far-reaching plans than it did to put a man on the moon, but the potential value is much greater. Even so, no future journey is likely to kindle the same historic excitement as the one that briefly united the world on July 20, 1969.

1970

Chile: Death of a Democracy

Salvador Allende's turbulent experiment in democratic Marxism ends in tragedy as Chile succumbs to a military coup.

If Allende wins, this will be the last election." Such was the prediction made by opponents of Salvador Allende during the stormy 1970 campaign for the Presidency of Chile. For many Chileans it rang dangerously true: Allende was the candidate of the Popular Unity coalition, an alliance of Socialists, Communists, and other leftist parties and groups; the most radical of his followers expressed open contempt for "bourgeois legality," seeing it as an obstacle to the sweeping political and economic changes they sought.

Most of his supporters, though, were not so militant, and Allende himself repeatedly stressed his commitment to a democratic, constitutional government. His goal, he told the voters, was to achieve socialism peacefully and legally by what he called *la vía Chilena*—"the Chilean road." "No one need fear," he proclaimed, "save for that tiny group that takes the great part of the national income."

At length, in the three-way election on September 4, 1970, Allende won a slim plurality: 36.6 percent of the vote as against 35.3 percent for an aging conservative opponent and 28.1 percent for the candidate of the ruling Christian Democratic Party. Since no one had won a majority, Chilean law called for Congress to name the President—traditionally the candidate with the largest vote. On October 24 Congress followed that tradition, and Salvador Allende was confirmed as the world's first freely elected Marxist President.

Slightly less than three years later, on September 11, 1973, Allende died in a military coup that also brought to a bloody conclusion both the oldest constitutional tradition in Latin America and one of the world's most unusual experiments in social change.

The rule of law had been a guiding principle in Chilean life since the nation first freed itself from Spain in 1817. Under Bernardo O'Higgins, Chile's liberator, the country's first constitution was written a year later, establishing a strong central government. In 1833 a new constitution was enacted that remained the foundation of Chilean government for almost a century, assuring a political continuity unique among the countries of Latin America. This constitution provided for a Congress, elected by the propertied elite, which in turn chose the country's President.

The latter years of the 19th century marked a period known as the Liberal Republic, during which progressive groups gradually gained ascendency over church-backed conservative forces. European immigrants were welcomed, and decades of peace and order attracted political and intellectual exiles from across South America to Santiago, Chile's capital. The nation grew rich in culture; newspapers and journals flourished. The University of Chile, founded in 1843, spawned many more institutions of higher learning. But, economically, the country was divided into fiefdoms; the old aristocracy maintained its grip on four-fifths of the arable land, while Chile's great mineral riches fell into the hands of foreigners.

By the late 19th century Chile was the world's leading producer of nitrates, but it was chiefly British capital that expanded and modernized the industry, and the bulk of all profits consequently went abroad.

Nitrate exports fell off sharply in the 1930's after the development of a synthetic substitute, but the void was more than filled by Chile's vast reserves of copper, for which there was a growing world demand. However, this industry was also developed and controlled by foreign concerns, especially U.S. mining companies, and the great majority of Chileans derived no benefit whatever from their country's most valuable resource.

Chile thus found itself in the kind of economic dilemma that has since become painfully familiar in developing nations. By tradition Chile was an agricultural country, yet her landless farmers were unable to earn a living on the great estates and flocked to the cities—only to become part of a chronically unemployed urban population. Those who did work found their wages eaten away by inflation, an economic disease that Chile had suffered since the 1880's. Infant mortality in the slums of Santiago was the highest in the Western Hemisphere. Even serious attempts at reform did little to improve the condition of Chile's poor. A liberal President, Arturo Alessandri, elected in 1920, persuaded the Congress to adopt a progressive new constitution that guaranteed the rights of labor, established social security laws, and separated church

After the fall: *Soldiers guard the ruins of La Moneda, Chile's Presidential palace (right), following the coup that ended the administration—and the life—of President Salvador Allende (inset) in September 1973. The military junta that staged the overthrow has since tightened its grip, largely through the use of terror and torture, on the country that had been South America's oldest democracy.*

Pro and con: The first anniversary of Allende's inauguration was celebrated by thousands of mineworkers and others (above) who supported his socialist programs. In stark contrast, the closing days of his regime were marked by angry strikes and demonstrations, typified by protests (above right) over severe food shortages and uncontrolled inflation.

from state. Though Alessandri and some of his successors pursued such reforms and encouraged industrial development, the underlying structure of the economy was largely unchanged.

In 1964 a moderate leftist, Eduardo Frei, was elected President of Chile with 56 percent of the vote—the largest majority ever won in Chile. His slogan was "Revolution in Freedom," and his promise was to institute reforms that would give the poor a greater share of their country's wealth.

Through Frei's program of "Chilenization" the government bought 51 percent of the shares of the U.S. copper corporations working in Chile and began parceling out the vast agricultural estates to their former tenants. Yet the condition of the poor did not improve as dramatically as had been hoped. In the meantime inflation continued and Chile became increasingly dependent on imported food.

Although Frei's hopes for a peaceful revolution were still unrealized at the end of his six-year term, expectations of progress had been aroused in millions of poor people, and in 1970 those expectations gave Allende his narrow margin of victory.

The New Regime

Sixty-two years old when he was sworn in, Allende was a familiar figure on Chile's political stage. A physician by training, he had been a founder of the Chilean Socialist Party, a Senator, Minister of Health, and four times Presidential candidate. Even his 33 years in government were scarcely an adequate preparation for the tensions that confronted him as he took office. Two days before the congressional vote confirming his election, members of a rightwing terrorist group assassinated Gen. René Schneider, commander in chief of the army, who had promised to aid in a smooth transfer of power. His murder might have plunged the country into chaos, but the army stood by its constitutional duty. In his inaugural address on November 3, before a wildly cheering crowd waving pictures of Che Guevara and Ho Chi Minh, the new President promised to "overthrow imperialist exploitation, to end the monopolies, to carry out a serious and profound agrarian reform, and to nationalize banking and credit . . ."

A few of Allende's promises were kept within his first year. Wages were increased by 35 percent and prices were frozen. U.S. copper companies were stripped of their 49 percent ownership in the Chilean mines with no compensation on the grounds that they had already taken excessive wealth out of the country. Farmworkers were organized into cooperatives and encouraged to demand higher wages; the attempts to expropriate land were accelerated—and in the process grew increasingly chaotic.

But from the beginning Allende faced enormous obstacles in his efforts to bring socialism to Chile. The first was an opposition Congress that after nationalizing the copper mines did little else to support him. In addition, Allende's election touched off a brief but damaging panic during which many wealthy Chileans

AFTER CHILE: NEW LIGHT ON THE CIA

After Salvador Allende's overthrow on September 11, 1973, repeated charges of CIA complicity helped focus public attention on the U.S. government's vast intelligence community and its covert operations overseas. In 1975 lengthy House and Senate inquiries revealed that between 1970 and 1973 the CIA had channeled at least $8 million into Chile to support opposition newspapers and political parties and, to a lesser extent, rightwing extremist groups (one of which was responsible for the murder of Gen. René Schneider, a strict constitutionalist and commander in chief of the Chilean Army). In broad terms, the House concluded that the CIA's covert action in Chile was "striking but not unique" and that similar programs (including elaborate plans to assassinate Cuban Premier Fidel Castro) had been conducted in many countries. In 1976 each of the committees published reports picturing the CIA and kindred agencies as virtually sovereign powers, habitually exceeding their statutory authority and conducting secret, and often illegal, activities at home and abroad without congressional consent. In an effort to remedy this, the Senate established, in May 1976, the Select Committee on Intelligence, a permanent body having sole authority over the CIA and sharing in the supervision of such other agencies as the National Security Agency, the Defense Intelligence Agency, and the FBI.

transferred their capital to banks in other countries, while scores of key mining technicians moved abroad, leaving behind almost no one qualified to manage the nation's copper industry; beyond that was the fear Allende produced in foreign nations—most prominently the United States, whose private investments totaled more than $1 billion. Following the seizure of the copper mines, the Nixon administration retaliated by pressuring financial institutions like the World Bank to refuse Chile further credit. At the same time the Pentagon kept close contact with Chile's armed forces, supplying funds for military equipment and training.

Finally, it was the Chilean people themselves against whom Allende stumbled. It had been easy to prophesy the fierce opposition of the upper and middle classes to a Socialist government, but even more difficult for Allende to handle were the suddenly militant demands of the impoverished. Spurring their newfound activism was the MIR (Movement of the Revolutionary Left), which under Frei had been an urban guerrilla group. In addition, the MIR found a potent ally in Senator Carlos Altamirano, the radical Secretary General of Allende's Socialist Party. From the outset Altamirano pressed Allende to move faster and further to the left and encouraged the illegal land takeovers that became epidemic in southern Chile.

Trouble From Within

In 1969 the MIR had begun to organize a number of "squatter" seizures. In mid-1970 a group of *los sin casa* ("homeless ones") occupied a tract of empty church-owned land on the outskirts of Santiago. Built of flimsy wood and cardboard, the *campamento* resembled the other hut-towns that ring Santiago; but under MIR direction it had a unique communal structure—an elected governing body, a medical clinic, a community kitchen, people's courts, and its own armed militia, prepared to fight off the police who constantly threatened eviction.

The new Allende regime recognized "Nueva La Habana," as its occupants named it, and gave the settlement money and materials for building houses and schools. Yet, while most of them admired Allende, the squatters did not trust his government and engaged the bureaucracy in a running battle of wills. Government bricks given to build a school were refused and better bricks demanded. Government teachers were sent away, and the settlers themselves became teachers so that their children would "understand the work of their fathers."

By the beginning of 1972 tensions between Allende and his once-ardent supporters were growing steadily more severe. In many areas the MIR-led peasants seized the land, forcing the government to choose between armed intervention against its own supporters and inaction in the face of blatant illegality. In some factories around Santiago the workers formed industrial militias, trained by the MIR and other extremist groups for the purpose of resisting any attempted rightwing coup. Daily the Socialist regime confronted workers whose expectations were more radical than anything the government considered possible. The result was an endless series of strikes, some aimed at the government, some in response to counteractions by the beleaguered middle class.

In December 1971 Santiago was shaken by the "March of the Empty Pots," the first large-scale anti-Allende demonstration. Organized by the Christian Democratic Party, some 5,000 women took to the streets, their march accompanied by the clang of spoons on empty pots—an angry dramatization of the food shortages that were plaguing the country. The march quickly turned into a riot, and Gen. Augusto Pinochet, commander of the Santiago garrison, warned that if the army came out, it would be to kill.

In early 1973 a 74-day strike of the copper workers cost the government $75 million in lost revenues. Then Chile's independent truck drivers, who had conducted a major strike the previous year, again refused to take their trucks out, paralyzing the country's transportation system. Food and fuel vanished; breadlines lengthened. Inflation reached stratospheric heights—300 percent in the first half of 1973. Hoping to reduce rightist opposition, Allende named several generals to his Cabinet; the army, which had stayed aloof from involvement in politics, was now at the stormy center.

The Generals Take Over

Allende had once observed that while the people held the government, they did not hold the power in Chile. The congressional elections of March 1973—and their aftermath—proved him tragically correct. In the elections his Popular Unity coalition won a significant increase, holding almost 44 percent of the vote; six months later the military struck with full force.

In the early hours of September 11, 1973, the Chilean Navy seized the port of Valparaiso and imprisoned some 3,000 inhabitants. At 7:00 a.m. radio broadcasts announced that a military junta, led by General Pinochet, had replaced the constitutional government. At 7:17 Allende—armed with a submachinegun given to him by Fidel Castro and accompanied by a few friends—prepared to defend the Presidential palace against a phalanx of tanks and fighter-bombers. By early afternoon Allende and several of his companions lay dead; others were assassinated soon after the army blasted its way inside. And in the streets of Santiago the army and the police fought large-scale sniper battles with Allende loyalists, killing over a thousand and imprisoning countless others.

Such was the nightmarish end of Chile's experiment with democratic socialism. There seems little doubt that Allende was doomed to failure. From a conservative viewpoint his own policies brought Chile to the brink of total economic collapse, making a coup inevitable. For those on the left the reasons for Allende's fall lay partly in the economic embargoes and subversion directed against Chile by the United States and partly in Allende's mistaken assumption that Chile's middle class would espouse his cause and that the powerful elite would have no alternative but to allow a redistribution of its wealth.

In fact, Allende's downfall was a complex process in which these factors and others all played a part. Investigations by the U.S. Congress have disclosed that during the Nixon administration the Central Intelligence Agency made various efforts to prevent Allende's election and, when that failed, to undermine his administration—chiefly through secret financial aid to his political opponents and to the organizers of the 1972 and 1973 truckers' strikes. Records also indicate that the CIA resisted pressure from several major U.S. companies to take more aggressive measures: The International Telephone and Telegraph Corporation, for example, offered to contribute $1 million for covert actions against Allende.

Such measures, however, could hardly have jeopardized a more stable government, and it seems inescapable that Allende's own political and tactical mistakes were the primary cause of his downfall. Most of his programs to nationalize industries and to redistribute farmland were carried out haphazardly and with too little thought of the practical consequences—which often involved a decline in productivity and profits, followed by a rise in unemployment. At the same time, his plan to improve the standard of living with wholesale pay raises—combined with a policy of covering the government's deficits simply by printing more money—pushed the inflation rate to staggering levels.

Such economic policies alone were a sufficient formula for disaster; allied with Allende's failure to impose a measure of discipline on his followers and the vigorous resistance of the well-to-do, they were fatal.

The history of Chile since the coup has been tragic. Two days after Allende's death Congress was dissolved by the military junta. Since then, the intention of the generals has manifestly not been "to restore institutional normality," as they have claimed, but to extinguish opposition by all the means available to a police state, including the imprisonment, torture, and execution of uncounted thousands. Reports in 1975 and 1976 by the U.N. Human Rights Commission charged the junta with "barbaric sadism," asserting that "inhuman, cruel and degrading treatment have . . . become a pattern of governmental policies in Chile."

Ironically, U.S. policy toward Chile underwent a noticeable change in the same period. Just a week before the coup Washington had turned down an urgent request to sell wheat-short Chile 300,000 tons of grain. A few weeks after the generals took over, the White House granted Chile $24.5 million in wheat credits. In the next two years the junta received some $2 billion in foreign credits from private banks (chiefly North American) and such international institutions as the World Bank that had refused to deal with Allende. Though this turnabout was officially explained as being based solely on economic factors, not politics, Chile's economic situation in fact grew steadily *worse* after the coup. Nevertheless, loans and investments continued to flow in—over the protests of labor, religious, and humanitarian groups—further strengthening the country's military regime.

On a continent increasingly vulnerable to the bayonet rule of strongmen, Chile's tragedy provides a bitter example. Its effects may be summed up in the decision of the now-outlawed (and once determinedly nonviolent) Chilean Communist Party to share its arms with other underground resistance groups. Finally, the Chilean experience may have convinced all South America's homeless ones that a bullet is more effective than a vote and that violence will sometimes accomplish what the law cannot.

Behind the dark glasses *is Gen. Augusto Pinochet (inset), leader of the 1973 coup and, subsequently, ruler of a police state flamboyant in its disregard for human rights.*

The streets of Santiago *were filled with scenes like the one below after September 11, 1973, as soldiers arrested virtually anyone considered unfriendly toward the new junta.*

1972

Earthwatch: A Strategy for Survival

The world environment conference in Stockholm adopts measures for the life and safety of our planet.

The watchful eye *of a NASA satellite photographed New York Bay in 1972, recording a zigzag trail of pollution. Rapid computer analysis of its spectral characteristics revealed the pollutant to be acid wastes dumped from a barge and gave clues to its density and probable rate of dispersion.*

One evening in June during the 1972 world environmental conference in Stockholm, a thousand young people staged a demonstration to celebrate the existence of the earth's largest animal, the whale. Marching through the streets behind a truck draped in black plastic to resemble the animal, they called for a moratorium on commercial whaling. Though no one knows how much the demonstrators may have swayed the 1,200 delegates to that first United Nations Conference on the Human Environment, the delegates did pass, the next day, a proposal calling for a 10-year ban on the hunting of whales.

Less than one month later the International Whaling Commission refused to accept the U.N. proposal, agreeing instead only to reduce the size of the 1973 catch from 40,000 to 34,000 whales. The refusal showed clearly how far efforts to preserve the environment and its endangered species were from being able to compete with commercial interests. It also showed that, however lofty its goals, the U.N. could not act in a binding way to protect the earth.

Nonetheless, representatives of 114 nations had come together that June to face a common problem. Their conference, hailed as a "new plateau" in man's awareness of his surroundings, was the most massive effort ever made to improve the declining quality of the environment. Yet most of the delegates knew that it would take more than a single conference to change attitudes as old as mankind itself, and one of the most realistic proposals made in Stockholm combined an awareness of the U.N.'s executive limitations with a knowledge of its capacity for collecting and disseminating information at a global level. Thus was Operation Earthwatch conceived, to evaluate data from a worldwide network of pollution monitoring stations and, when necessary, to sound the alert.

Heeding the Problem

Until 1962 the world had taken only passing notice of environmental problems. In that year Rachel Carson's *Silent Spring* was published, an alarming bestseller that brought to light the dangers of the pesticide DDT and made large segments of the government and the public aware for the first time that all living things depend on each other, and on a healthy environment, for survival. As evidence Carson pointed to the efforts of the city of East Lansing, Michigan, to wipe out the beetles that were killing its elm trees. The city sprayed the trees with DDT; in autumn the leaves fell to the ground and were eaten by worms; robins, returning in the spring, ate the worms; within a week almost all the robins in the city were dead.

"Our world," Carson wrote, summarizing the hazards posed by pesticides, "has been widely contaminated with the substances used in the control of insects—chemicals that have already invaded the water on which all living things depend have entered the soil and have spread a toxic film over vegetation. . . . Where the effects on man are already known, they are found to be destructive. Beyond these . . . is

Bearing tragic witness *to the dangers of pollution, victims of the Chisso-Minamata disease attended the 1972 Stockholm conference on the environment. They had eaten fish poisoned by methylmercury wastes dumped into Minamata Bay, Japan, by the Chisso corporation; the young girl, left, was poisoned while still in her mother's womb. So far, more than 100 people in the Minamata area have died from mercury poisoning, which attacks the central nervous system. To dramatize the threat, other victims have flown to Ontario, Canada, where mercury wastes are likewise poisoning fish, and where some Canadian Indians already have developed symptoms of the disease.*

the even more frightening prospect of damage that cannot be detected for years and of possible genetic effects that cannot be known for generations."

Agriculturists fought her vigorously, claiming that without pesticides crop yields could fall by as much as 90 percent. In response Carson urged the use of biological controls—fungi, bacteria, and other insects—to combat plant-eating pests.

Silent Spring prompted the U.S. Senate to review the issue of DDT and, ultimately, to declare a near-total ban on its use in the United States. Years later scientists discovered concentrations of the chemical in penguins and polar bears in the Antarctic, far from any area where insects had been sprayed. They also found DDT in whales raised off the coast of Greenland, hundreds of miles from the nearest farming areas.

Rachel Carson's book had sounded an alarm, and in the 1960's the nations of the world began to take stock of their land, rivers, and seas. Damage to the environment was clearly apparent all over the world. Soot from Germany's industrial Ruhr area was found to drop a gray tint on the snows of Norway. Spills from passing oil tankers covered the feet of bathers on the Ivory Coast. Of Europe's refuse-laden Rhine River an official said, "What was once 'Old Father Rhine' of celebrated beauty and romanticism has become a horrid sewer." And in major cities automobiles pumped tons of carbon monoxide, hydrocarbons, and nitrogen oxides into the air; combined with fog and the ultraviolet rays in sunlight, the chemicals formed dense—and increasingly dangerous—clouds of foul-smelling smog.

By the end of the decade the outlook was grim. A group of systems analysts, using mathematical formulas and computer processing to determine the world's ecological future, predicted nothing less than doom. Publishing their findings in *The Limits to Growth,* they claimed that existing trends would lead to catastrophic scarcities and severe pollution levels in 130 years. Although widely criticized as alarmist, the book won serious support. And things grew worse.

Scientists at the University of California, for example, were theorizing that the seemingly innocuous gas used in spray cans might ultimately increase the incidence of skin cancer. The fluorocarbon propellants, they said, eventually reached the upper atmosphere and cut into the layer of ozone that shields the earth from the sun's ultraviolet rays. A 5 percent decrease in the ozone level, said other researchers at the U.S. National Academy of Sciences, could result in some 8,000 more cases of skin cancer a year in the U.S.A.; at the rate aerosols were being used, this might happen by the year 2000.

Even the burning of oil and coal was said to be threatening the upper atmosphere, for the carbon dioxide thereby released was found to be gradually increasing the temperature of the stratosphere, creating a greenhouse effect and altering global weather patterns. By the mid-seventies prolonged drought in the Sahel region just south of the Sahara and floods in America's midwestern breadbasket states had combined to produce a famine that killed hundreds of thousands and threatened millions more in a wide dry swath from Senegal to Ethiopia.

Convergence in Stockholm

It was under such pressures that delegates went to Stockholm in 1972, hoping that otherwise contentious nations might yield to the urgency of the situation and learn to cooperate.

In fact, the politicians were playing their usual games even before the conference opened, with the Soviet Union screaming for a boycott because East Germany, not a U.N. member, had been denied a vote. Moreover, a deep rift between the developed and underdeveloped countries—the haves and the have-nots—threatened to stymie the conference altogether. If pollution is a byproduct of sorely needed industrialization, the developing nations argued, then so be it.

LOST FOREVER: THE FATEFUL TOLL

Since 1900 more than 80 different kinds of animals have disappeared forever. Today the rate of extinction—more than one species or subspecies of animal per year—is increasing, and 2.5 percent of all higher animals must now be considered endangered. In almost every case human activity has been the principal cause, and now only another kind of human activity—the protection of threatened environments, prohibitions on the hunting of endangered animals, and the preservation of rare species in zoos (even, perhaps, in tissue banks for future "resurrection")—can prevent the irreparable loss of creatures that are ultimately more precious than even the greatest works of human art.

The whooping crane totters at the brink of extinction, almost destroyed by hunters and the loss of its habitat.

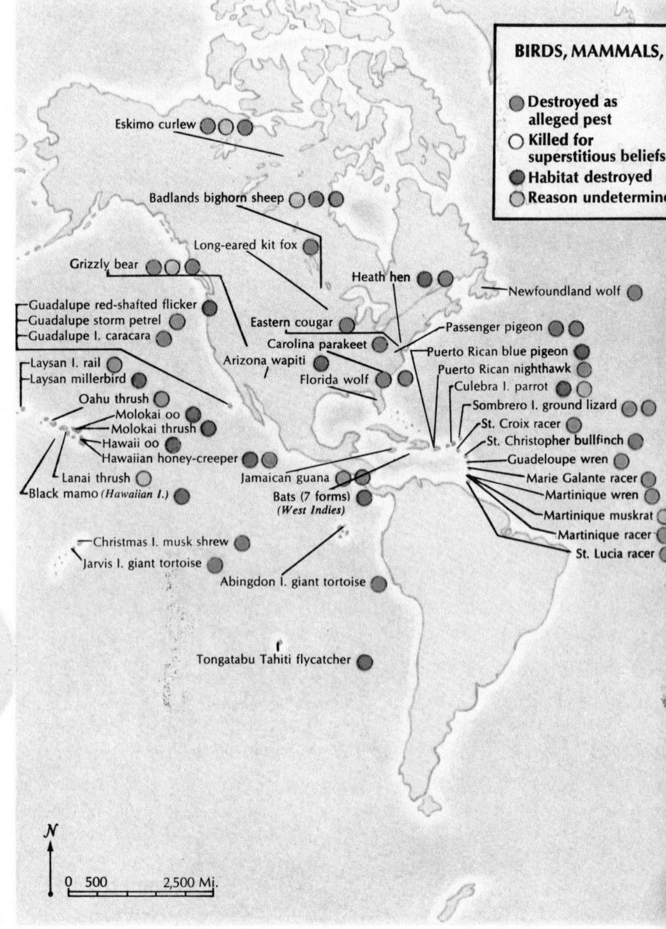

They also feared that wealthy nations would deduct the money spent fighting pollution from their foreign aid budgets and that any slowdown in the growth of industrialized nations would hurt the developing world by reducing the demand for its exports.

Maurice Strong of Canada, Secretary General of the U.N. environmental conference, had spent four years working on the problem, ever since the Swedish delegation had persuaded the U.N. General Assembly to endorse the idea of an international meeting on the environment. He had conducted a worldwide campaign to convince poor nations that they, too, had a stake in a clean environment and that with international help they could successfully attack such problems as impure water and sewage disposal in their cities. Strong also sought to convince them that the conference would deal seriously with such prime issues as soil erosion and the spread of deserts.

His success was limited. Indian Prime Minister Indira Gandhi spoke for Third World countries when she

OMENS OF DISASTER?

In the early 1970's the following ominous events occurred: Snow and ice increased worldwide by as much as 15 percent; a 100-year low-temperature record was set in Greenland; the Moscow region had its worst drought in centuries, and severe droughts hit Central America, South Asia, China, Australia, and the sub-Sahara; the United States had a series of floods. Some climatologists believe that a global cooling trend is taking place, and one study, commissioned by the U.S. Central Intelligence Agency and published in May 1976, forecasts catastrophic food shortages and major political and economic upheavals as a consequence. The role of pollution in this projected crisis is unknown, but most environmentalists agree that man's inadvertent modification of the climate may pose the most severe—and difficult to reverse—of all threats to his survival.

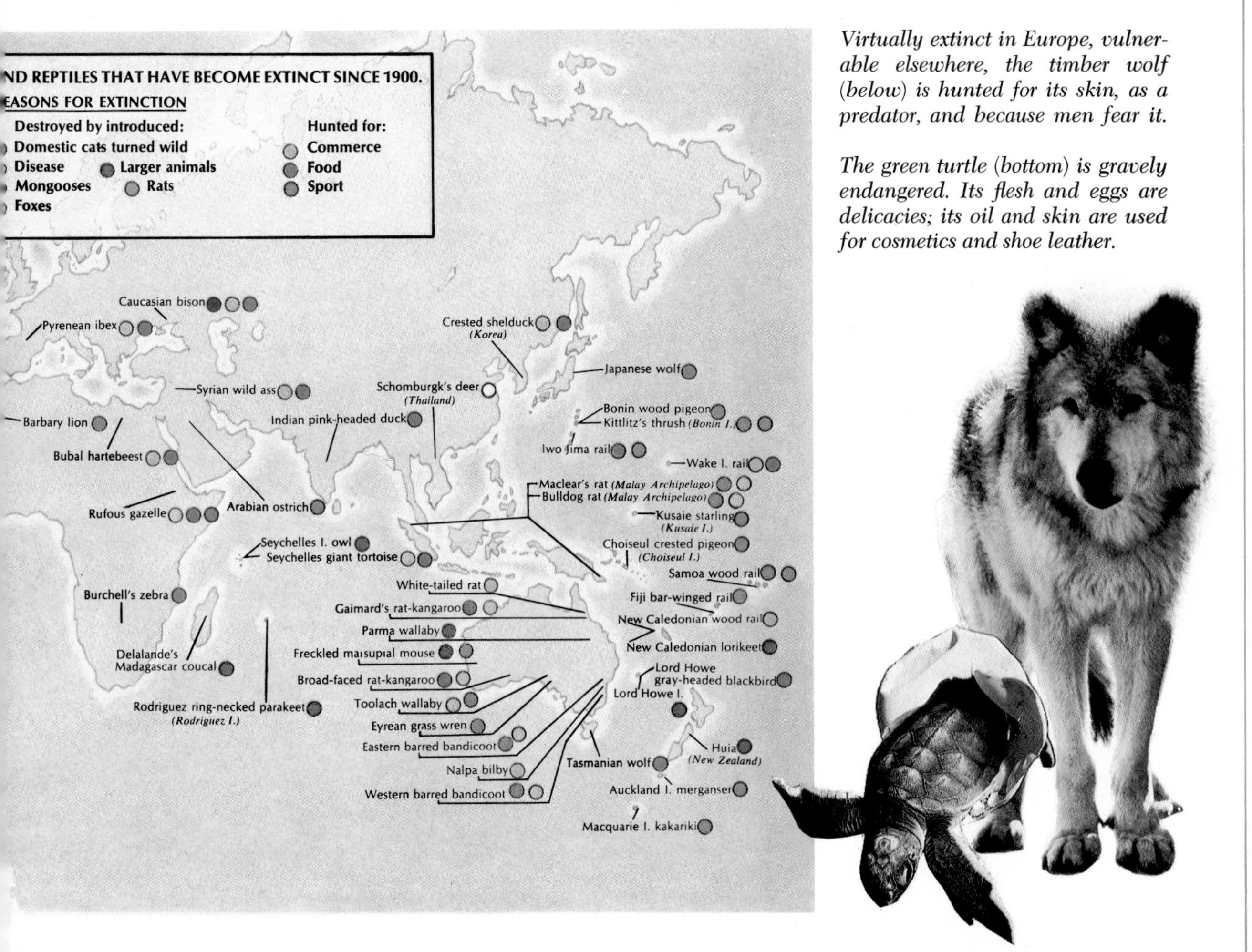

Virtually extinct in Europe, vulnerable elsewhere, the timber wolf (below) is hunted for its skin, as a predator, and because men fear it.

The green turtle (bottom) is gravely endangered. Its flesh and eggs are delicacies; its oil and skin are used for cosmetics and shoe leather.

said: "We cannot for a moment forget the grim poverty of large numbers of people. . . . How can we speak to those who live in villages and slums about keeping the oceans, the rivers, and the air clean when their own lives are contaminated at the source?"

Strong sympathized with the plight of the poorer nations and fought at the conference for resolutions that would encourage trade in natural commodities rather than in synthetic materials whose production causes pollution. "It is the height of effrontery," he said, "for the developed world to express surprise when developing countries identify smokestacks with progress. It's what we've been doing all along."

Down to Business

While the official delegates filed into the conference hall under a banner proclaiming "Only One Earth," thousands more gathered elsewhere in the city to have their own say. The U.N. had given almost 500 environmental groups a quasi-official status as nongovernmental observers. In their own declaration they compared the importance of the conference with that of the Copernican revolution four centuries earlier, which had compelled man to revise his entire sense of the earth's place in the cosmos.

Other groups were more politically direct. One chastised the industrialized nations for bringing economic despair to underdeveloped countries through relentless exploitation of their resources. Even the official conference itself got off to a highly political start: Prime Minister Olof Palme of Sweden joined the People's Republic of China in condemning the United States for "ecological warfare" in Vietnam, calling it the most outrageous environmental destruction in the history of man.

But the conference did manage to get down to the business at hand. After 15 formal meetings and countless informal sessions held over the 11 days of the conference, the delegates finally emerged on June 16 at 5 a.m. with a declaration: An environment "of a quality which permits a life of dignity and well-being" is a fundamental right of man, whose solemn responsibility it is to protect and improve his habitat; all states have a basic responsibility to avoid causing environmental damage to other states; rich nations should work to decrease the gap dividing them from the poor; safeguards must be provided against the exhaustion of unrenewable resources and against the pollution of the seas; all nuclear weapons should be eliminated. "A point has been reached in history," the document read, "where we must shape our actions throughout the world with a more prudent care for environmental consequences."

The delegates were quick to recognize that such lofty sentiments meant nothing without a program to carry them out. Backing the declaration was an action plan of 200 steps that could be taken almost immediately to reverse the decline of environmental quality. It authorized the establishment of a permanent environmental secretariat at the United Nations with a funding mechanism to sustain it and called for control of specific pollutants, such as mercury, and for the creation of genetic "zoos" to preserve the world's endangered animals and plants. It also established guidelines for Operation Earthwatch, linking over 100 monitoring stations across the globe to serve as an early warning system for pollution.

In December 1972 the General Assembly adopted the declaration as U.N. policy and set up a 58-member Secretariat for the Environment to start work on the action plan. The following June the new secretariat and its governing council convened, for the first time, in Geneva, and in 1974 they moved into permanent headquarters—a building designed to be as ecologically efficient as possible—in Nairobi, Kenya.

The Common Enemy

"The wonder of it all," said Sweden's Prime Minister Olof Palme, looking back on the two weeks in Stockholm and considering the practical steps taken there, "is that anything of substance should have come from a meeting that was so heavily politicized." Perhaps the most succinct assessment of the potential value of the U.N.'s initiatives was made by Maurice Strong a year after the conference. "The world," he said, "is not likely to unite behind a common ideology or a supergovernment. The only practical hope is that it will now respond to a common concern for its own survival, an acknowledgment of the essential interdependence of its peoples and an awareness that cooperative action can enlarge the horizons . . . of all peoples."

In trying to stimulate an ideology transcending concern for survival, the U.N. secretariat has helped create a worldwide sense of the environment's fragility. It has also helped to communicate a healthy awareness of the universal menace posed by pollution. For the poisons we have been pumping into the oceans and atmosphere are admirably democratic and eventually fall, like sunshine, equally on the rich and the poor, the warring and the peaceful, the innocent and the guilty. And sooner or later they will either compel man to unite in common defense against them, or they will unceremoniously shuffle him into oblivion, the ingenious victim of his own greed.

***The 20th century** has perhaps been the most momentous in the long history of mankind. As it draws to a close, a spirit new to our times begins to stir: a sense of interdependence among the peoples of the earth and a feeling of reverence for their planet—a fragile ark (right, against a backdrop of the great nebula in Orion) at sail in a universe whose vast wonders are only just beginning to be known.*

AN ALMANAC 1957-76

1957

Mar. 25 Six countries—France, West Germany, Italy, Belgium, the Netherlands, Luxembourg—sign treaty establishing European Common Market.

Oct. 4 Sputnik, first manmade satellite to orbit the earth, launched by Soviet Union. (See pp. 424–429.)

1958

Jan. 31 Explorer 1, first U.S. earth satellite, launched from Cape Canaveral, Florida; leads to discovery of Van Allen radiation belt 600 miles above earth.

Feb. 1 Egypt and Syria form United Arab Republic under President Gamal Abdel Nasser; union lasts until 1961.

May 13 French Army stages coup in Algeria following riots by French settlers; rightwing officers demand that Gen. Charles de Gaulle take power in France. De Gaulle takes office as Premier on June 1.

July 15 During civil war in Lebanon U.S Marines land at Beirut to safeguard independence of Lebanese government. When fighting stops, Marines begin to withdraw on Aug. 12.

Dec. 21 De Gaulle elected President of new Fifth Republic in France.

1959

Jan. 1 Fidel Castro's rebels take over Cuba as former dictator President Fulgencio Batista flees country. Castro becomes Cuban Premier Feb. 16.

Mar. 28-31 The Chinese Communists crush Tibetan revolt against them.

June 4 Cuba expropriates large landholdings and foreign-owned property.

1960

Jan. 1-Oct. 1 Seventeen former colonies of Britain, Belgium, and France become independent African states.

July 5 Congolese Army troops revolt against Belgian officers. Beginning of internal strife. (See pp. 442–449.)

Aug. 16 Cyprus gains independence, with Archbishop Makarios as President.

Nov. 8 Democratic candidate John F. Kennedy narrowly defeats Richard M. Nixon in U.S. Presidential election.

1961

Feb. 12 Murder of Congolese nationalist leader Patrice Lumumba accelerates Congo civil war.

Apr. 12 Soviet cosmonaut Yuri Gagarin becomes first man to orbit earth.

Apr. 17-20 Invasion of Cuba by 1,600 rebels, supported by U.S. government, crushed by Cuban Army at Bay of Pigs.

Apr. 21-26 Revolt by French rightwing generals in Algeria fails, as most of army remains loyal to De Gaulle.

May 31 South Africa cuts ties with Britain, becomes independent republic outside Commonwealth.

Aug. 17 Berlin Wall erected by East Germany to stop refugee flight across the border to the West.

Sept. 18 U.N. Secretary General Dag Hammarskjold dies in airplane crash. U Thant of Burma succeeds him.

1962

Feb. 20 John Glenn becomes first U.S. astronaut to orbit the earth.

Mar. 18 French government and Algerian rebel representatives sign ceasefire agreement ending seven-year war. Algeria becomes independent July 3.

Oct. 20 Fighting between Chinese and Indian soldiers erupts in border areas.

Oct. 22 U.S. President Kennedy announces air and naval quarantine of Cuba in response to the Soviet Union's installation of missile bases there.

Oct. 28 Soviet leader Khrushchev says that he has ordered removal of Soviet missiles from Cuba and the dismantling of all Soviet missile bases there.

Dec. 10 Nobel Prize for determining molecular structure of DNA shared by three scientists. (See pp. 454–461.)

1963

Aug. 5 Treaty banning nuclear test explosions in atmosphere signed by Britain, U.S.A., and Soviet Union.

Aug. 28 March on Washington, D.C., by 200,000 demonstrators dramatizes support for new civil rights legislation.

Oct. 16 Konrad Adenauer resigns as Chancellor of West Germany after 14 years in office; Ludwig Erhard elected Chancellor by Parliament.

Nov. 2 South Vietnamese President Ngo Dinh Diem killed in army coup.

Nov. 22 President Kennedy slain by sniper in Dallas, Texas. Lyndon B. Johnson becomes 36th U.S. President.

Dec. 4 Pope Paul VI authorizes use of vernacular, instead of Latin, in the Mass.

1964

Mar. 14 After riots and fighting between Greeks and Turks in Cyprus, U.N. peacekeeping force sent to island.

July 2 U.S. Civil Rights Act of 1964, prohibiting racial discrimination in public places, employment, unions, and federal programs, signed into law.

Aug. 2-5 U.S. Navy destroyers report attack by North Vietnamese gunboats in Gulf of Tonkin; in retaliation U.S. aircraft bomb four military bases. Incident provokes North Vietnamese to enter war in South Vietnam.

Oct. 15 Khrushchev ousted as Soviet leader and replaced as Premier by Alexei Kosygin and as First Secretary by Leonid Brezhnev.

Oct. 16 Harold Wilson becomes British Prime Minister after Labour Party wins general elections.

1965

Apr. 28-30 U.S. Marines sent to Dominican Republic to prevent Communist takeover during civil war.

Oct. 1 Indonesian Army crushes attempted Communist coup.

Nov. 11 Rhodesia declares its independence from Great Britain.

Dec. 8 Second Vatican Council ends after three years, having made numerous proposals for church reform. (See pp. 468–471.)

1966

Jan. 19 Mrs. Indira Gandhi, daughter of the late Prime Minister Nehru, becomes Prime Minister of India.

Feb. 24 Ghana's army ousts President Kwame Nkrumah; later expels foreign Communists from country.

Mar. 11 Indonesian President Sukarno overthrown by army; General Suharto assumes power Mar. 12.

Aug. 11 Indonesia and Malaysia officially end three-year undeclared war.

Aug. 13 Chinese Communist Central Committee endorses Chairman Mao Tse-tung's "proletarian cultural revolution." (See pp. 480–483.)

1967

Apr. 21 Coup by Greek colonels deposes Greece's civilian government.

May 30 Ibo region of Nigeria declares itself independent state of Biafra; fighting between Biafrans and Nigerian troops erupts July 6.

June 5-10 In Six-Day War Israel defeats Arab States. (See pp. 484–487.)

1968

Jan. 30 North Vietnam launches Tet (Lunar New Year) offensive in South Vietnam; leads to peace talks.

Apr. 4 U.S. black leader Martin Luther King, Jr., is assassinated; riots subsequently erupt in 126 U.S. cities.

Apr. 19 Pierre Elliott Trudeau succeeds retiring Lester B. Pearson as Prime Minister of Canada.

May 13 U.S.-North Vietnam peace talks begin in Paris.

June 5 U.S. Senator Robert F. Kennedy shot and mortally wounded by Sirhan Sirhan, an Arab militant.

Aug. 20 Soviet troops invade Czechoslovakia and end Communist Premier Alexander Dubcek's liberal reforms.

Nov. 5 Richard M. Nixon elected 37th U.S. President.

1969

Apr. 28 President De Gaulle resigns. Former Premier Georges Pompidou elected President of France on June 15.

July 20 U.S. astronauts Neil Armstrong and Edwin Aldrin are first to walk on the moon. (See pp. 498–503.)

Aug. 15-19 British troops sent into Northern Ireland to quell Catholic–Protestant violence.

Oct. 15 Nationwide Vietnam Moratorium Day participated in by antiwar demonstrators protesting U.S. involvement in South Vietnam.

1970

Jan. 12 Secessionist region of Biafra surrenders to Nigerian central government after 2½-year civil war.

Mar. 18 Cambodian Army coup deposes Prince Norodom Sihanouk.

June 18-19 Conservatives win British elections; Edward Heath becomes Prime Minister.

Sept. 6-12 Four jet airliners hijacked over Europe by Arab militants. Some 300 passengers are held as ransom for Arab prisoners. The planes are blown up Sept. 12, but most passengers are released.

Oct. 24 Salvador Allende Gossens elected President of Chile, first Marxist to head a South American country. (See pp. 504–509.)

Nov. 12-13 Most destructive cyclone and tidal wave of 20th century strikes East Pakistan coast, killing more than 500,000 persons.

1971

Oct. 25 Communist China is admitted to the United Nations, replacing Nationalist China (Taiwan).

Dec. 3-17 India and Pakistan war over revolt of Bangladesh (East Pakistan) against Pakistani rule. Bangladesh becomes independent nation.

1972

Jan. 22 European Common Market enlarged with admission of Great Britain, Denmark, Ireland, and Norway (Norway later rejects entry into Market in national referendum).

Feb. 21-28 U.S. President Nixon visits Communist China, establishing new ties after 22 years of mutual hostility.

May 22-29 President Nixon becomes first U.S. President to visit Moscow. He and Soviet leader Brezhnev sign arms limitation treaties and other accords.

June 5-16 United Nations Conference on Human Environment in Stockholm discusses how to meet the ecological complexities of the technological age. (See pp. 510–515.)

June 17 Five burglars are arrested in U.S. Democratic National Committee headquarters at Watergate office building in Washington, D.C. Their later identification as hirelings of the Committee to Reelect the President begins "Watergate affair," which involves White House aides in illegal acts and has wide political implications.

Aug. 12 Last U.S. troops pull out of Vietnam, although U.S. Air Force continues to bomb Communist-held areas.

Sept. 6 Arab terrorists kill 11 Israeli athletes during summer Olympic Games in Munich, Germany.

Nov. 7 U.S. President Nixon reelected, carrying record 49 states.

1973

Jan. 27 Formal peace accords are signed in Paris by North and South Vietnam, the U.S.A., and the National Liberation Front, ending 12 years of U.S. involvement in Vietnam war.

Oct. 6 Surprise attack on Israel launched by Egypt and Syria on Jewish holy day of Yom Kippur. This, Israel's fourth war, ends May 31, 1974.

Oct. 17 Arab oil-producing countries curtail oil shipments to industrial nations, deepening energy crisis.

1974

Apr. 2 French President Georges Pompidou dies. On May 19 Valéry Giscard d'Estaing elected.

Apr. 25 Portuguese military group under Gen. António de Spinola seizes government, ending more than 40 years of dictatorial rule. Spinola becomes President, begins democratic reforms.

July 1 Argentine President Juan Perón dies at age 78. His wife and Vice President, Isabel, succeeds him, becoming the first woman president in the Western Hemisphere. She is deposed by a military junta in March 1976.

July 16 Cypriot troops led by Greek officers depose Archbishop Makarios as President of Cyprus. On July 20 Turkey invades Cyprus. Makarios resumes Presidency in Dec. 1974, but Turks gain control of northern region.

July 24 Military rulers in Greece announce return of power to civilians.

Aug. 9 Richard M. Nixon, under threat of impeachment for obstruction of justice, becomes first U.S. President to resign. Vice President Gerald Ford assumes Presidency.

Sept. 9 Ford grants Nixon full pardon for any federal offenses he committed in office, setting off a national furor.

1975

Jan. 10 Angola granted independence, effective Nov. 11. Guerrilla fighting continues until victory of Soviet- and Cuban-backed faction in Feb. 1976.

Apr. 13 Fighting erupts in Lebanon between Muslims and Christians, beginning a long and bloody civil war.

Apr. 30 South Vietnamese government surrenders to Communists, ending 29 years of civil war.

June 25 Mozambique gains independence from Portugal.

June 26 Indian Prime Minister Indira Gandhi declares national state of emergency. Moves toward dictatorship approved by Parliament July 22–23.

July 17 U.S. spacecraft Apollo and Soviet Soyuz link in space, symbolizing new U.S.-Soviet cooperation.

Nov. 20 Gen. Francisco Franco dies, ending 36 years of dictatorship in Spain. Designated successor Prince Juan Carlos becomes King Nov. 22.

1976

Jan. 8 Chou En-lai, Premier of People's Republic of China (Communist China) since 1949, dies at age 78.

July 20 U.S. spacecraft Viking 1 makes first successful landing on Mars.

Sept. 9 Mao Tse-tung, Chinese Communist Party Chairman and leader of 1949 revolution, dies at age 82.

INDEX

*Page numbers in regular type refer to the text; those in **bold** type refer to illustrations and captions.*

A

B

Page numbers in regular type refer to the text; those in **bold** *type refer to illustrations and captions.*

C

*Page numbers in regular type refer to the text; those in **bold** type refer to illustrations and captions.*

D

E

F

Page numbers in regular type refer to the text; those in **bold** *type refer to illustrations and captions.*

G

H

Page numbers in regular type refer to the text; those in **bold** *type refer to illustrations and captions.*

I

J

K

L

*Page numbers in regular type refer to the text; those in **bold** type refer to illustrations and captions.*

M

N

*Page numbers in regular type refer to the text; those in **bold** type refer to illustrations and captions.*

P

*Page numbers in regular type refer to the text; those in **bold** type refer to illustrations and captions.*

R

T

*Page numbers in regular type refer to the text; those in **bold** type refer to illustrations and captions.*

U

V

W

XYZ

Page numbers in regular type refer to the text; those in **bold** *type refer to illustrations and captions.*

LIST OF MAPS

SUBJECT GUIDE TO MAPS

CREDITS & ACKNOWLEDGMENTS

The editors of Reader's Digest wish to thank the following writers and artists for their contributions to this book:

Writers

Edith E. Alston
James Cassidy
Peter Chaitin
Rebecca Chaitin
Crane Davis
Monte Davis
Ellen DeMaria
Thomas D. Dickey
George Friedman
Bernard S. Gresh
Bruce A. Kauffman
Jeff Magnes
Carol Mankin
Carolyn F. Rattray
John Reynolds
William Spencer
Charles S. Verral
Geoffrey C.Ward
Olie Westheimer
Fay Willey

Artists

Jim Alexander **69, 70, 71, 103, 105, 110, 112, 119, 120, 121, 123, 126, 127, 130, 151, 252, 263, 273, 289, 291, 300-301, 316, 329, 334, 340, 342, 345, 349, 351, 352, 399, 442, 445, 473, 486, 512-513**
John Batchelor **319**
John Ballantine **390, 432**
Dorothea Barlowe **40, 43, 213**
Howard Berelson **14, 20, 46, 58, 65, 86, 157, 159, 170**
Eva Cellini **93**
Donald Crowley **85**
Diamond Art Studio Ltd. **84, 179, 231, 362, 366, 370, 411, 440, 441**
Mort Drucker **483**
William Pène du Bois **81**
Mordicai Gerstein **81**
Robert L. Jones **305**
Steve Karchin **210**
George Kelvin **455, 456, 457, 458, 459**
Gabor Kiss **25, 28-29, 31, 52, 115, 164, 165, 209, 228-229, 264, 281, 297, 302, 368-369, 371, 438-439, 441-442, 453, 503**
Victor Lazzaro **44, 88-89, 108-109, 332-333**
Wesley McKeown **17, 32**
Harriet Pertchik **36, 90, 156, 157, 180, 234, 336, 337, 372-373**
Walter Rane **60-61**
Robert Ritter **37, 171**
Frank Schwarz **40, 213**

Special appreciation for invaluable help in picture research is extended to the following organizations and their staffs: Black Star, Brown Brothers, Keystone Press, Magnum, New York Public Library Picture Collection and Dance Collection at Lincoln Center, Sovfoto, Time/Life Picture Agency; and to the following individuals: Betsy Bird, Roberts Jackson of Culver Pictures, Sharon Mechling of the Museum of Modern Art, Josephine Ma'Arop of Pfizer, Inc., Gene Keesee of Photo Trends, Jack Novak of Photri, Vincent Di Prima of UPI, Lt. Mark Baker of the U.S. Navy Department, Dr. Albert S. Klainer of the West Virginia University Medical Center, and Donald Bowden of Wide World.

Photographs

4 Brown Brothers. **5** *left* UPI; *right* Culver Pictures. **6** *left* Pictorial Parade; *right* UPI. **7** NASA. **8-9** Brown Brothers. **10** Bildarchiv Preussischer Kulturbesitz. **12** Library of Congress. **13** Smithsonian Institution. **14** *top left* Musée de l'Air. **15** *left* Culver Pictures; *right* Library of Congress. **16** *left* Smithsonian Institution; *right* Curtiss-Wright Corp. **17** *top* Brown Brothers. **18** Museum of Modern Art, Film Stills Archive. **19** Library of Congress; *inset* The Museum of Modern Art, Film Stills Archive. **20** *bottom* The Museum of Modern Art. **21** Culver Pictures. **22** New York Public Library, Picture Collection. **23** *left* Phil Brodatz/© 1963 Time Inc.; *right* The Bettmann Archive. **24** Massachusetts Institute of Technology. **26** *left* Lyndhurst National Trust for Historic Preservation. **27** *right* Lyndhurst National Trust for Historic Preservation/Lawrence J. Majewski. **28** Joe Baker/FPG. **30** *ocean currents & river systems* NASA; *human eye* William Sonntag; *remainder* E. R. Degginger. **32-33** *bottom* Victoria & Albert Museum/Angelo Hornak. **34** *left* Ullstein GMBH Bilderdienst; *top right* New York Public Library, Picture Collection. **35** Culver Pictures. **38** © California Institute of Technology & Carnegie Institution of Washington. **39** Wide World. **41** Grant Heilman. **43** *top* E. R. Degginger. **45** Brown Brothers. **46** *right* Wide World. **47** *far left New York News; center left* Lone Ranger Television, Inc.; *center right* Wide World; *far right* UPI. **48** & **49** *center* New York Public Library at Lincoln Center, Dance Collection. **49** *top & bottom* Radio Times Hulton Picture Library. **50** *top* Van Abbemuseum Eindhoven, Holland. **50** *bottom* & **51** *top* The Museum of Modern Art, Lillie P. Bliss Bequest. **51** *bottom* Photo Musées Nationaux, Paris. **54** *top* Ullstein GMBH Bilderdienst; *bottom* Frankfurter Goethe-Museum. **55** Bildarchiv Preussischer Kulturbesitz; **56** *left* Musée du Louvre, Photo Musées Nationaux, Paris; *right* The Bettmann Archive. **57** *left* Rapho-Guillumette; *upper left* The Bettmann Archive; *right* Walker & Co. **58** *left* Culver Pictures; *right* Wide World. **59** © Institute of Psychiatry, Guttman-Maclay Collection, London/Photo Derek Bayes. **62** *upper left* Brown Brothers; *right* New York Public Library, Picture Collection; **62** *lower left,* **63** *top,* & **64** Courtesy of the Ford Archives, Dearborn Mich. **63** *inset* UPI. **65** *left* New York Public Library, Picture Collection. **66** *top* Culver Pictures; *bottom* Freer Gallery of Art, Smithsonian Institution. **67** British Museum. **68** Photoworld. **69** *left* Radio Times Hulton Picture Library. **70** *lower* Sovfoto. **71** *right* Ullstein GMBH Bilderdienst. **72** Giraudon. **73** *left* New York Public Library at Lincoln Center, Dance Collection; *Music Manuscript* © 1926 by Edition Russe de Musique. Copyright assigned 1947 to Boosey & Hawkes, Inc. Reprinted by permission. **74** *top* Paris Opera Library, Paris/Photo Germain; *bottom* New York Public Library, Picture Collection. **75** *left* Paris Opera Library, Bibliothèque Nationale; *right* Culver Pictures. **76** Radio Times Hulton Picture Library. **77** Sophia Smith Collection/Mark Sexton. **78** *top left & top center* New York Public Library, Picture Collection; *top right* Sophia Smith Collection; *bottom* Radio Times Hulton Picture Library. **79** Brown Brothers. **80** New York Public Library, Picture Collection. **81** *top Nice Little Girls* by Elizabeth Levy, illustrated by Mordicai Gerstein, published by Delacorte Press, © 1974; *bottom William's Doll* by Charlotte Zolotow, illustrated by William Pène du Bois, published by Harper & Row, © 1972. **82** & **83** *background* Gene Ahrens/Bruce Coleman, Inc. **83** *top right* Prof. Erwin W. Mueller, Pennsylvania State University; *center & lower right* Prof. J. Heslop-Harrison & Dr. Y. Heslop-Harrison. **86** *right* The Bettmann Archive. **90** *top* & **91** Culver Pictures. **92** *left* Brown Brothers; *right* K. Scholz/Shostal Associates. **94** *top* Kenneth Spencer Research Library, University of Kansas; *bottom* Sy Seidman/Photo Trends. **95** *left & lower right* Brown Brothers; *top right* Montgomery Ward and Company. **96** *top* Sy Seidman/Photo Trends. **96** *bottom left* & **97** *right* Brown Brothers. **96** *center* Culver Pictures; *bottom right* Museum of the City of New York, the Byron Collection. **97** *left* New York Public Library, Picture Collection. **98** *top* Ford Motor Company, Dearborn, Mich.; *lower left* Sy Seidman/Photo Trends. **98** *right* & **99** *right* Culver Pictures. **99** *left* UPI. **100-101** Collection of

Edward Vebell. **105** *upper left* New York Public Library, Picture Collection. **106** & **107** *left* Culver Pictures. **107** *right* Ullstein GMBH Bilderdienst. **110** *inset* Culver Pictures. **112** *bottom* Musée des Deux Guerres Mondiales (ECPA). **113** The New-York Historical Society. **115** *top* Library of Congress; *center left* Imperial War Museum; *lower left* Culver Pictures. **116** Radio Times Hulton Picture Library. **117** Culver Pictures. **118** Imperial War Museum. **119** *bottom right* & **121** *left* Ullstein GMBH Bilderdienst. **122** Culver Pictures. **123** *top L'illustration.* **124–125** Radio Times Hulton Picture Library. **126** *bottom left* Bildarchiv Preussischer Kulturbesitz; *right* Imperial War Museum. **128** *bottom* National Archives. **128–129** *top* Imperial War Museum/Angelo Hornak. **131** *photomontage* Ralph Crane & Alfred Eisenstaedt/Time-Life Picture Agency, © Time Inc. **132–133** *top* Sovfoto. **133** *bottom* Library of Congress. **134** & **135** Culver Pictures. **136** & **137** Charles Pickard/Camera Press. **138** & **139** Sovfoto. **142–143** UPI. **144** Archivi Edizioni del Gallo-Pizzi. **146** Radio Times Hulton Picture Library. **147** *left* The Bettmann Archive; *right* Bildarchiv Preussischer Kulturbesitz. **148** Sovfoto. **149** *upper* Bildarchiv Preussischer Kulturbesitz; *bottom* Private Collection. **150** Culver Pictures. **152** *left* Erich Salomon/Magnum; *right* UPI. **153** IPC Newspapers, Ltd. **154** & **155** *left* Bauhaus-Archiv. **155** *center* Ullstein GMBH Bilderdienst. **156** *left & upper center* Staatliche Kunstsammlungen, Weimar; *lower center* The Museum of Modern Art, Phyllis B. Lambert Fund; *right* Bauhaus-Archiv. **157** *left* The Museum of Modern Art, Abbe Aldrich Rockefeller Fund. **158** *upper* Shostal Associates. **158–159** *bottom* Lawrence Halprin & Associates. **160–161** *top* & **162** *bottom* Radio Times Hulton Picture Library. **160–161** *bottom* Wide World. **162** *top* Culver Pictures. **163** UPI. **166** *left* Brown Brothers; **166** *right* & **167** *top & bottom right* Private Collections. **167** *bottom left* The New-York Historical Society. **168** Ullstein GMBH Bilderdienst. **169** & **171** *right* Fototeca Storica Nazionale. **172** *left* Courtesy of *Vanity Fair,* © 1935 (renewed) 1963 by The Condé Nast Publications Inc.; *right* Library of Congress. **173** Ullstein GMBH Bilderdienst; *inset* Alfredo Zennaro. **174–175** Reprinted by permission of the estate of Morton Roberts. **176** *left* Culver Pictures. **176** *right*–**177** *center* Taken from *A Pictorial History of Jazz* by Orrin Keepnews and William Grauer, Jr., © 1955 by William Grauer, Jr., and Orrin Keepnews. Used by permission of Crown Publishers, Inc. **177** *right* Eliot Elisofon/Time-Life Picture Agency. **179** David Redfern. **180** *top* The Mansell Collection; *center* Princeton University Library; *bottom* Maritinie-Viollet. **181** *top* Brown Brothers; *lower* John T. Hopf. **182** *left & top right* Robert Capa/Magnum; *lower right* Brown Brothers. **183** Ernst Haas. **184** *top* Culver Pictures; *bottom* From the Metro-Goldwyn-Mayer release *Camille,* © 1937 Metro-Goldwyn-Mayer Distributing Corporation. Copyright renewed 1959 by Loew's Inc./Culver Pictures. **185** From the Metro-Goldwyn-Mayer release *Mata Hari,* © 1932 Metro-Goldwyn-Mayer Distributing Corporation. Copyright renewed 1959 by Loew's Inc./The Museum of Modern Art, Film Stills Archive. **186** & **187** The Museum of Modern Art. **188** *left* Philadelphia Museum of Art, the Louise & Walter Arensberg Collection; *right* Collection of Stanley R. Resor. **189** *top* From *Surrealism* by Patrick Waldberg, © 1971. Used with permission of McGraw-Hill Book Company; *lower right* The Museum of Modern Art, Gift of James Thrall Soby. **190** *left* Claude Spaak Collection, ADAGP, Paris, 1976/Photo Jacqueline Hyde. **190** *top right* & **191** *top* The Museum of Modern Art. **190–191** *center* Wadsworth Atheneum, Hartford, Conn., Ella Gallup & Mary Catlin Sumner Collection. **191** *bottom* William Douglas McAdams, Inc., for Roche Laboratories. **192** NASA. **193** *left* Smithsonian Institution; *upper right* Library of Congress; *bottom right* UPI. **195** *upper* Collection of Robert Lesser. **195** *bottom* & **196** NASA. **197** *left* Army News Features; *right* Smithsonian Institution. **198** *left* Wide World; *center & right* Culver Pictures. **199** *left* Brown Brothers; *right* Library of Congress. **200** *left* & **201** *bottom right* Culver Pictures; **200** *center & right* & **201** *right* Brown Brothers. **201** *upper right* Chicago Historical Society. **202** *left* UPI; *right New York News.* **203** *left* Brown Brothers; *center* New York Public Library, Picture Collection; *right* © 1929 by The New York Times Company; reprinted by permission. **204** *left* Private Collection. **204** *right* & **206** Sovfoto. **207** *left* UPI. **209** *bottom left Illustrated London News; bottom right* British Museum. **210** *bottom right* Pfizer, Inc.; *Nobel medal* Swedish Information Service; *remainder* Radio Times Hulton Picture Library. **212** & **213** *top left* Reprinted from *Agents of Bacterial Disease* by Albert S. Klainer by permission of Harper & Row. **214** & **215** *right* Pfizer, Inc. **215** *left* Grant Heilman. **218–219** Culver Pictures. **220** Private Collection. **222–223** Chicago Historical Society. **224** Collection of Charles J. Rosenblum. **225** *left* The Oakland Museum, Dorothea Lange Collection; *right* Culver Pictures. **226** & **227** *top* Radio Times Hulton Picture Library. **227** *bottom* Harlingue-Viollet. **230** *center left* Eric V. Grave/Photo Researchers; *lower left & center* Peter & Birgit Satir; *right* © 1974 by *Scientific American*, Inc. All rights reserved. **231** *upper left* Hale Observatories; *upper right* Wide World; *lower left* Helmut K. Wimmer; *bottom right* UPI. **232–233** *top* Bildarchiv Preussischer Kulturbesitz. **232** *bottom* Photoworld. **234** *top* Keystone; *bottom right* The Bettmann Archive. **236** Sovfoto. **237** Keystone. **238** *top* Roger-Viollet; *bottom* The Bettmann Archive. **241** *left* UPI; *right* Keystone. **242** *left* New York Public Library, Picture Collection; *right* UPI. **243** Wide World. **244** Bildarchiv Preussischer Kulturbesitz. **245** Ullstein Bilderdienst. **246** & **247** *bottom* Monte Davis. **247** *top* Nat Farbman/Time-Life Picture Agency, © Time Inc. **248** & **249** August Sander, courtesy of Gerd Sander Gallery. **250** Private Collection. **252** & **253** Culver Pictures. **253** *top* U.S. Army Photo; *lower left* Wide World; *right* UPI. **255** Camera Press. **256–257** *top* Dept. of the Interior; *bottom* Culver Pictures. **258** *bottom left* Culver Pictures; *remainder* Wide World. **259** Culver Pictures. **260** Robert Capa/Magnum. **261** Marc Riboud/Magnum. **263** *upper left* UPI; *lower left* Robert Capa/Magnum. **265** *upper* ADAGP; *bottom* Robert Capa/Magnum. **266** *left* Library of Congress; *right* Wide World. **267** *left & top right* Library of Congress; *lower right* Culver Pictures. **268** *top* UPI; *left & bottom right* Culver Pictures. **269** *left* Harris & Ewing/Photo Trends. **270** *top* Metro-Goldwyn-Mayer; *remainder* Culver Pictures. **271** *left* The Museum of Modern Art, Film Stills Archive; *top center* Culver Pictures; *right* Walt Disney Productions. **272** Bildarchiv Preussischer Kulturbesitz. **274** *left* UPI; *right* New York Public Library, Picture Collection. **275** UPI. **276** *left & bottom* Bildarchiv Preussischer Kulturbesitz; *center right* Wide World. **279** *top right* Courtesy of Children's Television Workshop; *center* RCA; (*Lucille Ball*) FPG; (*Edw. R. Murrow*) Culver Pictures; *remainder* Movie Star News. **284–285** Pictorial Parade. **286** New York Public Library, Picture Collection. **289** *bottom* & **290** UPI. **292** Keystone. **293** *top* Wide World; *bottom* Fox Photos. **294** *left* Popperfoto; *top right* Imperial War Museum; *lower right* Pictorial Parade. **295** Imperial War Museum. **298** *upper* Photri. **298** *bottom* & **299** *top* Keystone. **299** *bottom left* George C. Marshall Research Foundation/Photri; *remainder* From *The Codebreakers* by David Kahn, Macmillan, © 1967. **300–301** *top* Wide World. **301** *bottom* Reproduced by permission of *Esquire* magazine © 1942 by Esquire, Inc. **304** *left* Courtesy of Yivo Institute for Jewish Research; *upper right* Library of Congress. **305** *top* Doisneau-Rapho, Paris; *bottom* Rijksinstituut Voor Oorlogsdocumentatie, Amsterdam. **306** Pierre Boulat. **307** *top right* Photoworld. **307** *lower right* & **309** Wide World. **310–311** Sovfoto. **312** *left* Private Collection; *right* Sovfoto. **314** *upper left* Reproduced by permission of *Collier's* magazine © 1942; *bottom* National Archives. **317** Wide World. **319** *top* & **320** National Archives. **321** *left* Wide World; *right* U.S. Marine Corp./Photri. **322** *top* Anna L. Sobeck; *bottom* Library of Congress. **323** *left* Wide World; *top right* Library of Congress; *lower right* Brown Brothers. **324** *left* UPI; *top right* Bob Landry/*Life* magazine; *bottom right* National Archives. **325** *left* UPI. **325** *right* & **326** *left* Culver Pictures. **326** *upper middle* UPI. **326–327** *top center* Culver Pictures; *center* UPI. **327** *left* Courtesy of Norman Rockwell. **329** *bottom* Sovfoto. **330** Alfred Ott. **331** Bildarchiv Preussischer Kulturbesitz. **334** *middle right* Wide World; *bottom* Sovfoto. **338** & **341** UPI. **342** Pictorial Parade. **343** Private Collection. **344** Robert Capa/Magnum. **346** U.S. Army Photographs. **348** Robert Capa/Magnum. **350** U.S. Dept. of the Air Force. **352** & **356–357** UPI. **358** Private Collection. **361** & **362** *left* & **373** UPI. **362** *right*

Wide World. **364** UPI; *bottom right* Orion Press/Tom Stack & Assocs. **367** *upper left* Industrial Nucleonics; *bottom left* General Electric; *middle* U.S. Energy Research & Development Admin.; *upper right* Johnson & Johnson; *bottom right* Arco Chemical Co. **370** *right* Monte Davis. **371** *left* Reprinted by permission of Hawthorn Books, Inc., from *The Living Aura,* © 1975 by Kendall Johnson. All rights reserved; *center* The Metropolitan Museum of Art, the Carnarvon Collection, Gift of Edward S. Harkness; *right* UPI. **374** Wide World. **375** *left* UPI. **375** *right* & **376** United Nations. **379** Jon Brenneis for *Scientific American; inset* UPI. **380** *top* New York Public Library; *middle* IBM; *bottom* Erich Hartmann/Magnum. **383** *top left & center* Cornell University, Program of Computer Graphics; *top right* The New York Times Company, Terminal Information Bank; *lower left* NASA. **384** *left* The Solomon R. Guggenheim Museum; *right* The Museum of Modern Art. **385** Henri Cartier-Bresson/Magnum. **386** Hans Namuth. **387** Australian National Gallery, Canberra. **388** *left* Wide World; *right* Zoe Dominic. **390** *top* UPI; *bottom* P. R. Shinde/Black Star. **392** *top left & right & bottom left* Black Star; *center* Marc Riboud/Magnum. **393** *bottom* UPI. **394** *left* Harmit Singh/Black Star; *top* Marc Riboud/Magnum. **394–395** Pictorial Parade. **395** *right* Mike Peters/*The Dayton Daily News.* **396** John Phillips for *Life.* **397** *top left* UPI. **400** *upper left* Lasar Dunner; *bottom* Wide World. **401** Keystone. **402** © Arnold Newman. **403** Wide World. **404** *left* Margaret Bourke-White/Time-Life Picture Agency, © Time Inc. **404–405** *top* Andreas Feininger/Time-Life Picture Agency, © Time Inc. **405** *left* Bob Gomel/Time-Life Picture Agency, © Time Inc.; *upper right* Chevrolet Motor Division, General Motors Corp.; *lower right* Buick Motor Division, General Motors Corp. **406** *left* UPI; *upper right* Elliot Erwitt/Magnum; *bottom right* © 1971 *New York Review of Books.* **407** *left* © 1976 by Fred W. McDarrah; *right* R. W. Kelley/Time-Life Picture Agency, © Time Inc. **408** *left* Dennis Stock/Magnum; *bottom* UPI; *right* Museum of the City of New York. **409** *left* Milton Greene/Alskog, Inc.; *center* Andre de Dienes/Alskog, Inc.; *right* Brown Brothers. **411** *center* Bob Henriques/Magnum; *bottom right* UPI. **412** *left* Burt Glinn/Magnum; *right* Wide World. **413** *left* Bob Adelman/Magnum; *right* UPI. **414** *top left* Courtesy of Chris McNair; *top right* Courtesy of Alpha Robertson; *lower left* Wide World; *lower right* Courtesy of Mr. & Mrs. Claude A. Wesley. **415** *left* Bruce Anspach/Editorial Photocolor Archives; *right* Eve Arnold/Magnum. **416** *left* Bob Adelman/Magnum; *right* Daniel S. Brody/Editorial Photocolor Archives. **417** UPI. **420–421** NASA. **422** Queensborough Public Library. **424** Sovfoto. **426** (*inset*) NASA. **427** National Center for Atmospheric Research. **428** Fairchild Industries. **429** *left* Communications Satellite Corp.; *right* NASA. **430–431** *top* Bob Henriques/Magnum. **431** *bottom* UPI. **432** *top* Andrew St. George/Time-Life Picture Agency, © Time Inc.; *lower right* Joe Scherschel/Time-Life Picture Agency, © Time Inc. **434** & **435** Collection of Daniel Brown. **436** *upper* & **437** UPI. **436** *bottom* Photri. **440** *upper left* & *lower right* (*insets*) J. B. Gurdon. **442** *bottom* & **443** *middle far left* Keystone. **443** *upper left* Wide World; *top right* UPI; *lower right* United Nations; *bottom* Keystone. **446** George Rodger/Magnum. **447** *upper right* David McCullin/Magnum; *bottom* UPI. **448** J. P. Uetz/Black Star. **449** Ingeborg Lippman/*The New York Times.* **450** *top* Raghubir Singh/Woodfin Camp & Assocs.; *bottom* United Nations. **451** *upper* Courtesy of Syntex Corp. **452** Raghubir Singh/Woodfin Camp & Assocs. **455** *right* Charles E. Merrill Publishing Co. **461** *left Encyclopaedia Britannica.* **462** *top* Courtesy of PepsiCo, Inc., Purchase, N.Y. **462** *bottom* & **463** *left* Harry Redl/Black Star. **463** *right* Henri Cartier-Bresson/Magnum. **464** *left* Galleria Doria Pamphili, Rome/Guidotti-Grimoldi; *right* Hirshhorn Museum & Sculpture Garden. **465** From the artist's collection, photograph by Bevin Davies. **466** *upper* Laser Images, Inc. **466–467** *center* Gerhard Gscheidle/Magnum. **469** *top* Felici-Grimoldi; *bottom* Wide World. **470** *left* Dennis Brack/Black Star; *right* Greek Orthodox Archdiocese of North and South America. **471** *right* UPI; *bottom* Wide World. **473** *right* James Pickerell/Black Star. **474** & **475** Wide Wold. **476** *top* UPI; *lower right* Phillip Jones Griffiths/Magnum. **478** *left* UPI; *right* Charles Bonnay/Black Star. **481** *top left* Emil Schulthess/Black Star; *upper right* Bruno Barbey/Magnum; *bottom* Stern/Black Star. **482** Camera Press. **483** Mort Drucker. **485** *left* N. Gutman/Keystone. *top right* Marvin E. Newman/Woodfin Camp & Assocs.; *bottom* Charles Bonnay. **486–487** *bottom* Camera Press/Photo Trends. **487** *right* Michel Laurent/Gamma/Liaison Agency, Inc. **488** *top left* Wide World; *upper center* FPG; *upper right* Photoworld; *bottom left* Jim Marshall/Time-Life Picture Agency, © Time Inc. **489** *left* Leonard Freed/Magnum; *center* Myron Wood/Photo Researchers. **489** *right* & **490** *top* Wide World, **490** *middle* NASA; *bottom* UPI. **491** *left* Constantine Manos/Magnum; *right* Wide World. **492** *top* E. Landry/Magnum; *lower right* Wide World. **493** *left* Gatewood/Magnum; *center* George Kalinsky; *right* Monte Davis. **494** Helmut Wimmer © *Smithsonian* magazine. **496** *left* & *center* Lick Observatory; *right* © California Institute of Technology & Carnegie Institution of Washington. **499** *top* Reprinted from *Science Year, The World Book Science Annual,* 1976 © *The World Book Encyclopedia,* published by Field Enterprises Educational Corp., illustration by Donald E. Davis. **499** *bottom,* **500,** & **501** NASA. **502–503** *bottom* Reprinted from *Science Year, The World Book Science Annual,* 1976 © *The World Book Encyclopedia,* published by Field Enterprises Educational Corp., illustration by Frank Guidice. **503** *top* NASA; *lower right* Reprinted from *Science Year, The World Book Science Annual,* 1976 © *The World Book Encyclopedia,* published by Field Enterprises Educational Corp. **505** Naul J. Ojeda/Magnum; (*bottom inset*) Bruno Barbey/Magnum. **506** & **507** UPI. **509** *top* Charles Gerretson/Gamma/Liaison Agency Inc.; *bottom* Naul J. Ojeda/Magnum. **510** & **511** *left* Environmental Research Institute of Michigan. **511** *right* UPI. **512** Marty Stouffer/Bruce Coleman Inc. **513** *bottom* David Hughes/Bruce Coleman Inc.; *right* Pat Caulfield. **514** © California Institute of Technology & Carnegie Institution of Washington; (*inset*) NASA.